CONSTITUTIONAL LAW
OF THE
EUROPEAN UNION

CONSTITUTIONAL LAW
OF THE
EUROPEAN UNION

Second Edition

by

KOEN LENAERTS
Professor of European Law, Katholieke Universiteit Leuven,
Judge of the Court of Justice of the European Communities

and

PIET VAN NUFFEL
Legal secretary at the Court of Justice of the European Communities
Professor at the College of Europe, Natolin

ROBERT BRAY, EDITOR
Principal administrator, European Parliament

Published by
Sweet & Maxwell Limited
100 Avenue Road
Swiss Cottage
London NW3 3PF

(*http://www.sweetandmaxwell.co.uk*)

Typeset by J.P. Price, Chilcompton, Somerset
Printed in Great Britain

ISBN 0–421–88610–2

PREFACE

With the signature of the Treaty establishing a Constitution for Europe at the ceremony taking place in Rome on Friday, October 29, 2004, the European Union is poised to enter a stage when it will be founded upon a constitutive text whose title expressly reflects the function it is to fulfil. Yet it should not be forgotten that, according to the Court of Justice, the present Treaties already constitute "the constitutive charter of a [Union] based on the rule of law". Furthermore, since May 1, 2004 the Union is to be seen as the legal framework for the unification of Europe based on *"de facto* solidarity"—to use the words of Robert Schuman—which constitutes the core of the integration project. We have been at pains to take all these developments into account, while clearly distinguishing between the law as it stands and the changes announced in the Constitution for Europe.

What we have sought to do is to produce a truly systematic exposition of the constitutional law of the Union, in the broadest sense of the expression. Consequently, the description of the various competences, procedures and acts closely follows the structure of the EU and EC Treaties, being designed around the three pillars of the European Union—the Community pillar (or *acquis communautaire*) and the forms of co-operation between the Member States (common foreign and security policy and police and judicial co-operation in criminal matters) known as the second and third pillars. In considering each aspect of the law, we have endeavoured to raise the issues which lawyers are likely to encounter in practice, while amply referring to the internet as a source of materials for practitioners, academics and students worldwide.

Our work opens with a historical survey of the various paths taken towards integration in the European Union (Part I). This is followed by an outline of the Union's substantive, temporal and territorial jurisdiction (Part II). As far as the Community pillar of the Union is concerned, the starting point is the objectives and tasks of the Community, followed by the principles of conferral of powers, subsidiarity, proportionality, loyal co-operation and equal treatment, that is the legal framework for the exercise of Community powers in relation to those objectives and tasks. Next, Part II provides an extensive overview of substantive European law, which follows the arrangement of the Treaty and places particular emphasis on the free movement of goods, persons, services and capital and economic and monetary union. For reasons of space, discrete fields of study in their own right (such as competition law) are dealt with in outline, with copious references to learned articles and textbooks.

Part III identifies the actors which give shape to the European Union, in other words the institutions, the Member States and the citizens of the Union. Together with Part IV, which sets out the decision-making process in the European Union, this Part has been carefully adapted to reflect the composition of the institutions as from May 1, 2004 and the changes announced in the Constitution for Europe.

In the survey of the Union's sources of law (Part V), efforts have been made to provide clear practical guidance about the primacy and direct effect of Community law and the effects of non-Community law of the Union. Particular attention has been paid to the way in which the Member States ensure the application of Union law at national level. In this connection we are indebted to our colleagues from the new Member States who so generously gave of their time to explain the intricacies of their countries' constitutional systems.

As far as action by the European Union in the international arena is concerned, Part VI comprehensively explores both Community powers and non-Community foreign policy of the Union. The last chapter, prepared by Eddy De Smijter, administrator at the European Commission, deals with relations between the European Union and the rest of Europe, a matter of considerable topical relevance.

The question of judicial protection in the European Union is to be dealt with in a companion volume: Koen Lenaerts, Dirk Arts and Ignace Maselis; Robert Bray (ed.), *Procedural Law of the European Union,* Sweet & Maxwell.

This book reflects the state of the law on October 1, 2004. All views expressed are our own and cannot be ascribed to the institutions to which we belong.

Koen Lenaerts
Piet Van Nuffel
Robert Bray (editor)

Luxembourg and Brussels
October 1, 2004

FOREWORD TO THE FIRST EDITION

The title of this book *Constitutional Law of the European Union* might suggest that it is a modern day Dicey or Wade & Phillips of the Union, explaining only the structure and competences of the institutions, the Treaty rules which govern them and the conventions which have developed. It is that but it is far more. With its companion volume "Procedural Law of the European Union" it constitutes a veritable encyclopedia of Union law and practice.

To understand where we have got to it is necessary to have a succinct but accurate explanation of how and why everything began and why things were arranged as they were. No less important is it necessary to remember the changes to the basic Treaties of the European Community which have been made—the Merger Treaty of 1967, the Single European Act 1986, Maastricht 1992, Amsterdam 1997—and to relate what was being done in the Community to what was being done in Europe outside the Community—the Council of Europe, NATO, WEU, the European Council, European Political Co-operation, Schengen—as Europe moved towards Union with a more heterogenous institutional structure. This book begins with this in a way which will be of value not just to new "classes" of law students in the universities and new Member States but to the rest of us, at the least as a refresher course.

At the institutional level the book does not merely give a factual account of what is there. It shows why, for example, the Commission (as a body not democratically elected) was not given wider legislative powers; how the inter-relation of the Council of Ministers and the Parliament has changed; what is the constitutional significance of the Court; what are the basic functions of the European System of Central Banks and the European Central Bank; the importance of the European Social Fund.

Seekers for the substantive law will find a detailed account of so many areas. To take only the staple diet—free movement of goods, persons, services and capital—the cases are all there, the principles clearly explained with a wealth of detail. And much the same can be said about every other subject—the chapter headings show how far and wide the authors have travelled and I have not yet found anything which is not covered. But what is particularly striking about the book is the analysis of principles and underlying concepts. All too often the importance of considering what

Arts 2 and 3 of the Treaty say is overlooked—purposive interpretation may be impossible without them and here they are given due weight. Words which we take for granted without thinking them through—"*supra* nationality", "internal market" (as contrasted with "common market"); fundamental questions like the legal basis of powers, the extent (exclusive or otherwise) of Community competences; the meaning of subsidiarity, proportionality and the avoidance of discrimination—all are considered.

And the book is not just for legal issues; the economic and political consequences of what is happening are dealt with. "The elimination of internal frontiers for movements of goods, persons, services and capital renders the economies of the Member States so dependent on each other that any national economic policy decision has a direct cross-frontier effect." *(et seq.* para. 5–216). The budgets of the Union and the development of monetary union are clearly explained.

Those who know Koen Lenaerts—as professor, référendaire at the European Court and judge of the Court of First Instance—and his colleagues, will expect to find and will find not just clarity and accuracy of statement but a sense of intellectual excitement at what is happening. That is here. It is not lost in the breadth of the references not only to court decisions but to extensive academic and professional literature from everywhere. One puts the book down amazed that three people (even between them) could know so much and write so well.

With its companion volume it will become one of the pillars of every law school library; it should be readily available to judges and to practitioners.

Slynn of Hadley

CONTENTS

PART I: THE EUROPEAN UNION: DIFFERENT PATHS TOWARDS INTEGRATION

1. THE COMMUNITY INTEGRATION PATH

2. THE NON-COMMUNITY INTEGRATION PATH

3. BRINGING TOGETHER THE PATHS OF INTEGRATION INTO ONE EUROPEAN UNION

4. TOWARDS A "CONSTITUTION FOR EUROPE"

PART II: JURISDICTION OF THE EUROPEAN UNION

5. SUBSTANTIVE SCOPE OF THE COMMUNITY TREATIES

PART III: THE ACTORS OF THE EUROPEAN UNION

10. THE INSTITUTIONS AND BODIES OF THE UNION

PART V: SOURCES OF LAW OF THE EUROPEAN UNION

17. COMMUNITY LAW

**PART VI: THE EXTERNAL RELATIONS OF
THE EUROPEAN UNION**

19. THE POSITION IN INTERNATIONAL LAW OF THE
COMMUNITIES AND THE UNION

20. THE EXTERNAL POWERS OF THE COMMUNITIES AND THE UNION

INTRODUCTION TO THE SOURCE MATERIAL

A. OFFICIAL PUBLICATIONS

www.europa.eu.int/
The Internet is the easiest way to find information about the European Union. The "europa" website is a source of news and information about the history and activities of the Union and leads visitors to the websites of the various institutions and to several databases containing official information, including "Eur-Lex".

www.europa.eu.int/eur-lex
The "Eur-Lex" site is the starting point for any enquiry for legal information about the European Union. This site provides access in all official languages to the Treaties on which the Union is based and to legislation and to the case-law of the Court of Justice and the Court of First Instance. It is also a conduit to a number of other official documents.

I. Treaties

Under the heading "Treaties" of the "Eur-Lex" site, can be found the text of the EC Treaty, the EU Treaty and the amending treaties, including the (Draft) Treaty establishing a Constitution for Europe.

In the United Kingdom, the legislation necessary to implement EU Treaties and acts can be found on the site of Her Majesty's Stationery Office: *www.hmso.gov.uk*

2. Legislation

For some years, the "Eur-Lex" site has provided access free of charge to the *Official Journal of the European Union*, which is the official source for acts of the European Union (before February 1, 2003, its official name was *Official Journal of the European Communities*).

The *Official Journal* is published in all of the official languages (before May 1, 2004, the English version could be recognised by its mauve-coloured spine). As from the 1998 issues, it is available free of charge from "Eur-Lex". It is also available monthly or annually on CD ROM. The paper version is still available. Before 1968, the *Official Journal* appeared in one part, whose page numbers initially ran on from one issue to the next (*e.g.* OJ 1962, 1). Since July 1, 1967, the pagination of each volume starts from page 1 (*e.g.* [1967] O.J. 100/1). Since January 1, 1968, the Official Journal has been published in two parts and a supplement.

The *English Special Editions of the Official Journal* cover the period before the United Kingdom and Ireland joined the Community (until the end of 1972), but not all acts adopted were published therein.[1] Furthermore, there is no official list of English Special Editions and they have never been codified[2]

[1] If an English version of a measure exists, the *English Special Edition* is cited in the European Court Reports. Otherwise the practice is to cite the French *Journal Officiel* reference.
[2] However, the list below (drawn up by the English Translation Division of the ECJ over the years) is believed to be complete.

First series
1952–1958
1959–1962
1963–1964
1965–1966
1965–1972 (omissions)
1966–1972
1967
1968 (I)
1968 (II)
1969 (I)
1969 (II)
1970 (I)
1970 (II)
1970 (III)
1971 (I)
1971 (II)
1971 (III)
1972 (I)
1972 (II)
1972 (III)
1972 (March 27) = J.O. L73 (documents concerning accession)
1972 (October 10–31)
1972 (November)
1972 (December 1–8)
1972 (December 9–28)
1972 (December 28–30)
1972 (December 30–31) = J.O. L.297–299
1972 (31 December) = J.O. L.296
1972 (31 December) = J.O. L.300
1972 (31 December) = J.O. L.301
1972 (31 December) = J.O. L.302
1972 (31 December) = J.O. L.303 & 306
1972 (31 December) = J.O. L.307 (Budget 1973)
Supplement to the first series of Special Editions (1952–72) Consolidated edition of corrigenda

Second series
I   External Relations (2)
II   Agriculture and Food Aid
III   European Agricultural Guidance and Guarantee Fund
IV   Transport
V   Euratom
VI   Competition (a) and (b)
VII   Institutional Questions
VIII   European Coal and Steel Community
IX   Resolutions of the Council and of the Representatives of the Member States
X   Miscellaneous

Supplement
1959–1962 (Court of Justice)
(1959 J.O. 18 Rules of Procedure
1962 J.O. 34 Supplementary Rules
1960 J.O. 72 Instructions to the Registrar)

The *Official Journals* whose numbers are preceded by the letter L (*législation*, cited as [1999] O.J. L100/1) contain decisions of the institutions and bodies, divided into "acts whose publication is obligatory" (*inter alia*, regulations, directives and decisions addressed to all Member States) and "acts whose publication is not obligatory" (international agreements, other decisions and directives).

The *Official Journals* whose numbers are preceded by the letter C (*communications*, Information and Notices, cited as [1999] O.J. C100/1) publish preparatory acts, such as Commission proposals and common positions adopted by the Council in the course of the legislative procedure, together with minutes of the sittings of the European Parliament, written questions put by MEPs and their answers, a summary of the judgments of the Court of Justice and the Court of First Instance and notices of cases brought before the two courts. C-series issues indicated with a terminal "E" (*e.g.* [2002] O.J. C228E) exist only in electronic form.

The Supplement to the *Official Journal* publishes public procurement contracts exceeding specified limits. Since July 1998 the supplement may be consulted only electronically either through the "Eur-Lex" site (TED database) or on CD-ROM.

On the "Eur-Lex" site, the heading "Legislation" leads to the *Directory of Community legislation in force* and to consolidated legislation, which is available in full. The *Directory* is also published in paper form half-yearly with a chronological index and an index of key words.

The link on "Eur-Lex" to "Legislation in preparation" leads to proposals for legislation of the Commission and to opinions provided by other institutions and bodies in the legislative process. In order to find out where matters stand with a given proposal for legislation, it is possible to consult the "PreLex" database ("Monitoring the decision-making process between institutions") in any official language or "OEIL", the "legislative observatory" of the European Parliament (in English or French only).

3. Case law

Since June 1997 the most important decisions of the Court of Justice and the Court of First Instance have been available on the day of pronouncement from the Court's "curia" website: *www.curia.eu.int/en/content/juris/index__form.htm*

Pronouncements dating from before June 17, 1997 can be found on the "Eur-Lex" website under the heading "case law" (search for case number, date or the names of parties). For advanced searches recourse must be made to the CELEX database, which used to be subscription only, but has been available free of charge since July 1, 2004: *www.europa.eu.int/celex/htm/celex__en.htm*

A paper version of the case law of the Court of Justice and the Court of First Instance is published in all the official languages in the *Reports of Cases before the Court of Justice and the Court of First Instance (European Court Reports or ECR—*the English version is mauve).

Since 1990 the reports have been in two, separately paginated parts—Part I containing reports of cases of the Court of Justice, Part II those of the Court of First Instance. The case number is preceded by the letter C (*Cour*) where the proceedings were brought before the Court of Justice and by the letter T (*Tribunal*) where they were brought before the Court of First Instance. Where the case number is followed by "—P" (*pourvoi*), the case is an appeal against a decision of the Court of First Instance, where it is followed by "—R" (*référé*), the decision relates to an application for interim measures.

Since January 1, 1994 staff cases (proceedings brought by officials before the Court of First Instance under Community civil service law) have no longer been reported in the European Court Reports (except where they are of general interest or important in principle), but separately in the language of the case, with an abstract in the other languages, in the *European Court Reports—Reports of European Staff Cases (E.C.R.-S.C.)*.

The "curia" website is also a source of other useful information, including the weekly *Proceedings of the Court of Justice and the Court of First Instance*, which provides summaries of judgments and orders of both tiers of the Court and of Opinions of its Advocates General and notifies new cases brought before the Court. The Court's Research and Documentation Service publishes on the Internet a Digest of Community case law (systematic summaries of judgments and orders), an alphabetical index of subject matter and a useful survey of annotations of judgments.

4. Other documents

The "europa" portal guides the site visitor to a number of official documents which have been available for some years in both paper and electronic form.

Each month the Commission publishes the *Bulletin of the European Union* (EU Bull., prior to 1994: *Bulletin of the European Communities,* EC Bull.). That publication provides an overview of major events at Community level, describes the activities of the institutions and embodies a "documentation" section, including a list of infringement proceedings brought by the Commission against Member States alleged to be in breach of their obligations. Additionally, there are regular supplements to the *Bulletin* dealing with specific subjects. Issues of the *Bulletin* since 1996 are available in electronic form.

Each year the Commission issues a *General Report on the Activities of the European Union* (available in electronic form since 1997), together with other reports, including the *Report on Competition Policy,* which is available from the website of the Commission's Competition Directorate General: *www.europa.eu.int/comm/competition/*.

The Council publishes an annual *Review of the Council's Work.*

An interesting feature is the catalogue of the Commission's library, which contains references to more than 200,000 publications and gives access to a search engine: *www.europa.eu.int/eclas/*.

The historical archives may be consulted (partially also via the internet) at the European University Institute in Florence: *www.iue.it/ECArchives/.*

B. FURTHER INFORMATION

In most of the Member States there are a number of learned journals specialising in European law. Those published in English include principally *Common Market Law Review* (C.M.L.R.), *European Law Review* (E.L.Rev.), *Columbia Journal of European Law* (Col.J.E.L.) and *Legal Issues of European Integration* (L.I.E.I.). Among other journals, there are *Cahiers de droit européen* (C.D.E.), *Europarecht* (EuR.), *Journal des tribunaux—droit européen* (J.T.Dr.Eur.), *Revue du Marché Commun et de l'Union européenne* (R.M.C.U.E.), *Revue trimestrielle de droit européen* (R.T.D.E.) and *Sociaal-Economische Wetgeving* (S.E.W.). Major Community and national judicial decisions are reported in many of those journals and especially in *Common Market Law Reports* (C.M.L.R.). General and specialist law journals increasingly contain articles on European law. A number of daily newspapers, including *The Times* and the *Financial Times* regularly report cases of the Court of Justice.

Up-to-date information on the activities of the European Union can be found in *Europe,* a daily publication in several languages (including English) of the press agency *Agence Europe.* The weekly publication *European Voice* gives an excellent insight into current events on the European scene. The very latest news can be found on the web page *EU news,* which publishes press releases from the institutions as they are issued. This web page also provides links to the press services of the institutions and bodies: *www.europa.eu.int/news/index__en.htm.*

C. SOURCES CITED IN ABBREVIATED FORM

K. Lenaerts and D. Arts; editor R. Bray, *Procedural Law of the European Union,* 1st ed., 1999; 2nd ed., 2005, Sweet & Maxwell, London (K. Lenaerts, D. Arts and I. Maselis; editor R. Bray).

Accession Treaty 1972	Treaty of January 22, 1972 between the Member States of the European Communities, the Kingdom of Denmark, Ireland, the Kingdom of Norway and the United Kingdom of Great Britain and Northern Ireland concerning the accession of the Kingdom of Denmark, Ireland, the Kingdom of Norway and the United Kingdom of Great Britain and Northern Ireland to the European Economic Community and to the European Atomic Energy Community (see para. 1–021)

Accession Treaty 1979	Treaty of May 28, 1979 between the Member States of the European Communities and the Hellenic Republic concerning the accession of the Hellenic Republic to the European Economic Community and to the European Atomic Energy Community (see para. 1–021)
Accession Treaty 1985	Treaty of June 12, 1985 between the Member States of the European Communities and the Kingdom of Spain and the Portuguese Republic concerning the accession of the Kingdom of Spain and the Portuguese Republic to the European Economic Community and to the European Atomic Energy Community (see para. 1–021)
Accession Treaty 1994	Treaty of June 24, 1994 between the Member States of the European Union and the Kingdom of Norway, the Republic of Austria, the Republic of Finland and the Kingdom of Sweden concerning the accession of the Kingdom of Norway, the Republic of Austria, the Republic of Finland and the Kingdom of Sweden to the European Union (see para. 1–021)
Accession Treaty 2003	Treaty of April 16, 2003 between the Member States of the European Union and the Czech Republic, the Republic of Estonia, the Republic of Cyprus, the Republic of Latvia, the Republic of Lithuania, the Republic of Hungary, the Republic of Malta, the Republic of Poland, the Republic of Slovenia, the Slovak Republic, concerning the accession of the Czech Republic, the Republic of Estonia, the Republic of Cyprus, the Republic of Latvia, the Republic of Lithuania, the Republic of Hungary, the Republic of Malta, the Republic of Poland, the Republic of Slovenia and the Slovak Republic to the European Union (see para. 1–021)
Act of Accession 1972	Act appended to the 1972 Accession Treaty (see para. 1–021)
Act of Accession 1979	Act appended to the 1979 Accession Treaty (see para. 1–021)
Act of Accession 1985	Act appended to the 1985 Accession Treaty (see para. 1–021)

Act of Accession 1994	Act concerning the conditions of accession of the Republic of Austria, the Republic of Finland and the Kingdom of Sweden and the adjustments to the Treaties on which the Union is founded (see para. 1–021)
Act of Accession 2003	Act concerning the conditions of accession of the Czech Republic, the Republic of Estonia, the Republic of Cyprus, the Republic of Latvia, the Republic of Lithuania, the Republic of Hungary, the Republic of Malta, the Republic of Poland, the Republic of Slovenia and the Slovak Republic and the adjustments to the Treaties on which the European Union is founded (see para. 1–021)
Act on the Direct Election of the European Parliament	Act concerning the election of the European Parliament by direct universal suffrage (see para. 10–022)
Amsterdam Treaty	Treaty of Amsterdam of October 2, 1997 amending the Treaty on European Union, the Treaties establishing the European Communities and certain related acts (see para. 3–018)
Brussels Convention	Convention of September 27, 1968 on jurisdiction and the enforcement of judgments in civil and commercial matters (see para. 5–151)
Charter of Fundamental Rights	Charter of Fundamental Rights of the European Union of December 7, 2000 (see para. 17–083)
CFI Decision	Council Decision 88/591/ECSC, EEC, Euratom of October 24, 1988 establishing a Court of First Instance of the European Communities (see para. 10–072)
CFI Rules of Procedure	Rules of Procedure of the Court of First Instance of the European Communities (see para. 10–084)
Comitology Decision	Council Decision 1999/468/EC of June 28, 1999 laying down the procedures for the implementing powers conferred on the Commission (see para. 14–054)
Commission Rules of Procedure	Rules of Procedure of the Commission (see para. 10–067)
Conditions of Employment	Conditions of employment of other servants of the European Communities (see para. 10–152)

Council Rules of Procedure	Rules of Procedure of the Council (see para. 10–042)
Decision on Provisional Location	Decision of the Representatives of the Governments of the Member States on the provisional location of certain institutions and departments of the Communities (see para. 10–145)
EAEC Treaty	Treaty establishing the European Atomic Energy Community (see para. 1–007
EC Treaty	Treaty establishing the European Community (see para. 1–006)
ECHR	European Convention for the Protection of Human Rights and Fundamental Freedoms (see para. 2–004)
ECJ Rules of Procedure	Rules of Procedure of the Court of Justice of the European Communities (see para. 10–084)
ECJ Statute	Protocol on the Statute of the Court of Justice of the European Economic Community (see para. 10–072)
ECSC Treaty	Treaty establishing the European Coal and Steel Community (see para. 1–002)
EEA Agreement	Agreement on the European Economic Area (see para. 23–004)
EEC Treaty	Treaty establishing the European Economic Community (see para. 1–006)
EIB Statute	Protocol on the Statute of the European Investment Bank (see para. 10–105)
EMI Statute	Protocol on the Statute of the European Monetary Institute (see para. 10–101)
EP Rules of Procedure	Rules of Procedure of the European Parliament (see para. 10–026)
ESC Rules of Procedure	Rules of Procedure of the European Economic and Social Committee (see para. 10–095)
ESCB Statute	Protocol on the Statute of the European System of Central Banks and of the European Central Bank (see para. 10–102)
EU Constitution	Treaty establishing a Constitution for Europe (see para. 4–004)
EU Treaty	Treaty on European Union (see para. 3–011)
Financial Regulation	Financial Regulation of 21 December 1977 applicable to the general budget of the European Communities (see para. 10–116)

First Decision on Own Resources	Council Decision 70/243 of 21 April 1970 on the replacement of financial contributions from Member States by the Communities' own resources (see para. 10–121)
First Decision on the Seats of the Institutions	Decision of December 12, 1992 taken by common agreement between the Representatives of the Governments of the Member States on the location of the seats of the institutions and of certain bodies and departments of the European Communities (see para. 10–146)
First Treaty on Budgetary Provisions	Treaty of April 22, 1970 amending certain Budgetary Provisions of the Treaties establishing the European Communities and of the Treaty establishing a Single Council and a Single Commission of the European Communities (see para. 10–121)
Fourth Decision on Own Resources	Council Decision 94/728 of October 31, 1994 on the system of the Communities' own resources (see para. 10–121)
Fifth Decision on Own Resources	Council Decision 2000/597 of September 29, 2000 on the system of the Communities' own resources (see para. 10–121)
Merger Treaty	Treaty establishing a Single Council and a Single Commission of the European Communities (see para. 1–011)
Nice Treaty	Treaty of Nice of February 26, 2001 amending the Treaty on European Union, the Treaties establishing the European Communities and certain related acts (see para. 3–023)
Ombudsman Regulations	Decision of the European Parliament of March 9, 1994 on the regulations and general conditions governing the performance of the Ombudsman's duties (see para. 10–107)
Protocol on Privileges and Immunities	Protocol on the Privileges and Immunities of the European Communities (see para. 10–114)
Protocol on Seats	Protocol on the location of the seats of the institutions and of certain bodies and departments of the European Communities and of Europol (see para. 10–146)
Rome Convention	Convention of June 19, 1980 on the law applicable to contractual obligations (see para. 5–151)

Rules of Procedure—Court of Auditors	Rules of Procedure of the Court of Auditors (see para. 10–091)
Schengen Protocol	Protocol integrating the Schengen acquis into the framework of the European Union (see para. 5–164)
Second Decision on Own Resources	Council Decision 85/257 of May 7, 1985 on the system of the Communities' own resources (see para. 10–121)
Second Decision on the Seats of the Institutions	Decision of October 29, 1993 taken by common agreement between the Representatives of the Governments of the Member States, meeting at Head of State and Government level, on the location of the seats of certain bodies and departments of the European Communities and of Europol (see para. 10–147)
Second Treaty on Budgetary Provisions	Treaty of July 22, 1975 amending Certain Budgetary Provisions of the Treaties establishing the European Communities and of the Treaty establishing a Single Council and a Single Commission of the European Communities (see para. 10–130)
Single European Act	Single European act (para. 3–006)
Social Agreement	Agreement on social policy concluded between the Member States of the European Community with the exception of the United Kingdom of Great Britain and Northern Ireland (see para. 5–235)
Social Protocol	Protocol on social policy (see para. 5–235)
Staff Regulations	Staff Regulations of Officials of the European Communities (see para. 10–152)
Third Decision on Own Resources	Council Decision 88/376 of June 24, 1988 on the system of the Communities' own resources (see para. 10–121)
Third Decision on the Seats of the Institutions	Decision taken by common agreement between the Representatives of the Member States, meeting at Head of State or Government level, of December 13, 2003 on the location of the seats of certain offices and agencies of the European Union (see para. 10–147)

LIST OF ABBREVIATIONS

A.A.	Judgments of the Belgian *Arbitragehof/Cour d'arbitrage*
A.Ae.	Ars Aequi
ACP	African, Caribbean, Pacific
A.D.	*Actualités du droit*
A.J.C.L.	*American Journal of Comparative Law*
A.J.D.A.	*L'actualité juridique - droit administratif*
A.J.I.L.	*American Journal of International Law*
A.J.T.	*Algemeen Juridisch Tijdschrift*
Ann.Dr.Louv.	*Annales de droit de Louvain*
Ann.Dr.Lux.	*Annales du droit luxembourgeois*
Ann.Fac.Dr.Liège	*Annales de la Faculté de droit, d'économie et de sciences sociales de Liège*
A.ö.R.	*Archiv des öffentlichen Rechts*
Arr.Cass.	Judgments of the Belgian *Hof van Cassatie/Cour de Cassation*
A.Völkerr.	*Archiv des Völkerrechts*
B.S.	*Belgisch Staatsblad/Moniteur belge*
B.T.I.R.	*Belgisch Tijdschrift voor internationaal recht*
BVerfGE	Decisions of the *Bundesverfassungsgericht*
B.Y.I.L.	British Yearbook of International Law
Cambridge L.J.	*Cambridge Law Journal*
C.D.E.	*Cahiers de droit européen*
CFI	Court of First Instance of the European Communities
CFSP	common foreign and security policy
C.M.L.Rep.	*Common Market Law Reports*
C.M.L.R.	*Common Market Law Review*
Cm	Command Paper
Col.J.E.L.	*Columbia Journal of European Law*
Col.L.Rev.	*Columbia Law Review*
Coreper	Committee of Permanent Representatives
Cornell I.L.J.	*Cornell International Law Journal*

CSCE	Conference for Security and Cooperation in Europe
D.ö.V.	*Die öffentliche Verwaltung*
D.R.	Decisions and Reports of the European Commission on Human Rights
D.Vbl.	*Deutsches Verwaltungsblatt*
EAEC	European Atomic Energy Community
EBRD	European Bank for Reconstruction and Development
E.Bus.L.Rev.	*European Business Law Review*
E.Bus.Org.L.R.	*European Business Organisation Law Review*
EC	European Community
ECB	European Central Bank
EC Bull.	*Bulletin of the European Communities*
ECHR	European Convention for the Protection of Human Rights and Fundamental Freedoms
ECSC	European Coal and Steel Community
ECJ	Court of Justice of the European Communities
E.Comp.L.Rev.	*European Competition Law Review*
EDC	European Defence Community
E.C.R.	European Court Reports
EEA	European Economic Area
EEC	European Economic Community
E.Env.L.Rev.	European Environmental Law Review
EFTA	European Free Trade Association
E.For.Aff.Rev.	*European Foreign Affairs Review*
E.H.R.L.R.	*European Human Rights Law Review*
EIB	European Investment Bank
E.J.I.L.	*European Journal of International Law*
E.J.L.Ref.	*European Journal of Law Reform*
E.J.M.L.	*European Journal on Migration and Law*
E.J.Soc.Sec.	*European Journal of Social Security*
E.L.J.	*European Law Journal*
E.L.R.	*European Law Review*
EMI	European Monetary Institute
EMS	European Monetary System
EMU	economic and monetary union
Env.L.Rev.	*Environmental Law Review*
EPC	European Political Co-operation
EPC Bulletin	*European Political Co-operation Documentation Bulletin*
EPSO	European Personel Selection Office
E.Pub.L.	*European Public Law*

E.Rev.Priv.L.	*European Review of Private Law*
ERPL/REDP	*European Review of Private Law / Revue européenne de droit privé*
ESCB	European System of Central Banks
ESDP	European Security and Defence Policy
E.T.S.	European Treaty Series
EU	European Union
EU Bull.	*Bulletin of the European Union*
Eu.GR.Z.	*Europäische Grundrechte Zeitschrift*
EUMC	Military Committee of the European Union
EUMS	Military Staff of the European Union
EuR.	*Europarecht*
Euredia	*Revue Européenne de Droit Bancaire et Financier/European Banking and Financial Law Journal*
Eur.J.Soc.Sec.	*European Journal of Social Security*
Eur. L. F.	European Legal Forum
Europe	*Europe. Daily news bulletin*
Eu.Z.W.	*Europäische Zeitschrift für Wirtschaftsrecht*
E.W.S.	*Europäisches Wirtschafts- und Steuerrecht*
FAO	Food and Agricultural Organisation
Fordham I.L.J.	*Fordham International Law Journal*
GATT	General Agreement on Tariffs and Trade
GDP	gross domestic product
GNP	gross national product
G.J.	*Gaceta Jurídica*
G.Y.I.L.	*German Yearbook of International Law*
Harv.I.L.J.	*Harvard International Law Journal*
Human Rights L.J.	*Human Rights Law Journal*
I.C.L.Q.	*International and Comparative Law Quarterly*
IGC	Intergovernemental Conference
I.L.M.	International Legal Materials
ILO	International Labour Organisation
Int'l J.Comp.Lab.L.	*International Journal of Comparative Labour Law*
Ind.Rel.	*and Industrial Relations*
IMF	International Monetary Fund
IPRax.	*Praxis des Internationalen Privat- und Verfahrensrechts*
Ir.J.E.L.	*Irish Journal of European Law*
J.C.M.S.	*Journal of Common Market Studies*

J.C.P.	Jurisclasseur périodique—La semaine juridique
J.Env.L.	*Journal of Environmental Law*
JHA	justice and home affairs
J.I.E.L	*Journal of International Economic Law*
JRC	Joint Research Centre
J.T.	*Journal des tribunaux*
J.T.D.E.	*Journal des tribunaux—Droit européen*
J.T.T.	*Journal des tribunaux de travail*
Jura Falc.	*Jura Falconis*
J.W.T.	*Journal of World Trade*
J.Z.	*Juristen-Zeitung*
Kst.	*Kamerstukken* (Netherlands Parliament)
L.I.E.I.	*Legal Issues of European Integration* (since 2000: *Legal Issues of Economic Integration)*
Leiden J.I.L.	*Leiden Journal of International Law*
MEP	Member of the European Parliament
M.J.E.C.L.	*Maastricht Journal of European and Comparative Law*
Mich.L.Rev.	*Michigan Law Review*
Mod.L.Rev.	*Modern Law Review*
NATO	North Atlantic Treaty Organisation
N.I.L.R.	*Netherlands International Law Review*
N.J./A.B.	*Nederlandse Jurisprudentie. Administratiefrechte-lijke beslissingen*
N.J.B.	*Nederlands Juristenblad*
N.J.W.	*Neue Juristische Wochenschrift*
N.J.Wb.	*Nieuw Juridisch Weekblad*
Nordic J.I.L.	*Nordic Journal of International Law*
Not.U.Eur.	*Noticias de la Unión Europea*
N.T.B.	*Nederlands Tijdschrift voor bestuursrecht*
N.T.E.R.	*Nederlands Tijdschrift voor Europees Recht*
N.T.I.R.	*Nederlands Tijdschrift voor internationaal recht*
OECD	Organisation for Economic Cooperation and Development
OJ	*Official Journal of the European Union*
OLAF	European Anti-Fraud Office
OSCE	Organisation for Security and Cooperation in Europe
Pas.lux.	*Pasicrisie luxembourgeoise*

Pet.Aff.	*Les petites affiches*
PJCC	police and judicial cooperation in criminal matters
Publ. ECHR	Publications of the European Court of Human Rights
Pub.L.	*Public Law*
PSC	Political and Security Committee
R.A.E.	*Revue des affaires européennes*
R.B.D.C.	*Revue belge de droit constitutionnel*
R.C.C.	*Revue de la concurrence et de la consommation*
R.C.D.I.P.	*Revue critique de droit international privé*
R.D.Etr.	*Revue de droit des étrangers*
R.D.I.D.C.	*Revue de droit international et de droit comparé*
Rec.C.E.	*Recueil des décisions du Conseil d'Etat statuant au contentieux, du Tribunal des conflits et des jugements des Tribunaux administratifs*
Rec.Con.const.	*Conseil constitutionnel - Recueil des décisions*
Rec. Dalloz	*Recueil Dalloz-Sirey*
R.E.C.I.E.L.	*Review of European Community and International Environmental law*
R.D.U.E.	*Revue du droit de l'Union européenne*
R.D.ULB	*Revue du droit de l'Université Libre de Bruxelles*
R.D.Unif.	*Revue de droit uniforme/Uniform Law Review*
R.E.D.P.	*Revue européenne de droit public*
R.F.D.A.	*Revue française de droit administratif*
R.F.D.C.	*Revue française de droit constitutionnel*
R.G.D.I.P.	*Revue générale de droit international public*
R.I.D.C.	*Revue internationale de droit comparé*
R.I.E.J.	*Revue interdisciplinaire d'études juridiques*
Riv.D.E.	*Rivista di diritto europeo*
R.I.W.	*Recht der internationalen Wirtschaft*
R.M.C.	*Revue du Marché Commun*
R.M.C.U.E.	*Revue du Marché Commun et de l'Union européenne*
R.M.U.E.	*Revue du Marché Unique européen*
R.T.D.E.	*Revue trimestrielle de droit européen*
R.U.D.H.	*Revue universelle des droits de l'homme*
R.W.	*Rechtskundig Weekblad*
S.E.W.	*Sociaal-economische wetgeving. Tijdschrift voor Europees en economisch recht*
Stat.L.Rev.	*Statute Law Review*
Stb.	*Netherlands official gazette*
Stud. Dipl.	*Studia Diplomatica*
Swiss Rev.I.Comp.L.	*Swiss Review of International Competition Law*

T.B.H.	*Tijdschrift voor Belgisch handelsrecht*
T.B.P.	*Tijdschrift voor bestuurswetenschappen en publiekrecht*
Tilburg For.L.Rev.	*Tilburg Foreign Law Review*
T.O.R.B.	*Tijdschrift voor onderwijsrecht en onderwijsbeleid*
T.P.R.	*Tijdschrift voor privaatrecht*
Trb.	*Tractatenblad van het Koninkrijk der Nederlanden*
T.R.V.	*Tijdschrift voor rechtspersonen en vennootschappen*
Tulane E. & Civ. L. F.	*Tulane European and Civil Law Forum*
T.V.V.S.	*TVVS. Maandblad voor ondernemingsrecht en rechtspersonen*
UN	*United Nations*
U.N.T.S.	United Nations—Treaty Series
VAT	value added tax
WEAG	Western European Armaments Group
WEU	Western European Union
World Comp.	*World Competition*
WTO	World Trade Organization
W.u.W.	*Wirtschaft und Wettbewerb*
Y.ECHR	*Yearbook of the European Convention on Human Rights*
Y.E.L.	*Yearbook of European Law*
Z.a.ö.R.V.	*Zeitschrift für ausländisches öffentliches Recht und Völkerrecht*
Z.Eu.P.	*Zeitschrift für Europäisches Privatrecht*
Z.Eu.S.	*Zeitschrift für Europarechtliche Studien*
Z.f.RV.	*Zeitschrift für Rechtsvergleichung, internationales Privatrecht und Europarecht*
Z.H.W.	*Zeitschrift für das gesamte Handelsrecht und Wirtschaftsrecht*
Z.ö.R.	*Zeitschrift für öffentliches Recht*
Z.Vgl.RW.	*Zeitschrift für vergleichende Rechtswissenschaft*

NUMERICAL TABLE OF EUROPEAN CASES

EUROPEAN COURT OF JUSTICE

EFTA COURT

EUROPEAN COURT OF HUMAN RIGHTS

ALPHABETICAL TABLE OF EUROPEAN CASES

TABLE OF NATIONAL CASES

TABLE OF EU AND EC TREATIES, PROTOCOLS AND DECLARATIONS

Declarations annexed to the
EU Treaty

Protocol annexed to the
1994 Act of Accession

Declarations annexed to the
Treaty of Amsterdam

TABLE OF EUROPEAN UNION AND COMMUNITY ACTS

DIRECTIVES

COUNCIL DECISIONS AND DECISIONS OF REPRESENTATIVES OF MEMBER STATES

TABLE OF CONVENTIONS AND AGREEMENTS CONCLUDED BY THE EC OR EU

UK LEGISLATION

NON–UK LEGISLATION

Part I

THE EUROPEAN UNION: DIFFERENT PATHS TOWARDS INTEGRATION

CHAPTER 1

THE COMMUNITY INTEGRATION PATH

European Communities and European Union. The European Union is **1–001**
based on the three European Communities, which were established by
treaty: the European Coal and Steel Community (ECSC), the European
Community (EC) and the European Atomic Energy Community (Euratom
or EAEC). The EC (until 1992, the European Economic Community, or
EEC) is the most prominent of these international legal persons owing to
its general sphere of operation. The ECSC ceased to exist in 2002. Prior to
this "Community" integration process and in parallel thereto, European
States have engaged in other forms of co-operation. Indeed, the Member
States of the European Union have concluded agreements amongst
themselves concerning co-operation in areas falling outside the
Communities' sphere of operation with which they do not associate the
same legal consequences as they attach to Community action. In 1992, the
link which existed in practice between the two integration paths was
institutionalised by packaging them into the European Union, yet without
altering the specific legal character of either path. As a result, the
distinction remains between Community and non-Community action,
whereby only acts of the institutions based on one of the Community
Treaties constitute a source of "Community law".

The first part of this book describes the parallel emergence of the
Communities (Chapter 1) and the non-Community integration process
(Chapter 2), and explains how the European Union has combined the two
paths towards integration (Chapter 3). In 2004, the representatives of the
Member States agreed on a Treaty establishing a Constitution for Europe.
The proposed transformation of the existing Treaties into a genuine
Constitution seeks to confirm the constitutional nature of the current
Treaty structure. If this Constitution is ratified, the existing distinction
within the European Union between Community and non-Community
action will disappear (see Chapter 4).

I. THE ECSC TREATY

European Coal and Steel Community. On April 18, 1951 Belgium, France, **1–002**
Germany, Italy, Luxembourg and the Netherlands signed in Paris the
Treaty establishing the European Coal and Steel Community (ECSC

Treaty) for a period of 50 years (the ECSC entered into force on July 23, 1952 and came to an end on July 23, 2002).[1] The six ECSC Member States agreed to transfer the administration of two basic industries to an independent supranational institution, the High Authority, which was empowered to take decisions binding both on the Member States and on coal and steel undertakings. By accepting joint administration of sectors of their national economies, those States went further than the international consultation which had previously taken place within the Council of Europe (see para. 2–003). This new form of co-operation was referred to from the outset as "supranational" (see para. 1–013 *et seq.*).

1–003 Functional approach. The ECSC was based on a functional approach to the process of European integration which set specific aims and transferred genuine legislative power to the Community in designated fields in order to achieve them. The ECSC Treaty established a common market in coal and steel by abolishing and prohibiting within the Community all import and export duties and charges having equivalent effect and, likewise, all quantitative restrictions on the movement of products, together with all measures discriminating between producers, purchasers or consumers or interfering with the purchaser's free choice of supplier. Under the provisions of the Treaty, State aid and restrictive practices were prohibited. The ECSC institutions were given the task of ensuring an orderly supply to the market, equal access to sources of production, the lowest possible prices, the encouragement of more efficient and modernised production and resource utilisation, improved working conditions and the growth of international trade.[2]

The plan of commencing by pooling the coal and steel sectors came from the French Foreign Minister Robert Schuman, who, on May 9, 1950, launched an idea that had earlier been conceived by Jean Monnet, a senior French civil servant. It satisfied the French Government's concern to avoid a third resurgence of the German war machine and, at the same time, sought to reinforce the political clout of the western European States in the face of Soviet expansionism in central and eastern Europe.[3] Other European States did not respond to the invitation to attend the preparatory conference which opened in Paris on June 20, 1950. For the founding

---

[1] See Art. 97 of the ECSC Treaty. Upon the expiry of the Treaty, the net assets of the ECSC were earmarked for research in sectors related to the coal and steel industry; see the Protocol annexed to the EC Treaty by the Treaty of Nice [2001] O.J. C80/67 and Decision 2002/234/ECSC of the Representatives of the Governments of the Member States, meeting within the Council, of February 27, 2002 on the financial consequences of the expiry of the ECSC Treaty and on the research fund for coal and steel [2002] O.J. L79/42. See Obwexer, "Das Ende der Europäischen Gemeinschaft für Kohle und Stahl" (2002) Eu.Z.W. 517–524.

[2] For an evaluation of the extent to which these objectives were achieved, see Hosman, "Bij het afscheid van het EGKS-Verdrag: Droom en werkelijkheid" (2002) S.E.W. 134–144.

[3] For the background to the Schuman plan, see Kapteyn and VerLoren van Themaat, Gormley (ed.), *Introduction to the Law of the European Communities* (Kluwer Law International, London/The Hague, 1998), at 1–7.

fathers of the ECSC, this initiative constituted a first step in a process of integration which would develop further and was open to other States, as witness the recital in the preamble to the Treaty:

"recognising that *Europe* can be built only through practical achievements which will first of all create real solidarity, and through the establishment of common bases for economic development".[4]

ECSC Institutions. The ECSC Treaty was a textbook example of a **1–004** *traité-loi*. It contained virtually all the rules which the Member States deemed necessary for the smooth operation of a common market in the coal and steel sector. Since the Member States considered that their respective interests were sufficiently protected by the detailed Treaty provisions, they were prepared to place their confidence in an expert authority responsible for ensuring that those provisions were implemented. The Treaty therefore empowered a High Authority, composed of experts required to be independent *vis-à-vis* both the Member States and industry, to take binding decisions and make recommendations.[5]

The Treaty further set up a Special Council of Ministers, composed of representatives of the Member States, which was responsible for harmonising the action of the High Authority with the general economic policies of the Member States. The Contracting Parties limited the High Authority's autonomous power to take decisions to matters already extensively regulated by the Treaty and created a regulatory interaction between the High Authority and the Council where more fundamental political and economic options—often in specified circumstances—were to be decided upon.[6]

The ECSC Treaty also set up two supervisory institutions, a Common Assembly, composed of representatives from the national parliaments, and a Court of Justice which was given the task of ensuring that "in the interpretation and application of this Treaty, and of the rules laid down for the implementation thereof, the law is observed".[7]

---

[4] Emphasis supplied. This echoes the Schuman Declaration of May 9, 1950, "Europe will not be made all at once, or according to a single plan. It will be built upon concrete achievements which first create a de facto solidarity". See Fontaine, *Europe—A Fresh Start. The Schuman Declaration 1950–90* (Office for Official Publications of the European Communities, Luxembourg, 1990), at 44; Patijn, *Landmarks in European Unity* (Sijthoff, Leiden, 1970), at 46; *Selection of Texts concerning Institutional Matters of the Community from 1950–1982* (European Parliament Committee on Institutional Affairs, Luxembourg, 1982), at 47.

[5] ECSC Treaty, Arts 8 and 14.

[6] See, on the one hand, Art. 26 and, on the other, Arts 85 and 95, first para., of the ECSC Treaty. For a retrospective look at the application of those provisions, see Meunier, "La Communauté européenne du charbon et de l'acier est morte, vive la fédération européenne!" (2001) R.M.C.U.E. 509–515.

[7] See ECSC Treaty, Arts 24 and 31.

II. THE EEC TREATY AND THE EAEC TREATY

1–005 Spaak Report. The success of the ECSC initially led to plans to bring political matters, such as defence and foreign policy, also under the umbrella of a supranational organisation but, following the failure of the European Defence Community (see para. 2–005), the advocates of European integration switched to a more realistic economic and social approach. Starting from a plan which had been put forward by the Dutch Foreign Minister Johan Willem Beyen, the Benelux countries proposed establishing a common market and co–ordinating policy decisions relating to market support.

By the Resolution of Messina of June 2, 1955, the Member States subscribed to these proposals and charged an intergovernmental committee, chaired by the Belgian Foreign Minister Paul-Henri Spaak, with working out the still embryonic ideas. The Spaak Report amounted to an all-embracing programme for the establishment of a common market, which was too detailed to be enshrined in a treaty. The resultant broad substantive approach made it necessary to rethink the regulatory process capable of reacting to economic and social developments.

1–006 European Economic Community. The Treaty establishing the European Economic Community (EEC Treaty), which was signed in Rome on March 25, 1957 and entered into force on January 1, 1958,[8] took over the substantive aims and institutional structure proposed in the Spaak Report. The preamble and Arts 2 and 3 of the EEC Treaty set forth the objectives contemplated by the Contracting Parties. Article 2 of the EEC Treaty announces ambitious aims to be achieved through the establishment of a common market and the progressive approximation of the Member States' economic policies.[9] Article 3 of the EEC Treaty specifies those objectives by listing the tasks of the Community.

First, Art. 3 of the EEC Treaty looks forward to the achievement of four economic freedoms. Free movement of goods, persons, services, and capital (including payments) form the pillars on which the common market is based.[10] The "activities of the Community" also include "the approximation

---

[8] Art.8 of the Treaty on European Union of February 7, 1992 amended the Treaty establishing the European Economic Community so as to establish a European Community (EC). The abbreviation "EEC" is therefore used in this work only where express reference is made to the original EEC Treaty.

[9] Four of the dynamically formulated aims are of an economic and social nature—(1) harmonious development of economic activities throughout the Community, (2) continuous and balanced expansion, (3) an increase in stability, and (4) an accelerated raising of the standard of living—, whilst the fifth is simply a policy of seeking "closer relations between the States belonging to [the Community]".

[10] Free movement of goods (EEC Treaty, Arts 9–37) forms, together with free movement of persons, services and capital (EEC Treaty, Arts 48–73), the common agricultural policy (EEC Treaty, Arts 38–47) and the common transport policy (EEC Treaty, Arts 74–84), the "foundations of the Community" (Part Two of the EEC Treaty).

of the laws of Member States to the extent required for the proper functioning of the common market"[11] and "the establishment of a common customs tariff and of a common commercial policy towards third countries".[12] In order to prevent undertakings and Member States from frustrating the common market, free competition was to be secured.[13] Art. 3 further provides for the adoption of common policies in the spheres of agriculture and transport. Lastly, Art. 3 makes provision for the coordination of the Member States' economic policies.[14]

European Atomic Energy Community. At the same time as the EEC **1–007** Treaty, the Treaty establishing a European Atomic Energy Community (EAEC) was signed. It also entered into force on January 1, 1958. Its aim is to create the conditions necessary for the speedy establishment and growth of nuclear industries. To this end, Art. 2 of the EAEC Treaty provided for common policies on research, safety standards, investment and installations, supplies of ores and fuels, application of the nuclear industry, right of ownership in fissile materials and international relations in the field of nuclear energy, and introduced a common market.[15]

Traité-cadre. Since in principle[16] the EEC Treaty covers all sectors of the **1–008** economy and seeks to attain the chosen policy objectives progressively, it was impossible to lay down the requisite rules of law exhaustively in the Treaty itself. Accordingly, it is not a *traité-loi* but a *traité-cadre* containing provisions relating to the functioning of the institutions and decision-making, alongside basic substantive rules which have to be complied with by the Community and the Member States. Within the framework of the EEC Treaty—and pursuant thereto—a substantial corpus of rules has since been formulated, with the result that it may be said to be a *traité-fondation*[17] or a *traité-constitution* (see para. 1–020).

The EAEC Treaty does not embody the detailed market rules of the ECSC Treaty, but does share that Treaty's sectoral approach.

---

[11] See EEC Treaty, Arts 99–102.

[12] See the section "Setting up of the common customs tariff" (EEC Treaty, Arts 18–29) in the title on the free movement of goods and the chapter entitled "Commercial policy" (EEC Treaty, Arts 110–116) in the title on the economic policy of the Community.

[13] See EEC Treaty, Arts 85–98.

[14] This relates to conjunctural policy (EEC Treaty, Art. 103) and balance of payments (EEC Treaty, Arts 104–109). "Social policy" (EEC Treaty, Arts 117–122) is not mentioned as such in Art. 3, although it does refer to the "creation of a European Social Fund" (EEC Treaty, Arts 123–128) and to the "establishment of a European Investment Bank" (EEC Treaty, Arts 129 and 130). The last "activity of the Community" set out in Art. 3 is "association of the overseas countries and territories" (EEC Treaty, Arts 131–136).

[15] For a good description of the EAEC Treaty, see Cusak, "A Tale of Two Treaties: An Assessment of the Euratom Treaty in Relation to the EC Treaty" (2003) C.M.L.R. 117–142.

[16] See the discussion of Art. 305 of the EC Treaty, paras 1–011 and 15–015, *infra*.

[17] Lesguillons, *L'application d'un traité-fondation: le traité instituant la C.E.E.* (Librairie Générale de Droit et de Jurisprudence, Paris, 1968), 320 pp.

1–009 EEC and EAEC Institutions. The institutional structure of the EEC and the EAEC also consists of a Commission (the equivalent of the ECSC High Authority), a Council, an Assembly and a Court of Justice.[18] The parallel with the ECSC Treaty, however, does not extend any further than the organisational level, as the extensive programme to be achieved by the establishment of the EEC and the EAEC necessitated other roles for the institutions with decision-making powers.

The hub of the decision-making process was located in the Council. The Member States did not wish to vest any legislative powers in the Commission, because substantive policy choices had often been deliberately left open in the EEC Treaty. The ultimate policy choices were therefore to be determined by the Member States, within the Council. For those reasons, too, the role of the Assembly was not extended either.

The Commission's task, in principle at least, was confined to making proposals, implementing legislation and supervising compliance with Community law. The denial of legislative power to the Commission was also partly determined by the fact that it had no direct democratic legitimacy in any shape or form. In fact, compared with the Commission, the Council was a more democratic institution, given that it consisted of representatives of elected governments.

1–010 Subsequent Treaty amendments. The Community's objectives and competences laid down in the EEC Treaty have been supplemented by the Single European Act (SEA), the EU Treaty and the Treaty of Amsterdam. In contrast, the objectives and competences of the ECSC and the EAEC remained unchanged.

The Single European Act was signed by the Member States on February 17 and 28, 1986 (see para. 3–006). It conferred new competences on the Community,[19] but did not alter the general objectives of the Community (EEC Treaty, Art. 2) or the list of the Community's tasks (EEC Treaty, Art. 3). In addition, the SEA looked forward to the completion of the common market by adding an Art. 8a, which heralded the achievement by December 31, 1992 of an "internal market", defined as "an area without internal frontiers in which the free movement of goods, persons, services and capital is ensured in accordance with the provisions of this Treaty" (see now EC Treaty, Art. 14). At the institutional level, the SEA made decision-taking more flexible by introducing qualified majority voting in the Council.

---

[18] From the outset the latter two institutions were "common" to the three Communities (para. 1–011, *infra*).

[19] The most important areas entrusted to the Community by the SEA are: (1) increased Community competence with regard to social policy (EEC Treaty, Arts 118a and 118b); (2) economic and social cohesion (EEC Treaty, Arts 130a–130e); (3) research and technological development (EEC Treaty, Arts 130f–130q) and (4) the environment (EEC Treaty, Arts 130r–130t).

The introduction of the co-operation procedure (EEC Treaty, Art. 149, second para.; now EC Treaty, Art. 252) made for increased involvement of the Assembly, henceforward referred to in the Treaty as the European Parliament.

The Treaty on European Union of February 7, 1992 (EU Treaty; see para. 3–011) extended the sphere of action of the Community to such an extent that the title "European Economic Community" was replaced by "European Community". The competences of the Community were considerably enlarged, also outside the economic sphere.[20] What attracted the most attention was the decision to introduce, starting in 1997 and by no later than January 1, 1999, an economic and monetary union between Member States fulfilling the necessary conditions for the adoption of a single currency.[21] At the same time, the actual objectives of the Community were extended for the first time by expanding Arts 2 and 3 of the EC Treaty and introducing an Art. 3a (now EC Treaty, Arts 2, 3 and 4; see paras 5–003–5–004). At the institutional level, the EU Treaty advanced further into the territory opened up by the Single European Act. On the one hand, the EU Treaty further extended the scope of qualified majority voting in the Council.[22] On the other, further steps were taken to give the European Parliament a greater say in the legislative process, in particular through the introduction of a co-decision procedure (EC Treaty, Art. 189b, now Art. 251) and more extensive application of the co-operation procedure and procedures requiring the Parliament to give its assent or to deliver advisory opinions.[23]

---

[20] The EU Treaty conferred competence on the European Community with regard to (1) citizenship of the Union (EC Treaty, Arts 8–8e, now Arts 17–22); (2) common policy on visas (EC Treaty, Art. 100c, now repealed); (3) economic and monetary policy (EC Treaty, Arts 102a–109m, now Arts 98–124); (4) education (EC Treaty, Art. 126, now Art. 149); (5) culture (EC Treaty, Art. 128, now Art. 151); (6) public health (EC Treaty, Art. 129, now Art.152); (7) consumer protection (EC Treaty, Art. 129a, now Art. 153); (8) trans-European networks (EC Treaty, Arts 129b–129d, now Arts 154–156); (9) industry (EC Treaty, Art.130, now Art. 157); (10) development co-operation (EC Treaty, Arts 130u–130y, now Arts 177–181) and (11) extended powers in the social policy sphere as a result of the "Protocol on social policy", with the same status as the EC Treaty, and the "Agreement on social policy concluded between the Member States of the European Community with the exception of the United Kingdom of Great Britain and Northern Ireland" to which the Social Protocol refers. In addition, the EU Treaty clarified and extended the scope of existing Community powers under the original EEC Treaty and as added by the Single European Act. See Art. 127 (vocational training, now Art. 150), Arts 130a–130e (economic and social cohesion, now Arts 158–162), Arts 130f–130p (research and technological development, now Arts 163–173) and Arts 130r–130t (environment, now Arts 174–176) of the EC Treaty. See Lane, "New Community Competences under the Maastricht Treaty" (1993) C.M.L.R. 939–979.

[21] EC Treaty, Art. 109j [now Art. 121](3) and (4).

[22] See para. 14–011, *infra*.

[23] See EC Treaty, Art. 192, first para., for this enumeration (para. 14–020, *infra*). It is also noteworthy that the practice by which the nominated President and other Members of the Commission collectively are to be subject to a vote of approval by the European Parliament was enshrined in the Treaty (EC Treaty, Art. 214(2)).

The Treaty of Amsterdam of October 2, 1997 (see para. 3–011) further supplemented the objectives of the Community (see para. 5–003–5–004) and conferred some new areas of competence on it.[24]

Only limited changes were made to the institutional structure of the Community. The Amsterdam Treaty also simplified the three Community Treaties, most conspicuously by renumbering the articles of the EC Treaty.[25]

The Treaty of Nice of February 26, 2001 (see para. 3–022 *et seq.*) had the aim of further reforming the institutions with a view to enlargement. To this end, it adapted the composition of the Commission, the weighting of votes in the Council and the structure of the Court of Justice.

III. THE ORGANISATIONAL UNITY OF THE COMMUNITY TREATIES

1–011 Unity of the Communities. In principle, the broad field of competence of the EC Treaty also embraces the coal and steel and atomic energy sectors. Consequently, Art. 305 of the EC Treaty governs the interrelationship between that treaty and the EAEC Treaty and, before July 23, 2002, between the EC Treaty and the ECSC Treaty (see para. 17–059).

The differences between the Community Treaties in terms of the powers of the institutions and their substantive provisions are not reflected at the organisational level, since the institutions which each Treaty brought into being in parallel have been merged. Accordingly, the same institutions exercise different powers under each of the Treaties. This may be termed the organisational unity and functional diversity of the Communities.

As long ago as when the EEC Treaty and the EAEC Treaty came into being, the Member States concluded the Convention on certain institutions common to the European Communities.[26] That convention provided that there should be one Parliament and one Court of Justice serving the three Communities in accordance with the powers conferred on those institutions by the different Treaties (Convention, Arts 1–2 and 3–4). At the same time

---

[24] The areas of competence taken up in the EC Treaty are visas, asylum, immigration and other policies related to free movement of persons (Arts 61–69), employment (Arts 125–130) and customs co-operation (Art.135). At the same time, the powers conferred by the Social Protocol and the Social Agreement (n.20, *supra*) were incorporated into the EC Treaty (Arts 136–143) in place of the former Treaty provisions on social policy. See Golsalbo Bono, "Le Traité d'Amsterdam. Les politiques et actions communautaires" (1997) R.T.D.E. 769–800. Remarkably enough, the Amsterdam Treaty even made a minor amendment to the preamble of the EC Treaty (introduction of a recital concerning education, see para. 5–239, *infra*).

[25] See para. 3–021, *infra*.

[26] [1967] O.J. 152/5. Not printed in the English Special Edition of the O.J.; for the English text, see *European Union. Selected instruments taken from the Treaties*, Book I, Vol. I (Office for Official Publications of the European Communities, Luxembourg, 1995), at 683 *et seq.*

it was provided that one Economic and Social Committee was to perform such tasks as the EEC Treaty and the EAEC Treaty conferred on it (Convention, Art. 5). The Treaty establishing a Single Council and a Single Commission of the European Communities, known as the Merger Treaty, which was concluded on April 8, 1965 and entered into effect on July 1, 1967, was a further step in that direction.[27] The Council and the Commission continued to play the roles specifically ascribed to them by the various treaties. In addition, the Merger Treaty unified the Staff Regulations (Art. 24) and laid down the principle that there should be a single budget of the European Communities (Art. 20). According to its preamble, the Merger Treaty was intended to "effect the unification of the three Communities", but did not itself lead to that outcome (see also Art. 32(1)).[28]

The Convention and the Merger Treaty were repealed by Art. 9 of the Treaty of Amsterdam, although the aforementioned institutional arrangements still stand.[29]

Community law. Notwithstanding the incomplete nature of the Merger **1–012** Treaty and, consequently, the continued existence of separate Communities, the Court of Justice has consistently emphasised the connection between the Community Treaties.

For the sake of the coherence of Community law, the Court of Justice, when interpreting a provision of one of the Treaties, often looks to the other Treaties for assistance. Having regard to the single nature of the institutions the Court of Justice has interpreted the institutional provisions of the various Treaties in conjunction with each other, where necessary, reconciling them (see para. 17–059). In this way, the Treaties constitute the foundation of "Community law", which additionally consists of the legislative and implementing measures adopted on the basis of the Treaties and the judicial interpretation of those provisions, supplemented by the unwritten general principles of superior law.

IV. THE SUPRANATIONAL CHARACTER OF COMMUNITY LAW

Supranational organisation. The European Communities constitute an **1–013** "international" organisation since they stem from treaties concluded

---

[27] [1967] O.J. 152/2. Not printed in the English Special Edition of the O.J.; for the English text, see *European Union. Selected instruments taken from the Treaties* (see preceding n.) at 697 *et seq.*

[28] Linthorst Homan, "The Merger of the European Communities" (1965–66) C.M.L.R. 397–419; Bleckmann, "Die Einheit der Europäischen Gemeinschaftsrechtsordnung. Einheit oder Mehrheit der Europäischen Gemeinschaften" (1978) EuR. 95–104. As regards the merger idea, see also: Van Stempel, "Die Fusion der Organe der Europäischen Gemeinschaften", in Hallstein and Schlochauer (eds), *Zur Integration Europas. Festschrift für C.F. Ophüls* (Müller, Karlsruhe, 1965), at 229–241.

[29] Amsterdam Treaty, Art. 9(1), (2) and (3).

between sovereign States. As subjects of law, the Communities act *vis-à-vis* non-member countries in accordance with the rules of international law (see para. 19–002). In contrast, relations between Member States (within the field of application of Community law) and between Member States and the Communities are no longer governed by international law.[30] Community law governs the whole set of relationships between Member States, Community institutions and individuals in a "supranational" context,[31] of which the principal characteristics are as follows:

(a) the Community has institutions which act independently of the Member States in terms of their composition and manner of operation;

(b) the Community may take decisions by a majority, yet they will bind all the Member States;

(c) the institutions of the Community implement those decisions or are responsible for supervising that they are properly implemented by the Member States; and

(d) the founding treaty and decisions of the Community may give rise to rights and obligations on the part of individuals which are directly enforceable by courts in the Member States, even in the presence of conflicting provisions of national law.[32]

Consequently, the term "supranationalism" fits the *sui generis* nature of the European Communities perfectly. Nevertheless, it is useful to consider each of the above factors in more detail with a view to distinguishing more clearly from the Communities as such the other forms of international co-operation which have helped to shape European integration. In addition, those factors express the dynamic nature of the integration process which is taking place within the Communities.[33]

---

[30] See the different interpretation given by the Court of Justice to provisions of the EC Treaty and corresponding provisions of international agreements concluded by the Community on the basis of the more extensive objectives of the EC Treaty, the specific characteristics of decision-making within the Community and the possibilities of enforcing Community law: ECJ, Case 270/80 *Polydor* [1982] E.C.R. 329, paras 14–20; Opinion 1/91 *Draft agreement between the Community, on the one hand, and the countries of the European Free Trade Association, on the other, relating to the creation of the European Economic Area* [1991] E.C.R. I–6079, paras 13–21. For the EEA Agreement, see also para. 23–008, *infra*.

[31] The origin, meaning and application of the term "supranationality" are discussed extensively in von Lindeiner-Wildau, *La supranationalité en tant que principe de droit* (Sijthoff, Leiden, 1970), 178 pp.

[32] *cf., ibid.*, at 45–61; Schermers and Blokker, *International Institutional Law*, (Martinus Nijhoff, The Hague, 1995), para. 61, at 41–42 (who mentions, as additional requirements for supranational organisations, that the organisation should be financially independent and that participating States must have the approval of all the States and the supranational institutions in order to leave the organisation, wind it up or change its powers); Hay, *Federalism and Supranational Organisations, Patterns for New Legal Structures* (University of Illinois Press, Urbana/London, 1966), at 30–34 (who sets out additional political qualifications, such as the compass of the organisation's powers).

[33] Weiler,"The Community System: the Dual Character of Supranationalism" (1981) Y.E.L. 267–306.

(a) Independent institutions. The authentic French version of the ECSC **1–014** Treaty used the term "supranational" in referring to the independent status of the High Authority (the Commission).[34] As a result, the Commission is not made up of representatives of the governments of the Member States in the traditional manner of international institutions, as is still the case with the Council. Members of the European Parliament, the Court of Justice and the Court of Auditors are also independent of the governments of the Member States. In addition, the European Parliament is the only institution whose Members are not appointed by the national governments (or the Council) but directly elected.[35]

(b) Autonomous decision-making. In international law, there is a principle **1–015** of decision-making that States cannot be bound against their will. Although that principle is reflected in the contractual nature of the Treaties underlying the Communities and in the requirement that certain votes in the Council have to be unanimous, in many respects it does not apply in the Community legal order. In numerous cases a majority decision of the Council binds all Member States. In addition, the Court rejects the technique of international law whereby a State may enter a "reservation" when a decision is taken and so avoid being bound by a provision of a treaty or a decision. The Court stresses that measures of the Communities cannot be regarded as international agreements because of the independent institutional framework within which they are drawn up.[36] It further emphasises that the rules laid down by the common institutions must be interpreted in a uniform manner. That requirement would be detracted from if Community law were to take account of reservations or objections entered by Member States at the preparatory stage.[37]

(c) Implementation of decisions. Member States of the Communities must **1–016** take all necessary measures to ensure fulfilment of the obligations arising for them under Community law (EC Treaty, Art. 10; see para. 5–047). They are generally charged with implementing Community law, unless implementation is specifically entrusted to an institution of the Communities (see para. 14–046). Under Community law, Member States are subject to more far-reaching supervision than is generally the case under international law. Thus, the *exceptio non adimpleti contractus* (the

---

[34] See the original fifth and sixth paras of Art. 9 of the ECSC Treaty (removed by Art. 19 of the Merger Treaty and replaced by Art. 10 of that Treaty, the wording of which was introduced as the new Art. 9 of the ECSC Treaty by Art. 9(2) of the EU Treaty). For an earlier use of the term and for its intentional omission from the EEC and EAEC Treaties, see Hay (n.32, *supra*), at 29–30; Jaenicke, "Die Supranationalität der Europäischen Gemeinschaften", *Zur Integration Europas. Festschrift für C.F. Ophüls* (n.28, *supra*), 85, at 88.
[35] See para. 10–022, *infra*.
[36] ECJ, Case 38/69 *Commission v Italy* [1970] E.C.R. 47, paras 10–11.
[37] ECJ, Case 143/83 *Commission v Denmark* [1985] E.C.R. 427, paras 12–13 (para. 17–144, *infra*).

defence of a material breach of a treaty)[38] used in international law is not employed as a mechanism for enforcing reciprocal obligations; Community law has procedures of its own for determining infringements and imposing sanctions therefor.[39] The jurisdiction of the Court of Justice is compulsory and its judgments are binding throughout the Community. In contrast, within the international legal order, the International Court of Justice adjudicates only if there is voluntary—general or specific—acceptance of the court's jurisdiction on the part of the parties.

1–017 (d) Separate legal order. In common with every international organisation, the Communities constitute a legal order in their own right.[40] The Member States brought that legal order into being and at the same time limited their sovereignty:

> "[b]y creating a Community of unlimited duration, having its own institutions, its own personality, its own legal capacity and capacity of representation on the international plane and, more particularly, real powers [as a result of the Member States' having limited their own powers or transferred them to the Communities]".[41]

The essential characteristics of the Community legal order include the fact that individuals can rely in legal proceedings on a series of provisions of Community law and the primacy of Community law over the law of the Member States.[42] The Court of Justice established those basic principles in 1963 and 1964 in two ground-breaking judgments.[43]

---

[38] See Art. 60 of the Vienna Convention of May 23, 1969 on the Law of Treaties (for that Convention, see para. 17–103, *infra*).

[39] ECJ, Joined Cases 90 and 91/63 *Commission v Luxembourg and Belgium* [1964] E.C.R. 625, at 631–632; ECJ, Case C–5/94 *Hedley Lomas* [1996] E.C.R. I–2553, para. 20; ECJ, Case C–11/95 *Commission v Belgium* [1996] E.C.R. I–4115, paras 37–39; ECJ, Case C–14/96 *Denuit* [1997] E.C.R. I–2785, paras 34–35. Under Art. 292 of the EC Treaty, Member States must submit any dispute concerning the interpretation or application of the Treaty to the methods of resolution provided for therein.

[40] With a view to the coherence of Community law (para. 1–012, *supra*), the Community legal order is based on the three Treaties establishing the Communities, together with the annexes and protocols appended thereto, which form an integral part of them (ECSC Treaty, Art. 84; EC Treaty, Art. 311; EAEC Treaty, Art. 207), and the various treaties which have amended the founding treaties. See Louis, *The Community Legal Order* (3rd ed., Commission of the EC, Office for Official Publications, Brussels, 1995), 247 pp.

[41] ECJ, Case 6/64 *Costa* [1964] E.C.R. 585, at 593. Whereas that judgment and the judgment in *Van Gend & Loos* (para. 1–018, *infra*) refer to a limitation of sovereignty "within limited fields", Opinion 1/91 speaks of a limitation of sovereign rights "in ever wider fields": ECJ, Opinion 1/91 *Draft agreement between the Community, on the one hand, and the countries of the European Free Trade Association, on the other, relating to the creation of the European Economic Area* [1991] E.C.R. I–6079, para. 21.

[42] ECJ, Opinion 1/91, *ibid*.

[43] See, among others, Lecourt, "Quel eût été le droit des Communautés sans les arrêts de 1963 et 1964?", *L'Europe et le Droit, Mélanges en hommage à J. Boulouis*, Paris, Dalloz, 1991, at 349–361.

Rights for individuals. In *Van Gend & Loos*, the Court held for the first **1–018** time that Community law not only imposes obligations on individuals but is also intended to confer upon them "rights which become part of their legal heritage".[44] In so doing, it referred to "the spirit, the general scheme and the wording" of the EEC Treaty. The Court first considered that "[t]he objective of the EEC Treaty, which is to establish a Common Market, the functioning of which is of direct concern to interested parties in the Community, implies that this Treaty is more than an agreement which merely creates mutual obligations between the contracting States". The Court averred that this "view" was "confirmed" by "the preamble to the Treaty which refers not only to governments but to peoples" and "more specifically by the establishment of institutions endowed with sovereign rights, the exercise of which affects Member States and also their citizens". Two further *indicia* led the Court to conclude that "the Community constitutes a new legal order of international law for the benefit of which the States have limited their sovereign rights, albeit within limited fields, and the subjects of which comprise not only Member States but also their nationals". The first was the fact that "the nationals of the States brought together in the Community are called upon to cooperate in the functioning of this Community through the intermediary of the European Parliament and the Economic and Social Committee". The second was that "the task assigned to the Court of Justice under Article 177 [now Art. 234], the object of which is to secure uniform interpretation of the Treaty by national courts and tribunals, confirms that the States have acknowledged that Community law has an authority which can be invoked by their nationals before those courts and tribunals".

Van Gend & Loos had to come to terms with the view then held by the Member States that Community law constituted a form of international law and, accordingly, that only subjects of that law could take the initiative of seeking a declaration that the agreed rules had been breached. Van Gend & Loos, a Dutch company, had brought an action in the competent national court in which it sought to recover an import duty which it considered that the Netherlands tax authorities had charged contrary to (the former) Art. 12 of the EEC Treaty. The national court made a reference for a preliminary ruling on the interpretation of Art. 12, pursuant to what is now Art. 234 of the EC Treaty. The Belgian, Netherlands and German Governments argued before the Court that the reference was not concerned with the interpretation of the Treaty but with a Member State's compliance therewith. They contended that the Court could declare that national legislation was contrary to the Treaty only through the proper procedures provided for in Arts 226 and 227 of the EC Treaty. The Court's response was to hold that the fact that Arts 226 and 227 of the EC Treaty enabled the Commission and the Member States to bring an action did not

---

[44] ECJ, Case 26/62 *Van Gend & Loos* [1963] E.C.R. 1, at 12–13.

mean that individuals could not plead a Member State's infringement of Community law before a national court, which might result in a question being referred for an interpretation of Community law. The Court held that "[t]he vigilance of individuals concerned to protect their rights amounts to an effective supervision in addition to the supervision entrusted by Articles 169 and 170 [now Arts 226 and 227] to the diligence of the Commission and the Member States".

Consequently, the individual legal subject enforces his or her Community rights through the national courts which, in accordance with Art. 234 of the EC Treaty (or Art. 150 of the EAEC Treaty), "co-operate" with the Court of Justice with the aim of ensuring that Community law is applied in a uniform manner in all the Member States.[45] In this way, the Treaties establish a complete system of legal remedies in order to secure compliance with Community law by Community institutions, Member States and individuals.[46]

1-019 **Primacy of Community law.** Among the various legal orders which have been established by treaty, the Community legal order is special inasmuch as it takes away from Member States the freedom to determine the position of Community law *vis-à-vis* domestic law. National courts and tribunals are automatically required to apply Community law in the context of the national legal system. In the leading case of *Costa v ENEL* the Court inferred from "the integration into the laws of each Member State of provisions which derive from the Community, and more generally the terms and the spirit of the Treaty" that it is "impossible for the States, as a corollary, to accord precedence to a unilateral and subsequent measure over a legal system accepted by them on a basis of reciprocity".[47]

The Court was answering a preliminary question from an Italian court concerning the compatibility with the EEC Treaty of an Italian law of December 6, 1962 nationalising the electricity industry. The Italian Government submitted written observations to the Court in which it argued that the national court had no jurisdiction to make a reference under Art. 234 of the EC Treaty, because it was obliged to apply the national law. The Court rejected that argument on the ground that to take such a view would deprive the law stemming from the Treaty of its character as Community law and call in question the legal basis of the Community itself. "The executive force of Community law cannot vary from one State to another in

---

[45] ECJ, Case 16/65 *Schwarze* [1965] E.C.R. 877, at 886; ECJ, Case C–221/88 *Busseni* [1990] E.C.R. I–495, para. 13 (extension of co-operation under Art. 234 of the EC Treaty and Art.150 of the EAEC Treaty to preliminary rulings pursuant to Art. 41 of the ECSC Treaty). See, in addition, Lenaerts, "Form and Substance of the Preliminary Rulings Procedure" in Curtin and Heukels (eds), *Institutional Dynamics of European Integration Essays in Honour of Henry G. Schermers* Vol.II (Martinus Nijhoff, Dordrecht, 1994), at 355–380.
[46] ECJ, Case 294/83 *Les Verts v European Parliament* [1986] E.C.R. 1339, para. 23.
[47] ECJ, Case 6/64 *Costa v ENEL* [1964] E.C.R. 585, at 593–594.

deference to subsequent domestic laws, without jeopardising the attainment of the objectives of the Treaty set out in Article 5(2) [of the EEC Treaty, now Article 10 of the EC Treaty] and giving rise to the discrimination prohibited by Article 7 [now Art. 12]". The Court concluded from this that, if Member States were entitled to renounce their obligations unilaterally, those obligations would be merely contingent and the authorisation provisions which enable a Member State to derogate from the Treaty in particular cases would lose their purpose. Lastly, the Court expressed the view that "the precedence of Community law is confirmed by Article 189 [now Art. 249], whereby a regulation 'shall be binding' and 'directly applicable in the Member States' ".

Constitutional basis. As a result of its complete system of legal remedies, **1–020** the Community is a community based on the rule of law, whose foundation is the "constitutional charter" constituted by the Treaties.[48] For this reason, the texts of the Treaties are described as the constitution of the Communities[49] and the Court of Justice as a constitutional court.[50] The "constitutional law" of the European Communities consists of all the rules of Community law relating to the general objectives, the allocation of competences and the way in which the legislative, executive and judicial functions are performed within the Community. In view of the supranational character of the Communities, Community law employs concepts taken from international law[51] and national constitutional law,[52] in

---

[48] ECJ, Case 294/83 *Les Verts v European Parliament* [1986] E.C.R. 1339, para. 23; ECJ, Opinion 1/91 *Draft agreement between the Community, on the one hand, and the countries of the European Free Trade Association, on the other, relating to the creation of the European Economic Area* [1991] E.C.R. I–6079, para. 21 ("the EEC Treaty, albeit concluded in the form of an international agreement, none the less constitutes the constitutional charter of a Community based on the rule of law").

[49] Stein, "Lawyers, Judges, and the Making of a Transnational Constitution" (1981) A.J.I.L. 1–27; Hartley, "Federalism, Courts and Legal Systems: The Emerging Constitution of the European Community" (1986) A.J.C.L. 229–247; Ipsen, "Europäische Verfassung—Nationale Verfassung" (1987) EuR. 195–213; Lenaerts, *Le juge et la constitution aux Etats-Unis d'Amérique et dans l'ordre juridique européen* (Bruylant, Brussels, 1988), paras 243–245, at 257–263; Mancini, "The Making of a Constitution for Europe" (1989) C.M.L.R. 595; Lenaerts, "Constitutionalism and the Many Faces of Federalism" (1990) A.J.C.L. 205–263; Gerkrath, *L'émergence d'un droit constitutionnel pour l'Europe* (Editions de l'Université de Bruxelles, Brussels, 1997), 425 pp.

[50] See Lenaerts, Arts and Maselis, *Procedural Law of the European Union*, Ch.1.

[51] See the temporal (paras 7–001 and 7–010) and territorial scope (paras 8–001 and 8–012) of the Treaties; the privileges and immunities of the Communities in the national systems (para. 10–114); the legal concept of the direct effect of Treaty provisions (para. 17–047); the status of international law in the Community legal order (paras 17–091–17–106); the position in international law of the Communities and the Union (paras 19–002–19–014).

[52] See, for instance, the allocation of the three classic functions of a State (paras 13–012–13–014); the distinction between legislation and the implementation of legislation (paras 14–002–14–004); democratic legitimacy (paras 16–004–16–006) and the role of the Parliament (paras 16–008–16–014); citizenship (paras 12–004–12–013); the principle of equal treatment (paras 5–056–5–064) and other general principles of law (paras 17–065–17–067) and fundamental rights (paras 17–073–17–075); the rules on public

particular the constitutional law of federal States.[53] The constitutional law *of the European Union* extends the analysis to cover the areas in which the Union does not act as the Community.[54] In order to clarify the constitutional elements of the supranational legal order and confer greater democratic legitimacy on them, the European Parliament prepared on its own motion a formal Constitution of the European Union (see para. 3–017). Constitutional questions were also raised in the Declaration adopted by the European Council of December 14 and 15, 2001 at Laeken. That declaration led to the convening of a "Convention". That Convention ultimately produced a Draft Treaty establishing a Constitution for Europe, which was submitted to the Intergovernmental Conference. In June 2004, agreement was found on a Treaty establishing a Constitution for Europe, which will be submitted for ratification by the Member States (see para. 4–001 *et seq.*).

V. THE ENLARGEMENT OF THE COMMUNITIES (AND THE EUROPEAN UNION)

1–021 Five waves of accessions. In the meantime, the number of Member States of the Communities has been enlarged on five occasions.[55] After the UK accession negotiations foundered in January 1963 on the veto of the French President, General de Gaulle, it was not until June 1970 that accession

---

funding (paras 10–117–10–120); the procedure for concluding international agreements (paras 21–003–21–021).

[53] See the discussion of exclusive and non-exclusive competence (paras 5–021–5–026); the principles of subsidiarity (paras 5–028–5–029) and proportionality (paras 5–036–5–037); the duty to co-operate in good faith (para. 5–047 *et seq.*); the allocation of powers of implementation (para. 14–046 *et seq.*); the primacy of Community law (para. 17–003 *et seq.*); the relationship between the external powers of the Community and those of the Member States (paras 20–036–20–037 and paras 21–016–21–018).

[54] See, for example, VerLoren van Themaat, "De constitutionele problematiek van een Europese politieke Unie" (1991) S.E.W. 436–454; Curtin, "The Constitutional Structure of the Union: A Europe of Bits and Pieces" (1993) C.M.L.R. 17–69; Pliakos, "La nature juridique de l'Union européenne" (1993) R.T.D.E. 187–224; Favret, "Le traité d'Amsterdam: une révision *a minima* de la 'charte constitutionnelle' de l'Union européenne" (1997) C.D.E. 555–605; Snyder, "General Course on Constitutional Law of the European Union", in European University Institute, *Collected Courses of the Academy of European Law* (1995 — Volume VI–1), (Nijhoff, Dordrecht, 1998), 41–155; Weiler, *The Constitution of Europe*, (Cambridge University Press, 1999), 364 pp.; Piris, "Does the European Union have a Constitution? Does it need one?" (1999) E.L.Rev. 557–585; Arnold, "European Constitutional Law: Some Reflections on a Concept that Emerged in the Second Half of the Twentieth Century" (1999) Tulane E. & Civ. L.F. 49–64; Rossi, " 'Constitutionalisation' de l'Union européenne et des droits fondamentaux" (2002) R.T.D.E. 27–52.

[55] Three times in accordance with the procedures provided for in Art. 98 of the ECSC Treaty, Art.237 of the EEC Treaty and Art. 205 of the EAEC Treaty and once in accordance with that set out in Art. 49 of the EU Treaty, which lays down a single procedure for accession to the European Union (para. 8–006 *et seq., infra*).

negotiations started up again with Denmark, Ireland, Norway and the United Kingdom. On January 22, 1972 the six Member States concluded with those four States an accession treaty and signed related documents setting out the conditions of accession.[56] France made ratification of the treaty conditional upon the result of a referendum, which was held on April 23, 1972. Accession was also approved by referendum in Ireland (May 10, 1972) and Denmark (October 2, 1972). Following the adverse outcome of a national referendum held on May 24–25, 1972 in Norway (53.6 per cent against accession), on January 1, 1973 only Denmark, Ireland and the United Kingdom acceded to the three Communities.[57]

On May 28, 1979 the nine Member States concluded an accession treaty with Greece,[58] resulting in the Hellenic Republic becoming a member of the Communities on January 1, 1981.

A third enlargement took place on January 1, 1986, when Portugal and Spain joined the Communities following signature of the accession treaty on June 12, 1985.[59]

---

[56] Treaty of January 22, 1972 between the Member States of the European Communities, the Kingdom of Denmark, Ireland, the Kingdom of Norway and the United Kingdom of Great Britain and Northern Ireland concerning the accession of the Kingdom of Denmark, Ireland, the Kingdom of Norway and the United Kingdom of Great Britain and Northern Ireland to the European Economic Community and to the European Atomic Energy Community, [1972] O.J. Spec. Ed. 5, and the appended Acts, Protocols, Exchanges of letters, Final Acts and Declarations. For the accession to the ECSC, see the Decision of the Council of the European Communities of January 22, 1972 concerning the accession of the Kingdom of Denmark, Ireland, the Kingdom of Norway and the United Kingdom of Great Britain and Northern Ireland to the European Coal and Steel Community, [1972] O.J. Spec. Ed. 12. The treaty obligations were incorporated into domestic law in the United Kingdom by the European Communities Act 1972.

[57] See the Decision of the Council of the European Communities of January 1, 1973 adjusting the documents concerning the accession of the new Member States to the European Communities, [1973] O.J. L2/1. EC membership was the subject of a referendum in the United Kingdom on June 5, 1975, where the result was in favour of that country's remaining in the European Communities. In a referendum held on February 23, 1982 the population of Greenland expressed the wish to leave the European Communities. This wish was subsequently carried out by an amendment to the Treaties (see para. 8–002).

[58] Treaty of May 28, 1979 between the Member States of the European Communities and the Hellenic Republic concerning the accession of the Hellenic Republic to the European Economic Community and the European Atomic Energy Community, [1979] O.J. L291/9, and the appended Acts, Protocols, Final Acts and Declarations; Decision of the Council of the European Communities of May 24, 1979 on the accession of the Hellenic Republic to the European Coal and Steel Community, [1979] O.J. L291/5; this was incorporated into domestic law in the United Kingdom by the European Communities (Greek Accession) Act 1979.

[59] Treaty of June 12, 1985 between the Member States of the European Communities and the Kingdom of Spain and the Portuguese Republic concerning the accession of the Kingdom of Spain and the Portuguese Republic to the European Economic Community and the European Atomic Energy Community, [1985] O.J. L302/9, and the appended Acts, Protocols, Final Acts and Declarations; Decision of the Council of the European Communities of June 11, 1985 on the accession of the Kingdom of Spain and the Portuguese Republic to the European Coal and Steel Community, [1985] O.J. L302/5; this was incorporated into domestic law in the United Kingdom by the European Communities (Spanish and Portuguese Accession) Act 1985.

Since the entry into force of the EU Treaty, States become members of the Communities by acceding to the European Union (see para. 8–006). Following the signature of the EU Treaty in 1991, it was agreed to deal with the applications to accede made by the States which, as members of the European Free Trade Area (EFTA), had signed the Agreement on the European Economic Area (EEA) (see para. 23–004). The negotiations which started in February 1993 with Austria, Finland and Sweden and in April 1993 with Norway resulted in the accession treaty signed in Corfu on June 24, 1994.[60] The accession was approved by referendum in Austria on June 12, 1994 (66.36 per cent in favour), in Finland on October 16, 1994 (56.9 per cent in favour) and in Sweden on November 13, 1994 (52.2 per cent in favour). Following another adverse referendum in Norway on November 27 and 28, 1994 (52.5 per cent against), on January 1, 1995, only Austria, Finland and Sweden acceded to the European Union (EU).[61]

The European Council considered that negotiations on additional accessions to the Union could not commence until after the conclusion of the Intergovernmental Conference scheduled to open in 1996.[62] In accordance with the decision taken by the European Council in Luxembourg on December 12 and 13, 1997, the enlargement process was started on March 30, 1998 with 10 central and eastern European States and Cyprus.[63] On March 31, 1998 accession negotiations were commenced with Cyprus, the Czech Republic, Estonia, Hungary, Poland and Slovenia and on February 15, 2000 also with Bulgaria, Latvia, Lithuania, Malta, Romania and Slovakia.[64] The negotiations resulted in the Accession Treaty signed in Athens on April 16, 2003 by the Member States and ten applicant Member

---

[60] Treaty of June 24, 1994 between the Member States of the European Union and the Kingdom of Norway, the Republic of Austria, the Republic of Finland and the Kingdom of Sweden concerning the accession of the Kingdom of Norway, the Republic of Austria, the Republic of Finland and the Kingdom of Sweden to the European Union, [1994] O.J. C241/9, and the Act concerning the conditions of accession of the Republic of Austria, the Republic of Finland and the Kingdom of Sweden and the adjustments to the Treaties on which the European Union is founded, *ibid.*, p.9, and the Final Act, [1994] O.J. C241/371 (title amended by Decision 95/1 (see following n.), ratified in the United Kingdom by the European Union (Accessions) Act 1994.

[61] Decision 95/1/EC, Euratom, ECSC of the Council of the European Communities of January 1, 1995 adjusting the instruments concerning the accession of new Member States to the European Union, [1995] O.J. L1/1. Further particulars may be found in Jorna, "The Accession Negotiations with Austria, Sweden, Finland and Norway: A Guided Tour" (1995) E.L.Rev. 131–158; Goebel, "The European Union Grows: The Constitutional Impact of the Accession of Austria, Finland and Sweden" (1995) Fordham I.L.J. 1092–1190.

[62] See the European Council held in Corfu on June 24–25, 1994 ((1994) 6 EU Bull. point I.13), the European Council held in Essen on December 9–10, 1994 ((1994) 12 EU Bull. point I.13) and the European Council held in Cannes on June 26–27, 1995 ((1995) 6 EU Bull. point I.12).

[63] See (1997) 12 EU Bull. point I.2–6 (European Council) and (1998) 3 EU Bull. point 1.3.49. In Malta the government formed after the elections on October 26, 1996 "froze" the Maltese application to accede (*Europe*, No. 6860, November 25/26, 1996, 2); at the end of 1998 the application was "reactivated".

[64] For the negotiations, see Ott and Inglis (eds.), *Handbook on European Enlargement—A Commentary on the Enlargement process* (T.M.C. Asser Press, The Hague, 2002), 1150 pp.

States (Cyprus, the Czech Republic, Estonia, Hungary, Latvia, Lithuania, Malta, Poland, Slovenia and the Slovak Republic).[65] Referendums were held on accession in nine of the applicant countries. Each of them was in favour of joining the European Union: Malta on March 8, 2003 (53.6 per cent in favour), Slovenia on March 23, 2003 (89.6 per cent in favour), Hungary on April 12, 2003 (83.8 per cent in favour), Lithuania on May 10 and 11, 2003 (91.1 per cent in favour), the Slovak Republic on May 16 and 17, 2003 (92.5 per cent in favour), Poland on June 7 and 8, 2003 (77.4 per cent in favour), the Czech Republic on June 13 and 14, 2003 (77.3 per cent in favour), Estonia on September 14, 2003 (66.9 per cent in favour) and Latvia on September 20, 2003 (67 per cent in favour). On May 1, 2004 these States acceded to the European Union, which now has 25 Member States. Negotiations are under way with Bulgaria and Romania with a view to their acceding in 2007 (see para. 8–011).

---

[65] Treaty of April 16, 2003 between the Member States of the European Union and the Czech Republic, the Republic of Estonia, the Republic of Cyprus, the Republic of Latvia, the Republic of Lithuania, the Republic of Hungary, the Republic of Malta, the Republic of Poland, the Republic of Slovenia, the Slovak Republic, concerning the accession of the Czech Republic, the Republic of Estonia, the Republic of Cyprus, the Republic of Latvia, the Republic of Lithuania, the Republic of Hungary, the Republic of Malta, the Republic of Poland, the Republic of Slovenia and the Slovak Republic to the European Union, [2003] O.J. L236/17, together with the Act concerning the conditions of accession of the Czech Republic, the Republic of Estonia, the Republic of Cyprus, the Republic of Latvia, the Republic of Lithuania, the Republic of Hungary, the Republic of Malta, the Republic of Poland, the Republic of Slovenia and the Slovak Republic and the adjustments to the Treaties on which the European Union is founded, [2003] O.J. L236/33, and the Final Act, [2003] O.J. L236/959. For some rectifications to the Treaty, see [2004] O.J. L126. The Treaty was ratified in the United Kingdom by the European Union (Accessions) Act 2003 (c.35).

CHAPTER 2

THE NON-COMMUNITY INTEGRATION PATH

Intergovernmental co-operation. The post-war history of European **2–001** integration is made up of a succession of co-operation groupings set up to prepare for, or in parallel to, integration in the context of the Communities. The adjective "intergovernmental" appropriately describes those forms of international co-operation. The international agreements involved are generally made between representatives of the executives or of the "governments" (hence "governmental") of the States party to them. Where an organisation is set up by such agreements, it will generally operate on the basis of the voluntary participation of government representatives.[1] This distinguishes intergovernmental organisations from supranational ones, which operate with (relatively) independent institutions and may take their decisions by majority vote. Although some intergovernmental organisations have parliamentary assemblies or committees of experts, they play a purely advisory role. In contradistinction to decisions taken within supranational organisations, decisions of intergovernmental organisations do not in principle have the force of law within national legal systems unless they are specifically adopted therein, and generally do not confer any rights on individuals.[2]

I. THE ESTABLISHMENT OF THE COUNCIL OF EUROPE

European integration. The idea of "European integration", which was **2–002** contemplated on several occasions even before the First World War and in

---

[1] For an overview, see Schraepler, *European Handbook of Organisations* (Whurr, London, 1993), 177 pp.; Oschinsky and Jenard, *L'espace juridique et judiciaire européen* (Bruylant, Brussels, 1993), 860 pp. See also Schiavone, *International organisations. A Dictionary and Directory* (Macmillan, London, 1997), 350 pp. For an assessment of intergovernmental forms of co-operation in the light of experience of international organisations, see VerLoren van Themaat, "The Dialectic Relationship between Institutional Law and Substantive Tasks in and after the Treaty of Maastricht: Some Lessons from Henry G. Schermers and from Jean Monnet", in Curtin and Heukels (eds), *Institutional Dynamics of European Integration. Essays in Honour of Henry G. Schermers*, Vol.II (Martinus Nijhoff, Dordrecht, 1994), at 3–21.

[2] Schermers and Blokker, *International Institutional Law* (Martinus Nijhoff, The Hague, 1995), paras 58–59, at 39–40, and paras 1330–1331, at 819–820.

the inter-war period,[3] was brought back to the attention of the public on September 19, 1946 by a speech made by Winston Churchill at the University of Zürich in which he called for the establishment of "a kind of United States of Europe" on the continent.[4] On April 16, 1948 the Organisation for European Economic Co-operation (OEEC) was set up to co-ordinate economic recovery in Europe and in particular to distribute aid granted under the Marshall Plan.[5] In May 1948 prominent persons from different social, cultural and political circles meeting at the "Congress of Europe" held in The Hague passed a number of resolutions working out the idea of European integration in two ways. First, they called for a European organisation to be set up to safeguard the democratic systems of the European countries through multilateral supervision of compliance with human rights. Secondly, they called for a pooling of the crucial components of economic, industrial and—hence also to some extent—political life with a view to forestalling the threat of war in western Europe.

2–003 The Council of Europe. With the signature of the Statute of the Council of Europe on May 5, 1949, the ideas formulated at the Congress of Europe gave rise to an international organisation.[6] The Council of Europe, which is based in Strasbourg, has at present 46 member countries.[7] It may concern itself with all political, economic and social matters of European interest and hence has a more extensive field of activity than the European Communities.[8] The organisation has a Committee of Ministers, which is

---

[3] For a historical survey of ideas for European integration, see Beutler, Bieber, Pipkorn and Streil, *Die Europäische Union—Rechtsordnung und Politik* (Nomos, Baden-Baden, 1993), at 30–32.

[4] For the text of the speech, see Patijn, *Landmarks in European Unity* (Sijthoff, Leyden, 1970), 27, at 29.

[5] Convention on European Economic Co-operation, signed at Paris on April 16, 1948, UNTS (1949) 59, Cmnd. 7796. The OEEC was replaced on September 30, 1961 by the Organisation for Economic Cooperation and Development (OECD), which seeks to promote, alongside economic growth, employment and rising living standards in member countries, also the well-being of developing countries and other States. The Convention on the Organisation for Economic Cooperation and Development was signed at Paris on December 14, 1960, (1961) UNTS 21, Cmnd. 1646. Its website is at *www.oecd.org.* Art. 93 of the ECSC Treaty, Art. 304 of the EC Treaty and Art. 202 of the EAEC Treaty make provision for co-operation with the OECD.

[6] (1949) UNTS 61, Cmnd. 7778. The Council of Europe's website is at *www.coe.int.*

[7] The founder members were Belgium, Denmark, France, Greece (which withdrew from the Council of Europe in 1970 to be readmitted in 1974), Ireland, Italy, Luxembourg, the Netherlands, Norway, Sweden and the United Kingdom. The Federal Republic of Germany, Iceland and Turkey joined in 1950, Austria in 1956, Cyprus in 1961, Switzerland in 1963, Malta in 1965, Portugal in 1976, Spain in 1977, Liechtenstein in 1978, San Marino in 1988, Finland in 1989, Hungary in 1990, Poland in 1991, Bulgaria in 1992, the Czech Republic, Estonia, Lithuania, Romania, Slovakia and Slovenia in 1993 (Czechoslovakia had already joined as a unitary State in 1991), Andorra in 1994, Albania, Latvia, Macedonia, Moldova, the Ukraine and the Former Yugoslav Republic of Macedonia in 1995, Croatia and Russia in 1996, Georgia in 1999, Armenia and Azerbaijan in 2001, Bosnia and Herzegovina in 2002, Serbia and Montenegro in 2003 and Monaco in 2004.

[8] The Community Treaties call for co-operation with the Council of Europe (ECSC Treaty, Art. 94; EC Treaty, Art. 303, and EAEC Treaty, Art. 200). See Ouchterlony, "The European Communities and the Council of Europe" (1984) 1 L.I.E.I. 59–74.

advised by the Parliamentary Assembly (formerly the Consultative Assembly). Although the Assembly has been made up of delegates from the national parliaments since 1951, the Council of Europe is still organised on an intergovernmental model. It does not have any actual power to make laws. The two instruments employed in the context of the Council of Europe are non-binding resolutions and draft conventions, which take effect only between States which have ratified them. As a result, it has not evolved any further than a forum for discussion, providing interesting ideas for European co-operation, but not affording any genuine prospects of realising them.

European Convention on Human Rights. The most important convention **2–004** which has come into being under the auspices of the Council of Europe is the European Convention for the Protection of Human Rights and Fundamental Freedoms (ECHR) of November 4, 1950.[9] The distinct place occupied by the ECHR within the Council of Europe is clear from two special characteristics.

First and foremost, the Council of Europe is identified with the ECHR. No State can join the Council of Europe unless it agrees to accede to the ECHR. At the same time, States may accede to the ECHR only if they are also members of the Council of Europe (ECHR, Art. 59(1)). The preamble to the ECHR states that the central aim of the Council of Europe is "the collective enforcement of certain of the Rights stated in the Universal Declaration of Human Rights proclaimed by the General Assembly of the United Nations on 10th December 1948". Accordingly, every person within the jurisdiction of the Contracting States is *ipso facto* protected by the ECHR, irrespective of his or her nationality or place of residence.

The ECHR constitutes a first expression of supranationalism in the European integration process. With the creation of the European Court of Human Rights, the ECHR provides an enforcement structure which subjects the States to "European" supervision of their compliance with the provisions of the Convention. Ratification of the ECHR has the result that any Contracting Party may refer to the European Court of Human Rights the acts or omissions of another Contracting Party for its appraisal (ECHR, Art. 33). More importantly, any person, non-governmental organisation or group of individuals claiming to be the victim of a violation by one of the

---

[9] Cmnd. 8969. The ECHR and Protocols Nos 1 and 6 thereto are set out in Schedule to the Human Rights Act 1998. For an exhaustive discussion of the rights set out in the ECHR, see Jacobs and White, *The European Convention on Human Rights* (Clarendon Press, Oxford, 2002), 506 pp.; Van Dijk and Van Hoof, *Theory and Practice of the European Convention on Human Rights* (Kluwer Law International, Deventer, 1998), 850 pp.; Vande Lanotte, Haeck, Lathouwers, Tobback and Van de Putte, *Het Europees Verdrag tot bescherming van de rechten van de mens in hoofdlijnen*(Maklu, Antwerp, 1997) 293 pp.; Frowein and Peukert, *Europäische Menschenrechtskonvention—EMRK-Kommentar*, (Engel Verlag, Kehl am Rhein, 1996) 1042 pp.; Velu and Ergec, *La Convention européenne des droits de l'homme* (Bruylant, Brussels, 1990), 1185 pp.

Contracting Parties of the rights set forth in the ECHR may submit an application to the European Court of Human Rights (ECHR, Art. 34). The procedure for dealing with individual applications has been radically altered by Protocol No.11 to the ECHR, which has been in force since November 1, 1998.[10] If an individual application is not declared inadmissible by a committee of the Court consisting of three Judges, it will be referred to a Chamber of seven Judges which decides on its admissibility and merits (ECHR, Arts 28 and 29).[11] After the Chamber has given judgment, any party may request that the case be referred to the Grand Chamber of seventeen Judges (ECHR, Art. 43(1)). The Grand Chamber will accept such a request only if a panel of five Judges determines that the case raises a serious question affecting the interpretation or application of the Convention or the Protocols thereto, or a serious issue of general importance (ECHR, Art. 43(2)). Judgments of the Grand Chamber and—in so far no request is made to refer the case to the Grand Chamber or such a request is refused—of the Chambers are final and the Contracting Parties have to abide by them (ECHR, Arts 44 and 46).

As a result of Protocol No. 11 the Strasbourg procedure has come a long way from the original enforcement procedure, which severely limited direct access to the European Court of Human Rights by individual victims of violations. Originally, persons or groups of individuals lodged a complaint with the European Commission of Human Rights, which had to decide whether to consider the petition admissible and whether to remit the case to the Court of Human Rights. It could only do so if the Contracting State against which the petition was lodged had made a separate declaration that it recognised the competence of the Commission to receive such complaints and accepted the Court's jurisdiction. Under the present system, the individual right to submit applications and the jurisdiction of the Strasbourg Court is accepted by all the Contracting States.

---

[10] Protocol No. 11 to the European Convention for the Protection of Human Rights and Fundamental Freedoms restructuring the control machinery established thereby, signed on May 11, 1994. For the position of the United Kingdom, see now the Human Rights Act 1998. The Protocol is discussed in Drzemczewski and Meyer-Ladewig, "Principales caractéristiques du nouveau méchanisme de contrôle établi par la CEDH suite au Protocole N° 11, signé le 11 mai 1994" (1994) R.U.D.H. 81–113 (with the complete texts of the Protocol, the explanatory report and the adjusted version of the ECHR and the additional Protocols; see also *European Convention on Human Rights. Collected texts*, Council of Europe Press, 1995, 363 pp.); Schermers, "The Eleventh Protocol to the European Convention on Human Rights" (1994) E.L.Rev. 367–384; Wachsmann, Eissen and Flauss (eds), *Le Protocole N° 11 à la Convention européenne des droits de l'homme* (Bruylant, Brussels, 1995), 194 pp.; De Schutter, "La nouvelle Cour européenne des droits de l'homme" (1998) C.D.E. 319–352; Lawson, "Een nieuw Europees Hof voor de Rechten van de Mens" (1998) N.J.B. 1903–1907; Vande Lanotte and Haeck, "Het nieuwe Europees Hof te Straatsburg aan de vooravond van de 21e eeuw" (1999–2000) R.W. 1417–1448; Drzemczewski, "The European Human Rights Convention: Protocol No. 11—Entry into force and first year of application" (2000) Human Rights L.J. 1–17.
[11] In certain cases, the Chamber may, before it has rendered its judgment, relinquish jurisdiction in favour of the Grand Chamber of 17 judges, see ECHR, Art. 30.

II. PROPOSALS FOR FURTHER COLLABORATION BETWEEN THE MEMBER STATES OF THE COMMUNITIES

European Defence Community. After a functional approach to European 2–005 integration led to the ECSC (see para. 1–003), active international consultations took place with a view to transferring real powers in other areas to a common institution.

On May 27, 1952 the ECSC Member States signed the Treaty establishing the European Defence Community (EDC).[12] The Member States of the EDC were to make army divisions available to the European Defence Forces under a Commissariat. The EDC was also to have a Council, a Parliamentary Assembly (the ECSC Common Assembly plus nine delegates) and to use the Court of Justice of the ECSC. The EDC was based on a plan put forward by the French Minister of Defence René Pleven which offered a solution enabling a military security structure to be put in place in continental Europe as a counterweight to the expansion of communism—a present threat in view of the Korean War—yet without ignoring French resistance to German rearmament.

Prior to the entry into force of the EDC Treaty, the Ministers of Foreign Affairs of the ECSC decided to implement Art. 38 of the EDC Treaty, which charged the Common Assembly with considering any changes eventually to be made to the Treaty, having regard to the principle that "the final organisation which will replace the present provisional organisation should be so conceived as to be able to constitute one of the elements in a federal or confederal structure". The aim of the changes was to co-ordinate the agencies for European co-operation, already existing or which might be established, within the framework of a federal or confederal structure (EDC Treaty, Art. 38(1)). The Common Assembly of the ECSC—meeting as the "Ad Hoc Assembly"— proposed that a European Political Community should be set up to co-ordinate Member States' foreign policy and establish a common market. The institutional structure of the ECSC was to be taken over and more extensive powers were to be given to the "supranational" institutions, namely the independent policy institution and the Parliamentary Assembly.[13] Both the EDC Treaty and the draft Statute of the European Political Community expressly set out to establish a Community of a "supranational character".[14]

The whole plan fell through when, on August 29, 1954, the French National Assembly voted to postpone ratification of the EDC Treaty *sine die*. The Gaullists and Communists had opposed the EDC, the former

---

[12] See Fursdon, *The European Defence Community: A History* (Macmillan, London, 1980), 360 pp.

[13] For the draft text, see *Selection of Texts concerning Institutional Matters of the Community from 1950–1982* (European Parliament Committee on Institutional Affairs, Luxembourg, 1982), at 52.

[14] Art. 1 of the EDC Treaty; Art. 1 of the Draft Statute. See Von Lindeiner-Wildau, *La supranationalité en tant que principe de droit* (Sijthoff, Leiden, 1970), at 9.

fearful of surrendering French sovereignty, the latter shrinking from German rearmament.

2–006 **Defence co-operation.** In October 1954, a solution was found to the problem of growing German strength. The North Atlantic Treaty Organisation (NATO) accepted the Federal Republic of Germany as a member. In addition, Germany, together with Italy, joined the Western European Union (WEU).

NATO was set up by the North Atlantic Treaty of April 4, 1949.[15] It has a military and a civil structure. At present, all Member States, with the exception of Austria, Cyprus, Finland, Ireland, Malta and Sweden, are members.[16] However, France and Spain do not belong to the integrated military structure. Its most important civil institution is the North Atlantic Council which is attended regularly by the Ministers of Foreign Affairs and at times also by the heads of State or heads of government of the Member States. In addition, although there is no basis in the Treaty for this, members of the parliament from the various NATO countries meet in the North Atlantic Assembly.

France, the United Kingdom and the Benelux countries were already co-operating militarily as from the Brussels Treaty of March 17, 1948.[17] The Paris Protocol of October 23, 1954 amended the Brussels Treaty and set up the Western European Union (WEU).[18] At present, the WEU consists of ten EU Member States (Belgium, France, Germany, Greece, Italy, Luxembourg, the Netherlands, Portugal, Spain and the United Kingdom).[19] Co-operation with the WEU has been enshrined in the EU Treaty and has eventually resulted in its integration into the Union's common foreign and security policy (CFSP) (see para. 20–045). The WEU Council is composed of the Foreign Ministers and Defence Ministers. Alongside the Council, there is the WEU Assembly, consisting of members of parliament of the WEU States who sit in the Council of Europe's Parliamentary Assembly.[20] The WEU Assembly is advisory and does not alter in any way the strictly inter-governmental nature of the organisation. The WEU has accepted

---

[15] North Atlantic Treaty, (1949) UNTS 56, Cmnd. 7789. NATO's website is to be found at *www.nato.int.*

[16] Most recently, Estonia, Latvia, Lithuania, Slovakia and Slovenia (together with Bulgaria and Romania) joined NATO on March 29, 2004.

[17] Treaty between Belgium, France, Luxembourg, the Netherlands and the United Kingdom, (1949) UNTS 1, Cmnd. 7599.

[18] The Treaty establishing the Western European Union and Protocols thereto, signed in Paris on October 23, 1954 (1955) UNTS 39, Cmnd. 9498. See Dumoulin and Remacle, *L'Union de l'Europe occidentale. Phénix de la défense européenne* (Bruylant, Brussels, 1998), 604 pp. The WEU website is at *www.weu.int/.*

[19] Austria, Denmark, Finland, Ireland and Sweden have the status of observer members. The Czech Republic, Hungary and Poland are associated WEU members whereas Estonia, Latvia, Lithuania, the Slovak Republic and Slovenia are associate partners (see nn.21–22, *infra*).

[20] De Vree, Coffrey and Lauwaars, *Towards a European Foreign Policy—Legal, Economic and Political Dimensions* (Martinus Nijhoff, Dordrecht, 1987), at 250.

NATO States as associated members[21] and seven central and eastern European States as associate partners.[22] Unless a majority of WEU members object, those States may take part in WEU operations. They sit on the WEU Council, but cannot block a decision on which the WEU States agree.[23]

A subsequent development is the participation of all Member States of the European Union in the Conference for Security and Co-operation in Europe (CSCE), which met for the first time in 1973, resulting in the signing of the Helsinki Final Act.[24] The CSCE was institutionalised by the 1990 Charter of Paris[25] and has been renamed since January 1, 1995 the Organisation for Security and Co-operation in Europe (OSCE).[26] The OSCE consists of several institutions, including meetings of Heads of State or Government, a Ministerial Council (Ministers of Foreign Affairs), a Senior Council, which meets in Prague to prepare meetings of the Council of Ministers, a Permanent Council, in which permanent representatives to the OSCE meet in Vienna, a Chairman in Office, assisted by a Secretariat in Prague, a Parliamentary Assembly and, among other things, a High Commissioner on National Minorities and an Office for Democratic Institutions and Human Rights. The OSCE has 55 Member States, including virtually all the European countries (including all the republics of the former Soviet Union), the United States and Canada. In pursuance of

---

[21] Iceland, Norway and Turkey are associate members pursuant to the document approved at Rome on November 20, 1992. See also the related Declaration of the WEU Council of May 9, 1994, *Europe*, doc. No. 1884, May 11, 1994, at 7–8. Hungary, Poland and the Czech Republic have been associated members since March 23, 1999 (following their accession to NATO); see the declaration of the WEU Council of May 10–11, 1999, *Europe*, doc. No.2138, May 15, 1999. At the time of writing, it was not yet clear whether for those States having acceded to the EU, associated membership would be replaced by full membership.

[22] To this end, the WEU signed a Document on May 9, 1994 in Luxembourg with Bulgaria, Estonia, Latvia, Lithuania, Romania and Slovakia (as well as with Hungary, Poland and the Czech Republic, which have been associated members since 1999), *Europe*, doc. No. 1884, May 11, 1994, at 5–7. On June 25, 1996, the WEU also accepted Slovenia as an associate partner. Since then, all States concerned joined NATO. It is not clear whether the subsequent accession to NATO of all States concerned (and the accession to the EU of the majority them) would result in associated partnership being replaced by (associated) membership.

[23] *ibid.*

[24] Final Act of Helsinki of August 1, 1975, for the English text see *From Helsinki to Vienna. Basic documents of the Helsinki Process*, 1990, IEE/39 (the text was not subject to ratification). The Final Act consists of the conclusions of the Conference on Security and Cooperation in Europe, which opened in Helsinki on July 3, 1973. It embodies a political declaration setting out principles for the conduct of relations between the States party to it (including respect for human rights), a document on "confidence-building measures and certain aspects of security and disarmament", together with provisions on co-operation in the fields of economics, science and technology and of the environment.

[25] Charter of Paris of November 19–21, 1990 for a New Europe (1990) 11 EC Bull point 2.2.1.

[26] See the final declaration of the meeting of Heads of State or Government held on December 6, 1994 in Budapest, *Europe*, doc. No. 1917, December 28, 1994. OSCE's website is at *www.osce.org/*.

its task of preserving peace, security and stability, the OSCE has several dispute-resolution instruments.[27]

2–007 Benelux and EFTA. As from 1955, the way was open to a *relance européenne*, which, encouraged by the Benelux countries and the influential Action Committee for the United States of Europe, was to lead to the signature in 1957 of the EEC Treaty and the EAEC Treaty (see paras 1–005–1–007).

The Benelux countries took the necessary steps in order to convert their customs union founded in 1948 into an economic union in which their economic, financial and social policies were co-ordinated.[28] The Committee of Ministers of the Benelux Economic Union is assisted by a general secretariat and advisory bodies, including the Advisory Benelux Interparliamentary Council. A Benelux Court of Justice is responsible for ensuring the uniform interpretation of agreements concluded between the Benelux countries.[29]

Seven other western European countries decided to set up a free trade area, without common external tariffs or supplementary harmonisation of economic and social legislation,[30] when, on January 4, 1960, Austria, Denmark, Norway, Portugal, the United Kingdom, Sweden and Switzerland concluded the Convention establishing the European Free Trade

---

[27] For further particulars, see Decaux, *Sécurité et co-opération en Europe. Les textes officiels du processus de Helsinki (1973–1992)* (La Documentation française, Paris, 1992), 460 pp.; Oschinsky and Jenard (n.1, *supra*) at 27–33; McGoldrick, "The Development of the Conference on Security and Co-operation in Europe (CSCE) after the Helsinki 1992 Conference" (1993) I.C.L.Q. 411–432; Bertrand, "La nature juridique de l'Organisation pour la sécurité et la co-opération en Europe (OSCE)" (1998) R.G.D.I.P. 365–406.

[28] Treaty of The Hague of February 3, 1958 establishing a Benelux Economic Union (*UNTS* No. 5471,) which succeeded the Customs Convention between Belgium, Luxembourg and the Netherlands which was signed in London on September 5, 1944. The leading role played by Benelux (recognised in Art. 306 of the EC Treaty, para. 17–098, *infra*), especially in the field of free movement of persons (para. 2–017, *infra*) has now been largely assumed by the EC/EU: see Mortelmans, "Benelux 50 jaar: voorlopen, gelijklopen of doodlopen?" (1995) S.E.W. 399–403; Van den Oosterkamp, "Is er naast de Europese Unie nog toekomst voor de Benelux?" (2002) S.E.W. 237–240.

[29] Treaty on the establishment and statute of the Benelux Court of Justice, signed at Brussels on March 31, 1965, as supplemented by the Protocol of April 29, 1969. It has been in force since January 1, 1974. The Benelux Court of Justice—composed of Judges of the highest courts of each of the three countries—is itself a court against whose decisions there is no remedy under national law and hence is required by the third para. of Art. 234 of the EC Treaty to make a reference for a preliminary ruling to the Court of Justice of the EC whenever a question of Community law is raised before it: ECJ, Case C–337/95 *Parfums Christian Dior* [1997] E.C.R. I–6013, paras 15–31.

[30] According to Art. XXIV(8) of the General Agreement on Tariffs and Trade (GATT, para. 20–010, *infra*), a free-trade area is a group of two or more customs territories in which the duties and other restrictive regulations of trade are eliminated on substantially all the trade between the constituent territories in products originating in such territories. A free trade area differs from a customs union, in which the reciprocal abolition of restrictions on trade is coupled with a common external tariff; see the discussion in para. 5–086, *infra*.

Association (EFTA).[31] Later, Finland, Iceland and Liechtenstein joined,[32] but first Denmark and the United Kingdom, then Portugal, and finally Austria, Finland and Sweden left the organisation to accede to the Communities and the Union (see para. 23–001 *et seq.*). EFTA's Council of Ministers and Committee of Parliamentarians have been supplemented—as far as the EFTA States belonging to the European Economic Area (Iceland, Liechtenstein and Norway) are concerned—by a Standing Committee, a Joint Parliamentary Committee, a Surveillance Authority and a Court of Justice (see para. 23–016).

---

[31] *Convention establishing the European Free Trade Association*, signed at Stockholm on January 4, 1960, (1960) UNTS 30, Cmnd. 1026. EFTA's website is at *www.efta.int/*. The EFTA States did not only aim at removing barriers to trade between themselves, but also referred expressly to the EEC Member States as potential members of a future multilateral economic co-operation association: see Jacot-Guillarmod, "Expressions juridiques, au sein du système européen de libre-échange, du rapprochement de l'AELE et de la Communauté", in Capotorti, Ehlermann, Frowein, Jacobs, Joliet, Koopmans and Kovar (eds), *Du droit international au droit de l'intégration. Liber Amicorum P. Pescatore* (Nomos, Baden-Baden, 1987), at 317–318.

[32] Iceland became a member of EFTA on March 1, 1970, Finland (having been an associate member since 1961) on January 1, 1986 and Liechtenstein on September 1, 1991.

Figure 1: Integration among European States

		European Union	EU Accession Negotiations	Council of Europe	NATO	WEU*	EEA
		(see para. 1-021)	(see para. 8–011)	(see para. 2–003)	(see para. 2–006)	(see para. 2–006)	(see para. 23–005)
Member States	Austria	X		X			X
	Belgium	X		X	X	X	X
	Cyprus	X		X			X
	Czech Rep.	X		X	X	AM	X
	Denmark	X		X	X		X
	Estonia	X		X	X	AP	X
	Finland	X		X			X
	France	X		X	X	X	X
	Germany	X		X	X	X	X
	Greece	X		X	X	X	X
	Hungary	X		X	X	AM	X
	Ireland	X		X			X
	Italy	X		X	X	X	X
	Latvia	X		X	X	AP	X
	Lithuania	X		X	X	AP	X
	Luxembourg	X		X	X	X	X
	Malta	X		X			X
	Netherlands	X		X	X	X	X
	Poland	X		X	X	AM	X
	Portugal	X		X	X	X	X
	Slovak Rep.	X		X	X	AP	X
	Slovenia	X		X	X	AP	X
	Spain	X		X	X	X	X
	Sweden	X		X			X
	UK	X		X	X	X	X
Candidate Member States	Bulgaria		X	X	X	AP	
	Croatia			X			
	FYROM			X			
	Romania		X	X	X	AP	
	Turkey			X	X	AM	
EFTA	Iceland			X	X	AM	X
	Liechtenstein			X			X
	Norway			X	X	AM	X
	Switzerland			X			

* AM: Associate Member AP: Associate Partner

Fouchet Plan. After the first years of operation of the EEC and the EAEC, **2–008** plans began to emerge anew to extend integration to less socio-economically oriented areas.[33] The French President de Gaulle presented plans for forming a Political Union, which were discussed in 1961 and 1962 first at summit conferences and subsequently in the Fouchet Committee.[34] Under the structure proposed by de Gaulle, the Heads of State or of Government meeting within the Council of the Union would conduct common foreign and defence policy by unanimous vote and co-operate on culture, science and safeguarding human rights, fundamental freedoms and democracy. The Union was also to have a Political Commission and a Parliamentary Assembly, but no Court of Justice. Made up of national civil servants, the Political Commission was to confine itself to preparing and, where necessary, carrying out the decisions of the Council. The Parliamentary Assembly was to play an advisory role. Under the first proposal of November 1961, this *Union d'Etats* was to operate alongside the existing Communities. Under a subsequent proposal, this organisation was also to have powers in the economic field and foresaw the institutions of the Communities being bound by decisions of the Heads of State or of Government. The "Fouchet Plan" ultimately came to grief because of the fears of the smaller Member States that this would erode the powers and supranational character which the Communities had acquired. A further decisive factor was de Gaulle's refusal to resume negotiations with the United Kingdom.

III.   INTERGOVERNMENTAL CO-OPERATION BETWEEN THE MEMBER STATES

Co-operation between Member States. From the outset, the momentum of **2–009** supranational integration led the Member States to become involved in intergovernmental co-operation in areas which did not (as yet) fall within the competence of the Communities. As a result of their political connection with Community activities, those areas were gradually brought either within the competence of the Community (monetary policy) or within the sphere of the second and third pillars of the Union (foreign policy and police and judicial co-operation).

A.   EUROPEAN MONETARY CO-OPERATION

Initial steps. The initial successes of the Communities prompted the Heads **2–010** of State or of Government in December 1969 to investigate transforming

---

[33] Lang, "Die Bemühungen um die politische Einigung Europas seit dem Scheitern der Europäischen Verteidigungsgemeinschaft", in Hallstein and Schlochauer (eds), *Zur Integration Europas. Festschrift für C.F. Ophüls* (Müller, Karlsruhe, 1965), at 125–141.

[34] These plans are annexed to Bloes, *Le "Plan Fouchet" et le problème de l'Europe politique* (College of Europe, Bruges, 1970), at 487–510; see also *Selection of Texts concerning Institutional Matters of the Community from 1950–1982* (n.13, *supra*), at 109–121.

the customs union, which had only just been introduced, into an economic and monetary union (EMU).[35] The Council set up the Werner Committee, which put forward proposals in October 1970 for achieving EMU in stages.[36] With a view to achieving the first stage, a resolution of March 22, 1971 of the Council and the representatives of the governments of the Member States looked forward to increased co-ordination of economic and monetary policies and limitation of the fluctuation margins between the Member States' currencies.[37] Since not all the measures seemed feasible—the economic climate became more unfavourable after the oil crisis—EMU remained at the starting blocks. In the monetary sphere, the Council nevertheless set up the European Monetary Co-operation Fund as planned.[38] Following the collapse of the international system of fixed exchange rates (the Bretton Woods system), the Member States endeavoured, with varying degrees of success, to co-ordinate their intervention on the currency markets (the "Snake").

2–011 **European Monetary System.** Monetary co-operation as between the Member States came into being on the basis of the resolution of the European Council of December 5, 1978 on the establishment of the European Monetary System (EMS).[39] Within the EMS, bilateral exchange rates were set as between the various currencies. Initially, the EMS operated on the basis of the intergovernmental agreements contained in the resolution of the European Council and in agreements between the central banks. For the co-ordination of their general monetary policy, representatives of the central banks also met in institutions of the Communities, such as the Monetary Committee and the Committee of Governors of the central banks.[40] By a regulation, the Council subsequently entrusted the management of the EMS to the Monetary Co-operation Fund.[41] In 1978 the Council had adopted, in connection with monetary co-operation, a regulation introducing the ECU (European Currency Unit) as a unit of account for the exchange rate mechanism and a means of

---

[35] Final communiqué of the Conference (December 2, 1969), EC Bull., 1–1970, 16, point 8.
[36] The final report of the Werner Committee of October 8, 1970 was published in (1970) EC Bull. Suppl. 11, and in [1970] O.J. C136.
[37] Resolution of the Council and of the Representatives of the Governments of the Member States of March 22, 1971 on the attainment by stages of economic and monetary union in the Community, [1974] O.J. English Spec. Ed., Second Series, IX. Resolutions of the Representatives of the Member States, 40.
[38] Regulation (EEC) No. 907/73 of the Council of April 13, 1973 establishing a European Monetary Co-operation Fund, [1973] O.J. L89/2.
[39] Resolution of the European Council of December 5, 1978 on the establishment of the European Monetary System (EMS) and related matters (1978) 12 EC Bull. point 1.1.11.
[40] For these bodies, see the Rules governing the Monetary Committee, [1952–1958] O.J. English Spec. Ed. 60; Council Decision 64/300/EEC of May 8, 1964 on co-operation between the Central Banks of the Member States of the European Economic Community, [1963–1964] O.J. English Spec. Ed. 141.
[41] Council Regulation (EEC) No. 3181/78 of December 18, 1978 relating to the European Monetary System, [1978] O.J. L379/2.

settling transactions between national authorities and the Fund.[42] The ECU was a basket of currencies whose value was determined by the value of the national currencies, weighted according to their share of the basket. That share was fixed commensurately with each Member State's share of the Union's GNP and of internal Community trade. By means of a regulation, the Council introduced the ECU as the means of account for the Communities' budget.[43]

Economic and Monetary Union. The EU Treaty laid the foundations for **2–012** the introduction of economic and monetary Union. On December 31, 1998 the conversion rates between the common currency—now named the Euro—and the currencies of the Member States taking part in EMU were irrevocably fixed.[44] Since January 1, 1999 the Euro has been the currency of the Member States participating in EMU, namely Austria, Belgium, Finland, France, Germany, Ireland, Italy, Luxembourg, the Netherlands, Portugal and Spain. Those States were joined by Greece on January 1, 2001 (see paras 5–219—5–233).

B. EUROPEAN POLITICAL CO-OPERATION

EPC. The second field in which Member States agreed to co-ordinate their **2–013** policies outside the sphere of competence of the Communities was foreign policy, resulting in the emergence of European Political Co-operation (EPC).[45] At a meeting of the Council held in Luxembourg on October 27, 1970, the Foreign Ministers gave their approval to the Davignon Report, which proposed that there should be half-yearly meetings of the Foreign Ministers, to which a member of the Commission could also be invited.[46] It was in this way that European Political Co-operation came about. It was further developed on the basis of reports of the Foreign Ministers[47] and of the Heads of State or of Government.[48]

Initially, the Foreign Ministers deliberately kept their EPC meetings separate from meetings of the Council of the European Communities.[49] But

---

[42] Council Regulation (EEC) No. 3180/78 of December 18, 1978 changing the value of the unit of account used by the European Monetary Co-operation Fund [1978] O.J. L379/1.

[43] Council Regulation (EEC, Euratom) No. 3308/80 of December 16, 1980 on the replacement of the European unit of account by the ECU in Community legal instruments, [1980] O.J. L345/1.

[44] Council Regulation (EC) No. 2866/98 of December 31, 1998 on the conversion rates between the euro and the currencies of the Member States adopting the Euro, [1998] O.J. L359/1.

[45] De Schoutheete, *La co-opération politique européenne* (Nathan/Labor, Paris/Brussels, 1986), 334 pp.; Ifestos, *European Political Co-operation—Towards a Framework of Supranational Diplomacy?* (Avebury, Aldershot, 1987), 635 pp.

[46] Report of the Ministers of Foreign Affairs of the Member States on the question of political integration (1970) 11 EC Bull. 9–14.

[47] Copenhagen, 1973, (1973) 9 EC Bull. 13 and 20–23; London, 1981, (1981) EC Bull., Suppl.3, 14–18 (see also (1981) 10 EC Bull. point 2.2.59).

[48] Solemn Declaration of Stuttgart on European Union of June 19, 1983 (1983) 6 EC Bull. Point 1.6.1.

[49] The most striking example is one day in 1973 when the Foreign Ministers met in the morning in Copenhagen under EPC auspices and in the afternoon in Brussels as the Council of the European Communities.

gradually a link grew up between them.[50] Because having a special body for EPC was still reminiscent of the Political Committee proposed in the Fouchet Plan, the EPC secretariat was given purely administrative functions under the authority of the Presidency.

2–014 **Legal status.** All EPC decisions were taken by consensus and the Court of Justice had no jurisdiction to supervise the fulfilment by Member States of the obligations which they assumed in the context of EPC. Accordingly, the rules of conduct governing EPC constituted a species of soft law influencing the international action of the Member States. It was not until 1986 that the Member States gave EPC practice a legal basis under a treaty by means of the Single European Act (Art. 1; Art. 3(2); Art. 30 or Title III of the Single European Act). The EU Treaty converted EPC into the non-Community "second pillar" of the Union, the common foreign and security policy (CFSP; see paras 20–039—20–048).[51]

C. POLICE AND JUDICIAL CO-OPERATION

2–015 **First co-operation and agreements.** Thirdly, outside the ambit of the Communities, forms of co-operation grew up between ministerial departments of the Member States with regard to trans-frontier aspects of justice and home affairs. In December 1975, the European Council meeting in Rome approved the initiative of ministers from the Member States meeting twice a year in order to discuss questions of law and order, such as terrorism and other forms of international lawlessness.[52] Various other inter-governmental bodies co-ordinated and studied national police policy.[53] Agreements were also concluded between the Member States on police and judicial co-operation in criminal matters and on judicial co-operation in civil matters, including the Brussels Convention.[54] Similar

---

[50] See Nuttall, "Interaction between European Political Co-operation and the European Community" (1987) Y.E.L. 211–249.

[51] Title V of the EU Treaty. Art. 50(2) of the EU Treaty repealed Arts 2, 3(2) and 30 (Title III) of the Single European Act.

[52] (1975) 11 EC. Bull. point 1104. These meetings were known as the Trevi Group. "Trevi" refers to the Roman fountain and has been turned into an acronym for *Terrorisme, Radicalisme, Extrémisme et Violence Internationale*. For the structure and operation of Trevi, see Le Jeune, *La coopération policière européenne contre le terrorisme* (Bruylant, Brussels, 1992), at 105–148.

[53] For example, Celad (*Comité européen pour la lutte anti-drogue*), which was set up on the initiative of the French to co-ordinate national anti-drugs policies (1989) 12 EC Bull. point 1.1.9., and Interpol, an intergovernmental co-operative association which has been operating since 1923 not on the basis of a treaty. See Fijnaut, "The 'Communitisation' of Police Co-operation in Western Europe", in Schermers, Flinterman, Kellermann, Van Haersolte and Van de Meent (eds), *Free Movement of Persons in Europe. Legal Problems and Experiences* (Martinus Nijhoff, Dordrecht, 1993), at 75–92.

[54] Brussels Convention of September 27, 1968 on jurisdiction and the enforcement of judgments in civil and commercial matters (Accession Convention for Denmark, Ireland and the United Kingdom: [1978] O.J. L304/77; a codified text of the Convention can be found in [1998] O.J. C17/1), implemented in the United Kingdom by the Civil Jurisdiction

conventions are also concluded under the auspices of the Council of Europe.[55]

Co-operation extended to migration issues. The internal-market **2–016** programme (see para. 5–077) looked forward to the abolition of checks on persons at the internal frontiers of the Community by the end of 1992. Co-operation between the Member States in the sphere of customs controls and combating criminality therefore became essential. Free movement of persons meant that non-EC nationals could move freely within the Community once they had crossed the external frontiers. The Member States accordingly sought to arrive at forms of co-operation enabling a common control policy at the external frontiers and a uniform policy with regard to the access, movement and residence of nationals of third countries in the Community. The European Council meeting at Rhodes on December 2 and 3, 1988 set up a co-ordinators Group to co-ordinate the various activities in the sphere of the free movement of persons.[56] The activities of an ad hoc working group on immigration[57] resulted in agreements which have been submitted to the Member States for ratification. The Dublin Convention of June 15, 1990, which determines which Member State should examine applications for asylum, entered into force on September 1, 1997 (see para. 5–161). A draft Convention on the crossing of external borders of the Member States failed to be signed on account of differences between Spain and the United Kingdom relating to the application of the Convention to Gibraltar.[58]

Since the EU Treaty entered into force, intergovernmental co-operation between the Member States in the fields of the police and justice has been conducted on the basis of the non-Community third pillar of the Union, namely Title VI of the EU Treaty. In this way, a convention has been drawn up pursuant to the EU Treaty to supplement the Brussels

and Judgments Act 1982. The Brussels Convention has since been replaced, except as far as Denmark is concerned, by Council Regulation (EC) No. 44/2001 of December 22, 2000 on jurisdiction and the recognition and enforcement of judgments in civil and commercial matters ([2001] O.J. L12/1; implemented in the United Kingdom by the Civil Jurisdiction and Judgments Order 2001 (SI 2001/3929)); see para. 5–151, *infra*, and for the interpretation of the Brussels Convention by the Court of Justice, para. 17–097, *infra*. See also the Brussels Convention of May 25, 1987 abolishing the Legalisation of Documents in the Member States of the European Communities, (1987) 5 EC Bull. point 3.4.3, and the Rome Convention of November 6, 1990 between the Member States of the European Communities on the Simplification of Procedures for the Enforcement of Maintenance Payments (1990) Trb. 54.

[55] For an overview of those conventions, see Oschinsky and Jenard, n.1, *supra*.

[56] (1988) 12 EC Bull. point 1.1.3. The Co-ordinators Group drew a distinction as regards the various areas of co-operation between priority and ancillary measures. This resulted in the Palma document of June 1989, which was approved by the European Council held in Madrid in June 1989 (1989) 6 EC Bull. point 1.1.7.

[57] The ad hoc group consisted of national officials meeting in various working parties: policy on asylum, external frontiers, admission/deportation, visa policy and forged papers. See (1986) 10 EC Bull. point 2.4.7.

[58] See the discussion of movement of persons, para. 5–158, *infra*.

Convention as regards jurisdiction and the recognition and enforcement of judgments in matrimonial matters.[59] The Treaty of Amsterdam brought judicial co-operation in civil matters and immigration and asylum policy within the sphere of the EC Treaty (see para. 5–150 *et seq.*).

2–017 Schengen Agreements. Some Member States have already taken the decision to replace frontier controls amongst themselves by a common policy at their external frontiers. The Benelux Treaty of April 11, 1960 obtained that outcome with effect from July 1, 1960.[60] National courts in the Benelux countries may refer questions on the interpretation of that treaty to the Benelux Court of Justice (see para. 2–007).

On June 19, 1990, France, Germany and the Benelux countries concluded the Convention on the application of the Schengen Agreement of June 14, 1985 on the gradual abolition of checks at the common borders.[61] The Schengen Convention established free movement of persons without checks at internal borders and stepped up checks at the external borders of the Schengen countries. It introduced common rules on the grant of visas and a uniform visa for nationals of third States (*i.e.* non-EC nationals) intending to stay in the Schengen area for less than three months. In order to offset the disappearance of internal borders, the Convention introduced a system for the exchange of information and co-operation between police forces and the judicial authorities, together with the Schengen Information System (SIS), which enables authorities to consult personal data held by authorities in other States *via* a central computer in Strasbourg. Upon the entry into effect of the Amsterdam Treaty, all EU Member States, with the exception of Ireland and the United Kingdom, were parties to the Schengen Convention and the agreements concluded pursuant to it.[62] The "Schengen *acquis*" did not

---

[59] Convention of May 28, 1998, drawn up on the basis of the former Art. K.3 of the EU Treaty, on Jurisdiction and the Recognition and Enforcement of Judgments in Matrimonial Matters ([1998] O.J. C221/2; the "Brussels II Convention", see para. 5–151, *infra*).

[60] Agreement between the Kingdom of Belgium, the Grand Duchy of Luxembourg and the Kingdom of the Netherlands on the displacement of checks on persons to the external frontiers of the Benelux area, signed at Brussels on April 11, 1960 (B.S., July 1, 1960, Trb., 1960, 40). See Kruijtbosch, "Benelux Experiences in the Abolition of Border Controls", in *Free Movement of Persons in Europe. Legal Problems and Experiences* (n.53, *supra*), at 31–39.

[61] Schengen Convention of June 19, 1990 implementing the Schengen Agreement of June 14, 1985 between the Governments of the States of the Benelux Economic Union, the Federal Republic of Germany and the French Republic on the gradual abolition of checks at their common borders ([2000] O.J. L239/19; for the Schengen Agreement of June 14, 1985: *ibid.*, p.13). See the discussion in Schutte, "Schengen: Its Meaning for the Free Movement of Persons in Europe" (1991) C.M.L.R. 549–570; Fijnaut, Stuyck and Wytinck (eds), *Schengen: Proeftuin voor de Europese Gemeenschap?* (Kluwer/Gouda Quint, Antwerp/Arnhem, 1992), 212 pp.

[62] Italy signed the convention on November 27, 1990, Portugal and Spain on June 25, 1991, Greece on November 6, 1992, Austria on April 28, 1995 and Denmark, Finland and Sweden on December 19, 1996.

enter into effect in all the States at the same time.[63] Since Denmark, Finland and Sweden, together with Iceland and Norway, had already abolished checks on persons moving between them under the auspices of the Nordic Council, the Schengen *acquis* could not be applied until Iceland and Norway had been enabled to take part in the Schengen co-operation by means of an agreement concluded with the Community.[64] The Treaty of Amsterdam incorporated the Schengen *acquis* into the European Union (see para. 5–164).

D. THE EUROPEAN COUNCIL

Summit conferences. From 1961 onwards, the Heads of State or of **2–018.** Government of the Member States held regular meetings in order to discuss political sticking points in Community policy.[65] At the Paris summit conference on December 9 and 10, 1974, they decided to hold such meetings from then on at least three times a year, accompanied by the Foreign Ministers.[66] The institution created thereby, the European Council, was intended not only to give impetus to European Political Co-operation, but also to take political decisions regarding matters coming within the sphere of competence of the Communities.[67] Although the European Council also makes pronouncements about matters for which the Communities are competent, it does not play a formal role in Community decision-making and does not constitute an institution hierarchically superior to the Community institutions. The Single European Act caused the European Council to be acknowledged for the first time in the Treaties The EU Treaty conferred a number of tasks on the European Council in the context of the Community decision-making process and the CFSP. Consequently, since the EU Treaty and the Treaty of Amsterdam the European Council acts as a specific organ of the Union alongside the Community institutions (see para. 10–003 *et seq.*).

E. DECISIONS OF THE GOVERNMENTS OF THE MEMBER STATES

Ministers meeting in the Council. In all matters, Ministers of the Member **2–019** States, precisely as in the case of the Heads of State or of Government within the European Council, may jointly take decisions pursuant to their

---

[63] For the last States, see Council Decision 1999/848/EC of December 13, 1999 on the full application of the Schengen *acquis* in Greece, [1999] O.J. L327/58 (entry into force on January 1, 2000), and Council Decision 2000/777/EC of December 1, 2000 on the application of the Schengen *acquis* in Denmark, Finland and Sweden, and in Iceland and Norway, [2000] O.J. L309/24 (entry into force on March 25, 2001).

[64] para. 5–164, *infra*.

[65] Such summit conferences took place twice in 1961 (Paris and Bonn) and thereafter in 1967 (Rome), 1969 (The Hague), 1972 (Paris) and 1973 (Copenhagen), each time at the prompting of the French President.

[66] Communiqué of the Heads of State or of Government meeting in Paris on December 9 and 10, 1974 (1974) 12 EC. Bull. point 1104(3).

[67] See Tindemans, "Le Conseil européen: un premier bilan, quelques réflexions", *Mélanges Fernand Dehousse. II. La construction européenne* (Nathan/Labor, Paris/Brussels, 1979), at 167–173; Wessels, *Der Europäische Rat* (Europa Union, Bonn, 1980), 472 pp.

power to bind their respective States under international law. The result can be non-binding resolutions or binding agreements. The Ministers can take such decisions at normal meetings of the Council as "representatives of the Governments of the Member States meeting in the Council". They form an aspect of classical intergovernmental co-operation between States.[68]

Such decisions are often closely related to decisions taken by the Council pursuant to the Treaties and intend to achieve uniformity in Member States' policies on non-Community aspects of European integration. The Member States have recourse to this type of co-operation where efficient action by the Communities requires touching upon matters not cited in the Treaties as falling within the jurisdiction of the Communities.[69] Where a matter falls partly within the jurisdiction of the Member States and partly within the jurisdiction of the Communities (or where no consensus can be reached as to with whom jurisdiction lies), decisions often take the hybrid form of "decisions of the Council and of the Ministers of the Member States meeting in the Council".[70]

Recent amendments of the Treaties have brought some non-Community matters within the competence of the Communities, as a result of which earlier resolutions of the Ministers meeting in the Council could if necessary be elaborated into binding Community law. Thus, the Single European Act brought research and development and the environment within the ambit of the EC Treaty, whilst the EU Treaty did the same for education, culture, public health and consumer protection and the Amsterdam Treaty for employment and matters connected with the movement of nationals of third countries.

---

[68] For the legal force of such decisions, see para. 18–003 *et seq., infra.* In addition to the academic writings cited therein, see Kaiser, "Die im Rat Vereinigten Vertreter der Regierungen der Mitgliedstaaten", *Zur Integration Europas. Festschrift für C.F. Ophüls* (n.35, *supra*), at 107–124; Bebr, "Acts of Representatives of the Governments of the Member States" (1966) S.E.W. 529–545.

[69] See the influence of the common commercial policy on EPC (para. 2–013, *supra*), of the free movement of persons on internal security policy (para. 2–016, *supra*) and on education policy (para. 5–239, *infra*) and of the free movement of goods on cultural, public health and environmental policies (paras 5–103 and 5–110, *infra*). See for the dynamic development of Community powers and co-operation between Member States, the articles in Bieber and Ress (eds), *Die Dynamik des Europäischen Gemeinschaftsrechts/The Dynamics of EC Law* (Nomos, Baden-Baden, 1987), 457 pp.

[70] See also para. 18–011, *infra*.

CHAPTER 3

BRINGING TOGETHER THE PATHS OF INTEGRATION INTO ONE EUROPEAN UNION

I. PROPOSALS FOR A EUROPEAN UNION

Towards European Union. Ten years after the Fouchet Plan, there was a **3–001** resurgence of the idea of expanding the area of activity of the Communities and, at the same time, of unifying the existing Community and non-Community integration paths. At the Paris summit conference held in October 1972, the Heads of State or of Government set themselves the major objective of "transforming, before the end of the present decade and with the fullest respect for the Treaties already signed, the whole complex of the relations of the Member States into a *European Union*",[1] From that point on, the framework to be established was referred to as the "European Union", regardless of its legal nature.

Tindemans Report. At the Paris summit conference held in December **3–002** 1974, the Heads of State or Government of the Member States invited the then Prime Minister of Belgium, Leo Tindemans, to draw up a report on European Union on the basis of reports to be prepared by the European Parliament, the Commission and the Court of Justice and after consulting "with the governments and a wide range of public opinion in the Community".[2] The Tindemans Report on European Union of December 1975 listed policy priorities for the Communities, but did not propose any real institutional reforms. It did make the case for meetings dealing with European Political Co-operation (EPC) to coincide as far as possible with Council meetings and for conferring formal legal force on the procedures relating to EPC.[3] The only achievement of the report was that the European Council instructed the Commission and the Foreign Ministers to report once a year on progress made towards achieving European Union.[4]

---

[1] (1972) 10 EC Bull. 25, point 16 (italics supplied).
[2] (1974) 12 EC Bull. point 1104, No. 13.
[3] Tindemans Report (1976) EC Bull. Suppl. 1, 14–15.
[4] (1976) 11 EC Bull. 109, point 2501.

No more did the European Council follow up the "Report of the Three Wise Men" drawn up at its request in 1979.[5]

3–003 Stuttgart Declaration. In 1981 the German and Italian Foreign Ministers, Hans-Dietrich Genscher and Emilio Colombo came up with a Draft European Act.[6] The draft proposed unifying all decision-making procedures of the Communities and EPC by conferring competence for all matters on the European Council and various subdivisions of the Council, which would be answerable to the European Council. It was also proposed to give more powers to the European Parliament, including the right to be consulted on the appointment of the President of the Commission and on the conclusion of international agreements. In the end, the European Council held in Stuttgart on June 19, 1983 merely adopted a Solemn Declaration on European Union, which, on the institutional level, contained little that was of any substance or novelty.[7] The Declaration confirmed that the European Council acted within the ambit of the Communities and EPC and likewise in other spheres (culture, law and order and lawlessness were mentioned), but that in so doing Community matters and matters coming under the heading of EPC were to continue to be governed by their respective procedures.

3–004 Draft Treaty on European Union. The proposal which attracted the most interest was the Draft Treaty establishing the European Union which was approved by the European Parliament on February 14, 1984.[8] The Draft Treaty proposed to eliminate the distinction between the Communities and EPC. The European Communities were to be converted into a European Union which was to have general competence in respect of external relations, yet retain the intergovernmental method of decision-making alongside the supranational one. It was proposed that the European Union would conduct its policy through common action in some fields and through co-operation between the Member States in the European Council in others.

The Draft Treaty proposed that the European Council should be recognised as an institution of the Union alongside the four existing

---

[5] For a summary of that report, see (1979) 11 EC Bull. point 1.5.2. The "Wise Men" were Barend Biesheuvel, Edmund Dell and Robert Marjolin. For the Council's comments, see (1980) 12 EC Bull. point 1.1.11. See VerLoren van Themaat, "Enkele kanttekeningen bij de rapporten van drie Wijzen en van de Commissie Spierenburg" (1980) S.E.W. 144–153.

[6] Neville-Jones, "The Genscher-Colombo Proposals on European Union" (1983) C.M.L.R. 658–699.

[7] Solemn Declaration of Stuttgart on European Union of June 19, 1983 (1983) 6 EC Bull. Point 1.6.1.

[8] [1984] O.J. C77/33, and (1984) 2 EC Bull. point 1.1.2. For commentaries on the Draft Treaty, see Bieber, Jacqué and Weiler, *An ever closer Union—A critical analysis of the Draft Treaty establishing the European Union* (Commission of the EC, Brussels, 1985), 345 pp.; Capotorti, Hilf, Jacobs and Jacqué, *Le Traité d'Union européenne—Commentaire du project adopté par le Parlement européen* (Editions de l'Université de Bruxelles, Brussels, 1985), 307 pp. See also Nickel, "Le projet de traité instituant l'Union européenne élaboré par le Parlement européen" (1984) C.D.E. 511–542.

institutions (European Parliament, Council, Commission, Court of Justice). Common action of the Union would invariably have to be based on a law. In principle, legislative power would be exercised jointly by the Council and the European Parliament. The Union would obtain extensive powers in relation to economic policy (including conjunctural and credit policy) and to "societal policies" (consumer, environmental, education and research, cultural, and information policies). As far as external relations policy was concerned, it was proposed that the Union would undertake common actions in respect of aspects already falling within the competence of the Communities, but co-operation between the Member States would continue to apply to the remaining aspects. Obligations entered into by the Member States under mutual co-operation would not form part of the law of the Union, but would be governed by international law.

Adonnino and Dooge Committees. Although the Draft Treaty was not **3–005** approved, it did set in motion a political debate on amending the existing Treaties. The European Council held in Fontainebleau in June 1984 set up two ad hoc committees, one to prepare and co-ordinate measures "to strengthen and promote [the Community's] identity and its image for its citizens and for the rest of the world" (the Adonnino Committee) and the second on institutional affairs (the Dooge Committee).[9] The Dooge Committee concluded that negotiations should be held on a treaty to establish a European Union.[10] In June 1985, the Milan European Council decided to convene a conference of representatives of the governments of the Member States within the meaning of Art. 236 of the EEC Treaty to discuss amendments to the Treaties.[11] In September 1985 the proceedings of the Intergovernmental Conference began. Portugal and Spain, as candidates for accession, were involved from the outset. The result was the Single European Act.

II. THE SINGLE EUROPEAN ACT

Single European Act. On February 17, 1986, nine Member States signed **3–006** the Single European Act (SEA).[12] The Danish Government wished first to hold a referendum and both Greece and Italy decided to await the outcome

---

[9] (1984) 6 EC Bull. point 1.1.9. For the Adonnino Committee's report, see the discussion of citizenship, para. 12–005, *infra*.

[10] (1985) 3 EC Bull. point 3.5.1. See Lauwaars, "De Europese Unie: Het Ontwerp-Verdrag van het Europese Parlement en het rapport van het Comité-Dooge" (1985) S.E.W. 398–409.

[11] (1985) 6 EC Bull. point I.2.2.

[12] For a general discussion, see Nuttall, "European Political Co-operation and the Single European Act" (1985) Y.E.L. 203–232; Pescatore, "Some Critical Remarks on the Single European Act" (1986) C.M.L.R. 9–18; Edward, "The Impact of the Single European Act on the Institutions" (1986) C.M.L.R. 19–30; De Zwaan, "The Single European Act: Conclusion of a Unique Document" (1986) C.M.L.R. 747–765; Glaesner, "L'Acte unique européen" (1986) R.M.C. 307–321; Jacqué, "L'Acte unique européen" (1986) R.T.D.E. 575–612;

of that referendum before signing. Although the Danish Parliament voted to reject the Single European Act on January 21, 1986, the Danish people voted in a referendum on February 27, 1986 by 56.2 per cent to accept the results of the negotiations. On the following day, Denmark, Greece and Italy signed the SEA. Although in Ireland the Parliament (the Dail) had voted in favour of the Single European Act, the Government could not deposit the instrument of ratification because an action was brought challenging the constitutionality of the new treaty. Because the Supreme Court ruled that the SEA necessitated a change in the Constitution, the latter was amended after a referendum held on May 26, 1987.[13] As a result, the Single European Act did not enter into force until July 1, 1987.[14]

3–007 **EC and EPC.** The Single European Act is a heterogeneous text. First, it made major changes to the ECSC, EEC and EAEC Treaties (see para. 1–010). Secondly, it codified for the first time existing practice in the matter of European Political Co-operation (see para. 2–013). The form in which the Treaty provisions were to be combined was a delicate matter, which the Intergovernmental Conference did not tackle until the last moment. The SEA keeps the two integration paths separate in Title II (Arts 4–29) and Title III (Art. 30 only), respectively, but brings them together into one text, which is supplemented by common provisions (Title I: Arts 1, 2 and 3) and general and final provisions (Title IV: Arts 31–34).[15] The first para. of Art. 1 of the SEA states that the objective of the European Communities and European Political Co-operation is "to contribute together to making concrete progress towards European unity[16]". The SEA was therefore a step on the way to European Union covering "relations as a whole among [the Member] States", as stated at the 1972 Paris summit conference and reformulated in the preamble to the SEA.

3–008 **Separate bases for EC and EPC.** The SEA emphasises the differing legal bases of the European Communities and EPC (SEA, second and third paras of Art. 1) and the various conditions and purposes which the Community institutions and the EPC institutions and bodies have to take

---

Krenzler, "Die Einheitliche Europäische Akte als Schritt auf dem Wege zu einer Gemeinsamen Europäischen Außenpolitik" (1986) EuR. 384–391; VerLoren van Themaat, "De Europese Akte" (1986) S.E.W. 464–483; Bosco, "Commentaire de l'Acte unique européen des 17–28 février, 1986" (1987) C.D.E. 355–382; De Ruyt, *L'Acte unique européen* (Editions de l'Université de Bruxelles, Brussels, 1987), 355 pp.

[13] Temple Lang, "The Irish Court Case Which Delayed the Single European Act: *Crotty v An Taoiseach and others*" (1987) C.M.L.R. 709–718; Murphy and Cras, "L'affaire Crotty: la Cour Suprême d'Irlande rejette l'Acte Unique Européen" (1988) C.D.E. 276–305; McCutcheon, "The Irish Supreme Court, European Political Co-operation and the Single European Act" (1988) L.I.E.I. 93–100.

[14] Implemented in the UK by the European Communities (Amendment) Act 1986.

[15] Hence its title "Single European Act" (*Acte unique européen, Einheitliche Europäische Akte*).

[16] "European Union" (*Union européenne, Europäische Union, Europese Unie*) in other Community languages.

into account when taking action (SEA, Art. 3(1) and (2)). The SEA also provides for the two integration paths to develop in their own way. Art. 31 of the SEA denies any jurisdiction to the Court of Justice to rule on acts taken by EPC institutions or bodies or by Member States within the framework of EPC.[17] The Member States intended thereby to keep the last word on any further integration in the context of EPC. On the other hand, Art. 32 of the SEA provides that, apart from Art. 31 and the provisions amending the Community Treaties, nothing in the Act is to affect the Community Treaties. Neither intergovernmental co-operation under EPC nor the European Council (SEA, Art. 2) may go back on the *acquis communautaire*, that is, existing Community law as interpreted and applied by the Court of Justice. The Member States undertook to examine the need for any revision of the Treaty provisions relating to EPC five years after the entry into force of the SEA (SEA, Art. 30(12)).

Links between EPC and EC. Nevertheless, the Single European Act **3–009** established for the first time a number of institutional links between the two integration paths. The European Council was empowered to act in both spheres under Art. 2 of the SEA. The SEA made it easier for decision-making of the Communities and EPC to be concentrated within the Council on the initiative of the Member State holding the Presidency, with the permanent involvement of the Commission and the European Parliament. Above all, the establishment of the EPC secretariat in Brussels was of practical significance in this regard. At the same time, the SEA necessitated a contribution from the Community institutions on account of the consistency required to be shown by the external policies of the Communities and of EPC (SEA, Art. 30(5)). The Act shared responsibility for attaining that consistency by providing that both the Presidency and the Commission should have special responsibility in that regard "each within its own sphere of competence".

The incorporation of the two integration paths into a single treaty also had the effect of making the Communities and EPC into two firmly fixed pillars, on which the European Union would be built. EPC was enshrined in a treaty which was the outcome of a procedure initiated in the context of the Communities. All the Member States of the Communities thus became parties to EPC. In turn, Title III required the "High Contracting Parties" to EPC to be members of the European Communities (SEA, Art. 30(1)).

---

[17] Article 31 provides that the provisions of the ECSC Treaty, the EEC Treaty and the EAEC Treaty "concerning the powers of the Court of Justice of the European Communities and the exercise of those powers shall apply only to the provisions of Title II and to Art. 32; they shall apply to those provisions under the same conditions as for the provisions of the said Treaties". Consequently, that article rules out the common provisions (Title I), the provisions on European co-operation in the sphere of foreign policy (Title III) and the general and final provisions (Title IV), with the exception of Art. 32. For the lack of jurisdiction of the ECJ to rule on an act of the European Council, see CFI (order of July 14, 1994), Case T–584/93 *Roujansky v Council* [1994] E.C.R. II-585, paras 12–14, confirmed by ECJ (order of January 13, 1995), Case C–253/94 P *Roujansky* [1995] E.C.R. I–7.

III.   THE TREATY ON EUROPEAN UNION

A.   THE INTERGOVERNMENTAL CONFERENCES HELD IN 1990–1991

3–010 **Intergovernmental conference.** In December 1989 the European Council held in Strasbourg decided to convene "a conference of representatives of the governments of the Member States" within the meaning of Art. 236 of the EEC Treaty.[18] This intergovernmental conference was to determine the changes which needed to be made to the EEC Treaty in order to achieve economic and monetary union. The unification of Germany and political developments in central and eastern Europe, however, triggered debate about the further development of the Community's political dimension, both internally and externally. Following the collapse of the communist state machinery of the eastern bloc, the question arose as to whether the Member States could allow the new democracies to join the Community or whether it was necessary first to improve the Community's institutional structure.[19] Subjects were put forward from various quarters for an additional intergovernmental conference. Following a memorandum from the Belgian Government and a joint letter from the French President François Mitterand and Chancellor Helmut Kohl, addressed to the Irish Presidency, the Commission and the European Parliament also lodged proposals.[20] In June 1990, the European Council decided to hold both a Conference on Economic and Monetary Union and a Conference on Political Union.[21] These Intergovernmental Conferences were opened at the meeting of the European Council held in Rome on December 14–15, 1990.

The proceedings were rounded off at the European Council held in Maastricht on December 9–10, 1991.[22] The two texts on which the

---

[18] (1989) 12 EC Bull. point I.1.11.

[19] See the preamble to the EU Treaty, where the High Contracting Parties refer to "the historic importance of ending the division of the European continent and the need to create firm bases for the construction of the future Europe".

[20] All these texts are reproduced as annexes to Laursen and Vanhoonacker (eds), *The Intergovernmental Conference on Political Union* (European Institute of Public Administration/Martinus Nijhoff, Maastricht, 1992), 505 pp., and in Corbett, *The Treaty of Maastricht. From Conception to Ratification: A Comprehensive Reference Guide* (Longman, Harlow (Essex), 1993), 512 pp.

[21] (1990) 6 EC Bull. point I.1., No. I.11.

[22] For commentaries on the negotiations, see VerLoren van Themaat, "De constitutionele problematiek van een Europese politieke Unie" (1991) S.E.W. 436–454; VerLoren van Themaat, "Some Preliminary Observations on the Intergovernmental Conferences: The Relations between the Concepts of a Common Market, a Monetary Union, an Economic Union, a Political Union and Sovereignty" (1991) C.M.L.R. 291–318; Vignes, "Le project de la Présidence luxembourgeoise d'un Traité sur l'Union" (1991) R.M.C. 504–517; Reich, "Le développement de l'Union européenne dans le cadre des conférences intergouvernementales" (1991) R.M.C. 704–709; Corbett, "The Intergovernmental Conference on Political Union" (1992) J.C.M.S. 271–298.

European Council had reached agreement, namely provisions on Economic and Monetary Union and provisions on Political Union, were fused into one Treaty on European Union, which was signed on February 7, 1992 by all the Member States. Particular heed was paid during the conferences to the form in which the different texts were to be amalgamated. In April 1991, the Luxembourg Presidency compiled the views of the Member States in a non-paper, which traced out a structure in which the Union was based on three pillars, namely provisions on the Communities, provisions on a common foreign and security policy, and provisions on co-operation in the fields of justice and home affairs.[23] In September 1991, the Netherlands Presidency unexpectedly moved that discussion should proceed on the basis of a non-paper which assumed as its destination, not the "European Union", but the "European Community".[24] Under this proposal, both the common foreign and security policy and co-operation in the fields of justice and home affairs were to be brought within the sphere of competence of the European Community. This approach was supported by the European Parliament and the Commission. In the conference room, the Presidency was backed only by Belgium, with the result that preference was given to pursuing the negotiations on the basis of the Luxembourg proposal of a European Union founded on three pillars.

Ratification in Member States. The Treaty on European Union (EU **3–011** Treaty) was signed at Maastricht on February 7, 1992, but did not enter into force until November 1, 1993.[25] Just as in the case of the Single European Act, the entry into force of the EU Treaty was delayed by complications in the national ratification procedures.[26] In Denmark, 50.7 per cent of the votes cast in the referendum held on June 2, 1992 were against the Treaty, although the Danish Parliament had voted in favour on May 12, 1992.[27] The Treaty was approved, however, by referendum on June

---

[23] For the text of the non-paper, see *Europe*, No. 1709/1710, May 3, 1991.

[24] For the text of the Netherlands Draft Treaty, see *Europe*, No. 1734/1734, October 3, 1991.

[25] [1992] O.J. C191; implemented in the UK by the European Communities (Amendment) Act 1993. The Treaty was republished, together with a complete, revised text of the EC Treaty in [1992] O.J. C224. For general commentaries on the EU Treaty, see Everling, "Reflections on the Structure of the European Union" (1992) C.M.L.R. 1053–1077; Hartley, "Constitutional and Institutional Aspects of the Maastricht Agreement" (1993) I.C.L.Q. 213–237; Melchior, "Le Traité de Maastricht sur l'Union européenne (essai de présentation synthétique)" (1992) A.D. 1207–1255; Constantinesco, "La structure du Traité instituant l'Union européenne—Les dispositions communes et finales. Les nouvelles compétences" (1993) C.D.E. 251–294; Curtin, "The Constitutional Structure of the Union: A Europe of Bits and Pieces" (1993) C.M.L.R. 17–69; Cloos, Reinesch, Vignes and Weyland, *Le traité de Maastricht. Genèse, analyse, commentaires* (Bruylant, Brussels, 1994, 2nd ed.), 814 pp.

[26] For a survey of the national ratification procedures, see (1993) 10 EC Bull. point 2.3.1. See the discussion in Rideau, "Les procédures de ratification du traité sur l'Union Européenne" (1992) R.F.D.C. 611–624; Arts *et al.*, "Ratification Process of the Treaty on European Union" (1993) E.L.Rev. 228–253, 356–360, 448–451 and 541–544.

[27] For the situation after the referendum, see Kapteyn, "Denemarken en het Verdrag van Maastricht" (1992) N.J.B. 781–783. Without Danish ratification, the EU Treaty could not enter into force (see EU Treaty, Art. 52, 302, *infra*). *Cf.* Rideau, "La ratification et l'entrée en vigueur du Traité de Maastricht. Aspects internationaux" (1992) R.F.D.C. 479–491.

18, 1992 in Ireland (69.05 per cent voted yes) and on September 20, 1992 in France, albeit narrowly (51.05 per cent). In order to enable the Treaty to be ratified in Denmark, the European Council held in Edinburgh on December 11–12, 1992 laid down a number of special rules which would apply only to Denmark and enter into force at the same time as the Treaty itself.[28] Those rules are embodied, partly in a decision of the Heads of State or Government meeting within the European Council,[29] and partly in unilateral "declarations" of the European Council and Denmark itself.[30] The provisions helped to ease Denmark's obligations, yet without encroaching upon the EU Treaty. In a second referendum held on May 18, 1993, 56.8 per cent of Danes voted in favour of ratifying the EU Treaty.[31]

The Constitutions of Germany,[32] France,[33] Ireland,[34] Spain,[35]

---

[28] (1992) 12 EC Bull. points I.33-I.44.

[29] Decision of the Heads of State or Government, meeting within the European Council, concerning certain problems raised by Denmark on the Treaty on European Union, [1992] O.J. C348/2.

[30] Declarations of the European Council, [1992] O.J. C348/3; Unilateral Declarations of Denmark, to be associated to the Danish instrument of ratification of the Treaty on European Union and of which the 11 other Member States will take cognisance, [1992] O.J.C348/4.

[31] Gjørtler, "Ratifying the Treaty on European Union: An Interim Report" (1993) E.L.Rev. 356–360; Glistrup, "Le traité sur l'Union européenne: la ratification du Danemark" (1994) R.M.C.U.E. 9–16; Howarth, "The Compromise on Denmark and the Treaty on European Union: A Legal and Political Analysis" (1994) C.M.L.R. 765–805. For this and other Danish referendums concerning European integration, see Simoulin, "L'Europe au miroir danois" (2002) R.M.C.U.E. 83–88.

[32] For the amendment of the *Grundgesetz* (Basic Law), see Autexier, "Le traité de Maastricht et l'ordre constitutionnel allemand" (1992) R.F.D.C. 625–641; Hahn, *Der Vertrag von Maastricht als völkerrechtliche Übereinkunft und Verfassung* (Nomos, Baden-Baden, 1992), 141 pp.; Scholz, "Grundgesetz und europäische Einigung" (1992) N.J.W. 2593–2601; Arnold, "La loi fondamentale de la RFA et l'Union européenne: le nouvel article 23 de la loi fondamentale" (1993) R.I.D.C. 673–678; Scholz, "Europäische Union und Verfassungsreform" (1993) N.J.W. 1690–1692.

[33] For the judgment of the *Conseil constitutionnel* of April 9, 1992, which prompted the amendment of the Constitution, see (1993) C.M.L.R 345–358, the commentaries of Jacqué (1992) R.T.D.E. 251–264 and Genevois (1992) R.F.D.A. 373, and, in addition, Favoreu and Gaïa, "Les décisions du Conseil constitutionnel relatives au traité sur l'Union européenne" (1992) R.F.D.C. 389–412; Grewe, "La révision constitutionnelle en vue de la ratification du traité de Maastricht" (1992) R.F.D.C. 413–438; for the second judgment of the *Conseil constitutionnel* of September 2, 1992, see Genevois, "Le Traité sur l'Union européenne et la Constitution révisée" (1992) R.F.D.A. 937; for a discussion of those judgments and the third judgment of September 23, 1992, see L. Favoreu, "Le contrôle de constitutionnalité du traité de Maastricht et le développement du 'droit constitutionnel international'" (1993) R.G.D.I.P. 39–66; Blumann, "La ratification par la France du traité de Maastricht" (1994) R.M.C.U.E. 393–406; Oliver, "The French Constitution and the Treaty of Maastricht" (1994) I.C.L.Q. 1–25.

[34] Murphy, "Maastricht: Implementation in Ireland" (1994) E.L.Rev. 94, at 100.

[35] For the judgment of the *Tribunal constitucional* and the amendment of the Spanish Constitution, see Rubio Llorente, "La constitution espagnole et le traité de Maastricht" (1992) R.F.D.C. 651–662; Lopez Castillo and Polakiewicz, "Verfassung und Gemeinschaftsrecht in Spanien—Zur Maastricht-Erklärung des Spanischen Verfassungsgerichts" (1993) Eu.GR.Z. 277–285.

Luxembourg[36] and Portugal[37] were amended, principally to enable those countries to participate in economic and monetary union and to give the vote to nationals of other Member States. In Belgium and Italy the necessary constitutional changes were to be made after the event.[38] In the Netherlands the government considered that the EU Treaty was not incompatible with the Constitution.[39] In the United Kingdom[40] and Germany[41] ratification hinged on a judicial pronouncement on the constitutional implications of the EU Treaty.

B. THE ESTABLISHMENT OF THE EUROPEAN UNION

European Union. By the EU Treaty, the Contracting Parties established a **3–012** European Union, founded on the European Communities and supplemented by the policies and forms of co-operation established by the

[36] Delpérée, "La Constitution belge, la Constitution luxembourgeoise et le Traité sur l'Union européenne" (1993) Ann.Dr.Lux. 15–33; Arendt, "Le traité sur l'Union européenne et la Constitution du Grand-Duché de Luxembourg" (1993) Ann.Dr.Lux. 35–52; Frieden, "L'Union européenne et la Constitution luxembourgeoise: une cohabitation nécessaire" (1993) Ann.Dr.Lux. 53–63; Thewes, "La Constitution luxembourgeoise et l'Europe" (1993) Ann.Dr.Lux. 65–78.

[37] Miranda, "La constitution portugaise et le traité de Maastricht" (1992) R.F.D.C. 679–688; Alves Vieira, "Ratifying the Treaty on European Union" (1993) E.L.Rev. 448–451.

[38] Van Ginderachter, "De goedkeuring van het Verdrag van Maastricht" (1992–93) R.W. 670–673; Gaudissart, "La ratification du traité sur l'Union européenne: l'exemple de la Belgique" (1994) R.M.C.U.E. 86–93. See the opinion of the *Raad van State/Conseil d'Etat* (1991–1992) Gedr.St., Kamer, B.Z, No. 482/1, 69–89. The *Arbitragehof/Cour d'Arbitrage* (Belgian constitutional court) declared an application for annulment of the law approving the EU Treaty inadmissible on the ground that persons claiming that the introduction of voting rights for the non-Belgians would diminish the weight of their own votes had no specific interest: *Arbitragehof/Cour d'Arbitrage*, October 18, 1994, No. 76/94, (1994) A.A. 901–910. For the situation in Italy, see Luciani, "La Constitution italienne et les obstacles à l'intégration européenne" (1992) R.F.D.C. 663–676.

[39] Ter Kuile, "Tussen Brussel en Maastricht" (1992) N.J.B. 1040–1044; Brouwer, "Wijkt het Unie-Verdrag van Maastricht af van de Grondwet of van het Statuut?" (1992) N.J.B. 1045–1049; Besselink, "De constitutie van Europa: de verenigbaarheid van het Verdrag betreffende de Europese Unie met de Nederlandse Constitutie" (1993) T.B.P. 370–376. But see Heringa, "De verdragen van Maastricht in strijd met de Grondwet" (1992) N.J.B. 749–752. For the advice of the *Raad van State* to the Queen of May 27, 1992, see *Kst.*, Tweede Kamer, 1991–92, 22 647 (R1437), A.

[40] On July 30, 1993 the Divisional Court dismissed an action brought against the intended ratification of the EU Treaty: Marshall, "The Maastricht Proceedings" (1993) P.L. 402–407; Szyszczak, "Ratifying the Treaty on European Union: a final report" (1993) E.L.Rev. 541–544; Denza, "La ratification du traité de Maastricht par le Royaume-Uni" (1994) R.M.C.U.E. 172–180.

[41] The *Bundesverfassungsgericht* held on October 12, 1993 that the ratification of the EU Treaty did not raise any constitutional objections. For the relevant judgment, see para. 17–019, *infra*. On the following day, the Federal Republic of Germany deposited the instrument of ratification, it being the last Member State to do so, after which the EU Treaty entered into force on November 1, 1993 pursuant to Art. 52(2) of the EU Treaty. See the notice concerning the date of entry into force, [1993] O.J. L293/61. In a judgment of March 31, 1998, the *Bundesverfassungsgericht* further held that participation in Economic and Monetary Union was compatible with the German Basic Law; see (1998) EuR. 324–339 and Mengelkoch, "Bundesverfassungsgericht lässt Euro rollen" (1998) EuR. 563–570; see also Kempen, "Die Europäische Währungsunion und der Streit um die Geltung des Gemeinschaftsrechts" (1997) A.Völkerr. 273, at 290–292.

new Treaty (EU Treaty, Art. 1, first and third paras). The EU Treaty establishes a legal link between the Communities and the supplementary policies and forms of co-operation: henceforward, there is to be one procedure for acceding to the Union, supplanting the various accession procedures provided for in the ECSC, EEC and EAEC Treaties (EU Treaty, Art. 49) and one procedure for amending the various Treaties on which the Union is founded (EU Treaty, Art. 48). Yet the EU Treaty has not conferred legal personality on the Union as a whole.[42] It was initially suggested that the whole entity should be called a "Union with a federal mission", but some Member States were strongly opposed to this.[43] In the end, the Intergovernmental Conference characterised the Treaty as "a new stage in the process of creating an ever closer union among the peoples of Europe, in which decisions are taken as closely as possible to the citizen".[44]

Accordingly, the Contracting Parties did not regard the European Union as completing the integration process, but as a new step towards "union among the peoples of Europe", as mentioned already in the preamble to the EEC Treaty. In this way, the EU Treaty makes it clear that the Union is more than an organisation of States; it is of direct concern to the various regions and to the citizen. The third para. of Art. 1 of the EU Treaty confers on the Union the task of organising "in a manner demonstrating consistency and solidarity, relations between the Member States and between their peoples". The Union takes account of geographical and cultural diversity within the Member States,[45] alongside its obligation to "respect the *national* identities of its Member States" .[46] In order to secure the so-called principles of "diversity" and "proximity" in the continuing process of integration, the EU Treaty provides that the objectives of the Union are to be achieved "while respecting the principle of subsidiarity as defined in Art. 5 of the Treaty establishing the European Community" (Art. 2, second para., see para. 5–028 *et seq.*)

---

[42] For the factors on the basis of which the Union may since be considered to have legal personality, see para. 19–003.

[43] Principally, the UK, Denmark and Portugal strongly objected to the term "federal", often wrongly interpreting it as a synonym for centralism. See Lenaerts, "Federalism: Essential Concepts in Evolution—The Case of the European Union" (1998) Fordham I.L.J. 746–798.

[44] In 1997 the Treaty of Amsterdam added that "decisions are [to be] taken as openly as possible and as closely as possible to the citizen": EU Treaty, Art. 1, second para.

[45] The EU Treaty recognises regional diversity (see EC Treaty, Art. 151(1) and Art. 174(2)). See also the preamble to the EU Treaty, in which the Contracting Parties express their desire "to deepen the solidarity between their peoples while respecting their history, their culture and their traditions". For the question of cultural diversity, see also EC Treaty, Art. 151(4) (added by the Treaty of Amsterdam).

[46] EU Treaty, Art. 6(3) (italics supplied). See also the preamble to the Charter of Fundamental Rights of the European Union (see para. 17–083), which refers to " respecting the diversity of the cultures and traditions of the peoples of Europe as well as the national identities of the Member States and the organisation of their public authorities at national, regional and local levels".

The Union is founded on principles common to the Member States, namely liberty, democracy, respect for human rights and fundamental freedoms, and the rule of law (EU Treaty, Art. 6(1), as amended by the Amsterdam Treaty). It is to respect fundamental rights, as guaranteed by the European Convention for the Protection of Human Rights and Fundamental Freedoms signed in Rome on November 4, 1950 and as they result from the constitutional traditions common to the Member States, as general principles of Community law (EU Treaty, Art. 6(2); see para. 17–073 *et seq.*). The Union recognises nationals of the Member States as *citizens* of the Union (EC Treaty, Arts 17–22; see para. 12–007 *et seq.*).

Objectives. The first paragraph of Art. 2 of the EU Treaty provides that **3–013** the Union is to set itself the following objectives:

(1) to promote economic and social progress and a high level of employment and to achieve balanced and sustainable development;

(2) to assert the Union's identity on the international scene;

(3) to strengthen the protection of the rights and interests of nationals of Member States of the Union;

(4) to maintain and develop the Union as an area of freedom, security and justice, in which the free movement of persons is assured; and

(5) to maintain in full the *acquis communautaire* and build on it.[47]

The EU Treaty was the first of the Treaties to use the expression *acquis communautaire*. Whereas, generally speaking, that expression refers to existing Community law as interpreted and applied by the Court of Justice, here it denotes the specific institutional and substantive bases of the Community legal order, on which the Union may not go back.[48]

The Union is to provide itself with the means necessary to attain its objectives and carry through its policies (EU Treaty, Art. 6(4)). Article 2

---

[47] The objectives set out in Art. 2 of the EU Treaty have been supplemented by the Treaty of Amsterdam; para. 3–017, *infra*. In 1992 the EU Treaty had extended the objectives of the European Community (EC Treaty, Arts 2, 3 and 4) and conferred specific objectives on the CFSP (EU Treaty, Art. 11; para. 20–039, *infra*). In 1997 the Amsterdam Treaty further extended the objectives of the EC Treaty, while setting out aims for police and judicial co-operation in criminal matters (PJCC; EU Treaty, Art. 29); para. 6–006, *infra*. See Müller-Graff, "Einheit und Kohärenz der Vertragsziele von EG und EU" (1998) EuR. Beiheft 2 67–80.

[48] In the context of the accession of new Member States to the Union, *acquis communautaire* is used to describe the whole corpus of Community law which new Member States have to take over; para. 8–008, *infra*. For a critical view of the different meanings ascribed to this expression, see Delcourt, "The *acquis communautaire*: has the concept had its day?" (2001) C.M.L.R. 829–870.

sketches out a number of policy avenues, some of which were already being followed by the Communities, whilst others build on forms of co-operation which operated in parallel to the Communities. In order to promote economic and social progress and a high level of employment and to achieve balanced and sustainable development, the Union aims: (1) to create an area without internal frontiers, (2) to strengthen economic and social cohesion, and (3) to establish economic and monetary union, ultimately including a single currency.[49] In order to assert the Union's identity on the international scene, the Union is to implement a common foreign and security policy, including the progressive framing of a common defence policy, which might lead to a common defence.[50] As a means of protecting the rights and interests of nationals of the Member States, Union citizenship is introduced.[51] Maintaining and developing the Union as an area of freedom, security and justice, in which the free movement of persons is assured, is to be coupled with "appropriate measures with respect to external border controls, asylum, immigration and the prevention and combating of crime".[52] Respecting and building upon the *acquis communautaire* is the first task for the institutional framework of the Union (EU Treaty, Art. 3, first para.). In order to ensure the effectiveness of the mechanisms and the institutions of the Community, Art. 2 of the EU Treaty refers to the possibility of examining to what extent the "supplementary" policies and forms of co-operation (Art. 1, third para.) require revision.[53]

C. RETENTION OF DIFFERENT PATHS TOWARDS INTEGRATION

3–014 **Treaty structure.** The Communities and the supplementary policies and forms of co-operation subsist within the European Union as different integration paths. The type of integration is not immediately apparent from the structure of the EU Treaty, which contains, preceded by common

---

[49] The Single European Act already conferred powers on the Community with a view to attaining the internal market, which was described as an "area without internal frontiers" (EEC Treaty, Art. 8a, now EC Treaty, Art. 14; paras 5–077–5–081, *infra*), and to promoting economic and social cohesion (EEC Treaty, Arts 130a–130e, now EC Treaty, Arts 158–162; para. 5–247, *infra*) and announced economic and monetary union (EEC Treaty, Art. 102a; para. 5–127, *supra*). For European monetary co-operation, see para. 2–011, *supra*.

[50] Such policy is an extension of European Political Co-operation, para. 2–013, *supra*.

[51] For the developments leading up thereto, see paras 12–004–12–006, *infra*.

[52] As a result of this provision, the Treaty of Amsterdam replaced the objective introduced in 1992 of developing "close co-operation on justice and home affairs". The measures to which the provision refers relate to the activities carried out under Title VI of the original EU Treaty and by way of co-operation between most of the Member States under the Schengen Convention; para. 2–017, *supra*.

[53] This was done for the first time by the Treaty of Amsterdam; para. 3–019, *infra*.

provisions (Title I: Arts 1–7)[54] and followed by final provisions (Title VIII: Arts 46–53)[55]:

— provisions amending the Treaty establishing the European Economic Community with a view to establishing the European Community (Title II: Art. 8);

— provisions amending the Treaty establishing the European Coal and Steel Community (Title III: Art. 9);

— provisions amending the Treaty establishing the European Economic Energy Community (Title IV: Art. 10);

— provisions on a common foreign and security policy (Title V: Arts 11–28);

— provisions on police and judicial co-operation in criminal matters (Title VI: Arts 29–42); and

— provisions on closer co-operation (Title VII: Arts 43–45).

Separate pillars. Action on the part of the institutions listed in Art. 5 of **3–015** the EU Treaty pursuant to the EC Treaty and the EAEC Treaty constitutes the Community pillar of the Union. In contrast, the common foreign and security policy (CFSP, which replaced European Political Co-operation (EPC)[56]) exhibits the characteristics of an intergovernmental form of co-operation. In view of the task conferred on the Court of Justice with regard to police and judicial co-operation in criminal matters (PJCC or JHA[57]), this is less true of that form of co-operation, which was introduced

---

[54] The common provisions cover the establishment, definition, foundation and task of the Union (Art. 1), its objectives (Art. 2, first para.) and the manner of achieving them (Art. 2, second para.), the institutional framework and its tasks (Art. 3), the European Council (Art. 4), the manner in which the Community institutions exercise their powers (Art. 5), the principles respected by the Union (Art. 6(1), (2) and (3)), providing the Union with the necessary means (Art. 6(4)) and the possibility of imposing sanctions for a serious and persistent breach by a Member State of the principles of liberty, democracy, respect for human rights and fundamental freedoms, and the rule of law (Art. 7).

[55] The final provisions consist of rules on the powers of the Court of Justice (Art. 46), the relationship between the EU Treaty and the Community Treaties (Art. 47), the amendment of the Treaties on which the Union is founded (Art. 48), the admission of States to the Union (Art. 49), the repeal of Articles of the Merger Treaty and the Single European Act (Art. 50), the conclusion of the EU Treaty for an unlimited period (Art. 51), the ratification and entry into force of the EU Treaty (Art. 52) and the drawing up of the Treaty in 12 authentic versions (Art. 53).

[56] Art. 50(2) of the EU Treaty repealed Arts 2 and 3(2) and Title III of the Single European Act.

[57] Ever since the Treaty of Amsterdam, co-operation in the fields of justice and home affairs under Title VI of the EU Treaty has been confined to police and judicial co-operation in criminal matters. Since the expression "justice and home affairs" (JHA) bears on both the "communitarised" competences (EC Treaty, Title IV) and on non-Community co-operation in criminal matters (EU Treaty, Title VI), the authors have elected in this book to refer to co-operation pursuant to Title VI of the EU Treaty as police and judicial co-operation in criminal matters (PJCC) in line with the wording of the Treaty.

by the Treaty of Amsterdam in place of the characteristically intergovernmental co-operation in the fields of justice and home affairs.

The CFSP and PJCC operate in principle outside the ambit of the Communities. They take shape in accordance with the procedural rules and other provisions set out in Titles V and VI, respectively, and in the common provisions and the final provisions. Under the procedures set out in Title V and Title VI, decision-making is in the hands of the Council, and hence of the national governments collectively, although the European Parliament does have the right to be consulted on PJCC measures adopted by the Council.

As far as Union action under the CFSP is concerned, any supervision by the Court of Justice is ruled out. Article 46 of the EU Treaty confines the Court's jurisdiction to provisions amending the Community Treaties, the provisions of Title VI (under the conditions provided for by Art. 35 of the EU Treaty), the provisions of Title VII (under the conditions provided for by Arts 11 and 11A of the EC Treaty and Art. 40 of the EU Treaty), Art. 6(2) of the EU Treaty with regard to action of the institutions in so far as the Court has jurisdiction under the Community Treaties or the EU Treaty, the procedural provisions of Art. 7 of the EU Treaty and the final provisions (see para. 10–076). Consequently, the Court exercises no supervision over the fulfilment by Member States of obligations laid down in the common provisions and in the provisions concerning the CFSP (Title V) of the EU Treaty.[58] The Court also has no jurisdiction to rule whether an act of the Union is lawfully based on the common provisions or on the provisions of Title V of the EU Treaty.[59] Furthermore, it cannot give a preliminary ruling on the validity of such an act in the light of those provisions, on its interpretation or on the interpretation of the relevant Treaty provisions.[60] This also takes acts of the European Council, which as such does not adopt acts of Community law (see para. 10–007), outside the scope of judicial review.[61] As far as PJCC (Title VI) is concerned, although the Court of Justice is not empowered to review whether Member States have fulfilled their Treaty obligations, Art. 35 of the EU Treaty confers jurisdiction on it to review, under certain conditions, acts adopted by the Union under Title VI (see para. 10–077). Closer co-operation between Member States may also be the subject of judicial review on the conditions

---

[58] para. 18–019, *infra*; compare the powers of the Court of Justice under Arts 226–228 of the EC Treaty.

[59] Subject, however, to the enforcement by the Court of Art. 47 of the EU Treaty (see n.62, *infra*, and the associated text). See also para. 18–021, *infra*; compare the powers of the Court under Arts 230–233 of the EC Treaty.

[60] *cf.* the preliminary ruling procedure under Art. 234 of the EC Treaty. See ECJ (order of April 7, 1995), Case C–167/94 *Grau Gomis* [1995] E.C.R. I–1023, para. 6, where the Court held that it had no jurisdiction to interpret Art. 2 of the EU Treaty.

[61] See CFI (order of July 14, 1994), Case T–584/93 *Roujansky v Council* [1994] E.C.R. II–585, paras 12–14 (and the parallel order given on the same day in Case T–179/94 *Bonnamy v Council*, paras 10–12, unreported), upheld by ECJ (order of January 13, 1995), Case C–235/94 P *Roujansky* [1995] E.C.R. I–7.

laid down in Art. 35 as far as police and judicial co-operation is concerned; where such closer co-operation relates to matters coming under the EC Treaty, the provisions of that Treaty apply (EU Treaty, Art. 40(4), and EC Treaty, Art. 11(4); see para. 9–009).

Since the non-Community provisions of the EU Treaty may not affect the Community Treaties or the Treaties and acts modifying or supplementing them (EU Treaty, Art. 47), the Union must always respect the *acquis communautaire*. The Court of Justice can enforce compliance with that obligation using the proper procedures against institutions of the Communities acting for the Union and against Member States (Article 47 is among the final provisions of the EU Treaty which are enforceable by the Court).[62]

D. A SINGLE INSTITUTIONAL FRAMEWORK

Institutional framework. Institutional links between the Communities and **3–016** the supplementary policies and forms of co-operation make it possible to achieve the common objectives of the Union using a heterogeneous structure. Under the first paragraph of Art. 3 of the EU Treaty, the Union has an "institutional framework which shall ensure the consistency and the continuity of the activities carried out in order to attain its objectives while respecting and building upon the *acquis communautaire*." By that institutional framework is meant the European Council and the institutions of the Communities (the European Parliament, the Council, the Commission, the Court of Justice and the Court of Auditors; see Art. 5). The fact that there is a "single" institutional framework does not signify, however, that the institutions perform the same functions within each of the two integration paths.[63]

Article 4 of the EU Treaty gives the European Council the task of providing the Union with the necessary impetus for its development and of defining the general political guidelines.[64] The EU Treaty assigned the European Council with a few specific tasks in Title II (provisions amending

---

[62] See, to that effect, ECJ, Case C–170/96 *Commission v Council* [1998] E.C.R. I–2763, paras 12–18. See Isaac, "Le 'pilier' communautaire de l'Union européenne, un 'pilier' pas comme les autres" (2001) C.D.E. 45–89.

[63] *cf.* Curtin (n.25, *supra*), at 27–30, who referred to the single institutional framework as a "fiction" and as "being given the lie". As regards the logistical support provided by the Community for the non-Community forms of co-operation, see Isaac (n.62, *supra*), 49–63. With regard to the heterogeneous structure perpetuated by the Treaty of Amsterdam, see the commentaries in (1998) EuR. Beiheft 2: Koenig, "Die Europäische Union als bloßer materiellrechtlicher Verbundsrahmen", 159–150; Zuleeg, "Die Organisationsstruktur der Europäischen Union—Eine Analyse der Klammerbestimmungen des Vertrags von Amsterdam", 156–163; Von Bogdandy, "Die Europäische Union als einheitlicher Verband", 165–183. See also Von Bogandy, "The Legal Case for Unity: The European Union as a Single Organisation with a Single Legal System" (1999) C.M.L.R. 887–910.

[64] The second para. of Art. 4 of the EU Treaty codifies the existing composition of the European Council, the third para. defines the latter's relations with the European Parliament; paras 10–003–10–006, *supra*.

the EC Treaty) and Title V (CFSP), which have been supplemented by the Treaty of Amsterdam (see para. 10–003).

Henceforth, the Community institutions have not only the powers which they had under the Community Treaties, but also the task of determining and implementing the CFSP of the Union and the Member States and of organising PJCC among the Member States. As far as these policies and forms of co-operation are concerned, it is the Council, the most "intergovernmental" institution of the Communities, which is to organise consultations among the Member States, adopt common positions and joint actions (in the context of the CFSP) and adopt common positions, framework decisions and decisions, and establish conventions (in the context of PJCC)[65]; the Commission does not have an exclusive right of initiative and exercises no supervision as to the Member States' compliance with the obligations which they enter into; the European Parliament is entitled only to be consulted and kept informed.[66]

The second paragraph of Art. 3 of the EU Treaty charges the Council and the Commission also with ensuring consistency of the Union's external activities as a whole in the context of its external relations, security, economic and development policies, co-operating to that end, and, each in accordance with its respective powers, ensuring the implementation of those policies. Since the Union does not have legal personality, its external activities take the form of action by the Communities and/or joint action by the Member States.

Article 5 of the EU Treaty states that the Community institutions are to exercise their powers under the conditions provided for and in order to achieve the objectives laid down, on the one hand, in the Community Treaties and, on the other, in the other provisions of the EU Treaty. Consequently, in the context of Title V, Title VI and Title VII the institutions are to operate in accordance with the procedural rules laid down therein.[67] Under Art. 28(1), Art. 41(1) and Art. 44, respectively, of the EU Treaty, the composition and manner of operation of the European Parliament, the Council and the Commission as laid down in the EC Treaty are to apply to those functions, with the exception of the rules on voting in the Council. In addition, the Community budgetary procedure is to apply to all administrative and operational expenditure occasioned by actions taken under Title V or Title VI, unless the Council decides otherwise by a

---

[65] EU Treaty, Arts 14–16 (CFSP) and Art. 34 (PJCC).
[66] EU Treaty, Art. 18(4), Art. 21, Art. 22 and Art. 27 (CFSP) and Art. 34(2), Art. 36(2) and Art. 39 (PJCC).
[67] Thus, in principle the requirement that the Council must take decisions by a unanimous vote applies (EU Treaty, Art. 23 and Art. 34).

unanimous vote in the case of operational expenditure.[68] In this way, the European Parliament, which has a power of decision relating to non-compulsory expenditure (see para. 10–130), may exercise supervision over non-Community action on the part of the Union.

IV. THE TREATY OF AMSTERDAM

Intergovernmental conference. The EU Treaty of February 7, 1992 stated **3–017** that a conference of representatives of the governments of the Member States was to meet in 1996 to examine the provisions of the Treaty for which revision was provided.[69] Members of the European Parliament produced a proposal for consolidating the texts of the Treaties into a formal Constitution of the European Union, although it failed to trigger a political debate.[70] When the accession negotiations were being rounded off in 1994, the Member State governments committed themselves to

---

[68] EC Treaty, Art. 268, second para.; EU Treaty, Art. 28(2)–(4) and Art. 41(2)–(4). As far as the closer co-operation catered for in Title VII is concerned, Art. 44A(2) of the EU Treaty provides that operational expenditure is to be borne by the participating Member States, unless the Council, acting unanimously, decides otherwise. Pursuant to the powers which Arts 246 and 248 of the EC Treaty confer on the Court of Auditors for the purposes of verifying the Communities' accounts, that institution also exercises powers in connection with Title V, Title VI and Title VII of the EU Treaty. For an application of the original version of Art. 41 (the former Art. K.8(1)) of the EU Treaty, see CFI, Case T–174/94 *Svenska Journalistförbundet v Council* [1998] E.C.R. II–2289, para. 82.

[69] Art. N(2) of the original EU Treaty. The articles concerned were the original Art. B, last indent (policies and forms of co-operation introduced by the EU Treaty), Art. J.4(6) and Art J.10 (CFSP, particularly security policy) of the EU Treaty and the former Art. 189b(8) of the EC Treaty (scope of the co-decision procedure). See also the declarations annexed to the EU Treaty relating to the commitment to examining the incorporation into the EC Treaty of specific titles on energy, civil protection and tourism (Declaration No.1) and the establishment of a hierarchy between the different categories of Community Acts (Declaration No. 16). Reference was also made to the 1996 Intergovernmental Conference in a statement annexed to the Interinstitutional Agreement of October 29, 1993 on budgetary discipline and improvement of the budgetary procedure to the effect that the budgetary procedure should be reviewed at the Conference in order to achieve interinstitutional co-operation on a partnership basis ([1993] O.J. C331/10) and in the *modus vivendi* between the European Parliament, the Council and the Commission of December 20, 1994 concerning the implementing measures for acts adopted in accordance with the procedure laid down in Art. 189b [now Art. 251] of the EC Treaty ([1995] O.J. C43/40), where the three institutions referred to the review of the comitology question.

[70] Draft Constitution of the European Union, not approved by the European Parliament, but published as an annex to a resolution of February 10, 1994, [1994] O.J. C61/155. See Petersmann, "Proposals for a New Constitution for the European Union: Building-Blocks for a Constitutional Theory and Constitutional Law of the EU" (1995) C.M.L.R. 1123–1175; Gouad, "Le projet de Constitution européenne" (1995) R.F.D.C. 287–318.

discussing at the intergovernmental conference (IGC) scheduled for 1996 how the institutions should be adapted in order to operate effectively after the forthcoming and subsequent enlargements of the Union.[71] In order to prepare for the IGC, the European Council, meeting at Corfu on June 24 and 25, 1994, established a Reflection Group, consisting of representatives of the Ministers for Foreign Affairs, a representative of the President of the Commission and two representatives of the European Parliament.[72] On the basis of reports which the institutions had been asked to draw up on the functioning of the Union[73] and of the priorities sketched out by the European Council held in Cannes on June 26 and 27, 1995 with a view to responding to citizens' expectations,[74] the Reflection Group submitted its final report on December 5, 1995.[75] On March 29, 1996 the IGC opened, resulting in the Treaty on which the Heads of State or Government reached agreement on June 16 and 17, 1997 at Amsterdam.[76]

3–018 **Treaty of Amsterdam.** On October 2, 1997 the Treaty of Amsterdam amending the Treaty on European Union, the Treaties establishing the European Communities and certain related acts was signed.[77] The Treaty of

---

[71] (1993) 12 EU Bull. point I.18 and (1994) 3 EU Bull. point I.3.28. For the challenges facing the IGC, see Louis, "La réforme des institutions" (1995) 3 R.M.U.E. 233–242; Justus Lipsius, "The 1996 Intergovernmental Conference" (1995) E.L.Rev. 235–242; Chaltiel, "Enjeux et perspectives de la conférence intergouvernementale de 1996" (1995) R.M.C.U.E. 625–636; Dashwood, *Reviewing Maastricht issues for the 1996 IGC: Seminar series organised by the Centre for European Legal Studies Cambridge* (Sweet & Maxwell, London, 1996), 341 pp.

[72] (1994) 6 EU Bull. point I.25. The Reflection Group was chaired by a Spanish State Secretary, Carlos Westendorp.

[73] See the reports of the Council of April 10, 1995 ((1995) 4 EU Bull. point 1.9.1) and of the Commission of May 10, 1995 ((1995) 5 EU Bull. point 1.9.1), the resolution of the European Parliament of May 17, 1995 ([1995] O.J. C151/55; (1995) 5 EU Bull. point 1.9.2), the report of the Court of Justice of May 17, 1995 ((1995) EU Bull. point 1.9.3), the contribution of the Court of First Instance of May 17, 1995 ((1995) 5 EU Bull. point 1.9.4) and the report of the Court of Auditors ((1995) 6 EU Bull. point 1.9.4). See also the Opinions of the Economic and Social Committee of November 23, 1995 ([1995] O.J. C39/85) and of the Committee of the Regions of April 21, 1995 ([1996] O.J. C100/1). For commentaries on the contributions of the Court of Justice and the Court of First Instance, see Arnull (1995) E.L.Rev. 599–611, and Craig (1996) Pub.L. 13–17.

[74] (1995) 6 EU Bull. point I.28 (strengthening the CFSP and JHA co-operation, making the institutions more efficient, democratic and open; meeting the needs of citizens, who are concerned about employment and environment questions; putting the principle of subsidiarity into practice more effectively).

[75] (1995) 12 EU Bull. point 1.9.2 (for the text of the first part, "A Strategy for Europe", see point I.97 *et seq.*).

[76] (1997) 6 EU Bull. points I.3 and II.4. For further discussion of the IGC, see Lenaerts and De Smijter, "La conférence intergouvernementale de 1996" (1996) J.T.D.E. 217–229; Dehousse, "Evolution ou révolution des institutions européennes: le débat fondamental de la Conférence intergouvernementale de 1996" (1996) J.T. 593–596; Kortenberg, "Le Traité d'Amsterdam. La négotiation du Traité. Une vue cavalière" (1997) R.T.D.E. 709–719.

[77] [1997] O.J. C340/1 (available on the internet at *www.eurotreaties.com/amsterdamtext.html*). The Treaty of Amsterdam was enacted into UK law by the European Communities (Amendment) Act 1998. For commentaries, see Timmermans, "Het Verdrag van Amsterdam. Enkele inleidende kanttekeningen" (1997) S.E.W. 344–351; Blumann, "Le

Amsterdam was the subject of a referendum in Ireland on May 22, 1998 (61.7 per cent in favour) and in Denmark on May 28, 1998 (55.1 per cent in favour) and prompted an amendment of the Constitution in Austria, France and Ireland.[78] The Treaty entered into force on May 1, 1999.[79]

Pillar structure maintained. The Treaty of Amsterdam did not interfere **3–019** with the structure of the European Union as described above (paras 3–012–3–016). It amended the common and final provisions of the EU Treaty and each of the three Community Treaties, restructured the CFSP (EU Treaty, Title V) and radically reformed Title VI of the EU Treaty (now covering police and judicial co-operation in criminal matters).[80]

As far as the common and final provisions of the EU Treaty are concerned, States wishing to accede to the Union were henceforth expressly required to respect the principles of liberty, democracy, respect for human rights and fundamental freedoms, and the rule of law (EU Treaty, Art. 6(1) and Art. 49). In order to secure compliance therewith, the Treaty of Amsterdam made it possible, in the event of a Member State's committing a serious and persistent breach of those principles, to suspend certain of the

---

traité d'Amsterdam. Aspects institutionnels" (1997) R.T.D.E. 721–749; Petite, "Le traité d'Amsterdam: ambition et réalisme" (1997) 3 R.M.U.E. 17–52; Favret, "Le traité d'Amsterdam: une révision *a minima* de la 'charte constitutionnelle' de l'Union européenne" (1997) C.D.E. 555–605; Hilf and Pache, "Der Vertrag von Amsterdam" (1998) N.J.W. 705–713; Lenaerts and De Smijter, "Le traité d'Amsterdam" (1998) J.T.D.E. 25–36; Manin "The Treaty of Amsterdam" (1998) Col.J.E.L. 1–26, Sauron, "Le traité d'Amsterdam: une réforme inachevée?" (1998) Rec. Dalloz 69–78; De Zwaan, "Het Verdrag van Amsterdam. Etappe in het proces van Europese integratie" (1999) N.J.B. 492–500; Hummer, Obwexer and Schweitzer, "Die Europäische Union nach dem Vertrag von Amsterdam. Gegenwärtige Stand and künftige Entwicklung" (1999) Z.f.R.V. 132–146; Barents, *Het Verdrag van Amsterdam in werking* (Kluwer, Deventer, 1999), 452 pp.

[78] See the survey in Lepka and Terrebus, "Les ratifications nationales, manifestations d'un projet politique européen — la face cachée du Traité d'Amsterdam" (2003) R.T.D.E. 365–388; Hoffmeister, "Europäisches Verfassungsrecht nach Amsterdam" (1999) EuR. 280–288. In France the *Conseil constitutionnel* held on December 31, 1997 that some provisions of Title IV of the EU Treaty introduced by the Amsterdam Treaty conflicted with the Constitution, see Chaltiel, "Commentaire de la décision du Conseil constitutionnel relative au traité d'Amsterdam" (1998) R.M.C.U.E. 73–84. For the French law ratifying the Amsterdam Treaty, see Karagiannis, "Observations sur la loi française no. 99–229 du 23 mars 1999 autorisant la ratification du traité d'Amsterdam" (2001) R.T.D.E. 19–47. For the constitutional situation in Germany, see Bothe and Lohmann, "Verfahrensfragen der deutschen Zustimmung zum Vertrag von Amsterdam" (1998) Z.a.ö.R.V. 1–44.

[79] Under Art. 14 of the Amsterdam Treaty, it entered into force on the first day of the second month following that in which the instrument of ratification was deposited by the last signatory State to fulfil that formality. See information about the date of entry into force of the Treaty of Amsterdam, [1999] O.J. L114/56.

[80] Bardenhewer, "Die Einheitlichkeit der Organisationsstruktur der Europäischen Union" (1998) EuR. Beiheft 2, 125–138. See also Vedder, "Die Unterscheidung von Unionsrecht und Gemeinschaftsrecht nach dem Vertrag von Amsterdam" (1999) EuR. Beiheft 1, 7–44; Isaac (n.62, *supra*). For the first time, a Treaty also amended the preamble to the EU Treaty (references to fundamental social rights, sustainable development and the establishment of an area of freedom, security and justice; see Art. 1(1) to (3) of the Treaty of Amsterdam) and the preamble to the EC Treaty (reference to access to education; see Art. 2(1) of the Treaty of Amsterdam).

rights deriving from the application of the EU Treaty and the EC Treaty to the Member State in question (EU Treaty, Art. 7; see also EC Treaty, Art. 309).

The most important change made by the Amsterdam Treaty with regard to the Community Treaties was the introduction in the EC Treaty of powers relating to visas, asylum, immigration and other policies related to free movement of persons, to employment and to customs co-operation.[81] On the institutional level, the Amsterdam Treaty refined the co-decision procedure (EC Treaty, Art. 251), but deferred the promised review of the composition and functioning of the institutions to a subsequent intergovernmental conference.[82]

The provisions on the CFSP (EU Treaty, Title V) were completely redrafted. Primarily, the procedure and instruments for determining and implementing the CFSP were clarified. As a result of the incorporation in the EC Treaty of a number of fields relating to justice and home affairs which have to do with free movement of persons and customs, only police and judicial co-operation in criminal matters fell within the field of application of Title VI of the EU Treaty (PJCC). However, the Amsterdam Treaty did not confine such co-operation to that which was necessary in connection with the abolition of frontier checks, but placed it in the broader context of the Union's objective of providing "citizens with a high level of safety within an area of freedom, security and justice".[83] At the same time, maintaining and developing the Union as an area of freedom, security and justice continued to be an objective of the Union itself (EU Treaty, Art. 2, fourth indent; see para. 3–013), which was to be pursued both by Community policy and by action in the context of PJCC.[84] The Treaty of Amsterdam cautiously subjected action on the part of the Union to achieve this objective to review by the Court of Justice. On the one hand, Art. 35 of the EU Treaty conferred jurisdiction on the Court, subject to certain conditions, to give preliminary rulings on the validity and interpretation of acts of the institutions in connection with PJCC (see para. 10–077). On the other hand, review by the Court of the exercise of Community powers conferred in pursuance of this objective (EC Treaty,

---

[81] EC Treaty, Title IV (Arts 61–69, Title VIII (Arts 125–130) and Title X (Art. 135), respectively.

[82] Art. 2 of the Protocol annexed to the EU Treaty and the Community Treaties on the institutions with the prospect of enlargement of the European Union, [1997] O.J. C340/111. In addition, the promised review (see n.69, *supra*) of the incorporation into the EC Treaty of specific titles on energy, civil protection and tourism, the determination of a hierarchy between the different categories of Community acts and the question of comitology were also postponed. However, a declaration was annexed to the Amsterdam Treaty, calling on the Commission to submit a proposal for the revision of the existing Comitology Decision by no later than the end of 1998 ([1998] O.J. C340/137; on the basis of the proposal submitted by the Commission on July 16, 1998, the Council approved a new Comitology Decision on June 28, 1999, see para. 14–054 *et seq., infra*).

[83] See Art. 29, first para., of the EU Treaty.

[84] See Art. 61 of the EC Treaty, para. 5–159, *infra*.

Title IV) was limited, since the Court's jurisdiction to give preliminary rulings in this connection under Art. 234 was confined to requests from national courts and tribunals against whose decisions there is no judicial remedy.[85] In view of the fact that most of the provisions of Title IV of the EC Treaty require the Council to act, in a transitional period, by a unanimous vote and provide for only limited powers on the part of the Commission and the European Parliament in the decision-making process,[86] the Amsterdam Treaty accentuated the intergovernmental features of these Community provisions.

Closer co-operation. In addition, the Treaty of Amsterdam provided for **3–020** general mechanisms for Member States wishing to co-operate more closely with each other in Community matters or in matters covered by Title VI of the EU Treaty (PJCC), where not all the Member States show the same readiness to co-operate (EU Treaty, Title VII). These mechanisms enable Member States to co-operate more closely, under certain conditions, while using the institutions, procedures and mechanisms laid down by the EU Treaty and the EC Treaty (see para. 9–005).

Forms of co-operation in which not all the Member States take part had already materialised before (see paras 9–003–9–004) both outside the context of the EU Treaty (*e.g.* Schengen) and within it, particularly pursuant to the EC Treaty (EMU) or a protocol to that Treaty authorising Member States to engage in co-operation while using the Community institutions (Social Protocol); in some cases, existing co-operation is merely confirmed by the EU Treaty (WEU). The Amsterdam Treaty reordered some of these forms of co-operation. It incorporated the Schengen co-operation into the European Union by introducing Community powers in this sphere, enlarging the scope of Title VI of the EU Treaty and adopting the Schengen *acquis*, partly as Community law, partly as Union law (with Denmark being given a special status and with exceptions being provided for Ireland and the United Kingdom; see para. 5–164, *et seq.*). Furthermore, the Treaty repealed the Social Protocol and transformed the corresponding co-operation entirely into Community powers (see para. 5–235), while strengthening the role of the WEU in the area of the CFSP (see para. 20–045).

Renumbering. The most conspicuous change introduced by the **3–021** Amsterdam Treaty for practitioners and students is the renumbering of the articles, titles and sections of the EU Treaty and the EC Treaty in order to

---

[85] EC Treaty, Art. 68(1). For the jurisdiction of the Court of Justice under Title IV of the EC Treaty, see para. 10–075, *infra*.
[86] See EC Treaty, Art. 67(1) (the Commission did not have the sole right of initiative; requirement to "consult" the European Parliament), para. 14–069, *infra*.

reduce their complexity and make them more accessible.[87] In the course of this exercise, lapsed provisions of the EU Treaty and of the then three Community Treaties were deleted.[88]

V. THE TREATY OF NICE

3–022 **Intergovernmental conference.** The Protocol on the institutions with the prospect of enlargement of the European Union annexed to the Treaty of Amsterdam already signalled that it was necessary to reform the institutions with a view to enlargement.[89] That protocol provided that reform should take place in two stages. An initial limited adjustment was to take place upon entry into force of the subsequent accession treaties. At least one year before the membership of the European Union exceeded 20, a comprehensive review of the composition and functioning of the institutions was to be carried out.

The European Council held at Cologne on June 3 and 4, 1999 announced that a new Intergovernmental Conference (IGC) would be convened in early 2000 "[i]n order to ensure that the European Union's institutions can continue to work efficiently after enlargement". The European Council placed the emphasis on the following matters: size and composition of the Commission, weighting of votes in the Council, the possible extension of qualified majority voting in the Council and other necessary amendments to the Treaties arising as regards the European institutions in connection with those issues and in implementing the Treaty of Amsterdam.[90]

---

[87] Art. 12 of the Amsterdam Treaty, which refers to the tables of equivalences set out in the Annex thereto. A consolidated version of the EU Treaty and the EC Treaty has been published together with the Treaty of Amsterdam, [1997] O.J. C340/145 (EU Treaty) and [1997] O.J. C340/173 (EC Treaty). It is also available on the Internet *www.europa.eu.int/eur-lex/en/treaties/dat/EC—consol.pdf.*

[88] See Art. 6 (for the EC Treaty), Art. 7 (ECSC Treaty) and Art. 8 (EAEC Treaty) of the Amsterdam Treaty. Art. 9 repealed the Convention of March 25, 1957 on certain institutions common to the European Communities and the Merger Treaty of April 8, 1965 (see para. 1–011, *supra*). In order to ensure that the repeal or deletion of such provisions does not bring about any change in existing Community law, Art. 10 provides that there is to be no change in the legal effects of the provisions of the Treaties and acts adopted pursuant thereto. See the Explanatory Report from the General Secretariat of the Council on the simplification of the Community Treaties, [1997] O.J. C353/1, and Jacqué, "Le Traité d'Amsterdam. La simplification et la consolidation des traités" (1997) R.T.D.E. 903–913; for earlier proposals for the consolidation of the Treaties, see Von Bogdandy and Ehlermann, "Consolidation of the European Treaties: feasibility, costs and benefits" (1996) C.M.L.R. 1107–1116; Schmid, "Konsolidierung und Vereinfachung des europäischen Primärrechts—wissenschaftliche Modelle, aktueller Stand und Perspektiven" (1998) EuR. Beiheft 2, 17–38.

[89] For that protocol, see n. 82, *supra*. See also the Declaration by Belgium, France and Italy on the Protocol annexed to the EU Treaty and the Community Treaties on the institutions with the prospect of enlargement of the European Union ([1997] O.J. C340/144), in which those countries stated that the Treaty of Amsterdam did not meet the need for substantial progress towards reinforcing the institutions, this being an indispensable condition for the conclusion of the first accession negotiations.

[90] (1999) 6 EC Bull., point I.21.

The President of the Commission convened a group of experts under the chairmanship of the former Belgian Prime Minister, Jean-Luc Dehaene to report on the "institutional implications of enlargement". The group concluded that comprehensive reform was necessary and suggested that the agenda for the IGC should be extended to cover matters such as more extensive application of the co-decision procedure, simplification of closer co-operation, review of the tasks and functioning of the other institutions and bodies (Court of Justice and Court of First Instance, Court of Auditors, Committee of the Regions, Economic and Social Committee), extension of the Union's power of external representation and European Defence.[91] Following that report, the Commission pressed for wide-ranging reform.

On February 14, 2000 the Portuguese Presidency of the Council convened the Intergovernmental Conference,[92] after the Council had obtained the opinion of the Commission and the European Parliament.[93] The IGC concluded on December 10, 2000 at Nice when the Heads of State or of Government reached agreement on a new treaty.[94]

Treaty of Nice. On February 26, 2001 the Treaty of Nice amending the **3–023** Treaty on European Union, the Treaties establishing the European Communities and certain related acts was signed.[95] The Treaty was put to a first referendum in Ireland on June 7, 2001 and rejected by 53.87 per cent of votes. Following this, the Irish Government launched a national debate, which culminated in a second referendum on October 19, 2002, in which

---

[91] Report to the European Commission of October 18, 1999, "The Institutional Implications of Enlargement" (report of the Dehaene Working Group, whose members consisted of Jean-Luc Dehaene, Richard von Weizsäcker and Lord Simon of Highbury). See www.europa.eu.int/igc2000/repoct99—en.pdf.

[92] (2000) 1/2 EU Bull., point 1.1.5.

[93] See the resolution of the European Parliament on the convening of the Intergovernmental Conference ([2000] O.J. C309/85) and the Commission's opinion of January 26, 2000, "Adapting the institutions to make a success of enlargement" ((2000) EU Bull., Suppl. 2/2000), which was obtained by the Council under Art. 48 of the EU Treaty.

[94] (2000) 12 EU Bull., point 1.1.3. As to how the Treaty came about, see Wiedmann, "Der Vertrag von Nizza—Genesis einer Reform" (2001) EuR. 185–215.

[95] [2001] O.J. C80/1. The Treaty of Nice was ratified in the UK by the European Communities (Amendment) Act 2002. For general commentaries, see Lenaerts and Desomer, "Het Verdrag van Nice en het 'post-Nice'-debat over de toekomst van de Europese Unie" (2001–2002) R.W. 73–90; Bradley, "Institutional design in the Treaty of Nice" (2001) C.M.L.R. 1095–1124; Favret, "Le traité de Nice du 26 février 2001: vers un affaiblissement irréversible de la capacité d'action de l'Union européenne?" (2001) R.D.E. 271–304; Pieter Van Nuffel, "Le Traité de Nice. Un commentaire" (2001) R.D.U.E. 329–387; Louis, "Le Traité de Nice" (2001) J.T.D.E. 25–34; Hatje, "Die institutionelle Reform der Europäischen Union—der Vertrag von Nizza auf dem Prüfstand" (2001) EuR. 143–184; Shaw, "The Treaty of Nice: Legal and Constitutional Implications" (2001) E.Pub.L. 195–215. For critical commentaries, see Pescatore, "Nice—Aftermath" (2001) C.M.L.R. 265–271; De Zwaan, "Het Verdrag van Nice" (2001) S.E.W. 42–52.

62.89 per cent voted in favour.[96] The Treaty entered into effect on February 1, 2003.

3–024 **Changes.** For its part too, the Treaty of Nice did not change the structure of the European Union as it is laid down in the EU Treaty (see paras 3–012—3–016). The Treaty did not result in the comprehensive reform sought in some quarters, but was limited primarily to adjustments of the composition and operation of the European Parliament, the Council and the Commission following the accession of new Member States and to a reform of the Community judicature.

First, the Treaty provides that the Council may henceforward nominate the President of the Commission by a qualified majority vote.[97] The powers of the President of the Commission are also strengthened. In addition, the Treaty provided that from 2005 the number of Members of the Commission would be limited to one per Member State. Once the 27th Member State acceded, the number of Members of the Commission would be further limited insofar as the Member States having a national as a Member would be chosen by rotation.[98] By way of compensation for losing their right to have a second national as Member of the Commission, the large Member States demanded that the weighting of votes in the Council be adjusted. The upshot was a compromise whereby the weighted percentage of votes necessary to attain a qualified majority will be gradually increased.[99] At the same time, half of the Member States must vote in favour of any decision and any Member State may request verification that the Member States constituting the qualified majority represent at least 62 per cent of the total population of the Union.[100] The number of Members of the European Parliament will be gradually increased to 732, against the wishes of Parliament itself.[101] In this connection, a complex transitional regime is to apply for the 2004–2009 legislature.[102]

The Court of Justice and the Court of First Instance were radically reformed. Henceforward, both courts are in principle to sit as chambers. Institutions and Member States are still entitled to bring a case before the

---

[96] For these referendums, see Gilland, "Ireland's (First) Referendum on the Treaty of Nice" (2002) J.C.M.S. 527–535; Kämmerer, "Das Déjà-vu von Dublin—Gedanken zum Ausgang des zweiten irischen Referendums über den Vertrag von Nizza" (2002) N.J.W. 3596–3598. For ratification in France, see Chaltiel, "La ratification du Traité de Nice par la France" (2001) R.M.C.U.E. 442–446; for ratification in Germany, see Streinz, "(EG)-Verfassungsrechtliche Aspekte des Vertrags von Nizza" (2003) Z.ö.R. 137–161.

[97] EC Treaty, Art. 214(2).

[98] Art. 4 of the Protocol on the enlargement of the European Union, annexed to the EU Treaty and the Community Treaties by the Treaty of Nice.

[99] Art. 3 of the Protocol on the enlargement of the European Union. See also Declaration (No. 20) on the enlargement of the European Union and Declaration (No. 21) on the qualified majority threshold and the number of votes for a blocking majority in an enlarged Union.

[100] Protocol on the enlargement of the European Union, Art. 3(a)(ii).

[101] EC Treaty, Art. 189, second para.

[102] Protocol on the enlargement of the European Union, Art. 2.

"Grand Chamber" of the Court of Justice. The Court of Justice will sit as a full Court only in very exceptional circumstances.[103] The number of advocates general is still limited to eight, but they are to be involved only in cases where required by the Statute of the Court of Justice.[104] The possibility was created to set up specialised chambers ("judicial panels") for specific matters. An appeal will lie from those "judicial panels" to the Court of First Instance.[105] The Court of First Instance may see its range of tasks expanded, since the Treaty allows all direct actions to be concentrated in that court and enables requests for preliminary rulings to be referred to it in respect of certain matters to be indicated in the Statute.[106]

Lastly, the Treaty of Nice increased the possibilities for enhanced co-operation—although no use has been made of them as yet—, whilst laying down more flexible conditions.[107] For instance, the minimum number of Member States required for enhanced co-operation was reduced to eight. Enhanced co-operation is now also possible in the field of the common foreign and security policy, albeit on stricter conditions (see para. 9–005 *et seq.*).

In the margins of the Nice European Council, a Charter of Fundamental Rights[108] was adopted. That list of fundamental rights was not incorporated in the Treaty itself, but jointly proclaimed by the Presidents of the European Parliament, the Council and the Commission. Nevertheless, the Charter gained immediate acceptance as an authoritative description of the fundamental rights to which everyone in the European Union is entitled (see para. 17–012).

---

[103] EC Treaty, Art. 221, and Art. 16 of the Protocol on the Statute of the Court of Justice, annexed by the Treaty of Nice to the EU Treaty, the EC Treaty and the EAEC Treaty.
[104] EC Treaty, Art. 222.
[105] EC Treaty, Art. 225a.
[106] EC Treaty, Art. 225.
[107] EU Treaty, Arts 43–45.
[108] EU Bull. (2000) 12, point 1.2.2; for the text of the Charter, see *ibid.*, point 2.2.1 [2000] O.J. C364/1.

CHAPTER 4

TOWARDS A "CONSTITUTION FOR EUROPE"

I. THE CONVENTION ON THE FUTURE OF EUROPE

Laeken Declaration. When the Treaty of Nice was signed, it was clear that **4–001**
this text would be just another step in the ongoing process of reforming the
European Union.[1] In a declaration annexed to the Nice Treaty, the 2000
Intergovernmental Conference proposed that further discussion on the
future of the Union should cover four areas: a more precise delimitation of
competences between Member States and the Union, the status of the
Charter of Fundamental Rights, simplification of the Treaties and the role
of national parliaments.

As announced at the Nice European Council, the European Council held
in Laeken (Brussels) on December 14 and 15, 2001 adopted a Declaration
on the future of the European Union.[2] The "Laeken Declaration"
convened a "Convention" composed of representatives of the Heads of
State or of Government and the parliaments of the Member States and the
candidate Member States, the European Parliament and the Commission,
together with observers from the European Economic and Social
Committee, the Committee of the Regions, the European Ombudsman and
the European social partners.[3] The composition of the Convention, which
was largely inspired by the group which had drawn up the Charter of
Fundamental Rights (see para. 17–083), made it clear that there was a
genuine willingness to see the future of the Union debated in a broader and
more transparent way, rather than behind the closed doors of an

---

[1] Brand, "*Quo vadis* Europa? Thoughts on the Future of the Union" (2002) Tilburg
For.L.Rev. 106–143; Prechal, "Een constitutionele 'post-Nice' agenda?" (2001) N.J.B.
384–389; Touscoz, "Un large débat. L'avenir de l'Europe après la conférence
intergouvernementale de Nice (CIG-2000)" (2001) R.M.C.U.E. 225–236.

[2] For the text of this Declaration, see (2001) 12 EU Bull. point I.27. See also Lenaerts, "La
déclaration de Laeken : premier jalon d'une Constitution européenne?" (2002) J.T.D.E.
29–43.

[3] (2001) 12 EU Bull. point I.1. See also the resolution of the European Parliament of
November 29, 2001 on the constitutional process and the future of the Union ([2002] O.J.
C153E/310) and Rieder, "Der Konvent zur Zukunft Europas" (2002) Zeitschrift für
Rechtspolitik 241–280; Grawert, "Wie soll Europa organisiert werden?—Zur
konstitutionellen 'Zukunft Europas' nach dem Vertrag von Nizza" (2003) EuR. 971–991;
Hobe, "Bedingungen, Verfahren, und Chancen europäischer Verfassunggebung: Zur Arbeit
des Brüsseler Verfassungskonvents" (2003) EuR. 1–16.

inter-governmental conference.[4] According to the Laeken Declaration, the Convention's discussions and all official documents were to be in the public domain. Moreover, the Convention was to work in all the Union's working languages. The terms of reference given to the Convention by the Laeken Declaration expanded upon the four issues mentioned above, whilst adding the question whether the simplification and reorganisation of the Treaties might not lead in the long run to the adoption of a constitutional text for the Union.[5]

4-002 **Convention.** On February 28, 2002, the Convention on the future of Europe started its work, with Valéry Giscard d'Estaing acting as Chair and Giuliano Amato and Jean-Luc Dehaene as Vice-Chairs. The Praesidium of the Convention[6] steered the discussions, which were conducted in a number of working groups and discussion circles.[7] At the same time, the Convention gave rise to a broader debate in the Member States.[8] In order to give impetus to the discussion, a "Contribution to a Preliminary Draft Constitution of the European Union" was prepared in December 2000 at the request of the President of the Commission and the Commissioners participating in the Convention.[9] On the basis of the conclusions and suggestions of the working groups, the Praesidium of the Convention ultimately formulated a Draft Treaty establishing a Constitution for Europe, which obtained a broad consensus at the plenary session of the Convention held on June 13, 2003.[10]

---

[4] See Lenaerts and Desomer, "New Models of Constitution-Making in Europe: The Quest for Legitimacy" (2002) C.M.L.R. 1217, at 1234–1243; Walker, "Europe's constitutional passion play" (2003) E.L.Rev. 905–908.

[5] See De Witte, "Simplification and Reorganisation of the European Treaties" (2002) C.M.L.R. 1255–1287; Pache, "Eine Verfassung für Europa—Krönung oder Kollaps der europäischen Integration?" (2002) EuR. 767–784.

[6] Pursuant to the Laeken Declaration, the Praesidium was composed of the Convention Chair and Vice-Chairs, the representatives of the Spanish, Danish and Greek governments occupying the Presidency of the Council during the Convention, two representatives of national parliaments, two European Parliament representatives and two Commission representatives.

[7] Within the framework of the Convention, working groups were set up on "subsidiarity", the "Charter of Fundamental Rights of the European Union", "legal personality" of the Union, "national parliaments", "complementary competences", "economic governance", "external action", "defence", "simplification" of legislative procedures and instruments, the area of "freedom, security and justice", and "social Europe". In addition, discussion circles addressed the role of the Court of Justice, the budgetary procedure and own resources of the Union. See Barents, "Naar een Europese constitutie?" (2002) N.T.E.R. 305–311 and (2003) N.T.E.R. 39–47. All Convention documents can be consulted on the Convention's website: *www.european-convention.eu.int/bienvenue.asp?lang=EN&Content=*.

[8] In accordance with the Laeken Declaration, a forum was created in order to enable organisations representing civil society (*e.g.* the social partners, the business world, non-governmental organisations and academia) to be involved in the debate. Specific websites were created for this purpose: *www.europa.eu.int/futurum/index—en.htm*.

[9] This document, known as "Penelope", can be consulted on the Futurum website (see n.8, *supra.*) alongside the contributions from the Commission. For a commentary by the Chair of the working group that prepared the document, see Lamoureux, "La Constitution 'Penelope': une refondation pour en finir avec les replâtrages" (2003) R.D.U.E. 13–37.

[10] A draft of the 16 opening articles was presented in February 2003, see (2003) C.M.L.R. 267–277.

Draft Constitution. On June 20, 2003 the first two parts of the Draft Treaty **4–003** establishing a Constitution for Europe were submitted to the European Council meeting in Thessaloniki[11]; the third and fourth parts of the Draft Constitution were adopted by the Convention on July 10, 2003 and submitted to the Italian Presidency of the Council in Rome on July 18, 2003. The Draft Constitution was published in the *Official Journal*[12] and was widely debated by academics.[13]

II. The Intergovernmental Conference of 2003–2004

IGC. Given the fact that the Treaty establishing a Constitution for Europe **4–004** intends to amend the existing Treaties, it has to be adopted in accordance with the procedure for the amendment of the Treaties laid down in Art. 48 of the EU Treaty. As a result, the changes have to be approved by the representatives of the national governments meeting in an Intergovernmental Conference (IGC) and have to be ratified by all Member States in accordance with their respective constitutional requirements (see para. 7–004). On October 4, 2003, the Italian Presidency of the Council convened an IGC.[14] Under the Irish Presidency, the IGC reached agreement on the Treaty establishing a Constitution for Europe

---

[11] According to the European Council held in Thessaloniki on June 19 and 20, 2003, this marked "a historic step in the direction of furthering the objectives of European integration". Nevertheless, the European Council considered the text of the draft constitutional treaty to be no more than "a good basis" for starting the intergovernmental conference: (2003) 6 EU Bull. points I.3.2-I.3.5.

[12] [2003] O.J. C169.

[13] For general comments, see Kokott and Rüth, "The European Convention and its Draft Treaty establishing a Constitution for Europe: Appropriate Answers to the Laeken Questions?" (2003) C.M.L.R. 1315–1343; Dougan, "The Convention's Draft Constitutional Treaty: bringing Europe closer to its lawyers?" (2003) E.L.Rev. 763–793; Schwarze, "Ein pragmatischer Verfassungsentwurf—Analyse und Bewertung des vom Europäischen Verfassungskonvent vorgelegten Entwurfs eines Vertrags über eine Verfassung für Europa" (2003) EuR. 535–573; Epping, "Die Verfassung Europas?" (2003) J.Z. 821–831; Geelhoed, "Een Europawijde Europese Unie: een grondwet zonder staat?" (2003) S.E.W. 284–310; Eijsbouts, "Presidenten, parlementen, fundamenten—Europa's komende constitutie en het Hollands ongemak" (2003) N.J.B. 662–673; Lenaerts, Binon and Van Nuffel, "L'Union européenne en quête d'une Constitution: bilan des travaux de la Convention sur l'avenir de l'Europe" (2003) J.T.D.E. 289–299; Lenaerts and Gerard, "The structure of the Union according to the Constitution for Europe: the emperor is getting dressed" (2004) E.L.Rev. 289–322; Arnull, "The Member States of the European Union and Giscard's Blueprint for its Future" (2004) Fordham I.L.J. 503–543; Temple Lang; "The Main Issues After the Convention on the Constitutional Treaty for Europe" (2004) Fordham I.L.J. 544–589; Ruffert, "Schlüsselfragen der Europäischen Verfassung der Zukunft: Grundrechte—Institutionen—Kompetenz—Ratifizierung" (2004) EuR. 165–201.

[14] Pursuant to Art. 48 of the EU Treaty, the IGC was convened following consultation of the European Parliament (Resolution of September 24, 2003 on the draft Treaty establishing a Constitution for Europe and on the convening of the Intergovernmental Conference), the Commission (Opinion of September 17, 2003 "A Constitution for the Union", COM (2003) 548 final) and the European Central Bank (Opinion of September 19, 2003, [2003] O.J. C229/7), the Council having delivered an opinion in favour on September 29, 2003.

(the "EU Constitution") within the framework of the European Council held in Brussels on June 18, 2004. All references to the EU Constitution in this book refer to the text as it was published in August 2004.[15] After signature by the representatives of the Member States on October 29, 2004, the Treaty establishing a Constitution for Europe will be submitted for ratification to the Member States.

III. THE TREATY ESTABLISHING A CONSTITUTION FOR EUROPE

4–005 **New European Union.** The Treaty establishing a Constitution for Europe seeks to replace the EC Treaty and the EU Treaty by a new Treaty.[16] It is proposed that the new Treaty will be the "Constitution" of the new European Union, with legal personality, which will take the place of the European Community and the European Union (see para. 10–113). Only the European Atomic Energy Community will continue to exist as a separate legal entity. The Convention refrained from discussing possible amendments to or the repeal of the EAEC Treaty as this might only too easily have degenerated into a discussion about the desirability of pursuing policies based on nuclear energy.[17]

4–006 **Four parts.** As has already been mentioned, the EU Constitution consists of four parts. Part I sets out the objectives of the Union, refers to fundamental rights and citizenship of the Union, catalogues the Union's competences, describes its institutions and the way how the Union's competences are to be exercised (institutionally and financially) and sets forth the conditions for membership of the Union. Part II of the EU Constitution incorporates the Charter of Fundamental Rights of the Union, virtually unmodified. Part III of the EU Constitution enters at length into the policies and functioning of the Union. It takes over the various legal bases from the EC Treaty and the EU Treaty—with or without amendments and additions—and contains detailed provisions on the operation and internal organisation of the institutions and bodies of the Union. The general and final provisions of Part IV determine the territorial scope of the Constitution, the procedure for amending it and the conditions under which the Constitution will enter into force.

---

[15] On August 6, 2004, the Intergovernmental Conference published the "Treaty establishing a Constitution for Europe" (CIG 87/04), together with Protocols and Annexes I and II annexed to the Treaty establishing a Constitution for Europe (CIG 87/04 ADD1) and Declarations to be annexed to the Final Act of the Intergovernmental Conference and the Final Act (CIG 87/04 ADD2). A Working Party of IGC Legal Experts, chaired by Jean-Claude Piris, took care of editorial and legal adjustments to the successive "draft" versions of the EU Constitution.

[16] See the repeal of earlier Treaties by Art. IV–437 of the draft EU Constitution.

[17] The Protocol annexed to the EU Constitution amending the Treaty establishing the European Atomic Energy Community confines itself to replacing the institutional and financial provisions of the EAEC Treaty by the arrangements set out in the EU Constitution with regard to the European Union.

Initially, the idea was to give a different status to the various parts of the Constitution with the principal aim of enabling Part III to be more easily amended than Part I. Ultimately, however, the EU Constitution did not introduce any hierarchy as between the various parts. As a result, a single amendment procedure applies to all four parts of the Constitution (see para. 7–007). By the same token, the Union's objectives enumerated in Part I are to be read in conjunction with the specific objectives listed in other parts of the Constitution, in particular the provisions of Part III empowering the Union to take action in its various policy areas (see para. 5–007).

Simplified structure. The EU Constitution is designed to simplify the legal **4–007** structure of the Union by abolishing the pillar structure and by merging the Union's intergovernmental field of action with the field currently covered by the Community.

The Union's powers in the field of police and judicial co-operation in criminal matters (PJCC), currently based on Title VI of the EU Treaty, are to be incorporated into Part III of the Constitution, together with the present Community powers on "visa, asylum, immigration and other policies related to the free movement of persons" (EC Treaty, Part Three, Title IV), resulting in a single chapter on the "area of freedom, security and justice" (see para. 6–014). It is proposed that the PJCC will be fully subject to the Community method—namely legislation is to be adopted by the European Parliament and the Council under the co-decision procedure, whilst there will be the possibility of judicial review by the Court of Justice, even though PJCC decision-making will retain some specific characteristics of its own (see para. 15–015).

Part III of the EU Constitution also brings the common foreign and security policy (CFSP, Title V of the EU Treaty) and the existing external competences of the Community together in a single Title on the Union's external action (see para. 20–041). In the field of the CFSP, decision-making continues to exhibit significant features of intergovernmentalism (see para. 15–009). In this field, the Union's action will be subject to judicial review by the Court of Justice solely as regards restrictive measures against natural or legal persons (see para. 18–022). In any event, the Union's CFSP action will be governed by fundamental principles of Union law, such as the principle of primacy of Union law. Together with the fact that judicial review will no longer be altogether excluded, this means that the CFSP is no longer to be regarded as a completely different form of legal co-operation, but rather as an aspect of the Union's foreign policy in respect of which judicial review is to be restricted having regard to its specifically "political" nature.[18]

---

[18] *cf.* the doctrine of *"political questions"* which are excluded from judicial review under US constitutional law.

4–008   Constitutional innovations. On top of this, the EU Constitution introduces some remarkable innovations. In the first place, it updates the values and objectives of the Union (see para. 5–007) and incorporates the Charter of Fundamental Rights of the Union as a catalogue of rights, freedoms and principles to be respected by the Union and by the Member States when implementing Union law (see para. 17–086). Next, the EU Constitution sets forth the democratic principles on which the functioning of the Union is based (see para. 16–004 *et seq.*). A notable novelty lies in the fact that any Member State that no longer subscribes to the objectives and/or policies of the Union will have the right to withdraw from the Union (see para. 8–013). This right of withdrawal has a clear symbolic value. Even if, on the face of it, the right of withdrawal may seem to endanger the internal cohesion of the Union, it also underscores the deliberate choice made by each Member State belonging to the Union. In order to strengthen the Union's identity, the EU Constitution expressly refers to the existing symbols of the Union, namely its flag, anthem, motto, the euro as its currency and May 9 as Europe Day (see para. 12–005).[19]

Secondly, the EU Constitution clarifies the allocation of competences as between the Union and the Member States, as well as the extent to which the institutions of the Union can make use of the Union's competences. To this end, the EU Constitution classifies the Union's competences, largely on the basis of principles elaborated in the case-law of the Court of Justice (see paras 5–008–5–027). Henceforth, the principle of primacy of Union law over the law of the Member States will be enshrined in the Constitution (see para. 17–002). As to the legal instruments of the Union, the EU Constitution makes an unambiguous distinction between legislative acts and other acts. Pursuant to the EU Constitution, all legislative acts will be adopted, in principle, by the European Parliament and the Council under the co-decision procedure—the "ordinary legislative procedure" (see para. 14–013). The EU Constitution also extends the substantive scope of application of this procedure. Legislative acts will take the form of a "European law" or a "European framework law", corresponding to the present regulation and directive, respectively (see para. 17–145 *et seq.*). As regards other acts to be adopted by the Union for the implementation of the Constitution or for the implementation of legislative acts or other implementing acts, the EU Constitution reorganises the division of powers between the institutions (see para. 14–053) and defines new kinds of instruments ("European regulations" and "European decisions"; see para. 17–147).

---

[19] For the EU Constitution as a step towards the building of a "European" identity, see von Bogdandy, "Europäische Verfassung und europäische Identität" (2004) J.Z. 53–104; for the link between the EU Constitution and the citizens of Europe, see Schmitz, "Das europäische Volk und seine Rolle bei einer Verfassunggebung in der Europäischen Union" (2003) EuR. 217–243.

Thirdly, the EU Constitution reinforces the arrangements on the basis of which the Union is to pursue its external policies.[20] As already mentioned, the EU Constitution will bring together all external policies in one title on the Union's external action, for which specific objectives are to be formulated. In order to ensure consistency between the various external policies, the EU Constitution provides for the appointment of a Union Minister for Foreign Affairs who will conduct the CFSP and be responsible, at the same time, as Vice-President of the Commission, for handling external relations and co-ordinating other aspects of the Union's external action (see para. 15–009). The Union Minister for Foreign Affairs is to chair the meetings of the Foreign Affairs Council. In addition, the EU Constitution creates a single procedure for the negotiation and conclusion of international agreements which will apply in the field of CFSP as well as in all other fields of external action (see para. 21–015). Moreover, the EU Constitution takes a number of significant steps towards a European security and defence policy. The EU Constitution extends the list of tasks that can be accomplished by the Union in this respect and consolidates the Member States' commitment to make civilian and military capabilities available to the Union. Furthermore, it provides for a species of "structured co-operation" among those Member States which are capable of contributing thereto (see para. 20–046).

Fourthly, with respect to the procedure for future amendments of the Constitution, the EU Constitution determines that the intergovernmental stage of the amendment procedure will be preceded by a Convention composed of representatives of the national governments, the national parliaments, the European Parliament and the Commission (see para. 7–006).

Institutional changes. Last, the EU Constitution proposes some **4–009** amendments to the institutional framework of the Union.[21] First, the European Council is to be formally recognised as an institution of the Union in its own right, even though its function will continue to be confined to issuing general policy guidelines without any participation in the legislative process (see para. 10–008). The European Council will elect its President. Secondly, the EU Constitution makes some changes which will step up the role played by the European Parliament in the legislative and budgetary process (see para. 10–031). More important—and more

---

[20] See Pernice and Thym, "A New Institutional Balance for European Foreign Policy?" (2002) E.For.Aff.Rev. 369–400; Thym, "Reforming Europe's Common Foreign and Security Policy" (2004) E.L.J. 5–22.

[21] See Moussis, "For a drastic reform of European institutions" (2003) E.L.Rev. 250–258; Huber, "Das institutionnelle Gleichgewicht zwischen Rat und Europäischem Parlament in der künftigen Verfassung für Europa" (2003) EuR. 574–599; Chaltiel, "Une Constitution pour l'Europe, an I de la République européenne" (2003) R.M.C.U.E. 493–501; Smulders, "Kritische kanttekeningen bij de gevolgen van het 'ontwerp-Verdrag tot vaststelling van een grondwet voor Europa' voor het institutionele evenwicht" (2003) N.T.E.R. 246–252.

controversial—changes directly affect the balance of power between the Member States, in particular the arrangements relating to the presidency of the Council formations, the number of votes required for the Council to take decisions by a qualified majority (see para. 10–054) and the question whether or not the college of Commissioners should comprise at least one national of every Member State (see para. 10–070).

IV. WILL THE EUROPEAN UNION BE ENDOWED WITH A CONSTITUTION?

4–010 **Focus for debate.** As has already been mentioned, the EU Constitution is to replace the existing Treaties only if it is ratified by all the Member States in accordance with their respective constitutional requirements. It is likely that in several Member States ratification of the Constitution will be made dependent on the positive outcome of a referendum. As a result, the Constitution for Europe will remain a focus for debate. It is interesting to note that, at governmental level at least, neither the integration of the Community and non-Community paths towards integration nor the actual idea of a Constitution seemed to pose any difficulties. The political breaking points were as ever the arrangements directly affecting the allocation of competences between the Member States and the Union, the extent of qualified majority voting and the status and justiciability of the Charter of Fundamental Rights.

4–011 **Constitutional framework.** Within some years, the EC Treaty and the EU Treaty are thus to be replaced by the Treaty establishing a Constitution for Europe. It emerges fairly clearly from the contents of the EU Constitution that, even if it is embodied in a "Treaty", this document is genuinely constitutional in nature. This is because it contains the fundamental rules governing the exercise of public authority at Union level, together with a well-balanced allocation of authority as between the different functions carried out by a State (legislative, executive and judicial) and the various levels of governance (Union and Member States). At the same time, the document identifies the basic principles which the authorities must respect in their relations with citizens, in particular citizens' fundamental rights. It is clear from the case-law of the Court of Justice that similar constitutional tasks are already being performed by the EC Treaty as far as the Community is concerned (see para. 1–020). In view of the significant innovations introduced by the EU Constitution by comparison with the existing Treaties—including an express classification of competences and the incorporation of the Charter of Fundamental Rights—the future Constitution will have even more reason to be known as the constitutional charter of the European Union. There is no doubt that this document will become an important legal and political point of reference in each of the Member States, if only because, in the course of ratification by each Member State, the "Constitution" will become part and parcel of the arrangements regarded as being of a "constitutional" nature in every Member State. In this way, the European Constitution will supplement the national constitutional arrangements as a common constitutional framework within whose confines each Member State will organise its own domestic legal order.

Part II

JURISDICTION OF THE EUROPEAN UNION

CHAPTER 5

SUBSTANTIVE SCOPE OF THE COMMUNITY TREATIES

Jurisdiction. The jurisdiction of the European Union is laid down in the **5–001** Community Treaties (EC Treaty and EAEC Treaty) and in Titles V, VI and VII of the EU Treaty.[1] The first matter to be dealt with is the substantive scope of the Community Treaties, namely the powers that those treaties confer on the EC and the EAEC (this chapter). Subsequently, a survey will be given of the fields of action covered by Title V (common foreign and security policy) and Title VI (police and judicial co-operation in criminal matters) of the EU Treaty (Chapter 6). Within the jurisdiction of the Union, individual Member States may engage in enhanced co-operation (EU Treaty, Title VII; see para. 9–004 *et seq.*). The survey of the substantive scope of the Community Treaties and the EU Treaty is followed by a discussion of the temporal (Chapter 7) and territorial (Chapter 8) scope of those treaties and a survey of the exceptions to the general application of the Treaties (Chapter 9).

The proposed EU Constitution will integrate the Union's fields of action into a single Treaty providing a common foundation for the entire range of action of the Union. As a result, the main principles governing the division of powers between the Community and its Member States—set out below—will be extended to the Union's powers in the fields of the common foreign and security policy and police and judicial co-operation in criminal matters (see paras 6–014 and 20–041). The latter fields of action will still be treated differently, in so far as "specific provisions" will apply both to the substance of the Union's action and to the decision-making process.[2] However, those "specific provisions" will not prevent the general principles which the EU Constitution lays down for the allocation and exercise of the Union's powers from being applicable in full to all of the Union's policy areas.

---

[1] The Community Treaties, together with the Treaties modifying and supplementing them and the protocols annexed to the Treaties by common agreement between the Member States, constitute primary Community law (para. 17–056 *et seq.*). A number of protocols are annexed to both the EU Treaty and the Community Treaties: see Protocol (No. 6) introduced by the original EU Treaty (n.737 to para. 5–170, *infra*); seven protocols annexed by the Treaty of Amsterdam, [1997] O.J. C340/93–102 and 111–114, and two protocols annexed by the Treaty of Nice, [2001] O.J.C80/49–66. For the status of Title V, Title VI and Title VII of the EU Treaty, see para. 18–001 *et seq.*
[2] EU Constitution, Arts I–40—I–43.

I. PRINCIPLES

5–002 Functional approach. The Community Treaties set the Communities "tasks" with a view to attaining clearly circumscribed objectives. Accordingly, the task of the ECSC was to "contribute . . . through the establishment of a common market . . . to economic expansion, growth of employment and a rising standard of living in the Member States" (ECSC Treaty, Art. 2, first para.). Article 3 of the ECSC Treaty briefly indicated what this entailed (see para. 1–003). Article 2 of the EC Treaty likewise prescribes objectives and tasks, which are enlarged upon in Arts 3 and 4 of that treaty (paras 5–003–5–004). By the same token, Art. 1 of the EAEC Treaty provides that the EAEC is to "contribute to the raising of the standard of living in the Member States and to the development of relations with other countries by creating the conditions necessary for the speedy establishment and growth of nuclear industries", this task being enlarged upon in Art. 2 (see para. 1–007).

Following this description of objectives and tasks, each of the Treaties sets out the legal rules pursuant to which the tasks indicated are to be carried out (the "legal basis" for Community action).[3] In addition, the Treaties contain a supplementary legal basis for Community action for which specific provision is not made therein but which is necessary to attain one of the objectives of the Communities (EC Treaty, Art. 308; EAEC Treaty, Art. 203). Consequently, Community competence is not divided up according to subject-matter, but "functionally" limited to what is required by the objectives and tasks of the Communities.[4] It is further subject to compliance with the principles of subsidiarity (where the competence in question is non-exclusive) and proportionality.[5] The same approach will basically be adopted by the EU Constitution in so far as it will set out a whole range of objectives that will apply both to the present Community competences and to the present non-Community fields of action (see para. 5–007).

The discussion of Community competences below briefly indicates the changes that the EU Constitution will make to the field of application of the Community Treaties. Since, in principle, the broad field of action of the Community also covers the nuclear sector (see para. 1–011), the remainder of the section is confined to discussing the substantive scope of the EC Treaty.

---

[3] ECSC Treaty: Title III, "Economic and social provisions"; EC Treaty: the 20 titles of Part Three, "Community policies"; EAEC Treaty: Title II, "Provisions for the encouragement of progress in the field of nuclear energy".

[4] See Reimer, "Ziele und Zuständigkeiten—Die Funktionen der Unionszielbestimmungen" (2003) EuR. 992–1012.

[5] At least within the field of application of the EC Treaty: see the discussion of Art. 5; paras 5–009–5–035, *infra*.

A. OBJECTIVES AND TASKS OF THE COMMUNITY

Objectives. Article 2 of the EC Treaty provides that the objectives[6] of the **5–003** Community are as follows: to promote throughout the Community: (1) a harmonious, balanced and sustainable development of economic activities, (2) a high level of employment and of social protection, (3) equality between men and women, (4) sustainable and non-inflationary growth, (5) a high degree of competitiveness and convergence of economic performance, (6) a high level of protection and improvement of the quality of the environment, (7) the raising of the standard of living and quality of life, and (8) economic and social cohesion and solidarity among Member States. These objectives, which were amended for the first time by the EU Treaty,[7] are connected with the Union's aim of "promot[ing] economic and social progress and a high level of employment and [achieving] balanced and sustainable development" (EU Treaty, Art. 2, first indent; see para. 3–013)

As a result of the EU Treaty, Art. 2 of the EC Treaty introduced objectives, such as economic and social cohesion and environmental protection, which the Member States already regarded as important for Community policy and for which Community action already had an express legal basis in the Treaty as a result of the Single European Act.[8] By adopting the objectives of non-inflationary growth and a high level of employment and social protection, the Community followed in the direction already taken by co-operation between the Member States and Community social policy.[9] Convergence of economic performance and improvement of the "quality of life" constituted completely new objectives. The Treaty of Amsterdam made promoting equality between men and women—a general principle of Community law—a Community task,[10] added a high degree of competitiveness to the task of promoting economic convergence, and enlarged upon the existing principles of sustainable growth and protection of the environment.

---

[6] Although Art. 2 refers to the "task" of the Community, Art. 3(1) of the EC Treaty uses the expression "the purposes set out in Art. 2". However, the terminology used in the various languages differs.

[7] For the objectives set out in Art. 2 of the EEC Treaty, see para. 1–006, *supra*. For a study of their ideological background and their contemporary relevance, see Weiler, "Fin-de-siècle Europe: On Ideals and Ideology in Post-Maastricht Europe", in Curtin and Heukels (eds), *Institutional Dynamics of European Integration. Essays in Honour of Henry G. Schermers*, Vol.II (Martinus Nijhoff, Dordrecht, 1994), at 23–41. See also Müller-Graff, "Einheit und Kohärenz der Vertragsziele von EG und EU" (1998) EuR. Beiheft 2, 67–80.

[8] As far as economic and social cohesion is concerned, see the reference to "reducing the differences existing between the various regions and the backwardness of the less-favoured regions" in the preamble to the EEC Treaty and Arts 130a–130e of that treaty. As for environment protection, see the declaration of the Paris Summit Conference held in October 1972, which launched an environmental policy (1972) 10 EC Bull. 21, point 8; the recognition of environmental protection as "one of the Community's essential objectives" in ECJ, Case 240/83 *Procureur de la République v ADBHU* [1995] E.C.R. 531, para. 13, and Arts 130r–130t of the EEC Treaty.

[9] See Art. 104 of the EEC Treaty, which required the Member States "to ensure a high level of employment and a stable level of prices" in their economic policies, the first para. of Art. 117 and Art. 118a(1) of the EEC Treaty (social policy).

[10] For that principle of law, see para. 5–056, *infra*.

Article 2 of the EC Treaty does not set any objectives for international action on the part of the Community, unlike the preamble.[11] The objective of the Union's asserting its identity on the international scene (EU Treaty, Art. 2, second indent) is enlarged upon only in specific provisions of the EC Treaty[12] and the Treaty provisions relating to the common foreign and security policy.[13]

5–004 Instruments. Article 2 of the EC Treaty affords the Community three instruments for achieving the aforementioned objectives. First, the Community is to establish a common market. This entails the abolition of barriers to the free movement of goods, persons, services and capital in order to create an internal market without internal frontiers (see para. 5–071 *et seq.*). Secondly, the Community is to establish economic and monetary union (see para. 5–214 *et seq.*) by gradually approximating Member States' economic and monetary policies. The introduction of a common currency is the most tangible achievement in this regard. Lastly, the Community carries out flanking common policies and activities (see paras 5–235–5–253).

5–005 Tasks. Those instruments are enlarged upon in Art. 3(1) of the EC Treaty, which provides an overview in its 21 paragraphs of the Community's activities, and in Art. 4, which gives an outline of the economic, monetary and exchange rate policies which the Member States and the Community are to conduct. The EC Treaty expands on all these tasks in the 21 titles of Part Three, "Community Policies" (see paras 5–071—5–255).

Article 3 of the original EEC Treaty conferred on the Community only policy areas connected with the establishment and functioning of the common market.[14] In contrast, following its amendment by the EU Treaty, Art. 3 of the EC Treaty lists ancillary areas in which the Community is to pursue policies: social policy, environment policy and development-co-operation policy.[15] In addition, the Community is to *promote co-ordination* between employment policies of the Member States,[16] act to *strengthen* economic and social cohesion and the competitiveness of Community industry,[17] *promote* research and

---

[11] In the preamble to the EC Treaty, the Contracting Parties express the desire "to contribute, by means of a common commercial policy, to the progressive abolition of restrictions on international trade", "to confirm the solidarity which binds Europe and the overseas countries", "to ensure the development of their prosperity, in accordance with the principles of the Charter of the United Nations" and "by thus pooling their resources to preserve and strengthen peace and liberty, and calling upon the other peoples of Europe who share their ideal to join in their efforts".

[12] See, for example, EC Treaty, Art. 131, first para., Art. 177 and Arts 300 and 301.

[13] EU Treaty, Art. 11(1).

[14] For the limited policy goal undertaken in Art. 3 of the EEC Treaty, see para. 1–006, *supra*.

[15] EC Treaty, Art. 3(1)(j), (l) and (r), respectively.

[16] EC Treaty, Art. 3(1)(i).

[17] EC Treaty, Art. 3(1)(k) and (m), respectively.

technological development,[18] *encourage* the establishment and development of trans-European networks[19] and *contribute* to the attainment of a high level of health protection, education and training of quality and to the flowering of the cultures of the Member States, and to the strengthening of consumer protection.[20] The wording used to describe the method of acting suggests in itself that the Community is to perform a preparatory and supplementary task in these fields and that Community policies will not replace, or be conducted independently of, national policies. This is specified in the provisions of Part Three of the Treaty. No further legal basis exists for the measures in the spheres of energy, civil protection or tourism contemplated by Art. 3(1)(u) of the EC Treaty.[21] Rules on the association of overseas countries and territories are set out in Part Four of the EC Treaty.[22]

The EU Treaty reformulated the tasks of the Community: it extended the instruments set out in Art. 2 of the EEC Treaty, retouched the list of tasks in Art. 3 of the EEC Treaty, extended it by including the tasks resulting from the powers conferred by the Single European Act and the EU Treaty itself and added an Art. 3a [now Art. 4].[23] The Treaty of Amsterdam added the new power to co-ordinate Member States' employment policies as a task.[24]

The Treaty of Amsterdam gave prominence to two principles which the Community must take into account in all its activities: eliminating inequalities, and promoting equality, between men and women (EC Treaty, Art. 3(2)) and environmental protection requirements, in particular with a view to promoting sustainable development (EC Treaty, Art. 6).[25] The EC Treaty mentions other values or objectives which the Community must

---

[18] EC Treaty, Art. 3(1)(n).

[19] EC Treaty, Art. 3(1)(o).

[20] EC Treaty, Art. 3(1)(p), (q) and (t), respectively.

[21] In Declaration (No. 1) on civil protection, energy and tourism annexed to the EU Treaty, the Commission declared that Community action in those spheres would be pursued on the basis of the present provisions of the Treaties establishing the European Communities. However, neither the Amsterdam Treaty nor the Treaty of Nice gave effect to the declaration of the 1992 Intergovernmental Conference that, upon a subsequent amendment of the Treaty, titles on those spheres might be included. See paras 5–252–5–253, *infra*.

[22] See para. 20–016, *infra*.

[23] The list, formerly contained in Art. 3 of the EEC Treaty (para. 1–006, *supra*), no longer includes the "establishment of a common customs tariff", which has already been achieved, or the reference to the "establishment" or "institution" of certain common policies (agriculture, transport, competition). The common policy in the sphere of "agriculture" was specified by the addition of the term "fisheries". The definition of the economic policy of the Member States and the Community in Art. 3a [now Art. 4] replaced the expression "the application of procedures by which the economic policies of Member States can be co-ordinated and disequilibria in their balances of payments remedied" formerly contained in Art. 3(g) of the EEC Treaty.

[24] See EC Treaty, Art. 3(1)(i).

[25] Wasmeier, "The integration of environmental protection as a general rule for interpreting Community law" (2001) C.M.L.R. 159–177; Schumacher, "The environmental integration clause in Art. 6 of the EU Treaty: prioritising environmental protection" (2001) Env.L.Rev. 29–43.

invariably take into account in its activities: a high level of protection with regard to health, safety, environmental protection and consumer protection (Art. 95(3)), a high level of employment (Art. 127(2)), cultural aspects (Art. 151(4)), a high level of human health protection (Art. 152(1), first subpara.), consumer protection requirements (Art. 153(2)), development co-operation objectives (Art. 177) and the welfare of animals (as "sentient beings").[26]

5–006 Legal status. According to the Court of Justice, the aims on which the establishment of the Community is based cannot have the effect of "imposing legal obligations on the Member States or of conferring rights on individuals".[27] They depend for their implementation on the policies pursued by the Community and the Member States, with the result that their legal impact is limited to guiding the interpretation of Community law.[28] In that sense, the Court of Justice has relied on several occasions on Arts 2 and 3 of the EC Treaty in determining the requirements entailed by the establishment of the common market. Thus, Community competence is often inferred from specific Treaty provisions read together with the "objectives of the Community" or the "requirements of the common market" enshrined in Art. 3 of the EC Treaty.[29] The Court interprets the Treaty provisions "in the light of the Community's objectives and activities as defined by Arts 2 and 3 of the EEC Treaty".[30] Accordingly, the Court has inferred from Art. 3(g) of the EC Treaty, read in conjunction with Arts 10, 81 and 82, an obligation for Member States not to adopt any measures which may render ineffective the competition rules for undertakings set out in Arts 81 and 82.[31] Conversely, an objective such as

---

[26] See Protocol (No. 33) on protection and welfare of animals, annexed to the EC Treaty by the Treaty of Amsterdam ([1997] O.J. C340/110). Ensuring the welfare of animals does not for all that constitute a general principle of Community law: ECJ, Case C–189/01 *Jippes and Others* [2001] E.C.R. I–5689, paras 71–79. For the objectives of environmental and animal protection, see Van Calster and Deketelaere, "Amsterdam, the Intergovernmental Conference and Greening the EU Treaty" (1998) 12 E.Env.L.Rev. 17–19; Camm and Bowles, "Animal Welfare and the Treaty of Rome—A Legal Analysis of the Protocol on Animal Welfare and Welfare Standards in the European Union" (2000) J.Env.L. 197–205.

[27] ECJ, Case C–339/89 *Alsthom Atlantique* [1991] E.C.R. I–107, para. 9; ECJ, Case C–9/99 *Echirolles Distribution* [2000] E.C.R. I–8207, para. 25. For their legal force, see Reimer (n.4, *supra*); Durand, "Les principes", in de Cockborne, Defalque, Durand, Prahl and Verdersanden, *Commentaire Mégret—Le droit de la CEE. 1. Préambule. Principes. Libre circulation des marchandises* (Editions de l'Université de Bruxelles, Brussels, 1992), Nos 12–18, at 13–19; Pescatore, "Les objectifs de la Communauté européenne comme principes d'interprétation dans la jurisprudence de la Cour de Justice", *Miscellanea W.J. Ganshof van der Meersch* (Bruylant, Brussels, 1972), Part II, at 325–369.

[28] ECJ, Case C–149/96 *Portugal v Council* [1999] E.C.R. I–8395, paras 86–87 (objective of economic and social cohesion).

[29] For the common transport policy, see ECJ, Case 22/70 *Commission v Council* [1971] E.C.R. 263, para. 20; for compliance with the conditions of competition, see ECJ, Case 97/78 *Schumalla* [1978] E.C.R. 2311, para. 6.

[30] ECJ, Case 270/80 *Polydor* [1982] E.C.R. 329, para. 16.

[31] ECJ, Case 311/85 *VVR v Sociale Dienst van de Plaatselijke en Gewestelijke Overheidsdiensten* [1987] E.C.R. 3801, para. 24; ECJ, Case 267/86 *Van Eycke* [1988] E.C.R. 4769, para. 20 (see para. 5–195, *infra*).

an "open market economy with free competition" (EC Treaty, Art. 4) must be read in conjunction with the provisions of the Treaty designed to implement it.[32]

Constitution. The EU Constitution will replace the list of Community 5–007 objectives, instruments and tasks by an introductory title that sets out the values of the Union (Art. I–2: respect for human dignity, liberty, democracy, equality, the rule of law and respect for human rights, including the rights of persons belonging to minorities)[33] and provides the Union with a shopping list of objectives (Art. I–3).

It follows from this list of objectives that the EU Constitution focuses on non-economic goals to a far greater extent than the EC Treaty. The Union's first aim is to promote peace, the Union's values and the well-being of its peoples. Next, the EU Constitution refers to "an area of freedom, security and liberty without internal frontiers, and an internal market where competition is free and undistorted", to "the sustainable development of Europe based on balanced economic growth and price stability, a highly competitive social market economy, aiming at full employment and social progress, and with a high level of protection and improvement of the quality of the environment", to the promotion of scientific and technological advance, to combating social exclusion and discrimination, to the promotion of social justice and protection, equality between women and men, solidarity between generations and protection of the rights of the child, to the promotion of economic, social and territorial cohesion, and solidarity among Member States, to respect for the Union's rich cultural and linguistic diversity and to the safeguarding and enhancement of Europe's cultural heritage.[34]

Unlike the EC Treaty, the EU Constitution also provides the Union with specific objectives as to its external action.[35] Furthermore, the EU Constitution mentions in Art. I–4 free movement of persons, services, goods and capital, freedom of establishment and the principle of non-discrimination on grounds of nationality. These objectives have to be complemented by further objectives, laid down in the "provisions of general application" of Part III, that the Union must take into account in the implementation of its policies: the elimination of inequalities and the promotion of equality between men and women, combating all forms of

---

[32] ECJ, Case C–9/99 *Echirolles Distribution* [2000] E.C.R. I–8207, para. 24.

[33] The EU Constitution adds that these values are common to the Member States "in a society in which pluralism, non-discrimination, tolerance, justice, solidarity and equality between women and men prevail" (Art. I–2). A highly debated issue in civil society has been the request made in some quarters to emphasise the Christian roots of European civilisation in (the preamble to) the EU Constitution, see, for example, Mattera, "L'européanité est-elle chrétienne?" (2003) R.M.C.U.E. 325–342. The preamble to the EU Constitution refers to the Contracting Parties "drawing inspiration from the cultural, religious and humanist inheritance of Europe".

[34] EU Constitution, Art. I–3(1) to (3).

[35] EU Constitution, Arts I–3(4) and III–292(1) and (2).

discrimination referred to in Art. III–118 and respect for requirements relating to the promotion of a high level of employment and adequate social protection, environmental protection, consumer protection and animal welfare.[36]

All these objectives are to be treated on equal footing with the objectives set for the Union in other specific provisions of the EU Constitution. In accordance with Art. III–115 of the EU Constitution, the Union shall indeed ensure consistency between its different policies and activities "taking all of its objectives into account".

B. THE POWERS OF THE COMMUNITY

5–008 **Fundamental principles.** The Union may act only within the limits of the competences conferred upon it by the Treaties (the principle of conferral). Furthermore, the exercise by the Union of its competences is governed by the principles of subsidiarity and proportionality. These fundamentals regarding the division of powers between the Community and the Member States are confirmed in the EU Constitution as "fundamental principles" applicable to the entire field of action of the Union.

1. Need for a legal basis

5–009 **Principle of conferral.** The first para. of Art. 5 of the EC Treaty provides that "[t]he Community shall act within the limits of the powers conferred upon it by this Treaty and of the objectives assigned to it therein". This signifies that the Community has only conferred powers, which is known as the principle of "attribution of powers" or principle of conferral (see also EU Constitution, Art. I–11). This principle must be respected in both the internal action and the international action of the Community.[37] All Community action must be founded upon a legal basis laid down in the

---

[36] See Arts III–116—III–121 of the EU Constitution. On the relevance of such "integration principle" to environmental policy, see Jans and Scott, "The Convention on the Future of Europe: An Environmental Perspective" (2003) J.Env.L. 323–339.

[37] ECJ, Opinion 2/94, *Accession by the Communities to the Convention for the Protection of Human Rights and Fundamental Freedoms* [1996] E.C.R. I–1759, para. 24; ECJ, Opinion 2/00, *Carthagena Protocol* [2001] E.C.R. I–9713, para. 5. For legal basis as the precondition for legislative and executive action on the part of the Community, see Triantafyllou, *Des compétences d'attribution au domaine de la loi. Etude sur les fondements juridiques de l'activité administrative communautaire* (Bruylant, Brussels, 1997), 432 pp.; Van Ooik, *De keuze van rechtsgrondslag voor besluiten van de Europese Unie* (Kluwer, Deventer, 1999), 483 pp. See also Lauwaars, *Lawfulness and Legal Force of Community Decisions* (Sijthoff, Leiden, 1973), at 56–105; Lenaerts, *Le juge et la constitution aux Etats-Unis d'Amérique et dans l'ordre juridique européen* (Bruylant, Brussels, 1988), No. 300, at 346–349, and Nos 309–311, at 357–362; Bradley, "The European Court and the Legal Basis of Community Legislation" (1988) E.L.Rev. 379–402; Barents, "The Internal Market Unlimited: Some Observations on the Legal Basis of Community Legislation" (1993) C.M.L.R. 85–109; Lenaerts and van Ypersele, "Le principe de subsidiarité et son contexte: étude de l'article 3 B du traité CE" (1994) C.D.E. 13–30 and 35–44; Peter, "La base juridique des actes en droit communautaire" (1994) R.M.C.U.E. 324–333; Emiliou, "Opening Pandora's Box: The Legal Basis of Community Measures Before the Court of Justice" (1994) E.L.Rev. 488–507.

Treaty. Naturally, the legal basis for Community acts may also be found in another Community act which they are designed to implement. In those circumstances, too, an institution or a body cannot act unless its action is based on a basic act having a legal basis in the Treaty which: (1) defines the Community's competence *ratione materiae*; and (2) specifies the means of exercise of that competence, that is to say, the legislative instruments and the decision-making procedure.[38]

(1) Vertical division of powers. In the first place, the legal basis determines **5–010** a division of competence between the Community and the Member States: where the Community is not empowered to act, such action comes within the residuary competence of the Member States.[39]

The first para. of Art. 5 of the EC Treaty draws a distinction between Community powers depending on their legal basis. The Community exercises "the powers conferred upon it by this Treaty" where the action undertaken falls, expressly or impliedly, within one of the tasks listed in Arts 3 and 4 of the EC Treaty and the power is expanded upon in one of the subsequent titles of the Treaty. The expression "objectives assigned to [the Community]" refers to competence to act which does not as such follow from a Treaty provision, but appears necessary in order to attain one of the objectives assigned to the Community by the Treaty (EC Treaty, Art. 308; for this difference between legal bases, see paras 5–013–5–020). This "suppletive" legal basis of Art. 308 and the teleological interpretation which the Court of Justice has given to various legal bases mean that the principle of conferred powers has in practice placed few limits on the action of the Community.[40]

The second paragraph of Art. 5 uses the expression "exclusive competence" to make the distinction between the situation where the Community alone has jurisdiction or the situation where it shares it with the Member States (see paras 5–021–5–027).

The attribution of ever more competences to the Community has given rise to a continual debate about the most appropriate distribution of competence as between the Community and the Member States, which has

---

[38] Unlike, for instance, Dutch, which uses the same term for both (*bevoegdheid*), other official languages of the Community sometimes employ different terms for competence *ratione materiae* (*compétence, Zuständigkeit*) and the means available to exercise it (*pouvoirs, powers, Befugnisse*). For the distinction, see Constantinesco, *Compétences et pouvoirs dans les Communautés européennes* (Librairie Générale de Droit et de Jurisprudence, Paris, 1974), 492 pp. For a recent analysis of types of powers, see Von Bogdandy and Bast, "Die vertikale Kompetenzordnung der Europäischen Union—Rechtsdogmatischer Bestand und verfassungsrechtliche Reformperspektiven" (2001) Eu.GR.Z. 441–458.

[39] This corollary of the principle of conferred powers is expressly mentioned in Art. I–11(2) of the EU Constitution ("Competences not conferred upon the Union in the Constitution remain with the Member States").

[40] See Van Nuffel, *De rechtsbescherming van nationale overheden in het Europees recht* (Kluwer, Deventer, 2000), 84–102. Nevertheless, the Council can use the "suppletive" legal basis of Art. 308 of the EC Treaty only if it remains within the limits traced by the Treaty; see para. 5–018.

found expression in particular in the introduction of principle of subsidiarity (see para. 5–028 *et seq.*) and in the call for a more precise delimitation of powers.[41] The EU Constitution has partially responded to this call in so far as it codifies in the Constitution some of the principles that are to be found at present only in the case law of the Court of Justice and sets out a limitative list of exclusive competences (see para. 5–027).[42]

5–011 **(2) Horizontal division of powers.** In addition, the legal basis determines the way in which the Community exercises its competence *ratione materiae* (together with the principle of subsidiarity, para. 5–028, and the principle of proportionality, para. 5–036). As far as the appropriate legislative instrument is concerned, some Treaty articles restrict action on the part of the Community to "directives", "directives or regulations", "recommendations" or "incentive measures", whilst others authorise any "measures" to be taken.[43] As far as the decision-making procedure is concerned, the Treaty articles determine what institutions are to be involved in the adoption of an act and how this is to take place.[44] A dispute as to the correct legal basis for an act is not a purely formal one inasmuch as a different decision-making procedure may affect the determination of the content of the act adopted.[45] This will be the case, for example, where a Treaty article requiring the Council to decide by unanimity rather than by qualified majority is wrongly used.[46] However, an argument contesting the legal basis of an act may indeed have only formal significance where the legal basis argued for does not entail any stricter procedural requirements than the one on which the act is actually founded.[47]

The decision-making procedure and any limitation as to the legislative instruments which may be used determine the horizontal allocation of

---

[41] See the call for a wide debate in Declaration (No. 23) on the future of the Union, annexed to the Treaty of Nice ([2001] O.J. C80/85) and the "Declaration of Laeken" of the European Council of December 14 and 15, 2001. For the question of lack of transparency in the delimitation of powers, see para. 16–007. For further discussion of the delimitation of powers as between the Community/Union and the Member States, see Von Bogdandy and Bast, "The European Union's Vertical Order of Competences: The Current Law and Proposals for its Reform" (2002) C.M.L.R. 227–268.

[42] See Davies, "The post-Laeken division of competences" (2003) E.L.Rev. 686–698; Michel, "2004: Le défi de la répartition des compétences" (2003) C.D.E. 17–86; Hanf and Baumé, "Vers une clarification de la répartition des compétences entre l'Union et ses États membres? Une analyse du projet d'articles du Présidium de la Convention" (2003) C.D.E. 135–156.

[43] See the lists of instruments in Arts 249 and 300(1) of the EC Treaty and the discussion of acts of the institutions and bodies, para. 17–113 *et seq.*

[44] See the discussion of decision-making, para. 14–006 *et seq.*

[45] See, *e.g.* ECJ Case 45/86 *Commission v Council* [1987] E.C.R. 1493, para. 12; ECJ, Case 68/86 *UK v Council* [1988] E.C.R. 855, para. 6; ECJ, Case 131/86 *UK v Council* [1988] E.C.R. 905, para. 11.

[46] *e.g.* ECJ (judgment of September 11, 2003), Case C–211/01 *Commission v Council*, not yet reported, para. 52.

[47] ECJ, Case 165/87 *Commission v Council* [1988] E.C.R. 5545, para. 19; ECJ, Case C–268/94 *Portugal v Council* [1996] E.C.R. I–6177, para. 79; ECJ, Case C–491/01 *British American Tobacco (Investments) and Imperial Tobacco* [2002] E.C.R. I–11453, paras 97–98.

powers among the Community institutions according to which "[e]ach institution shall act within the limits of the powers conferred upon it by this Treaty" (EC Treaty, Art. 7(1), second subpara.). At the same time, this allocation of powers influences the vertical relationship between the Community and the Member States. Where an institution is entitled to adopt a regulation, it may restrict the power of the Member States to a greater degree than where it is empowered only to adopt directives, since, in principle, a directive leaves the Member States with more latitude than a regulation. Where the decision-making procedure requires there to be a unanimous vote in the Council, each Member State has a right of veto. The EU Constitution will re-order the available legislative instruments and introduce a degree of uniformity into the various decision-making procedures. However, each enabling clause will still determine the specific instruments to be used and the particular procedure to be followed where action is to be taken on the basis of the Article in question.[48]

Choice of legal basis. Given the consequences of the legal basis in terms of **5–012** substantive competence and the procedure, the choice of the correct legal basis is of constitutional importance.[49] The choice of the legal basis for an act does not turn on the relevant institution's conviction as to the objective pursued but must be "based on objective factors which are amenable to judicial review",[50] such as the aim and content of the measure.[51] The Community must make the aim of the act completely clear.[52] It is an essential procedural requirement of any Community act that it should state its legal basis.[53] The absence of such a statement is tolerated only if the legal basis of the act may be determined unambiguously from other factors.[54] However, an error as to the legal basis will not affect the validity of the act in question where the persons affected enjoyed all of the procedural guarantees which may have been applicable and the error did not have any adverse effect on their legal position.[55]

---

[48] See EU Constitution, Art. I–12(6).

[49] ECJ, Opinion 2/00 *Carthagena Protocol* [2001] E.C.R. I–9713, para. 5.

[50] ECJ, Case 45/86 *Commission v Council* [1987] E.C.R. 1493, para. 11.

[51] ECJ, Case C–300/89 *Commission v Council* [1991] E.C.R. I–2867, para. 10. For the practical interpretation of the "objective factors", see Van Nuffel (n.40, *supra*), 180–211.

[52] The choice of aim is reviewed only marginally by the Court. The Community is free to determine whether the measure is suitable for the purpose of achieving the intended aim and the Court will consider only whether the Community was guilty of an error, manifestly exceeded its powers or misused its powers: ECJ, Case C–331/88 *Fedesa* [1990] E.C.R. I–4023, para. 8; see also para. 5–039. Where the act affects the residuary powers of the Member States, the principles of subsidiarity and proportionality require the aim and content of the act and likewise the choice of legislative instrument to be specifically reasoned, paras 5–033 and 5–044.

[53] ECJ, Case C–325/91 *France v Commission* [1993] E.C.R. I–3283, para. 26.

[54] ECJ, Case 45/86 *Commission v Council* [1987] E.C.R. 1493, para. 9; CFI, Case T–70/99 *Alpharma v Council* [2002] E.C.R. II–3495, paras 110–121.

[55] CFI, Case T–213/00 *CMA CGM v Commission* [2003] E.C.R. II–913, paras 65–103. For the possibility that a dispute concerning the legal basis has merely formal significance, see also para. 5–011.

Institutions, Member States and, to a lesser extent, individuals have often challenged the legal basis of Community acts, with the parties adopting a stance reflecting their differing (political) interests. In such cases, the Court of Justice acts as a constitutional court, reviewing the horizontal and vertical division of powers within the Communities.[56] In this way, the Court of Justice annulled a directive of the European Parliament and the Council on tobacco advertising on the ground that those institutions had adopted a piece of legislation—at the Commission's proposal—which exceeded the bounds set by the Treaty for harmonisation.[57]

2. Powers differ depending on the legal basis

a. Powers conferred expressly or impliedly by the Treaty

5–013 **Legal basis.** Action by the Community is founded in principle on a "specific" provision of the Treaty which confers the power to act. Competence to act is defined by the list of its aims and the means which may be employed in order to attain them.[58] The aims and means mentioned act as the demarcation of the power as it ensues from the Treaty provision in question. Some Treaty articles allow the Community to act in so far as certain policy areas of the Member States are respected[59] or there is no harmonisation of national laws and regulations.[60]

The Treaty also contains "general" provisions empowering the Community to issue, in any field, "directives for the approximation of such

---

[56] Lenaerts (n.37, *supra*), Nos 309–311, at 357–362.

[57] ECJ, Case C–376/98 *Germany v European Parliament and Council* [2000] E.C.R. I–8419; see commentaries by Barents, "De tabaksrichtlijn in rook opgegaan" (2000) N.T.E.R. 327–331; Mortelmans and Van Ooik, "Het Europese verbod op tabaksreclame: verbetering van de interne markt of verbetering van de volksgezondheid?" (2001) A.A. 114–130; Hervey, "Up in Smoke? Community (anti-)tobacco law and policy" (2001) E.L.Rev. 101–125; Cornides, "Eine Richtlinie löst sich in Rauch auf" (2001) Z.f.RV. 130–135; Usher (2001) C.M.L.R. 1519–1543; Gosalbo Bono, "L'arrêt 'tabac' ou l'apport de la Cour de justice au débat sur la délimitation de compétences" (2001) R.T.D.E. 790–808; Amtenbrink and Appeldoorn, "Is er leven na het Tabaksreclamearrest?" (2000) S.E.W. 413–420.

[58] *cf.* ECJ, Case 242/87 *Commission v Council* [1989] E.C.R. 1425, paras 6–37.

[59] See, *e.g.* the areas reserved to the Member States in Arts 135 and 280 (national criminal law and national administration of justice) and in Art. 149(1) (content of teaching and organisation of education systems) and Art. 150(1) (content and organisation of vocational training) of the EC Treaty. See in this regard Van Nuffel (n.40, *supra*), at 102–121. See also the areas in which the application of certain legal bases is precluded, particularly Art. 18(3) (passports, identity cards, residence permits or any other such document or provisions on social security or social protection), Art. 137(4) (fundamental principles of national social security systems) and (5) (pay, the right of association, the right to strike and the right to impose lock-outs) and Art. 157(3), second subpara. (tax provisions and provisions relating to the rights and interests of employed persons) of the EC Treaty.

[60] See Art. 129 (employment), Art. 149 (education), Art. 150 (vocational training), Art. 151 (culture) and Art. 152 (public health) of the EC Treaty; Van Nuffel (n.40, *supra*), at 267–268. The Treaty of Nice added areas in this respect: Art. 13(2) (action to combat discrimination) and Art. 137(2), first subpara. , indent (a) (social policy), of the EC Treaty. As far as the external powers of the Community are concerned, this is confirmed in Art. 133(6), first subpara. , of the EC Treaty (common commercial policy).

laws, regulations or administrative provisions of the Member States as directly affect the establishment or functioning of the common market" (EC Treaty, Art. 94)[61] or to adopt "measures for the approximation of the provisions laid down by law, regulation or administrative action in Member States which have as their object the establishment and functioning of the internal market" (EC Treaty, Art. 95(1)). Such provisions may not, however, be used as a legal basis in order to circumvent an express exclusion of harmonisation laid down in specific articles of the EC Treaty.[62]

In many instances, a measure is intended to attain objectives set out in a specific Treaty article, whilst at the same time influencing the functioning of the common or internal market (e.g. an environment protection measure harmonising product or production standards and thereby promoting the free movement of goods and/or free competition). If the measure has a manifold objective or if several aspects are involved, the legal basis must be determined on the basis of the Treaty article corresponding to the main aim or the main aspect of the act. Where, for example, harmonisation of national legislation is only an incidental effect of a measure which primarily pursues another objective, the measure must be adopted only on the basis of the specific Treaty article which corresponds to its principal characteristic.[63] Conversely, a general Treaty article, such as Art. 95 of the EC Treaty, constitutes a sufficient legal basis where a measure aims to harmonise national measures, even if that measure also seeks, in a subordinate manner, to attain an aim sought by specific Treaty articles.[64] The same is true of the Community's external powers where agreements coming under the common commercial policy, development co-operation or environment protection are based on Treaty provisions relating to the chief subject-matter of the agreement.[65]

---

[61] The first para. of Art. 100 as it was worded in the EEC Treaty empowered the Council to issue "directives for the approximation of such provisions laid down by law, regulation or administrative action in Member States as directly affect the establishment or functioning of the common market".

[62] ECJ, Case C–376/98 *Germany v European Parliament and Council* [2000] E.C.R. I–8419, para. 79 (for commentaries, see n.57, *supra.*).

[63] ECJ, Case 68/86 *UK v Council* [1988] E.C.R. 855, paras 14–16: ECJ, Case C–70/88 *European Parliament v Council* [1991] E.C.R. I–4529, paras 16–18; ECJ, Case C–155/91 *Commission v Council* [1993] E.C.R. I–939, paras 18–20; ECJ, Case C–187/93 *European Parliament v Council* [1994] E.C.R. I–2857, paras 23–26; ECJ, Case C–426/93 *Germany v Council* [1995] E.C.R. I–3723, para. 33; ECJ, Case C–271/94 *European Parliament v Council* [1996] E.C.R. I–1689, paras 28–32; ECJ, Case C–84/94 *UK v Council* [1996] E.C.R. I–5755, paras 11–12 and 22; ECJ, Joined Cases C–164–165/97 *European Parliament v Council* [1999] E.C.R. I–1339, para. 16; ECJ, Case C–36/98 *Spain v Council* [2001] E.C.R. I–779, para. 59; ECJ, Case C–281/01 *Commission v Council* [2002] E.C.R. I–12649, paras 33–49; ECJ (judgment of April 29, 2004), Case C–338/01 *Commission v Council*, not yet reported, para. 55. See Lenaerts, "The Principle of Subsidiarity and the Environment in the European Union: Keeping the Balance of Federalism" (1994) Fordham I.L.J. 846, at 871–873.

[64] ECJ, Case C–377/98 *Netherlands v European Parliament and Council* [2001] E.C.R. I–7079, paras 27–28; ECJ, Case C–491/01 *British American Tobacco (Investments) and Imperial Tobacco* [2002] E.C.R. I–11453, paras 93–94.

[65] ECJ, Opinion 2/00 *Carthagena Protocol* [2001] E.C.R. I–9713, paras 22–44 (environment protection). See also paras 20–002 (common commercial policy) and 20–027 (development co-operation).

5–014 Multiple legal bases. Where a measure has several contemporaneous objectives which are indissolubly linked with each other without one being secondary and indirect in respect of the others, the measure must be based on the various relevant Treaty provisions[66] unless this is impossible on account of the mutual incompatibility of the decision-making procedures laid down by the provisions.[67] In that event, it must be determined in the light of the general scope of the Treaty which Treaty provision affords the appropriate legal basis by itself.[68]

5–015 Implied power. Where the Community acts on the basis of a specific or a general Treaty provision, it exercises its powers using the means and by the procedure laid down in the relevant provision. Some Treaty provisions do not expressly provide for all necessary means in order to attain the objectives of the relevant competence *ratione materiae.* In such cases, the Court of Justice has recognised that it is implicit in the Community competence that additional means may be used in order to achieve the objectives.

In this way, it fell to the Court to determine whether the Community had the power to negotiate and conclude the European Agreement concerning the work of crews of vehicles engaged in international road transport (AETR).[69] By judgment of March 31, 1971, it held that although the Treaty provisions empowering the Community to take measures within the framework of the common transport policy:

"do not expressly confer on the Community authority to enter into international agreements, nevertheless the bringing into force . . . of

---

[66] ECJ, Case 165/87 *Commission v Council* [1988] E.C.R. 5545, para. 11.

[67] ECJ, Case C–300/89 *Commission v Council* [1991] E.C.R. I–2867, paras 17–21. In that case, the Court of Justice held that the directive which the Council had adopted on the basis of Art. 130s of the EEC Treaty on procedures for harmonising the programmes for the reduction and eventual elimination of waste from the titanium dioxide industry displayed, "in view of its aim and content, . . . the features both of action relating to the environment with which Art. 130s of the Treaty is concerned and of a harmonising measure which has as its object the establishment and functioning of the internal market, within the meaning of Art. 100a of the Treaty". It was impossible to have such a dual legal basis, however, because then the co-operation procedure with the European Parliament required by Art. 100a would be jeopardised (see the discussion of the co-operation procedure in para. 14–029). The Court went on to hold that Art. 100a was the proper legal basis, thereby giving preference to the provision which afforded the European Parliament the greater say in the legislative process. See also ECJ (judgment of April 29, 2004), Case C–338/01 *Commission v Council,* not yet reported, para. 58 (Art. 95 cannot be applied in conjunction with Arts 93 and 94 of the EC Treaty since unanimity is required for the adoption of a measure on the basis of Arts 93 and 94 whereas a qualified majority is sufficient for a measure to be adopted on the basis of Art. 95). *Cf.* ECJ, Case C–491/01 *British American Tobacco (Investments) and Imperial Tobacco* [2002] E.C.R. I–11453, paras 103–111 (the fact that the co-decision procedure laid down by Art. 95 of the EC Treaty was combined with the qualified majority vote prescribed by Art. 133 did not prejudice the substance of the legislative procedure).

[68] ECJ, Case C–300/89 *Commission v Council* [1991] E.C.R. I–2867, paras 21–25.

[69] ECJ, Case 22/70 *Commission v Council* [1971] E.C.R. 263. The acronym "AETR" stands for "Accord européen sur les transport routiers" (European Agreement on Road Transport).

Regulation No. 543/69 of the Council on the harmonisation of certain social legislation relating to road transport . . . necessarily vested in the Community power to enter into any agreements with third countries relating to the subject-matter governed by that regulation".[70]

Whenever Community law has conferred on the institutions powers within the internal system of the Community for the purpose of attaining a specific objective, the Community has authority to enter into the international commitments necessary for the attainment of that object even in the absence of an express provision concerning the matter.[71]

Implied competence. An implied competence provides the Community **5-016** with an ancillary substantive basis for powers and must therefore be distinguished from the implicit powers which the Community has available to it in connection with a particular substantive competence (see preceding section). French lawyers refer to *compétences implicites* (implicit competence) as opposed to *pouvoirs implicites* (implicit powers).

The Community is entitled to rely on an implied competence only where it is necessary in order to supplement an express competence.[72] The close relationship between the two must be shown by objective evidence which the Court of Justice can review. Thus, the Court held that the professional and social integration of workers from non-member countries was directly linked with the social questions for which the former Art. 118 of the EEC Treaty provided for co-operation between the Member States.[73]

Procedure. The Treaty provision providing for the express competence **5-017** with which the implied competence is associated determines the decision-making procedure which the Community has to follow in exercising that competence. Accordingly, whenever the Community legislates on the right of residence of students and dependants pursuant to an implied competence contained in Art. 12 of the EC Treaty, which empowers the Community to adopt rules designed to prohibit any discrimination on grounds of nationality, it has to do so in accordance with the procedure prescribed by the second para. of Art. 12 of the EC Treaty.[74]

The Treaty article which indirectly provides the legal basis for the implied competence does not always prescribe the means necessary for

---

[70] *ibid.*, para. 28.
[71] ECJ, Opinion 1/76 *Draft Agreement establishing a European laying-up fund for inland waterway vessels* [1977] E.C.R. 741, para. 3. See also the discussion of the external powers of the Community: para. 20–032, *infra*.
[72] ECJ, Case C–295/90 *European Parliament v Council* [1992] E.C.R. I–4193, paras 18–20. See also ECJ, Case 9/74 *Casagrande* [1974] E.C.R. 773, paras 4–6.
[73] ECJ, Joined Cases 281/85, 283–285/85 and 287/85 *Germany, France, Netherlands, Denmark and UK v Commission* [1987] E.C.R. 3203. However, the Court found no legal basis for the cultural integration of such workers in that former Community power on the ground that the link was "extremely tenuous", *ibid.*, para. 22.
[74] *cf.* ECJ, Case C–295/90 *European Parliament v Council* [1992] E.C.R. I–4193, paras 18–20.

exercising that power. Accordingly, the Court of Justice accepts that an implied competence, just like an express competence (see para. 5–015), is capable of entailing the necessary powers, which are not specifically mentioned in the Treaty Article serving as the legal basis (*pouvoirs implicites*).[75]

b. Supplementary competence to achieve Community objectives (EC Treaty, Art. 308)

5–018 **Supplementary competence.** Article 308 of the EC Treaty gives the Community an ancillary legal basis in order to take the appropriate measures "if action by the Community should prove necessary to attain, in the course of the operation of the common market, one of the objectives of the Community and this Treaty has not provided the necessary powers". Consequently, action pursuant to Art. 308 is justified only where no other Treaty provision gives the Community the necessary express or implied competence.[76] However, Art. 308 may not be used to supplement a specific Treaty provision which limits Community competence by excluding coverage of certain policy areas or the use of certain instruments, such as harmonisation measures.[77] In addition, the action must be necessary to attain one of the objectives of the Community. For a long time, it was assumed that it fell to the Council to determine (by unanimous vote) that action was necessary and that its decision to this effect was in principle not justiciable.[78] But in a 1996 opinion the Court of Justice unambiguously held that Art. 308 "cannot serve as a basis for widening the scope of Community powers beyond the general framework created by the provisions of the Treaty as a whole and, in particular, by those that define the tasks and the activities of the Community".[79] Since the institutional system of the Community is based on the principle of conferred powers, Art. 308 cannot

---

[75] See ECJ, Joined Cases 281/85, 283–285/85 and 287/85 *Germany, France, Netherlands, Denmark and UK v Commission* [1987] E.C.R. 3203, paras 27–29.

[76] ECJ, Case 45/86 *Commission v Council* [1987] E.C.R. 1493, para. 13. See also ECJ Case 242/87 *Commission v Council* [1989] E.C.R. 1425, in which the Court of Justice dismissed an application for annulment of the decision by which the Council had adopted the European Community action scheme for the mobility of university students (Erasmus) on the basis of Arts 128 and 235 of the EEC Treaty (Art. 235 EEC Treaty being the predecessor of Art. 308 EC Treaty). The Court held that the dual legal basis of Arts 128 and 235 was lawful inasmuch as the decision also concerned scientific research. This fell outside the scope of Art. 128, which—as it was worded in the EEC Treaty—authorised the Council to adopt "a common vocational training policy". The Council adopted a second Erasmus decision solely on the basis of Art. 128 of the EEC Treaty following the omission of the research aspect from the Commission proposal. *Cf.* ECJ Joined Cases C–51/89, C–90/89 and C–94/89 *UK v Council* [1991] E.C.R. I–2757. For the extension of Community competence made possible by that Art. 308, see Bungenberg, "Dynamische Integration, Art. 308 und die Fordering nach dem Kompetenzkatalog" (2000) EuR. 819–900.

[77] See Van Nuffel (n.40, *supra*), 90, No. 117.

[78] For the latitude which the Court allows the Council in assessing "necessity", see ECJ, Case 8/73 *Massey-Ferguson* [1973] E.C.R. 897, para. 3.

[79] ECJ, Opinion 2/94, *Accession by the Communities to the Convention for the Protection of Human Rights and Fundamental Freedoms* [1996] E.C.R. I–1759, para. 30.

be used as the legal basis for the adoption of provisions whose effect would, in substance, be to amend the Treaty without following the procedure which it provides for that purpose.[80] Article 308 of the EC Treaty creates a supplementary competence and does not contain any obligation for the Community to use it.[81]

Procedure. Article 308 lays down the precise decision-making procedure **5–019** which the Community must follow whenever it exercises this supplementary competence. The article does not specify any particular types of legislative measure ("the appropriate measures"), as a result of which all means are possible and recourse will never have to be made to implicit powers.

Constitution. The EU Constitution retains this supplementary competence **5–020** in the form of a "flexibility clause" allowing the Council, within the framework of the policies defined in Part III, to take action to attain one of the objectives set by the Constitution if the Constitution has not provided the necessary powers (Art. I–18). Whereas Art. 308 EC Treaty requires the European Parliament only to be consulted, Art. I–18 makes action of the Union dependent upon the consent of the European Parliament.

3. Exclusive and non-exclusive competence

Classification. Depending on their relationship to the powers of the **5–021** Member States, the Community's competences are subdivided into exclusive and non-exclusive competences (see the second paragraph of Art. 5 of the EC Treaty and Art. 43(d) of the EU Treaty). Non-exclusive competences are sometimes referred to as "shared" (see the second subparagraph of Art. 133(6) of the EC Treaty), "parallel" or "concurrent" competences. The EU Constitution will delimit exclusive competences for the first time on a constitutional basis and also introduce new categories of non-exclusive competences (see para. 5–027).

Exclusivity. Exclusive competence comprises powers which have been **5–022** definitively and irreversibly forfeited by the Member States by reason of their straightforward transfer to the Community. In that event, Member States may act only to implement measures adopted by the Community. A Community power is exclusive where it appears from the wording or the context of the Treaty provisions in question that any parallel action by the Member States would conflict therewith. Accordingly, in Opinion 1/75 the Court of Justice recognised the exclusive nature of the common commercial

---

[80] *ibid.* (Opinion holding that the accession of the Community to the ECHR would exceed the limits of Art. 308; see also para. 17–082, *infra*).

[81] ECJ, Case 22/70 *Commission v Council* [1971] E.C.R. 263, para. 95 ("Although Article 235 empowers the Council to take any "appropriate measures" . . . it does not create an obligation, but confers on the Council an option, failure to exercise which cannot affect the validity" of a decision).

policy with regard to trade in goods covered by Art. 133 of the EC Treaty in the following terms:

"Such a policy is conceived in that article in the context of the operation of the common market, for the defence of the common interests of the Community, within which the particular interests of the Member States must endeavour to adapt to each other. Quite clearly, however, this conception is incompatible with the freedom to which the Member States could lay claim by invoking a concurrent power, so as to ensure that their own interests were separately satisfied in external relations, at the risk of compromising the effective defence of the common interests of the Community. In fact any unilateral action on the part of the Member States would lead to distortions in the conditions for the grant of export credits, calculated to distort competition between undertakings of the various Member States in external markets. Such distortion can be eliminated only by means of a strict uniformity of credit conditions granted to undertakings in the Community, whatever their nationality. . . . The provisions of Arts 113 and 114 [now Art. 133] . . . show clearly that the exercise of concurrent powers by the Member States and the Community in this matter is impossible. To accept that the contrary were true would amount to recognising that, in relations with third countries, Member States may adopt positions which differ from those which the Community intends to adopt, and would thereby distort the institutional framework, call into question the mutual trust within the Community and prevent the latter from fulfilling its task in the defence of the common interest."[82]

5–023 Pre-emption. Nevertheless, most Treaty provisions allow Member States to act with a view to attaining the objectives of the Treaty. That power only ceases to exist once the Community actually exercises its own competence (the "pre-emption" principle).[83] In that event, the national rule must give way to the Community provision in so far as there is a conflict between them (primacy of Community law: see para. 17–005). In this connection, it must be determined to what extent Community action in a particular area still leaves room for the Member States to legislate. Accordingly, the Court of Justice held in the *AETR* case that the Community's exercise of its powers in regard to the common transport policy "excludes the possibility of concurrent powers on the part of the Member States, since any steps taken outside the framework of the Community institutions would be

---

[82] ECJ, Opinion 1/75 *Draft OECD Understanding on a Local Cost Standard* [1975] E.C.R. 1355, at 1363–1364.

[83] For comparisons with the pre-emption principle in the constitutional law of the US, see Lenaerts (n.37, *supra*), Nos 436–468, at 525–566 (for the doctrine of pre-emption, see Nos 167–174, at 176–185); Cross, "Pre-emption of Member State Law in the European Economic Community: A Framework for Analysis" (1992) C.M.L.R. 447–472.

incompatible with the unity of the common market and the uniform application of Community law".[84] Action on the part of the Community restricts the power of the Member States to such an extent that they can only act in future in conformity with the Community provision. Depending upon the extent to which the Community exercises its power, it may confer upon it an "exclusive nature",[85] even though exclusive competence has not been transferred to the Community within the meaning of the second paragraph of Art. 5 of the EC Treaty.[86]

Repeal. The EC Treaty precludes Member States from establishing closer **5–024** co-operation between themselves in areas which fall within the exclusive competence of the Community (see EU Treaty, Art. 43(d)). Furthermore, the Community cannot transfer a field in which it has exclusive competence back to the Member States because the text of the Treaty itself definitively rules out competence on the part of the Member States. In an area of non-exclusive competence, the Community may in principle repeal the Community measure, leaving the Member States in a position to exercise their powers in full again. The repeal must accord, however, with the objectives of the Treaty provision forming the legal basis of the measure and with the principle of subsidiarity (see para. 5–032).

Exclusive powers. Virtually all Community powers are non-exclusive. **5–025** Nevertheless, the Court of Justice has recognised two exclusive competences. The first is the power under Art. 133 of the EC Treaty to conduct a common commercial policy *vis-à-vis* third countries with regard to trade in goods.[87] The second is the competence conferred by Art. 102 of the 1972 Act of Accession, which empowers the Community to determine conditions for fishing with a view to ensuring protection of fishing grounds and the conservation of the biological resources of the sea.[88] In addition, it is accepted that, as a result of the introduction of the common customs

---

[84] ECJ, Case 22/70 *Commission v Council* [1971] E.C.R. 263, para. 31.

[85] ECJ, Opinion 2/91 *Convention No. 170 of the International Labour Organisation concerning safety in the use of chemicals at work* [1993] E.C.R. I–1061, para. 9; see also ECJ, Opinion 1/94 *Agreement establishing the World Trade Organisation* [1994] E.C.R. I–5267, paras 72–105; ECJ, Opinion 2/92 *Third Revised Decision of the OECD on national treatment* [1995] E.C.R. I–521, paras 31–36 (para. 20–036, *infra*).

[86] See ECJ, Case C–491/01 *British American Tobacco (Investments) and Imperial Tobacco* [2002] E.C.R. I–11453, para. 179 (competence to harmonise under Art. 95 is not exclusive). For these so-called *compétences exclusives par exercice*, see also Lenaerts and van Ypersele (n.37, *supra*), at 20–28.

[87] ECJ, Opinion 1/75 *Draft OECD Understanding on a Local Cost Standard* [1975] E.C.R. 1355, at 1363–1365 (para. 5–022, *supra*); ECJ, Case 41/76 *Donckerwolcke* [1976] E.C.R. 1921, para. 32; ECJ, Opinion 1/78 *International Agreement on Natural Rubber* [1979] E.C.R. 2871, paras 52–60; ECJ, Opinion 2/91 *Convention No. 170 of the International Labour Organisation concerning safety in the use of chemicals at work* [1993] E.C.R. I–1061, para. 8.

[88] ECJ, Joined Cases 3–4/76 and 6/76 *Kramer* [1976] E.C.R. 1279, paras 39–41; ECJ, Case 804/79 *Commission v UK* [1981] E.C.R. 1045, paras 17–18; ECJ, Opinion 2/91 (n.87, *supra*), para. 8.

tariff, Art. 26 of the EC Treaty on the customs union precludes any parallel competence on the part of the Member States. The same is true of monetary policy as regards the Member States participating in the third stage of Economic and Monetary Union (see para. 5–214 *et seq.*).

5–026 **Authorisation.** Where the Community has exclusive competence, this means that any action by a Member State in the same field is *a priori* in conflict with the Treaty. This is liable to raise problems. If the Community omits to act, a measure deemed to be necessary may remain untaken in the absence of any other competent authority. Furthermore, changed political and economic circumstances may make action on the part of the Member States desirable. Accordingly, the exclusive character of a Community competence should remain limited to what is essential in order to attain the objectives of the Community.

The fact that a particular competence is exclusive does not preclude the Community from delegating certain means of exercising that competence to the Member States. In so doing, the Member States may act as agents of the Community pursuant to a "specific authorisation".[89] In such a case, the Community specifies in what way and according to what procedure the Member States are to act.[90] Accordingly, the Court of Justice was prepared in principle to accept Member States taking measures to preserve fish stocks "as trustees of the common interest" since the Council had not yet formulated any policy following the entry into effect of Art. 102 of the 1972 Act of Accession. They had to do so "as part of a process of collaboration with the Commission and with due regard to the general task of supervision which Art. 155 of the EEC Treaty . . . gives to the Commission".[91] In 1986 the Court went very far in this direction when it decided that the United Kingdom had a "specific authorisation" to prohibit oil exports to Israel by derogation from the exclusive competence with regard to the common commercial policy. It inferred that authorisation from the fact that there was no express prohibition of export restrictions in the EEC-Israel Agreement and that oil was excluded from the Council regulation establishing common rules for exports.[92] However, where a specific authorisation can exist without the Community's having genuinely endorsed the national measures taken, the very exclusivity of the relevant competence is called in question.[93]

---

[89] ECJ, Case 41/76 *Donckerwolcke* [1976] E.C.R. 1921, para. 32.
[90] Lenaerts, "Regulating the Regulatory Process: 'Delegation of Powers' in the European Community" (1993) E.L.Rev. 23–49, in particular at 27–32.
[91] ECJ, Case 804/79 *Commission v UK* [1981] E.C.R. 1045, para. 30.
[92] ECJ, Case 174/84 *Bulk Oil* [1986] E.C.R. 559, paras 15–19 and 33.
[93] See Lenaerts, "Les répercussions des compétences de la Communauté européenne sur les compétences externes des Etats membres et la question de la 'preemption'", in Demaret, *Relations extérieures de la Communauté européenne et marché intérieur: aspects juridiques et fonctionnels* (College of Europe/Story, Bruges, 1988), 39, at 47–54. For the "specific authorisation" by which the Community export rules permit Member States to subject

Constitution. The case law of the Court of Justice will be confirmed by the **5–027** proposed EU Constitution. The EU Constitution defines exclusive competence as the situation where "only the Union may legislate and adopt legally binding acts, the Member States being able to do so themselves only if so empowered by the Union or for the implementation of Union acts" (Art. I–12(1)). As regards the competences that the Union shares with the Member States, the EU Constitution states that "the Union and the Member States may legislate and adopt legally binding acts" and—in accordance with the principle of pre-emption—that "Member States shall exercise their competence to the extent that the Union has not exercised, or has decided to cease exercising, its competence" (Art. I–12(2)).

Next, the EU Constitution sums up the Union's exclusive competences. In addition to the policy areas mentioned above (the common commercial policy, the conservation of marine biological resources under the common fisheries policy, the customs union and monetary policy—for the Member States whose currency is the euro), the EU Constitution grants exclusive competence to establish the competition rules necessary for the functioning of the common market[94] (Art. I–13(1)). As far as the common commercial policy is concerned, no distinction is made between goods or services, implying that both are covered by the exclusive competence. The EU Constitution confirms the case law of the Court of Justice by establishing an 'exclusive competence' for the Union to conclude an international agreement where its conclusion is provided for in a legislative act of the Union or is necessary to enable the Union to exercise its external competence, or in so far as its conclusion may affect common rules or alter their scope (Art. I–13(2)).[95] The non-exclusive competences of the Union make up the areas of "shared competence" (Art. I–14(1)), which are in principle subject to the principle of pre-emption. By means of a non-exhaustive list[96] Article I–14(2) of the EU Constitution enumerates the most important competences that the Union shares with the Member States (*e.g.* the internal market, social policy, agriculture, environment, the area of freedom, security and justice).

According to the EU Constitution, some competences of the Union to support, co-ordinate or complement action by the Member States do not fall within the areas of shared competence.[97] The areas in question are

---

dual-use goods to export controls, see paras 20–004–20–007, *infra*. Another example is Council Decision 1999/405/EC of June 10, 1999 authorising the Kingdom of Spain to accede to the Convention establishing the Inter-American Tropical Tuna Commission on a temporary basis (IATTC), [1999] O.J. L155/37.

[94] The exclusive character of the Union's competence to legislate in this matter does not affect the Member States' competence to implement the Union's rules on competition (see paras 5–196–5–197, *infra*) or to take legislative action themselves with respect to situations that fall outside the "competition rules necessary for the functioning of the internal market" (thus, Arts 81 and 82 EC Treaty apply only if trade between Member States is affected: paras 5–196 and 5–199, *infra*).

[95] *cf.* para. 20–032, *infra*, for a comparison with the current regime.

[96] Art. I–14(2) of the EU Constitution refers in this respect to "the following principal areas".

[97] EU Constitution, Art. I–17 in conjunction with Art. I–14(1).

protection and improvement of human health, industry, culture, tourism, education, youth, sport and vocational training, civil protection and administrative co-operation, which therefore constitute a third category of competences. Within this category of competences, the Union may legislate but its legally binding acts may not entail harmonisation of Member States' law or regulations (EU Constitution, Art. I–12(5)). Some other competences fall within the category of "shared competences" but are nonetheless also protected—in the same way as the competences co-ordinating, complementary and supporting action—from the application of the principle of pre-emption.[98]

Finally, the EU Constitution mentions two other policy areas (co-ordination of economic and monetary policies and common foreign and security policy), for which no further classification is given.[99] These areas can only be classified as falling within the general category of shared competences.

C. THE PRINCIPLE OF SUBSIDIARITY

1. Role played by the principle

5–028 **Limit to the exercise of power.** The second paragraph of Art. 5 of the EC Treaty defines the following principle of law:

"In areas which do not fall within its exclusive competence, the Community shall take action, in accordance with the principle of subsidiarity, only if and in so far as the objectives of the proposed action cannot be sufficiently achieved by the Member States and can therefore, by reason of the scale or effects of the proposed action, be better achieved by the Community".[100]

---

[98] In the areas of research, technological development and space (Art. I–14(3)) and development co-operation and humanitarian aid (Art. I–14(4)), the exercise by the Union of its competences "may not result in Member States being prevented from exercising theirs". Compare Art. I–12(5) of the EU Constitution ("the Union shall have competence to carry out actions to support, co-ordinate or supplement the actions of the Member States without thereby superseding their competence in these areas"). However, pursuant to the principles of primacy of Union law and of sincere co-operation (EU Constitution, Arts I–5(2) and I–6), the principle of pre-emption will appear to apply if a Member State adopts measures putting at a risk the uniform application of the acts adopted by the Union in the area concerned.

[99] EU Constitution, Art. I–12(3) in conjuction with Art. I–15 and Art. I–12(4) in conjunction with Art. I–16.

[100] See Lenaerts and van Ypersele (n.37, *supra*), at 3–85. See also for general discussions, Bribosia, "Subsidiarité et répartition des compétences entre la Communauté et ses Etats membres. Commentaire sur l'article 3 B du traité de Maastricht" (1992) R.M.U.E. 165–188; Emiliou, "Subsidiarity: An Effective Barrier against 'the Enterprises of Ambition'?" (1992) E.L.Rev. 383–407; Toth, "The Principle of Subsidiarity in the Maastricht Treaty" (1992) C.M.L.R. 1079–1105; Lambers, "Subsidiarität in Europa—Allheilmittel oder juristische Leerformel?" (1993) EuR. 229–242; Bermann,

In this way the principle of subsidiarity constitutes a filter between Community competence and the possibility of exercising that competence. When the Community has competence, it can nonetheless act only "in accordance with the principle of subsidiarity". The EU Treaty introduced the principle into the EC Treaty as a reaction to a degree of dissatisfaction in some Member States about the way in which the Community was exercising its powers. Above all, following the extension of majority voting in the Council, there was a growing feeling that the Member States might be caught unaware by Community action markedly restricting their freedom to frame their own policies, even in areas not directly targeted by that action. In federal Member States, moreover, the constituent entities felt the loss of "national" sovereignty rather as an encroachment of the Community on their powers, whilst they themselves had no say in the matter.

When the Single European Act conferred competence on the Community with regard to the environment, Art. 130r(4) of the EEC Treaty at the same time laid down the principle that the Community was to take action relating to the environment "to the extent to which the objectives . . . can be attained better at Community level than at the level of the individual Member States".[101] The EU Treaty deleted this specific mention of the principle of subsidiarity when the principle set out in general terms in Art. 5 of the EC Treaty was introduced for all Community competences. The principle of subsidiarity formulated in Art. 5 of the EC Treaty constitutes a guide as to how powers at Community level have to be exercised, as was emphasised in the criteria for applying the principle set forth by the European Council held at Edinburgh on December 11 and 12, 1992[102] and subsequently incorporated in a protocol annexed to the EC Treaty by the Treaty of Amsterdam.[103] The EU Constitution has retained this approach (see para. 5–035).

"Taking Subsidiarity Seriously: Federalism in the European Community and the United States" (1994) Col.L.Rev. 331–456; von Börries, "Das Subsidiaritätsprinzip im Recht der Europäischen Union" (1994) EuR. 263–300; de Areilza Carvajal, "El principio de subsidiariedad en la construcción de la Unión europea" (1995) 45 Revista Española de Derecho Constitucional 53–93; Winter, "Subsidiarität und Deregulierung im Gemeinschaftsrecht" (1996) EuR. 247–269.

[101] See also Art. 12(2) of the Draft Treaty establishing the European Union (para. 3–004, supra), [1984] O.J. C77/33. As to the success of this principle, see Cass, "The Word that Saves Maastricht? The Principle of Subsidiarity and the Division of Powers Within the European Community" (1992) C.M.L.R. 1107–1136; Emiliou (n.100, supra), at 384–399; Hummer, "Subsidiarität und Föderalismus als Strukturprinzipien der Europäischen Gemeinschaften?" (1992) Z.f.R.V. 81–91.

[102] Overall approach to the application by the Council of the subsidiarity principle and Art. 3b [now Art. 5 of the EC Treaty] (1992) 12 EC Bull. points I.15–I.22, which was adopted by the European Council held in Edinburgh on December 11 and 12, 1992 even before what is now Art. 5 of the EC Treaty entered into force (ibid., point I.4). The European Council had been provided with the Commission's communication to the Council and the European Parliament of October 27, 1992 on the principle of subsidiarity (1992) 10 EC Bull. point 2.2.1; for a commentary, see Ehlermann, "Quelques réflexions sur la communication de la Commission relative au principe de subsidiarité" (1992) 4 R.M.U.E. 215–220.

[103] Protocol (No. 30), annexed to the EC Treaty, on the application of the principles of

5–029 Limit to conferral of power. At the same time, subsidiarity is formulated in the Treaties as a political principle which does not govern the exercise of powers which have been conferred but oversees the actual conferment of powers.[104] The principle arose in a socio-economic context as limiting intervention by the authorities to such matters as the persons or groups concerned could not deal with themselves. Later, it acquired the additional meaning of an obligation for the authorities whenever taking action to weigh up the different levels of authority at which action may be taken.[105] It is above all pursuant to the latter idea that the process of European integration must respect the diversity of regional cultures and come as close as possible to the citizen.[106] In order to achieve this, various amendments to the Treaties and in particular the EU Treaty, on the one hand, enlarged Community competence to cover areas where a Community contribution appeared to be absolutely essential,[107] yet, on the other hand, safeguarded the powers of the Member States in those areas where a national contribution was required in some respect.[108]

In this sense, subsidiarity already permeated the original EEC Treaty,[109] both in the choice of powers which were conferred on the Community

---

subsidiarity and proportionality, [1997] O.J. C340/105. See Constantinesco, "Le traité d'Amsterdam. Les clauses de 'coopération renforcée'. Le protocole sur l'application des principes de subsidiarité et de proportionalité" (1997) R.T.D.E. 751–767; Feral, "Le principe de subsidiarité: progrès ou statu quo après le traité d'Amsterdam?" (1998) 1 R.M.U.E. 95–117. Point 2 of the Protocol states that the application of the principles of subsidiarity and proportionality must not affect the principles developed by the Court of Justice regarding the relationship between national and Community law and should take into account Art. 6(4) of the EU Treaty, which requires the Union to provide itself with the means necessary to attain its objectives and carry through its policies.

[104] For the two aspects, see Constantinesco, "La subsidiarité comme principe constitutionnel de l'intégration européenne" (1991) Aussenwirtschaft 439–459; Jacqué, "Centralisation et décentralisation dans les projets d'Union européenne" (1991) Aussenwirtschaft 469–483; Van Gerven, "De beginselen 'subsidiariteit, evenredigheid en samenwerking' in het Europese gemeenschapsrecht" (1991–1992) R.W. 1241–1246. For a somewhat critical view of the utility of the principle, see Geelhoed, "Het subsidiariteitsbeginsel: een communautair principe?" (1991) S.E.W. 422–435; Pennings, "Is the Subsidiarity Principle Useful to Guide the European Integration Process?" (1993) Tilburg For.L.Rev. 153–163.

[105] For the origin of the subsidiarity principle, see Wilke and Wallace, *Subsidiarity: Approaches to Power-sharing in the European Community* (Royal Institute of International Affairs, London, 1990), 43 pp.; Adonis and Jones, "Subsidiarity and the European Community's Constitutional Future" (1991) Staatswissenschaft und Staatspraxis 179–196; Millon-Delsol, *L'Etat subsidiaire. Ingérence et non-ingérence de l'Etat: le principe de subsidiarité aux fondements de l'histoire européenne* (Presses Universitaires de France, Paris, 1992).

[106] Para. 3–012, *supra.*

[107] See, *e.g.* economic and monetary union, para. 5–214 *et seq.* (a formulation of the subsidiarity principle was already contained in the Report of the Delors Committee; para. 5–218).

[108] See the wording of the new legal bases; para. 5–034. In a broader context, see Handoll, "The Protection of National Interests in the European Union" (1994) Ir.J.E.L. 221–246.

[109] See Kapteyn, "Community Law and the Principle of Subsidiarity" (1991) R.A.E. 35, at 38–39; Berger, "Le principe de subsidiarité en droit communautaire" (1992) 79 Pet.Aff. 40–44; for a somewhat different view, see Toth (n.100, *supra*), at 1080–1086. For the role played by subsidiarity in the system of legal protection, see Chaltiel, "Le principe de subsidiarité dix ans après de traité de Maastricht" (2003) R.M.C.U.E. 365, at 370–371.

(common commercial policy, abolition of obstacles to free movement, common agricultural policy, common transport policy, etc. or else in the choice of areas in which the Community itself implements its policies, such as competition policy or anti-dumping policy) and in the determination of the areas of competence left to the Member States (implementation of Community legislation by Member States: see para. 11–011; decentralised enforcement of Community law by national courts in co-operation with the Court of Justice: see para. 11–012; legislation by directives having to be transposed by the Member States: see para. 17–120). As a political principle, subsidiarity guides the development of the constitutional system and is therefore incapable of being enforced by a court within that system. As will be explained below, the position is different as far as the legal principle defined in Art. 5 of the EC Treaty is concerned.

2. The requirements of subsidiarity

Definition. Wherever the Community does not possess exclusive **5–030** competence, it may take action only *"if* and *in so far as* the objectives of the proposed action cannot be sufficiently achieved by the Member States and can therefore, by reason of the scale or effects of the proposed action, be better achieved by the Community" (second paragraph of Art. 5 of the EC Treaty—emphasis supplied). This definition tests Community action against both a decentralisation criterion and an efficiency criterion: the Community acts *only* if the proposed objectives cannot be sufficiently achieved by the Member States and if they can be *better* achieved by the Community. According to the Protocol on the application of the principles of subsidiarity and proportionality, Community action is justified only if both aspects of the subsidiarity principle are met.[110] It sets out the following guidelines for use in examining whether that condition is fulfilled:

(1) the issue under consideration has transnational aspects which cannot be satisfactorily regulated by action by Member States;

(2) actions by Member States alone or lack of Community action would conflict with the requirements of the Treaty (such as the need to correct distortions of competition or avoid disguised restrictions on trade or strengthen economic and social cohesion) or would otherwise significantly damage Member States' interests; and

(3) action at Community level would produce clear benefits by reason of its scale or effects compared with action at the level of the Member States.[111]

It should be noted that the expression "in so far as" makes Community action subject to an additional requirement of proportionality (see para. 5–042).

---

[110] Protocol (No. 30), annexed to the EC Treaty, on the application of the principles of subsidiarity and proportionality ([1997] O.J. C340/105), point 5, first para.

[111] *ibid.*, point 5, second para. (reiterating the guidelines set out in the European Council's overall approach—n.102, *supra*—point I.18).

5–031 Impact. The limitation placed on Community action by the principle of subsidiarity is not large if it is principally considered whether such action affords "clear benefits" or is "better" than action at national level. This is because Community action is invariably tested against the objectives which the Community purports to achieve. If Community action is tested against objectives such as the achievement of uniform or coherent rules or the equal treatment of EU citizens or legal persons, it is obvious that Community action will be more efficient than individual action by Member States or voluntary co-ordination of national policies.[112] The principle of subsidiarity therefore makes sense above all in so far as it compels consideration of whether the objective sought by the Community or the matter dealt with is in itself such that national action would inevitably fall short (with the result that Community action is necessarily "better").[113] Community action will conflict with the principle of subsidiarity only where it can be shown that the objective sought can be achieved just as much in all Member States either by individual action or by co-operation between the Member States concerned.[114] In this regard, it makes little difference whether the comparison with Community action is carried out at the level of the Member State or at the level of decentralised authorities: this is because in either case there will be a breach of the principle where the objective sought can be sufficiently achieved in all Member States and it is irrelevant by whose intervention or at what level of policy it is achieved within the Member States.[115] Where the application of the principle of subsidiarity leads to no action being taken by the Community, Member States are required in their action to comply with the general rules laid down in Art. 10 of the EC Treaty, by taking all appropriate measures to ensure fulfilment of their obligations under the Treaty and by abstaining from any measure which could jeopardise the attainment of the objectives of the Treaty.[116]

The subsidiarity principle does not authorise Member States to avoid Community obligations.[117] Nor may the principle be interpreted as meaning that intervention by the Community authorities must be confined to what is strictly necessary where the result would be that private associations could

---

[112] See, *e.g.* ECJ, Case C–377/98 *Netherlands v European Parliament and Council* [2001] E.C.R. I–7079, para. 32; ECJ, Case C–491/01 *British American Tobacco (Investments) and Imperial Tobacco* [2002] E.C.R. I–11453, paras 180–183; ECJ, Case C–103/01 *Commission v Germany* [2003] E.C.R. I–5369, para. 47.

[113] Van Nuffel, *De rechtsbescherming van nationale overheden in het Europees recht* (Kluwer, Deventer, 2000), at 364–388.

[114] The *acquis communautaire* would be affected if the Community had to justify its action against possible intergovernmental action on the part of all Member States: Lenaerts and van Ypersele, "Le principe de subsidiarité et son contexte: étude de l'article 3 B du traité CE" (1994) C.D.E. 13–30 and 35–44, at 45–57; Van Nuffel (see n.113, *supra*), at 394–396.

[115] Van Nuffel (see n.113 *supra*.), at 396–400.

[116] Protocol (No. 30), annexed to the EC Treaty, on the application of the principles of subsidiarity and proportionality ([1997] O.J. C340/105), point 8.

[117] See ECJ, Case C–11/95 *Commission v Belgium* [1996] E.C.R. I–4115, paras 51–53.

adopt rules restricting the exercise of rights conferred on individuals by the Treaty.[118]

3. Application of the principle of subsidiarity

Scope. The second para. of Art. 5 of the EC Treaty requires the **5–032** Community to comply with the principle of subsidiarity in "areas which do not fall within its exclusive competence". This applies equally to the first measure which the Community adopts and to existing measures where they are tightened (*e.g.* where a recommendation or a communication is replaced by a binding measure) or made stricter (*e.g.* a regulation replacing a directive). The principle of subsidiarity is a dynamic concept which allows Community action to be expanded where circumstances so require and, conversely, to be restricted or discontinued where it is no longer justified.[119] Nevertheless, movement in either direction is constrained by the requirement for a legal basis and by the principle of proportionality: both an expansion of Community action and a restriction thereof must seek to achieve the objectives of the Treaty and be essential for achieving the intended aim.

In contrast, where the Community has exclusive competence, it does not have to take account of the principle of subsidiarity set out in the second para. of Art. 5, although it does have to have regard to the principle of proportionality set out in the third paragraph.[120]

Institutional implementation. In exercising the powers conferred on it, **5–033** each institution has to ensure that the principle of subsidiarity is complied with.[121] Just before the EU Treaty entered into effect, the European Parliament, the Council and the Commission concluded an Interinstitutional Agreement on procedures for implementing the principle of subsidiarity,[122] the thrust of which was incorporated in 1997 into the Protocol on the application of the principles of subsidiarity and proportionality. For any proposed Community legislation, the reasons on which it is based are to be stated with a view to justifying its compliance with the principles of subsidiarity and proportionality.[123] The Commission

---

[118] ECJ, Case C–415/93 *Bosman* [1995] E.C.R. I–4921, para. 81.

[119] Protocol on the application of the principles of subsidiarity and proportionality (n.116, *supra*), point 3.

[120] Para. 5–043, *infra*. Non-exclusive competences obtaining an "exclusive character" following their exercise by the Community should not remain outside the scope of the subsidiarity principle and do not constitute "exclusive competences" within the meaning of the second para. of Art. 5 of the EC Treaty. If they would, the Community would be able, through its own action, to restrict the very principle which is intended to limit Community action.

[121] Protocol on the application of the principles of subsidiarity and proportionality, point 1.

[122] (1993) 10 EC Bull. point 1.6.3; for the text of the Agreement, see point 2.2.2 (or [1993] O.J. C329/135).

[123] Protocol on the application of the principles of subsidiarity and proportionality, point 4. Accordingly, the reasons for concluding that a Community objective cannot be sufficiently achieved by the Member States but can be better achieved by the Community must be substantiated by qualitative or, whenever possible, quantitative factors (already stipulated in point I.18 of the European Council's overall approach, see n.102, *supra*).

should justify the relevance of its proposals with regard to the principle of subsidiarity, providing details whenever necessary in the explanatory memorandum.[124] The European Parliament and the Council have to consider whether Commission proposals (and any amendments envisaged by either of those institutions) are consistent with Art. 5 of the EC Treaty. This scrutiny is not to take place in a prior or parallel decision-making procedure dealing with the aspects of subsidiarity and proportionality, but as "an integral part of the overall examination of Commission proposals".[125] The Commission is to report annually to the European Council, the European Parliament and the Council on the application of Art. 5.[126]

After considering its pending proposals and existing legislation, the Commission decided in the early 1990s to withdraw some proposals and to make new proposals adapting existing legislation.[127] The Commission stated that it was prepared to withdraw certain initiatives after consulting interested parties[128] and hence interprets subsidiarity also as the political principle whereby public intervention is weighed against private initiative.

Judicial review of the validity of Community acts extends to compliance with the principle of subsidiarity.[129] Since, when considering Community action, the institutions make a judgment of complex practical and political circumstances, the courts will carry out a marginal review of that judgment as it is set out in the statement of reasons of the act concerned.[130]

---

[124] *ibid.*, point 9, second indent (which also requires an explanation to be given of the financing of Community action in whole or in part from the Community budget).

[125] *ibid.*, point 11 (already stipulated in point I.22 of the European Council's overall approach, see n.102).

[126] *ibid.*, point 9, fourth indent; already provided for in point 2.2.2 of the interinstitutional agreement (para. 5–033, *supra*).

[127] See the Commission's answer of February 15, 1995 to question E–370/95 (Crampton), [1995] O.J. C175/38, and the lists of proposals which have already been withdrawn, [1995] O.J. C344/2, and [1997] O.J. C2/2.

[128] (1992) 12 EC Bull. point I.23.

[129] See, *e.g.* ECJ, Case C–377/98 *Netherlands v European Parliament and Council* [2001] E.C.R. I–7079, paras 30–33; ECJ, Case C–491/01 *British American Tobacco (Investments) and Imperial Tobacco* [2002] E.C.R. I–11453, paras 180–183. See Chaltiel, "Le principe de subsidiarité dix ans après le traité de Maastricht" (2003) R.M.C.U.E. 365, at 368–370.

[130] See ECJ, Case C–233/94 *Germany v European Parliament and Council* [1997] E.C.R. I–2405, paras 22–29; ECJ, Case C–377/98 *Netherlands v European Parliament and Council* [2001] E.C.R. I–7079, para. 33; subsidiarity was considered summarily in ECJ, Case C–84/94 *UK v Council* [1996] E.C.R. I–5755, paras 80–81, with a case note by Van Nuffel (1997) Col.J.E.L. 298–309. For an exposition of this duty to provide a statement of reasons, see Lenaerts and van Ypersele (n.114, *supra*), at 75–80, and Van Nuffel, *De rechtsbescherming van nationale overheden in het Europees recht* (Kluwer, Deventer, 2000), at 412–424; for the duty to state grounds in general, see para. 17–109, *infra*. A call for more extensive judicial review is to be found in König and Lorz, "Stärkung des Subsidiaritätsprinzips" (2003) J.Z. 167–173. The Court of Justice has also used the principle of subsidiarity as an aid to interpretation; see ECJ (judgment of September 11, 2003), Case C–114/01 *AvestaPolarit Chrome Oy*, not yet reported, paras 56–57.

Dual dimension. The principle of subsidiarity may possibly constitute an **5–034** important restriction where the Community acts to achieve the broadly framed objectives already contained in the original EEC Treaty.[131] On the other hand, various provisions introduced by the EU Treaty and the Amsterdam Treaty already limit action on the part of the Community to encouraging and "if necessary" supporting and supplementing action on the part of the Member States.[132]

The subsidiarity principle has a dual dimension in the Treaty provisions on social policy (see para. 5–236). Not only do those provisions reflect the subsidiary nature of Community action in relation to that of the Member States (Art. 137(1), (2) and (4)), they also give a role to management and labour in the formulation or implementation of measures at Community level (Art. 138). Since Art. 5 of the EC Treaty limits the action of the Community only *vis-à-vis* action taken by the Member States, considerations of subsidiarity cannot detract from the Community's powers to adopt measures without the agreement of management and labour.

4. The principle of subsidiarity in the EU Constitution

Control by national parliaments. The EU Constitution preserves the **5–035** current definition of the principle of subsidiarity, although it does make it clear that this principle applies where the objectives of the intended action are not sufficiently achieved by the Member States "either at central level or at regional and local level" (Art. I–11(3), first subparagraph).[133] The guidelines on the basis of which the protocol on the application of the principles of subsidiarity and proportionality has made the subsidiarity test somewhat more concrete (see para. 5–030) will not be taken over in the

---

[131] For a possible application in the field of *competition policy* (in addition to the recent "decentralisation" of supervision of compliance with Arts 81 and 82 of the EC Treaty; para. 10–010, *infra*), see Alford, "Subsidiarity and Competition: Decentralised Enforcement of EU Competition Law" (1994) Cornell I.L.J. 271–302; Van den Bergh, "Economic Criteria for Applying the Subsidiarity Principle in the European Community: The Case of Competition Policy" (1996) Int'l Rev. of Law & Econ. 363–383; Wesseling, "Subsidiarity in Community Antitrust Law: Setting the Right Agenda?" (1997) E.L.Rev. 35–54; Van den Bossche, "Subsidiariteit in werking: het einde van de parallelle toepassing van nationaal en Europees mededingsrecht?" (1998) T.B.H. 488–507; for *internal-market policy*, see Schmidhuber and Hitzler, "Binnenmarkt und Subsidiaritatsprinzip" (1993) Eu.Z.W. 8–10; for a possible application in the field of *social policy*, see Spicker, "The Principle of Subsidiarity and the Social Policy of the European Community" (1991) Journal of European Social Policy 3–14; for *environmental policy*, see Brinkhorst, "Subsidiarity and European Community Environmental Policy. A Panacea or a Pandora's Box?" (1993) E.Env.L.Rev. 16–24; Lenaerts, "The Principle of Subsidiarity and the Environment in the European Union: Keeping the Balance of Federalism" (1994) Fordham I.L.J. 846–895; Wils, "Subsidiarity and EC Environmental Policy: Taking People's Concerns Seriously" (1994) J.Env.L. 85–91. See also Bernard, "The Future of European Economic Law in the Light of the Principle of Subsidiarity" (1996) C.M.L.R. 633–666.

[132] See EC Treaty, Arts 126–129 (employment), Art. 149(1) (education); Art. 151(2) (culture) and Art. 152(1) (public health); paras 5–237—5–243, *infra*. See Lenaerts, "Subsidiarity and Community Competence in the Field of Education" (1994/95) Col.J.E.L. 1–28.

[133] This does not make any difference to the application of the test: para. 5–031, *supra*.

new protocol on the application of the principles of subsidiarity and proportionality annexed to the EU Constitution. The new protocol confirms the Commission's duty to justify its proposals in the light of the principle of proportionality, including its obligation, in that connection, to assess every proposal for the adoption of a framework law in the light of the implications that it may have for the rules to be put in place by Member States.[134]

The major change introduced by the new protocol on the principles of subsidiarity and proportionality concerns the control that national parliaments may exercise over the application of the principle of subsidiarity.[135] First, any Commission proposal or other draft legislative act, as well as any position taken by the European Parliament and the Council in the course of the legislative process will be sent to the national parliaments. If the Commission proposes to base its action on the flexibility clause (now Art. 308 of the EC Treaty), it must draw the national parliaments' attention specifically to the proposed use of that article.[136] Within six weeks of the date of transmission of a draft legislative act, any national parliament (or any chamber of a national parliament) may issue an opinion stating the reasons for which it considers that the draft in question does not comply with the principle of subsidiarity. If the draft legislative act concerns a matter for which, under national law, competence exists with regional parliaments with legislative powers, the national parliament must consult the regional parliaments concerned.[137] The Commission, the European Parliament and the Council must take account of the reasoned opinions issued by national parliaments. The draft legislative act must be reviewed where reasoned opinions on non compliance with the principle of subsidiarity represent at least one-third of all the votes of the national parliaments (one-fourth in the case of a Commission proposal or an initiative initiating from a group of Member States related to police co-operation or judicial co-operation in criminal matters).[138] To calculate the threshold of one-third or one-fourth of the votes, every national parliament will have two votes, shared out on the basis of the national parliamentary system. In the case of a bicameral parliamentary system, each of the two chambers will have one vote.[139] After having reviewed its draft

---

[134] Protocol annexed to the EU Constitution on the application of the principles of subsidiarity and proportionality, Art. 5.

[135] See Davies (n.42, *supra*), 691–697; Mager, "Die Prozeduralisierung des Subsidiaritäts-prinzips im Verfassungsentwurf des Europäischen Konvents—Verbesserte Schutz vor Kompetenzverlagerung auf die Gemeinschaftsebene?" (2003) Z.Eu.S. 471–484.

[136] EU Constitution, Art. I–18(2).

[137] Protocol annexed to the EU Constitution on the application of the principles of subsidiarity and proportionality, Art. 6 (imposes this obligation on national parliaments or chambers of a national parliament "where appropriate").

[138] *ibid*., Art. 7, first and third para. (refers for the threshold of "one-fourth" to Art. III–264 of the EU Constitution).

[139] *ibid*., Art. 7, second para.

legislative act, the Commission may decide to maintain, amend or withdraw it, while giving its reasons therefor.[140]

With respect to the enforcement of the principle of subsidiarity by the Court of Justice, the new protocol makes it clear that Member States may bring an action for annulment against a legislative act on grounds of infringement of the principle of subsidiarity on behalf of their national parliament or of one of its chambers.[141] According to the protocol, the Committee of the Regions may also bring such action against legislative acts where the Constitution provides that it must be consulted.[142]

D. THE PRINCIPLE OF PROPORTIONALITY

1. Role played by the principle

Limit to exercise of power. The principle of proportionality restricts the   5–036
authorities in the exercise of their powers by requiring a balance to be struck between the means used and the intended aim (or result reached).[143] It is a general principle of law which affects the exercise of powers by Member States as well as by the Community. In the case law, the principle of proportionality serves principally to assess the legality of an exercise of power where an admittedly legitimate aim is pursued, but at the same time other objectives deserving of protection are damaged.[144] The exercise of power in such a case will be regarded as lawful only if it is appropriate to attain the intended aim and also indispensable in that alternative forms of exercise of power—which would inflict no or less damage on other objectives worthy of protection—would not be capable of achieving the intended aim.

Applications. Accordingly, it falls to the Court of Justice to adjudge   5–037
whether national measures which impede the free movement of goods, persons or services or the freedom of establishment—central objectives of the common market—can be justified where they seek to attain objectives

---

[140] *ibid.*, Art. 7, fourth para.

[141] *ibid.*, Art. 8, first para. (refers to an action brought "in accordance with their legal order"). This possibility already exists today in so far as it is up to any Member State to determine the domestic authorities on behalf of which it brings an action before the Court. See Van Nuffel, "What's in a Member State? Central and decentralised authorities before the Community Courts", (2001) C.M.L.R. 871, at 879.

[142] *ibid.*, Art. 8, second para. (see also para. 10–096, *infra*).

[143] For general discussions, see Jans, "Evenredigheid: ja, maar waartussen?" (1992) S.E.W. 751–770; Van Gerven, "Principe de proportionnalité, abus de droit et droits fondementaux" (1992) J.T. 305–309; de Búrca, "The Principle of Proportionality and its Application in EC Law" (1993) Y.E.L. 105–150; Emiliou, *The Principle of Proportionality in European Law—A Comparative Study* (Kluwer, London/The Hague, 1996), 288 pp; Kischel, "Die Kontrolle der Verhältnismässigkeit durch den Europäischen Gerichtshof" (2000) EuR. 380–402; Jans, "Proportionality Revisited" (2000) L.I.E.I. 239–265.

[144] The principle is also applied in connection with the imposition of sanctions, para. 17–070, *infra*.

accepted by Community law. In this connection, the Court of Justice will have regard in particular to whether the national measures pursue their objectives in a proportional manner.[145] As far as the implementation of Community legislation is concerned, it follows from the principle of proportionality that whilst Member States may employ means which enable them effectively to attain the objectives pursued by their domestic laws, they must make sure that those means are the least detrimental to the objectives and principles laid down by the relevant Community legislation.[146]

In the same way, the Court tests the action of the Community against the principle of proportionality where the objective of the action conflicts with other Community objectives. It does so where the objectives of various Treaty articles[147] or aims defined within a given Treaty article[148] cannot be achieved concurrently. Some Treaty articles require the Community to take account of particular objectives irrespective of the field in which they are acting.[149] Since those Treaty articles do not provide for any ranking order of the various Community objectives, they certainly increase the importance of the principle of proportionality, which seeks to settle the conflict between them.

The principle of proportionality also guides the Court of Justice in resolving alleged conflicts between objectives of Community law and fundamental rights[150] or between procedural rights, such as providing confidential treatment for business secrets and the *inter partes* nature of court proceedings.[151] The principle of proportionality is likewise in evidence in competition law when the prohibition contained in Art. 81(1) of the EC

---

[145] Paras 5–104 and 5–112 (trade in goods), 5–134, 5–139 and 5–143–5–144 (movement of persons) and 5–175—5–179 (freedom to supply services), *infra*.

[146] ECJ, Joined Cases C–286/94, C–340/95, C–401/95 and C–47/96 *Molenheide* [1997] E.C.R. I–7281, paras 46–49.

[147] See, *e.g.* for a case in which the free movement of goods (EC Treaty, Arts 28–30) had to be balanced against the aim of a directive adopted pursuant to Arts 37 and 94 to protect agricultural products against harmful organisms, see ECJ, Case 37/83 *Rewe-Zentrale* [1984] E.C.R. 1229, paras 18–20.

[148] See, *e.g.* as regards the various objectives enumerated in Art. 33 of the EC Treaty (agricultural policy), ECJ, Case 5/73 *Balkan-Import-Export* [1973] E.C.R. 1091, para. 24; ECJ Case 29/77 *Roquette* [1977] E.C.R. 1835, para. 30; ECJ, Case C–311/90 *Hierl* [1992] E.C.R. I–2061, para. 13; ECJ, Joined Cases C–133/93, C–300/93 and C–362/93 *Crispoltoni* [1994] E.C.R. I–4863, para. 32, and ECJ Case C–280/93 *Germany v Council* [1994] E.C.R. I–4973, paras 47–51.

[149] See para. 5–005, *supra*.

[150] For instance, the balancing of the right of property and effective enforcement of Community law obligations carried out by the Court of Justice in considering whether the sanction of forfeiture of security was proportional to the relevant infringement of agricultural law: ECJ, Case 181/84 *Man (Sugar)* [1985] E.C.R. 2889, paras 20–30; ECJ, Case C–199/90 *Italtrade* [1991] E.C.R. I–5545, paras 12–15; the balancing of the right of property and of freedom to pursue a trade or profession against a common organisation of the market: ECJ, Case 44/79 *Liselotte Hauer* [1979] E.C.R. 3727, para. 23; ECJ, Case 265/87 *Schräder* [1989] E.C.R. 2237, para. 15.

[151] See CFI (order of November 15, 1999), Joined Cases T–1/89–T–4/89 and T–6/89–T–15/89 *Rhône-Poulenc v Commission* [1990] E.C.R. II–637, para. 22.

Treaty is declared, pursuant to Art. 81(3), to be inapplicable to certain agreements or concerted practices in so far as they impose only restrictions on competition which are "indispensable" to the attainment of the objectives set out in Art. 81(3).[152]

2. The requirements of proportionality

Requirements. As has already been mentioned, the action must be "appropriate" to attain its objectives and at the same time "indispensable". **5–038**

Appropriateness. Action is appropriate where it is capable of attaining the intended objective. The Court of Justice leaves a large measure of discretion to the authority concerned and only considers whether it was not guilty of a manifest error. Accordingly, the Court responded to the argument that protective measures taken in the context of the common market were inappropriate in the following terms: **5–039**

> "[s]ince in the present case it is a question of complex economic measures, which for the purpose of their efficacy necessarily require a wide discretion and moreover as regards their effects frequently present an uncertainty factor, the observation suffices that these measures do not appear on issue as obviously inappropriate for the realisation of the desired object".[153]

Accordingly, the Court does not replace the assessment of the authority concerned by its own *ex post facto* assessment.

Indispensability. Action is indispensable where it cannot be replaced by some alternative form of action which would have equal effectiveness (*effet utile*) having regard to the intended aim and be less detrimental to another aim or interest protected by Community law. An appropriate measure may consequently not entail needless adverse effects. The Court of Justice **5–040**

---

[152] Art. 81(3)(a) of the EC Treaty. See ECJ, Joined Cases 56 and 58/64 *Consten and Grundig v Commission* [1966] E.C.R. 299, at 347–350; ECJ, Case 258/78 *Nungesser v Commission* [1982] E.C.R. 2015, paras 76–78; CFI, Case T–66/89 *Publishers Association v Commission* [1992] E.C.R. II–1995, para. 98; CFI, Joined Cases T–39/92 and T–40/92 *CB and Europay v Commission* [1994] E.C.R. II–49, paras 111–114. With regard to the control of concentrations, see Schwarze, "Die Bedeutung des Grundsatzes der Verhältnismässigkeit bei der Behandlung von Verpflichtszusagen nach der europäischen Fusionskontrollverordnung" (2002) Eu.Z.W. 741–746.

[153] ECJ, Case 40/72 *Schroeder v Germany* [1973] E.C.R. 125, para. 14. See also ECJ, Case 265/87 *Schräder* [1989] E.C.R. 2237, para. 22; ECJ, Joined Cases C–133/93, C–300/93 and C–362/93 *Crispoltoni* [1994] E.C.R. I–4863, paras 43–48, and Case C–280/93 *Germany v Council* [1994] E.C.R. I–4973, paras 89–95; CFI, Joined Cases T–481/93 and T–484/93 *Exporteurs in Levende Varkens v Commission* [1995] E.C.R. II–2941, paras 116–120; Dony, "L'affaire des bananes" (1995) C.D.E. 461, at 477–487. For the discretion which exists where the legislature has to make "social policy choices and complex assessments", see ECJ, Case C–84/94 *UK v Council* [1996] E.C.R. I–5755, para. 58.

respects the aim which the authority seeks to achieve through its action and, as a rule, does not take account of other measures which would not achieve it to a sufficient extent, even if such measures would have no or less effect on a protected aim or interest. Consequently, the Court generally does not weigh generally the detriment done to the aim or interest deserving of protection against the advantages of the action for the aim pursued.[154] If it did so, the Court would be able to allow different aims to prevail from those which the authority concerned chose and so introduce its own hierarchy of legitimate aims.[155] There is only one area in which the Court takes the view that the aim chosen by the authority must yield to a higher objective. This is the field of fundamental rights, where the Court regards a measure as disproportionate to the intended aim if it impinges upon the "substance" of fundamental rights.[156]

3. Application of the principle of proportionality

5–041 **Scope.** The third paragraph of Art. 5 of the EC Treaty expresses the principle of proportionality as a limitation on action by the Community, "which shall not go beyond what is necessary to achieve the objectives of this Treaty". The second paragraph of Art. 5 further specifies that principle with regard to the non-exclusive competence of the Community. Those two provisions constitute two expressions of the principle of proportionality, but, naturally, do not detract from the general application of the principle in Community law.

5–042 **Protecting national powers.** The second paragraph of Art. 5 of the EC Treaty provides that the Community is to take action only "in so far as" the objectives of the proposed action cannot be sufficiently achieved by the Member States and can therefore be better achieved by the Community. That provision embodies a specific application of the principle of proportionality with a view to protecting the residuary powers of the Member States. Any Community action must be appropriate and indispensable to supplement the insufficient capabilities of the Member States. Community action must first be "appropriate" to achieve the proposed objectives, which does not automatically follow from the fact that the Member States appear not to be capable. In addition, the action must be "indispensable" and therefore incapable of being replaced by measures which have less of an effect on the residual powers of the Member States.

---

[154] In the few cases in which the Court of Justice has weighed interests generally, the test has been confined to what is appropriate and necessary and the weighing of interests conducted by the Community authority has been constantly followed; see, *e.g.* ECJ, Case C–189/01 *Jippes* [2001] E.C.R. I–5689, paras 80–100. See Van Nuffel (n.130, *supra.*), at 311–320.

[155] See, with regard to environment protection, Notaro, "The New Generation Case Law on Trade and Environment" (2000) E.L.Rev. 467, at 486–487.

[156] ECJ, Case 44/79 *Liselotte Hauer* [1979] E.C.R. 3727, paras 23 and 30 (para. 17–090, *infra*). For the problems raised by the overall balancing of interests, see Lenaerts and van Ypersele (n.114, *supra*), at 56–60, and Van Nuffel (n.130, *supra*), at 320–328.

Where the Member States are in a position to achieve the contemplated objectives in part, the Community must encourage and support them and oblige them to do what they are capable of and, where necessary, take supplementary action where they fall short.

The Protocol on the application of the principles of subsidiarity and proportionality requires the form of Community action to be as simple as possible and preference to be given to directives over regulations and to framework directives over detailed measures.[157] Regarding the nature and the extent of Community action, Community measures should leave as much scope for national decisions as possible, consistent with securing the aim of the measure and observing the requirements of the Treaty. Well-established national arrangements and the organisation and working of Member States' legal systems should be respected. Where appropriate and subject to the need for proper enforcement, Community measures should provide Member States with alternative ways to achieve the objectives of the measures.[158] Where appropriate, the Community may leave the administration of, or supervision of compliance with, Community measures to the Member States.[159]

Protecting legitimate interests. The third paragraph of Art. 5 of the EC **5–043** Treaty limits Community action to "what is necessary to achieve the objectives of this Treaty". However, action founded upon a legal basis afforded by the Treaty can hardly go beyond the objectives *of this Treaty* without at the same time exceeding the confines of the legal basis in question, which would mean that the action would be *ultra vires*. Rather, the principle of proportionality requires a given action not to go beyond what is necessary to achieve the objectives *of that action*. In that sense, the principle, as it is expressed in the third paragraph of Art. 5 of the EC Treaty, provides protection for Member States, regional and local authorities, trade and industry, and citizens against Community action involving obligations or burdens which are not proportionate to the

---

[157] Protocol on the application of the principles of subsidiarity and proportionality, point 6; see the guidelines set out by the European Council in its overall approach (n.102 to para. 5–028, *supra*), point I.19.

[158] *ibid.*, point 7. For a case in which alternative ways of achieving the objectives of a particular measure (directive on working time) were weighed up, see ECJ, Case C–84/94 *UK v Council* [1996] E.C.R. I–5755, paras 50–66, with a case note by Van Nuffel (1997) Col.J.E.L. 298–309.

[159] An advance application of the second para. of Art. 5 of the EC Treaty may already be identified in a judgment of September 18, 1992 in which the Court of First Instance agreed with the Commission in rejecting a complaint in the field of competition law on the grounds that it did not disclose a "sufficient" Community interest and that the national court before which the matter was already pending was in a position to protect the rights of the undertakings affected by the practices in restraint of competition which were at issue: CFI, Case T–24/90 *Automec v Commission* [1992] E.C.R. II–2223, paras 77–98. For a case in which the proportionality of Community action as compared with possible national action was weighed in the balance, see ECJ, Case C–352/92 *Germany v Council* [1994] E.C.R. I–3681, paras 42–50.

proposed objective. Such legal subjects may plead infringement of the third paragraph of Art. 5 of the EC Treaty where the Community unreasonably affects their interests.

Even where the Community exercises exclusive powers, it must take account of Member States' potential to help to achieve the proposed objective. Although the actual principle of the exercise of Community powers in such a case does not have to be justified (the subsidiarity principle being inapplicable), the third paragraph of Art. 5 nevertheless imposes similar requirements in point of proportionality to the second paragraph.

5–044 Institutional implementation. The Protocol on the application of the principles of subsidiarity and proportionality annexed to the EC Treaty by the Amsterdam Treaty requires the institutions to take proportionality into account to the same extent as subsidiarity when lodging, discussing and approving proposals (see para. 5–033). Every measure must state the reasons for which it is appropriate to achieve the proposed aims and indispensable to that end. In its reports to the European Council on adjustment of existing legislation in the light of the principle of subsidiarity, the Commission pointed to a number of proposals for legislation which, for reasons of proportionality, should be withdrawn or revised, and listed existing legislation which could be revised, simplified or repealed.[160] The intention to simplify legislation indicates how subsidiarity and proportionality fit into the process designed to make Community legislation more transparent (see para. 16–015 *et seq.*).

4. The principle of proportionality in the EU Constitution: protection of national sovereignty?

5–045 Substance and form. Article I–11(4) of the EU Constitution states that, under the principle of proportionality, the content and form of Union action shall not exceed what is necessary to achieve the objectives of the Constitution. Accordingly, the EU Constitution confirms that the principle of proportionality may restrict not only the substance but also the form of legislative action. Nevertheless, the protocol annexed to the EU Constitution on the application of the principles of subsidiarity and proportionality (see para. 5–035) no longer contains the concrete guidance that the current protocol gives in that respect (see para. 5–042). The new protocol, however, does confirm that the institutions are under a duty to ensure respect for the principle of proportionality and to justify their action in that regard.[161]

5–046 Respect for national identities. It follows that, in the EU Constitution, the principle of proportionality will continue to debar the Union from imposing unnecessary restrictions on the exercise by the Member States of their

---

[160] para. 5–033, *supra*.
[161] Protocol annexed to the EU Constitution on the application of the principles of subsidiarity and proportionality, Arts 1–4.

residual and shared competences. In this respect, it should be mentioned that Art. I–5(1) of the EU Constitution will require the Union to respect the "national identities [of the Member States], inherent in their fundamental structures, political and constitutional, inclusive of regional and local self-government" as well as "their essential State functions, including those for ensuring the territorial integrity of the State, and for maintaining law and order and safeguarding national security". This clause does not prevent the Union from taking measures requiring the Member States to adapt their political and constitutional structures or the way in which they organise the essential functions of a State. However, the clause certainly emphasises some elements of national sovereignty that the Union should not unnecessary restrict.[162]

E. THE PRINCIPLE OF SINCERE CO-OPERATION OR CO-OPERATION IN GOOD FAITH

1. Role played by the principle

Definition. Article 10 of the EC Treaty requires Member States to "take all 5–047 appropriate measures, whether general or particular, to ensure fulfilment of the obligations arising out of this Treaty or resulting from action taken by the institutions of the Community" (first paragraph) and, at the same time, to "abstain from any measure which could jeopardise the attainment of the objectives of this Treaty" (second paragraph). This provision, formulated in terms of a positive and a negative obligation, expresses the duty to co-operate in good faith (sometimes referred to as the duty of loyal or sincere co-operation) to which the Member States are subject in their dealings with the Community and as between themselves (see also EAEC Treaty, Art. 192). Since the duty to co-operate in good faith is an expression of Community solidarity,[163] it is not the same as the principle of international law that States are required to implement in good faith the treaties which they conclude.[164] The principle of co-operation in good faith is a reflection of the principle of "federal good faith" which is designed to secure mutual respect of the powers of the legislative, executive and judicial

---

[162] Compare the equivalent protection of the Member States' "national identity" in Art. 6 of the EU Treaty, which, however, cannot be enforced by the Court of Justice (para. 10–076, *infra*). See Van Nuffel (n.130, *supra*), at 271 *et seq.*

[163] See ECJ, Joined Cases 6 and 11/69 *Commission v France* [1969] E.C.R. 523, para. 16.

[164] For Art. 10 (formerly Art. 5) of the EC Treaty, see Constantinesco, "L'article 5 CEE, de la bonne foi à la loyauté communautaire", in Capotorti, Ehlermann, Frowein, Jacobs, Joliet, Koopmans and Kovar (eds), *Du droit international au droit de l'intégration. Liber amicorum P. Pescatore* (Nomos, Baden-Baden, 1987), at 97–114. For a general discussion, see Blanquet, *L'article 5 du traité CEE. Recherche sur les obligations de fidélité des Etats membres de la Communauté* (Librairie Générale de Droit et de Jurisprudence, Paris, 1994), 502 pp.; Temple Lang, "Community Constitutional Law: Art. 5 EEC Treaty" (1990) C.M.L.R. 645–681; Temple Lang, "The duties of co-operation of national authorities and courts under Art. 10 E.C.: two more reflections" (2001) E.L.Rev. 84–93.

bodies of different levels of authority within a federal system and readiness to co-operate.[165] Article 10 of the EC Treaty is binding on "all the authorities of Member States",[166] including, for matters within their jurisdiction, the courts[167] and decentralised authorities.[168]

Article 10 of the EC Treaty does not have direct effect in itself, but it can be used as an additional argument where the Member State in question is alleged to have breached an unconditional and sufficiently precise obligation.[169] In such a case, the national court, as an institution of its Member State, has to refrain from applying the provisions of domestic law which prevent Community law from having its full effect (see para. 5–054).

5–048 Scope. Since it is chiefly the national authorities which have to implement Community law, most of the decided cases concerning the duty to co-operate in good faith are concerned with the application of the principle to the Member States. Nevertheless, increasing activity on the part of the Community has made it clear that the Community institutions are also subject to the duty to co-operate in good faith in their relations both with Member States and with each other.[170] However, the adoption of a legislative measure by the Council cannot constitute a breach of the duty to co-operate in good faith attaching to either the Council or the Member States, which defend their interests in that institution.[171]

---

[165] Van Gerven with the collaboration of Gilliams, "Gemeenschapstrouw: goede trouw in E.G.-verband" (1989–90) R.W. 1158, at 1159. However, the Community principle does not alter the division of powers between the Community and the Member States. See Due, "Artikel 5 van het EEG-Verdrag. Een bepaling met een federaal karakter?" (1992) S.E.W. 355, at 366. For examples from Belgium, see Verhoeven, "The application in Belgium of the duties of loyalty and co-operation" (2000) S.E.W. 328–340.

[166] ECJ, Case 80/86 *Kolpinghuis Nijmegen* [1987] E.C.R. 3969, para. 12.

[167] *ibid.* See also the earlier case ECJ, Case 14/83 *Von Colson and Kamann* [1984] E.C.R. 1891, para. 26. For Art. 86 of the ECSC Treaty, see ECJ, Case C–341/94 *Allain* [1996] E.C.R. I–4631, para. 25.

[168] For municipal bye-laws, see ECJ, Case 85/85 *Commission v Belgium* [1985] E.C.R. 1149, paras 22–23.

[169] See ECJ, Case 9/73 *Schlüter* [1973] E.C.R. 1135, para. 39, and ECJ, Case 10/73 *Rewe-Zentral* [1973] E.C.R. 1175, para. 26; ECJ, Case 44/84 *Hurd v Jones* [1986] E.C.R. 29, paras 47–48; ECJ, Joined Cases C–72 and C–73/91 *Sloman Neptun* [1993] E.C.R. I–887, para. 28. Cf. Dauses, "Quelques réflexions sur la signification et la portée de l'article 5 du traité CEE", in Bieber and Ress (eds), *Die Dynamik des Europäischen Gemeinschaftsrechts/The Dynamics of EC-Law* (Nomos, Baden-Baden, 1987), 229, at 233–235.

[170] ECJ, Case 230/81 *Luxembourg v European Parliament* [1983] E.C.R. 255, para. 37 ("the rule imposing on Member States and the Community institutions mutual duties of sincere co-operation, as embodied in particular in Article 5 of the EEC Treaty [now Art. 10 of the EC Treaty]"). See, *inter alia*, ECJ, Case 44/84 *Hurd v Jones* [1986] E.C.R. 29, para. 38, and ECJ, Case 52/84 *Commission v Belgium* [1986] E.C.R. 89, para. 16; ECJ, Case C–65/93 *European Parliament v Council* [1995] E.C.R. I–643, para. 23; ECJ, Case C–319/97 *Kortas* [1999] E.C.R. I–3143, para. 35; ECJ, Case C–29/99 *Commission v Council* [2002] E.C.R. I–11221, para. 69. See also Declaration (No. 3) annexed to the Treaty of Nice on Art. 10 of the EC Treaty, [2001] O.J. C80/77.

[171] ECJ, Joined Cases C–63/90 and C–67/90 *Portugal and Spain v Council* [1992] E.C.R. I–5073, para. 53.

Constitution. These principles are to be codified by Art. I–5(2) of the EU **5–049** Constitution, which provides that "[p]ursuant to the principle of sincere co-operation, the Union and the Member States shall, in full mutual respect, assist each other in carrying out tasks which flow from the Constitution". The EU Constitution does not only confirm the obligation imposed on the Member States in terms of a duty to act or refrain from acting[172] but also explicitly refers to the duty incumbent upon the institutions of the Union to practise sincere mutual co-operation.[173]

2. The requirements of the duty of sincere co-operation

Twofold duty. The substance of the duty to co-operate in good faith **5–050** "depends in each individual case on the provisions of the Treaty or on the rules derived from its general scheme".[174] Where a provision of Community law contains a specific obligation for Member States, a finding that there has been a failure to fulfil the obligation in question may unquestionably be made.[175] Where, in contrast, there is no such obligation, a Member State's conduct may nonetheless constitute a breach of the duty to co-operate in good faith. This is because the Court of Justice has gradually broadened its interpretation of the "obligations arising out of this Treaty or resulting from action taken by the institutions of the Community" and of the requirement not to "jeopardise the attainment of the objectives of the Treaty" (EC Treaty, Art. 10). The upshot is: (1) ancillary obligations with which the Member States and the institutions must comply in implementing a specific provision of Community law or even independently of such implementation (supplementary function of the duty to co-operate in good faith)[176]; and (2) a prohibition on Member States or institutions acting where to act would constitute a misuse of powers (the so-called "derogatory function" of the duty to co-operate in good faith).[177]

a. Supplementary requirements

Duty of care. In the first place, Art. 10 of the EC Treaty puts the Member **5–051** States under a duty to take all measures necessary to implement provisions of Community law (see para. 14–047 *et seq.*). In so doing, they have to lay down the necessary sanctions in so far as the actual Community provisions themselves do not provide for any.[178] In addition, the Member States are under a general duty of care in implementing Community law. They have to

---

[172] EU Constitution, Arts I–5(2), second subpara.
[173] *ibid.*, Art. I–19(2).
[174] ECJ, Case 78/70 *Deutsche Grammophon* [1971] E.C.R. 487, para. 5.
[175] See, *e.g.* ECJ, Case C–48/89 *Commission v Italy* [1990] E.C.R. I–2425.
[176] Failure to comply with an undertaking to remedy an infringement of the Treaty itself constitutes a breach of Art. 10 of the EC Treaty: ECJ, Case C–374/89 *Commission v Belgium* [1991] E.C.R. I–367, paras 12–15.
[177] *cf.* Van Gerven with the collaboration of Gilliams (n.165, *supra*), at 1160–1162.
[178] For sanctions, see para. 14–049, *infra*.

take all appropriate measures to guarantee the full scope and effect of Community law. They must also deal with any irregularities as quickly as possible.[179] The conduct of other Member States or apprehension of internal difficulties cannot justify a failure to apply Community law correctly.[180] Where the implementation of Community law raises special difficulties, the Member States should submit them to the Commission and work together with it in good faith with a view to overcoming the difficulties.[181] Where Member States wish to derogate from a harmonisation measure pursuant to Art. 95(4) and (5) of the EC Treaty, the principle of co-operation in good faith puts them under a duty to notify the derogating measures as soon as possible.[182] They are under a duty to facilitate the Commission's supervisory task and therefore have to provide it with all such information as it might request to that end.[183] In implementing the competition rules, the national courts and the Commission must collaborate with each other with a view to overcoming the problems arising and to co-operate in the implementation of the investigation decision ordered by the Commission.[184]

In accordance with the principle of co-operation, the national courts are entrusted with securing the legal protection which citizens derive from the direct effect of provisions of Community law.[185] The courts must also ensure that provisions of Community law not endowed with direct effect are given *effet utile*, since they must refrain from applying conflicting

---

[179] ECJ, Case C–34/89 *Italy v Commission* [1990] E.C.R. I–3603, para. 12; ECJ, Case C–28/89 *Germany v Commission* [1991] E.C.R. I–581, para. 31; ECJ, Case C–277/98 *France v Commission* [2001] E.C.R. I–8453, para. 40.

[180] ECJ, Case C–265/95 *Commission v France* [1997] E.C.R. I–6959, paras 55 and 63.

[181] ECJ, Case 52/84 *Commission v Belgium* [1986] E.C.R. 89, para. 16, at 105; ECJ, Case 94/87 *Commission v Germany* [1989] E.C.R. 175, para. 9, at 192; ECJ, Case C–217/88 *Commission v Germany* [1990] E.C.R. I–2879, para. 33; ECJ, Case C–75/97 *Commission v Belgium* [1999] E.C.R. I–3671, para. 88; ECJ, Case C–404/97 *Commission v Portugal* [2000] E.C.R. I–4897, para. 40; ECJ, Case C–261/99 *Commission v France* [2001] E.C.R. I–2537, para. 24; ECJ, Case 378/98 *Commission v Belgium* [2001] E.C.R. I–5107, para. 31; ECJ, Case C–499/99 *Commission v Spain* [2002] E.C.R. I–6031, para. 24. Where a Member State notifies difficulties in transposing a directive, no obligation can be inferred from Art. 10 of the EC Treaty for the Commission to submit a proposal to amend the directive or to delay bringing an action for failure to fulfil obligations: ECJ, Case C–239/99 *Commission v Belgium* [2000] E.C.R. I–5657, paras 25–29.

[182] ECJ, Case C–319/97 *Kortas* [1999] E.C.R. I–3143, para. 35. For the correlative obligation on the Commission, see para. 5–053.

[183] ECJ, Case 96/81 *Commission v Netherlands* [1982] E.C.R. 1791, para. 7; ECJ, Case 240/86 *Commission v Greece* [1988] E.C.R. 1835, paras 25–28; ECJ, Case 272/86 *Commission v Greece* [1988] E.C.R. 4875, paras 30–32. See also ECJ, Case C–69/90 *Commission v Italy* [1991] E.C.R. I–6011, paras 11–15 (where a directive requires Member States to inform the Commission of implementing provisions adopted, a Member State must also notify the Commission of existing national provisions which allegedly already ensure full application of the directive in question).

[184] ECJ, Case C–94/00 *Roquette Frères* [2002] E.C.R. I–9011, paras 91–94 (the competent national court must obtain the necessary information from the Commission or the national competition authority which the Commission must procure as rapidly as possible).

[185] ECJ, Case 33/76 *Rewe* [1976] E.C.R. 1989, para. 5, and ECJ, Case 45/76 *Comet* [1976] E.C.R. 2043, para. 12.

national provisions (see para. 5–054). Member States must make sure that procedural conditions applicable to claims seeking to assert rights derived from Community law are not less favourable than those relating to similar domestic claims and are not such as in practice to make it impossible or excessively difficult to enforce those rights.[186] As far as Member States' implementation of the legal instruments referred to in Art. 249 of the EC Treaty is concerned, Art. 10 constitutes an additional ground for the duty of Member States to repeal national provisions incompatible with a Community regulation[187] and for the direct effect of non-implemented directives which are unconditional and sufficiently precise.[188] In particular, Art. 10 puts all national authorities, including the courts, under a duty to interpret national law in the light of the wording and purpose of Community directives.[189] More generally, the national courts must, as far as is at all possible, interpret national law in a way which accords with the requirements of Community law.[190]

The principle of co-operation in good faith obliges all national authorities to remedy any unlawful consequences of an infringement of Community law (see para. 17–012). Although the principle of legal certainty precludes an administrative authority going back on a decision which has become final when it subsequently becomes clear that it is based on a wrong interpretation of Community law, an administrative body which has the power to revise a decision which has become definitive may be obliged in certain circumstances to review that decision pursuant to the principle of co-operation in good faith.[191] Where individuals suffer loss or damage as a result of breaches of Community law for which the State can be held responsible, it is inherent in the "system of the Treaty" and Art. 10 of the EC Treaty that the Member State in question must allow a claim to be made against the public authorities.[192]

As regards legal protection against Community acts, the Member States are under a duty, together with the Community Courts, to establish a system of legal remedies and procedures which ensure respect for the right to effective judicial protection. In that context, in accordance with the principle of co-operation in good faith, national courts are required, so far as possible, to interpret and apply national procedural rules governing the

---

[186] *Rewe* (cited in preceding n.86, *supra.*), para. 5; *Comet* (cited in preceding n.86, *supra.*), paras 13–16; see also para. 17–011, *infra*.

[187] ECJ, Case 74/86 *Commission v Germany* [1988] E.C.R. 2139, paras 10–12.

[188] See ECJ, Case 190/87 *Oberkreisdirektor des Kreises Borken* [1988] E.C.R. 4689, paras 22–24.

[189] See ECJ, Case 14/83 *Von Colson and Kamann* [1984] E.C.R. 1891, para. 26; ECJ, Case C–106/89 *Marleasing* [1990] E.C.R. I–4135, para. 8 (interpretation of national law in the light of the wording and purpose of the directive, para. 17–131, *infra*).

[190] ECJ, Case C–262/97 *Engelbrecht* [2000] E.C.R. I–7321, para. 39 (see para. 17–006).

[191] ECJ (judgment of January 13, 2004), Case C–453/00 *Kühne & Heitz*, not yet reported, paras 20–28. For a critical comment, see Jans and de Graaf, "Bevoegdheid = verplichting?" (2004) N.T.E.R. 98–102.

[192] ECJ, Joined Cases C–6/90 and C–9/90 *Francovich* [1991] E.C.R. I–5357, paras 33–36; see also para. 17–012, *infra*.

exercise of rights of action in a way that enables natural and legal persons to challenge before the courts the legality of any decision or other national measure relative to the application to them of a Community act of general application—which they cannot contest under Art. 230 of the EC Treaty—, by pleading the invalidity of such an act.[193]

5–052 **Duty to co-operate.** Article 10 of the EC Treaty puts each Member State and the Commission under a duty to co-operate in good faith with institutions of other Member States responsible for implementing Community law.[194] As a result of the obligation mutually to facilitate the implementation of Community law, Member States must recognise the equivalence of each other's product tests, diplomas and evidence of professional qualifications in the context of the free movement of goods, persons and services.[195]

Where the Community is empowered to conduct a particular policy but does not succeed in doing so on account of differences of opinion within the Council, the duty of co-operation in good faith requires the Member States to take the necessary conservation measures, which they must notify to the Commission for its approval.[196] Such measures must also be notified to the other Member States.[197] They may only be temporary and provisional and must be abrogated as soon as Community measures are adopted.[198] The Member States are subject to obligations to co-operate in particular in the situation where the Commission has already submitted proposals to the Council.[199] In such case, the Member States, as "trustees of the common interest", may act only as part of the process of collaboration with the Commission (positive obligation) and may certainly not take any measures

---

[193] ECJ, Case C–50/00 P *Unión de Pequeños Agricultores v Council and Commission* [2002] E.C.R. I–6677, para. 42.

[194] ECJ, Case C–251/89 *Athanasopoulos* [1991] E.C.R. I–2797, para. 57; ECJ, Case C–165/91 *Van Munster* [1994] E.C.R. I–4661, para. 32 (see para. 5–149, *supra.*); ECJ, Case C–202/97 *Fitzwilliam Executive Search* [2000] E.C.R. I–883, paras 51–59; ECJ, Case C–178/97 *Banks* [2000] E.C.R. I–2005, paras 38–45. Where a bilateral agreement between Member States is liable to impede the application of a provision of Community law, the Member States concerned are under a duty to assist each other in order to facilitate the application of the relevant provision: ECJ, Case 235/87 *Matteucci* [1988] E.C.R. 5589, paras 17–19.

[195] See with regard to the free movement of goods: ECJ, Case 25/88 *Wurmser* [1989] E.C.R. 1105, para. 18 (para. 5–104, *infra*); with regard to the free movement of persons: ECJ, Case 71/76 *Thieffry* [1977] E.C.R. 765, paras 15–19; ECJ, Case C–340/89 *Vlassopoulou* [1991] E.C.R. I–2357, para. 14 (self-employed persons), and ECJ, Case 222/86 *Unectef v Heylens* [1987] E.C.R. 4097, para. 12 (workers) (para. 5–134, *infra*). For similar rulings concerning free movement of services, see para. 5–179, *infra*.

[196] See with regard to the conservation of fish stocks ECJ, Case 32/79 *Commission v UK* [1980] E.C.R. 2403, paras 10–15 and para. 25; ECJ, Case 804/79 *Commission v UK* [1981] E.C.R. 1045, para. 30 (para. 5–026, *supra*).

[197] ECJ, Case 141/78 *France v UK* [1979] E.C.R. 2923, paras 8–12.

[198] ECJ, Joined Cases 47–48/83 *Pluimveeslachterij Midden-Nederland and Van Miert* [1984] E.C.R. 1721, para. 23; ECJ, Case C–158/89 *Dietz-Matti* [1990] E.C.R. I–2013, para. 13.

[199] ECJ, Case 804/79 *Commission v UK* [1981] E.C.R. 1045, para. 28.

in spite of objections, reservations or conditions which might have been formulated by the Commission (negative obligation).[200]

The duty to co-operate further puts Member States under an obligation to consult the Community institutions where they propose adopting measures affecting the Staff Regulations of Community officials.[201]

Duties for institutions. Pursuant to the duty to co-operate in good faith, **5–053** the Commission, for its part, has to display the necessary diligence where a Member State notifies the wish to derogate from a harmonisation measure under Art. 95(4) and (5) of the EC Treaty.[202] The institutions are also under a duty to collaborate with the Member States' judicial authorities. As far as the Court of Justice is concerned, that collaboration takes the form of the preliminary ruling procedure provided for in Art. 234 of the EC Treaty. Furthermore, every Community institution—especially the Commission in view of its duty of ensuring that Community law is applied—must give its active assistance to a national court conducting a preliminary judicial inquiry into breaches of a Community provision which makes a request for information concerning potential evidence of such breaches.[203]

In principle, the same mutual duties of co-operation in good faith apply between the institutions as govern relations between the institutions and the Member States.[204] That is true in particular of decision-making procedures based on interinstitutional dialogue.[205] Where the Council is under a duty to consult the Parliament, it should avail itself of all the openings afforded by the Treaty and the Parliament's Rules of Procedure in order to obtain the Parliament's prior opinion. In turn, the Parliament should comply with a justified request from the Council to deal with a particular proposal urgently (see para. 14–025). If the Parliament fails to do so, the Council is entitled to adopt the relevant act without awaiting the Parliament's opinion.[206] The Court of Justice has held that in such a case the "essential procedural requirement of Parliamentary consultation was not complied with because of the Parliament's failure to discharge its obligation to co-operate sincerely with the Council".[207] Another example of an application of the duty to co-operate in good faith is the obligation for

---

[200] *ibid.*, paras 30–31. See also ECJ, Case 325/85 *Ireland v Commission* [1987] E.C.R. 5041, paras 15–16.

[201] ECJ, Case 186/85 *Commission v Belgium* [1987] E.C.R. 2029, para. 39.

[202] ECJ, Case C–319/97 *Kortas* [1999] E.C.R. I–3143, paras 35–36.

[203] ECJ, Case C–2/88 Imm. *Zwartveld* [1990] E.C.R. I–3365, paras 17–22; ECJ, Case C–234/89 *Delimitis* [1991] E.C.R. I–935, para. 53. The Commission may refuse to provide information in order to avoid any interference with the functioning and independence of the Community or to safeguard its interests; see ECJ, Case C–275/00 *Frist and Franex* [2002] E.C.R. I–10943, para. 49.

[204] ECJ, Case 204/86 *Greece v Council* [1988] E.C.R. 5323, para. 16.

[205] ECJ, Case C–65/93 *European Parliament v Council* [1995] E.C.R. I–643, para. 23, with case notes by Heukels (1995) C.M.L.R. 1407–1426 and Van Nuffel (1995) Col.J.E.L. 504, at 511–515.

[206] *ibid.*, para. 28.

[207] *ibid.*

the Council to ensure in approving an international agreement that such approval enables the other institutions to comply with international law (see para. 20–037).

b. Derogatory requirements

5–054 Respect for Community interest. As has already been mentioned, Art. 10 of the EC Treaty prohibits any measure which could jeopardise the attainment of the objectives of the Treaty. Accordingly, under that provision in conjunction with Art. 3(g) of the EC Treaty, Member States are precluded from reinforcing agreements in restraint of competition concluded by undertakings contrary to Art. 81.[208] More generally, Member States must allow measures preventing Community rules from having full force and effect (*effet utile*) to be set aside. A national court which has to apply Community law must therefore have jurisdiction to do everything necessary to set aside provisions of (even constitutional) law which might prevent Community rules from having full effect.[209]

Article 10 of the EC Treaty puts Member States under a duty to respect the division of powers between the Community and the Member States. Where a Community measure is adopted, conflicting national measures must be set aside pursuant to the principle of the primacy of Community law. The extent to which Member States' action is restricted depends on the scope of the Community measure (see para. 17–005). Member States must not exercise their powers (in particular in the field of international relations) in such a way as to affect the Community measure or alter its scope.[210] During the period for transposition of a directive, Member States must refrain from adopting measures which would jeopardise the achievement of what is provided for in the directive.[211] In situations in which Member States take action because the Community has failed to act,

---

[208] See the judgments cited in the discussion of competition in para. 5–195, *infra*. However, such a requirement exists only where there is already a clear Community policy: ECJ, Case 229/83 *Leclerc* [1985] E.C.R. 1, para. 20.

[209] ECJ, Case C–213/89 *Factortame* (*Factortame I*) [1990] E.C.R. I–2433, para. 20 (setting aside the rule of the British Constitution to the effect that a court may not give interim relief against the Crown especially in the form of an order setting aside the application of an act of Parliament). See also the earlier case ECJ, Case 106/77 *Simmenthal* [1978] E.C.R. 629, para. 22, containing no express reference to Art. 5 [now Art. 10] of the EC Treaty (the national court has to refuse to apply any conflicting provision of national law of its own motion and does not have to await a ruling of its national Constitutional Court as required by its national legal system on the constitutionality of the domestic provision). See also the discussion of the primacy of Community law, paras 17–007—17–011. There is no obligation, however, to disapply a national provision where the issue before the national court concerns a situation which lies outside the scope of Community law: ECJ, Case C–264/96 *ICI* [1998] E.C.R. I–4695, paras 31–35.

[210] ECJ, Case 22/70 *Commission v Council* [1971] E.C.R. 263, para. 22 (AETR case). See also para. 20–036, *infra*, regarding limitations on the international action of the Member States.

[211] Para. 17–123, *infra*; for a general discussion of standstill obligations, see Meyring, "Europarechtliche Stillhalteverpflichtungen bei der nationalen Gesetzgebung" (2003) EuR. 949–959.

the principle of co-operation in good faith requires them to refrain from adopting measures which do not have regard to the common interest. This applies to any action of Member States in areas which do not fall within the exclusive competence of the Community. The same is true *a fortiori* where Member States take action exceptionally in areas which do fall within the exclusive competence of the Community, *e.g.* during a transitional period[212] or where temporary conservation measures are necessary.[213]

Respect for institutional balance. Lastly, the duty to co-operate in good **5–055** faith requires Member States to refrain from taking measures which might jeopardise the independence of the Community institutions and hence the institutional balance.[214] A Member State must avoid taking any measure which would result in officials and other servants of the Communities directly or indirectly losing the benefit of the privileges and immunities to which they are entitled under the relevant Protocol.[215] Member States are also not entitled to adopt any measures which would result in a charge on the EU budget.[216]

F. THE PRINCIPLE OF EQUAL TREATMENT

1. Field of application

General principle of law. The principle of equal treatment requires persons **5–056** in the same situation to be treated in the same way. It is a general principle of Community law,[217] which is enshrined in the Charter of Fundamental Rights of the European Union[218] and finds expression in the EC Treaty in

---

[212] See the fisheries policy during the transitional period provided for in Art. 102 of the 1972 Act of Accession: ECJ, Joined Cases 3, 4 and 6/76 *Kramer* [1976] E.C.R. 1279, paras 40–45; ECJ, Case 61/77 *Commission v Ireland* [1978] E.C.R. 417, paras 63–67. See also the judgments discussed above (see n.196 to para. 5–052, *supra*): ECJ, Case 32/79 *Commission v UK* [1980] E.C.R. 2403, paras 10–15; ECJ, Case 141/78 *France v UK* [1979] E.C.R. 2923, paras 7-9.

[213] See the judgment on fisheries after the expiry of the transitional period: ECJ, Case 804/79 *Commission v UK* [1981] E.C.R. 1045, para. 30 (see nn.196 and 199 to para. 5–052, *supra*, together with the discussion of powers in para. 5–026, *supra*).

[214] ECJ, Case 208/80 *Lord Bruce of Donington* [1981] E.C.R. 2205; ECJ, Case 230/81 *Luxembourg v European Parliament* [1983] E.C.R. 255. See also ECJ, Case C–345/95 *France v European Parliament* [1997] E.C.R. I–5215.

[215] ECJ, Case 85/85 *Commission v Belgium* [1986] E.C.R. 1149, paras 22–23.

[216] See the judgments concerning the European Schools, para. 10–111, *infra*.

[217] For a general discussion, see Arnull, *The General Principles of EEC Law and the Individual* (Leicester University Press, Leicester, 1990), 300 pp.; Lenaerts, "L'égalité de traitement en droit communautaire: un principe unique aux apparences multiples" (1991) C.D.E. 3–41; Demaret, "L'égalité de traitement" (1994) A.D. 165–208; Lenaerts and Arts, "La personne et le principe de l'égalité en droit communautaire et dans la Convention européenne de sauvegarde des droits de l'homme et des libertés fondamentales", *La personne humaine, sujet de droit* (Presses Universitaires de France, Paris, 1994), at 101–134.

[218] Chapter III of the Charter, which deals with equality before the law (Art. 20), non-discrimination (Art. 21), cultural, religious and linguistic diversity (Art. 22), equality between men and women (Art. 23), the rights of the child (Art. 24), the rights of the elderly (Art. 25) and integration of persons with disabilities (Art. 26).

the form of the aim of eliminating inequalities between men and women (EC Treaty, Art. 3(2); see also Art. 141) and the prohibition of discrimination on grounds of nationality (EC Treaty, Art. 12).[219] A number of Treaty provisions refer to the obligation to treat market participants in the same way.[220] For instance, the second subparagraph of Art. 34(2) of the EC Treaty provides that the common organisation of the agricultural markets shall "exclude any discrimination between producers or consumers within the Community". The Court of Justice has declared that "the prohibition of discrimination laid down in the aforesaid provision is merely a specific enunciation of the general principle of equality which is one of the fundamental principles of Community law [and] requires that similar situations shall not be treated differently unless differentiation is objectively justified".[221]

5–057 Scope. Within the scope of application of Community law, the principle of equal treatment is binding not only on Member States and individuals, but also on the Community institutions, which may not adopt any criteria in breach of that principle.[222] The Court of Justice declared Art. 73(2) of Regulation No. 1408/71 invalid because, for the purpose of determining the amount of family benefits for migrant workers with family members living in another Member State, it made a distinction between workers who were subject to French legislation and workers subject to the legislation of another Member State. Consequently, that provision was "not of such a nature as to secure the equal treatment laid down by Art. 48 of the EEC Treaty [now, EC Treaty, Art. 39]".[223]

---

[219] Martin, "'Discriminations', 'entraves' et 'raisons impérieuses' dans le traité CE: trois concepts en quête d'identité" (1998) C.D.E. 261–318 and 561–637.

[220] See EC Treaty, Art. 34(2), second subpara. ; Art. 81(1)(d); Art. 82, second para. , indent (c).

[221] ECJ, Joined Cases 117/76 and 16/77 *Ruckdeschel* [1977] E.C.R. 1753, para. 7. Where a common organisation of the market covers economic operators who are neither producers nor consumers, the prohibition of discrimination also applies to all other categories of operators subject to the common organisation: ECJ, Case C–280/93 *Germany v Council* [1994] E.C.R. I–4973, para. 68.

[222] See with regard to the prohibition of indirect discrimination on grounds of sex: ECJ, Case 20/71 *Sabbatini v European Parliament* [1972] E.C.R. 345, para. 13.; ECJ (judgment of September 9, 2003), Case C–25/02 *Rinke*, not yet reported, paras 25–28.

[223] ECJ, Case 41/84 *Pinna* [1986] E.C.R. 1, paras 22–25; for another provision of Regulation No. 1408/71 which was declared to be in breach of the principle of equal treatment enshrined in Art. 39 of the EC Treaty, see ECJ, Case 20/85 *Roviello* [1988] E.C.R. 2805, paras 14–18. For Regulation No. 1408/71, see para. 5–148, *infra*. Accordingly, the Council infringed the principle of equal treatment by applying the Staff Regulations differently with regard to institutions which were in the same situation: CFI, Case I–164/97 *Busaca v Court of Auditors* [1998] E.C.R.-S.C. I–1699, paras 48–61 (upheld on appeal: ECJ, Case C–434/98 P *Council v Busaca and Court of Auditors* [2000] E.C.R. I–8577). The European Central Bank was found to have infringed the principle of equal treatment by granting an education allowance only to staff in receipt of expatriation allowance: CFI (judgment of January 8, 2003), Joined Cases T–94/01, T–125/01 and T–286/01 *Hirsch v ECB*, not yet reported (staff case), paras 45–72.

Constitution. The EU Constitution presents the principle of equality as **5–058** one of the "values" of the Union while at the same time it includes among the Union's objectives the fight against discrimination and the promotion of equality between women and men (Arts I 2 and I–3(3)). As indicated below, the EU Constitution makes several other references to the prohibition of discrimination on grounds of nationality or on grounds of sex, as well as to other prohibited forms of discrimination. A novel expression of the principle of equality is to be found in the obligation incumbent on the Union to respect "the equality of Member States before the Constitution" (Art. I–5(1)).

a. Prohibition of discrimination on grounds of the nationality of a Member State

Article 12 EC Treaty. The first para. of Art. 12 of the EC Treaty prohibits **5–059** any discrimination on grounds of nationality "[w]ithin the scope of application of this Treaty" and "without prejudice to any special provisions contained therein".[224] In a situation governed by Community law, a Member State must treat nationals of other Member States and its own nationals in the same way. Thus, a Member State may not make the award of a right subject to the condition that the person concerned holds a residence permit or is a national of a country which has entered into a reciprocal agreement with that Member State.[225] Individuals too are subject to the prohibition of discrimination on grounds of nationality, in particular where a group or organisation exercises a certain power over individuals and is in a position to impose on them conditions which adversely affect the exercise of the fundamental freedoms guaranteed under the Treaty.[226] Every citizen of the Union has the right not to suffer discrimination on grounds of nationality within the scope of application *ratione materiae* of the Treaty.[227] In some circumstances, however, a difference in treatment may be objectively justified, for example an obligation imposed only on non-residents to pay security in respect of infringements given the absence

---

[224] See Rossi, "Das Diskriminierungsverbot nach Art. 12 EGV" (2000) EuR. 197–217. Art. 12 of the EC Treaty, which lays down the general principle of the prohibition of discrimination on grounds of nationality, applies independently only to situations governed by Community law in respect of which the Treaty lays down no specific prohibition of discrimination: ECJ, Case C–193/94 *Skanavi and Chryssanthakopoulos* [1996] E.C.R. I–929, para. 20; ECJ, Case C–131/96 *Mora Romero* [1997] E.C.R. I–3659, para. 10. Within the scope of application of the EC Treaty and of the EU Treaty any discrimination on grounds of nationality is also prohibited by Art. 21(2) of the Charter of Fundamental Rights of the European Union.

[225] ECJ, Case 186/87 *Cowan* [1989] E.C.R. 195, para. 13.

[226] ECJ, Case C–411/98 *Ferlini* [2000] E.C.R. I–8081, para. 50; see also ECJ, Case C–281/98 *Angonese* [2000] E.C.R. I–4139, paras 30–36.

[227] ECJ, Case C–85/96 *Martínez Sala* [1998] E.C.R. I–2691, paras 54–65; ECJ, Case C–184/99 *Grzelczyk* [2001] E.C.R. I–6193, para. 32; ECJ, Case C–224/98 *D'Hoop* [2002] E.C.R. I–6191, paras 27–28; ECJ (judgment of October 2, 2003), Case C–148/02 *Garcia Avello*, not yet reported, paras 22–23. In any event, within the scope of application of Community law, citizens of the Union have a general right to equal treatment, see para. 12–008.

of international or Community instruments to ensure that a fine may if necessary be enforced in another Member State[228] or a residence requirement which places a Member State's own nationals at an advantage but is based on objective considerations that are independent of the nationality of the persons concerned and proportionate to the legitimate aim of the national provisions.[229] The words "special provisions" in Art. 12 refer to other Treaty provisions specifying the principle set forth in that article as regards a number of specific situations. Those provisions express the basic condition of the common market, namely that all factors of production, irrespective of the nationality of persons[230] or the origin of goods,[231] services[232] and capital,[233] may participate in the market.

5–060   Scope of application. In order to determine the scope of application of the EC Treaty, within which the principle of non-discrimination enshrined in Art. 12 applies, the Court of Justice gives a broad interpretation to the rights which persons derive from Community law. Thus, the Court declared in *Cowan* with regard to free movement of services that:

> "[w]hen Community law guarantees a natural person the freedom to go to another Member State the protection of that person from harm in the Member State in question, on the same basis as that of nationals and persons residing there, is a corollary of that freedom of movement. It follows that the prohibition of discrimination is applicable to recipients of services within the meaning of the Treaty as regards protection against the risk of assault and the right to obtain financial compensation provided for by national law when that risk materialises".[234]

In addition, a person falls within the scope *ratione personae* of the provisions of the Treaty if he or she, being a national of a Member State and thus a citizen of the Union, lawfully resides in the territory of another Member State.[235]

The situations which fall within the scope *ratione materiae* of Community law include those involving the exercise of the fundamental freedoms guaranteed by the Treaty and those involving the freedom to move and reside within the territory of the Member States conferred by Art. 18 of the EC Treaty.[236] Accordingly, a job-seeker in another Member State may

---

[228] ECJ, Case C–224/00 *Commission v Italy* [2002] E.C.R. I–2965, paras 20–24.
[229] See ECJ (judgment of March 23, 2004), Case C–138/02 *Collins*, not yet reported, paras 65–73.
[230] See EC Treaty, Art. 31(1); Art. 39(2); Art. 43, second para. ; Art. 72 and Art. 184(5).
[231] See EC Treaty, Art. 30, last sentence; Art. 75(1); Art. 90, first para.
[232] See EC Treaty, Art. 50, third para. , and Art. 54.
[233] See EC Treaty, Art. 58(3).
[234] ECJ, Case 186/87 *Cowan* [1989] E.C.R. 195, para. 17. See also ECJ, Case C–45/93 *Commission v Spain* [1994] E.C.R. I–911, paras 5–10.
[235] ECJ, Case C–85/96 *Martínez Sala* [1998] E.C.R. I–2691, para. 61.
[236] ECJ, Case C–224/98 *D'Hoop* [2002] E.C.R. I–6191, para. 29; ECJ (judgment of October 2, 2003), Case C–148/02 *Garcia Avello*, not yet reported, para. 24; ECJ (judgment of April 29, 2004), Case C–224/02 *Antero Pusa*, not yet reported, para. 17.

claim equal treatment with regard to the grant of a financial benefit designed to facilitate access to the employment market in that Member State.[237] The Court also ruled that nationals of a Member State who, in accordance with Art. 18, make use of their right to move to another Member State and reside there are in principle entitled, pursuant to Art. 12 of the EC Treaty, to treatment no less favourable than that accorded to nationals of the host State so far as concerns the use of languages which are spoken there[238] or entitlement to a social benefit such as a child-raising allowance[239] or a minimum subsistence allowance.[240] The Court of Justice likewise links Art. 12 of the EC Treaty with the Treaty provisions which empower the Community to act, even if it has not yet exercised the power. In the judgment in *Gravier*, the Court held that the requirement to pay a fee in order to study cartoon art fell within the ambit of the "common vocational training policy" referred to in Art. 128 of the EEC Treaty. Consequently, it is contrary to the principle of non-discrimination for a Member State to distinguish, as regards the level of educational fees, between students who are its nationals and students who are nationals of other Member States.[241] Since the principle of non-discrimination also covers the treatment of different situations in the same way, Union citizens may rely on Art. 12 in order to contest a Member State's refusal to take account of their specific situation. Accordingly, a Member State must make it possible in its legislation on surnames for nationals having dual nationality of that State and of another Member State to bear the surname to which they are entitled according to the law of the second Member State.[242]

It follows from the case law that even when a particular matter falls within the competence of the Member States (*e.g.* the rules governing a person's surname), Community law sets certain limits to their power and national legislative provisions "may not discriminate against persons to whom Community law gives the right to equal treatment or restrict the

---

[237] See ECJ (judgment of March 23, 2004), Case C–138/02 *Collins*, not yet reported, paras 54–64.

[238] ECJ, Case C–274/96 *Bickel and Franz* [1998] E.C.R. I–7637, paras 13–31 (for the question of the justification under cultural policy, see para. 5–242, *infra*).

[239] ECJ, Case C–85/96 *Martínez Sala* [1998] E.C.R. I–2691, para. 57.

[240] ECJ, Case C–184/99 *Grzelczyk* [2001] E.C.R. I–6193, paras 29–46; ECJ (judgment of September 7, 2004), Case C–456/02 *Trojani*, not yet reported.

[241] ECJ, Case 293/83 *Gravier* [1985] E.C.R. 593, paras 11–26; ECJ, Case 24/86 *Blaizot* [1988] E.C.R. 379, paras 10–24; ECJ, Case C–47/93 *Commission v Belgium* [1994] E.C.R. I–1593. See also ECJ, Case 309/85 *Barra* [1988] E.C.R. 355, paras 16–21 (repayment of undue registration fees); ECJ, Case 39/86 *Lair* [1988] E.C.R. 3161, paras 11–16; ECJ Case 197/86 *Brown* [1988] E.C.R. 3205, paras 14–19, and Case C–357/89 *Raulin* [1992] E.C.R. I–1027, paras 25–29 (grant to cover costs of access to a course); ECJ, Case 42/87 *Commission v Belgium* [1988] E.C.R. 5445, paras 7–9 (funding of educational establishments).

[242] ECJ (judgment of October 2, 2003), Case C–148/02 *Garcia Avello*, not yet reported, paras 30–45.

fundamental freedoms guaranteed by Community law".[243] Accordingly, national legislative provisions are subject to the prohibition of discrimination laid down by Art. 12 where they fall within the scope of application of the Treaty by reason of their effects on free movement of persons (including the aforementioned exercise of rights accruing to a person as a citizen of the Union) or their effects on intra-Community trade in goods and services.[244] The ambit of the Treaty also extends to agreements concluded as between Member States pursuant to Art. 293 of the EC Treaty. Since such agreements are concluded on the basis of that article and within the framework defined by it, they are linked with the EC Treaty in such a way that if they are applied in a discriminatory manner, this will constitute an infringement of Art. 12 of that Treaty.[245] Even in the case of the application of an agreement with non-member countries, the principle of equal treatment requires a Member State to grant nationals of other Member States the benefits accruing from the agreement for its own nationals (see para. 17–097).

A disparity in treatment between Member States resulting simply from differences existing between their laws does not constitute discrimination within the meaning of Art. 12 of the EC Treaty, so long as the differences affect all persons subject to them in accordance with objective criteria and without regard to their nationality.[246] As regards matters of civil law which fall outside the scope of the Treaty, it is not contrary to Art. 12 for persons to be treated differently on grounds of their nationality as a result of the fact that the private international law of a Member State takes nationality as the connecting factor for determining the applicable substantive law.[247]

5–061 Combating discrimination. The second para. of Art. 12 of the EC Treaty empowers the European Parliament and the Council, acting under the co-decision procedure, to adopt "rules designed to prohibit such

---

[243] See also ECJ, Case 186/87 *Cowan* [1989] E.C.R. 195, para. 19 (right to compensation of a person who is a victim of an offence, which comes under the French law of criminal procedure and, as a result, within the competence of the Member State); ECJ, Joined Cases C–92/92 and C–326/92 *Phil Collins* [1993] E.C.R. I–5145, paras 19–28; ECJ, Case C–360/00 *Ricordi & Co. Bühnen- und Musikverlag* [2002] E.C.R. I–5089, paras 24–34 (concerning copyrights and related rights); ECJ, Case C–43/95 *Data Delecta and Forsberg* [1996] E.C.R. I–4461, paras 10–22; ECJ, Case C–323/95 *Hayes* [1997] E.C.R. I–1711, paras 13–17; ECJ, Case C–122/96 *Saldanha and MTS* [1997] E.C.R. I–5325, paras 16–24 (concerning requirements to furnish security for costs); ECJ (judgment of April 29, 2004), Case C–224/02 *Antero Pusa*, not yet reported, para. 22–35 (rules on enforcement for the recovery of debts).

[244] ECJ, Case C–323/95 *Hayes* [1997] E.C.R. I–1711, para. 16; ECJ, Case C–122/96 *Saldanha and MTS* [1997] E.C.R. I–5325, para. 20. However, there are limits to the scope of Community law, see ECJ, Case C–291/96 *Grado and Bashir* [1997] E.C.R. I–5531, paras 13–14.

[245] ECJ, Case C–398/92 *Mund & Fester* [1994] E.C.R. I–467, paras 10–13. Likewise, a bilateral agreement between Member States may not encroach upon the right of Community workers and their families to equal treatment: ECJ, Case 235/87 *Matteucci* [1988] E.C.R. 5589, para. 14.

[246] See ECJ, Case C–177/94 *Perfili* [1996] E.C.R. I–161, para. 71.

[247] ECJ, Case C–430/97 *Johannes* [1999] E.C.R. I–3475, paras 26–29.

discrimination". This means that the Council may take (in co-decision with the European Parliament only since the Treaty of Amsterdam) the necessary measures to prohibit all forms of discrimination on grounds of nationality. The measures need not be confined to the right to equal treatment flowing from the first para. of Art. 12, but may also deal with ancillary aspects which ought to be settled in order to secure effective exercise of that right. The Court of Justice has held that Art. 12 was the only proper legal basis for the Council directive on students' right of residence on the ground that equal treatment in the matter of access to vocational training requires that students have the right to reside in the Member State where they have been admitted to vocational training.[248]

Constitution. The EU Constitution will prohibit discrimination on grounds **5–062** of nationality within the entire field of application of the Constitution and so this principle will cover areas outside the scope of the present EC Treaty (Art. I–4(2)).[249]

b. Prohibition of discrimination on grounds of sex/gender

Sex and gender. An important application of the prohibition of **5–063** discrimination is the obligation that men and women must be treated equally.[250] The Court of Justice has referred to equal treatment of men and women as one of the fundamental human rights whose observance it has a duty to ensure.[251] The principle is also enshrined in Art. 23 of the Charter of Fundamental Rights of the European Union. The principle of equal treatment prohibits the Community and the Member States from discriminating on grounds of sex. This is also expressed in the EC Treaty in form of the principle that male and female workers should receive equal

---

[248] ECJ, Case C–295/90 *European Parliament v Council* [1992] E.C.R. I–4193, paras 15–20.

[249] See also Art. II–81(2) of the EU Constitution (Art. 21 of the Charter of Fundamental Rights). Art. III–123 of the EU Constitution provides the Union with a legal basis to take legislative action in this regard.

[250] See Prechal and Burrows, *Gender Discrimination Law of the European Community* (Dartmouth, Aldershot, 1990), 351 pp.; Langenfeld, *Die Gleichbehandlung von Mann und Frau im Europäischen Gemeinschaftsrecht* (Nomos, Baden-Baden, 1990), 322 pp.; Ellis, "The Definition of Discrimination in European Community Sex Equality Law" (1994) E.L.Rev. 563–580; Hervey and O'Keeffe (eds), *Sex Equality Law in the European Union* (John Wiley & Sons, Chichester, 1996), 427 pp.; Drijber and Prechal, "Gelijke behandeling van mannen en vrouwen in horizontaal perspectief" (1997) S.E.W. 122–167; Mancini and O'Leary, "The New Frontiers of Sex Equality Law in the European Union" (1999) E.L.Rev. 331–353; Jacqmain, "Egalité entre travailleurs féminins et masculins" (2000) J.T.D.E. 201–210.

[251] ECJ, Case C–185/97 *Coote* [1998] E.C.R. I–5199, para. 23. For a survey of the case-law, see Ellis, "Recent Developments in European Community Sex Equality Law" (1998) C.M.L.R. 379–408 and "The Recent Jurisprudence of the Court of Justice in the Field of Sex Equality" (2000) C.M.L.R. 1403–1426; see also Pager, "Strictness vs. Discretion: The European Court of Justice's Variable Vision of Gender Equality" (2003) A.J.C.L. 553–609.

pay for equal work or work of equal value (EC Treaty, Art. 141(1)).[252] The Community law requirement for equal treatment of men and women applies to access to employment and, consequently, in principle also to military occupations.[253] However, the Member States' choices of military organisation for the defence of their territory or of their essential interests do not necessarily fall within Community law. Accordingly, Community law does not preclude compulsory military service being reserved to men.[254] As a result of the prohibition of discrimination on grounds of sex, a worker may not be discriminated against because he or she or his or her partner wishes to undergo a gender-reassignment operation or has undergone such an operation.[255] The Court of Justice considers, however, that discrimination on grounds of sexual orientation does not fall within the prohibition of discrimination on grounds of sex.[256]

In many areas, the Community law principle of equal treatment of men and women has prompted better protection for women against unjustified discrimination.[257] Article 3(2) of the EC Treaty provides that, in all its activities, "the Community shall aim to eliminate inequalities, and to promote equality, between men and women".[258] Equality between men and

---

[252] See the discussion of indirect discrimination, para. 5–067, *infra*, and the discussion of social policy, para. 5–236. For a blatant example, see ECJ, Case C–206/00 *Mouflin* [2001] E.C.R. I–10201, paras 28–31. Until the Treaty of Amsterdam, Art. 119 [now Art. 141] referred only to "equal work"; the principle was extended to "the same work" by Council Directive 75/117/EEC of February 10, 1975 on the approximation of the laws of the Member States relating to the application of the principle of equal pay for men and women, [1975] O.J. L45/19.

[253] ECJ, Case C–273/97 *Sirdar* [1999] E.C.R. I–7403, paras 11–29; ECJ, Case C–285/98 *Kreil* [2000] E.C.R. I–69, paras 15–32 (in spite of the constitutional ban on military service for women); the exclusion of women from service in special commando units may, however, be justified on the basis of Directive 76/207 (n.62, *infra*): *Sirdar*, paras 21–32.

[254] ECJ, Case C–186/01 *Dory* [2003] E.C.R. I–2479, paras 29–42 (see also para. 8–012, *infra*).

[255] ECJ, Case C–13/94 *P.* [1996] E.C.R. I–2143, paras 13–24, with a case note by Brems (1996) Col.J.E.L. 339–345; ECJ (judgment of January 7, 2004), Case C–117/01 *K.B.*, not yet reported.

[256] ECJ, Case C–249/96 *Grant v South-West Trains Ltd* [1998] E.C.R. I–621, paras 24–47, with a case note by McInnes (1999) C.M.L.R. 1043–1058. See also para. 5–064.

[257] The principle also opposes the discriminatory effects of legislation intended to protect women; see, *inter alia*, the case-law rejecting a national ban on night work by women: ECJ, Case C–345/89 *Stoeckel* [1991] E.C.R. I–4047; ECJ, Case C–158/91 *Levy* [1993] E.C.R. I–4287. See De Vos, "Le travail de nuit: La 'Realpolitik' de l'égalité!" (1993) J.T. 1–7 and, in addition, Masselot and Berthou, "La CJCE, le droit de la maternité et le principe de non-discrimination—vers une clarification?" (2000) C.D.E. 637–656; Caracciolo di Torella and Masselot, "Pregnancy, maternity and the organisation of family life: an attempt to classify the case law of the Court of Justice" (2001) E.L.Rev. 239–260; Foubert, *The legal protection of the pregnant worker in the European Community: sex equality, thoughts of social and economic policy and comparative leaps to the United States of America* (Kluwer, The Hague, 2002), 389 pp.

[258] See also the reference to "equality between men and women" as a task of the Community in Art. 2 of the EC Treaty (introduced by the Treaty of Amsterdam). *Cf.* Council Recommendation 96/694 adopted by the Council pursuant to Art. 235 [now Art. 308] of the EC Treaty, on the balanced participation of women and men in the decision-making process ([1996] O.J. L319/11); Commission Decision 2000/407/EC of June 19, 2000 relating to gender balance within the committees and expert groups established by it ([2000] O.J.

women with regard to labour market opportunities and treatment at work is also among the objectives of Community social policy (see EC Treaty, Article 137(1)(i)).[259] Article 141(3) of the EC Treaty empowers the European Parliament and the Council, acting under the co-decision procedure, to adopt measures to ensure the application of the principle of equal opportunities and equal treatment for men and women in matters of employment and occupation, including the principle of equal pay for equal work or work of equal value. The Community had already adopted directives to ensure men and women equal treatment as regards access to employment, vocational training, promotion and working conditions,[260] and in the field of social security.[261]

All this does not mean that the Member States are not entitled to take measures embodying "positive discrimination". The guarantee of equal access to employment and of equal promotion opportunities for men and women does not preclude measures to enhance equal opportunity for men and women which are intended, *inter alia*, to eliminate actual instances of inequality which affect women's opportunities.[262] However, this exception does not authorise a Member State to adopt or tolerate measures which guarantee absolute and unconditional priority for women in the matter of promotion or employment. Where both male and female candidates are equally qualified and where there are fewer women than men at the level of the relevant post, priority may be given to the promotion of female candidates if it is not excluded for one or more criteria specific to individual candidates—which may not be such as to discriminate against

---

L154/34); Regulation (EC) No. 806/04 of the European Parliament and the Council of April 21, 2004 on promoting gender equality in development co-operation ([2004] O.J. L143/40).

[259] Art. 137 takes over the wording of Art. 2 of the Social Agreement (para. 5–235, *infra*), pursuant to which the Council adopted, on December 15, 1997, Directive 97/80/EC on the burden of proof in cases of discrimination based on sex, [1998] O.J. L14/6.

[260] Council Directive 76/207/EEC of February 9, 1976 on the implementation of the principle of equal treatment for men and women as regards access to employment, vocational training and promotion, and working conditions, [1976] O.J. L39/40. See also Council Directive 86/613/EEC of December 11, 1986 on the application of the principle of equal treatment between men and women engaged in an activity, including agriculture, in a self-employed capacity, and on the protection of self-employed women during pregnancy and motherhood, [1986] O.J. L359/56.

[261] Council Directive 79/7/EEC of December 19, 1978 on the progressive implementation of the principle of equal treatment for men and women in matters of social security, [1979] O.J. L6/24. See also Council Directive 86/378/EEC of July 24, 1986 on the implementation of the principle of equal treatment for men and women in occupational social security schemes, [1986] O.J. L225/40. For a survey of the case-law, see Cousins, "Equal Treatment and Social Security" (1994) E.L. Rev. 123–145.

[262] Art. 2(4) of Directive 76/207, n.62, *supra*. This applied where, in order to tackle the under-representation of women, a ministry reserved nursery places in principle for women employees: ECJ, Case C–476/99 *Lommers* [2002] E.C.R. I–2891, paras 31–50. This was not the case, however, where a measure entitled female employees with children alone to a service credit for the purpose of calculating their pensions: ECJ, Case C–366/99 *Griesmar* [2001] E.C.R. I–9383, paras 62–67 (the measure was in breach of the principle of equal pay and consequently discriminated against men).

female candidates—to tilt the balance in favour of some male candidates.[263] Article 141(4) of the EC Treaty provides, with a view to ensuring full equality in practice between men and women in working life, that the principle of equal treatment shall not prevent any Member State from maintaining or adopting measures providing for specific advantages in order to make it easier for the underrepresented sex to pursue a vocational activity or to prevent or compensate for disadvantages in professional careers.

The EU Constitution reproduces the wording of Arts 3(2) and 141 of the EC Treaty and of Art. 23 of the Charter of Fundamental Rights.[264]

c. Other prohibited forms of discrimination

5–064 **Forbidden grounds.** Under Art. 13 of the EC Treaty (introduced by the Amsterdam Treaty), the Council, acting unanimously on a proposal from the Commission and after consulting the European Parliament, is to take appropriate action within the limits of the powers conferred upon the Community by the EC Treaty to combat discrimination based on sex, racial or ethnic origin, religion or belief, disability, age or sexual orientation. Accordingly, the Council has adopted directives prohibiting discrimination on the basis of racial or ethnic origin[265] and a general framework for

---

[263] ECJ, Case C–409/95 *Marschall* [1997] E.C.R. I–6363, paras 21–35, with a case note by Brems (1998) Col.J.E.L. 668–675; ECJ, Case C–158/97 *Badeck* [2000] E.C.R. I–1875, paras 13–67; ECJ, Case C–407/98 *Abrahamsson* [2000] E.C.R. I–5539, paras 39–65; EFTA Court, Case E–1/02 *EFTA Surveillance Authority v Norway*, (2003) Reports of the EFTA Court 1, with a note by Tobler (2004) C.M.L.R. 245–260. In *Marschall*, the Court qualified an earlier judgment according to which rules giving priority to equally-qualified female candidates for promotion or employment in sectors of public employment where they were underrepresented were precluded by Directive 76/207: ECJ, Case C–450/93 *Kalanke* [1995] E.C.R. I–3051, paras 15–24. That judgment came in for severe criticism, see Brems (1995/96) Col.J.E.L. 172–179; Loenen and Veldman (1995) N.J.B. 1521–1527; De Schutter and Renauld (1996) J.T.T. 125–129; Moore (1996) E.L.Rev. 156–161; Charpentier (1996) R.T.D.E. 281–303; Prechal (1996) C.M.L.R. 1245–1259. See also Caruso, "Limits of the Classic Method: Positive Action in the European Union After the New Equality Directives" (2003) Harv.I.L.J. 331–386; Hauquet, "L'action positive, instrument de l'égalité des chances entre hommes et femmes" (2001) R.T.D.E. 305–333; Suhr, "Grenzen der Gleichbehandlung: Zur Vereinbarkeit von Frauenquoten mit dem Gemeinschaftsrecht" (1998) Eu.GR.Z. 121–128; Barnard, "The Principle of Equality in the Community Context: *P., Grant, Kalanke* and *Marschall*: Four Uneasy Bedfellows?" (1998) Cambridge L.J. 352–373.

[264] EU Constitution, Arts III–2, III–116 and III–214 and Art. II–83, respectively.

[265] Council Directive 2000/43/EC of June 29, 2000 implementing the principle of equal treatment between persons irrespective of racial or ethnic origin, [2000] O.J. L180/22. See Jones, "The Race Directive: Redefining Protection from Discrimination in EU Law" (2003) E.H.R.L.R. 515–526; Bell, "Beyond European Labour Law? Reflections on the EU Racial Equality Directive" (2002) E.L.J. 384–399; Mahlmann, "Gleichheitsschutz und Privatautonomie—Probleme und Perspektiven der Umsetzung der Richtline 2000/43/EG gegen Diskriminierungen aufgrund von Rasse und etnischer Herkunft" (2002) Z.Eu.S. 407–425; Nickel, "Handlungsaufträge zur Bekämpfung von ethnischen Diskriminierungen in der neuen Gleichbehandlungsrichtlinie 2000/43/EC" (2001) N.J.W. 2668–2672; Sewandono, "De Rassenrichtlijn en de Algemene Wet gelijke behandeling" (2001) S.E.W.

combating discrimination on the grounds of religion or belief, disability, age or sexual orientation as regards employment and occupation.[266] The Treaty of Nice made it possible for the European Parliament and the Council to adopt, under the co-decision procedure, incentive measures, excluding any harmonisation of the laws and regulations of the Member States, to support action taken by the Member States (EC Treaty, Art. 13(2)).[267] The EU Constitution confirms these powers of the Union, but also introduces the requirement that the Council is to adopt measures to combat discrimination only after obtaining the consent of the European Parliament (Art. III–124(1)).

Where a person suffers discrimination outside that context on the basis of the specified (or other) criteria, he or she can bring an action on the basis of the general principle of equal treatment.[268] This remains the case

218–226; Rodrigues, "De richtlijn tegen rassendiscriminatie bezien vanuit polderperspectief" (2000) N.T.E.R. 279–284. For the origins of the directive, see Tyson, "The Negotiation of the European Community Directive on Racial Discrimination" (2001) E.J.M.L. 199–229. Pursuant to Arts 213 and 235 [now Arts 284 and 308] of the EC Treaty, the European Monitoring Centre on Racism and Xenophobia was set up in Vienna (para. 10–110, *infra*). See also the first para. of Art. 29 of the EU Treaty (on PJCC) and Joint Action 96/443/JHA of July 15, 1996 adopted by the Council on the basis of the former Art. K.3 of the Treaty on European Union, concerning action to combat racism and xenophobia, [1996] O.J. L185/5. See Rosenberg, "La lutte contre le racisme et la xénophobie dans l'Union européenne" (1999) R.T.D.E. 201–238; Espósito, "The European Union Response Towards Racism" (2000) R.A.E. 118–127. See also Bell, "Mainstreaming Equality Norms into European Union Asylum law" (2001) E.L.Rev. 20–34.

[266] Council Directive 2000/78/EC of November 27, 2000 establishing a general framework for equal treatment in employment and occupation, [2000] O.J. L303/16. See also Council Decision 2000/750/EC of November 27, 2000 establishing a Community action programme to combat discrimination (2001 to 2006), [2000] O.J. L303/23; Council Decision 2001/51/EC of December 20, 2000 establishing a Programme relating to the Community framework strategy on gender equality (2001–2005), [2001] O.J. L17/22. For general considerations, see Waddington and Bell, "More Equal than Others: Distinguishing European Union Equality Directives" (2001) C.M.L.R. 587–611; Goldschmidt, "De hete adem van Europa. Implementatie van nieuw gelijke behandelingsrecht in Nederland" (2001) N.J.B. 983–990; Bayart, "De opmars van het discriminatierecht in de arbeidsverhoudingen" (2002) J.T.T. 309–329; Dollat, "Vers la reconnaissance généralisée du principe de l'égalité de traitement entre les personnes dans l'Union européenne" (2002) J.T.D.E. 57–64; see also Flynn, "The Implications of Art. 13 EC—After Amsterdam, Will Some Forms of Discrimination Be More Equal Than Others?" (1999) C.M.L.R. 1127–1152; Bell and Waddington, "Reflecting on inequalities in European equality law" (2003) E.L.Rev. 349–369. For Community competence with regard to the integration of persons with disabilities, see Sarapas, "Les droits des personnes handicappées dans le domaine des transports européens" (2000) R.M.C.U.E. 395–406. See also Council Decision 2001/903/EC of December 3, 2001 on the European Year of People with Disabilities 2003 ([2001] O.J. L335/15).

[267] See the Community action programme to promote organisations active at European level in the field of equality between men and women, established by Decision 848/2004/EC of the European Parliament and of the Council of April 29, 2004, [2004] O.J. L157 (republished with corrigendum: [2004] O.J. L195/7).

[268] See Lenaerts, "Le respect des droits fondementaux en tant que principe constitutionnel de l'Union européenne", in *Mélanges Michel Waelbroeck* (Bruylant, Brussels, 1999), I, 423–457. See also Art. 21(1) of the Charter of Fundamental Rights of the European Union, which, in addition to the grounds for discrimination mentioned in Art. 13 of the EC Treaty, prohibits discrimination on grounds of colour, social origin, genetic features, language, political or any other opinion, membership of a national minority, property and birth.

under the EU Constitution, which adds only that the Union shall itself aim to combat discrimination on the grounds specified (Art. III–118).[269] So far, the Community Courts did not regard unequal treatment of married couples and homosexual couples as prohibited discrimination.[270] According to the most recent Staff Regulations, Community officials in a non-marital relationship recognised by a Member State as a stable partnership who do not have legal access to marriage should be granted the same range of benefits as married couples.[271] Likewise, recent Community legislation on the right of citizens of the Union and their family members to move and reside freely within the territory of the Member States includes among the "family member" of a citizen the registered partner if the legislation of the host Member State treats registered partnership as equivalent to marriage.[272] It is also contrary to the principle of equal treatment for the Community institutions to make the grant of an allowance for an official's children who have lost their other parent dependent upon the condition that the official was married to that other parent.[273]

---

[269] In addition, Art. I–45 of the EU Constitution proclaims the general principle of the equality of citizens of the Union before the Union's institutions, bodies, offices and agencies (principle of democratic equality).

[270] The Courts referred to the legislator's power to make societal choices connected with the assessment of such discrimination: ECJ, Case C–249/96 *Grant* [1998] E.C.R. I–621, para. 48 (n.256, *supra*); CFI, Case T–264/97 *D. v Council* [1999] E.C.R.-S.C. II–1, para. 32. The Court of Justice did not consider that the situation of a married official was comparable to the same-sex partnerships recognised by some Member States: ECJ, Joined Cases C–122/99 P and C–125/99 P *D. v Council* [2001] E.C.R. I–4319, paras 47–52; for a critical view, see Berthou and Masselot, "Le mariage, les partenariats et la CJCE: ménage à trois" (2000) C.D.E. 679–694. For earlier articles, see Weyembergh, "Les droits des homosexuels devant le juge communautaire" (1998) J.T.D.E. 110–113; Guiguet, "Le droit communautaire et la reconnaissance des partnenaires de même sexe" (1999) C.D.E. 537–567; Jessurun d'Oliveira, "Vrijheid van verkeer voor geregisteerde partners in de Europese Unie" (2001) N.J.B. 205–210.

[271] Council Regulation (EC, Euratom) No. 723/2004 amending the Staff Regulations of officials of the European Communities and the Conditions of Employment of other servants of the European Communities ([2004] O.J. L124/1) makes certain benefits formerly granted only to married couples available to an official who is registered as a stable non-marital partner, provided that the couple produces a legal document recognised as such by a Member State, or any competent authority of a Member State, acknowledging their status as non-marital partners, neither partner is in a marital relationship or in another non-marital partnership, the partners are not related in specified ways and the couple has no access to legal marriage in a Member State (Art. 1d(1) and Annex VII, Art. 1(2)(c)). For previous treatment of such a partnership in the same way as marriage, see the Commission's answers of October 15, 2001 to question P-2438/01 (Buitenweg), [2002] O.J. C93E/131, and of March 12, 2002 to question E-3261/01 (Swiebel), [2003] O.J. C28E/2, and Jessurun d'Oliveira, "De Europese Commissie erkent het Nederlands huwelijk" (2001) N.J.B. 2035–2040. *Cf.* the refusal to accord equal treatment in the Council's answer of December 17, 2001 to question E–1830/01 (Van der Laan), [2002] O.J. C115E/16.

[272] Directive 2004/38 on the right of the citizen of the Union and their family members to move and reside freely within the territory of the Member States, [2004] O.J. L158/77 (on that Directive, paras 5–127 and 12–009).

[273] CFI (judgment of January 30, 2003), Case I–307/00 *C. v Commission*, not yet reported, paras 48–56.

2. Content

a. Substantive discrimination

Definition. In Community law, the prohibition of discrimination does not **5–065** only require equal treatment formally to be complied with, but also that no inequality is caused in practice. Where that occurs, there is substantive discrimination. According to the Court of Justice, it is specifically prohibited to treat "either similar situations differently or different situations identically".[274] In order to categorise cases as "similar" or "different", they must be considered in the light of the aims of the measure in question. Substantive discrimination will be tolerated only if the difference in treatment (or, conversely, the absence of differential treatment in the presence of differing cases) is justified.[275] In order for this to be so, the "unequal" treatment must be proportionate to the objective sought by the authority.[276] Often, the reason given in justification is considered together with the question whether the cases in question are similar or different.[277]

b. Direct and indirect discrimination

Definition. Discrimination is direct where a measure employs a prohibited **5–066** distinguishing criterion (*e.g.* nationality) or subjects different cases to formally similar rules.

Indirect discrimination arises where, although not making use of an unlawful distinguishing criterion, a provision has effects coinciding with or approaching those of such a distinguishing criterion as a result of its use of other distinguishing criteria which are not as such prohibited.[278] Accordingly, the Court of Justice has held that "[t]he rules regarding

---

[274] ECJ, Case 13/63 *Italy v Commission* [1963] E.C.R. 165; see also ECJ, Case 8/82 *Wagner v Balm* [1983] E.C.R. 371, para. 18. For instances in which dissimilar situations required differing measures, see ECJ, Case 230/78 *Eridania* [1979] E.C.R. 2749, paras 18–19, at 2767–2768; CFI, Case T–47/91 *Auzat v Commission* [1992] E.C.R. II–2535 and Case T–75/91 *Scaramuzza v Commission* [1992] E.C.R. II–2557.

[275] ECJ, Joined Cases 117/76 and 16/77 *Ruckdeschel* [1977] E.C.R. 1753, para. 7. For a case in which unequal treatment arising out of uniform rules (establishment of a common organisation of the market in bananas) laid down for differing situations was justified by the aim of integrating the national markets, see ECJ, Case C–280/93 *Germany v Council* [1994] E.C.R. I–4973, para. 74; this judgment was criticised in Everling, "Will Europe Slip on Bananas? The Banana Judgment of the Court of Justice and National Courts" (1996) C.M.L.R. 401, at 415–416. For unequal treatment which is justified on grounds of environment protection, see para. 5–111.

[276] For different treatment which was objectively justified but not proportional, see ECJ, Case C–29/95 *Pastoors and Trans-Cap* [1997] E.C.R. I–285, paras 19–26.

[277] See, *e.g.* ECJ, Case 35/80 *Denkavit Nederland* [1981] E.C.R. 45, paras 16–17. Accordingly, it is possible to find that the principle of equality has been infringed where a difference in treatment does not have regard to the principle of proportionality: see ECJ, Case C–323/95 *Hayes* [1997] E.C.R. I–1711, paras 24–25.

[278] For a general discussion, see Garronne, "La discrimination indirecte en droit communautaire: vers une théorie générale" (1994) R.T.D.E. 425–449.

equality of treatment, both in the Treaty and in Article 7 of Regulation No. 1612/68, forbid not only overt discrimination by reason of nationality but also all covert forms of discrimination which, by the application of other criteria of differentiation, lead in fact to the same result".[279] Thus, for instance, the criterion of residence may in fact produce the same result as discrimination on grounds of nationality.[280] A measure will also be indirectly discriminatory where it distinguishes only formally between different cases, but in reality treats them the same.

5–067 Indirect discrimination. The Court of Justice has repeatedly had to consider cases of indirect sex discrimination, particularly when interpreting the "principle of equal pay for male and female workers for equal work or work of equal value" enshrined in Art. 141 of the EC Treaty.[281] Thus, the question arose whether a difference in the level of pay for work carried out part time and the same work carried out full time was capable of constituting discrimination where the category of part-time workers was exclusively or predominantly comprised of women. The Court of Justice held that different treatment was acceptable "in so far as the difference in pay between part-time work and full-time work is attributable to factors which are objectively justified and are in no way related to any discrimination based on sex".[282] It is for the national court, which has jurisdiction to make findings of fact and interpret the national legislation, to determine whether a pay policy of a given employer or a statutory provision which in fact affects women more than men can be objectively justified. The measures chosen in the policy or provision must correspond to a real need on the part of the undertaking or a necessary aim of a national social policy and be in proportion to the objective pursued (that is to say, appropriate and indispensable in order to attain that objective).[283] Also in other circumstances in which a national or a Community measure is couched in neutral terms but women are in fact disadvantaged, it must be examined whether the criterion employed is justified by objective factors independent of any discrimination on grounds of sex.[284]

---

[279] ECJ, Case 152/73 *Sotgiu* [1974] E.C.R. 153, para. 11. See also ECJ, Case 41/84 *Pinna* [1986] E.C.R. 1, para. 23; ECJ, Case 33/88 *Allué* [1989] E.C.R. 1591, paras 11–12.

[280] See, *e.g.* ECJ, Case C–29/95 *Pastoors and Trans-Cap* [1997] E.C.R. I–285, paras 17–18.

[281] See also para. 5–063. For this and other instances of indirect discrimination, see, *e.g.* Hervey, "Justification for Indirect Sex Discrimination in Employment: European Community and UK Law Compared" (1990) I.C.L.Q. 807–826; Adinolfi, "Indirect Discrimination on Grounds of Sex in Collective Labour Agreements" (1992) C.M.L.R. 637–645; Prechal, "Combating Indirect Discrimination in Community Law Context" (1993) L.I.E.I. 81–97.

[282] ECJ, Case 96/80 *Jenkins* [1981] E.C.R. 911, paras 11–12.

[283] See, by way of example, ECJ, Case 170/84 *Bilka* [1986] E.C.R. 1607, para. 36 (wages policy of an employer); ECJ, Case 171/88 *Rinner Kühn* [1989] E.C.R. 2743, paras 14–15 (national provision). The Court of Justice held that there was a justified national social policy objective in Case C–229/89 *Commission v Belgium* [1991] E.C.R. I–2205, paras 19–26. For the temporal effects of Art. 141 of the EC Treaty, see para. 17–049, *infra*.

[284] ECJ (judgment of September 9, 2003), Case C–25/02 *Rinke*, not yet reported, paras 36–42.

c. Reverse discrimination

Internal situations. The Community prohibition of discrimination cannot **5-068** be applied to purely internal matters of a Member State which have no connection with a situation to which Community law applies. Accordingly, a national of a Member State may in principle rely on the provisions relating to the free movement of goods, persons, services and capital only in so far as he or she is not in a purely internal situation.[285] In such a situation, a Member State may adopt measures which treat its own nationals less favourably than nationals of other Member States. So a Member State may obviously treat its nationals differently from nationals of other Member States where it enacts legislation for vessels flying the national flag outside its territorial waters, since, under the rules of public international law, it may exercise its jurisdiction beyond territorial sea limits only over vessels flying its flag.[286] In a purely domestic situation falling outside the field of application of Community law, a Member State is also not debarred under that law from exercising "reverse discrimination" by treating its own subjects or national situations less favourably than nationals of other Member States or situations stemming from other Member States.[287] Any discrimination which this would cause must then be dealt with within the framework of the internal legal system of the State in question.[288]

Free movement. Such "reverse discrimination" is prohibited by Community **5-069** law where it threatens the aims of the Treaty. This will be the case in practice where a situation cannot be regarded as purely internal from the point of view of the Member State concerned. Thus, the fundamental freedoms relating to establishment and the provision of services do not admit of interpretation:

> "so as to exclude from the benefit of Community law a given Member State's own nationals when the latter, owing to the fact that they have lawfully resided on the territory of another Member State and have there acquired a trade qualification which is recognised by provisions of Community law, are, with regard to their State of origin, in a situation

---

[285] cf. the stricter requirement for a transborder situation for the application of the provisions on free movement of persons and services (see paras 5-125 and 5-171, *infra*) with the relatively ready acceptance of a transborder factor in applying the provisions on free movement of goods (see paras 5-088 and 5-100).

[286] ECJ, Case C-379/92 *Peralta* [1994] E.C.R. I-3453, para. 47.

[287] *ibid.*, para. 27; ECJ, Case C-132/93 *Steen* [1994] E.C.R. I-2715, paras 8-11. See also, Nicolaysen, "Inländerdiskriminierung im Warenverkehr" (1991) EuR. 95-120; Münnich, "Art. 7 und Inländerdiskriminierung" (1992) Z.f.R.V. 92-100; Weyer, "Freier Warenverkehr, rein innerstaatliche Sachverhalte und umgekehrte Diskriminierung" (1998) EuR. 435-461.

[288] ECJ, Joined Cases C-45/96 and C-46/96 *Uecker and Jacquet* [1997] E.C.R. I-3171, para. 23 (which makes it clear that the introduction of citizenship of the Union makes no difference to this position). See also König, "Das Problem der Inländerdiskriminierung—Abschied von Reinheitsgebot, Nachtbackverbot und Meisterprüfung?" (1993) A.ö.R. 591-616.

which may be assimilated to that of any other persons enjoying the rights and liberties guaranteed by the Treaty".[289]

When the Dutchman Knoors applied to the Netherlands authorities for an authorisation to carry on the trade of a plumber in his own country on the ground of the skills which he had acquired in Belgium, the Netherlands had to recognise those skills pursuant to Directive 64/427 relating to attainment of freedom of establishment and freedom to provide services.[290] There is no question of there being a purely internal situation where a national holds a professional diploma issued in another Member State, not even if the diploma is not actually recognised by a provision of Community law.[291] This also applies to nationals wishing to use a diploma which does not afford access to employment or self-employment, but nevertheless affords advantages for the exercise of a profession.[292] According to the Court of Justice, there is no question of there being an internal situation where a national can rely on a right to free movement against his own Member State.[293] EU nationals, as citizens of the Union, may not be disadvantaged simply because they have exercised their right to free movement, for example by studying in or moving to another Member State.[294] As a result of the increasing range of circumstances in which persons may derive rights from Community law with regard to the Member State of which they are nationals,[295] it will become more difficult for Member States to apply reverse discrimination.[296]

5–070 Circumvention. However, Community law does not allow of a person using free movement in order to evade the legislation of his Member State. A Member State may have a legitimate interest in preventing its nationals from wrongly evading the application of national legislation as regards training for a trade[297] or the manner of exercise of an activity, by means of facilities created under the Treaty.[298]

---

[289] ECJ, Case 115/78 *Knoors* [1979] E.C.R. 399, para. 24. See also para. 5–125, *infra*.

[290] For Directive 64/427, see n.622 to para. 5–145, *infra*.

[291] ECJ, Case C–61/89 *Bouchoucha* [1990] E.C.R. I–3551, paras 11 and 14.

[292] See, for the use of an LLM degree, ECJ, Case C–19/92 *Kraus* [1993] E.C.R. I–1663, paras 17–18.

[293] ECJ, Case C–378/97 *Wijsenbeek* [1999] E.C.R. I–6207, paras 18–23.

[294] ECJ, Case C–224/98 *D'Hoop* [2002] E.C.R. I–6191, paras 27–35; ECJ (judgment of April 29, 2004), Case C–224/02 *Antero Pusa*, not yet reported, para. 17. See Staples, "Heeft omgekeerde discriminatie zijn langste tijd gehad?" (2002) N.T.E.R. 205–209.

[295] See, with regard to the free movement of workers, ECJ, Case C–281/98 *Angonese* [2000] E.C.R. I–4139 (discussed in para. 5–125, *supra*).

[296] See De Beys, "Le droit européen est-il applicable aux situations purement internes? A propos des discriminations à rebours dans le marché unique" (2001) J.T.D.E. 137–144; Papadopoulou, "Situations purement internes et droit communautaire: un instrument jurisprudentiel à double fonction ou une arme à double tranchant?" (2002) C.D.E. 95–129.

[297] ECJ, Case 115/78 *Knoors* [1979] E.C.R. 399, para. 25. That was the case in ECJ, Case C–61/89 *Bouchoucha* [1990] E.C.R. I–3551.

[298] ECJ, Case C–148/91 *Veronica Omroep Organisatie* [1993] E.C.R. I–487, paras 12–14; ECJ, Case C–23/93 *TV10* [1994] E.C.R. I–4795, paras 17–22, with a case note by Straetmans and Goemans (1995) Col.J.E.L. 319–331; ECJ, Case C–212/97 *Centros* [1999] E.C.R. I–1459, paras 23–30.

II. The Common/Internal Market

A. Establishment of a Common/Internal Market

Common market. The establishment of a common market continues to be **5–071** the Community's most important task. Although the Treaty does not define the expression "common market", a number of provisions make reference to it. Thus, the common market is mentioned as having to be progressively established during a specific transitional period,[299] after which its operation and development is to be maintained.[300] To that end, all practices impeding the establishment of the common market are to be eliminated as far as possible[301] and the Community may intervene to assist where necessary.[302] The expression "common market" also helps to define the (geographical) scope of the Community rules.[303] The scope of the common market may be inferred from the list of tasks set out in Art. 3 of the EC Treaty and the provisions contained in Part Three of the EC Treaty. Problems in achieving the common market have led to the introduction of the concept of the "internal market" to supplement that of the common market (EC Treaty, Art. 14). The EU Constitution will replace the expression "common market" by "internal market" throughout.

1. Scope of the common market

Elimination of obstacles to trade. The establishment of the common **5–072** market includes first the elimination, as between Member States, of customs duties and quantitative restrictions on the import and export of goods, and of all other measures having equivalent effect (Art. 3(1)(a))[304] and, more generally, obstacles to the free movement of goods, persons, services and capital (Art. 3(1)(c), which refers in that connection to "an internal market"). The Court of Justice has described the common market as involving "the elimination of all obstacles to intra-Community trade in order to merge the national markets into a single market bringing about conditions as close as possible to those of a genuine internal market".[305] The Treaty breaks down the establishment of the common market into the free movement of goods (Part Three, Title I) and the free movement of

---

[299] See EC Treaty, Art. 32 (2) and Art. 71(2).

[300] See EC Treaty, Art. 3(1)(h); Art. 32(1) and (4); Art. 88(1); Art. 119(1), first subpara.; Art. 120(1); Art. 136, third para.; Art. 211; Art. 267; Art. 297 and Art. 308.

[301] See EC Treaty, Art. 15, second para.; Art. 81(1); Art. 82, first para.; Art. 87(1), (2) and (3); Art. 88(2) and (3) and Art. 134, third para.

[302] See EC Treaty, Art. 94 and Art. 308.

[303] See EC Treaty, Art. 81(1); Art. 82, first para.; Art. 84; Art. 96, first para.; Art. 296(1)(b) and Art. 298, first para.

[304] As a result of the simplification introduced by the Treaty of Amsterdam, Art. 3(1)(a) of the EC Treaty no longer refers to the "elimination" but to the "prohibition" of customs duties, quantitative restrictions and measures having equivalent effect.

[305] ECJ, Case 15/81 *Schul* [1982] E.C.R. 1409, para. 33.

persons, services and capital (Part Three, Title III). The intention of the relevant provisions is that every market participant should be able to deploy his or her labour and capital, sell or buy goods and perform or receive services across the Community's "internal" frontiers without being impeded by national rules maintaining or reintroducing frontiers by means of trade restrictions. As a result, all discrimination on grounds of nationality is also prohibited within the field of application of the Treaty (EC Treaty, Art. 12).[306]

Free movement of goods, together with the abolition of customs duties as between the Member States, led to the introduction of a common customs tariff for goods coming from non-member countries. From the outset, the resulting customs union was set within the framework of a common commercial policy (Art. 3(1)(b); see Title IX of Part Three of the EC Treaty). Free movement of persons has not directly given rise to any common policy on persons from non-Community countries wishing to enter the territory of the Member States. It was not until the Amsterdam Treaty that the Community was empowered to adopt "measures concerning the entry and movement of persons" (EC Treaty, Art. 3(1)(d); see Title IV of the EC Treaty).

5–073 **Positive integration.** In the agricultural and transport sectors the common market could not be attained by abolishing all national restrictions on trade between Member States. In all the Member States, government had taken those sectors outside the mechanism of the free market, *inter alia*, through guaranteed prices for agricultural products, investment in transport infrastructure and State operation of means of transport. Since the rules on the free movement of goods and services could not be declared to be applicable in full to those sectors, the market could be unified only by bringing national policies into alignment. As a result, the Treaty provides for a common policy in the sphere of agriculture and fisheries (Art. 3(1)(e)) and a common policy in the sphere of transport (Art. 3(1)(f)). After the title on free movement of goods, the Treaty embodies a title on "agriculture" (Title II of Part Three) and, after the title on free movement of persons, services and capital, a title on "transport" (Title V of Part Three). It is clear from this that the establishment of the common market does not constitute a purely negative form of integration, *i.e.* the enforcement of prohibitory provisions. It also requires the Community institutions to fulfil their Treaty obligations to act.[307]

5–074 **Free competition.** A third component of the common market is constituted by the rules ensuring that competition is not distorted (Art. 3(1)(g)).[308] A common market in which internal frontiers no longer impeded free trade

---

[306] See para. 5–059 *et seq.*
[307] For the Council's obligations with regard to the common transport policy, see ECJ, Case 13/83 *European Parliament v Council* [1985] E.C.R. 1513, para. 53 and paras 64–71 (see para. 5–194, *infra*).
[308] ECJ, Case 32/65 *Italy v Council and Commission* [1966] E.C.R. 389, at 405.

would not remain intact if the internal frontiers were to be retained or reintroduced by the action of undertakings or Member States. That might arise where an undertaking had a dominant position on a particular market, where undertakings formed cartels or where a Member State itself operated an undertaking or granted aid to its own undertakings. In order to obviate distortions of competition, Title VI of Part Three contains provisions applying to undertakings (EC Treaty, Arts 81–85) and provisions relating to public involvement in industry (EC Treaty, Art. 86) and State aid to undertakings (EC Treaty, Arts 87, 88 and 89).

Approximation of legislation. Lastly, the Treaty foresaw that the common **5–075** market could not be attained merely by prohibiting trade restrictions, discrimination and distortions of competition. The unequal position of traders in the market is often ascribable to differences in national legislative or administrative provisions that are not as such incompatible with the provisions of the Treaty. Consequently, action by the Community includes the general task of positive integration (alongside the common agricultural and transport policies), which consists in approximating the laws of the Member States to the extent required for the functioning of the common market (Art. 3(1)(h), which is enlarged upon in Title VI of Part Three, that is to say, Arts 93–97 of the EC Treaty). It is also possible for the Member States to conclude supplementary treaties (EC Treaty, Art. 293) and for the Community to take supplementary action (EC Treaty, Art. 308).

2. From common market to internal market

Transitional period. According to Art. 8 of the EEC Treaty, the common **5–076** market was to be established over a transitional period of 12 years. That period could be extended in certain circumstances to a maximum of 15 years. The Council decided that the first of the three transitional stages had been completed on December 31, 1961.[309] The second and third stages ended automatically, with the result that the transitional period was over on December 31, 1969. Economic growth during the Community's early years produced even quicker results: by means of the so-called "acceleration decisions" of May 12, 1960 and May 15, 1962, the Member States introduced the customs union earlier than had been anticipated.[310] By Council Decision of July 26, 1966, the customs union for industrial products was brought into being with effect from July 1, 1968, one and a half years

---

[309] Council Decision of January 14, 1962 concerning the transition to the second stage of the transitional period, J.O. 164/62.

[310] Decision of May 12, 1960 of the representatives of the Member States of the European Economic Community meeting within the Council on quickening the pace for achieving the objectives of the Treaty, J.O. 1217/60; Decision of May 15, 1962 of the representatives of the Member States of the European Economic Community meeting within the Council on quickening the pace for achieving the objectives of the Treaty, J.O. 1284/62.

before the expiry of the transitional period laid down by Art. 14 of the EEC Treaty.[311]

Nevertheless the Community did not succeed in achieving the common market in all its component parts before the end of the transitional period. Technical complications and political sensitivities stood in the way of adopting measures to secure the right of establishment and liberalise capital movements. The accession of new Member States, budgetary disagreements and economic recession produced *euro-sclerosis*, bringing the achievement of the common market to a standstill. Admittedly, the Court of Justice had given a broad interpretation to the provisions on free movement, but residual disparities between national legislation could be harmonised only in so far as they directly affected the establishment or functioning of the common market, and this required a unanimous vote in the Council (EEC Treaty, Art. 100).

5–077 **White Paper.** At the European Council held in Copenhagen in December 1982, the Commission succeeded in persuading the Heads of State or Government that work had to be carried out on "priority measures . . . to reinforce the internal market".[312] At the European Council's request, the Commission adopted in June 1985 the White Paper entitled *Completing the internal market*, setting out an extensive programme with a view to eliminating all the remaining barriers.[313] The White Paper classed the barriers in three categories: physical, technical and fiscal. The physical barriers encompassed frontier checks, which existed principally because of technical and fiscal differences as between Member States. According to the White Paper, if those differences disappeared any frontier check would become superfluous, provided that ancillary measures were taken for the security of citizens, immigration and the control of drugs. Technical barriers were the result of the differing requirements to which Member States subjected products and services with a view to protecting, for instance, safety, health or the environment. Rather than harmonising these requirements, the Commission proposed fostering the equivalence and mutual recognition of national legislation. The Commission regarded the abolition of fiscal barriers as an important part of the internal market, but recognised that abolition was a controversial question. Consequently, the White Paper confined itself to proposing that efforts should be made towards mutual adjustment of national legislation. The White Paper

---

[311] Council Decision 66/532/EEC of July 26, 1966 concerning the abolition of customs duties and the prohibition of quantitative restrictions as between Member States and the application of the common customs tariff duties to products not mentioned in Annex II [now Annex I] to the Treaty, J.O. 2971/66.

[312] (1982) 12 EC Bull. point 1.2.3.

[313] Commission of the European Communities, *Completing the Internal Market: White Paper from the Commission to the European Council (Milan, 28–29 June, 1985)*, June 14, 1985, COM (85) 310 final. The Milan European Council broadly welcomed the White Paper (1985) 6 EC Bull. point 1.2.5.

announced some 300 measures (later reduced to 279 but expanded again in 1990 to 282 measures) to be adopted in accordance with a detailed timetable by no later than 1992 in order to abolish the barriers in question.

Objective 1992. The Single European Act added Arts 8a, 8b and 8c to the **5–078** EEC Treaty, which committed the Community to adopting measures "with the aim of progressively establishing the internal market over a period expiring on 31 December, 1992".[314] In the present version of the EC Treaty, Art. 14(2) defines the "internal market" as "an area without internal frontiers in which the free movement of goods, persons, services and capital is ensured in accordance with the provisions of this Treaty". Article 14(1) refers to potential legal bases for the measures listed in the White Paper.[315] Above all, Art. 95 [formerly Art. 100a](1) of the EC Treaty is important in this regard. It empowers the Council to adopt by a qualified majority measures for the "approximation of the provisions laid down by law, regulation or administrative action in Member States which have as their object the establishment and functioning of the internal market" (see paras 5–209—5–210).[316] The introduction of this legal basis went hand in hand with a new approach to harmonisation policy (see para. 5–212). The attainment of the internal market also included a drive for better knowledge of the activities of the Community and of Community law.[317]

Scope of internal market. The "internal market" concentrates on **5–079** abolishing, as between Member States, obstacles to the free movement of goods, persons, services and capital (EC Treaty, Art. 3(1)(c)) and thus has a more limited scope than the common market. The White Paper which launched the internal market does not cover competition, agricultural or transport policy. Accordingly, the harmonisation rules contemplated by Art. 95 of the EC Treaty constitute only part of the harmonisation of legislation entailed by the attainment of the common market (see EC Treaty, Art.

---

[314] As a result of the EU Treaty, Arts 8a–8c of the EEC Treaty became Arts 7a–7c of the EC Treaty; see now Art. 14(1) of the EC Treaty.

[315] The Community is to adopt measures "in accordance with the provisions of this Article and of Articles 15, 26, 47(2), 49, 80, 93 and 95 and without prejudice to the other provisions of this Treaty".

[316] The Single European Act made not only for more flexible decision-making but also for a greater role for the European Parliament by providing in Art. 100a(1) of the EEC Treaty for the (new) procedure of co-operation with the Parliament. The EU Treaty maintained this trend by replacing the procedure provided for in Art. 100a [now Article 95](1) of the EC Treaty by the new co-decision procedure. Article 95(2) of the EC Treaty does, however, preclude the application of Art. 95(1) to fiscal provisions, to those relating to the free movement of persons and to those relating to the rights and interests of employed persons.

[317] On the ground that effective application of Community law is essential for the proper functioning of the internal market, Art. 95 of the EC Treaty constituted the legal basis for, *inter alia*, Decision No. 1496/98/EC of the European Parliament and of the Council of June 22, 1998 establishing an action programme to improve awareness of Community law within the legal professions (Robert Schuman project), [1998] O.J. L196/24.

3(1)(h)). In fact, the internal market realises the core of the common market within the meaning of Art. 2 of the EC Treaty by means of a more flexible harmonisation procedure.[318]

5–080 Checks at internal borders. At the same time, the definition of the internal market as an "area without internal frontiers" shows that the intended result is more ambitious than the establishment of a "common market", which merely sets out to achieve "open" internal frontiers, but does not affect the relevance of those frontiers. In a 1976 judgment, the Court of Justice held that "[b]y creating the principle of freedom of movement for persons and by conferring on any person falling within its ambit the right of access to the territory of the Member States, for the purposes intended by the Treaties, Community law has not excluded the power of Member States to adopt measures enabling the national authorities to have an exact knowledge of population movements affecting their territory".[319] In contrast, the internal market "without internal frontiers" requires any formality imposed upon entry into the territory of a Member State from another Member State to be abolished.

From January 1, 1993 checks at internal borders in principle disappeared; only identity checks continued in being provisionally for movements of persons. Unlike in the case of movements of goods, the Commission deemed it appropriate to leave the formulation of measures enabling free movement of persons to take place largely to intergovernmental co-operation. Such co-operation had been set up by some Member States within the framework of the Schengen Convention (see para. 2–017). Despite the adoption of some Community measures in this field,[320] certain Member States denied that the Community was in general empowered to adopt the necessary measures of co-operation in the fields of police and judicial co-operation to accompany the complete liberalisation of

---

[318] For the relationship between the common market and the internal market, see Mortelmans, "The Common Market, the Internal Market and the Single Market, What's in a Market" (1998) C.M.L.R. 101–136. For the meaning of the term "internal market", see also Forwood and Clough, "The Single European Act and Free Movement—Legal Implications of the Provisions for the Completion of the Internal Market" (1986) E.L.Rev. 383–408; Steindorff, "Gemeinsamer Markt als Binnenmarkt" (1986) Z.H.R. 687–704; Pescatore, "Some Critical Remarks on the 'Single European Act'" (1987) C.M.L.R. 9–18; Ehlermann, "The Internal Market Following the Single European Act" (1987) C.M.L.R. 361–404; Dehousse and Demaret, "Marché unique, significations multiples" (1992) J.T. 137–141; Müller-Graff, "Die Verdichtung des Binnenmarktsrechts zwischen Handlungsfreiheiten und Sozialgestaltung" (2002) EuR. Beiheft 1, 7–73.

[319] ECJ, Case 118/75 *Watson and Belmann* [1976] E.C.R. 1185, para. 17.

[320] The Commission White Paper proposed that directives should be adopted to align national law on weapons and drugs and for the co-ordination of provisions relating to the status of nationals of non-member countries, the law relating to asylum, the status of refugees, national visa policy and extradition. Nevertheless, Community measures were adopted only on weapons and drugs.

movements of persons.[321] The EU Treaty did not settle the debate with regard to Community competence, but merely conferred express Community powers with regard to policy on visas.[322] Intergovernmental co-operation was not, however, successful in making, as of January 1, 1993,[323] identity checks at all internal frontiers[324] redundant. Article 14 of the EC Treaty does not embody any prohibition with direct effect which can be relied on against the imposition of frontier checks.[325] The Court of Justice made it clear that so long as the rules on the crossing of external borders have not been harmonised, the Member States retain in general the right to carry out identity checks at internal borders; it must be possible to establish the nationality even of nationals of Member States.[326] The expiry of the date of December 31, 1992 prescribed by Art. 14 of the EC Treaty therefore did not automatically entail an obligation for the Member States to abolish all identity checks at the internal borders.[327] The European Parliament sought to infer from Art. 14 an obligation on the Community to act and repeatedly urged the Commission to put forward proposals for Community rules.[328] In August 1995 the Commission submitted proposals for directives on various aspects of free movement of persons.[329] Ultimately,

---

[321] For this debate, see Plender, "Competence, European Community Law and Nationals of Non-Member States" (1990) I.C.L.Q. 559–610; Timmermans, "Free Movement of Persons and the Division of Powers Between the Community and its Member States", in Schermers, Flinterman, Kellermann, Van Haersolte and Van de Meent (eds), *Free Movement of Persons in Europe. Legal Problems and Experiences* (Martinus Nijhoff, Dordrecht, 1993), 352–368; O'Keeffe, "The Free Movement of Persons and the Single Market" (1992) E.L.Rev. 3–19. For interesting reservations about the link made between migration and security, see Huysmans, "The European Union and the Securitisation of Migration" (2000) J.C.M.S. 751–777.

[322] EC Treaty, former Art. 100c; see para. 5–160, *infra*. Title VI of the EU Treaty also organised co-operation in the fields of justice and home affairs (JHA co-operation), including policy regarding nationals of third countries, albeit "without prejudice to the powers of the European Community" (former Art. K.1, first para., of the EU Treaty).

[323] See the delay in bringing the agreements which have been made into force, para. 2–016, *supra*.

[324] The Schengen Agreements did not enter into force as between all Member States, para. 2–017, *supra*.

[325] As regards the legal effects of Art. 14 of the EC Treaty, see Schermers, "The Effect of the Date 31 December, 1992" (1991) C.M.L.R. 275–289; Schockweiler, "Les conséquences de l'expiration du délai imparti pour l'établissement du marché intérieur" (1991) R.M.C.U.E. 882–886.

[326] ECJ, Case C–378/97 *Wijsenbeek* [1999] E.C.R. I–6207, paras 39–43. The Court added, however, that Member States may not prescribe a disproportionate penalty for failure to comply with the obligation to produce an identity document; *ibid.*, para. 44.

[327] *ibid.*, para. 40.

[328] The Commission elected to await the outcome of the intergovernmental initiatives, whereupon on November 18, 1993 the Parliament brought an action against the Commission (EC Treaty, Art. 232) for failure to act ([1994] O.J. C1/12). As a result of the submission of proposals for directives (see following n.), the proceedings were held to be no longer to any purpose: ECJ (order of July 11, 1996), Case C–445/93 *European Parliament v Commission*, unreported.

[329] For the proposals based on Art. 94 of the EC Treaty, see [1995] O.J. C289/16 and C306/5, and [1997] O.J. C139/6 and C140/21; for proposals based on Arts 40, 44(2) and 52(2) of the EC Treaty, see [1995] O.J. C307/18. See in this connection the editorial "Legislating Free Movement: An Over-ambitious Commission Package?" (1996) C.M.L.R. 1–5.

the Commission's proposals were not adopted, but the Intergovernmental Conference of 1996–1997 elected by means of the Amsterdam Treaty to take over the "Schengen *acquis*" as EU legislation.

The Treaty of Amsterdam brought the debate about competence to an end by empowering the Community to adopt measures "with a view to ensuring, in compliance with Article 14, the absence of any controls on persons, be they citizens of the Union or nationals of third countries, when crossing internal borders" (EC Treaty, Art. 62(1)). By means of the powers relating to visas, asylum, immigration and other measures in the field of free movement of persons set out in the new Title IV of the EC Treaty, the Community aims to maintain and develop "an area of freedom, security and justice" (Art. 61, reiterating the objective added by the Amsterdam Treaty to Art. 2, fourth indent, of the EU Treaty). The 1996–1997 Intergovernmental Conference succeeded in agreeing on this Community power by simultaneously confirming in a Protocol annexed to the EC Treaty and the EU Treaty the right of the United Kingdom and Ireland to carry out border controls on travellers.[330] Title IV of the EC Treaty empowers the Community to adopt flanking measures with respect to the abolition of border controls on persons and measures to achieve a Community policy at its external borders with regard to entry into and residence in the territory of the Union for third-country nationals (see para. 5–158). In this way, the achievements of the Schengen co-operation could be integrated into Community law; that part of the "Schengen *acquis*" which could not be so integrated has been incorporated as Union law in the context of police and judicial co-operation in criminal matters (PJCC, Title VI of the EU Treaty).[331] Under protocols annexed to the EC Treaty and the EU Treaty,[332] the Schengen *acquis* is not to apply to the United Kingdom and Ireland and those two countries, together with Denmark, will, in principle, not take part in further Community action under Title IV of the EC Treaty (see paras 5–165–5–166).

5–081 **Non-economic integration.** Furthermore, through the abolition of internal frontiers, the EC Treaty no longer seeks to attain merely an open market but an "area". The use of this term makes it clear that integration is not confined to economic factors of production, but extends to the whole of life in society. This political scope also warrants the reference to the expression "area without internal frontiers" as a means of achieving one of the

---

[330] Protocol (No. 3) annexed to the EU Treaty and the EC Treaty on the application of certain aspects of Art. 14 of the Treaty establishing the European Community to the UK and Ireland; para. 5–166, *infra*.

[331] See Protocol (No. 2) annexed to the EU Treaty and the EC Treaty integrating the Schengen *acquis* into the framework of the European Union; para. 5–164, *infra*.

[332] See Protocol (No. 4) annexed to the EU Treaty and the EC Treaty on the position of the UK and Ireland and Protocol (No. 5) annexed to the EU Treaty and the EC Treaty on the position of Denmark; paras 5–165—5–166, *infra*.

objectives of the Union (EU Treaty, Art. 2, first indent).[333] Following the extension of Community powers and the amendment of Title VI of the EU Treaty, the Amsterdam Treaty added the idea of the Union as "an area of freedom, security and justice" (EU Treaty, Art. 2, fourth indent).[334] According to the Court of Justice, EU nationals who are not economically active (or nationals of non-member countries) cannot derive a right of residence or a right to free movement from the articles on free movement.[335] However, the Council has introduced a general right of residence for all EU nationals on the basis of the power to attain the objective set out in Art. 14 of the EC Treaty.[336] As citizens of the Union, EU nationals may also assert the right to free movement enshrined in Art. 18 of the EC Treaty (see para. 12–009).

3. The internal market in the EU Constitution

Changes. The concept of the common market will disappear in the EU 5–082 Constitution. The EU Constitution simply preserves the concept of the internal market as "an area without internal frontiers in which the free movement of persons, services, goods and capital is ensured in accordance with the Constitution" (Art. III–130). In the chapter on the "Internal market", Part III of the EU Constitution covers not only the free movement of persons, services, goods and capital but also the rules on competition and the harmonisation clauses, whereas the provisions on agriculture, fisheries and transport are moved to the chapter on "Policies in other specific areas".[337] The provisions on border checks, asylum, immigration and other policies relating to the free movement of persons are brought together with the provisions on police and judicial co-operation in criminal matters in a single chapter on the "area of freedom, security and justice".[338]

B. THE TREATY PROVISIONS ON FREE MOVEMENT

Four freedoms. The foundations of the common market are the Treaty 5–083 provisions on the free movement of goods (Arts 23–31) and the free movement of persons, services and capital (Arts 39–60). The prohibition on

---

[333] Compare the definition of "internal market" in a restricted sense in Art. 3(1)(c) of the EC Treaty with the broader "area without internal frontiers" in the second para. of Art. 14 of the EC Treaty and in the first indent of Art. 2 of the EU Treaty.

[334] Labayle, "Le Traité d'Amsterdam. Un espace de liberté, de sécurité et de justice" (1997) R.T.D.E. 813, at 824–825.

[335] See ECJ, Case C–292/89 *Antonissen* [1991] E.C.R. I–745, paras 16 and 22 (para. 5–122, *infra*).

[336] Council Directive 90/364/EEC of June 28, 1990 on the right of residence, [1990] O.J. L180/26 (para. 5–128, *infra*).

[337] EU Constitution, Part III, Title III (Internal policies and action), Chapter I "Internal market" (Arts III–130 to III–176) and Chapter III "Policies in other specific areas" (Arts III–203 to III–256).

[338] EU Constitution, Part III, Title III, Chapter IV (Arts III–257—III–277).

Member States' discriminating against goods, persons (employees and self-employed persons), services and capital from other Member States is intended to secure the ability freely to deploy factors of production across frontiers. The Court of Justice also emphasises in its interpretation of the "four freedoms" the consumer's right freely to purchase goods and receive services in other Member States.[339] As far as goods are concerned, the rules on "free movement" encompass since the judgment in *Dassonville* (1974) not only the prohibition of discrimination but also a prohibition of other—even potential—barriers to free movement. The Court's case law has gradually extended that broad interpretation also to the rules on the supply of services and, subsequently, also to the rules on the movement of persons and capital.[340] At the same time, the Court has held, also in respect of the free movement of persons, services and capital, that a Member State may impose non-discriminatory restrictions on free movement only if they pursue an aim in the general interest and comply with the principle of proportionality. In other words, it has extended the *Cassis de Dijon* case law on free movement of goods to cover the other freedoms.[341] The provisions on the free movement of services which are provided across border without the provider or the recipient of the services moving are increasingly being interpreted in parallel with the provisions on free movement of goods.[342] As to the obligations flowing from the Treaty with regard to the treatment of providers of services from other Member States, they frequently match the obligations which apply in regard to employees or self-employed persons established from other Member States.[343] In order to promote free movement of goods and services, harmonisation is carried out of national provisions relating to the production and distribution of goods and services;

---

[339] paras 5–100 and 5–171, *infra*.

[340] *cf.* paras 5–009 (goods) and 5–134 (persons), 5–174 (services) and 5–181 (capital).

[341] *cf.* paras 5–107 *et seq.* (goods) and 5–143—5–144 (persons), 5–176—5–179 (services) and para. 5–185 (capital). For the convergence of the four freedoms, see Jarass, "Elemente einer Dogmatik der Grundfreiheiten II" (1995) EuR. 202–226 and (2000) EuR. 705–723; Bernard, "Fitting the remaining pieces into the goods and persons jigsaw?" (2001) E.L.Rev. 35–59. For the convergence of the four freedoms and competition law, see Mortelmans, "Towards Convergence in the Application of the Rules on Free Movement and on Competition?" (2001) C.M.L.R. 613–649; Steinberg, "Zur Konvergenz der Grundfreiheiten auf der Tatbestands- und Rechtfertigungsebene" (2002) Eu.GR.Z. 13–25; O'Loughlin, "EC Competition Rules and Free Movement Rules: An Examination of the Parallels and their Furtherance by the ECJ *Wouters* Decision" (2003) E.Comp.L.Rev. 62–69.

[342] For a joint application of trade in goods and trade in services, see ECJ, Case C–390/99 *Canal Satélite Digital* [2002] E.C.R. I–607, paras 39–41. If one of the freedoms is entirely secondary in relation to the other and may be considered together with it, the Court of Justice will in principle examine the national measure in question in relation to the latter freedom only: *ibid.*, para. 31.

[343] For the parallel treatment of two freedoms, see ECJ, Case C–439/99 *Commission v Italy* [2002] E.C.R. I–305, paras 35–41; ECJ, Case C–294/00 *Deutsche Paracelsus Schulen für Naturheilverfahren* [2002] E.C.R. I–6515, paras 38–52. To make the supply of services conditional upon the satisfaction of requirements which apply for establishment in a Member State is, however, a denial of the freedom to offer services in a Member State from an establishment in another Member State: para. 5–179, *infra*.

the free movement of persons is further assisted by the harmonisation and mutual recognition of diplomas and professional rules.[344]

As such, the Treaty provisions on free movement impose obligations only on Member States; however, as far as the free movement of persons and services is concerned, the Court of Justice has made it clear that the prohibition of discrimination also entails obligations for private groups or organisations which exercise a degree of authority over individuals.[345]

From the outset, the EC Treaty supplemented the provisions on the free movement of goods within the Community by the Community's competence to determine, by means of a uniform customs policy and a common commercial policy, the conditions on which goods from non-member countries can enter into circulation in the Community.[346] Recent Treaty amendments have also given the Community competence (alongside the competence retained by the Member States in the relevant areas) to lay down rules on the entry of persons into the Community and on the conditions on which services and capital from non-member countries can be deployed within the Community.[347]

The EU Constitution will not change to any significant degree the Treaty provisions on the free movement of persons, services, goods and capital, although it will rearrange those provisions in a new order. As noted above, the provisions on the status of third-country nationals will be moved to a new chapter on the area of freedom, security and justice (see para. 5–167).

1. Free movement of goods

Treaty rules. In principle, the realisation of free movement of goods **5–084** requires Member States to abolish all measures constituting a barrier to trade within the Community.[348] Abolition of restrictive national measures of a fiscal nature is the corollary of the establishment of a customs union, entailing prohibition of duties on imports and exports and any charges having equivalent effect in trade between Member States (EC Treaty, Art. 25; see paras 5–086–5–094) and the setting-up of the Common Customs Tariff *vis-à-vis* non-member countries (EC Treaty, Arts 26 and 27; see para.

---

[344] For professional rules and diplomas, see paras 5–145—5–147, *infra*; for harmonisation, see also paras 5–207—5–212, *infra*.

[345] paras 5–115 and 5–169, *infra*.

[346] paras 5–086 and 5–097, *infra*.

[347] paras 5–158—5–166, 5–180 and 5–186, *infra*.

[348] For an exhaustive discussion of free movement of goods, see de Cockborne, Defalque, Prahl and Vandersanden, "La libre circulation des marchandises" in de Cockborne, Defalque, Durand, Prahl and Verdersanden, *Commentaire Mégret—Le droit de la CEE. 1. Préambule. Principes. Libre circulation des marchandises* (Editions de l'Université de Bruxelles, Brussels, 1992), at 65–355; Oliver, *Free Movement of Goods in the European Community under Articles 30–36 of the EC Treaty* (Sweet & Maxwell, London, 1996), 455 pp; see also Mayer, "Die Warenverkehrsfreiheit im Europarecht—Eine Rekonstruktion" (2003) EuR 793–824.

5–095).[349] Non-fiscal measures, namely quantitative restrictions on imports and exports and measures having equivalent effect, are prohibited by Arts 28–30 of the EC Treaty,[350] which form the basis for a comprehensive body of case law (see paras 5–097–5–113). For the sake of completeness, it should be noted that Art. 31 of the EC Treaty requires Member States to organise any State monopolies of a commercial character so as to preclude any discrimination between Member State nationals regarding conditions under which goods are procured and marketed.[351]

Since all the Treaty provisions laying down prohibitions have had direct effect since the end of the transitional period,[352] individuals may enforce the free movement of goods *vis-à-vis* Member States. Those prohibitions are also binding on the institutions of the Community itself,[353] although the case law allows the Community a degree of discretion in balancing free movement of goods against other legitimate policy objectives.[354] In principle, restrictive measures agreed between individuals are not caught by those prohibitions.[355] Taken in conjunction with Art. 10 of the EC Treaty, however, the prohibiting provisions require Member States also to take all necessary and appropriate measures to eliminate barriers to free movement of goods the cause of which lies outside the sphere of the State.[356] The

---

[349] The Treaty of Amsterdam deleted from the chapter entitled "The Customs Union" the rules on the progressive abolition of customs duties between the Member States (the former Arts 13–17 of the EC Treaty) and on the establishment of the common customs tariff (the former Arts 18–27).

[350] The Treaty of Amsterdam amended the title of the chapter "Elimination of quantitative restrictions between Member States" to "Prohibition of quantitative restrictions between Member States" and repealed the transitional provisions (the former Arts 31–33 and 35 of the EC Treaty).

[351] ECJ, Case 59/75 *Manghera* [1976] E.C.R. 91; ECJ, Case C–347/88 *Commission v Greece* [1990] E.C.R. I–4747; ECJ, Case C–387/93 *Banchero* [1995] E.C.R. I–4663; ECJ, Case C–189/95 *Franzén* [1997] E.C.R. I–5909, paras 30–66 In the event of an infringement of Art. 31, it is no longer possible to rely on the exception provided for in Art. 30; see ECJ, Case C–157/94 *Commission v Netherlands* [1997] E.C.R. I–5699, para. 24.

[352] See the discussion of the Treaty articles in paras 5–087, 5–088 and 5–097, *infra*.

[353] ECJ, Joined Cases 80 and 81/77 *Commissionaires Réunis* [1978] E.C.R. 927, para. 35; ECJ, Case C–108/01 *Consorzio del Prosciutto di Parma* [2003] E.C.R. I–5121, paras 53–59.

[354] *e.g.* ECJ, case 37/84 *Rewe-Zentrale* [1984] E.C.R. 1229, para. 20; ECJ, Case C–51/93 *Meyhui* [1994] E.C.R. I–3879, para. 21; ECJ, Case C–233/94 *Germany v European Parliament and Council* [1997] E.C.R. I–2405, para. 43. See Mortelmans, "The Relationship Between the Treaty Rules and Community Measures for the Establishment and Functioning of the Internal Market—Towards a Concordance Rule" (2002) C.M.L.R. 1303–1346.

[355] ECJ, Case C–159/00 *Sapod Audic* [2002] E.C.R. I–5031, para. 74. For the addressees of the prohibitions (and the question whether they may be individuals), see Mortelmans, "Excepties bij non-tarifaire intracommunautaire belemmeringen: assimilatie in het nieuwe EG-Verdrag?" (1997) S.E.W. 182, at 185–186.

[356] ECJ, Case C–265/95 *Commission v France* [1997] E.C.R. I–6959, paras 30–32. (concerning acts taken by individuals against products from other Member States); ECJ, Case C–112/00 *Schmidberger* [2003] E.C.R. I–5659, paras 57–64 (individuals blocking traffic on the Brenner motorway). See also Ronkes Agerbeek (2004) E.L.Rev. 255–266; Jaeckel, "The duty to protect fundamental rights in the European Community" (2003) E.L.Rev. 508–527.

Council has specified this obligation in a regulation, under which the Commission is responsible for monitoring compliance.[357]

Goods concerned. Free movement of goods applies both to "products **5–085** originating in Member States" and to "products coming from third countries which are in free circulation in Member States" (EC Treaty, Art. 23(2); see also EC Treaty, Art. 24).[358] The Court of Justice has defined "goods" as "products which can be valued in money and which are capable, as such, of forming the subject of commercial transactions".[359] As a result, the rules on free movement of goods are applicable to articles of artistic, historic, archaeological or ethnographic value[360] and also to non-recyclable waste.[361]

a. The customs union

Customs union. The abolition of customs duties as between Member **5–086** States goes against the most-favoured nation clause enshrined in Art. I of the General Agreement on Tariffs and Trade (GATT), which puts contracting parties under an obligation to accord any preferential treatment of any product originating in or destined for any other country to the like product originating in or destined for the territories of all other GATT countries. All Member States are contracting parties to GATT and the World Trade Organisation (WTO), which replaced the GATT in 1995 and took over the basic rules of the original General Agreement.[362] GATT accepts, however, as an exception to the most-favoured nation clause, the establishment of a customs union, which is defined as an area within which customs duties and other restrictive regulations of commerce are eliminated with respect to substantially all the trade between the constituent territories of the Member States and in which substantially the same duties and other regulations of commerce are applied *vis-à-vis* third countries (GATT, Art. XXIV). GATT does impose conditions to the effect

---

[357] Council Regulation (EC) No. 2679/98 of December 7, 1998 on the functioning of the internal market in relation to the free movement of goods among the Member States, [1998] O.J. L337/8. See Mattera, "Un instrument d'intervention rapide pour sauvegarder l'unicité du Marché intérieur: le règlement 2679/98. De nouveaux pouvoirs pour la 'Commission Prodi' " (1999) R.M.U.E. 9–33; Gimeno Verdejo, "La réponse communautaire aux blocages des réseaux de transport: application et perspectives d'avenir du règlement n° 2679/98 en vue de la protection du marché intérieur" (2002) C.D.E. 45–93.

[358] ECJ, Case 41/76 *Donckerwolcke* [1976] E.C.R. 1921, paras 15–21; ECJ, Case 125/88 *Nijman* [1989] E.C.R. 3533, para. 11.

[359] ECJ, Case 7/68 *Commission v Italy* [1968] E.C.R. 423, at 428.

[360] *ibid.* See Mattera, "La libre circulation des oeuvres d'art à l'intérieur de la Communauté et la protection des trésors nationaux ayant une valeur artistique, historique ou archéologique" (1993) 2 R.M.U.E. 9–31.

[361] ECJ, Case C–2/90 *Commission v Belgium* [1992] E.C.R. I–4431, paras 23–28, with a note by De Sadeleer (1993) C.D.E. 672–698; see also De Sadeleer, "La circulation des déchets et le Marché unique européen" (1994) 1 R.M.U.E. 71–116.

[362] For the General Agreement on Tariffs and Trade (GATT) and the World Trade Organisation, see para. 20–010 *et seq.*

that the transitional period for achieving such a customs union must follow a schedule for the formation of the customs union within a reasonable length of time and that the customs union taken as a whole must not introduce higher duties for non-Member States.[363] The EC Treaty set out a timetable for the stage-by-stage introduction of a customs union. Whenever Member States have acceded to the Community, a new transitional period has been laid down for the abolition of customs duties and charges having equivalent effect as between Member States. The culmination of the customs union envisaged by the Treaty is the establishment and uniform application of a common customs tariff *vis-à-vis* third countries.[364]

(1) *Prohibition of customs duties on imports and exports and charges having equivalent effect*

5–087 **Customs duties.** In trade in goods between Member States, customs duties on imports and exports and charges having equivalent effect are prohibited. This prohibition also applies to customs duties of a fiscal nature (EC Treaty, Art. 25).[365] It means that charges collected by a Member State where goods cross its border are prohibited. This embraces not only import and export duties, but also transit charges.[366] By Council decision of July 26, 1966 customs duties were completely abolished as from July 1, 1968.[367] Those prohibitions have had direct effect ever since the end of the transitional period.[368]

5–088 **Charges having equivalent effect.** Article 25 of the EC Treaty couples the ban on customs duties on imports and exports with a prohibition of charges having equivalent effect. The Court of Justice interprets that expression very broadly: "any pecuniary charge, however small and whatever its designation and mode of application, which is imposed unilaterally on

---

[363] For the significance of Art. XXIV of GATT for the customs union within the Community and free trade agreements with third countries, see Cremona, "Rhetoric and Reticence: EU External Commercial Policy in a Multilateral Context" (2001) C.M.L.R. 359–396.

[364] See also Art. 131 of the EC Treaty, which stresses the positive contribution of the customs union to world trade. See Starink, "Veertig jaar EU-douane-unie" (1998) S.E.W. 241–252.

[365] Art. 12 of the EC Treaty before the Treaty of Amsterdam. The Amsterdam Treaty repealed the obligation to abolish existing duties (the former Arts 13 and 16 of the EC Treaty) and replaced the ban on the introduction of new duties or the increase of existing duties (stand-still provision) set out in the former Art. 12 of the EC Treaty by a straightforward prohibition of customs duties and charges having equivalent effect. For import duties, charges having equivalent effect and permitted charges, see Schön, "Die freie Warenverkehr, die Steuerhoheit der Mitgliedstaaten und der Systemgedanke im europäischen Steuerrecht" (2001) EuR. 216–233 and 341–362.

[366] ECJ, Case 266/81 *SIOT* [1983] E.C.R. 731, paras 16–19.

[367] Council Decision 66/532/EEC of July 26, 1966 abolishing customs duties and prohibiting quantitative restrictions as between Member States and applying the duties of the common customs tariff to products not mentioned in Annex II to the Treaty, J.O. 2971/66.

[368] ECJ, Case 26/62 *Van Gend & Loos* [1963] E.C.R. 1, at 13. The obligation to abolish existing charges having equivalent effect under the former Art. 13(2) (ECJ, Case 33/70 *SACE* [1970] E.C.R. 1213, paras 9–10) and the former Art. 16 of the EC Treaty (ECJ, Case 18/71 *Eunomia* [1971] E.C.R. 811, paras 6–7) have also been held to have direct effect.

domestic and foreign goods by reason of the fact that they cross a frontier, and which is not a customs duty in the strict sense, constitutes a charge having equivalent effect [. . .], even if it is not imposed for the benefit of the State, is not discriminatory or protective in effect or if the product on which the charge is imposed is not in competition with any domestic product".[369] Charges collected on crossing "regional" borders within a Member State are likewise prohibited, even where they are levied on goods coming from another region of the same Member State.[370]

Accordingly the Court has held the following to be contrary to the Treaty: a charge imposed to cover the cost of compiling statistics on movements of goods across frontiers[371]; pecuniary charges imposed on grounds of sanitary inspection of goods when they cross the frontier,[372] and charges imposed for compulsory quality controls on exports.[373] A Member State may not charge traders taking part in intra-Community trade the cost of inspections and administrative formalities carried out by customs offices.[374] Even if such a charge is imposed, not by virtue of a unilateral measure adopted by the authorities, but as a result of a series of private contracts, it will be caught by the prohibition laid down in Arts 23 and 25 of the EC Treaty.[375]

(2) *Permissible charges*

Three types. The broad interpretation of "charges having equivalent **5–089** effect" reduces the number of permissible pecuniary charges on Intra-Community trade in goods to such an extent that only three types of charges satisfy the Community law test.

Consideration for service rendered. In the first place, Member States may **5–090** charge for a service provided to the importer or exporter by the authorities ("consideration"). The Court of Justice has hedged this possibility about with strict conditions. The consideration may not exceed either the value or the cost of the service actually rendered to the importer or exporter and may be charged only in "special cases". Administrative activity intended to

---

[369] ECJ, Joined Cases 2 and 3/69 *Sociaal Fonds Diamantarbeiders* [1969] E.C.R. 211, para. 15/18, at 222.
[370] ECJ, Case C–163/90 *Legros* [1992] E.C.R. I–4625, paras 10–18; ECJ, Joined Cases C–363/93, C–407/93, C–408/93, C–409/93, C–410/93 and C–411/93 *Lancry* [1994] E.C.R. I–3957, paras 25–32 (charge levied on imports); ECJ, Joined Cases C–485/93 and C–486/93 *Simitzi* [1995] E.C.R. I–2655, paras 10–22 (charges levied on imports and exports). See Slotboom, "L'application du Traité CE au commerce intraétatique? Le cas de l'octroi de mer" (1996) C.D.E. 9–29; Graser, "Eine Wende im Bereich der Inländerdiskriminierung? Zur Entscheidung des EuGH in der Rechtssache *Lancry*" (1998) EuR. 571–579.
[371] ECJ, Case 24/68 *Commission v Italy* [1969] E.C.R. 193, paras 14–17.
[372] ECJ, Case 29/72 *Marimex* [1972] E.C.R. 1309, para. 8; ECJ, Case 87/75 *Bresciani* [1976] E.C.R. 129, paras 4–9.
[373] ECJ, Case 63/74 *Cadsky* [1975] E.C.R. 281, paras 2–8.
[374] ECJ, Case 340/87 *Commission v Italy* [1989] E.C.R. 1483, para. 17.
[375] ECJ, Case C–16/94 *Dubois and Général Cargo Services* [1995] E.C.R. I–2421, paras 13–21.

maintain a system imposed in the general interest (*e.g.* a phyto-sanitary or plant-health examination) cannot be regarded as a service rendered to the importer or exporter such as to justify the imposition of a pecuniary charge.

The Court of Justice accepted that the placing of goods, at the importer's request, in temporary storage in the special stores of public warehouses constituted a service rendered to importers that could give rise to the payment of charges commensurate with the service thus rendered. The Court held, however, that when payment of storage charges was demanded solely in connection with the completion of customs formalities, this constituted a "charge having equivalent effect".[377]

5–091 Charges forming part of Community system. Charges imposed for the purposes of implementing a Community system constitute a second exception to the extensive prohibition of charges having equivalent effect. For instance, the Court of Justice has held that certain charges imposed in connection with the common agricultural policy[378] and fees charged for inspections required by a Community directive[379] do not constitute charges having an effect equivalent to import or export duties.

5–092 Internal taxation. Thirdly, a charge may not be characterised as a charge having equivalent effect if it forms part of a general system of internal dues applying systematically to categories of products according to objective criteria applied without regard to the origin of the products. In that case the charge will come within the scope of Art. 90 of the EC Treaty.[380] As far as internal taxation is concerned, Art. 90 requires Member States not to impose directly or indirectly on products from other Member States any taxation in excess of that imposed on similar domestic products or impose internal taxation of such a nature as to afford protection to other domestic products. The criterion for testing whether a tax is caught by Art. 90 is therefore the discrimination or protection resulting therefrom.[381] The prohibition of discrimination also covers discrimination between national products which are processed and marketed on the domestic market and national products which are exported in an unprocessed state to other

---

[376] ECJ, Case 39/73 *Rewe-Zentralfinanz* [1973] E.C.R. 1039, para. 4.

[377] ECJ, Case 132/82 *Commission v Belgium* [1983] E.C.R. 1649, paras 10–14.

[378] ECJ, Case 106/81 *Kind v EEC* [1982] E.C.R. 2885, para. 21.

[379] ECJ, Case 46/77 *Bauhuis v Netherlands* [1977] E.C.R. 5, para. 31.

[380] See Schön, "Die freie Warenverkehr, die Steuerhoheit der Mitgliedstaaten und der Systemgedanke im europäischen Steuerrecht" (2001) EuR. 341–362. One and the same charge cannot be caught both by the provisions on charges having equivalent effect and by the prohibition of discriminatory internal taxation laid down in Art. 90: ECJ, Case 94/74 *IGAV* [1975] E.C.R. 699, para. 12–13.

[381] ECJ, Joined Cases C–149/91 and C–150/91 *Sanders Adour and Guyomarc'h Orthez Nutrition animale* [1992] E.C.R. I–3899, para. 19. Art. 90 of the EC Treaty does not preclude "reverse discrimination" arising where a Member State imposes internal taxation on its domestic products which is higher than that imposed on similar products imported from other Member States: ECJ, Case 86/78 *Peureux* [1979] E.C.R. 897, para. 32.

Member States.[382] The prohibition of discrimination applies to internal taxation "of any kind" (*e.g.* excise duty, VAT, registration charges, road fund taxes, etc.). Article 90 has direct effect.[383]

Identification of discrimination. The application of Art. 90 of the EC **5–093** Treaty requires a demarcation of the market for the national products with which the products imported (or to be exported) compete. It must therefore be considered which domestic products are similar or substitutable for the relevant imported products.[384] Then, it needs to be examined to what extent the taxation imposed on the products imported (or to be exported) protects domestic products. The comparison ranges over all aspects of the imposition of the tax (determination of the basis of assessment, determination of rates, methods of collection of amounts due) and is not confined to a formal inquiry. Thus, the Court of Justice held that a special French tax imposed on vehicles with a power rating of more than 16 fiscal horsepower which was higher than the differential tax charged on other vehicles was contrary to Art. 90. The Court held that the power rating determining liability to the special tax had been fixed at a level such that only imported cars were subject to the special tax whereas French cars were liable to the distinctly more advantageous differential tax.[385] The Court held that the special tax discriminated against imported vehicles in favour of cars of domestic manufacture because it resulted in a much larger increase in taxation than passing from one category of car to another in the system of differential taxation.[386]

Burden offset or justified. For the purposes of the legal categorisation of a **5–094** tax which is imposed in accordance with the same criteria on domestic products and on products imported (or to be exported), it is necessary to take account of the destination of the proceeds of the taxation. Taxation is incompatible with Art. 90 of the EC Treaty and therefore prohibited where

---

[382] ECJ, Case C–234/99 *Nygård* [2002] E.C.R. I–3657, para. 20.

[383] For the first para. of Art. 90 of the EC Treaty, see ECJ, Case 57/65 *Lütticke* [1966] E.C.R. 205, at 211; for the second para. of Art. 90, see Case 27/65 *Fink Frucht* [1968] E.C.R. 223, at 232.

[384] See ECJ, Case 170/78 *Commission v UK* [1980] E.C.R. 417, paras 12–24, and [1983] E.C.R. 2265, paras 7–28; ECJ, Case 356/85 *Commission v Belgium* [1987] E.C.R. 3299, paras 9–21 (consideration whether higher taxation on wine promoted the domestic consumption of beer). In the absence of similar or substitutable domestic products, the taxation is not in breach of Art. 90 of the EC Treaty: ECJ, Case 158/82 *Commission v Denmark* [1983] E.C.R. 3573, para. 22; ECJ, Case C–383/01 *De Danske Bilimportører* [2003] E.C.R. I–6065, paras 38–42.

[385] ECJ, Case 112/84 *Humblot* [1985] E.C.R. 1367, para. 14.

[386] *ibid.*, para. 15; *cf.* ECJ, Case C–113/94 *Casarin* [1995] E.C.R. I–4203, paras 17–26 (new French system of progressive taxation on motor vehicles held to be compatible with Art. 90); ECJ, Case C–421/97 *Tarantik* [1999] E.C.R. I–3633, paras 20–32; ECJ, Case C–265/99 *Commission v France* [2001] E.C.R. I–2305, paras 40–51. See also ECJ, Case C–345/93 *Fazenda Pública* [1995] E.C.R. I–479, paras 12–20; ECJ, Case C–393/98 *Gomes Valente* [2001] E.C.R. I–1327, paras 20–44.

it discriminates against the product imported (or to be exported). This may be the case where the revenue from such taxation is intended to finance activities from which domestic products primarily benefit as a result of which the fiscal burden on domestic products is neutralised by the advantages which the charge is used to finance whilst the charge on the products imported (or to be exported) constitutes a net burden.[387] If the proceeds of the charge fully offset the burden borne by the domestic products, the burden is in fact borne exclusively by products imported (or to be exported) and the charge must be regarded as a charge having equivalent effect prohibited by the Treaty.[388] Within these limits, a Member State may differentiate a charge on the basis of objective criteria, such as the nature of the raw materials used or the production processes employed, provided that the differentiation pursues policy objectives which are compatible with Community law (*e.g.* environment protection[389]).

(3) *The Common Customs Tariff*

5–095 **Customs tariffs.** Further to the abolition of customs duties in intra-Community trade in goods, the Council adopted Regulation No. 950/68 on the basis of Arts 28 and 111 of the EEC Treaty, which introduced a Common Customs Tariff for goods from non-member countries as from July 1, 1968.[390] Article 26 of the EC Treaty provides that the Council is to fix Common Customs Tariff duties. In the meantime, major changes have been made in the customs tariff, *inter alia*, as a result of the ratification of agreements reducing tariffs which have arisen in the multilateral trade negotiations under the auspices of the GATT. The legal basis for these "conventional" alterations to the Common Customs Tariff is to be found in the provisions concerning the common commercial policy (Art. 111 of the EEC Treaty during the transitional period, now Art. 133 of the EC Treaty). In pursuance of the Council regulations, the Commission has to draw up the customs tariff in force on the basis of a detailed nomenclature. The Commission has to adopt each year, by means of a regulation, the complete version of the nomenclature, together with the autonomous and conventional rates of duty in force.[391] The Community has exclusive competence with regard to the establishment of the customs

---

[387] ECJ, Case 73/79 *Commission v Italy* [1980] E.C.R. 1533, paras 15–16 (discrimination against imported products); ECJ, Case C–234/99 *Nygård* [2002] E.C.R. I–3657, paras 21–22 (discrimination against products to be exported).

[388] ECJ, Joined Cases C–78/90–C–83/90 *Compagnie commerciale de l'Ouest* [1992] E.C.R. I–1847, para. 27.

[389] ECJ, Case C–213/96 *Outokumpu* [1998]E.C.R. I–1777, paras 30–41. For the relationship between a discriminatory tax system and State aid incompatible with the common market, see ECJ, Case C–234/99 *Nygård* [2002] E.C.R. I–3657, paras 50–65.

[390] Council Regulation (EEC) No. 950/68 of June 28, 1968 on the Common Customs Tariff, [1968] O.J. English Spec. Ed. (I) 275; replaced by Council Regulation (EEC) No. 2658/87 of July 23, 1987 on the tariff and statistical nomenclature and on the Common Customs Tariff, [1987] O.J. L256.

[391] Art. 12 of Regulation No. 2658/87 (see preceding n.390, *supra*).

union (see para. 5–025 and, for the situation under the EU Constitution, para. 5–027).

Alongside the general Common Customs Tariff, the Community also applies preferential tariffs in force under association agreements, free trade agreements or general tariff preferences.[392]

In order to secure uniform application of the common tariffs, it was necessary to harmonise the Member States' differing customs legislation. The Council has adopted directives and regulations pursuant to other Treaty provisions (EC Treaty, Art. 94 and, as far as regulations are concerned, Art. 308 and/or the provisions concerning the common commercial policy) relating to such matters as determining the origin of goods, customs value, the various customs arrangements (bringing into free circulation, warehousing, inward and outward processing, temporary import/export, etc.), exemption from customs duties and payment of customs debt.[393]

(4) *Customs co-operation*

Co-operation between customs authorities. Customs co-operation is one of **5–096** the areas in which the Member States had already adopted joint actions[394] and drawn up conventions[395] in the context of co-operation in the fields of justice and home affairs (pursuant to the former Art.K.3 of the EU Treaty). Police and judicial co-operation in criminal matters (PJCC, Title VI of the EU Treaty) now provides a framework for these activities. The Treaty of Amsterdam also conferred competence on the Community in this field. Within the scope of application of the EC Treaty, the European Parliament and the Council are to take measures in accordance with the co-decision

---

[392] para. 20–009, *infra*.

[393] With effect from January 1, 1994, most of these rules have been replaced by Regulation (EEC) No. 2913/92 of October 12, 1992 establishing the Community Customs Code ([1992] O.J. L302/1), which the Council adopted on the basis of Arts 28, 100a and 113 [now Arts 26, 95 and 133] of the EC Treaty. See also Lasok, *The Trade and Customs Law of the European Union* (Kluwer Law International, The Hague, 1998), 470 pp.

[394] See, *e.g.* the Joint Actions adopted by the Council on November 29, 1996 (96/698/JHA) on co-operation between customs authorities and business organisations in combating drug trafficking ([1996] O.J. L322/3) and on June 9, 1997 (97/372/JHA) for the refining of targeting criteria, selection methods, etc., and collection of customs and police information ([1997] O.J. L159/1). See also the Council Resolutions of November 29, 1996 on the drawing up of police/customs agreements in the fight against drugs ([1996] O.J. C375/1) and of June 9, 1997 concerning a handbook for joint customs surveillance operations ([1997] O.J. C193/4).

[395] See the Convention of July 26, 1995 on the use of information technology for customs purposes ([1995] O.J. C316/34; for its provisional application between certain Member States, see [1995] O.J. C316/58), as supplemented by the Protocol of May 8, 2003 ([2003] O.J. L139/1) and the Convention of December 18, 1997 on mutual assistance and co-operation between customs administrations ([1998] O.J. C24/2; with an explanatory report in [1998] O.J. C189/1). A Protocol of November 29, 1996 drawn up on the basis of the former Art. K.3 of the EU Treaty confers jurisdiction on the Court of Justice to interpret, by way of preliminary rulings, the Convention on the use of information technology for customs purposes ([1997] O.J. C151/16) (para. 18–009, *infra*).

procedure in order to strengthen customs co-operation between the Member States and between the latter and the Commission (EC Treaty, Art. 135). Such Community measures may not, however, concern the application of national criminal law or the national administration of justice (*ibid.*). That restriction will be removed by the EU Constitution (Art. III–152).

b. Prohibition of non-tariff restrictions

5–097 **Non-tariff barriers.** The GATT includes non-tariff barriers among the trade restrictions to be abolished in a customs union. In addition to the chapter on the customs union, Title I of the EC Treaty includes a chapter on prohibition of quantitative restrictions between Member States (see also the EU Constitution, Arts III–153–III–155). Thus, Art. 28 prohibits "quantitative restrictions on imports and all measures having equivalent effect" and Art. 29 of the EC Treaty "quantitative restrictions on exports and all measures having equivalent effect". Art. 30 of the EC Treaty, however, permits such restrictions and measures where they are justified on grounds of public morality, public policy or public security; the protection of health and life of humans, animals or plants; the protection of national treasures possessing artistic, historic or archaeological value; or the protection of industrial and commercial property, provided that they do not constitute a means of arbitrary discrimination or a disguised restriction on trade between Member States. The provisions prohibiting quantitative restrictions and measures having equivalent effect have direct effect.[396] Art. 28 does not solely prohibit measures emanating from the State which, in themselves, create restrictions on trade between Member States, it may also apply where a Member State abstains from adopting the measures required in order to eliminate or prevent obstacles to the free movement of goods which are created by actions taken by individuals on its territory aimed at products originating in other Member States.[397] In such case, it has to be considered whether the Member State concerned can rely on the grounds which may be pleaded in justification of trade restrictions under Community law.[398]

The need to invoke these prohibitory provisions diminishes in practice where the national measures which might otherwise hinder trade in goods have been harmonised at Community level and made subject to a system of mutual recognition (see paras 5–207–5–212).

---

[396] For Art. 28, see ECJ, Case 74/76 *Iannelli* [1977] E.C.R. 557, para. 13; for Art. 29, see ECJ, Case 83/78 *Pigs Marketing Board* [1978] E.C.R. 2347, para. 66.

[397] ECJ, Case C–265/95 *Commission v France* [1997] E.C.R. I–6959, paras 30–32 (which refers to Member States' obligations under Art. 10 of the EC Treaty, see para. 5–051, *infra*).

[398] *ibid.*, paras 33–66 (consideration of possible justificatory grounds and of the proportionality of the national measures which were in fact taken).

(1) *Prohibition of quantitative restrictions and measures having equivalent effect*

Quantitative restrictions. The Court of Justice has defined "quantitative **5–098** restrictions" as "measures which amount to a total or partial restraint of, according to the circumstances, imports, exports or goods in transit".[399] These are measures which introduce a limitation depending upon the quantity or the value of the goods concerned. Since most trade "quotas" had already been abolished before the EEC Treaty entered into effect under the auspices of the OECD,[400] the prohibition of quantitative restrictions raises *per se* only a few problems.

Measures having equivalent effect. However, alongside quantitative **5–099** restrictions, all measures having equivalent effect are also prohibited. This ancillary prohibition came to have great significance owing to its broad scope. The original interpretation given to that prohibition by the Commission[401] opened the way to a broad interpretation by the Court of Justice.

Indeed, in the 1974 judgment in *Dassonville*, the Court of Justice held that "[a]ll trading rules enacted by Member States which are capable of hindering, directly or indirectly, actually or potentially, intra-Community trade are to be considered as measures having an effect equivalent to quantitative restrictions".[402] In that case, the Court categorised as a measure having equivalent effect a Belgian provision prohibiting the import of Scotch whisky without a certificate of origin. Importers, such as Dassonville, which obtained the product from another Member State where it was in free circulation, found it less easy to get hold of that certificate than importers who obtained it directly from the country of origin. Thus, the Court of Justice interpreted the concept of measures having equivalent effect in the broadest possible manner. The test was no longer, as the Commission had suggested, the distinction made by the relevant national provision between domestic and imported products, but simply whether the measure directly or indirectly, actually or potentially, hindered the free movement of goods.

The implications of *Dassonville*. That definition of "measures having **5–100** equivalent effect" takes in a complete range of legislative and administrative measures which are applicable without distinction to

---

[399] ECJ, Case 2/73 *Geddo* [1973] E.C.R. 865, para. 7.

[400] On January 14, 1955 the Council of Ministers of the Organisation for European Economic Co-operation (now OECD, see para 2–002, *supra*) adopted, pursuant to Art. 4 of the OEEC Treaty, a Code with a list of products for which liberalisation was required to be achieved.

[401] Commission Directive 70/50/EEC of December 22, 1969 on the abolition of measures which have an effect equivalent to quantitative restrictions on imports and are not covered by other provisions adopted in pursuance of the EEC Treaty, [1970] O.J. English Spec. Ed.(I) 17.

[402] ECJ, Case 8/74 *Dassonville* [1974] E.C.R. 837, para. 5.

domestic and imported products, yet have a—sometimes minimal—effect on potential sales of imported products and hence on the free movement of goods. Accordingly, the Court of Justice held that an unlawful measure having an effect equivalent to a quantitative restriction was involved in the case of a Belgian provision which, in order to protect consumers from confusing butter and margarine, provided that margarine could be marketed only in cubic form. Although the provision drew no distinction between domestic and imported products, it was nevertheless of such a nature as to render the marketing of imported products "more difficult or more expensive either by barring them from certain channels of distribution or owing to the additional costs brought about by the necessity to package the products in question in special packs which comply with the requirements in force on the market of their destination".[403] There will also be a restriction of imports where a measure does not affect trade in products imported or reimported through parallel channels in the same way as trade in products manufactured in the home market or imported into that market by approved distributors.[404] Free movement of goods concerns not only traders but also consumers. It requires that consumers resident in one Member State may travel freely to the territory of another Member State to shop under the same conditions as the local population.[405]

The same touchstone is used to assess national provisions governing import and export formalities, requirements to be fulfilled by products (such as requirements relating to the name, form, dimensions, weight, composition, presentation, labelling or packaging),[406] price rules, methods of sale[407] and advertising, conditions for public tenders and intellectual property rights.

Once any link can be made between a national measure and the import of goods, the application of Art. 28 of the EC Treaty is not precluded on the sole ground that all the facts of the specific case are confined to a single Member State.[408]

---

[403] ECJ, Case 261/81 *Rau* [1982] E.C.R. 3961, para. 13.

[404] ECJ, Case C–240/95 *Schmit* [1996] E.C.R. I–3179, paras 16–22.

[405] ECJ, Case C–362/88 *GB-INNO-BM* [1990] E.C.R. I–667, para. 8 (consumers may not be deprived of access to advertising available in the country where purchases are made).

[406] See the survey in Capelli, "La libre circulation des produits alimentaires à l'intérieur du marché commun" (1993) R.M.C.U.E. 790–811.

[407] But see para. 5–113, *infra*.

[408] ECJ, Joined Cases C–321–C–324/94 *Pistre* [1997] E.C.R. I–2343, paras 44–45; ECJ, Case C–448/98 *Guimont* [2000] E.C.R. I–10663, paras 21–24. Only the application of the measure to imported products is prohibited: *Guimont*, paras 15–21. See De Beys, "Le droit européen est-il applicable aux situations purement internes? A propos des discriminations à rebours dans le marché unique" (2001) J.T.D.E. 137–144; Papadopoulou, "Situations purement internes et droit communautaire: un instrument jurisprudentiel à double fonction ou une arme à double tranchant?" (2002) C.D.E. 95–129. In certain cases, the Court has held that the restrictions on trade in goods were too "uncertain and indirect" to hinder trade between Member States: ECJ, Case C–69/88 *Krantz* [1990] E.C.R. I–583, para. 11; ECJ, Case C–93/92 *CMC Motorradcenter* [1993] E.C.R. I–5009, para. 12; ECJ, Case C–379/92 *Peralta* [1994] E.C.R. I–3453, para. 24; see to the same effect, ECJ, Case 155/80 *Oebel* [1981]

Export restrictions. In contradistinction to the broad interpretation of the **5–101** concept of measures having effect equivalent to quantitative restrictions on imports (EC Treaty, Art. 28), the Court of Justice regards as measures having effect equivalent to quantitative restrictions on exports (EC Treaty, Art. 29):

> "national measures which have as their specific object or effect the restriction of patterns of exports and thereby the establishment of a difference in treatment between the domestic trade of a Member State and its export trade in such a way as to provide a particular advantage for national production or for the domestic market of the State in question at the expense of the production or of the trade of other Member States".[409]

An example of such a restriction on exports is where a Member State requires wine protected by a designation of origin to be bottled in the region of production.[410] Measures which are applicable without distinction to domestic and export trade fall outside the scope of Art. 29 of the EC Treaty.[411]

(2) Exceptions

Exceptions and justifications. The *Dassonville* definition of measures **5–102** having equivalent effect brings within the prohibition set out in Art. 28 of the EC Treaty a whole series of national measures which pursue policy

---

E.C.R. 1993, paras 11–21; ECJ, Case 75/81 *Blesgen* [1982] E.C.R. 1211, para. 9; ECJ, Case 145/85 *Forest* [1986] E.C.R. 3499, para. 19; ECJ, Case C–23/89 *Quietlynn and Richards* [1990] E.C.R. I–3059, paras 10–11; ECJ, Joined Cases C–140/94, C–141/94 and C–142/94 *DIP* [1995] E.C.R. 3257, para. 29; ECJ, Case C–134/94 *Esso Española* [1995] E.C.R. I–4233, para. 24.

[409] ECJ, Case 15/79 *Groenveld* [1979] E.C.R. 3409, para. 7. Since the Treaty provisions on free movement of goods also apply to the Community institutions, Community measures may also constitute measures having equivalent effect: ECJ, Case C–469/00 *Ravil* [2003] E.C.R. I–5053, paras 40–44, and ECJ, Case C–108/01 *Consorzio del Prosciutto di Parma* [2003] E.C.R. I–5121, paras 54–59.

[410] ECJ, Case C–388/95 *Belgium v Spain* [2000] E.C.R. I–3123, paras 36–42. For the justification identified by the Court of Justice in the good reputation of the wine in question, see Blanchi, "La mise en bouteille obligatoire des vins de qualité dans la région de production" (2001) R.M.C.U.E. 343–350.

[411] ECJ, Case 155/80 *Oebel* [1981] E.C.R. 1993, paras 15–16; ECJ, Case 237/82 *Jongeneel Kaas* [1984] E.C.R. 483, paras 22–27; ECJ, Case 15/83 *Denkavit Nederland* [1984] E.C.R. 2171, paras 16–18. For further applications, see ECJ, Case C–302/88 *Hennen Olie* [1990] E.C.R. I–4625, paras 17–18; ECJ, Case C–339/89 *Alsthom Atlantique* [1991] E.C.R. I–107, paras 13–16; ECJ, Case C–332/89 *Marchandise* [1991] E.C.R. I–1027, paras 16–17; ECJ, Case C–47/90 *Delhaize and Le Lion* [1992] E.C.R. I–3669, paras 11–27. For the distinction between this case law and that on Art. 28, see Roth, "Wettbewerb der Mitgliedstaaten oder Wettbewerb der Hersteller?" (1995) Z.H.W. 78–95; Weatherill, "After *Keck*: Some Thoughts on How to Clarify the Clarification" (1996) C.M.L.R. 885, at 902–903. A measure does not constitute a measure having equivalent effect to a restriction on exports where its effect on exports is too "uncertain and indirect": ECJ, Case C–412/97 *ED and Fenocchio* [1999] E.C.R. I–3845, para. 11 (with a reference to the case law cited in n.408, *supra*.).

objectives in the general interest and thereby restrict trade. In so far as the policy in question cannot be justified on the basis of Art. 30 of the EC Treaty, strict application of Art. 28 would make it impossible to pursue those goals. As a result, pending harmonisation of such national provisions—which would neutralise their effect of hampering trade—the Court of Justice has accepted in the *Cassis de Dijon* case law an additional exception which allows measures to be reconciled with Art. 28 of the EC Treaty where they protect legitimate interests in a reasonable manner (the rule of reason). It is for the Member State to prove that its measure which restricts trade (or its failure to prevent a restriction of trade) comes within one of the exceptions provided for in Art. 30 or that it is covered by the rule of reason.[412] In addition, the Court of Justice has, by the judgment in *Keck and Mithouard*, taken all national provisions on methods of sale without discriminatory effects outside the scope of the *Dassonville* definition of measures having equivalent effect.[413]

(i) Article 30 of the EC Treaty

5–103 Grounds for justification. The exceptions provided for in Art. 30 of the EC Treaty relate to measures of a non-economic nature[414] and are strictly interpreted by the Court of Justice.[415] Only those interests listed in the Treaty Article (protection of public morality, public policy, public security, health and life of humans, animals or plants, national treasures possessing artistic, historic or archaeological value, and industrial and commercial property) are capable of justifying a measure restricting trade.[416] Article 30 does not amount to a constitutionally protected core of residuary powers of the Member States. A Member State may no longer justify a measure on the basis of Art. 30 of the EC Treaty where the national legislation intended to protect the specific interest concerned has been harmonised.[417]

---

[412] But see the view taken in Directive 70/50 (para. 5–099, *supra*) and the *Keck and Mithouard* case law on sales methods (para. 5–113, *infra*), where the burden of proof has to be discharged by the person arguing for protection of the free movement of goods.

[413] The consideration that such provisions have only a minimal impact on intra-Community trade (para. 5–113, *infra*) also underlies the judgments cited in n.408, *supra*.

[414] ECJ, Case 7/61 *Commission v Italy* [1961] E.C.R. 317, at 329; ECJ, Case 238/82 *Duphar v Netherlands* [1984] E.C.R. 523, para. 23; ECJ, Case 288/83 *Commission v Ireland* [1985] E.C.R. 1761, para. 28. This does not mean that rules justified by objective circumstances may not also make it possible to achieve additional objectives of an economic nature sought by the Member State: ECJ, Case 72/83 *Campus Oil* [1984] E.C.R. 2727, para. 36.

[415] Case 13/68 *Salgoil* [1968] E.C.R. 453, at 463.

[416] ECJ, Case 113/80 *Commission v Ireland* [1981] E.C.R. 1625, paras 7–8.

[417] ECJ, Case 148/78 *Ratti* [1979] E.C.R. 1629, para. 36. A harmonising directive precludes recourse to Art. 30 even if the directive itself does not lay down any Community procedure for monitoring compliance or any penalties: ECJ, Case C–5/94 *Hedley Lomas* [1996] E.C.R. I–2553, paras 18–20, with a case note by Van Calster (1996/97) Col.J.E.L. 132–145; ECJ, Case C–1/96 *Compassion in World Farming* [1998] E.C.R. I–1251, paras 47–64 (in view of the full harmonisation measure existing, it is not possible to rely on Art. 30 in respect of a ban on the *export* of calves); see Van Calster, "Export restrictions—a watershed for Art. 30"

Conditions. In addition, the measure may not constitute "a means of **5–104** arbitrary discrimination or a disguised restriction on trade between Member States". This means that the measure must be proportionate to the aim sought. The interest may not be capable of being as effectively protected by measures which do not restrict intra-Community trade so much.[418]

A Member State is not entitled unnecessarily to subject products to tests where the Member State in which they originated has already carried out tests which satisfy the requirements of health protection and the results are available.[419] Accordingly, the Commission challenged French rules prohibiting the marketing of woodworking machines imported from other Member States on the ground that they did not comply with safety standards. The Court of Justice held that it was contrary to the principle of proportionality for "imported products to [be required] to comply strictly and exactly with the provisions or technical requirements laid down for products manufactured in the Member State in question when those imported products afford users the same level of protection".[420] Nevertheless, the Court acknowledged that the French rules' approach to protection differed from that of the rules of other Member States, notably Germany. The French legislation was based on the idea that users of machines must be protected from their own mistakes and that the machine must be designed so that the users' intervention is limited to the strict minimum. In contrast, the basic principle in Germany was that the worker should receive thorough and continuing training. The difference sufficed in order for France to be able to impose its rules on importers of woodworking machines manufactured and lawfully marketed in other Member States.[421] In more recent case law, the Court of Justice has confirmed that, in the absence of harmonisation, it is for the Member State to decide on the level of protection of human health and life they wish to ensure.[422] In the event that a Member State wishes to rely on Art. 30 in order to justify a measure restricting the free movement of goods, it must be able to show that the measure is based on a detailed assessment of the risk, based on the most recent reliable scientific data available. Where it

---

(2000) E.L.Rev. 335–352. Where harmonisation of national legislation has been carried out pursuant to Art. 95 of the EC Treaty, account must be taken of Art. 95(4) to (7); para. 5–210, *infra*.

[418] ECJ, Case 104/75 *De Peijper* [1976] E.C.R. 613, para. 17. For a very flexible application, see ECJ, Case C–320/93 *Ortscheit* [1994] E.C.R. I–5243, paras 17–20.

[419] ECJ, Case 272/80 *Frans-Nederlandse Maatschappij voor Biologische Produkten* [1981] E.C.R. 3277, paras 14–15; ECJ, Case 25/88 *Wurmser* [1989] E.C.R. 1105, para. 18: "That rule is a particular application of a more general principle of mutual trust between the authorities of the Member States". See also ECJ, Case 373/92 *Commission v Belgium* [1993] E.C.R. I–3107, paras 8–10; ECJ, Case C–293/94 *Brandsma* [1996] E.C.R. I–3159, paras 10–13.

[420] ECJ, Case 188/84 *Commission v France* [1986] E.C.R. 419, para. 16.

[421] *ibid.*, paras 18–22.

[422] *e.g.*, ECJ (judgment of February 5, 2004), Case C–95/01 *Greenham and Abel*, not yet reported, para. 37.

proves to be impossible to determine with scientific certainty the existence or extent of the alleged risk to public health, a Member State may take protective measures on the basis of the precautionary principle without having to await full proof that the risk actually exists and is a major one.[423]

5–105 Discrimination. In the absence of harmonisation and if the national measure does not exceed what is necessary to attain one of the objectives listed in Art. 30, that article will justify the measure, even if it embodies formal discrimination or has a discriminatory effect.

5–106 Intellectual property. The exception provided for in Art. 30 of the EC Treaty for "protection of industrial and commercial property" (such as patents, drawings and designs, copyrights and trademarks) has obliged the Court of Justice to strike a balance between the principle of free movement of goods and protection of the rights in question. The Treaty does not affect the existence of exclusive rights recognised under national legislation with regard to industrial and commercial property (see EC Treaty, Art. 295), but does set limitations to the exercise of such rights. Art. 30 only admits derogations from free movement of goods to the extent to which they are justified for the purpose of safeguarding rights which constitute the "specific subject-matter" of such property.[424] The "exhaustion" doctrine expounded by the Court of Justice states that the owner of the right cannot rely on his exclusive right in order to prevent the importation and marketing of a product which has been marketed in another Member State by himself, with his consent, or by a person economically or legally dependent on him.[425] Where a patentee is legally bound under national law

---

[423] *ibid.*, paras 39–50. For the precautionary principle, see para. 17–070.

[424] For rights related to copyrights, see ECJ, Case 78/70 *Deutsche Grammophon* [1971] E.C.R. 487, paras 11–13; for trademarks, ECJ, Case 192/73 *Van Zuylen* [1974] E.C.R. 731, paras 7–10, reconsidered in ECJ, Case C–10/89 *Hag GF* [1990] E.C.R. I–3711, paras 10–20; ECJ, Case C–9/93 *IHT Internationale Heiztechnik and Danzinger* [1994] E.C.R. I–2789, paras 40–46; ECJ, Case 16/74 *Centrafarm* [1974] E.C.R. 1183, paras 7–8; ECJ, C–317/93 *Deutsche Renault* [1993] E.C.R. I–6227, paras 30–39; for patents, ECJ, Case 15/74 *Centrafarm* [1974] E.C.R. 1147, paras 8–9. For copyrights, see Joined Cases 55 and 57/80 *Musik-Vertrieb membran* [1981] E.C.R. 147, paras 11–13 (as regards free movement of services, see previously ECJ, Case 62/79 *Coditel* [1980] E.C.R. 881, paras 12–14); for designations and indications of origin, see ECJ, Case 12/74 *Commission v Germany* [1975] E.C.R. 181, paras 7–18; ECJ, Case C–3/91 *Exportur* [1992] E.C.R. I–5529, paras 23–38; ECJ, Case C–388/95 *Belgium v Spain* [2000] E.C.R. I–3123, paras 47–75; for designs and models, see ECJ, Case 53/87 *CICRA and Maxicar* [1988] E.C.R. 6039, para. 11, and ECJ, Case 238/87 *Volvo* [1988] E.C.R. 6211, para. 8.

[425] In addition to the judgments cited in the preceding note see as regards patents: ECJ, Case 187/80 *Merck* [1981] E.C.R. 2063, paras 9–14; as regards trademarks: ECJ, Case 119/75 *Terrapin* [1976] E.C.R. 1039, paras 5–8 (also the right to a trade name); ECJ, Case 102/77 *Hoffmann-La Roche* [1978] E.C.R. 1139, paras 6–14; ECJ, Case 3/78 *Centrafarm* [1978] E.C.R. 1823, paras 7–22; ECJ, Joined Cases C–427/93, C–429/93 and C–436/93 *Bristol-Myers Squibb* [1996] E.C.R. I–3457; ECJ, Joined Cases C–71/94, C–72/94 and C–73/94 *Eurim-Pharm* [1996] E.C.R. I–3603; ECJ, Case C–232/94 *MPA Pharma* [1996] E.C.R. I–3671; as regards copyrights: ECJ, Case 158/86 *Warner Brothers* [1988] E.C.R. 2605, paras 1–19; with regard to designs, see ECJ, Case 144/81 *Keurkoop* [1982] E.C.R. 2853, paras 22–29.

or Community law to market his or her products in a Member State, he or she cannot be deemed to have given his or her consent to the marketing of the products concerned. He or she is therefore entitled to oppose importation and marketing of those products by a third party in the State where they are protected.[426]Putting a product on the market outside the European Economic Area does not entail exhaustion of the right to contest importation without consent.[427] It should be noted that Arts 30 and 295 of the EC Treaty do not reserve an exclusive power to the Member States to regulate the law on intellectual property and hence do not preclude harmonisation measures on the part of the Community.[428]

(ii) The rule of reason

5–107 Cassis de Dijon. In the leading *Cassis de Dijon* judgment of February 20, 1979, the Court of Justice opened the door to certain "reasonable" national measures in restraint of trade being regarded as compatible with Art. 28 of the EC Treaty on grounds other than those listed in Art. 30. The Court had been called upon to rule on a provision of German law requiring various alcoholic beverages to have a minimum alcoholic strength. The requirement for fruit liqueurs to have a minimum of 25 per cent alcohol content prevented *Cassis de Dijon*, which contained only 15 to 20 per cent alcohol and was freely marketed in France, from being imported into Germany. The Court accepted that, in the absence of common rules, it was for Member States to "regulate all matters relating to the production and marketing of alcohol and alcoholic beverages on their own territory". The Court went on to state that:

"[o]bstacles to movement within the Community resulting from disparities between the national laws relating to the marketing of the products in question must be accepted in so far as those provisions may be recognised as being necessary in order to satisfy mandatory requirements relating in particular to the effectiveness of fiscal supervision, the protection of public health, the fairness of commercial transactions and the defence of the consumer".[429]

---

[426] ECJ, Case 19/84 *Pharmon v Hoechst* [1985] E.C.R. 2281, paras 22–27 (compulsory licence); ECJ, Joined Cases C–267/95 and C–268/95 *Merck and Beecham* [1996] E.C.R. I–6285, paras 26–54.

[427] ECJ, Case C–355/96 *Silhouette International Schmied* [1998] E.C.R. I–4799, para. 26; ECJ, Case C–173/98 *Sebago and Maison Dubois* [1999] E.C.R. I–4103, para. 21; ECJ, Joined Cases C–414/99–C–416/99 *Zino Davidoff and Others* [2001] E.C.R. I–8691, paras 30–67.

[428] ECJ, Case C–350/92 *Spain v Council* [1995] E.C.R. I–1985, paras 12–24. For Community harmonisation measures, see para. 5–207, *infra*.

[429] ECJ, Case 120/78 *Rewe v Bundesmonopolverwaltung für Branntwein* [1979] E.C.R. 649, para. 8. Later the Court of Justice was to refer to that case as follows (in Case 302/86 *Commission v Denmark* [1988] E.C.R. 4607, para. 6): "[I]n the absence of common rules relating to the marketing of the products in question, obstacles to free movement within the Community

5–108 Four conditions. In individual cases concerning the application of Art. 28 of the EC Treaty, the Court of Justice requires the given national measure invariably to satisfy four requirements.

5–109 (1) Absence of harmonisation. First, the Court allows a Member State to apply a measure restricting trade only in so far as there is no legislation at Community level. In fact, the rule of reason constitutes an exception to the prohibition of measures having equivalent effect pending the adoption of Community legislation. Once national legislation has been harmonised, a Member State may in principle no longer deviate from the Community rule.[430]

5–110 (2) Mandatory requirements. Next, the measure adopted by the Member State must be justified by a "mandatory requirement" (*exigence impérative*) recognised or to be recognised by the Court of Justice, such as protection of consumers,[431] fairness of commercial transactions,[432] effectiveness of fiscal supervision,[433] combating fraud,[434] completion of the internal market by establishing statistics on the trading of goods between Member States,[435] protection of public health,[436] protection of the environment,[437] road safety,[438] proper functioning of the public telecommunications network,[439] protection of cultural works[440] and maintenance of press diversity with a view to safeguarding freedom of expression.[441] This list is not exhaustive, but may be supplemented by other non-economic policy aims in the general interest.[442] A restriction of the free movement of goods may also be justified on the ground of the need to protect fundamental rights, such as freedom of expression and freedom of assembly.[443]

---

resulting from disparities between the national laws must be accepted in so far as such rules, applicable to domestic and imported products without distinction, may be recognised as being necessary in order to satisfy mandatory requirements recognised by Community law. Such rules must also be proportionate to the aim in view. If a Member State has a choice between various measures for achieving the same aim, it should choose the means which least restricts the free movement of goods." *Cf.* Art. 95 of the EC Treaty, which refers to "major needs".

[430] *e.g.* ECJ, Case C–221/00 *Commission v Austria* [2003] E.C.R. I–1007, para. 42. But see Art. 95 (4) and (5) of the EC Treaty; para. 5–210, *infra*.

[431] ECJ, Case 27/80 *Fietje* [1980] E.C.R. 3839, paras 10–11.

[432] ECJ, Case 6/81 *Industrie Diensten Groep* [1982] E.C.R. 707, paras 7–9.

[433] ECJ Case 823/79 *Carciati* [1980] E.C.R. 2773, para. 9.

[434] See also ECJ, Case C–184/96 *Commission v France* [1998] E.C.R. I–6197, paras 23–37.

[435] ECJ, Case C–114/96 *Kieffer and Thill* [1997] E.C.R. I–3629, paras 29–31.

[436] ECJ, Case 120/78 *Rewe* [1979] E.C.R. 649, paras 8–11.

[437] ECJ, Case 302/86 *Commission v Denmark* [1988] E.C.R. 4607, paras 7–9. See Notaro, "The New Generation Case Law on Trade and Environment" (2000) E.L.Rev. 467–491.

[438] ECJ, Case C–314/98 *Snellers Auto's* [2000] E.C.R. I–8633, para. 55.

[439] ECJ, Joined Cases C–388/00 and C–429/00 *Radiosistemi* [2002] E.C.R. I–5845, para. 44.

[440] ECJ, Joined Cases 60–61/84 *Cinéthèque* [1985] E.C.R. 2605, para. 23.

[441] ECJ, Case C–368/95 *Familiapress* [1997] E.C.R. I–3689, para. 18.

[442] A risk of seriously undermining the financial balance of the social security system may possibly constitute a mandatory requirement: ECJ, Case C–120/95 *Decker* [1998] E.C.R. I–1831, para. 39; ECJ (judgment of December 11, 2003), Case C–322/01 *Deutscher Apothekerverband*, not yet reported, para. 122.

[443] ECJ, Case C–112/00 *Schmidberger* [2003] E.C.R. I–5659, para. 74.

(3) Application without distinction. A Member State can comply with **5–111** "mandatory requirements" only by means of a measure which is applicable without distinction to domestic and imported products, even if it is indirectly discriminatory,[444] in particular where it will be more difficult for imported products than for domestic products to conform to the measure or where the particular nature of the imported products would have necessitated a derogating measure. In this way, the Court of Justice has had to consider whether the Belgian measure requiring margarine to be packaged in cubes was justified[445] and, in *Cassis de Dijon*, the German minimum alcoholic strength requirement, which did not involve foreign products being treated differently from domestic ones, but in practice kept foreign spirits off the German market.[446]

A measure which makes a distinction between domestic and imported products and so directly discriminates against the latter may be tolerated only if it satisfies Art. 30 of the EC Treaty. Such a measure ceases to be discriminatory, however, where the distinction is due to particular characteristics of the product. Accordingly, preferential treatment for domestic, as opposed to imported, waste may be justified by the principle that environmental damage should as a matter of priority be remedied at source.[447] In such a case, the "non-discrimination" requirement is satisfied and the rule of reason may be applied.[448]

(4) Proportionality. Lastly, the national measure must be proportionate to **5–112** the intended aim. If a Member State has a choice between different measures to attain the same objective it should choose the means which least restricts the free movement of goods.[449] Consequently, a national measure must not only be appropriate in order to achieve an aim in the

---

[444] For this expression, see para. 5–066, *supra*.

[445] ECJ, Case 261/81 *Rau* [1982] E.C.R. 3961, paras 16–20 (see also para. 5–100, *supra*).

[446] para. 5–107, *supra*. Another example is ECJ, Case 302/86 *Commission v Denmark* [1988] E.C.R. 4607, where what was at issue was a deposit-and-return system under which containers for beer and soft drinks not approved by a national agency might be used for only a maximum quantity of 3,000 hectolitres a year. Although the system did not distinguish between domestic and foreign producers, it impeded the import of drinks from other Member States in otherwise than approved containers. *cf.* ECJ, Case C–237/94 *O'Flynn* [1996] E.C.R. I–2617, para. 18, in which the Court of Justice held that measures which are applicable without distinction in terms of nationality must be regarded as indirectly discriminatory if they can be more easily satisfied by national workers than by migrant workers or where there is a risk that they may operate to the particular detriment of migrant workers.

[447] ECJ, Case C–2/90 *Commission v Belgium* [1992] E.C.R. I–4431, para. 34.

[448] In some cases, the Court of Justice appears not to rule out a justification on grounds of "mandatory requirements" even in the case of discriminatory measures, *e.g.* ECJ, Case C–203/96 *Dusseldorp* [1998] E.C.R. I–4075, paras 44–50; ECJ, Case C–386/96 *Aher-Waggon* [1998] E.C.R. I–4473, paras 18–19; ECJ, Case C–209/98 *Sydhavnens Sten & Grus* [2000] E.C.R. I–3473, paras 48–50 (environmental protection and public health). See Notaro, "The New Generation Case Law on Trade and Environment" (2000) E.L.Rev. 467, at 489.

[449] See, *e.g.* ECJ, Case C–51/94 *Commission v Germany* [1995] E.C.R. I–3599, paras 32–37; ECJ, Case C–114/96 *Kieffer and Thill* [1997] E.C.R. I–3629, paras 31–38.

general interest (which is regarded as a "mandatory requirement"), but it must also be indispensable in the sense that there are no less restrictive means available of achieving the intended aim.[450] In the *Cassis de Dijon* case, the Court of Justice accordingly held that it would go too far to "regard the mandatory fixing of minimum alcohol requirements as being an essential guarantee of the fairness of commercial transactions, since it is a simple matter to ensure that suitable information is conveyed to the purchaser by requiring the display of an indication of origin and of the alcohol content on the packaging of products".[451] The Court further referred to reciprocal recognition of national provisions as a particular application of the principle of proportionality when it held that "[t]here is therefore no valid reason why, provided that they have been lawfully produced and marketed in one of the Member States, alcoholic beverages should not be introduced into any other Member State".[452] A Member State wishing to apply a measure restricting trade must show that the aim sought by the measure is not already achieved by the legislation in force in the Member State from which the imported product originates. The burden of proof in fact requires the Member State to show why its own situation differs so much from that of other Member States as to necessitate a specific measure.[453] Accordingly, Art. 28 of the EC Treaty precludes a national rule which does not allow a trader to show that an imported product satisfied the prescribed requirements already in its State of origin.[454]

(iii) Rules governing selling arrangements

5–113   ***Keck and Mithouard.*** The *Dassonville* interpretation of Art. 28 of the EC Treaty raised questions about the permissibility of national legislation relating to selling arrangements, which, although not intended to regulate trade in goods between Member States, nevertheless affect the volume of sales within the Member State concerned and hence also impede the sale of products from other Member States. In this way, the Court of Justice delivered a number of controversial rulings on Sunday-trading legislation.[455]

---

[450] See the discussion of the principle of proportionality, paras 5–038–5–039, *supra*.

[451] ECJ, Case 120/78 *Rewe* [1979] E.C.R. 649, para. 13. The Court has also referred to labelling requirements as a less restrictive means of preventing confusion arising between butter and margarine than cubic packaging: ECJ, Case 261/81 *Rau* [1982] E.C.R. 3961, para. 17.

[452] *Rewe*, cited in the preceding n.451, *supra* para. 14.

[453] See Mattera, "L'article 30 du traité CEE, la jurisprudence 'cassis de Dijon' et le principe de la reconnaissance mutuelle" (1992) 4 R.M.U.E. 13–71, and "L'Union européenne assure le respect des identités nationales, régionales et locales, en particulier par l'application et la mise en oeuvre du principe de la reconnaissance mutuelle" (2002) R.D.U.E. 217–239.

[454] *e.g.* ECJ, Joined Cases C–388/00 and C–429/00 *Radiosistemi* [2002] E.C.R. I–5845, paras 44–46.

[455] See ECJ, Case C–145/88 *Torfaen Borough Council* [1989] E.C.R. I–3851; ECJ, Case C–312/89 *Conforama* [1991] E.C.R. I–997 and Case C–332/89 *Marchandise* [1991] E.C.R. I–1027; ECJ, Case C–169/91 *Council of the City of Stoke-on-Trent and Norwich City Council* [1992] E.C.R. I–6635.

The question arose as to whether such indirect influence on free movement of goods sufficed in order for the legislation concerned to be regarded as unlawful measures having equivalent effect.[456]

"In view of the increasing tendency of traders to invoke Article 30 of the Treaty as a means of challenging any rules whose effect is to limit their commercial freedom even where such rules are not aimed at products from other Member States", the Court considered in the judgment of November 24, 1993 in *Keck and Mithouard* that it was "necessary to re-examine and clarify its case law on this matter".[457] Within the class of measures applicable without distinction to domestic and imported products, the Court introduced a distinction between provisions laying down requirements which products have to satisfy and provisions restricting or prohibiting certain selling arrangements. The Court then declared that:

"contrary to what has previously been decided, the application to products from other Member States of national provisions restricting or prohibiting certain selling arrangements is not such as to hinder directly or indirectly, actually or potentially, trade between Member States within the meaning of the *Dassonville* judgment . . ., so long as those provisions apply to all relevant traders operating within the national territory and so long as they affect in the same manner, in law and in fact, the marketing of domestic products and of those from other Member States".[458]

---

[456] Some commentators advocated restricting the concept of "measures having equivalent effect": Van der Woude, "The Limits of Free Circulation: The Torfaen Borough Council Case" (1990) Leiden J.I.L. 57–63; Mortelmans, " Art. 30 of the EEC Treaty and Legislation Relating to Market Circumstances: Time to Consider a New Definition?" (1991) C.M.L.R. 115–136; Steiner, "Drawing the Line: Uses and Abuses of Art. 30 EEC" (1992) C.M.L.R. 749–774. Others argued for retaining its broad scope: Gormley, "Recent Case Law on the Free Movement of Goods: Some Hot Potatoes" (1990) C.M.L.R. 825–857; Arnull, "What shall we do on Sunday?" (1991) E.L.Rev. 112–124. See also the appraisal by Wils, "The Search for the Rule in Art. 30 EEC: Much Ado About Nothing?" (1993) E.L.Rev. 475–492 and the survey of the debate by Straetmans, *Consument en markt* (Kluwer, Deurne, 1998), 323–326.

[457] Joined Cases C–267/91 and C–268/91 *Keck and Mithouard* [1993] E.C.R. I–6097, para. 14.

[458] *ibid.*, para. 16 (in that case the Court considered that Art. 28 did not apply to a French provision imposing a blanket ban on resale at a loss; *ibid.*, para. 18). For some commentaries on the judgment, see Becker, "Von 'Dassonville' über 'Cassis' zu 'Keck'—Der Begriff der Maßnahmen gleicher Wirkung in Art. 30 EGV" (1994) EuR. 162–174; Chalmers, "Repackaging the Internal Market: The Ramifications of the *Keck* Judgment" (1994) E.L.Rev. 385–403; Mattera, "De l'arrêt 'Dassonville' à l'arrêt 'Keck': l'obscure clarté d'une jurisprudence riche en principes novateurs et en contradictions" (1994) 1 R.M.U.E. 117–160; Poiares Maduro, "*Keck*: The End? The Beginning of the End? Or Just the End of the Beginning?" (1994) Ir.J.E.L. 30–43; Picod, "La nouvelle approche de la Cour de justice en matière d'entraves aux échanges" (1998) R.T.D.E. 169–189; González Vaqué, "La jurisprudencia relativa al artículo 28 CE (antiguo artículo 30 TCE) sobre la libre circulación de mercancías después de *Keck y Mithouard*" (2000) G.J. 24–38.

Accordingly, a measure governing selling arrangements which may affect trade between Member States, yet does not discriminate either "in law" or "in fact" against traders from other Member States, is no longer regarded as a measure having equivalent effect. In addition to the ban on selling at a loss or for a low margin,[459] the Court of Justice has accepted that "selling arrangements" cover, for example, rules relating to sales outlets,[460] making sales on rounds,[461] shop-opening hours,[462] advertising[463] and promotions.[464] Rules on packaging and labelling, for example, do not constitute selling arrangements.[465] The Court of Justice has held that a discriminatory effect ensues, for example, from a blanket prohibition on the advertising of alcoholic beverages, because such a ban is liable to impede access to the market by products from other Member States more than it impedes access by domestic products, with which consumers are instantly more familiar.[466] If it can be shown that a measure governing selling arrangements has discriminatory effects, it may still be justified in accordance with the *Cassis de Dijon* criteria in so far as it is applicable without distinction to domestic and imported products[467]; a

---

[459] See, in addition to *Keck and Mithouard* (see preceding ns), ECJ, Case C–63/94 *Belgapom* [1995] E.C.R. I–2467, paras 8–15.

[460] ECJ, Case C–391/92 *Commission v Greece* [1995] E.C.R. I–1621, paras 9–21; ECJ, Case C–387/93 *Banchero* [1995] E.C.R. I–4663, paras 32–44; ECJ, Case C–189/95 *Franzén* [1997] E.C.R. I–5909, paras 69–72 (system of import licences); ECJ (judgment of December 11, 2003), Case C–322/01 *Deutscher Apothekerverband*, not yet reported, paras 68–76 (concerning a ban on mail order sales).

[461] ECJ, Case C–254/98 *TK-Heimdienst Sass* [2000] E.C.R. I–151, paras 24–37.

[462] ECJ, Joined Cases C–401/92 and C–402/92 *Tankstation 't Heukske and Boermans* [1994] E.C.R. I–2199, paras 10–12; ECJ, Joined Cases C–69/93 and C–258/93 *Punto Casa and PPV* [1994] E.C.R. I–2355, paras 12–14; ECJ, Joined Cases C–418–C–421/93, C–460–C–462/93, C–464/93, C–9–C–11/94, C–14–15/94, C–23–24/94 and C–332/94 *Semeraro Casa Uno* [1996] E.C.R. I–2975, paras 9–28.

[463] ECJ, Case C–292/92 *Hünermund* [1993] E.C.R. I–6787, paras 17–24; ECJ, Case C–320/93 *Ortscheit* [1994] E.C.R. I–5257, para. 9; ECJ, Case C–412/93 *Société d'Importation Leclerc-Siplec* [1995] E.C.R. I–179, paras 18–24; ECJ, Joined Cases C–34–36/95 *De Agostini and TV Shop* [1997] E.C.R. I–3843, paras 40–47; ECJ, Case C–405/98 *Gourmet International Products* [2001] E.C.R. I–1795, paras 18–25; ECJ (judgment of March 25, 2004), Case C–71/02 *Karner*, not yet reported, paras 38–39. Legislation imposing requirements with regard to the products themselves is not covered, see ECJ, Case C–315/92 *Verband Sozialer Wettbewerb* [1994] E.C.R. I–317, paras 17–24; ECJ, Case C–470/93 *Mars* [1995] E.C.R. I–1923, paras 11–14; see the case notes by Ballon (1995) Col.J.E.L. 523–530 and Straetmans, *Consument en markt*, (Kluwer, Deurne, 1998), 341–346. Naturally, advertising in itself also constitutes a provision of a service, see Kugelmann, "Werbung als Dienstleistung" (2001) EuR. 363–375 and Drijber, "Les communications commerciales au carrefour de la dérégulation et de la réglementation" (2002) C.D.E. 529–610.

[464] This does not apply to rules relating to sales promotions which are liable to alter the content of the product: ECJ, Case C–368/95 *Familiapress* [1997] E.C.R. I–3689, paras 11–12, with a case note by Ballon (1998) Col.J.E.L. 172–178.

[465] *e.g.* ECJ, Case C–12/00 *Commission v Spain* [2003] E.C.R. I–459, para. 76.

[466] ECJ, Case C–405/98 *Gourmet International Products* [2001] E.C.R. I–1795, paras 19–21. For the importance of "market access" as a criterion, see the commentary by Straetmans (2002) C.M.L.R. 1407–1421.

[467] ECJ, Joined Cases C–34–36/95 *De Agostini and TV Shop* [1997] E.C.R. I–3834, paras 44–45.

formally discriminatory measure may be retained only under one of the exceptions provided for in Art. 30 of the EC Treaty.[468]

c. Common commercial policy

External trade in goods. Alongside the customs policy, commercial policy **5–114** also determines the conditions under which goods from non-member countries may be brought into free circulation in the Member States and goods from Member States may be exported to non-member countries. The Community conducts a common commercial policy pursuant to Art. 133 of the EC Treaty and a number of scattered Treaty provisions.[469] The common commercial policy covers independent measures which the Community adopts unilaterally (changes in tariff rates, export policy, measures to protect trade) and contractual measures adopted in agreement with third countries or international organisations (see the discussion of the common commercial policy and other external powers in para. 20–002 *et seq.*). The common commercial policy removes from the Member States the power to influence imports and exports to the benefit of national industry, thereby constituting a sphere of competence exclusive to the Community (see para. 5–022). The Council decides on a proposal from the Commission by a qualified majority (Art. 133(2) and (4)). As far as trade-related aspects of intellectual property are concerned, the Council decides in some cases on a proposal from the Commission by a unanimous vote and the Community does not have exclusive competence (Art. 133(5) and (6); see paras 20–003–20–004). The EU Constitution modifies many of these points in certain respects (see para. 20–006).

2. Free movement of persons

a. General scope

Treaty rules. The Treaty provisions on free movement of persons seek to **5–115** attain an optimum allocation of supply and demand in the Community market through complete movement of economic operators.[470] They are

---

[468] See, *e.g.* ECJ, Case C–320/93 *Ortscheidt* [1994] E.C.R. I–5243, paras 9–22; ECJ, Case C–189/95 *Franzén* [1997] E.C.R. I–5909, paras 69–7; ECJ, Case C–254/98 *TK-Heimdienst Sass* [2000] E.C.R. I–151, para. 36; ECJ (judgment of December 11, 2003), Case C–322/01 *Deutscher Apothekerverband*, not yet reported, paras 68–76.

[469] See, *inter alia*, Arts 26 and 27 of the EC Treaty on the common customs tariff (para. 5–095, *supra*) and Arts 34 and 37, pursuant to which commercial policy measures were taken in the context of the common agricultural policy.

[470] For general discussions, see Aussant, Fornasier, Louis, Séché, and Van Raepenbusch, *Commentaire Mégret—Le droit de la CEE. 3. Libre circulation des personnes, des services et des capitaux. Transports* (Editions de l'Université de Bruxelles, Brussels, 1990), at 9–149; Schermers, Flinterman, Kellermann, Van Haersolte and Van de Meent (eds), *Free Movement of Persons in Europe. Legal Problems and Experiences* (Martinus Nijhoff, Dordrecht, 1993), 641 pp.; Van Dijk, "Free Movement of Persons: Towards European Citizenship" (1992) S.E.W. 277–307; de Lary, *La libre circulation des personnes dans la CEE*

therefore intended to "facilitate the pursuit by Community citizens of occupational activities of all kinds throughout the Community".[471] Free movement of persons precludes Member States from discriminating against or imposing restrictions on both workers (EC Treaty, Art. 39) and self-employed persons (EC Treaty, Art. 43) who are nationals of another Member State. The Treaty provides for exceptions on grounds of public policy, public security or public health (EC Treaty, Art. 39(3) and Art. 46) where the Community may adopt implementing regulations (EC Treaty, Art. 39(3)(d)) or co-ordinating directives (Art. 46(2)), and also as regards employment in the public service (EC Treaty, Art. 39(4) and Art. 45). The provisions of the Treaty laying down prohibitions have direct effect,[472] not only *vis-à-vis* Member States in respect of action of public authorities, but also *vis-à-vis* associations or organisations not governed by public law in respect of acts resulting from the exercise of their legal autonomy creating obstacles to free movement of persons.[473] Accordingly, the prohibition of discrimination on grounds of nationality applies in cases where a group or organisation exercises a certain power over individuals and is in a position to impose on them conditions which adversely affect the exercise of the fundamental freedoms guaranteed under the Treaty.[474] The Court of Justice has held that the prohibition of discrimination enshrined in Art. 39 of the EC Treaty applies to an individual employer.[475] However, it is not certain whether the prohibition of non-discriminatory restrictions can be invoked against individual private persons.[476]

5–116 Legislation. The Treaty gives the Community the task of issuing directives or making regulations to facilitate free movement of workers (EC Treaty, Art. 40) and directives securing freedom of establishment (EC Treaty, Art.

(Presses Universitaires de France, Paris, 1992), 127 pp.; Fallon, "Les droits accessoires à l'exercice des droits économiques de la personne dans la Communauté" (1993) Ann.Dr.Louv. 235–253; Minor-De Pauw, "The Abolition of Non-Discriminatory Obstacles to Free Movement" (1994) A.D. 210–225. For a survey of recent case law, see Castro Oliveira, "Workers and other persons: step-by-step movement to citizenship—case law 1995–2001" (2002) C.M.L.R. 77–127.

[471] ECJ, Case 143/87 *Stanton* [1988] E.C.R. 3877, para. 13, and ECJ, Joined Cases 154 and 155/87 *RSVZ* [1988] E.C.R. 3897, para. 13.

[472] See for Art. 39(1) to (3) of the EC Treaty, ECJ, Case 41/74 *Van Duyn* [1974] E.C.R. 1337, paras 5–7; see for Art. 43 of the EC Treaty, ECJ, Case 2/74 *Reyners* [1974] E.C.R. 631, para. 30.

[473] ECJ, Case 36/74 *Walrave* [1974] E.C.R. 1405, paras 15–23 (para. 21 states in general terms that "Article 48 [now Art. 39], relating to the abolition of any discrimination based on nationality as regards gainful employment, extends likewise to agreements and rules which do not emanate from public authorities"); ECJ, Case C–415/93 *Bosman* [1995] E.C.R. I–4921, paras 82–87. For the question of the horizontal effect of the prohibiting provisions, see Mortelmans, "Excepties bij non-tarifaire intracommunautaire belemmeringen: assimilatie in het nieuwe EG-Verdrag?" (1997) S.E.W. 182, at 185–186.

[474] ECJ, Case C–411/98 *Ferlini* [2000] E.C.R. I–8081, para. 50 (concerning Art. 12 of the EC Treaty).

[475] ECJ, Case C–281/98 *Angonese* [2000] E.C.R. I–4139, paras 30–36.

[476] For a critical view in a case note on the judgment in *Angonese*, see Körber (2000) EuR 932, at 940–952; Stuyck (2001) S.E.W. 112–118; for a less critical view, see Van der Steen (2001) N.T.E.R. 4–9; Lengauer (2001) Z.f.RV. 57–65.

44(2)). As far as workers are concerned, Art. 42 of the EC Treaty contemplates ancillary measures in the social security field. As regards taking up and pursuing activities as self-employed persons, Art. 47 provides for directives for the mutual recognition of diplomas, certificates and other evidence of formal qualifications. The EU Constitution will not modify the rights that workers and self-employed persons may derive from the Treaties. It does however adapt the legislative instruments which may be used and, to a certain extent, the decision-making process by which the institutions are to facilitate free movement pursuant to the relevant Treaty provisions (see Arts III–133 to III–143).[477]

Workers and self-employed persons. As a result, workers and **5–117** self-employed persons are subject to different Treaty rules. In view of the common objective of the free movement of persons and of the fact that Community legislation frequently confers identical rights on workers and the self-employed, both sets of rules will be discussed together.[478] Ultimately, these provisions give shape to the "fundamental right" of citizens to freedom to seek employment, to work, to exercise the right of establishment and to provide services in any Member State.[479]

b. Beneficiaries

Conditions. The rules on free movement of workers and the right of **5–118** establishment, respectively, apply to workers and self-employed persons who are nationals of a Member State who find themselves in a situation warranting a connection with Community law.

(1) Nationals of a Member State

Nationality. Free movement of workers and the right of establishment **5–119** apply in principle only to nationals of a Member State.[480] Each Member State determines the conditions on which a natural person acquires and

---

[477] Thus, the Council will no longer have to decide by unanimity when laying down measures to co-ordinate national social security systems (compare Art. III–136(1) of the EU Constitution with Art. 42 of the EC Treaty) or measures governing the professions with respect to training and conditions of access for natural persons (compare Art. III–141(1)(b) of the EU Constitution with Art. 47(2) of the EC Treaty). As far as the co-ordination of social security systems is concerned, however, Art. III–136(2) provides that a Member State may request that the matter be referred to the European Council, as a result of which the co-decision procedure will be suspended. This possibility of having the matter referred to the European Council is similar to the "alarm bell" procedure which applies in the field of judicial co-operation in criminal matters, except for the fact that Art. III–136(2) does not provide that, where it is not possible to find agreement on a new draft framework law, Member States wishing to proceed with enhanced co-operation on the basis of that draft, will be authorised to do so (cf. para. 15–015, infra).

[478] See ECJ, Case C–107/94 Asscher [1996] E.C.R. I–3089, para. 29. See specifically as regards free movement of workers, Verschueren, Internationale arbeidsmigratie (Die Keure, Bruges, 1991), at 279–333; Martin, "Réflexions sur le champ d'application matériel de l'article 48 du Traité CE" (1993) C.D.E. 555–596.

[479] See Art. 15(2) of the Charter of Fundamental Rights of the European Union.

[480] See Art. 39(2) and Art. 43 of the EC Treaty: ECJ, Case 238/83 Meade [1984] E.C.R. 2631, para. 7.

loses its nationality (for companies, see para. 5–124). A Member State must recognise the conferral of nationality by another Member State without imposing additional conditions (see para. 12–007). As a result, the scope of application of free movement of persons varies with every change in the nationality law of Member States.

5–120 Third-country nationals covered. Nevertheless, persons other than workers or self-employed persons having the nationality of a Member State enjoy the advantages of free movement.[481] Community legislation has extended enjoyment of certain rights to members of the families of employed persons,[482] self-employed[483] persons and other persons on whom Community law confers a right of residence,[484] regardless of their nationality. Agreements concluded with non-member countries have also conferred rights on nationals of third countries and members of their families (see para. 5–157).

(2) *Qualifying workers*

5–121 Community definition. Article 39 (2) of the EC Treaty prohibits "any discrimination based on nationality between workers of the Member States". Consequently, alongside each Member State's legislation on nationality, the concept of "worker" determines who qualifies for free movement of workers. The term "worker" employed in Arts 39–42 of the EC Treaty is a concept of Community law with an independent Community meaning. If the definition of that term could be determined unilaterally by national law, it would be possible for each Member State to eliminate at will the protection afforded by the Treaty to certain categories of person.[485] In view of the fact that the Treaty does not define the term "worker", the Court of Justice has clarified its scope by taking the view that it defines the field of application of one of the fundamental freedoms guaranteed by the Treaty and, as such, may not be interpreted restrictively.[486]

---

[481] For a survey, see Carlier, "Le droit d'entrée et de séjour des ressortissants des Etats membres" (1994) A.D. 143, at 147–160. Free movement also applies to workers (regardless of their nationality) of a provider of services established in a Member State, who must be able to move within the Community together with the provider of services: ECJ, Case C–113/89 *Rush Portuguesa* [1990] E.C.R. I–1417, para. 12; ECJ, Case C–43/93 *Van der Elst* [1994] E.C.R. I–3803, para. 21.

[482] ECJ, Case 40/76 *Kermaschek v Bundesanstalt für Arbeit* [1976] E.C.R. 1669, para. 9. See Directive 68/360 and Regulations Nos 1612/68 and 1251/70; paras 5–127 and 5–131, *infra*. For a discussion, see Ziekow, "Der gemeinschaftsrechtliche Status der Familienangehörigen von Wanderarbeitnehmer" (1991) D.ö.V. 363–370.

[483] See Directives 73/148 and 75/34, since replaced by Directive 2004/38; nn.509–514 to para. 5–127, *infra*.

[484] See para. 5–128.

[485] ECJ, Case 75/63 *Hoekstra (née Unger)* [1964] E.C.R. 177, at 184.

[486] ECJ, Case 53/81 *Levin* [1982] E.C.R. 1035, para. 13.

Objective criteria. The Court of Justice bases itself on objective criteria **5–122** which distinguish the employment relationship by reference to the rights and duties of the persons concerned. The essential feature of an employment relationship is that "for a certain period of time a person performs services for and under the direction of another person in return for which he receives remuneration".[487] This must be determined in each case on the basis of all the factors and circumstances characterising the arrangements between the parties, such as the sharing of the commercial risks of the business and the freedom for a person to choose his own working hours and to engage his own assistants.[488]

The type of work is irrelevant, provided that an economic—that is, a remunerated—activity is involved.[489] Furthermore, it is not necessary that the remuneration received in exchange for the work performed should cover the costs of subsistence of the person concerned (and his dependants). Thus, free movement of workers applies to employment relationships where the remuneration provided for genuine work is under the minimum subsistence level laid down in the Member State of employment,[490] even if the person concerned claims supplementary benefit in the Member State concerned in order to supplement his remuneration.[491] Free movement also covers persons carrying out genuine part-time work.[492]

The protection of free movement also extends to job-seekers in another Member State, but only as long as they are potential participants in the labour market. The principle of free movement of workers requires only that the legislation of a Member State give the persons concerned a reasonable time in which to apprise themselves, in the territory of the Member State concerned, of offers of employment corresponding to their occupational qualifications and to take, where appropriate, the necessary steps in order to be engaged. The job-seeker may, however, be required to leave the territory of that State if he has not found employment there after six months, unless the person concerned provides evidence that he is

---

[487] ECJ, Case 66/85 *Lawrie-Blum* [1986] E.C.R. 2121, para. 17. Even an official of the European Communities (or of another international organisation) who is a national of Member State other than that in which he or she is employed must be regarded as a migrant worker: ECJ, Case C–411/98 *Ferlini* [2000] E.C.R. I–8081, para. 42.

[488] ECJ, Case C 3/87 *Agegate* [1989] E.C.R. 4459, para. 36. The fact that a person is related by marriage to the director and sole owner of the undertaking does not mean that that person cannot be regarded as being a worker within the meaning of Art. 39 of the EC Treaty if he or she pursues an effective and genuine activity in a relationship of subordination: ECJ, Case C–337/97 *Meeusen* [1999] E.C.R. I–3289, paras 14–16.

[489] *e.g.* professional cyclists: ECJ, Case 36/74 *Walrave* [1974] E.C.R. 1405, paras 4–7; professional footballers: ECJ, Case 13/76 *Donà* [1976] E.C.R. 1333, para. 12, and ECJ, Case C–415/93 *Bosman* [1995] E.C.R. I–4921, paras 73–76 (paras 5–130 and 5–134, *infra*). See also (commercial) activities carried out by members of a community based on religion or another form of philosophy: ECJ, Case 196/87 *Steymann* [1988] E.C.R. 6159, paras 12–14.

[490] ECJ, Case 53/81 *Levin* [1982] E.C.R. 1035, para. 15.

[491] ECJ, Case 139/85 *Kempf* [1986] E.C.R. 1741, para. 14.

[492] ECJ, Case 53/81 *Levin* [1982] E.C.R. 1035, para. 17.

continuing to seek employment and that he has genuine chances of being engaged.[493]

Free movement of workers (especially in connection with unemployment insurance) applies only to persons who have already participated in the employment market by exercising an effective and genuine occupational activity, which has conferred on them the status of workers within the Community meaning of that term.[494]

5–123 Employers. Reliance may be made on the provisions relating to free movement of workers by others, in particular employers. In order to be truly effective, the right of workers to be engaged and employed without discrimination necessarily entails as a corollary the employer's entitlement to engage them in accordance with the rules governing freedom of movement for workers.[495]

(3) *Self-employed persons and companies qualifying*

5–124 Establishment. The right of establishment relates to activities not carried out by way of gainful employment. This means economic activities carried on by a person outside any relationship of subordination with regard to the conditions of work or remuneration and under his own personal responsibility.[496] "Establishment" of a natural or legal person within the meaning of the Treaty involves the actual pursuit of an economic activity through a fixed establishment in another Member State for an indefinite period.[497] If an occupational activity is not carried out in a lasting way, it may constitute the supply of a service (see para. 5–172). The first paragraph of Art. 43 of the EC Treaty refers to "freedom of establishment of nationals of a Member State in the territory of another Member State". For the purposes of the application of freedom of establishment, Art. 48 equates companies or firms "formed in accordance with the law of a Member State and having their registered office, central administration or principal place of business within the Community" with natural persons

---

[493] ECJ, Case C–292/89 *Antonissen* [1991] E.C.R. I–745, paras 16 and 22. Accordingly, a Member State cannot automatically oblige job-seekers to leave their territory after their time has expired: ECJ, Case C–344/95 *Commission v Belgium* [1997] E.C.R. I–1035, paras 12–18. For the reasonable time enjoyed by a Turkish national in order to seek work under the relevant Association Agreement, see ECJ, Case C–171/95 *Tetik* [1997] E.C.R. I–329, paras 27–48.

[494] ECJ, Case C–278/94 *Commission v Belgium* [1996] E.C.R. I–4307, para. 40; ECJ, Case C–224/98 *D'Hoop* [2002] E.C.R. I–6191, para. 18. For the differing position of workers and job-seekers, see ECJ (judgment of March 23, 2004), Case C–138/02 *Collins*, not yet reported, paras 30–31. However, after exercising his or her rights of free movement, a job-seeking citizen of the Union may not suffer discrimination on grounds of nationality: *D'Hoop*, paras 27–40 (see para. 5–059).

[495] ECJ, Case C–350/96 *Clean Car Autoservice* [1998] E.C.R. I–2521, paras 19–20.

[496] ECJ, Case C–268/99 *Jany* [2001] E.C.R. I–8615, paras 34–50 (definition applied to prostitution).

[497] ECJ, Case C–221/89 *Factortame Limited* (*Factortame II*) [1991] E.C.R. I–3905, para. 20. See also paras 5–135 *et seq.*

who are nationals of Member States. Art. 48 does not apply to "non-profit-making" companies or firms (see the second para. of that article).

(4) *Connection with Community law*

Transfrontier situation. A person may rely on the Treaty provisions on **5–125** free movement of workers or the right of establishment only where his or her situation exhibits a genuine transfrontier factor. The Treaty provisions cannot be applied to situations wholly internal to a Member State.[498] For instance, a transfrontier situation exists where a person works in the territory of a Member State other than the one in which he or she resides and of which he or she is a national.[499] The fact that an employment relationship is potentially of a transfrontier nature is insufficient to cause Community law to apply. When Moser, a German national, argued that the refusal of the *Land* of Baden-Württemberg to let him undertake teacher-training on the ground that he was a member of the Communist Party made it impossible for him to apply for teaching posts in another Member State, the Court of Justice held that a purely hypothetical prospect of employment in another Member State did not establish a sufficient connection with Community law to justify the application of Art. 39 of the EC Treaty.[500]

A Member State is entitled to impose stricter requirements upon its own nationals than upon nationals of other Member States. Nevertheless, the Court of Justice explained in *Knoors* (see para. 5–069) that a Member State may not operate "reverse" discrimination against nationals who, by taking advantage of the facilities existing in the matter of freedom of movement and establishment, are in a situation which may be assimilated to that of any other person enjoying the rights and liberties guaranteed by the Treaty.[501] Any Community national who, irrespective of his or her place of residence or nationality, has worked in another Member State falls within the scope of free movement of workers or freedom of establishment.[502] In

---

[498] ECJ, Case 175/78 *Saunders* [1979] E.C.R. 1129, para. 11; ECJ, Case C–152/94 *Van Buynder* [1995] E.C.R. I–3981, paras 10–12; ECJ, Case C–134/94 *Esso Española* [1995] E.C.R. I–4223, paras 13–16; ECJ, Joined Cases C–225–C–227/95 *Kapasakalis* [1998] E.C.R. I–4239, para. 22. See, with regard to the Community provisions governing the right of residence of nationals of other Member States and their spouses: ECJ, Joined Cases C–297/88 and C–197/89 *Dzodzi* [1990] E.C.R. I–3763, para. 28.

[499] ECJ, Case C–336/96 *Gilly* [1998] E.C.R. I–2793, para. 21.

[500] ECJ, Case 180/83 *Moser* [1984] E.C.R. 2539, para. 18.

[501] ECJ, Case 115/78 *Knoors* [1979] E.C.R. 399, paras 20 and 24. A person is not entitled to rely on Community law where his or her professional activity is impeded in some way in his or her own Member State, merely because he or she lives in another Member State: ECJ, Case C–112/91 *Werner* [1993] E.C.R. I–429, paras 16–17.

[502] ECJ, Case C–419/92 *Scholz* [1994] E.C.R. I–505, para. 9. *Cf.* ECJ, Case C–19/92 *Kraus* [1993] E.C.R. I–1663, paras 16–22 (para. 5–134, *infra*); ECJ, Case C–443/93 *Vougioukas* [1995] E.C.R. I–4033, para. 38; ECJ, Case C–107/94 *Asscher* [1996] E.C.R. I–3089, paras 31–34; ECJ, Case C–18/95 *Terhoeve* [1999] E.C.R. I–345, paras 27–28. See also the discussion of reverse discrimination, para. 5–069, *supra*.

addition, the Court of Justice considered that an Italian who had studied in Austria could rely on the provisions relating to the free movement of workers as against an Italian employer who, as proof of knowledge of German, accepted only a certificate issued locally.[503]

The applicability of the free movement of workers or the right of establishment is also important for the members of the family of such a worker or self-employed person. When a national who has availed himself or herself of the right of free movement or freedom of establishment returns to his or her country of origin, his or her spouse must enjoy at least the same rights of entry and residence there as would be granted to him or her under Community law if the national in question chose to enter and reside in another Member State, even if the spouse is not a national of a Member State.[504] If the Community national in question has never exercised the right to free movement within the Community, members of his or her family cannot necessarily rely on Community law.[505]

5–126 Territorial aspects. An employment relationship must exhibit not only a transfrontier element but also a sufficiently close link with the territory of the Community.[506] A national of a Member State who works for an undertaking of another Member State continues to enjoy the protection of Community law while working temporarily outside the Community, provided that he or she was working on behalf of the undertaking.[507] Community law is also applicable to a national of a Member State working for an embassy of another Member State in a non-member country as regards those aspects of his or her employment relationship which are governed by the law of the second Member State.[508]

---

[503] ECJ, Case C–281/98 *Angonese* [2000] E.C.R. I–4139. See Stuyck (2001) S.E.W. 112–118, who criticises the judgment for failing to find that this was a purely internal situation.

[504] ECJ, Case C–370/90 *Surinder Singh* [1992] E.C.R. I–4265, paras 21 and 23. Community law can guarantee this only where the spouse who is a national of a non-Member State had a valid right to remain in the Member State from which he or she returns together with the EU national: ECJ (judgment of September 23, 2003), Case C–109/01 *Akrich*, not yet reported, paras 50–54. Where the spouse is not lawfully resident in that Member State, regard must still be had to the right of respect for family life enshrined in Art. 8 of the ECHR: *ibid.*, paras 58–60 (in which reference is made to case law of the Court of Human Rights recognising a right of residence on this basis).

[505] ECJ, Joined Cases C–64/96 and C–65/96 *Uecker and Jacquet* [1997] E.C.R. I–3171, paras 16–21.

[506] See, *e.g.* ECJ, Case C–248/96 *Grahame and Hollanders* [1997] E.C.R. I–6407, para. 36 (work in the territory of an overseas territory of a Member State).

[507] ECJ, Case 237/83 *Prodest* [1984] E.C.R. 3153, para. 7. See also ECJ, Case C–60/93 *Aldewereld* [1994] E.C.R. I–2991, paras 14–15 and 20–24.

[508] ECJ, Case C–214/94 *Boukhalfa* [1996] E.C.R. I–2253, paras 15–17. Consequently, the connection is not only with the territory but also with the law of a Member State, see the case note by Lhoest (1998) C.M.L.R. 247–267.

c. Substance of the free movement of persons

(1) *Right to enter, leave and reside*

Entry and residence rights. Effective exercise of the right to obtain **5–127** employment in another Member State is conditional upon the worker or the job-seeker being able readily to enter or leave the host country and reside there. This also applies to persons wishing to engage in self-employed activities in another Member State.

The rights enshrined in Art. 39(3)(b), (c) and (d) of the EC Treaty have been enlarged upon in Directive 68/360, adopted by the Council on the basis of Art. 40 of the EC Treaty, which was only recently replaced by Directive 2004/38 of the European Parliament and of the Council.[509] Persons qualifying for free movement (workers and members of their families) may enter the territory of another Member State simply on production of a valid identity card or passport.[510] According to Art. 4 of Directive 68/360, their right of residence in the host State was to be evidenced—but not determined—by production of a "Residence Permit for a National of a Member State of the EEC".[511] Under Directive 2004/38, a Member State may require Union citizens to register with the relevant authorities in the case of residence for periods longer than three months (Art. 8). The right of residence of a qualifying worker extends to his or her spouse (since Directive 2004/38: also the registered partner) and their descendants who are under the age of 21 years (since Directive 2004/38: or are dependants), as well as to dependent relations in the ascending line of the worker and his or her spouse (or registered partner), irrespective of their nationality (Directive 2004/38, Art. 2; previously Art. 10 of Regulation No. 1612/68; see para. 5–131). Workers who have been employed in a Member State, and members of their families, are entitled to remain in the

---

[509] Council Directive 68/360/EEC of October 15, 1968, on the abolition of restrictions on movement and residence for workers of Member States and their families, [1968] O.J. English Spec. Ed. II 485. See para. 12–009, *infra*, for Directive 2004/38/EC of the European Parliament and of the Council of April 29, 2004 on the right of citizens of the Union and their family members to move and reside freely within the territory of the Member States amending Regulation (EEC) No. 1612/68 and repealing Directives 64/221/EC, 68/360/EC, 72/194/EC, 73/148/EC, 75/34/EC, 75/35/EC, 90/364/EC, 90/365/EC and 93/96/EC, [2004] O.J. L158/77 (adopted on the basis of Arts 12, 18, 40, 44 and 52 of the EC Treaty).

[510] Directive 68/360, Art. 3; see also Directive 2004/38, Art. 5(1). In view of the importance which the Community legislature attaches to the protection of family life, a third-country national married to an EU national may not be sent back because he or she has no valid identity card, passport or visa, where the person in question is able to prove his or her identity and the conjugal ties: ECJ, Case C–459/99 *MRAX* [2002] E.C.R. I–6591, paras 53–62. See also ECJ, Case C–68/89 *Commission v Netherlands* [1991] E.C.R. I–2637, para. 12. See also Directive 2004/38, Art. 5(4).

[511] See also *MRAX, ibid.*, paras 89–91 (a Member State cannot refuse a national of a non-Member State who is married to an EU national a residence permit merely because that third-country national entered the territory unlawfully or because his or her visa expired before an application was made for a residence permit). For the prohibition on more extensive administrative obstacles in granting that right of residence, see ECJ, Case C–344/95 *Commission v Belgium* [1997] E.C.R. I–1033, paras 20–34.

territory of that State (Art. 39(3)(d) of the EC Treaty, as enlarged upon by Commission Regulation No. 1251/70).[512]

At the same time, the Council has adopted directives in order to secure the right to enter a Member State and reside there for nationals of a Member State and members of their families wishing to establish themselves there (or provide or receive services).[513] Member States must recognise the right of residence of members of a family even if the latter are not nationals of a Member State.[514] These directives have also been replaced by Directive 2004/38.

5–128 **Extension to non-economically active persons.** Free movement of workers and freedom of establishment (and likewise freedom to provide services) entail a right of residence for economically active persons and their dependants. On June 28, 1990, the Council adopted three directives governing the right of residence for Member State nationals generally,[515] for employed and self-employed persons who have stopped working[516] and for students.[517] The directives conferred a right of residence on Member State nationals and members of their families who had no such right under other provisions, subject to the proviso that they were covered by sickness insurance in respect of all risks in the host State and had sufficient resources. Consequently, part of the rules on free movement of persons also applied to nationals of Member States who are not economically active.[518] The residence rights laid down in these directives, together with

---

[512] Regulation (EEC) No. 1251/70 of the Commission of June 29, 1970 on the right of workers to remain in the territory of a Member State after having been employed in that State, [1970] O.J. English Spec. Ed. (II), 402.

[513] Council Directive 73/148/EEC of May 21, 1973 on the abolition of restrictions on movement and residence within the Community for nationals of Member States with regard to establishment and the provision of services, [1973] O.J. L172/14; Council Directive 75/34/EEC of December 17, 1974 concerning the right of nationals of a Member State to remain in the territory of another Member State after having pursued therein an activity in a self-employed category, [1975] O.J. L14/10.

[514] In view of the fundamental right to respect for family life, a Member State must grant such a right of residence to a national of a non-member country who is married to a EU national established in that Member State where the latter falls under Directive 73/148 because he or she provides services for persons established in other Member States: ECJ, Case C–60/00 *Carpenter* [2002] E.C.R. I–6279, paras 28–46.

[515] Council Directive 90/364/EEC of June 28, 1990 on the right of residence, [1990] O.J. L180/26.

[516] Council Directive 90/365/EEC of June 28, 1990 on the right of residence for employees and self-employed persons who have ceased their occupational activity, [1990] O.J. L180/28.

[517] Council Directive 90/366 on the right of residence for students, [1990] O.J. L180/30, which was annulled by the Court of Justice on the ground that its legal basis should have been the second para. of Art. 7 of the EEC Treaty [now Art. 12 of the EC Treaty], and not Art. 235 [now Art. 308 of the EC Treaty] as in the case of the two aforementioned directives on the right of residence: ECJ, Case C–295/90 *European Parliament v Council* [1992] E.C.R. I–4193. However, the legal effects of the annulled directive were left in force until December 31, 1993, the last date for implementing Council Directive 93/96/EEC of October 29, 1993 on the right of residence for students, [1993] O.J. L317/59, which was based on the second paragraph of Art. 7 of the EEC Treaty.

[518] See also the introduction of the internal market as an area without internal frontiers (para. 5–081, *supra*) and citizenship of the Union (para. 12–001 *et seq.*).

the residence rights conferred by other Community instruments on persons engaged in economic activities, have been codified in Directive 2004/38 of the European Parliament and of the Council.[519] This directive grants Union citizens who are not engaged in economic activities the right to reside in another Member State if they have sufficient resources for themselves and their family members and comprehensive sickness insurance cover in the host State. In addition, this directive grants Union citizens who have resided legally for a continuous period of five years in the host Member State the right of permanent residence there (see para. 12–009).

(2) Prohibition of discriminatory and non-discriminatory obstacles

Contents. Article 39(2) of the EC Treaty provides that freedom of **5–129** movement for workers is to entail "the abolition of any discrimination based on nationality between workers of the Member States as regards employment, remuneration and other conditions of work and employment". In addition, the first paragraph of Art. 43 states that "restrictions on the freedom of establishment of nationals of a Member State in the territory of another Member State shall be prohibited". The Court of Justice has made it clear that the Treaty precludes, not only any form of discrimination in the exercise of free movement of workers (see paras 5–130–5–131) and the right of establishment (see paras 5–132–5–133), but also measures which are applicable without distinction to a Member State's own nationals and nationals from other Member States if they treat persons less favourably where they exercise their right of free movement or of freedom of establishment in a Member State other than their own (see para. 5–134).

Prohibited discrimination against workers. The Court of Justice considers **5–130** that Art. 39(2) of the EC Treaty prohibits all direct or indirect discrimination[520] between nationals of a given Member State and nationals of other Member States.[521]

In some cases, the place of residence is held to be an unjustifiable criterion.[522] Accordingly, the Court of Justice has held that "[e]ven though the criterion [applied by Luxembourg] of permanent residence in the national territory . . . in connection with obtaining any repayment of an over deduction of tax applies irrespective of the nationality of the taxpayer concerned, there is a risk that it will work in particular against taxpayers

---

[519] See n.509, *supra*.
[520] For these terms, see paras 5–065–5–067, *supra*.
[521] ECJ, Case 152/73 *Sotgiu* [1974] E.C.R. 153, paras 10–13; ECJ, Case 33/88 *Allué* [1989] E.C.R. 1591, paras 11–12; ECJ, Case C–90/96 *Petrie* [1997] E.C.R. I–6527, paras 53–56. Use of the criterion of nationality does not invariably constitute prohibited discrimination, see ECJ, Case C–336/96 *Gilly* [1998] E.C.R. I–2793, paras 30–34 (double taxation of frontier workers).
[522] See, *e.g.* ECJ, Case C–350/96 *Clean Car Autoservice* [1998] E.C.R. I–2521, paras 26–43.

who are nationals of other Member States. It is often such persons who will in the course of the year leave the country or take up residence there."[523] Nevertheless, a Member State may, in principle, tax the income of a taxpayer who is employed in that State but has his residence elsewhere more heavily than the income of a "resident" with the same income. Generally, this will not involve any discrimination since there are objective differences between residents and non-residents justifying a difference in treatment, in particular as far as concerns taking account of the taxpayer's personal and family circumstances when making an assessment to tax.[524] This will result in unjustified discrimination, however, where a non-resident receives the major part of his income in the Member State in which he works and insufficient income in the State of his residence to enable his personal and family circumstances to be taken into account for taxation purposes.[525] Such discrimination may take place both against beneficiaries of free movement of workers and beneficiaries of freedom of establishment.[526]

Since free movement of workers holds good for all forms of gainful employment, discrimination on grounds of nationality is also prohibited in principle in professional sport. Nevertheless, the Court of Justice has accepted that foreign players may be excluded from certain matches for reasons of a non-economic nature which relate to the particular nature and context of such matches and are thus of sporting interest only, such as matches between national teams from different countries.[527] In *Bosman* the

---

[523] ECJ, Case C–175/88 *Biehl* [1990] E.C.R. I–1779, para. 14. See also ECJ, Case C–111/91 *Commission v Luxembourg* [1993] E.C.R. I–817, paras 9–10 and para. 23; ECJ, Case C–151/94 *Commission v Luxembourg* [1995] E.C.R. I–3685, paras 12–22.

[524] ECJ, Case C–279/93 *Schumacker* [1995] E.C.R. I–225, paras 30–35; ECJ, Case C–336/96 *Gilly* [1998] E.C.R. I–2793, paras 47–50; ECJ, Case C–391/97 *Gschwind* [1999] E.C.R. I–5451, paras 20–32.

[525] *Schumacker* (cited in the preceding n.524. *supra*), paras 36–47. For a case of discrimination against foreign companies, see ECJ, Case C–311/97 *Royal Bank of Scotland* [1999] E.C.R. I–2651, paras 28–31 (discrimination as compared with national companies in a like situation); ECJ, Joined Cases C–397/98 and C–410/98 *Metallgesellschaft* [2001] E.C.R. I–1727, paras 37–76 (discrimination against subsidiaries of foreign companies as compared with subsidiaries of domestic companies).

[526] ECJ, Case C–80/94 *Wielockx* [1995] E.C.R. I–2493, paras 20–27. See also the (unjustified) indirect discrimination in ECJ, Case C–107/94 *Asscher* [1996] E.C.R. I–3089, paras 37–49. See Vanistendael, "The Consequences of *Schumacker* and *Wielockx*: Two Steps Forward in the Tax Procession of Echternach" (1996) C.M.L.R. 255–269; Keeling and Shipwright, "Some Taxing Problems concerning Non-Discrimination and the EC Treaty" (1995) E.L.Rev. 580–597; Lenaerts and Maselis, "Inkomstenbelasting en non-discriminatie in de Europese Unie" in *Liber Amicorum Jean-Pierre Lagae*, (Ced. Samson, Diegem, 1998), at 477–495; Van Thiel, "Removal of income tax barriers to market integration in the European Union: litigation by the Community citizen instead of harmonisation by the Community legislature?" (2003) EC Tax Review 4–19; Farmer, "The Court's case law on taxation: a castle built on shifting sands?" (2003) EC Tax Review 75–81; Vanistendael, "The compatibility of the basic economic freedoms with the sovereign national tax systems of the Member States" (2003) EC Tax Review 136–143; Wattel, "Red Herrings in Direct Tax Cases before the ECJ" (2004) L.I.E.I. 81–95; for testing tax rules against the right of establishment, see also para. 5–138, *infra*.

[527] ECJ, Case 13/76 *Donà* [1976] E.C.R. 1333, paras 14–15.

Court made it clear that nationality clauses are contrary to Art. 39 of the EC Treaty for matches between football clubs composed of professional players.[528]

Equal treatment for migrant workers. Council Regulation No. 1612/68 of **5–131** October 15, 1968 defines the fundamental prohibition of discrimination with regard to migrant workers.[529] The regulation guarantees equal treatment within a given Member State of national workers and workers who are nationals of other Member States as regards all conditions of employment and work, in particular as regards remuneration, dismissal and, in the event of unemployment, reinstatement or re-employment (Art. 7(1)); social and tax advantages (Art. 7(2)); access to vocational training schools and retraining centres (Art. 7(3)); membership of trade unions and the exercise of trade-union rights, including the right to vote (Art. 8(1)), and housing (Art. 9). The regulation confers on the worker's spouse and dependent children the right to take up any activity as an employed person.[530] In addition, migrant workers' children must be admitted to general educational, apprenticeship and vocational training courses under the same conditions as nationals of the host Member State (Art. 12).

The Court of Justice has associated application of the requirement for equal treatment primarily with the expression "social and tax advantages" (Art. 7(2) of the Regulation), defining it very broadly as all advantages "which, whether or not linked to a contract of employment, are generally granted to national workers primarily because of their objective status of workers or by virtue of the mere fact of their residence on the national territory and the extension of which to workers who are nationals of other Member States therefore seems suitable to facilitate their mobility within the Community".[531] Accordingly, the Court of Justice counted as a social advantage the migrant worker's right to use his own language—in proceedings not linked to his employment relationship—before the courts of the Member State in which he resided, on the ground that this played

---

[528] ECJ, Case C–415/93 *Bosman* [1995] E.C.R. I–4921, paras 127–137 (for the ruling on transfer fees, see para. 5–134, *infra*). Nationals of non-member countries can also invoke the prohibition of discrimination on the basis of association agreements concluded by the Community with third countries, see ECJ, Case C–438/00 *Kolpak* [2003] E.C.R. I–4135, paras 24–58 (concerning a Slovakian handball player), and Pautot, "La liberté de circulation des sportifs professionnels en Europe" (2001) R.M.C.U.E. 102–105. For the controversial case of *Bosman*, see Defalque (1996) J.T. 539–546; Hilf and Pache (1996) N.J.W. 1169–1177; Weatherill (1996) C.M.L.R. 991–1033; Van Nuffel (1996) Col.J.E.L. 345–359, and a number of articles in (1996) 1 R.M.C.U.E. For sport, see also para. 5–238, *infra*.

[529] Council Regulation (EEC) No. 1612/68 of the Council of October 15, 1968 on freedom of movement for workers within the Community, [1968](II) O.J. English Spec. Ed. II 475.

[530] Regulation No. 1612/68, Art. 11, now replaced by Art. 23 of Directive 2004/38 (see para. 5–127, *supra*).

[531] ECJ, Case 207/78 *Even* [1979] E.C.R. 2019, para. 22. For the concept of "social advantages", see Ellis, "Social Advantages: A New Lease of Life?" (2003) C.M.L.R. 639, at 642–652.

"an important role in the integration of a migrant worker and his family into the host country".[532] In the same spirit, Art. 7(2) of the Regulation puts a Member State which allows its nationals to obtain permission for foreign unmarried companions to reside with them under a duty to afford the same opportunity to nationals of another Member State.[533] Nevertheless, the Court of Justice has held that Member States are entitled to rely on any objective difference there may be between their own nationals and those of other Member States when they lay down the conditions under which leave to remain indefinitely in their territory is to be granted to the spouses of such persons.[534] However, the grant of a social advantage may not be made dependent on the condition that the worker or members of his family dependent upon him be resident within the territory of the Member of State of employment.[535]

5–132 Prohibited discrimination with respect to establishment. As far as freedom of establishment is concerned, the Court of Justice held in *Reyners* that Art. 43 of the EC Treaty constituted a particular embodiment of the general prohibition of discrimination on grounds of nationality and hence considered that "[a]fter the expiry of the transitional period the directives provided for by the Chapter on the right of establishment have become superfluous with regard to implementing the rule on nationality, since this is henceforth sanctioned by the Treaty itself with direct effect."[536] Accordingly, Belgium had to allow Reyners, a Dutchman with a Belgian diploma of *docteur en droit*, to be inscribed on the roll of *avocats*. The Court referred to the transitional period, during which the Council had drawn up, pursuant to Art. 54 of the EEC Treaty, a General Programme for the Abolition of Restrictions on Freedom of Establishment, which advocated liberalisation of the rules on entry to and residence in other Member States by means of directives.[537] The General Programme went on

---

[532] ECJ, Case 137/84 *Mutsch* [1985] E.C.R. 2681, paras 16–17. For the extension of this right to all persons who exercise their right of free movement, see ECJ, Case C–274/96 *Bickel and Franz* [1998] E.C.R. I–7637, paras 13–31 (see para. 5–060, *infra*).

[533] ECJ, Case 59/85 *Reed* [1986] E.C.R. 1283, paras 28–29. See also the fact that grant of funding for studying has been recognised as a social advantage, n.1130 to para. 5–239, *infra*. Other examples of "social advantages" are: a funeral payment (ECJ, Case C–237/94 *O'Flynn* [1996] E.C.R. I–2617, paras 17–30); unemployment benefits paid to young people who have just completed their studies ("tideover allowances") and are the dependents of workers resident in Belgium (ECJ, Case C–278/94 *Commission v Belgium* [1996] E.C.R. I–4307, paras 25–31); a benefit conditional on residence (ECJ, Case C–57/96 *Meints* [1997] E.C.R. I–6689, paras 44–48). See the note by Peers to *O'Flynn* and *Commission v Belgium* (1997) E.L.Rev. 157–165.

[534] ECJ, Case C–356/98 *Kaba* [2000] E.C.R. I–2623, paras 31–34 (a Member State may require the spouse of a non-national to be resident for a longer period). For a critical commentary, see Peers, "Dazed and Confused: Family Members' Residence Rights and the Court of Justice" (2001) E.L.Rev. 76–83.

[535] ECJ, Case C–337/97 *Meeusen* [1999] E.C.R. I–3289, paras 21–25.

[536] ECJ, Case 2/74 *Reyners* [1974] E.C.R. 631, para. 30.

[537] General Programme for the Abolition of Restrictions on Freedom of Establishment, December 18, 1961 [1961] English O.J. Spec. Ed., Second Series, IX. Resolutions of the Council and of the Representatives of the Member States, p.7.

to cite by way of restrictions to be abolished that access to self-employment might not be made subject to a period of prior residence or training in the host country and that the latter might not impose taxation or other financial burdens, such as the provision of security. Towards the end of the transitional period, the Council had not adopted all the necessary directives.[538] The Court of Justice, however, construed the obligation to abolish restrictions on freedom of establishment "by progressive stages" (EEC Treaty, Art. 52) as having the same implications as the prohibition of discrimination laid down for workers in Art. 39 of the EC Treaty. In the present version of this provision, Art. 43 of the EC Treaty consequently speaks of the "prohibition" of restrictions on freedom of establishment.[539]

Prohibited indirect discrimination. Article 43 of the EC Treaty also **5–133** prohibits indirect discrimination, such as the refusal of the Paris Bar to admit a Belgian who held a Belgian diploma recognised by a French university as equivalent to the requisite French degree and had also fulfilled the French vocational training requirements for persons not holding a French diploma.[540] Article 43 prohibits any national rule which places nationals of another Member State in a less favourable situation than nationals of the State in question in the exercise of a self-employed activity. Accordingly, German legislation obliging a Greek hydrotherapist to have his name entered in the registers of civil status in a form modifying its pronunciation and thereby causing potential clients possibly to confuse him with other persons was held to be contrary to Art. 43.[541] Freedom of establishment also means that self-employed persons from other Member States may not be discriminated against in the grant of social advantages to which they would be entitled under Regulation No. 1612/68 (see para. 5–131) if they were workers.[542]

In the absence of any Community legislation on the matter, a Member State may impose certain administrative formalities in respect of the exercise of freedom of establishment, but any sanction for failing to comply

---

[538] The Council adopted directives on the right of residence (n.509 to para. 5–127, *supra*) and various others on agriculture, trade, industry and crafts (n.623 to para. 5–145, *infra*), but did not, for example, adopt all the necessary directives on transport and the liberal professions.

[539] In this way, the Amsterdam Treaty replaced the references to the abolition in progressive stages of the restrictions in question during the transitional period; at the same time, it removed the stand-still provision set out in the former Art. 53 of the EC Treaty (prohibition on Member States' introducing new restrictions) and the first paragraph of the former Art. 54, which referred to the General Programme.

[540] ECJ, Case 71/76 *Thieffry* [1977] E.C.R. 765, para. 19. For architects, see ECJ, Case 11/77 *Patrick* [1977] E.C.R. 1199, para. 18; for employees, see ECJ, Case 222/86 *Heylens* [1987] E.C.R. 4097, paras 11–12 (football trainer).

[541] ECJ, Case C–168/91 *Konstantinidis* [1993] E.C.R. I–1191, para. 17.

[542] ECJ, Case C–111/91 *Commission v Luxembourg* [1993] E.C.R. I–817, paras 16–18 and 33. ECJ, C–337/97 *Meeusen* [1999] E.C.R. I–3289, paras 26–30.

with such a formality may not be so disproportionate to the gravity of the infringement as to become an obstacle to free movement of persons. Accordingly, where a person obtained a driving licence in a Member State and could have exchanged it for a driving licence issued by another Member State where he was established, but failed to do so within the time-limit prescribed, it is contrary to Art. 43 of the EC Treaty to treat that person as if he were driving without a licence, thereby incurring criminal penalties.[543]

Since national law can determine, *inter alia*, the nationality of companies from the place of their seat, indirect discrimination will arise where a Member State employs a criterion which is liable to work more particularly to the disadvantage of companies having their seat in other Member States.[544] The prohibition of direct or indirect discrimination on grounds of nationality must also be taken into account in registering vessels. Such grant of "nationality" to a vessel is a condition for the exercise of the right of establishment which cannot be made to depend on the nationality of the owners or charterers and, in the case of a company, on the nationality of the shareholders or directors, or on their place of residence or domicile.[545]

The Court has held that it is a "corollary" of free movement of persons, in particular the right to pursue an employed or self-employed activity in another Member State and to reside there after having pursued such an activity, that there should be access to leisure activities available in that State. Consequently, French legislation under which only French nationals could register a leisure craft in France was held not to be compatible with free movement.[546] It clearly emerges from this case law that the Court of Justice treats the Treaty provisions on free movement of workers and freedom of establishment as having to be read together in governing free movement of persons.

---

[543] ECJ, Case C–193/94 *Skanavi and Chryssanthakopoulos* [1996] E.C.R. I–929, paras 31–39. The restriction on Member States' power to impose criminal sanctions as a result of the free movement of persons does not apply, however, to a national of a third country who cannot rely on the rules governing free movement of persons: ECJ, Case C–230/97 *Awoyemi* [1998] E.C.R. I–6781, paras 28–30. Now Council Directive 91/439/EEC of July 29, 1991 on driving licences ([1991] O.J. L237/1, as amended by Council Directive 96/47/EC of July 23, 1996, [1996] O.J. L235/1) requires mutual recognition of driving licences and there is no need to exchange the driving licence issued by one Member State for the driving licence of the State of residence.

[544] ECJ, Case C–330/91 *Commerzbank* [1993] E.C.R. I–4017, paras 13–15 (residence for tax purposes); ECJ, Case C–101/94 *Commission v Italy* [1996] E.C.R. I–2691, paras 8–28 (corporate seat).

[545] ECJ, Case C–221/89 *Factortame Limited* (*Factortame II*) [1991] E.C.R. I–3905, paras 22–33; the same form of words is to be found in ECJ, Case C–246/89 *Commission v UK* [1991] E.C.R. I–4585, paras 23–31; ECJ, Case C–93/89 *Commission v Ireland* [1991] E.C.R. I–4569, paras 10–11; ECJ, Case C–334/94 *Commission v France* [1996] E.C.R. I–1307, paras 12–19; ECJ, Case C–62/96 *Commission v Greece* [1997] E.C.R. I–6275, paras 17–18.

[546] ECJ, Case C–334/94 *Commission v France* [1996] E.C.R. I–1307, paras 21–23; ECJ, Case C–151/96 *Commission v Ireland* [1997] E.C.R. I–3327, paras 11–16; ECJ, Case C–62/96 *Commission v Greece* [1997] E.C.R. I–6725, paras 19–20.

Non-discriminatory obstacles. For a long time, it was assumed that the **5–134** Treaty provisions on free movement of persons did not preclude a restriction of the mobility of economic operators if the restriction applied without distinction to a State's own nationals and nationals of other Member States. The Court of Justice seemed not to recognise free movement of persons (employees and self-employed persons) as having the same scope as free movement of goods and services.[547]

In the 1988 judgment in *Wolf*, the Court of Justice went further, however, by declaring incompatible with the principles of free movement of persons a national measure which both in law and in fact was applicable in the same way to nationals of the Member State in question and to nationals of other Member States but nevertheless restricted free movement of persons because it treated *all* Community nationals less favourably where they had been employed in the territory of more than one Member State.[548] The 1993 judgment in *Kraus* took the further step of aligning the effect of the provisions on free movement of persons very closely with the rules on free movement of goods and services. The Court of Justice held that Arts 39 and 43 of the EC Treaty preclude any national measure which, even though it is applicable without discrimination on grounds of nationality, is liable to hamper or to render less attractive the exercise by a national of any Member State of fundamental freedoms guaranteed by the Treaty.[549] Kraus, a German national, challenged a German provision requiring German nationals (and nationals of other Member States) to apply for authorisation in order to use an academic title of Master of Laws (LL.M.) obtained in another Member State. The Court of Justice held that this would accord with Arts 39 and 43 of the EC Treaty only in so far as the obligation was proportionate to the aim of protecting the public and intended solely to verify that the title was properly awarded.[550] By the same token, the Court of Justice declared, with regard to a requirement to have a second language, that although the requirement for applicants to show that they had the requisite level of linguistic knowledge through possession of a diploma could be legitimate, the fact that it was impossible to submit proof of the required linguistic knowledge by means other than one particular diploma issued only in one particular province of a Member State must be considered disproportionate in relation to the aim in view.[551]

---

[547] For a description of how the case law developed, see Behrens, "Die Konvergenz der wirtschaftlichen Freiheiten im europäischen Gemeinschaftsrecht" (1992) EuR. 145–162; Jarass, "Elemente einer Dogmatik der Grundfreiheiten" (1995) EuR. 202–226; Bernard, "Discrimination and Free Movement in EC Law" (1996) I.C.L.Q. 82–108; Daniele, "Non-Discriminatory Restrictions to the Free Movement of Persons" (1997) E.L.Rev. 191–200; Straetmans, *Consument en markt* (Kluwer, Deurne, 1998), 312–323.

[548] ECJ, Joined Cases 154–155/87 *Wolf* [1988] E.C.R. 3897, paras 9–14. See also ECJ, Case 143/87 *Stanton* [1988] E.C.R. 3877, paras 9–14, delivered on the same date.

[549] ECJ, Case C–19/92 *Kraus* [1993] E.C.R. 1663, para. 32; case notes by Roth (1993) C.M.L.R. 1251–1258, and Denys (1994) C.D.E. 638–662.

[550] *Kraus*, cited in the preceding n.549, *supra* paras 32–38.

[551] ECJ, Case C–281/98 *Angonese* [2000] E.C.R. I–4139, paras 37–46.

Provisions which preclude or deter a national of a Member State from leaving the country in which he or she is pursuing an economic activity in order to exercise the right to freedom of movement constitute an obstacle to that freedom even if they apply without regard to the nationality of the worker concerned.[552] With regard to free movement of workers, the Court of Justice has held that such an obstacle exists only where a provision affects access of workers to the labour market.[553] In *Bosman* the Court of Justice declared an obstacle to free movement of workers transfer rules adopted by sports associations according to which, at the expiry of his contract, a professional footballer could be taken on by a new club only if it paid his old club a transfer fee.[554]

An obstacle to free movement of persons may be justified by pressing reasons of public interest, provided that it applies without distinction as to nationality, is appropriate and does not exceed what is necessary to attain its intended objective (see para. 5–144). In this way, the proportionality test takes the place of any inquiry into the existence of discrimination.[555]

(3) *Primary and secondary right of establishment*

5–135 Definition of establishment. According to the second paragraph of Art. 43 of the EC Treaty, freedom of establishment includes "the right to take up and pursue activities as self-employed persons and to set up and manage undertakings, in particular companies and firms within the meaning of the second para. of Art. 48, under the conditions laid down for its own nationals by the law of the country where such establishment is effected". The term "establishment" is broadly construed in the case law so as to allow a Community national to participate, on a stable and continuous basis, in the economic life of a Member State other than his or her State of origin and to profit therefrom, so contributing to economic and social interpenetration within the Community in the sphere of activities as self-employed persons.[556] However, the substance of freedom of establishment is not the same in the case of natural persons as it is for legal persons.

---

[552] ECJ Case C–18/95 *Terhoeve* [1999] E.C.R. I–345, paras 36–41; ECJ (judgment of October 2, 2003), Case C–232/01 *Van Lent*, not yet reported, paras 15–21.

[553] ECJ, Case C–190/98 *Graf* [2000] E.C.R. I–493, para. 23 (if not there would only be a "too uncertain and indirect" possibility within the meaning of the caselaw on free movement of goods cited in n.408, *supra, ibid.*, para. 25). See Ranocher, "Grundfreiheiten und Spürbarkeitstheorie" (2001) Z.f.R.V. 95–107.

[554] ECJ, Case C–415/93 *Bosman* [1995] E.C.R. I–4921, paras 94–104 (for commentaries, see n.526 *supra*). See also Blanpain, "Transfers van voetballers naar nationaal en Europees recht, recente ontwikkelingen" (2000–2001) R.W. 763–768.

[555] Huglo, "Droit d'établissment et libre prestation des services" (1993) R.T.D.E. 655, at 660–662. See also ECJ, Case C–111/91 *Commission v Luxembourg* [1993] E.C.R. I–817, paras 9–18, where proportionality was weighed in the balance in considering indirect discrimination.

[556] ECJ, Case C–55/94 *Gebhard* [1995] E.C.R. I–4165, para. 25, with case notes by Ballon (1996/97) Col.J.E.L. 145–151; Goffin (1996) C.D.E. 723–743.

Natural persons. As far as natural persons are concerned, freedom of **5–136** establishment encompasses, alongside the right to create a first establishment in the territory of another Member State (the primary right of establishment), a second right of establishment in order to "set up and maintain, subject to observance of the professional rules of conduct, more than one place of work within the Community".[557] Accordingly, a self-employed person may open a second office in another Member State or participate in setting up a company.[558] Article 43 of the EC Treaty provides that progressive abolition of restrictions on freedom of establishment is also to apply to restrictions on the "setting-up of agencies, branches or subsidiaries by nationals of any Member State established in the territory of any Member State".

Companies. Community law recognises a secondary right of establishment **5–137** as far as concerns companies incorporated under the law of a Member State, but not the primary right to move their seat. Unlike natural persons, companies exist only by virtue of the law determining the conditions governing their formation and operation. Member States' legislation differs considerably in terms of the connection required to exist with the national territory when setting up a company under national law and with regard to changing that connection.[559] Hence, Art. 48 of the EC Treaty recognises three criteria for conferring the "nationality" of a Member State on a company (see para. 5–124). In addition, Art. 293 of the EC Treaty calls on Member States to enter into negotiations with each other with a view to securing mutual recognition of companies and firms, the retention of legal personality in the event of the transfer of their seat from one country to another and the possibility of mergers between companies or firms governed by the laws of different countries. To date, no agreement to this effect has entered into force,[560] although the Council has created European corporate bodies, which, subject to certain conditions, can transfer their statutory seat to another Member State (see para. 5–145). In the absence of rules laid down by legislation or convention, the Court of Justice has held that Arts 43 and 48 of the EC Treaty do not confer on companies

---

[557] ECJ, Case 107/83 *Klopp* [1984] E.C.R. 2971, para. 19.

[558] In *Klopp* (see n.557, *supra*), the Court of Justice held that a lawyer was entitled to open a second set of chambers in another Member State. See also ECJ, Case C–55/94 *Gebhard* [1995] E.C.R. I–4165, para. 24; ECJ, Case C–53/95 *Kemmler* [1996] E.C.R. I–703, paras 10–14. See, with regard to auditors, ECJ, Case C–106/91 *Ramrath* [1992] E.C.R. I–3351, para. 22, and with regard to doctors, dentists and veterinary surgeons, ECJ, Case C–351/90 *Commission v Luxembourg* [1992] E.C.R. I–3945, para. 24.

[559] See Halbhuber, "National Doctrinal Structures and European Company Law" (2001) C.M.L.R. 1385–1420.

[560] Pursuant to Art. 220 of the EEC Treaty, the Member States concluded the Brussels Convention of February 29, 1968 on the mutual recognition of companies and bodies corporate (see (1969) Bull.EC Suppl.2), which has not entered into force. For a rather better unofficial English translation, see Stein, *Harmonisation of European Company Laws*, 1971.

incorporated under the laws of a Member State a right to transfer their central management and control and their central administration to another Member State while retaining their status as companies incorporated under the legislation of the first Member State.[561] But Arts 43 and 48 of the EC Treaty preclude requiring a company formed in one Member State to be re-incorporated in another Member State in order for it to retain legal capacity in that Member State.[562]

5–138 Secondary right of establishment. The upshot is that Community law confers only a secondary right of establishment on companies incorporated under the laws of a Member State to set up agencies, branches and subsidiaries in other Member States.[563] According to the Court of Justice, it is inherent in the exercise of freedom of establishment that a national of a Member State who wishes to set up a company may choose to form it in the Member State whose rules of company law seem to him the least restrictive and then to set up branches in other Member States. The fact that a company is incorporated in a particular Member State in order to take advantage of more favourable legislative rules therefore does not in itself constitute an abuse of the right of establishment.[564] Consequently, a Member State cannot impose conditions on setting up a branch solely on the ground that the parent company does not conduct any business in the Member State in which it is established and pursues its activities only in the Member State where its branch is established.[565] Moreover, all restrictions imposed on grounds of imperative requirements in the general interest (*e.g.* in relation to combating fraud or protecting creditors) must

---

[561] ECJ, Case 81/87 *Daily Mail and General Trust PLC* [1988] E.C.R. 5483, para. 24.

[562] ECJ, Case C–208/00 *Überseering* [2002] E.C.R. I–9919, paras 52–94 (a Member State cannot deny a company legal capacity on the basis of the presumption that it has moved its actual centre of administration to its territory). See Roth, "From Centros to Überseering: Free Movement of Companies, Private International Law, and Community Law" (2003) I.C.L.Q. 177–208; Jonet, "Sociétés commerciales—La théorie du siège réel à l'épreuve de la liberté d'établissement" (2003) J.T.D.E. 33–37; Rammeloo, "The Long and Winding Road Towards Freedom of Establishment for Legal Persons in Europe" (2003) M.J.E.C.L. 169–196; Lombardo, "Conflict of Law Rules in Company Law after *Überseering*: An Economic and Comparative Analysis of the Allocation of Policy Competence in the European Union" (2003) E.Bus.Org.L.R. 301–336; Ballarino, "Les règles de conflit sur les sociétés commerciales à l'épreuve du droit communautaire d'établissement" (2003) R.C.D.I.P. 373–402. For a survey of the constraints which Community law places on the "emigration" and "immigration" of companies, see Wymeersch, "The Transfer of the Company's Seat in European Company Law" (2003) C.M.L.R. 661–695.

[563] See Drury, "Migrating Companies" (1999) E.L.Rev. 354–372; Roussos, "Realising the Free Movement of Companies" (2001) E.Bus.L.Rev. 7–25.

[564] ECJ, Case C–212/97 *Centros* [1999] E.C.R. I–1459, paras 18–27; ECJ (judgment of September 30, 2003), Case C–167/01 *Inspire Art*, not yet reported, paras 95–98 and 136–138. However, in so far as such action does not conflict with freedom of establishment, a Member State is entitled to take measures designed to prevent certain of its nationals from attempting, under cover of the rights created by the Treaty, improperly to circumvent their national legislation: *Centros, ibid.*, paras 24–25; *Inspire Act, ibid.*, para. 136.

[565] ECJ, Case C–212/97 *Centros* [1999] E.C.R. I–1459, para. 29; ECJ (judgment of September 30, 2003), Case C–167/01 *Inspire Art*, not yet reported.

satisfy the requirement of proportionality.[566] One upshot of the secondary right of establishment is that the registration or operation with a view to carrying out an economic activity in a Member State of vessels owned by a legal person may not be made conditional on the seat of that legal person being located in that Member State. Such a condition would preclude the operation of such vessels by agencies, branches or subsidiaries.[567] Art. 43 likewise precludes national legislation which, in the case of companies established in that State belonging to a consortium, makes a form of tax relief subject to the requirement that the holding company's business consist wholly or mainly of the holding of shares in subsidiaries established in the Member State concerned.[568]

d. Permitted restrictions on the free movement of persons

(1) Restrictions on grounds of public policy, public security and public health

Justificatory grounds. Under Art. 39(3) of the EC Treaty, Member States **5–139** may place limitations on the free movement of workers on grounds of public policy (*ordre public*), public security or public health. Individuals may also rely on these justificatory grounds.[569] Restrictions may also be imposed on freedom of establishment on the same grounds (EC Treaty, Art. 46). The Council fleshed out the relevant concepts in Directive 64/221 of February 25, 1964.[570] Although the directive was based on Art. 56(2) of the EC Treaty, it applied to any national of a Member State who resided in or travelled to another Member State, either in order to pursue a gainful

---

[566] See, *e.g.* ECJ, Case C–212/97 *Centros* [1999] E.C.R. I–1459, paras 34–38; ECJ (judgment of September 30, 2003), Case C–167/01 *Inspire Art*, not yet reported, paras 133–134. See De Wulf, "*Centros*: vrijheid van vestiging zonder *race to the bottom*" (1999) Ondernemingsrecht 318–324; Forsthoff, "Niederlassungsrecht für Gesellschaften nach dem *Centros*-Urteil des EuGH: Eine Bilanz" (2000) EuR. 167–196; Ebke "*Centros*—Some Realities and Some Mysteries" (2000) A.J.C.L. 623–660; Behrens, "Reactions of Member State Courts to the *Centros* Ruling by the ECJ" (2001) E.Bus.Org.L.J. 159–174; Wouters, "Private International Law and Companies' Freedom of Establishment" (2001) E.Bus.Org.L.R. 101–139.

[567] ECJ, Case C–334/94 *Commission v France* [1996] E.C.R. I–1307, paras 16 and 19; see also ECJ, Case C–221/89 *Factortame Limited* (*Factortame II*) [1991] E.C.R. I–3905, para. 35. See, with regard to aircraft, ECJ, Case C–203/98 *Commission v Belgium* [1999] E.C.R. I–4899.

[568] ECJ, Case C–264/96 *ICI* [1998] E.C.R. I–4695, paras 22–30. See Travers, "Residence Restraints on the Transferability of Corporate Trading Losses and the Right of Establishment in Community Law" (1999) E.L.Rev. 403–425. For other tax rules held to be contrary to Art. 43 of the EC Treaty, see, *e.g.* ECJ, Case C–254/97 *Baxter* [1999] E.C.R. I–4809 (tax deductibility of costs of research carried out in the Member State); ECJ, Case C–200/98 *X and Y* [1999] E.C.R. I–8261 (relief from corporation tax dependent on the place where the subsidiary was established); ECJ, Case C–251/98 *Baars* [2000] E.C.R. I–2787 (exemption from wealth tax for shareholdings in domestic companies); ECJ, Case C–141/99 *AMID* [2000] E.C.R. I–11619 (loss not capable of being set off against the profit made during previous years in so far as the profit came from a permanent establishment abroad).

[569] ECJ, Case C–415/93 *Bosman* [1995] E.C.R. I–4921, para. 86; ECJ, Case C–350/96 *Clean Car Autoservice* [1998] E.C.R. I–2521, para. 24.

[570] Council Directive 64/221/EEC of February 25, 1964 on the co-ordination of special measures concerning the movement or residence of foreign nationals which are justified on grounds of public policy, public security or public health, [1963–1964] O.J. English Spec. Ed. 117.

activity (as an employed or self-employed person or as a supplier of services) or as a recipient of services. The Community legislation fleshing out the right of residence also allowed for exceptions on public policy, public security or public health grounds. The same exceptions have been laid down in Directive 2004/38, which codifies all existing Community legislation on the right of citizens of the Union to reside within the territory of the Member States and replaces Directive 64/221.[571] The Directive makes it clear that a measure may only be justified on one of those grounds in so far as it is proportional to the aim pursued thereby.[572]

5–140 Conditions. The right of Member States to restrict freedom of movement for persons on grounds of public policy, public security or public health is not intended to exclude economic sectors or occupations from the application of that principle, but to allow Member States to refuse access to their territory or residence there to persons whose access or residence would in itself constitute a danger for public policy, public security or public health.[573] The rights associated to the citizenship of the Union demand that any such derogation from the principle of free movement be interpreted strictly.[574] By virtue of Art. 39(3) of the EC Treaty a Member State may refuse to allow a worker who is a national of another Member State to enter its territory or reside therein only on the ground that his or her presence or conduct constitutes a genuine and sufficiently serious threat to the requirements of public policy,[575] affecting one of the fundamental interests of society.[576] Although Community law does not impose upon the Member States a uniform scale of values, it does not permit a Member State to apply an arbitrary distinction to the detriment of nationals of other Member States. In the 1974 judgment in the *Van Duyn* case, the Court of Justice had accepted that a Member State was entitled, on grounds of public policy, to prevent a national of another Member State from taking gainful employment within its territory with an organisation which it regarded as socially harmful, even though no similar restriction was placed on its own nationals.[577] In 1982, the Court of Justice held, however, that

---

[571] Directive 2004/38 (n.509, *supra*), Art. 27(1).

[572] *ibid.*, Art. 27(2). This principle has been developed in the case law of the Court of Justice, see ECJ, Case C–101/94 *Commission v Italy* [1996] E.C.R. I–2691, paras 25–26; ECJ, Case C–294/00 *Deutsche Paracelsus Schulen für Naturheilverfahren* [2002] E.C.R. I–6515, paras 38–66.

[573] ECJ, Case 131/85 *Gül* [1986] E.C.R. 1573, para. 17; ECJ, Case C–114/97, *Commission v Spain* [1998] E.C.R. I–6717, para. 42; ECJ (judgment of September 20, 2003), Case C–405/01 *Colegio de Oficiales de la Marina Mercante Espanola*, not yet reported, para. 48, and ECJ (judgment of September 20, 2003), Case C–47/02 *Anker*, not yet reported, para. 67.

[574] ECJ (judgment of April 29, 2004), Joined Cases C–482/01 and C–493/01 *Orfanopoulos*, not yet reported, para. 65.

[575] ECJ, Case 36/75 *Rutili* [1975] E.C.R. 1291, para. 28. See now Directive 2004/38, Art. 27(2), second subpara.

[576] ECJ, Case 30/77 *Boucherau* [1977] E.C.R. 1999, para. 35. See now Directive 2004/38, Art. 27(2), second subpara.

[577] ECJ, Case 41/74 *Van Duyn* [1974] E.C.R. 1337, paras 20–24.

conduct on the part of nationals of other Member States is not a sufficiently serious threat where similar conduct by nationals of the Member State in question does not give rise to repressive measures or other genuine and effective measures intended to combat such conduct.[578] A genuine and sufficiently serious threat affecting one of the fundamental interests of society is also required where public policy or public security is invoked as the justification for limitations on freedom of establishment or to provide services, such as a rule that managers of an undertaking or the seat of an undertaking must be established in the Member State in question.[579]

In common with Directive 64/221, Directive 2004/38 requires measures taken on grounds of public policy or public security to be "based exclusively on the personal conduct of the individual concerned".[580] Previous criminal convictions are not in themselves to constitute grounds for the taking of such measures.[581] Moreover, for a person to be expelled, the "genuine threat" must in principle remain until the moment of his or her expulsion.[582] The Directive formulates procedural requirements for the exercise of the public policy reservation by Member States.[583] In this way, the requirements and prohibitions laid down by the directive constitute a restriction of the Member State's residuary power in the sphere of public policy.[584]

---

[578] ECJ, Joined Cases 115 and 116/81 *Adoui and Cornuaille v Belgium* [1982] E.C.R. 1665, para. 8; See also ECJ, Case 249/86 *Commission v Germany* [1989] E.C.R. 1263, paras 17–20; ECJ, Case C–363/89 *Roux* [1991] E.C.R. I–273, paras 29–31; ECJ, Case C–268/99 *Jany* [2001] E.C.R. I–8615, paras 55–62; ECJ, Case C–100/01 *Oteiza Oluzubul* [2002] E.C.R. I–10981, paras 27–45.

[579] ECJ, Case C–114/97 *Commission v Spain* [1998] E.C.R. I–6717, paras 44–47; ECJ, Case C–355/98 *Commission v Belgium* [2000] E.C.R. I–1221, paras 27–34.

[580] Directive 2004/38, Art. 27(2), first subpara.; see previously Directive 64/221, Art. 3(1).

[581] Directive 2004/38, Art. 27(2), first subpara.; see previously Directive 64/221, Art. 3(2). Thus, automatic expulsion from the territory is not permitted of nationals of other Member States found guilty on that territory of drug offences: ECJ, Case C–348/96 *Calfa* [1999] E.C.R. I–11, paras 16–29; ECJ (judgment of April 29, 2004), Joined Cases C–482/01 and C–493/01 *Orfanopoulos*, not yet reported, paras 66–71. *Cf.* ECJ, Case C–340/97 *Nazli* [2000] E.C.R. I–957, paras 50–64 (the same applies to workers deriving rights from association agreements).

[582] ECJ (judgment of April 29, 2004), Joined Cases C–482/01 and C–493/01 *Orfanopoulos*, not yet reported, paras 79 and 82.

[583] Directive 2004/38, Arts 30–33. See, previously, with respect to the procedural safeguards laid down by Directive 64/221: ECJ, Case 36/75 *Rutili* [1975] E.C.R. 1291, paras 33–39; ECJ, Case 30/77 *Bouchereau* [1977] E.C.R. 1999, paras 15–30; ECJ, Case 131/79 *Santillo* [1980] E.C.R. 1585, paras 11–19; ECJ, Joined Cases 115 and 116/81 *Adoui and Cornuaille* [1982] E.C.R. 1665, paras 14–19; ECJ, Joined Cases C–297/88 and C–197/89 *Dzodzi* [1990] E.C.R. I–3763, paras 57–69; ECJ, Case C–175/94 *Gallagher* [1995] E.C.R. I–4253, paras 1–26; ECJ, Joined Cases C–65/95 and C–111/95 *Shingara and Radiom* [1997] E.C.R. I–3343, paras 1–45; ECJ, Case C–357/98 *Nana Yaa Konadu Yiadom* [2000] E.C.R. I–9265, paras 17–43; ECJ, Case C–459/99 *MRAX*, [2002] E.C.R. I–6591, paras 100–104.

[584] Hubeau, "L'exception d'ordre public et la libre circulation des personnes en droit communautaire" (1981) C.D.E. 207–256; Peers, "National Security and European Law" (1996) Y.E.L. 363–404. For further consideration of the development of the concept of "ordre public", see Karydis, "L'ordre public dans l'ordre juridique communautaire: un concept à contenu variable" (2002) R.T.D.E. 1–26; Chaltiel, "L'ordre public devant la Cour de justice des Communautés européennes" (2003) R.M.C.U.E. 120–123.

(2) *Employment in the public service and exercise of public authority*

5–141 Public service. According to Art. 39(4) of the EC Treaty, the provisions of that article do not apply to "employment in the public service". This exception applies only to posts "which involve direct or indirect participation in the exercise of powers conferred by public law and duties designed to safeguard the general interests of the State or of other public authorities", since such posts presume "the existence of a special relationship of allegiance to the State and reciprocity of rights and duties which form the foundation of the bond of nationality".[585] Other posts cannot be reserved for a Member State's own nationals, not even for considerations relating to the preservation of national identity.[586]

This functional interpretation of the expression "public service" means that a large number of posts which do not involve the exercise of public authority, but where the employer is a public authority, are not taken outside the scope of the Treaty.[587] The legal categorisation of the employment relationship between the employee and the administration—that is to say, whether the relationship is governed by private or public law—is irrelevant for this purpose.[588] Accordingly, the Court of Justice has held that civil servants' and public employees' posts in public water, gas and electricity distribution services,[589] public-sector research, education, health, postal and telecommunications services [590] and

---

[585] ECJ, Case 149/79 *Commission v Belgium* [1980] E.C.R. 3881, para. 10.

[586] ECJ, Case C–473/93 *Commission v Luxembourg* [1996] E.C.R. I–3207, para. 35 (there are less far-reaching means of protecting that interest recognised by Art. 6(3) of the EU Treaty). For the impact of Community law on national civil-service law, see Kämmerer, "Europäisierung des öffentlichen Dienstrechts" (2001) EuR. 27–48.

[587] A number of guidelines were set out in the Commission communication on its action in respect of the application of Art. 48 [now Art. 39](4) of the EC Treaty: [1988] O.J. C72/2; see Handoll, "Article 48(4) EEC and Non-National Access to Public Employment" (1988) E.L.Rev. 223–241; Guillén and Fuentetaja, "Free Movement of Workers and Public Administration: The ECJ Doctrine on the Interpretation of the Scope of Article 39(4) EC" (1999) ERPL/REDP 1567–1593.

[588] ECJ, Case 152/73 *Sotgiu* [1974] E.C.R. 153, paras 5–6. However, Art. 39(4) of the EC Treaty does not cover employment by a private natural or legal person: ECJ, Case C–283/99 *Commission v Italy* [2001] E.C.R. I–4363, para. 25.

[589] ECJ, Case C–473/93 *Commission v Luxembourg* [1996] E.C.R. I–3207, para. 31; Case C–173/94 *Commission v Belgium* [1996] E.C.R. I–3265, para. 17; Case C–290/94 *Commission v Greece* [1996] E.C.R. I–3285, para. 34. For an early case, see ECJ, Case 149/79 *Commission v Belgium* [1982] E.C.R. 1845, paras 8–9 (drivers and manual workers employed by railways).

[590] ECJ, Cases C–473/93 and C–290/94, *ibid*. According to the Court of Justice, the following do *not* fall within the exception: various manual occupations, crèche nurses and children's nurses employed by local authorities (ECJ, Case 149/79 *Commission v Belgium* [1982] E.C.R. 1845, paras 8–9; although the exception was held to cover controllers, night watchmen and local authority architects); nurses in public hospitals (ECJ, Case 307/84 *Commission v France* [1986] E.C.R. 1725, para. 13); medical specialists working in the public service (ECJ, Case C–15/96 *Schöning-Kougebetopoulou* [1998] E.C.R. I–47, para. 13); directors and teachers in institutions specialising in supplementary instruction and music and dancing schools (ECJ, Case 147/86 *Commission v Greece* [1988] E.C.R. 1637, paras 19–21); foreign-language assistants at universities (ECJ, Case 33/88 *Allué* [1989]

radio and television,[591] and some seamen's occupations,[592] private security posts[593] and members of an occupational guild[594] do not fall within the exception. Even where persons are granted powers conferred by public law, it is still necessary that such powers are exercised on a regular basis by their holders and do not represent a very minor part of their activities in order for them to fall within Art. 39(4).[595]

Exercise of public authority. Nationals of a Member State have no right of **5–142** establishment in another Member State in respect of "activities which in that State are connected, even occasionally, with the exercise of official authority" (EC Treaty, Art. 45). This exception relates only to activities which "taken on their own, constitute a direct and specific connection with the exercise of official authority" and not the profession as such of which those activities form a part.[596] Consequently, the profession of a lawyer (*avocat*) cannot be reserved to nationals, since the most typical activities of that profession, such as consultation and legal assistance and representation and defence of parties in courts, cannot be regarded as participating in the

---

E.C.R. 1591, para. 9); primary school teachers (ECJ, Case C–473/93 *Commission v Luxembourg* [1996] E.C.R. I–3207, paras 32–34); secondary school teachers (ECJ, Case C–4/91 *Bleis* [1991] E.C.R. I–5627, para. 7); trainee teachers (ECJ, Case 66/85 *Lawrie-Blum* [1986] E.C.R. 2121, paras 27–29) and researchers at a national research institution (Case 225/85 *Commission v Italy* [1987] E.C.R. 2625, para. 9; although the exception was held to cover posts involving management duties or advising the State).

[591] ECJ Case C–290/94 *Commission v Greece* [1996] E.C.R. I–3285, para. 34 (which mentions also musicians in municipal and local orchestras and opera houses).

[592] ECJ, Case C–37/93 *Commission v Belgium* [1993] E.C.R. I–6295, paras 1–6. As far as masters and chief mates are concerned, the Court of Justice has since held that their powers conferred by public law were too incidental to warrant application of the exception: ECJ (judgment of September 20, 2003), Case C–450/01 *Colegio de Oficiales de la Marina Mercante Espanola*, not yet reported, paras 42–45, and ECJ (judgment of September 20, 2003), Case C–47/02 *Anker*, not yet reported, paras 61–64.

[593] ECJ, Case C–114/97 *Commission v Spain* [1998] E.C.R. I–6717, para. 33; ECJ, Case C–355/99 *Commission v Belgium* [2000] E.C.R. I–1221, para. 26; ECJ, Case C–283/99 *Commission v Italy* [2001] E.C.R. I–4363, para. 20.

[594] ECJ, Case C–213/90 *ASTI* [1991] E.C.R. I–3507, paras 19–20; Case C–171/01 *Wählergruppe Gemeinsam* [2003] E.C.R. I–4301, paras 90–93.

[595] ECJ (judgment of September 20, 2003), Case C–405/01 *Colegio de Oficiales de la Marina Mercante Espanola*, not yet reported, para. 44, and ECJ (judgment of September 20, 2003), Case C–47/02 *Anker*, not yet reported, para. 63.

[596] ECJ, Case 2/74 *Reyners* [1974] E.C.R. 631, paras 45–46. The following activities have been held not to constitute the exercise of public authority: the establishment of institutions for supplementary instruction and vocational training schools and giving private lessons at home (ECJ, Case 147/86 *Commission v Greece* [1988] E.C.R. 1637, paras 8–10), the design, programming and operation of data-processing systems (ECJ, Case C–3/88 *Commission v Italy* [1989] E.C.R. 4035, para. 13), the activities of experts on traffic accidents (ECJ, Case C–306/89 *Commission v Greece* [1991] E.C.R. I–5863, para. 7), the post of "approved commissioner" with Belgian insurance undertakings (ECJ, Case C–42/92 *Thijssen* [1993] E.C.R. I–4047, paras 16–22), the concession for a lottery computerisation system (ECJ, Case C–272/91 *Commission v Italy* [1994] E.C.R. I–1409, paras 6–13), and the activities of private security undertakings and their staff (ECJ, Case C–114/97 *Commission v Spain* [1998] E.C.R. I–6717, paras 34–39; ECJ, Case C–355/98 *Commission v Belgium* [2000] E.C.R. I–1221, para. 26; ECJ, Case C–283/99 *Commission v Italy* [2001] E.C.R. I–4363, para. 20).

exercise of official authority.[597] Sitting as a substitute judge, say, could certainly be restricted to nationals.[598] It is uncertain whether such a restriction could be placed on other legal professions, such as that of notary, which does not exist (or at least does not have the same connotations) in all Member States.[599]

(3) Restrictions arising on other justificatory grounds

5–143 Public-interest requirements. So long as the requirements for access to a given occupation have not been harmonised, Member States may themselves determine what knowledge and skills are needed in order to exercise it, and require diplomas or a professional qualification. The case law accepts that the obstacles to free movement of persons created by such requirements may be justified by public-interest requirements, provided that the restriction does not go beyond what is appropriate and indispensable in order to satisfy those requirements.[600] One upshot of this is that, in processing applications for recognition of foreign diplomas and vocational qualifications, the national authorities must inquire into the equivalence of the knowledge and qualifications obtained abroad (see para. 5–147). Furthermore, a public body recruiting staff for posts or assessing seniority for personnel (not falling within the scope of Art. 39(4) of the EC Treaty) which takes account of previous employment in the public service may not make a distinction according to whether such employment was in the public service of the particular State or in the public service of another Member State.[601]

5–144 Rule of reason. More generally, the Court of Justice declares—in terms similar to those employed in its case law on the movement of goods and services—that national measures liable to hinder or render less attractive the exercise of free movement of persons may be compatible with the

---

[597] *Reyners*, cited in the preceding note, *supra*, para. 52.

[598] This is probably also true of (Bavarian) lay assessors according to the view taken by the Commission in its answer of September 5, 1996 to question No. E–1580/96 (Sakellariou), [1996] O.J. C356/61.

[599] See Schiller, "Freier Personenverkehr im Bereich der freiwilligen Gerichtsbarkeit?" (2004) EuR. 27–51; Demaret, "L'égalité de traitement" (1994) A.D. 165, at 203–204. The European Parliament considered that the notary's profession came within the exception; see the resolution of January 18, 1994 on the state and organisation of the profession of notary in the 12 Member States of the Community, [1994] O.J. C44/36, at point 4.

[600] See ECJ, Case 96/85 *Commission v France* [1986] E.C.R. 1475. para. 11 (self-employed persons); ECJ, Case C–204/90 *Bachmann* [1992] E.C.R. I–249, para. 28 (employees).

[601] ECJ, Case C–419/92 *Scholz* [1994] E.C.R. I–505, paras 11–12; ECJ, Case C–15/96 *Schöning-Kougebetopoulou* [1998] E.C.R. I–47, paras 21–28; ECJ, Case C–187/96 *Commission v Greece* [1998] E.C.R. I–1095, paras 17–23; Case C–195/98 *Österreichischer Gewerkschaftsbund—Gewerkschaft öffentlicher Dienst* [2000] E.C.R. I–1097, paras 33–51; ECJ (judgment of September 30, 2003), Case C–224/01 *Köbler*, not yet reported, paras 70–87.

freedoms guaranteed by the Treaty if they satisfy the following conditions (rule of reason).[602]

(1) The measures must be applied in a non-discriminatory manner from the point of view of nationality (even if they are indirectly discriminatory).[603]

(2) The measures must be justified by imperative requirements in the general interest. These may consist of rules relating to organisation, qualifications, professional ethics, supervision and liability[604] and with regard to the knowledge of languages required in order to exercise the professional activity,[605] or even policy aims accepted by the case law in the areas of trade in goods and services, such as consumer protection,[606] protection of public health,[607] road traffic safety,[608] effectiveness of fiscal controls[609] and the need to preserve the cohesion of the tax system[610] (but not avoiding loss of tax revenue[611] or administrative considerations[612]), overriding requirements relating to the general interest, such as the protection of the interests of creditors, minority shareholders, employees or the taxation authorities,[613] maintaining or promoting the use of an

---

[602] For a list of the conditions, see ECJ, Case C–55/94 *Gebhard* [1995] E.C.R. I–4165, para. 37 (which refers to ECJ, Case C–19/92 *Kraus* [1993] E.C.R. I–1663, para. 32). See Tesauro, "The Community's Internal Market in the Light of the Recent Case-Law of the Court of Justice" (1995) Y.E.L. 1, at 7–10. Naturally, national measures must also comply with the fundamental rights of the persons concerned, see para. 17–078, *infra*.

[603] For this expression, see para. 5–066, *supra*. Most instances which have arisen before the Court of Justice have been concerned with national measures which, albeit not making any distinction as to nationality, nevertheless place nationals of other Member States indirectly at a disadvantage. Sometimes the Court uses the expression "indirect discrimination" to denote more specifically the type of measures which cannot be justified in the case at issue, *cf.* ECJ, Case C–237/94 *O'Flynn* [1996] E.C.R. I–2617, paras 18–20.

[604] ECJ, Case C–55/94 *Gebhard* [1995] E.C.R. I–4165, para. 35, following ECJ, Case 71/76 *Thieffry* [1977] E.C.R. 765, para. 12. See also ECJ, Case C–340/89 *Vlassopoulou* [1991] E.C.R. I–2357, para. 9 (ensuring that a person has the knowledge and skills required in order to pursue a particular occupation); ECJ, Case C–106/91 *Ramrath* [1992] E.C.R. I–3351, para. 35 (rules relating to the integrity and independence of auditors); ECJ, Case C–101/94 *Commission v Italy* [1996] E.C.R. I–2691, paras 19–24 (rules for the supervision of securities dealers); ECJ, Case C–19/92 *Kraus* [1993] E.C.R. I–1663, para. 35 (protection of the public against the unlawful use of academic titles).

[605] ECJ, Case C–424/97 *Haim* [2000] E.C.R. I–5123, paras 50–61.

[606] ECJ, Case C–204/90 *Bachmann* [1992] E.C.R. I–249, para. 16.

[607] ECJ, Case 96/85 *Commission v France* [1986] E.C.R. I–1475, para. 10.

[608] ECJ, Case C–246/00 *Commission v Netherlands* [2003] E.C.R. I–7485, para. 67.

[609] ECJ, Case C–204/90 *Bachmann* [1992] E.C.R. I–249, para. 18 (see also the parallel judgment of the same date, ECJ, Case C–300/90 *Commission v Belgium* [1992] E.C.R. I–305, para. 11); ECJ, Case C–264/96 *ICI* [1998] E.C.R. I–4695, para. 26.

[610] ECJ, Case C–204/90 *Bachmann* [1992] E.C.R. I–249, para. 21, and ECJ, Case C–300/90 *Commission v Belgium* [1992] E.C.R. I–305, para. 14 (where this ground was accepted as a justification); ECJ, Case C–264/96 *ICI* [1998] E.C.R. I–4695, para. 29 (where this ground was not accepted as a justification).

[611] ECJ, Case C–264/96 *ICI* [1998] E.C.R. I–4695, para. 28.

[612] ECJ, Case C–18/95 *Terhoeve* [1999] E.C.R. I–345, paras 44–45 (the aim of simplifying and co-ordinating the levying of taxes and contributions is not a justification).

[613] ECJ, Case C–208/00 *Überseering* [2002] E.C.R. I–9919, para. 92.

official language,[614] respecting fundamental rights[615] and, in view of the social importance of sport, maintaining a balance between football clubs and supporting the search for talent and the training of young players.[616]

(3) Lastly, there is the requirement for proportionality: the measures must be appropriate for achieving the aim sought and must not exceed what is necessary in order to attain that aim.[617] The fact that the fact that one Member State imposes less strict rules than another Member State does not mean that the latter's rules are disproportionate.[618]

e. Harmonisation and recognition of professional rules

5–145 Harmonisation. Freedom of establishment is made more difficult by rules which differ from one Member State to another and are applicable without distinction to nationals and to subjects of other Member States. Art. 44 of the EC Treaty makes provision for harmonisation of such rules. Accordingly, the Council has adopted a series of directives pursuant to Art. 44(2)(g)—since the entry into force of the EU Treaty, acting with the European Parliament under the co-decision procedure—on the harmonisation of the law relating to the stock exchange[619] and company

---

[614] ECJ, Case C–379/87 *Groener* [1989] E.C.R. 3967, para. 19.

[615] ECJ, Case C–112/00 *Schmidberger* [2003] E.C.R. I–5659, paras 71–74 (the case concerns free movement of goods, but refers generally to "a fundamental freedom guaranteed by the Treaty").

[616] ECJ, Case C–415/93 *Bosman* [1995] E.C.R. I–4921, paras 106–110 (transfer fees not appropriate for achieving these aims).

[617] See—alongside the cases cited—ECJ, Case C–106/91 *Ramrath* [1992] E.C.R. I–3351, paras 29–31.

[618] ECJ, Case C–108/96 *Mac Quen* [2001] E.C.R. I–837, paras 33–34; ECJ (judgment of July 11, 2002), Case C–294/00 *Deutsche Paracelsus Schulen für Naturheilverfahren*, not yet reported, paras 44–50. See also the caselaw on the provision of services, para. 5–179, *infra*.

[619] The directives adopted by the Council pursuant to Art. 44 of the EC Treaty have since been replaced by directives adopted by the European Parliament and the Council pursuant to Art. 95 (possibly in combination with Art. 44) of the EC Treaty: Directive 2001/34/EC of May 28, 2001 on the admission of securities to official stock exchange listing and on information to be published on those securities ([2001] O.J. L184/1), Directive 2003/6/EC of January 28, 2003 on insider dealing and market manipulation (market abuse) ([2003] O.J. L96/16) and Directive 2003/71/EC of November 4, 2003 on the prospectus to be published when securities are offered to the public or admitted to trading and amending Directive 2001/34/EC ([2003] O.J. L345/64) ; see also Directive 2004/25/EC of April 21, 2004 on takeover bids ([2004] O.J. L142/12), based on Art. 44 EC Treaty. The Council has further adopted, on the basis of Art. 47(2) of the EC Treaty, Directive 85/611/EEC of December 20, 1985 (collective investment undertakings, [1985] O.J. L375/3), Directive 93/6/EEC of March 15, 1993 (capital adequacy of investments firms and credit institutions, [1993] O.J. L141/1 and Directive 2004/39/EEC of April 21, 2004, (markets in financial instruments), [2004] O.J. L145/1. Further coordination of the securities markets has since been taking place in accordance with a new approach whereby the competent authorities consult with each other in a Committee of European Securities Regulators and a European Securities Committee; see Commission Decisions 2001/527/EC and 2001/528/EC of June 6, 2001 ([2001] O.J. L191/43 and 45, respectively) and Berger and Altemir Mergelina, "Un nouveau

law.[620] In 2001 a European form of company, the Societas Europea (SE), was introduced under Art. 308 of the EC Treaty which allows companies incorporated under the laws of different Member States to merge or to set up a holding company or a common subsidiary.[621] In 2003, the Council, acting under the same article of the Treaty, made it possible for natural or legal persons coming under the laws of different Member States to establish a European Cooperative Society (SCE).[622]

In order to "make it easier" for self-employed activities to be taken up and pursued, the Council (acting with the Parliament under the co-decision procedure) is empowered to adopt directives for the mutual recognition of diplomas, certificates and other evidence of formal qualifications (EC Treaty, Art. 47(1)) and for the co-ordination of provisions concerning the taking-up and pursuit of activities as self-employed persons (EC Treaty, Art. 47(2)). Accordingly, some Council directives aim at ensuring that pursuit of an occupation in a Member State for a certain period is accepted as sufficient evidence that the person concerned has the knowledge and

---

système de régulation communautaire des marchés de valeurs mobilières dans l'Union européenne" (2001) R.M.C.U.E. 529–534; Moloney, "New Frontiers in EC Capital Markets Law: From Market Construction to Market Regulation" (2003) C.M.L.R. 809–843; Janin, "Le premier cas pratique d'approche 'Lamfalussy'—Les mesures d'exécution de la directive sur les opérations d'initiés et les manipulations de marché (abus de marché)" (2003) R.M.C.U.E. 658–669.

[620] See the First Directive (68/151/EEC) of March 9, 1968, [1968] O.J. English Spec. Ed. 41; the Second Directive (77/91/EEC) of December 13, 1976 (formation and alteration of capital), [1977] O.J. L26/1; the Fourth Directive (78/660/EEC) of July 25, 1978 (annual accounts), [1978] O.J. L222/11; the Third Directive (78/855/EEC) of October 9, 1978 (mergers), [1978] O.J. L295/36; the Sixth Directive (82/891/EEC) of December 17, 1982 (division of companies), [1982] O.J. L378/47; the Seventh Directive 83/349/EEC of June 13, 1983 (consolidated annual accounts), [1983] O.J. L193/1; the Eighth Directive (84/253/EEC) of April 10, 1984 (auditing), [1984] O.J. L126/20; the Eleventh Directive (89/666/EEC) December 21, 1989 (disclosure requirements of branches of foreign companies), [1989] O.J. L395/36; the Twelfth Directive (89/667/EEC) of December 21, 1989 (single-member companies), [1989] O.J. L395/40. See also the directives adopted pursuant to Art. 94 of the EC Treaty, 90/434/EEC and 90/435/EEC (tax treatment of mergers, divisions and parent/subsidiary companies, respectively), [1990] O.J. L25/1 and 6. See Edwards, *European Company Law* (Clarendon, Oxford, 1999), 431 pp.; Wouters, "European Company Law: *Quo Vadis?*" (2000) C.M.L.R. 257–307. For a general assessment, see Winter, "EU Company Law on the Move" (2004) L.I.E.I. 97–114; Timmermans, "Europees vennootschapsrecht" (2002) S.E.W. 248–252.

[621] Council Regulation (EC) No. 2157/2001 of October 8, 2001 on the Statute for a European company (SE) ([2001] O.J. L294/1), as supplemented by Council Directive 2001/86/EC of October 8, 2001 with regard to the involvement of employees ([2001] O.J. L294/22). See Edwards, "The European Company—Essential Tool or Reviscerated Dream?" (2003) C.M.L.R. 443–464; Fouassier, "Le statut de la 'société européenne': Un nouvel instrument juridique au service des entreprises" (2001) R.M.C.U.E. 85–88; Blanquet, "Enfin la société européenne" (2001) R.D.U.E. 65–109, and "La société européenne n'est plus un mythe" (2001) R.D.I.D.C. 139–170; Roelvink, "De Europese vennootschap na Nice" (2001) S.E.W. 162–165; Hopt, "The European Company (SE) under the Nice Compromise: Major Breakthrough or Small Coin for Europe?" (2000) Euredia 465–475.

[622] Council Regulation (EC) No. 1435/2003 of July 22, 2003 on the Statute for a European Cooperative Society (SCE) ([2003] O.J. L207/1), as supplemented by Council Directive 2003/72/EC of July 22, 2003 with regard to the involvement of employees ([2003] O.J. L207/25).

competence to carry on that occupation in another Member State.[623] In the banking and insurance sectors, directives have resulted in a substantial liberalisation of the right of establishment (on the basis of Art. 47 of the EC Treaty) and of the supply of services (on the basis of Art. 47 in conjunction with Art. 55 of the EC Treaty[624]).[625]

---

[623] See, *e.g.* Council Directive 64/427/EEC of July 7, 1964 laying down detailed provisions concerning transitional measures in respect of activities of self-employed persons in manufacturing and processing industries falling within ISIC Major Groups 23–40 (Industry and small craft industries), [1963–1964] O.J. English Spec. Ed. 148. See the judgment in *Knoors*, para. 5–069, *supra*. For an attempt at simplifying and amending these rules, see Directive 1999/42/EC of the European Parliament and of the Council of June 7, 1999 establishing a mechanism for the recognition of qualifications in respect of the professional activities covered by the Directives on liberalisation and transitional measures and supplementing the general systems for the recognition of qualifications, [1999] O.J. L201/77 (corrigendum in [2002] O.J. L23/48). See Fouassier, "Une tentative de simplification et d'amélioration de la législation communautaire: la directive 1999/42/CE relative à la reconnaissance mutuelle des qualifications professionnelles" (2000) R.M.C.U.E. 601–608.

[624] See also the discussion of free movement of services, paras 5–169—5–179, *infra*.

[625] See Directive 2000/12/EC of the European Parliament and the Council of March 20, 2000 relating to the taking up and pursuit of the business of credit institutions ([2000] O.J. L126/1), codifying, *inter* alia, Directive 73/183/EEC of June 28, 1973 (adopted on the basis of Arts 44, 51 and 52 of the EC Treaty), [1973] O.J. L194/1, and the co-ordinating directives, adopted on the basis of Art. 47 of the EC Treaty, 77/780/EEC of December 12, 1977, [1977] O.J. L322/30, and Directive 89/646/EEC of December 15, 1989, [1989] O.J. L386/1. See Alpa, "The Harmonisation of the EC Law of Financial Markets in the Perspective of Consumer Protection" (2002) E.Bus.L.Rev. 523–540; Moreiro Gonzalez, "La codification de la réglementation communautaire relative à l'activité des établissements de credit et son exercice" (2001) R.T.D.E. 529–550; Garcia Collados, "La codification des directives bancaires" (2000) Euredia 313–319; Strivens, "The Liberalisation of Banking Services in the Community" (1992) C.M.L.R. 283–307. For the application of the rule of reason in this connection, see the Commission interpretative communication, Freedom to provide services and the interest of the general good in the Second Banking Directive, [1997] O.J. C209/6. See also Directive 94/19/EC of the European Parliament and the Council of May 30, 1994, [1994] O.J. L135/5, and Directive 2000/46/EC of the European Parliament and of the Council of September 18, 2000 on the taking up, pursuit of and prudential supervision of the business of electronic money institutions, [2000] O.J. L275/39. For electronic commerce, see Roeges, "Quelques réflexions critiques sur le cadre légal pour la libre prestation de services bancaires et financiers" (2000) Euredia 149–156. A new approach is now being applied to co-ordinating supervision of the banking and insurance sectors (as for the securities industry: see n.619, *supra*), involving consultation through the Committee of European Banking Supervisors, the Committee of European Insurance and Occupational Pensions Supervisors, the European Banking Committee and the European Insurance and Occupational Pensions Committee, all of which were set up by Commission Decisions of November 5, 2003 ([2004] O.J. L3/28 to 36); see also Mogg, "Regulating Financial Services in Europe: A New Approach" (2002) Fordham I.L.J. 58–82. For the liberalisation of insurance, see, as regards establishment, the "first generation" co-ordination directives 74/239/EEC of July 24, 1973 (indemnity insurance), [1973] O.J. L228/3, and 79/267/EEC of March 5, 1979 (life assurance), [1979] O.J. L63/1; as regards the supply of services, the "second generation" co-ordinating directives 88/357/EEC of June 22, 1988 (indemnity insurance), [1988] O.J. L172/1, and 90/619/EEC of November 8, 1990 (life assurance), [1990] O.J. L330/50, and the "third generation" directives 92/49/EEC of June 18, 1992 (indemnity insurance), [1992] O.J. L228/1, and 92/96/EEC of November 10, 1992 (life assurance), [1992] O.J. L360/1. The provisions on life assurance were revised by Directive 2002/83/EC of the European Parliament and of the Council of November 5, 2002 ([2002] O.J. L345/1). See also Directive 2001/17/EC of the European Parliament and of the Council of March 19, 2001 on the reorganisation and winding-up of insurance undertakings,

Mutual recognition of diplomas. In some sectors, the Council has adopted **5–146** directives dealing with the mutual recognition of diplomas with a view to access to an occupation (not "academic" recognition) for both employed and self-employed persons (as a result of which Art. 40 serves as the legal basis for these directives, alongside Art. 47(1)). They are aimed at medical and paramedical diplomas[626] and architects' diplomas.[627] Directive 89/48/EEC of December 21, 1988 which introduced a general system for the recognition of higher-education diplomas awarded on completion of at least three years' professional education and training[628] marked the abandonment of the sectoral approach. That Directive applies to any national of a Member State wishing to pursue a "regulated profession" in a self-employed capacity or as an employed person, where the profession is not yet the subject of a specific directive, in a Member State other than the one in which he or she obtained his or her diploma (Art. 2).[629] Employment

[2001] O.J. L110/28, and Directive 2002/92/EC of the European Parliament and of the Council of December 9, 2002 on insurance mediation, [2003] O.J. L9/3. The emergence of financial groups offering services and products in various financial sectors led to the need for appropriate supervision, resulting in Directive 2002/87/EC of the European Parliament and of the Council of December 16, 2002 on the supplementary supervision of credit institutions, insurance undertakings and investment firms in a financial conglomerate ([2003] O.J. L35/1).

[626] In the case of a number of medical and paramedical diplomas, each directive on mutual recognition was coupled with a directive co-ordinating the study curricula. Doctors: Directives 75/362/EEC and 75/363/EEC of June 16, 1975, [1975] O.J. L167/1 and 14, together with Directive 84/457/EEC of September 15, 1986 (training in general medical practice), which have been repealed and replaced by (one) Directive 93/16/EEC of April 15, 1993, [1993] O.J. L165/1; nurses: Directives 77/452 and 77/453/EEC, [1977] O.J. L176/1 and 8; dental practitioners, Directives 78/686 and 78/687/EEC of June 27, 1977, [1978] O.J. L233/1 and 10; veterinary surgeons, Directives 78/1026/EEC and 78/1027/EEC of December 18, 1978, [1978] O.J. L362/1 and 7; midwives, Directives 80/154/EEC of July 25, 1978 and 80/155, [1980] O.J. L33/1 and 8; pharmacists, Directives 85/432 and 85/433/EEC of September 16, 1985, [1985] O.J. L253/34 and 37.

[627] Directive 85/384/EEC of June 10, 1985, [1985] O.J. L223/15.

[628] Council Directive 89/48/EEC of December 21, 1998 on a general system for the recognition of higher-education diplomas awarded on completion of professional education and training of at least three years' duration, [1989] O.J. L19/16, supplemented by Council Directive 92/51/EEC of June 18, 1992 on a second general system for the recognition of professional education and training, [1992] O.J. L209/25. For the difference between this and the sectoral approach based on minimum harmonisation of training, see ECJ, Case C–110/01 *Tennah-Durez* [2003] E.C.R. I–6239, paras 29–81. For a survey, see Obwexer and Happacher Brezinka, "The Recognition of Diplomas within the Internal Market" (2000/01) Eur.L.F. 377–386; Pertek (ed.), *La reconnaissance des qualifications dans un espace européen des formations et des professions* (Bruylant, Brussels, 1998), 370 pp.; Favret, "Le système général de reconnaissance des diplômes et des formations professionnelles en droit communautaire: l'esprit et la méthode. Règles actuelles et développements futurs" (1996) R.T.D.E. 259–280; Pertek, "Une dynamique de la reconnaissance des diplômes à des fins professionnelles et à des fins académiques: réalisations et nouvelles réflexions" (1996) R.M.U.E. 89–176. The Commission proposes to consolidate all directives concerning the recognition of professional qualifications in a single Directive of the European Parliament and of the Council on the recognition of professional qualifications (see the amended proposal of April 20, 2004, COM (2004) 317 final).

[629] The Directive does not apply to persons who have not studied or worked in a Member State other than their Member State of origin: ECJ, Joined Cases C–225—C–227/95 *Kapasakalis* [1998] E.C.R. I–4239, paras 18–24.

in the public service may also constitute a regulated profession where access thereto is dependent upon passing a final examination after at least three years' training.[630] A Member State must recognise a diploma which is prescribed in another Member State in order to be admitted to the profession in question (Art. 3(a)).[631] The host Member State may require evidence of professional experience where the duration of the education and training in the other Member State is shorter, or completion of an adaptation period or aptitude test where the education and training received in the other Member State differs substantially in respect of the matters covered (Art. 4). The directive therefore proceeds on the basis of the principles of minimum harmonisation and reciprocal recognition set out in the Commission's White Paper (see para. 5–212).[632] Additionally, the right of establishment and freedom to supply services have been facilitated for some occupations and professions by specific provisions contained in the directive governing the recognition of the diploma required[633] or in separate directives (such as those concerning lawyers).[634]

5–147 Comparison of qualifications. The national authorities are generally obliged to examine to what extent the knowledge and qualifications attested by a diploma obtained in another Member State correspond to those required by its own rules.[635] The obligation to compare abilities already acquired with the knowledge and qualifications required by the national rules also applies with regard to persons in possession of a diploma in an area for which a directive on the mutual recognition of diplomas has been

---

[630] ECJ (judgment of September 9, 2003), Case C–285/01 *Burbaud*, not yet reported, paras 38–58 (this applies even where the final examination leads to an appointment to a permanent post without the award of a formal diploma).

[631] The Directive does not apply where a diploma is not recognised by the Member State in which it was obtained: CFI, Case I–16/90 *Panagiotopoulou v European Parliament* [1992] E.C.R. II–89, para. 45.

[632] Since a diploma obtained in a non-member country does not necessarily satisfy the harmonised minimum requirements, a Member State does not automatically have to recognise it—not even if other Member States do: ECJ, Case C–154/93 *Tawil-Albertini* [1994] E.C.R. I–451, paras 11–13.

[633] See the mutual recognition directives on (para)medical diplomas listed in n.634 *infra*.

[634] Directive 98/5/EC of the European Parliament and of the Council of February 16, 1998 to facilitate practice of the profession of lawyer on a permanent basis in a Member State other than that in which the qualification was obtained, [1998] O.J. L77/36. The Court of Justice upheld the validity of that directive in Case C–168/98 *Luxembourg v European Parliament and Council* [2000] E.C.R. I–9131. See also the earlier Council Directive 77/249/EEC of March 22, 1977 to facilitate the effective exercise by lawyers of freedom to provide services, [1977] O.J. L78/17. Diplomas in law are covered by the general harmonisation directive, Directive 89/48. See Dal and Defalque, "La directive 'établissement avocats' 98/5/CE du février 16, 1998" (1999) J.T. 693–695; Pertek, "L'Europe des professions d'avocat après la directive 98/5 sur l'exercice permanent dans un autre Etat membre" (2001) R.M.C.U.E. 106–111.

[635] ECJ, Case 222/86 *Heylens* [1987] E.C.R. 4097, paras 10–13 (access to gainful employment, as a football trainer); ECJ, Case C–340/89 *Vlassopoulou* [1991] E.C.R. I–2357, paras 9–21 (access to self-employment, as a lawyer). See also ECJ, Case C–19/92 *Kraus* [1993] E.C.R. I–1663, paras 32–38 (authorisation required in order to use the title LL.M. obtained in another Member State, para. 5–134, *supra*).

adopted who, nevertheless, cannot rely on the automatic recognition introduced by the directive in question.[636] If the diplomas correspond only partially, the national authorities in question are entitled to require the person to prove that he or she has acquired the knowledge and qualifications which are lacking.[637] The mutual-recognition directives ensure admission to the selection and recruitment procedures for a regulated profession, but do not themselves afford any right to be recruited.[638] However, it is contrary to the Treaty provisions on free movement of persons for a recruitment procedure to require a person to pass an examination giving access to training organised by the State where that procedure does not enable account to be taken of qualifications that a candidate has already obtained in another Member State by completing such training.[639]

f. Social security and the free movement of persons

Co-ordination of social security systems. Article 42 of the EC Treaty **5–148** requires the Council to adopt such measures in the field of social security as are necessary to provide freedom of movement for workers. The article refers to arrangements to secure for migrant workers and their dependants aggregation of all periods taken into account under the laws of the several countries for acquiring benefits and payment of benefits to persons resident in the territories of Member States. Such arrangements have been laid down in Regulation (EEC) No. 1408/71 of June 14, 1971,[640] which was recently replaced by Regulation (EC) No. 883/2004 of April 29, 2004.[641] Acting on the basis of Art. 308 of the EC Treaty, the Council had extended

---

[636] See ECJ, Case C–238/98 *Hocsman* [2000] E.C.R. I–6623, para. 23 (diploma obtained in a non-member country); ECJ, Case C–31/00 *Dreessen* [2002] E.C.R. I–663, para. 28 (the diploma fell outside the scope of the directive). See also ECJ (judgment of May 16, 2002), Case C–232/99 *Commission v Spain*, not yet reported, paras 18–41.

[637] ECJ, Case C–340/89 *Vlassopoulou* [1991] E.C.R. I–2357, paras 16–23, in which the Court of Justice applied the principles of Directive 89/48 to facts dating back to before the end of the period prescribed for implementing the directive. See, to the same effect, ECJ, Case C–234/97 *Fernández de Bobadilla* [1999] E.C.R. I–4773.

[638] The fact that a person has been successful in a recruitment examination in one Member State does not entitle that person to be recruited in another Member State: ECJ (judgment of September 9, 2003), Case C–285/01 *Burbaud*, not yet reported, paras 85–93.

[639] *ibid.*, paras 94–112.

[640] Regulation (EEC) No. 1408/71 of the Council of June 14, 1971 on the application of social security schemes to employed persons and their families moving within the Community, [1971] O.J. Spec. Ed. 416 (adopted on the basis of Arts 2, 7 and 51 of the EEC Treaty [now articles 2, 12 and 42 of the EC Treaty]), and the implementing Council Regulation (EEC) No. 574/72 March 21, 1972 [1972] O.J. English Spec. Ed. 159. These regulations had been codified by Council Regulation (EEC) No. 118/97 of December 2, 1996, [1997] O.J. L28/1 (on the basis of Arts 42 and 308 of the EC Treaty).

[641] Regulation (EC) No. 883/2004 of the European Parliament and of the Council of April 29, 2004 on the co-ordination of social security systems, [2004] O.J. L166/1; republished with corrigendum: [2004] O.J. L200/1 (adopted on the basis of Arts 42 and 308 of the EC Treaty). See Pennings, "The European Commission Proposal to Simplify Regulation 1408/71" (2001) Eur.J.Soc.Sec. 45–60.

the scope of Regulation No. 1408/71 to cover self-employed persons and members of their families,[642] students and special schemes for civil servants.[643] Regulation No. 883/2204, which has been adopted on the basis of Art. 42 (now requiring the Council to act in co-decision with the European Parliament) and Art. 308 of the EC Treaty, likewise applies to all nationals of a Member State, stateless persons and refugees resident in the territory of a Member State who are or have been subject to the social security legislation of one or more Member States, as well as to the members of their families and to their survivors.[644] According to this regulation, migrant workers and their families retain rights which they have acquired in one Member State, with benefits being paid elsewhere in the Community.[645] The Regulation also entitles them to enjoy the same benefits as nationals of the host State (Art. 4, Regulation No. 883/2004; see previously Art. 3(1) of Regulation No. 1408/71). Acceptance of an employment relationship in another Member State therefore has no (or only minimal) adverse effect on the social security status of the worker concerned. The regulation enshrines the principle that a worker is to be subject to the legislation of a single Member State only, and indicates by means of a number of conflict-of-law rules what legislation is to be applicable (Title II of Regulation No. 883/2004). Title III of the regulation

---

[642] Regulation 1390/81, [1981] O.J. L143/1.

[643] Council Regulation (EEC) No. 1606/98 of June 29, 1998, [1998] O.J. L209/1, and Council Regulation (EC) No. 307/99 of February 8, 1999, [1999] O.J. L38/1. Civil servants' supplementary pension rights are covered by Council Directive 98/49/EC of June 29, 1998 on safeguarding the supplementary pension rights of employed and self-employed persons moving within the Community, [1998] O.J. L209/46. See also the extension of Regulations Nos 1408/71 and 574/72 pursuant to Art. 63(4) of the EC Treaty to nationals of third countries legally resident in the territory of the Member States: Council Regulation (EC) No. 859/2003 of May 14, 2003, [2003] O.J. L124/1.

[644] As to Regulation No. 1408/71, the Court of Justice held that stateless persons and refugees also fell within that regulation in view of the international obligations incumbent on Member States to treat stateless persons and refugees in the same way as their own nationals for the purposes of social security: ECJ, Joined Cases C–95/99–C–98/99 and C–180/99 *Khalil* [2001] E.C.R. I–7413, paras 39–58. See Baquero Cruz, "Khalil e.a.: Les réfugiés et les apatrides face au droit communautaire" (2002) C.D.E. 501–516.

[645] As a sample of the extensive caselaw on the content of entitlements acquired and the calculation thereof, see ECJ, Case 21/75 *Petroni* [1975] E.C.R. 1149, paras 10–21 (pensions); ECJ, Case 320/82 *D'Amario* [1983] E.C.R. 3811, paras 4–10 (orphans' benefits); ECJ, Case 242/83 *Patteri* [1984] E.C.R. 3171, paras 7–11 (family allowances); ECJ, Case C–131/96 *Mora Romero* [1997] E.C.R. I–3659, paras 27–36 (legislation providing for payment of orphan's benefit to be extended for a period equal to the duration of military service also has to be applied where the military service was carried out by a national of another Member State in that State). See also Van Raepenbusch, "Le régime de sécurité sociale applicable aux travailleurs et à leur famille se déplaçant dans la Communauté", in Aussant, Fornasier, Louis, Séché and Van Raepenbusch, *Commentaire Mégret—Le droit de la CEE. 3. Libre circulation des personnes, des services et des capitaux. Transports* (Editions de l'Université de Bruxelles, Brussels, 1990), at 97–149; for a survey of the case law, see Moore, "Freedom of Movement and Migrant Workers' Social Security: An Overview of the Court's Jurisprudence 1992–1997" (1998) C.M.L.R. 409–457 and "Freedom of Movement and Migrant Workers' Social Security: An Overview of the Case Law of the Court of Justice 1997–2001" (2002) C.M.L.R. 807–839.

sets out specific provisions relating to different sorts of benefits.[646] After the adoption of the EU Constitution, the need to have recourse to the supplementary clause of competence equivalent to the present Art. 308 of the EC Treaty will decrease since Art. III–136 of the EU Constitution (corresponding to Art. 42 of the EC Treaty) will be applicable to "employed and self-employed migrant workers and their dependants".

The Court of Justice has held that even if the Council has not carried out any co-ordination in respect of a social security scheme, Arts 39–42 of the EC Treaty require social security benefits to which a worker is entitled under that system not to be affected as a result of the fact that the work was performed in another Member State. Where the adverse effects experienced by a worker can be overcome without Community co-ordination measures, the national authorities may have to apply the rules of Regulation No. 1408/71 by analogy. This was the case where national legislation provided that only periods of employment completed in national public hospitals might be recognised as pensionable because the fact that comparable periods completed in public hospitals in other Member States might not be recognised as such dissuaded workers from exercising their right to freedom of movement and discriminated against workers who had exercised that right.[647]

Facilitating free movement. Article 42 of the EC Treaty leaves in being **5–149** differences between the Member States' social security systems and hence in the rights of persons working in the Member States. Subject to the limits imposed by free movement of goods, persons, services and capital, the Member States still have the power to determine the conditions under which a person may become affiliated to a social security scheme and entitled to social security benefits.[648] Where a social security entitlement of

---

[646] Namely: sickness, maternity and equivalent paternity benefits, benefits in respect of accidents at work and occupational diseases, death grants, invalidity benefits, old-age and survivors' pensions, unemployment benefits, pre-retirement benefits, family benefits and special non-contributory cash benefits. However, the Court held, as regards Regulation No. 1408/71, that it did not apply to situations which are confined in all respects within a single Member State: ECJ, Joined Cases C–95/99–C–98/99 and C–180/99 *Khalil* [2001] E.C.R. I–7413, paras 39–58. For a critical view, see Mavridis, "La sécurité sociale et les promesses des droits fondamentaux dans l'Union européenne" (2002) C.D.E. 643–677.

[647] ECJ, Case C–443/93 *Vougioukas* [1995] E.C.R. I–4033, paras 39–42. For a case in which it was held that the negative consequences of working in another Member State could be overcome only by recourse to co-ordination measures adopted by the Council, see ECJ, Case C–360/97 *Nijhuis* [1999] E.C.R. I–1919, paras 28–32.

[648] See, with regard to the conditions imposed by a social security institution for the reimbursement to the insured person of costs incurred in another Member State: ECJ, Case C–120/95 *Decker* [1998] E.C.R. I–1831 (rules making reimbursement of costs incurred for medical products (spectacles) in another Member State dependent on prior authorisation held contrary to free movement of goods); ECJ, Case C–158/96 *Kohll* [1998] E.C.R. I–1931 and ECJ, Case C–385/99 *Müller-Fauré and van Riet* [2003] E.C.R. I–4509, paras 93–108 (requirement for prior authorisation of dental treatment as an outpatient and for non-hospital care, respectively, in another Member State held contrary to freedom to

a migrant worker falls under two different statutory schemes (*e.g.* a right to a pension after being employed in two Member States), the application of one set of national rules to a migrant worker may give rise to unforeseen consequences, hardly compatible with Arts 39–42 of the EC Treaty. According to the Court of Justice, the national authorities should ascertain whether their legislation can be applied literally to migrant workers, in exactly the same way as to non-migrant workers, without causing migrant workers to lose a social security advantage.[649] In addition, the national court concerned should interpret its own legislation in the light of the aims of those articles and, as far as possible, prevent its interpretation from being such as to discourage a migrant worker from actually exercising his right to freedom of movement.[650] Where it is impossible to apply national law in conformity with Community law in this way, the national court must fully apply Community law and disapply any provision which would lead to a result contrary to Community law.[651]

g. Judicial co-operation in civil matters

5–150 Scope. In so far as necessary for the proper functioning of the internal market, the Council is empowered to take measures in the field of judicial co-operation in civil matters having cross-border implications (EC Treaty, Arts 61(c) and 65).[652] The Treaty of Amsterdam introduced this

---

supply services); ECJ, Case C–157/99 *Smits and Peerbooms* [2001] E.C.R. I–5473 and ECJ, Case C–385/99 *Müller-Fauré and van Riet* [2003] E.C.R. I–4509, paras 66–92 (requirement for prior authorisation for hospital treatment in another Member State held in certain circumstances not to conflict with freedom to provide services); ECJ, Case C–368/98 *Vanbraekel* [2001] E.C.R. I–5363 (limitation of reimbursement of hospital treatment received in another Member State to the lower level applicable in that State held incompatible with freedom to provide services). For *Decker* and *Kohll*, see Van Raepenbusch (1998) C.D.E. 683–697; for *Müller-Fauré*, see Flear (2004) C.M.L.R. 209–233; see also Hatzopoulos, "*Killing* National Health and Insurance Systems but *Healing* Patients? The European Market for Health Care Services after the Judgments of the ECJ in *Vanbraekel* and *Peerbooms*" (2002) C.M.L.R. 683–729; Nowak, "Zur grundfreiheitlichen Inanspruchnahme von Gesundheitsleistungen im europäischen Binnenmarkt" (2003) EuR. 644–656.

[649] ECJ, Case C–165/91 *Van Munster* [1994] E.C.R. I–4661, para. 33; ECJ, Case C–202/97 *Fitzwilliam Executive Search* [2000] E.C.R. I–883, paras 51–59; ECJ, Case C–178/97 *Banks* [2000] E.C.R. I–2005, paras 38–45. If the national authorities cannot reach agreement on the applicable national legislation, they must initiate proceedings under Art. 227 of the EC Treaty: *Fitzwilliam Executive Search*, para. 58, and *Banks*, para. 45. See Van Zeben and Donders, "Coordination of Social Security: Developments in the Area of Posting" (2001) Eur.J.Soc.Sec. 107–116.

[650] *Van Munster*, cited in n.649, *supra*, para. 34.

[651] ECJ, Case C–262/97 *Engelbrecht* [2000] E.C.R. I–7321, para. 40.

[652] For general discussions, see Basedow, "The Communitarisation of the Conflict of Laws under the Treaty of Amsterdam" (2000) C.M.L.R. 687–708; Remien, "European Private International Law, the European Community and its Emerging Area of Freedom, Security and Justice" (2001) C.M.L.R. 53–86. For the relationship with the Hague Conference on Private International Law and the question whether Art. 65 implies the power to conclude agreements with non-member countries, see Traest, "Development of a European Private International Law and the Hague Conference" (2003) Yearbook of Private International

competence with regard to private (international) law. Although private law is primarily within the competence of the Member States, the Council adopts measures pursuant to Art. 65 of the EC Treaty which restrict national policy options and, just as in other Community policy areas, may in some cases preclude any parallel exercise of competence by the Member States.[653] Since the entry into force of the Treaty of Nice, the Council is to take such measures in accordance with the co-decision procedure, with the exception of aspects relating to family law.[654] Art. 68 limits the jurisdiction of the Court of Justice to give preliminary rulings in connection with the interpretation of Art. 65 of the EC Treaty and the validity and interpretation of acts adopted pursuant thereto (see para. 10–075).

Cross-border actions. What is involved is, first, measures for improving **5–151** and simplifying: (i) the system for cross-border service of judicial and extrajudicial documents; (ii) co-operation in the taking of evidence; and (iii) the recognition and enforcement of decisions in civil and commercial cases, including decisions in extrajudicial cases (Art. 65(a), first, second and third indents). In these areas, regulations have been adopted on the basis of Arts 61(c) and 67(1) of the EC Treaty to replace and build upon agreements concluded as between the Member States under Art. 293 of the Treaty or outside the Community framework which the Court of Justice had jurisdiction to interpret (see paras 18–008—18–009).[655]

As far as cross-border service of documents is concerned, a regulation has replaced the convention concluded by the Member States in the context

---

Law 223–259; Kotuby, "External Competence of the European Community in the Hague Conference on Private International Law: Community Harmonisation and Worldwide Unification" (2001) N.I.L.R. 1–30; Israël, "Europees internationaal privaatrecht. De EG, een *comitas Europea* en vrijheid, veiligheid en rechtvaardigheid" (2001) Nederlands Internationaal Privaatrecht 135–149.

[653] Thus, Regulation No. 1347/2000 (n.660, *infra*) and Regulation No. 44/2001 (n. 658, *infra*) preclude any parallel competence on the part of the Member States within the meaning of the *AETR* case law (see para. 5–023, *supra*), which confers an "exclusive nature" on the Community in the relevant areas. This means that the Member States may no longer act internationally in the fields covered by these Regulations without the authorisation of the Community; see Council Decision 2003/93/EC of December 19, 2002 authorising the Member States, in the interest of the Community, to sign the 1996 Hague Convention on jurisdiction, applicable law, recognition, enforcement and co-operation in respect of parental responsibility and measures for the protection of children ([2003] O.J. L48/1) and Council Decision 2003/882/EC of November 27, 2003 authorising the Member States which are Contracting Parties to the Paris Convention of July 29, 1960 on Third Party Liability in the Field of Nuclear Energy to sign, in the interest of the European Community, the Protocol amending that Convention ([2003] O.J. L338/30). See Boele-Woelki and Van Ooik, "De ingrijpende communautisering van het internationale privaatrecht" (2002) S.E.W. 394–407; Traest, "Harmonisation du droit international privé: relation entre la Communauté européenne et la Conférence de La Haye" (2003) R.D.Unif. 499–507.

[654] For these aspects, the Council continues to act by unanimous vote on a proposal from the Commission after consulting the European Parliament: EC Treaty, Art. 67(1) in conjunction with (5), second indent (see para. 14–069, *infra*).

[655] See Traest, "Internationaal privaatrecht in verordeningen: een verdere stap in de ontwikkeling van Europees internationaal privaatrecht" (2000–2001) A.J.T. 537–564; Van Houtte and Pertegás Sender (eds), *Het nieuwe Europese IPR: van verdrag naar verordening* (Intersentia, Antwerp, 2001), 303 pp.

of co-operation in the fields of justice and home affairs.[656] For the purpose of the taking of evidence in civil and commercial matters, a Council regulation has introduced a system of co-operation between the courts of the Member States.[657] Moreover, as regards recognition and enforcement of judgments in civil and commercial matters, a regulation has been adopted to deal with the recognition and enforcement of judicial decisions while laying down common rules as to jurisdiction.[658] That regulation took over from the Brussels Convention (or Brussels I), which the Member States concluded as long ago as 1968 pursuant to Art. 220 [now Art. 293] of the EC Treaty.[659] A similar regulation has been adopted on jurisdiction and the recognition and enforcement of judgments in matrimonial matters and

---

[656] Council Regulation (EC) No. 1348/2000 of May 29, 2000 on the service in the Member States of judicial and extrajudicial documents in civil or commercial matters ([2000] O.J. L160/37; for the Member States' notification of the central bodies and transmitting agencies, see [2001] O.J. C151/4) See Ekelmans, "Le règlement 1348/2000 relatif à la signification et à la notification des actes judiciaires et extrajudiciaires" (2001) J.T. 481–488; Heß, "Die Zustellung von Schriftstücken im europäischen Justizraum" (2001) N.J.W. 15–23. See, formerly, the Convention of May 26, 1997 on the service in the Member States of the European Union of judicial and extrajudicial documents in civil or commercial matters, [1997] O.J. C261/26 (explanatory report in [1997] O.J. C261/26). See Paulino Pereira, "La Convention relative à la signification et à la notification dans les Etats membres de l'Union européenne des actes judiciaires et extrajudiciaires en matière civile et commerciale" (1998) R.M.C.U.E. 111–115; Stadler, "Neues europäisches Zustellungsrecht" (2001) UPRIX 514–521. For the interpretation of the Convention by the Court of Justice, see para. 18–009, infra.

[657] Council Regulation (EC) No. 1206/2001 of May 28, 2001 on co-operation between the courts of the Member States in the taking of evidence in civil or commercial matters, [2001] O.J. L174/1; Berger, "Die EG-Verordnung über die Zusammenarbeit der Gerichte auf dem Gebiet der Beweisaufnahme in Zivil- und Handelssachen (EuBVO)" (2001) IPRax. 522–527; Mougenot, "Le règlement européen sur l'obtention des preuves" (2002) J.T. 17–21; Van het Kaar, "De Europese Bewijsverordening wordt op 1 januari 1 2004 van kracht" (2003) N.T.E.R. 287–291.

[658] Council Regulation (EC) No. 44/2001 of December 22, 2000 on jurisdiction and the recognition and enforcement of judgments in civil and commercial matters ([2001] O.J. L12/1); Nuyts, "La communautarisation de la Convention de Bruxelles" (2001) J.T. 913–922; Schmidt, "De EEX-Verordening: de volgende stap in het Europese procesrecht" (2001) Nederlands Internationaal Privaatrecht 150–172; Piltz, "Vom EuGVÜ zur Brüssel-I-Verordnung" (2002) N.J.W. 789–794; Droz and Gaudemet-Tallon, "La transformation de la Convention de Bruxelles du 27 septembre 1968 en Règlement du Conseil concernant la compétence judiciaire, la reconnaissance et l'exécution des décisions en matière civile et commerciale" (2001) R.C.D.I.P. 601–652. See also the draft programme of measures for implementation of the principle of mutual recognition of decisions in civil and commercial matters, [2001] O.J. C12/1.

[659] Brussels Convention of September 27, 1968 on jurisdiction and the enforcement of judgments in civil and commercial matters (Accession Convention for Denmark, Ireland and the UK: [1978] O.J. L304/77), implemented in the UK by the Civil Jurisdiction and Judgments Act 1982; see the consolidated text of the Convention in [1998] O.J. C27/1. See Van Houtte and Pertegás Sender (eds), Europese IPR-verdragen (Acco, Leuven, 1997), 410 pp; Briggs and Rees, Civil Jurisdiction and Judgments (Lloyd's of London Press, London, 1997), 472 pp. For the way in which the Convention came about and entered into force, see paras. 15–016—15–017, infra; for its interpretation by the Court of Justice, see para. 18–008, infra. The scope of these arrangements was extended to the EFTA States by the Lugano Convention, nn. to para. 23–004, infra.

in matters of parental responsibility for children of both spouses.[660] That regulation replaced a convention concluded by the Member States in the context of co-operation in the fields of justice and home affairs with regard to judicial decisions in matrimonial matters ("Brussels II").[661] Another regulation has created the possibility for a judgment on uncontested claims to be certified as a European Enforcement Order, which allows the judgment to be recognised and enforced in another Member State without any intermediate proceedings needing to be brought in that State.[662] None of these regulations, however, apply to Denmark.[663] The recognition and enforcement of orders freezing property or evidence in criminal matters are the subject of Council decisions adopted in the context of police and judicial co-operation in criminal matters (see para. 6–009).

Where the Member States have not harmonised a particular area or introduced a system of reciprocal recognition, the Treaty provisions on free movement of persons may require national authorities to accept certificates and analogous documents relative to personal status issued by the competent authorities of the other Member States, unless their accuracy is seriously undermined by concrete evidence relating to the individual case in question. This will be the case in particular where workers have to prove facts set out in registers of civil status (in their Member State of origin) in

---

[660] Council Regulation (EC) No. 2201/2003 of November 27, 2003 concerning jurisdiction and the recognition and enforcement of judgments in matrimonial matters and the matters of parental responsibility ([2003] O.J. L338/1: "Brussels IIa"), which replaced Council Regulation (EC) No. 1347/2000 of May 29, 2000 on jurisdiction and the recognition and enforcement of judgments in matrimonial matters and in matters of parental responsibility for children of both spouses ([2000] O.J. L160/19; corrigendum in [2000] O.J. C219/6: "Brussels II"). See Watté and Boularbah, "Les nouvelles règles de conflits de juridictions en matière de désunion des époux. Le règlement communautaire 'Bruxelles II' " (2001) J.T. 369–378; Drouet, "La communautarisation de 'Bruxelles II': chronique d'une mutation juridique" (2001) R.M.C.U.E. 247–257; Kohler, "Internationales Verfahrensrecht für Ehesachen in der Europäischen Union: Die Verordnung 'Brüssel II' " (2001) N.J.W. 10–15; Ancel and Muir Watt, "La désunion européenne: le Règlement dit 'Bruxelles II' " (2001) R.C.D.I.P. 403–457; Sumampouw, "Ouderlijke verantwoordelijkheid onder de Verordening Brussel II" (2002) Nederlands Internationaal Privaatrecht 1–8; McEleavy, "The Brussels II Regulation: How the European Community has Moved into Family Law" (2002) I.C.L.Q. 883–908.
[661] Convention of May 28, 1998 on jurisdiction and the recognition and enforcement of judgments in matrimonial matters (Second Brussels Convention, [1998] O.J. C221/2). See Paulino Pereira, "La reconnaissance mutuelle des decisions de divorce et de responsabilité parentale dans l'Union européenne (Convention de Bruxelles II)" (1999) R.M.C.U.E. 484–489; Boele-Woelki, "Brüssel II: Die Verordnung über die Zuständigkeit und die Anerkennung von Entscheidungen in Ehesachen" (2001) Z.f.RV 121–130; Mostermans, "De wederzijdse erkenning van echtscheidingen binnen de Europese Unie" (2002) N.I.P.R. 263–273; Bigot, "La responsabilité parentale après désunion du couple en Europe" (2003) R.M.C.U.E 111–119. For its interpretation by the Court of Justice, see para. 18–009, infra.
[662] Regulation (EC) No. 805/2004 of the European Parliament and of the Council of April 21, 2004 creating a European Enforcement Order for uncontested claims, [2004] O.J. L143/15.
[663] The Brussels I Convention applies in relations between Denmark and the other Member States. The Lugano Convention also continues to apply (n. 659, supra).

order to assert entitlements to social security benefits in another Member State.[664]

5–152 Conflict of laws. In addition, the Council is to take measures to promote the compatibility of the rules applicable in the Member States concerning conflict of laws and of jurisdiction (EC Treaty, Art. 65(b)). Apart from rules on jurisdiction, this relates to instruments such as the Rome Convention concluded by the Member States in 1980 on the law applicable to contractual obligations (the Rome Convention).[665] Rules have been laid down by regulation on jurisdiction and the applicable law with regard to cross-border insolvency proceedings and the recognition of judgments delivered on the basis of such proceedings.[666]

5–153 Civil procedure. Lastly, Art. 65(c) of the EC Treaty provides for measures to eliminate obstacles to the good functioning of civil proceedings, if necessary by promoting the compatibility of the rules on civil procedure applicable in the Member States. In this way, the Council has laid down minimum standards for legal aid in cross-border disputes for persons without sufficient financial means.[667]

5–154 European judicial network. In this connection, the Council has also adopted other measures which help to eliminate obstacles to judicial co-operation in civil matters, in particular the establishment of a European

---

[664] ECJ, Case C–336/94 *Dafeki* [1997] E.C.R. I–6761, paras 8–21.

[665] Rome Convention of June 19, 1980 on the law applicable to contractual obligations ([1980] O.J. L266/1; ratified in the UK by the Contracts (Applicable Law) Act 1990; see the consolidated version in [1998] O.J. C27/34). For the way in which the Convention came about and its entry into force, see paras 15–016—15–017, *infra*; for its interpretation by the Court of Justice, see para. 18–008, *infra*. For this Convention, see Van Houtte and Pertegás Sender (eds), *Europese IPR-verdragen* (Acco, Leuven, 1997), at 189–320; Plender, *The European Contracts Convention* (Sweet & Maxwell, London, 1991), 351 pp; Martigny, "Internationales Vertragsrecht im Schatten des Europäischen Gemeinschaftsrechts" (2001) Z.Eu.P. 308–366. It is also contemplated to harmonise the conflict rules with regard to the law applicable to non-contractual obligations (see the Commission's proposal of July 22, 2003 ("Rome II") (COM (2003) 427 final) and the law applicable to matrimonial cases. For the harmonisation of the rules of private international law, see also Jayme and Kohler, "Europäisches Kollisionsrecht 2001: Anerkennungsprinzip statt IPR" (2001) IPRax. 501–514; for the extent to which Community law influences the application of national conflicts rules, see Wilderspin and Lewis, "Les relations entre le droit communautaire et les règles de conflits de lois des Etats membres" (2002) R.C.I.P. 1–37.

[666] Council Regulation (EC) No. 1346/2000 of May 29, 2000 on insolvency proceedings, [2000] O.J. L160/1 (not applicable to Denmark). See Bos, "The European Insolvency Regulation and the Harmonisation of Private International Law in Europe" (2003) N.I.L.Rev. 31–57 and "De Europese insolventieverordening" (2000) N.T.E.R. 295–299; Bureau, "La fin d'un îlot de résistance—Le règlement du Conseil relatif aux procédures d'insolvabilité" (2002) R.C.D.I.P. 613–679. A convention on insolvency proceedings was adopted on November 23, 1995 but did not enter into force since it was not signed by all Member States.

[667] Council Directive 2002/8/EC of January 27, 2003 to improve access to justice in cross-border disputes by establishing minimum common rules relating to Legal Aid for such disputes ([2003] O.J. L26/41; the Directive does not apply to Denmark).

judicial network in civil and commercial matters and other forms of collaboration between legal practitioners.[668]

Constitution. In the EU Constitution, the Union's competence with **5–155** respect to judicial co-operation in civil matters having cross-border implications is included amongst the provisions on the "area for freedom, security and justice" (Art. III–269). In so far as mutual recognition and enforcement of judgments and decisions in extrajudicial cases are concerned, this competence is no longer limited to "civil and commercial matters". Furthermore, the Union will be given the competence to enact measures aimed at ensuring effective access to justice, the development of alternative methods of dispute settlement and support for the training of the judiciary and judicial staff (EU Constitution, Art. III–269(2)(e), (g) and (h)). The co-decision procedure will be applicable to the enactment of European "laws" and "framework laws", but not to measures concerning family law.[669]

h. Administrative co-operation in connection with free movement of persons

Administrative co-operation. In order to secure co-operation between **5–156** departments of the administrations of the Member States responsible for the areas of free movement of persons covered by Title IV of the EC Treaty and between those departments and the Commission, the Council may take measures under Art. 61(d) and Art. 66 of the EC Treaty.[670] The

---

[668] Council Decision 2001/470/EC of May 28, 2001 establishing a European Judicial Network in civil and commercial matters, [2001] O.J. L174/25 (adopted on the basis of Art. 61(c) and (d) and Art. 66 of the EC Treaty; not applicable to Denmark) and Council Regulation (EC) No. 290/2001 of February 12, 2001 extending the programme of incentives and exchanges for legal practitioners in the area of civil law (Grotius civil), [2001] O.J. L43/1 (not applicable to Denmark). The latter regulation extended a JHA Joint Action in the field of civil law (for its extension in the field of criminal law, see n. 20 to para. 6–008). Council Regulation (EC) No. 743/2002 of April 25, 2002 established a general Community framework of activities to facilitate the implementation of judicial co-operation in civil matters, [2002] O.J. L115/1 (not applicable to Denmark).

[669] In the area of family law, European laws or framework laws are to be adopted by the Council, acting unanimously on a proposal of the Commission and after consulting the European Parliament. On a proposal of the Commission and after consulting the Parliament, the Council, acting unanimously, may however determine aspects of family law with cross-border implications that may be regulated according to the co-decision procedure (Art. III–269(3) of the EU Constitution).

[670] See Council Decision 2002/463/EC of June 13, 2002 adopting an action programme for administrative co-operation in the fields of external borders, visas, asylum and immigration (ARGO programme), [2002] O.J. L161/11 (following on from the Odysseus programme introduced by Council Joint Action 98/244/JHA of March 19, 1998, [1998] O.J. L99/2) and Council Regulation (EC) No. 377/2004 of February 19, 2004 on the creation of an immigration liaison officers network ([2004] O.J. L64/1; not applicable to Denmark). See also Council Decision 2001/470/EC of May 28, 2001 (cited in preceding n.) and Council Regulation (EC) No. 2424/2001 of December 6, 2001 on the development of the second generation Schengen Information System (SIS II), [2001] O.J. L328/4 (not applicable to Denmark; see also n.716 *infra* to para. 5–164).

Council acts by a qualified majority on a proposal from the Commission after consulting the European Parliament.[671] As in the case of Art. 65, the jurisdiction of the Court of Justice is limited by Art. 68 of the EC Treaty. This limitation will disappear as a result of the EU Constitution.[672]

i. Movement of nationals of third countries

(1) *Rights to free movement*

5–157 Third-country nationals. The Treaty provisions on free movement of persons do not apply to nationals of third countries, unless they have the right of free movement as members of the family of a Community worker or self-employed person.[673] Third-country nationals may also obtain certain rights where the Community concludes an agreement with their country which confers rights on them.[674] In this way, the association agreements with the Maghreb countries and some decisions of the EC-Turkey Association Council[675] confer on nationals of those countries who are lawfully employed in the Member States the right to be treated in the same way as their own nationals as regards conditions of employment, remuneration and social security.[676] This also applies as regards association

---

[671] This is the procedure as from May 1, 2004 by virtue of the Protocol annexed by the Treaty of Nice to the EC Treaty on Art. 67 of the EC Treaty ([2001] O.J. C80/69).

[672] In the EU Constitution, the competence to ensure administrative co-operation in this respect is to be found in Art. III–263 of the chapter on the "Area of freedom, security and justice" (see para. 5–167, *infra*).

[673] See para. 5–120, *supra*. For discussions of their status, see Barrett, "Family-Matters: European Community Law and Third-Country Members" (2003) C.M.L.R. 369–421 and also Akandji-Kombé, "Les droits des étrangers et leur sauvegarde dans l'ordre communautaire" (1995) C.D.E. 351–381; Hedemann-Robinson, "Third-Country Nationals, European Union Citizenship, and Free Movement of Persons: A Time for Bridges rather than Divisions" (1996) Y.E.L. 321–362.

[674] Hedemann-Robinson, "An Overview of Recent Legal Developments at Community Level in Relation to Third Country Nationals Resident within the European Union, with Particular Reference to the Case Law of the European Court of Justice" (2001) C.M.L.R. 525–586.

[675] For these association agreements and decisions, see para. 20–020, *infra*.

[676] This also applies to resident family members who qualify for benefit under the legislation of a Member State: ECJ, Case C–18/90 *Kziber* [1991] E.C.R. I–199, para. 28; ECJ, Case C–126/95 *Hallouzi-Choho* [1996] E.C.R. I–4807, paras 21–40; ECJ, C–179/98 *Mesbah* [1999] E.C.R. I–7955, paras 42–48 (Co-operation Agreement with Morocco); ECJ, Case C–103/94 *Krid* [1995] E.C.R. I–719, paras 21–24; ECJ, Case C–113/97 *Babahenini* [1998] E.C.R. I–183, paras 19–31 (Co-operation Agreement with Algeria). However, the agreement with Morocco embodies more limited rights than the agreement with Turkey, which is supplemented by association decisions: ECJ, Case C–416/96 *El-Yassini* [1999] E.C.R. I–1209, paras 33–67. For examples of rights arising under Decisions 2/76 and 1/80 of the EEC-Turkey Association Council, see ECJ, Case C–192/89 *Sevince* [1990] E.C.R. I–3461, paras 27–33; ECJ, Case C–237/91 *Kus* [1994] E.C.R. I–6781, paras 11–36; ECJ, Case C–188/00 *Kurz* [2002] E.C.R. I–10691, paras 26–70; ECJ, Case C–171/01 *Wählergruppe Gemeinsam* [2003] E.C.R. I–4301, paras 68–94. For Decision 3/80, see, *e.g.* ECJ, Case C–277/94 *Taflan-Met* [1996] E.C.R. I–4085; ECJ, Case C–262/96 *Sürül* [1999] E.C.R. I–2685, paras 75–105; ECJ, Joined Cases C–102/98 and C–211/98 *Kocak and Örs* [2000] E.C.R. I–1287, paras 32–55. For Art. 41(1) of the Additional Protocol to the agreement with

agreements with Central European States, which likewise require equal treatment with respect to establishment, albeit the Member States retain the right to apply to nationals of these States their legislation concerning entry, residence and establishment.[677] According to the Charter of Fundamental Rights of the European Union, nationals of third countries who are authorised to work in the territories of the Member States are entitled to working conditions equivalent to those of citizens of the Union.[678]

(2) *Access to and residence in the territory: frontier controls, visas, immigration and asylum*

(i) *Rules regarding access to the territory and establishment of an area of freedom, security and justice*

Community competence. There was protracted discussion as to whether the **5–158** Community was competent to adopt measures relating to third-country nationals' access to and residence in the territory of the Member States. The discussion took off as efforts to achieve the internal market programme began. That programme set out to eliminate controls on the movement of persons within the Community and looked forward to measures in the field of police and judicial co-operation which were to accompany the abolition of checks on persons (see para. 5–080). The EU Treaty conferred on the Community some powers with regard to policy on visas (the former Arts 100c and 100d of the EC Treaty), whilst also bringing the question within the ambit of co-operation in the field of justice and home affairs (JHA co-operation, see the former Art. K.1 of the EU Treaty). In the meantime, most Member States applied common rules in

---

Turkey (on establishment and services), see ECJ, Case C–37/98 *Savas* [2000] E.C.R. I–2927, paras 56–71; ECJ (judgment of October 21, 2003), Joined Cases C–317/01 and C–369/01 *Abatay*, not yet reported, paras 58–117. Nationals of non-member countries do not as a result obtain the right to free movement within the Community: ECJ, Case C–179/98 *Mesbah* [1999] E.C.R. I–7955, para. 356. See also Stangos, "La jurisprudence récente de la Cour de justice des Communautés européennes concernant les travailleurs migrants, ressortissants de pays tiers" (2000) R.A.E. 107–117; Tezcan, "Le droit du travail et le droit de séjour des travailleurs turcs dans l'Union européenne à la lumière des arrêts récents de la Cour de justice des Communautés européennes" (2001) R.M.C.U.E. 117–128. With regard to the direct effect of such provisions, see para. 17–094, *infra*.

[677] See ECJ, Case C–63/99 *Gloszczuk and Gloszczuk* [2001] E.C.R. I–6369, paras 39–86 (agreement with Poland); ECJ, Case C–235/99 *Kondova* [2001] E.C.R. I–6427, paras 40–91 (agreement with Bulgaria); ECJ, Case C–257/99 *Barkoci and Malil* [2001] E.C.R. I–6557, paras 40–84 (agreement with the Czech Republic). See also ECJ, Case C–268/99 *Jany* [2001] E.C.R. I–8615, paras 25–31; ECJ, Case C–162/00 *Pokrzeptowicz-Meyer* [2002] E.C.R. I–1049, paras 31–45; ECJ, Case C–438/00 *Kolpak* [2003] E.C.R. I–4135, paras 31–58 (agreements with Poland, the Czech Republic and Slovakia, respectively) and the commentaries in Hillion (2003) C.M.L.R. 465–491 and Weiss, "The Chapter II on Establishment in the Europe Agreements" (2001) E. For.Aff.Rev. 243–281. For these agreements, see paras 23–027 *et seq.*

[678] Charter of Fundamental Rights of the European Union, Art. 15(3). *Cf.* the "citizens" right, para. 5–117, *supra*.

the context of the Schengen Convention with regard to controls at the external borders and the grant of visas for extended stays of no more than three months (the Schengen *acquis*, see para. 2–017). Outside the Schengen and JHA accords, the conditions for an extended stay on the part of nationals of non-Community countries and asylum policy remained largely determined by each of the Member States themselves.[679]

5–159 Treaty of Amsterdam. As a result of the incorporation of Title IV into the EC Treaty, the Treaty of Amsterdam brought this discussion to a close. Title IV of the EC Treaty empowers the Community to adopt measures relating to the whole policy field of aliens in order to establish progressively "an area of freedom, security and justice" (EC Treaty, Art. 61).[680] This includes measures to permit the abolition of border checks at the internal borders and directly related flanking measures with respect to external border controls, asylum and immigration (EC Treaty, Arts 61, 62 and 63). During a period of five years after the entry into force of the Treaty of Amsterdam,[681] the Council was to act unanimously, on proposals from the Commission or on the initiative of a Member State, after consulting the European Parliament; since May 1, 2004, the co-decision procedure is to apply in most cases (EC Treaty, Art. 67, see para. 14–069). Under Art. 61 of the EC Treaty, the Council is to supplement the Community measures by flanking measures in the area of police and judicial co-operation in criminal matters (PJCC) aimed at a high level of security by preventing and combating crime within the Union (EU Treaty, Title VI, see paras

---

[679] See, *e.g.* Hailbronner, "Perspectives of a Harmonisation of the Law of Asylum After the Maastricht Summit" (1992) C.M.L.R. 917–939; O'Keeffe, "The Emergence of a European Immigration Policy" (1995) E.L.Rev. 20–36. The draft Convention on the crossing of external borders of the Member States (para. 2–016, *supra*) failed to be signed.

[680] See Hailbronner, "European Immigration and Asylum Law under the Amsterdam Treaty" (1998) C.M.L.R. 1047–1067; Hailbronner and Thiery, "Amsterdam— Vergemeinschaftlichung der Sachbereiche Freier Personenverkehr, Asylrecht und Einwanderung sowie Überführung des Schengen-Besitzstands auf EU-Ebene" (1998) EuR. 583–615; Peers, "Building Fortress Europe: The Development of EU Migration Law" (1998) C.M.L.R. 1235–1272; Pollet, "The Amsterdam Treaty and Immigration and Asylum Policies: A Legal Analysis" (2000) R.A.E. 57–80; Wollenschläger, "'Das Asyl- und Einwanderungsrecht der EU" (2001) Eu.GR.Z. 354–364. See also Bell, "Mainstreaming Equality Norms into European Union Asylum law" (2001) E.L.Rev. 20, at 30–34. For discussions of Community powers in connection with JHA co-operation, see Labayle, "Le Traité d'Amsterdam. Un espace de liberté, de sécurité et de justice" (1997) R.T.D.E. 813–881; Bribosia, "Liberté, sécurité et justice: l'imbroglio d'un nouvel espace" (1998) 1 R.M.U.E. 27–54; Donner, "De derde pijler en de Amsterdamse doolhof" (1997) S.E.W. 370–378; Harings, "Die Zusammenarbeit in den Bereichen Justiz und Inneres" (1998) EuR. Beiheft 2, 81–97. On December 3, 1998, the Council adopted an Action Plan on how best to implement the provisions of the Treaty of Amsterdam on an area of freedom, security and justice, [1999] O.J. C19/1. In this connection, the European Council called for a common European asylum and migration policy, facilitated access to courts, enhanced mutual recognition of judicial decisions and judgments, greater convergence of civil law and the combating of crime through prevention and co-operation: Conclusions of the European Council held in Tampere on October 15 and 16, 1999 (1999) 10 EU.Bull point 1.6.1.

[681] The five-year period did not apply to measures adopted under Art. 63(2)(b), (3)(a) or (4) (EC Treaty, Art. 63, third paragraph).

6–006–6–013). Accordingly, the procedural framework for the development of the Schengen information system has been laid down in decisions adopted in parallel on the basis of Title IV of the EC Treaty and Title VI of the EU Treaty.[682] The EU Constitution will bring the Community and non-Community powers together in a single chapter covering the Union's competence to establish an area of freedom, security and justice (see para. 5–167).

(ii) *Measures relating to border checks*

Visa policy. In the Member States which have taken over the Schengen **5–160** *acquis,* border checks at the internal borders have in principle been abolished.[683] Pursuant to Art. 62(1) of the EC Treaty, the Community may adopt "measures with a view to ensuring, in compliance with Art. 14, the absence of any controls on persons, be they citizens of the Union or nationals of third countries when crossing internal borders". Community measures on the crossing of the external borders are to establish standards and procedures to be followed by Member States in carrying out checks on persons at such borders (EC Treaty, Art. 62(2)(a))[684] and rules on visas for extended stays of no more than three months (Art. 62(2)(b)). The latter rules cover matters for which the Community already had competence under the former Arts 100c and 100d of the EC Treaty; the procedure for adopting them is somewhat more flexible.[685] They include:

(i) the list of third countries whose nationals must be in possession of visas when crossing the external borders and those whose nationals are exempt from that requirement;[686]

(ii) the procedures and conditions for issuing visas by Member States;[687]

---

[682] See n. to para. 5–164, *infra*.

[683] For the possibility of introducing temporary border checks, see Groenendijk, "Reinstatement of Controls at the Internal Borders of Europe; Why and Against Whom?" (2004) E.L.J. 150–170.

[684] See previously the Joint Action (96/197/JHA) of March 4, 1996, which the Council had adopted on the basis of the former Art. K.3 of the EU Treaty, on airport transit arrangements, [1996] O.J. L63/8. The Court of Justice dismissed an action brought by the Commission for the annulment of this joint action on the ground that it should have been based on the former Art. 100c of the EC Treaty: ECJ, Case C–170/96 *Commission v Council* [1998] E.C.R. I–2763. The Court held in interpreting the former Art. 100c of the EC Treaty that "crossing the external borders of the Member States" refers to access to the territory of a Member State: *ibid.*, paras 21–26; see the case note by Oliveira (1999) C.M.L.R. 149–155.

[685] EC Treaty, Art. 67 (3) and (4) (see para. 14–069, *infra*).

[686] See, most recently, Council Regulation (EC) No. 539/2001 of March 15, 2001 listing the third countries whose nationals must be in possession of visas when crossing the external borders and those whose nationals are exempt from that requirement, [2001] O.J. L81/1 (this regulation, however, does not apply to Ireland and the UK). See also Hailbronner, "Visa Regulations and Third-Country Nationals in EC Law" (1994) C.M.L.R. 969–995; Peers, "The Visa Regulation: Free Movement Blocked Indefinitely" (1996) E.L.Rev. 150–155.

[687] See Council Regulation (EC) No. 415/2003 of February 27, 2003 on the issue of visas at the border, including the issue of such visas to seamen in transit, [2003] O.J. L64/1 (not binding on Denmark, Ireland and the UK).

(iii) a uniform format for visas;[688] and

(iv) rules on a uniform visa.[689]

The Council is further to adopt measures setting out the conditions under which nationals of third countries are to have the freedom to travel within the territory of the Member States during a period of no more than three months (Article 62(3)).[690] As a result of the integration of the Schengen *acquis*, the criteria agreed for the grant of short-term visas between the Schengen States apply within the Community in this regard. In the sphere of visa applications and border surveillance, the Council granted itself implementing powers in order to amend provisions of the incorporated Schengen *acquis*.[691] The Member States which acceded on May 1, 2004 are to adopt the Schengen *acquis* in two stages, whereby checks on persons at the new internal borders will be abolished only if the Schengen acquis has been sufficiently put into effect in those Member States.[692] Some Member States may qualify for temporary assistance to finance investment for the purposes of carrying out checks at the new external frontiers of the Union.[693]

---

[688] See Council Regulation (EC) No. 1683/95 of May 29, 1995—adopted under the former Art. 100c(1) of the EC Treaty—laying down a uniform format for visas, [1995] O.J. L164/1, as amended, pursuant to Art. 62 of the EC Treaty, by Council Regulation (EC) No. 334/2002 of February 18, 2002 [2002] O.J. L53/7 (not binding on Ireland).

[689] For the specific situation of third-country nationals who have to travel through one or more Member States in order to move between two non-contiguous parts of their countries (as in the case of Russians, who have to travel through Lithuania in order to reach Kaliningrad), see the specific Facilitated Transit Document and the Facilitated Rail Transit Document governed by Council Regulations (EC) Nos 693/2003 and 694/2003 of April 14, 2003, [2003] O.J. L99/8 and 15 (not binding on Denmark, Ireland and the UK.) See Potemkina, "Some Ramifications of Enlargement on the EU-Russia Relations and the Schengen Regime" (2003) E.J.M.L. 229–247.

[690] See the initiative of the Portuguese Republic with a view to adopting the Council Regulation on the period during which third-country nationals exempt from visa requirements are free to travel within the territory of the Member States, [2000] O.J. C146/6.

[691] See Council Regulations (EC) No. 789/2001 of April 24, 2001 reserving to the Council implementing powers with regard to certain detailed provisions and practical procedures for examining visa applications and 790/2001 reserving to the Council implementing powers with regard to certain detailed provisions and practical procedures for carrying out border checks and surveillance ([2001] O.J. L116/2 and 5, respectively), against which the Commission has brought an action for annulment on the ground that the Council had infringed Art. 202 of the EC Treaty and Art. 1 of the Comitology Decision: Case C–257/01, [2001] O.J. C245/15. For those provisions, see Peers, "Key Legislative Developments on Migration in the European Union" (2001) EJ.Migr.L. 231, at 245–248. The detailed rules are set out in the Common Consular Instructions on visas for the diplomatic missions and consular posts ([2003] O.J. C310/1) and in the Common Manual ([2003] O.J. C313/97).

[692] See Art. 3 of the 2003 Act of Accession. See, in particular, Piorko and Sie Dhian Ho, "Integrating Poland in the Area of Freedom, Security and Justice" (2003) E.J.M.L. 175–199.

[693] Art. 35 of the, 2003 Act of Accession (the "Schengen Facility" available to Estonia, Latvia, Lithuania, Hungary, Poland, Slovakia and Slovenia).

(iii) *Measures relating to asylum*

Asylum-seekers and displaced persons. As regards asylum, in the first **5–161** place the Council is to adopt measures containing criteria and mechanisms for determining which Member State is responsible for considering an application for asylum submitted by a national of a third country in one of the Member States (EC Treaty, Art. 63(1)(a)), together with "minimum standards" on the reception of asylum seekers in Member States, on the qualification of nationals of third countries as refugees and on procedures in Member States for granting or withdrawing refugee status (EC Treaty, Art. 63(1)(b) to (d)). The Council is to adopt such measures "in accordance with" the Geneva Convention of July 28, 1951 and the Protocol of January 31, 1967 relating to the status of refugees and other relevant treaties.[694] The right to asylum, together with protection in the event of removal, expulsion or extradition, is enshrined in the Charter of Fundamental Rights of the European Union.[695] In order to determine which State is to be responsible for examining applications for asylum in a given case, the Member States established the Dublin Convention in 1990, which entered into effect in 1997.[696] Pursuant to Art. 63(1)(a), of the EC Treaty, that convention has been replaced since September 1, 2003 by a regulation which determines the Member State responsible for examining an asylum application lodged

---

[694] Geneva Convention relating to the Status of Refugees, signed on July 28, 1951 (*TS* 39 (1954); Cmd. 9171), which has been ratified by all the Member States of the European Union. According to Declaration (No. 17) annexed to the Treaty of Amsterdam on Art. 63 of the Treaty establishing the European Community ([1997] O.J. C340/134), consultations are to be established with the United Nations High Commissioner for Refugees and other relevant international organisations on matters relating to asylum policy. So as to ensure harmonised application of Art. 1 of the Geneva Convention, the Council defined a Joint Position (96/196/JHA) on March 4, 1996 on the definition of the term "refugee", [1996] O.J. L63/2. For an analysis of the substance of policy on asylum, see Guild, "Seeking asylum: storm clouds between international commitments and EU legislative measures" (2004) E.L.Rev. 198–218; Harvey, "The Right to Seek Asylum in the European Union" (2004) E.H.R.L.R. 17–36, and "The European Regulation of Asylum: Constructing a Regional Solidarity?" (1998) E.Pub.L. 561–592.

[695] Art. 18 (referring to the Geneva Convention and the Protocol) and Art. 19 of the Charter of Fundamental Rights of the European Union. See Peers, "Immigration, Asylum and the European Union Charter of Fundamental Rights" (2001) E.J.M.L. 141–169.

[696] Convention determining the State responsible for examining applications for asylum lodged in one of the Member States of the European Communities; for the text see (1990) 6 EC Bull. point 2.2.2 or [1997] O.J. C254/1 (for its entry into effect on September 1, 1997, see the notice in [1997] O.J. L242/63; for recent Member States to accede, see the notice in [1998] O.J. L176/39). Implementing provisions were adopted by the Committee set up by Art. 18 of the Convention, *e.g.* Decision No. 1/97 of September 9, 1997 concerning provisions for the implementation of the Convention and Decision No. 2/97 of the same date establishing the Committee's Rules of Procedure ([1997] O.J. C281/1 and 26, respectively). See Hailbronner and Thiery, "Schengen II and Dublin: Responsibility for Asylum Applications in Europe" (1997) C.M.L.R. 957–989; Marx, "Adjusting the Dublin Convention: New Approaches to Member State Responsibility for Asylum Applications" (2001) E.J.Migr.L. 7–22. From April 1, 2001, Iceland and Norway had acceded to the system set out in the Dublin Convention by means of an agreement concluded with the Community, approved by Council Decision of March 15, 2001, [2001] O.J. L93/38.

in one of the Member States by a third-country national.[697] Acting under the same legal basis, the Council has adopted a system for the identification of asylum seekers.[698] The minimum standards for the reception of asylum seekers laid down under Art. 63(1)(b) are designed to ensure them a dignified standard of living and comparable living conditions in all Member States.[699] For all legal and practical purposes in relation to asylum matters, Member States are to be regarded as constituting safe countries of origin; according to a protocol annexed to the EC Treaty, in principle applications for asylum made by a national of a Member State will be regarded as inadmissible for processing by another Member State or admitted only in expressly stated cases.[700]

As far as refugees and displaced persons are concerned, the Council is to adopt "minimum standards" for giving temporary protection to displaced persons from third countries who cannot return to their country of origin and persons who otherwise need international protection (EC Treaty, Art. 63(2)(a)) and take measures promoting a balance of effort between

---

[697] Council Regulation (EC) No. 343/2003 of February 18, 2003 establishing the criteria and mechanisms for determining the Member State responsible for examining an asylum application lodged in one of the Member States by a third-country national, [2003] O.J. L50/1 (not binding on Denmark—the Dublin Convention remains in force between Denmark and the other Member States).

[698] Council Regulation (EC) No. 2725/2000 of December 11, 2000 concerning the establishment of 'Eurodac' for the comparison of fingerprints for the effective application of the Dublin Convention, [2000] O.J. L316/1 (not applicable in Denmark). See Bell, "Mainstreaming Equality Norms into European Union Asylum law" (2001) E.L.Rev. 20, at 26–28; Peers, "Key Legislative Developments on Migration in the European Union" (2001) EJ.Migr.L. 231, at 235–236.

[699] Council Directive 2003/9/EC of January 27, 2003 laying down minimum standards for the reception of asylum seekers ([2003] O.J. L31/18—not binding on Denmark and Ireland).

[700] Sole Article of Protocol (No. 29) to the EC Treaty on asylum for nationals of Member States of the European Union, annexed by the Treaty of Amsterdam to the EC Treaty ([1997] O.J. C340/103), which mentions, alongside cases where the Member State avails itself of Art. 15 of the ECHR (derogation in the event of war or other public emergency) and the procedure referred to in Art. 7 of the EU Treaty (see para. 9–012, *infra*), the case in which a Member State so decides "unilaterally in respect of the application of a national of another Member State", in which event the Council is to be informed and the application "shall be dealt with on the basis of the presumption that it is manifestly unfounded without affecting in any way, whatever the cases may be, the decision-making power of the Member State". What prompted this protocol was Spain's unhappiness with Belgium's refusal to surrender suspected Basque terrorists who had asked to be recognised as refugees. According to a Declaration (No. 48) annexed to the Treaty of Amsterdam on Protocol (No. 29), the Protocol does not prejudice the right of each Member State to take the organisational measures it deems necessary to fulfil its obligations under the Geneva Convention of July 28, 1951 relating to the status of refugees ([1997] O.J. C340/141). For the tense relationship between the Protocol and the Geneva Convention, see the Commission's answer of December 8, 1997 to question No. E–3441/97 (Van Dijk), [1998] O.J. C174/58 (the Commission considered it "unfortunate" that the Protocol was included in the Amsterdam Treaty, but was pleased to note that the Protocol nevertheless sought to respect the objectives of the Geneva Convention) and Bribosia and Weyembergh, "Le citoyen européen privé du droit d'asile?" (1997) J.T.D.E. 204–206. Belgium made a unilateral declaration on the Protocol in which it stated that it would carry out an "individual examination" of any asylum request made by a national of another Member State ([1997] O.J. C340/144).

Member States in receiving and bearing the consequences of receiving refugees and displaced persons (Art. 63(2)(b)).[701]

(iv) *Measures relating to immigration policy*

Immigration. As far as immigration policy is concerned, the Council is to **5–162** adopt measures on entry and residence and standards on procedures for the issue by Member States of long-term visas and residence permits, including those for the purpose of family reunion (EC Treaty, Art. 63(3)(a)),[702] and on illegal immigration and residence, including repatriation of illegal residents (EC Treaty, Art. 63(3)(b)).[703] The Council is further to adopt measures defining the rights and conditions under which nationals of third countries who are legally resident in a Member State may reside in other Member States (EC Treaty, Art. 63(4)).[704]

Following expiry of the period prescribed for implementing the relevant directives, a Member State is to grant long-term resident status to third-country nationals who have resided legally and continuously within its territory during the previous five years and have sufficient resources and

---

[701] Council Directive 2001/55/EC of July 20, 2001 on minimum standards for giving temporary protection in the event of a mass influx of displaced persons and on measures promoting a balance of efforts between Member States in receiving such persons and bearing the consequences thereof, [2001] O.J. L212/12 (this directive does not apply to Denmark or Ireland); Van Selm, "Temporarily Protecting Displaced Persons or Offering the Possibility to Start a New Life in the European Union" (2001) E.J.Migr.L 23–35. See also Council Decision 2000/596/EC of September 28, 2000 establishing a European Refugee Fund, [2000] O.J. L252/12 (Denmark alone did not participate in the Fund); see Peers, "Key Legislative Developments on Migration in the European Union" (2001) EJ.Migr.L. 231, at 233–235.

[702] See Council Regulation (EC) No. 1091/2001 of May 28, 2001 on freedom of movement with a long-stay visa, [2001] O.J. L150/4 (this regulation is not binding on Denmark, Ireland or the UK), Council Regulation (EC) No. 1030/2002 of June 13, 2002 laying down a uniform format for residence permits for third-country nationals, [2002] O.J. L157/1 (this regulation is not binding on Ireland or Denmark), Council Directive (EC) No. 2003/86 of September 22, 2003 on the right to family reunification, [2003] O.J. L251/12 (this directive is not binding on Denmark, Ireland or the UK) and Council Directive 2003/109/EC of November 25, 2003 concerning the status of third-country nationals who are long-term residents, [2004] O.J. L16/44 (this directive is not binding on Denmark, Ireland or the UK). See further Groenendijk and Guild, "Converging Criteria: Creating an Area of Security of Residence for Europe's Third Country Nationals" (2001) E.J.Migr.L. 37–59.

[703] See Council Directive 2001/40/EC of May 28, 2001 on the mutual recognition of decisions on the expulsion of third country nationals, [2001] O.J. L149/34, and, by way of compensation for the financial imbalances resulting from the application of this directive, Council Decision 2004/19/EC of February 23, 2004, [2004] O.J. L60/55 (neither the directive nor the decision applies to Ireland and Denmark); see also Council Directive 2002/90/EC of November 28, 2002 defining the facilitation of unauthorised entry, transit and residence, [2002] O.J. L328/17 (this directive does not apply to Denmark) and Council Regulation (EC) No. 377/2004 of February 19, 2004 on the creation of an immigration liaison officers' network, [2004] O.J. L64/1 (this regulation does not apply to Denmark).

[704] On this basis, the application of Council Regulations Nos 1408/71 and 574/72 on the co-ordination of social security systems has been extended to third-country nationals legally residing in the territory of the Member States. This remains true after the replacement of Regulation 1408/71 by Regulation No. 883/2004 (see para. 5–148), see Art. 90(1)(a) of the latter regulation.

sickness insurance cover for themselves and their dependants.[705] The status may be refused on grounds of public policy or public security.[706] Subject to certain conditions, long-term residents are to enjoy equal treatment with nationals of the host State as regards access to employment and self-employed activities, conditions of employment and working conditions, education and vocational training, recognition of professional diplomas, certificates and other qualifications, social security, tax benefits, access to goods and services and the supply of goods and services made available to the public and freedom of association.[707]

(v) *Particular rules relating to Community policy pursuant to Title IV of the EC Treaty*

5–163 **Member States' discretion.** Measures adopted by the Council pursuant to Art. 63(3) and (4) of the EC Treaty do not prevent any Member State from maintaining or introducing in the areas concerned national provisions which are compatible with that Treaty and with international agreements (EC Treaty, Art. 63, second para.). At first sight, this would appear to authorise Member States to retain or adopt provisions potentially deviating from measures adopted by the Council in the same field, provided that they respect "this Treaty" and "international agreements". However, that interpretation is hard to square with the precedence which Council measures ought to enjoy as Community law. This problem is avoided as far as Art. 62(2)(a) (checks on persons at external borders) is concerned, since a protocol confirms the Member States' power to conclude agreements with third countries "as long as they respect Community law and other relevant international agreements".[708] The reference to Community law covers all measures adopted by the Council in the field. These Treaty provisions may perhaps be coherently construed as not precluding all powers of the Member States in the areas covered by Title IV of the EC Treaty and as therefore conferring non-exclusive powers on the Community (see para. 5–023).

---

[705] Council Directive 2003/109/EC of November 25, 2003 concerning the status of third-country nationals who are along-term residents (n.702, *supra*), Arts 4 and 5. Stricter conditions apply with respect to the right of a long-term resident to reside in the territory of Member States other than the one which granted him or her the long-term resident status, for a period exceeding three months: *ibid.*, Arts 14–23. This Directive is to be implemented by January 23, 2006 at the latest.

[706] *ibid.*, Art. 6(1).

[707] *ibid.*, Art. 11(1). According to Art. 11(3), Member States may retain restrictions to access to employment or self-employed activities where these activities are reserved to nationals, EU or EEA citizens. Whereas Art. 11(1) also mentions social assistance and social protection, Art. 11(4) allows member States to limit equal treatment in these fields to core benefits.

[708] Protocol (No. 31) to the EC Treaty on external relations of the Member States with regard to the crossing of external borders, annexed by the Treaty of Amsterdam to the EC Treaty ([1997] O.J. C340/108). This is confirmed as regards Art. 63(3)(a) of the EC Treaty by Declaration (No. 18) annexed to the Treaty of Amsterdam ([1997] O.J. C340/134).

The EC Treaty further declares that Title IV does not affect the exercise of the responsibilities incumbent upon Member States with regard to the maintenance of law and order and the safeguarding of internal security (EC Treaty, Art. 64(1)).[709] These policy aspects are also excluded from the jurisdiction of the Court of Justice with regard to measures or decisions taken pursuant to Art. 62(1) (EC Treaty, Art. 68(2)).[710] Moreover, the Court's jurisdiction to give preliminary rulings is subject to the limitation laid down in Art. 68 of the EC Treaty, as in the case of the other provisions of Title IV (see para. 10–075).

In the event of one or more Member States being confronted with an emergency situation characterised by a sudden inflow of nationals of third countries, the Council may, acting by a qualified majority on a proposal from the Commission, adopt provisional measures of a duration not exceeding six months for the benefit of the Member States concerned (EC Treaty, Art. 64(2)).

(vi) *Incorporation of the Schengen acquis*

Schengen *acquis.* The provisions of Title IV of the EC Treaty provide the **5–164** Community with a legal basis for transposing the Schengen obligations into Community law. A protocol to the EU Treaty and the EC Treaty empowers the Member States involved in the Schengen co-operation (the United Kingdom and Ireland are not participating; see para. 2–017) to integrate the whole of that co-operation within the framework of the European Union[711]: existing provisions or decisions may be converted and developed as Community law under Title IV of the EC Treaty or as "Union law" under Title VI of the EU Treaty. The Schengen Protocol declares the Schengen *acquis* (including decisions of the Executive Committee) applicable from the date of entry into force of the Treaty of Amsterdam (Schengen Protocol, Art. 2(1), first subpara.). Pursuant to the Schengen Protocol, the Council has determined for each provisions or decision of the

---

[709] There is an identical provision in Art. 33 of the EU Treaty. *cf.* the provisions on free movement of workers and the right of establishment, paras 5–139—5–140, *supra*, and freedom to provide services, para. 5–175, *supra*. See Peers, "National Security and European Law" (1996) Y.E.L. 363, at 365–371 (free movement) and paras 10–055—10–060 (measures relating to justice and home affairs).

[710] *i.e.* measures relating to the elimination of controls on persons at internal borders. The Court's jurisdiction is similarly excluded by Art. 2(1), third subpara. , of Protocol (No. 2) to the EU Treaty and the EC Treaty integrating the Schengen *acquis* into the framework of the European Union ([1997] O.J. C340/93) and by Art. 35(5) of the EU Treaty. As to whether such measures are justiciable, see Peers, "National Security and European Law" (1996) Y.E.L. 363, at 398–403.

[711] Protocol (No. 2) to the EU Treaty and the EC Treaty integrating the Schengen *acquis* into the framework of the European Union, [1997] O.J. C340/93.

Schengen *acquis* the (Community or non-Community) legal basis.[712] Depending upon the choice of legal basis, the Court of Justice has the jurisdiction conferred upon it by either the EC Treaty or the EU Treaty (Schengen Protocol, Art. 2(1), second and third subparas).[713] It is the intention that measures to be adopted by the Council with regard to the abolition of checks at common borders should provide "at least the same level of protection and security" as the Schengen provisions.[714]

Schengen co-operation continues on the basis of the provisions of Title IV of the EC Treaty and Title VI of the EU Treaty (PJCC), as appropriate.[715] The Schengen countries can consult personal data relating to nationals of other States through the central Schengen Information System, of which a newer version (SIS II) was developed in 2001.[716] The Council takes the place of the Executive Committee (Schengen Protocol, Art. 5(1), first subpara.). Denmark, in common with the United Kingdom and Ireland, is in a special position (see below). In a sense, the participating Member States engage in a form of "enhanced co-operation" as provided for in Art. 11 of the EC Treaty and Art. 40 of the EU Treaty, respectively.

---

[712] Council Decision 1999/436/EC of May 20, 1999 determining, in conformity with the relevant provisions of the Treaty establishing the European Community and the Treaty on European Union, the legal basis for each of the provisions or decisions which constitute the Schengen *acquis*, [1999] O.J. L176/17. To this end, the Council had to list the provisions which form part of the Schengen *acquis*, see Council Decision 1999/435/EC of May 20, 1999 concerning the definition of the Schengen acquis for the purpose of determining, in conformity with the relevant provisions of the Treaty establishing the European Community and the Treaty on European Union, the legal basis for each of the provisions or decisions which constitute the *acquis*, [1999] O.J. L176/1 (it names those provisions for which it is unnecessary or inappropriate to determine a legal basis) and the publication of those provisions in [2000] O.J. L239 (corrigendum in Council Decision 2000/645/EC of October 17, 2000, [2000] O.J. L272/24). For the extension of PJCC provisions to Iceland and Norway, see, for example, n.717, *infra*. See, in this regard, Kuijper, "Some Legal Problems Associated with the Communitarisation of Policy on Visas, Asylum and Immigration Under the Amsterdam Treaty and Incorporation of the Schengen Acquis" (2000) C.M.L.R. 345, at 346–350; Den Boer, "Not Merely a Matter of Moving House: Police Co-operation from Schengen to the TEU" (2000) M.J.E.C.L. 336–357.

[713] So long as the Council had not taken such measures, the Schengen provisions and decisions were to be regarded as acts based on Title VI of the EU Treaty (Schengen Protocol, Art. 2(1), fourth subpara.).

[714] See Declaration (No. 15) annexed to the Amsterdam Treaty on the preservation of the level of protection and security provided by the Schengen *acquis* ([1997] O.J. C340/134).

[715] As a result the Council, acting under Art. 63 of the EC Treaty, amended Art. 1of the 8, 1990 Schengen Convention by Regulation (EC) No. 1091/2001 of May 28, 2001 (n.702 to para. 5–162, *supra*) and supplemented Art. 26 of that Convention (relating to carriers' obligation to return third-country nationals) by means of Directive 2001/51/EC of June 28, 2001 ([2001] O.J. L187/45). Further, acting under Arts 32 and 34 of the EU Treaty, the Council amended Art. 40(1) and (7) of the Schengen Convention by Decision 2003/725/JHA (so as to extend cross-border surveillance), [2003] O.J. L260/37.

[716] This second-generation Schengen Information System is based on the dual EU/EC legal basis of Council Decision 2001/886/JHA of December 6, 2001 and Council Regulation (EC) No. 2424/2001 of December 6, 2001 ([2001] O.J. L328/1 and 4, respectively. This also applies to the related system for the exchange of information between the national "Sirene offices" in accordance with the "Sirene Manual"; see the procedures for amending the Sirene Manual laid down in Council Regulation (EC) No. 378/2004 of February 19, 2004 and Decision 2004/201/JHA ([2004] O.J. L64/5 and 45, respectively).

Iceland and Norway, which were associated with Schengen co-operation, continue to be associated with the implementation of the Schengen *acquis* and its further development in accordance with procedures agreed by those States and the Council on May 18, 1999.[717] New Member States have to accept the Schengen *acquis* in full in any event as part of the *acquis communautaire* (Schengen Protocol, Art. 8). As a result, the provisions of the Schengen *acquis* are binding on all the Member States which acceded on May 1, 2004. Since accession the bulk of the existing rules (in particular on visa and asylum policy) has been in force; the remainder of the *acquis* (including the elimination of checks on persons at the internal borders) will become applicable when the Council has verified that the Member States concerned meet the necessary conditions.[718]

(vii) *Exceptional status of Denmark, Ireland and the United Kingdom*

Denmark. Denmark is bound by the Schengen *acquis* and so has agreed to **5–165** the elimination of checks on persons at the internal borders and to the arrangements regarding checks at the external borders and entry for a short stay. However, as far as Denmark is concerned, the integration of the Schengen *acquis* does not give the decisions and provisions concerned the force of Community law: those parts of the *acquis* that are determined to have their legal basis in Title IV of the EC Treaty do not create any new rights or obligations for that country *vis-à-vis* the other States (Schengen Protocol, Art. 3; see para. 18–005). Under a separate protocol to the EU Treaty and the EC Treaty, in principle Denmark will not take part in the further adoption by the Council of measures pursuant to Title IV of the EC Treaty, will not be bound by such measures (or by decisions of the Court of Justice interpreting them), and is not to bear the financial consequences

---

[717] Agreement with the Republic of Iceland and the Kingdom of Norway concerning the latters' association with the implementation, application and development of the Schengen *acquis*, [1999] O.J. L176/35 (corrigendum for certain language versions in [2000] O.J. L58/31). For provisions implementing that agreement, see Council Decision 1999/437/EC of May 17, 1999, [1999] O.J. L176/31. The Council concluded a further agreement with Iceland and Norway on June 30, 1999 on the establishment of rights and obligations between Ireland and the United Kingdom of Great Britain and Northern Ireland, on the one hand, and the Republic of Iceland and the Kingdom of Norway, on the other, in areas of the Schengen *acquis* which apply to these States, [2000] O.J. L15/2. See Kuijper, "Some Legal Problems Associated with the Communitarisation of Policy on Visas, Asylum and Immigration Under the Amsterdam Treaty and Incorporation of the Schengen *acquis*" (2000) C.M.L.R. 345, at 350–354; Den Boer, "Not Merely a Matter of Moving House: Police Co-operation from Schengen to the TEU" (2000) M.J.E.C.L. 336, at 350–351. The Schengen *acquis* entered into effect for the Nordic countries on March 25, 2001: Council Decision 2000/777/EC of December 1, 2000 on the application of the Schengen *acquis* in Denmark, Finland and Sweden, and in Iceland and Norway, [2000] O.J. L309/24.

[718] Accordingly, Art. 3 of the 2003 Act of Accession refers to the acts listed in Annex I to the Act; Art. 3(2) of the Act provides that the provisions not so listed, while binding on the new Member States, shall only apply in a new Member State pursuant to a Council decision to that effect after verification in accordance with the applicable Schengen evaluation procedures that the necessary conditions have been met.

ensuing therefrom.[719] It is so to participate when the Council takes measures establishing the list of third countries whose nationals must be in possession of visas when crossing the external borders and the uniform format for visas.[720] Denmark may nevertheless decide to implement in national law a Council decision to build upon the Schengen *acquis*. If it decides to do so, its decision will create "an obligation under international law" between Denmark and the other participating Member States.[721] Denmark will maintain its specific position when the EU Constitution enters into force.[722]

5–166 Ireland and United Kingdom. Unlike Denmark, Ireland and the United Kingdom are not Schengen States and are not bound by the Schengen *acquis* following its integration into the framework of the European Union. The United Kingdom retains the right to conduct controls on persons at its frontiers in order to verify that persons purportedly having the right to enter the United Kingdom do in fact have such a right and to determine whether or not to grant other persons permission to enter the country.[723] Since the United Kingdom and Ireland have arrangements between themselves relating to the movement of persons between their territories ("the Common Travel Area"), Ireland also has the right to carry out such controls as long as the arrangements are maintained.[724] The other Member States are entitled to exercise controls on persons seeking to enter their territories from the United Kingdom or Ireland.[725] Pursuant to the Schengen Protocol, both the United Kingdom and Ireland have made

---

[719] Arts 1–3 of Protocol (No. 20) to the EU Treaty and the EC Treaty on the position of Denmark ([1997] O.J. C340/101). For the special decision-making procedure, see para. 14–070, *supra*. Denmark may relinquish its separate status by informing the other Member States: *ibid.*, Art. 7. Denmark does not have separate status with regard to measures adopted by the Council pursuant to Title VI of the EU Treaty. The second para. of Art. 3 of the Schengen Protocol provides that Denmark continues to have the "same rights and obligations" as the other signatories with regard to those parts of the Schengen *acquis* that are determined to have their legal basis in Title VI of the EU Treaty. This covers, among other things, the judicial review provided for by Art. 35 of the EU Treaty (para. 10–077, *infra*).

[720] *ibid.*, Art. 4. See, *e.g.* the participation of Denmark in the adoption of Regulation 539/2001 (n.686, *supra*).

[721] *ibid.*, Art. 5 (see para. 18–005, *infra*).

[722] See the adjusted Protocol on the position of Denmark, annexed to the EU Constitution.

[723] Art. 1 of Protocol (No. 3) to the EU Treaty and the EC Treaty on the application of certain aspects of Art. 7a [now Art. 14] of the Treaty establishing the European Community to the UK and to Ireland ([1997] O.J. C340/97), which states that nothing in Art. 14 of the EC Treaty or in any other Treaty provisions shall prejudice the right of the UK to adopt or exercise such controls.

[724] *ibid.*, Art. 2. See Ryan, "The Common Travel Area between Britain and Ireland" (2001) Mod.L.Rev. 855–874.

[725] *ibid.*, Art. 3.

requests to take part in specific provisions of the Schengen *acquis*.[726] In principle, however, they do not take part in the adoption by the Council of measures based on Title IV of the EC Treaty which do not build on those provisions, they are not bound by such measures (or by decisions of the Court of Justice relating thereto) and they do not to bear the financial consequences of such measures.[727] If the United Kingdom or Ireland so wishes, it may notify the Council of its intention to take part in the adoption and application of a proposed measure.[728] Under the EU Constitution, Ireland and the United Kingdom will preserve their specific position with respect to judicial co-operation in civil matters and policy-making on border controls, asylum and immigration.[729]

(3) *The area of freedom, security and justice in the EU Constitution*

Change in structure. Under the title "the area of freedom, security and **5–167** justice", the EU Constitution brings together all competences of the Union with regard to border checks, asylum, immigration, judicial co-operation in civil and criminal matters and police co-operation. In all those areas, legislation will be enacted, in principle, under the ordinary legislative procedure (co-decision), whereas action by the Union and the Member States will be fully subject to judicial review by the Court of Justice. For the competences based at present on Title IV of the EC Treaty, this means that the "specific rules" discussed in para. 5–163 will disappear, except for the reservation on the exercise of the responsibilities incumbent upon Member States with regard to maintaining law and order and safeguarding internal

---

[726] Schengen Protocol (para. 5–164, *supra*), Art. 4. For the participation of the UK, see Council Decision 2000/365/EC of May 29, 2000 ([2000] O.J. L131/43); for the participation of Ireland, see Council Decision 2002/192/EC of February 28, 2002 ([2002] O.J. L64/20—which includes a virtually identical list of Schengen measures). As a result of that decision, a number of decisions are also binding on Ireland, even though that State, unlike the UK, did not take part in their adoption, *e.g.* Directive 2001/51/EC (n.715, *supra*) and Council Regulation (EC) No. 2424/2001 of December 6, 2001 on the Schengen Information System (n.716, *supra*). Neither the UK nor Ireland adopted, for instance, Regulation 539/2001 listing the third countries whose nationals must be in possession of visas when crossing the external borders and those whose nationals are exempt from that requirement (n.686, *supra*), with the result that they are free to draw up their own lists.

[727] Arts 1, 2 and 5 of Protocol (No. 4), annexed to the EU Treaty and the EC Treaty by the Amsterdam Treaty, on the position of the UK and Ireland, [1997] O.J. C340/99. Ireland may notify the Council that it no longer wishes to be covered by this Protocol: *ibid.*, Art. 8.

[728] *ibid.*, Art. 3. *e.g.* the notification given by the UK (and not Ireland) that it would participate in Regulation No. 1030/2002 (n.702, *supra;* see recital 14 in the preamble thereto) and the notification given by Ireland and the UK that they would participate in Regulation No. 343/2003 (n.697, *supra;* see recital 17 in the preamble thereto). For the decision-making procedure and for the possibility of accepting a measure, even after it has been adopted, under the "enhanced co-operation" procedure, see para. 14–070, *infra*. A similar procedure governs the potential participation of the UK and Ireland in the adoption of measures by the Council under Title VI of the EU Treaty; see para. 15–014, *infra*.

[729] See the Protocol on the position of the UK and Ireland on policies in respect of border controls, asylum and immigration, judicial co-operation in civil matters and on police co-operation, and the Protocol on the Schengen *acquis* integrated into the framework of the European Union, both annexed to the EU Constitution.

security (EU Constitution, Art. III–262). For the competences based at present on Title VI of the EU Treaty, the institutional changes involved are even more radical (see para. 6–014).

5–168 Substantive changes. On the substantive level, existing competences will not only be brought together in a specific title, there will also be specific extensions of the Union's field of action.

As regards border checks, the Union will be given the competence gradually to establish an integrated management system for external borders (EU Constitution, Art. III–265(2)(d)).[730]

As far as asylum is concerned, the EU Constitution will modify the existing Community competence to establish "minimum standards" with respect to the categorisation of refugees or persons otherwise entitled to international protection, the reception of such persons and the granting or withdrawal of refugee status. Under the EU Constitution, the Union will have the competence to set up a common European asylum system involving a uniform status of asylum or a uniform status of subsidiary protection for nationals of third countries who, without obtaining European asylum, are in need of international protection, as well as common procedures for the granting or withdrawal of such status and common standards concerning the conditions for the reception of applicants for asylum or subsidiary protection (EU Constitution, Art. III–266).

With respect to immigration, the existing competences will be embedded in a "common immigration policy" aimed at ensuring the efficient management of migration flows, fair treatment of third-country nationals residing legally in the Member States, and enhanced measures to combat illegal immigration and trafficking in human beings (EU Constitution, Art. III–267(1)). In addition, the Union may establish measures to provide incentives and support for the action of Member States with a view to promoting the integration of third-country nationals residing legally in their territories, but without carrying out any harmonisation of the laws and regulations of Member States (Art. III–267(4)). It will be up to the Member States to determine the number of third-country nationals who may be admitted to their territory in order to seek work (Art. III–267(5)).

The aforementioned policies of the Union are to be governed by the principles of solidarity and fair sharing of responsibility (which includes the financial implications) between the Member States (EU Constitution, Art. III–268). Furthermore, the Union may co-operate with third countries for the purpose of managing inflows of applicants for asylum or subsidiary or temporary protection and for the readmission to their countries of origin or provenance of third-country nationals who do not or who no longer fulfil the conditions for entry, presence or residence in the territory of one of the Member States (EU Constitution, Arts III–266(2)(g) and III–267(3)).

---

[730] Moreover, one of the objectives set for the policy of the Union will be "carrying out checks on persons and efficient monitoring of the crossing of external borders" (EU Constitution, Art. III–265(1)(b)).

3. Freedom to provide of services

Treaty rules. Under Art. 49 of the EC Treaty, restrictions on freedom to **5–169** provide services within the Community are prohibited within the framework of the provisions set out thereafter.[731] Article 55 states that Arts 45–48 are to apply to services. Consequently, free movement of services is subject to the same exceptions as the provisions on free movement of persons with regard to the exercise of public authority (EC Treaty, Art. 45; see para. 5–142) and public policy, public security and public health (EC Treaty, Art. 46; see para. 5–139), and is to be facilitated by the mutual recognition of diplomas, certificates and other evidence of formal qualifications and by further co-ordinating directives (EC Treaty, Art. 47; see paras 5–145–5–147). Just as in the case of the provisions on free movement of persons, the provisions on the free movement of services not only apply to the action of public authorities but extend also to associations or organisations not governed by public law where they lay down collective rules in the exercise of their legal autonomy.[732] The case law interprets the provisions on free movement of services and free movement of goods in a parallel manner, in particular where services are provided across border without the provider or the recipient moving.

a. Definition and beneficiaries

Services. The first paragraph of Art. 50 of the EC Treaty regards as **5–170** "services" those which are "normally provided for remuneration, in so far as they are not governed by the provisions relating to freedom of movement for goods, capital and persons". What is therefore covered is activities, for instance of an industrial or commercial character, of craftsmen or of the professions (see EC Treaty, Art. 50, second para.), which "normally" yield an economic consideration or "remuneration".[733] Consequently, services which are normally remunerated, but sporadically provided free of charge, are not excluded. Services do not necessarily have to be paid for by the person for whom they are performed,[734] although they do have to be paid for primarily with private money. Accordingly, tuition provided in an educational institution which is principally funded by the State does not constitute a service within the meaning of the Treaty.[735]

---

[731] Before the simplification carried out by the Amsterdam Treaty, the EC Treaty debarred Member States from introducing any new restrictions (EC Treaty, former Art. 62) and existing restrictions had to be gradually abolished over a transitional period (EC Treaty, former Art. 59, first para.). Just as in the case of freedom of establishment, the provision of services was to be liberalised on the basis of a general programme and implementing directives (EC Treaty, former Art. 63, first para.).

[732] ECJ, Joined Cases C–51/96 and C–191/97 *Deliège* [2000] E.C.R. I–2549, para. 47 (referring to the judgments in *Walrave* and *Bosman*, see para. 5–115).

[733] ECJ, Joined Cases C–51/96 and C–191/97 *Deliège* [2000] E.C.R. I–2549, paras 49–59 (public and private sponsoring as remuneration for sporting activities).

[734] ECJ, Case 352/85 *Bond van Adverteerders* [1988] E.C.R. 2085, para. 16.

[735] ECJ, Case C–109/92 *Wirth* [1993] E.C.R. I–6447, paras 15–19.

Medical treatment in or outside a hospital which is paid directly by a sickness insurance fund on a flat-rate basis does constitute a service.[736] An activity will be regarded as a service, even if it is strictly regulated or even forbidden in some Member States. Accordingly, medical termination of pregnancy which in one Member State is prohibited constitutes a service when lawfully carried out in another Member State.[737] National legislation requiring profits from such an activity (*e.g.* a lottery) to be paid to the State or used for specific ends, does not cause that activity to lose its economic character.[738]

Article 50 regards as "services" only activities not falling under the other freedoms. Thus, the transmission of television signals is a service, but the material, sound recordings, films, apparatus and other products used for the diffusion of television signals are subject to the rules relating to freedom of movement for goods.[739]

5–171 Service providers and recipients. According to Art. 49 of the EC Treaty, the beneficiaries of free movement of services are "nationals of Member States who are established in a State of the Community other than that of the person for whom the services are intended". The provider of the service (not the recipient) must be a national of a Member State (or a company or firm formed in accordance with the law of a Member State; see Art. 48 in conjunction with Art. 55 of the EC Treaty) and established in a Member State. Freedom to provide services may be relied upon not only by the provider and recipient of services, but also in certain circumstances by the employees of the service provider.[740]

---

[736] ECJ, Case C–157/99 *Smits and Peerbooms* [2001] E.C.R. I–5473, paras 56–59 and the case-law cited in n.649 to para. 5–149, *supra*.

[737] ECJ, Case C–159/90 *Society for the Protection of Unborn Children Ireland* [1991] E.C.R. I–4685, paras 18–21 (also known as the *Grogan* case). Art. 40.3.3. of the Irish Constitution prohibits abortion. In order to safeguard that prohibition, a Protocol (No. 7) was appended to the EU Treaty and the Community Treaties, declaring that nothing in the Treaties shall affect the application in Ireland of that provision of its Constitution ([1992] O.J. C224/130). Following the turmoil caused by the application of this prohibition in February 1992, the Irish Government secured the adoption by the Contracting Parties as an annex to the EU Treaty of a Declaration, made in Guimarâes on May 1, 1992, in which they give the following "legal interpretation" of Protocol No. 7: "[I]t was and is their intention that the Protocol shall not limit freedom to travel between Member States or, in accordance with conditions which may be laid down, in conformity with Community law, by Irish legislation, to obtain or make available in Ireland information relating to services lawfully available in Member States". As a result of a referendum held on November 25, 1992, Art. 40.3.3 of the Constitution was amended by the addition of particulars recognising the freedom to travel to another Member State and to obtain and disseminate information regarding lawful abortion elsewhere. See Curtin, note to the *Grogan* judgment of the Court of Justice (1992) C.M.L.R. 583–603; Murphy, "Maastricht: Implementation in Ireland" (1994) E.L.Rev. 94–104. Since then, Protocol No. 7 on abortion in Malta, annexed to the 2003 Act of Accession, specifies that nothing in the Treaties shall affect the application in the territory of Malta of national legislation relating to abortion ([2003] O.J. L236/947).

[738] ECJ, Case C–275/92 *Schindler* [1994] E.C.R. I–1039, paras 31–35.

[739] ECJ, Case 155/73 *Sacchi* [1974] E.C.R. 409, paras 6–7.

[740] ECJ (judgment of October 21, 2003), Joined Cases C–371/01 and C–369/01 *Abatay* not yet reported, para. 106.

The transfrontier element mentioned in the article is that the provider and recipient of the service must be established in different Member States. Nevertheless, in practice the transfrontier element also assumes other forms. The Treaty refers only to the situation in which a provider of services "temporarily pursue[s] his activity in the State where the service is provided" (EC Treaty, Art. 50, third para.). However, the Court of Justice has regarded "the freedom, for the recipients of services to go to another Member State in order to receive a service there" as a natural corollary of the provision of services "which fulfils the objective of liberalising all gainful activity not covered by the free movement of goods, persons and capital".[741] Consequently, tourists, persons receiving medical treatment and persons travelling for the purpose of education or business may invoke freedom to provide services.[742] In this connection, the provider and the recipient of the service do not necessarily have to be established in different Member States. Where a travel agent takes tourists from its own country to another Member State and makes use of a guide who may be established in another Member State or in its own country, the rules on freedom to provide services are applicable in either case, since services are being provided in a Member State other than the one in which the provider of the services is established.[743]This is because both the provider and the recipient of the service move from their Member State to another. In the case of maritime transport between Member States, the service is provided on behalf of persons who may or may not be established in another Member State, but the service is offered in either case—at least in part on the territory of another Member State.[744] This is a sufficient transfrontier element in itself.

In addition, the rules on free movement of services apply where the provider of the service and the recipient remain in the countries where they are established and only the service crosses the border. Thus, the transmission of television signals across a frontier falls under the free movement of services both as regards the service provided by cable network operators relaying television programmes sent out by broadcasters in other Member States and as regards the service provided by the broadcasters transmitting advertisements to the public in another Member State on

---

[741] ECJ, Joined Cases 286/82 and 26/83 *Luisi and Carbone* [1984] E.C.R. 377, paras 10 and 16.
[742] *ibid.*, para. 16. As regards tourists, see, ECJ, Case 186/87 *Cowan* [1989] E.C.R. 195, paras 15–17; ECJ, Case C–45/93 *Commission v Spain* [1994] E.C.R. I–911, paras 5–10; Van der Woude and Mead, "Free Movement of the Tourist in Community Law" (1988) C.M.L.R. 117; Tichadou, "Der Schutz des Touristen in der Rechtsprechung des Europäischen Gerichtshofs" (2002) Z.Eu.S. 299–319. As regards medical activities, see ECJ, Case C–159/90 *Society for the Protection of Unborn Children Ireland* [1991] E.C.R. I–4685, para. 18.
[743] ECJ, Case C–154/89 *Commission v France* [1991] E.C.R. I–659, para. 11; Case C–180/89 *Commission v Italy* [1991] E.C.R. I–709, para. 10; Case C–198/89 *Commission v Greece* [1991] E.C.R. I–727, para. 11.
[744] ECJ, Case C–381/93 *Commission v France* [1994] E.C.R. I–5145, paras 14–15.

behalf of advertisers established in that State.[745] Another case to which those rules apply is that of a service offered by a service provider over the telephone or the Internet to potential recipients in another Member State without the provider leaving the Member State where he or she is established.[746]

However, the Treaty provisions on freedom to provide services cannot be applied to activities which are confined in all respects within a single Member State.[747] Freedom to provide services may be relied upon by an undertaking as against the Member State in which it is established if the services are provided for persons established in another Member State.[748] The same applies to intermediaries established in the Member State of the potential recipients of the services who make it easier for a supplier of services to offer his or her services across borders.[749]

5–172 Temporary nature. Where the provider of the service goes to the Member State of the recipient of the service, freedom to provide services differs from freedom of establishment by reason of its temporary nature. Free movement of services cannot be relied upon where a national of a Member State goes to reside in the territory of another Member State and establishes his principal residence there in order to provide or receive services there for an indefinite period.[750] The temporary nature of the activities in question has to be determined in the light, not only of the duration of the provision of the service, but also of its regularity, periodicity or continuity. A provider of services within the meaning of the Treaty may equip himself or herself with some form of infrastructure in the host Member State (including an office, chambers or consulting rooms) in so far as such infrastructure is necessary for the purposes of performing the

---

[745] ECJ, Case 352/85 *Bond van Adverteerders* [1988] E.C.R. 2085, paras 14–15. See also ECJ, Joined Cases C–34–36/95 *De Agostini and TV Shop* [1997] E.C.R. I–3843, para. 29, with a case note by Verhoeven (1997/98) Col.J.E.L. 479–491. For advertising, see also n. to para. 5–113, *supra*.

[746] ECJ, Case C–384/93 *Alpine Investments* [1995] E.C.R. I–1141, paras 20–22 (services offered by telephone); ECJ (judgment of November 6, 2003), Case C–243/01 *Gambelli*, not yet reported, paras 53–54 (services offered on the Internet).

[747] ECJ, Joined Cases C–29/94–C–35/94 *Aubertin* [1995] E.C.R. I–301, para. 9.

[748] ECJ, Case C–384/93 *Alpine Investments* [1995] E.C.R. I–1141, paras 29–31, with case notes by Hatzopoulos (1995) C.M.L.R. 1427–1445 and Straetmans (1995/96) Col.J.E.L. 154–164. See also ECJ, Case C–224/97 *Ciola* [1999] E.C.R. I–2517, paras 10–13; ECJ, Case C–60/00 *Carpenter* [2002] E.C.R. I–6279, para. 29. For the cross-border nature of services, see Straetmans, *Consument en markt* (Kluwer, Deurne, 1998), 296–303.

[749] ECJ (judgment of November 6, 2003), Case C–243/01 *Gambelli*, not yet reported, para. 58.

[750] ECJ, Case 196/87 *Steymann* [1988] E.C.R. 6159, para. 17; ECJ, Case C–70/95 *Sodemare* [1997] E.C.R. I–3395, paras 38–40.

services in question.[751] Services within the meaning of the Treaty may cover services which a business established in a Member State supplies with a greater or lesser degree of frequency or regularity, even over an extended period, to persons established in one or more other Member States, for example the giving of advice or information for remuneration. The Court holds that the Treaty does not afford a means of determining, in an abstract manner, the duration or frequency beyond which the supply of a service in another Member State can no longer be regarded as the provision of services within the meaning of the Treaty.[752]

b.   Substance of the freedom to provide services

Prohibited discrimination. Direct effect attaches to the principle of **5–173** non-discrimination enshrined in the first para. of Art. 49 and the third para. of Art. 50 of the EC Treaty "in so far as they seek to abolish any discrimination against a person providing a service by reason of his nationality or of the fact that he resides in a Member State other than that in which the service is to be provided".[753] The Court of Justice recognised the direct effect of those provisions after a transitional period, in which the Council adopted, just as in the case of freedom of establishment, a General Programme for the abolition of restrictions on entry, exit and residence imposed on nationals established in one Member State who wish to receive or provide services in another Member State. The Council adopted legislation pursuant to that programme.[754] Under these rules, persons providing or receiving services have a right of residence of equal duration to the period during which the services are provided.[755]

In *Van Binsbergen*, the Court of Justice held that the Netherlands could not restrict the right to represent parties in legal proceedings to persons

---

[751] ECJ, Case C–55/94 *Gebhard* [1995] E.C.R. I–4165, para. 27. See with regard to lawyers, ECJ, Case C–145/99 *Commission v Italy* [2002] E.C.R. I–2235, paras 22–23. In 1986 the Court still held that an insurance company which maintains a "permanent presence" in another Member State cannot rely on the freedom to provide services "even if that presence does not take the form of a branch or agency, but consists merely of an office managed by the undertaking's own staff or by a person who is independent but authorised to act on a permanent basis for the undertaking, as would be the case with an agency": ECJ, Case 205/84 *Commission v Germany* [1986] E.C.R. 3755, para. 21.

[752] ECJ (judgment of December 11, 2003), Case C–215/01 *Schnitzer*, not yet reported, paras 30 and 31; ECJ (judgment of April 29, 2004) C–171/02, *Commission v Portugal*, not yet reported, paras 26–27.

[753] ECJ, Case 33/74 *Van Binsbergen* [1974] E.C.R. 1299, para. 27.

[754] General Programme for the Abolition of Restrictions on Freedom to Provide Services, [1962] O.J. English Spec. Ed., Second Series, IX. Resolutions of the Council and of the Representatives of the Member States, p.3, adopted on the basis of the former Art. 63 of the EC Treaty, and see Council Directive 73/148/EEC of May 21, 1973 on the abolition of restrictions on movement and residence within the Community for nationals of Member States with regard to establishment and the provision of services, [1973] O.J. L172/14 (see also para. 5–127, *supra*).

[755] Art. 4(2) Directive 73/148/EEC. These rules have been replaced by the general system of residence rights for Union citizens laid down in Directive 2004/38/EC, see para. 12–009, *infra*.

established in that country. This was because freedom to provide services prohibited all restrictions "imposed on the person providing the service by reason in particular of his nationality or of the fact that he does not habitually reside in the State where the service is provided, which do not apply to persons established within the national territory or which may prevent or otherwise obstruct the activities of the person providing the service".[756] Thus, the Treaty provisions on freedom to provide services preclude making the supply of services conditional upon obtaining a prior authorisation or licence, unless this can be justified objectively (see paras 5–175 *et seq.*). An obligation that a particular activity may be carried out only under a contract of employment likewise constitutes a restriction on trade in services, for which the Member State concerned must provide justification.[757] Trade in services is also restricted where a service provider is required to have a particular legal form or status or to conduct his business on an exclusive basis and of a prohibition of pursuing profit.[758] This is because such requirements often discriminate indirectly against service providers from other Member States.[759] Similarly, it has been held, for example, that the freedom to supply services as a lawyer is impeded where, if a party was successful in a dispute in which he or she was represented by a lawyer established in another Member State, that party cannot obtain reimbursement, from the unsuccessful party, of the fees of the lawyer practising before the court seised with whom, under national law, the lawyer from another Member State had to work in conjunction.[760] Equal treatment of nationals of other Member States wishing to pursue activities other than those of an employed person extends so far that they must have the same right as nationals of the host State to purchase or lease housing built or renovated with the help of public funds and to obtain reduced-rate mortgage loans.[761] Providers of services (in the same way as self-employed persons) must be able to take part in legal and economic transactions locally in the same way as nationals of the host State, even as regards aspects which are not directly connected with their occupational activities. Accordingly, persons who go to another Member State where they intend or are likely to receive services are likewise entitled in principle to treatment no less favourable than that accorded to nationals of the host State as regards the right to protection against criminal offences and the right to use in court proceedings the languages spoken there (see para. 5–060).

---

[756] ECJ, Case 33/74 *Van Binsbergen* [1974] E.C.R. 1299, para. 10.

[757] ECJ, Case C–398/95 *SETTG* [1997] E.C.R. I–3091, paras 14–19.

[758] ECJ, Case C–439/99 *Commission v Italy* [2002] E.C.R. I–305, para. 32.

[759] Thus, the Court of Justice will investigate whether different tax treatment of residents and non-residents constitutes indirect discrimination against service providers established abroad; see, for example, ECJ, Case C–234/01 *Gerritse* [2003] E.C.R. I–5933, paras 23–55 (see also para. 5–130, *supra*) on the right of establishment).

[760] ECJ (judgment of December 11, 2003), Case C–289/02 *AMOK Verlags*, not yet reported, paras 36–39.

[761] ECJ, Case 63/86 *Commission v Italy* [1988] E.C.R. 29, paras 16–20.

Non-discriminatory obstacles. In more recent case law, the Court of **5–174** Justice has made it clear that freedom to provide services does not require only the abolition of all overt and covert[762] discrimination against the provider of the services by reason of his nationality or the place at which he is established, "but also the abolition of any restriction, even if it applies without distinction to national providers of services and to those of other Member States, when it is liable to prohibit or otherwise impede the activities of a provider of services established in another Member State where he lawfully provides similar services".[763] In this way, in 1991 the Court applied *Dassonville* (1974), which was concerned with free movement of goods (see para. 5–099), to freedom to provide services: national legislation which, although applicable irrespective of the nationality of the provider of services, has the effect of making the provision of services between Member States more difficult than the provision of services purely within one Member State, no longer withstands the test of Community law.[764] Accordingly, the Court of Justice held that a municipal tax on satellite dishes was contrary to freedom to supply services because it constituted a charge on the reception of broadcasts from foreign operators and therefore impeded the activities of foreign operators more than those of operators established in the Member State in question.[765]

c. Permitted restrictions on freedom to provide services

(1) *Restrictions pursuant to Arts 45 and 46 of the EC Treaty*

Justificatory grounds. A Member State may impose restrictions on **5–175** freedom to provide services which are dependent on the origin of the service and hence discriminate only on the basis of the derogating provisions of Art. 45 (public authority; see para. 5–142) and Art. 46 of the EC Treaty (public policy, public security and public health; see paras 5–139–5–140).[766] Objectives of an economic nature cannot constitute public policy grounds.[767]

Restrictions must be limited to what is necessary in order to protect the interests which they seek to safeguard. This was held not to be the case with the general prohibition in the Netherlands on distributing radio and television programmes broadcast from other Member States containing

---

[762] ECJ, Joined Cases 62 and 63/81 *Seco* [1982] E.C.R. 223, para. 8.

[763] ECJ, Case C–76/90 *Säger* [1991] E.C.R. I–4221, para. 12. For the prohibition of restrictive conditions imposed on members of staff of a provider of services who are not nationals of a Member State, see the judgments cited in n.481 to para. 5–120, *supra*.

[764] See also ECJ, Case C–381/93 *Commission v France* [1994] E.C.R. I–5145, paras 17–21.

[765] ECJ, Case C–17/00 *De Coster* [2001] E.C.R. I–9445, paras 31–35.

[766] See, *e.g.* ECJ, Case C–484/93 *Svensson and Gustavsson* [1995] E.C.R. I–3955, paras 12 and 15.

[767] ECJ, Case C–211/91 *Commission v Belgium* [1992] E.C.R. I–6757, paras 9–11; ECJ, Case C–17/92 *Distribuidores Cinematográficos* [1993] E.C.R. I–2239, paras 16–21; ECJ, Case C–224/97 *Ciola* [1999] E.C.R. I–2517, paras 15–17; ECJ, Case C–388/01 *Commission v Italy* [2003] E.C.R. I–721, paras 18–19.

advertisements intended for the public in that country or subtitled in Dutch. Although in the final analysis the aim of the rule in question was not to secure for a public foundation all the revenue from advertising, but to safeguard the non-commercial and, thereby, pluralistic nature of the Netherlands broadcasting system, that objective could be achieved by means of a less restrictive measure, such as making the advertising restrictions imposed on national broadcasters generally applicable.[768]

(2) Restrictions based on the rule of reason

5–176 Rule of reason. In *Van Binsbergen*, the Court of Justice held that: "taking into account the particular nature of the services to be provided, specific requirements imposed on the person providing the service cannot be considered incompatible with the Treaty where they have as their purpose the application of professional rules justified by the general good—in particular rules relating to organisation, qualifications, professional ethics, supervision and liability—which are binding upon any person established in the State in which the service is provided, where the person providing the service would escape from the ambit of those rules being established in another Member State".[769] Following the *Cassis de Dijon* line of cases on free movement of goods (see paras 5–107–5–112), the Court has formulated conditions for allowing exceptions in respect of freedom to provide services on the basis of a rule of reason.[770] The distinction drawn in *Keck and Mithouard* with regard to selling arrangements does not apply, particularly where access to the market in services in another Member State is restricted.[771]

5–177 Application without distinction. In the first place, the restrictions on trade in services must apply without distinction to all providers of services, regardless of their nationality or of the Member State in which they are established (even if the restrictions discriminate indirectly).

5–178 Public-interest requirements. Secondly, the restrictions must be justified in the public interest, which does not necessarily relate to the protection of the occupation as such, but can also be designed to secure protection for

---

[768] ECJ, Case 352/85 *Bond van Adverteerders* [1988] E.C.R. 2085, paras 34–37. See also ECJ, Case C–11/95 *Commission v Belgium* [1996] E.C.R. I–4115, para. 92.

[769] ECJ, Case 33/74 *Van Binsbergen* [1974] E.C.R. 1299, para. 12.

[770] ECJ, Case 205/84 *Commission v Germany* [1986] E.C.R. 3755, paras 27–29; ECJ, Case C–154/89 *Commission v France* [1991] E.C.R. I–659, paras 14–15; ECJ, Case C–180/89 *Commission v Italy* [1991] E.C.R. I–709, paras 17–18; ECJ, Case C–198/89 *Commission v Greece* [1991] E.C.R. I–727, paras 18–19; ECJ, Case C–288/89 *Collectieve Antennevoorziening Gouda* [1991] E.C.R. I–4007, paras 13–15; ECJ, Case C–353/89 *Commission v Netherlands* [1991] E.C.R. I–4069, paras 17–19. See also the commentaries cited in n.547 to para. 5–134, *supra*, and Becker, "Vorraussetzungen und Grenzen der Dienstleistungsfreiheit" (1996) N.J.W. 179–181.

[771] ECJ, Case C–384/93 *Alpine Investments* [1995] E.C.R. I–1141, paras 32–39 (for commentaries, see n. 748, *supra*); see also with regard to access to the employment market, ECJ, Case C–415/93 *Bosman* [1995] E.C.R. I–4921, paras 102–103.

the recipient of the service,[772] consumer protection,[773] protection of employees,[774] protection of investors' confidence in the domestic financial markets,[775] fair trading,[776] the maintenance of order in society,[777] combating fraud,[778] protection of creditors or safeguarding the sound administration of justice in relation to the provision of litigation services on a professional basis,[779] ensuring the cohesion of the tax system[780] and the financial balance of the social security system[781] including maintaining a balanced medical service open to all,[782] road safety,[783] protection of intellectual property,[784] conservation of the national historical and artistic heritage,[785] proper appreciation of places and things of historical interest and the widest possible dissemination of knowledge of a country's artistic and cultural heritage,[786] the maintenance of a certain level of (television) programme quality,[787] cultural policy intended to safeguard freedom of expression[788] and respecting fundamental rights generally.[789] "Maintaining industrial peace" as a means of preventing labour disputes from having any adverse effects on an economic sector is not acceptable as a public-interest ground.[790] Neither can a Member State rely on the need to ensure tax

---

[772] ECJ, Joined Cases 110–111/78 *Van Wesemael* [1979] E.C.R. 35, para. 28.

[773] ECJ, Case 205/84 *Commission v Germany* [1986] E.C.R. 3755, paras 30–33.

[774] ECJ, Case 279/80 *Webb* [1981] E.C.R. 3305, paras 18–19; ECJ, Joined Cases 62 and 63/81 *Seco* [1982] E.C.R. 223, para. 14.

[775] Case C–384/93 *Alpine Investments* [1995] E.C.R. I–1141, paras 42–44.

[776] ECJ, Joined Cases C–34–36/95 *De Agostini and TV Shop* [1997] E.C.R. I–3834, para. 53.

[777] ECJ, Case 15/78 *Société Générale Alsacienne de Banque* [1978] E.C.R. 1971, para. 5; ECJ, Case C–275/92 *Schindler* [1994] E.C.R. I–1039, paras 57–58. This includes, for example, the prevention of both fraud and incitement to squander on gaming; see ECJ (judgment of November 6, 2003), Case C–243/01 *Gambelli*, not yet reported, para. 67.

[778] ECJ, Case C–275/92 *Schindler* [1994] E.C.R. I–1039, paras 60–63.

[779] ECJ, Case C–3/95 *Reisebüro Broede* [1996] E.C.R. I–6511, para. 36.

[780] ECJ, Case C–204/90 *Bachmann* [1992] E.C.R. I–249, para. 33.

[781] ECJ, Case C–204/90 *Kohll* [1998] E.C.R. I–1931, para. 41.

[782] This objective may also fall within the public health derogation provided for in Art. 46: *ibid*, paras 50–51; ECJ, Case C–157/99 *Smits and Peerbooms* [2001] E.C.R. I–5473, paras 73–74.

[783] ECJ, Case C–55/93 *Van Schaik* [1994] E.C.R. I–4837, para. 19.

[784] ECJ, Case 62/79 *Coditel v Ciné Vog Films* [1980] E.C.R. 881, para. 15.

[785] ECJ, Case C–180/89 *Commission v Italy* [1991] E.C.R. I–709, para. 20.

[786] ECJ, Case C–154/89 *Commission v France* [1991] E.C.R. I–659, para. 17; ECJ, Case C–198/89 *Commission v Greece* [1991] E.C.R. I–727, para. 21.

[787] ECJ, Case C–288/89 *Collectieve Antennevoorziening Gouda* [1991] E.C.R. I–4007, para. 27; ECJ, Case C–6/98 *ARD* [1999] E.C.R. I–7599, para. 50.

[788] ECJ, Case C–288/89 *Collectieve Antennevoorziening Gouda* [1991] E.C.R. I–4007, paras 22–23; and ECJ, Case C–353/89 *Commission v Netherlands* [1991] E.C.R. I–4069, para. 30 (both judgments were prompted by the Dutch Media Law; see also ECJ, Case C–148/91 *Veronica Omroep Organisatie* [1993] E.C.R. I–487; ECJ, Case C–23/93 *TV10* [1994] E.C.R. I–4795).

[789] ECJ, Case C–112/00 *Schmidberger* [2003] E.C.R. I–5659, paras 71–74 (the case concerns free movement of goods, but refers generally to "a fundamental freedom guaranteed by the Treaty").

[790] ECJ, Case C–398/95 *SETTG* [1997] E.C.R. I–3091, para. 23 (referring to *Collectieve Antennevoorziening Gouda* (n.788, *supra*), in which economic aims were held to be incapable of constituting a justificatory ground under Art. 46 of the EC Treaty).

revenue.[791] Aims of a purely economic nature cannot constitute overriding reasons in the general interest.[792]

5-179 Proportionality. Restrictions placed on freedom to provide services must in addition be "objectively justified" by the need to comply with such objectives in the public interest.[793] Restrictions may be imposed only if the public interest is not already protected by the rules of the State of establishment of the provider of services and the same result cannot be obtained by less restrictive rules.[794] The restrictions must also be suitable for achieving those objectives, for example by restricting the activities in question in a consistent and systematic manner.[795] The same principles of proportionality and reciprocal recognition apply as in the field of the free movement of goods. Accordingly, the Court of Justice has held that a Member State may require agencies to hold a licence for the provision of manpower on account of its particularly sensitive nature from the social point of view, but that it may not impose conditions which would lead to unnecessary duplication of the evidence and guarantees already produced by the provider of services in the Member State in which he is established.[796] In the context of road safety, a Member State may subject a service provider who is already subject to technical inspections in another Member State to additional testing only if the first Member State subjects domestic service providers to the same inspections in the same circumstances.[797] For the same reasons, a Member State may not impose unnecessary requirements when it places restrictions upon the possibility to receive a service in another Member State, for example in connection with the reimbursement of medical treatment received abroad.[798]

---

[791] *e.g.* ECJ (judgment of November 6, 2003), Case C–243/01 *Gambelli*, not yet reported, para. 61.

[792] ECJ, Case C–388/01 *Commission v Italy* [2003] E.C.R. I–721, para. 21.

[793] ECJ, Joined Cases 110 and 111/78 *Van Wesemael* [1979] E.C.R. 35, para. 29.

[794] ECJ, Case C–154/89 *Commission v France* [1991] E.C.R. I–659, para. 15. See, with regard to the imposition of a minimum wage, ECJ, Case C–165/98 *Mazzoleni* [2001] E.C.R. I–2189, paras 25–39.

[795] Accordingly, a Member State may not rely on public policy in order to restrict the organisation of gaming when it is at the same time encouraging consumers to participate in games of chance: ECJ (judgment of November 6, 2003), Case C–243/01 *Gambelli and Others*, not yet reported, paras 67–69.

[796] ECJ, Case 279/80 *Webb* [1981] E.C.R. 3305, paras 18–20. Social legislation designed to protect an interest which is already similarly protected in the Member State in which the provider of services is established conflicts with free movement of services: ECJ, Case C–272/94 *Guiot* [1996] E.C.R. I–1905, paras 9–2; ECJ, Joined Cases C–369/96 and C–376/96 *Arblade* [1999] E.C.R. I–8457, paras 32–80; see also Joined Cases C–49/98, C–50/98 to C–54/98, C–68/98 to C–71/98 *Finalarte Sociedade de Construçao Civil* [2001] E.C.R. I–7831, paras 28–83; ECJ, Case C–279/00 *Commission v Italy* [2002] E.C.R. I–1425, paras 19–25 and 33–35. See Giesen, "Posting: Social Protection of Workers vs. Fundamental Freedoms?" (2003) C.M.L.R. 143–158.

[797] ECJ, Case C–451/99 *Cura Anlagen* [2002] E.C.R. I–3193, para. 46.

[798] ECJ, Case C–158/96 *Kohll* [1998] E.C.R. I–1931, para. 35; ECJ, Case C–368/98 *Vanbraekel* [2001] E.C.R. I–5363 and ECJ, Case C–157/99 *Smits and Peerbooms* [2001] E.C.R. I–5473, paras 45 and 62–69; ECJ (judgment of March 18, 2004), Case C–8/02 *Leichtle*, not yet reported, paras 27–51.

The fact that less strict provisions apply in one Member State than in another does not signify in itself that provisions in force in the latter Member State are disproportionate and hence incompatible with Community law.[799]

A requirement for prior authorisation or permission may constitute a justified restriction on freedom to provide services where national rules on the receipt or performance of the relevant services have not (yet) been harmonised. A prior authorisation scheme must, in any event, be based on objective, non-discriminatory criteria which are known in advance.[800] Such a prior administrative authorisation scheme must likewise be based on a procedural system which is easily accessible and capable of ensuring that a request for authorisation will be dealt with objectively and impartially within a reasonable time and refusals to grant authorisation must also be capable of being challenged in legal proceedings.[801] Provided that it is objectively justified, a Member State may impose on service providers a requirement to have a particular legal form or status. The requirement to have a permanent establishment in the territory of the Member State is the "very negation of that freedom" and can therefore be accepted only if it is "indispensable for attaining the objective pursued".[802]

A Member State may not make the provision of services in its territory subject to compliance with all the conditions required for establishment. This would deprive the right freely to provide services of all practical effectiveness.[803] The Treaty does not require a provider also to offer services in the Member State in which it is established.[804] If, however, providers of services direct their activities entirely or principally towards the territory of a neighbouring State for the purpose of avoiding its professional rules of conduct, the Member State concerned may apply its rules relating to the right of establishment and not to the provision of services.[805] Accordingly, a Member State may prohibit national undertakings from participating in undertakings established in another Member State from which they provide services which would frustrate national legislation,[806] or subject such providers of services to the same conditions as providers

---

[799] ECJ, Case C–384/93 *Alpine Investments* [1995] E.C.R. I–1141, para. 51; ECJ, Case C–3/95 *Reisebüro Broede* [1996] E.C.R. I–6511, para. 42.

[800] ECJ, Case C–205/99 *Analir* [2001] E.C.R. I–1271, para. 38; ECJ, Case C–157/99 *Smits and Peerbooms* [2001] E.C.R. I–5473, para. 90.

[801] ECJ, Case C–157/99 *Smits and Peerbooms* [2001] E.C.R. I–5473, para. 90.

[802] ECJ, Case 205/84 *Commission v Germany* [1986] E.C.R. 3755, para. 52; ECJ, Case C–101/94 *Commission v Italy* [1996] E.C.R. I–2691, para. 31; ECJ (judgment of January 15, 2002), Case C–439/99 *Commission v Italy*, not yet reported, para. 30. The Court of Justice accepted a requirement for a permanent establishment for example in Case C–204/90 *Bachmann* [1992] E.C.R. I–249, paras 32–33.

[803] ECJ, Case C–154/89 *Commission v France* [1991] E.C.R. I–659, para. 12; ECJ, Case C–76/90 *Säger* [1991] E.C.R. I–4221, para. 13.

[804] ECJ, Case C–56/96 *VT4* [1997] E.C.R. I–3143, para. 22.

[805] ECJ, Case 33/74 *Van Binsbergen* [1974] E.C.R. 1299, para. 13; see also Case 115/78 *Knoors* [1979] E.C.R. 399, para. 25 (para. 5–070, *supra*).

[806] ECJ, Case C–148/91 *Veronica Omroep Organisatie* [1993] E.C.R. I–487, paras 12–14.

established on its own territory.[807] A Member State may not prohibit altogether the provision of certain services by operators established in other Member States, as that would be tantamount to abolishing the freedom to provide services.[808] However, a domestic prohibition on the provision of particular services may make it necessary to ban the same services provided from other Member States.[809]

d. Services and the common commercial policy

5–180 **External trade in services.** Unlike in the case of the free movement of goods, the Treaty does not directly provide for a common policy *vis-à-vis* non-member countries. However, where the Community harmonises the conditions for the supply of services and/or the right of establishment within the Community, it often regulates the status of natural and legal persons from non-member countries.[810] In addition, the status of Community nationals in third countries and of third-country nationals within the Community is the subject of various agreements concluded by the Community with non-member countries on the basis of the external competence provided for in the EC Treaty (see paras 5–157 and 20–001 *et seq.*). Initially, Art. 133 of the EC Treaty (common commercial policy) afforded a legal basis for the provision of services across frontiers—*i.e.* between the Community and a third country—where neither the provider nor the recipient of the service moved, but not for services supplied through a natural person or a commercial presence in the country of the recipient of the services or following the movement of the recipient of the services to the country of the service provider. However, the Treaty of Nice has extended the scope of Art. 113 to cover the negotiation and conclusion of agreements in the field of trade in services (see para. 20–003). Unlike the common commercial policy, this power is not exclusive to the Community (see para. 20–004).

4. Free movement of capital and payments

a. Definition and substance

5–181 **Context.** Article 56 of the EC Treaty prohibits all restrictions on the movement of capital and payments between Member States and between Member States and third countries. That prohibition is part of the chapter which, since the beginning of the second stage of economic and monetary union (January 1, 1994), has replaced the former Arts 67–73 of the EEC

---

[807] ECJ, Case C–23/93 *TV10* [1994] E.C.R. I–4795, paras 20–22.
[808] ECJ, Case C–211/91 *Commission v Belgium* [1992] E.C.R. I–6757, para. 12; ECJ, Case C–11/95 *Commission v Belgium* [1996] E.C.R. I–4115, para. 65.
[809] ECJ, Case C–275/92 *Schindler* [1994] E.C.R. I–1039, paras 61–62. See also ECJ, Case 15/78 *Société Générale Alsacienne de Banque* [1978] E.C.R. 1971, para. 5.
[810] See Tiedje, "La libre prestation de services et les ressortissants de pays tiers" (1999) R.M.C.U.E. 73–105.

Treaty. The prohibitive provision of Art. 56 of the EC Treaty has direct effect.[811]

Capital movement. Free movement of capital constitutes a necessary **5–182** support for the freedoms discussed above: a transaction in goods or services or establishment in another Member State will often require investment necessitating a capital movement to another Member State. Nevertheless, the Treaty provided only for the gradual abolition over a transitional period of restrictions on capital movements and of discrimination on grounds of nationality or place of establishment/investment. National policy on capital movements is intermeshed with Member States' economic and monetary policies and could be liberalised only when the economic policy options of the Member States were more attuned to each other. Article 67(1) of the EEC Treaty required liberalisation "to the extent necessary to ensure the proper functioning of the common market". The Court of Justice made it clear that restrictions on capital movements, unlike those on the free movement of goods and services and on the right of establishment, could not be regarded as having been abolished at the end of the transitional period.[812] Consequently, Art. 67 and the stand-still provision of Art. 71 of the EEC Treaty were not held to have direct effect. This was because it was still open to the Council to adopt on the basis of Art. 69 of the EEC Treaty "the necessary directives for the progressive implementation of the provisions of Article 67". Following the adoption of a first directive on May 11, 1960, the Council introduced a gradual liberalisation of the various categories of capital movements, culminating in the general liberalisation requirement laid down by Directive 88/361/EEC of June 24, 1988, which entered into force on July 1, 1990.[813] Article 56 of the EC Treaty goes further than the Directive in that it also liberalises in principle capital movements with third countries.[814] The prohibition of restrictions on

---

[811] ECJ, Joined Cases C–163/94, C–165/94 and C–250/94 *Sanz de Lera* [1995] E.C.R. I–4821, paras 40–48 (EC Treaty, Art. 56(1) in conjunction with Arts 57 and 58(1)(b)). For a survey of the case-law, see Flynn, "Coming of Age: The Free Movement of Capital Case Law 1993–2002" (2002) C.M.L.R. 773–805.

[812] ECJ, Case 203/80 *Casati* [1981] E.C.R. 2595, paras 10–13.

[813] Council Directive 88/361/EEC of June 24, 1988 for the implementation of [the former] Art. 67 of the Treaty, [1988] O.J. L178/5. The directive allowed Spain, Portugal, Greece and Ireland a longer transitional period (Art. 5, Art. 6(2) and Annexes II and III). Member States may still adopt protective measures in respect of certain capital movements, but only with the Commission's authorisation and for a maximum six-month period (Art. 3).The first steps towards liberalisation were taken with the First Council Directive of May 11, 1960 for the implementation of [the former] Art. 67 of the Treaty, [1959–1962] O.J. Spec. Ed. 49, and the Second Council Directive (63/21/EEC) of December 18, 1962 adding to and amending the First Directive for the implementation of [the former] 'Art. 67 of the Treaty, [1963–1964] O.J. English Spec. Ed. 5. No further steps were taken until the programme for achieving the internal market. See Louis, "La libre circulation des capitaux", in Aussant, Fornasier, Louis, Séché and Van Raepenbusch, *Commentaire Mégret—Le droit de la CEE. 3. Libre circulation des personnes, des services et des capitaux. Transports* (Editions de l'Université de Bruxelles, Brusels, 1990), at 171–189.

[814] Art. 7(1) of Directive 88/361 contains only a commitment on the part of the Member States to endeavour to achieve this end.

movements of capital aims at more than eliminating discrimination based on nationality on the financial markets and precludes all rules which make free movement of capital illusory by preventing market participants from investing in other Member States. Accordingly, national measures dissuading nationals of the Member State in question from taking out loans or making investments in other Member States[815] or making direct foreign investment dependent on authorisation[816] are incompatible with the free movement of capital.

5–183 Payments. Free movement of payments relates to transfers of foreign exchange as consideration for a transaction and not, as in the case of capital movements, to investment of the funds in question.[817] Art. 106(1) of the EEC Treaty required Member States to liberalise payments connected with the movement of goods, persons, services or capital to the extent that the underlying transactions had been liberalised.[818] Accordingly, the attainment of free movement of goods, persons and services entailed liberalisation of the resultant payments. Consequently, until such time as capital movements were liberalised, it was important to distinguish in financial transactions between capital movements and payments.[819] Since January 1, 1994, all payments have been liberalised in currencies of Member States, in euros (ECUs) or in currencies of third countries.

b. Permitted restrictions on the free movement of capital and payments

5–184 Permitted restrictions. Restrictions on the free movement of capital may be justified on grounds of general interest, including the grounds for exceptions set out in Art. 58 of the EC Treaty.[820] Furthermore, in certain

---

[815] ECJ, Case C–484/93 *Svensson and Gustavsson* [1995] E.C.R. I–3955, paras 9–10; ECJ, Case C–222/97 *Trummer and Mayer* [1999] E.C.R. I–1661, para. 26; ECJ, Case C–439/97 *Sandoz* [1999] E.C.R. I–7041, para. 19. See also ECJ, Case C–478/98 *Commission v Belgium* [2000] E.C.R. I–7587, para. 20 (prohibition of acquisition of securities for loans issued abroad); ECJ, Case C–367/98 *Commission v Portugal* [2001] E.C.R. I–5107, paras 45–46; ECJ, Case C–483/99 *Commission v France* [2002] E.C.R. I–4781, paras 40–42 ("golden shares"; requirement for approval of the acquisition of holdings in privatised companies); ECJ, Case C–98/01 *Commission v UK* [2003] E.C.R. I–4641, paras 38–50 (restriction on the possibility of buying voting shares in a privatised company); ECJ (judgment of September 7, 2004), Case C–319/02 *Manninen* not yet reported.

[816] ECJ, Joined Cases C–163/94, C–165/94 and C–250/94 *Sanz de Lera* [1995] E.C.R. I–4821, paras 24–25; ECJ, Case C–302/97 *Konle* [1999] E.C.R. I–3099, paras 23 and 38–39; ECJ, Case C–54/99 *Eglise de scientologie* [2000] E.C.R. I–1335, para. 14.

[817] ECJ, Joined Cases 286/82 and 26/83 *Luisi and Carbone* [1984] E.C.R. 377, para. 21.

[818] Art. 106(1) of the EEC Treaty was in force until January 1, 1994 as the former Art. 73h of the EC Treaty. For current payments connected with the movement of capital, see former Art. 67(2) of the EEC Treaty.

[819] ECJ, Joined Cases 286/82 and 26/83 *Luisi and Carbone* [1984] E.C.R. 377, paras 33–34.

[820] Moreover, Protocol (No. 16) on the acquisition of property in Denmark, appended to the EC Treaty by the EU Treaty ([1992] O.J. C224/104) and Protocol No. 6 on the acquisition of secondary residences in Malta, annexed to the 2003 Act of Accession ([2003] O.J. L236/947) allow these Member States to maintain in force restrictions on the acquisition and holding of immovable property for secondary residence purposes. In the case of Malta, this applies to nationals of the Member States who have not legally resided in that State for at least five years.

circumstances, restrictions may be imposed on capital movements (EC Treaty, Arts 57 and 59) or on capital movements and payments (EC Treaty, Art. 60) to or from third countries.

Public-interest requirements. Article 58(1) of the EC Treaty sets out a **5–185** general mitigation of the liberalisation principle enshrined in Art. 56 to be relaxed generally so as to enable Member States:

(a) to apply provisions of their tax law which justifiably "distinguish between taxpayers who are not in the same situation with regard to their place of residence or with regard to the place where their capital is invested"[821] and

(b) to take "all requisite measures"

  (i) to prevent infringements of national law and regulations, in particular in the tax field and in regard to the prudential supervision of financial institutions,

  (ii) to lay down procedures for the declaration of capital movements for the purposes of administrative or statistical information and

  (iii) to take measures justified on grounds of public policy or public security.[822]

Furthermore, the provisions of the Chapter of the Treaty on capital and payments are stated to be without prejudice to the applicability of restrictions on the right of establishment which are compatible with the Treaty (Art. 58(2)).[823]

A parallel may be drawn with the requirement of proportionality applying to permissible derogations from free movement of goods and services, since the "measures and procedures referred to in Art. 58(1) and (2) shall not constitute a means of arbitrary discrimination or a disguised

---

[821] Declaration (No. 7), annexed to the EU Treaty, on Art. 73d [now Art. 58] of the Treaty establishing the European Community makes it clear that Member States are entitled to apply the derogation in respect of capital movements and payments between Member States only as far as provisions in force at the end of 1993 are concerned.

[822] See ECJ, Case C–439/97 *Sandoz* [1999] E.C.R. I–7041, paras 24–37; ECJ, Case C–54/99 *Eglise de scientologie* [2000] E.C.R. I–1335, para. 19; ECJ, Case C–423/98 *Albore* [2000] E.C.R. I–5965, paras 17–25; ECJ, Case C–478/98 *Commission v Belgium* [2000] E.C.R. I–7587, paras 37–38. For restrictions on capital movements in connection with public security, in particular in order to secure energy supplies in a crisis, *cf.* ECJ, Case C–367/98 *Commission v Portugal* [2002] E.C.R. I–5107, paras 52–54, and ECJ, Case C–483/99 *Commission v France* [2002] E.C.R. I–4781, paras 47–54 (requirement for the approval of the acquisition of holdings in privatised companies held to be in breach of free movement of capital) with ECJ, Case C–503/99 *Commission v Belgium* [2002] E.C.R. I–4809, paras 46–55 (more specifically defined restriction held not to be in breach of free movement of capital).

[823] For the relationship between free movement of capital, the right of establishment and freedom to supply services, see Landsmeer, "Het kapitaalverkeer en overige vrijheden" (2001) S.E.W. 434–439.

restriction on the free movement of capital and payments" (EC Treaty, Art. 58(3); *cf.* Art. 30). Accordingly, on grounds of public policy (*e.g.* preventing illegal activities such as tax evasion, money laundering, drug trafficking or terrorism), a Member State may make the export of foreign currency conditional on a prior declaration, but not on prior authorisation, which would make capital movements conditional upon the consent of the administrative authorities.[824] The Court of Justice is further prepared to inquire into whether a restriction on capital movements can be justified on grounds of general interest other than those mentioned in Art. 58(1) of the EC Treaty. Accordingly, restrictions are held to be permissible provided that they are not applied in a discriminatory manner and do not exceed what is necessary in order to achieve an objective in the general interest (rule of reason),[825] for instance in connection with town and country planning.[826] Economic grounds cannot afford a valid justification.[827] Prior authorisation for foreign investment cannot be regarded as a proportionate measure where the same objective can be achieved by prior notification and the associated possibilities for supervision and imposing sanctions.[828] In any event, any authorisation system must be based on objective, non-discriminatory criteria which are known in advance to the undertakings concerned, and all persons affected by a restrictive measure of that type must have a legal remedy available to them.[829]

5–186 Movement to and from third countries. As far as capital movements to and from third countries are concerned, restrictions existing on December 31, 1993[830] under national or Community law in respect of direct investment (including investment in real estate), establishment, the provision of financial services or the admission of securities to capital markets may continue to be applied (EC Treaty, Art. 57(1)). In order to secure compliance with such restrictions, Member States are entitled to verify the nature and reality of the transactions and transfers in question by means of

---

[824] ECJ, Joined Cases C–163/94, C–165/94 and C–250/94 *Sanz de Lera* [1995] E.C.R. I–4821, paras 23–30. This was already the case under Directive 88/361: ECJ, Joined Cases C–358/93 and C–416/93 *Bordessa* [1995] E.C.R. I–361, paras 16–31.

[825] See ECJ, Case C–35/98 *Verkooijen* [2000] E.C.R. I–4071, paras 42–61; ECJ, Case C–367/98 *Commission v Portugal* [2002] E.C.R. I–5107, para. 49, ECJ, Case C–483/99 *Commission v France* [2002] E.C.R. I–4708, para. 45, and ECJ, Case C–503/99 *Commission v Belgium* [2002] E.C.R. I–4809, para. 45.

[826] See ECJ, Case C–302/97 *Konle* [1999] E.C.R. I–3099, paras 36–49; ECJ, Joined Cases C–515/99, C–519–524/99, C–526–540/99 *Reisch* [2002] E.C.R. I–2157, para. 34; ECJ, Case C–300/01 *Salzmann* [2003] E.C.R. I–4899, para. 42. See Glöckner, "Grundverkehrsbeschränkungen und Europarecht" (2000) EuR. 592–622.

[827] ECJ, Case C–367/98 *Commission v Portugal* [2002] E.C.R. I–5107, para. 52.

[828] *e.g.* ECJ, Joined Cases C–515/99, C–519–524/99, C–526–540/99 *Reisch* [2002] E.C.R. I–2157, paras 35–39.

[829] ECJ, Case C–367/98 *Commission v Portugal* [2002] E.C.R. I–5107, para. 50; ECJ, Case C–483/99 *Commission v France* [2002] E.C.R. I–4781, para. 45, and ECJ, Case C–503/99 *Commission v Belgium* [2002] E.C.R. I–4809, para. 46.

[830] As far as Estonia and Hungary are concerned, the date is December 31, 1999 (see Art. 18 of the 2003 Act of Accession).

a prior declaration.[831] The Council may adopt measures on such capital movements and even, by unanimous vote, introduce new restrictions (EC Treaty, Art. 57(2)).[832] In addition, the Council may take such safeguard measures as are strictly necessary where, "in exceptional circumstances, movements of capital to or from third countries cause, or threaten to cause, serious difficulties for the operation of economic and monetary union" (EC Treaty, Art. 59). The European Central Bank must be consulted and the measures may not go on for more than six months. Art. 60(1) of the EC Treaty defines the Council's power to take economic sanctions in the sphere of capital movements and payments. In urgent cases, a Member State may take such measures itself, provided that the Commission and the other Member States are informed. Subsequently, the Council may decide that such unilateral measures should be amended or abolished (EC Treaty, Art. 60(2)). In the EU Constitution, economic sanctions in the sphere of capital movement will be covered by the general provision on restrictive measures (see para. 20–054) but a legal basis will be introduced for the Union to act in the context of the fight against terrorism and related activities (Art. III–160).

C. AGRICULTURE AND FISHERIES

Common agricultural policy. Article 32(2) of the EC Treaty provides that **5–187** the rules laid down for the establishment of the common market are to apply to agricultural products, save as otherwise provided in Arts 33–38. Art. 36 of the EC Treaty lays down that the rules on competition are to apply to production of and trade in agricultural products only to the extent determined by the Council, which made it necessary for the Council to adopt an implementing regulation.[833] The operation and development of the common market for agricultural products must be accompanied by the establishment of a common agricultural policy (CAP) (EC Treaty, Art.

---

[831] ECJ, Joined Cases C–163/94, C–165/94 and C–250/94 *Sanz de Lera* [1995] E.C.R. I–4821, paras 37–38. See also Ståhl, "Free movement of capital between Member States and third countries" (2004) EC Tax Review 47–56. For a complete picture of the framework for investments from non-member countries, see Vadcar, "Un cadre communautaire pour l'investissement?" (2001) R.M.C.U.E 332–342.

[832] In this field, the EU Constitution will provide for the application of the co-decision procedure, except for measures introducing new restrictions on the movement of capital, on which the European Parliament will still be only consulted (compare Art. III–157(2) and (3) of the EU Constitution with Art. 57(2) of the EC Treaty).

[833] Council Regulation (EEC) No. 26 applying certain rules of competition to production of and trade in agricultural products, [1959–1962] O.J. English Spec. Ed. 129. For the application of Community competition law, see, *e.g.* ECJ, Joined Cases C–319/93, C–40/94 and C–224/94 *Dijkstra* [1995] E.C.R. I–4471, paras 15–24; for an application of national competition law, see ECJ (judgment of September 9, 2003), Case C–137/00 *R. v The Competition Commission*, not yet reported, paras 57–67. For the priority enjoyed by agriculture over the objectives in respect of competition, see ECJ, Case C–280/93 *Germany v Council* [1994] E.C.R. I–4973, paras 59–61, and the discussion in Dony, "L'affaire des bananes" (1995) C.D.E. 461, at 470–471.

32(4)).[834] Both national organisations of agricultural markets and the common organisations of the markets by which the Community replaces them must adapt themselves to the rules on free trade and free competition within the common market.[835]

Where an agricultural product comes under a common organisation of the market, the only action open to Member States is to adopt measures implementing the agricultural policy. Additional aid to the agricultural sector is subject to the rules on State aid set forth in Arts 87, 88 and 89 of the EC Treaty.[836] In some cases, Community legislation leaves a measure of discretion to Member States.[837]

5–188 Products concerned. The common agricultural policy relates to "the products of the soil, of stockfarming and of fisheries and products of first-stage processing directly related to these products", as listed in "Annex I" to the EC Treaty (EC Treaty, Art. 32(1) and (3)).[838]

5–189 Objectives. The objectives of the common agricultural policy are listed in Art. 33(1) of the EC Treaty: (a) increased agricultural productivity; (b) a fair standard of living of the agricultural community; (c) stable markets; (d) secured supplies and (e) reasonable prices. Together with the objectives set in other policy spheres,[839] the agricultural policy is to take account of the particular nature of agricultural activity, the need to effect the necessary adjustments by degrees and the close links between the sector and the economy as a whole (EC Treaty, Art. 33(2)). Every measure cannot

---

[834] For an exhaustive discussion of the CAP, see Usher, *EC Agricultural Law* (Oxford University Press, Oxford, 2002), 207 pp.; Barents, *The Agricultural Law of the EC* (Kluwer, Deventer, 1994), 417 pp.; Olmi, *Commentaire Mégret—Le droit de la CEE. 2. Politique agricole commune* (Editions de l'Université de Bruxelles, Brussels, 1991), 383 pp. For a potential simplification of the rules, see Bianchi, "Simplifier la politique agricole communautaire? C'est possible!" (2003) R.T.D.E. 51–90.

[835] ECJ, Case 48/74 *Charmasson* [1974] E.C.R. 1383, paras 6–20 (national organisation of agricultural markets); ECJ, Joined Cases 80 and 81/77 *Commissionaires Réunis* [1978] E.C.R. 927, paras 22–38 (common organisation of the market).

[836] Dehousse and Ghilain, "Les règles de concurrence sur les aides d'Etat dans le secteur de l'agriculture" (2000) Stud. Dipl. 41–58.

[837] Sometimes, for example, the Member State can choose the method of calculation or determine the level of premiums within a set "bracket". Moreover, structural policy is based on initiatives emanating from Member States.

[838] "Annex II" until the Treaty of Amsterdam.

[839] *e.g.* environmental protection (EC Treaty, Art. 6), public health (EC Treaty, Art. 152(1), first subpara.) and economic and social cohesion (EC Treaty, Arts 158 and 159, first para.). See in this connection, Gencarelli, "La politique agricole commune et les autres politiques communautaires: la nouvelle frontière" (2001) R.D.U.E. 173–188; Bianchi, "La politique agricole commune au lendemain du traité d'Amsterdam" (2001) R.T.D.E. 371–395. For environment protection, see also Jack, "Protecting the European environment from the Community: the case of agriculture" (2001) Env.L.Rev. 44–60; Born, "La conservation de la biodiversité dans la politique agricole commune" (2001) C.D.E. 341–401.

invariably take all the objectives into account.[840] Over the years, the emphasis has gradually shifted from helping to make good the shortfall in satisfying the Community's own needs to concern to maintain farmers' incomes, overproduction notwithstanding. The Council is empowered to adopt regulations, directives, decisions and recommendations by a qualified majority vote on a proposal from the Commission and after consulting the European Parliament (EC Treaty, Art. 37(2), third subpara.). Following the adoption of the EU Constitution, legislative acts will be adopted by the European Parliament and the Council under the co-decision procedure (*e.g.* in relation to the establishment of a common organisation of the market), whereas some specific implementing measures are to be taken by the Council on a proposal from the Commission (EU Constitution, Art. III–231(2) and (3)).[841]

The common agricultural policy is made up primarily of the common organisations of the markets and rural development actions. Under Art. 34(3), the European Agricultural Guidance and Guarantee Fund was set up,[842] of which the Guarantee Section funds the common organisations of the markets and actions underpinning rural development and the Guidance Section other rural development actions ("structural policy").[843]

Market organisations. The Council has adopted common organisations of 5–190 the market for most agricultural products by means of some 20 basic regulations.[844] The management of the common organisations is delegated

---

[840] For the requisite weighing of interests, see ECJ, Case 68/86 *UK v Council* [1988] E.C.R. 855, paras 10–14; ECJ, Case C–122/94 *Commission v Council* [1996] E.C.R. I–881, paras 23–25; for the necessary proportionality in achieving the objectives, see n.146 *supra*. For a number of case studies, see Dehousse and Lewalle, "La crise de la dioxine: un révélateur des faiblesses de la réglementation alimentaire nationale" (2000) Stud. Dipl. 5–27; Barents, "De commautaire maatregelen ter bestrijding van mond- en klauwzeer" (2001) N.T.E.R. 169–177; Mortelmans and Van Ooik, "De Europese aanpak van mond- en klauwzeer en de rechtmatigheid van het preventieve vaccinatieverbod" (2001) A.Ae. 911–927.

[841] See Bianchi, "Une PAC 'dénaturée', 'délaissée' et 'malmenée'? Plaidoyer en faveur d'une politique agricole moderne dans le projet de Constitution européenne" (2004) R.T.D.E. 71–95.

[842] See Council Regulation (EEC) No. 25 of April 4, 1962 on the financing of the common agricultural policy, [1959–1962](I) O.J. English Spec. Ed. 118, and Council Regulation (EEC) No. 729/70 of the Council of April 21, 1970 on the financing of the common agricultural policy, [1970](I) O.J. Spec. Ed. 218 (before the Treaty of Amsterdam, para. 3 was numbered 4).

[843] For the present rules, see Council Regulation (EC) No. 1258/1999 of May 17, 1999 on the financing of the common agricultural policy, [1999] O.J. L160/103. See also the provisions on economic and social cohesion, para. 5–247, *infra*.

[844] See the Council Regulations (EEC) on the establishment of a common organisation of the market in live trees and other plants, bulbs, roots and the like, cut flowers and ornamental foliage (Regulation No. 234/68 of February 27, 1968, [1968] O.J. English Spec. Ed. (I) 26), certain products listed in Annex I to the Treaty (Regulation No. 827/68 of June 28, 1968, [1968] O.J. English Spec. Ed. (I) 209), hops (Regulation No. 1696/71 of July 26, 1971, [1971] O.J. English Spec. Ed. (II) 634), seeds (Regulation No. 2358/71 of October 26, 1971, [1971] O.J. English Spec. Ed. (III) 894), pigmeat (Regulation No. 2759/75 of October 29, 1975, [1975] O.J. L282/1), eggs (Regulation No. 2771/75 of October 29, 1975, [1975] O.J.

to the Commission. Of the forms of market organisation provided for in Art. 34(1) of the EC Treaty, the Community has invariably opted for "a European market organisation" (indent (c)).[845] Every common organisation of the market proceeds on the basis of the principles of a unified market (free movement of agricultural products and uniform prices), "Community preference" (utmost self-sufficiency) and financial solidarity within the Community (the Community manages and distributes agricultural expenditure).

There are, however, large differences in terms of the methods of market organisation. Since a high level of prices guarantees producers' income, most of the market organisations provide for price intervention. In order to eliminate the competitive advantage of producers from non-Community countries, the Community imposes import duties and other import levies to cover the difference between the world market price and a "threshold price". Producers exporting surplus products outside the Community are entitled to additional "export refunds". Within the Community market, supply and demand determine the price of a given product, but at the same time it has a "target price" (sometimes known as a "reference" or "guide" price). If the market price deviates from the target price to such an extent as to reach the "intervention price", intervention agencies may or must buy in the product. The uniform agricultural prices are expressed in the Community's unit of account (which was the ECU since the introduction of the European monetary system and is henceforward the euro). In order to avoid changes in the ratio between the unit of account and national currencies (devaluations and revaluations) giving rise to differences in agricultural prices, provision was made for a system of monetary compensatory amounts. Following the exchange rate turbulence in 1992, the Council introduced a new system to deal with the problem of conversion into national currencies.[846] Since the introduction of the euro,

---

L282/49), poultrymeat (Regulation No. 2777/75 of October 29, 1975, [1975] O.J. L282/77), raw tobacco (Regulation No. 2075/92 of June 30, 1992, [1992] O.J. L215/70), bananas (Regulation No. 404/93 of February 13, 1993, [1993] O.J. L47/1), fruit and vegetables (Regulation No. 2200/96 of October 28, 1996, [1996] O.J. L297/1), processed fruit and vegetable products (Regulation No. 2201/96 of October 28, 1996, [1996] O.J. L297/29), beef and veal (Regulation No. 1254/1999 of May 17, 1999, [1999] O.J. L160/21), milk and milk products (Regulation No. 1225/1999 of May 17, 1999, [1999] O.J. L160/48), wine (Regulation No. 1493/1999 of May 17, 1999, [1999] O.J. L179/1), flax and hemp (Regulation No. 1673/2000 of July 27, 2000, [2000] O.J. L193/16), sugar (Regulation No. 1260/2001 of June 19, 2001, [2001] O.J. L178/1), sheepmeat and goatmeat (Regulation No. 2529/2001 of December 19, 2001, [2001] O.J. L341/3), cereals (Regulation No. 1784/2003 of September 29, 2003, [2003] O.J. L270/78), rice (Regulation No. 1785/2003 of September 29, 2003, [2003] O.J. L270/96), dried fodder (Regulation No. 1786/2003 of September 29, 2003, [2003] O.J. L270/114) and olive oil and table olives (Regulation No. 865/2004 of April 29, 2004, [2004] O.J. L161, republished with corrigendum: [2004] O.J. L203/37).

[845] The other forms provided for in Art. 34(1) are "common rules on competition" and "compulsory co-ordination of the various national market organisations".

[846] Council Regulation (EEC) No. 3813/92 of December 28, 1992 on the unit of account and the conversion rates to be applied for the purposes of the common agricultural policy, [1992] O.J. L387/1.

there is a risk of loss of income owing to exchange-rate fluctuations only for producers from Member States not belonging to the euro zone; under the new agrimonetary system, any loss of income suffered by them will be replaced by direct aid.[047] In addition to intervention with respect to prices, the agricultural policy also makes provision for product subsidies and general quality standards.

Since the agricultural policy makes the income support of farmers depend on the quantities produced, this has encouraged structural surpluses constituting a heavy burden on the Community budget, which no longer result in increased incomes. Accordingly, in May 1992 the Council set in train a reform of the common agricultural policy, something which the Commission had been proposing for some time.[848] The Community is lowering farm prices towards world market prices. This is accompanied by increasing direct income support for farmers, which is no longer calculated on the basis of production and dependent on restrictions of the acreage in use or herd size. Further reforms took place in the context of Agenda 2000 (preparation for the accession of new Member States; see para. 23–032).

Structural policy. Structural policy consists, among other things, of **5–191** measures for the modernisation and expansion of agricultural holdings, aid upon the cessation of farming and, since the Single European Act, support for the least-favoured regions.[849] In the measures for rural development, the reformed agricultural policy emphasises environmental measures, afforestation of agricultural land and structural improvements through early retirement, while seeking at the same time to improve the safety and quality of foodstuffs. The Community confines itself to making a financial contribution to the cost of programmes submitted by Member States and regions.[850]

Fisheries. Fishery measures form part of the common agricultural policy. **5–192** The power conferred by Art. 102 of the 1972 Act of Accession to determine conditions for fishing with a view to ensuring protection of the fishing grounds and conservation of the biological resources of the sea, falls within the exclusive competence of the Community (see paras 5–025–5–026). In 1983 a common fisheries policy was established, which has been reformed

---

[847] Council Regulation (EC) No. 2799/98 of December 15, 1998 establishing agrimonetary arrangements for the euro, [1998] O.J. L349/1.

[848] Viscardini Dona, "La politique agricole commune et sa réforme" (1992) R.M.U.E. 13–48; Blumann, "La réforme de la PAC" (1993) R.T.D.E. 247–298.

[849] See Gonzales, "Het EG-landbouwstructuurbeleid: integrerend onderdeel van het gemeenschappelijk landbouwbeleid?" (1997) S.E.W. 7–19.

[850] Council Regulation (EC) No. 1257/1999 of May 17, 1999 on support for rural development from the European Agricultural Guidance and Guarantee Fund (EAGGF) and amending and repealing certain Regulations, [1999] O.J. L160/80.

at the end of 2002. Its most important aim is to preserve fish stocks, for the purpose of which catch quotas and specific preservation measures have been laid down.[851] At the same time, it has to ensure the viability of the fishery industry and create a fair standard of living for those who depend on fishing activities. Therefore, the Community is pursuing a common structural policy for the fishery sector[852] whereas a common organisation of the market in fishery products is in operation.[853]

D. TRANSPORT

5–193 **Treaty rules.** Article 70 of the EC Treaty requires Member States to pursue the objectives of the Treaty within the framework of a common transport policy.[854] Actions in the transport sector come under the general rules of the Treaty, especially the rules on the establishment of the common market, unless the Treaty provides otherwise.[855] Accordingly, Art. 51(1) of the EC Treaty provides that freedom to provide services in the field of transport shall be governed by the provisions of the Title relating to transport. This has not prevented freedom to supply services from being established in the field of transport. The Treaty rules on competition also apply in the transport sector.[856] The provisions of the Title of the Treaty

---

[851] See Council Regulation (EC) No. 2371/2002 of December 20, 2002 on the conservation and sustainable exploitation of fisheries resources under the Common Fisheries Policy, [2002] O.J. L358/59.

[852] See Council Regulation (EC) No. 2792/1999 of December 17, 1999 laying down the detailed rules and arrangements regarding Community structural assistance in the fisheries sector, [1999] O.J. L337/10, as amended by Council Regulation (EC) No. 2369/2002 of December 20, 2002, [2002] O.J. L358/49, and supplemented with Council Regulation (EC) No. 2370/2002 of December 20, 2002 establishing an emergency Community measure for scrapping fishing vessels, [2002] O.J. L358/57. For the Financial Instrument for Fisheries Guidance, see Council Regulation (EC) No. 1263/1999, [1999] O.J. L161/54.

[853] Council Regulation (EC) No. 104/2000 of December 17, 1999 on the common organisation of the markets in fishery and aquaculture products, [2000] O.J. L17/22.

[854] For an exhaustive discussion, see Tromm, *Juridische aspecten van het communautair vervoerbeleid* (T.M.C. Asser Institute, The Hague, 1990), 534 pp.; Aussant and Fornasier, "La politique commune des transports", in Aussant, Fornasier, Louis, Séché and Van Raepenbusch, *Commentaire Mégret—Le droit de la CEE. 3. Libre circulation des personnes, des services et des capitaux. Transports* (Editions de l'Université de Bruxelles, Brussels, 1990), at 191–328.

[855] ECJ, Case 167/73 *Commission v France* [1974] E.C.R. 359, paras 24–28.

[856] ECJ, Case 156/77 *Commission v Belgium* [1978] E.C.R. 1881, para. 10 (application of rules relating to aid); ECJ, Joined Cases 209–213/84 *Asjes* [1986] E.C.R. 1425, paras 35–42 (likewise Arts 81–86). However, the Council ruled out the application of Regulation No. 17/62 (which has itself since been replaced by Regulation No. 1/2003; see para. 5–197, *infra*) to the transport sector by Regulation (EEC) No. 141/62 [1959–1962] O.J. English Spec. Ed. 291. Subsequently, the Council adopted Regulation (EEC) No. 1017/68 applying rules of competition to transport by rail, road and inland waterway, [1968](I) O.J. Spec. Ed. 302. As far as transport by sea and air is concerned, the Council did not adopt equivalent rules implementing Art. 83 of the EC Treaty until later: Regulation 4056/86 laying down detailed rules for the application of Arts 85 and 86 [now Arts 81 and 82] of the Treaty to maritime transport, [1986] O.J. L378/4; Regulation (EEC) No. 3975/87 of December 14, 1987 on laying down the procedure for the application of the rules on competition to undertakings in the air transport sector, [1987] O.J. L374/1—since repealed by Regulation (EC) No.

headed "Transport" apply to transport by rail, road and inland waterway (EC Treaty, Art. 80(1)). This was not automatically so as regards sea and air transport. First, the Council had to decide, by a qualified majority, whether, to what extent and by what procedure appropriate provisions might be laid down. In so doing, the Council is to comply with the general decision-making procedures applicable to transport (EC Treaty, Art. 80(2) and Art. 71).[857]

Member States may not introduce any provisions which are less favourable for carriers of other Member States (EC Treaty, Art. 72).[858] The Treaty debars carriers from discriminating on grounds of the country of origin or of destination of the goods transported and empowers the Council to introduce checks on the part of the Community (EC Treaty, Art. 75(1) and (3), respectively).[859] The Member States are debarred from imposing rates and conditions involving any element of support or protection in the interest of one or more particular undertakings or industries, unless authorised by the Commission (EC Treaty, Art. 76(1)). The Commission may authorise such rates and conditions provided that they comply with Art. 76(2) of the EC Treaty. For the rest, aid measures are caught by the rules set out in Arts 87, 88 and 89 of the EC Treaty (see para. 5–203), unless they can be justified under Art. 73 of the EC Treaty on the ground that they meet the needs of co-ordination of transport or they represent reimbursement for the discharge of certain obligations inherent in the concept of a public service.

Common transport policy. In the context of the common transport policy, **5–194** the Council is empowered to adopt any measures which it deems appropriate, *inter alia*, in relation to international transport, the conditions

---

411/2004 of February 26, 2004, [2004] O.J. L98/1 (which subjects all air transport to the general implementing rules laid down in Regulation No. 1/2003).

[857] For the application of freedom to provide services to maritime transport between Member States and between Member States and third countries, see Council Regulation (EEC) No. 4055/86 of December 22, 1986, [1986] O.J. L378/1; for maritime transport within Member States (maritime cabotage), see Regulation 3577/92 of December 7, 1992, [1992] O.J. L364/7. For the application of freedom to supply services in air transport, see most recently the Council Regulations of July 23, 1992 on licensing of air carriers (Regulation (EEC) No. 2407/92, [1992] O.J. L240/1), on access for Community air carriers to intra-Community air routes (Regulation (EEC) No. 2408/92, [1992] O.J. L240/8) and on fares and rates for air services (Regulation (EEC) No. 2409/92, [1992] O.J. L240/15). For the extent to which Community action places limits on the differential treatment of sea transport to non-Community and Community ports, see ECJ, Case C–435/00 *Geha Naftiliaki EPE* [2002] E.C.R. I–10615, paras 21–22.

[858] Art. 76 may be relied upon to contest any amendment to national legislative provisions but also any change in an administrative practice which may disadvantage carriers from other Member States: ECJ, Joined Cases C–184/91 and C–221/91 *Oorburg and van Messem* [1993] E.C.R. I–1633, paras 12–15.

[859] Council Regulation (EEC) No. 11 of June 27, 1960 concerning the abolition of discrimination in transport rates and conditions, in implementation of Art. 79 [now Art. 75](3) of the Treaty establishing the European Economic Community, [1959–1962] O.J. English Spec. Ed. 60.

under which non-resident carriers may operate transport services and transport safety, while taking account of "the distinctive features of transport" (EC Treaty, Art. 71(1); see also Art. 74). In a 1985 judgment, the Court of Justice held that there was not yet a coherent set of rules which might be regarded as a common transport policy. Yet it did not regard this as a failure to act on the part of the Council, on the ground that that institution had a discretion, for example, to decide whether action in the transport sector must first deal with relations between the railways and the public authorities or with competition between road and rail.[860] On the other hand, the Council had failed to fulfil its obligations in the fields of international transport and of the conditions under which non-resident carriers might operate transport services in a Member State, since those obligations were sufficiently well-defined in the Treaty.[861] Since then, the Council has phased in a Community licensing system for carriage of goods by road to replace the system of national quotas[862] and has set its sights on a gradual liberalisation of domestic goods and passenger transport (*cabotage*).[863]

The achievement of the common transport policy, also for sea and air transport, goes hand in hand with the abolition of frontier controls between Member States and harmonisation of technical and social rules.

E. Competition

5-195 Undertakings and Member States. The Community is based on an open market economy with free competition, "favouring an efficient allocation of resources" (EC Treaty, Art. 98 and Art. 105(1)). The "rules on competition" comprise rules prohibiting distortion of competition by undertakings (EC Treaty, Arts 81–86) and rules restricting State aid granted to undertakings (EC Treaty, Arts 87, 88 and 89). A brief overview of the scope of these rules is set out below.[864] The EU Constitution will leave these rules virtually unchanged.[865]

---

[860] ECJ, Case 13/83 *European Parliament v Council* [1985] E.C.R. 1513, paras 46–50.
[861] *ibid.*, paras 64–68.
[862] See, in particular, Council Regulation (EEC) No. 881/92 of March 26, 1992 on access to the market in the carriage of goods by road within the Community to or from the territory of a Member State or passing across the territory of one or more Member States, [1992] O.J. L95/1.
[863] For the determination of the conditions under which non-resident carriers may transport goods or passengers by inland waterway in a Member State in which they are not established, see Council Regulation (EEC) No. 3921/91 of December 16, 1991, [1991] O.J. L373/1, and Council Regulation (EEC) No. 1356/96 of July 8, 1996, [1996] O.J. L175/7; the equivalent regulations for road passenger services and road haulage services are Council Regulation (EC) No. 12/98 of December 11, 1997, [1998] O.J. L4/10, and Council Regulation (EEC) No. 3118/93 of October 25, 1993, [1993] O.J. L279/1.
[864] For further information on this area, see, among other works, Bellamy and Child and Others, *Common Market Law of Competition* (Sweet & Maxwell, London, 2001), 1339 pp.; Whish, *Competition Law* (Butterworths, London, 2001), 913 pp.; Korah, *An introductory guide to EC competition law and practice* (Hart, Oxford, 2000), 404 pp.; Faull and Nikpay, *The EC Law of Competition* (Oxford University Press, London, 1999), 961 pp.; Waelbroeck

In competition law, the concept of an undertaking encompasses every entity engaged in an economic activity, regardless of the legal status of the entity and the way in which it is financed.[866] Although Arts 81 and 82 of the EC Treaty are directed at undertakings, the second para. of Art. 10 requires Member States to abstain from any measure which could detract from the effectiveness of those provisions. This is the case, for example, where a Member State requires or favours the adoption of agreements contrary to Art. 81 or reinforces their effects or deprives its own legislation of its official character by delegating to private traders the responsibility for taking decisions affecting the economic sphere.[867] Consequently, it has been held that a Member State infringes Arts 10 and 81 of the EC Treaty by obliging the national council of customs agents to set a uniform tariff for all customs agents.[868] In such a case, the national authorities must disapply the provisions conflicting with Art. 81 or 82.[869] If those provisions preclude the possibility of competition, no penalties may be imposed on the undertakings concerned in respect of the period preceding the finding of an

---

and Frignani, *Commentaire Mégret. Le droit de la CE. 4. Concurrence* (Editions de l'Université de Bruxelles, Brussels, 1997), 1098 pp. ; Van Gerven, Gyselen, Maresceau, Stuyck and Steenbergen, *Beginselen van Belgisch Privaatrecht. XIII. Handels- en economisch Recht. Deel 2. Mededingingsrecht. B. Kartelrecht* (Story-Scientia, Antwerp, 1996), 1089 pp.

[865] For the changes, see mainly Art. III–122 (on services of general economic interest, para. 5–201, *infra*) and Arts III–165(3) and III–168(4), which confirm the Council's present practice of determining the categories of agreements or aid measures, respectively, in respect of which the Commission may grant a "block exemption" (see paras 5–198 and 5–203, *infra*).

[866] For the definition of the term "undertaking", see ECJ, Case C–41/90 *Höfner and Elser* [1991] E.C.R. I–1979, paras 21–22; ECJ, Case C–244/94 *Fédération française des sociétés d'assurance* [1995] E.C.R. I–4013, paras 14–22; ECJ, Case C–343/95 *Diego Calì & Figli* [1997] E.C.R. I–1547, paras 16–25. This does not encompass an institution charged with the management of a social security system on the basis of the principle of solidarity (ECJ, Joined Cases C–159/91 and C–160/91 *Poucet and Pistre* [1993] E.C.R. I–637, paras 17–20; ECJ, Case C–218/00 *Cisal di Battistello Veneziano* [2002] E.C.R. I–691, paras 31–46; ECJ (judgment of March 16, 2004), Joined Cases C–264/01, C–306/01, C–354/01 and C–355/01 *AOK Bundesverband*, not yet reported) or an organisation entrusted by Member States with the exercise of powers which are typically those of a public authority, such as the control and supervision of air space (ECJ, Case C–364/92 *Eurocontrol* [1994] E.C.R. I–43, paras 18–31). The same criteria apply to an "association of undertakings" within the meaning of Art. 81(1) of the Treaty, see ECJ, Case C–309/99 *Wouters* [2002] E.C.R. I–1577, paras 56–71 (where a Bar association was regarded as being an "association of undertakings").

[867] ECJ, Case 13/77 *INNO* [1977] E.C.R. 2115, paras 30–33; ECJ, Joined Cases 209–213/84 *Asjes* [1986] E.C.R. 1425, paras 70–77; ECJ, Case 311/85 *Vereniging van Vlaamse Reisbureaus* [1987] E.C.R. 3801, para. 10; ECJ, Case 267/86 *Van Eycke* [1988] E.C.R. 4769, para. 16; ECJ, Case C–2/91 *Meng* [1993] E.C.R. I–5751, para. 14; ECJ, Case C–185/91 *Reiff* [1993] E.C.R. I–5801, para. 14; ECJ, Case C–245/91 *Ohra* [1993] E.C.R. I–5851, para. 10; ECJ, Case C–35/99 *Arduino* [2002] E.C.R. I–1529, para. 35; ECJ (judgment of September 9, 2003), Case C–198/01 *Consorzio Industrie Fiammiferi*, not yet reported, para. 46.

[868] ECJ, Case C–35/96 *Commission v Italy* [1998] E.C.R. I–3851, paras 33–60. See also Ballarino and Bellodi, "Contraintes étatiques en matière de concurrence" (2003) R.D.U.E. 555–589; Schwarze, "Der Staat als Adressat des europäischen Wettbewerbsrechts" (2000) Eu.Z.W. 613–627.

[869] ECJ (judgment of September 9, 2003), Case C–198/01 *Consorzio Industrie Fiammiferi*, not yet reported, paras 48–51.

infringement of Art. 81 or 82. But penalties may be imposed for any future conduct in breach of the competition rules. If, however, the national provisions merely encourage or make it easier for undertakings to engage in autonomous anti-competitive conduct, those undertakings have themselves to bear the consequences of the infringement of Arts 81 and 82 of the EC Treaty.[870]

1.   Rules for undertakings

a.   Article 81 of the EC Treaty

5–196   Prohibited agreements. Article 81(1) of the EC Treaty prohibits "all agreements between undertakings, decisions by associations of undertakings and concerted practices which may affect trade between Member States and which have as their object or effect the prevention, restriction or distortion of competition within the common market".[871] The prohibited agreements, decisions or concerted practices, of which Art. 81(1) of the EC Treaty lists some examples, cover both horizontal "agreements" between competitors and vertical "agreements" between producers, suppliers and customers.[872] In order to be caught by the prohibition, the agreements must also affect trade between Member States. This does not mean that the undertakings concerned have to operate in different Member States: intra-Community trade may also be adversely affected where the agreement is between undertakings from one Member State[873] or even between undertakings from non-Community countries where they implement the agreement in the Community.[874]

---

[870] *ibid.*, paras 52–57.

[871] For the distinction between "agreements between undertakings", "decisions by associations of undertakings" and "concerted practices", see, *inter alia*, CFI, Case T–1/89 *Rhône-Poulenc v Commission* [1991] E.C.R. I–867, paras 118–128. *Cf.* Pais Antunes, "Agreements and Concerted Practices under EEC Competition Law: Is the Distinction Relevant?" (1992) Y.E.L. 57–77.

[872] Agreements concluded in the context of collective negotiations between management and labour to improve conditions of work and employment are not caught by Art. 81: ECJ, Case C–67/96 *Albany* [1999] E.C.R. I–5751, paras 53–60 (see also the judgments of the same date in ECJ, Joined Cases C–115–C–117/97 *Brentjens' Handelsonderneming* [1999] E.C.R. I–6025 and ECJ, C–219/97 *Drijvende Bokken* [1999] E.C.R. I–6121); ECJ, Case C–222/98 *van der Woude* [2000] E.C.R. I–7111, paras 24–27. However, Art. 81 does cover collective agreements between self-employed persons or members of a liberal profession: ECJ, Joined Cases C–180–C–184/98 *Pavlov* [2000] E.C.R. I–6451, paras 67–70; ECJ, Case C–309/99 *Wouters* [2002] E.C.R. I–1577, paras 44–71. See Van den Bergh and Camesasca, "Irreconcilable Principles? The Court of Justice Exempts Collective Labour Agreements from the Wrath of Antitrust" (2000) E.L.Rev. 492–508; Evju, "Collective Agreements and Competition Law. The *Albany* Puzzle, and *van der Woude*" (2001) Int'l J.Comp.Lab.L.Ind.Rel. 165–184; Boni and Manzini, "National Social Legislation and EC Antitrust Law" (2001) World Comp. 239–255; O'Loughlin, "EC Competition Rules and Free Movement Rules: An Examination of the Parallels and their Furtherance by the ECJ *Wouters* Decision" (2003) E.Comp.L.Rev. 62–69.

[873] ECJ, Case 8/72 *Cementhandelaren v Commission* [1972] E.C.R. 977, paras 26–31.

[874] ECJ, Joined Cases 89, 104, 114, 116–177 and 125–129/85 *Åhlström v Commission* [1988] E.C.R. 5193, paras 16–17. See also the Commission Notice—Guidelines on the effect on trade concept contained in Arts 81 and 82 of the Treaty ([2004] O.J. C101/81).

Prohibited agreements or decisions are automatically void (Art. 81(2)), which means that they have no validity retroactively or *vis-à-vis* third parties. Nevertheless, the prohibition is not absolute in that Art. 81(3) of the EC Treaty affords an opportunity for Art. 81(1) to be declared inapplicable. To that end, that provision requires the agreement, decision or concerted practice in question to have beneficial effects (it must contribute to improving the production or distribution of goods or promote technical or economic progress, while giving consumers a share of the benefit), not to impose disproportionate restrictions on the undertakings concerned and afford some opportunity for competition.

Decentralised enforcement. The prohibition set out in Art. 81 of the EC **5–197** Treaty has direct effect and may therefore be relied upon before national courts, which are to consider whether an agreement, decision or concerted practice within the meaning of Art. 81(1) satisfies the requirements of Art. 81(3).[875] Before the national courts, compensation may be claimed for loss caused by a prohibited agreement, even by an individual who was party to the agreement.[876] The Treaty also requires the Commission and the national competition authorities to supervise compliance with the competition rules (Arts 84 and 85). That supervision is carried out in accordance with provisions adopted by the Council pursuant to Art. 83 of the EC Treaty. Of those provisions, Regulation No. 1/2003 is of prime importance because of its general scope.[877] Originally, only the Commission was empowered to apply Art. 81(3) and undertakings had to notify all agreements conflicting with Art. 81(1) to it in order to have the prohibition declared inapplicable or, in the event that this was not possible, to avoid the

---

[875] For the direct effect of Art. 81(1) of the EC Treaty, see ECJ, Case 127/73 *BRT* [1974] E.C.R. 51, para. 16. Arts 1–6 of Regulation No. 1/2003 (see below) confirm the direct effect of Art. 81(3) of the EC Treaty, which, before May 1, 2004, was precluded by the fact that the Commission had been granted exclusive competence to apply Art. 81(3) (Art. 9 of Regulation No.17/62; see also below).

[876] ECJ, Case C–453/99 *Courage* [2001] E.C.R. I–6297, paras 17–28. However, a Member State may debar a party from relying on his own unlawful actions to obtain damages where it is established that that party bears significant responsibility for the distortion of competition: *ibid.*, paras 29–36. See Komninos, "New Prospects for Private Enforcement of EC Competition Law: *Courage v Crehan* and the Community Right to Damages" (2002) C.M.L.R. 447–487; Mäsch, "Private Ansprüche bei Verstössen gegen das europäische Kartellverbot—*Courage* und die Folgen" (2003) EuR. 825–846.

[877] Council Regulation (EC) No. 1/2003 of December 16, 2002 on the implementation of the rules on competition laid down in Arts 81 and 82 of the Treaty, [2003] O.J. L1/1. Regulation No. 1/2003 is generally applicable unless a separate implementing regulation has been adopted for a particular sector (see the exceptions for the transport sector listed in Art. 32 of Regulation No. 1/2003, and the regulations mentioned in n.857, *supra*).

imposition of a fine.[878] With effect from May 1, 2004, Regulation No. 1/2003 abolished the notification system. Undertakings must henceforth work out for themselves whether their agreements conflict with Art. 81 and the whole of that article (including as a result para. 3) may be applied by the national courts and the national competition authorities.[879] Responsibility for supervising that Art. 81 is complied with is vested primarily in the national courts and the national competition authorities in order that the Commission can concentrate on investigating the most serious infringements.[880]

The national competition authorities together with the Commission form the "European Network of Competition Authorities".[881] They are to inform the Commission of the steps they take in investigating infringements of Art. 81 (and Art. 82) and exchange information amongst themselves and with the Commission.[882] Once the Commission has initiated a procedure of its own, the national competition authorities are relieved of their

---

[878] This system was set up by Regulation No.17: First Regulation implementing Arts 85 and 86 [now Arts 81 and 82] of the Treaty, [1959–1962] O.J. English Spec. Ed. 87.

[879] See, however, the Commission Notices on informal guidance relating to novel questions concerning Arts 81 and 82 of the EC Treaty that arise in individual cases (guidance letters) and on the handling of complaints by the Commission under Arts 81 and 82 of the EC Treaty ([2004] O.J. C101/78 and 65, respectively). Moreover, where the Community public interest so requires, the Commission, acting on its own initiative, may by decision find that Art. 81 of the Treaty is not applicable to an agreement; see Art. 10 of Regulation No. 1/2003.

[880] See Venit, "Brave New World: The Modernisation and Decentralisation of Enforcement under Arts 81 and 82 of the EC Treaty" (2003) C.M.L.R. 545–580; Gilliams, "Modernisation: From Policy to Practice" (2003) E.L.Rev. 451–474; Nyssens, "Le règlement 1/2003 CE: vers une décentralisation et privatisation du droit de la concurrence" (2003) T.B.H. 286–294; Lavagne, "La réforme du droit des ententes—Le règlement du 13 Décembre 2002" (2003) R.M.C.U.E. 526–529; Paulis and Gauer, "La réforme des règles d'application des articles 81 et 82 du Traité" (2003) J.T.D.E. 65–73; Cooke, "Centralised Subsidiary: The Reform of Competition Law Enforcement" (2001) 10 Ir.J.E.L. 4–21. The debate which culminated in this "decentralisation" started with the White Paper on modernisation of the rules implementing Arts 81 and 82 of the EC Treaty ([1999] O.J. C132/1). Compare the critical observations in Möschel, "Guest Editorial: Change of Policy in European Competition Law" (2000) C.M.L.R. 495–499 with Ehlermann, "The Modernisation of EC Antitrust Policy: A Legal and Cultural Revolution" (2000) C.M.L.R. 537–590 and the commentaries in (2001) C.D.E. 134–236. For the extent to which national authorities continue to have the power to apply national competition law, see Art. 3 of Regulation No.1/2003. For the openings for arbitrators, see Komninos, "Arbitration and the Modernisation of European Competition Law Enforcement" (2001) World Comp. 211–238.

[881] A division of work is set out in the Joint Statement of the Council and the Commission on the functioning of the Network of Competition Authorities, entered in the Council minutes upon the adoption of Regulation No. 1/2003 (document No.15435/EDD, available on the Internet at *register.consilium.eu.int/pdf/en/02/st15/15435-a1en2.pdf* See also Böge and Scheidgen, "Das neue Netzwerk der Wettbewerbsbehörden in der Europäischen Union" (2002) E.W.S. 201–206.

[882] See Arts 11, 12 and 13 of Regulation No. 1/2003 and the Commission Notice on co-operation within the Network of Competition Authorities ([2004] O.J. C101/43). Only where the national competition authority constitutes a "court or tribunal of a Member State" may it refer a question to the Court of Justice for a preliminary ruling under Art. 234 of the EC Treaty; see Komninos, "Art. 234 EC and National Competition Authorities in the Era of Decentralisation" (2004) E.L.Rev. 106–114.

competence to apply Arts 81 and 82.[883] This does not apply to national courts before which reliance is made on Art. 81 or Art. 82. Where the Commission has initiated a procedure itself, the national court must, however, avoid taking a decision which would conflict with the decision contemplated by the Commission[884] The national court may, if necessary, stay proceedings and enter into consultations with the Commission.[885] Where the Commission has taken a decision, the national court may not take a decision conflicting with that of the Commission.[886] Where an action for annulment has been brought against the Commission decision, it is for the national court to decide whether it should stay proceedings until a definitive decision has been given by the Community Court.[887]

Investigation by the Commission. In order to track down infringements of **5–198** Arts 81 and 82, Regulation No. 1/2003 confers broad powers of investigation on the Commission, including the power to inspect business premises (Arts 17–21). Acting under Regulation No. 1/2003, the Commission may make a finding that there has been an infringement of Art. 81 or Art. 82 of the EC Treaty and require the undertakings concerned to bring it to an end (Art. 7(1)). The Commission may also impose fines or periodic penalty payments (Regulation No. 1/2003, Arts 23 and 24).[888] During the procedure, hearings take place of interested parties in accordance with Art. 27 of Regulation No. 1/2003 and detailed implementing rules drawn up by the Commission.[889] Article 31 of Regulation No. 1/2003 confers on the Court of Justice (the Court of First Instance) unlimited jurisdiction to review decisions whereby the Commission has fixed a fine or periodic penalty payment.

---

[883] Regulation No. 1/2003, Art. 11(6).
[884] Regulation No. 1/2003, Art. 16(1), and the Commission Notice on the co-operation between the Commission and the courts of the EU Member States in the application of Arts 81 and 82 EC ([2004] O.J. C101/54). See Lenaerts and Gerard, "Decentralisation of EC Competition Law Enforcement: Judges in the Frontline" (Sept. 2004) World Comp.
[885] ECJ, Case C–234/89 *Delimitis* [1991] E.C.R. I–935, paras 43–55. The national court may also make a reference to the Court of Justice for a preliminary ruling: ECJ, Case 127/73 *BRT* [1974] E.C.R. 51, paras 20–23; ECJ, Joined Cases C–319/93, C–40/94 and C–224/94 *Dijkstra* [1995] E.C.R. I–4471, paras 25–36.
[886] Regulation No. 1/2003, Art. 16(1).
[887] ECJ, Case C–344/98 *Masterfoods and HB Ice Cream* [2000] E.C.R. I–11369, paras 45–60. If it has doubts as to the validity of the Commission decision, the national court may always make a reference for a preliminary ruling to the Court of Justice: *ibid.*, para. 57. See Fierstra (2001) N.T.E.R. 159–163; O'Keefe (2001) E.L.Rev. 301–311; Malferrari (2001) EuR. 605–616.
[888] For the setting of fines, see the Commission's guidelines in [1998] O.J. C9/3.
[889] See the Commission Regulation (EC) No. 773/2004 of April 7, 2004 relating to the conduct of proceedings by the Commission pursuant to Arts 81 and 82 of the EC Treaty ([2004] O.J. L123/18).

The Council has empowered the Commission to grant exemptions by regulation in respect of categories of agreements.[890] If an agreement satisfies the requirements for "block exemption", as it is termed, the undertakings concerned may, under the regulation, rely directly on exemption from the prohibition set out in Art. 81.[891] In order to simplify compliance with Art. 81, the Commission has clarified in guidelines in what circumstances vertical agreements (between producer, supplier or buyer) and horizontal agreements (between competitors), in its view, do not have an appreciable effect on competition or satisfy the requirements of Art. 81(3).[892] In addition, the Commission publishes policy statements concerning categories of agreements in respect of which it does not consider it necessary to take action.[893]

b. Article 82 of the EC Treaty

5-199 Abuse of dominant position. Article 82 of the EC Treaty prohibits one or more undertakings from abusing a dominant position within the common market or in a substantial part of it in so far as it may affect trade between Member States. In common with the prohibition laid down by Art. 81, the corresponding provision of Art. 82 has direct effect[894] and is subject to

---

[890] For the Council's authorisation, see Council Regulation (EEC) No. 19/65 of March 2, 1965 on application of Art. 85 [now Art. 81](3) of the Treaty to certain categories of agreements and concerted practices ([1965–1966] O.J. Spec. Ed. 36), as amended by Council Regulation 1215/1999, ([1999] O.J. L148/1), and Council Regulation (EEC) No. 2821/71 of December 20, 1971 on application of Art. 85 [now Art. 81](3) of the Treaty to categories of agreements, decisions and concerted practices ([1971](III) O.J. English Spec. Ed. 1032). For authorisations for individual sectors, see Council Regulation (EEC) No. 1534/91 of May 31, 1999 (insurance sector), [1991] O.J. L143/1, Council Regulations (EEC) Nos 4056/86 and 479/92 (sea transport and liner shipping companies, respectively ([1986] O.J. L378/13, and [1992] O.J. L55/3; n.857 to para. 5–193 *supra*) and Council Regulation (EEC) No. 3976/87 of December 14, 1987 (air transport), [1987] O.J. L374/9).

[891] The Commission has drawn up block exemptions for agreements in Regulation (EC) No. 2790/1999 of December 22, 1999, [1999] O.J. L336/21 (vertical agreements in general), Regulation (EC) No. 2658/2000 of November 29, 2000, [2000] O.J. L304/3 (specialisation agreements), Regulation 2659/2000 of November 29, 2000, [2000] O.J. L304/7 (research and development agreements), Regulation (EC) No. 1400/2002 of July 31, 2002 [2002] O.J. L203/30 (agreements in the motor vehicle sector) and Regulation (EC) No. 772/2004 of April 27, 2004, [2004] O.J. L123/11 (technology transfer agreements). On the first, see Whish, "Regulation (EC) No. 2790/99of April 27, 2004: The Commission's 'New Style' Block Exemption for Vertical Agreements" (2000) C.M.L.R. 887–924.

[892] See, accompanying the block exemptions listed in the preceding note, the Guidelines on Vertical Restraints ([2000] O.J. C291/1), on the applicability of Art. 81 of the EC Treaty to horizontal co-operation agreements ([2001] O.J. C3/2) and on the application of Art. 81 of the EC Treaty to technology transfer agreements ([2004] O.J. C101/2). In addition, see the Commission's Notice—Guidelines on the application of Art. 81(3) of the Treaty ([2004] O.J. C101/97) as well as the guidelines mentioned in n.800, *supra*.

[893] See, *e.g.* the Commission Notice on agreements of minor importance which do not appreciably restrict competition under Art. 81(1) of the Treaty establishing the European Community (*de minimis*) ([2001] O.J. C368/13).

[894] ECJ, Case 155/73 *Sacchi* [1974] E.C.R. 409, para. 18.

supervision by the national courts, the national competition authorities and the Commission in accordance with the provisions of Regulation No. 1/2003.

A dominant position is determined by defining the relevant market both from the geographic point of view and from the standpoint of the product and by evaluating the market power (not solely market share) of the undertaking or undertakings.[895] Article 82 lists some instances of prohibited abuse of a dominant position (including limiting of production, markets or technological development or "tying" the conclusion of contracts to the acceptance by parties of supplementary obligations without necessary connection with the subject of the contracts).[896]

Article 82 also applies where an undertaking holding a dominant position on a particular market has such freedom of conduct on a neighbouring but separate market compared with the other economic operators on that market that, even without its holding a dominant position there, it bears a special responsibility to maintain genuine undistorted competition.[897]

c. Control of concentrations

Merger control. Initially, supervision of mergers or concentrations of **5–200** undertakings was confined to the Commission's control of compliance with Art. 82 of the EC Treaty, since the Court of Justice held that an undertaking abuses its dominant position if it strengthens its position in such a way that the degree of dominance reached substantially fetters competition, *i.e.* with the result that only undertakings remain in the market whose behaviour depends on the dominant one.[898] Ever since September 21, 1990, all concentrations of undertakings with a Community dimension have been subject to the obligatory prior notification and control introduced by Regulation No. 4064/89,[899] which has been replaced with effect from May 1, 2004 by Regulation No. 139/2004.[900]

---

[895] ECJ, Case 22/76 *United Brands v Commission* [1978] E.C.R. 207, paras 10–129; CFI, Case I–51/89 *Tetra Pak v Commission* [1990] E.C.R. I–309. See the Commission notice on the definition of relevant market for the purposes of Community competition law, [1997] O.J. C372/5.

[896] For an example, see CFI, Case I–228/97 *Irish Sugar v Commission* [1999] E.C.R. II–2969.

[897] CFI, Case T–83/91 *Tetra Pak v Commission* [1994] E.C.R. II–755, paras 112–122, as upheld by ECJ, Case C–333/94P *Tetra Pak v Commission* [1996] E.C.R. I–5951.

[898] ECJ, Case 6/72 *Europemballage and Continental Can v Commission* [1973] E.C.R. 215, para. 26.

[899] Council Regulation (EEC) No. 4064/89 of December 21, 1989 on the control of concentrations between undertakings, [1989] O.J. L395/1.

[900] Council Regulation (EC) No. 139/2004 of January 20, 2004 on the control of concentrations between undertakings (the EC Merger Regulation), [2004] O.J. L24/1. See Brunet and Girgenson, "La double réforme du contrôle communautaire des concentrations" (2004) R.T.D.E. 1–31; see also, more generally, Navarro, Font, Folguera and Briones, *Merger Control in the European Union* (Oxford University Press, Oxford, 2002), 926 pp.; Cook and Kerse, *E.C. Merger Control* (Sweet & Maxwell, London, 2000), 376 pp.; Hawk and Husher, *European Community Merger Control: A Practitioner's Guide* (Kluwer Law International, The

The Community dimension is determined by means of thresholds in terms of the aggregate worldwide turnover of the undertakings concerned and the aggregate Community-wide turnover of the two largest undertakings concerned (Regulation No. 139/2004, Art. 1(2)). The requirement for a Community dimension is also satisfied where a concentration meets—lower—thresholds which have a significant impact in at least three Member States (Regulation No. 139/2004, Art. 1(3)).[901] In accordance with these criteria, the concentration regulation may also be applied to undertakings which are not established in a Member State and carry out their production activities outside the Community.[902] Following notification, the Commission must reach a decision on the compatibility of the concentration with the common market within the time-limits fixed by Regulation 139/2004. Concentrations which would significantly impede effective competition, in the common market or in a substantial part of it, in particular as a result of the creation or strengthening of a dominant position, are declared incompatible with the common market and may not be put into effect.[903]

Hague, 1996), 511 pp.; Broberg, *The European Commission's Jurisdiction to Scrutinise Mergers* (Kluwer Law International, The Hague, 1998), 394 pp.

[901] For the notifications, time limits and hearings of parties concerned and third parties, see Commission Regulation (EC) No. 802/2004 of April 7, 2004 implementing Council Regulation (EC) No. 139/2004 on the control of concentrations between undertakings, [2004] O.J. L133/1.

[902] See CFI, Case T–102/96 *Gencor v Commission* [1999] E.C.R. II–753, paras 78–88 (concerning the same thresholds in Regulation No. 4064/89). Under international law, it must be foreseeable that a proposed concentration will have an immediate and substantial effect in the Community: *ibid.*, paras 90–101. See in this regard Slot (2001) C.M.L.R. 1573–1586.

[903] Regulation No. 139/2004, Art. 2(3) and Art. 8(3). Under Regulation No. 4064/89, only concentrations which created or strengthened a dominant position were incompatible with the common market. For the control criteria, see CFI, Case T–3/93 *Air France v Commission* [1994] E.C.R. II–121, paras 87–108 (in connection with the Community dimension); CFI, Case T–2/93 *Air France v Commission* [1994] E.C.R. II–323, paras 54–72 (as regards the type of concentration) and paras 78–87 (the relevant market); CFI, Case T–342/99 *Airtours v Commission* [2002] E.C.R. II–2585, paras 19–20 and 26 (relevant market). See also the Commission's Guidelines on the assessment of horizontal mergers under the Council Regulation on the control of concentrations between undertakings ([2004] O.J. C31/5) and the Commission notices on the concepts "full-time joint ventures" ([1998] O.J. C66/1), "concentration" ([1998] O.J. C66/5), "undertakings concerned" ([1998] O.J. C66/14), calculation of turnover under Regulation No. 4064/89 ([1998] O.J. C66/25), acceptable remedies ([2001] O.J. C68/3) and on restrictions directly related and necessary to concentrations ([2001] O.J. C188/5). As regards the substantive control which the Commission has to carry out in relation to concentrations, see ECJ, Joined Cases C–68/94 and C–30/95 *France and Others v Commission* [1998] E.C.R. I–1375, paras 90–250; CFI, Case T–5/02 *Tetra Laval v Commission* [2002] E.C.R. II–4381, paras 119–338 (against which an appeal has been lodged: Case C–12/03 P, [2003] O.J. C70/7); see also Bailey, "Standard of Proof in EC Merger Proceedings: A Common Law Perspective" (2003) C.M.L.R. 845–888. For the application of the principle of proportionality, see n.152 to para. 5–037.

d. Public undertakings and services of general interest

Public undertakings. Under Community competition law, Member States **5–201** may establish or operate public undertakings, namely publicly-owned undertakings or undertakings to which the State grants special or exclusive rights.[904]

According to Art. 86(1) of the EC Treaty, public undertakings have to comply with the rules of the Treaty, including the principle of equality and the competition rules.[905] The establishment or operation of public undertakings carrying out economic activities will therefore be incompatible with the Treaty where the undertakings have exclusive rights such that their exercise must be regarded as the abuse of a dominant position and that abuse is liable to affect trade between Member States.[906] Accordingly, the Court of Justice has held that Art. 86(1) is infringed by a Member State which grants a monopoly to public placement offices where those offices are unable to satisfy demand on the employment market, placement of employees by private companies is rendered impossible and the placement activities in question could extend to the nationals or the territory of other Member States.[907] The creation of a dominant position through the grant of an exclusive right within the meaning of Art. 86(1) is not as such incompatible with Art. 82 of the EC Treaty.[908] A Member State is in breach of the prohibitions set out in those two provisions only if the undertaking in question, merely by exercising the exclusive right granted to it, cannot avoid abusing its dominant position[909] or where the grant of exclusive rights is liable to create a situation in which the undertaking concerned is led to infringe Art. 82 of the EC Treaty.[910] An exclusive right which restricts the freedom of establishment of nationals of another Member State will be contrary to Arts 43 and 86 of the EC Treaty where that restriction is not

---

[904] For a survey of the status of public undertakings, see Weiss, "Öffentliche Unternehmen und EGV" (2003) EuR. 165–190; Buendía Sierra, *Exclusive rights and state monopolies under EC law* (Clarendon, Oxford, 1999), 458 pp.; Blum and Logue, *State Monopolies under EC Law* (Wiley, Chichester, 1998), 402 pp.; Burgi, "Die öffentlichen Unternehmen im Gefüge des primären Gemeinschaftsrechts" (1997) EuR. 261–290; Stuyck and Vossestein (eds), *State Entrepreneurship, National Monopolies and European Competition Law* (Kluwer Law and Taxation, Deventer, 1993), 129 pp.

[905] Art. 86(1) refers to Art. 12 of the EC Treaty.

[906] An undertaking with a statutory monopoly may be regarded as occupying a dominant position within the meaning of Art. 82 of the EC Treaty and the territory of the Member State covered by that monopoly may constitute a substantial part of the common market: ECJ, Case 311/84 *CBEM* [1985] E.C.R. 3261, para. 16.

[907] ECJ, Case C–55/96 *Job Centre* [1997] E.C.R. I–7119, para. 38.

[908] ECJ, Case 311/84 *CBEM* [1985] E.C.R. 3261, para. 17.

[909] ECJ, Case C–41/90 *Höfner and Elser* [1991] E.C.R. I–1979, para. 29.

[910] ECJ, Case C–260/89 *ERT* [1991] E.C.R. I–2925, paras 37–38; see also ECJ, Case C–320/91 *Corbeau* [1993] E.C.R. I–2533, paras 9–12, and the case note by Hancher in (1994) C.M.L.R. 105–122. For the determination of abuse and adverse effects on trade between Member States, see also ECJ, Case C–179/90 *Merci convenzionali porto di Genova* [1991] E.C.R. I–5889, paras 14–22; ECJ, Case C–18/88 *GB-INNO-BM* [1991] E.C.R. 5941, paras 17–27; ECJ, Case C–163/96 *Raso* [1998] E.C.R. I–533, paras 25–33.

appropriate and necessary to satisfy requirements of overriding public interest.[911]

Derogations from the rules on free trade and competition are possible only on the basis of the exceptions provided for in Art. 86(2) of the EC Treaty for undertakings entrusted with the operation of services of general economic interest or having the character of a revenue-producing monopoly.[912] Examples arise in the fields of transport, (tele)communications, postal services, energy and other utilities. The exceptions apply in so far as the application of the Treaty rules would obstruct the performance, in law or in fact, of the particular tasks assigned to the undertakings in question[913] and to the extent that the development of trade is not affected contrary to the interests of the Community.[914] The national court has to determine whether the conduct of a public undertaking contrary to Treaty provisions may be justified under Art. 86(2) of the EC Treaty.[915] Consequently, the provisions of Art. 86(1) and (2) have direct effect.

The Treaty of Amsterdam has emphasised the role played by services of general interest, yet without associating this with any limitation to the application of the competition rules. Thus, Art. 16 of the EC Treaty declares that the Community and the Member States are to take care that such services operate on the basis of principles and conditions which enable them to fulfil their missions "[w]ithout prejudice to Arts 73, 86 and 87", "given the place occupied by services of general economic interest in the shared values of the Union as well as their role in promoting social and territorial cohesion".[916] As far as the public service remit of broadcasting

---

[911] CFI, Case T–266/97 *VTM v Commission* [1999] E.C.R. II–2329, paras 105–123.

[912] ECJ, Case 155/73 *Sacchi* [1974] E.C.R. 409, para. 13 (derogation from the competition rules); ECJ, Case C–157/94 *Commission v Netherlands* [1997] E.C.R. I–5699, para. 32; ECJ, Case C–158/94 *Commission v Italy* [1997] E.C.R. I–5789, para. 43; ECJ, Case C–159/94 *Commission v France* [1997] E.C.R. I–5815, para. 49 (derogation from Art. 31). See Kovar, "Droit communautaire et service public: esprit d'orthodoxie ou pensée laïcisée" (1996) R.T.D.E. 215–242 and 493–533.

[913] ECJ, Case C–320/91 *Corbeau* [1993] E.C.R. I–2533, paras 13–20; ECJ, Case C–340/99 *TNT Traco* [2001] E.C.R. I–4109, paras 54–58; ECJ, Case C–475/99 *Firma Ambulanz Glöckner* [2001] E.C.R. I–8089, paras 55–56.

[914] For a discussion of this exception and its relationship with grounds justifying restrictions on free movement, see Wachsmann and Berrod, "Les critères de justification des monopoles: un premier bilan après l'affaire *Corbeau*" (1994) R.T.D.E. 39–61.

[915] ECJ, Case 66/86 *Ahmed Saeed Flugreisen* [1989] E.C.R. 803, paras 53–56; ECJ, Case C–260/89 *ERT* [1991] E.C.R. I–2925, para. 34.

[916] Art. 73 is concerned with State aid in respect of transport, Art. 87 with State aid generally (see also paras 5–203 *et seq.*). For commentaries on Art. 16 and services of general interest, see Schwintowski, "The common good, public subsistence and the functions of public undertakings in the European internal market" (2003) E.Bus.Org.L.R. 353–382 ; Rojanski, "L'Union européenne et les services d'intérêt général" (2002) R.D.U.E. 735–773; Frenz, "Dienste von allgemeinem wirtschaftlichen Interesse" (2000) EuR. 901–925; Rodrigues, "Les services publics et le traité d'Amsterdam. Genèse et portée juridique du projet de nouvel article 16 du traité CE" (1998) R.M.C.U.E. 37–46. It should be noted in this connection that Declaration (No.13) annexed to the Treaty of Amsterdam confirms that

organisations is concerned, a protocol to the EC Treaty confirms that the Member States have competence to provide for the public funding of public service broadcasting.[917] The EU Constitution will provide the Union with a legal basis to define common principles and conditions within whose limits services of general economic interest must fulfil their missions.[918]

Liberalisation. Article 86(3) of the EC Treaty empowers the Commission **5–202** to address directives or decisions to the Member States. As a result, the Commission may act individually by decision against public undertakings and Member States (alongside its supervisory powers under Art. 226 of the EC Treaty),[919] but may also issue general rules specifying the Member States' Treaty obligations by directives.[920] On this basis the Commission has adopted directives for the liberalisation of sectors of the economy which in most Member States were the province of publicly-owned corporations or monopoly undertakings, such as telecommunications and energy.[921] In parallel with these liberalisation measures, the Council has adopted

---

Art. 16 is to be implemented with full respect for the jurisprudence of the Court of Justice, *inter alia* as regards the principles of equality of treatment, quality and continuity of public services ([1997] O.J. C340/133). Declaration (No.37) to the Treaty of Amsterdam is concerned with services of general economic interest provided by public credit institutions existing in Germany ([1997] O.J. C340/138). See also the Communication from the Commission, "Services of general interest in Europe", [2001] O.J. C17/4.

[917] Protocol (No.32) annexed to the EC Treaty on the system of public broadcasting in the Member States, [1997] O.J. C340/109. See also the Resolution of the Council and of the representatives of the Governments of the Member States, meeting within the Council, of January 25, 1999 concerning public service broadcasting, [1999] O.J. C30/1.

[918] EU Constitution, Art. III–122, which otherwise reproduces the wording of Art. 16 of the EC Treaty, while adding that any European law will be "without prejudice to the competence of the Member States, in compliance with the Constitution, to provide, to commission and to fund such services". See Rodrigues, "Vers une loi européenne des services publics. De brèves considérations et une proposition à propos de l'article III–6 du projet de traité établissant une Constitution pour l'Europe" (2003) R.M.C.U.E. 503–512.

[919] ECJ, Joined Cases C–48/90 and C–66/90 *Netherlands v Commission* [1992] E.C.R. I–565, paras 27–37. See also Lenaerts and Arts, *Procedural Law of the European Union*, Ch.5.

[920] For the Commission's discretion, see CFI, Case T–32/93 *Ladbroke Racing v Commission* [1994] E.C.R. II–1015, paras 36, 37 and 38 and 44; for the first application of Art. 86(3) of the EC Treaty, see Commission Directive 80/723 of June 25, 1980 on the transparency of financial relations between Member States and public undertakings, [1980] O.J. L195/35.

[921] See Directive 88/301/EEC of May 16, 1988 on competition in the markets in telecommunications terminal equipment ([1988] O.J. L131/73) and Directive 90/388/EEC of June 28, 1990 on competition in the markets for telecommunications services ([1990] O.J. L192/10), since replaced by Directive 2002/77/EEC of September 16, 2002 on competition in the markets for electronic communications networks and services, [2002] O.J. L249/21. The Commission's competence was confirmed by the Court of Justice following actions for annulment brought by Member States: ECJ, Joined Cases 188–190/80 *France, Italy and UK v Commission* [1982] E.C.R. 2545 (Directive 80/723/EEC); ECJ, Case C–202/88 *France v Commission* [1991] E.C.R. I–1223, para. 14 (Directive 88/301/EEC); ECJ, Joined Cases C–271/90, C–281/90 and C–289/90 *Spain v Commission* [1992] E.C.R. I–5833 (Directive 90/388/EEC). As regards the Commission's competence, see Hocepied, "Les directives article 90, paragraphe 3: une espèce juridique en voie de disparition?" (1994) 2 R.A.E. 49–63. For the energy sector, see Fiquet, "Vers une réconciliation entre l'Europe et les services publics: l'exemple de l'électricité" and Lombart, "Le service public du gaz sous les feux de l'actualité juridique" (1998) A.J.D.A. 864–872 and 873–883, respectively.

harmonisation directives pursuant to Art. 95 of the EC Treaty, which especially emphasise opening up non-discriminatory access to infrastructure, for instance in telecommunications.[922]

2. State aid

5–203 Prohibited aid. Free competition in the common market requires a prohibition in principle of aid funded out of the public purse which distorts or threatens to distort competition by favouring certain undertakings or the production of certain goods and adversely affects trade between Member States (EC Treaty, Art. 87(1)).[923] By way of exception the Treaty lists three types of aid which are, by operation of law, compatible with the common market (EC Treaty, Art. 87(2)) and refers to other types of aid measures which *may* be compatible with the common market[924] (Art. 87(3)). Even where aid is compatible with the common market, it may not be "misused" (EC Treaty, Art. 88(2)).

The prohibition of aid covers not only positive benefits, such as subsidies, loans and public shareholdings, but also interventions which, in various forms, mitigate the charges which are normally included in the budget of an undertaking and which, without therefore being subsidies in the strict

---

[922] See, for example, the directives of the European Parliament and of the Council of March 7, 2002 on a common regulatory framework for electronic communications networks and services: Framework Directive 2002/21/EC and Directive 2002/19/EC (access), Directive 2002/20 (authorisation) and Directive 2002/22 (universal service), [2002] O.J. L108/7, 21 and 51, respectively. For "open network provision" or OPN, see, *inter alia*, Council Directive 90/387/EEC of June 28, 1990, ([1990] O.J. L192/1). See Bavasso, "Electronic Communications: A New Paradigm for European Regulation" (2004) C.M.L.R. 87–118; De Streil, Queck and Vernet, "Le *nouveau cadre réglementaire européen des réseaux et services de communications électroniques*" (2002) C.D.E. 243–341; Franzius, "Strukturmodelle des europäischen Telekommuikationsrechts" (2002) EuR. 660–690; Garzaniti, *Telecommunications, Broadcasting and the Internet: EU Competition Law and Regulation* (Sweet & Maxwell, London, 2000), 365 pp.; for universal service, see Karayannis, "Le service universel de télécommunications en droit communautaire: entre intervention publique et concurrence" (2002) C.D.E. 315–375. For the relationship between liberalisation of the markets and the privatisation carried out by the Member States, see Edward and Hoskins, "Art. 90: Deregulation and EC Law. Reflections arising from the XVI Fide Conference" (1995) C.M.L.R. 157–186; Verhoeven, "Privatisation and EC Law: Is the European Commission 'neutral' with respect to Public versus Private Ownership of Companies?" (1996) I.C.L.Q. 861–887.

[923] For further particulars, see Quigley and Collins, *EC State Aid Law and Policy* (Hart, Oxford, 2003), 381 pp.; Hancher, Ottervanger and Slot, *EC State Aids* (Sweet & Maxwell, London, 1999), 669 pp.; Keppenne, *Guide des aides d'Etat en droit communautaire. Réglementation, jurisprudence et pratique de la Commission* (Bruylant, Brussels, 1999), 693 pp; Evans, *EC Law of State Aid* (Clarendon Press, Oxford, 1997), 484 pp. With regard to the definition of State aid, see, for instance, Ross, "State Aids and National Courts: Definitions and Other Problems—A Case of Premature Emancipation?" (2000) C.M.L.R. 401–423; Bacon, "The Concept of State Aid: The Developing Jurisprudence in the European and UK Courts" (2003) E.Comp.L.Rev. 54–61.

[924] This list may be supplemented by the Council acting by a qualified majority vote on a proposal from the Commission (EC Treaty, Art. 87(3)(e)).

meaning of the word, are similar in character and have the same effect.[925] Where the public authorities intervene, as shareholders, creditors or contractors *vis-à-vis* an undertaking, that public intervention will constitute State aid only where in similar circumstances a private shareholder, creditor or contractor, would not have so intervened.[926] Compensation for services performed by an undertaking in discharging public-service obligations does not constitute aid within the meaning of Art. 87.[927] In any event, an economic benefit for an undertaking is in the nature of aid only if it can be imputed to the State and is directly or indirectly paid out of public funds.[928] Moreover, a general measure must not be involved, but a benefit which, by displaying a degree of selectivity, is such as to favour "certain undertakings or the production of certain goods".[929] According to the Court of Justice, a measure results in a distortion of competition or threatens to distort competition as soon as it enables an undertaking to reduce its costs and therefore strengthens its competitive position compared with other undertakings.[930] Intra-Community trade is regarded as being affected by aid which strengthens the position of an undertaking compared with other undertakings competing in intra-Community trade.[931]

---

[925] ECJ, Case 30/59 *De Gezamenlijke Steenkolenmijnen in Limburg v High Authority* [1961] E.C.R. 1, at 40; ECJ, Case C–387/92 *Banco Exterior de Espana* [1994] E.C.R. I–877, para. 13; ECJ, Case C–39/94 *SFEI* [1996] E.C.R. I–3547, paras 57–62.

[926] ECJ, Case 234/84 *Commission v Belgium* [1986] E.C.R. 2263, para. 14, and ECJ, Case 40/85 *Commission v Belgium* [1986] E.C.R. 2321, para. 13. See Karydis, "Le principe de l'opérateur économique privé', critère de qualification des mesures étatiques, en tant qu'aides d'Etat, au sens de l'article 87 para. 1 du traité CE" (2003) R.T.D.E. 389–413.

[927] ECJ, Case 53/00 *Ferring* [2001] E.C.R. I–9067, para. 27; ECJ, Case C–280/00 *Altmark Trans and Regierungspräsident Magdeburg* [2003] E.C.R. I–7747, para. 87. The following conditions apply: (1) the recipient undertaking must actually have clearly defined public service obligations to discharge; (2) the parameters on the basis of which the compensation is calculated must be established in advance in an objective and transparent manner; (3) the compensation cannot exceed what is necessary to cover all or part of the costs incurred in the discharge of public service obligations, taking into account the relevant receipts and a reasonable profit for discharging those obligations; and (4) where the undertaking which is to discharge public service obligations, in a specific case, is not chosen pursuant to a public procurement procedure which would allow for the selection of the tenderer capable of providing those services at the least cost to the community, the level of compensation needed must be determined on the basis of an analysis of the costs which a typical undertaking, well run, would have incurred in discharging those obligations, taking into account the relevant receipts and a reasonable profit for discharging the obligations: *Altmark Trans and Regierungspräsident Magdeburg*, paras 88–94. See Louis and Vallery (2004) World Comp. 53–74; Nicolaides (2003) E.Comp.L.Rev. 561–573; Leibenath (2003) EuR. 1052–1066; Drijber and Sanen-Siebenga (2003) N.T.E.R. 253–258; Thouvenin and Lorieux (2003) R.M.C.U.E. 633–641; Bracq (2004) R.T.D.E. 33–70.

[928] See, in particular, ECJ, Case C–482/99 *France v Commission* [2002] E.C.R. I–4397, paras 21–59; ECJ, Case C–317/98 *PreussenElektra* [2001] E.C.R. I–2099, paras 57–66.

[929] *e.g.* ECJ, Case C–241/94 *France v Commission* [1996] E.C.R. I–4551, paras 22–40; ECJ, Case C–143/99 *Adria-Wien Pipeline and Wietersdorfer & Peggauer Zementwerke* [2001] E.C.R. I–8357, para. 34.

[930] ECJ, Case 730/79 *Philip Morris v Commission* [1980] E.C.R. 2671, para. 11; ECJ, Case 259/85 *France v Commission* [1987] E.C.R. I–4393, para. 24.

[931] ECJ, Case 730/79 *Philip Morris v Commission* [1980] E.C.R. 2671, para. 11; CFI, Case T–214/95 *Vlaams Gewest v Commission* [1998] E.C.R. I–717, para. 50.

Pursuant to Art. 89 of the EC Treaty, the Council has empowered the Commission to grant exemptions for certain categories of aid.[932]

5–204 Centralised supervision. All State aid which falls within the prohibition set out in Art. 87(1) of the EC Treaty is subject to the supervision of the Commission in accordance with the procedure codified in Regulation No. 659/1999.[933] It is for the Commission alone to determine whether an aid measure is compatible with the common market, subject to review by the Court of Justice and the Court of First Instance.[934] The Commission has indicated in a number of communications the conditions under which it regards aid for particular regions or activities as being compatible with the common market.[935] A national court may rule on whether or not action by a public authority constitutes State aid, but has no jurisdiction to rule on whether an aid measure is compatible or incompatible with the common market.[936]

---

[932] Council Regulation (EC) No. 994/98 of May 7, 1998 on the application of Arts 92 and 93 [now Arts 87 and 88] of the Treaty establishing the European Community to certain categories of horizontal State aid, [1998] O.J. L142/1, implemented by the Commission through Regulation (EC) No. 68/2001 of January 12, 2001, [2001] O.J. L10/20 (training aid), Regulation (EC) No. 70/2001 of January 12, 2001, [2001] O.J. L10/33 (aid to SMEs outside the agricultural sector), Regulation (EC) No. 2204/2002 of December 12, 2002, [2002] O.J. L337/3 (aid for employment—corrigendum in [2002] O.J. L349/126), Regulation (EC) No. 1/2004 of December 23, 2003, [2004] O.J. L1/1 (aid to SMEs in the agricultural sector) and Regulation (EC) No. 1595/2004 of September 8, 2004, [2004] O.J. L291/3 (aid to SMEs in the fisheries sector). Moreover, pursuant to Regulation No. 994/98, the Commission has declared that aid not exceeding a ceiling of €100,000 over any period of three years does not affect trade between Member States and/or does not distort competition: Regulation (EC) No. 69/2001 of January 12, 2001 on the application of Arts 87 and 88 of the EC Treaty to *de minimis* aid ([2001] O.J. L10/30). See Sinnaeve, "Block Exemptions for State Aid: More Scope for State Aid Control by Member States and Competitors" (2001) C.M.L.R. 1479—1501 and "Die ersten Gruppenfreistellungen: Dezentralisierung der Beihilfenkontrolle?" (2001) Eu.Z.W. 69—77; Bartosch, "Die neuen Gruppenfreistellungensverordnungen im EG-Beihilfenrecht" (2001) N.J.W. 921–927.

[933] Council Regulation (EC) No. 659/1999 of March 22, 1999 laying down detailed rules for the application of Art. 93 [now Art. 88] of the EC Treaty, [1999] O.J. L83/1. See Sinnaeve and Slot, "The New Regulation on State Aid Procedures" (1999) C.M.L.R. 1153–1194; Rivas Andrés and Gutiérrez Gisbert, "Un comentario crítico al Reglamento procedimental en materia de ayudas de Estado" (2000) G.J. 40–58.

[934] ECJ, Case 78/76 *Steinike und Weinlig* [1977] E.C.R. 595, para. 9. The Commission has a broad discretion and this limits, but does not eliminate, the scope for judicial review, see CFI, Joined Cases T–471/94 and T–494/94 *British Airways v Commission* [1998] E.C.R. II–2405.

[935] For the Commission's communications and guidelines, in particular for aid for regional development, employment, research and development, protection of the environment, rescue and restructuring of firms in difficulty, see the link "State aid" on the website of the Commission's DG Competition (*www.europa.eu.int/comm/competition/index—en.html*).

[936] ECJ, Case 78/76*Steinike & Weinlig v Germany* [1977] E.C.R. 595, paras 10–15; ECJ, Case C–44/93 *Namur-Les Assurances du Crédit* [1994] E.C.R. I–3829, para. 17, at I–3871. For the distribution of tasks as between the national courts and the Commission, see Struys and Abbott, "The role of national courts in State aid litigation" (2003) E.L.Rev. 172–189.

Procedure. For the purposes of the Commission's supervision of State aid, **5–205** the rules differ depending on whether existing aid or aid which Member States wish to introduce or to alter is concerned.[937]

Existing systems of aid are kept under constant review by the Commission. In this connection, the Commission is to propose any appropriate measures required by the progressive development or the functioning of the common market (EC Treaty, Art. 88(1)). If the Member State concerned does not accept the proposed modification, the Commission initiates the formal *inter partes* investigation procedure (by notice published in the *Official Journal*) which culminates in a decision by which the Commission determines either that the measure—subject, where appropriate, to certain conditions—is not aid or is compatible with the common market or that the measure is incompatible with the common market.[938] If the Commission finds that an existing aid is incompatible with the common market having regard to Art. 87 or that such aid is being misused, it is to decide that the Member State concerned must abolish or alter the aid within such time as the Commission shall determine (EC Treaty, Art. 88(2), first subpara.). An action may be brought directly before the Court of Justice, by way of derogation from Arts 226 and 227, by the Commission or any interested Member State against a Member State in breach of that obligation (EC Treaty, Art. 88(2), second subpara.).

There is a procedure for new aid without which no aid may be regarded as lawful. Any plans to grant or alter aid must be notified to the Commission in time for it to submit its comments (EC Treaty, Art. 88(3)).[939] If, after an initial examination, the Commission should find that the notified measure is not aid or that no doubts are raised as to its compatibility with the common market, it adopts a decision to that effect.[940] If, in contrast, the Commission should consider that the measure notified raises doubts as to its compatibility with the common market, it must initiate without delay the *inter partes* procedure provided for by Art. 88(2).[941] If it does so, the Member State concerned is debarred under the last sentence of Art. 88(3) from putting its proposed measure into effect until the procedure has resulted in a final decision by which the

---

[937] As far as the States which acceded on May 1, 2004 are concerned, "existing aid" on accession is defined in Annex IV to the 2003 Act of Accession pursuant to Art. 22 of that Act ([2003] O.J. L236/797).

[938] Regulation No. 659/1999 (para. 5–204, *supra*), Art. 7 in conjunction with Art. 19(2).

[939] The obligation to notify the Commission does not apply to categories of aid which the Commission has declared to be compatible with the common market pursuant to Regulation No. 994/98; n.932, *supra*. Compulsory notification forms have been laid down in Commission Regulation (EC) No. 794/2004 of April 21, 2004 implementing Council Regulation No. 659/1999, [2004] O.J. L140/1.

[940] Regulation No. 659/1999 (para. 5–204, *supra*), Art. 4(2) and (3).

[941] EC Treaty, Art. 88(3) and Regulation No. 659/1999, Art. 4(4). For that obligation, see, for instance, ECJ, Case C–294/90 *British Aerospace and Rover v Commission* [1992] E.C.R. I–493, paras 10–15; ECJ, Case C–225/91 *Matra v Commission* [1993] E.C.R. I–3203, para. 33.

Commission finds that the measure is not aid or is compatible with the common market. If the Commission determines in its final decision that the measure is aid incompatible with the common market, the measure may not be put into effect.[942] Pending a final decision, a proposed aid measure may be implemented only if the Commission, after being informed of it, fails to carry out the examination involving interested parties and sufficient time has elapsed for the preliminary examination, provided that the Member State gives the Commission prior notice—after which the aid measure comes under the rules relating to existing aid.[943]

Since the last sentence of Art. 88(3) has direct effect,[944] the national courts are empowered to determine whether a measure which has not been notified to the Commission nevertheless has to be regarded as a new aid measure which, in the absence of notification, must be considered to infringe Community law (even if it subsequently transpires that the aid is compatible with the common market).[945] If the national court entertains doubts about the categorisation of the measure at issue it may seek clarification from the Commission or request the Court of Justice for a preliminary ruling on the interpretation of Art. 87 of the EC Treaty.[946]

Under the third subpara. of Art. 88(2) of the EC Treaty, a Member State may apply to the Council, which may declare existing or proposed aid compatible with the common market by a unanimous vote "if such a decision is justified by exceptional circumstances".[947] If the Commission has initiated the *inter partes* procedure, the fact that the State concerned has made its application to the Council will have the effect of suspending that procedure for a period of three months (EC Treaty, Art. 88(2), third and fourth subpara.). Where that period has expired, the Council is no longer competent to adopt a decision in relation to the aid concerned. If the

---

[942] Regulation No. 659/1999, Art. 7(5).

[943] ECJ, Case 120/73 *Lorenz* [1973] E.C.R. 1471, para. 4. For this first investigation, which the Commission has two months to carry out, see ECJ, Case C–99/98 *Austria v Commission* [2001] E.C.R. I–1101, paras 34–37.

[944] ECJ, Case 6/64 *Costa* [1964] E.C.R. 585, at 596.

[945] ECJ, Case 78/76 *Steinike und Weinlig* [1977] E.C.R. 595, para. 14; ECJ, Case C–44/93 *Namur-Les Assurances du Crédit* [1994] E.C.R. I–3829, para. 16; ECJ, Case C–295/97 *Industrie Aeronautique e Meccaniche Rinaldo Piaggio* [1999] E.C.R. I–3735, paras 44–50. By the same token, a national court may consider whether a (non-notified) aid falls within the categories of aid measures which are exempted by the Commission. If the measure does not satisfy the requirements for exemption, the national court may only find in an appropriate case that the duty to notify has been infringed; it cannot itself rule on the compatibility of the aid with the common market.

[946] ECJ, Case C–39/94 *SFEI* [1996] E.C.R. I–3547, paras 50–51. If the national court considers it necessary in order to safeguard the interests of the parties, it may order interim relief, such as suspension of the measures at issue (*ibid.*, para. 52), or order non-notified aid which has already been disbursed to be repaid (*ibid.*, para. 70).

[947] For the broad discretion of the Council in this connection, see ECJ, Case C–122/94 *Commission v Council* [1996] E.C.R. I–881, paras 7–25. See, *e.g.* Council Decisions 2002/361/EC, 2002/362/EC and 2002/363/EC of May 3, 2002 on the granting of a national aid in favour of road transport undertakings by the authorities of the Netherlands, Italy and France, respectively, [2002] O.J. L131/12, 14 and 15.

Member State concerned has made no application to the Council before the Commission declares the aid in question incompatible with the common market and thereby closes the *inter partes* procedure, the Council is no longer authorised to declare such aid compatible with the common market.[948]

Repayment of unlawfully granted aid. The Commission can require **5–206** unlawfully granted aid to be repaid; the procedures for recovering it are left to national law.[949] An undertaking to which aid has been granted cannot resist the recovery of aid by claiming that it had a legitimate expectation that it was lawful if the procedure laid down in Art. 88 was not complied with when the aid was granted.[950]

A Member State and an undertaking in receipt of the aid are entitled to challenge a Commission decision on aid measures in proceedings before the Court of Justice or the Court of First Instance, respectively (EC Treaty, Art. 230).[951] Once the time-limit laid down has expired, the validity of the decision may no longer be called in question by the Member State concerned (*e.g.* in infringement proceedings before the Court of Justice under the second subpara. of Art. 88(2)).[952] Nor may it be challenged in the national court by the recipient of the aid who has been notified of the decision by the Member State (*e.g.* after steps have been taken to recover the unlawful aid).[953]

F HARMONISATION OF NATIONAL LEGISLATION

Legal bases for harmonisation. Specific Treaty provisions empower the **5–207** Community to bring divergent national laws more in line with each other, even though they are completely compatible with Community law, where

---

[948] ECJ (judgment of June 29, 2004), Case C–110/02 *Commission v Council*, not yet reported, paras 28–36 (annulment of a decision by which the Council declared compatible with the common market an aid designed to compensate farmers for the repayment of unlawful aid which the Commission had previously declared incompatible with the common market).

[949] See Priess, "Recovery of Illegal State Aid: An Overview of Recent Developments in the Case Law" (1996) C.M.L.R. 69–91; Karpenschif, "La récupération des aides nationales versées en violation du droit communautaire à l'aune du règlement no 659/1999: du mythe à la réalité?" (2001) R.T.D.E. 551–596.

[950] ECJ, Case C–5/89 *Commission v Germany* [1990] E.C.R. I–3437, para. 14; ECJ, Case C–169/95 *Spain v Commission* [1997] E.C.R. I–135, paras 51–54; ECJ, Case C–24/95 *Alcan Deutschland* [1997] E.C.R. I–1591, paras 22–54. For defences of Member States and recipients of aid, see Montaldo and Medina Palomino, "Aides d'Etat et moyens de défense des entreprises" (1991) 4 R.M.C.U.E 11–48.

[951] ECJ, Case 730/79 *Philip Morris v Commission* [1980] E.C.R. 2671, para. 5. For other interested parties entitled to contest Commission decisions relating to State aid, see ECJ, Case C–367/95 P *Commission v Sytraval and Brink's France* [1998] E.C.R. I–1719, paras 33–49; Lenaerts and Arts, *Procedural Law of the European Union*, Ch.7; Winter, "The Rights of Complainants in State Aid Cases: Judicial Review of Commission Decisions Adopted under Art. 88 (ex 93) EC" (1999) C.M.L.R. 521–568.

[952] ECJ, Case 156/77 *Commission v Belgium* [1978] E.C.R. 1881, paras 21–24; ECJ, Case C–183/91 *Commission v Greece* [1993] E.C.R. I–3131, para. 10.

[953] ECJ, Case C–188/92 *TWD Textilwerke Deggendorf* [1994] E.C.R. I–833, paras 17–26.

the disparities between the legislation result in market participants being placed in differing positions from the point of view of competition.[954] Thus, the Treaty supplements the provisions on free movement of goods, persons, services and capital by providing a legal basis for harmonisation, co-ordination, approximation and mutual recognition of national legislation or administrative provisions.[955] In some cases, harmonisation of national legislation is necessary where the Community intends to pursue a policy of its own.[956] In addition, Arts 94–97 of the EC Treaty afford general bases for powers for "approximation of legislation", together with the supplementary legal basis of Art. 308 of that Treaty[957] and the additional power of Member States to conclude agreements between themselves (see EC Treaty, Art. 293[958]). The proposed EU Constitution preserves these general bases for harmonisation (except for the power of the Member States to conclude agreements between themselves), whilst enlarging their scope somewhat (see para. 5–213).

1. The impact of Community harmonisation measures

5–208 Expanding Community law. As a result of the harmonisation of national legislation, Community law penetrates into areas which do not form a direct part of the Community's competence.[959] Thus the Member States had to adapt their administrative rules to suit directives co-ordinating national procedures for the award of public works contracts[960] and the

---

[954] Slot, "Harmonisation" (1996) E.L.Rev. 378–397; Vignes, "Le rapprochement des législations", in Calleja, Vignes and Wägenbaur, *Commentaire Mégret. Le droit de la CEE. 5. Dispositions fiscales. Rapprochement des législations* (Editions de l'Université de Bruxelles, Brussels, 1993), at 299–379; for the political implications, see Dougan, "Minimum harmonisation and the internal market" (2000) C.M.L.R. 853–885.

[955] With regard to the free movement of goods, see Art. 83 (indirect taxation); as regards free movement of persons and services, see Arts 40 and 42, Art. 44, in particular para. 2(g), and Arts 46, 47 and 52. For the free movement of capital, see the former Art. 70 of the EC Treaty.

[956] See Arts 34 and 35 of the EC Treaty relating to agriculture; Art. 71 relating to transport; Art. 99 for the co-ordination of Community economic policy and Art. 109 on preparation for the common monetary policy; Art. 132 as regards the common commercial policy; Art. 137 as regards social policy.

[957] paras 5–018—5–019, *supra*.

[958] For agreements concluded on the basis of Art. 293 and other agreements concluded between the Member States, see para. 15–016, *infra* (non-Community decision-making) and para. 18–008, *infra* (legal force).

[959] See Usher, "Maastricht and English Law" (1993) Stat.L.Rev. 27, at 35–39.

[960] See, most recently, Directive 2004/18/EC of the European Parliament and of the Council of March 31, 2004 on the co-ordination of procedures for the award of public works contracts, public supply contracts and public service contracts ([2004] O.J. L134/114), adopted pursuant to Arts 47(2), 55 and 95 of the EC Treaty and replacing previous Council Directives on public works contracts (93/37/EEC of June 14, 1993, [1993] O.J. L199/54), public supply contracts (93/36/EEC of June 14, 1993, [1993] O.J. L199/1) and public service contracts (92/50/EEC of June 18, 1992, [1992] O.J. L209/1). See Wainwright, "Marchés publics—refonte des directives" (2001) R.M.C.U.E. 394–399; Mattera, "Vers un Code européen des marchés publics" (2000) R.D.U.E. 523–570. Since the water, energy, transport and telecommunications sectors do not invariably come under public law, the Council

relevant review procedures[961] in order to guarantee free movement of goods, persons and services in connection with the award of public contracts.[962] In addition, the Community has adopted rules for the co-ordination of national law on intellectual property[963] and—acting on the basis of Art. 308 of the EC Treaty—has introduced Community intellectual property rights.[964] Also there was harmonisation in the field of

adopted specific directives relating to them; see, most recently, Directive 2004/17/EC of the European Parliament and Council of March 31, 2004 co-ordinating the procurement procedures of entities operating in the water, energy, transport and postal services sectors ([2004] O.J. L134/1). Purchasing by the telecommunications sector is no longer covered in view of the liberalisation of this sector and the resultant opening to competition (see recital 5 in the preamble to Directive 2004/17).

[961] See the Council directives adopted pursuant to Art. 100a [now Art. 95] of the EC Treaty: Directive 89/665/EEC of December 21, 1989 on the application of review procedures to the award of public supply and public works contracts, [1989] O.J. L395/33, and, specifically as regards the sectors referred to in n.960, *supra* Directive 92/13/EEC of February 25, 1992 on the application of Community rules on procurement procedures, [1992] O.J. L76/14.

[962] Bovis, "Recent Case Law Relating to Public Procurement: A Beacon for the Integration of Public Markets" (2002) C.M.L.R. 1025–1056; Cassia, "Contrats publics et principe communautaire d'égalité de traitement" (2002) R.T.D.E. 413–449; Millett, "Les marchés publics en droit communautaire" (2001) R.M.C.U.E. 622–630; Mahler, "Europese aanbestedingen: een open deur?" (1997) S.E.W. 97–108. For the review procedures, see Boyenga-Bofala, "L'impact des directives-recours sur l'organisation des voies de droit internes et les modalités d'exercice par le juge administratif français de son office" (2002) R.T.D.E. 499–525. See also the Commission interpretative communications on concessions under Community law ([2000] O.J. C121/2) and on the possibilities for integrating environmental considerations and social considerations into public procurement ([2001] O.J. C333/12 and 17, respectively).

[963] Council Directive 87/54/EEC of December 16, 1986 on the legal protection of topographies of semiconductor products ([1987] O.J. L24/36); First Council Directive 89/104/EEC of December 21, 1988 to approximate the laws of the Member States relating to trade marks ([1989] O.J. L40/1); Council Directive 91/250/EEC of May 14, 1991 on the legal protection of computer programs ([1991] O.J. L122/42); Council Directive 92/100/EEC of November 19, 1992 on rental right and lending right and on certain rights related to copyright in the field of intellectual property ([1992] O.J. L346/61); Council Directive 93/83/EEC of September 27, 1993 on the co-ordination of certain rules concerning copyright and rights related to copyright applicable to satellite broadcasting and cable retransmission ([1993] O.J. L248/15); Council Directive 93/98 of October 29, 1993 harmonising the term of protection of copyright and certain related rights ([1993] O.J. L290/9); Directive 96/9/EC of the European Parliament and of the Council of March 11, 1996 on the legal protection of databases ([1996] O.J. L77/20); Directive 98/44/EC of the European Parliament and of the Council of July 6, 1998 on the legal protection of biotechnological inventions ([1998] O.J. L213/13); Directive 98/71/EC of the European Parliament and of the Council of October 13, 1998 on the legal protection of designs ([1998] O.J. L289/28); Directive 2001/29/EC of the European Parliament and of the Council of May 22, 2001 on the harmonisation of certain aspects of copyright and related rights in the information society ([2001] O.J. L167/10); Directive 2001/84/EC of the European Parliament and of the Council of September 27, 2001 on the resale right for the benefit of the author of an original work of art ([2001] O.J. L275/32).

[964] Council Directive 40/94/EC of December 20, 1993 on the Community trade mark ([1994] O.J. L11/1); Council Regulation (EC) No. 2100/94 of July 27, 1994 on Community plant variety rights ([1994] O.J. L227/1) and Council Regulation 6/2002 (EC) No. of December 12, 2001 on Community designs ([2002] O.J. L3/1). See also, pursuant to Art. 100a [now Art. 95] of the EC Treaty, Council Regulation (EEC) No. 1768/92 of June 18, 1992 concerning the creation of a supplementary protection certificate for medicinal products ([1992] O.J. L182/1) (for the Community's competence: ECJ, Case C–350/92 *Spain v Council* [1995] E.C.R. I–1985, paras 25–41); see further, pursuant to Art. 95, Regulation (EC) No. 1610/96

tourism.[965] As a result of its action to protect tourists and other consumers, in particular with regard to financial services (see paras 5–145 and 5–244), and its action with respect to cross-border collaboration in civil matters (see para. 5–150), the Community is becoming involved in increasing areas of private law, such as the law of contractual and non-contractual liability, procedural law and family law.[966]

In some cases, a harmonisation measure allows the Member States to adopt or maintain stricter rules in its national legislation than those required by the harmonisation itself. Where the harmonisation measure does not expressly so provide, it has to be inferred from the wording, purpose and structure of the measure to what extent complete harmonisation is intended or whether it leaves the Member States any margin to deviate from a requirement or a level of protection laid down by

---

of the European Parliament and of the Council of July 23, 1996 concerning the creation of a supplementary protection certificate for plant protection products ([1996] O.J. L198/30) and Directive 2004/48 of the European Parliament and of the Council on the enforcement of intellectual property rights ([2004] O.J. L157/45; republished with corrigendum: [2004] O.J. L195/16). See also the Commission's proposal for a Directive of the European Parliament and of the Council on the patentability of computer-implemented inventions (COM (2002) 92 final). For further particulars, see Prime, *European Intellectual Property Law* (Ashgate, Aldershot, 2000), 320 pp.

[965] Even before "tourism" was incorporated as one of the policy spheres listed in Art. 3 of the EC Treaty, the Council adopted on December 22, 1986 a Decision (86/664/EEC) establishing a consultation and co-operation procedure in the field of tourism ([1986] O.J. L384/52) and resolutions on standardised information in existing hotels (86/665/EEC, [1986] O.J. L384/54) and fire safety in existing hotels (86/666/EEC, [1986] O.J. L384/60). See also the most recent Community action plan to assist tourism, Council Decision 92/421/EEC of July 31, 1992 ([1992] O.J. L231/26).

[966] Communications from the Commission to the Council and the European Parliament on European contract law, [2001] O.J. C255/1, and on a more coherent European contract law—An action plan, [2003] O.J. C63/1; see von Bahr and Swann, "Response to the Action Plan on European Contract Law: A More Coherent European Contract Law" (2003) ERPL 595–622; Kenny, "The 2003 Action Plan on European Contract Law: Is the Commission Running Wild?" (2003) E.L.Rev. 538–550; Weatherill, "The Commission's Options for Developing EC Consumer Protection and Contract Law: Assessing the Constitutional Basis" (2002) E.Bus.L.Rev. 497–515 and "European Contract Law: Taking the Heat Out of Questions of Competence" (2004) E.Bus.L.Rev. 23–32. Discussion is under way on the utility of a wider ranging harmonisation of private law, see the commentaries in (2002) E.Bus.L.Rev. 491 *et seq.* and also Betlem and Hondius, "European Private Law after the Treaty of Amsterdam" (2001) E.Rev.Priv.L. 3–20; Basedow, "Codification of Private Law in the European Union: the making of a Hybrid" (2001) E.Rev.Priv.L. 35–49; Sturm, "Der Entwurf eines Europäisches Vertragsgesetzbuchs" (2001) J.Z. 1097–1102; Van Gerven, "A Common Law for Europe: The Future Meeting the Past?" (2001) E.Rev.Priv.L. 485–503 and "Codifying European private law? Yes, if . . .!" (2002) E.L.Rev. 156–176; Grundmann, "The Structure of European Contract Law" (2001) E.Rev.Priv.L. 505–528; Alpa, "The European Civil Code: 'E Pluribus Unum" (1999) Tulane E. & Civil L.F. 1–14; Racine, "Pourquoi unifier le droit des contrats en Europe? Plaidoyer en faveur de l'unification" (2003) R.D.U.E. 369–407. For a critical view of the effect of existing harmonisation measures, see Niglia, "The Non-Europeanisation of Private Law" (2001) E.Rev.Priv.L. 575–599. For the influence of the case-law of the Court of Justice on family law, see Caracciolo di Torello and Masselot, "Under construction: EU family law" (2004) E.L.Rev. 32–51.

the measure.[967] Because of the primacy of Community law, once legislation has been harmonised, it can no longer be amended or replaced by national rules. In policy areas where this influence on national law is not desired, the EC Treaty has expressly precluded any power to harmonise on the part of the Community.[968] In view of the political implications of harmonisation, disputes often arise with regard to the proper legal basis for the relevant Community legislation, with general legal bases or specific Treaty provisions being argued for, depending on the different voting procedures in the Council or the input of the European Parliament (see paras 5–013—5–014).

2. Harmonisation under Arts 94 and 95 of the EC Treaty

Harmonisation within the internal market. "Approximation of laws, **5–209** regulations and administrative provisions" of the Member States may be based on Art. 94 of the EC Treaty where they "directly affect the establishment or functioning of the common market" or on Art. 95(1) where they "have as their object the establishment and functioning of the internal market". The manner in which the decision is taken to effect such approximation of national legislation differs sharply: under Art. 94 of the EC Treaty, the Council is to act unanimously after consulting the European Parliament; under Art. 95, the Council and the European Parliament decide in accordance with the co-decision procedure (EC Treaty, Art. 251), which requires only a qualified majority in the Council. The legal instruments differ also: only directives may be issued under Art. 94, whereas Art. 95 authorises the adoption of any "measures". Although preference is to be given to directives under Art. 95,[969] the Council may impose harmonisation of national legislation also by regulation.[970] In addition, Art. 95—and not Art. 94—allows Member States to maintain or

---

[967] See, *e.g.* with regard to liability for defective products: ECJ, Case C–52/00 *Commission v France* [2002] E.C.R. I–3827, paras 13–24, ECJ, Case C–154/00 *Commission v Greece* [2002] E.C.R. I–3879, paras 9–20, and ECJ, Case C–183/00 *González Sanchez* [2002] E.C.R. I–3901, paras 23–34. For the differing intensity of harmonisation, see Kurcz, "Harmonisation by means of Directives—never-ending story?" (2001) E.Bus.L.Rev. 287–307; Rott, "Minimum Harmonisation for the Completion of the Internal Market? The Example of Consumer Sales Law" (2003) C.M.L.R. 1107–1135.

[968] See para. 5–013, *supra*.

[969] See the declaration annexed to the Single European Act that the Commission shall give preference to the use of the instrument of a directive in its proposals pursuant to Art. 95(1) if harmonisation involves the amendment of legislative provisions in one or more Member States.

[970] Depending on the harmonising instrument, the Community legislation itself gives rise to obligations on individuals (regulations) or does so only after it has been transposed into national law (directives); see ECJ, Case C–91/92 *Faccini Dori* [1994] E.C.R. I–3325, para. 24 (concerning Directive 85/577, n.1100 *infra*). See also para. 17–128, *infra*.

introduce national provisions derogating from a Community harmonisation measure.[971]

The first paragraph of Art. 95 of the EC Treaty applies "for the achievement of the objectives set out in Article 14" "[b]y way of derogation from Article 94 and save where otherwise provided in this Treaty". Although formulated as a *lex specialis* in relation to Art. 94, the provision has a broad sphere of application as a result of the definition set out in Art. 14. Nevertheless, it does not confer a general power on the Community to regulate the internal market. In the judgment by which the Court of Justice annulled the tobacco advertising directive, the Court held that the measures referred to in Art. 95 of the Treaty must genuinely have as their object the improvement of the conditions for the establishment and functioning of the internal market.[972] Where such a measure has the aim of preventing the emergence of future obstacles to trade resulting from multifarious development of national laws, the emergence of such obstacles must be likely and the measure in question must be designed to prevent them.[973] In addition, in assessing the legality of a measure adopted on the basis of Art. 95, the Court of Justice verifies whether the distortion of competition which the measure purports to eliminate is appreciable.[974] Finally, it is clear from the very wording of Art. 95(1) that it applies only if the Treaty does not otherwise provides. It follows that, if the Treaty contains a more specific provision that is capable of constituting the legal basis for the measure in question, that measure must be founded on such provision.[975]

Article 94 continues to be relevant above all for the three areas which Art. 95(2) excludes from the application of Art. 95(1). However, the practical significance of Art. 94 of the EC Treaty is not so great given that harmonisation may be carried out in these areas also on the basis of other Treaty Articles. The first category listed in Art. 95(2) consists of "fiscal provisions". This covers all areas and aspects of taxation, whether substantive rules or procedural rules, including arrangements for the collection of such taxes.[976] In this field, Art. 94 is relevant primarily to

---

[971] para. 5–210, *infra*. For the fact that Art. 94 refers to the "common market" whereas Art. 95 to the "internal market", see Gormley, "Competition and Free Movement: Is the Internal Market the Same as a Common Market?" (2002) E.Bus.L.Rev. 517–522.

[972] ECJ, Case C–376/98 *Germany v European Parliament and Council* [2000] E.C.R. I–8419, paras 83–84 (for commentaries, see n.57, *supra*).

[973] *ibid.*, para. 86; ECJ, Case C–377/98 *Netherlands v European Parliament and Council* [2001] E.C.R. I–7079, paras 15–18; ECJ, Case C–491/01 *British American Tobacco (Investments) and Imperial Tobacco* [2002] E.C.R. I–11453, paras 60–61.

[974] ECJ, Case C–376/98 *Germany v European Parliament and Council* [2000] E.C.R. I–8419, para. 106. For limits on the power to harmonise, see Möstl, "Grenzen an der Rechtsangleichung im europäischen Binnenmarkt" (2002) EuR. 318–350; Selmayr, Kamann and Ahlers, "Die Binnenmarktkompetenz der Europäischen Gemeinschaft" (2003) E.W.S. 49–61.

[975] ECJ (judgment of April 29, 2004), Case C–338/01 *Commission v Council*, not yet reported, paras 59–60.

[976] *ibid.*, paras 63–67.

harmonisation of direct taxation,[977] since indirect taxation may be harmonised pursuant to Art. 93 of the EC Treaty (the procedure is the same as for Art. 94). The second category is provisions "relating to the free movement of persons". This refers above all to aspects of free movement of not economically active persons which do not fall within Title IV of the EC Treaty, since national provisions may be harmonised as regards persons coming under rules on workers, self-employed persons, providers of services or recipients of services under specific articles of the Treaty.[978] The third category is provisions "relating to the rights and interests of employed persons", in respect of which specific articles likewise permit harmonisation in some cases.[979]

In some areas, approximation of national legislation is not sufficient to attain a single market. As a result, the Council may empower the Commission, in a harmonising measure adopted pursuant to Art. 95(1), to adopt a decision requiring Member States to take temporary measures where the objectives sought by the harmonising measure can be ensured only by supplementary action at Community level.[980]

Authorised derogations. Harmonisation of national legislation decided by **5–210** the Council acting by a qualified majority vote constitutes a threat to Member States where their legislation is based on a higher degree of protection than that afforded in most Member States. Accordingly, Art. 95(3) provides that, in its proposals concerning health, safety, environmental protection and consumer protection, the Commission is to take as its base a high level of protection, taking into account in particular any new development based on scientific facts.[981] In the event that the

---

[977] *e.g.* Council Directive 2003/48/EC of June 3, 2003 on taxation of savings income in the form of interest payments, [2003] O.J. L157/38. See Dassesse, "The EU Directive 'on taxation of savings': the provisional end of a long journey?" (2004) EC Tax Review 41–46; Malherbe and Hermand, "La nouvelle directive du juin 3, 2003 sur la fiscalité de l'épargne: éléments d'actualité" (2004) J.T. 145–150; Berlin, "La fiscalité de l'épargne dans l'Union européenne. Histoire d'une harmonisation en voie de disparition" (2003) J.T.D.E. 162–168; Merland, "La co-ordination de la fiscalité: un exemple de la difficulté de la construction européenne" (2003) R.T.D.E. 637–656. For the competence to harmonise tax, see Vanistendael, "Memorandum on the taxing powers of the European Union" (2002) EC Tax Review 120–129; Laule, "Harmonisierung der Steuern in Europa" (2002) Z.Eu.S. 381–405. For the toilsome harmonisation of direct taxation, see also the Conclusions of the ECOFIN Council Meeting on December 1, 1997 concerning taxation policy and the annexed Resolution of the Council and the Representatives of the Governments of the Member States, meeting within the Council of December 1, 1997 on a code of conduct for business taxation—Taxation of savings, together with the Annex on taxation of savings ([1998] O.J. C2/1) and Bratton and McCahery, "Tax Coordination and Tax Competition in the European Union: Evaluating the Code of Conduct on Business Taxation" (2001) C.M.L.R. 677–718.

[978] See n. 955, *supra*.

[979] See Art. 137(2) of the EC Treaty, para. 5–236, *infra*.

[980] ECJ, Case C–359/92 *Germany v Council* [1994] E.C.R. I–3681, paras 30–37 (accordingly, the Court of Justice rejected the action brought by Germany for annulment of Council Directive 92/59/EEC of June 29, 1992 on general product safety ([1992] O.J. L228/24), which has since been replaced; for the new directive, see n. to para. 5–244, *infra*).

[981] According to Declaration (No. 22) annexed to the Treaty of Amsterdam, account must also be taken of the needs of persons with a disability ([1997] O.J. C340/135).

Commission adopts the high level of protection of a Member State, that State may prevent the Council from setting a lower level.[982] In addition, a harmonising measure may embody a safeguard clause authorising Member States to take provisional measures on one or more of the grounds listed in Art. 30 of the EC Treaty (EC Treaty, Art. 95(10)).[983]

Lastly, there are the exceptional provisions set out in Art. 95(4) and (5) of the EC Treaty, which enable a Member State to apply national provisions when the Council or the Commission has adopted a harmonisation measure. In the first place, a Member State may maintain existing measures which it deems necessary on grounds of major needs referred to in Art. 30 or relating to the protection of the environment or the working environment (Art. 95(4)). Accordingly, a Member State may base an application to maintain its already existing national provisions on an assessment of the risk to public health different from that accepted by the Community legislature when it adopted the harmonisation measure from which the national provisions derogate. To that end, it must prove that those national provisions ensure a level of health protection which is higher than the Community harmonisation measure and that they do not go beyond what is necessary to attain that objective.[984] Next, on grounds of a problem specific to a Member State arising after the adoption of the harmonisation measure, the Member State concerned may apply (new) national provisions based on new scientific evidence relating to the protection of the environment or the working environment (Art. 95(5)). In this particular instance, grounds other than protection of the environment or the working environment cannot justify a derogation.[985] In both instances, the Member State has to notify the Commission of the provisions maintained or introduced and of the grounds for maintaining or introducing them.[986] Within six months of notification, the Commission is to approve or reject the national provisions after having verified whether or

---

[982] This is because the Council may only amend a Commission proposal by a unanimous vote (EC Treaty, Art. 250(1)). See also the requirement for a high level of Community protection in EC Treaty, Art. 152(1), first subpara. (public health), Art. 153(1), first subpara. (consumer protection) and Art. 174(2), first subpara. (the environment).

[983] See De Sadeleer, "Procedures for Derogations from the Principle of Approximation of Laws under Art. 95 EC" (2003) C.M.L.R. 889–915 and "Les clauses de sauvegarde prévues à l'article 95 du traité CE" (2002) R.T.D.E. 53, at 55–57.

[984] ECJ, Case C–3/00 *Denmark v Commission* [2003] E.C.R. I–2643, paras 63–65.

[985] For the difference between those two situations, see ECJ Case C–512/99 *Germany v Commission* [2003] E.C.R. I–845, para. 41; ECJ, Case C–3/00 *Denmark v Commission* [2003] E.C.R. I–2643, paras 57–62.

[986] By analogy with the third sentence of Art. 88(3) (see para. 5–205, *supra*), it follows from Art. 95(5) that the Member State is debarred from applying "proposed measures" which deviate from the harmonisation measure. See Barents, "Het Verdrag van Amsterdam en het Europees gemeenschapsrecht" (1997) S.E.W. 351, at 354. Paras 4–9 of Art. 95 of the EC Treaty were added by the Treaty of Amsterdam to specify para. 4 of the former Art. 100a of the EC Treaty, see Bähr and Albin, "The 'Environmental Guarantee' on the Rise? The Amended Art. 95 after the Revision through the Treaty of Amsterdam" (2000) E.J.L.Rev. 119–134; De Sadeleer "Les clauses de sauvegarde prévues à l'article 95 du traité CE" (2002) R.T.D.E. 53, at 58–73.

not they are a "means of arbitrary discrimination or a disguised restriction on trade between Member States and whether or not they . . . constitute an obstacle to the functioning of the internal market" (Art. 95(6)).[987] In the absence of a decision by the Commission, the national provisions in question are deemed to have been approved.[988] Rejection or approval constitutes a Commission decision against which an action will lie (*e.g.* where the national provisions confirmed are considered not to be proportional to the major needs referred to in Art. 95(4)).

When a Member State is authorised to maintain or introduce national provisions derogating from a harmonisation measure, the Commission is to examine immediately whether to propose an adaptation to that measure (Art. 95(7)). In the event that the Commission or a Member State considers that another Member State is making improper use of the powers conferred by Art. 95, it may bring the matter directly before the Court of Justice by way of derogation from the procedure laid down in Arts 226 and 227 of the EC Treaty (Art. 95(9)).[989] Such misuse would be present if a Member State continued to apply the diverging national provisions after the Commission had rejected them or if it went beyond the limits of the approval granted by the Commission.

---

[987] See, *e.g.* the series of Decisions of October 26, 1999 ([1999] O.J. L329) by which the Commission approved national provisions on the marketing and use of creosote (notified by the Netherlands, Germany, Sweden and Denmark) but not national provisions on the use of sulphites, nitrites and nitrates in foodstuffs (notified by Denmark) and concerning mineral wool (notified by Germany). See Verheyen, "Article 95 EC Treaty in practice: The European Commission decisions on creosote, sulphite, nitrates and nitrites" (2000) R.E.C.I.E.L. 71–75. The action brought by Denmark against the decision addressed to that Member State resulted in its partial annulment: ECJ, Case C–3/00 *Denmark v Commission* [2003] E.C.R. I–2643 (as regards nitrites and nitrates); Germany's action against the decision addressed to that Member State was declared unfounded: ECJ, Case C–512/99 *Germany v Commission* [2003] E.C.R. I–845.

[988] In the pre-Amsterdam Treaty version, Art. 100a of the EC Treaty referred in general terms to provisions which a Member State wished to "apply" and the Commission could "confirm". Pursuant thereto, on August 2, 1991 the Federal Republic of Germany notified the Commission of its decision to apply a stricter ban on pentachlorophenol (PCP) than that embodied in Council Directive 91/713/EEC of March 21, 1991 amending Directive 76/769 relating to the marketing and use of certain dangerous substances and preparations, [1991] O.J. L85/34, which Germany had voted against in the Council. On December 2, 1992, the Commission adopted a decision "confirming" the national provisions, [1992] O.J. C334/8. On an application from France, the Court of Justice annulled that decision for failure to satisfy the obligation to state the reasons on which it was based (EC Treaty, Art. 253) by judgment of May 17, 1994 in Case C–41/93 *France v Commission* [1994] E.C.R. I–1829, paras 31–37. By Decision 94/783/EC of September 14, 1994, the Commission re-confirmed the derogation granted to Germany, [1994] O.J. L316/43. The former Art. 100a(4) of the EC Treaty did not contain any time within which the Commission had to take a decision. Failure by the Commission to react to a notification made by a Member State constituted a breach of the principle of co-operation in good faith enshrined in Art. 10 of the EC Treaty, but did not affect the applicability of the directive in question: ECJ, Case C–319/97 *Kortas* [1999] E.C.R. I–3143, paras 33–38.

[989] For a comparison of the former Art. 110a(4) with the procedure laid down in Art. 88(2) of the EC Treaty, see Flynn, "How Will Art. 100a(4) Work? A Comparison with Art. 93" (1987) C.M.L.R. 689.

5-211 Distortion of trade. Where a difference between national legislation affects the conditions of competition in such a way as to give rise to "distortion", the Council does not have to act by means of the procedures laid down in Art. 94 or 95 of the EC Treaty, but may issue the "necessary directives" pursuant to Art. 96 on a proposal from the Commission by a qualified majority. In order to avoid an amendment of national legislation giving rise to distortion, the Commission is to make recommendations to the Member State concerned (EC Treaty, Art. 97).[990]

In practice, national measures impeding trade in goods in non-harmonised areas often prompt the Commission to bring proceedings before the Court of Justice or national courts to make references for preliminary rulings in connection with the obligations arising under Art. 28 of the EC Treaty. In order to deal with such problems more expeditiously, the Community has introduced a procedure obliging Member States to notify the Commission of measures constituting an obstacle to trade.[991] Where a Community measure has carried out an exhaustive harmonisation of the grounds on which obstacles to trade may be justified, any national measure relating thereto must be assessed in the light of the provisions of that harmonising measure and not of Arts 28 EC and 30 of the EC Treaty.[992]

3. New approach to Community harmonisation

5-212 Harmonising essential standards. Harmonisation of national legislation becomes protracted where unanimity has to be achieved on detailed rules. Since the 1980s, a major part of harmonisation has taken a new approach: only minimum requirements are harmonised, after which the Member States must recognise each other's legislation. That approach links up with the *Cassis de Dijon* case law, which prohibits Member States, in the absence of harmonisation, from imposing restrictions on the marketing of products which are lawfully marketed in another Member State, unless such restrictions are necessary in order to protect "mandatory [or overriding] requirements" (see para. 5-112).

As early as 1985, the Council advocated laying down by directive only the fundamental safety standards for products and leaving it to other bodies (*e.g.* standardisation institutes) to specify them in technical standards. Every

---

[990] After such distortion has arisen, the Council is not entitled to apply Art. 96 to the other Member States in order to require them to amend their own legislation or to apply it in favour of a Member State which has caused distortion detrimental only to itself (EC Treaty, Art. 97(2)). For a general discussion, see Van Grinsven, "Het distorsiebegrip bij voortschrijdende Europese integratie" (1991) S.E.W. 173–193.

[991] Decision No. 3052/95/EC of the European Parliament and of the Council of December 13, 1995 establishing a procedure for the exchange of information on national measures derogating from the principle of the free movement of goods, [1995] O.J. L321/1 (adopted on the basis of Art. 95 of the EC Treaty).

[992] ECJ, Case C–221/00 *Commission v Austria* [2003] E.C.R. I–1007, para. 42 (see paras 5–103 and 5–109, *supra*).

administration would then have to accept that products complying with those technical standards also complied with the basic safety standards.[993] Likewise, in its White Paper on completing the internal market, the Commission put forward a "new strategy", whereby harmonisation designed to eliminate technical barriers would be limited to requirements for which the mutual recognition of national legislation alone did not produce a satisfactory result (see also paras 5–145–5–147).[994] The Community also seeks to forestall measures restricting trade. Community information procedures require Member States to notify any draft technical regulations and standards to the Commission and to take account of any observations submitted by the Commission or other Member States.[995]

4. Powers to harmonise in the EU Constitution

Changes. Some of the changes that the EU Constitution will introduce in specific policy areas will result in an extension of the Union's powers to harmonise national law.[996] The conferral of a specific ground for harmonisation may make recourse to the "flexibility clause" (the present Art. 308 of the EC Treaty) unnecessary. This is the case with intellectual property rights, since the EU Constitution lays down a specific power for the Union to provide uniform protection throughout the Union by introducing European instruments and setting up centralised Union-wide authorisation, co-ordination and supervision arrangements.[997] In addition,

5–213

---

[993] Council Resolution of May 7, 1985 on a new approach to technical harmonisation and standards, [1985] O.J. C136/1. The following standardisation bodies operate at European level: CEN (European Committee for Standardisation), Cenelec (European Committee for the Coordination of Electrical Standards) and ETSI (European Telecommunications Standards Institute); see also the Council resolutions of October 28, 1999 on the role of standardisation in Europe and on mutual recognition, [2000] O.J. C141/1 and 5, respectively. See also Waelbroeck, "L'harmonisation des règles et normes techniques dans la CEE" (1988) C.D.E. 243–275; MacMillan, "La 'certification', la reconnaisance mutuelle et le marché unique" (1991) 2 R.M.U.E. 181–211; Andrieu, "La normalisation européenne, instrument de cohésion—quelques points de repère" (1992) R.M.C.U.E. 627–630; Ehricke, "Dynamische Verweise in EG-Richtlinien auf Regelungen privater Normungsgremien" (2002) Eu.Z.W. 746–753.

[994] Commission of the European Communities, *Completing the internal market: Commission white paper for the European Council* (*Milan, June 28–29, 1985*), June 14, 1985, COM (85) 310 final, 19, s.65.

[995] See Directive 98/34/EC of the European Parliament and of the Council of June 22, 1998 laying down a procedure for the provision of information in the field of technical standards and regulations and of rules on Information Society services, [1998] O.J. L204/37 (as amended by Directive 98/48, [1998] O.J. L217/18), replacing Council Directive 83/189/EEC of March 28, 1983 for the provision of information in the field of technical standards and regulations, [1983] O.J. L109/8. For the inapplicability of non-notified provisions, see n.22 to para. 17–007, *infra*.

[996] See, *e.g.* the extended powers with respect to customs co-operation (see para. 5–096, *supra*), co-ordination of national social security law (see para. 5–148, *supra*), and immigration laws (see para. 5–168, *supra*).

[997] These measures may be established by European law or framework law, *i.e.* under the co-decision procedure. There is an exception for language arrangements for the European instruments, on which the Council's decision is to take the form of a European law, adopted by unanimity after consulting the European Parliament (Art. III–176, second para. of the EU Constitution).

the EU Constitution enables the Member States to set up "open methods of co-ordination" with the Commission in various policy areas. Where there is an open method of co-ordination, the Member States will be encouraged to submit national policies to periodic monitoring and evaluation against guidelines and indicators established in common.[998] In some cases this voluntary co-ordination of national policies will make formal harmonisation unnecessary.[999]

As far as the general bases for harmonisation are concerned, the EU Constitution preserves the power of the European Parliament and the Council, acting under the co-decision procedure for the purposes of achieving the objectives of the internal market, to establish measures for the "approximation of the provisions laid down by law, regulation or administrative action in Member States which have as their object the establishment and functioning of the internal market" (Art. III–172, which largely reproduces the wording of Art. 95 of the EC Treaty). In areas excluded from the scope of application of that legal basis, it is the Council, acting unanimously after consulting the European Parliament, which is empowered to enact harmonisation measures (Art. III–173, which is largely based on Art. 94 of the EC Treaty). In this connection, the EU Constitution refers, in both provisions, to the "establishment [and/or] functioning of the internal market".[1000]

As regards harmonisation of indirect taxation, the Convention had proposed to enable the Council to take a decision by qualified majority on matters relating to administrative co-operation or combating tax fraud and tax evasion. As far as direct taxation was concerned, a specific power had been proposed for the harmonisation of company taxation subject to the same conditions.[1001] Since these proposals did not meet with general approval in the Intergovernmental Conference, the EU Constitution provides only for indirect taxation to be harmonised by European law or framework law of the Council, acting unanimously after consulting the European Parliament, "provided that such harmonisation is necessary to ensure the establishment and the functioning of the internal market and to avoid distortion of competition" (EU Constitution, Art. III–171, which is largely based on Art. 93 of the EC Treaty).

---

[998] See Art. III–210, second para. (on social policy, see also para. 5–235, *infra*), Art. III–250(2) (on research and technological development), Art. III–278(2), second subpara. (on public health) and Art. III–279(2) (on industrial policy). *Cf.* the formal co-ordination of national economic policies on the basis of Art. 99 of the EC Treaty (see para. 5–225, *infra*) and of national employment policies on the basis of Art. 128 of the EC Treaty (see para. 5–237, *infra*).

[999] For this method, see de Búrca, "The constitutional challenge of new governance in the European Union" (2003) E.L.Rev. 814–839.

[1000] The EU Constitution also maintains the difference between Arts 94 and 95 of the EC Treaty as to the legislative instruments which may be used: European framework laws in Art. III–173 and European laws or framework laws in Art. III–172.

[1001] See Arts III–62(2) and 63 of the draft EU Constitution. In both cases, it would have been up to the Council, acting unanimously on a proposal from the Commission, to determine whether the measures concerned relate to administrative co-operation or combating tax fraud or tax evasion.

III. Economic and Monetary Policy

Treaty rules. In addition to establishing "a common market", Art. 2 of the **5–214**
EC Treaty refers to "economic and monetary union" as an instrument for
achieving the Community's objectives in place of "progressively
approximating the economic policies of Member States" as referred to in
the original Art. 2 of the EEC Treaty. Article 4 of the EC Treaty provides a
definition of the economic and monetary union which the Community is to
establish. The economic aspect is described as "an economic policy which is
based on the close co-ordination of Member States' economic policies, on
the internal market and on the definition of common objectives, and
conducted in accordance with the principle of an open market economy
with free competition" (EC Treaty, Art. 4(1)). Although that policy is
conducted by action on the part of the Member States and the Community,
the definition shows that any economic policy must square with the free
movement of goods, persons, services and capital and with general
objectives, such as economic and social cohesion, and competition policy.
The monetary policy includes "the irrevocable fixing of exchange rates
leading to the introduction of a single currency, the [euro], and the
definition and conduct of a single monetary policy and exchange-rate policy
the primary objective of both of which shall be to maintain price stability
and, without prejudice to this objective, to support the general economic
policies in the Community, in accordance with the principle of an open
market economy with free competition" (EC Treaty, Art. 4(2)). Unlike the
economic policy, the monetary policy entails a definitive transfer of powers
from the national level to the Community.[1002] Article 4(3) of the EC Treaty
underlines the guiding principles of EMU: stable prices, sound public
finances and monetary conditions and a sustainable balance of payments.

In Title VII of Part Three of the EC Treaty, economic and monetary
union is dealt with in separate chapters on economic policy and monetary
policy (Chapters 1 and 2) and on the institutional framework of EMU
(Chapter 3).[1003] The transitional provisions set out in Chapter 4 deal with

---

[1002] In Protocol (No. 4), annexed by the EU Treaty to the EC Treaty, on certain provisions
relating to the UK of Great Britain and Northern Ireland, the United Kingdom retained the
right not to move to the third stage as a result of which Art. 4(2) of the EC Treaty does not
apply to it (para. 5–233, *infra*).

[1003] For a general discussion of the Treaty provisions relating to EMU (which were not
amended by the Amsterdam Treaty), see Louis, "L'Union économique et monétaire"
(1992) C.D.E. 251–305; Pipkorn, "Legal Arrangements in the Treaty of Maastricht for the
Effectiveness of the Economic and Monetary Union" (1994) C.M.L.R. 263–291; Roth, "Der
rechtliche Rahmen der Wirtschafts- und Währungsunion" and Pipkorn, "Der rechtliche
Rahmen der Wirtschafts- und Währungsunion —Vorkehrungen für die Währungspolitik"
(1994) EuR., Beiheft 1, 45–83 and 85–95, respectively (and see the discussion at 97–100);
Lardoux, "L'Union économique et monétaire: génèse, mise en place, perspectives" (1998)
R.M.C.U.E. 429–436; Louis, "A Legal and Institutional Approach for Building a Monetary
Union" (1998) C.M.L.R. 33–76; Partsch, "De quelques questions juridiques relatives au

the procedure and criteria for determining which Member States were to take part in the third stage of EMU as from January 1, 1999 or at a later date. Not all the provisions of Chapters 1 to 3 apply to the Member States not taking part (Denmark, the United Kingdom, Sweden and the ten Member States which acceded on May 1, 2004). These provisions are virtually unaffected by the EU Constitution.

A. PREPARATION OF ECONOMIC AND MONETARY UNION

5–215 **Monetary co-operation.** Under the original EEC Treaty, the maintenance of stable prices, sound public finances and monetary conditions and a sustainable balance of payments was left to national economic policy, which Member States were to co-ordinate in close co-operation with the institutions of the Community "to the extent necessary to attain the objectives of this Treaty".[1004] Member States were to regard their conjunctural and monetary policies as "a matter of common concern".[1005] The Treaty prescribed in the first place consultation between the Member States and the Commission, but also conferred powers on the Council to set the co-operation in motion and to adopt measures relating to conjunctural policy.[1006] Accordingly, the Council set up a system for the co-ordination of economic policy and developed financial instruments, including the possibility for Member States to obtain loans from the Community or the European Investment Bank. In the monetary sphere, the Treaty had already set up an advisory Monetary Committee to keep under review the monetary and financial situation of the Member States and of the Community and the general payments systems and to deliver opinions and the Council arranged for co-operation to take place between the Central Banks through the Committee of Central-Bank Governors.[1007] A first plan for enlarging the economic and monetary powers of the Community and ultimately achieving economic and monetary union was adopted as long ago as 1970 in the report of the Werner Committee, which was never completely implemented (see para. 2–010). On the basis of a resolution of the European Council of December 5, 1978, the European Monetary

---

passage à la troisième phase de l'Union économique et monétaire et au fonctionnement de celle-ci" (1998) R.T.D.E. 35–74; Seidel, "Konstitutionelle Schwächen der Währungsunion" (2001) EuR. 861–878. For the institutional framework, see (in addition to paras 10–101—10–104, *infra*, on the European Central Bank), Slot, "The Institutional Provisions of the EMU", in Curtin and Heukels (eds), *Institutional Dynamics of European Integration. Essays in Honour of Henry G. Schermers*, Vol.II (Martinus Nijhoff, Dordrecht, 1994), at 229–249; Andenas and others (eds), *European Economic and Monetary Union: The Institutional Framework* (Kluwer Law International, London, 1997), 565 pp.

[1004] See Art. 12(1) of the EEC Treaty.

[1005] EEC Treaty, Art. 103(1) and Art. 107(1), respectively.

[1006] EEC Treaty, Arts 103(1) and (2) and Art. 105(1).

[1007] See EEC Treaty, Art. 105(2) and para. 2–011, *supra*. In the third stage of EMU, the Monetary Committee was replaced by an Economic and Financial Committee (EC Treaty, Art. 114(2)). The Committee of Central-Bank Governors has been dissolved since the beginning of the second stage of EMU.

System was started and subsequently the ECU was introduced as the unit of account for the exchange rate mechanism and as a means of settling transactions between the Community and the Member States (see para. 2–011).

Internal market. In a 1973 judgment, the Court of Justice held that "one **5–216** of the cardinal aims of the Treaty is to create a single economic region, free from internal restrictions in which economic and customs union may be progressively achieved. This requires the parities between the currencies of the various Member States to remain fixed; as soon as this requirement ceases to be met, the process of integration envisaged by the Treaty will be retarded or prejudiced".[1008] The integration of the markets necessitated a greater degree of co-ordination at Community level of the Member States' economic and monetary policies. This became clear above all in the course of the implementation of the internal-market programme.[1009]

The elimination of internal frontiers for movements of goods, persons, services and capital renders the economies of the Member States so dependent on each other that any national economic policy decision has a direct cross-frontier effect. Thus, a Member State cannot pursue a policy of stimulating its own economy if expenditure stimuli only give rise to increased imports from other Member States, resulting in a balance-of-payments deficit.[1010] Furthermore, the internal market has accentuated existing regional and structural disequilibria within the Community, especially differences in production costs, price stability and budget deficits. The disequilibria have brought strong pressure to bear on Member States' exchange rates. A high degree of co-ordination of economic policies by the Community was likely to result in uniform growth within the Member States and at the same time might decrease the pressure on Member States' monetary policies.

A monetary union should make fixed exchange rates possible and eliminate the economic cost of uncertain exchange rates. Liberalisation of capital movements and integration of financial markets made it impossible for many Member States to pursue an independent monetary policy. Consequently, effective supervision of the currency and of financial and capital markets had to be ensured at Community level.

Economic union and monetary union were to be achieved in parallel. A centralised monetary policy could not be pursued in the presence of sharply divergent national economies. On the other hand, monetary policy constituted one of the available instruments for intervening in the economy.

[1008] ECJ, Case 10/73 *Rewe-Zentral* [1973] E.C.R. 1175, para. 26.

[1009] See Louis, "A Monetary Union for Tomorrow?" (1989) C.M.L.R. 301–326; VerLoren van Themaat, "Some Preliminary Observations on the Intergovernmental Conferences: The Relations Between the Concepts of a Common Market, a Monetary Union, an Economic Union, a Political Union and Sovereignty" (1991) C.M.L.R. 291–318.

[1010] For an example, see the policy of the French Mauroy administration in 1981–1982, referred to by Lauwaars and Timmermans, *Europees recht in kort bestek*, (W.E.J. Tjeenk Willink, Deventer, 1999), at 305.

5–217 Single European Act. The Single European Act contained a reference to economic and monetary union.[1011] At the monetary level, the EEC Treaty merely adverted to existing co-operation within the framework of the European Monetary System[1012] and in developing the ECU.[1013] Article 102a(2) of the EEC Treaty did, however, announce a formal amendment of the Treaty "in so far as further development in the field of economic and monetary policy necessitates institutional changes".

5–218 Delors Committee. Economic and Monetary Union (EMU) gained new impetus when the European Council held in Hanover on June 27 and 28, 1988 set up a committee under the chairmanship of the President of the Commission, Jacques Delors, with the task of studying and proposing concrete stages leading towards economic and monetary union.[1014] The Delors Committee proposed that economic and monetary union should be attained in three stages.[1015] According to the Committee, a single currency was not strictly necessary to monetary union, but commended itself for its economic, psychological and political advantages. A single currency would reinforce the irreversible nature of EMU, facilitate Community monetary policy, avoid transaction costs in exchanging currencies and, provided that stability was ensured, have more weight internationally than the individual currencies of the Member States.[1016]

B. Introduction of Economic and Monetary Union

5–219 Three stages. On the basis of the Report of the Delors Committee, the Madrid European Council decided in June 1989 that the first stage of EMU should start on July 1, 1990.[1017] The EU Treaty made the necessary changes

---

[1011] The title of the new Ch. 1 ("Co-operation in economic and monetary policy") of Title II ("Economic policy") of the EEC Treaty (Art. 102a) included in brackets the words "economic and monetary union". According to the Court of Justice, it appeared therefrom that the Community aimed at integration which would result in economic and monetary union: ECJ, Opinion 1/91 *Draft Agreement between the Community, on the one hand, and the countries of the European Free Trade Association, on the other, relating to the creation of the European Economic Area* [1991] E.C.R. I–6079, para. 17.

[1012] At the start of the EMS, all the then Member States, with the exception of the UK took part. The Spanish peseta was accepted into the exchange rate system in July 1989, the pound sterling in October 1990 and the Portuguese escudo in April 1999. Following financial turbulence in September 1992, the pound sterling and the Italian lira suspended their participation in the mechanism. The Austrian schilling acceded on January 9, 1995, the Finnish markka on October 14, 1996 and the Greek drachma on March 16, 1998; the Italian lira re-entered the exchange rate mechanism on November 25, 1996. The Swedish krona never joined the mechanism. The Member States which did not participate in the exchange rate mechanism had acceded to the agreements with regard to the EMS.

[1013] The ECU developed into a parallel currency which was used above all on financial markets for the issue of bonds and gradually introduced itself into banking transactions.

[1014] (1988) 6 EC Bull. point 3.4.1.

[1015] Committee for the Study of Economic and Monetary Union, *Report on Economic and Monetary Union in the European Community* (Official Publications Office of the European Communities, Luxembourg, 1989) [hereinafter "Report of the Delors Committee"]; also published in *Europe*, doc. 1550/1551, April 20, 1989.

[1016] Report of the Delors Committee, s.23. See also Gnos, "La transition vers l'Union économique et monétaire" (1992) R.M.C.U.E. 621–626.

[1017] (1989) 6 EC Bull. point 1.1.11. See the Report of the Delors Committee, s.43.

to the EC Treaty to make the second and third stages of EMU possible "as provided in this treaty and in accordance with the timetable [and procedures] set out therein" (EC Treaty, Art. 4(1) and (2)). Just as in the case of the internal market, EMU would ensure that a partial aspect of the common market was completed, namely free movement of capital, while embodying a programme of policies which, upon the introduction of the single currency, would go further than the intended common market. However, not all the Member States were prepared to subscribe to this programme in full. Denmark and the United Kingdom obtained exceptional status in the EU Treaty, as a result of which they are free to decide whether or not to accede to EMU (see para. 5–233).

First stage. The first stage of EMU comprised, on the economic level, **5–220** achieving the internal market (free movement of persons, goods, services and capital), reinforcing the Community's regional and structural policies[1018] and introducing new procedures for supervising national economic policies, incorporating specific rules for co-ordinating budgetary policy (which were to become binding only in the final stage).[1019] On the monetary level, the initial stage required the complete liberalisation of capital transactions,[1020] all Member States had to join the European Monetary System,[1021] all barriers to the private use of the ECU were to disappear and the Committee of Central-Bank Governors was to obtain additional consultative powers.[1022]

Second stage. The timetable for introducing the second and third stages—a **5–221** matter left open in the Report of the Delors Committee—was determined by the EU Treaty in the transitional provisions of Title VII of the EC Treaty. The second stage began on January 1, 1994 (EC Treaty, Art. 116(1)). Capital and payments movements were liberalised and the economic policies of the Member States and the Community had to comply with the supervisory procedure and rules laid down in the Treaty, albeit without any binding sanctions.[1023] Each Member State prepared the status of its central bank for the third stage (EC Treaty, Art. 116(5)). Monetary

---

[1018] See, *inter alia*, the reform of the structural funds effected by Council Regulation (EEC) 2052/88 of June 24, 1988 on the tasks of the Structural Funds and their effectiveness and on the co-ordination of their activities between themselves and with the operations of the European Investment Bank and the other existing financial instruments, [1988] O.J. L185/9.

[1019] Council Decision 90/141/EEC of March 12, 1990 on the attainment of progressive convergence of economic policies and performance during stage one of economic and monetary union, [1990] O.J. L78/23.

[1020] Council Directive 88/361/EEC of June 24, 1988 for the implementation of [the former] Art. 67 of the Treaty, [1988] O.J. L178/5; para. 5–182, *supra*.

[1021] However, not all Member States were participating in the exchange rate mechanism, see n.1012, *supra*.

[1022] Council Decision 90/142/EEC of March 12, 1990 amending Decision 64/300/EEC (see the discussion of the Committee of Central-Bank Governors; para. 2–011, *supra*), [1990] O.J. L78/25. See also Art. 117(8) of the EC Treaty.

[1023] See the Council measures mentioned in paras 5–224—5–225 and 5–229, *infra*.

policy remained for the time being in the hands of the Member States, but the currency composition of the ECU was frozen (EC Treaty, Art. 118).[1024] The European Monetary Institute (EMI)—the precursor of the European Central Bank—monitored the operation of the EMS, organised consultations between the central banks and prepared the instruments for the third stage of EMU (EC Treaty, Art. 117). The national governments decided at the European Council held in Madrid on December 15 and 16, 1995 that the term "ECU" used in the EC Treaty to refer to the European currency unit was a generic term. They agreed to call the European currency unit the "euro" and to interpret all Treaty provisions mentioning the ECU as referring to the euro.[1025]

5–222 Third stage. On January 1, 1999 the third stage started as between the eleven Member States which satisfied the conditions for the adoption of a single currency.[1026] In anticipation of that date, the European Central Bank was set up, replacing the EMI from June 1, 1998 (EC Treaty, Art. 123(1) and (2)).[1027] Before July 1, 1998, the Council had to decide which States fulfilled the conditions for the adoption of a single currency.[1028] The situation in a given Member State had to be assessed primarily by reference to four convergence criteria, more closely formulated in a Protocol:

(1) a rate of inflation not exceeding by more than 1.5 percentage points that of the three best performing Member States in terms of price stability;

(2) a deficit which was not excessive within the meaning of Art. 104;

[1024] See Vissol, "L'écu dans la phase de transition vers UEM" (1994) R.M.C.U.E. 425–436.

[1025] Conclusions of the Presidency (1995) 12 EU Bull. point I.3. An action was brought against the Commission on the ground that it had used the term "Euro" when the Treaty referred to ECUs, but it was declared inadmissible on the ground that it was directed against a proposal for legislation: CFI (order of May 15, 1997), Case T–175/96 *Berthu v Commission* [1997] E.C.R. II–811.

[1026] To do this, the Council, meeting in the special composition of the Heads of State or Government, had to decide by a qualified majority by no later than December 31, 1996. In December 1996 the Council found that there was not a majority of Member States which fulfilled the conditions. Under Art. 121(4) of the EC Treaty, the third stage was then to start automatically on January 1, 1999 as between the Member States fulfilling the conditions, regardless as to their number. See Council Decision 96/736/EC of December 13, 1996 in accordance with Art. 109j [now Art. 121](3) of the Treaty establishing the European Community, on entry into the third stage of economic and monetary union, [1996] O.J. L335/48.

[1027] See Decision 98/345/EC taken by common accord of the Governments of the Member States adopting the single currency at the level of Heads of State or Government of May 26, 1998 appointing the President, the Vice-President and the other members of the Executive Board of the European Central Bank, [1998] O.J. L154/33.

[1028] This assessment by the Council, meeting in the special composition of the Heads of State or Government, was made by a qualified majority vote following a procedure in which first the EMI and the Commission reported to the Council (in its usual composition) and the Council drew up by a qualified majority vote a recommendation, on a recommendation from the Commission, which then went to the Council in its special composition, together with an opinion from the European Parliament (EC Treaty, Art. 121(1) and (2)).

(3) the normal fluctuation margins of the EMS had to have been complied with for at least the preceding two years; and

(4) the average long-term interest rate must not have exceeded by more than two percentage points that of the three best performing Member States in terms of price stability.[1029]

On May 3, 1998 the Council held by decision that Austria, Belgium, Germany, Finland, France, Ireland, Italy, Luxembourg, the Netherlands, Spain and Portugal fulfilled the conditions for the adoption of the single currency on January 1, 1999.[1030] Greece and Sweden did not fulfil the conditions; the United Kingdom and Denmark were not subjected to assessment in view of their having notified the intention not to move to the third stage.[1031] Since, Greece has also fulfilled the criteria and has taken part in the third stage of EMU as from January 1, 2001 (see para. 5–232). In Sweden—as in Denmark and the United Kingdom—the political will is lacking to introduce the euro.[1032] The 2003 Accession of Act confers on each of the Member States which acceded on May 1, 2004 the status of Member State with a derogation.[1033]

The euro. Article 123(4) of the EC Treaty provided that, on the starting **5–223** date of the third stage, the Council, acting by a unanimous vote of the Member States without a derogation, was to adopt the conversion rates at which their currencies would be irrevocably fixed, rendering the Euro a currency in its own right, together with the other measures necessary for the rapid introduction of the euro in place of the national currencies. In order to facilitate the introduction of the euro, the Council had already

---

[1029] First subpara. of Art. 121(1) of the EC Treaty and Protocol (No. 21) annexed to the EC Treaty on the convergence criteria referred to in Art. 109j [now Art. 121] of the Treaty establishing the European Community.

[1030] Art. 1 of Council Decision 98/317/EC of May 3, 1998 in accordance with Art. 109j [now Art. 121](4) of the Treaty, [1998] O.J. L139/30, by which the Council, meeting in the composition of the Heads of State or Government, adopted the identically worded recommendation drawn up that weekend and submitted to the European Parliament for its opinion: Recommendation 98/316 in accordance with Art. 109j [now Art. 121](2) of the Treaty, [1998] O.J. L139/21.

[1031] See recitals 4 to 7 in the preamble to Decision 98/317/EC, *ibid.* As far as Greece was concerned, the Council found that it did not fulfil any of the four convergence criteria set out in the four indents of Art. 121(1). As for Sweden, it had never participated in the exchange rate mechanism and its national legislation, including the statute of the national central bank, was not compatible with the EC Treaty. It should be noted that the Swedish Parliament had expressly spoken out against participation in EMU (*Europe* No. 7115, December 6, 1997, p.7). For a commentary on the May 1998 decisions, see the editorial "The Birth of the Euro" (1998) C.M.L.R. 585–594; Smits, "Het begin van de muntunie: besluitvorming en regelgeving" (1999) S.E.W. 2–21.

[1032] On September 14, 2003 the Swedish people came out against the introduction of the single currency in a referendum in which 56.1 per cent voted against ((2003) 9 EU Bull. point 1.3.2).

[1033] Act of Accession 2003, Art. 4.

determined the content of those measures.[1034] In addition, the Commission issued recommendations (based on Art. 211 of the EC Treaty) with a view to resolving practical problems connected with the switch to the euro.[1035] On December 31, 1998 the Council fixed the conversion rates between the euro and the currencies of the eleven participating Member States.[1036] Although the participating currencies were replaced by the euro as of January 1, 1999, the use of the euro was confined to transfer payments. From January 1, 2002, euro-denominated banknotes and coins were brought into circulation. National banknotes continued to circulate as legal tender for a short transitional period and had to be completely replaced by the euro in all participating States by no later than six months afterwards.[1037] Article 123(4) of the EC Treaty empowers the Council to

---

[1034] On May 3, 1998 the Council, the Commission and the EMI reached agreement on the method for determining the irrevocable conversion rates and laid down the bilateral conversion rates which would be used to that end, see the Joint Communiqué by the Ministers and Central Bank Governors of the Member States adopting the euro as their single currency, the Commission and the European Monetary Institute on the determination of the irrevocable conversion rates for the euro, [1998] O.J. C160/1. In order to create certainty about the legal framework for the euro, the Council adopted as from June 17, 1997 a number of provisions on the basis of Art. 235 [now Art. 308] concerning the introduction of the euro: Regulation No. 1103/97, [1997] O.J. L162/1 (applicable with effect from January 1, 1999). Pursuant to Art. 123(4), third sentence, of the EC Treaty the Council adopted on May 3, 1998 Regulation No. 974/98 on the introduction of the euro ([1998] O.J. L139/1), which took effect on January 1, 1999 but had already been published as a draft in an annex to the Resolution of the European Council of July 7, 1997 on the legal framework for the introduction of the euro, [1997] O.J. C236/7.

[1035] See the Recommendations of April 23, 1998: Recommendation 98/286 concerning banking charges for conversion to the euro, [1998] O.J. C130/22; Recommendation 98/287 concerning dual display of prices and other monetary amounts, [1998] O.J. L130/26; Recommendation 98/288 on dialogue, monitoring and information to facilitate the transition to the euro, [1998] O.J. L130/29.

[1036] Council Regulation (EC) No. 2866/98 of December 31, 1998 on the conversion rates between the euro and the currencies of the Member States adopting the euro, [1998] O.J. L359/1 (for the ECB's opinion of the same date on the Commission's proposal, see [1998] O.J. C142/1). Under the regulation, conversion rates (to six significant figures) were adopted as one euro expressed in terms of each of the national currencies of the participating countries (1 Euro = 13.7603 Austrian Schillings; 40.3399 Belgian Francs; 5.94573 Finnish Markkas; 6.55957 French Francs; 1.95583 Deutsche Mark; 0.787564 Irish Pounds; 1936.27 Italian Lira; 40.3399 Luxembourg Francs; 2.20371 Dutch Guilders; 200.482 Portuguese Escudo, and 166.386 Spanish Pesetas). Furthermore, 1 Euro = 340.750 Greek Drachmas (Council Regulation (EC) No. 1478/2000 of June 19, 2000, [2000] O.J. L167/1). The euro is also the currency of a number of non-member countries; see para. 5–231, *infra*.

[1037] In accordance with the scenario approved by the European Council in Madrid on December 15 and 16, 1995 ((1995) EU Bull. 12, points I.3 and I.49). For the transitional provisions on the 2002 cash changeover, see Guideline ECB/2001/1 of the ECB of January 10, 2001, [2001] O.J. L55/80. For the status of the euro, see Malferrari, "Le statut juridique de l'euro dans la perspective du droit allemand, européen et international" (1998) C.D.E. 509–560; Botter, Van Kuijk, Van Olffen and Verdam, "Invoering van de euro in de verschillende lidstaten" (1998) T.V.V.S. 361–367; Sunt, "Juridische aspecten van de invoering van de euro" (1998–99) R.W. 761–778; Block, "Les incidences du passage à l'euro en procédure civile" (1999) J.T. 97–105; Usher, "Legal Background of the Euro" (1999) S.E.W. 12–23; Koppenol-Laforce, "De euro: enkele (internationaal) privaatrechtelijke aspecten" (November, 2000) Mededelingen van de Nederlandse vereniging voor internationaal recht 1–67; Ruiz Ruiz, "L'introduction de l'euro et la continuité des contrats sur les obligations

take the measures necessary for the rapid introduction of the euro as the single currency of the Member States.[1038]

C. ECONOMIC POLICY

Economic guidelines. Member State's economic policies must contribute to **5–224** the achievement of the objectives of the Community as defined in Art. 2 of the EC Treaty. The Member States and the Community are to act in accordance with the principle of an open market economy with free competition, favouring an efficient allocation of resources, and in compliance with the principles set out in Art. 4 of the EC Treaty (EC Treaty, Art. 98). Economic policy may require direct intervention on the part of the Community (EC Treaty, Art. 100(1), although it nevertheless consists primarily of measures of the Member States, which are to regard their economic policies as a matter of common concern and to co-ordinate them within the Council (EC Treaty, Art. 99(1)).[1039] To this end, the Council is to adopt "broad guidelines" in accordance with a procedure whereby the Council, acting by a qualified majority on a recommendation from the Commission, submits draft guidelines to the European Council and, subsequently, on the basis of the latter's conclusion, is to adopt a recommendation by a qualified majority setting out the broad guidelines. The Council has to inform the European Parliament of its recommendations (EC Treaty, Art. 99(2)).[1040] At the same time, the European Council has reached agreements on the co-ordination of economic policy in the third stage of EMU.[1041]

Stability and growth pact. The Member States' economic policies are to be **5–225** co-ordinated by means of multilateral surveillance of economic developments in each of the Member States and in the Community and of

---

pécuniaires" (2000) R.T.D.E. 705–726; Delpérée, "De invoering van de euro in de Belgische wetgeving" (2000–2001) R.W. 720–725. See also Denters, "Volkenrechtelijke aspecten van de introductie van de euro" (November 2000) Mededelingen van de Nederlandse vereniging voor internationaal recht 69–114.

[1038] The utility of this legal basis is not confined to measures for the introduction of the euro, see para. 5–231, *infra*.

[1039] Louis, "The Eurogroup and Economic Policy Co-ordination" (2001–2002) Euredia 19–43. Under Art. 202 of the EC Treaty, it falls to the Council to ensure co-ordination of the general economic policies of the Member States.

[1040] See the recommendations on the broad guidelines of the economic policies of the Member States and of the Community which the Council adopted on the basis of conclusions of the European Council on December 22, 1993 ([1994] O.J. L7/9), July 11, 1994 ([1994] O.J. L200/38), July 10, 1995 ([1995] O.J. L191/24; also (1995) 7/8 EU Bull. point 2.2.1), July 8, 1996 ([1996] O.J. L179/46; also (1996) 7/8 EU Bull. point 2.4.1), July 7, 1997 ([1997] O.J. L209/12; also (1997) 7/8 EU Bull. point 2.2.1), July 6, 1998 ([1998] O.J. L200/34; also (1998) 7/8 EU Bull. point 2.3.1), July 12, 1999 ([1999] O.J. L217/34), June 19, 2000 ([2000] O.J. L210/1), June 15, 2001 ([2001] O.J. L179/1), June 21, 2002 ([2002] O.J. L182/1) and June 26, 2003 ([2003] O.J. L195/1). See Buzelay, "De la co-ordination des politiques économiques nationales au sein de l'Union européenne" (2003) R.M.C.U.E. 235–241.

[1041] See points 1–6 of the Resolution of the European Council of December 13, 1997 on economic policy co-ordination in stage 3 of EMU and on Treaty Arts 109 and 109b [now Arts 111 and 112], [1998] O.J. C35/1.

their consistency with the broad guidelines. Economic policy co-ordination also affects the Member States which are not taking part in the third stage of EMU. This is intended to secure sustained convergence of the economic performance of the Member States. For the purpose of multilateral surveillance, Member States are obliged to forward information to the Commission about important measures taken by them in the field of their economic policy and such other information as they deem necessary. Pursuant to a stability and growth pact agreed in 1997, the Member States have to show each year by means of stability or convergence programmes that their budgetary situation provides an adequate basis for price stability and sustainable growth or that they are taking adjustment measures to that end.[1042] The Commission is to report to the Council, which has regularly to assess the situation (EC Treaty, Art. 99(3)). The President of the Council and the Commission have to report to the European Parliament on the results of multilateral surveillance (EC Treaty, Art. 99(4), second subpara., first sentence).

In the event that the economic policies of a Member State are not consistent with the broad guidelines or they risk jeopardising the proper functioning of EMU, the Council may, acting by qualified majority (the Member State concerned being entitled to vote), make the necessary—secret—recommendations to the Member State concerned.[1043] The Council may, acting by a qualified majority on a proposal from the Commission, decide to make its recommendation public (Art. 99(4), first subpara.),[1044] in which case the President of the Council may be invited to appear before the competent committee of the European Parliament (EC Treaty, Art. 99(4), second subpara., second sentence).

[1042] See Council Regulation (EC) No. 1466/97 of July 7, 1997 adopted on the basis of Art. 103(5), on the strengthening of the surveillance of budgetary positions and the surveillance and co-ordination of economic policies ([1997] O.J. L209/1), which requires Member States taking part in EMU to submit a stability programme and the others a convergence programme. The stability and growth pact, on which the European Council reached agreement in Dublin as long ago as December 1996 (see (1996) 12 EU Bull. point I.3), was elaborated on by Regulation No. 1466/97 and Council Regulation No. 467/97 on speeding up and clarifying the implementation of the excessive deficit procedure ([1997] O.J. L209/6) and the Resolution of the Amsterdam European Council of June 17, 1997 on the stability and growth pact ([1997] O.J. C236/1). For a recent assessment, see Gellhoed, "Het stabiliteitspact, zin en onzin" (2003) S.E.W. 42–49; see, further, Amtenbrink and De Haan, "Economic Governance in the European Union: Fiscal Policy Discipline Versus Flexibility" (2003) C.M.L.R. 1075–1106; Hahn, "The Stability Pact for European Monetary Union: Compliance with Deficit Limit as a Constant Legal Duty" (1998) C.M.L.R. 77–106; Martenczuk, "Der Europäische Rat und die Wirtschafts- und Währungsunion" (1998) EuR. 151, at 158–165, Amtenbrink, De Haan and Sleijpen, "Stability and Growth Pact: Placebo or Panacea?" (1997) E.Bus.L.Rev. 202–210 and 233–238.

[1043] The EU Constitution introduces an intermediate stage, in which the Commission may address a warning to the Member State concerned (Art. III–179(4), first subpara.).

[1044] See also, as regards the stability and growth pact, Art. 6 of Council Regulation (EC) No. 1466/97 (n.1042, *supra*). See the Council Recommendation of February 12, 2001 with a view to ending the inconsistency with the broad guidelines of the economic policies in Ireland ([2001] O.J. L69/22) and the Recommendation of January 21, 2003 with a view to giving early warning to France in order to prevent the occurrence of an excessive deficit ([2003] O.J. L34/18).

Community measures. On the basis of Art. 100, which empowers the **5–226** Council, acting by a qualified majority vote on a proposal from the Commission, to "decide upon the measures appropriate to the economic situation", the Council itself can pursue an economic policy. In particular, Art. 100(2) of the EC Treaty provides that "Community financial assistance" may be granted to a Member State in the event of severe difficulties "caused by natural disasters or exceptional occurrences beyond its control". The President of the Council has to inform the European Parliament of the decision taken.

Prohibitions. The Treaty imposes specific prohibitions in regard to **5–227** economic policy. They are contained in Art. 101(1), Art. 102(1) and Art. 103(1) of the EC Treaty (see para. 5–228), which have been in force for the Community and the Member States since the second stage entered into effect,[1045] and in Art. 104 of the EC Treaty (see para. 5–229).

No bail out. Article 101(1) of the EC Treaty prohibits monetary financing **5–228** of Community institutions or bodies, central governments, regional, local or other public authorities, other bodies governed by public law or public undertakings of the Member States, with the result that neither the European Central Bank (ECB) nor the national central banks may grant them credit or overdraft facilities or purchase their debt instruments directly from them.[1046] Article 102(1) of the EC Treaty precludes the same entities from having privileged access to financial institutions, unless this is based on prudential considerations. Article 103(1) declares that neither the Community nor a particular Member State may be made liable for the commitments of any (other) Member State (the "no bail out" rule).[1047]

Excessive deficits. Article 104(1) of the EC Treaty provides that the **5–229** Member States are to avoid excessive government deficits.[1048] The Commission is to monitor the development of the budgetary situation and of the stock of government debt in the Member States having regard, *inter alia*, to the ratio of government deficit and government debt, respectively,

---

[1045] EC Treaty, Art. 113(3).

[1046] This does not prevent central banks from supplying publicly owned credit institutions with liquidity in the same way as private credit institutions (EC Treaty, Art. 101(2)).

[1047] The Council is entitled to lay down definitions for the purpose of the application of these prohibitory provisions. Thus, on December 13, 1993, the Council adopted Regulation No. 3604/93, pursuant to Art. 104a [now Art. 102], specifying definitions for the application of the prohibition of privileged access referred to in Art. 104a [now Art. 102] of the Treaty, [1993] O.J. L332/4, and Regulation No. 3603/93, pursuant to Art. 104b [now Art. 103](2), specifying definitions for the application of the prohibitions referred to in Arts 104 and 104b(1) [now Arts 101 and 103(1)] of the Treaty, [1993] O.J. L332/1, as amended by Regulation No. 475/2000, [2000] O.J. L58/1.

[1048] This provision applies to Member States participating in the third stage of EMU. In the second stage, "Member States shall endeavour to avoid excessive deficits" (EC Treaty, Art. 116(3) and (4)).

to gross domestic product. Those ratios may not exceed reference values specified in a Protocol annexed to the Treaty (Art. 104(2)).[1049]

In the event that a Member State does not satisfy a given criterion or the Commission considers that there is a risk of an excessive deficit, the Commission is to prepare a report, on which the Economic and Financial Committee formulates an opinion. Where appropriate, the Commission is to address an opinion to the Council (Art. 104(3)–(5)). After hearing any observations from the Member State concerned and deciding by a qualified majority whether an excessive deficit exists, the Council makes recommendations (which are not made public) to the Member State (Art. 104(6) and (7)).[1050] Any Member State is at liberty to publish a recommendation concerning it.[1051] If the Member State takes no effective action in response to the recommendations, the Council itself may make them public (Art. 104(8)).

If a Member State persists in failing to put into practice the Council's recommendations, the Council may give it notice to take remedial measures

---

[1049] Protocol (No. 20)—annexed by the EU Treaty to the EC Treaty—on the excessive deficit procedure provides that the planned or actual government deficit may not exceed 3 per cent of gross domestic product and that government debt may not exceed 60 per cent of gross domestic product. Art. 104(2)(a) of the EC Treaty allows the reference values to be overshot where the deficit or debt is declining and comes close thereto. In assessing government deficit, the Commission takes account of all relevant factors, including the ratio between the deficit and investment expenditure and the medium-term economic and budgetary situation (EC Treaty, Art. 104(3), first subpara.). For clarifications of the terms employed in Art. 104, see Art. 2 of Regulation No. 1467/97, (n.1042, *supra*).

[1050] On September 26, 1994 the Council found, in accordance with the Commission's opinion, that such a deficit existed in all the Member States with the exception of Luxembourg and Ireland ((1994) 9 EU Bull. point 1.2.11), and consequently made recommendations to each of the other Member States ((1994) 11 EU Bull. point 1.2.11). On July 10, 1995 the Council abrogated the decision on the existence of an excessive deficit in Germany and found that such a deficit existed in the three new Member States ((1996) 7/8 EU Bull. points 1.3.8–9). On July 27, 1996 the Council abrogated the decision on the existence of an excessive deficit in Denmark (Decision 96/420/EC, [1996] O.J. L172/25), but found that Germany once more had such a deficit (Decision 96/421/EC, [1996] O.J. L172/26). On June 30, 1997 the Council abrogated the decisions on the existence of an excessive deficit in the Netherlands and Finland (Decisions 97/416/EC and 97/417/EC, [1997] O.J. L177/23 and 24), on May 1, 1998 in respect of Belgium, Germany, Austria, France, Italy, Spain, Portugal, Sweden and the UK (Decisions 98/307/EC–98/315/EC, [1998] O.J. L139/9 to 20) and on December 17, 1999 in respect of Greece (Decision 2000/33/EC, [2000] O.J. L12/24). Excessive deficits were again found for Portugal on November 5, 2002 (Decision 2002/923/EC, [2002] O.J. L322/30), Germany on January 21, 2003 (Decision 2003/89/EC, [2003] O.J. L34/16) and France on June 3, 2003 (Decision 2003/487/EC, [2003] O.J. L165/29). The Council also sent on the same date to each of those States, pursuant to Art. 104(7), a recommendation on how to remedy the situation (the recommendations may be found on the website of the Commission's DG for Economic and Financial Affairs). In May 2004, the Commission launched the procedure to decide on excessive deficits with respect to several of the Member States which acceded on May 1.

[1051] This was agreed in the Council (1994) 10 EU Bull. point 1.2.3. However, the European Council invited the Member States to make public such recommendations on their own initiative: see the Resolution of the Amsterdam European Council of June 17, 1997 on the stability and growth pact, [1997] O.J. C236/1. Accordingly, the publication of the recommendations to France and Germany (see n.1050, *supra*) refers to those States' having consented to publication.

within a specified time-limit (Art. 104(9)).[1052] As long as a Member State fails to comply therewith, the Council may decide to apply "one or more of the following measures:—to require the Member State concerned to publish additional information, to be specified by the Council, before issuing bonds and securities;—to invite the European Investment Bank to reconsider its lending policy towards the Member State concerned;—to require the Member State concerned to make a non-interest-bearing deposit of an appropriate size with the Community until the excessive deficit has, in the view of the Council, been corrected;—to impose fines of an appropriate size" (Art. 104(11); the President of the Council is to inform the European Parliament of the decisions taken).[1053] Pursuant to the stability and growth pact, the Council has laid down strict time-limits for this procedure.[1054] It has also determined that the sanction which it would apply for an excessive deficit would be to require the offending Member State to make a non-interest-bearing deposit with the Commission. The deposit would be converted into a fine if the excessive deficit was not corrected within two years.[1055] Member States not taking part in the third stage of EMU are not subject to any sanctions for excessive general government deficits (see para. 5–232).

The right of the Commission or a Member State to bring an action against a Member State under Arts 226 and 227 of the EC Treaty may not be exercised within the framework of paras 1 to 9 of Art. 104 (Art. 104(10)). That right may, however, be exercised in order judicially to enforce sanctions imposed under Art. 104(11).

The Council takes the decisions referred to on a recommendation from the Commission.[1056] This means that the Council may adopt a decision different from that recommended by the Commission but cannot subsequently modify its decision without a fresh recommendation from the Commission.[1057] The Council adopts the decisions mentioned in paras 7–9

[1052] On November 25, 2003 the Council did not take up the Commission's recommendation to address a recommendation to France and Germany pursuant to Art. 104(8) and (9) of the EC Treaty. The Council evaluated in "conclusions" the measures taken by those Member States. The "conclusions" have been annulled by ECJ (judgment of July 13, 2004), Case C–27/04 *Commission v Council*, not yet reported (see nn. 1057 and 1061 and accompanying text, *infra*).

[1053] Once the deficit has been corrected, the Council is to abrogate its decisions; where public recommendations have been made, a public statement has to be given (Art. 104(12)). By the same token, the Council published the decisions abrogating decisions finding an excessive deficit: see n.1050, *supra*.

[1054] Council Regulation (EC) No. 1467/97 (n.1042, *supra*), Arts 3–8.

[1055] *ibid.*, Arts 11–16.

[1056] EC Treaty, Art. 104(6) and (13). The IGC failed to agree on the Convention's proposal to have both the Council decision as to whether an excessive deficit exists and the Council recommendation addressed to the Member State concerned adopted on a "proposal" from the Commission (see the initial version of Art. III–76(6) of the draft EU Constitution).

[1057] ECJ (judgment of July 13, 2004), Case C–27/04 *Commission v Council*, not yet reported, paras 91–92 (annulment of Council "conclusions" that modified a Council recommendation without a recommendation from the Commission and not in accordance with the voting rules prescribed).

and 11 and 12 of Art. 104 (*i.e.* not the actual decision finding an excessive deficit) by a special majority, excluding the votes of the representative of the Member State concerned.[1058] Further provisions on the implementation of the procedure described in Art. 104 are set out in the Protocol on the excessive deficit procedure, to which reference has already been made (Art. 104(14))[1059] and in the stability and growth pact as elaborated by the Council.[1060] The Council cannot have recourse to an alternative procedure, for example in order to adopt a measure that would not be the very decision envisaged at a given stage or that would be adopted in conditions different from those required by the applicable provisions.[1061]

D. MONETARY POLICY

5–230 Price stability. Monetary policy in the Member States participating in EMU is fully determined by the European System of Central Banks (Eurosystem or ESCB), a network of central banks, each possessing legal personality: the European Central Bank (ECB), which has legal personality by virtue of Art. 107(2) of the EC Treaty, and the central banks of the Member States, established under national law. Both the ECB and the national central banks operate within the ESCB complete independently of the national or Community political authorities.[1062] The primary objective of the ESCB is to maintain price stability and it is to support the general economic policies in the Community with a view to contributing to the achievement of the objectives of the Community as laid down in Art. 2 of the EC Treaty, in accordance with the principles prescribed for economic policy (EC Treaty, Art. 105(1); see Art. 98).[1063]

[1058] EC Treaty, Art. 104(13) refers to "two-thirds of the votes of its members weighted in accordance with Art. 205(2)".

[1059] n.1049, *supra*. The Council, acting unanimously on a proposal from the Commission and after consulting the European Parliament and the ECB, may replace the said Protocol (EC Treaty, Art. 104(14), second subpara.). The Council was entitled, before January 1, 1994, to lay down detailed rules and definitions for the application of the Protocol (Art. 104(14), third subpara.): Council Regulation (EC) No. 3605/93 of November 22, 1993 on the application of the Protocol on the excessive deficit procedure annexed to the Treaty establishing the European Community, [1993] O.J. L332/7.

[1060] See Council Regulation (EC) No. 1467/97, (n.1042, *supra*), adopted pursuant to Art. 104(14) of the EC Treaty.

[1061] ECJ (judgment of July 13, 2004), Case C–27/04 *Commission v Council*, not yet reported, paras 81–97 (Council "conclusions" annulled in so far as they contained a decision to hold the excessive deficit procedure in abeyance and a decision modifying the recommendation previously adopted by the Council).

[1062] Art. 108 of the EC Treaty and the Statute of the ECB, see para. 10–102. Each Member State has to ensure that its national legislation is compatible with the Treaty and the Statute of the ESCB (EC Treaty, Art. 109); see the provisions with regard to the term of office of the Governor of a national central bank (ESCB Statute, Art. 14.2) and special functions of national central banks (ESCB Statute, Art. 14.4, and Protocol (No. 22) on Denmark— annexed by the EU Treaty to the EC Treaty—which authorises the National Bank of Denmark to continue to carry out its existing tasks concerning those parts of the Kingdom of Denmark which are not part of the Community).

[1063] See Herdegen, "Price Stability and Budgetary Restraints in the Economic and Monetary Union: The Law as Guardian of Economic Wisdom" (1998) C.M.L.R. 9–32.

Monetary policy. The ESCB's four "basic tasks" are (Art. 105(2) and (3)): **5–231**

(1) to define and implement the monetary policy of the Community;

(2) to conduct foreign exchange operations;

(3) to hold and manage the official foreign reserves of the Member States, without prejudice to the governments of the Member States holding and managing working balances in foreign exchange; and

(4) to promote the smooth operation of payment systems.

The Statute of the ESCB defines the "monetary functions and operations of the ESCB".[1064]

The ECB draws up the necessary guidelines for the conduct of the common monetary policy, with which the national central banks have to comply.[1065] In so far as it is necessary for the performance of its tasks, the ECB may adopt regulations and decisions, make recommendations and deliver opinions.[1066] In its fields of competence, the ECB must be consulted on any proposed Community or draft national legislation[1067] and may itself submit opinions to the appropriate authorities (Art. 105(4)). It has certain reporting obligations.[1068]

The ECB is also responsible for developing an exchange rate system for the euro in relation to non-Community currencies. The Council takes its decisions in this connection, on a recommendation from the ECB or after consulting it (following a recommendation from the Commission), "in an endeavour to reach a consensus consistent with the objective of price

---

[1064] Protocol (No. 18)—annexed to the EC Treaty by the EU Treaty—on the Statute of the European System of Central Banks and of the European Central Bank, Arts 17–24.

[1065] For the monetary policy instruments and procedures of the Eurosystem, see Guideline ECB/2000/776 of the European Central Bank of August 31, 2000, [2000] O.J. L310/1, as most recently amended by ECB Guideline 2004/202/EC of December 1, 2003, [2004] O.J. L69/1. For the ECB's role within the ESCB, see Seidel, "Im Kompetenzkonflikt: Europäisches System der Zentralbanken (ESZB) versus EZB" (2000) Eu.Z.W 552–554; Weiss, "Kompetenzverteilung in der Währungspolitik und Außenvertretung des Euro" (2002) EuR. 165–191.

[1066] e.g. with regard to credit institutions, Regulation (EC) No. 2818/98 of December 1, 1998 of the European Central Bank on the application of minimum reserves, [1998] O.J. L356/1.

[1067] The obligation to consult applies to legislation relating to specific functions exercised by the ECB in the Community framework for which, by virtue of the high degree of expertise that it enjoys, the ECB is particularly well placed to play a useful role in the legislative process envisaged: ECJ, Case C–11/00 *Commission v European Central Bank* [2003] E.C.R. I–7147, paras 110–111 (no obligation in the case of legislation on combating fraud). The national authorities' obligation to consult the ECB has been fleshed out, in accordance with Art. 105(4), by Council Decision 98/415/EC of June 29, 1998 on the consultation of the European Central Bank by national authorities regarding draft legislative provisions, [1998] O.J. L189/42.

[1068] See EC Treaty, Art. 113(3) and Art. 122(2); ESCB Statute, Art. 15.

stability".[1069] Accordingly, the Council adopted rules entitling Monaco, San Marino, the Vatican City and certain overseas territories to use the Euro as their currency unit.[1070]

The ESCB is also to be responsible for contributing to the smooth conduct of policies pursued by the competent authorities relating to the prudential supervision of credit institutions and the stability of the financial system (Art. 105(5)). The Council, acting unanimously on a proposal from the Commission after consulting the ECB and receiving the assent of the European Parliament, may confer on the ECB specific tasks concerning policies relating to the prudential supervision of credit institutions and other financial institutions (but not insurance undertakings) (Art. 105(6)).

The ECB has the exclusive right to authorise the issue of banknotes within the Member States participating in the third stage of EMU. The ECB and the national central banks may issue such notes. They are the only banknotes to have the status of legal tender within the participating Member States (Art. 106(1)).[1071] The ECB and the central banks of the

---

[1069] The Council is empowered to conclude agreements on an exchange-rate system for the euro in relation to non-Community currencies (EC Treaty, Art. 111(1)). The Council decides by a unanimous vote on a recommendation from the ECB or the Commission after consulting the ECB and the European Parliament. The Council may, acting by a qualified majority on a recommendation from the ECB or from the Commission, and after consulting the ECB in an endeavour to reach a consensus consistent with the objective of price stability, adopt, adjust or abandon the central rates of the ecu within the exchange-rate system. The European Parliament is only informed after the event (*ibid.*). See the commitments already set out in points 7–10 of the Resolution of the European Council of December 13, 1997 on economic policy co-ordination in stage 3 of EMU and on Treaty Arts 109 and 109b [now Arts 111 and 113], [1998] O.J. C35/1. For policy with regard to the currencies of the Member States not taking part in the third stage of EMU, see para. 5–232, *infra*.

[1070] See the monetary agreements concluded by Italy on behalf of the Community with San Marino and the Vatican City ([2001] O.J. C209/1, and C299/1, respectively; see the amendments approved by the Council to the agreement with the Vatican City, [2003] O.J. L267/27) and by France on behalf of the Community with Monaco ([2002] O.J. C142/59). Under Council Decision 1999/95/EC of December 31, 1998 ([1999] O.J. L30/29), the euro is the currency unit of Saint-Pierre-et-Miquelon and Mayotte, which have the status of French overseas territories (TOMs) (see para. 20–016, *supra*). See the authorisations given by the Council to Portugal and France to conclude agreements with regard to the Cape Verde Escudo and with regard to the CFA and Comorian Franc, respectively, securing parity between the euro and those currencies: Decision 98/683/EC of November 23, 1998 ([1998] O.J. L320/58) and Decision 98/744/EC of December 21, 1998 ([1998] O.J. L358/111). For the use of the euro as domestic means of payment in other countries not belonging to the EU, see Stumpf, "The introduction of the euro to States and territories outside the European Union" (2003) E.L.Rev. 283–292, and the Commission's answer of March 18, 2002 to question E–0088/02 (Meijer), [2002] O.J. C309E/9. The Commission has been authorised to conclude an agreement with Andorra to that effect, see Council Decision 2004/548/EC of May 11, 2004 [2004] O.J. L244/47.

[1071] See the Decision ECB/2003/4 of the European Central Bank of March 20, 2003 on the denominations, specifications, reproduction, exchange and withdrawal of euro banknotes ([2003] O.J. L78/16) and Decision ECB/2001/15 of the ECB of December 6, 2001 on the issue of euro banknotes ([2001] O.J. L337/52).

participating Member States put banknotes denominated in euros into circulation as from January 1, 2002.[1072] The participating Member States have issued euro and cent coins from that date.[1073] Only the Member States are authorised to issue coins. However, the volume of coins issued must be approved by the ECB (Art. 106(2)).[1074] Pursuant to Art. 106(2), the Council has harmonised the denominations and technical specifications of euro coins.[1075] Accordingly, all euro coins have one common face and one face with a national design.[1076] Pursuant to the third subpara. of Art. 123(4) of the EC Treaty, the Council is to take the measures necessary for the introduction of the euro (since the Treaty of Nice by a qualified majority vote).[1077] In this way, it adopts the necessary measures to protect the euro against counterfeiting.[1078]

[1072] Art. 10 of Council Regulation (EC) No. 974/98 of May 3, 1998 on the introduction of the Euro, [1998] O.J. L139/1. Banknotes are denominated in the range 5 Euros to 500 Euros.

[1073] *ibid.*, Art. 11.

[1074] For the prior authorisation by the ECB of the volume of coin issuance as from 2000, see Decisions ECB/1999/11 of December 23, 1999 ([2000] O.J. L4/18), ECB/2001/17 of December 14, 2000 ([2000] O.J. L336/118), ECB/2002/19 of December 20, 2001 ([2001] O.J. L334/89), ECB/2002/12 of December 19, 2002 ([2002] O.J. L358/144) and ECB/2003/15 of November 28, 2003 ([2003] O.J. L324/57).

[1075] Council Regulation (EC) No. 975/98 of May 3, 1998 on denominations and technical specifications of euro coins intended for circulation, [1998] O.J. L139/6 (the text of which had already been determined, see the Annex to the Council Resolution of January 19, 1998 on denominations and technical specifications of Euro coins intended for circulation, [1998] O.J. C35/5).

[1076] Photographs of the common face and the national faces together with a description of their designs may be found in the Commission communication: "The visual characteristics of the euro coins", [2001] O.J. C373/1.

[1077] See Servais, Vigneron and Ruggeri, "Le Traité de Nice. Son impact sur l'Union économique et monétaire" (2000) Euredia 477, at 483. The EU Constitution provides for such a legal basis in Art. III–191. In order to make cross-border payments cheaper with the introduction of the euro, the European Parliament and the Council adopted on December 19, 2001, pursuant to Art. 95 of the EC Treaty, Regulation No. 2560/2001 on cross-border payments in euro, [2001] O.J. L344/13. See Allix, "Le règlement sur les paiements transfrontaliers en euros: les bases de l'espace unique de paiement" (2002) R.D.U.E. 485–511.

[1078] For those Member States which have adopted the euro as their currency unit, the Council uses Art. 123(4) of the EC Treaty; since the Euro has to enjoy the same protection in the other Member States, the Council has extended those measures to the other Member States on the basis of Art. 308 of the EC Treaty, see Council Regulation (EC) No. 1338/2001 and extending Council Regulation (EC) No. 1339/2001 both of June 28, 2001 ([2001] O.J. L181/6 and 11) and the "Pericles" action programme establishing an exchange, assistance and training programme for the protection of the Euro against counterfeiting, established by Council Decision 2001/923/EC and extending Decision 2001/924/EC of December 17, 2001 ([2001] O.J. L339/50 and 55). For co-operation between the European and national central banks, Europol and Eurojust, see Council Decision 2001/887/JHA of December 6, 2001 on the protection of the euro against counterfeiting ([2001] O.J. L329/1) and the Agreement of December 13, 2001 between the European Police Office (Europol) and the European Central Bank (ECB) ([2002] O.J. C23/11); for the Counterfeit Monitoring System (CMS), see Decision 2001/912/EC of the European Central Bank of November 8, 2001 ([2001] O.J. L337/49). See also Van den Berghe, "Valsemunterij en de euro" (2002) S.E.W. 3–10.

E.   POSITION OF MEMBER STATES NOT BELONGING TO THE EURO ZONE

5–232 **Derogations.** Member States not fulfilling the requisite conditions for adoption of a single currency fall under a derogating system, conduct their own monetary policies, retain their own currencies and will not take part in the Council's international monetary action. Major rules in force for the third stage of EMU do not apply to them: they cannot have sanctions imposed upon them by the Council on account of excessive budget deficits; they are not subject to decisions of the ECB (and their undertakings are not liable to have fines or periodic penalty payments imposed on them by the ECB), and they are not entitled to vote for members of the Executive Board of the ECB.[1079] Accordingly, they are not able to vote in the Council or the ECB when decisions are taken in this connection (see para. 14–071). Nevertheless, they must avoid excessive deficits (EC Treaty, Art. 104(1)) and submit an annual convergence programme to this end.[1080] In order to foster convergence of their economies and to obtain support for their monetary policies, these Member States may voluntarily take part in an exchange rate mechanism ("ERM II" or "EMS 2"), linking their currencies with the euro.[1081] That exchange rate mechanism is based on central rates against the euro, with the ECB and the non-euro-zone Member States' central banks being committed to intervene at the margins.[1082] Decisions on central rates and the standard fluctuation band are taken by mutual agreement of the euro-zone Member States, the ECB and the ministers and central bank governors of the non-euro-zone Member States participating in ERM II following a procedure involving the Commission and after

---

[1079] See the provisions listed in Art. 122(3) and (4), Art. 123(1) and Art. 124(2) of the EC Treaty. Member States with a derogation may have recourse to protective measures within the meaning of Arts 119 and 120 (EC Treaty, Art. 122(6)).

[1080] para. 5–225, *supra*.

[1081] See the Resolution of the Amsterdam European Council of June 16, 1997 on the establishment of an exchange rate mechanism in the third stage of economic and monetary union ([1997] O.J. C236/5), as effectuated by the Agreement of September 1, 1998 between the European Central Bank and the national central banks of the Member States outside the euro area laying down the operating procedures for an exchange rate mechanism in stage three of Economic and Monetary Union, [1998] O.J. C345/6 (amended in view of the accession of 10 new Member States by Agreement of April 29, 2004, [2004] O.J. C135/3). Those arrangements are to be enlarged upon in an agreement between the ECB and the central banks of the Member States concerned. The Danish krone, which took part in the first European Monetary System (EMS; see para. 2–011, *supra*), is taking part in EMR II. Estonia, Lithuania and Slovenia joined EMR II in June 2004. Cyprus intends to take part in ERM II early 2005; Hungary, Latvia, Malta and the Slovak Republic intend to join in the course of 2005, Poland in 2008–2009 and the Czech Republic in 2009–2010. *Europe*, No.8700, May 6, 2004, at 11.

[1082] There is one standard fluctuation band of plus or minus 15 per cent around the central rate fixed against the euro: Resolution of the European Council of June 16, 1997, *ibid.*, point 2.1. At the request of EMS 2 Member States, even narrower bands may be fixed: *ibid.*, point 2.3. As a result, the band for the Danish Krone has been set at plus or minus 2.25 per cent (*Europe* No.7375, January 4–5, 1999, 7).

consultation of the Economic and Financial Committee.[1083] Member States not participating in ERM II from the outset may join at a later date.[1084]

At least every two years or at the request of a Member State with a derogation, the Commission and the ECB are to report to the Council, which is to decide which Member States with a derogation have fulfilled the necessary conditions in the meantime. The Council will sit in its normal composition when taking that decision, but it must first consult the European Parliament and discuss the matter in the Council meeting in the composition of the Heads of State or Government. Member States with derogation will take part in the vote, which requires a qualified majority (Art. 122(2)). In this way, the Council decided on June 19, 2000 to abrogate the derogation with regard to Greece with effect from January 1, 2001.[1085] In the event that the Council abrogates the derogation of a Member State, it is to adopt, by a unanimous vote of the Member States without a derogation and the Member State concerned, the rate at which the euro is to be substituted for its currency, and the necessary accompanying measures (Art. 123(5)).[1086]

United Kingdom and Denmark. The United Kingdom and Denmark are **5–233** covered by special protocols.[1087] Those Member States enjoy a measure of latitude as to whether or not they take part in the third stage of EMU, even if they do fulfil the requisite conditions. Before the Council made its assessment of all the Member States, Britain and Denmark were entitled to make their intentions clear.

By giving notice that it did not intend to take part in the third stage[1088] Denmark was granted an exemption, resulting in its obtaining the status of a Member State with a derogation in the third stage. Unlike other Member States with derogation, the exemption may be abrogated only at Denmark's request, in which case the procedure set out in Art. 122(2) of the EC Treaty

---

[1083] *ibid.*, points 2.3–2.4. The ministers and central bank governors of Member States not taking part in EMS 2 participate in the procedure but have no vote: *ibid.*

[1084] *ibid.*, point 1.6. The exchange rate of the euro in the currencies of the non-participating Member States is established daily and published in the *Official Journal* (Financial Regulation, Art. 11(5)). This is done also for the currencies of major trading partners.

[1085] Council Decision 2000/427/EC of June 19, 2000, [2000] O.J. L167/19.

[1086] For the conversion rate between the euro and the Greek Drachma, see Regulation No.1478/2000: see n.1036, *supra*.

[1087] Protocol (No.25) annexed to the EC Treaty on certain provisions relating to the United Kingdom of Great Britain and Northern Ireland; Protocol (No.26) annexed to the EC Treaty on certain provisions relating to Denmark. The two protocols were annexed to the EC Treaty by the EU Treaty. See Vigneron and Mollica, "La différenciation dans l'union économique et monétaire—Dispositions juridiques et processus décisionnel" (2000) Euredia 197–231.

[1088] Section B of the Decision of the Heads of State and Government, meeting within the European Council on December 11 and 12, 1992, concerning certain problems raised by Denmark on the Treaty on European Union, [1992] O.J. C348/2.

will be followed.[1089] In a referendum held on September 28, 2000, 53.1 per cent of Danes voted against the introduction of the common currency.[1090]

The United Kingdom also notified the Council that it did not intend to enter the third stage. That country not only retains its monetary powers, it also does not have to subscribe to the actual objective of monetary union (EC Treaty, Art. 4(2)) or to a number of essential obligations which Member States with a derogation accept completely in the third stage: the United Kingdom will only have to "endeavour" to overcome excessive government deficits,[1091] will not have to consult the ECB on draft monetary/economic legislation and would not have to remove political control from the Bank of England (although it has in fact done so).[1092] The Protocol also authorises the United Kingdom so long as it does not participate in the third stage to continue not to comply with the prohibition of monetary financing of public authorities laid down in Art. 101 of the EC Treaty.[1093] If the United Kingdom gives notice that it wishes to take part in EMU, the Council is to decide on its request in accordance with the procedure laid down in Art. 122(2) of the EC Treaty and adopt the necessary measures pursuant to Art. 123(5) of the EC Treaty.[1094]

IV. OTHER AREAS OF COMMUNITY POLICY

5–234 Flanking policies. In addition to the aforementioned policy areas, the Third Part of the EC Treaty mentions other fields in which the Community intends to pursue (internal) policies: employment, social policy, education, vocational training and youth, culture, public health, consumer protection, Trans-European networks, industry, economic and social cohesion, research and technological development and the environment. A description of the scope of these policy areas is set out below. The external powers

---

[1089] Arts 3 and 4 of Protocol (No.26) on certain provisions relating to Denmark. As a result of Section E of the December 1992 decision, Denmark may "at any time" inform other Member States that it no longer wishes to avail itself of all or part of that decision, upon which Denmark will "apply in full all relevant measures then in force taken within the framework of the European Union".

[1090] *Europe*, September 30, 2000, p.4.

[1091] However, the obligations of the stability and growth pact continue to be applicable: see the third and fourth recitals in the preambles to Regulation Nos 1466/97 and 1467/97 (n.1042, *supra*).

[1092] See the list of Articles of the EC Treaty and the Statute of the ESCB in Arts 5–8 of the Protocol relating to the UK. For the independence of the Bank of England, see the Bank of England Act 1997.

[1093] Art. 11 of the Protocol relating to the UK which refers to the ways and means facility with the Bank of England.

[1094] Art. 10(a) and (c) of the Protocol relating to the UK. An act of Parliament is required before the UK Government may give such notice; see the European Communities (Amendment) Act 1993 (reproduced in Denza, "La ratification du traité de Maastricht par le Royaume Uni" (1994) R.M.C.U.E. 172, at 180).

(development co-operation and other forms of co-operation with third countries) are discussed in Part VI.

Those internal powers will be confirmed without significant alterations in the EU Constitution. Certain policy areas will be categorised, however, as "areas where the Union may take co-ordinating, complementary or supporting action" (these are public health, industry, culture, education, vocational training, youth and sport). The EU Constitution will also include some new policy areas in this category (tourism, civil protection and administrative co-operation), whilst "energy" will be listed, as a new policy area, among the general category of shared competences set out in Art. I–14(2).

A. SOCIAL POLICY AND EMPLOYMENT

Social policy. The harmonisation of national legislation which the **5–235** Community has carried out pursuant to specific or general Treaty provisions in order to realise the common market, has often affected Member States' social policy.[1095] The third para. of Art. 136 of the EC Treaty reflects the Member States' belief that social progress will ensue "not only from the functioning of the common market, which will favour the harmonisation of social systems, but also from the procedures provided for in this Treaty and from the approximation of provisions laid down by law, regulation or administrative action" Harmonisation measures have been adopted pursuant to Arts 94, 95 and 308 of the EC Treaty.[1096] In addition, the Community has had the possibility from the outset of pursuing its own social policy and this was widened by the addition of a special "social" harmonisation power in Art. 118a of the EEC Treaty.[1097]

The Heads of State or Government of eleven Member States (not including the United Kingdom) concluded on December 9, 1989 the

---

[1095] See EC Treaty, Art. 33(1)(b) (agriculture); Arts 40 and 42 (free movement of workers); Art. 150 (vocational training).

[1096] See, *e.g.* the directives on equal treatment of men and women (all listed in nn.260–262, to para. 5–063, *supra*), adopted pursuant to Art. 100 [now Art. 94] of the EC Treaty (Directive 75/117), Art. 235 [now Art. 308] of the EC Treaty (Directives 76/207 and 79/7) or both articles (Directives 86/613 and 86/378). For directives adopted on the basis of Art. 100 [now Art. 94], see also Council Directive 98/59/EC of July 20, 1998 on the approximation of the laws of the Member States relating to collective redundancies ([1998] O.J. L225/16) and those cited in n.1105 to para. 5–236, *infra*.

[1097] Pursuant to the former Art. 118a of the EC Treaty, the Council adopted directives setting out minimum requirements with a view to improving the working environment and protecting workers' health and safety. For the scope of Art. 118a and the review in the light of that provision of Council Directive 93/104/EC of November 23, 1993 concerning certain aspects of the organisation of working time ([1993] O.J. L307/18), see ECJ, Case C–84/94 *UK v Council* [1996] E.C.R. I–5755, paras 11–45, with a case note by Van Nuffel (1997) Col.J.E.L. 298–309; see also Banks, "L'article 118 A—Element dynamique de la politique communautaire" (1993) C.D.E. 537–554.

Charter of Fundamental Social Rights of Workers.[1098] At the 1990–1991 Intergovernmental Conference, the United Kingdom alone opposed the incorporation into the EC Treaty of broader objectives and instruments for the purpose of giving effect to the Charter. The other Member States agreed on more extensive powers to be exercised using the Community institutions pursuant to a protocol annexed to the EC Treaty and in accordance with an agreement which they concluded (the "Social Agreement").[1099] Depending upon the objective and content of the proposed action and the expected standpoint of the United Kingdom, the Community therefore based its social policy either on the EC Treaty or on the Social Agreement. In the Treaty of Amsterdam, the United Kingdom agreed to incorporate the broader powers provided for by the Social Agreement in the EC Treaty as the new Arts 136–143 (and to repeal the Social Agreement and the Social Protocol[1100]). At the same time, the Contracting Parties emphasised the promotion of employment as a prime objective of the Community (EU Treaty, Art. 2, first indent) and added a new title to the Treaty for the co-ordination of national employment policies.[1101] Various fundamental social rights have now been recognised in the chapter on "solidarity" of the Charter of Fundamental Rights of the European Union.[1102]

[1098] (1989) 12 EC Bull. point 1.1.10; the text may be found in Commission of the European Communities, *Social Europe*, 1/90; see also Blanpain and Engels, *European Labour Law* (Kluwer Law International, The Hague, 1998), at 441–448; Bercusson, "The European Community's Charter of Fundamental Social Rights of Workers" (1990) M.L.R. 624–642; Hepple, "The Implementation of the Community Charter of Fundamental Social Rights" (1991) M.L.R. 643–654; Watson, "The Community Social Charter" (1991) C.M.L.R. 37–68.

[1099] See Protocol (No.14) on social policy, annexed by the EU Treaty to the EC Treaty ([1992] O.J. C224/126) and the Agreement on social policy concluded between the Member States of the European Community with the exception of the UK of Great Britain and Northern Ireland ([1992] O.J. C224/127). The Social Agreement was accepted as it stood by the Member States which joined the Community in 1995. For the construction brought about by the Social Protocol and the Social Agreement, see para. 9–003, *infra*.

[1100] Treaty of Amsterdam, Art. 2(58).

[1101] For a general discussion of Community social policy, see Barnard, *EC Employment Law* (Wiley, Chichester, 2000), 600 pp.; Lenaerts and Foubert, "De plaats van de sociale politiek in het Europees Gemeenschapsrecht" in *Liber Amicorum Prof. Dr. Roger Blanpain* (Die Keure, Bruges, 1998), at 15–36; Flynn, "EC Labour Law after Maastricht: A Critical Evaluation" (1996) Ir.J.E.L. 164–188; Martin, "Le droit social communautaire: droit commun des Etats membres de la Communauté européenne en matière sociale" (1994) R.T.D.E. 609–630; Watson, "Social Policy After Maastricht" (1993) C.M.L.R. 481–513; Whiteford, "Social Policy After Maastricht" (1993) E.L. Rev. 202–222.

[1102] See workers' right to information and consultation within the undertaking (Art. 27), the right of collective bargaining and action (Art. 28), the right of access to placement services (Art. 29), the right to protection in the event of unjustified dismissal (Art. 30), the right to fair and just working conditions, including the right to paid leave (Art. 31), the prohibition of child labour and protection of young people at work (Art. 32), the right to family and professional life, including the right to be paid maternity leave and to parental leave (Art. 33), and entitlement to social security and social assistance (Art. 34). See De Schutter, "La contribution de la Charte des droits fondamentaux de l'Union européenne à la garantie des droits sociaux dans l'ordre juridique communautaire" (2000) R.U.D.H. 33–47; McGlynn, "Families and the European Union Charter of Fundamental Rights: progressive change or entrenching the status quo?" (2001) E.L.Rev. 582–598.

The EU Constitution does not propose to confer new competences on the Union in the social sphere. On the contrary, the EU Constitution emphasises that the Commission may have recourse to an open method of co-ordination so as to submit national social policies to periodic monitoring and evaluation on the basis of guidelines and indicators established in common and for the purposes of the exchange of information.[1103]

Minimum harmonisation. As objectives of the social policy of the **5–236** Community and the Member States, Art. 136 of the EC Treaty refers to the promotion of employment, the steady improvement of living and working conditions, proper social protection, dialogue between management and labour, the development of human resources, lasting high employment and the combating of exclusion.[1104] The Community and the Member States are to take account of the diverse forms of national practices, in particular in the field of contractual relations, and the need to maintain the competitiveness of the Community economy (Art. 136, second para.).

In order to support and complement Member States' activities, the Council is to adopt directives embodying minimum requirements relating to:

(a) improvement of the working environment (with a view to protecting workers' health and safety);

(b) working conditions;

(c) social security and social protection of workers;

(d) protection of workers where their employment contract is terminated;

(e) the information and consultation of workers;

(f) representation and collective defence of the interests of workers and employers;

(g) conditions of employment for third-country nationals legally residing in Community territory;

(h) the integration of persons excluded from the labour market; and

(i) equality between men and women with regard to labour market opportunities and treatment at work (Art. 137(1) and (2), first subpara., indent (b)).

[1103] EU Constitution, Art. III–213, second para. This method already applies in relation to employment policy, see para. 5–237, *infra*. For this "open method of co-ordination", see para. 5–213, *supra*; for the utility of this method as far as social policy is concerned, see Vandenbroucke, *The EU and Social Protection: What Should the European Convention Propose*, MPIfG Working Paper 02/6, June 2002, at 2.1.

[1104] EC Treaty, Art. 136, first para. The former Art. 117 referred only to improving the standard of living and working conditions, although a high level of employment and social protection was already mentioned in the former Art. 2 of the EC Treaty. For a practical expression of these objectives, see the European Social Agenda approved by the European Council of December 7–9, 2000 in Nice, [2001] O.J. C157/4.

Such directives are to avoid holding back the creation and development of small and medium-sized undertakings (Art. 137(2)(b)). In this way, directives have been adopted requiring Community-scale undertakings and groups of undertakings to introduce a European Works Council or an information and consultation procedure and establishing a general framework for informing and consulting employees.[1105] The Council may adopt measures for encouraging co-operation between Member States in these areas and also with a view to combating social exclusion and modernising systems of social protection, without proceeding to any harmonisation of national laws or regulations (Art. 137(2), first subparagraph, indent (a)).[1106] Such directives and other measures are not to affect the right of Member States to define the fundamental principles of their social security systems and must not significantly affect the financial equilibrium of those systems. In addition, those measures do not prevent any Member State from maintaining or introducing more stringent protective measures (Art. 137(4)). In principle, the Council adopts the measures in question under the co-decision procedure with the European Parliament; in cases (c), (d), (f) and (g) the Council has to act unanimously after consulting the European Parliament. However, the Treaty provides that the Council, acting unanimously on a proposal from the Commission, after consulting the European Parliament, may decide to render the co-decision procedure applicable to cases (d), (f) and (g) (Art. 137(2), second subpara.). In some cases, Art. 137 is inapplicable, namely in the case

---

[1105] Council Directive 94/45/EC of September 22, 1994 on the establishment of a European Works Council or a procedure in Community-scale undertakings and Community-scale groups of undertakings for the purposes of informing and consulting employees ([1994] O.J. L254/64); Directive 2002/14/EC of the European Parliament and of the Council of March 11, 2002 of the European Parliament and of the Council establishing a general framework for informing and consulting employees in the European Community ([2002] O.J. L80/219). See Pélissier, "Le droit à l'information et à la consultation des travailleurs" (1997) R.M.C.U.E. 203–212; Blanpain (ed.), *Labour Law and Industrial Relations in the European Union* (Kluwer Law International, The Hague, 1998), 238 pp.; Rojot, Le Flanchec and Voynnet-Fourboul, "European Collective Bargaining, New Prospects or Much Ado about Little?" (2001) Int'l J. Comp.Lab.L. Ind. Rel. 345–370. For further applications of Art. 2(2) of the Social Agreement—whose wording is the basis of Art. 137 of the EC Treaty—, see Council Directive 97/80/EC of December 15, 1997 on the burden of proof in cases of discrimination based on sex ([1998] O.J. L14/6); Council Directive 96/34/EC of June 3, 1996 on the framework agreement on parental leave concluded by UNICE, CEEP and the ETUC, [1996] O.J. L145/4; Council Directive 97/81/EC of December 15, 1997 concerning the Framework Agreement on part-time work concluded by UNICE, CEEP and the ETUC, [1998] O.J. L14/9. These directives have been extended to cover the UK pursuant to Art. 100 [now Art. 94] of the EC Treaty by Council Directive 97/74/EC of December 15, 1997, [1998] O.J. L10/22 (for Directive 94/45/EC); Council Directive 97/75/EC of December 15, 1997, [1998] O.J. L10/24 (for Council Directive 96/34/EC); Directive 98/23/EC of April 7, 1998, [1998] O.J. L131/10 (for Council Directive 97/81) and Council Directive 98/52/EC of July 13, 1998, [1998] O.J. L205/66 (for Directive 97/80).

[1106] See the Community action programme to encourage co-operation between Member States to combat social exclusion, adopted by Decision 50/2002/EC of the European Parliament and of the Council of December 7, 2001 ([2002] O.J. L10/1), and Schoukens, "How the European Union Keeps the Social Welfare Debate on Track: A Lawyer's View of the EU Instruments Aimed at Combating Social Exclusion" (2002) E.J.Soc.Sec. 117–150.

of pay, the right of association, the right to strike and the right to impose lock-outs (EC Treaty, Art. 137(5)).

The EC Treaty encourages management and labour themselves to conclude agreements at Community level and they may be charged with the implementation of directives adopted by the Council (see paras 14–041–14–042). The Commission is charged to promote dialogue between management and labour at European level (Art. 138(1)) and to encourage co-operation between the Member States by making studies, delivering opinions and arranging consultations on a variety of subjects (Art. 140).[1107]

The task of the European Social Fund is to render the employment of workers easier, to increase their geographical and occupational mobility and to facilitate their adaptation to industrial changes and changes in production systems, in particular through vocational training and retraining (Art. 146; see also Art. 150 as regards vocational training).[1108] The European Parliament and the Council adopt implementing decisions relating to the Fund (EC Treaty, Art. 148); it is administered by the Commission, assisted by a committee composed of representatives of governments, trade unions and employers' associations (EC Treaty, Art. 147).[1109]

Article 141 of the EC Treaty puts Member States under a duty to ensure the application of the principle that men and women should receive equal pay for equal work or work of equal value. That principle has direct effect.[1110] Through the many questions which national courts have referred for preliminary rulings, the Court of Justice has given a broad interpretation to the term "pay" and has clarified several instances of direct and indirect discrimination.[1111] The Community also pursues a general policy on equal opportunities for men and women (see para. 5–063).

[1107] The Council set up, pursuant to Art. 235 [now Art. 308] of the EC Treaty, a European Foundation for the Improvement of Living and Working Conditions (Council Regulation (EEC) No. 1365/75 of May 26, 1975, [1975] O.J. L139/1) and a European Agency for Safety and Health at Work (Council Regulation (EC) No. 2062/94 of July 18, 1994, [1994] O.J. L216/1), which principally carry out studies and exchange information between Member States.

[1108] Council Decision 83/516/EEC of October 17, 1983 on the tasks of the European Social Fund, [1983] O.J. L289/38.

[1109] See Regulation (EC) No. 1784/1999 of the European Parliament and of the Council of July 12, 1999 on the European Social Fund, [1999] O.J. L213/5.

[1110] ECJ, Case 43/75 *Defrenne* [1976] E.C.R. 445, paras 24 and 40. See the discussion of the principle of equal treatment, in paras 5–063 and 5–067, *supra*. In the light of the recognition of the principle of non-discrimination as a fundamental right, the original economic aim pursued by Art. 119 [now Art. 141] of the EC Treaty, namely the elimination of distortions of competition between undertakings established in different Member States, is secondary to the social aim pursued by that provision of the Treaty; see ECJ, Case C–50/96 *Schröder* [2000] E.C.R. I–743, paras 53–57, and ECJ, Joined Cases C–270/97 and C–271/97 *Sievers and Schrage* [2000] E.C.R. I–929, paras 53–57.

[1111] para. 5–067, *supra*. For the temporal effect of Art. 141 following the judgments in *Defrenne* and *Barber*, see para. 17–153, *infra*.

5–237 Employment. In order to achieve the objective of a high level of employment, the Member States and the Community are to work towards a co-ordinated strategy for employment and particularly for promoting a skilled and adaptable workforce and labour markets responsive to economic change (EC Treaty, Art. 125).[1112]

The Member States are to regard promoting employment as a matter of common concern "having regard to national practices related to the responsibilities of management and labour". Their employment policies are to be consistent with the broad guidelines of their economic policies (see para. 5–224) and they are to co-ordinate their action in this respect within the Council (EC Treaty, Art. 126(1) and (2)). To this end, the Council is to draw up separate "guidelines" each year as the culmination of a procedure in which the Council and the Commission submit a joint annual report to the European Council on the employment situation, on the basis of which the latter is to adopt conclusions. The conclusions are to be used in turn as the basis for the guidelines, which are to be adopted by the Council by a qualified majority on a proposal from the Commission and after consulting the European Parliament and the advisory Employment Committee (EC Treaty, Art. 128(1) and (2)).[1113] Article 128(2) provides that these social guidelines have to be consistent with the broad economic-policy guidelines adopted pursuant to Art. 99 of the EC Treaty, which, however, provides for less of a say on the part of the other institutions.[1114] On the basis of annual reports furnished by the Member States, the Council is to carry out an examination of the implementation of national employment policies in the light of the employment guidelines. This so-called "Luxembourg Process" results in exposing national politicies to peer review with the aim of learning from examples of 'best practices'.[1115] If the Council considers it appropriate, it may,

---

[1112] See Szyszczak, "The New Paradigm for Social Policy: A Virtuous Circle?" (2001) C.M.L.R. 1125–1170; Euzéby, "La Communauté européenne face au défi de l'emploi" (2001) R.M.C.U.E. 185–192; Kenner, "Employment and Macroeconomics in the EC Treaty: A Legal and Political Symbiosis?" (2000) M.J.E.C.L. 375–397; Martin, "Le traité d'Amsterdam inaugure-t-il une politique communautaire de l'emploi?" (2000) R.T.D.E. 47–65; Martinelli, "La stratégie européenne en faveur de l'emploi" (1998) 1 R.M.U.E. 55–75.

[1113] See the guidelines for Member States' employment policies for the year 2000 (Council Decision of March 13, 2000, [2000] O.J. L72/15), for 2001 (Council Decision of January 19, 2001, [2001] O.J. L22/18), for 2002 (Council Decision of February 18, 2002, [2002] O.J. L60/60), and for 2003 (Council Decision of July 22, 2003, [2003] O.J. L197/13).

[1114] Thus, under Art. 99 of the EC Treaty the European Council adopts conclusions, not on the basis of a joint report of the Council and the Commission, but in the light of a report drawn up by the Council acting on a recommendation from the Commission; moreover, other institutions are not consulted—the European Parliament is only informed after the event: para. 5–224, *supra*).

[1115] See Ashiagbor, "Soft Harmonisation: The 'Open Method of Co-ordination' in the European Employment Strategy" (2004) E.Pub.L. 305–332. In anticipation of the ratification of the Amsterdam Treaty which was to introduce in the EC Treaty the provisions on employment, the European Council meeting on November 20 and 21, 1999 in Luxembourg had called for the immediate implementation of those new provisions: (1997) 11 EU Bull. points I.2.3 and I.4.20.

by a qualified majority, make recommendations to the Member States on the basis of a recommendation of the Commission (Art. 128(4)).[1116]

Community employment policy sets out primarily to complement national policies and encourage co-operation. Accordingly, the EC Treaty provides that the competences of the Member States are to be respected (Art. 127(1)).[1117] Article 129 empowers the European Parliament and the Council, acting under the co-decision procedure, to adopt "incentive measures" designed to encourage co-operation between Member States and to support their action in the field of employment, but makes no provision for harmonisation of national administrative and statutory provisions.[1118] In addition, the Community has to take the objective of a high level of employment into consideration in the formulation and implementation of other Community policies and activities (EC Treaty, Art. 127(2)).

B. EDUCATION, VOCATIONAL TRAINING, YOUTH AND SPORT

Community competence. The Community is empowered to adopt measures to supplement Member States' policy in the field of education and vocational training.[1119] Articles 149 and 150 of the EC Treaty were introduced by the EU Treaty to replace Art. 128 of the EEC Treaty, which provided only for "a common vocational training policy".[1120] The Court of Justice paved the way for an actual educational policy for the Community, first by construing the expression "vocational training" in Art. 128 of the EEC Treaty as covering most educational curricula[1121] and secondly by

5–238

[1116] See the Council Recommendations on the implementation of Member States' employment policies of February 14, 2000 ([2000] O.J. L52/32), January 19, 2001 ([2001] O.J. L22/27), February 18, 2002 ([2002] O.J. L60/70) and July 22, 2003 ([2003] O.J. L197/22).

[1117] This does not preclude Community competence under other Treaty provisions; see *e.g.* before the introduction of Title VIII of the EC Treaty, the decision taken by the Council pursuant to Art. 308 of the EC Treaty on February 23, 1998 on Community activities concerning analysis, research and co-operation in the field of employment, [1998] O.J. L63/26 (which further refers in its preamble to the new title on employment to be incorporated by the Amsterdam Treaty and to the fact that the European Council "indicated that the Council should seek to make the relevant provisions of this Title immediately effective").

[1118] See Decision 1145/2002/EC of the European Parliament and of the Council of June 10, 2002 on Community incentive measures in the field of employment, [2002] O.J. L170/1.

[1119] For a survey of this power, see Lenaerts, "Education in European Community Law after 'Maastricht' " (1994) C.M.L.R. 7–41; Bekemans and Balodimos, "Le traité de Maastricht et l'éducation, la formation professionnelle et la culture" (1993) 2 R.M.U.E. 99–142; Frazier, "L'éducation et l'Union européenne" (1997) R.M.C.U.E. 476–491. For international powers (EC Treaty, Arts 149 and 150(1) and (3)), see para. 20–034, *infra.*

[1120] Admittedly, the Council adopted positions in the form of "resolutions" or "conclusions" of the "Council and the Ministers of Education, meeting within the Council". For the previous powers of the Community in the sphere of education, see De Witte, "The Scope of Community Powers in Education and Culture in the Light of Subsequent Practice", in Bieber and Ress (eds), *Die Dynamik des Europäischen Gemeinschaftsrechts/The Dynamics of EC-Law* (Nomos, Baden-Baden, 1987), at 261–281; De Witte (ed.), *European Community Law of Education* (Nomos, Baden-Baden, 1989), 159 pp.

[1121] ECJ, Case 293/83 *Gravier* [1985] E.C.R. 593, paras 19–31 (para. 5–060, *supra*); ECJ, Case 24/86 *Blaizot* [1988] E.C.R. 379, paras 15–21; ECJ, Case 263/86 *Humbel* [1988] E.C.R. 5365, paras 8–20.

regarding also Community action programmes requiring co-operation between the Member States as "an application of a common policy".[1122] The addition of Art. 149 to the EC Treaty made recourse to the provisions on vocational training unnecessary for educational questions which, according to the case law of the Court of Justice, could be regarded as "vocational training".[1123]

In the EU Constitution the Union's competence with respect to education and vocational training comes within the areas of "co-ordinating, complementary or supporting action" (see para. 5–027). The only substantive change brought about by the EU Constitution is that the Union's field of action is extended to cover sport.[1124] This does not mean that the sports sector is to be protected against the application of the Treaty rules.[1125]

5–239 Education. As far as education is concerned, Art. 149(1) of the EC Treaty refers to the Community contributing to the development of quality education by encouraging co-operation between Member States and supporting and supplementing their action. The preamble to the EC Treaty also lists (since the Amsterdam Treaty) access to education and its continuous updating as means of promoting the highest possible level of knowledge of the peoples of the Community. The list of Community tasks set out in Art. 149(2) of the EC Treaty is based on the existing action programmes and mentions primarily language teaching and transfrontier aspects of education and work with young people.[1126] In this connection, the

---

[1122] ECJ, Case 242/87 *Commission v Council* [1989] E.C.R. 1425 (n.76, *supra*). See also the interpretation of the principle of non-discrimination contained in Art. 7 of the EEC Treaty in conjunction with Art. 128 of that Treaty: ECJ, Case 295/90 *European Parliament v Council* [1992] E.C.R. I–4193, paras 15–20 (para. 5–017, *supra*).

[1123] Some Community action programmes embodying elements of education and of vocational training must be based on both Arts 149 and 150: see, *e.g.* the Lingua Programme and its continuation, cited in the following n.1124, *infra*.

[1124] According to Art. III–282(1)(g) of the EU Constitution, Union action is to aim at developing the European dimension in sport, by promoting fairness and openness in sporting competitions and co-operation between bodies responsible for sport and by protecting the physical and moral integrity of sportsmen and sportswomen, especially young sportsmen and sportswomen. The Union is to take account of the "specific nature" of sport, "its structures based on voluntary activity and its social and educational function" (EU Constitution, Art. III–282(1), second subpara.).

[1125] For the application of the Treaty provisions on the free movement of persons, see paras 5–130 and 5–134, *supra*, and also Weatherill, " 'Fair Play Please': Recent Developments in the Application of EC Law to Sport" (2003) C.M.L.R. 51–93; Dubey and Dupont, "Droit européen et sport: Portrait d'une cohabitation" (2002) J.T.D.E. 1–15; Parret, "EG-recht en sport: is sport anders?" (2001) S.E.W. 53–61. Declaration (No.29) annexed to the Amsterdam Treaty ([1997] O.J. C340/136) had already emphasised the "social significance of sport, in particular its role in forging identity and bringing people together". The Intergovernmental Conference of 1997 therefore called on the bodies of the European Union to "listen to" sports associations when important questions affecting sport are at issue (*ibid.*).

[1126] See the early Council Decision adopted on the basis of Arts 128 and 235 of the EEC Treaty, Decision 87/327/EEC of June 15, 1987 adopting the European Community Action Scheme

Treaty makes it clear what boundaries have to be drawn for Community action. First, the Community has to respect the Member States' responsibility for the content of teaching and the organisation of educational systems and their cultural and linguistic diversity (Art. 149(1); see also para. 5–242). Secondly, the Community's action is to consist of (a) "incentive measures" which the European Parliament and the Council adopt by means of the co-decision procedure, "excluding any harmonisation of the laws and regulations of the Member States",[1127] and (b) "recommendations" adopted by the Council by a qualified majority vote on a proposal from the Commission (Art. 149(4)).[1128] It is noteworthy that the majority of Member States are now co-ordinating their higher-education policy pursuant to the Sorbonne and Bologna declarations of intent and hence agree, outside the Community framework, on a measure of harmonisation of education systems.[1129] In addition, the Community has long been tackling aspects of education in the context of its

---

for the Mobility of University Students (Erasmus), [1987] O.J. L166/20 (replaced by Decision 89/663/EEC of December 14, 1989, based on Art. 128 of the EEC Treaty, [1989] O.J. L395/23; see the discussion of its legal basis in n.76, *supra*) and Council Decision 89/489/EEC of July 28, 1989 establishing an action programme to promote foreign language competence in the European Community (Lingua), [1989] O.J. L239/24, adopted on the basis of Arts 128 and 235 of the EEC Treaty. Since January 1, 1995 these programmes have been continued in the form of a new action programme "Socrates", adopted by the European Parliament and the Council on the basis of Arts 149 and 150 of the EC Treaty: Decision 819/95/EC of March 14, 1995, [1995] O.J. L87/10 (see the joint statement by the European Parliament, the Council and the Commission, [1995] O.J. L132/18). The Socrates programme has been extended until 2006 by Decision 253/2000/EC of the European Parliament and of the Council of January 24, 2000 ([2000] O.J. L28/1). See also the "Erasmus Mundus" programme for the enhancement of quality in higher education and the promotion of intercultural understanding through co-operation with third countries established for 2004–2008 by Decision No.2317/2003/EC of the European Parliament and of the Council of December 5, 2003, [2003] O.J. L345/1, and the Trans-European Mobility Scheme for University Studies (Tempus), adopted by the Council by Decision 90/223/EEC of May 7, 1990, [1990] O.J. L131/21), on the basis of Art. 235 of the EEC Treaty, which has been extended until 2006 by Council Decision 1999/311/EC of April 29, 1999 ([1999] O.J. L120/30) and enlarged from the Balkan States, the new independent States of the former Soviet Union and Mongolia to cover countries in the Mediterranean by Council Decision 2002/601/EC of June 27, 2002 ([2002] O.J. L195/34).

[1127] See Decision 1031/2000/EC of the European Parliament and of the Council of April 13, 2000 establishing the 'Youth' Community action programme ([2000] O.J. L117/1), which, for the period 2000–2006, *inter alia*, co-ordinates activities relating to the Youth for Europe and European voluntary service programmes. For the exclusion of harmonisation, see Hablitzel, "Harmonisierungsverbot und Subsidiaritätsprinzip im Europäischen Bildungsrecht" (2002) D.ö.V. 407–414.

[1128] *e.g.* the Recommendation of the European Parliament and of the Council of July 10, 2001 on mobility within the Community for students, persons undergoing training, volunteers, teachers and trainers, [2001] O.J. L215/30. See also Pertek and Sleiman, "Les étudiants et la Communauté: l'esquisse d'un statut de l'étudiant en mobilité" (1998) R.M.C.U.E. 306–321. See also the Commission Recommendation of March 11, 2002 on a common European format for *curricula vitae* (CVs), [2002] O.J. L79/66, based on Arts 149, 150 and 211 of the EC Treaty.

[1129] See Pertek, "L'action communautaire en matière d'éducation et le processus de Bologne" (2004) J.T.D.E. 65–70; Verbruggen, "De Bolognaverklaring kritisch getoest aan het Europees onderwijsbeleid" (2003) S.E.W. 199–212.

policy on equal educational opportunities for migrant workers' children (EC Treaty, Art. 40)[1130] and mutual recognition of diplomas (EC Treaty, Art. 47).[1131]

5–240 Vocational training. As far as vocational training is concerned, the Community pursues a policy of its own, although it is designed to support and supplement the action of the Member States, which remain responsible for the content and organisation of such training (Art. 150(1)). The European Parliament and the Council adopt measures, "excluding any harmonisation of the laws and regulations of the Member States", by the co-decision procedure (Art. 150(4)).[1132] As long ago as 1975, the Council set up under Art. 308 of the EC Treaty a European Centre for the Development of Vocational Training (Cedefop) to promote and co-ordinate vocational training in the Member States. It has also set up a European Training Foundation, which is to contribute to the development of vocational training in central and eastern Europe, the Balkans, the former Soviet Union, Mongolia and Mediterranean third countries and areas.[1133]

C. CULTURE

5–241 Community competence. The Community's powers in the cultural field (introduced by the EU Treaty), like those in the sphere of education, are conceived as supplementary, that is, as contributing to the flowering of the cultures of the Member States, whilst emphasising the common cultural heritage yet respecting national and regional cultural diversity (EC Treaty,

---

[1130] See Art. 12 of Regulation No. 1612/68 (para. 5–131, *supra*). As long ago as 1974 the Court of Justice held that, although the determination of the conditions for admission to education is a matter of national law, Community law requires that they must be applied without discrimination between national workers' children and those of migrant workers: ECJ, Case 9/74 *Casagrande* [1974] E.C.R. 773, para. 14. See also the caselaw according to which a grant awarded for maintenance and training with a view to the pursuit of university studies leading to a professional qualification constitutes a "social advantage" within the meaning of Art. 7(2) of Regulation No.1612/68: ECJ, Case 39/86 *Lair* [1988] E.C.R. 3161, para. 28. See Verbruggen, "Toegang tot het onderwijs en studiefinanciering" (1993) T.O.R.B. 282–289.

[1131] paras 5–145—5–147, *supra*.

[1132] See the "Leonardo da Vinci" Action Programme established for the period 2000–2006 by Council Decision 1999/382/EC of April 26, 1999 ([1999] O.J. L146/33), the training programme for professionals in the European audiovisual programme industry (MEDIA-Training), established for 2001–2005 by Decision 163/2001/EC of the European Parliament and of the Council of January 19, 2001 ([2001] O.J. L26/1) and the multiannual programme "eLearning" for the effective integration of information and communication technologies (ICT) in education and training systems in Europe established for 2004–2006 by Decision 2318/2003/EC of the European Parliament and of the Council of December 5, 2003 ([2003] O.J. L345/9).

[1133] Council Regulation (EEC) No. 337/75 of February 10, 1975 establishing a European Centre for the Development of Vocational Training, [1975] O.J. L39/1; Council Regulation (EEC) No. 1360/90 of May 7, 1990, establishing a European Training Foundation, [1990] O.J. L131/1, as extended in particular recently by Council Regulation (EC) No. 2666/2000 of December 5, 2000, ([2000] O.J. L306/1).

Art. 151(1)).[1134] Article 151(2) enumerates the areas in which the European Parliament and the Council may adopt, under the co-decision procedure, incentive measures,[1135] excluding any harmonisation of the laws and regulations of the Member States, and the Council may adopt recommendations, albeit in both cases by a unanimous vote (Art. 151(5)).[1136] The Community is to take cultural aspects into account in its action in other spheres, in particular in order to respect and to promote the diversity of its cultures (Art. 151(4)).[1137] All this remains valid for the EU Constitution, although there will no longer be a requirement for a unanimous vote in the Council in order for the Union to act in the field of culture.[1138]

Cultural diversity. Community action in the cultural field is to remain **5–242** complementary on the ground that each Member State wishes to conduct its own cultural policy with its own emphases. Accordingly, the conferral of clearly circumscribed powers on the Community in regard to both culture and education also operates as a protection under Treaty law of the "national identities" of the Member States (see EU Treaty, Art. 6(3)).

[1134] See Nettesheim, "Das Kulturverfassungsrecht der Europäischen Union" (2002) J.Z. 157–166; Albers, *Europees Gemeenschapsrecht en cultuur: eenheid en verscheidenheid* (Kluwer, Deventer, 1999), 460 pp. For the incorporation of the competence in respect of culture by the EU Treaty, see Loman, Mortelmans, Post and Watson, *Culture and Community law. Before and After Maastricht* (Kluwer, Deventer, 1992), 258 pp.; Cornu, *Compétences culturelles en Europe et principle de subsidiarité* (Bruylant, Brussels, 1993), 231 pp.; Missir di Lusignano, "Communauté et culture" (1994) R.M.C.U.E. 181–194; Niedobitek, "Die kulturelle Dimension im Vertrag uber die Europäische Union" (1995) EuR. 349–376; Niedobitek (trans. Benn and Bray), *The Cultural Dimension in EC Law*, (Kluwer Law International, London/The Hague, 1997), 344 pp.

[1135] See Decision 508/2000/EC of the European Parliament and of the Council of February 14, 2000 establishing the Culture 2000 programme ([2000] O.J. L63/1), which constitutes the framework for the period 2000–2004 for the cultural policy formerly implemented through the following programmes: Kaleidoscope (Decision 719/96/EC of the European Parliament and of the Council of March 29, 1996 establishing a programme to support artistic and cultural activities having a European dimension, [1996] O.J. L99/20), Ariane (Decision 2085/97/EC of the European Parliament and of the Council of October 6, 1997 establishing a programme of support, including translation, in the field of books and reading, [1997] O.J. L291/26) and Raphael (Decision 2228/97/EC of the European Parliament and of the Council of October 13, 1997 establishing a Community action programme in the field of cultural heritage, [1997] O.J. L305/31). See also Decision 1419/1999/EC of the European Parliament and of the Council of May 25, 1999 establishing a Community action for the European Capital of Culture event for the years 2005 to 2019 ([1999] O.J. L166/1).

[1136] In view of the need for the free expression of culture, the Community's action is not restricted to cultural expressions with a European dimension, see Britz, "Die Freiheit der Kunst in der europäischen Kulturpolitik" (2004) EuR. 1–26.

[1137] See also the Council Resolution of January 20, 1997 on the integration of cultural aspects into Community actions, [1997] O.J. C36/4, and the resolution of the European Parliament relating thereto of January 30, 1997, [1997] O.J. C55/37. For an argument in favour of a broad interpretation, see Cunningham, "In Defence of Member State Culture: The Unrealised Potential of Art. 151(4) of the EC Treaty and the Consequences for EC Cultural Policy" (2001) Cornell I.L.J. 119–163. Art. 87(3)(d) of the EC Treaty mentions the promotion of culture and heritage conservation as a possible justification for State aid, see paras 5–203 *et seq.*). See also Protocol (No.32) annexed to the EC Treaty on the system of public broadcasting in the Member States, para. 5–201, *supra.*

[1138] EU Constitution, Art. III–280(5).

For some time now, the Court of Justice has recognised cultural aims as overriding or mandatory requirements in view of which Member States may place reasonable restrictions on the free movement of goods, persons and services.[1139] Accordingly, the Court of Justice accepted the fact that Ireland required a Dutch lecturer to have a certificate of knowledge of Irish in order to teach art full time in Ireland, even though the teaching was conducted essentially in English.[1140] This was not precluded by free movement of workers. The Court of Justice held that the EC Treaty "does not prohibit the adoption of a policy for the protection and promotion of a language of a Member State which is both the national language and the first official language" and recognised the importance of education for the implementation of such a policy "provided that the level of knowledge required is not disproportionate in relation to the objective pursued".[1141] Moreover, protection of an ethno-cultural minority (such as German-speakers in northern Italy) constitutes a legitimate aim, provided that it is not pursued in a disproportionate manner.[1142] As far as the use of languages in product labelling is concerned, such policy considerations did not initially prevail. The Court considered that a requirement to use the official language or languages in the part of the country in which the products were marketed was compatible with free movement of goods only in so far as a particular statement in the language or languages in question was necessary in order to ensure that the consumer was adequately informed.[1143] Where a directive provides that the Member States are to ensure that particulars about foodstuffs provided on labelling must appear "in a language easily understood by purchasers", the Court held that this does not mean that Member States may make use of the language or languages of the linguistic region compulsory, even if they do not preclude

---

[1139] See, e.g. paras 5–110 (goods), 5–144 (persons) and 5–175 and 5–178 (services), *supra*; Karydis, "Le juge communautaire et la préservation de l'identité culturelle nationale" (1994) R.T.D.E. 551–560.

[1140] ECJ, Case C–379/87 *Groener* [1989] E.C.R. 3967.

[1141] *Groener*, paras 19–21.

[1142] ECJ, Case C–274/96 *Bickel and Franz* [1998] E.C.R. I–7637, paras 23–30 (discrimination where nationals of other Member States who do not reside in the Member State concerned are precluded from the right conferred on the minority to use their language in judicial proceedings); ECJ, Case C–281/98 *Angonese* [2000] E.C.R. I–4139, paras 37–45 (discrimination where proof of bilingualism is conditional upon possession of a language diploma that may be obtained only in the national territory). For the situation of minorities under Community law, see also von Arnauld, "Minderheitenschutz im Recht der Europäischen Union" (2004) A.Völkerr. 111–141; Hilpold, "Minderheiten im Unionsrecht" (2001) A.Völkerr. 432–471.

[1143] ECJ, Case C–369/89 *Piageme* [1991] E.C.R. I–2971, paras 14–16 (a rule allowing only the official language or languages of the Member State to be used on labelling is incompatible with free movement of goods); ECJ, Case C–51/93 *Meyhui* [1994] E.C.R. I–3879, paras 18–21 (an obligation to use a particular language or languages will be lawful if a clearly specified definition in that language or languages is necessary for the protection of consumers), case note by Temmink (1995) S.E.W. 615–620.

inclusion of the relevant particulars also in other languages.[1144] The directive in question was subsequently amended in order to allow the Member States to impose such an obligation.[1145] The question remains, however, as to whether, in the absence of Community legislation on the matter, the principle of free movement of goods may limit the Member States' power to regulate the use of languages. In view of the respect for national and regional diversity required by the EC Treaty, national and regional authorities may most probably impose reasonable limitations on free movement (of goods) also in order to protect language and culture.[1146] However, this consideration in itself does not authorise a Member State from deviating from harmonisation measures adopted by the Community.[1147]

On the other hand, the requirement to take account of diversity in and as between the Member States means that the Community has to take account in its educational and cultural policies also of the special characteristics of regions and geographical and cultural minorities.[1148]

D. PUBLIC HEALTH

Health policy. Before the EU Treaty added to the EC Treaty Title XIII **5–243** "Public health", the Council had already adopted a number of measures to protect public health, principally on the basis of Art. 100a (para. 3 of which

---

[1144] ECJ, Case C–85/94 *Piageme and Others* [1995] E.C.R. I–2955, paras 14–21, with a case note by Verbruggen (1995/96) Col.J.E.L. 164–171; ECJ, Case C–366/98 *Geffroy and Casino France* [2000] E.C.R. I–6579, paras 24–28. The Court took the view that the national court has to determine in each individual case whether the compulsory particulars given in a language other than the language mainly used in the Member State or region concerned can be easily understood by consumers in that State or region: *Piageme and Others*. paras 28–30; ECJ, Case C–385/96 *Goerres* [1998] E.C.R. I–4431, paras 16–25. See also Candela Soriano "Les exigences linguistiques: une entrave légitime à la libre circulation?" (2002) C.D.E. 9–44.

[1145] Directive 97/4/EC of the European Parliament and of the Council of January 17, 1997 amending Directive 79/112 on the approximation of the laws of the Member States relating to the labelling, presentation and advertising of foodstuffs, [1997] O.J. L43/21 (replaced by Directive 2000/13/EC of the European Parliament and of the Council of March 20, 2000, [2000] O.J. L109/29).

[1146] See Pieter Van Nuffel, note to the first *Piageme* judgment (n.1143, *supra*) (1992) S.E.W. 397, at 400. The free movement of goods remains for the present the chief concern: see ECJ, Case C–33/97 *Colim and Bigg's Continent Noord* [1999] E.C.R. I–3175, paras 36–42 (a measure requiring the use of a language which consumers can readily understand must not exclude the possible use of other means of informing them and must be restricted to the information made mandatory by the Member State concerned) and the Commission's answer of June 15, 2000 to question E–0614/00 (Staes), [2001] O.J. C46E/19. To place this in the broader context of the protection of national values *vis-à-vis* Community law, see De Witte, "Community Law and National Constitutional Values" (1992) 2 L.I.E.I. 1, at 15–18.

[1147] See, *e.g.* ECJ, Case C–11/95 *Commission v Belgium* [1996] E.C.R. I–4115, para. 50.

[1148] See, *e.g.* the concern for minority languages in the Socrates and Ariane programmes (see n.1126, *supra*) and the suggestions made by the European Parliament in its resolution of February 9, 1994 on cultural and linguistic minorities in the European Communities, [1994] O.J. C61/110. Linguistic diversity is also covered by Community industrial policy; see Council Decision 2001/48/EC of December 22, 2000, [2001] O.J. L14/32 (n.1170, *infra*), and ECJ, Case C–42/97 *European Parliament v Council* [1999] E.C.R. I–869. See further Donders, "The Protection of Cultural Rights in Europe: None of the EU's Business?" (2003) M.J.C.E.L. 117–147.

required the Commission to take as its base a high level of protection of public health) and Art. 235 of the EEC Treaty.[1149] Thus the Council set up pursuant to that provision of the EEC Treaty a European Monitoring Centre for Drugs and Drug Addiction, which provides and processes information.[1150] The Council and the Ministers of Public Health, meeting in the Council, agreed on common positions in the form of "resolutions" and "conclusions".

The specific title in the EC Treaty on public health (as revised by the Treaty of Amsterdam) sees Community action as complementing national policies and as directed towards improving public health, preventing human illness and diseases, and obviating sources of danger to human health (EC Treaty, Art. 152(1), second subpara.).[1151] In addition to the fight against major health scourges, such action is to cover promotion of research and health information and education. The Commission, together with the Member States, is to co-ordinate their policies and programmes (Art. 152(2)). The European Parliament and the Council are to adopt "incentive measures"[1152] under the co-decision procedure "excluding any harmonisation of the laws and regulations of the Member States" (Art. 152(4)(c)); since the Amsterdam Treaty, the European Parliament and the Council are also empowered nevertheless to adopt harmonisation measures addressing some safety concerns under the same procedure (see Art. 152(4)(a) and (b)).[1153] In this way, the Community has harmonised foodstuffs legislation and set up the European Food Safety Authority with the task of providing scientific advice and scientific and technical support for the Community's legislation and policies in all fields which have a direct

---

[1149] See, *inter alia*, Council Directive 89/105/EEC of December 21, 1988 relating to the transparency of measures regulating the prices of medicinal products for human use and their inclusion in the scope of national health insurance systems ([1989] O.J. L40/8) and Council Directive 89/107/EEC of December 21, 1988 on the approximation of the laws of the Member States concerning food additives authorised for use in foodstuffs intended for human consumption ([1989] O.J. L40/27).

[1150] Regulation (EEC) No. 302/93 of February 8, 1993, [1993] O.J. L36/1.

[1151] For the division of powers, see Hervey, "Community and National Competence in Health after *Tobacco Advertising*" (2001) C.M.L.R. 1421–1446. For a general discussion, see also Dubois, "L'Europe de la santé" (1993) Ann.Dr.Louv. 143–164; Bourgoignie and Fraselle, "La santé des personnes et la politique communautaire de protection des consommateurs à l'épreuve du marché intérieur" (1993) Ann.Dr.Louv. 195–206; Van Schwanenflügel, "Gesundheit in Europa" (1998) EuR. 210–218; Hervey, "Mapping the Contours of European Union Health Law and Policy" (2002) E.Publ.L. 69–105.

[1152] See, *e.g.* Decision 1786/2002/EC of the European Parliament and of the Council of September 23, 2002 adopting a programme of Community action in the field of public health (2003–2008), [2002] O.J. L271/1; Decision 803/2004 of the European Parliament and of the Council of April 21, 2004 adopting a programme of Community action (2004–2008) to prevent and combat violence against children, young people and women and to protect victims and groups at risk (the Daphne II programme), [2004] O.J. L143/1.

[1153] Measures and recommendations may concern: (a) setting high standards of quality and safety of organs and substances of human origin, blood and blood derivatives (although Member States are not precluded from maintaining or introducing more stringent measures), and (b) measures in the veterinary and phytosanitary fields which have as their direct object the protection of public health.

or indirect impact on food and feed safety.[1154] Pursuant to Art. 152(4)(b), the Community also established a European Medicines Agency and a European Centre for disease prevention and control.[1155] The Council may also adopt recommendations by a qualified majority vote on a proposal from the Commission (Art. 152(4), second subpara.).[1156] In taking such action, the Community must fully respect the "responsibilities of the Member States for the organisation and delivery of health services and health care" (Art. 152(5)).[1157]

Under Art. 152(1) all Community policies and activities are to ensure a high level of protection of human health. Consequently, the Community may adopt under Art. 95 of the EC Treaty measures which are designed to eliminate obstacles to the functioning of the internal market and, at the same time, have an eye to the protection of public health.[1158]

The EU Constitution will include the field of public health among the areas where the Union may take co-ordinating, complementary or supporting action (see para. 5–027). The only exception is constituted by "common safety concerns in public health matters", which Art. I–14(2) of the EU Constitution includes within the general category of the Union's

---

[1154] Regulation (EC) No. 178/2002 of the European Parliament and of the Council of January 28, 2002 laying down the general principles and requirements of food law, establishing the European Food Safety Authority and laying down procedures in matters of food safety, [2002] O.J. L31/1 (adopted on the basis of Arts 37, 95, 133 and 152(4)(b) of the EC Treaty). See Dehousse, Engelstadt and Gevers, "La sécurité alimentaire et le principe de la précaution (2000) Stud. Dipl. 95–112; Beurdeley, "La sécurité alimentaire au sein de l'Union européenne: un concept en gestation" (2002) R.M.C.U.E. 89–103.

[1155] Regulation (EC) No. 726/2004 of the European Parliament and of the Council of March 31, 2004 laying down Community procedures for the authorisation and supervision of medicinal products for human and veterinary use and establishing a European Medicines Agency, [2004] O.J. L136/1; Regulation (EC) No. 851/2004 of the European Parliament and of the Council of April 21, 2004 establishing a European Centre for disease prevention and control, [2004] O.J. L142/1.

[1156] e.g. Council Recommendation of June 5, 2001 on the drinking of alcohol by young people, in particular children and adolescents, [2001] O.J. L161/38.

[1157] According to this provision, measures referred to in para. 4(a) shall not affect national provisions on the donation or medical use of organs and blood. Under the EU Constitution, the responsibilities of the Member States include "the management of health services and medical care and the allocation of the resources assigned to them" (Art. III–278(7)).

[1158] ECJ, Case C–376/98 Germany v European Parliament and Council [2000] E.C.R. I–8419, para. 88 (by which, however, a general prohibition of all forms of tobacco advertising and sponsoring, even where the tobacco product was not named, was annulled on the ground that Arts 47(2), 55 and 95 did not afford a sufficient legal basis). See Hervey, "Up in Smoke? Community (anti-)tobacco law and policy" (2001) E.L.Rev. 101–125. Arts 47(2), 55 and 95 of the EC Treaty were nevertheless used as the legal basis for an adapted tobacco advertising ban in Directive 2003/33/EC of the European Parliament and the Council of May 26, 2003, ([2003] O.J. L152/16), which has been contested in particular by Germany (Case C–380/03, [2003] O.J. C275/31). Other examples are Directives 2001/82/EC of the European Parliament and the Council of November 6, 2001 and 2001/83/EC of the European Parliament and the Council of November 6, 2001 on the Community code relating to veterinary medicinal products and on the Community code relating to medicinal products for human use ([2001] O.J. L311/1 and 67, respectively). See also the Council resolution of November 18, 1999 on ensuring health protection in all Community policies and activities ([2000] O.J. C86/3).

shared competences. This concerns the same substantive matters in respect of which the European Parliament and the Council are already entitled to adopt harmonisation measures under the existing provisions of the EC Treaty.[1159]

E. CONSUMER PROTECTION

5–244 Consumer policy. In order to promote the interests of consumers and to ensure a high level of consumer protection, the Community is to contribute to protecting the health, safety and economic interests of consumers, as well as to promoting their right to information, education and to organise themselves in order to safeguard their interests (EC Treaty, Art. 153(1)).[1160] The means employed are harmonising measures adopted pursuant to Art. 95[1161] and measures supporting, supplementing and monitoring the policy pursued by the Member States, which the European Parliament and the Council are to adopt under the co-decision procedure (EC Treaty, Art.

[1159] Compare Art. III–278(4) of the EU Constitution with Art. 152(4)(a) and (b) of the EC Treaty.

[1160] For general discussions, see, for instance, Howells and Wilhelmsson, "EC Consumer Law: Has it Come of Age?" (2003) E.L.Rev. 370–388; Stuyck, "European Consumer Law after the Treaty of Amsterdam: Consumer Policy in or Beyond the Internal Market?" (2000) C.M.L.R. 367–400; Dehousse and Iotsova, "La politique européenne des consommateurs: un succès méconnu de la construction européenne" (2000) Stud. Dipl. 113–170; Straetmans, *Consument en markt* (Kluwer, Deurne, 1998), 197–465.

[1161] See Directive 97/7/EC of the European Parliament and of the Council of May 20, 1997 on the protection of consumers in respect of distance contracts, [1997] O.J. L144/19; Directive 98/27/EC of the European Parliament and the Council of May 19, 1998 on injunctions for the protection of consumers' interests, [1998] O.J. L166/5; Directive 1999/44/EC of the European Parliament and of the Council of May 25, 1999 on certain aspects of the sale of consumer goods and associated guarantees, [1999] O.J. L171/12; Directive 2000/31/EC of the European Parliament and of the Council of June 8, 2000 on certain legal aspects of information society services, in particular electronic commerce, in the Internal Market ("Directive on electronic commerce"), [2000] O.J. L178/1; Directive 2001/95/EC of the European Parliament and of the Council of December 3, 2001 on general product safety, [2002] O.J. L11/4. For the role of the directive on electronic commerce in the context of other Community legislation, see Walden, "Regulating electronic commerce: Europe in the global E-conomy" (2001) E.L.R. 529—547. Directives were adopted on the basis of Art. 100a of the EEC Treaty even before specific competence was introduced in the matter of consumer protection: see, *e.g.* Council Directive 88/314/EEC of June 7, 1988 on consumer protection in the indication of the prices of non-food products, [1988] O.J. L142/19; Council Directive 93/13/EEC of April 5, 1993 on unfair terms in consumer contracts, [1993] O.J. L95/29. See also the directives adopted by the Council pursuant to Art. 100 of the EEC Treaty on the approximation of the laws, regulations and administrative provisions of the Member States concerning misleading advertising and comparative advertising (Directive 84/450/EEC of September 10, 1984, [1984] O.J. L250/17, as amended under Art. 100a [now Art. 95] by Directive 97/55/EC of the European Parliament and of the Council of October 6, 1997, [1997] O.J. L 290/18), liability for defective products (Directive 85/374/EEC of July 25, 1985, [1985] O.J. L210/29, extended by Directive 1999/34/EC of the European Parliament and of the Council of May 10, 1999, [1999] O.J. L141/20) and protection of the consumer in respect of contracts negotiated away from business premises (Directive 85/577/EEC of December 20, 1985, [1985] O.J. 1985 L372/31).

314

153(3) and (4)).[1162] As far as measures adopted on the basis of Art. 95 (or Art. 94) are concerned,[1163] Member States may maintain or introduce more stringent measures, provided that they are compatible with the Treaty and that the Commission is notified of them (Art. 153(5)). Consumer protection requirements must be taken into account in defining and implementing other Community policies and activities (EC Treaty, Art. 153(2)).

F. TRANS-EUROPEAN NETWORKS

Interconnection. Since the EU Treaty, the Treaty provisions on **5–245** "trans-European networks" have supplemented the existing Community competence to promote economic and social cohesion. The Community is to contribute to the development of infrastructure networks in the areas of transport, telecommunications and energy by promoting the interconnection and "interoperability" of national networks and access to those networks.[1164] Importance is attached to linking island, landlocked and peripheral regions with the central regions of the Community. The intention behind Community action is to help to attain the objectives of the single market and economic and social cohesion in such a way that not only economic operators, but also communities and citizens, benefit (EC Treaty, Art. 154). Member States are to co-ordinate their policies among themselves, in liaison with the Commission (Art. 155(2)). The Council is to adopt guidelines covering the objectives, priorities and broad lines of measures envisaged, identifying projects of common interest.[1165] In addition, the Community is to adopt such (harmonisation) measures as may prove necessary to ensure the interoperability of networks, for example by arranging for a ".eu" domain on the Internet.[1166] It may also support projects of common interest financially supported by Member States (Art.

[1162] Prior to the Amsterdam Treaty, Art. 129a of the EC Treaty referred to "specific action", see Directive 98/6/EC of the European Parliament and the Council of February 16, 1998 on consumer protection in the indication of the prices of products offered to consumers ([1998] O.J. L80/27, corrigendum in [1998] O.J. L190/86), which was adopted on the basis of that provision and the general framework for Community activities in favour of consumers established by Decision 283/1999/EC of the European Parliament and of the Council of January 25, 1999, [1999] O.J. L34/1.

[1163] ECJ, Case C–52/00 *Commission v France* [2002] E.C.R. I–3827, para. 15.

[1164] Roggenkamp, "Transeuropese netwerken. Op weg naar een communautair infrastructuur-beleid?" (1998) S.E.W. 416–423.

[1165] Guidelines and projects have to be approved by the Member State to whose territory they relate (EC Treaty, Art. 156, second para.). See the Decisions of the European Parliament and of the Council laying down guidelines for trans-European energy networks (Decision 1229/2003/EC of June 26, 2003, [2003] O.J. L176/11), for the development of the trans-European transport network (Decision 1692/96/EC of July 23, 1996, [1996] O.J. L228/1) and for trans-European telecommunications networks (Decision 1336/97 of June 17, 1997, [1997] O.J. L183/12). The guidelines need not necessarily have been preceded by a separate measure adopted beforehand: ECJ, Case C–22/96 *European Parliament v Council* [1998] E.C.R. I–3231, para. 34.

[1166] Regulation (EC) No. 733/2002 of the European Parliament and the Council of April 22, 2002 on the implementation of the EU Top Level Domain, [2002] O.J. L113/1.

155(1)).[1167] The guidelines and measures are drawn up under the co-decision procedure (Art. 156, first para.). Article 155 constitutes, together with Art. 156, the specific legal basis for measures ensuring interoperability of networks, even where the measures also cover objectives pursued by the single market.[1168]

G. INDUSTRY

5–246 Competitiveness. Article 157(1) of the EC Treaty lists aims for fostering competitiveness of Community industry. The Member States are to address their policies to this, where necessary co-ordinating their action, possibly at the initiative of the Commission (Art. 157(2)). The Community endeavours to attain those objectives by means of policies and action based on other provisions of the Treaties.[1169] The addition by the EU Treaty of a title "Industry" in the EC Treaty does not confer on the Community competence to conduct its own industrial policy, but enables the European Parliament and the Council to adopt, under the co-decision procedure on a proposal from the Commission, "specific measures" in support of action taken in the Member States (Art. 157(3), first subpara.).[1170] Any Community measure may in no event lead to a distortion of competition or contain tax provisions or provisions relating to the rights and interests of employed persons (Art. 157(3), second subpara.). Whilst retaining these restrictions, the EU Constitution includes the provisions on industry among the areas where the Union may take "co-ordinating, complementary or supporting action" (see para. 5–027).

[1167] The Community may contribute through the Cohesion Fund (para. 5–247, *infra*) to the financing of projects (EC Treaty, Art. 155(1), third indent). For general rules for the granting of Community financial aid in the field of trans-European networks, see Council Regulation (EEC) No. 2236/95 of September 18, 1995 [1995] O.J. L228/1.

[1168] ECJ, Case C–271/94 *European Parliament v Council* [1996] E.C.R. I–1689, paras 13–35 (annulment of a decision based on Art. 308 of the EC Treaty; the decision was subsequently replaced by a decision based on Art. 156, [1996] O.J. L327/34). See also Council Directive 96/48/EC of July 23, 1996 on the interoperability of the trans-European high-speed rail system, [1996] O.J. L235/6; Directive 2001/16/EC of the European Parliament and the Council of March 19, 2001 on the interoperability of the trans-European conventional rail system, [2001] O.J. L110/1.

[1169] See Commission of the European Communities, *European Industrial Policy for the Nineties* (1991) EC Bull. Suppl.3. For an overview, see Nicolaides, *Industrial Policy in the European Community* (European Institute of Public Administration, Maastricht, 1993), 134 pp.

[1170] See Council Decision 2000/819/EC of December 20, 2000 on a multiannual programme for enterprise and entrepreneurship, and in particular for small and medium-sized enterprises (SMEs) (2001–2005), [2000] O.J. L333/84; Council Decision 2000/821/EC of December 20, 2000 on the implementation of a programme to encourage the development, distribution and promotion of European audiovisual works (MEDIA Plus Development, Distribution and Promotion) (2001–2005), [2001] O.J. L13/34; Council Decision 2001/48/EC of December 22, 2000 adopting a multiannual Community programme to stimulate the development and use of European digital content on the global networks and to promote linguistic diversity in the information society, [2001] O.J. L14/32; Decision 2256/2003/EC of the European Parliament and of the Council of November 17, 2003 adopting a multiannual programme (2003–2005) for the monitoring of the Europe 2005 action plan, dissemination of good practices and the improvement of network and information security (Modinis), [2003] O.J. L336/1.

H. ECONOMIC, SOCIAL AND TERRITORIAL COHESION

Least-favoured regions. Economic and social cohesion aims to reduce **5–247** disparities between the levels of development of the various regions and the backwardness of the least-favoured regions or islands, including rural areas (EC Treaty, Art. 158). The title "Economic and social cohesion" was only incorporated into the EC Treaty as a result of the Single European Act. Since the EU Treaty, cohesion has constituted an express objective for the Community (EC Treaty, Art. 2) and the Union (EU Treaty, Art. 2, first indent) in that provision is made for the implementation and co-ordination of Member States' economic policies and for the determination and implementation of Community policy.[1171] The EU Constitution will take over the provisions of the EC Treaty under the heading of "economic, social and territorial cohesion".[1172]

The Community grants aid through the Structural Funds (the European Agricultural Guidance and Guarantee Fund, Guidance Section,[1173] the European Social Fund[1174] and the European Regional Development Fund[1175]), the European Investment Bank[1176] and other financial instruments (EC Treaty, Art. 159, first para.). The Council, acting unanimously on a proposal from the Commission and after obtaining the assent of the European Parliament, is responsible for defining the tasks, priority objectives and the organisation of the Structural Funds, which may involve grouping the Funds, and for laying down the general rules for co-ordinating the Funds with one another and with the other financial instruments[1177] (Art. 161, first para.).[1178] The Council radically reformed the

---

[1171] For a survey, see Evans, *The EU Structural Funds* (Oxford University Press, Oxford, 1999), 348 pp.; Comijs, *Europese structuurfondsen* (Kluwer, Deventer, 1998), 319 pp. Mestre and Petit, "La cohésion économique et sociale après le Traité sur l'Union européenne" (1995) C.D.E. 207–243; Kenner, "Economic and Social Cohesion—The Rocky Road Ahead" (1994) 1 L.I.E.I. 1–37.

[1172] EU Constitution, Arts III–220 to III–224. See David, "Territorialer Zusammenhalt: Kompetenzzuwachs für die Raumordnung auf europäischer Ebene oder neues Kompetenzfeld?" (2003) D.ö.V. 146–155.

[1173] para. 5–189, *supra*.

[1174] para. 5–236, *supra*.

[1175] According to Art. 160 of the EC Treaty, that fund is intended to help redress regional imbalances through participation in the development and structural adjustment of regions whose development is lagging behind and in the conversion of declining industrial regions. The European Parliament and the Council adopt implementing decisions relating to the Fund by the co-decision procedure (EC Treaty, Art. 162, first para.). See Regulation (EEC) No. 1783/1999 of the European Parliament and of the Council of June 12, 1999 on the European Regional Development Fund, [1999] O.J. L213/1.

[1176] paras 10–105–10–106, *infra*.

[1177] *e.g.* the Financial Instrument for Fisheries Guidance, see Council Regulation (EC) No. 1263/1999 of June 21, 1999, [1999] O.J. L161/54.

[1178] Under the Treaty of Nice, the Council may act by a qualified majority if the 2007–2013 financial perspective and the Interinstitutional Agreement relating thereto have been adopted: EC Treaty, Art. 161, third para.

existing funds in 1988.[1179] A further reform was carried out in 1999 with an eye to the accession of new Member States. A new reform was carried out in 1999 with a view to preparing for the accession of the new Member States (Agenda 2000).[1180] In addition, the Cohesion Fund[1181] provides a financial contribution to projects in the fields of the environment and trans-European networks in the area of transport infrastructure (Art. 161, second para.), but only in Member States fulfilling the criteria set out in a Protocol annexed to the EC Treaty.[1182] The Commission reports every three years on progress made towards achieving economic and social cohesion.

If "specific actions" prove necessary outside the Funds, the European Parliament and the Council may adopt them under the co-decision procedure (Art. 159, third para.). In this way, a Solidarity Fund has been set up which can provide rapid assistance to Member States in the event of a major natural disaster.[1183]

I. RESEARCH AND TECHNOLOGICAL DEVELOPMENT

5–248 Community support. Although the Community has long been providing support for research and technological development, for instance by means of measures based on Art. 308 of the EC Treaty, the title "Research and technological development" was introduced for the first time into the EC Treaty by the Single European Act. Title XVIII deals with the Community's activities in this field with the objective of strengthening the

---

[1179] Council Regulation (EEC) No. 2052/88 of June 24, 1988 on the tasks of the Structural Funds and their effectiveness and on co-ordination of their activities between themselves and with the operations of the European Investment Bank and the other existing financial instruments, [1988] O.J. L185/9. The regulation classified the tasks of the various financial instruments by reference to five objectives, which were increased to six by Protocol No.6 to the 1994 Act of Accession. See Célimène, "La réforme de l'action des fonds structurels européens" (1991) A.J.D.A. 251–266.

[1180] Council Regulation (EC) No. 1260/1999 of June 21, 1999 laying down general provisions on the Structural Funds ([1999] O.J. L161/1). Its principal aims were: (1) promoting the development and structural adjustment of regions whose development is lagging behind; (2) supporting the economic and social conversion of areas facing structural difficulties; (3) supporting the adaptation and modernisation of policies and systems of education, training and employment.

[1181] Council Regulation (EC) No. 1164/94 of May 16, 1994 establishing a Cohesion Fund, [1994] O.J. L130/1, as amended by Council Regulation (EC) No. 1264/1999of June 21, 1999, [1999] O.J. L161/57.

[1182] Protocol (No.28) annexed to the EC Treaty on economic and social cohesion ([1992] O.J. C224/130) requires the Member State concerned to have a *per capita* GNP of less than 90 per cent of the Community average (which, up to 2004, limited qualifying Member States to Greece, Ireland, Portugal and Spain) and to have a programme for the fulfilment of the economic convergence criteria set out in Art. 104 of the EC Treaty.

[1183] See Council Regulation (EC) No. 2012/2002 of November 11, 2002 establishing the European Union Solidarity Fund ([2002] O.J. L311/3). This regulation is based on the third para. of Art. 159 of the EC Treaty (which, prior to the Treaty of Nice, required only consultation of the European Parliament) and Art. 308 of the EC Treaty (so as to make the regulation also applicable to candidate countries). For the financing of the fund, see the Interinstitutional Agreement of November 7, 2002 between the European Parliament, the Council and the Commission ([2002] O.J. C283/1) supplementing the Interinstitutional Agreement of May 6, 1999 (see para. 10–127).

scientific and technological bases of Community industry and hence of making it more competitive internationally, whilst promoting research into other areas covered by the Treaty (Art. 163).[1184] Action by the Community is simply to complement activities undertaken by Member States. It is to cover programmes fostering co-operation between undertakings, research centres and universities, together with international co-operation, disseminating and optimising the results of research and stimulating the training and mobility of researchers (Art. 164).

The Commission is empowered to take any useful initiative to promote co-ordination of national policies and Community policy (Art. 165). The European Parliament and the Council, acting under the co-decision procedure, are to adopt multiannual framework programmes setting out all the activities of the Community (Art. 166(1)).[1185] The Council, acting by a qualified majority on a proposal from the Commission after consulting the European Parliament, may then adopt specific programmes for the implementation of the framework programmes (Art. 166(3) and (4)). Other procedures apply where implementation is carried out by means of supplementary programmes in which only some Member States take part,[1186] Community participation,[1187] international co-operation[1188] or the creation of joint undertakings by the Community.[1189]

The EU Constitution will supplement the existing provisions on research and technological development by adding a legal basis which will allow the Union to draw up a European space policy, including a European space programme (Art. III–254). It should be noted, moreover, that the Union's competence on research and technological development will not fall under the areas where the Union may take only "co-ordinating, complementary or supporting action".[1190]

J. ENVIRONMENT

Sustainable development. Ever since the Single European Act, the 5–249 Community has had express powers in regard to environment policy under

---

[1184] See Commission of the European Communities, *Research after Maastricht: a balance sheet, a strategy* (1992) EC Bull. Suppl.2.

[1185] See Decision 1513/2002/EC of the European Parliament and of the Council of June 27, 2002 concerning the sixth framework programme of the European Community for research, technological development and demonstration activities, contributing to the creation of the European Research Area and to innovation (2002–2006), [2002] O.J. L232/1. See Dévoué, "La co-ordination des politiques de recherche-développement: le cas européen" (2002) R.M.C.U.E. 688–695.

[1186] EC Treaty, Art. 168 and Art. 172, second para.

[1187] EC Treaty, Art. 169 and Art. 172, second para.

[1188] EC Treaty, Art. 170 and Art. 300 (para. 20–031, *infra*).

[1189] EC Treaty, Art. 171 and Art. 172, first para. (para. 10–110, *infra*).

[1190] However, it follows from Art. I–14(3) that it is not the intention of the EU Constitution that the exercise by the Union of its powers should prevent the Member States from pursuing their own space policy (see para. 5–027, *supra*).

the title of the EC Treaty headed "Environment".[1191] The aim of the Community's policy is to preserve, protect and improve the environment, protect human health, ensure prudent and rational use of natural resources, and promote an international approach to regional or worldwide environmental problems (Art. 174(1)). The policy aims at a high level of protection taking account of the diversity of situations in the various regions of the Community (Art. 174(2), first subpara.).[1192] In this connection, the Member States are to co-operate with third countries and with the competent international organisations.[1193] The Treaty lists the principles on which its environment policy is based as follows: preventive action; environmental damage to be rectified as a priority at source; "the polluter should pay".[1194] Environmental requirements must be integrated

---

[1191] For a discussion of environment policy, see Jans, *European Environmental Law* (Europa Law International, Groningen, 2000), 464 pp.; Krämer, *EC Environmental Law* (Sweet & Maxwell, London, 2000), 368 pp.; Scott, *EC Environmental Law* (Longman, London, 2000), 329 pp; London, "Droit communautaire de l'environnement" (1997) R.T.D.E. 629–652. For the formal recognition of environmental protection as a Community objective, see para. 5–003, *supra*, and the action programmes adopted in 1973 ([1973] O.J. C112), 1977 ([1983] O.J. C139), 1983 ([1977] O.J. C46), 1987 ([1987] O.J. C328) and 1993 ([1993] O.J. C138/1) in the form of a declaration or resolution of the Council and representatives of the Member State Governments, meeting in the Council. As early as April 2, 1979, the Council adopted, pursuant to Art. 235 [now Art. 308] of the EC Treaty, Directive 79/409 on the conservation of wild birds, [1979] O.J. L103/1. For the development of Community powers, see Lenaerts, "The Principle of Subsidiarity and the Environment in the European Union: Keeping the Balance of Federalism" (1994) Fordham I.L.J. 846–895; Van Calster and Deketelaere, "Amsterdam, the Intergovernmental Conference and Greening the EC Treaty" (1998) E.Env.L.Rev. 12–25; Scheuing, "Regulierung und Marktfreiheit im Europäischen Umweltrecht" (2001) EuR. 1–26; for a study of the real impact of environmental concerns, see Stetter, "Maastricht, Amsterdam and Nice: the Environmental Lobby and Greening the Treaties" (2001) E.Env.L.Rev. 150–159; Bär and Klasing, "Fit for Enlargement? Environmental Policy after Nice" (2001) E.Env.L.Rev. 212–220; for recent caselaw, see Scheuing, "Das Europäische Umweltverfassungsrecht als Masstab gerichtlicher Kontrolle" (2002) EuR. 619–659; Krämer, "Die Rechtsprechung der EG-Gerichte zum Umweltrecht 20und 00, 2001" (2002) Eu.GR.Z. 438–498.

[1192] Under Art. 174(3) of the EC Treaty, the Community is to take account, *inter alia*, of environmental conditions in the various regions and the balanced development of the regions, together with the economic and social development of the Community as a whole. In order to be able to take available scientific and technological data into consideration, the European Environment Agency collects all useful environmental data and supplies them to the Commission and the Member States, in particular through the Environment Information and Observation Network: Council Regulation (EEC) No. 1201/90 of May 7, 1990, [1990] O.J. L120/1, as amended by Regulation No. 933/1999, [1999] O.J. L117/1.

[1193] EC Treaty, Art. 174(4); para. 20–031, *infra*.

[1194] See De Sadeleer, *Les principes du pollueur-payeur, de prévention et de précaution* (Bruylant, Brussels, 1999), 437 pp.; Vandekerckhove, "The Polluter Pays Principle in the European Community" (1993) Y.E.L. 201–262. For the principle that environmental damage should be rectified at source and the polluter-pays principle: ECJ, Case C–293/97 *Standley, Metson* [1999] E.C.R. I–2603, paras 51–53 (testing Community law against these principles); ECJ, Joined Cases C–175/98 and C–177/98 *Lirussi and Bizarro* [1999] E.C.R. I–6881, para. 51; ECJ, Case C–318/98 *Fornasar* [2000] E.C.R. I–4785, para. 38 (interpretation of Community law in the light of those principles); for the precautionary principle, see para. 17–070. Art. 174(3) of the EC Treaty refers to the process of weighing potential benefits and costs which must take place before the Community takes any decision in this field.

into Community policies in other spheres, in particular with a view to promoting sustainable development (EC Treaty, Art. 6).[1195] In principle, it is for the Member States to finance and implement the environment policy (Art. 175(4)).

Environment policy. The European Parliament and the Council, acting **5–250** under the co-decision procedure, are to decide what action is to be taken by the Community in order to achieve the objectives of the environment policy (Art. 175(1)).[1196] In the case of a number of matters, the Council is to take its decisions unanimously on a Commission proposal after consulting the European Parliament (Art. 175(2)).[1197] In other areas, the European Parliament and the Council are to adopt general action programmes in accordance with the co-decision procedure (Art. 175(3)).[1198] If a measure based on Art. 175(1) involves disproportionate costs for a given Member State, the Council may apply a temporary derogation or provide for financial support from the Cohesion Fund (Art. 175(5)). Member States

---

[1195] See London, "Droit communautaire de l'environnement—Interaction environnement et santé: état des lieux" (2001) R.T.D.E. 139–154. According to Declaration (No.12) annexed to the Treaty of Amsterdam, the Commission undertakes to prepare environmental impact assessment studies when making proposals which may have significant environmental implications ([1997] O.J. C340/133).

[1196] See, *e.g.* Regulation (EC) No. 1655/2000 of the European Parliament and of the Council of July 17, 2000 concerning the Financial Instrument for the Environment (LIFE), [2000] O.J. L192/1; Directive 2001/42 of the European Parliament and of the Council of June 27, 2001 on the assessment of the effects of certain plans and programmes on the environment, [2001] O.J. L197/30; Decision 1411/2001/EC of the European Parliament and of the Council of June 27, 2001 on a Community framework for co-operation to promote sustainable urban development, [2001] O.J. L191/1; Directive 2004/35/EC of the European Parliament and of the Council of April 21, 2004 on environmental liability with regard to the prevention and remedying of environmental damage, [2004] O.J. L143/56. Each successive amendment of the Treaty has altered the procedure laid down in Art. 175(1). In the version embodied in the EEC Treaty, all environmental measures required a Council decision taken by a unanimous vote after consultation of the European Parliament. After the EU Treaty, the co-operation procedure was applied, which was replaced by the co-decision procedure as a result of the Treaty of Amsterdam.

[1197] These are: (a) provisions primarily of a fiscal nature; (b) measures affecting:—town and country planning,—quantitative management of water resources or affecting, directly or indirectly, the availability of those resources,—land use, with the exception of waste management; and (c) measures significantly affecting a Member State's choice between different energy sources and the general structure of its energy supply. The extension of the expression "quantitative management of water resources" by the Treaty of Nice accords with the way in which the Court of Justice confined the areas under (b) to measures relating to the management of limited resources in its quantitative aspects: ECJ, Case C–36/98 *Spain v Council* [2001] E.C.R. I–779, paras 50–53. However, the Council may define (by a unanimous vote) such of those matters as may be decided on by a qualified majority (Art. 175(2), second subpara). Art. 175(2) applies "without prejudice to Art. 95", which may serve as the legal basis for Community measures intended (in part) to protect the environment (para. 5–013, *supra*).

[1198] See Decision 1600/2002/EC of the European Parliament and of the Council of July 22, 2002 laying down the Sixth Community Environment Action Programme, [2002] O.J. L242/1. The Council is to adopt the measures necessary for the implementation of general action programmes by the procedure laid down in para. 1 or 2 of Art. 175, depending on the case (EC Treaty, Art. 175(3), second subpara.).

wishing to maintain or introduce more stringent measures may do so provided that they are compatible with the Treaty and notified to the Commission (Art. 176).[1199] At the same time, harmonisation measures are to include a safeguard clause allowing Member States to take provisional measures for non-economic environmental reasons, subject to a Community inspection procedure (Art. 174(2), second subpara.).

K. DEVELOPMENT CO-OPERATION AND OTHER FORMS OF CO-OPERATION WITH THIRD COUNTRIES

5–251 Third countries. The EC Treaty provided from the outset for structures for co-operation with third countries. Alongside association with overseas countries and territories of the Member States (Arts 182–188 or Part Four of the EC Treaty), there are the associations of the Community and various third countries concluded pursuant to Art. 310 of the EC Treaty (see paras 20–015 *et seq.*). In addition, the Community may contribute to the development of third countries through measures adopted under the common commercial policy and also through measures based on Art. 308 of the EC Treaty (see paras 20–009 and 20–027). The EU Treaty conferred on the Community a specific competence to define its own development co-operation policy, complementary to the corresponding policies of the Member States. The aim of the policy is to support the economic and social development of the developing countries, foster their integration into the world economy and support the campaign against poverty, while promoting democracy and the rule of law and respect for human rights and fundamental freedoms (EC Treaty, Art. 177(1) and (2); see paras 20–026 *et seq.*). The Treaty of Nice has added a specific competence pursuant to which the Council may adopt measures for economic, financial and technical co-operation with third countries (EC Treaty, Art. 181a; see para. 20–029). Such measures must be complementary to those carried out by the Member States and consistent with the development policy of the Community (EC Treaty, Art. 181a(1)). Where Community action in other areas is likely to affect developing countries, it must take its development policy objectives into account (EC Treaty, Art. 178). In the EU Constitution, the provisions on development co-operation will be integrated, together with a new legal basis for humanitarian aid, into a Title specifically dedicated to the Union's external action, for which specific objectives are to be formulated (see para. 20–028).

L. ENERGY, TOURISM AND CIVIL PROTECTION

5–252 Energy. In a sense, energy has been a central feature of European integration from the outset: coal in the ECSC Treaty and nuclear energy in

---

[1199] For a general discussion of the Member States' discretion, see Somsen, "Discretion in European Community Environmental Law: An Analysis of ECJ Case Law" (2003) C.M.L.R. 1413–1453.

the EAEC Treaty. The EC Treaty did not, however, confer on the Community any specific competence to lay down the "measures in the [sphere] of energy" mentioned in Art. 3 of that Treaty (see para. 5–005). Nevertheless, national energy policies have been affected by numerous Community measures in the fields of agriculture, transport and the environment and national energy markets have been harmonised and liberalised as part of the establishment of the internal market.[1200]

The EU Constitution proposes to endow the Union with express powers in the area of energy. Union action will aim to ensure the functioning of the energy market, to ensure security of energy supply in the Union, and to promote energy efficiency and saving and the development of new and renewable forms of energy.[1201] Such action may not however affect the Member States' right to determine the conditions for exploiting their energy resources, their choice between different energy sources or the general structure of their energy supply.[1202]

Tourism and civil protection. As regards tourism and civil protection, the **5–253** EC Treaty does not contain any specific competence to lay down the measures mentioned by Art. 3 in this connection (see para. 5–005). Nevertheless, various aspects of tourism have been the subject of Community harmonisation measures adopted on the basis of Arts 95 and 308 of the EC Treaty (see para. 5–208). As for civil protection, the Council has used Art. 308 of the EC Treaty as the legal basis for setting up a mechanism for co-operation between the Member States and likewise for civil protection assistance interventions.[1203]

The EU Constitution will create a specific competence for civil protection, which will enable the Union to encourage co-operation between the Member States with a view to improving the effectiveness of systems for preventing and protecting against natural or man-made disasters (Art. III–284). As for tourism, the Convention did not propose any specific legal basis. However, in the course of the Intergovernmental Conference it has been agreed to confer on the Union an express power to improve the

---

[1200] For this liberalisation, see para. 5–202, *supra*. For energy, see already Council Decision 1999/21/EC, Euratom of December 14, 1998 adopting a multiannual framework programme for actions in the energy sector (1998–2002) and connected measures ([1999] O.J. L7/16), together with specific programmes adopted on the basis of Art. 308 of the EC Treaty. For the relationship between EC and EAEC powers, see Trüe, "Legislative competences of Euratom and the European Community in the energy sector: the 'Nuclear Package' of the Commission" (2003) E.L.Rev. 664–685.

[1201] EU Constitution, Art. III–256(1).

[1202] EU Constitution, Art. III–256(2), second subpara.

[1203] See Council Decision 1999/847/EC of December 9, 1999 establishing a Community action programme in the field of civil protection ([1999] O.J. L327/53) and Council Decision 2001/792/EC, Euratom of October 23, 2001 establishing a Community mechanism to facilitate reinforced co-operation in civil protection assistance interventions ([2001] O.J. L297/7).

competitiveness of undertakings in the sector of tourism (see Art. III–281 of the EU Constitution). Like civil protection, tourism will be regarded as an area where the Union may take "co-ordinating, complementary or supporting action", with the result that any harmonisation of the laws and regulations of the Member States is ruled out (see para. 5–027).

M. Administrative co-operation

5–254 Implementing Union law. Effective implementation of Union law by the Member States is essential for the proper functioning of the Union and is therefore regarded as being a matter of common interest. The EU Constitution provides a legal basis which will enable the Union to support Member States' efforts to improve their administrative capacity to implement Union law (Art. III–285). In this connection, the EU Constitution mentions facilitating the exchange of information and exchanges of civil servants and supporting training schemes.

N. Implementation of the solidarity clause

5–255 Solidarity clause. In the wake of the attacks of March 11, 2004 in Madrid, the Heads of State or Government of the Member States adopted a declaration on combating terrorism[1204] which refers to the solidarity clause contained in Art. I–43 of the EU Constitution. Pursuant to that clause the Union and the Member States are to act jointly in a spirit of solidarity if a Member State is the victim of a terrorist attack or of a natural or man-made disaster. Under the EU Constitution, this will entail Member States co-ordinating between themselves in the Council. The Council may have recourse to the structures developed under the common security and defence policy.[1205] The Union is to mobilise "all the instruments at its disposal, including the military resources made available by the Member States".[1206] The Council, acting by qualified majority on a joint proposal by the Commission and the Union Minister for Foreign Affairs, is to define the arrangements for the implementation of the solidarity clause. The European Parliament will then be informed.[1207]

[1204] See the Declaration annexed to the Conclusions of the European Council held in Brussels on March 25 and 26, 2004 (referring to then Art. I–42 of the draft EU Constitution).
[1205] EU Constitution, Art. III–329(1) and (2).
[1206] EU Constitution, Art. I–43(1).
[1207] The Council is to decide unanimously where its decision has defence implications: EU Constitution, Art. III–329(2), first subpara., in conjunction with Art. I–23(3).

CHAPTER 6

SUBSTANTIVE SCOPE OF TITLES V AND VI OF THE EU TREATY

CFSP and PJCC. The EU Treaty empowered the institutions of the Union **6–001** to pursue policies outside the scope of the Communities in two areas, that is to say, common foreign and security policy (CFSP, based on Title V of the EU Treaty) and police and judicial co-operation in criminal matters (PJCC, based on Title VI of the EU Treaty). The basic principles and the substantive scope of these policy areas will be described below (as far as the CFSP is concerned, the reader is referred chiefly to the discussion in Part VI). When the EU Constitution enters into force, there will be a change in the status of both fields of action. This is because the present distinction between Community and non-Community powers of the Union will disappear and both PJCC and the CFSP will come within the competences of the Union (for PJCC, see para. 6–014; for the CFSP, see para. 20–041). For both fields of action, the EU Constitution will nonetheless lay down some "specific provisions", which mainly concern the decision-making procedure in the case of the CFSP.[1]

I. PRINCIPLES

Non-Community policies. Title V (CFSP) and Title VI (PJCC) of the EU **6–002** Treaty confer specific fields of activity on the Union. The Union has to realise the objectives of the Treaty and is given some specific tasks to perform, especially in connection with PJCC. As far as the CFSP is concerned, the Treaty rules primarily indicate the instruments for action and the decision-making procedure for employing those instruments. In principle, the Council may not act on the basis of Title V or Title VI where the conditions for application of the EC Treaty are fulfilled.[2] Since the Union action pursuant to Title V or Title VI falls outside the sphere of

---

[1] para. 15–009, *infra*. For the specific institutional features of PJCC, see para. 15–015, *infra*.

[2] ECJ, Case C–170/96 *Commission v Council* [1998] E.C.R. I–2763, paras 13–17. Accordingly, a Community act may be enforced by criminal sanctions in the Member States; however, in order to harmonise criminal law provisions (type and level of sanctions), action under Title VI of the EU Treaty is required. For the question as to whether Community measures may also impose criminal law enforcement, see Comijs, "Communautair strafrecht?" (2001) N.T.E.R. 267–271 and the articles mentioned in ns to para. 5–096, *supra*.

competence of the Communities, such action of the Union is based on consultation and co-operation between the Member States[3] or on action on the part of the Union itself in the form of common positions, joint (or common) actions, framework decisions, decisions, conventions and implementing measures adopted by the Council (see paras 18–014 et seq.).[4] To date, Council measures have generally been based on Title V or Title VI of the EU Treaty; sometimes, measures are adopted pursuant to both Titles[5] or even on the basis of "the EU Treaty".[6] Since acts of the Council pursuant to Title V do not have the force of Community law, conflicts in the event of action by the Union clashing with that of a Member State will have to be resolved by recourse to the rules of international law.[7] As far as PJCC is concerned, Art. 35 of the EU Treaty confers on the Court of Justice jurisdiction, subject to certain conditions, to determine disputes on the interpretation or application of PJCC acts.[8]

6–003 Constraining principles. As a result of the final paragraph of Art. 2 of the EU Treaty, the principle of subsidiarity as defined in Art. 5 of the EC Treaty also applies to action taken by the Union pursuant to Title V and Title VI of the EU Treaty. Action of the Union pursuant to Title V and Title VI must comply with the principle of proportionality in the event of conflicting objectives, since Art. 6 authorises only the "necessary" means to be used. Action must also respect the national identities of the Member States and fundamental rights, as guaranteed by the ECHR and as they result from the constitutional traditions common to the Member States, as general principles of Community law (EU Treaty, Art. 6(2) and (3), see para. 17–079).

II. THE COMMON FOREIGN AND SECURITY POLICY (TITLE V)

6–004 Framework. Title V of the EU Treaty constitutes the legal basis for the Union's common foreign and security policy (CFSP). That policy replaced European Political Co-operation between the Member States in 1993

---

[3] See EU Treaty, Art. 16 and Art. 34(1).

[4] Before the Treaty of Amsterdam, Title VI was concerned with co-operation in the field of justice and home affairs (JHA co-operation), see para. 5–181, *infra*.

[5] See Joint Action 96/668/CFSP of November 22, 1996 adopted by the Council on the basis of the former Arts J.3 and K.3 of the Treaty on European Union concerning measures protecting against the effects of the extra-territorial application of legislation adopted by a third country, and actions based thereon or resulting therefrom, [1996] O.J. L309/7, and Council Common Positions 2001/930/CFSP and 2001/931/CFSP of December 27, 2001, adopted pursuant to Arts 15 and 34 of the EU Treaty, on combating terrorism and on the application of specific measures to combat terrorism, ([2001] O.J. L344/90 and 93, respectively).

[6] This is true of non-binding measures such as the Council Recommendation of December 6, 2001 setting a common scale for assessing threats to public figures visiting the European Union ([2001] O.J. C356/1).

[7] For the legal force of CFSP decisions of the Council, see para. 18–014 et seq.; for the relationship between international action on the part of the Union and such action undertaken by Member States, see para. 22–009, *infra*.

[8] See the discussion of the jurisdiction of the Court of Justice, para. 10–077, *infra*, and of PJCC acts, paras 18–019 et seq.

(EPC; see para. 2–013) and is based both on action by the institutions of the Union and on co-operation between the Member States. Article 11(1) of the EU Treaty sets out objectives supplementing the general objectives of Art. 2 of the EU Treaty (see para. 20–039). Title V of the EU Treaty does not determine in greater detail how the CFSP is to take substantive shape, but elaborates the procedures and instruments pursuant to which the institutions and the Member States may conduct a foreign and security policy (Arts 12 to 15). Pursuant to general guidelines and common strategies determined by the European Council, the Council adopts joint actions, common positions or other decisions and concludes agreements with third countries and international organisations (for a survey of the CFSP, see paras 20–039–20–049). The Member States are to consult one another on any matter of foreign and security policy of general interest (EU Treaty, Art. 16). The CFSP covers all matters bearing on the security of the Union and might lead to a "common defence", should the European Council so decide (EU Treaty, Art. 17(1); see para. 20–045). The EU Constitution will place the CFSP alongside the other external powers of the Union, while making some changes to the decision-making procedure and to the choice of legislative instruments which may be used (see paras 15–009 and 18–021). In addition, the EU Constitution will extend the Union's scope of action with respect to the common security and defence policy (see para. 20–046).

Differentiated participation. According to the EU Treaty, the CFSP is to **6–005** respect the obligations of Member States under the North Atlantic Treaty and the policy established within NATO. At the same time, the policy of the Union must not prejudice the specific character of the security and defence policy of certain Member States (EU Treaty, Art. 17(1), second subpara.). Moreover, the CFSP decision-making procedure allows Member States to make a formal declaration that they abstain in a given vote. They will then not be obliged to apply the relevant decision (EU Treaty, Art. 23(1), see para. 15–002). In this way, Denmark does not participate in the elaboration and implementation of decisions and actions of the Union which have defence implications.[9] On the other hand, the EU Treaty does not prevent the development of enhanced co-operation between two or more Member States on a bilateral level, provided that such co-operation does not run counter to or impede the CFSP (EU Treaty, Art. 17(4); see para. 20–048). Since the Treaty of Nice, two or more Member States may also engage in enhanced co-operation in the field of the CFSP relating to implementation of a joint action or a common position, although such co-operation may not relate to matters having military or defence implications (EU Treaty Arts 27a–27e; see para. 9–007).

---

[9] Art. 6 of Protocol (No. 5) on the position of Denmark, annexed by the Treaty of Amsterdam to the EC Treaty and the EU Treaty ([1997] O.J. C340/101); see para. 20–047, *infra*.

III. Police and Judicial Co-operation in Criminal Matters (Title VI)

A. Co-operation in Criminal Matters and Creation of an Area of Freedom, Security and Justice

6–006 Scope of PJCC. Title VI of the EU Treaty provides the framework for police and judicial co-operation in criminal matters between Member States (PJCC).[10] PJCC covers the area retained by the Treaty of Amsterdam from the matters of common interest which had been listed in the EU Treaty under the heading "co-operation in the fields of justice and home affairs" ("JHA co-operation"—the area originally covered by Title VI).[11] JHA co-operation contemplated primarily such police and judicial co-operation as was necessary to accompany the liberalisation of the movement of persons in the internal market.[12] The 1996 Intergovernmental Conference decided to extend the aim of this "third pillar" of the European Union to cover the provision of a high level of freedom, security and justice for citizens (see para. 3–019). The Treaty of Amsterdam conferred on the Community competence to adopt measures with respect to visas, asylum, immigration and other areas connected with free movement of persons (EC Treaty, Arts 61–69; see para. 5–158 *et seq.*), customs co-operation (EC Treaty, Art. 135; see para. 5–096) and countering fraud (EC Treaty, Art. 280; see para. 10–114). Co-operation in criminal matters under Title VI of the EU Treaty is therefore directed towards preventing and combating crime, organised or otherwise (EU Treaty, Art. 29, second para.). The EU Treaty further mentions preventing and combating racism and xenophobia as a means—without prejudice to the powers of the Community—of achieving the Union's objective of "providing citizens with a high level of safety within an area of freedom, security and justice" (Art. 29, first para.).[13]

---

[10] In decisions adopted pursuant to Title VI of the EU Treaty, the—less precise—abbreviation "JHA" is used even after the Treaty of Amsterdam. For a discussion of the PJCC provisions, see Margue, "La coopération européenne en matière de lutte contre la criminalité organisée dans le contexte du traité d'Amsterdam" (1997) 3 R.M.U.E. 91–117; Monar, "Justice and Home Affairs in the Treaty of Amsterdam: Reform at the Price of Fragmentation" (1998) E.L.R. 320–335. See also the action plan and the discussions thereof cited in n.680.

[11] See Müller-Graff, "The Legal Base of the Third Pillar and its Position in the Framework of the Union Treaty" (1994) C.M.L.R. 493–503. These matters were also the subject of intergovernmental co-operation between the Member States before the EU Treaty entered into force (see paras 2–015—2–017).

[12] For the first results and the need to reform the third pillar, see Den Boer, "Police Co-operation in the TEU: Tiger in a Trojan Horse?" (1995) C.M.L.R. 555–578; Lepoivre, "Le domaine de la justice et des affaires intérieures dans la perspective de la Conférence intergouvernementale" (1995) C.D.E. 323–349; O'Keeffe, "Recasting the Third Pillar" (1995) C.M.L.R. 893–920; Labayle, "La coopération européenne en matière de justice et d'affaires intérieures et la Conférence intergouvernementale (1997) R.T.D.E. 1–35. Compare Vignes, "Plaidoyer pour le IIIème pilier" (1996) R.M.C.U.E. 273–281, with Dehousse and Van den Hende, "Plaidoyer pour la réforme du troisième pilier" (1996) R.M.C.U.E. 714–718.

[13] For non-Community and Community actions against racism, see para. 5–064, *supra.*

Article 42 of the EU Treaty provides that action in areas referred to in Art. 29 of the EU Treaty may be brought within the scope of Title IV of the EC Treaty. In the event that this is done, the Council is to determine the relevant voting conditions.[14] On similar lines the EU Constitution will bring the Union's powers with respect to police and judicial co-operation in criminal matters and the competences now contained in Title IV of the EC Treaty together in a single chapter on the "area of freedom, security and justice" (see para. 6–014).

European criminal law. Pursuant to Title VI of the EU Treaty, the Union **6–007** may now act in various ways in order to prevent and combat crime, organised or otherwise, in particular terrorism, trafficking in persons and offences against children, illicit drug trafficking and illicit arms trafficking, corruption and fraud (see EU Treaty, Art. 29, second para.).[15] As a result, the European Union has become the pre-eminent forum for bringing Member States' criminal law policy closer together and to make a start with European criminal law.[16] Title VI of the EU Treaty constitutes part of the legal basis for integrating the Schengen *acquis* into the European Union and its further development (see para. 5–164).

B. POLICE CO-OPERATION

Europol. Title VI of the EU Treaty provides for closer co-operation **6–008** between police forces, customs authorities and other competent authorities in the Member States, both directly and through the European Police Office (Europol).[17] Under Art. 30(1) of the EU Treaty, common action in the field of police co-operation includes:

(a) operational co-operation between national law enforcement services in relation to the prevention, detection and investigation of criminal offences[18];

---

[14] para. 7–008, *infra*. The Council is to adopt such decision by a unanimous vote on the initiative of the Commission or a Member State, after consulting the European Parliament, and is to recommend the Member States to adopt it in accordance with their respective constitutional requirements.

[15] Margue, "La coopération en matière de prévention et de lutte contre le crime dans le cadre du nouveau troisième pilier" (2000) R.D.U.E. 729 747; Mitsilegas, "Defining organised crime in the European Union: the limits of European criminal law in an area of 'freedom, security and justice'" (2001) E.L.Rev. 565–581.

[16] See also Harding, "Exploring the intersection of European law and national criminal law" (2000) E.L.Rev. 374–390; Van der Wilt, "Harmonisatie van strafrecht in Europa: gewogen en te licht bevonden" (2002) N.J.B. 747–752; von Bubnoff, "Institutionelle Kriminalitätsbekämpfung in der EU—Schritte auf dem Weg zu einem europäischen Ermittlungs- und Strafverfolgungsraum" (2002) Z.Eu.S. 185–237; Guild, "Crime and the EU's Constitutional Future in an Area of Freedom, Security and Justice" (2004) E.L.J. 218–234.

[17] See Heckler, "Europäisches Verwaltungskooperationsrecht am Beispiel der grenzüberschreitenden polizeilichen Zusammenarbeit" (2001) EuR 826–845.

[18] See Council Framework Decision 2002/465/JHA of June 13, 2002 on joint investigation teams, [2002] O.J. L162/1, and Council Decision 2002/956/JHA of November 28, 2002 setting up a European Network for the Protection of Public Figures, [2002] O.J. L333/1.

(b) collection, storage, processing, analysis and exchange of relevant information[19];

(c) co-operation and joint initiatives in training, the exchange of liaison officers, secondments, the use of equipment and forensic research; and

(d) the common evaluation of particular investigative techniques in relation to the detection of serious forms of organised crime.[20]

In recent measures, particular attention has been paid to the prevention of offences.[21] National police training institutions work together within the framework of the European Police College (CEPOL), which has now legal personality.[22]

The Council also promotes co-operation through Europol (EU Treaty, Art. 30(2); see also para. 10–112). This European Police Office was

---

[19] *e.g.* Council Decision 2000/261/JHA of March 27, 2000 on the improved exchange of information to combat counterfeit travel documents, [2000] O.J. L81/1; Council Decision 2000/642/JHA of October 17, 2000 concerning arrangements for co-operation between financial intelligence units of the Member States in respect of exchanging information, [2000] O.J. L271/4; Council Decision 2001/886/JHA of December 6, 2001 on the second-generation Schengen Information System, [2001] O.J. L328/1 (see para. 5–164, *supra*) and Council Decision 2002/348/JHA of April 25, 2002 concerning security in connection with football matches with an international dimension, [2002] O.J. L121/1.

[20] See Council Decision 2002/630/JHA of July 22, 2002 establishing a framework programme on police and judicial co-operation in criminal matters (AGIS) ([2002] O.J.L203/5), which co-ordinates for the period 2003 to 2007 existing exchange, training and co-operation programmes for legal practitioners and other legal occupations (Council Decision 2001/512/JHJA of 28 June 2001 "Grotius—criminal law", [2001] O.J. L186/1, extending in the field of criminal law Joint Action 96/636/JHA of October 28, 1996, [1996] O.J. L287/3;—for the civil side, see n. to para. 5–154, *supra*), for law enforcement authorities (Council Decision 2001/513/JHA of June 28, 2001—"Oisin II", [2001] O.J. L186/4, extending Joint Action 97/12/JHA of December 20, 1996—"Oisin", [1997] O.J. L7/5), and for persons responsible for combating trade in human beings and the sexual exploitation of children (Council Decision 2001/514/JHA of June 28, 2001 "Stop II", [2001] O.J. L186/7, extending Joint Action 96/700/JHA of November 29, 1996 "Stop", [1996] O.J. L322/7) as well as in the field of crime prevention (Council Decision 2001/515/JHA of June 28, 2001 "Hippocrates", [2001] O.J. L186/11). Prior to the Treaty of Amsterdam, see the exchange programmes in the field of identity documents (Joint Action 96/637/JHA of October 28, 1996—"Sherlock", [1996] O.J. L287/7) and for combating organised crime (Joint Action 98/245/JHA of March 19, 1998—Falcone programme, [1998] O.J. L99/8) and for asylum and immigration policy (Joint Action 98/244/JHA of March 19, 1998 "Odysseus", [1998] O.J. L99/2).

[21] See Council Decision 2001/427/JHA of May 28, 2001 setting up a European crime prevention network, [2001] O.J. L153/1.

[22] Council Decision 2000/820/JHA of December 22, 2000 establishing a European Police College (CEPOL) ([2000] O.J. L336/1). The college was provisionally established at Brøndby (Denmark); the Third Decision on Seats (para. 10–147, *infra*) fixed its seat in Bramshill (UK) following which Council Decision 2000/820/JHA was amended (see [2004] O.J. L251/20). For its legal personality, see [2004] O.J. L251/19.

established by convention concluded between the Member States pursuant to the former Art. K.3 of the EU Treaty. The Convention entered into force on October 1, 1998 (Europol Convention).[23] Europol is to improve the effectiveness and co-operation of the competent authorities in the Member States in preventing and combating serious forms of international crime where there are factual indications or reasonable grounds for believing that an organised criminal structure is involved and two or more Member States are affected in such a way as to require a common approach by the Member States owing to the scale, significance and consequences of the offences concerned. It is concerned in particular with terrorism, unlawful drug trafficking, illegal money-laundering activities, trafficking in nuclear and radioactive substances, illegal immigrant smuggling, trade in human beings and motor vehicle crime.[24] Article 30(2) of the EU Treaty lists tasks which the Council is to carry out within five years of the entry into force of the Treaty of Amsterdam in order to promote police co-operation through Europol.[25]

C. JUDICIAL CO-OPERATION IN CRIMINAL MATTERS

Eurojust. Alongside police co-operation, the EU Treaty also provides for **6–009** closer co-operation in the judicial sphere between the national competent authorities, in particular through the intervention of Eurojust, the European Judicial Co-operation Unit (EU Treaty, Art. 31). The Union is empowered to adopt measures:

---

[23] Convention of July 26, 1995 on the establishment of a European Police Office (Europol Convention), [1995] O.J. C316/1 (concluded pursuant to the former Art. K.3 of the EU Treaty). For the interpretation by the Court of Justice of the Europol Convention, see para. 18–009, *infra*. For the operation of Europol, see Ellermann, "Von Sammler zu Jäger—Europol auf dem Weg zu einem 'europäischen FBI'?" (2002) Z.Eu.S. 561–585. Europol started work on June 1, 1999 following the entry into force of the Protocol on privileges and immunities and the agreements on privileges and immunities of liaison officers, see the notice in [1999] O.J. C185/1.

[24] Europol Convention, Art. 2(2), as amended by the Protocols drawn up by Council Act of November 30, 2000 ([2000] O.J. C358/1) and Council Act of November 27, 2003 ([2004] O.J. C2/1). For these phenomena, see Weyembergh, "L'Union européenne et la lutte contre la traite des êtres humains" (2000) C.D.E. 215–251; Barbé, "L'Union européenne face au blanchiment du produit du crime" (2001) R.M.C.U.E. 161–163. In anticipation of the establishment of Europol, the Member States set up a Europol Drugs Unit (EDU) in 1993 in The Hague, where Europol is also based ((1993) 6 EC Bull. point 1.4.19). Its mandate was laid down by Joint Action 95/73/JHA of March 10, 1995 ([1995] O.J. L62/1) and extended by Joint Action 96/748/JHA of December 16, 1996, [1996] O.J. L342/4. See Subhan, "L'Union européenne et la lutte contre la drogue" (1999) R.M.C.U.E. 196–201.

[25] See, *e.g.* the Council Recommendations to Member States of September 28, 2000 in respect of requests made by Europol to initiate criminal investigations in specific cases ([2000] O.J. C289/8) and of November 30, 2000 in respect of Europol's assistance to joint investigative teams set up by the Member States ([2000] O.J. C357/7).

(a) concerning co-operation between ministries and judicial or equivalent authorities in relation to proceedings and the enforcement of decisions[26];

(b) facilitating extradition between Member States[27];

(c) ensuring compatibility in rules applicable in the Member States to the extent necessary to improve co-operation; and

(d) preventing conflicts of jurisdiction between Member States.

The Council promotes co-operation between national authorities through Eurojust (EU Treaty, Art. 31(2)). Eurojust is a unit composed of prosecutors, magistrates or police officers seconded from each Member State to facilitate the co-ordination of national prosecution authorities and support criminal investigations into organised crime.[28] As a result, Eurojust constitutes the embryonic beginnings of a genuine European public prosecutor's office.[29] In co-operation with the existing network of judicial contact points (the European Judicial Network), Eurojust has in particular to facilitate the execution of letters rogatory and the implementation of

---

[26] See the Convention of May 29, 2000 on Mutual Assistance in Criminal Matters between the Member States of the European Union established by Council Act of the same date in accordance with Art. 34 of the EU Treaty ([2000] O.J. C197/1; for the explanatory report, see [2000] O.J. C379/7) and the protocol to this convention of October 16, 2001 ([2001] O.J. C326/1; for the explanatory report, see [2002] O.J. C257/1). Both parts have been extended to Iceland and Norway; see the agreement concluded by the European Union with those States to that end on December 19, 2003, approved by Council Decision 2004/79/EC of December 17, 2003 ([2004] O.J. L26/1). See Denza, "The 2000 Convention on Mutual Assistance in Criminal Matters" (2003) C.M.L.R. 1047–1074. See also Council Framework Decision 2003/577/JHA of July 22, 2003 on the execution in the European Union of orders freezing property or evidence ([2003] O.J. L196/45). For a critical view of the principle of mutual recognition in criminal matters, see Peers, "Mutual Recognition and Criminal Law in the European Union: Has the Council Got it Wrong?" (2004) C.M.L.R. 5–36.

[27] See formerly the Convention of March 10, 1995, adopted on the basis of the former Art. K.3 of the EU Treaty, on simplified extradition procedure between the Member States of the European Union ([1995] O.J. C78/2) and the Convention of September 27, 1996 relating to extradition between the Member States of the European Union ([1996] O.J. C313/12; for the explanatory report, see [1997] O.J. C191/13). See Paulino Pereira, "Convention relative à la procédure simplifiée d'extradition entre les Etats membres de l'Union européenne" (1995) R.M.C.U.E. 521–524. For the interpretation of the Convention by the Court of Justice, see para. 18–009, *infra*.

[28] Council Decision 2002/187/JHA of February 28, 2002 setting up Eurojust with a view to reinforcing the fight against serious crime ([2002] O.J. L63/1), pursuant to Declaration (No. 2) annexed to the Treaty of Nice on Art. 31(2) of the EU Treaty ([2001] O.J. C80/77). Until Eurojust was set up, a Provisional Judicial Co-operation Unit operated by virtue of Council Decision 2000/799/JHA of December 14, 2000 ([2000] O.J. L324/2).

[29] See Veldt, "Een Europees Openbaar Ministerie: de oplossing voor de EU-fraude?" (2001) J.J.B. 666–671; Fijnaut and Groenhuijsen, "Een Europees openbaar ministerie: kanttekeningen bij het Groenboek" (2002) N.J.B. 1234–1241. For the relationship between Eurojust and Europol, see Berthelet and Chevallier-Govers, "Quelle relation entre Europol et Eurojust? Rapport d'égalité ou rapport d'autorité?" (2001) R.M.C.U.E. 468–474. See also Van Gerven, "Constitutional Conditions for a Public Prosecutor's Office at the European Level" (2000) European Journal of Crime, Criminal Law and Criminal Justice 296–318.

extradition requests.[30] The creation of the European arrest warrant is noteworthy in this connection.[31]

D. ALIGNMENT OF NATIONAL CRIMINAL PROVISIONS

Definition of criminal offences. Lastly, where necessary the Union is to **6–010** bring Member States' national criminal provisions into line with each other. Article 31(e) of the EU Treaty refers to the progressive adoption of measures establishing minimum rules relating to the constituent elements of criminal acts and to penalties in the fields of organised crime, terrorism and illicit drug trafficking. On this basis, the Council has, for example, defined crimes in the areas of fraud and forgery, corruption, trafficking in human beings and sexual exploitation.[32] Following the terrorist attacks of September 11, 2001, the Council adopted measures to ensure that any

---

[30] See EU Treaty, Art. 31(2). The European Judicial Network was set up by the Council by Joint Action 98/428/JHA of June 29, 1998 ([1998] O.J. L191/4).

[31] Council Framework Decision 2002/584/JHA of June 13, 2002 on the European arrest warrant and the surrender procedures between Member States ([2002] O.J. L190/1). See Benoit, "Le mandat d'arrêt européen" (2003) R.M.C.U.E. 106–110; Barbé, "Une triple étape pour le troisième pilier de l'Union européenne" (2002) R.M.C.U.E. 5–9; Flore, "Le mandat d'arrêt européen: première mise en oeuvre d'un nouveau paradigme de la justice pénale européenne" (2002) J.T. 273–281; Monville, "Le mandat d'arrêt européen: remise en cause du mécanisme de la simple remise . . ." (2003) J.T.D.E. 168–173; for a somewhat critical view, see Alegre and Leaf, "Mutual Recognition in European Judicial Co-operation: A Step Too Far Too Soon? Case Study—the European Arrest Warrant" (2004) E.L.J. 200–217; Peers (n.26, *supra*). For the amendment to the Constitution necessitated by this framework decision in France, see Monjal, "La décision-cadre instaurant le mandat d'arrêt européen et l'ordre juridique français: la constitutionnalité du droit dérivé de l'Union européenne sous contrôle du Conseil d'Etat" (2003) R.D.U.E. 109–187.

[32] See Council Framework Decision 2000/383/JHA of May 29, 2000 on increasing protection by criminal penalties and other sanctions against counterfeiting in connection with the introduction of the Euro ([2000] O.J. L140/1); Council Framework Decision 2001/413/JHA of May 28, 2001 combating fraud and counterfeiting of non-cash means of payment ([2001] O.J. L149/1); Council Framework Decision 2001/500/JHA of June 26, 2001 on money laundering, the identification, tracing, freezing, seizing and confiscation of instrumentalities and the proceeds of crime ([2001] O.J. L182/1); Council Framework Decision 2002/629/JHA of July 19, 2002 on combating trafficking in human beings ([2002] O.J. L203/1); Council Framework Decision 2002/946/JHA of November 28, 2002 on the strengthening of the penal framework to prevent the facilitation of unauthorised entry, transit and residence ([2002] O.J. L328/1); Council Framework Decision 2003/568/JHA of July 22, 2003 on combating corruption in the private sector ([2003] O.J. L192/54); Council Framework Decision 2004/68/JHA of December 22, 2003 on combating the sexual exploitation of children and child pornography ([2004] O.J. L13/44), and Council Decision 2000/375/JHA of May 29, 2000 to combat child pornography on the Internet ([2000] O.J. L138/1). For commentaries, see Obokata, "EU Council Framework Decision on Combating Trafficking in Human Beings: A Critical Appraisal" (2003) C.M.L.R. 917–936. See also to this effect the definition of "fraud" in the Convention on the protection of the European Communities' financial interests, para. 10–144, *infra*, the Convention of June 17, 1998, drawn up on the basis of the former Art. K.3 of the EU Treaty, on driving disqualifications, [1998] O.J. C216/2, and the Joint Actions adopted by the Council on the basis of the former Art. K.3 of the EU Treaty on making it a criminal offence to participate in a criminal organisation (98/733/JHA of December 21, 1998, [1998] O.J. L351/1) and on corruption in the private sector (98/742/JHA of December 22, 1998, [1998] O.J. L358/2).

assistance to acts of terrorism would be criminal offences.[33] The Council has also determined in a framework decision environmental offences which the Member States must regard as criminal offences in their legislation, even though the Commission had proposed to criminalise such offences pursuant to the environmental competence provided for in Art. 250 of the EC Treaty.[34] The Council has also adopted measures concerning criminal proceedings in particular with a view to improving the standing of victims of crime.[35]

E. SPECIFIC RULES FOR POLICE AND JUDICIAL CO-OPERATION IN CRIMINAL MATTERS

6–011 **Member State responsibilites.** The Council is to lay down the conditions and limitations under which the police and judicial authorities may operate in the territory of another Member State in liaison and in agreement with the authorities of that State (EU Treaty, Art. 32). The EU Treaty specifies that it is not to affect the exercise of the responsibilities incumbent upon Member States with regard to the maintenance of law and order and the safeguarding of internal security (EU Treaty, Art. 33).

6–012 **Institutional framework.** The Council is to arrange for the flow of information and consultation between the Member States in all the above-mentioned areas (EU Treaty, Art. 34(1)).[36] The Council is also to adopt common positions defining the Union's approach to particular matters, adopt framework decisions for the purpose of the approximation of national laws and regulations, and adopt decisions (and measures

---

[33] Council Framework Decision 2002/475/JHA of June 13, 2002 on combating terrorism ([2002] O.J. L164/3), which builds on Council Common Position 2001/930/JHA of December 27, 2001 on combating terrorism ([2001] O.J. L344/90). Specific measures were adopted against named persons in Council Common Position 2001/931/JHA of December 27, 2001 on the application of specific measures to combat terrorism ([2001] O.J. L344/93), as supplemented by Regulation 2580/2001 on specific restrictive measures directed against certain persons and entities with a view to combating terrorism ([2001] O.J. L344/70). See Margue, "Les initiatives menées par l'Union dans la lutte antiterroriste dans le cadre du troisième pilier (Justice et afffaires intérieures)" (2002) R.D.U.E. 261–281; Dubois, "The Attacks of 11 September: EU-US Co-operation Against Terrorism in the Field of Justice and Home Affairs" (2000) E.For.Aff.Rev. 317–335.

[34] Council Framework Decision 2003/80/JHA of January 27, 2003 on the protection of the environment through criminal law ([2003] O.J. L29/55). Since the Commission considers that Art. 175 of the EC Treaty affords the correct legal basis for such a measure, it has brought proceedings for the annulment of the framework decision: Case C–176/03, [2003] O.J. C135/21. See Compte, "Droit pénal de l'environnement et compétence communautaire" (2002) R.D.U.E. 775–799.

[35] Council Framework Decision 2001/220/JHA of March 15, 2001 on the standing of victims in criminal proceedings, [2001] O.J. L82/1. In order to ensure access to compensation to crime victims in cross-border situations, the Council adopted Directive 2004/80/EC of April 29, 2004 ([2004] O.J. L 261/15) pursuant to Art. 308 of the EC Treaty.

[36] See, *e.g.* Council Decision 2002/996/JHA of November 28, 2002 establishing a mechanism for evaluating the legal systems and their implementation at national level in the fight against terrorism ([2002] O.J. L349/1).

implementing them) for any other purpose than the approximation of legislation (EU Treaty, Art. 34(2)(a), (b) and (c)).[37] At the same time, it may establish Conventions (and measures implementing them) between the Member States (Art. 34(2)(d)) and conclude agreements with non-member countries and international organisations (Art. 38).[38] If a comparison is made with the procedure which applied to JHA co-operation, it stands out that in the case of PJCC the Council does not invariably have to decide by a unanimous vote and the Commission (alongside the Member States) can put forward initiatives in all areas.[39] Unlike in the case of JHA co-operation, the Council must now always consult the European Parliament before adopting a framework decision or a decision and before establishing a convention or an implementing measure.[40] Article 35 of the EU Treaty confers on the Court of Justice jurisdiction to give rulings on the validity and interpretation of framework decisions, decisions and implementing measures and on the interpretation of conventions in so far as the Member State concerned accepts the Court's jurisdiction.[41]

Enhanced co-operation. The original JHA co-operation did not prevent **6–013** the establishment or development of closer co-operation between two or more Member States in so far as such co-operation did not conflict with or impede the co-operation envisaged by Title VI of the EU Treaty (EU Treaty, former Art. K.7). There is no such provision in the context of PJCC, although the EU Treaty does specify the conditions and procedures under which Member States may establish enhanced co-operation among themselves, making use of the institutions, procedures and mechanisms laid down by the Treaties (see paras 9–005–9–009).

---

[37] Examples of "decisions" and "framework decisions" are set out in the notes above; see, *e.g.* also Council Common Position 2000/130/JHA of January 31, 2000 on the proposed protocol against the illicit manufacturing of and trafficking in firearms, their parts and components and ammunition, supplementing the United Nations Convention against transnational organised crime ([2000] O.J. L37/1). For these legal instruments, see paras 18–014—18–023, *infra*.

[38] See the Convention of May 29, 2000 on Mutual Assistance in Criminal Matters between the Member States of the European Union and the Agreement with Iceland and Norway on the application of certain provisions of that Convention to Iceland and Norway (n.26, *supra*); see also the Agreements of June 25, 2003 on extradition and mutual legal assistance in criminal matters concluded by the European Union with the United States of America ([2003] O.J. L181/27 and 34, respectively). See Genson, "Les accords d'extradition et d'entraide judiciaire signés le 25 juin 2003 à Washington entre l'Union européenne et les Etats d'Amérique" (2003) R.M.C.U.E. 427–432.

[39] For a discussion of decision-making within the sphere of PJCC, see paras 15–010—15–013, *infra*. In the case of JHA co-operation, the Commission was not entitled to take the initiative in proposing a common position, a joint action or a draft convention on judicial co-operation in the fields of criminal matters, customs co-operation or police co-operation.

[40] para. 15–011, *infra*. In the case of JHA co-operation, the Parliament was merely regularly informed and consulted.

[41] EU Treaty, Art. 35(1), (2) and (3). On certain conditions, Member States and the Commission may submit a dispute to the Court of Justice and bring before it an application for annulment of PJCC framework decisions and decisions. For the jurisdiction of the Court of Justice in the sphere of PJCC, see para. 10–077, *infra*.

F. POLICE AND JUDICIAL CO-OPERATION IN CRIMINAL MATTERS IN THE EU CONSTITUTION

6–014 New framework. As noted earlier, the EU Constitution will conjoin the powers of the Union in the field of police and judicial co-operation in criminal matters with the competences at present contained in Title IV of the EC Treaty. In the areas which aim at establishing an "area of freedom, security and justice", the Union's action will take shape through European laws and framework laws, which are to be adopted, in principle, by the European Parliament and the Council under the co-decision procedure. As far as police and judicial co-operation in criminal matters is concerned, this means that the specific institutional arrangements discussed in para. 6–012 will disappear. Some sensitive matters will, however, still be decided by the Council acting unanimously after consulting the European Parliament or, in some cases, after obtaining the consent of the European Parliament. Moreover, where a Member State considers that a draft European framework law would affect fundamental aspects of its criminal justice system, it may request that the draft framework law be referred to the European Council (see para. 15–015).

The EU Constitution will also maintain some other arrangements which will enable the Member States to exercise a measure of control over policy making, that is to say the right of initiative conferred on (a group of at least a quarter of) the Member States and the specific mechanisms enabling national parliaments to supervise action on the part of the Union (see para. 15–015 and, as regards compliance with the principle of subsidiarity, para. 5–035). In any event, the Union's action in the field of police and judicial co-operation in criminal matters will be amenable in full to judicial review by the Court of Justice.

6–015 Substantive changes. At the substantive level, the EU Constitution significantly extends the Union's power to take action in the field of judicial co-operation in criminal matters in so far as it will enable the Union to lay down measures aimed at harmonising not only the definition of certain types of criminal offences and sanctions but also aspects of criminal procedure.

First, the EU Constitution provides the Union with a fully fledged competence to establish rules and procedures to secure the recognition throughout the Union of judgments and judicial decisions and to facilitate co-operation between judicial or equivalent authorities of the Member States in relation to proceedings in criminal matters and the enforcement of decisions (Art. III–270(1)). To that end, the Union will be given the competence to establish minimum rules concerning the mutual admissibility of evidence, the rights of individuals in criminal procedure, the rights of victims of crime and such other specific aspects of criminal procedure as are identified in advance by the Council, acting unanimously after obtaining the consent of the European Parliament. These minimum rules must take into account the differences between the legal traditions and systems of the Member States (EU Constitution, Art. III–270(2)).

Next, the EU Constitution will enable the Union to establish minimum rules on the definition of criminal offences and sanctions in the area of "particularly serious crime with a cross-border dimension resulting from the nature or impact of such offences or from a special need to combat them on a common basis" (Art. III–271(1), first subpara.). The offences in question are terrorism, trafficking in human beings and sexual exploitation of women and children, illegal drug trafficking, illegal arms trafficking, money laundering, corruption, counterfeiting of means of payment, computer crime and organised crime, as well as other areas of crime to be identified by the Council, acting unanimously after obtaining the consent of the European Parliament (EU Constitution, Art. III–271(1), second and third subpara.).

In addition, the Union will be empowered to accompany its harmonisation measures by minimum rules with regard to the definition of criminal offences and sanctions in the area concerned. If it proves essential in order to ensure the effective implementation of a Union policy, a European framework law may be established to this end in accordance with the same procedure as was used to adopt the harmonisation measure (EU Constitution, Art. III–271(2)).

The Union will further be able to establish measures to promote and support the action of Member States in the field of crime prevention. These measures may not, however, extend to approximation of Member States' legislative and regulatory provisions (EU Constitution, Art. III–272).

European Public Prosecutor. Remarkably, the EU Constitution provides **6–016** not only for measures relating to the operation, scope of action and tasks of Eurojust, but also holds out the prospect of setting up a European Public Prosecutor's Office in order to combat crimes affecting the Union's financial interests (Art. III–274(1)). The European Public Prosecutor's Office may be established by the Council, acting unanimously after obtaining the consent of the European Parliament. The European Public Prosecutor's Office will be responsible for investigating, prosecuting and bringing to judgment the perpetrators of offences against the Union's financial interests and their accomplices. In relation to those offences the European Public Prosecutor's Office will act as prosecutor in the competent courts of the Member States (EU Constitution, Art. III–274(2)). The Convention had proposed to confer on the European Public Prosecutor's Office powers with respect to other "serious crimes having a cross-border dimension". The Intergovernmental Conference agreed however only on a clause leaving it to the European Council to determine whether its powers should be extended to include serious crimes affecting more than one Member State (Art. III–274(4) of the EU Constitution).

6–017 Police operations. As far as police co-operation and Europol are concerned, the EU Constitution takes over the existing competences, whilst enabling the European Parliament and the Council to enact European laws and framework laws under the co-decision procedure. It is for the Council, acting unanimously after consulting the European Parliament, to decide on operational co-operation between law enforcement services and to determine the conditions and limitations under which national authorities may operate in the territory of another Member State (EU Constitution, Arts III–275(3) and III–277). Operational actions by Europol will be possible solely in liaison and in agreement with the authorities of the Member State concerned. In this sphere, the competent national authorities have the exclusive responsibility to apply coercive measures (EU Constitution, Art. III–276(3)).

CHAPTER 7

TEMPORAL SCOPE OF THE TREATIES

I. ENTRY INTO EFFECT OF THE TREATIES

Entry into force. Each of the Treaties stipulates the conditions and time of **7–001** its entry into force. The entry into effect of the ECSC, EEC, EAEC and EU Treaties was conditional upon their ratification by all the Contracting Parties in accordance with their respective constitutional requirements and the deposit of the instruments of ratification.[1] Ratification by all Member States is also a requirement for the entry into force of Treaties amending those Treaties (see para. 7–005) and of Treaties governing the accession of new Member States (see para. 8–009). Each Treaty specifies the exact day following the deposit of the last instrument of ratification on which it is to enter into force.[2] Unless otherwise provided, such a Treaty will apply to the future effects of situations arising prior to the date on which it entered into effect.[3] Where a Treaty (or a protocol thereto) makes it necessary to adopt

---

[1] ECSC Treaty, Art. 99; EEC Treaty, Art. 247; EAEC Treaty, Art. 224; Single European Act, Art. 33; EU Treaty, Art. 52; Treaty of Amsterdam, Art. 14; Treaty of Nice, Art. 12; see also EU Constitution, Art. IV–447. The ECSC Treaty provided for the instruments of ratification to be lodged with the French Government; the instruments of ratification of the subsequent Treaties were to be lodged with the Italian Government.

[2] The same day under Art. 99 of the ECSC Treaty (namely July 23, 1952); the first day of the following month under Art. 247 of the EEC Treaty, Art. 224 of the EAEC Treaty (since the Benelux countries deposited their instruments of ratification last on December 13, 1957, this was January 1, 1958) and Art. 33 of the Single European Act. The Treaty of Amsterdam entered into force under Art. 14 on the first day of the second month following the deposit of the instrument of ratification by the last signatory State (namely May 1, 1999). The same arrangements applied to the Treaty of Nice by virtue of Art. 12 thereof (entry into force on February 1, 2003) and will apply to the EU Constitution by virtue of Art. IV–447 thereof. Under Art. 52(2), the earliest date for the entry into force of the EU Treaty was January 1, 1993, failing which it was to enter into force on the first day of the month following the deposit of the instrument of ratification by the last State to do so (this was November 1, 1993). The Accession Treaties also laid down a fixed (earliest) date for their entry into force: January 1, 1973 in the second paragraph of Art. 2 of the Accession Treaty of January 22, 1972 ([1972] O.J. English Spec. Ed. 5); January 1, 1981 in the second paragraph of Art. 2 of the Accession Treaty of May 28, 1979 ([1979] O.J. L291/9); January 1, 1986 in the first subparagraph of Art. 2(2) of the Accession Treaty of June 12, 1985 ([1985] O.J. L302/9); January 1, 1995 in the first subpara. of Art. 2(2) of the Accession Treaty of June 24, 1994 ([1994] O.J. C241/13); May 1, 2004 in Art. 2(2) of the Accession Treaty of April 16, 2003 ([2003] O.J. L236/17). For full references to the Accession Treaties, see para. 1–021, *supra*.

[3] ECJ, Case C–122/96 *Saldanha and MTS* [1997] E.C.R. I–5325, para. 14; ECJ, Case C–321/97 *Andersson and Andersson* [1999] E.C.R. I–3551, paras 35–46; ECJ, Case C–512/99 *Germany v Commission* [2003] E.C.R. I–845, para. 46. For the resolution of intermediate temporal

implementing measures, the principle of good administration requires the preliminary work leading to the adoption of those measures to be started before the entry into force of the Treaty, in order for them to be applicable from a date as close as possible to that of the entry into force.[4]

Unless all the Contracting Parties have ratified the Treaty, it cannot enter into force.[5] Since, however, it is impossible to tell beforehand whether an Accession Treaty will be approved in all the would-be Member States, such Treaty will generally contain a provision empowering the Council to make the necessary adjustments in the event that a smaller number of States actually join.[6] No such adjustments may be made in the case of an amendment of the Treaties. Consequently, the rejection of the EU Treaty by a referendum held in Denmark held up its entry into force until that country proceeded to ratify it after a positive vote in a new referendum.[7] The problem recurred with the Treaty of Nice, which Ireland could not ratify until after the positive outcome of a second referendum.[8] The EU Constitution will contain a clause that seeks to avoid future amendments to the Constitution coming up against such impasse (see para. 7–007).

II. DURATION OF THE TREATIES

7–002 **Unlimited period.** Only the ECSC Treaty was concluded for a specific period: it expired on July 23, 2002 (ECSC Treaty, Art. 97). This is because the Contracting Parties regarded the ECSC as a provisional first step

---

problems (in particular in connection with the entry into force of Accession Treaties, see Kaleda, "Immediate Effects of Community Law in the New Member States: Is There a Place for a Consistent Doctrine?" (2004) E.L.J. 102–122.

[4] CFI, Joined Cases T–164/99, T–37/00 and T–38/00 *Leroy v Council* [2001] E.C.R. II–1819, para. 82.

[5] Nevertheless, in theory, a treaty may enter into force between some of the parties if it allows for this possibility (Art. 24(2) of the Vienna Convention on the Law of Treaties of May 23, 1969, para. 17–103, *infra*). The second paragraph of Art. 82 of the Draft Treaty establishing the European Union (para. 3–004, *supra*) would have allowed the Treaty to enter into force as soon as it had been ratified by a majority of the Member States of the Communities whose population represented two-thirds of the total population of the Communities. In that case, the governments of the Member States which had ratified the Treaty were to meet in order to decide by common accord on the procedures by and the date on which the Treaty should enter into force and to decide on their relations with the other Member States ([1984] O.J. C77/52). Art. 47 of the 1994 Draft Constitution of the European Union was similar, although it provided for a majority of four-fifths of the total population of the Union; para. 3–017, *supra*.

[6] Pursuant to the third paragraph of Art. 2 of the 1972 Accession Treaty and the second subparagraph of Art. 2(2) of the 1994 Accession Treaty, the Council adopted a decision each time Norway found it impossible to ratify the Accession Treaty (on January 1, 1973 and January 1, 1995, respectively), adjusting the instruments concerning the accession of new Member States to the European Communities/European Union ([1973] O.J. L2/1, and [1995] O.J. L1/1). See also the second subpara. of Art. 2(2) of the 1985 Accession Treaty and the second subparagraph of Art. 2(2) of the 2003 Accession Treaty.

[7] Para. 3–011, *supra*. The procedure for Treaty amendment laid down in Art. 236 of the EEC Treaty did not allow the EU Treaty to enter into force as between the other Member States: Rideau, "La ratification et l'entrée en vigueur du traité de Maastricht" (1992) R.F.D.C. 479–491. Art. 48 of the EU Treaty also requires all the Member States to ratify the amendments before the amended Treaty can enter into force, para. 7–005, *infra*.

[8] Para. 3-023, *supra*.

towards European integration (see para. 1–003). Since the tasks of the ECSC could be taken over by the EC, the ECSC Treaty was not extended.[9]

The subsequent Treaties were concluded for an unlimited period (EEC Treaty, Art. 240, and EAEC Treaty, Art. 208; see also EU Treaty, Art. 51, the Treaty of Amsterdam, Art. 13, and the Treaty of Nice, Art. 11). The fact that a Community, having its own institutions and powers, was established for an unlimited duration demonstrates that the Member States intended to create a new legal order, which binds both their subjects and themselves.[10] In order to bring about the abrogation of the Treaties and, with them, the Communities or the Union, the Member States may not rely unconditionally on the rule of international law that a treaty may be terminated if the parties conclude a subsequent treaty between them.[11] It appears to be contrary to Community law for the Member States simply to bring an end to European integration by means of an amendment to the Treaties or in some other manner.[12] The Treaty establishing a Constitution for Europe follows the same pattern by laying down in Art. IV–446 that the Treaty is concluded for an unlimited period.

III. AMENDMENT OF THE TREATIES

Amendment. An amendment to the Treaties enables amending or **7–003** supplementing provisions to be adopted that the same legal force as the original Treaty provisions.[13] In this way, the original Community Treaties were amended and supplemented by the Single European Act and the EU Treaty. Both the Community Treaties as so amended and the provisions which the EU Treaty added to them were subsequently amended by the Treaty of Amsterdam and the Treaty of Nice (and soon also by the EU Constitution). Alongside the general amendment procedure, the Treaties make provision for altering specific provisions by means of a special procedure. After a discussion of these procedures, it will be considered whether the Treaties subject their amendment, not only to procedural, but also to substantive constraints.

---

[9] See the resolution of the Council of the European Union and the representatives of the governments of the Member States, meeting within the Council of July 20, 1998 concerning the expiry of the Treaty establishing the European Coal and Steel Community, [1998] O.J. C247/5.

[10] ECJ, Case 6/64 *Costa v ENEL* [1964] E.C.R. 585, at 593 (para. 1–017, *supra*).

[11] For this rule, see Art. 54 of the 1969 Vienna Convention (para. 17–103, *infra*).

[12] This question is directly related to the possible substantive limitations on amending the Treaties, para. 7–011, *infra*.

[13] Para. 17–057, *infra*.

A. PROCEDURE FOR AMENDING THE TREATIES

1. General amendment procedure

7–004 General scope. Article 48 of the EU Treaty defines the procedure for amending "the Treaties on which the Union is founded". This procedure therefore applies both to the amendment of the Community Treaties and to the amendment of the non-Community provisions introduced by the EU Treaty. It replaces the different manners of amendment originally contained in the ECSC Treaty (Art. 96), the EEC Treaty (Art. 236) and the EAEC Treaty (Art. 204).[14] The Treaty of Amsterdam and the Treaty of Nice were concluded under the procedure laid down by Art. 48 of the EU Treaty and it is that procedure which applies to the amendment that is to replace the Treaties by a Treaty establishing a Constitution for Europe.

7–005 Two stages. Under Art. 48 of the EU Treaty, an amendment to the Treaties requires action on the part of the Community institutions (the Community stage) and is determined by a conference of representatives of the Member State governments, the "intergovernmental conference" or IGC (the intergovernmental stage).

Any Member State government or the Commission may submit proposals for amendment. The Council has to consult the European Parliament[15] and, provided that it did not make the proposal, the Commission. In the event that institutional changes in the monetary area are proposed, the European Central Bank must also be consulted by the Council.[16] The amendment becomes possible if the Council "delivers an opinion in favour" of calling an intergovernmental conference. Since Art. 48 does not require the vote to be taken by any particular majority, the Council may take its decision by a simple majority.[17]

The President of the Council convenes the conference. The representatives of the Member State governments determine by common accord the amendments to be made to the Treaties. The amendments do not enter into force until they have been ratified by all the Member States in accordance with their respective constitutional requirements. The assent

---

[14] These articles were repealed by Art. 9(21), Art. 8(86) and Art. 10(28), respectively, of the EU Treaty.

[15] Only Art. 96 of the ECSC Treaty did not contain this requirement.

[16] The EU Treaty introduced that requirement into the revision procedure. Art. 102a(2) of the EEC Treaty, however, already required the Monetary Committee and the Committee of Central Bank Governors to be consulted on such amendments.

[17] By analogy with Art. 205(1) of the EC Treaty, which applied to the procedure laid down in Art. 236 of the EEC Treaty. Accordingly, the decision to convene an intergovernmental conference pursuant to that article was adopted in June 1985 despite the opposition of Denmark, Greece and the UK. See Pescatore, "Some Critical Remarks on the 'Single European Act'" (1987) C.M.L.R. 9, at 14. The Council took that decision within the framework of the European Council; see n.16 to para. 10–007, *infra*. Only Art. 96 of the ECSC Treaty required a two-thirds majority in the Council for such a decision.

of the European Parliament is therefore not required.[18] In order to increase the likelihood of ratification by each Member State, an amending Treaty will often contain opt-out provisions for particular Member States (see para. 9–003).

"Convention" method. In December 2001, the European Council meeting **7–006** in Laeken (Brussels) decided that the intergovernmental conference to be set up for the next amendment of the Treaties would be prepared by a "Convention" consisting of representatives of the national governments, the national parliaments, the European Parliament and the Commission. The discussions in the Convention resulted in the EU Constitution, which was submitted to the Intergovernmental Conference and approved by it on June 18, 2004 (see para. 4–004).

Since the participants felt that the Convention constituted an improvement over the traditional procedure for amending the Treaties, an obligatory "convention stage" has been enshrined in the EU Constitution for every future amendment of the Constitution. Under the new amendment procedure to be introduced by the EU Constitution, not only the government of any Member State and the Commission, but also the European Parliament, may take the initiative to seek an amendment of the Constitution (Art. IV–443(1)). If the European Council, after consulting the European Parliament and the Commission, decides in favour of examining the proposed amendments, the President of the European Council is to convene a Convention composed of representatives of the national parliaments, the Heads of State or Government of the Member States, the European Parliament and the Commission. The European Council may equally decide, however, after obtaining the consent of the European Parliament, that the extent of the proposed amendments does not justify convening a Convention.[19] The Convention is to adopt by consensus a recommendation to a conference of representatives of the governments of the Member States (EU Constitution, Art. IV–443(2)). As under the existing system, the intergovernmental conference will be convened by the President of the Council for the purpose of determining by

---

[18] At most, the Framework Agreement on Relations between the European Parliament and the Commission of July 5, 2000 ((2000) 7/8 EU Bull. point 2.2.1) provides that "[t]he Commission shall ensure, within its means, that the European Parliament is kept informed and is fully associated with the preparation and conduct of intergovernmental conferences" (point 6). Art. 84 of the European Parliament's Draft Treaty establishing the European Union provided for a revision procedure whereby the "two arms of the legislative authority" (European Parliament and Council) had to approve any "draft law amending one or more provisions of this Treaty". Such amendments could be submitted by a representation in the Council or one-third of MEPs or the Commission. The draft law was to come into force when all the Member States had ratified it ([1984] O.J. C77/52). The 1994 Draft Constitution of the European Union would also have involved the European Parliament and the Council in making the amendment. Such an amendment would have to be made by a "constitutional law" on the initiative of the European Parliament, the Commission, the Council or a Member State. See Art. 32 of the Draft Constitution; para. 3–017, *supra*.

[19] The European Council will decide by a simple majority (Art. IV–443(2), second subpara.).

common accord the amendments to be made to the Constitution, which will then need to be ratified by all the Member States in accordance with their respective constitutional requirements.

7-007 **Amendment of EU Constitution.** Even under the EU Constitution, every amendment to the Constitution will continue to depend on the national governments reaching agreement among themselves and on subsequent ratification by all Member States. Indeed, it has not been possible to agree on a less cumbersome procedure for amending certain provisions of the Constitution, for instance by making a distinction between essential and non-essential provisions. Such a system would have the advantage that consensus among the Member States would be required solely for amendments to the "constitutional core" of the Union, whilst agreement among a broad majority of the Member States would suffice to adapt the detailed provisions relating to the Union's various policy areas in order to take account of changed social or economic circumstances.[20] The amending procedure has been simplified only to the extent that the provisions of Title III of Part III of the Constitution on the internal policies of the Union may be amended by a decision of the European Council, acting unanimously, instead of having to convene a conference of the representatives of the Member States (see para. 7-008). That method of amendment still depends on an agreement among the Heads of State or Government of the Member States and the subsequent ratification of the amending decision by the Member States.[21]

The only "relaxation" of the requirement for consensus in the EU Constitution is the obligation for the European Council to consult if, two years after the signature of a Treaty amending the Constitution, one or more Member States encounter difficulties in proceeding with its ratification and such Treaty has already been ratified by four-fifths of the Member States (EU Constitution, Art. IV-443(4)). In that event, consultations in the European Council may perhaps create the appropriate political climate for the Member States to proceed with ratification. However, it does not alter the fact that an amendment to the Constitution can not enter into force unless it is ratified by all the Member States.[22]

---

[20] For a proposal to this effect, see the Report to the European Commission of October 18, 1999, "The Institutional Implications of Enlargement", section 3 (for this report, see para. 3-022, *supra*).

[21] Both conditions also have to be fulfilled in the case where the European Council is to decide on changes in the decision-making procedure or the voting requirement in the Council (see Art. IV-444 of the EU Constitution), where the decision of the European Council, acting unanimously, comes into force only if no national parliament makes known its opposition, see para. 7-009, *infra*.

[22] Pursuant to a declaration in the final act of signature of the Treaty establishing a Constitution for Europe, such system will be applied as from the ratification of the Constitution: if, two years after the signature of the Treaty establishing a Constitution for Europe, four fifths of the Member States have ratified it and one or more Member States have encountered difficulties in proceeding with ratification, the "matter" will be referred to the European Council.

2. Special procedures for specific Treaty amendments

Without intergovernmental conference. Alongside the general amendment **7–008** procedure laid down in Art. 48 of the EU Treaty, some articles of the Treaties may be amended without convening an intergovernmental conference. In such a case, the Council determines the amendment by a unanimous vote pursuant to an ad hoc decision-making procedure. Nevertheless, under the Treaty, the entry into force of the amendment in question is dependent upon its "adoption [by the Member States] in accordance with their constitutional requirements".[23] There are five cases in which this may be done. First, the Council may, on a proposal from the Commission and after consulting the European Parliament, strengthen or add to the rights attaching to citizenship of the Union (EC Treaty, Art. 22, second para.). Second, the Council, after obtaining the assent of the European Parliament, which is to act by a majority of its component members, lays down the provisions for the election of the European Parliament by direct universal suffrage in accordance with a uniform procedure in all Member States (EC Treaty, Art. 190(4), second subpara.).[24] Third, the Council, acting unanimously on a proposal from the Commission and after consulting the European Parliament, may adopt provisions to confer jurisdiction on the Court of Justice in disputes relating to Community industrial property rights (EC Treaty, Art. 229a). Fourth, the Council, acting on a proposal from the Commission and after consulting the European Parliament, lays down provisions relating to the system of own resources of the Community (EC Treaty, Art. 269, second para.).[25] Fifth, the Council, acting on the initiative of the Commission or a Member State, may decide that action in areas of police and judicial

---

[23] For the legal force of such a Council decision, see para. 17–064, *infra*. Denmark has notified the constitutional procedure which has to be followed in this connection in two cases: decisions taken under Art. 22 of the EC Treaty and Art. 42 of the EU Treaty, "in the case of a transfer of sovereignty, as defined in the Danish Constitution, require either a majority of 5/6 of Members of the Folketing or both a majority of Members of the Folketing and a majority of voters in a referendum". For Art. 22 of the EC Treaty, see the Unilateral Declarations to be annexed to the Danish act of ratification of the EU Treaty of which the other Member States will take cognisance ([1992] O.J. C348/4); for Art. 42 of the EU Treaty, see the Declaration by Denmark on Article K.14 of the Treaty on European Union, annexed to the Treaty of Amsterdam ([1997] O.J. C340/143).

[24] See also Art. 108(3), second subpara. , of the EAEC Treaty. For the amendments made by the Treaty of Amsterdam to Art. 108 of the EAEC Treaty and Art. 190 of the EC Treaty, see para. 10–022, *infra*. On the basis of those Treaty articles, the Council adopted Decision 76/787/ECSC, EEC, Euratom of September 20, 1976 and the Act annexed to it concerning the election of the representatives of the Assembly by direct universal suffrage ([1976] O.J. L278/1 and 5, respectively). This decision was approved in all the Member States (for the UK, see the 1978 European Parliamentary Elections Act). In accordance with the procedure laid down in the Treaty, the Act was amended by Council Decision of February 1, 1993 ([1993] O.J. L33/15), which adjusted the number of seats of each Member State in the European Parliament (para. 10–023, *infra*) and by Council Decision of June 25, 2002 and September 23, 2002 laying down common principles for the election procedure in the Member States ([2002] O.J. L283/1) (para. 10–022, *infra*).

[25] See the "own-resources" decisions; para. 10–121, *infra*.

co-operation in criminal matters is to fall under Title IV of the EC Treaty, rather than be the subject of non-Community co-operation (EU Treaty, Art. 42).

The EU Treaty provides for a similar procedure for decisions taken by the European Council for the realisation of a common defence whereby the European Council recommends to the Member States the adoption of a decision in accordance with their respective constitutional requirements (Art. 17(1), first subpara.). However, the decisions in question are policy decisions and do not amend the Treaty itself.[26]

Under the EU Constitution, all or part of the provisions of Title III of Part III on the internal policies of the Union may be revised by the European Council, acting unanimously after consulting the European Parliament and the Commission, and the European Central Bank in the case of institutional changes in the monetary area. The European decision amending the provisions in question shall not come into force until it has been approved by the Member States in accordance with their respective constitutional requirements (Art. IV–445(2)). Article IV–445(3) of the Treaty establishing a Constitution provides that that decision may not increase the competences conferred on the Union by that Treaty.

7–009 **Without national ratification.** The Treaties also allow amendments to be fully implemented at Community level without ratification by the Member States. Under the "minor amendments procedure" laid down in Arts 76, 85 and 90 of the EAEC Treaty, the Council may amend the chapters "Special provisions", "Safeguards" and "Property ownership", respectively, in exceptional circumstances on the initiative of a Member State or the Commission. Such an amendment has to be adopted unanimously by the Council on a proposal from the Commission and after consulting the European Parliament.[27]

The EC Treaty permits the Council to extend the field of application of Art. 133 by a unanimous vote on a proposal from the Commission and after consulting the European Parliament (common commercial policy, see para. 20–003) and also the application of the co-decision procedure.[28] On the basis of a similar procedure, the Council can also amend technical provisions, for instance by making additions to the lists annexed to

---

[26] Moreover, Art. 17(5) of the EU Treaty refers to the procedure laid down in Art. 48 for the purposes of reviewing the provisions of that article.

[27] The second paragraph of Art. 76 of the EAEC Treaty further requires the Council to apply the provisions of Chapter VI in accordance with the same procedure in the event that it fails to confirm them within seven years of their entry into force. The fact that the Council did not proceed to confirm or amend the provisions in question does not mean that they must have lapsed: ECJ, Case 7/71 *Commission v France* [1971] E.C.R. 1003, paras 18–29.

[28] Art. 137(2), second subparagraph (social policy, see para. 5–236). See also the procedure laid down (without the right of proposal on the part of the Commission) in Art. 67(2), second indent, of the EC Treaty (policy on visas, asylum and migration; see para. 14–069).

the Treaty[29] or regarding the early introduction of the customs union.[30] The Council may also amend provisions of a number of the Protocols annexed to the Treaty, acting unanimously in accordance with specific procedures,[31] and confer new powers on the ECB.[32] The Council, acting unanimously, may alter the number of Members of the Commission (EC Treaty, Art. 213(1), second subpara.) and the numbers of Advocates General of the Court of Justice (EC Treaty, Art. 222, first para.) and create judicial panels with particular jurisdiction (EC Treaty, Art. 225a, first para.).[33]

The EU Constitution will enable the European Council to adopt a European decision authorising the Council to act by a qualified majority in an area or case where Part III of the Constitution provides for the Council to act unanimously (Art. IV–444(1)).[34] Likewise, the European Council may adopt a European decision allowing for the adoption of European laws or framework laws according to the ordinary legislative procedure where Part III of the Constitution provides for European laws and framework laws to be adopted by the Council according to a special legislative procedure (Art. IV–444(2)). Any initiative taken by the European Council in this connection shall be notified to the national parliaments. The European decision shall not be adopted if a national parliament makes known its opposition within six months of the date of notification of the initiative. In the absence of opposition, the European Council may adopt its decision, acting unanimously after obtaining the consent of the European Parliament, which shall be given by a majority of its component members (Art. IV–444(3)).

B.   LIMITS TO THE POSSIBILITY TO AMEND THE TREATIES

Procedural constraints. Under international law, a treaty may be amended **7–010** at any time by agreement between the parties.[35] Some commentators take

---

[29] See Art. 38(3) of the EEC Treaty (the present Art. 32(3) of the EC Treaty no longer permits "Annex I" to be amended). See also Art. 215(2) of the EAEC Treaty concerning modification of a research programme referred to in Annex V to that Treaty.

[30] See Art. 14(7) and Art. 33(8) of the EEC Treaty and Art. 95 of the EAEC Treaty.

[31] See the second subparagraph of Art. 104(14) (Protocol (No. 20) annexed to the EC Treaty on the excessive deficit procedure; n.1049 to para. 5–559, *supra*); Art. 107(5) (ESCB Statute, to be amended by a qualified majority on the recommendation of the ECB; para. 10–102, *infra*); Art. 245 of the EC Treaty (Statute of the Court of Justice; para. 10–072, *infra*); Art. 266, third para. of the EC Treaty (EIB Statute).

[32] EC Treaty, Art. 105(6) (para. 5–231, *supra*).

[33] For the Council decisions altering the number of Members of the Commission and of the Court of Justice, see the discussion of the composition of those institutions (paras 10–062 and 10–080, *infra*); see also Council Decision 74/584/EEC, Euratom, ECSC of November 26, 1974 on the adjustment of Art. 32 of the ECSC Treaty, Art. 165 of the EEC Treaty and Art. 137 of the Euratom Treaty, [1974] O.J. L318/22.

[34] This possibility does not apply to decisions with military implications or those in the area of defence: Art. IV–7a(1), second subparagraph.

[35] See Art. 39 of the 1969 Vienna Convention (para. 17–103, *infra*).

the view that it is implicit in the rules embodied in the Community legal order that the Member States as "masters of the Treaties" may amend the Community Treaties without having to comply with the procedure set out in Art. 48 of the EU Treaty.[36] It is a fact that the ECSC Treaty has been amended on two occasions outwith Art. 96 of the ECSC Treaty.[37] The amendments were made during the transitional period in which it was not possible to amend the Treaty pursuant to Art. 96.[38] Nevertheless, the Court of Justice has held that the Member States cannot amend provisions of Community law by means of Art. 308 of the EC Treaty,[39] a joint resolution[40] or an agreement jointly concluded with third countries[41] and that the Treaty rules regarding the manner in which the Community institutions arrive at their decisions are not at the disposal of the Member States.[42] The fact that the Member States are subject in their "constituent" function to the rules governing the amendment of the Treaties ensues from the specific character of the Community legal order. The Court of Justice has ruled that, "apart from any specific provisions, the Treaty can only be modified by means of the amendment procedure carried out in accordance with Article 236 [of the EEC Treaty]".[43]

---

[36] Deliège-Sequaris, "Révision des traités européens en dehors des procédures prévues" (1980) C.D.E. 539–552; Zuleeg, "Der Bestand der Europäischen Gemeinschaft", in Bieber, Bleckmann, Capotori *et al.* (eds), *Das Europa der zweiten Generation. Gedächtnisschrift für C. Sasse* (Nomos, Baden-Baden, 1981), Vol.2, at 58–59. But see the commentary by Louis (1980) C.D.E. 553–558; Everling, "Sind die Mitgliedstaaten der Europäischen Gemeinschaften noch Herren der Verträge?", *Völkerrecht als Rechtsordnung. Internationale Gerichtsbarkeit. Menschenrechte. Festschrift H. Mosler* (Springer, Berlin, 1983), 173, at 186–190; König and Pechstein, "Die EU-Vertragsänderung" (1998) EuR. 130–150 (who argue that the resultant treaty would be valid only under international law).

[37] Treaty of October 27, 1956 amending the ECSC Treaty (change in the distribution of votes in Art. 28 following the cession of the Saar to the Federal Republic of Germany) and the Convention of March 25, 1957 on certain institutions common to the European Communities (para. 1–011, *supra*).

[38] In the debate held in the Dutch Second Chamber prior to the Law approving the Treaty of October 27, 1956, the Second Chamber passed a motion deploring the fact that it was possible for the Community Treaties to be amended otherwise than by recourse to the procedures provided for in the Treaties themselves to that end (*Handelingen*, Tweede Kamer, 1957–58, Annex I, 1957–58, 4763 No. 9) and the government stated that it would in practice comply with the motion (*Handelingen*, Tweede Kamer, 1957–58, 1092). See Van der Goes van Naters, "La révision des traités supranationaux" in *N.T.I.R.* (*Varia Ius Gentium. Liber Amicorum J.P.A. François*) (Sijthoff, Leyden, 1959), at 120–131.

[39] ECJ, Opinion 2/94 *Accession by the Communities to the Convention for the Protection of Human Rights and Fundamental Freedoms* [1996] E.C.R. I–1759, para. 30.

[40] ECJ, Case 59/75 *Manghera* [1976] E.C.R. 91, paras 19–21; ECJ, Case 43/75 *Defrenne* [1976] E.C.R. 455, paras 57–58.

[41] ECJ, Case 22/70 *Commission v Council* [1971] E.C.R. 263, paras 17 and 22.

[42] ECJ, Case 68/86 *UK v Council* [1988] E.C.R. 855, para. 38.

[43] ECJ, Case 43/75 *Defrenne* [1976] E.C.R. 455, para. 58. In Opinion 1/92, the Court of Justice observed that "[t]he powers conferred on the Court by the Treaty may be modified pursuant only to the procedure provided for by Article 236 of the Treaty", ECJ, Opinion 1/92 *Draft Agreement between the Community, on the one hand, and the countries of the European Free Trade Association, on the other, relating to the creation of the European Economic Area* [1992] E.C.R. I–2821, para. 32.

Substantive constraints. A further question is whether there are also **7–011** substantive, in addition to procedural, limits imposed by Community law on amendments to the Treaties. Where a Treaty article provides for a specific amendment procedure, the amendment remains confined to the content of that article. In addition, it appears from the Treaty articles which refer to the "irrevocable" fixing of exchange rates and of the value of the Euro for the third stage of EMU[44] that any later revision of the Treaty reversing that situation is precluded.

Some commentators take the view that Community law debars the Member States from introducing amendments detracting from the fundamental values of respect for human rights, democracy and the rule of law or amendments affecting the identity and the very existence of the Community.[45] Although the Court of Justice has not ruled on any principles or specific Treaty articles which are purportedly not open to amendment, it nevertheless stresses the importance of the Court's function under Art. 220 of the EC Treaty of guaranteeing the autonomy of the Community legal order, alongside other "foundations of the Community".[46]

Judicial review. Since an amending Treaty concluded between the Member **7–012** States is not an act of the institutions and has the same legal force as the Treaty sought to be amended, the Court of the Justice is not entitled to review the legality or validity of an amending Treaty.[47] However, the Commission is entitled to bring a Member State which has failed to fulfil its obligations under the Treaty before the Court of Justice. That Court also reviews the conduct of all the governments of the Member States for compliance with their Treaty obligations.[48] The commentators in question infer from this that the Court of Justice is entitled to act against the

---

[44] See Art. 4(2), Art. 118, second paragraph, and Art. 123(4) of the EC Treaty and Art. 52 of the Protocol (No. 18) annexed to the EC Treaty on the Statute of the ESCB and of the ECB.

[45] Bieber, "Les limites matérielles et formelles à la révision des traités établissant la Communauté européenne" (1993) R.M.C.U.E. 343–350; Da Cruz Vilaça and Piçarra, "Y a-t-il des limites matérielles à la révision des traités instituant les Communautés européennes?" (1993) C.D.E. 3–37; Curti Gialdino, "Some Reflections on the *Acquis Communautaire*" (1995) C.M.L.R. 1089, at 1109–1114. See also Heintzen, "Hierarchisierungsprozesse innerhalb des Primärrechts der Europäischen Gemeinschaft" (1994) EuR. 35–49 (who regards only the principles of democracy and the rule of law at Community level as inviolable on the ground that the Member States themselves are constituted on the basis thereof).

[46] ECJ, Opinion 1/91 *Draft Agreement between the Community, on the one hand, and the countries of the European Free Trade Association, on the other, relating to the creation of the European Economic Area* [1991] E.C.R. I–6079, paras 35 and 69–72; see also ECJ, Opinion 1/00 *Proposed agreement between the European Community and non-Member States on the establishment of a European Common Aviation Area* [2002] E.C.R. I–3493, para. 5.

[47] See CFI (order of July 14, 1994), Case T–584/93 *Roujansky v Council* [1994] E.C.R. II–585, para. 15 (para. 17–058, *infra*).

[48] See ECJ, Case 230/81 *Luxembourg v European Parliament* [1983] E.C.R. 255, paras 36–37.

Member States as a whole in the event that they should disregard the procedural or substantive limits set with regard to the revision of the Treaties. They also argue that the Court would construe an amending Treaty which transgresses the substantive limits in such a way as to keep that Treaty within the bounds of Community law.[49]

---

[49] Bieber (n.45, *supra*), at 348–349; see also Da Cruz Vilaça and Piçarra (n.45, *supra*), at 17–18. See further König and Pechstein, "Die EU-Vertragsänderung" (1998) EuR. 130, at 138–142 (who argue that such an amendment of the Treaties would be inapplicable).

CHAPTER 8

TERRITORIAL SCOPE OF THE TREATIES

I. TERRITORIAL APPLICATION

Jurisdiction of Member States. Each Community Treaty determines its **8–001** territorial scope in so far as it declares that it is applicable to all the Member States (EC Treaty, Art. 299; EAEC Treaty, Art. 198; see also EU Constitution, Art. IV–440).[1] The EU Treaty does not define its territorial scope, but simply employs the expression "Member States". The upshot is that the territorial field of application of the Treaties is constituted by the EU Member States. Under international law, the Treaties therefore apply to all areas which are under the sovereignty or within the jurisdiction of the Member States.

The Treaties are therefore applicable in principle to the Member States' overseas territories (see, however, also para. 8–002).[2] The application of the Treaties extends to the airspace and maritime waters which come under the sovereignty or within the jurisdiction of the Member States: territorial waters and, in so far as the Member State concerned lays claim to it, the fishing zone or exclusive economic zone, together with the continental shelf.[3] The Community itself accepted the international rules adopted in

---

[1] For a discussion of the various meanings of territoriality, see Groux, " 'Territorialité' et droit communautaire" (1987) R.T.D.E. 5–33.

[2] See expressly the first paragraph of Art. 198 of the EAEC Treaty, which provides that that Treaty shall apply to the European territories of the Member States and to non-European territories under their jurisdiction.

[3] Most Member States limit their territorial waters to 12 nautical miles from the baseline, but some apply a limit of three (Denmark, Germany, Ireland) or six nautical miles (Greece). In accordance with the Council Resolution of November 3, 1976 ([1981] O.J. C105/1), the Member States concerned have set their fishing zone or an exclusive economic zone in the North Sea and the North Atlantic Ocean at 200 nautical miles. See Scovazzi, "La liberté de navigation dans la zone économique exclusive confrontée à l'attitude des Etats membres de la CEE en matière de prévention de la pollution", in Lebullenger and Le Morvan (eds), *La Communauté européenne et la mer* (Economica, Paris, 1990), at 307–315. Where a State has exclusive rights over the continental shelf in respect of the exploration and the exploitation of the natural resources of the sea-bed and subsoil of the shelf, it also has exclusive fishing rights in an exclusive economic zone (*cf.* Arts 77–81 and 55–73 of the Convention on the Law of the Sea, see n.4, *infra*). For the contested general application of Community law to the continental shelf, see Michael, "L'application du droit communautaire au plateau continental des Etats membres et ses conséquences" (1983) R.M.C. 82–90; Van der Mensbrugghe, "La CEE et le plateau continental des Etats membres", *Mélanges F. Dehousse* (Nathan/Labor, Paris/Brussels, 1979), Vol.II, at 311–317. For the limitations imposed by customary international law on Community competence, see ECJ, Case C–286/90 *Poulsen*

1982 in the Convention on the Law of the Sea.[4] As long as the territory of Cyprus is partitioned, the *acquis communatunaire* applies, according to a protocol annexed to the 2003 Act of Accession only to those (southern) areas in which the Government of the Republic of Cyprus exercises effective control.[5]

The Treaties are also stated to be applicable to European territories for whose external relations a Member State is responsible,[6] which boils down in practice to Gibraltar.[7] The 1972 Act of Accession provided that major areas of Community law should not apply to Gibraltar,[8] in particular free

---

and Diva Navigation [1992] E.C.R. I–6019, paras 21–34; for its competence in respect of the conservation of the fishery resources of the high seas, see *ibid.*, paras 9–11, and ECJ, Case C–405/92 *Mondiet* [1993] E.C.R. I–6133, paras 12–15; ECJ, Case C–25/94 *Commission v Council* [1996] E.C.R. I–1469, para. 44.

[4] United Nations Convention on the Law of the Sea, signed at Montego Bay on December 10, 1982, which was ratified by the Community (together with the Agreement of July 28, 1994 relating to the implementation of Part XI thereof) by Council Decision 98/392/EC of March 23, 1998, [1998] O.J. L179/1. See Garzón Clariana, "L'Union européenne et la Convention de 1982 sur le droit de la mer" (1995) B.T.I.R. 36–45.

[5] Art. 1 of Protocol No. 10 on Cyprus annexed to the 2003 Act of Accession suspends the application of the *acquis* in those areas of the Republic of Cyprus in which the Government of the Republic of Cyprus does not exercise effective control. Since Cyprus became independent in 1960, there have been tensions between the Greek and Turkish Cypriot communities, which led to Turkish military intervention in 1974. The two communities are partitioned *de facto* by a UN buffer zone and there has been no general free movement of goods, persons or services between them. Since the Community and the Member States goods, persons or services between them. Since the Community and the Member States recognise only the "Greek" Republic of Cyprus (and not the Turkish Republic of Northern Cyprus), under the EC-Cyprus Association Agreement, Member States were to accept only movement and phytosanitary certificates issued by the competent authorities of the Republic of Cyprus in respect of the import of products from the part of Cyprus located to the north of the buffer zone: ECJ, Case C–432/92 *Anastasiou* [1994] E.C.R. I–3087. According to the European Council held at Luxembourg on December 12 and 13, 1997, the accession negotiations would contribute positively to the search for a political solution to the Cyprus problem: (1997) 12 EU Bull. Point I.28. Nevertheless, no solution has yet been found. On the eve of accession, the plan for reunification proposed by the United Nations' Secretary General was rejected in a referendum (of the Greek Community, 75.83 per cent voted against; of the Turkish Community 64.9 per cent voted in favour). See Yakemtchouk, "Chypre : la réunification avortée" (2004) R.M.C.U.E. 239–296; Klebes-Pelissier, "L'adhésion de la République de Chypre à l'Union européenne" (2003) R.T.D.E. 441–469: Berramdane, "Chypre entre adhésion à l'Union européenne et réunification" (2003) R.D.U.E. 87–108. See para. 8–003 for the procedure for bringing this exceptional regime to an end.

[6] EC Treaty, Art. 229(4); EAEC Treaty, Art. 198, second para. For the EU Treaty, see n.7, *infra*.

[7] The Treaties expressly exclude other territories, which could qualify (*e.g.* the Channel Islands and the Isle of Man; para. 8–002, *infra*). Nor are they considered to apply to Andorra (for the EC-Andorra Agreement, see para. 20–009, *infra*). Since the EU Treaty is not stated to be applicable to territories for the foreign relations of which a Member State is responsible, acts adopted pursuant to the EU Treaty are, where appropriate, expressly declared to be applicable to Gibraltar; see, *e.g.* Council Decision 2003/642/JHA of July 22, 2003 concerning the application to Gibraltar of the Convention on the fight against corruption involving officials of the European Communities or officials of Member States of the European Union ([2003] O.J. L226/27).

[8] See Art. 28 (exclusion of measures relating to certain agricultural products and to the harmonisation of turnover tax) and Annex I(I) (customs legislation) of the 1972 Act of Accession.

movement of goods and harmonisation measures adopted for that purpose by the Community under Arts 94 and 95 of the EC Treaty.[9]

Within that framework, the Treaties apply to legal relationships which can be located "within the territory of the Community", by reason of the place where they are entered into or of the place where they take effect[10] or by reason of a sufficiently close link with the law of a Member State and thus the relevant rules of Community law.[11]

Territories with specific status. The Treaties provide for certain overseas **8–002** territories to have a special status. As far as the French Overseas Departments (Guadeloupe, Guyana, Martinique and Réunion), the Azores, Madeira and the Canary Islands are concerned, the provisions of the Treaties apply in principle, although the Council may adopt specific measures making the application of the EC Treaty subject to certain conditions in view of the structural economic and social situation of those areas (EC Treaty, Art. 299(2)).[12] Part Four of the Treaty (Arts 182–188)

---

[9] ECJ (judgment of September 23, 2003), Case C–30/01 *Commission v UK*, not yet reported, paras 47–59 (this follows from Gibraltar's exclusion from the customs territory of the Community). According to Annex II to the Act of September 20, 1976 on the direct election of the European Parliament (see para. 10–022), that act applies only to the UK. However, the Court of Human Rights considered that the exclusion of Gibraltar was contrary to Art. 3 of Protocol No. 1 to the ECHR; see para. 17–081, *infra*, and further De Schutter and Lhoest, "La Cour européenne des droits de l'homme juge du droit communautaire: Gibraltar, l'Union européenne et la Convention européenne des droits de l'homme" (2000) C.D.E. 141, at 146–164.

[10] See ECJ, Case 36/74 *Walrave* [1974] E.C.R. 1405, para. 28; ECJ, Case 237/83 *Prodest* [1984] E.C.R. 3153, paras 6–7 (para. 5–126, *supra*); ECJ, Joined Cases 89, 104, 114, 116–117 and 125–129/85 *Åhlström v Commission* [1988] E.C.R. 5193, paras 16–17 (para. 5–196, *supra*); CFI, T–102/96 *Gencor v Commission* [1999] E.C.R. II–753, paras 89–108 (para. 5–200, *supra*).

[11] ECJ, Case C–214/94 *Boukhalfa* [1996] E.C.R. I–2253, para. 15 (para. 5–126, *supra*). For a definition of the legal subjects of the Community, see also Vanhamme, *Volkenrechtelijke beginselen in het Europees recht*, (Europa Law, Groningen, 2001), 131–148.

[12] See Sermet, "La notion juridique de l'ultrapériphéricité communautaire", *Europe—Editions du Juris-Classeur*, June 2002, at 3–6; Omarjee, "Le traité d'Amsterdam et l'avenir de la politique de différenciation en faveur des départements français d'outre-mer" (1998) R.T.D.E. 515–533; Puissochet, "Aux confins de la Communauté européenne: les régions ultrapériphériques" in Rodriguez-Iglesias, Due, Schintgen and Elsen (eds), *Mélanges en hommage à Fernand Schockweiler* (Nomos, Baden-Baden, 1999), 491–509; Brial, "La place des régions ultrapériphériques au sein de l'Union européenne" (1998) C.D.E. 639–659. Under the former Art. 227(2) of the EC Treaty, that Treaty was to be fully applicable to the French *départements d'outre mer* (DOMs) only after two years; see, *inter alia*, ECJ, Case 148/77 *Hansen* [1978] E.C.R. 1787, paras 7–10. The third subpara. of the former Art. 227(2) likewise authorised the Council to determine specific conditions of application without derogating from the Treaty provisions mentioned in the first subparagraph of that provision. Consequently, the Council was not empowered to authorise France to collect charges in a DOM—contrary to "free movement of goods" mentioned in the first subparagraph—on products coming from other French departments (ECJ, Joined Cases C–363/93 and C–407/93 to C–411/93 *Lancry* [1994] E.C.R. I–3957, paras 36–38), but this did not prevent the Council from authorising exemptions from those charges subject to strict conditions (ECJ, Case C–212/96 *Chevassus-Marche* [1998] E.C.R. I–743, paras 1–54). For other decisions, see the Commission's answer of February 4, 1985 to question 1839/84

353

introduced special association arrangements for the overseas countries and territories listed in Annex II to the EC Treaty (Art. 299(3); see para. 20–016).[13] Most of the countries and territories originally concerned have since become parties, as independent States, to the ACP-EC Conventions (see para. 20–021). In accordance with a Protocol to the EEC Treaty, the Netherlands declared that that Treaty is not applicable to Surinam and the Netherlands Antilles.[14] An amendment to the Treaties caused them not to apply to Greenland as from February 1, 1985.[15] The Treaties exclude the Faroe Islands[16] from their scope and provide for special arrangements for the UK Sovereign Base Areas in Cyprus (Akrotiri and Dhekelia),[17] the Åland Islands (located between Sweden and Finland),[18] and the Channel Islands and the Isle of Man, which are Crown dependencies, but not part of the United Kingdom.[19]

(Poniatowski), [1985] O.J. C263/1. The derogation provided for in Art. 25 of the 1985 Act of Accession and Protocol No. 2 thereto applied to the Canary Islands, just as it applied to Ceuta and Melilla. See ECJ, Case C–45/94 *Ayuntamiento de Ceuta* [1995] E.C.R. I–4385, paras 14–21 and para. 42.

[13] For the list of those areas (including the French *territoires d'outre mer* or TOMs), see para. 20–016, *infra*. For the purposes of the application of certain provisions of Community legislation, work performed in such an area may be equated with work carried out in the territory of the Member State concerned: ECJ, Case C–248/96 *Grahame and Hollanders* [1997] E.C.R. I–6407, para. 36 (see para. 5–126, *infra*). The second subparagraph of Art. 299(3) excludes countries and territories having special relations with the UK which are not listed in Annex II; this referred only to Hong Kong.

[14] Since then, Surinam, which became independent on June 16, 1976, has acceded to the ACP-EC Convention. As far as the Netherlands Antilles are concerned, the association arrangements provided for in Part Four of the EC Treaty apply by virtue of the Convention of November 13, 1962 amending Part Four of the EEC Treaty, O.J. 2414/64. The association arrangements also apply to Aruba.

[15] Treaty of March 13, 1984 amending, with regard to Greenland, the Treaties establishing the European Communities, [1985] O.J. L29/1. In a referendum held on February 23, 1982, the people of Greenland expressed the desire to leave the Community, whereupon the Danish Government applied to have the Treaty amended. However, Greenland remains part of Denmark and therefore falls by virtue of Arts 2, 3 and 4 of the Treaty under the association arrangements provided for in Part Four of the EC Treaty.

[16] EC Treaty, Art. 299(6)(a), and EAEC Treaty, Art. 198, fourth paragraph, indent (a); the EU Treaty removed from those articles Denmark's option, which was open to it until the end of 1975 but was never exercised, to declare the Treaties applicable to the Faroe Islands.

[17] Art. 299(6)(b) of the EC Treaty (as amended by Protocol No. 3 to the 2003 Act of Accession, [2003] O.J. L236/940) provides that the Treaty is to apply to the "United Kingdom Sovereign Base Areas of Akrotiri and Dhekelia in Cyprus" only to the extent necessary to ensure the implementation of the exceptional arrangements set out in that protocol. After Cyprus became independent in 1960, the UK has continued to maintain two military bases in southern Cyprus; see the Commission's Opinion on Cyprus's application to accede (1993) EC Bull. Suppl.5, 12.

[18] EC Treaty, Art. 299(5), and EAEC Treaty, Art. 198, third paragraph, provide that the Treaties are applicable to the Åland Islands in accordance with the provisions of Protocol No. 2 to the 1994 Act of Accession (see [1995] O.J. L75/18).

[19] EC Treaty, Art. 299(6)(c), and EAEC Treaty, Art. 198, fourth paragraph, indent (c). The Treaties apply to the Channel Islands and the Isle of Man only to the extent necessary to ensure the implementation of the special arrangements for those islands set out in Protocol No. 3 to the 1972 Act of Accession. See ECJ, Case C–171/96 *Pereira Roque* [1998] E.C.R. I–4605, paras 34–58.

Change in territorial jurisdiction. Apart from those specific arrangements **8–003** for particular areas, the application of the Treaties coincides with the territorial jurisdiction of the Member States under international law. Community law is automatically applicable to areas acquired by a Member State as a result of a change in its frontiers and it deals with territories ceded by a Member State in the same way as it would with a third country. Such changes do not require any amendment of the Treaties,[20] but consultation as between the Member States is advisable.[21] Accordingly, the European Council decided that it was unnecessary to amend the Treaties when the *Länder* of the former German Democratic Republic acceded to the Federal Republic of Germany on October 3, 1990 and therefore to the Communities.[22] The Council adopted a number of adjusting and transitional measures in the light of German reunification.[23] A similar solution is foreseen for Cyprus in the event that a settlement is found for bringing the partition of the island to an end. By means of a protocol annexed to the 2003 Act of Accession, the Council, acting unanimously, is then to decide on the adaptations to the terms concerning the accession of Cyprus with regard to the Turkish Cypriot Community.[24] The territorial

---

[20] The Community accepted the independence of Algeria in 1962 without amending Art. 227(2) of the EEC Treaty, which treated that country as a French overseas department. The EU Treaty deleted the reference to Algeria. The transfer of the Saar to the Federal Republic of Germany necessitated an amendment to the Treaties, since Germany sought a change in the allocation of votes (n.37 to para. 7–010, *supra*).

[21] For the general obligation to consult other Member States, see Ehlermann, "Mitgliedschaft in der Europäischen Gemeinschaft—Rechtsproblem der Erweiterung, der Mitgliedschaft und der Verkleinerung" (1984) EuR. 113, at 118–119.

[22] See the conclusions of the Dublin European Council of April 28, 1990 (1990) 4 EC Bull. point I.5. Under the Protocol annexed to the EEC Treaty on German internal trade and connected problems, the FRG was entitled to regard trade with the GDR as part of German internal trade. Nevertheless, the GDR did not form part of the Community and goods from the GDR were not regarded as originating in the FRG: ECJ, Case 14/74 *Norddeutsches Vieh- und Fleischkontor* [1974] E.C.R. 899, para. 6.

[23] See the package of legislation adopted by the Council on October 4, 1990, [1990] O.J. L/353; Westlake, "The Community Express Service: The Rapid Passage of Emergency Legislation on German Unification" (1991) C.M.L.R. 599–614. See also Glaesner, "Les problèmes de droit communautaire soulevés par l'unification allemande" (1990) R.M.C. 647–654; Jacqué, "L'unification de l'Allemagne et la Communauté européenne" (1990) R.G.D.I.P. 997–1018; Drobnig, "Die Eingliederung der ehemaligen DDR in die Europäischen Gemeinschaften" (1991) Z.f.R.V. 321–332; Grabitz, "L'unité allemande et l'intégration européenne" (1991) C.D.E. 423–441.

[24] Protocol No. 10 on Cyprus annexed to the 2003 Act of Accession, Art. 4. See also the literature cited in n. 5, *supra*. After the rejection of the proposed plan for reunification, on the eve of accession, the Council laid down measures to facilitate trade and other links between the northern and southern areas of the island, whilst ensuring that appropriate standards of protection are maintained as to the security of the European Union with regard to illegal immigration, threats to public order and public health. See Council Regulation 866/2004 2004 on a regime under Art. 2 of Protocol No. 10 of the Act of Accession, [2004] O.J. L161/128 (republished with *corrigendum*: [2004] O.J. L206/51). For the extraordinary elections of the representatives in the European Parliament to be held in the whole of Cyprus in the event of a settlement of the Cyprus problem, see Council Decision 2004/511/EC of June 10, 2004 concerning the representation of the people of Cyprus in the European Parliament in the case of a settlement of the Cyprus problem, [2004] O.J. L211/22.

field of application of the Treaties also adjusts itself where a Member State changes the status of a territory under its sovereignty.[25] Nevertheless, in some of these cases the Member States have revised the Treaties.[26] This not only ensures acceptance on the part of the Member States, but also provides a democratic foundation for the acceptance into the Union, or the loss, of what is often a substantial population. Where a new State wishes to join the Union, this can occur only in accordance with the accession procedure laid down in Art. 49 of the EU Treaty (see para. 8–006).

8–004 **Acts with specific territorial scope.** Acts of the Community institutions in principle cover the same geographical field of application as the Treaty on which they are based. Member States' extension of their exclusive fishing zones to 200 miles off their North Sea and North Atlantic coasts therefore resulted in a commensurate extension of the field of application of Community measures relating to a structural policy for the fishing industry.[27] Nevertheless, secondary Community legislation often defines its own field of application. For instance, customs law does not apply to certain areas coming under the jurisdiction of a Member State.[28] The fact that particular areas have an exceptional status under the Treaties does not mean that the Court of Justice has no jurisdiction to give preliminary rulings on questions referred by courts in those areas, even though Community law is only partially in force there.[29] Conversely, secondary Community law may also be applicable in areas which do not belong to the Member States. For instance, Monaco comes within the customs territory of the Community,[30] other Community acts are declared by agreement to

---

[25] In 1976 France granted Saint-Pierre-et-Miquelon, which were associated with the Community as *territoires d'outre mer* (TOMs), the status of *départements d'outre mer* (DOMs) by Law No. 76–664 of July 19, 1976. As a result, the islands became part of the Community by virtue of Art. 227(2) of the EEC Treaty. Similarly, they left the Community in 1985 when, by Law No. 85–595 of June 11, 1985, the islands resumed the status of TOMs. Under the EU Constitution the European Council is to decide, acting unanimously on the initiative of the Member State concerned, on the amendment of the status, with regard to the Union, of the French, Netherlands or Danish countries or territories in question (Art. IV–440(7)).

[26] See the Convention on the Netherlands Antilles (n.14, *supra*), by which the Member States sought to introduce in a Protocol to the EEC Treaty special arrangements for imports of petroleum products refined in the Netherlands Antilles (J.O. 2416/64) and the Treaty on the withdrawal of Greenland (n.15, *supra*).

[27] ECJ, Case 61/77 *Commission v Ireland* [1978] E.C.R. 417, paras 45–50. See also ECJ, Joined Cases 3, 4 and 6/76 *Kramer* [1976] E.C.R. 1279, para. 30/33.

[28] For the customs territory of the Community, see Art. 3 of Regulation 2913/92 establishing the Community Customs Code, [1992] O.J. L302/1 (n.32 to para. 5–095, *supra*).

[29] ECJ, Joined Cases C–100/89 and C–101/89 *Kaefer and Procacci* [1990] E.C.R. I–4647, paras 8–10 (Polynesia, a *territoire d'outre mer*); ECJ, Case C–355/89 *Barr and Montrose Holdings* [1991] E.C.R. I–3479, paras 6–10 (Isle of Man).

[30] Under Art. 3(2) of Regulation No. 2913/92 (see n.390 to para. 5–095), the Principality of Monaco, as its territory is defined in a bilateral convention signed with France, forms part of the customs territory. Before a customs agreement was signed with the EC (para. 20–009, *infra*), San Marino also belonged to the customs territory of the Community. The Vatican City and Andorra do not belong to the customs territory (but see the EC-Andorra Agreement, para. 19–013, *infra*).

be applicable to Monaco[31] and Community legislation on euro banknotes and coins applies in Monaco, San Marino, the Vatican City and some other areas which have obtained by agreement the right to use the Euro as their currency unit.[32] As a result of agreements with non-member countries, a substantial part of Community law also applies in third countries, in particular the States belonging to the European Economic Area (see paras 23–004 *et seq.*).

Extraterritorial effects. The application of Community law sometimes **8–005** depends on factors situated outside the territorial jurisdiction of the Member States. That is generally the case with independent or conventional measures of Community commercial policy. Community measures may impose obligations—even on non-Community undertakings—having to be complied with outside the territory of the Community.[33] Community competition policy may be applied to undertakings which are established outside the Community and not incorporated under the laws of one of the Member States but which act in the Community (see paras 5–196 and 5–200).

II. ACCESSION OF MEMBER STATES

Accession. Article 49 of the EU Treaty governs the accession of States to **8–006** the European Union. It repeals the respective provisions of Art. 98 of the ECSC Treaty, Art. 237 of the EEC Treaty and Art. 205 of the EAEC Treaty.[34] As a result, the accessions to the Communities in 1973 (Denmark, Ireland and the United Kingdom), 1981 (Greece) and 1985 (Portugal and Spain) were based on the specific rules contained in each of the Community Treaties, whereas the accessions to the European Union in 1995 (Austria, Finland and Sweden) and in 2004 (Cyprus, Estonia, the Czech Republic, Hungary, Latvia, Lithuania, Malta, Poland, Slovenia and Slovakia) were based on Art. 49 of the EU Treaty. By becoming a member of the Union, a State accedes to all the Treaties on which the Union is based. Likewise,

---

[31] See the Agreement on the application of certain Community acts on the territory of the Principality of Monaco, approved by Council Decision 2003/885/EC of November 17, 2003 ([2003] O.J. L332/41).

[32] See para. 5–231. On the monetary level, special relations existed between France and Monaco and between Italy and San Marino and the Vatican City. On behalf of the Community, France and Italy conducted the respective negotiations as a result of which those three States obtained the right to use the Euro as their currency unit.

[33] See, for example, ECJ, Case C–177/95 *Ebony Maritime and Loten Navigation* [1997] E.C.R. I–1135, paras 15–27 (sanction imposed in respect of conduct of vessels on the high seas —conduct giving good reason to believe that a breach of sanctions imposed on Yugoslavia might result—irrespective of whether the vessels were flying the flag of a Member State).

[34] Repealed by EU Treaty, Arts 9(21), 8(83) and 10(28), respectively.

before the EU Treaty, a would-be Member State always had to accede to all three Communities because of their institutional and political unity. The EU Constitution takes over the procedure for accession in Art. I–58.

A. CONDITIONS FOR ACCESSION TO THE EUROPEAN UNION

8–007 Essential conditions. Article 49 of the EU Treaty provides that "[a]ny European State which respects the principles set out in Article 6(1)" may apply to become a member of the Union. In the words of the EU Constitution, the Union is to be open "to all European States which respect its values and are committed to promoting them together".[35]

As far as what is meant by "European" is concerned, it should be mentioned that in 1987 the Council did not accede to Morocco's request to join the Communities in all probability because Morocco was not regarded as a European State.[36] The Commission takes the view that not only geographical, but also historical, factors contribute to the "European identity" and that the essence of that notion is likely to be regarded differently by each succeeding generation.[37]

The requirement that a candidate State should "respect the principles set out in Article 6(1)" was introduced by the Treaty of Amsterdam and refers to the principles of liberty, democracy, respect for human rights and fundamental freedoms, and the rule of law. Even before that provision was added to the Treaty, it was deemed to be a fundamental requirement for accession to the Communities.[38] In a Joint Declaration of April 5, 1977, the European Parliament, the Council and the Commission stressed "the prime importance they attach to the protection of fundamental rights, as derived in particular from the constitutions of the Member States and the European Convention for the Protection of Human Rights and Fundamental Freedoms".[39] The European Council, meeting in Copenhagen on April 7 and 8, 1978, associated itself with that declaration and affirmed

---

[35] EU Constitution, Arts I–1(2) and I–58(1).

[36] See the wording of the application (1987) 7/8 EC Bull. point 2.2.35, and the Council's veiled answer (1987) 9 EC Bull. point 2.2.19. See also Dorau, "Die Öffnung der Europäischen Union für europäische Staaten. 'Europäisch' als Bedingung für einen EU-Beitritt nach Art. 49 EUV" (1999) EuR. 736–753.

[37] Commission of the European Communities, *Europe and the challenge of enlargement* (1992) EC Bull., Suppl.3, 11.

[38] In the preamble to the EEC Treaty, the Contracting Parties called upon "the other peoples of Europe who share their ideal" to join in their efforts towards integration. Admittedly, the Court of Justice held in 1978 that it had no jurisdiction to answer questions referred for a preliminary ruling on the form and content of the conditions for accession to the Community on the ground that "the legal conditions for such accession remain to be defined in the context of [the procedure laid down by Art. 237 of the EEC Treaty] without its being possible to determine the content judicially in advance" (ECJ, Case 93/78 *Mattheus* [1978] E.C.R. 2203, para. 8).

[39] Joint Declaration by the European Parliament, the Council and the Commission, [1977] O.J. C103/1 (para. 17–074, *infra*).

that "respect for and maintenance of representative democracy and human rights in each Member State are essential elements of membership of the European Communities".[40] The European Council took over that requirement at Copenhagen on June 21 and 22, 1993 and coupled it with other criteria which candidate countries had to fulfil. First, membership of the Union requires that the candidate country has achieved stability of institutions guaranteeing democracy, the rule of law, human rights, and respect for and protection of minorities. Secondly, there must be the existence of a functioning market economy as well as the capacity to cope with competitive pressures and market forces within the Union. Thirdly, the candidate country must have the ability to take on the obligations of membership, including adherence to the aims of political, economic and monetary union.[41]

Other requirements. Membership implies acceptance of the *acquis* **8–008** *communautaire*, which the Commission defines as "the rights and obligations, actual and potential, of the Community system and its institutional framework".[42] The would-be Member State has to accept the provisions of the Treaties, the decisions taken by the institutions pursuant to the Treaties (including agreements concluded by the Communities or the Union) and the case law of the Court of Justice. It has to accede to the declarations, resolutions, decisions and agreements made by the Member States, meeting within the Council, in the European Council, in the Council or elsewhere which relate to the Communities or the Union. At the same time, it must undertake to accede to agreements concluded by the Member States which affect the functioning of the Union or are closely connected with action by the Union, the agreements referred to in Art. 293 of the EC Treaty and other agreements which cannot be divorced from areas connected with the objectives of the Community (and the Protocols relating to their interpretation by the Court of Justice), international agreements concluded by the Member States jointly with one of the Communities and agreements concluded between the Member States relating to such

---

[40] (1978) 3 EC Bull. 5–6.
[41] European Council meeting at Copenhagen on June 21 and 22, 1993 ((1993) 6 EC Bull. Point I.13); *Europe and the challenge of enlargement*, (n.37, *supra*), 12; Katz, "Les critères de Copenhague" (2000) R.M.C.U.E. 483–486. See also Hoffmeister, "Changing requirements for membership" in A. Ott and K. Inglis (eds.), *Handbook on European Enlargement—A Commentary on the Enlargement Process*, (T.M.C. Asser Press, The Hague, 2002), at 90–102; Williams, "Enlargement of the Union and human rights conditionality: a policy of distinction?" (2000) E.L.Rev. 601–617; Šarčević, "EU-Erweiterung nach Art. 49 EUV: Ermessensentscheidungen und Beitrittsrecht" (2002) EuR. 461–482; Nettesheim, "EU-Beitritt und Unrechtsaufarbeitung" (2003) EuR. 36–64.
[42] *Europe and the challenge of enlargement*, (n.37, *supra*), 12. For the origin and meaning of the term *acquis communautaire* in this context, see Goebel, "The European Union Grows: The Constitutional Impact of the Accession of Austria, Finland and Sweden" (1995) Fordham I.L.J. 1092, at 1140–1157.

agreements or implementing them.[43] Candidate States also accede to the provisions of the Schengen *acquis* as integrated into Community law or EU law and the acts building upon it or otherwise related to it.[44] Difficulties of adjustment are resolved by temporary derogations and transitional measures.

The establishment of the internal market means that transitional measures which might have the effect of maintaining the frontiers between established and new Member States must be kept to the strict minimum. Countries applying to accede to the Union are to take the necessary measures to satisfy the conditions of accession in good time. After the Act of Accession has been signed, they must refrain from adopting measures interfering with the functioning of the Community.[45]

B. PROCEDURE FOR ACCEDING TO THE EUROPEAN UNION

8–009 **Application and negotiations.** The accession procedure begins with an application to become a member of the Union. The request is to be addressed to the Council. Under Art. 49 of the EU Treaty, the Council is to take its decision by a unanimous vote after consulting the Commission and receiving the assent of the European Parliament acting by an absolute majority of its component Members.[46] The Member States and the applicant Member State agree intergovernmentally on the terms of accession and the resulting application of the Treaties.[47]

In practice the Commission delivers an initial Opinion and the Council takes an initial decision to open the procedure. The actual Opinion of the Commission and the decisions of the European Parliament and the Council are not given until after the negotiations with the applicant Member State have been concluded. In accordance with the working procedure adopted by the Council on June 8 and 9, 1970, the applicant State negotiates in fact

---

[43] See Arts 2–4 of the 1972, 1979 and 1985 Acts of Accession, Arts 2–5 of the 1994 Act of Accession and Arts 2–6 of the 2003 Act of Accession. For further discussion of the legal force of the various instruments which new Member States have to accept, see para. 17–142 and 18–009—18–021, *infra*.

[44] 2003 Act of Accession, Art. 3(1) (see para. 5–164).

[45] See ECJ, Case C–27/96 *Danisco Sugar* [1997] E.C.R. I–6653, paras 24–31 (see also para. 17–103, *infra*).

[46] The Single European Act introduced the requirement for assent of the European Parliament in Art. 237 of the EEC Treaty. The accession procedures laid down in Art. 98 of the ECSC Treaty and Art. 205 of the EAEC Treaty required the Council only to seek the opinion of the Commission. During the procedure for the accession of Portugal and Spain, the Economic and Social Committee delivered an own-initiative Opinion ([1984] O.J. C23/51). Since the Council had consulted the European Parliament in accordance with point 2.3.7 of the Solemn Declaration of Stuttgart, the Parliament gave its views on the conclusion of the negotiations with Portugal and Spain in a resolution, [1985] O.J. C141/130.

[47] Under the procedure laid down by Art. 98 of the ECSC Treaty, the Council was to determine the terms of accession by a unanimous vote. As a result, the three rounds of accession negotiations prior to the entry into force of EU Treaty resulted in a Council decision on accession to the ECSC alongside a Treaty between the Member States and the applicant Member State with regard to accession to the EC and the EAEC.

with the Community institutions (and therefore not with the Member States as such): the Council negotiates on the basis of common positions which it determines beforehand and, as far as some matters are concerned, it requires the Commission to negotiate with the applicant State.[48] The final agreement is concluded between the Member States and all the applicant Member States, and enters into force after ratification by all the States in accordance with their various constitutional provisions.[49]

The conditions for accession and the resulting adjustments to the Treaties are laid down in an Act annexed to the Accession Treaty, as supplemented by Protocols, Declarations and a Final Act.[50] For every enlargement by which several countries accede, a single Accession Treaty has been drawn up which stipulates that the new Member States are to become members of the European Union subject to the conditions set out in an Act of Accession annexed to the Treaty.[51] In the course of ratification by each of the Member States, the national parliaments (and, in the event of a referendum, the people) cannot therefore confine their approval to only some of the new Member States mentioned in the Accession Treaty.

Accession Treaty. The agreement contains the "conditions of admission **8–010** and the adjustments to the Treaties on which the Union is founded which such admission entails" (EU Treaty, Art. 49). In 1978, the Commission argued that the adjustments could encompass amendments of the Treaties going further than mere technical adjustments.[52] Nevertheless, the 1972, 1979, 1985, 1994, and 2003 Accession Treaties confined the institutional

---

[48] For the procedure, see Puissochet, *L'élargissement des Communautés européennes: présentation et commentaire du Traité et des Actes relatifs à l'adhésion du Royaume-Uni, du Danemark et de l'Irlande* (Editions techniques et économiques, Paris, 1974), at 21–22; for the application of the procedure during the most recent accession negotiations, see Joly, "Le processus de l'élargissement de l'Union européenne" (2002) R.M.C.U.E. 239–246; Landaburu, "The Fifth Enlargement of the European Union: The Power of Example" (2002) Fordham I.L.J. 1–11; Maurer, "Negotiations in progress" and "Progress of the negotiations" in A. Ott and K. Inglis (eds.), *Handbook on European Enlargement—A Commentary on the Enlargement Process,* (T.M.C. Asser Press, The Hague, 2002), at 113–129; for the preceding enlargement of the Union, see Booss and Forman, "Enlargement: Legal and Procedural Aspects" (1995) C.M.L.R. 95, at 104–109.

[49] For where all the applicant States do not ratify the Treaty, see para. 7–001, *supra.* The European Parliament's draft Treaty (Art. 2) and its 1994 Draft Constitution (Art. 45) would make accession to the Union dependent on the conclusion of a treaty by the applicant State directly with the Union.

[50] For full references to the documents relating to preceding accessions, see para. 1–021, *supra.*

[51] See the Council's answer of December 19, 2002 and the Commission's answer of August 20, 2002 to questions E–2069/02 and E–2070/02, respectively (Van den Bos and Van der Laan), [2003] O.J. C92E/131, and C192E/47, respectively.

[52] See the Communication of the Commission to the Council (supplementing its Communication of April 20, 1978 (1978) EC Bull., Suppl.1), *Enlargement of the Community—Transitional period and institutional implications* (1978) EC Bull. Suppl.2, points 30–53.

amendments to an appropriate representation of the new Member States in the institutions and bodies of the Communities. The Court of Justice takes the view that the conditions of admission and the adjustments to the Treaties entailed thereby include adjustments to Community secondary legislation agreed by the Member States upon accession.[53]

8–011 **Pending applications.** Various countries have applied for membership. Following the accession of ten new Member States on May 1, 2004, the following countries' applications remain outstanding: Turkey (April 14, 1987), Switzerland (May 26, 1992), Romania (June 22, 1995), Bulgaria (December 14, 1995), Croatia (February 21, 2003) and the Former Yugoslav Republic of Macedonia (March 22, 2004). An application from Norway led to negotiations which culminated in the 1972 Accession Treaty, which, however, was rejected by a majority of voters in a referendum (see para. 1–021). The same thing happened with the negotiations on Norway's second application, which resulted in the 1994 Accession Treaty.[54]

As long as there is no majority in Switzerland for joining the EEA, it is difficult to see it acceding to the Union (see para. 23–005).

As far as Bulgaria and Romania are concerned, the Commission gave its opinion on their accession on July 15, 1997—together with its opinion on the applications for membership submitted by other central and eastern European States having applied to join the Union, which was accompanied by a programme ("Agenda 2000") covering the adjustments which enlargement would necessitate.[55] After the opening of accession negotiations with six countries on March 31, 1998, the negotiations were extended to six other countries, including Bulgaria and Romania, on February 15, 2000. On April 16, 2003, an accession treaty was signed with the ten countries which acceded on May 1, 2004. January 2007 is proposed for the accession of Bulgaria and Romania.[56]

As far as Turkey is concerned, there is a pre-accession strategy but no date has been set for the opening of accession negotiations (see para. 23–033). Croatia, the Former Yugoslav Republic of Macedonia and the other countries participating in a stabilisation and association process are recognised as being potential candidates for membership of the Union (see para. 23–034). Whether they accede or not will depend upon whether they

---

[53] ECJ, Joined Cases 31–35/86 *LAISA and Another v Council* [1988] E.C.R. 2285, paras 9–12, with a critical note by Vandersanden (1989) C.M.L.R. 551–561.

[54] para. 1–021, *supra*. Norway had applied to join on November 25, 1992. See also Booss and Forman (n.48, *supra*), at 95–130.

[55] European Commission: *Agenda 2000—For a stronger and wider Union* (1997) EU Bull. Suppl.5, which has been enlarged upon in some 20 specific proposals, see (1998) 3 EU Bull. points I.2 to I.22 (para. 23–032, *infra*).

[56] See the conclusions of the European Council held in Brussels on June 17 and 18, 2004, point 20–24.

comply with the general accession criteria and upon the progress they make in the stabilisation and association process. In June 2004, the European Council declared that Croatia meets the requisite conditions to start accession negotiations in 2005.[57]

III. MEMBER STATES LEAVING THE UNION

Current situation. Since the Treaties (with the exception of the ECSC **8–012** Treaty) were concluded for an unlimited time, Member States are not entitled unqualifiedly to revoke their membership. Within the European Union, which, under its main pillar, the European Community, confers enforceable rights directly on Member States and individuals, possesses institutions entitled to deal with economic, social and political issues and has a compulsory system for the judicial resolution of disputes, revocation of membership is also not a possibility on grounds of the specific reasons accepted by international law as justifying the unilateral termination of a relationship established by treaty, namely breach of the Treaty by other Member States, supervening impossibility of performance on the part of the Member State seeking to withdraw, or fundamental change of circumstances with respect to those existing at the time when the Treaty was concluded.[58] A Member State could leave the Union only following "amendment" of the Treaty (procedure set out in Art. 48 of the EU Treaty).

Constitution. This will change when the EU Constitution enters into force. **8–013** From then, any Member State may withdraw voluntarily from the European Union (Art. I–60).[59] If a Member State has taken the decision to withdraw, in accordance with its own constitutional requirements, it has to notify the European Council of its intention and negotiate and conclude an agreement with the Union, setting out the arrangements for its withdrawal and taking account of the framework for its future relationship with the Union (Art. I–60(2)). That agreement is to be concluded on behalf of the Union by the Council, acting by a qualified majority after obtaining the consent of the European Parliament. In this connection, it will have to be

---

[57] *ibid.*, points 31–36.

[58] See Arts 60, 61 and 62 of the 1969 Vienna Convention on the Law of Treaties (para. 17–103, *infra*). However, for agreements concluded by the Community with third countries, see para. 17–103, *infra*. Moreover, a Member State cannot unilaterally change the delimitation of powers between the Community and its Member States: see the Commission's answer of September 7, 2001 to question E–2399/01 (Huhne), [2001] O.J. C364E/252.

[59] See Friel,"Secession from the European Union: Checking out of the Proverbial 'Cockroach Motel' " (2004) Fordham I.L.J. 590–641; Bruha and Nowak, "Recht auf Austritt aus der Europäischen Union?" (2004) A. Völkerr. 1–25.

determined to what extent rights and obligations stemming from Union law may continue to apply to citizens of the withdrawing Member State. Under the EU Constitution, a Member State cannot be forced to await the outcome of the negotiations on the conditions accompanying its withdrawal. In the absence of any agreement, the Constitution will cease to apply to the State in question two years after the notification of the intention to withdraw, unless the European Council, in agreement with the Member State concerned, unanimously decides to extend this period (Art. I–60(3)).

CHAPTER 9

EXCEPTIONS TO THE APPLICATION OF THE TREATIES

I. SAFEGUARD CLAUSES

Substantive derogations. Various articles of the Treaty empower the **9–001**
Commission to authorise a Member State temporarily not to comply in full
with its Treaty obligations.[1] Articles 296–298 of the EC Treaty allow the
Member States themselves to deviate from their general Treaty obligations
on grounds of internal or external security.[2] The EU Constitution will take
over these provisions.[3] Just as in the case of the exceptions provided for in
the Treaty with regard to the free movement of goods, persons, services
and capital (see Arts 30, 39(3) and (4), 45–46 and 58 of the EC Treaty), the
articles in question must be strictly construed.[4] They do not take away from
the Community any substantive competence to deal with security aspects in
a Community act. Moreover, a measure taken on grounds of public security
does not necessarily fall outside the scope of Community law. Accordingly,
decisions taken by the Member States with regard to the organisation of
their armed forces are not outside the application of Community law,
notably where it is a question of respecting the principle of the equal
treatment of men and women in employment relationships, in particular
with regard to access to military occupations.[5] Nevertheless, the Court of
Justice makes an exception for the application of Community law to

---

[1] See EC Treaty, Art. 95(6); Art. 119(3); Art. 134, first and second paragraphs; Art. 298, first
paragraph. See Mortelmans, "Excepties bij non-tarifaire intracommunautaire
belemmeringen: assimilatie in het nieuwe EG-Verdrag?" (1997) S.E.W. 182, at 185–186.
[2] See Peers, "National Security and European Law" (1996) Y.E.L. 363, at 379–387; Trybus,
"The Limits of European Community Competence for Defence" (2004) E.For.Aff.Rev.
189–217 and "The EC Treaty as an Instrument of European Defence Integration: Judicial
Scrutiny of Defence and Security Exceptions" (2002) C.M.L.R. 1347–1372. For the limited
derogation authorised by Art. 60(2) of the EC Treaty, see para. 20–051, *infra*.
[3] For Art. 296 of the EC Treaty, see Art. III–436 of the EU Constitution; for Arts 297 and 298
of the EC Treaty, see Arts III–131 and III–132 of the EU Constitution.
[4] ECJ, Case 13/68 *Salgoil* [1968] E.C.R. 453, at 463. For the exceptional nature of Art. 296 of
the EC Treaty, see ECJ, Case C–414/97 *Commission v Spain* [1999] E.C.R. I–5585, para. 21;
for the exceptional nature of Art. 297, see Case 222/84 *Johnston* [1986] E.C.R. 1651,
paras 25–26.
[5] ECJ, Case C–273/97 *Sirdar* [1999] E.C.R. I–7403, para. 19, and ECJ, Case C–285/98 *Kreil*
[2000] E.C.R. I–69, para. 16.

decisions of Member States relating to military organisation whose aim is the defence of their territory or of their essential interests.[6] Where the Community itself has acted, however, it may be hard for a Member State to invoke exceptional circumstances.[7]

Articles 296 and 297 authorise a Member State to take unilateral measures where "the essential interests of its security" are at stake (Art. 296(1)) or "in the event of serious internal disturbances affecting the maintenance of law and order, in the event of war, serious international tension constituting a threat of war" or in order to carry out obligations entered into by the Member State for the purpose of maintaining peace and international security (Art. 297). In such a situation, a Member State may withhold information which it would otherwise be bound to provide (Art. 296(1)(a)) or take such measures as it considers necessary which are connected with the production of or trade in weapons, munitions and war material (Art. 296(1)(b)). On April 15, 1958 the Council adopted a list, by a unanimous vote, of the products to which Art. 296 applies.[8] One example of the effects of this exceptional provision is that where a Member State adopts an aid measure in favour of activities relating to products appearing on that list, the Commission cannot initiate an investigation procedure under Art. 88 of the EC Treaty.[9] Article 297 refers to Member States consulting each other with a view to taking together steps to prevent the functioning of the common market being affected by a measure which a Member State feels itself called upon to take. Depending on the type of problem involved, the consultation with other Member States takes place in

---

[6] ECJ, Case C–186/01 *Dory* [2003] E.C.R. I–2479, paras 35–42 (Germany's decision to ensure its defence in part by compulsory military service limited to men is the expression of a choice of military organisation to which Community law is not applicable). For critical observations, see Trybus (2003) C.M.L.R. 1269–1280; for a somewhat favourable view, see Koutrakos (2003) Mod.L.Rev. 759–768; Anagnostaras (2003) E.L.Rev. 713–722; Dietrich (2003) D.ö.V. 883–889.

[7] See ECJ, Case C–124/95 *Centro-Com* [1997] E.C.R. I–81, para. 46 (where exceptions to the Community export regime were relied on; see para. 20–007, *infra*). See also Gilsdorf, "Les réserves de sécurité du traité CEE, à la lumière du traité sur l'Union européenne" (1994) R.M.C.U.E. 17, at 18–19 and 23–25, where it is argued that a CFSP joint action may also raise the hurdles which a Member State must overcome in order to invoke such safeguard clauses.

[8] The list was published as the Council's answer of September 27, 2001 to question E-1324/01 (Staes), [2001] O.J. C364E/85; a detailed list was published in connection with a CFSP Code of Conduct for Weapons Exports; see the common list of military equipment covered by the European Union code of conduct on arms export, adopted by the Council on November 12, 2003 ([2003] O.J. C314/1), replacing the list of June 13, 2000 ([2000] O.J. C191/2). See Trybus, *European Defence Procurement* (Kluwer Law International, The Hague, 1999), 331 pp.; Lhoest, "La production et le commerce des armes, et l'article 223 du traité instituant la Communauté européenne" (1993) B.T.I.R. 176–207. The export regime adopted by the Council on "dual-use goods" (civil and military use) expressly provides that it does not affect Art. 296 of the EC Treaty: Art. 22 of Regulation No. 1334/2000; para. 20–007, *infra*. See Vincentelli-Meria, "Vers une normalisation de l'application de l'article 296 du TCE dans le secteur des industries d'armement" (2001) R.M.C.U.E 96–101.

[9] See CFI (judgment of September 30, 2003), Case T–26/01 *Fiocchi munizioni v Commission*, not yet reported, paras 58–59.

accordance with the provisions of Title V or Title VI of the EU Treaty and may make unilateral national measures unnecessary should the outcome of the consultation be a decision to adopt a joint action pursuant to these Treaty provisions or Community action.[10]

Articles 296 and 297 of the EC Treaty leave Member States free to a degree to estimate themselves whether there is a risk to security and to what extent the risk justifies departing from the obligations laid down by the Treaty. However, the Court of Justice can review whether such action is manifestly disproportionate to the alleged risk to security.[11] If the national measures have the effect of distorting the conditions of competition, the Commission, together with the State concerned, will examine how these measures can be adjusted to the rules laid down in the Treaty (Art. 298, first para.).[12] In the event that the Member State makes "improper use" of the powers provided for in Arts 296 and 297, the Commission[13] or any Member State may bring the matter directly before the Court of Justice, by way of derogation from the procedure laid down in Arts 226 and 227. The Court is to give its ruling *in camera* (Art. 298, second para.). Pending its decision on the substance, the Court of Justice may make an order prescribing interim measures.[14]

Transitional derogations. During the transitional period a Member State **9–002** could apply to the Commission for authorisation to take protective measures if difficulties arose which were serious and liable to persist in any sector of the economy or which could bring about serious deterioration in

---

[10] Gilsdorf (n.7, *supra*), at 21; Kotrakos, "Is Article 297 EC a 'Reserve of Sovereignty'?" (2000) C.M.L.R. 1339–1362. For the application of Art. 297 of the EC Treaty in the case of economic sanctions, see para. 20–050, *infra*.

[11] Trybus "The EC Treaty as an Instrument of European Defence Integration: Judicial Scrutiny of Defence and Security Exceptions" (2002) C.M.L.R. 1347, at 1364–1369. According to the Court of Justice, the Member State must prove that reliance on Art. 296 is necessary to protect the essential interests of its security: ECJ, Case C–414/97 *Commission v Spain* [1999] E.C.R. I–5585, para. 22.

[12] This will be the case, *e.g.* where a national aid measure benefits activities connected with products not on the Council's list of April 15, 1958 or having a "dual use": CFI (judgment of September 30, 2003), Case T–26/01 *Fiocchi munizioni v Commission*, not yet reported, para. 63. For the Commission's powers in this connection, see *ibid.*, paras 74–75.

[13] In this connection, the Commission has to look after the Community's interests, not those of third countries: ECJ (order of June 29, 1994), Case C–120/94 R *Commission v Greece* [1994] E.C.R. I–3037, paras 99–101.

[14] *ibid.*, paras 38–45 (with a case note by Vanhamme (1994/95) Col.J.E.L. 134–139). In this first application of Art. 298, the Commission accused Greece of having infringed rules of the common commercial policy without being in one of the situations for which Art. 297 provides for exceptions, by imposing a ban on imports and trade in products from the former Yugoslav Republic of Macedonia. The Court of Justice did not have to rule on the substance, since the Commission discontinued the proceedings in view of the conclusion of an agreement between Greece and Macedonia, see ECJ (order of March 19, 1996), Case C–120/94 *Commission v Greece* [1996] E.C.R. I–1513. Advocate General F.G. Jacobs took the view that Greece had not abused Art. 297: *ibid.*, at I–1525–1533; see also Peers (n.2, *supra*), at 384–387.

the economic situation of a given area .[15] Every Accession Treaty provides for similar protective measures to be taken during the transitional period on the request of an acceding Member State.[16]

III. DIFFERENTIATED SCOPE OF THE TREATIES

A. GRANT OF EXCEPTIONAL STATUS TO A MEMBER STATE

9–003 **Differentiated integration.** In certain circumstances the application of Community law may lead to difficulties in certain Member States or parts of Member States. In order to avoid or resolve such difficulties, provisions of Community law sometimes contain exceptions, which are to respect the principles of equal treatment and proportionality.[17] There are also the safeguard clauses for which the EC Treaty makes provision (see para. 9–001). As a result, the process of European integration is not needlessly hampered on account of difficulties in one or more Member States. As long as all Member States fully subscribe to the objectives of the integration process, Member States struggling with generally acknowledged difficulties may be authorised temporarily not to take part in Community policy in certain areas, whilst the other Member States provide support in order to enable the Member State or States concerned to get back to grips.[18] Such differentiated integration can be traced back to the transitional arrangements applied on the accession of Member States (see para. 8–008) and the derogations granted to Member States not fulfilling the criteria for entry to the third stage of EMU (see para. 5–232). The technique is also frequently invoked in connection with the possible accession of new

---

[15] EEC Treaty, Art. 226(1); for applications, see ECJ, Case 13/63 *Italy v Commission* [1963] E.C.R. 165, at 175–179; ECJ, Joined Cases 73 and 74/63 *Handelsvereniging Rotterdam* [1964] E.C.R. 1, at 11–14; ECJ, Case 37/70 *Rewe-Zentrale* [1971] E.C.R. 23, paras 2–19; ECJ, Case 72/72 *Einfuhr- und Vorratsstelle Getreide* [1973] E.C.R. 377, paras 4–20.

[16] See Art. 135 of the 1972 Act of Accession; Art. 130 of the 1979 Act of Accession; Art. 379 of the 1985 Act of Accession; Art. 152 of the 1994 Act of Accession; Art. 37 of the 2003 Act of Accession. See Garcia-Duran Huet, "Le traité d'Athènes, un traité d'adhésion comme les autres?" (2004) R.M.C.U.E. 290–292; Van Haersolte, "Het Toetredingsverdrag 2003 (alias het Verdrag van Athene)" (2003) N.T.D.E. 301, at 308–310.

[17] For the principle of equal treatment, see ECJ, Case 153/73 *Holtz & Willemsen v Council and Commission* [1974] E.C.R. 675, paras 13–14, and para. 5–056, *supra*; for the principle of proportionality, see paras 5–038 *et seq.*

[18] See the Tindemans Report on European Union (1976) EC Bull. Suppl.1, 22 (new approach proposed to economic and monetary policy); Grabitz and Langeheine, "Legal Problems Related to a Proposed 'Two-Tier System' of Integration within the Community" (1981) C.M.L.R. 33–48; Langeheine, "Abgestufte Integration" (1983) EuR. 227–280; Ehlermann, "How Flexible is Community Law? An Unusual Approach to the Concept of 'Two Speeds'" (1984) Michigan L.Rev. 1274–1293.

Member States which are not yet in a position to implement all the Community obligations.[19]

In addition, the Member States have accepted forms of integration whereby some Member States may permanently withdraw from the realisation of intended objectives.[20] The EU Treaty allowed Denmark and the United Kingdom to opt out from participating in the third stage of EMU (see para. 5–233). The United Kingdom, Ireland and Denmark have the right not to take part in Community measures adopted pursuant to Title IV of the EC Treaty (see paras 5–165–5–166). By virtue of a protocol, Denmark is not to participate in the elaboration and implementation of the European Security and Defence Policy (ESDP), and in particular in CFSP measures adopted pursuant to Title V of the EU Treaty which have defence implications (see para. 6–005). In so far as the exceptional status of the Member State concerned stems from a political decision on its part not to collaborate with the other Member States in the field in question, it may become involved simply by intimating the wish to do so.[21] Where decision-making is confined to particular Member States, the voting requirements in the Council have to be adjusted, but the other institutions and bodies of the Community retain their usual composition and mode of operation (see para. 14–067). Consequently, the Court of Justice can rule in its normal composition on disputes concerning the validity and interpretation of Community acts adopted in this way.[22]

In order to provide the United Kingdom with an opt-out *vis-à-vis* the social policy which the other Member States wished to pursue, the EU Treaty created a legal structure whereby a protocol to the EC Treaty (signed by all the Member States) authorised the Member States, with the

---

[19] See, *inter alia*, Fastenrath, "Die Struktur der erweiterten Europäischen Union" and Lautenschlager, "Die Struktur der erweiterten Europäischen Union" (1994) EuR. Beiheft 1, 101–126 and 127–146, respectively (and the discussion at 147–150, *ibid.*). For the problems associated with differentiated integration, see Ehlermann, "Différenciation accrue ou uniformité renforcée?" (1995) 3 R.M.U.E. 191–218; Maillet, "Convergence et géométrie variable; l'organisation du fonctionnement de l'Union européenne diversifiée est à repenser" (1995) R.M.C.U.E. 145–159.

[20] For some critical comments, see Curtin, "The Constitutional Structure of the Union: A Europe of Bits and Pieces" (1993) C.M.L.R. 17, at 51–52; Whiteford, "Social Policy After Maastricht" (1993) E.L.Rev. 216–217 (concerning the Social Agreement).

[21] This is the case with Denmark and its exceptional position on defence policy and Title IV of the EC Treaty (see para. 5–165, *supra*); the same is true of Ireland as regards Title IV of the EC Treaty (see para. 5–166, *supra*). In the negotiations, the UK did not consider it necessary to press for such an option. As far as participation in EMU is concerned, however, the Member States which have opted out have to satisfy the requisite criteria if they should wish to participate; see paras 5–232—5–233, *supra*.

[22] *cf.* Koenig, "Die Europäische Sozialunion als Bewährungsprobe der supranationalen Gerichtsbarkeit" (1994) EuR. 175–195 (concerning the Social Agreement). As far as Title IV of the EC Treaty is concerned, account must be taken of the limitations which Art. 68 of the EC Treaty puts on the jurisdiction of the Court of Justice (para. 10–075, *infra*). In principle, courts in the Member States with an opt-out would be concerned with applying the acts in question might refer questions to the Court of Justice for a preliminary ruling on their validity and interpretation and the States enjoying an opt-out could bring actions for the annulment of such measures. See Curtin (n.20, *supra*), at 60.

exception of the United Kingdom, to "have recourse to the institutions, procedures and mechanisms of the Treaty" for the purpose of taking and applying the acts and decisions required for giving effect to the "Agreement on Social Policy" annexed to the protocol, which was concluded only between those Member States (the "Social Protocol" and the "Social Agreement").[23] Under the more extensive powers provided for in the Social Agreement, the other Member States adopted directives—using Community institutions and procedures—which had the same legal force as other Community directives for all the Member States with the exception of the United Kingdom.[24] At the 1996 Intergovernmental Conference, the (new) British government voted to adopt the more extensive powers enshrined in the Social Agreement in the form of the new Treaty provisions on social policy (see para. 5–235). Following the European Council held in Amsterdam on June 16 and 17, 1997, the United Kingdom was already involved in discussion of the directives which were still to be adopted pursuant to the Social Agreement.[25] In addition, the Council adopted directives on the basis of Art. 100 of the EC Treaty, which extended the directives adopted pursuant to the Social Agreement to the United Kingdom.[26]

---

[23] See Schuster, "Rechtsfragen der Maastrichter Vereinbarungen zur Sozialpolitik" (1992) Eu.Z.W. 178–187; Watson, "Social Policy After Maastricht" (1993) C.M.L.R. 481–513; Whiteford (n.20, *supra*), at 202–222.

[24] For the directives adopted pursuant to the Social Agreement, see n.1105 to para. 5–236, *supra*. Those directives have the same status as other directives, see, *e.g.* the interpretation in ECJ, Case C–366/99 *Griesmar* [2001] E.C.R. I–9383, paras 62–67.

[25] (1997) 6 EU Bull. point I.8; for the first occasion, see the Social Affairs Council held on June 27, 1997 (*Europe* Nos 7004–7006 of June 27, 28 and 30, 1997, at p.8).

[26] See the directives mentioned in n.1105 to para.5–236, *supra*. According to the preamble of each of these directives, the fact that the directive is not applicable to the UK has a direct effect on the functioning of the internal market and the implementation of the directive in all the Member States is to improve the operation of the internal market.

Figure 2: Differentiation within the European Union and the European Economic Area

		EMU	Schengen-*acquis*		ESDP	EEA
		(see para. 5-222)	(see paras 5–164–5–166)		(see para. 20–047)	(see para. 23–005)
			Integration existing *acquis*	Further development *acquis*		
EU Member States	Austria	X	X	X	X	X
	Belgium	X	X	X	X	X
	Cyprus		X	X	X	X
	Czech Rep.		X	X	X	X
	Denmark	(opt-out)	X	(opt-in)		X
	Estonia		X	X	X	X
	Finland	X	X	X	X	X
	France	X	X	X	X	X
	Germany	X	X	X	X	X
	Greece	X	X	X	X	X
	Hungary		X	X	X	X
	Ireland	X	(opt-in)		X	X
	Italy	X	X	X	X	X
	Latvia		X	X	X	X
	Lithuania		X	X	X	X
	Luxembourg	X	X	X	X	X
	Malta		X	X	X	X
	Netherlands	X	X	X	X	X
	Poland		X	X	X	X
	Portugal	X	X	X	X	X
	Slovak Rep.		X	X	X	X
	Slovenia		X	X	X	X
	Spain	X	X	X	X	X
	Sweden		X	X	X	X
	UK	(opt-out)	(opt-in)		X	X
EFTA	Iceland		X	X		X
	Liechtenstein					X
	Norway		X	X		X
	Switzerland					

B. ENHANCED CO-OPERATION BETWEEN MEMBER STATES

9–004 Previous examples. Some Member States have taken steps towards enhanced (formerly "closer") co-operation by means of mutual agreements and/or conventions. These non-Community forms of integration are differentiated in that Member States accede thereto when they deem it appropriate to do so. Examples are the European Monetary System (see para. 2–011) and the Schengen Convention (see para. 2–017), which came into being between those Member States which wished to bring their national monetary policies and police and judicial policies into closer alignment in the absence of, or as a precursor to, a Community policy.[27] Clearly, Member States may not enter into such forms of co-operation in a manner contrary to their obligations under Community law (EC Treaty, Art. 10).[28]

The CFSP was based on such a relationship of co-operation between some of the Member States when it charged the Western European Union (WEU) with the elaboration and implementation of decisions and actions with defence implications.[29] However, the Treaty of Nice integrated the activities of the WEU into the Union's CFSP (see para. 20–045).

9–005 General framework. The Treaty of Amsterdam created a general framework for enhanced co-operation between Member States which is enshrined in the new Title VII of the EU Treaty.[30] The "provisions on enhanced co-operation" allow Member States to make use of the institutions, procedures and mechanisms laid down in the EC Treaty or the EU Treaty or both treaties. Depending on the subject-matter of the co-operation, the Member States involved in the enhanced co-operation apply the Community, the CFSP or the PJCC decision-making procedure

---

[27] See also Benelux co-operation, para. 2–007, *supra*.

[28] para. 5-054, *supra*. Accordingly, the Schengen Convention took account of the fact that conventions concluded between the Member States may replace or adapt provisions of that convention (Art. 142(1), first subparagraph). Provisions of the Schengen Convention which prove to conflict with such conventions would have to be adapted in any event (Art. 142(1), third subparagraph), although the Schengen Convention could provide for more extensive co-operation than that resulting from such a convention (Art. 142(1), second subparagraph). For Benelux co-operation, see EC Treaty, Art. 306 (para. 17–098, *infra*).

[29] See EU Treaty, Art. 17(3) in the version prior to the changes introduced by the Treaty of Nice. In such case Member States which were not WEU members were to be entitled to participate fully in the tasks carried out by the WEU.

[30] Constantinesco, "Le traité d'Amsterdam. Les clauses de 'coopération renforcée'. Le protocole sur l'application des principes de subsidiarité et de proportionalité" (1997) R.T.D.E. 751–767; Ehlermann, "Differentiation, Flexibility, Closer Cooperation: The New Provisions of the Amsterdam Treaty" (1998) E.L.J. 246–270 and "Engere Zusammenarbeit nach dem Amsterdamer Vertrag: Ein neues Verfassungsprinzip?" (1998) EuR. 362–397; Chaltiel, "Le traité d'Amsterdam et la coopération renforcée" (1998) R.M.C.U.E. 289–293; Kortenberg, "Closer Co-operation in the Treaty of Amsterdam" (1998) C.M.L.R. 833–854; Gaja, "How Flexible is Flexibility under the Amsterdam Treaty?" (1998) C.M.L.R. 855–870. See also Bribosia, "Différenciation et avant-gardes au sein de l'Union européenne" (2000) C.D.E 57–115; Tuytschaever, "Nauwere samenwerking volgens het Verdrag van Nice" (2001) S.E.W. 375–387.

(EU Treaty, Art. 44(1); see paras 14–017 and 15–014, respectively). Member States apply, as far as they are concerned by enhanced co-operation, the acts and decisions adopted for the implementation of the enhanced co-operation in which they participate. Such acts and decisions are binding only on those Member States which participate in such co-operation and, as appropriate, are directly applicable only in those States (EU Treaty, Art. 44(2)). Non-participating Member States may not impede the implementation of such acts and decisions by the participating States. Prior to the Treaty of Nice, enhanced co-operation was possible in the context of the EC Treaty and JHA co-operation but was not put into practice. The Treaty of Nice introduced the possibility of having enhanced co-operation also for the CFSP and made the conditions for such co-operation more flexible.[31]

Member States proposing to embark on enhanced co-operation may do so only if the co-operation satisfies the requirements laid down in Arts 43, 43a and 43b of the EU Treaty. It must concern at least eight Member States and be used only as a last resort, when it has been established within the Council that the objectives of such co-operation cannot be attained within a reasonable period by applying the relevant provisions of the Treaties.[32] The co-operation must be open to all Member States and allow them to become parties to it at any time, provided that they comply with the basic decision and with the decisions taken within that framework.[33] The Commission and the Member States participating in enhanced co-operation are to ensure that as many Member States as possible are encouraged to take part.[34] From the substantive viewpoint, the co-operation must be aimed at furthering the objectives of the Union and the Community and at protecting and serving their interests and at reinforcing their process of integration. It must further respect the EU and EC Treaties and the single institutional framework of the Union and likewise the *acquis communautaire* and the measures adopted under the other provisions of those Treaties, must remain within the limits of the powers of the Union or the Community and must not concern the areas which fall within the exclusive competence of the Community.[35] In addition, enhanced co-operation may not constitute a barrier to or discrimination in trade between the Member States, distort competition between them, undermine the Internal Market or economic and social cohesion, or affect the Schengen Protocol. At the same time, it must respect the competences, rights, obligations and interests of those Member States which do not

---

[31] See Fines, "La réforme des coopérations renforcées" (2001) R.A.E. 359–373; Bribosia, "Les coopérations renforcées au lendemain du traité de Nice" (2001) R.D.U.E. 111–171; Rodrigues, "Le traité de Nice et les coopérations renforcées au sein de l'Union européenne" (2001) R.M.C.U.E. 11–16.
[32] EU Treaty, Art. 43(g) and Art. 43a.
[33] EU Treaty, Art. 43(j) and Art. 43b.
[34] EU Treaty, Art. 43b, *in fine*.
[35] EU Treaty, Art. 43(a)–(d).

participate therein.[36] As far as the CFSP is concerned, enhanced co-operation must also comply with the specific additional criteria laid down in Art. 27a of the EU Treaty. As regards enhanced co-operation within the framework of the EC Treaty, the CFSP and PJCC, authorisation must be granted by the Council in accordance with the procedures laid down by Art. 11 of the EC Treaty, Art. 27a of the EU Treaty or Art. 40 of the EU Treaty, as the case may be.[37] Acts and decisions adopted under enhanced co-operation do not form part of the Union *acquis*.[38]

9–006 Community matters. As regards matters coming under the EC Treaty, Member States may establish enhanced co-operation after receiving authorisation from the Council (EC Treaty, Art. 11(1) and (2)). Member States intending to establish enhanced co-operation are to address a request to the Commission, which may then submit a proposal to the Council.[39] If the Commission submits a proposal, the Council takes its decision by a qualified majority, after consulting the European Parliament (EC Treaty, Art. 11(2)).[40] When enhanced co-operation relates to an area covered by the co-decision procedure, the assent of the European Parliament is required (EC Treaty, Art. 11(2)). A member of the Council may request that the matter be referred to the European Council. After that matter has been raised before the European Council, the Council may take a decision by a qualified majority.[41]

Another procedure is applied where a non-participating Member State notifies its intention to take part in an existing form of enhanced co-operation. In such case, the Commission decides on the request and on such specific arrangements as it may deem necessary (EC Treaty, Art. 11a; see para. 14–072).

9–007 Common foreign and security policy. As far as the CFSP is concerned, there is another form of enhanced co-operation between Member States where a Member State formally abstains from voting and hence does not have to apply the decision concerned, even though it accepts that it commits the Union ("constructive abstention" as provided for by Art. 23(1), second subpara.; see para. 15–002). The EU Treaty further allows for enhanced co-operation in the field of the CFSP. Such enhanced co-operation must aim at safeguarding the values and serving the interests

---

[36] EU Treaty, Art. 43(e), (f), (h), (i) and (j).

[37] EU Treaty, Art. 44(1).

[38] EU Treaty, Art. 44(1), *in fine*.

[39] EC Treaty, Art. 11(1). If the Commission does not submit a proposal, it is to inform the Member States concerned of the reasons for not doing so (*ibid.*).

[40] The European Parliament considers that the Commission must undertake to withdraw any proposal for enhanced co-operation where the European Parliament delivers a negative opinion; see the resolution of the European Parliament of July 16, 1998 on the implementation of the Amsterdam Treaty: implications of closer co-operation, point 13 ([1998] O.J. C292/143).

[41] EC Treaty, Art. 11(2), *in fine*.

of the Union as a whole by asserting its identity as a coherent force on the international scene (EU Treaty, Art. 27a(1)).[42] The potential for enhanced co-operation is limited, however, in that it may relate only to implementation of a joint action or a common position (EU Treaty, Art. 27b). It may not relate to matters having military or defence implications (EU Treaty, Art. 27b, *in fine*). Article 27a of the EU Treaty further requires that enhanced co-operation respect the principles, objectives, general guidelines and consistency of the CFSP and the decisions taken within the framework of that policy, the powers of the European Community, and consistency between all the Union's policies and its external activities.

The procedure for establishing enhanced co-operation with regard to the CFSP is based on the procedure which applied prior to the Treaty of Nice for JHA co-operation.[43] Authorisation to establish enhanced co-operation is given by the Council, but not in the same way provided for in Art. 11 of the EC Treaty. This is because, under Art. 27c, first para., of the EU Treaty, the Member States make their request directly to the Council. After consulting the Commission on whether the proposed co-operation is consistent with Union policies, the Council takes its decision in principle by a qualified majority. However, if a member of the Council declares that, for important and stated reasons of national policy, it intends to oppose the adoption of the decision, no vote is taken. In that case, the Council may, acting by a qualified majority, request that the matter be referred to the European Council for decision by unanimity. The European Parliament is not consulted; the request is merely forwarded to it for information (EU Treaty, Art. 27c, second para.).

Where another Member State wishes to participate in enhanced CFSP co-operation which has already been established, it must notify its intention to the Council and inform the Commission. The Council (namely the Member States taking part in the enhanced co-operation[44]) takes the decision on the request and on such specific arrangements as it may deem necessary (EU Treaty, Art. 27e, first para.; see para. 15–008).

Police and judicial co-operation in criminal matters. In the case of **9–008** enhanced co-operation under the auspices of police and judicial co-operation in criminal matters (PJCC), Art. 40(1) of the EU Treaty requires, not only that the criteria set out in Art. 43 be satisfied, but also that the proposed co-operation respect the powers of the Community and

---

[42] For the openings for enhanced co-operation within the CFSP, see Jaeger, "Enhanced Co-operation in the Treaty of Nice and Flexibility in the Common Foreign and Security Policy" (2002) E.For.Aff.Rev. 297–316; Pernice and Thym, "A New Institutional Balance for European Foreign Policy?" (2003) E.For.Aff.Rev. 369, at 380–386.

[43] See the former Art. 40(2) of the EU Treaty.

[44] The Council acts by a qualified majority, defined as the same proportion of the weighted votes and the same proportion of the number of the members of the Council concerned as those laid down in the third subpara. of Art. 23(2) of the EU Treaty (EU Treaty, Art. 27e, third para.).

the objectives of PJCC. It also provides that the co-operation must have the aim of enabling the Union to develop more rapidly into an area of freedom, security and justice.

Authorisation to establish enhanced co-operation under PJCC is also granted by the Council. Under Art. 40a(1) of the EU Treaty, the Member States concerned are to address their request directly to the Commission, which may submit a proposal to the Council. In the event that the Commission does not submit a proposal, the Member States may submit their initiative directly to the Council. The Council decides by a qualified majority[45] on a proposal of the Commission or on the initiative of at least eight Member States, and after consulting the European Parliament (EU Treaty, Art. 40a(2)). Also in the case of PJCC, a Member State may request that the matter be referred to the European Council (the Treaty does not require any specific "reasons"). After that matter has been raised before the European Council, the Council may act by a qualified majority (EU Treaty, Art. 40a(2), second subpara.).

If a Member State wishes to become a party to an existing form of PJCC enhanced co-operation, it must notify its intention to the Council and to the Commission. The Council (composed of the parties to the enhanced co-operation) then decides on the request and on such specific arrangements as it may deem necessary after consulting the Commission (EU Treaty, Art. 40b; see para. 15–014).

9–009 **Judicial review.** The conditions which the Treaty provisions impose on the establishment of enhanced co-operation are a specific expression of the obligation to co-operate in good faith imposed on the Member States by Art. 10 of the EC Treaty. In order to safeguard the *acquis communautaire*, Art. 46 of the EU Treaty recognises the jurisdiction of the Court of Justice with regard to the provisions of Title VII of the EU Treaty under the conditions provided for in Art. 11 and 11a of the EC Treaty and Art. 40 of the EU Treaty. In the case of enhanced co-operation under Art. 11 of the EC Treaty, the Court of Justice exercises the powers conferred on it by the EC Treaty.[46] As far as PJCC enhanced co-operation is concerned, Art. 40(3) of the EU Treaty provides that the provisions of the EC Treaty concerning the powers of the Court of Justice and the exercise of those powers shall apply to Art. 40 and Arts 40a and 40b. This means that the Court of Justice may also exercise supervision in respect of PJCC as regards Council authorisation to engage in enhanced co-operation (including compliance with the requirements set out in Arts 40 and 43–43b of the EU

---

[45] Votes of members of the Council are to be weighted in accordance with Art. 205(2) of the EC Treaty (EU Treaty, Art. 40(2), third subpara.).
[46] See also Art. 11(3) of the EC Treaty, which provides that "The acts and decisions necessary for the implementation of enhanced co-operation activities" are to be subject to all the relevant provisions of EC Treaty, save as otherwise provided in that Article and in Arts 43–45 of the EU Treaty.

Treaty) and as regards decisions to allow a Member State to participate in co-operation after it has been established. Articles 29–41 of the EU Treaty apply to the implementation of PJCC enhanced co-operation (EU Treaty, Art. 40(2)), which signifies that the Court of Justice may review the relevant acts—including the aspect of their compatibility with the aforementioned requirements[47]—subject to the conditions set out in Art. 35 of the EU Treaty (see para. 10–077).

Constitution. The EU Constitution retains the framework for Member **9–010** States wishing to establish enhanced co-operation amongst themselves and makes the applicable conditions the same for all the various policy areas of the Union.[48] Consequently, the present restrictions on enhanced co-operation in the field of the CFSP will disappear. Once the Constitution is in force, enhanced co-operation will require the participation of at least one-third of the Member States (EU Constitution, Art. I–44(2)). On the procedural level, the EU Constitution distinguishes between, on the one hand, enhanced co-operation outside the scope of the CFSP—requiring a request to be addressed to the Commission and authorisation from the Council after obtaining the consent of the European Parliament—and, on the other hand, enhanced co-operation in the field of the CFSP—requiring a request to be addressed to the Council, which is to decide after receiving an opinion from the Commission and from the Union Minister for Foreign Affairs (EU Constitution, Art. III–419). The possibility for a Member State to have the matter referred to the European Council will no longer exist. The authorisation to proceed with enhanced co-operation will be deemed to be granted within the framework of the "alarm bell" procedure provided for in Arts III–270(4) and III–271(4) of the EU Constitution (see para. 15–015). Any Member State wishing to participate in an existing form of enhanced co-operation has to notify its intention to the Council and the Commission and, in the field of the CFSP, also to the Union Minister for Foreign Affairs (EU Constitution, Art. III–420). As far as concerns judicial review of action of the institutions and the Member States within the framework of enhanced co-operation, the powers of the Court of Justice will be restricted only in so far as the CFSP is concerned (see para. 10–086).

III. SUSPENSION OF TREATY RIGHTS AND OBLIGATIONS

No unilateral suspension. Member States may not suspend their own **9–011** Treaty obligations *vis-à-vis* a Member State which is in persistent breach. No more do the Treaties permit a Member State to be excluded or

---

[47] See Donner, "De derde pijler en de Amsterdamse doolhof" (1997) S.E.W. 370, at 376.
[48] For this form of co-operation and other possible forms, see Shaw, "Flexibility in a 'reorganised' and 'simplified' Treaty" (2003) C.M.L.R. 279–311.

compelled to leave the Union.[49] A Member State which fails to fulfil its obligations may be brought before the Court of Justice by the Commission or another Member State, and possibly fined (EC Treaty, Arts 226–228).[50] Commentators have been divided as to whether a unilateral suspension of Treaty obligations may be justified under international law where no solution can be found using the dispute-settlement procedures or the safeguard clauses of Arts 296–298 of the EC Treaty.[51]

9–012 **Suspension of Treaty rights.** If a Member State commits a "serious and persistent breach" of the principles mentioned in Art. 6(1) of the EU Treaty, the Council may decide to suspend certain of its rights deriving from the application of the EU and the EC Treaties (EU Treaty, Art. 7, and EC Treaty, Art. 309; see also Art. I–59 of the EU Constitution)). The principles are liberty, democracy, respect for human rights and fundamental freedoms, and the rule of law.[52] The Council determines such a breach after inviting the government of the Member State in question to submit its observations. It makes that determination unanimously (not counting the vote of the representative of the Member State concerned) meeting in the composition of the Heads of State or Government at the proposal of one-third of the Member States or the Commission, after obtaining the assent of the European Parliament (EU Treaty, Art. 7(2) and (5)).[53]

---

[49] Thus, when Denmark was unable to ratify the EU Treaty after a negative vote in a first referendum, the other Member States could not exclude it from the Community or replace the Community by some other organisation: Rideau, "La ratification et l'entrée en vigueur du traité de Maastricht" (1992) R.F.D.C. 479, at 490–491; see to the same effect, Kapteyn, "Denemarken en het Verdrag van Maastricht" (1992) N.J.B. 781–783.

[50] For further details, see Lenaerts and Arts, *Procedural Law of the European Union,* Ch.5. In the event of an excessive deficit, the Council, excluding the representative of the Member State concerned, may impose sanctions (EC Treaty, Art. 104(11); para. 5–229, *supra*).

[51] For further literature and a number of scenarios for exceptional measures, see Ehlermann, "Mitgliedschaft in der Europäischen Gemeinschaft—Rechtsproblem der Erweiterung, der Mitgliedschaft und der Verkleinerung" (1984) EuR. 113, at 120–121. The view that such measures would run counter to the Community legal order is discussed in Everling, "Sind die Mitgliedstaaten der Europäischen Gemeinschaften noch Herren der Verträge?", *Völkerrecht als Rechtsordnung. Internationale Gerichtsbarkeit. Menschenrechte. Festschrift H. Mosler*, Berlin, Springer, 1983, 173–191.

[52] For the violation of fundamental rights, see Wachsmann, "Le traité d'Amsterdam. Les droits de l'homme" (1997) R.T.D.E. 883, at 895–897; for breaches of the principle of democracy, see Verhoeven, "How Democratic Need European Union Members Be? Some Thoughts After Amsterdam" (1998) E.L.Rev. 217–234. Art. I–59 of the EU Constitution mentions a serious and persistent breach by a Member State of "the values mentioned in Art. I-2", thereby referring to the same list of values complemented by "respect for human dignity, including the rights of persons belonging to minorities" (see para. 5–007, *supra*).

[53] For a detailed study of the possibility of suspending Member States, see Schmitt von Sydow, "Liberté, démocratie, droits fondementaux et Etat de droit: analyses de l'article 7 du traité EU" (2001) R.D.U.E. 285–328. The Commission is convinced that this possibility should not have to be applied, see the Commission's communication to the Council and the European Parliament of October 15, 2003 on Art. 7 of the EU Treaty: "Respect for and promotion of the values on which the Union is based" (COM (2003) 606 final). Abstentions by members of the Council present in person or by representative do not prevent the adoption of a decision under Art. 7(2) (Art. 7(5)). The European Parliament acts by a two-thirds majority of the votes cast, representing a majority of its members (Art. 7(6)).

The Treaty of Nice supplemented this procedure by a warning procedure under which the Council may determine that there is a "clear risk" of a serious breach by a Member State of the said principles and address appropriate recommendations to that State. This requires a reasoned proposal by one-third of the Member States, by the European Parliament or by the Commission which the Council (in its usual composition and again without taking into account the vote of the representative of the government of the Member State in question) must adopt by a majority of four-fifths of its members after obtaining the assent of the European Parliament (new first para. of Art. 7 of the EU Treaty). The Council must hear the Member State concerned and must regularly verify that the grounds on which such a determination was made continue to apply. Under this protracted procedure, the Council may also call on independent persons to submit within a reasonable time limit a report on the situation in the Member State in question. This procedure affords a legal basis for Member States to act where the political situation in a Member State is at risk of no longer affording all the guarantees for the protection of fundamental rights.[54]

Within one month from the date of the determination that there is a "clear risk" of a "serious and persistent breach", the Court of Justice may, at the request of the Member State concerned, rule on whether the purely procedural stipulations of Art. 7 have been complied with (EU Treaty, Art. 46, point (e)). The Treaty does not specify that there must have been a determination of a clear risk of a serious breach of the principles set out in Art. 6(1) before the Council can determine that a serious and persistent breach exists.

When the Council has determined that there is a serious and persistent breach, it may decide by a qualified majority to suspend certain rights.[55] Under Art. 7(3) of the EU Treaty, the Council can decide to suspend

---

[54] A rather extreme example is afforded by the reaction of 14 Member States on January 31, 2000 following the formation of a government including an extreme right-wing party in Austria where bilateral contacts with members of the Austrian Government were broken off. See Gilliaux, "L'Union européenne à l'épreuve de gouvernements liberticides?" (2000) J.T. 449–454; Schmahl, "Die Reaktionen auf den Einzug der Freiheitlichen Partei Österreichs in das österreichische Regierungskabinett" (2000) EuR 819–835; Leidenmühler, "Zur Legalität der Massnahmen gegen die österreichische Bundesregierung" (2000) Zeitschrift für öffentliches Recht 299–322; Regan, "Are EU Sanctions Against Austria Legal?" (2000) Zeitschrift für öffentliches Recht 323–336. Following a situation report drawn up by a number of "wise men", these "sanctions" were lifted. See Adamovich, "Juristische Aspekte der 'Sanktionen' der EU-14 und des 'Weisenberichtes'" (2001) Eu.GR.Z. 89–92; Hummer, "The End of EU Sanctions Against Austria—A Precedent for New Sanctions Procedures?" (2000/01) European Legal Forum 77–83; Burchill, "The Promotion and Protection of Democracy by Regional Organisations in Europe: The Case of Austria" (2001) E.Pub.L. 79–102.

[55] The Council decides without taking into account the vote of the representative of the government of the Member State in question. Art. 7 of the EU Treaty and Art. 309 of the EC Treaty define the applicable "qualified majority" as the same proportion of the weighted votes of the members of the Council concerned as is laid down in Art. 205(2) of the EC Treaty.

certain of the rights deriving from the application of that Treaty, including the voting rights of the representative of the government in question in the Council. Where voting rights are suspended in this way, they are also suspended with regard to the EC Treaty (EC Treaty, Art. 309(1)). Under Art. 309(2) of the EC Treaty, the Council may also suspend certain of the rights deriving from the application of the EC Treaty (also by a qualified majority vote).

The Council has to take into account the possible consequences of such a suspension on the rights and obligations of natural and legal persons. The obligations of the Member State in question under the EU and EC Treaties continue in any case to be binding on that State (EU Treaty, Art. 7(3), and EC Treaty, Art. 309(2)). Subsequently, the Council may decide by a qualified majority to vary or revoke the suspension of rights in response to changes in the situation which led to its being imposed (EU Treaty, Art. 7(4), and EC Treaty, Art. 309(3)).

Part III

THE ACTORS OF THE EUROPEAN UNION

CHAPTER 10

THE INSTITUTIONS AND BODIES OF THE UNION

Institutional framework. The Union is served by a single institutional **10–001** framework (EU Treaty, Art. 3). The institutions of the Union are the institutions and bodies established by or by virtue of the EC Treaty and the EAEC Treaty and the bodies established by or by virtue of the EU Treaty ("Community" as opposed to "non-Community" institutions and bodies).

The "institutions" in the strict sense of the EC Treaty are the European Parliament, the Council, the Commission, the Court of Justice and the Court of Auditors (EC Treaty, Art. 7(1), first subpara.; EAEC Treaty, Art. 3(1), first subpara.; see para. 10–009 *et seq.*). They do not have legal personality, but act on behalf of the Communities.[1] The Council and the Commission are assisted by a European Economic and Social Committee and a Committee of the Regions (EC Treaty, Art. 7(2)). Other advisory or consultative committees sometimes have a specific role to play (see para. 10–099).

The EC Treaty established other bodies which carry out their duties as legal persons in their own right: the European Central Bank (ECB; EC Treaty, Art. 8), and the European Investment Bank (EIB; EC Treaty, Art. 9). In addition, the Communities have a number of bodies, established by or pursuant to the Treaties and with or without legal personality. Since both those bodies and the ECB and the EIB are bodies of the Community, their acts are subject to judicial review by the Court of Justice in the same way as those of the institutions.[2]

In so far as the Treaties or the statutes annexed to them do not regulate their operation and establishment, Community institutions and bodies have the power to organise their internal operation.

Some Union bodies are not based on the Community Treaties, but have been established by or by virtue of the EU Treaty, in particular the European Council, some committees within the Council, Europol and Eurojust (see para. 10–112).

---

[1] For the position of the Communities in the legal systems of the Member States, see para. 10–113, *infra*, and at international level, see para. 19–002 *et seq.*

[2] ECJ, Case 294/83 *Les Verts v European Parliament* [1986] E.C.R. 1339, para. 23; ECJ, Case C–15/00 *Commission v European Investment Bank* [2003] I–7281, para. 75; for the bodies of the Community, see paras 14–064 and 14–066, *infra*.

10–002 Constitution. The EU Constitution will put all the institutions and bodies of the Union on a uniform legal footing. Under the EU Constitution, the institutional framework of the Union will consist of the European Parliament, the European Council, the Council, the Commission and the Court of Justice.[3] As a result, the European Council will be included among the "institutions" of the Union. Although this list does not include the Court of Auditors, that body is nevertheless referred to as an "institution" of the Union, likewise the European Central Bank.

I. THE EUROPEAN COUNCIL

10–003 Tasks. Since 1974 the Heads of State or Government of the Member States meet a few times a year at "summit conferences" (see para. 2–018). Art. 2 of the Single European Act enshrined this meeting in the Treaties under the name of the "European Council".[4] The EU Treaty conferred on the European Council the task of providing "the Union with the necessary impetus for its development" and of defining "the general political guidelines" (Art. 4, first para.). In addition, the European Council has some specific tasks in the context of the Communities' decision-making process[5] and in the context of the CFSP.[6]

10–004 Composition. The second para. of Art. 4 of the EU Treaty lays down the composition of the European Council, which, since 1983, has consisted of the Heads of State or Government of the Member States and the President of the Commission, assisted by the Ministers of Foreign Affairs of the Member States and a Member of the Commission.[7] That provision

---

[3] EU Constitution, Art. I–19(1).

[4] For a detailed discussion of the European Council, see Werts, *The European Council* (Amsterdam, Asser Institute, 1992), 377 pp.; Taulegne, *Le Conseil européen* (Presses Universitaires de France, Paris, 1993), 504 pp.; Glaesner, "Der Europäische Rat" (1994) EuR. 22–34.

[5] It is to discuss a conclusion on the broad lines of the economic policies of the Member States and the Community (EC Treaty, Art. 99(2)) and to adopt conclusions on the employment situation in the Community (EC Treaty, Art. 128(1)); see Martenczuk, "Der Europäische Rat und die Wirtschafts- und Währungsunion" (1998) EuR. 151–177. The European Central Bank has to give it an annual report on the activities of the European System of Central Banks and monetary policy (EC Treaty, first subpara. of Art. 113(3)). It also has to receive annual reports from the Commission and the Council on the employment situation in the Community and on the implementation of the guidelines for employment (EC Treaty, Art. 128(5)) and from the Commission on the application of Art. 5 of the EC Treaty pursuant to the fifth indent of point 9 of the Protocol (No.30) annexed to the EC Treaty on the application of the principles of subsidiarity and proportionality ([1997] O.J. C340/105).

[6] The European Council shall define the principles of and general guidelines for the common foreign and security policy (EU Treaty, Art. 13(1) and (2)). The European Council may decide on the progressive framing of a common defence policy, which might lead to a common defence. In that event, it is to recommend to the Member States the adoption of the relevant decisions in accordance with their respective constitutional requirements (EU Treaty, Art. 17(1)).

[7] See the Solemn Declaration of Stuttgart, June 19, 1983 ((1983) 6 EC Bull. point 2.1.1) and Art. 2 of the Single European Act. The European Council is to be distinguished from the "Council meeting in the composition of the Heads of State or Government", para. 10–039, *infra*.

confirmed the practice that the European Council "shall meet at least twice a year, under the chairmanship of the Head of State or Government of the Member State which holds the Presidency of the Council". The President of the European Council invites the Economic and Finance Ministers to participate in European Council meetings when the European Council is discussing matters relating to economic and monetary union.[8] The European Council has laid down its own rules of procedure.[9] Irrespective of the matter in question, the European Council invariably takes its decisions by consensus. Each Member State presiding over the Council used to organise meetings of the European Council in its own territory. From 2002 onwards, one European Council meeting per Presidency was to be held in Brussels. As from the most recent accession of new Member States, it is the intention that all European Council meetings will be held in Brussels.[10]

Operation. The European Council is not an institution of the Communities **10–005** and (apart from the exceptions mentioned above) takes no formal part in Community decision-making. The institution of the European Council therefore does not mean that the Community institutions are subject to a higher-ranking intergovernmental institution. As long ago as 1974, the European Council stated that the arrangements regarding the European Council did not in any way affect the rules and procedures laid down in the Community Treaties.[11]

On the political level, the institutionalisation of the meetings of the Heads of State or of Government did pose a threat to the position of the Commission and the Council. The subjects on which the European Council was to confer were initially prepared by national civil servants, whilst the Commission was involved in the meetings only passively, even so far as Community matters were concerned. From 1985 onwards, the Commission itself began to take more initiatives within the European Council.[12] In addition, the Council's role was also weakened in that crucial decisions which that institution was empowered to take in principle by a majority vote were often left to the European Council, which had to find a consensus. The trend became even clearer after 1987 when decision-making in the Council was no longer by consensus, as a result of the 1966

---

[8] See Declaration No.4 of the signatories of the EU Treaty on Part Three, Title VI [now Title VII], of the Treaty establishing the European Community.

[9] See Annex I to the Conclusions of the European Council held on June 21 and 22, 2002 in Seville ((2002) 6 EU Bull. point I.27); before then, see the Communiqué of the Heads of State or Government meeting in Paris on December 9 and 10, 1974 ((1974) 12 EC Bull. point 1104(3)); Decision of the European Council meeting in London ((1977) 6 EC Bull. point 2.3.1); Solemn Declaration of Stuttgart (n.7, *supra*), point 1.6.1.

[10] See Declaration (No. 22) annexed to the Treaty of Nice on the venue for European Councils ([2001] O.J. C80/85), according to which this would be the case "when the Union comprises 18 members".

[11] Communiqué of the Heads of State of or Government meeting in Paris on December 9 and 10, 1974 (n.9, *supra*), (3).

[12] Werts (n.4, *supra*), s.56, at 140–151.

"Luxembourg compromise".[13] The Treaty of Amsterdam institutionalised this practice as regards the CFSP by providing that a vote is not to be taken if a member of the Council declares that, for important and stated reasons of national policy, it intends to oppose a measure which would otherwise be adopted by a qualified majority; the Council, acting by a qualified majority, may then request that the matter be referred to the European Council for decision by unanimity.[14]

10–006 Parliamentary control. The European Parliament is informed after the event of the European Council's activities. Initially, the European Parliament obtained information about the activities of the European Council only on the occasion of the report which the Minister of Foreign Affairs of the Member State holding the Presidency and the President of the Commission make before the Parliament at the end of each Presidency. Starting in 1981, the Head of State or Government occupying the Presidency of the European Council has come before Parliament to report, initially half-yearly, at present after every European Council.[15] Under the third para. of Art. 4 of the EU Treaty, the European Council is under a duty to submit to the European Parliament a report after each of its meetings and a yearly written report on the progress achieved by the Union.

10–007 Status of decisions. The legal force of the "acts" which the European Council adopts differs depending on the subject-matter in question. In areas coming within the sphere of competence of the Communities, the European Council does not take decisions of Community law. In theory, the European Council may act as the Council, because it is composed of a representative at ministerial level of each Member State (*cf.* EC Treaty, Art. 203, first para.; see para. 10–039). What is then required is that the procedural rules laid down in the Treaties are complied with, in particular a vote on the basis of a Commission proposal, having regard to the prerogatives of the European Parliament. In practice, the European Council has never applied the decision-making procedures laid down in the Treaties and decisions of the European Council are transformed by Community institutions into decisions of Community law.[16]

---

[13] See the discussion of the operation of the Council, para. 10–046, *infra*.
[14] EU Treaty, Art. 23(2), second subpara. (CFSP, see para. 15–002); EU Treaty, Art. 27c, second para. (enhanced co-operation in connection with the CFSP, see para. 9–007).
[15] Werts (n.4, *supra*), s.58, at 158–159. See also the Solemn Declaration of Stuttgart (n.7, *supra*), point 2.1.4.
[16] Admittedly the European Council held in Milan on June 29, 1985 adopted by a majority vote against a minority the decision to initiate the procedure provided for in Art. 236 of the EEC Treaty and to consult the Parliament on amending the Treaty. In so doing, it disregarded the Council's Rules of Procedure, which provide that an agenda item must be already on the agenda before a decision can be taken. However, the formal decision was taken by the Council, after consulting the Parliament, in July 1985. See De Ruyt, *L'Acte unique européen* (Editions de l'Université de Bruxelles, Brussels, 1987) at 62.

The "impetus" and "guidelines" which, according to the first paragraph of Art. 4 of the EU Treaty, the European Council is to give, are not legally binding on the institutions of the Communities, since the incorporation of the European Council into the EU Treaty did not change the powers conferred on the institutions by the Community Treaties.[17] A decision of the European Council therefore does not prevent a Member State from taking up the matter again within the Council.[18] This is also the case where, in the context of the Union's CFSP, the Council takes a decision "on the basis of the general guidelines adopted by the European Council" (EU Treaty, Art. 13(3)) or implements common strategies decided on by the European Council (EU Treaty, Art. 13(2) and (3)). Nevertheless, it is clear in practice that, in all these cases, the Council only gives legal effect to what the European Council has decided on the political level.[19] Also in the sphere of economic and monetary policy, some European Council resolutions embody in practice determinative policy choices which direct the action of the Community institutions and the Member States.[20] Moreover, CFSP action on the part of the European Council has legal effects inasmuch as whenever the European Council has decided on a common strategy, the Council may implement it by a qualified majority vote.[21]

The European Council may also pronounce and take a decision on other fields deemed to be of interest for the purposes of European integration. Although agreements may be concluded in this connection or other binding

---

[17] See Art. 47 of the EU Treaty, para. 3–015, *supra*. See also Curtin, "The Constitutional Structure of the Union: A Europe of Bits and Pieces" (1993) C.M.L.R. 17, at 27; VerLoren van Themaat, "De constitutionele problematiek van een Europese politieke Unie" (1991) S.E.W. 436, at 442. Nevertheless, Art. 99(2) of the EC Treaty provides for the adoption by the Council of a recommendation setting out the broad guidelines of the economic policies of the Member States and the Community "on the basis of" the European Council's conclusion on those guidelines. Although, in view of its composition, the Council will perhaps be at the same view as the European Council, it is not under a legal obligation to be so. See Everling, "Reflections on the Structure of the European Union" (1992) C.M.L.R. 1053, at 1062. This is also true of the Council where it draws up guidelines for employment policy "on the basis of the conclusions of the European Council" (EC Treaty, Art. 128(2)).

[18] See, *inter alia*, Werts (n.4, *supra*), s.53, at 125–130.

[19] See also the provision whereby common strategies are to set out their objectives and duration, together with "the means *to be made available* by the Union and the Member States" (EU Treaty, Art. 13(2), second subpara. —emphasis added).

[20] See the resolutions of the European Council of June 16, 1997 on the establishment of an exchange-rate mechanism in the third stage of economic and monetary union ([1997] O.J. C236/5), on the Stability and Growth Pact ([1997] O.J. C236/1), on economic policy co-ordination in Stage 3 of EMU and on Treaty Arts 109 and 109b [now Arts 111 and 113] of the EC Treaty ([1998] O.J. C35/1) and of January 19, 1998 on denominations and technical specifications of Euro coins intended for circulation ([1998] O.J. C35/5). The scenario for the changeover to the single currency approved by the European Council on December 15 and 16, 1995 at Madrid also turned out to be of major importance ((1995) 12 EU Bull. points I–3 and I.49). For the growing importance of this type of resolution, see Martenczuk (n.5, *supra*), at 174–175.

[21] EU Treaty, Art. 13(2). See Timmermans, "Het Verdrag van Amsterdam. Enkele inleidende kanttekeningen" (1997) S.E.W. 344, at 347.

instruments adopted, as yet all the decisions taken by the European Council have been "resolutions" of a non-binding nature.[22]

10–008 Constitution. As noted above, the EU Constitution includes the European Council among the "institutions" of the Union. In order to avoid confusion between the European Council and the Council, the EU Constitution makes it clear that the European Council provides impetus and defines general political directions and priorities but "shall not exercise legislative functions" (Art. I–21(1)).[23]

After the entry into force of the Constitution, the European Council will consist of the Heads of State or Government of the Member States, together with its President and the President of the Commission (EU Constitution, Art. I–21(2)). The President of the European Council will not be a Head of State or Government of a Member State, but is to be elected by the European Council, by a qualified majority, for a term of two and a half years, renewable once (EU Constitution, Art. I–22(1)). The EU Constitution will leave it to the members of the European Council to decide whether they wish to be assisted by a Minister or, in the case of the President of the Commission, by a European Commissioner. The Union Minister for Foreign Affairs will be entitled to take part in the work of the European Council (EU Constitution, Art. I–21(2)). Since the President of the European Council may not hold a national mandate (EU Constitution, Art. I–22(3)), he or she will perform a full-time job, which will consist mainly of preparing the work of the European Council and chairing it (EU Constitution, Art. I–22(2)).

The European Council will take its decisions by consensus "[e]xcept where the Constitution provides otherwise" (EU Constitution, Art. I–21(4)). In fact, it may take some decisions by a unanimous vote or by a qualified majority.[24] When a vote is held, neither its President nor the

---

[22] The decision that the European Council meeting in Edinburgh on December 11 and 12, 1992 took concerning certain problems raised by Denmark on the Treaty on European Union (para. 3–011, *infra*) has certain legal effects and is therefore entitled "decision of the Heads of State or Government, meeting within the European Council". See Curtin and van Ooik, "De bijzondere positie van Denemarken in de Europese Unie" (1993) S.E.W. 675, at 677–678.

[23] At the substantive level, the European Council will continue to have the task of defining general guidelines (although this task will be extended to the "area of freedom, security and justice" and the Union's external action in general: Arts III–258 and III–293(1)) and of deciding on certain institutional matters (*e.g.* EU Constitution, Arts I–20(2), second subpara., I–24(4), I–26(6), I–27(1) and I–28(1)). In addition, the European Council is to act as the "constituent authority" in so far as it may decide, in respect of certain provisions of Part III, to replace a special legislative procedure by the ordinary legislative procedure and voting by unanimity by qualified majority voting (EU Constitution, Arts I–40(7), III–300(3) and IV–444).

[24] Voting in the European Council will be subject to the same arrangements as apply (in their amended version) to voting by unanimity and qualified majority voting in the Council (para. 10–054, *infra*): EU Constitution, Art. I–25(3); compare Art. III–341(1) with Arts III–343(1) and (3).

President of the Commission may vote.[25] This system will allow the European Council to take the decisions that the EC Treaty at present reserves to the Council (where the Commission has no right to vote) meeting in the composition of the Heads of State or Government. At the administrative level, the European Council will be assisted by the General Secretariat of the Council (EU Constitution, Art. III–341(4)).

II. THE INSTITUTIONS OF THE UNION

Institutions. As noted above, five bodies have the status of "institutions" **10–009** (the European Parliament, the Council, the Commission, the Court of Justice and the Court of Auditors)[26] and, as a result, special legal status.[27] The powers, composition and manner of operation of each institution are governed by the Treaties. Both in the Community and non-Community spheres, the institutions act within the limits of the powers conferred on them by the Treaties (EU Treaty, Art. 5; see also EC Treaty, Art. 7(1), second subpara.). An overview will be given below of each institution's powers, composition, operation and internal organisation, including a brief account of the changes proposed by the EU Constitution.[28] It is recalled that under the EU Constitution, the European Council will also have the status of an "institution" (see para. 10–002).

A. THE EUROPEAN PARLIAMENT

Designation. The European Parliament[29] was originally established as the **10–010** "Common Assembly" of the ECSC and as the "Assembly" of the EEC and the EAEC, which the Convention on certain institutions common to the European Communities (see para. 1–011) merged as long ago as 1957 into

---

[25] EU Constitution, Art. I–25(4). Having regard to the heading of this provision ("Definition of qualified majority within the European Council and the Council"), it could also be argued that the President of the European Council and the President of the Commission will be precluded from voting only where the European Council decides by a qualified majority.

[26] See ECJ (order of March 17, 2004), Case C–176/03 *Commission v Council*, not yet reported (the European Economic and Social Committee does not constitute an "institution" entitled to be joined in proceedings before the Court of Justice pursuant to Art. 40 of the ECJ Statute).

[27] Any institution is entitled to bring an action for failure to act in the Court of Justice pursuant to the first para. of Art. 232 of the EC Treaty. In addition, indent (b) of the first para. of Art. 234 of the EC Treaty confers jurisdiction on the Court of Justice to give preliminary rulings on the validity and interpretation of acts of the institutions. Nevertheless, the Treaties often confer the same legal position on other Community bodies: see, for example, the ECB in Arts 232 and 234 of the EC Treaty and the extension of privileges and immunities to cover other bodies: paras 10–151 and 10–153, *infra*.

[28] The EU Constitution does not provide for any notable changes as far as the Court of Auditors is concerned.

[29] See in general Corbett, Jacobs and Shackleton, *The European Parliament* (Harper, London, 2000) 363 pp. For the website of the European Parliament, see *www.europarl.eu.int/*.

a single Assembly for the three Communities. It was not long before the Assembly started to refer to itself as the "European Parliament".[30] The title "European Parliament" did not gain general acceptance until the Single European Act provided that the institutions of the European Communities were to be "henceforth designated as referred to hereafter" (Single European Act, Art. 3(1)).[31] Since then, the title has been used in all acts and has been systematically introduced into other Treaty provisions by the EU Treaty.

1. Powers

a. Nature

10–011 Representative assembly. Within the institutional framework of the ECSC Treaty, the European Parliament played the modest role of supervising the High Authority.[32] Since the adoption of the EEC and EAEC Treaties[33] and the subsequent amendments of and additions to the Community Treaties and the EU Treaty, the European Parliament's powers are:

(1) to advise;

(2) to take part in Community and Union decision-making;

(3) to pronounce upon certain matters relating to the Union's external relations;

(4) to adopt the EU budget in co-operation with the Council; and

(5) to supervise other institutions and bodies of the Union.

A brief analysis follows of these powers on the basis of which the European Parliament secures at Union level respect for the fundamental democratic principle that "the peoples should take part in the exercise of power through the intermediary of a representative assembly".[34]

10–012 Voice of citizens. Nevertheless the European Parliament's role does not lie only in giving political expression to the will of the democratic majority within the Union, it also gives citizens of the Union and other persons affected by action taken by the Union a means of making their views known on the policy which is being conducted.

---

[30] Resolutions of March 20, 1958, [April 20, 1958] J.O. 6 ("European Parliamentary Assembly") and of March 30, 1962, [1962] J.O. 1045 ("European Parliament").

[31] See Bieber, Pantalis and Schoo, "Implications of the Single Act for the European Parliament" (1986) C.M.L.R. 767, at 770–772.

[32] ECSC Treaty, Art. 20.

[33] See Art. 137 of the EEC Treaty and Art. 107 of the EAEC Treaty: "The Assembly . . . shall exercise the advisory and supervisory powers which are conferred upon it by this Treaty".

[34] ECJ, Case 138/79 *Roquette Frères v Council* [1980] E.C.R. 3333, para. 33, and ECJ, Case 139/79 *Maïzena v Council* [1980] E.C.R. 3393, para. 34; ECJ, Case C–300/89 *Commission v Council* [1991] E.C.R. I–2867, para. 20. For the (growing) say of the European Parliament in decision-making, see also paras 14–020 *et seq.*

In the first place, Members of the European Parliament ("MEPs") may be informed of problems personally. Secondly, citizens of the Union and any natural or legal person residing or having its registered office in a Member State has the right to petition the European Parliament (EC Treaty, Art. 21 and Art. 194). As a result, the EC Treaty has transformed a "custom"[35] into a right of petition protected by the Treaty.[36] Beneficiaries of the right may "address, individually or in association with other citizens or persons, a petition to the European Parliament on a matter which comes within the Community's fields of activity and which affects him, her or it directly".[37] Pursuant to its power of internal organisation, the European Parliament also entertains petitions from other persons and petitions which do not comply with all the requirements of Art. 194 of the EC Treaty.[38] Lastly, persons qualifying to exercise the right of petition under the Treaty may also submit complaints of maladministration in the activities of Community institutions or bodies to the European Ombudsman, who is closely connected with the European Parliament (EC Treaty, Art. 195; see para. 10–107).

As the voice of the citizens of the Union, the European Parliament represents their interests in the exercise of its various powers.

b. Survey of powers

(1) *Provision of advice*

Resolutions. The European Parliament is entitled to give advice on any **10–013** question concerning the Communities and to adopt resolutions on such

---

[35] See the exchanges of letters between the European Parliament, the Council and the Commission of the European Communities of April 12, 1989 on the right to petition, [1989] O.J. C120/90. The Rules of Procedure of the European Parliament govern the right of petition.

[36] See Guckelberger, "Das Petitionsrecht zum Europäischen Parlament sowie das Recht zur Anrufung des Europäischen Bürgerbeauftragten im Europa der Bürger" (2003) D.ö.V. 829–838; Maniatis, "Le règlement des pétitions au Parlement européen" (2002) R.D.U.E. 133–145; Baviera, "Les pétitions au Parlement européen et le médiateur européen" (2001) R.M.C.U.E. 129–135; Marias, "The Right to Petition the European Parliament after Maastricht" (1994) E.L.R. 169–183; Pliakos, "Les conditions d'exercice du droit de pétition" (1993) C.D.E. 317–350. *cf.* Art. 44 of the Charter of Fundamental Rights; see Holdscheidt, "Die Ausgestaltung des Petitionsrechts in der EU-Grundrechtecharta" (2002) EuR. 441–448.

[37] The responsible parliamentary committee decides whether a given petition is admissible (EP Rules of Procedure, r.189(5) and (6)). The formal requirements for the admissibility of a petition are that it must show each petitioner's name, nationality and permanent address and must be written in one of the official languages (or a translation or summary drawn up in an official language must be attached) (EP Rules of Procedure, r.189(2) and (3)).

[38] As far as the substantive admissibility of petitions is concerned, the responsible parliamentary committee simply ascertains whether petitions "fall within the sphere of activities of the *European Union*" (EP Rules of Procedure, r.189(5), emphasis supplied). Art. 194 of the EC Treaty does not cover the non-Community matters dealt with in Titles V and VI of the EU Treaty (see also Art. 28(1) and Art. 41(1) of the EU Treaty). On the subject of the liberal approach taken to the former admissibility requirements, see the works cited in n. 36, *supra*. Petitions addressed by other persons are registered and filed separately (see EP Rules of Procedure, r.189(10)). See the European Parliament's resolution of May 15, 2001 on the petition at the dawn of the 21st Century, [2002] O.J. C34E/89.

questions.[39] By virtue of its power of internal organisation, the European Parliament itself determines when it meets and fixes its agenda. Even where the power to act lies with other institutions or with national governments, the European Parliament is entitled to "invite them to act".[40] This also applies to the Union's non-Community policy, in respect of which the EU Treaty expressly provides for the European Parliament to hold an annual debate (Art. 21, second para., and Art. 39(3)).

(2) Participation in decision-making

10–014 **Various procedures.** The European Parliament "participate[s] in the process leading up to the adoption of Community acts by exercising its powers under the procedures laid down in Art. 251 [co-decision] and Art. 252 [co-operation] and by giving its assent or delivering advisory opinions" (EC Treaty, Art. 192, first para.). Which of this range of procedures affording the Parliament a greater or lesser say in decision-making applies in practice is determined by the Treaty article constituting the legal basis of the proposed act (see paras 14–020 et seq.). The Court of Justice has held that participation of the European Parliament in Community decision-making is an essential procedural requirement with which other institutions must comply, failing which the act adopted may be annulled.[41]

The European Parliament may, acting by a majority of its Members, request the Commission to submit any appropriate proposal on matters on which it considers that a Community act is required for the purpose of implementing the Treaty (EC Treaty, Art. 192, second para.), but this does not amount to a genuine right to initiate legislation (see para. 14–018). Since the European Parliament does not have a general right of initiative and participation in decision-making, it does not have fully-fledged legislative powers. However, the European Parliament is sufficiently involved in the specific legislative processes leading to the passage of legislation under Arts 251 and 252 of the EC Treaty, and is sufficiently involved in the general democratic supervision of the activities of the European Community, to constitute part of the "legislature" for the purposes of Art. 3 of Protocol No. 1 to the ECHR.[42]

In decision-making with regard to the CFSP, the European Parliament has only an (unenforceable) right to be consulted on "the main aspects and the basic choices"; in the case of PJCC, the Council consults the European

---

[39] ECJ, Case 230/81 *Luxembourg v European Parliament* [1983] E.C.R. 255, para. 39.
[40] *ibid.* (with regard to national governments).
[41] See ECJ, Case 138/79 *Roquette Frères* [1980] E.C.R. 3333 and Case 139/79 *Maïzena* [1980] E.C.R. 3393 (n.34, *supra*) on breaches of the right to be consulted.
[42] Judgment of the European Court of Human Rights of February 18, 1999 in Case No.24833/94 *Matthews v UK. cf.* the joint dissenting opinion relying on Dashwood, "The Limits of European Community Powers" (1996) E.L.R. 113, at 127, "the Community has no legislature only a legislative process in which the different political institutions have different parts to play" (see the dissenting opinion, paras 4–7).

Parliament before adopting framework decisions, decisions, conventions and measures implementing conventions.[43]

Neither does the European Parliament have a decisive say in the procedure for amending the Treaties.[44] The role of "constituent assembly" falls in full to the Member States.[45]

(3) Involvement in external relations

International agreements. As far as the Union's external relations are **10–015** concerned, it was only as a result of the Single European Act and, subsequently, the EU Treaty that the European Parliament was given significant powers in this field, in particular in connection with the conclusion by the Community of international agreements. Since the Single European Act entered into force, the European Parliament has to give its assent to association agreements (EC Treaty, Art. 300(3), second subpara., and Art. 310) and to the accession of new Member States to the Community, now the Union (Art. 237 of the EEC Treaty, replaced by Art. 49 of the EU Treaty). The EU Treaty extended the requirement for the European Parliament to give its assent to international agreements establishing a specific institutional framework, having important budgetary implications for the Community (now the EU budget) or entailing amendment of an act adopted under the co-decision procedure (EC Treaty, Art. 300(3), second para.). In addition, the European Parliament is consulted on the conclusion of all other international agreements, with the exception of those coming under the common commercial policy (EC Treaty, Art. 300(3), first para.). Since the Treaty of Nice the European Parliament may also obtain the opinion of the Court of Justice as to whether an international agreement envisaged is compatible with the EC Treaty (EC Treaty, Art. 300(6)).

Outside the ambit of the Community pillar of the Union, the European Parliament's prerogatives in the field of external relations are also confined to the right to be consulted and informed and to ask questions of the Council and make recommendations to it (EU Treaty, Art. 21 and Art. 39).

(4) Budgetary authority

Finances. Ever since the First Treaty on Budgetary Provisions, the **10–016** European Parliament and the Council have together formed the budgetary

---

[43] See EU Treaty, Art. 21, first para. and Art. 39(1). Art. 192 of the EC Treaty does not apply to decision-making in connection with the CFSP or PJCC (EU Treaty, Art. 28(1) and Art. 41(1)).

[44] At most, the European Parliament must be consulted, except in the case of one specific constitutional procedure where its assent is required (EC Treaty, Art. 190(4)). See paras 7–004–7–009, *supra*.

[45] The procedure for amending the Treaties (EU Treaty, Art. 48) and some other specific procedures require ratification by the Member States "in accordance with their respective constitutional requirements"; see paras 11–002–11–003, *infra*.

authority of what is now the Union (for the adoption of the budget, see para. 10–130 *et seq.*). The European Parliament has the last word on non-compulsory expenditure and may also reject the budget in its entirety. It has made use of these powers on several occasions in order to assert its views in respect of the most diverse policy matters.

These powers also enable the European Parliament to increase its limited say in decision-making with regard to the CFSP and PJCC where action of the Union is charged to the EU budget.[46]

The European Parliament's power to give a discharge to the Commission in respect of the implementation of the budget reinforces the European Parliament's supervision of the Commission.

(5) *Supervision of other institutions and bodies*

10–017 **Supervision of Commission.** The Commission is politically answerable to the European Parliament. This is reflected in the first place in the European Parliament's right to put oral or written questions to the Commission (EC Treaty, Art. 197, third para.). Oral questions are placed on the agenda for a Parliamentary sitting and must be referred to the Commission at least a week beforehand.[47] The Commission is obliged to have one of its Members answer them. Written questions must be answered within six weeks and the answers are published together with the questions.[48] Question time is held at each part-session, at which a Member of the Commission briefly answers questions submitted in advance and two concise supplementary questions.[49]

The Commission is also required to draw up an annual report on the activities of the European Union and other reports for presentation to the European Parliament[50] and to keep it regularly informed about the CFSP and PJCC.[51] The Commission is also under a duty to submit a number of reports to the European Parliament and to give it hearings in connection with the latter institution's supervision of the implementation of the budget.[52] At the request of the President of the European Parliament, the

---

[46] para.10–114, *infra*.

[47] EP Rules of Procedure, r.108(1) and (2).

[48] EP Rules of Procedure, r.110. They are published in the *Official Journal* (Part C). Questions requiring an immediate answer but no detailed research (priority questions) should be answered within three weeks, other questions within six: r.110(4) and (5).

[49] r.109 and the guidelines on the conduct of question time set out in Annex II to the EP Rules of Procedure.

[50] For the general report, see EC Treaty, Arts 200 and 212, and EAEC Treaty, Art. 125. See also Art. 145 of the EC Treaty, which requires a separate chapter on social developments to be included. There are other reports as well; see n.230, *infra*.

[51] EU Treaty, Art. 21, first para., and EP Rules of Procedure, r.89; EU Treaty, Art. 39(2).

[52] EC Treaty, Art. 275 (see para. 10–140, *infra*) and Art. 276 (see para 10–143, *infra*).

Commission is to provide all information necessary for the exercise of the European Parliament's supervisory tasks.[53]

The European Parliament has the right to pass a motion of censure on the activities of the Commission (EC Treaty, Art. 201). Such a motion may be submitted by a tenth of its Members.[54] However, a vote cannot—publicly—be held on such a motion until at least three days after it has been submitted. In order for a motion to be carried, it must obtain a two-thirds majority of the votes cast, representing a majority of MEPs. If such a motion is carried, the Members of the Commission have to resign as a body. Pending their replacement, they continue to deal with current business only. Owing to the onerous requirement for a majority and the collective nature of the sanction, this method of control is in the realm of what is only theoretically possible[55] and has to be kept in reserve for genuinely exceptional situations.[56] Following the collective resignation of the Commission in March 1999 (see para. 10–066), a discussion was

---

[53] For the procedures, see Annex III (Forwarding of confidential information to the European Parliament) to the framework agreement of July 5, 2000 on relations between Parliament and the Commission ([2001] O.J. C121/122, and (2000) 7/8 EU Bull. point 2.2.1), which is itself appended to the EP Rules of Procedure as Annex XIII. That agreement does not limit the right of Members of Parliament to put questions to the Commission, see CFI (order of January 17, 2002), Case T–236/00 *Stauner v European Parliament and Commission* [2002] E.C.R. II–135, paras 59–62. For criticism of the Council, see Rodriques, "La paix des braves? A propos du nouvel accord-cadre 'Commission-Parlement européen'" (2000) R.M.C.U.E. 590, at 592.

[54] EP Rules of Procedure, r.100(1).

[55] The European Parliament has held eight votes on motions of censure, but a motion has never been carried: see Debates of the European Parliament, 1972, 156, p.8, and 156, p.52 (motion withdrawn without being put to a vote), 1976, 204, p.121 (no majority), 1976, 210, p.287 (motion withdrawn without being put to a vote), 1977, 215, p.63 (no majority), 1990, 386, p.85, and 386, p.316 (no majority), [1991] O.J. C240/167 (no majority), [1993] O.J. C21/30, and C21/124 (no majority), [1997] O.J. C85/103 (following a report of a committee of inquiry on "mad cow disease": no majority), [1999] O.J. C104/97 (following allegations of fraud, mismanagement and nepotism made against individual Commissioners of the Santer Commission: no majority) and *Europe*, No.8699, May 5, 2004, p.7 (following allegations of mismanagement in Eurostat: no majority). On January 14, 1999, the European Parliament failed by a relatively narrow margin to obtain the necessary majority to pass the motion of censure on the Santer Commission. As a result, the Parliament proposed that a committee of independent experts be set up under the auspices of the Parliament and the Commission to examine the way in which the Commission detected and dealt with fraud, mismanagement and nepotism and to review Commission practices in the awarding of financial contracts (Resolution of January 14, 1999). The Committee submitted its first report to the President of the Commission on allegations regarding fraud, mismanagement and nepotism in the European Commission on March 15, 1999. Thereupon the Santer Commission decided to resign as a body (see para. 10–066).

[56] Lenaerts, "Some Reflections on the Separation of Powers in the European Community" (1991) C.M.L.R. 11, at 23. In a 1988 judgment the Court of Justice referred to the motion of censure as a means available to the European Parliament to put political pressure on the Commission to defend the Parliament's prerogatives: ECJ, Case 302/87 *European Parliament v Council* [1988] E.C.R. 5638, para. 12. In a 1990 judgment, the Court of Justice qualified its earlier judgment and held that the Parliament was entitled to bring an action for annulment to safeguard its prerogatives, in order, *inter alia*, that it should not be dependent on compelling the Commission to act: ECJ, Case C–70/88 *European Parliament v Council* [1990] E.C.R. I–2041, para. 19 (for these judgments, see n.79, *infra*).

initiated as to the possibility of compelling individual Commissioners to resign.[57] The Commission has accepted that, where the European Parliament expresses lack of confidence in a Commissioner, the President of the Commission will "examine seriously" whether he or she should request that Member to resign.[58]

Since the EU Treaty entered into force, the European Parliament has to approve the Members of the Commission proposed for nomination by the Member States; since the Amsterdam Treaty, the Parliament has first to approve the nomination of the person whom the Member States propose to appoint as President of the Commission, after which the national governments may select, in agreement with the person nominated President, the other Members of the Commission (see para. 10–063). That vote of approval, together with the possibility of a motion of censure being carried against the Commission, constitutes the cornerstone of the Commission's political accountability to the European Parliament.[59]

10–018 **Relations with the Council.** The Community Treaties do not confer any general power of supervision on the European Parliament as far as the Council is concerned. The reason for this is that members of the Council are accountable to their national parliaments. The fourth para. of Art. 197 of the EC Treaty merely provides for the Council to be "heard by the European Parliament in accordance with the conditions laid down by the Council in its Rules of Procedure".[60] Nevertheless, members of the Council customarily came before the European Parliament in order to answer questions. In 1973 the Council converted that practice into an obligation,[61] which has subsequently been extended to cover matters relating to European Political Co-operation (EPC).[62] The EU Treaty codified the right to put questions on the CFSP and JHA co-operation and it has been confirmed that the same right exists in respect of PJCC.[63] The European

---

[57] See the resolution of the European Parliament of March 23, 1999 on the resignation of the Commission and the appointment of a new Commission, [1999] O.J. C177/19.

[58] Point 10 of the framework agreement of July 5, 2000 (n.53, *supra*). See Rodriques (n.53, *supra*), at 592–594; Coutron, "Le principe de la collégialité au sein de la Commission européenne après le Traité de Nice" (2003) R.T.D.E. 247, at 265.

[59] Rules 98 and 99 of the EP Rules of Procedure refer to the "election" of the President and Members of the Commission. For a critical discussion, see Raworth, "A Timid Step Forwards: Maastricht and the Democratisation of the European Community" (1994) E.L.R. 16, at 31–32.

[60] See Council Rules of Procedure, Art. 26.

[61] See the letter from the President of the Council of March 6, 1973 on the introduction of question time ((1973) 3 EC Bull. point 2402) and the communication from the Council to the European Parliament of October 16, 1973 ((1973) 34 EP Bull.); see also the Solemn Declaration of Stuttgart, June 19, 1983 ((1986) 6 EC Bull. point 1.6.1., under 2.3.3).

[62] See the decision of the Ministers for Foreign Affairs, meeting within the framework of European Political Co-operation, of February 28, 1986 ((1986) 1 EPC Bulletin point I.86, at 108 (document No.86/090)).

[63] Art. 21, second para., and Art. 39(3). Rules 85 and 87 of the EP Rules of Procedure provide that the High Representative for the CFSP should be invited to make statements to the Parliament prior and after his or her appointment and answer questions.

Parliament has adopted rules governing written and oral questions put to the Council during question time in much the same manner as questions put to the Commission.[64]

In addition, the President of the Council has a number of obligations to provide information to the European Parliament, in particular in connection with the CFSP and PJCC.[65]

Relations with other bodies. The supervision exercised indirectly by the **10–019** European Parliament over other institutions and bodies takes the form of its right to appoint the European Ombudsman and its right to be consulted on the appointment of Members of the Court of Auditors, Members of the Executive Board of the ECB and the Director of OLAF.[66] The European Parliament further has the right to obtain information from the Court of Auditors by way of assistance in exercising its powers of control over the budget[67] and to have an annual report from the ECB.[68] The competent committee of the European Parliament is also entitled to hold hearings of the President of the ECB and of the other members of its Executive Board.[69] The European Council has to submit a report to the European Parliament after each of its meetings and on an annual basis.[70]

Inquiries . Lastly, the European Parliament's right of supervision extends **10–020** to the right to hold inquiries into alleged contraventions of Community law or maladministration in its implementation (see EC Treaty, Art. 193, first para.). Complaints relating thereto may arrive at the European Parliament *inter alia* in the form of information from other institutions or bodies,

---

[64] para. 10–017, *supra*. Questions for oral answer must, however, be submitted to the Council three weeks before the sitting. No time-limits are prescribed for questions on matters coming under Titles V and VI of the EU Treaty and the Council must reply with sufficient promptness to keep the Parliament properly informed (EP Rules of Procedure, r.108(2) and (3)).

[65] EU Treaty, Art. 21, first para., and Art. 39(2). As far as concerns the European Parliament's access to sensitive information in the field of security and defence policy, the rules laid down in the Interinstitutional Agreement between the European Parliament and the Council of November 20, 2002 apply (see para. 15–004, *infra*). In addition, the President reports on multilateral economic surveillance, just as the Commission does, and may be invited to appear before the competent parliamentary committee if the Council has made its recommendations public (EC Treaty, Art. 99(4), second subpara.). He or she is to inform the Parliament of any decision of the Council pursuant to Art. 60(2) of the EC Treaty that a Member State must amend or abolish national measures and of any sanctions imposed (EC Treaty, Art. 104(11)).

[66] See the further discussion of these Community bodies in paras 10–089, 10–103, 10–108 and 10–109, *infra*. The European Parliament expressed a wish to be involved in the appointment of Members of the Court of Justice and asked for arrangements to be made for its (former) Committee on Legal Affairs and Citizens' Rights to meet with prospective Members of the Court prior to their appointment: resolution of February 9, 1994 ([1994] O.J. C61/126).

[67] EC Treaty, Art. 248(1) and (4) and Art. 276(1) (paras 10–142–10–143, *infra*).

[68] EC Treaty, Art. 113(3), first subpara.

[69] EC Treaty, Art. 113(3), second subpara. See also Rules 106 and 111 of the EP Rules of Procedure (r.111 provides for the possibility of putting written questions to the ECB).

[70] EU Treaty, Art. 4, third para.

petitions or complaints made to the European Ombudsman.[71] Even the conduct of national authorities in implementing Community law may be the subject of an inquiry by the European Parliament.[72]

The European Parliament may organise hearings, dispatch MEPs to establish the facts of the situation *in situ* and request the Commission to submit documents, supply information and grant it access to its facilities.[73] Where the European Parliament deems it appropriate, it may refer the matter in question to the European Ombudsman.[74] At the request of a quarter of its Members, the Parliament may set up a temporary committee of inquiry. The EU Treaty took over the procedure already in use at the Parliament in Art. 193 of the EC Treaty.[75] Agreement was not reached between the Parliament, the Council and the Commission on how the Parliament's right of inquiry was to be exercised until April 1995.[76] The European Parliament determines the composition and the rules of procedure of committees of inquiry.[77]

In any event, the Member States are under a duty to co-operate with any inquiries which the European Parliament is entitled to carry out.[78]

---

[71] See the right of petition provided for in Art. 194 of the EC Treaty (para. 10–012, *supra*) and the regulations governing the European Ombudsman provided for by Art. 195 of the EC Treaty (para. 10–107, *infra*). The right of petition entails a corresponding obligation on the Parliament to accept petitions satisfying the admissibility requirements and to deal with them effectively. See Pliakos (n.36, *supra*), at 335–337.

[72] The European Parliament has no right to conduct an inquiry where "the alleged facts are being examined before a court and while the case is still subject to legal proceedings" (EC Treaty, Art. 193, first para.). The European Ombudsman is not entitled to carry out an inquiry where "the alleged facts are or have been the subject of legal proceedings" (EC Treaty, Art. 195(1), second subpara.).

[73] See EP Rules of Procedure, r.190(3) and (4) on the examination of petitions.

[74] EP Rules of Procedure, r.189(9).

[75] See the former r.109 of the EP Rules of Procedure, now r.174.

[76] Decision 95/167/EC, Euratom, ECSC of the European Parliament, the Council and the Commission of April 19, 1995 on the detailed provisions governing the exercise of the European Parliament's right of inquiry ([1995] O.J. L113/2), appended to the EP Rules of Procedure as Annex VIII.

[77] *ibid.*, Art. 2(1), second subpara. See r.174 of the EP Rules of Procedure, as amended in the light of the aforementioned decision, [1995] O.J. C269/34 (with amendment in [1995] O.J. C308/106). The European Parliament set up a committee of inquiry to consider allegations of offences committed or of maladministration under the Community transit system ([1996] O.J. C7/1; identical version in C17/47) and in connection with bovine spongiform encephalopathy (BSE or "mad cow disease") ([1996] O.J. C239/1). For the recommendations made by those committees, see (1997) 3 EU Bull. point 2.2.1 and (1997) 1/2 EU Bull. point 2.2.1, respectively. See also Beckedorf, "Das Untersuchungsrecht des Europäischen Parlaments. Eine erste Bestandsaufnahme nach zwei parlamentarischen Untersuchungen" (1997) EuR. 237–260; Blanquet, "Le contrôle parlementaire européen sur la crise de la 'vache folle'" (1998) R.M.C.U.E. 457–470.

[78] See EC Treaty, Art. 10. For co-operation with the examination of complaints, see the works cited in n.36, *supra*. However, the powers of inquiry conferred by Arts 193–195 of the EC Treaty do not apply to action pursuant to the CFSP or (with the exception of Art. 195 on the European Ombudsman) to PJCC (EU Treaty, Art. 28 and Art. 41(1)).

Legal proceedings. The European Parliament may bring proceedings **10–021** before the Court of Justice for the annulment of acts of the Council, the Commission or the ECB.[79] The Parliament may also bring an action in the Court of Justice for failure to act against the Council, the Commission or the ECB.[80] However, the prerogatives which it exercises in connection with the common foreign and security policy (CFSP; EU Treaty, Title V) and police and judicial co-operation in criminal matters (PJCC; EU Treaty, Title VI) may not be enforced by bringing proceedings in the Court of Justice.[81]

2. Composition

Direct elections. The European Parliament consists of "representatives of **10–022** the peoples of the States brought together in the Community" (EC Treaty, Art. 189). Since 1979, MEPs have been elected by direct universal suffrage. This gives the institution a democratic legitimacy which others lack.

Initially, the Parliament consisted of delegates designated by the respective national parliaments from among their members.[82] Nevertheless, the EEC Treaty itself looked forward to the direct election of the Parliament in accordance with a uniform procedure in all Member States. Art. 190(4) of the EC Treaty requires the European Parliament to draw up "proposals" to this end, after which the Council, acting unanimously and—since the EU Treaty—with the assent of the Parliament, which is to act by a majority of its component Members, is to lay down the appropriate provisions. Those provisions are then to be recommended to the Member States for adoption in accordance with their respective constitutional requirements.[83] Using this procedure, the Council adopted the Decision of

---

[79] The Treaty of Nice abolished the requirement that an action brought by the European Parliament must seek to safeguard its prerogatives. Subject to that condition, the EU Treaty had codified in Art. 230 of the EC Treaty the European Parliament's right to bring proceedings as recognised by the Court of Justice: see ECJ, Case C–70/88 *European Parliament v Council* [1990] E.C.R. I–2041, paras 11–31. That right was not embodied in Art. 173 of the EEC Treaty and had not been accepted in an earlier judgment of the Court of Justice: ECJ, Case 302/87 *European Parliament v Council* [1988] E.C.R. 5638, paras 8–28. A first example of an action not brought to safeguard prerogatives is the Parliament's application for the annulment of a number of provisions of Council Directive 2003/86 on the right to family reunification (Case C–540/03, [2004] O.J. C47/21).

[80] EC Treaty, Art. 232, first para. See ECJ, Case 13/83 *European Parliament v Council* [1985] E.C.R. 1513, paras 13–19.

[81] EU Treaty, Art. 46; as far as PJCC is concerned, Art. 35 of the EU Treaty provides that the Court of Justice has jurisdiction to give preliminary rulings on the validity and interpretation of acts of the Union, but the European Parliament is not given the right to contest the legality of such acts by bringing an action in the Court (Art. 35(6) confers such a right only on the Member States and the Commission).

[82] EEC Treaty, Art. 138(1). The choice which Art. 21 of the ECSC Treaty left to each Member State to have members of the Assembly directly elected or designated by the national parliaments was abolished when in 1958 the Assembly merged into the Common Assembly of the three Communities, constituted in accordance with Art. 138 of the EEC Treaty.

[83] See also EAEC Treaty, Art. 108(3). The EU Treaty introduced the input from the European Parliament into these Treaty articles.

September 20, 1976 and the Act annexed thereto concerning the election of the representatives of the Assembly by direct universal suffrage.[84] The Act did not set out a uniform procedure for elections, but did apportion the number of seats among the Member States and determine the term of office of MEPs. The Council was to determine the period for the first elections.[85] Since then, elections have always been held in the period starting on a Thursday morning and ending on the following Sunday evening corresponding to the same period five years before,[86] except where the Council decided to hold the elections (not more than one month) later or earlier.[87]

The 1976 Act was amended in 2002, after the Treaty of Amsterdam had weakened the aim of Art. 190 of the EC Treaty that elections by direct universal suffrage were to take place in accordance with a uniform procedure in all Member States or "in accordance with principles common to all Member States". The amendments which the Council made to the Act on direct elections on the basis of a draft submitted by the European Parliament[88] entered into force after they had been approved by the

---

[84] Decision 76/787/ECSC, EEC, Euratom of the representatives of the Member States meeting in the Council relating to the Act concerning the election of the representatives of the Assembly by direct universal suffrage, [1976] O.J. L278/1. The European Parliament had regard to the first draft convention of May 17, 1960 ([1960] J.O. 834) in drawing up the Patijn draft convention of January 14, 1975, [1975] O.J. C32/15. Pursuant to the second subpara. of para. 3 of Art. 190 of the EC Treaty and Art. 108 of the EAEC Treaty, the Act declared that paras 1 and 2 of those articles had lapsed, without, however, introducing the "uniform procedure" referred to in para. 3, first subpara.

[85] Council Decision 78/639/Euratom, ECSC, EEC of July 25, 1978 ([1978] O.J. L205/75) prescribed the period June 7–10, 1979.

[86] Such as from June 10–13, 1999. Voting takes place on the Thursday in two Member States (the Netherlands and the UK), on the Friday in Ireland, on the Saturday in Latvia and Malta, on the Friday and the Saturday in the Czech Republic and on a Sunday in the rest of the Community.

[87] See the periods June 14–17, 1984 (Council Decision 83/285/EEC, Euratom, ECSC of June 2, 1983, [1983] O.J. L155/11) and June 15–18, 1989 (Council Decision 88/435/ECSC, EEC, Euratom of July 26, 1988, [1988] O.J. L210/25). In 1994 the elections were held on June 9 and 12.

[88] Council Decision 2002/772/EC, Euratom of June 25, 2002 and September 23, 2002 amending the Act concerning the election of the representatives of the European Parliament by direct universal suffrage, annexed to Decision 76/787/ECSC, EEC, Euratom, [2002] O.J. L283/1 (corrigendum to certain language versions in [2004] O.J. L64/48). In referring to the Act hereinafter, use will consistently be made of the new numbering introduced by that decision. Earlier drafts of the European Parliament were less successful; see the draft of March 10, 1982 ([1982] O.J. C87/61) and the resolutions of October 10, 1991 ([1992] O.J. C280/141) and March 10, 1993 ([1993] O.J. C115/121), as a result of which it was held unnecessary to proceed to judgment in proceedings brought against the European Parliament for failure to fulfil its Treaty obligations: ECJ (order of June 10, 1993), Case C–41/92 The Liberal Democrats v European Parliament [1993] E.C.R. I–3153. For the Council's reaction, see the Council's answer of January 17, 1997 to question E–2205/96 (De Vries), [1997] O.J. C83/8. See also De Vries, "La procédure électorale uniforme du Parlement européen: un pas pour rapprocher l'Europe des citoyens" (1996) R.M.C.U.E. 417–421.

Member States in accordance with their constitutional provisions.[89] The amended Act provides that members of the European Parliament are to be elected on the basis of proportional representation, using the list system or the single transferable vote (Act, Art. 1(1)). Member States may opt for a preferential list system (Act, Art. 1(2)), may establish constituencies or other subdivisions for elections (Art. 2) and may set a minimum threshold for the distribution of seats (Art. 3) and ceilings for candidates' election expenses (Art. 4).[90] The rules on the election period remain virtually unchanged.[91] Subject to the provisions of the Act, the electoral procedure is to be governed in each Member State by its national provisions, which, however, may not affect the essentially proportional nature of the voting system.[92]

Number of MEPs. Article 190(2) of the EC Treaty provides that each **10–023** Member State is to have a number of representatives reflecting its population size. The allocation of parliamentary seats to the various countries has been amended upon each accession of new Member States and following German reunification.[93] As from the 2004–2009 electoral

---

[89] See Art. 3 of Decision 2002/772/EC. Art. 14 of the Act (there was a corresponding provision also in the original version) empowers the Council to adopt any necessary implementing measures unanimously, in accordance with an unusual procedure: the Council acts on a proposal from the Parliament, after consulting the Commission, and after endeavouring to reach agreement with the Parliament in a conciliation committee consisting of the Council and representatives of the Parliament.

[90] In the absence of a uniform election procedure, there are also no uniform rules on the reimbursement of election expenses: see Joliet and Keeling, "The Reimbursement of Election Expenses: A Forgotten Dispute" (1994) E.L.R. 243–267.

[91] Act, Arts 10 and 11 (Art. 11(2) allows the Council to set the election period two months earlier or one month later than the normal period).

[92] Act, Art. 8. Usually in Member States where there is no obligation to go to the polls, the turnout for elections to the European Parliament is low. For ideas to improve this situation, see Lodge, "Making the Election of the European Parliament Distinctive: Towards E–Uniform Election Procedure" (2000) E.J.L.Ref. 191–215.

[93] EC Treaty Art. 190, as most recently amended by Art. 11 of the 2003 Act of Accession. In a Protocol on the enlargement of the Union, annexed by the Treaty of Nice to the EU Treaty and the Community Treaties ([2001] O.J. C80/49), it had already been agreed to reduce the total number of representatives for the 15 Member States, whilst at the same time a new distribution was laid down for the number of representatives *per* Member State. In Declaration (No.20) annexed to the Treaty of Nice on the enlargement of the Union ([2001] O.J. C80/80), the Member States at that time determined a distribution of the seats of the applicant countries—in the form of a common position that the Member States were to adopt during the accession negotiations—with a view to a Union of 27 Member States (no account was taken of Turkey as an applicant country). After it became clear that Bulgaria and Romania would not be acceding in 2004, the European Council held in Brussels on October 24 and 25, 2002 decided to apportion the seats in the European Parliament from 2004 by distributing the 50 seats allocated to Bulgaria and Romania by Declaration No.20 proportionately to the other Member States in accordance with that declaration (see the conclusions of the European Council in (2002) 10 EU Bull. point I.14). It is intended to apply the allocation of seats established by this declaration annexed to the Treaty of Nice from 2009. Initially, the allocation of seats was laid down in Art. 2 of the Act on the direct election of the European Parliament (now repealed), as amended by Art. 10 of the Acts of Accession of 1979 ([1979] O.J. L291/17) and 1985 ([1985] O.J. L302/23), by Council

period, Germany has 99 seats, France, Italy and the United Kingdom 78 each, Poland and Spain 54 each, the Netherlands 27, Belgium, the Czech Republic, Greece, Hungary and Portugal 24 each, Sweden 19, Austria 18, Denmark, Finland and Slovakia 14 each, Ireland and Lithuania 13, Latvia 9, Slovenia 7, Cyprus, Estonia and Luxembourg 6, and Malta 5. For the short period in 2004 between the date of accession and the beginning of the new parliamentary term, transitional arrangements were provided for whereby the new Member States were represented in the European Parliament by members of their national parliaments.[94]The Treaty of Amsterdam fixed the maximum number of MEPs at 700, which the Treaty of Nice raised to 732.[95] This is the number of MEPs for the 2004–2009 parliamentary term. MEPs are elected for a five-year term (EC Treaty, Art. 190(3)).

10–024 **Right to participate in elections.** The fact that the electoral procedure is determined in each Member State by its national provisions does not prevent Art. 19 of the EC Treaty from granting each citizen of the Union the right in principle to take part in the elections.[96] Any citizen of the Union who is resident in a Member State of which he is not a national enjoys the right to vote and stand as a candidate in European elections on the same terms as nationals of that State under Council Directive 93/109/EC of December 6, 1993, which was adopted pursuant to Art. 19 of the EC Treaty.[97] A person having the right to vote may exercise it either in

---

Decision of February 1, 1993 ([1993] O.J. L33/15) and by Art. 11 of the 1994 Act of Accession (as amended by Council Decision of January 1, 1995, [1995] O.J. L1/1). The Treaty of Amsterdam incorporated the distribution of seats set out in the Act in Art. 190 of the EC Treaty. Note that before the 1994 elections, the new German Länder were represented by only 18 observers. See also ECJ, Case C–25/92 *Miethke v European Parliament* [1993] E.C.R. I–473.

[94] 2003 Act of Accession, Art. 25. During that period, the European Parliament had 788 members: this is because the new Member States had the number of seats laid down for the 2004–2009 parliamentary term, whereas the 15 existing Member States still had the (larger) number of representatives allocated to them by Art. 190 of the EC Treaty before the accession: Germany 99 representatives (the same), but France, Italy and the UK 87 each, Spain 64, the Netherlands 31, Belgium, Greece and Portugal 25 each, Sweden 22, Austria 21, Denmark and Finland 16 each, Ireland 15; Luxembourg already had 6 representatives.

[95] EC Treaty, Art. 189, second para.

[96] In response to the ruling of the European Court of Human Rights in *Matthews* (see para. 17–081, *infra*), the UK has given Commonwealth citizens residing in Gibraltar the right to vote in the 2004 elections for the European Parliament (see European Parliament (Representation) Act 2003). Spain has brought an action against the UK alleging that this extension of the electorate goes against the Treaty and the 1976 act: Case C–145/04, [2004] O.J. C106/43. In Cyprus, elections for the 2004–2009 term were held only in the (southern) part in which the Government of Cyprus exercises effective control. See further Council Decision 2004/511/EC of June 10, 2004 concerning the representation of the people of Cyprus in the European Parliament in the case of a settlement of the Cyprus problem, [2004] O.J. L211/22.

[97] Council Directive 93/109/EC of December 6, 1993 laying down detailed arrangements for the exercise of the right to vote and stand as a candidate in elections to the European Parliament for citizens of the Union residing in a Member State of which they are not

the Member State of residence or in his or her home Member State; a person eligible to stand as a candidate may do so in only one Member State (Directive 93/109, Art. 4). If a Member State requires candidates to have been nationals for a certain minimum period, Union citizens are deemed to satisfy that condition if they have been nationals of a Member State for that period (Directive 93/109, Art. 3). Where nationals of the Member State in question are required to have spent a certain minimum period as a resident in the electoral territory of that State in order to be able to vote or stand for election, Union citizens satisfy that condition if they have resided for an equivalent period in other Member States. Nevertheless, this does not apply in the case of a Member State which imposes specific conditions as to length of residence in a given constituency or locality (Directive 93/109, Art. 5). Where, in a given Member State, the proportion of Union citizens of voting age who reside in it but are not nationals of it exceeds 20 per cent of the total number of Union citizens residing there who are of voting age, the directive authorises the Member State in question to restrict non-nationals' right to vote and stand in elections to those who have been resident in that State for a specified minimum period (Directive 93/109, Art. 14; implemented by Luxembourg).[98] As far as the right to stand for election is concerned, account obviously must be taken of the restrictions which national criminal law may impose in relation to eligibility.[99]

Conditions for exercise of office. MEPs are to vote on an individual and **10–025** personal basis, are not bound by any instructions and do not receive a binding mandate (Act on the Direct Election of the European Parliament, Art. 6(1)).[100] Since they represent citizens directly and not their Member States, they form a genuine supranational institution. This means that all MEPs may participate in debates and decision-making even in policy spheres in which not all Member States of the Union participate.[101]

The European Parliament is to lay down the regulations and general conditions governing the performance of the duties of its Members after consulting the Commission and with the approval of the Council, acting by a qualified majority, except for the tax arrangements for Members or

nationals, [1993] O.J. L329/34, implemented in the UK by the European Parliamentary Elections (Changes to the Franchise and Qualification of Representatives) Regulations 1994, amending the European Parliamentary Elections Act 1978. For a discussion of this right to stand and vote (and its application for the first time in 1994), see Oliver, "Electoral Rights under Art. 8b [*now Art. 19*] of the Treaty of Rome" (1996) C.M.L.R. 473–498.

[98] Luxembourg requires nationals of other Member States to have resided in its territory for at least five of the last six years in order to be able to vote and for at least 10 of the last 12 years in order to be able to stand as a candidate: see the law of January 28, 1994, JO du Grand-Duché de Luxembourg, January 31, 1994.

[99] For the European Parliament's power to take notice of a communication from a Member State that a MEP is disqualified as a result of a criminal conviction, see CFI, Case T–353/00 *Le Pen v European Parliament* [2003] E.C.R. II–1729. See also Art. 13 of the Act.

[100] See Böttger, "Die Rechtsstellung des Abgeordneten des Europäischen Parlaments" (2002) EuR. 898–916.

[101] Resolution of the European Parliament of January 19, 1994, [1994] O.J. C44/88.

former Members, for which unanimity is required (EC Treaty, Art. 190(5)).[102] The Act provides only that the holding of a number of offices is incompatible with being an MEP; member of the Government of a Member State; member of another Community institution; member of the Board of Directors of the European Central Bank; member of the European Economic and Social Committee or the Committee of the Regions; member of committees or other bodies set up to manage Community funds or to carry out a permanent direct administrative task; European Ombudsman; member of the Board of Directors or Management Committee of the EIB, or active official or servant of the Communities or of the ECB (Act, Art. 7(1)).[103] Originally, the Act expressly provided that an MEP might also be a member of a national parliament.[104] With effect from the election of the European Parliament in 2004, the capacity of MEP is incompatible with the office of national member of parliament (Act, Art. 7(2), which provides for temporary exceptions for Ireland and the United Kingdom). It should be noted that national rules may prescribe other incompatibilities.[105]

---

[102] On December 3, 1998 the European Parliament adopted a Draft Statute for Members of the European Parliament ([1998] O.J. C398/24). See Rothley, "Vers un statut unique des députés européens" (1999) R.M.C.U.E. 559–563.

[103] Since members of a government of a federated State or of a devolved legislative body may represent that Member State in the Council since the EU Treaty entered into force, holding such an office would also appear to be incompatible with membership of the European Parliament. According to the White Papers, *Scotland's Parliament* (Cm.3658) and *A Voice for Wales*, Ministers of the Scottish Executive and Welsh Assembly Secretaries will be able to participate in Council meetings and speak for the UK, most especially where there is a strong Scottish or Welsh interest. Hence it would appear that holding such office is incompatible with being an MEP (but not mere membership of the Scottish Parliament or of the Welsh Assembly: see Scotland Act 1998, s.15 (and s.81(1)(b) on reduction of Members' remuneration to take account of remuneration as an MEP) and Government of Wales Act 1998, s.12 (and s.17(1)(b) on remuneration)). Moreover, Art. 263, fourth paragraph, of the EC Treaty provides that membership of the Committee of the Regions is incompatible with being an MEP.

[104] In this context, the question arose as to whether a Member State could prohibit such a dual mandate. See, *e.g.* Art. 42 of the Belgian Law of March 23, 1989 on elections to the European Parliament, *Belgisch Staatsblad/Moniteur belge*, March 5, 1989 (as amended by laws of July 16, 1993 and April 11, 1994, *Belgisch Staatsblad/Moniteur belge*, July 20, 1993 and April 16, 1994). As to whether a Member State was entitled to prohibit dual mandates, see Question 2102/86 (De Gucht), [1987] O.J. C112/45.

[105] Para. 5 of Schedule 1 to the European Parliamentary Elections Act 1978 provides that a person is disqualified for the office of MEP if he or she is disqualified, whether under the House of Commons Disqualification Act 1975 or otherwise, for membership of the House of Commons, or if he or she is a Lord of Appeal in Ordinary. However, by virtue of subpara. 3 and in contradistinction to the position with regard to the House of Commons, peers, members of the clergy, holders of an office mentioned in s.4 of the House of Commons Disqualification Act 1975 (stewardship of the Chiltern Hundreds, etc.) and holders of an office described in Pt II or Pt III of Schedule 1 to that Act, provided they are designated by the Secretary of State as non-disqualifying offices in relation to the European Parliament, may stand for election to the European Parliament. See also the incompatibilities set out in Art. 3 of the draft statute (n.102, *supra*).

3. Operation

Rules of Procedure. In so far as the Treaty does not provide otherwise, the **10–026** European Parliament operates in accordance with its Rules of Procedure, adopted by a majority of its members (EC Treaty, Art. 199, first subpara.).[106] Pursuant to the power to determine its own internal organisation, the Parliament is entitled to "adopt appropriate measures to ensure the due functioning and conduct of its proceedings".[107] Its annual "session" meets on the second Tuesday in March (EC Treaty, Art. 196, first para.) and lasts in practice until the session of the following year or until the first meeting of a newly elected Parliament.[108] If the Parliament does not close the session earlier, there will be no need to hold an extraordinary session (see EC Treaty, Art. 196, second para.) and MEPs enjoy the immunities conferred upon them for the whole of the year.[109] The session includes meetings of committees and political groups and plenary sessions (sometimes referred to as "sittings").[110]

Seat. Meetings of the European Parliament are held in accordance with **10–027** the provisions of the Treaties (EP Rules of Procedure, r.127(1)). Pursuant to Art. 289 of the EC Treaty, the governments of the Member States have determined in the First Decision on the Seats of the Institutions of December 12, 1992 that the European Parliament has its seat in Strasbourg, where the twelve periods of monthly plenary sessions, including the budget session, are to be held. Additional plenary sessions are to be held in Brussels, where the parliamentary committees also meet. The general secretariat and its departments have remained in Luxembourg.[111] By requiring that the European Parliament should meet in principle every month in Strasbourg, the governments endorsed that institution's previous practice. In determining its internal organisation, the Parliament must respect the national governments' competence to determine its seat. Only if the European Parliament holds its twelve ordinary part sessions, including the budgetary part session, in Strasbourg may it hold additional part

---

[106] Rules of Procedure of the European Parliament [EP Rules of Procedure], as restructured on March 9, 2004 to enter into force after the 2004 elections: see the European Parliament's website.

[107] ECJ, Case 230/81 *Luxembourg v European Parliament* [1983] E.C.R. 255, para. 38.

[108] The newly elected Parliament meets for the first time on the first Tuesday in the month after the end of the election period (Act on the Direct Election of the European Parliament, Art. 11(3)).

[109] ECJ, Case 101/63 *Wagner* [1964] E.C.R. 195; ECJ, Case 149/85 *Wybot* [1986] E.C.R. 2391, paras 15–27. For the immunity of MEPs, see para. 10–149, *infra*.

[110] See EP Rules of Procedure, r.125.

[111] Art. 1(a) of the First Decision on the Seats of the Institutions of December 12, 1992, para. 10–146, *infra*.

sessions in Brussels.[112] By incorporating the Decision on the Seats of the Institutions into the Protocol on the location of the seats of the institutions and of certain bodies and departments of the European Communities and of Europol (Protocol on Seats, see para. 10–146), the Treaty of Amsterdam has given these rules the status of Treaty law.

10–028 Proceedings. Before each part-session (*i.e.* the meeting convened as a rule each month and divided into daily sittings) the European Parliament draws up its agenda.[113] The Commission is entitled to attend meetings.[114] Members of the Commission, the Council and the European Council may make statements to the European Parliament.[115] For its part, the Commission ensures that the responsible Commissioner is present at the plenary session or in committee when the European Parliament requests his or her presence.[116] Save as otherwise provided in the Treaty, the European Parliament acts by an absolute majority of the votes cast (EC Treaty, Art. 198, first para.). A number of Treaty Articles require it to act by a majority of its component Members[117] or by a two-thirds or three-fifths majority of the votes cast.[118] The Parliament is quorate when one-third of its component Members are present in the Chamber (EP Rules of Procedure, r.147(2)). Debates in the house are public (EP Rules of

---

[112] The Court of Justice annulled the European Parliament's vote to hold only 11 part-sessions in Strasbourg in 1996 on the ground that it infringed the First Decision on the Seats of the Institutions: ECJ, Case C–345/95 *France v European Parliament* [1997] E.C.R. I–5215, paras 13–35. An action brought against a similar vote relating to the calendar of part sessions for 1997 (Case C–267/96 *France v European Parliament*, lodged on August 5, 1996, [1996] O.J. C269/21) was removed from the register following the judgment in Case C–345/95 (order of December 19, 1997, [1998] O.J. C94/17). The Court held that the constraints as regards the organisation of parliamentary work imposed by the Decision on the Seats of the Institutions did not conflict with the Parliament's power of internal organisation (Case C–345/95, *ibid.*, paras 30–32). See also para. 10–145, *infra*.

[113] EP Rules of Procedure, r.131(1). The draft agenda drawn up by the Conference of Presidents (para. 10–030, *infra*) may be amended at that time at the proposal of a committee, a political group or at least 40 MEPs (*ibid.*).

[114] EC Treaty, Art. 197, second para.

[115] See EC Treaty, Art. 197, fourth para., and EP Rules of Procedure, r.103(1). See also points 23–24 of the framework agreement of July 5, 2002 (n.53, *supra*), which provide that the Commissioner may also be heard at his or her request in a parliamentary committee.

[116] Points 19 and 24 of the framework agreement of July 5, 2000 (*ibid.*) and point 8 of the Interinstitutional Agreement of December 16, 2003 on better law-making ([2003] O.J. C321/1). For that commitment, see also the Commission's answer of February 8, 1990 to question No.1207/89 (McMahon), [1990] O.J. C125/44.

[117] See EC Treaty, Art. 190(4); Art. 192, second para.; Art. 196, second para.; Art. 199, first para.; Art. 201, second para.; Art. 251(2)(b) and (c); Art. 252(c); Art. 272(4), second subpara., (6), (8) and (9), fifth subpara.; Art. 273, third para.; EU Treaty, Art. 7(6) and Art. 49.

[118] Two-thirds: EC Treaty, Art. 201, second para.; Art. 272(8); EU Treaty, Art. 7(6). Three-fifths: EC Treaty, Art. 272(6) and (9), fifth subpara.; Art. 273, third para. Other, different majorities are laid down in the Rules of Procedure.

Procedure, r.96(2)). MEPs prepare decisions to be adopted at the plenary session in parliamentary committees.[119]

In some legislative procedures, a delegation from the European Parliament meets with members of the Council or their representatives in a Conciliation Committee, which is presided over jointly by the Presidents of the Parliament and the Council.[120] The two delegations have the same number of members, equal to the number of members of the Council. The European Parliament delegation consists of three Members appointed by the political groups as permanent members of successive delegations for a period of twelve months and other Members appointed for each particular conciliation case, preferably from among the members of the committees concerned.[121]

4. Internal organisation

Internal bodies. The European Parliament elects a President and a Bureau **10–029** from among its Members (EC Treaty, Art. 197, first para.). The Bureau consists of the President and the Vice-Presidents of Parliament, together with the Quaestors sitting in an advisory capacity (EP Rules of Procedure, r.21). The President, Vice-Presidents and Quaestors are elected in that order by MEPs for a term of office of two-and-a-half years (see EP Rules of Procedure, rr.11–16). The President presides over parliamentary proceedings and represents the Parliament in its relations with the outside world (EP Rules of Procedure, r.19). The Rules of Procedure entrust the Bureau with financial, administrative and organisational tasks (EP Rules of Procedure, r.22); the Quaestors are responsible for purely administrative and financial matters (EP Rules of Procedure, r.25). The Bureau appoints a Secretary-General to head the Secretariat (see EP Rules of Procedure, r.195). The Secretariat has a staff of 4,000 and is divided into a legal service and seven directorates-general.[122]

---

[119] 20 standing committees have been set up pursuant to r.172 of the EP Rules of Procedure, as amended. For temporary committees of inquiry, see para. 10–020, *supra*. For the manner of operation of these committees, see Mamadouh and Raunio, "The Committee System: Powers, Appointments and Report Allocation" (2003) J.C.M.S. 335–351.

[120] See the co-decision procedure provided for by Art. 251 of the EC Treaty (para 14–030 *et seq.*, *infra*) and the conciliation procedure (para. 14–039, *infra*).

[121] See EP Rules of Procedure, r.64(3) (which provides that the chairman and the rapporteur of the committee responsible in each particular case are members of the delegation in any event). Meetings are held alternately in the premises of the Parliament and those of the Council and are chaired alternately by one of the two co-chairmen. The secretariat of the Conciliation Committee is provided jointly by the General Secretariats of the Council and the Parliament, in collaboration with the General Secretariat of the Commission. See the Joint Declaration of the European Parliament, the Council and the Commission on practical arrangements for the new co-decision procedure (Art. 251 of the Treaty establishing the European Community), [1999] O.J. C148/1.

[122] The Secretariat had 3,367 permanent posts and 594 temporary posts as at December 31, 2003. See Commission of the European Communities, *General Report on the Activities of the European Union 2003*, Brussels/Luxembourg, 2004, at 501.

10–030 Political groups and parties. Most MEPs belong to political groups; the remainder are referred to as non-attached.[123] A political group can only be set up on the basis of political affinity.[124] The President of the Parliament exercises certain powers together with the chairmen of the political groups as the Conference of Presidents.[125] In some political groups, the members have underpinned their political co-operation by forming a European political party.[126] Art. 191 of the EC Treaty declares that political parties at European level are "important as a factor for integration within the Union". The European Parliament and the Council, acting under the co-decision procedure, lay down the regulations governing political parties at European level and in particular the rules regarding their funding (EC Treaty, Art. 191, second para.).[127] According to the Treaty, political parties at European level "contribute to forming a European awareness and to expressing the political will of the citizens of the Union" (Art. 191, first para.).[128] However, so far the existence of European political parties has not prevented political debate at European level from attracting less attention from public opinion than national political discussions. European elections tend all to soon to be dragged in the wake of national issues and it

---

[123] EP Rules of Procedure, rr.29, 30 and 31. A political group must comprise Members from more than one Member State. Before July 2004 the minimum number of MEPs required to form a political group was 23 if they came from two Member States, 18 if they came from three Member States and 14 if they came from four or more Member States; from that date, a political group must have members from at least one-fifth of the Member States and at least 19 members (EP Rules of Procedure, r.29(2)). See further Nessler, "Die Fraktion im Europäischen Parlament" (1997) EuR 311–320.

[124] EP Rules of Procedure, r.29. This requirement ensues from social and political circumstances peculiar to parliamentary democracies and from the specific features and responsibilities of the European Parliament: CFI, Joined Cases T–222/99, T–327/99 and T–329/99 *Martinez v European Parliament* [2001] E.C.R. II–2823, paras 145–148, confirmed on the merits by ECJ (order of November 11, 2003), Case C–488/01 P *Martinez v European Parliament*, not yet reported, and set aside, as to the admissibility of the action brought by a political party, by ECJ (judgment of June 29, 2004), Case C–486/01 P *Front National v European Parliament*, not yet reported. This does not preclude members of a group in their day-to-day conduct from expressing different political opinions on any particular subject: CFI, *ibid.*, paras 80–94.

[125] See EP Rules of Procedure, r.24. The Conference replaced the enlarged Bureau, consisting of the members of the Bureau and the presidents of the political groups.

[126] See the Party of European Socialists (PES) (established in 1974), the European Liberal Democrat and Reform Party (ELDR) and the European People's Party (EPP) (both set up in 1976) and the European Green Party (set up in 2004).

[127] Regulation (EC) No. 2004/2003 of the European Parliament and of the Council of November 4, 2003 on the regulations governing political parties at European level and the rules regarding their funding, [2003] O.J. L297/1. Implementing rules have been laid down by Decision of the Bureau of the European Parliament of March 29, 2004, [2004] O.J. C155/1.

[128] See also Art. 12(2) of the Charter of Fundamental Rights of the European Union. See also Tsatsos, "Europäische politische Parteien? Erste Überlegungen zur Auslegung des Parteienartikels des Maastrichter Vertrages—Art. 138a EGV" (1994) Eu.GR.Z. 45–53; Stentzel, "Der normative Gehalt des Art. 138a EGV—Rechtlicher Grundstein eines europäischen Parteiensystems?" (1997) EuR. 174–191; Huber, "Die politischen Parteien als Partizipationsinstrument auf Unionsebene" (1999) EuR. 579–596; Bieber, "Les perspectives d'un statut pour les parties politiques européens" (1999) R.T.D.E. 349–362.

is often hard to regard them as being any indication of voters' views on future European policy choices.

5. Changes proposed in the EU Constitution

Extended powers. Article I–20 of the EU Constitution makes it clear that **10–031** the European Parliament not only is to exercise the functions of political control and consultation and to elect the President of the Commission but also has to fulfil, jointly with the Council, legislative and budgetary functions. As far as those functions are concerned, the EU Constitution takes further steps towards putting the European Parliament on an equal footing with the Council. First, the co-decision procedure will become the "ordinary legislative procedure" for the adoption of legislative acts and, as such, will be applicable to an extended list of substantive matters (see para. 14–030). As regards external policy, the European Parliament will have a general right to be consulted and will have to give its consent to all agreements in fields which are subject internally to the ordinary legislative procedure (see para. 21–015). As far as the adoption of the budget is concerned, the European Parliament will have the final say over all categories of expenditure (see para. 10–129).

As far as concerns the composition of the European Parliament, for the 2004–2009 Parliament the EU Constitution will draw on the arrangements laid down in the Treaty of Nice, as subsequently amended upon the accession of the new Member States.[129] The composition of the following Parliament will have to be established by the European Council, acting by unanimity, at the initiative of the European Parliament and with its consent (EU Constitution, Art. I–20(2)). In so doing, the European Council must respect the principles set out in the Constitution, including a maximum number of representatives of 750, a degressively proportional system of representation, a minimum threshold of six members and a maximum of 96 members per Member State.

B. THE COUNCIL

Designation. As a result of Art. 1 of the Merger Treaty, this institution, as **10–032** the "Council of the European Communities", replaced the Special Council of Ministers of the ECSC, the Council of the EEC and the Council of the EAEC. Following the entry into effect of the EU Treaty, the Council[130] decided that henceforth it would be known as the "Council of the European Union".[131]

---

[129] See Art. 1(2) of the Protocol annexed to the draft EU Constitution on the transitional provisions relating to the institutions and bodies of the Union.

[130] See in general Westlake, *The Council of the European Union* (Harper, London, 1999) 417 pp. For the Council's website, see *www.consilium.eu.int/*.

[131] Decision 93/591/EU, Euratom, ECSC, EC of November 8, 1993, [1993] O.J. L281/18 (corrigendum L285/41). The Merger Treaty has since been repealed by Art. 9 of the Treaty of Amsterdam.

1. Powers

10–033 **Survey.** The Council's powers are defined in Art. 202 of the EC Treaty as co-ordination, decision-making and implementing tasks carried out in order to "ensure that the objectives set out in this Treaty are attained". Art. 115 of the EAEC Treaty places the emphasis on co-ordination and exercising powers of decision. The EU Treaty provides for similar powers in respect of the Union's non-Community activities. As far as the CFSP is concerned, the (Presidency of the) Council is entrusted with representing the Union externally.

a. Decision-making

10–034 **Policy choices.** First, the Council makes the policy choices intended to attain the objectives set out in the Treaties. In many cases, the Council has to assess complex economic situations and has a discretion as to what priorities should be given to these policies,[132] the actual aim of any given action and the suitability of its action in order to achieve that aim,[133] the nature and scope of such action and, to a certain extent, the determination of basic data.[134] Community decision-making is carried out virtually always via the Council, which adopts most legislation on the basis of a Commission proposal. In addition, the Council decides on the general budget of the Union together with the European Parliament, although the Council has the last word on compulsory expenditure (see paras 10–130 *et seq.*). As far as external action is concerned, the Council concludes international agreements negotiated by the Commission on behalf of the Communities and the Council and the Commission are responsible for ensuring the consistency of the Union's external activities as a whole (EU Treaty, Art. 3, second para.). Decision-making in connection with the CFSP and PJCC falls, however, almost entirely to the Council.

b. Co-ordination

10–035 **Co-ordination.** The Council may adopt non-binding measures *vis-à-vis* the Member States in order to co-ordinate their "general economic policies" (EC Treaty, Art. 202) and, more generally, to bring national policies and Community action into line with each other.[135] The EC Treaty further gives the Council a specific power to co-ordinate the Member States' economic policies and it may impose sanctions in this connection.[136] Also as regards

---

[132] See, for example, ECJ, Case 13/83 *European Parliament v Council* [1985] E.C.R. 1513, para. 50.

[133] paras 5–012 and 5–039, respectively, *supra*.

[134] ECJ, Case 138/79 *Roquette Frères v Council* [1980] E.C.R. 3333, paras 25–26.

[135] See Art. 115 of the EAEC Treaty, which refers to harmonising or co-ordinating Community and national policies.

[136] EC Treaty, Art. 99 (paras 5–224–5–225, *supra*) and Art. 104(9) and (11) (para. 5–229, *supra*).

the CFSP and PJCC, Member States' policies are co-ordinated in the Council (EU Treaty, Arts 16 and 34(1)).

c. Implementation

Implementing powers. Article 202 of the EC Treaty confers Community **10–036** implementing powers in principle on the Commission, yet it also allows the Council to impose certain requirements in respect of the exercise of those powers or to reserve the right "in specific cases" to exercise implementing powers itself (see para. 14–051). The Treaties confer certain implementing powers expressly on the Council, in particular with regard to economic monitoring (EC Treaty, Art. 99(3) and Art. 104), the implementation of the CFSP (EU Treaty, Art. 13(3))—involving the Presidency and the Secretary General (EU Treaty, Arts 18(2) and 26)—and the implementation of PJCC (EU Treaty, Art. 34(2)).

d. Representation

External representation. With regard to the CFSP, the Union is **10–037** represented *vis-à-vis* third parties by the Presidency of the Council and the Secretary General, High Representative for the CFSP (EU Treaty, Arts 18(1) and 26).

e. Relationship to other institutions and bodies

Appointments. Because it is made up of representatives of the Member **10–038** States, the Council has a number of prerogatives which enable it to influence, to some extent, the operation of the other institutions, with the exception of the European Parliament.[137] Thus, the Council appoints the members of the Commission and the Court of Auditors,[138] may alter the number of Members of the Commission and of Advocates General at the Court of Justice,[139] and determines the emoluments of members of those institutions.[140] The Council also appoints members of other bodies and adopts the rules governing their organisation.[141] The Council is further entitled to exercise some control over the activities of the Commission: it can ask it to carry out studies and make proposals[142] and participates in

---

[137] Even though, after the Treaty of Amsterdam, the Council has to approve by a unanimous vote the "regulations and general conditions governing the performance of the duties" of the Members of the European Parliament (EC Treaty, Art. 190(5)).

[138] EC Treaty, Arts 214 and 247(3).

[139] EC Treaty, Art. 213(1), second subpara., and Art. 222, first para., respectively.

[140] EC Treaty, Art. 210. In addition, the Council has to approve amendments to the Statute of the Court of Justice, the Rules of Procedure established by the Court of Justice and the Court of First Instance (EC Treaty, Art. 223, sixth para., Art. 224, fifth para., and Art. 245, second para.) and the Rules of Procedure of the Court of Auditors (EC Treaty, Art. 248(4), fifth subpara.).

[141] This applies *inter alia* to the European Economic and Social Committee (para. 10–094, *infra*) and the Committee of the Regions (para. 10–097, *infra*). See also EC Treaty, Art. 209 (para. 10–100, *infra*).

[142] EC Treaty, Art. 208; EAEC Treaty, Art. 122 (para. 14–018, *infra*).

controlling the Commission's implementation of the budget.[143] The Council is entitled to consult the Court of Auditors, the European Economic and Social Committee and the Committee of the Regions.[144] It is also entitled to an annual report from the ECB[145] and may monitor its policy by having its President attend meetings of the ECB's Governing Council.[146]

Lastly, the Council has the right to bring actions for annulment or for failure to act in the Court of Justice.[147]

2. Composition

10–039 **Configurations.** The Council consists of a representative of each Member State at ministerial level, authorised to commit the government of that State (EC Treaty, Art. 203, first para.). Each Member State itself determines the person of ministerial rank who is to represent it. Depending on the subject-matter under discussion, the Council can meet in various "configurations". Alongside the General Affairs and External Relations Council, there are at present eight configurations of the Council:

(1) Economic and Financial Affairs;

(2) Justice and Home Affairs;

(3) Employment, Social Policy, Health and Consumer Affairs;

(4) Competitiveness (Internal Market, Industry and Research);

(5) Transport, Telecommunications and Energy;

(6) Agriculture and Fisheries;

(7) Environment; and

(8) Education, Youth and Culture.

The Council in its General Affairs and External Relations configuration fixes the list of configurations.[148] In some instances, the EC Treaty requires the Council to meet in the composition of the Heads of State or Government. In practice, meetings of this configuration of the Council generally coincide with those of the "European Council", although legally

---

[143] para. 10–143, *infra*.

[144] EC Treaty, Art. 248(4), second subpara.; Art. 262; Art. 265.

[145] EC Treaty, Art. 113(3).

[146] EC Treaty, Art. 113(1). The President of the Council may submit a motion for deliberation, *ibid.*

[147] EC Treaty, Art. 230, second para.; Art. 232, first para.

[148] Council Rules of Procedure, Art. 2(1) and the list in Annex I to the Rules. This "practice" was laid down for the first time when the Council Rules of Procedure were amended on June 5, 2000 ([2002] O.J. L230/7), and confirmed in the Council Rules of Procedure of July 22, 2002, which reduced the number of configurations (for the earlier more extensive list, see [2000] O.J. C174/2) and transformed the General Affairs Council into the General Affairs and External Relations Council.

there is a difference: the European Council consists of the Heads of State or Government, together with the President of the Commission, and it always takes its decisions by consensus (see para. 10–004).

The General Affairs and External Relations Council has two main areas of activity.[149] On the one hand, it is responsible for the preparation for and follow-up to the European Council meetings, overall co-ordination of policies, institutional and administrative questions, horizontal dossiers which affect several of the Union's policies and any dossier entrusted to it by the European Council. On the other, it holds separate meetings dealing with the whole of the Union's external action, namely common foreign and security policy, European security and defence policy, foreign trade, development co-operation and humanitarian aid. In the General Affairs and External Relations Council, each Member State is represented by the Minister or State Secretary of its choice.[150] Sometimes, the General Affairs Council meets together with another configuration (a "jumbo" Council) or specialised configurations ("Special Councils") meet jointly.

As a result of the EU Treaty, the General Affairs Council has surrendered some of its co-ordinating influence. This is because, as far as matters relating to Economic and Monetary Union are concerned, the Intergovernmental Conference put the emphasis on the ECOFIN Council.[151] Meetings of the ECOFIN Council attended only by representatives of Member States taking part in the third stage of EMU constitute the "Euro Council".[152] In addition, increasing reliance is being placed on decisions which the Council takes in the configuration of the Heads of State or Government. The EU Treaty introduced this procedure for some decisions relating to EMU.[153] The Treaties of Amsterdam and Nice conferred on the Council in the configuration of the Heads of State or

---

[149] Council Rules of Procedure, Art. 2(2). For the tasks of the former "General Affairs" Council, see Gomez and Peterson, "The EU's Impossibly Busy Foreign Ministers: 'No One is in Control' " (2001) E.For.Aff.Rev. 53–74.

[150] See Annex I to the Council Rules of Procedure. In practice, it is generally the Member States' Ministers of Foreign Affairs or Ministers or State Secretaries responsible for European Affairs.

[151] See Declaration (No.3) on Part Three, Titles III and VI [now Titles III and VII], of the EC Treaty, which was adopted when the EU Treaty was signed, and Declaration (No. 4) on Part Three, Title VI [now Title VII], of the EC Treaty. Under Art. 2(2)(a) of the Council Rules of Procedure, tasks are to be assigned to the General Affairs Council "having regard to operating rules for the Economic and Monetary Union".

[152] See para. 14–071. The procedures in the Council are adapted thereto. See Art. 16 of the Council Rules of Procedure and the annex thereto.

[153] See EC Treaty, Art. 121(2), (3) and (4) (decision on entry into the third stage of EMU) and Art. 122(2) (discussion of which Member States with a derogation may take part in EMU). In the first case, the Council decided by a qualified majority vote in the composition of the Heads of State or Government on the basis of a recommendation made by the Council meeting in its normal composition; in the second case, the Council discusses the matter in the composition of the Heads of State or Government, after which the Council meeting in its normal composition takes the decision. For the application of these provisions, see Council Decision 96/736/EC of December 13, 1996 in accordance with Art. 109j [now Art. 121](3) of the Treaty establishing the European Community, on entry into the third stage of economic and monetary union, [1996] O.J. L335/48.

Government the power to take some major constitutional decisions.[154] As a result, policy is co-ordinated increasingly at Head of State or Government level, within or without the European Council.[155]

10–040 Representatives at ministerial level. Before the EC Treaty entered into force, each government had to delegate "one of its members" to the Council.[156] However, in federal Member States, such as Germany and Belgium, the federal government shares powers with the governments of the federated states or regions. At the insistence of those Member States, the EU Treaty altered the composition of the Council so as to allow members of government of federated states or regions to represent their Member State in the Council. Since each Member State has only one representative in the Council, a federal Member State has to determine who is delegated to the Council and how that representative defends as one view in the Council what may be conflicting views within the Member State.[157] The composition of the Council as it is defined in Art. 203 of the EC Treaty also confirms the practice whereby a Member State is represented by junior ministers who under domestic law do not form part of the government, but are nevertheless deemed to be of "ministerial level".

10–041 Presidency of the Council. Each Member State occupies the Presidency of the Council in rotation for a period of six months.[158] The second para. of Art. 203 of the EC Treaty (as amended by Art. 12 of the 1994 Act of Accession) requires the Council to determine the order by unanimous vote.[159] Accordingly, in 2004 Ireland and the Netherlands occupy the Presidency, in 2005 it will be Luxembourg and the United Kingdom and in

---

[154] See EC Treaty, Art. 214(2), first subpara. (nomination of the President of the Commission) and Art. 7(2) of the EU Treaty (determination of the existence of a serious and persistent breach by a Member State of principles mentioned in Art. 6(1)). See also Art. 10.6 of the ESCB Statute (see para. 10–104, *infra*). For a decision taken in the event that a Member State declares that it intends to oppose the grant of authorisation for Member States to establish a form of enhanced co-operation, Art. 11(2) of the EC Treaty provides that the matter may be referred to the European Council (without providing for any right of decision of the European Council; *cf.* Art. 23(2), second subpara., of the EU Treaty). For a critical commentary, see Dashwood, "The Constitution of the European Union after Nice: law-making procedures" (2001) E.L.R. 215, at 234–236.

[155] See Martenczuk, "Der Europäische Rat und die Wirtschafts- und Währungsunion" (1998) EuR. 151, at 175–176; Mayer, "Nationale Regierungsstrukturen und europäische Integration" (2002) Eu.GR.Z. 111–124.

[156] Merger Treaty, Art. 2, first para., repealed by Art. 50 of the EU Treaty.

[157] para. 11–015, *infra*. When the Council decides by a qualified majority and each Member State has more than one vote, the number of votes cast is always expressed as a single block. If a single view cannot be reached within a Member State, its representative may abstain. For the various effects of abstention, see para 10–045, *infra*.

[158] See Hummer and Obwexer, "Die 'EU-Präsidentschaft'" (1999) EuR. 401–451.

[159] Before Art. 12 of the 1994 Act of Accession entered into force, Art. 203, second para., of the EC Treaty laid down a cycle determined by the alphabetical order of the names of the Member States in their respective languages. In the subsequent cycle, the same list was taken but the order of each pair of Member States on the list was inverted.

2006 Austria and Finland.[160] From 2007 the Member States which acceded as from 2004 will take part in this rotating system.[161] In order to ensure continuity in the Council's activities the Presidency is assisted if need be by the next Member State to hold the Presidency.[162] In the past, there was the practice of the "troika", whereby the previous and the next President of the Council assisted the holder of the office for the time being.[163] The EU Treaty formally enshrined this practice for the purposes of the external representation of the Union and the implementation of the CFSP.[164] In order to ensure that the troika had sufficient weight internationally, the order of succession of the Member States was constructed in such a way that the troika virtually always included one "large" Member State.[165] The Treaty of Amsterdam departed from this practice by entrusting the international representation of the Union to the Presidency, assisted by a High Representative for the CFSP (EU Treaty, Art. 18(3)).[166]

3. Operation

Rules of Procedure. The Council operates in accordance with the **10–042** provisions of the Treaty and the Rules of Procedure which it adopted pursuant to Art. 207(3) of the EC Treaty and Art. 121(3) of the EAEC Treaty.[167] The Council is not entitled to depart from its Rules of Procedure

---

[160] See Council Decision 95/2/EC, Euratom, ECSC of January 1, 1995 determining the order in which the office of President of the Council shall be held ([1995] O.J. L1/220). As a result, France and Spain held the Presidency in 1995, after which it was to be occupied for successive six-month periods as follows: Italy and Ireland (1996), Netherlands and Luxembourg (1997), UK and Austria (1998), Germany and Finland (1999), Portugal and France (2000), followed by Sweden and Belgium (2001), Spain, Denmark (2002) and Greece and, again, Italy (2003) (Art. 1(1)). The Council, acting unanimously on a proposal from the Member State concerned, may decide that a Member State may hold the Presidency during a period other than that resulting from the above order (Art. 1(2)). Accordingly, the order of the Presidencies of Germany and Finland have been reversed for 2006–2007 at their request by Council Decision 2002/105/EC, ECSC, Euratom of January 28, 2002, [2002] O.J. L39/17. As a result, in 2007 in principle first Germany and then Portugal should occupy the Presidency.

[161] See the conclusions of the European Council held in Brussels on October 24 and 25, 2002, which, in order to give the new Member States the necessary time to prepare, confirmed the present system of rotation until 2006 (conclusions of the European Council in (2002) 10 EU Bull. point I.14).

[162] EU Treaty, Art. 18(4) and Council Rules of Procedure, Art. 20(2).

[163] For the first occurrence of this, see the London report on European Political Co-operation (1981) EC Bull. Suppl.3, 14–18, especially point 10.

[164] Art. J.5(3) of the original EU Treaty.

[165] See the Council Decision of January 1, 1995 (n.160, supra), as agreed at the European Council held in Brussels on December 12 and 13, 1993 ((1993) 12 EC Bull. point I.18, 17–18), upon entry into force of the 1994 Accession Treaty.

[166] Javier Solana was appointed first Secretary-General of the Council, High Representative for the CFSP; see the Council Decision of September 13, 1999, [1999] O.J. L284/33.

[167] See the current Rules of Procedure, adopted by the Council by decision of March 22, 2004 ([2004] O.J. L106/22), replacing the Rules of July 22, 2002 ([2002] O.J. L230/7), of June 5, 2000 ([2000] O.J. L149/21), and the previous versions of May 31, 1999 ([1999] O.J. L147/13), of December 6, 1993 ([1993] O.J. L304/1; corrigendum [1994] O.J. L71/26; amended by [1995] O.J. L31/14 and [1998] O.J. L337/40) and of July 24, 1979 ([1979] O.J. L268/1, as amended on July 20, 1987 ([1987] O.J. L291/27).

without formally amending them.[168] The President convenes the Council on his or her own initiative or at the request of one of its members or the Commission (EC Treaty, Art. 204). Dates for meetings of the Council are made known to the Member States before the beginning of each Presidency (Council Rules of Procedure, Art. 1(2)). Where a rapid decision is required in matters coming under the CFSP, the President may convene an extraordinary Council meeting within 48 hours or, in an emergency, at even shorter notice (EU Treaty, Art. 22(2)). Meetings take place in Brussels, except in April, June and October, when the Council meets in Luxembourg, or, if the Council so decides by a unanimous vote, elsewhere.[169] The Commission is invited to take part in Council meetings, unless the Council decides by a majority vote to deliberate in its absence. The same applies to the European Central Bank (Council Rules of Procedure, Art. 5(2)). Members of the Council and the Commission may be accompanied by civil servants (Council Rules of Procedure, Art. 5(3)). Exceptionally, a representative of other bodies may be invited to a meeting concerning matters falling within the remit of the body in question. The EC Treaty confers this right on the President of the ECB.[170]

10–043 Public nature of deliberations. In principle, Council meetings are not public (Council Rules of Procedure, Art. 5(1)). A major exception is where the Council deliberates as legislator under the co-decision procedure. In such cases, the presentation by the Commission of its legislative proposals, the ensuing debate in the Council, together with the vote on legislative acts, the final Council deliberations leading to that vote and the explanations of voting accompanying it are open to the public (Council Rules of Procedure, Art. 8(1)). Policy debates on the Council's annual operational programme and, where the Council or Coreper so decides by a qualified majority vote, debates on important legislative proposals and other issues are also open to the public (Council Rules of Procedure, Art. 8(2) and (3)). Public access is secured by relaying the Council meeting to another room by audiovisual means.[171] Where the Council acts in a legislative capacity, it publishes in any event the results of its votes, together with explanations of votes and

---

[168] ECJ, Case 68/86 *UK v Council* [1988] E.C.R. 855, para. 48. Non-compliance with the Rules of Procedure may constitute an infringement of an essential procedural requirement within the meaning of Art. 230, second para., of the EC Treaty (para. 49 of that judgment).

[169] Sole Art. 1, para. (b), of the Protocol on Seats, para. 10–146, *infra*, and Art. 1(3) of the Council Rules of Procedure.

[170] EC Treaty, Art. 113(2).

[171] Council Rules of Procedure, Art. 8(1), second and third subparas, (2) and (3), fourth subpara. See already the Council's answer of May 8, 1996 to question E–1095/96 (Moorhouse), [1996] O.J. C385/6.

statements in the minutes (EC Treaty, Art. 207(3), second subpara.).[172] The Council defines the cases in which it is to be regarded as acting in a legislative capacity in its Rules of Procedure.[173] Results of votes, explanations of votes and the statements in the Council minutes are also published where the Council establishes a PJCC convention (Council Rules of Procedure, Art. 9(1)(c)). The result of other votes may be made public at the request of a member of the Council ((Council Rules of Procedure, Art. 9(2)(c)).[174] In all those cases, results of votes and declarations of vote may be consulted on the Internet; the minutes are available from the Council's website.[175] The Council adopts the necessary rules on security to cover matters where secrecy is required.[176]

Vote. A valid vote may be held in the Council if a majority of the members **10–044** of the Council who are, under the Treaties, entitled to vote are present (Council Rules of Procedure, Art. 11(4)). Decisions taken under Art. 44a of the EU Treaty must, however, be taken by a unanimous vote of all the members. Although a Member State may be represented by persons other than ministers (*e.g.* by its Permanent Representative; see para. 10–049), such a representative may not vote. The right to vote may be delegated only to another member of the Council (EC Treaty, Art. 206; Council Rules of Procedure, Art. 11(3)). Members of the Council vote in the order in which the Member States hold the Presidency (Council Rules of Procedure, Art. 11(2)).

Unanimity and qualified majority. As far as voting in the Council is **10–045** concerned, there exist, alongside specific rules, four types of majorities

---

[172] Under the first subpara. of Art. 9(1) of the Council's Rules of Procedure, the items in the Council minutes relating to the adoption of legislative acts are also to be made public. The same applies to results of votes and explanations of votes, as well as the statements in the Council minutes and the items in those minutes relating to the adoption of a common position pursuant to Art. 251 or 252 of the EC Treaty, results of votes and explanations of votes by members of the Council or their representatives on the Conciliation Committee set up by Art. 251 of the EC Treaty, as well as the statements in the Council minutes and the items in those minutes relating to the Conciliation Committee meeting (Council Rules of Procedure, Art. 9(1)).

[173] Under Art. 7 of the Council Rules of Procedure, the Council acts in its legislative capacity when it adopts rules which are legally binding in or for the Member States, by means of regulations, directives, framework decisions or decisions, on the basis of the relevant provisions of the Treaties. Exceptions are discussions leading to the adoption of internal measures, administrative or budgetary acts, acts concerning interinstitutional or international relations or non-binding acts (such as conclusions, recommendations or resolutions).

[174] In the case of action pursuant to Title V or a common position within the meaning of Title VI of the EU Treaty, the Council must so decide by a unanimous vote (Council Rules of Procedure, Art. 9(2) (a) and (b)). Explanations of votes are made public at the request of the Council members concerned "with due regard for these Rules of Procedure, legal certainty and the interests of the Council"; a Council decision is also required to make public statements entered in the Council minutes and items in those minutes (Council Rules of Procedure, Art. 9(2), second and third subparas.).

[175] For the Council website, see n.130, *supra*.

[176] Art. 24 of the Council Rules of Procedure, as implemented by Council Decision 2001/264/EC of March 19, 2001, [2001] O.J. L101/1.

which have to be attained depending on the Treaty article serving as the legal basis for the act to be adopted.[177] If the article in question does not specify that the Council has to vote by a particular majority, the act has to be adopted by a majority of its members (EC Treaty, Art. 205(1)). If the Treaty article in question requires a qualified majority,[178] a weighted vote applies for each Member State, together with differing majority thresholds. In order to obtain a qualified majority, a particular number of votes must be obtained and, at the same time, a majority of the Member States representing at least 62 per cent of the population of the Union must vote in favour (EC Treaty, Art. 205(2)). Where the Treaty article serving as the legal basis requires the Council to vote unanimously, the act cannot be adopted if any Member State votes against.[179] Abstentions make it more difficult to achieve a qualified majority, but are not regarded as votes cast against the proposal where a unanimous vote is required (EC Treaty, Art. 205(3)).[180]

For votes by a qualified majority, a number of votes is granted depending on the country's population size, but corrected to give more weight to the smaller Member States.[181] The allocation of votes among the Member States was adjusted with a view to the accession of ten new Member States by a Protocol on the enlargement of the Union annexed to the EC Treaty by the Treaty of Nice, and subsequently by the Act of Accession.[182] From

---

[177] For special requirements as to majorities, see para. 14–011, *infra*, where Community decision-making is discussed. For matters in relation to which not all Member States take part in decision-making, the voting right of the Member State concerned is suspended and the requirement for unanimity or a particular majority vote is amended accordingly; see paras 14–068, 14–071 and 14–072, *infra*.

[178] See the articles listed in n.17 to the discussion of decision-making in para. 14–011, *infra*.

[179] Unanimity is required for numerous Community decisions of a general nature (para. 14–011, *infra*) and for some decisions taken at the request of the Court of Justice (EC Treaty, Art. 222, first para.; Art. 225a, first para., and Art. 245, second para.), at the request of the EIB (EC Treaty, Art. 266, third para.) or on the Council's own initiative (EC Treaty, Art. 213(1), second para.). In principle, unanimity is required for decisions taken in connection with the CFSP and PJCC (see EU Treaty, Art. 23(1), first subpara., and Art. 34(2)).

[180] This is also the rule for votes on matters relating to the CFSP and PJCC, see EU Treaty, Art. 23(1), first subpara., and Art. 41(1) (which refers to Art. 205(3) of the EC Treaty).

[181] The final allocation of votes is not based on objective criteria, but reflects the influence in decision-making which the Member States in fact allow each other: De l'Ecotais, "La pondération des voix au Conseil de ministres de la Communauté européenne" (1996) R.M.C.U.E. 388–393 and 617–620 and (1997) R.M.C.U.E. 324–327. See also Vignes, "Le calcul de la majorité qualifiée, un casse-tête pour 1996" (1994) R.M.C.U.E. 561–563; Bangemann, "Le vote majoritaire pour l'Union européenne élargie" (1995) 3 R.M.U.E. 175–180.

[182] EC Treaty, Art. 205(1) as amended by Art. 12 of the 2003 Act of Accession. The Protocol on the enlargement of the Union annexed to the EC Treaty by the Treaty of Nice (n.93, *supra*) already determined the number of votes for the 15 existing Member States; as regards the number of votes for the new Member States, the Protocol referred to Declaration (No. 20) annexed to the Treaty of Nice on the enlargement of the European Union (n.93, *supra*), which was adjusted by the European Council held in Brussels on October 24 and 25, 2002 to take account of the fact that Bulgaria and Romania would not be acceding in 2004. That declaration annexed to the Treaty of Nice determined that

November 1, 2004, France, Germany, Italy and the United Kingdom each have 29 votes, Spain and Poland 27, the Netherlands 13, Belgium, the Czech Republic, Greece, Hungary and Portugal 12 each, Austria and Sweden 10 each, Denmark, Finland, Ireland, Lithuania and Slovakia seven each, Cyprus, Estonia, Latvia, Luxembourg and Slovenia four each and Malta three. A qualified majority is attained where the Commission proposal obtains 232 out of 321 weighted votes (or 72.27 per cent) and, at the same time, the majority of the members of the Council vote in favour (EC Treaty, Art. 205(2), second subpara.). This means that at least 13 Member States must vote in favour and that a 90-vote minority can block the adoption of the act. Where the Council does not vote on a Commission proposal, a qualified majority consists of 232 weighted votes in favour out of 321, which must be cast by at least two-thirds of the members.[183] In any case, a member of the Council may request verification that the Member States constituting the qualified majority represent at least 62 per cent of the total population of the Union. If that condition is shown not to have been met, the decision in question shall not be adopted (EC Treaty, Art. 205(4)). This decision-making system with differing thresholds for majorities was agreed when the Treaty of Nice was approved.[184] It replaces the method whereby in the case of acts adopted on the basis of a Commission proposal it only had to be ascertained whether a certain number of weighted votes had been obtained.[185] Transitional arrangements

Romania would have 14 votes and Bulgaria 10 and provided for a maximum threshold of 258 out of 345 votes or 74.78 per cent for a Union of 27 Member States. See also Declaration (No. 21) annexed to the Treaty of Nice on the qualified majority threshold and the number of votes for a blocking minority in an enlarged Union (which, unlike the Protocol, provides that when the Union consists of 27 Member States, the voting requirement is to be adjusted to 255 out of 345 votes or 73.91 per cent). For the correct "maximum" threshold, compare Pieter Van Nuffel, "Le Traité de Nice. Un commentaire" (2001) R.D.U.E. 329, at 356–358 (threshold specified in Declaration No. 21) with Bradley, "Institutional design in the Treaty of Nice" (2001) C.M.L.R. 1095, at 1112 (threshold to be derived from Declaration No. 20).

[183] See the decisions listed separately in n.17 to para. 14–011, *infra*. The stricter requirement in terms of the majority required reflects the fact that a Commission proposal has already weighed up the interests of, *inter alia*, the smaller Member States, see De l'Ecotais (n.181, *supra*), at 392–393.

[184] Art. 3(1) of the Protocol on the enlargement of the Union (n.93, *supra*) announced that this system would take effect on January 1, 2005. However, that article was repealed by Art. 12(2) of the Act of Accession, which introduced the system of differing majority thresholds with effect from November 1, 2004.

[185] Before May 1, 2004, France, Germany, Italy and the UK each had 10 votes, Spain eight, Belgium, Greece, the Netherlands and Portugal five each, Austria and Sweden four each, Denmark, Finland and Ireland three each, and Luxembourg two. There was a qualified majority if the Commission proposal received 62 out of the 87 weighted votes or 71.26 per cent (hence the blocking minority consisted of 26 votes). Where the Council did not vote on a Commission proposal, there was already a dual requirement in order to attain a qualified majority: 62 weighted votes in favour out of 87, which had to be cast by at least 10 out of 15 members.

based on the previous method apply to the period between May 1, 2004 (date of the accession of the new Member States) and October 31, 2004.[186]

10–046 Luxembourg compromise. For a long time the rules on (qualified) majority voting laid down by the Treaty did not reflect reality. In July 1965 the Community was struck by a serious crisis when France refused to take part in Council meetings (the "empty chair" policy) and complained about majority voting on Council decisions bearing on fundamental policy choices, even though the Treaty allowed this to take place with regard to matters such as agricultural policy after the second stage of the transitional period (January 1, 1966). In order to break out of the impasse, the Council, meeting on January 17 and 18 and January 28 and 29, 1966 adopted the so-called "Luxembourg Compromise", in which the Member States declared, *inter alia*, that where—in cases where acts could be adopted by a majority vote on a proposal from the Commission—"very important interests" of one or more of the partners were at stake, the members of the Council would try within a reasonable time-limit to find a solution acceptable to all of them "while respecting their mutual interests and those of the Community, in accordance with Art. 2 of the Treaty".[187] Subsequently, delegations to the Council found that there were differences of opinion as to what had to be done when divergent views could not be reconciled fully. Although the "Compromise" did not renounce the principle of majority voting, it did found a practice whereby almost all Council acts, with the exception of budgetary measures, had to be adopted by a unanimous vote. This practice became further entrenched following the accession of the United Kingdom, which attached constitutional importance to the Compromise, since it was partly on the strength of it that Britain joined the Community. Nevertheless, it has been possible from time to time for acts to be adopted against the will of a minority.[188]

10–047 Increased importance of qualified majority. As a result of the Single European Act, the number of Treaty articles prescribing a vote by qualified majority increased dramatically. Accordingly, it appeared essential to rein in the previous practice. The Council succeeded in so doing by means of an

---

[186] See Art. 26 of the 2003 Act of Accession, which lays down an allocation of votes such that a qualified majority is obtained where the Commission proposal obtains 88 out of 124 weighted votes or 70.9 per cent (which means that the blocking minority is 37 votes). Where the Council does not act on a Commission proposal, a qualified majority is attained where the double majority of 88 out of 124 weighted votes and two-thirds of the members voting in favour is attained.

[187] Luxembourg Compromise, Part B, s.1 (1966) 3 Bull. CE 10.

[188] Thus, in May 1982 the farm prices were determined for the first time by a qualified majority vote. For the practical significance of the "Compromise", see Vasey, "Decision-making in the Agriculture Council and the 'Luxembourg Compromise'" (1988) C.M.L.R. 725–732; see the Council's answer of June 3, 1996 to question No. E–0317/96 (Moorhouse), [1996] O.J. C217/22; corrigendum: [1996] O.J. C345/117).

amendment to its Rules of Procedure adopted on July 20, 1987.[189] As a result, the President is required, at the request of a member of the Council or of the Commission, to open a voting procedure, provided that a majority of the Council's members so decides (see Council Rules of Procedure, Art. 11(1), second subpara.). This means that negotiations must be continued in the Council only if most Member States object to a vote being held. Once the Commission is persuaded that a given proposal has the support of a certain majority, it can call for a vote and get the proposal adopted. This rule was not affected by the political decision taken by the Council when it determined the weighted votes to be given to the new Member States which were to join the Union on January 1, 1995, the "Ioannina Compromise".[190]

"A" and "B" items. In practice, the Council does not have to take a formal **10–048** vote on many acts, since the decision is prepared by the national delegations and the Commission in working parties and in the Committee of Permanent Representatives (Coreper; see para. 10–049). All matters on which Coreper has already reached agreement appear on the agenda for Council meetings as "A" items. The Council approves them without further ado unless a member requests that the particular item be subjected to further discussion (Council Rules of Procedure, Art. 3(6) and (8)). In that event, the agenda item in question is generally sent back to Coreper. Matters on which Coreper has not reached agreement but which are nevertheless up for decision may be placed on the agenda as "B" items by a member of the Council or the Commission. The Council then endeavours to reach agreement or to get a sufficient majority behind the proposal, after which it may be sent back to Coreper to be finalised. It then comes back on the agenda for the Council meeting for approval as an "A" item. Urgent

---

[189] For that decision see n. 167, *supra*.

[190] Council Decision of March 29, 1994 concerning the taking of a Decision by qualified majority by the Council ([1994] O.J. C105/1, adapted because only three new Member States acceded to the Union on January 1, 1995, [1995] O.J. C1). In the Union of 15 Member States, this compromise applied when Member States representing a total of 23 to 25 votes indicated their intention to oppose the adoption by the Council of a decision by qualified majority. In such case, the Council would "do all in its power" to reach an agreed solution, within a reasonable time and without prejudicing obligatory time-limits laid down by the Treaties (*e.g.* EC Treaty, Arts 251 and 252) and by secondary law, which could be adopted by at least 65 votes. The Compromise required the President to undertake, with the assistance of the Commission and members of the Council, any initiative necessary to facilitate a wider basis of agreement in the Council in compliance with the Council's Rules of Procedure. For a comparison with the Luxembourg Compromise, see "Editorial Comments: the Ioannina Compromise—Towards a Wider and Weaker European Union?" (1994) C.M.L.R. 453–457. See also De l'Ecotais (n.181, *supra*), at 324–327. The Ioannina compromise is incompatible with the changes made to the voting procedure by the Treaty of Nice and the 2003 Act of Accession and since May 1, 2004 can no longer be applied. For the significance of a "right of veto", see also Van Nuffel, *De rechtsbescherming van nationale overheden in het Europees recht* (Kluwer, Deventer, 2000) 453–458.

matters may be dealt with by a written vote.[191] That procedure is also used for routine matters.[192] The formal vote on an act takes place in the Council, not in the working party or in Coreper. The latter only carry out the preparatory work and determine whether or not there is a consensus or a sufficient majority. If there is no consensus or an insufficient majority, the Council has to cut the Gordian knot.[193]

4. Internal organisation

10–049 **Coreper.** The Committee of Permanent Representatives (Coreper) prepares the work of the Council and carries out tasks assigned to it by that institution (EC Treaty, Art. 207(1)).[194] In this context, Coreper is to ensure consistency of the Union's policies and actions and see to it that the principles of legality, subsidiarity, proportionality and providing reasons for acts are respected, together with the rules establishing the powers of Union institutions and bodies, budgetary provisions and the rules on procedure, transparency and the quality of drafting.[195] Coreper is an auxiliary body and cannot exercise the decision-making powers conferred by the Treaty on the Council.[196] In the cases mentioned in Art. 19(7) of the Council's Rules of Procedure, Coreper is entitled to adopt procedural decisions (EC Treaty, Art. 207(1)). Each Member State delegates to it a Permanent Representative, who has the status of an ambassador based in Brussels, together with a Deputy Permanent Representative, who has the diplomatic

---

[191] The Council or Coreper decides by a unanimous vote whether to take advantage of this possibility; if the President proposes recourse to written votes, such a vote may take place if all Member States agree (Council Rules of Procedure, Art. 12(1)). The Commission's agreement is required to the use of that procedure where the written vote is on a matter brought before the Council by that institution (Council Rules of Procedure, Art. 12(2)). For the purposes of implementing the CFSP, there exists a simplified written procedure which makes use of COREU (*correspondance européenne*), a confidential communications network linking the national Foreign Ministries, the Commission and the Council's General Secretariat (Council Rules of Procedure, Art. 12(4)). Under that procedure, a proposal made by the Presidency is deemed adopted if no member of the Council objects within a period laid down by the Presidency.

[192] See De Zwaan, *The Permanent Representatives Committee: Its Role in European Decision-making* (Elsevier, Amsterdam, 1995) 322pp., who also describes in detail the use of the "A" and "B" item procedures.

[193] So as to preserve efficient decision-taking with delegations of 25 Member States around the table, the Council adopted on March 22, 2004 "Working methods for an enlarged Council" (see Annex IV to the Council Rules of Procedure, [2004] O.J. L106/42). They call upon delegations to avoid pointless presentations and keep their interventions short, substantive and to the point (see points 6–13). For an inquiry into the decisive nature of the final vote in the Council, see Van Schendelen, " 'De Raad beslist'. Beslist de Raad?" (1995) S.E.W. 706–721. For a survey by Member State of abstentions and votes cast against, see the Council's answer of June 26, 2000 to question E–917/00 (Huhne), [2001] O.J. C26E/131.

[194] For this Committee, usually known as "Coreper", an abbreviation of *Comité des représentants permanents*, see Hayes-Renshaw, Lequesne and Mayor Lopez, "The Permanent Representations of the Member States to the European Communities" (1989) J.C.M.S. 119–137; De Zwaan (n.192, *supra*).

[195] Council Rules of Procedure, Art. 19(1).

[196] ECJ, Case C–25/94 *Commission v Council* [1996] E.C.R. I–1469, paras 25–28.

rank of minister. The Permanent Representatives head the Member States' Permanent Representations to the European Union, which are in continual contact with the ministries in their respective Member States. Coreper has two parts, which are not in a hierarchical relationship. Part I consists of the Deputy Permanent Representatives. It deals chiefly with matters concerning the internal market and technical and economic questions. Part II, which comprises the Permanent Representatives themselves, discusses general issues and questions of foreign policy. A special committee discharges Coreper's tasks in the field of agricultural policy.[197]

Working groups. Various committees and working parties, consisting of national civil servants and representatives of the Commission, operate under the auspices of Coreper.[198] Some working parties are brought together on an ad hoc basis, others are permanent. The first discussions of Commission proposals for legislation generally take place within these working groups. They report to Coreper, which in turn refers the matters on to the Council.[199] **10–050**

Preparatory committees. The Treaties expressly entrust a number of committees with the task of preparing the work of the Council, without prejudice to Coreper's general competence. As far as financial and monetary questions are concerned, the Economic and Financial Committee does the preparatory work for the Council (EC Treaty, Art. 114(2), third indent; see para. 10–099). For the purposes of promoting co-ordination of employment and social policies, the advisory Employment and Social Protection Committees contribute to the preparation of Council proceedings (EC Treaty, Arts 130 and 144; see para. 10–099). As for PJCC, a Coordinating Committee consisting of senior national officials plays both a co-ordinating and an advisory role (EU Treaty, Art. 36(1)). That co-ordinating committee deals with technical aspects of policy relating to PJCC, whilst the broader political and institutional implications are left to Coreper, which also covers co-ordination with other policy areas for which **10–051**

---

[197] Art. 5(4) of the Decision of May 12, 1960 of the representatives of the Member States of the European Economic Community meeting within the Council on quickening the pace for achieving the objectives of the Treaty, [1960] J.O. 1217, and the Council Decision of July 20, 1960 setting up the committee (1960) 5 EC Bull. 74–75.

[198] See, *inter alia*, the "133 Committee" set up pursuant to Art. 133 of the EC Treaty; the Committee on Cultural Affairs set up by Resolution of the Council of the Ministers responsible for cultural affairs meeting within the Council of May 27, 1988 ([1988] O.J. C197/1) and the Financial Services Committee set up by Council Decision 2003/165/EC of February 18, 2003 ([2003] O.J. L67/17). A list of committees may be found, together with the structure of the Council and the composition of the Permanent Representations in the *Council Guide* (Official Publications Office of the European Communities, Luxembourg) issued annually in three volumes by the General Secretariat of the Council of the European Union.

[199] See Council Rules of Procedure, Art. 19(3) and 21. In the case of agricultural affairs, reports are made to the Special Agriculture Committee.

the Council is responsible.[200] For advice on the implementation of the CFSP, the Council has a Political and Security Committee (EU Treaty, Art. 25, first para.) consisting of the "Political Directors" from the Member States or their deputies.[201] This committee plays a central role in European security and defence policy, including crisis management. It exercises, under the responsibility of the Council, political control and strategic direction of crisis management operations and may be authorised, for the purpose and for the duration of a crisis management operation, to take the relevant decisions (EU Treaty, Art. 25, second and third paras; see para. 15–007).

10–052 **Presidency of committees and groups.** Coreper is chaired by the Permanent Representative of the Member State holding the Presidency or by his or her Deputy; the various committees and working parties are chaired by a delegate of that Member State (Council Rules of Procedure, Art. 19(4)). This enables the Member State holding the Presidency to make an impression on Council policy through its diplomats and civil servants for a six-month period. The Presidency is to take all necessary steps to have work advanced between meetings of Coreper, working parties or committees, for example, by organising bilateral consultations and by requesting the delegations of the Member States to take position on specific proposals for amendment of the documents discussed.[202] The Commission is represented, not only at Council meetings, but also on Coreper and the working parties.[203] As a result, it plays a dynamic role in the legislative process (see para. 14–017).

10–053 **General Secretariat.** The Council's administrative structure is its General Secretariat (EC Treaty, Art. 207(2)), which is based in Brussels. The Secretary-General is the High Representative for the CFSP and is assisted

[200] See the Council's answer of March 17, 1994 to question E–3815/93 (Van Outrive), [1994] O.J. C102/26. The original Art. K.4 of the EU Treaty created this committee (known as the "K.4 Committee"). The K.4 Committee replaced the Co-ordinators' Group (para. 2–016, *supra*), which was wound up after the EU Treaty entered into effect. For a discussion of the organisation plan for JHA co-operation within the Council, see Lepoivre, "Le domaine de la justice et des affaires intérieures dans la perspective de la Conférence intergouvernementale de 1996" (1995) C.D.E. 323, at 339–340 and 349.

[201] Council Decision 2001/78/CFSP of January 22, 2001 setting up the Political and Security Committee, [2001] O.J. L27/1. The Political and Security Committee is assisted by the Committee for civilian aspects of crisis management (set up by Council Decision 2000/354/CFSP of May 22, 2000, [2000] O.J. L127/1) and by the Military Committee of the European Union (set up by Council Decision 2001/79/CFSP of January 22, 2001, [2001] O.J. L127/4). See also para. 15–003, *infra*. For a brief period, there was an Interim Political and Security Committee (Council Decision 2000/143/CFSP of February 14, 2000, [2000] O.J. L49/1) and an Interim Military Body (Council Decision 2000/144/CFSP of February 14, 2000, [2000] O.J. L49/2).

[202] See also the tasks entrusted to the Presidency in so far as the preparation for meetings is concerned in Annex IV of the Council Rules of Procedure ("Working methods for an enlarged Council", n.193, *supra*).

[203] See Ponzano, "Les relations entre le Coreper et la Commission européenne" (2000)1 Il Diritto dell'Unione Europea 23–38.

by a Deputy Secretary-General, who is responsible for running the General Secretariat. The General Secretariat is divided into seven Directorates-General (A–G) and a legal service. It employs about around 2,700 staff.[204] The General Secretariat organises meetings of the Council, Coreper and the working parties, translates and distributes documents, assists the President and deals with the Council's relations with the other institutions.[205]

5. Changes proposed in the EU Constitution

Constitutional changes. The EU Constitution expressly states that the **10–054** Council is to meet in different configurations (Art. I–24(1)). Although it does mention some Council configurations by name,[206] the EU Constitution leaves it to the European Council—therefore no longer the Council itself—to determine the other configurations in which the Council may meet (Art. I–24(4)). The Council formations will continue to be chaired by representatives of the Member States on the basis of equal rotation. The European Council will establish the conditions of such rotation (EU Constitution, Art. I–24(7)). In June 2004, the Intergovernmental Conference agreed that the Presidency of the Council, with the exception of the Foreign Affairs configuration, will be held by pre-established groups of Member States for a period of 18 months.[207] In order to make up such groups of Member States, account is to be taken of "their diversity and geographical balance within the Union". Each member of the group will in turn chair for a six month period all configurations of the Council, with the exception of the Foreign Affairs configuration, while being assisted by the other members of the group.[208] In contrast, the Foreign Affairs Council will be chaired by the Union Minister for Foreign Affairs (EU Constitution, Art. I–28(3)).

The Union Minister for Foreign Affairs is to conduct the common foreign and security policy and will also be responsible as a Vice-President of the Commission, for external relations and the co-ordination of the Union's external action (see para. 10–071). Since the Union Minister for Foreign Affairs will take over the tasks of the Secretary-General of the Council, High Representative for the common foreign and security policy, the responsibility for the running of the General Secretariat of the Council will revert to its Secretary-General (EU Constitution, Art. III–344(2)).

As far as the functioning of the Council is concerned, the EU Constitution provides that the Council is to take decisions by a qualified

---

[204] As at December 31, 2003, the Council had 2487 established posts and 51 temporary posts: *General Report on the Activities of the European Union 2003* (n.122, *supra*) at 505.

[205] Egger, *Das Generalsekretariat des Rates der EU* (Nomos, Baden-Baden, 1994) 359 pp.

[206] In particular, the General Affairs Council and the Foreign Affairs Council (EU Constitution, Art. I–24(2)–(3)).

[207] See Art. 1(1) of the Draft Decision of the European Council on the exercise of the Presidency of the Council of Ministers, which has been annexed by the IGC to the EU Constitution with a view to being approved after signature of the EU Constitution

[208] *ibid.*, Art. 1(2).

majority, except where the Constitution provides otherwise (Art. I–23(3)). The system of calculating votes has been one of the issues on which the Intergovernmental Conference (IGC) reached agreement only at the very end. The Convention had proposed to relinquish the initial method for calculating the qualified majority laid down in Art. 205 of the EC Treaty (based on the attainment of a specific number of weighted votes) and retain only the two additional conditions—albeit in a slightly adapted version—introduced as from November 1, 2004 (that is to say, a majority of the Member States representing 60 per cent of the total population of the Union). Starting from that proposal, the IGC ultimately adopted a system which will be based on higher majority thresholds. With respect to decisions taken by the Council (or by the European Council) by a qualified majority, the EU Constitution will provisionally retain the present system for calculating votes. From November 1, 2009, all decisions taken by a qualified majority will require at least 55 per cent of the members of the Council, comprising at least fifteen of them, and representing Member States comprising at least 65 per cent of the population of the Union. In addition, a blocking minority is to include at least four members of the Council, failing wich the qualified majority shall be deemed attained (EU Constitution, Art. I–25(1)).[209] The EU Constitution will require decisions which the Council or the European Council is to take by a qualified majority and not on the basis of a proposal from the Commission (or from the Union Minister of Foreign Affairs) to be approved by at least 72 per cent of the members of the Council representing Member States comprising at least 65 per cent of the population of the Union (Art. I–25(2)). Moreover, the IGC agreed to having the adoption of an act by a qualified majority delayed if a certain number of Member States, which do not, as such, constitute a blocking minority, express their opposition.[210] In much the same way as the 1994 Ioannina Compromise (see para. 10–047), the Council will then be required to "do all in its power" to reach, within a reasonable time and without prejudicing obligatory time limits, a "satisfactory solution" to address "concerns" raised by the members of the Council which indicated their opposition.[211]

In order to enable the Council to meet in public when it deliberates and votes on a draft legislative act, each Council meeting will be divided into

---

[209] Until October 31, 2009, the present system will apply on the basis of Art. 2 of the Protocol on the transitional provisions relating to the institutions and bodies of the Union (n.129, *supra*).

[210] Art. 1 of the Draft Council Decision relating to the implementation of Art. I–25, annexed to the EU Constitution which, however, is to be formally adopted by the Council on the day the EU Constitution enters into force, provides that "[i]f members of the Council, representing (a) at least three-quarters of the population, or (b) at least three quarters of the number of Member States necessary to constitute a blocking minority resulting from the application of Art. I–25(1), indicate their opposition to the Council adopting an act by a qualified majority, the Council shall discuss the issue".

[211] *ibid.*, Art. 2. It will be up to the President of the Council, with the assistance of the Commission, to undertake any initiative necessary to "facilitate a wider basis of agreement in the Council": *ibid.*, Art. 3.

two parts, dealing respectively with deliberations on legislative acts and non-legislative activities (EU Constitution, Art. I–24(6)).

C. THE COMMISSION

Designation. As a result of Art. 9 of the Merger Treaty, the "Commission **10–055** of the European Communities" replaced the High Authority of the ECSC, the Commission of the EEC and the Commission of the EAEC. Following the entry into force of the EU Treaty, the Commission[212] refers to itself by the short title of the "European Commission".[213]

1. Powers

Survey. Article 211 of the EC Treaty lists the tasks which the Commission **10–056** is to carry out "in order to ensure the proper functioning and development of the common market" (see also Art. 124 of the EAEC Treaty, which refers to the "development of nuclear energy"). Its supervisory powers, participation in decision-making and implementing powers are fleshed out in other Treaty articles, together with powers with regard to the Communities' external relations policy. As far as non-Community action on the part of the Union is concerned, the Commission has virtually no supervisory power, its participation in decision-making is limited and, apart from the implementation of the budget, has only such tasks of implementation and representation as the Council delegates to it.

a. Supervision

Guardian of the Treaties. The Commission ensures that the provisions of **10–057** the Community Treaties and the measures taken pursuant thereto by the institutions are applied (see EC Treaty, Art. 211, first indent, and EAEC Treaty, Art. 124, first indent). It therefore checks that the other Community institutions (the Council and the European Parliament), Community bodies and agencies, the Member States and natural and legal persons comply with Community law.[214] To this end it receives information in the shape of informal or formal complaints and information with which it has to be provided pursuant to specific provisions.[215] Where Community provisions

---

[212] For the Commission's website, see *www.europa.eu.int/comm/index—en.htm.*

[213] *Europe,* No. 6130, November 8/9, 1993, 7.

[214] For a survey, see Van Rijn, "The Investigative and Supervisory Powers of the Commission" in Curtin and Heukels (eds), *Institutional Dynamics of European Integration. Essays in Honour of Henry G. Schermers,* Vol.II (Martinus Nijhoff, Dordrecht, 1994), 409–421. For some critical comment, see Palacio Vallelersundi, "La Commission dans son rôle de gardienne des Traités" (2001) R.D.U.E. 901–907.

[215] See the annual reports of the Court of Auditors (EC Treaty, Art. 248(4), first subpara.) and of the ECB (EC Treaty, Art. 113(3)). See the obligations to provide information imposed on the Member States by, *inter alia,* EC Treaty, Art. 60(2), first subpara.; Art. 88(3); Art. 95(4), (5) and (8); Art. 99(3), second subpara.; Art. 120(2); Art. 128(3); Art. 176. As far as natural and legal persons are concerned, see, *inter alia,* the obligation to notify certain concentrations of undertakings; para. 5–200, *supra.*

so provide (*e.g.* with regard to competition law), the Commission is obliged to respond to complaints from natural or legal persons.[216] In the event of failure to comply with Community law on the part of national authorities, citizens may submit a complaint to the Commission.[217] However, there is no formal procedure obliging the Commission to take any action in response to citizens' complaints.[218]

In order to perform its tasks, the Commission also has the right—under Art. 284 of the EC Treaty— to collect any information and carry out any checks required within the limits and under conditions laid down by the Council.[219] It falls to the European Parliament and the Council, acting under the co-decision procedure, to adopt measures for the production of statistics necessary for the performance of the Community's activities (EC Treaty, Art. 285(1)).[220]

In the event that the Commission finds that the European Parliament, the Council or certain bodies have infringed Community law, it may bring an action for annulment or for failure to act in the Court of Justice (EC Treaty, Arts 230 and 232).[221]

If a Member State fails to fulfil its obligations, the Commission puts it on notice, giving it the opportunity to rectify matters and submit any observations. If necessary, it will then deliver a reasoned opinion, with which the Member State has to comply within a specified period. If the Member State does not do so, the Commission may bring the matter before the Court of Justice (EC Treaty, Art. 226).[222] Exceptionally, the Commission may even summon a Member State directly before the Court

---

[216] See the complaints relating to breaches of Arts 81 and 82 of the EC Treaty under Art. 7 of Regulation No. 1/2003 (para. 5–197, *supra*); as for other formal complaints, there are in particular the questions put by members of the European Parliament (para. 10–107, *supra*).

[217] A standard form is to be found in [1999] O.J. C119/5. The Commission undertakes to comply with the rules set out in the annex to the Commission communication to the European Parliament and the European Ombudsman on relations with the complainant in respect of infringements of Community law ([2002] O.J. C166/3). See Harden, "A quel avenir la mise en application centralisée du droit communautaire peut-elle s'attendre?" (2002) R.D.U.E. 461–483.

[218] See the discussion of the action for failure to fulfil obligations (EC Treaty, Art. 226) in Lenaerts and Arts, *Procedural Law of the European Union*, Ch.5. The European Ombudsman has argued for a more extensive right to complain, see Söderman, "Le citoyen, l'Etat de droit et le principe de transparence" (2001) R.D.U.E. 889–900.

[219] See Council Regulation (Euratom, EEC) No. 1588/90 of June 11, 1990 on the transmission of data subject to statistical confidentiality to the Statistical Office of the European Communities (based on Art. 284 of the EC Treaty), [1990] O.J. L151/1.

[220] See, *e.g.* Decision 507/2001/EC of the European Parliament and of the Council of March 12, 2001 concerning a set of actions relating to the trans-European network for the collection, production and dissemination of statistics on the trading of goods within the Community and between the Community and non-member countries (Edicom), [2001] O.J. L76/1. The production of Community statistics must not entail excessive burdens on economic operators, see EC Treaty, Art. 285(2).

[221] The Commission can also bring an action against the ECB (EC Treaty, Art. 230, third para., and Art. 232, fourth para.) and against decisions of the Board of Governors and the Board of Directors of the EIB (EC Treaty, Art. 237(b) and (c)).

[222] The EC Treaty precludes such supervision in connection with the obligation (in the third stage of EMU) to avoid excessive government deficits (EC Treaty, Art. 104(10)).

of Justice.[223] If the Court of Justice finds that the Member State has infringed Community law, the Member State is required to take the necessary measures to comply with the Court's judgment, failing which the Commission may repeat the procedure and ask the Court to order payment of a lump sum or a penalty payment (EC Treaty, Art. 228). The Commission determines the amount of the sanction sought in the light of the required deterrent effect and the seriousness and duration of the infringement.[224] As far as the Court of Justice is concerned, the suggested sanctions are a "useful point of reference", but not binding on the Court.[225] A penalty payment is likely to encourage the Member State in infringement to put an end as soon as possible to the breach that has been found. The frequency of the proposed penalty payment, whether its amount should stay the same or decrease and the exact calculation of its amount must be determined on a case-by-case basis.[226] According to the Court, the basic criteria which must be taken into account in order to ensure that penalty payments have coercive force are, in principle, the duration of the infringement, its degree of seriousness and the ability of the Member State to pay. In applying those criteria, regard should be had in particular to the effects of failure to comply on private and public interests and to the urgency of getting the Member State concerned to fulfil its obligations.[227]

In certain circumstances, the Commission is entitled to impose fines on natural or legal persons for infringements of competition law.[228]

Non-Community policies. The EU Treaty does not give the Commission 10–058 the task of supervising that the obligations entered into under the CFSP and PJCC are complied with (see paras 15–006 and 15–013). The only power that the Commission has in this respect is the right to bring an action

---

[223] See the direct remedies provided for in Art. 95(9) and Art. 298, second para., of the EC Treaty and the procedure related to Art. 226 provided for in Art. 88(2) of the EC Treaty.

[224] For the position adopted by the Commission, see the Communication from the Commission—Memorandum on applying Art. 171 [now Art. 228] of the EC Treaty, [1996] O.J. C242/6; for the method of calculating penalty payments under Art. 228, see [1997] O.J. C63/2.

[225] ECJ, Case C–387/97 *Commission v Greece* [2000] E.C.R. I–5047, para. 89. As a result of that judgment, Greece was the first Member State to be ordered to pay a penalty payment (€20,000) for each day of delay in implementing measures to comply with a 1992 judgment from the date of delivery of the judgment ordering payment. The Commission had claimed that it should pay a penalty payment of €24,600. See Hilson (2001) Env.L.Rev. 131–138; Härtel, "Durchsetzbarkeit von Zwangsgeld-Urteilen des EuGH gegen Mitgliedstaaten" (2001) EuR. 617–630. For the implementation of the judgment, see the Commission's answer of September 18, 2001 to question P–1760/01 (Trakatellis), [2002] O.J. C93E/26.

[226] ECJ (judgment of November 25, 2003), Case C–278/01 *Commission v Spain*, not yet reported, paras 42–61 (whereby Spain was the second Member State to be ordered to pay a penalty payment).

[227] ECJ, Case C–387/97 *Commission v Greece* [2000] E.C.R. I–5047, para. 92. According to the Court of Justice, taking account both of the gross domestic product of the Member State concerned and of the number of its votes in the Council enables that Member State's ability to pay to be reflected while keeping the variation between Member States within a reasonable range: *ibid*, para. 88.

[228] paras 5–198—5–200, *supra*.

for annulment against PJCC framework decisions and decisions of the Council (EU Treaty, Art. 35(6)).

b. Participation in decision-making

10–059 **Proposals and recommendations.** The EC Treaty empowers the Commission to formulate recommendations or deliver opinions on matters dealt with in the Treaty if it expressly so provides or if the Commission considers it necessary (Art. 211, second indent).[229] The Commission draws up numerous reports in pursuance of its duty to keep other institutions informed[230] and on its own initiative,[231] and is entitled to consult the Court of Auditors, the European Economic and Social Committee and the Committee of the Regions.[232]

In some cases, the Commission has the power to take decisions with regard to Community matters (see EC Treaty, Art. 211, third indent). That decision-making power consists mainly[233] of means whereby the Commission, as the guardian of Community law, assesses whether Member States have complied with their Treaty obligations and permits them in

---

[229] For an application of Art. 211, see para. 5–223, *supra*. See also the recommendations (provided for in, *inter alia*, EC Treaty, Art. 53, second para.; Art. 77, third para.; Art. 97(1); Art. 119(1), first subpara.; Art. 134, first para.) and opinions addressed to Member States (EC Treaty, Art. 140); for recommendations and opinions addressed to the Council, see para. 14–014, *infra*.

[230] Alongside the General Report on the Activities of the European Union intended for the European Parliament (n.50, *supra*), the Commission also makes three-yearly reports to the European Parliament, the Council and the European Economic and Social Committee on citizenship (EC Treaty, Art. 20, first para.) and economic and social cohesion (EC Treaty, Art. 159, second para.: the latter report is also to be forwarded to the Committee of the Regions); an annual report to the European Parliament and the Council on social policy (EC Treaty Art. 143, first para.: the latter report is also to be forwarded to the European Economic and Social Committee), on research and technological development (EC Treaty, Art. 173) and on measures taken for countering fraud (EC Treaty, Art. 280(5)); reports to the European Parliament on particular social problems (EC Treaty, Arts 143 and 145, the second para. thereof) and on the results of multilateral economic surveillance (EC Treaty, Art. 99(4), second subpara.) and a number of reports to the Council on matters relating to Economic and Monetary Union (EC Treaty, Art. 99(3), first subpara.; Art. 104(3), first subpara.; Art. 116(2)(b); Art. 121(1), first subpara.; Art. 122(2)). See also the annual report for the European Council, the European Parliament and the Council on the application of Art. 5 of the EC Treaty (point 9, fourth indent of Protocol (No. 30) to the EC Treaty on the application of the principles of subsidiarity and proportionality, [1997] O.J. C340/105; that report is also to be sent to the Committee of the Regions and the European Economic and Social Committee). The Commission, together with the Council, also produces an annual report on the employment situation in the Community (EC Treaty, Art. 128(5)).

[231] The Commission has committed itself to issuing annual reports on competition policy, the application of Community law and the completion of the internal market.

[232] EC Treaty, Art. 248(4), second subpara.; Art. 262; Art. 265.

[233] See, however, the powers to adopt decisions of a general nature provided for, *inter alia*, in EC Treaty, Art. 39(3)(d) and Art. 86(3) (para. 5–201, *supra*).

appropriate cases to deviate from their obligations[234] or takes steps for the purpose of co-ordinating Member States' policies.[235]

A further important aspect is the Commission's participation "in the shaping of measures taken by the Council and by the European Parliament in the manner provided for in this Treaty" (EC Treaty, Art. 211, third indent). What this signifies in the first place is the Commission's virtually exclusive right to initiate legislation in Community matters (see para. 14–014). In non-Community matters, the Commission shares the right to submit proposals with the Member States (see para. 15–003 and 15–011). At the same time, it is the Commission which submits the preliminary draft EU budget (EC Treaty, Art. 272(2); see para. 10–131). In view of its decisive role in the decision-making process, the Commission may take part in sessions of the European Parliament (see para. 10–028) and in meetings of the Council (see para. 10–042).

c. Implementation

Implementing powers. The Commission has extensive powers of **10–060** implementation. In Community matters, the Council determines in the measures which it adopts the conditions under which the Commission is to implement the rules which it lays down (EC Treaty, Art. 211, fourth indent, and Art. 202, third indent; see para. 14–051 *et seq.*). As regards activities in connection with the CFSP and PJCC, the Commission is "associated" therewith,[236] which in practice often means that it is entrusted with implementation tasks (see paras 15–006 and 15–012). In any event, the Commission has the task of implementing the EU budget (EC Treaty, Art. 274; see para. 10–140).

d. Representation

Representation. The Commission represents the Community in legal **10–061** transactions within each Member State (EC Treaty, Art. 282; see para. 10–113) and, as a rule, also in international transactions (see para. 19–009). In non-Community matters, the Union is generally represented, however, by the Presidency of the Council, which may "associate" the Commission therewith (see para. 19–011 *et seq.*).

2. Composition

Number of Commissioners. The Commission which will take up its **10–062** functions on November 1, 2004 will have 25 Members (often referred to as

---

[234] For the power to grant derogations, see para. 9–001, *supra*. See also the supervision provided for in EC Treaty, Art. 76(2), second subpara.; Art. 88(1) and (2) (para. 5–204, *supra*).

[235] See EC Treaty, Art. 152(2); Art. 155(2); Art. 157(2); Art. 165(2); Art. 180(2). As far as social provisions are concerned, see its task of promoting dialogue between management and labour (EC Treaty, Art. 138) and its power to organise consultations between the Member States (EC Treaty, Art. 140).

[236] See EU Treaty, Arts 18(4), 27 and 36(2).

"Commissioners"). This because, since May 1, 2004, the rule applies that a each Member State will have one of its nationals as a member of the Commission (EC Treaty, Art. 213(1), second subpara.).[237] Before the rule was that the Commission included at least one national of each of the Member States,[238] but could not include more than two nationals of any given country. In practice, the five large Member States were entitled to two Members each and the small countries to one. Accordingly, the former Commission had 20 Members (between May 1 and October 30, 2004 30 members).[239] When the Union consists of 27 Member States, a system will be introduced whereby the number of Members of the Commission is smaller than the number of Member States and Member States will have nationals of their own as Commissioners according to a rotation system based on the principle of equality.[240] The Council may alter the number of Members of the Commission by unanimous vote.[241]

10–063 Appointment. Since the Treaty of Nice, Members of the Commission are to be appointed by the Council by a qualified majority vote. Before, they were appointed by the Member State Governments "by common accord". The European Parliament's say in the appointment of the President and Members of the Commission has been gradually increased, first by the EU Treaty and subsequently by the Amsterdam Treaty (see EC Treaty, Art. 214). The Council, meeting in the composition of Heads of State or Government and acting by a qualified majority, nominates the person it intends to appoint as President of the Commission; the nomination has to be approved by the European Parliament. Then, the Council, in its normal

---

[237] EC Treaty, Art. 213(1), as amended by Art. 4(1) of the Protocol on the enlargement of the Union (n.93, *supra*). The date of January 1, 2005 mentioned by the Protocol was changed to November 1, 2004 by Art. 45(2)(d) of the 2003 Act of Accession.

[238] EC Treaty, Art. 215, second para., provides for an exception thereto in the event that the Council should decide unanimously not to fill a vacancy.

[239] Originally, the High Authority of the ECSC and the Commission of the EEC had nine Members and the Commission of the EAEC five. With the Merger Treaty, the number of Members of the single Commission came to nine (after a transitional period when it had 14 Members: Merger Treaty, Art. 32). Since then the number of Members has been increased to 13 (Council Decision of January 1, 1973, [1973] O.J. L2/28), to 14 (1979 Act of Accession, Art. 15, [1979] O.J. L291), to 17 (1985 Act of Accession, Art. 15, [1985] O.J. L302) and to 20 (1994 Act of Accession, Art. 16, as amended by Council Decision of January 1, 1995, [1995] O.J. L1/4). As a result of Art. 42(2)(a) of the 2003 Act of Accession, the Commission has been enlarged by one Member for each new Member State.

[240] Art. 4 of the Protocol on the enlargement of the European Union (n.93, *supra*), which heralded further amendments to Art. 213(1) of the EC Treaty and further provides how the Council has to determine the number of Members of the Commission and the system of rotation. For reservations, see Bradley (n.182, *supra*), at 1117–1119; Georgopoulos and Lefèvre, "La Commission après le traité de Nice: métamorphose ou continuité? (2001) R.T.D.E. 597, at 600–602.

[241] EC Treaty, Art. 213(1), third subpara. (before the amendment made by the Protocol on the enlargement of the Union: Art. 213(1), second subpara.). See, *e.g.* the Council Decision of January 1, 1973, n. 239, *supra*. See Temple Lang, "How Much Do the Smaller Member States Need the European Commission? The Role of the Commission in a Changing Europe" (2002) C.M.L.R. 315–335.

composition, acting by a qualified majority and by common accord with the nominee for President, adopts the list of the other persons whom it intends to appoint as Members of the Commission. That list consists of names put forward by the Member States (EC Treaty, Art. 214(2), first and second subparas). Pursuant to its Rules of Procedure, the Parliament requests the nominee for President and, subsequently, the nominees for the various posts of Commissioners to appear before the appropriate committees according to their prospective fields of responsibility. This occurs in a public hearing where each nominee is invited to make a statement and answer questions.[242] The President and the other Members of the Commission thus nominated are put to a vote of approval by the European Parliament, following which they are appointed by the Council, acting by a qualified majority (EC Treaty, Art. 214(2), third subpara.).[243] After obtaining the approval of the College, the President appoints Vice-Presidents from among its Members (EC Treaty, Art. 217(3)).[244]

---

[242] EP Rules of Procedure, rr.98(1) and 99(1)–(2).

[243] See Karagiannis, "Le Président de la Commission" (2000) C.D.E. 9, at 12–36. The European Parliament pressed for a say in the appointment of the Commission ever since the early days of the Community: see the resolution of June 27, 1963, [1963] J.O. 1916. As long ago as 1983, the European Council decided in the Solemn Declaration of Stuttgart (n.7, *supra*) that, before appointing the President of the Commission, the Member State governments would seek the opinion of the enlarged Bureau of the European Parliament and that, after the Members of the Commission had been appointed, the European Parliament would vote on the Commission's proposed programme (point 2.3.5). See Louis, "La désignation de la Commission et ses problèmes", in Louis and Waelbroeck (eds), *La Commission au coeur du système institutionnel des Communautés européennes* (Editions de l'Université de Bruxelles, Brussels, 1989) at 9–23. The EU Treaty added the obligation for the Parliament to be *consulted* on the person whom the governments wished to appoint as President; at the same time, the national governments had to nominate the other persons whom they wished to appoint as Members of the Commission *in consultation with* the nominee for President and the appointment of the President and Members of the Commission as a body depended on the European Parliament's approval. So Jacques Santer was nominated in the Decision of the representatives of the Governments of the Member States of July 26, 1994 ([1994] O.J. L203/20) which was only adopted after the European Parliament had delivered its opinion on July 21, 1994 (even though the governments had already agreed on the person to be appointed on July 15, 1994 at an extraordinary meeting of the European Council in Brussels). The Treaty of Amsterdam made the appointment of the President depend upon the *approval* of the European Parliament and required the governments to reach *agreement* with the nominee President on the other persons whom they intended to appoint as Commissioners. Lastly, the Treaty of Nice introduced a qualified majority vote for the nomination of the President and the appointment of the President and Members of the Commission and replaced "governments of the Member States" by "the Council". As far as the Members from the new Member States appointed on May 1, 2004 were concerned, a simplified procedure was applied whereby the Members were appointed by the Council, acting by qualified majority and by common accord with the President of the Commission (2003 Act of Accession, Art. 45(2)(a)).

[244] The Treaty of Nice amended Art. 217 of the EC Treaty, which, since the EU Treaty, provided that the President could appoint one or two Vice-Presidents. Prior to that, Art. 14 of the Merger Treaty provided that the President and six Vice-Presidents were to be appointed by the Member State governments from amongst the Members of the Commission.

10–064 **Term of office.** The EU Treaty increased Commissioners' (renewable) term of office from four to five years (EC Treaty, Art. 214(1)), with the result that it is the same as that of the European Parliament. This means that the legislative work need be interrupted only once every five years when the membership of the institutions changes. This association of the term of office of Members of the Commission with the election of the European Parliament enables the political outcome of the elections to be reflected to some extent in the composition of the Commission. Nevertheless, Commissioners have to be chosen on the grounds of their general competence and their independence must be beyond doubt (EC Treaty, Art. 213(1), first subpara.).

10–065 **Independence.** Members of the Commission have to be "completely independent" in performing their duties "in the general interest of the Community" (EC Treaty, Art. 213(2), first subpara.). This applies in the first place to the Commission as an institution, which has to weigh the different interests of groups and Member States against the general interest of the Community. As far as individual Members of the Commission are concerned, this means that they may not seek or take instructions from any government or any other body, that they may not in principle engage in any other gainful or other occupation and that they must take care in accepting certain appointments or benefits even after they have ceased to hold office. When entering upon their duties they give a solemn undertaking that they will respect these obligations.[245] In the event of a breach of these obligations, the Commission itself and the Council may apply directly to the Court of Justice, which may order the Member concerned to be retired (EC Treaty, Art. 213(2), second and third subparas).[246] The Member States also

---

[245] This is done at a solemn sitting of the Court of Justice.
[246] The Council brought an action for the first time against a former Member of the Commission who resigned in order to take up an appointment with a company active in the sector for which he had been competent (telecommunications): see the Council Decision of July 9, 1999 ([1999] O.J. L192/55; for the application, see Case C–290/99 *Council v Bangemann*, [1999] O.J. C314/2); see also the resolution of the European Parliament of July 22, 1999 ([1999] O.J. C301/34). The application was withdrawn after Mr Bangemann gave an assurance that he would not take up any appointment with any undertaking in the sector for a certain period (see the Council Decision of December 17, 1999 on the settlement of the Bangemann case, [2000] O.J. L16/73), subject to the proviso that Mr Bangemann would withdraw his action against the Council Decision of July 9, 1999 (Case T–208/99, [1999] O.J. C314/14). See also CFI, Joined Cases T–227/99 and T–134/00 *Kvaerner Warnow Werft v Commission* [2002] E.C.R. II–1205, paras 47–60 (validity of a Commission decision unaffected by the fact that Mr Bangemann had taken leave of absence after his announcement that he had accepted an appointment outside the Commission before the Council's decision not to replace him) and ECJ, Case C–334/99 *Germany v Commission* [2003] E.C.R. I–1139, paras 17–27 (following the Commission's decision to grant Mr Bangemann "leave of absence" until the Council decided whether to replace him, the composition of the Commission was lawful, since that decision had no influence on Mr Bangemann's status as Member of the Commission).

undertake to respect the independence of Members of the Commission. As a matter of fact, they can assert their national interests in the Council.[247]

Voluntary or compulsory retirement. Apart from formal replacement, or **10–066** death, a Member of the Commission gives up his or her duties on voluntary or compulsory retirement. Compulsory retirement takes place where the European Parliament decides for political reasons to pass a motion of censure requiring the Commission to resign as a body (EC Treaty, Art. 201; see para. 10–017) or where the Court of Justice compulsorily retires a Member on an application by the Council or the Commission on the ground that he or she no longer fulfils the conditions required for the performance of his or her duties or if he or she has been guilty of serious misconduct (EC Treaty, Art. 216). A Member of the Commission also has to resign if the President so requests, after obtaining the approval of the College (EC Treaty, Art. 217(4)).[248] In each of these cases, the Council appoints a replacement by a qualified majority vote (without any formal involvement of the European Parliament) or decides that the vacancy is not to be filled.[249] It is only if the President has to be replaced that the procedure laid down in Art. 214(2) has to be applied (see EC Treaty, Art. 215).

In the event that the Commission as a body is made to resign by the European Parliament, it remains in office under Art. 201 of the EC Treaty to deal with current business until it is replaced. If a Member voluntarily retires, he or she remains in office until his or her successor has been appointed or a decision has been taken not to fill the vacancy (EC Treaty, Art. 215, fourth para.). The Members of the Commission who resigned as a body on March 16, 1999 declared that, although under the Treaty their powers were not limited in the circumstances obtaining (voluntary resignation), they had decided to exercise their powers in a restrictive manner until such time as they were replaced, *i.e.* to deal with current and urgent business, and to comply with their institutional and legal obligations, but not to take fresh political initiatives.[250] Nevertheless, in the case of

---

[247] For problems arising in practice, see, *e.g.* the Commission's answers of September 13, 1996 to question E–1776/96 (Schreiner), [1996] O.J. C385/36, and of December 4, 1996 to question E–2837/96 (Wiebenga), [1997] O.J. C72/84. According to the Commission, Members of the Commission are politicians carrying out a political function, who, while honouring the obligations imposed by this function, remain free to express their personal opinions quite independently and on their own responsibility: see the answer of February 7, 2000 to questions E–2459/99, E–2600/99 and E–2628/99, [2000] O.J. C255E/139.

[248] See Coultron (n.58, *supra*), at 263–265.

[249] *e.g.* if the Commission's term of office is coming to an end, the Council may take a unanimous decision under Art. 215, second para., of the EC Treaty that there is no need to fill the vacancy. See, for example, Council Decision 1999/493/EC, ECSC, Euratom of July 9, 1999 on the composition of the Commission, [1999] L192/53.

[250] Press communiqué of March 17, 1999, doc. IP/99/186. See Rodrigues, "Quelques réflexions juridiques à propos de la démission de la Commission européenne—de la responsabilité des institutions communautaires comme 'manifestation ultime de la démocratie'?" (1999) R.M.C.U.E. 472–483; Tomkins, "Responsibility and Resignation in the European Commission" (1999) Mod.L.Rev. 744–765.

voluntary resignation, the resigning Members of the Commission continue to have their full powers until such time as they are replaced.[251]

So long as the national governments have not appointed new Members to the Commission at the end of its term of office, the old Commission remains in office, but its powers are limited to dealing with current business.[252]

3. Operation

10–067 Rules of Procedure. The Commission has to act collectively in accordance with the Treaties and its Rules of Procedure, adopted pursuant to Art. 218(2) of the EC Treaty.[253] It works under the political guidance of its President, who is to decide on its internal organisation in order to ensure that it acts consistently, efficiently and on the basis of collegiality (EC Treaty, Art. 217(1)).[254] The President of the Commission convenes the Commission to meet at least once a week (Commission Rules of Procedure, Art. 5). Its meetings are not public and its discussions are confidential (Commission Rules of Procedure, Art. 9). The Secretary-General attends its meetings and, exceptionally, other persons may be heard (Commission Rules of Procedure, Art. 10).

10–068 Collective responsibility. The Commission acts by a majority of its Members (EC Treaty, Art. 219, first para.). It is quorate if a majority of its Members is present (EC Treaty, Art. 219, second para., and Commission

---

[251] Therefore, after their decision of March 16, 1999 to resign as a body, the Commission's powers were not confined to dealing with current business: CFI (judgment of December 17, 2003), Case T–219/99 *British Airways v Commission*, not yet reported, paras 46–56. In an earlier case, the Court of First Instance did not rule on whether or not the Commission's powers were limited after March 16, 1999: CFI, Joined Cases T–228/99 and T–233/99 *Westdeutsche Landesbank Girozentrale v Commission* [2003] E.C.R. II–435, paras 94–100 (a decision by which the Commission declared State aid incompatible with the common market falls in any event under the heading of "current business").

[252] This is the view taken by the Commission's Legal Service, see *Europe*, No. 6396, January 12, 1995. 6. This situation occurred after the expiry of the term of office of the Commission presided over by Jacques Delors on January 6, 1995 because the European Parliament wished to pronounce on the nominated President (Santer) and other Members of the Commission at its first plenary session which MEPs from the Member States which acceded on January 1, 1995 were to attend. After it was approved by the European Parliament on January 18, 1995, the Santer Commission was appointed by decision of the representatives of the Governments of the Member States of January 23, 1995, [1995] O.J. L19/51.

[253] See also EAEC Treaty, Art. 131, second para. The present Rules of Procedure were adopted by the Commission on November 29, 2000 ([2000] O.J. L308/26). Previous versions date from September 18, 1999 ([1999] O.J. L252/41) and February 17, 1993 ([1993] O.J. L230/16, adopted pursuant to Art. 16 of the Merger Treaty) and January 31, 1963 (provisionally retained after the Merger Treaty entered into force by decision of July 6, 1967, [1967] J.O. 147/1). The provisions on security (Commission Decision of November 29, 2001, [2001] O.J. L317/1), the detailed rules on public access to documents (Commission Decision of December 5, 2001, [2001] O.J. L345/94) and the provisions on document management (Commission Decision of January 23, 2002, [2002] O.J. L21/23) are annexed to the Rules of Procedure.

[254] See Karagiannis (n.243, *supra*), at 36–55.

Rules of Procedure, Art. 7). However, decisions may be taken by means of a written procedure whereby a proposal made by one or more Members is deemed to have been adopted if no Member enters a reservation within a specified period or asks that the proposal be discussed at a meeting.[255] The fact that Commissioners participate equally in decision-making is indicative of the collegiate nature of the Commission, which means that "decisions should be the subject of a collective deliberation and that all the Members of the college of Commissioners bear collective responsibility on the political level for all decisions adopted".[256] In a framework agreement between the European Parliament and the Commission, it is stated, however, that, without prejudice to the principle of Commission collegiality, each Member of the Commission is to take political responsibility for action in the field for which he or she is responsible.[257]

Provided that the principle of collective responsibility is fully respected, the Commission may empower one or more of its Members to take management or administrative measures on its behalf and subject to such restrictions and conditions as it shall impose.[258] The Commission may

---

[255] Commission Rules of Procedure, Art. 12. According to that Article, the procedure in question may be employed only if the Directorates-General involved are in agreement and the proposal has been endorsed by the Commission's Legal Service.

[256] ECJ, Case 5/85 *AKZO Chemie v Commission* [1986] E.C.R. 2585, para. 30. For the principle of collegiality, see also Mistò, "La collégialité de la Commission européenne" (2003) R.D.U.E. 189–255; Coutron (n.58, *supra*), at 247–266.

[257] Framework agreement on relations between Parliament and the Commission of July 5, 2000 (n.53, *supra*), point 9. See also Mehde, "Responsibility and Accountability in the European Commission" (2003) C.M.L.R. 423–442.

[258] Commission Rules of Procedure, Art. 13, first para. According to the Court of Justice, the system of delegation of authority remains within the Commission's power of internal organisation since the Commission does not thereby divest itself of powers (the decisions may still be the subject of judicial review as Commission decisions and the Commission may always reserve certain decisions for itself) and the procedure is necessary for the sound functioning of the Commission's decision-making power: ECJ, Case 5/85 *AKZO Chemie v Commission* [1986] E.C.R. 2585, paras 35–37; ECJ, Joined Cases 97–99/87 *Dow Chemica Ibérica v Commission* [1989] E.C.R. 3165, para. 58. See the earlier recognition of the delegation of the power of signature for management and administrative measures: ECJ, Case 48/69 *ICI v Commission* [1972] E.C.R. 619, paras 12–14, and ECJ, Case 52/69 *Geigy v Commission* [1972] E.C.R. 787, para. 5; ECJ, Case 8/72 *Cementhandelaren v Commission* [1972] E.C.R. 977, paras 11–13; ECJ, Joined Cases 43 and 63/82 *VBVB and VBBB v Commission* [1984] E.C.R. 19, paras 12–14. No management or administrative measure constitutes a decision finding an infringement of Art. 81(1) of the EC Treaty in the authentic language: CFI, Joined Cases T–79/89, T–84/89, T–85/89, T–86/89, T–89/89, T–91/89, T–92/89, T–94/89, T–96/89, T–98/89, T–102/89 and T–104/89 *BASF v Commission* [1992] E.C.R. II–315, paras 57–59; ECJ, Case C–137/92 P *Commission v BASF* [1994] E.C.R. I–2555, paras 62–65; CFI, Joined Cases T–80/89, T–81/89, T–83/89, T–87/89, T–88/89, T–90/89, T–93/89, T–95/89, T–97/89, T–99/89, T–100/89, T–101/89, T–103/89, T–105/89, T–107/89 and T–112/89 *BASF v Commission* [1995] E.C.R. II–729, paras 96–102. With regard to State aid, see CFI, Case T–435/93 *ASPEC v Commission* [1995] E.C.R. II–1281, paras 100–104, and CFI, Case T–442/93 *AAC v Commission* [1995] E.C.R. II–1329, paras 81–95. Neither does a decision to issue a reasoned opinion or to commence infringement proceedings before the Court of Justice constitute a measure of administration or management: ECJ, Case C–191/95 *Commission v Germany* [1998] E.C.R. I–5449, paras 33–37. Powers conferred by delegation may be subdelegated to the Directors-General and Heads of Service unless this is expressly prohibited in the empowering decision (Commission Rules of Procedure, Art. 13, third para.).

likewise instruct one or more of its Members, with the President's agreement, to adopt the definitive text of any instrument or of a proposal for submission to other institutions if the substance of the act or proposal has already been determined.[259] Accordingly, the Commission may authorise one of its Members to amend a proposal before the Council in a particular way.[260] Where the Commission itself takes the final decision, the principle of collective responsibility requires that the operative part of that final decision and its statement of reasons should be adopted in its definitive written form by the Commission as a body, which means that only simple corrections of spelling and grammar may be made to the text of an act after its formal adoption.[261] Since 2001, the Commission may, provided the principle of collective responsibility is fully respected, delegate the adoption of management or administrative measures to the Directors-General and Heads of Service, acting on its behalf and subject to such restrictions and conditions as it shall impose.[262]

4. Internal organisation

10–069 **Directorates-General.** The President of the Commission decides on its internal organisation. He or she structures the responsibilities incumbent upon the Commission, allocates them among its Members and may reshuffle the allocation of those responsibilities during the Commission's term of office (EC Treaty, Art. 217(1) and (2)). Accordingly, the President assigns to Members of the Commission special fields of activity with regard to which they are specifically responsible for the preparation of Commission work and the implementation of its decisions.[263] The President

---

[259] Commission Rules of Procedure, Art. 13, second para., taking over Art. 11 of the 1993 Rules of Procedure, as amended following the judgment of the Court of First Instance of February 27, 1992 in *BASF v Commission* (n.258, *supra*) and again following the judgment of the Court of Justice of June 15, 1994 in *Commission v BASF* (*ibid*; for the amendment, see [1995] O.J. L97/82). As a result, it appears that the Commission may not authorise one of its Members to adopt the text of a definitive decision in other authentic languages.

[260] ECJ (judgment of September 11, 2003), Case C–445/00 *Austria v Council*, not yet reported, paras 40–42.

[261] ECJ, Case C–137/92 P *Commission v BASF* [1994] E.C.R. I–2555, paras 66–70. The Court of Justice mitigated these formal requirements as regards decisions to issue a reasoned opinion or to commence infringement proceedings. Such decisions must be the subject of collective deliberation by the college of Commissioners; accordingly, the information on which they are based must be available to the Members of the college; however, the college itself does not have to decide formally on "the wording of the acts which give effect to those decisions and put them into final form": ECJ, Case C–191/95 *Commission v Germany* [1998] E.C.R. I–5449, paras 41–48. See also ECJ, Case C–272/97 *Commission v Germany* [1999] E.C.R. I–2175, paras 16–22; ECJ, Case C–198/97 *Commission v Germany* [1999] E.C.R. I–3257, paras 19–22; ECJ, Case C–1/100 *Commission v France* [2001] E.C.R. I–9989, paras 79–86.

[262] Commission Rules of Procedure, Art. 14.

[263] Commission Rules of Procedure, Art. 3, first para. Commissioners have their own *cabinets* (private offices) and give policy directions to one or more directorates-general (or certain directorates) and other departments. See also Georgopoulos and Lefèvre (n.240, *supra*), at 602–608. The hierarchical link between a Commissioner and the administration is not legally determined; see Mehde (n.257, *supra*), at 429–433.

of the Commission is to notify the European Parliament immediately of any decision concerning the allocation of responsibilities to any of the Members of the Commission.[264] The Members of the Commission are to carry out the duties devolved upon them by the President under his or her authority (EC Treaty, Art. 217(2)). The Commission's administrative services consist of Directorates-General and equivalent departments (Commission Rules of Procedure, Art. 19). The Directorates-General (DGs), which are subdivided into directorates, each deal with a specific area of policy under the leadership of a Director-General.[265] Other departments include the General Secretariat, the Legal Service, the translation service, and a number of offices.[266] The Commission's seat is in Brussels, but a number of its departments are established in Luxembourg.[267] With more than 22,000 officials (of which approximately 1200 are in the translation service), the Commission constitutes the largest of the institutions.[268]

5. Changes proposed in the EU Constitution

Composition. Without modifying the role of the Commission, Art. I–26(1) **10–070** of the EU Constitution sets out a detailed description of the roles played by that institution, in particular in initiating legislation and monitoring the application of the law, together with its budgetary powers, executive powers

---

[264] Point 11 of the framework agreement of July 5, 2000 (n.53, *supra*), which also provides that in the case of substantial changes affecting an individual Commissioner, he or she shall appear before the relevant parliamentary committee at its request.

[265] For internal policy: DG Customs and Indirect Taxation (TAXUD), DG Competition (COMP), DG Economic and Financial Affairs (ECFIN), DG Energy and Transport (TREN), DG Health and Consumer Protection (SANCO), DG Information Society (INFOSO), DG Internal Market (MARKT), DG Justice and Home Affairs (JAI), DG Agriculture (AGRI), DG Environment (ENV), DG Enterprise (ENTR), DG Education and Culture (EAC), DG Research (RTD), DG Regional Policy (REGIO), DG Fisheries (FISH) and DG Employment and Social Affairs (EMPL). For external relations: DG External Relations (RELEX), DG Trade (TRADE), DG Development (DEV). For internal services: DG Budget (BUDG), DG Personnel and Administration (ADMIN) and DG Financial Control (FC). For external contacts: DG Press and Communication (PRESS). Before the Prodi Commission, the Directorates-General were designated by numbers (*e.g.* DG IV for DG Competition). For the internal modernisation implemented by the Prodi Commission, see O'Sullivan, "La réforme de la Commission européenne" (2000) R.D.U.E. 723–728.

[266] Such as the Official Publications Office (EUR-OP or OPOCE), the Statistical Office (Eurostat), the European Anti-Fraud Office (OLAF), the European Community Humanitarian Office (ECHO), the Internal Audit Service (IAS), the Enlargement Service (ELARG), the Europe Aid Co-operation Office (AIDCO), the Joint Research Centre (JRC), the Joint Interpretation and Conference Centre and the Group of Policy Advisors.

[267] See the sole Article, para. (c), of the Protocol on Seats (para. 10–146, *infra*), which refers, as regards the departments to remain in Luxembourg, to the list in the Decision on Provisional Location of April 8, 1965 (para. 10–145, *infra*). See also ECJ, Case C–137/92 P *Commission v BASF* [1994] E.C.R. I–2555, paras 41–42 (for the purpose of the extension of procedural time-limits on account of distance, the Commission has its "habitual residence" in Brussels).

[268] As at December 31, 2003 the Commission's establishment plan (which includes a number of agencies) consisted of 21,850 permanent posts and 634 temporary posts: *General Report on the Activities of the European Union 2003* (n.122, *supra*), at 507.

and powers of representation. In this connection, the EU Constitution confirms that the Union's legislative acts can be adopted only on the basis of a Commission proposal, except where the Constitution provides otherwise (Art. I–26(2)). As far as concerns the Commission's role in supervising Member States' compliance with their obligations, the EU Constitution will make it easier for the Commission to bring an action before the Court of Justice against any Member State failing to fulfil its obligation to notify measures transposing a European framework law. The Commission may obtain the imposition of a lump sum or penalty payment without any need to bring a second action against the Member State concerned (EU Constitution, Art. III–362(3)). In other cases of non-fulfilment by a Member State of its obligations, the EU Constitution simplifies the procedure whereby the Commission may bring a second action before the Court of Justice (EU Constitution, Art. III–362(2)).[269]

As for the composition of the Commission, the Convention had proposed that the Commission would consist of a President, the Union Minister for Foreign Affairs and 13 "European Commissioners" selected on the basis of a system of equal rotation between the Member States. In addition, the Commission would have comprised non-voting "Commissioners", coming from the Member States that would not have one of their nationals selected as European Commissioner. Several Member States insisted, however, on preserving the right for each Member State to have one of its nationals appointed as a full member of the Commission. The Intergovernmental Conference struck the following compromise. The first Commission appointed under the provisions of the Constitution will consist of one national of each Member State, including its President and the Union Minister for Foreign Affairs who will be one of its Vice-Presidents (EU Constitution, Art. I–26(5)). Thereafter, the Commission will consist of a number of Members, including its President and the Union Minister for Foreign Affairs, corrresponding to two thirds of the number of Member States, unless the European Council, acting unanimously, decides to alter this figure. The members of the Commission will be selected on the basis of a system of equal rotation between the Member States (draft EU Constitution, Art. I–26(6)).

As far as the appointment of the President of the Commission is concerned, the current procedure whereby the Council, meeting in the composition of the Heads of State or Government and acting by a qualified majority, nominates a candidate who has to be approved by the European Parliament, will be replaced by a system under which the European Council, acting by a qualified majority, will propose a candidate for the Presidency who will then have to be elected by the European Parliament (EU Constitution, Art. I–27(1)). That proposal must take the elections to the European Parliament into account.[270] The Council, acting

---

[269] As a result, the Commission does not have to deliver another reasoned opinion.
[270] EU Constitution, Art. I–27(1).

by a qualified majority and in common accord with the President-elect, is to adopt the list of the other persons whom it intends to appoint as Members of the Commission on the basis of the suggestions made by Member States (EU Constitution, Art. I–27(2)). Next, the President, the Union Minister for Foreign Affairs and the other Members of the Commission will be submitted collectively to a vote of approval by the European Parliament. On the basis of this approval, the Commission will be appointed by the European Council, acting by a qualified majority (EU Constitution, Art. I–27(2)).

Within the College, the President of the Commission will retain the power to decide on the internal organisation of the Commission and every Member of the Commission will be under duty to resign if so requested by the President. The Commission will continue to be collectively accountable to the European Parliament (EU Constitution, Art. I–26(8)).

Union Minister for Foreign Affairs. The Union Minister for Foreign **10–071** Affairs will be part of the College of Commissioners, as one of the Commission's Vice-Presidents, but the Minister's status will be somewhat singular owing to his or her dual role. On the one hand, the Minister will conduct the Union's common foreign policy and common security and defence policy as the mandatory of the Council. On the other hand, he or she will be responsible within the Commission for handling external relations and for co-ordinating other aspects of the Union's external action. As befits this dual role, the Minister will be appointed by the European Council, acting by a qualified majority, with the agreement of the President of the Commission, and will also be submitted, together with the President and the other Members of the Commission, to a vote of approval by the European Parliament (EU Constitution, Arts I–28(1) and I–27(2)). This dual role also explains why, as far as the CFSP is concerned, the Union Minister for Foreign Affairs will be answerable to the European Council, which may end his or her tenure by the same procedure by which he or she is appointed. In contrast, when the Minister carries out the tasks entrusted to him or her as a Member of the Commission, he or she will be bound by Commission procedures (EU Constitution, Art. I–28(1) and (4)).[271]

D. THE COURT OF JUSTICE AND THE COURT OF FIRST INSTANCE

Two courts. When the EEC Treaty and the EAEC Treaty entered into **10–072** force, one institution, the Court of Justice of the European Communities,[272]

---

[271] Art. I–28(4) of the EU Constitution provides that the Minister is bound by Community procedures "to the extent that this is consistent with paragraphs 2 and 3". Likewise, where the President of the Commission requests the Minister to resign, he or she will have to do so "in accordance with the procedure set out in Art. I–28(1)" (EU Constitution, Art. I–27(3)). Where a motion of censure is carried and the Commission is to resign as a body, the Minister will be under a duty only to "resign from the duties that he or she carries out in the Commission" (EU Constitution, Art. I–26(8)).

[272] For the website of the Court of Justice, see *www.curia.eu.int.*

took the place of the existing Court of Justice of the ECSC. The Court of Justice exercised jurisdiction in accordance with each of the three Community Treaties and the protocols on the Statute of the Court appended thereto. Since September 1, 1989, the institution known as the Court of Justice has consisted of two independent courts, one bearing that name, the other entitled the Court of First Instance.[273] The Treaty of Nice considerably altered the jurisdiction of the Court of Justice and the Court of First Instance and made it possible for the Council to attach judicial panels to the Court of First Instance to exercise judicial competence in certain specific areas (EC Treaty, Art. 220, second para.).[274] The Council is to decide thereon unanimously on a proposal from the Commission and after consulting the European Parliament and the Court of Justice or at the request of the Court of Justice and after consulting the European Parliament and the Commission (EC Treaty, Art. 225a(1)).[275] By means of a new Protocol on the Statute of the Court of Justice, the Treaty of Nice introduced a single Statute for the Court of Justice and the Court of First Instance,[276] which the Council may amend by unanimous vote in order, for instance, to implement Art. 225 and 225a of the EC Treaty that contemplate amendments to the respective jurisdictions of the Court of Justice and the Court of First Instance and the judicial panels (see para. 10–079). Unless the Statute of the Court of Justice or the decision establishing a judicial panel provide otherwise, the provisions of the Treaty

---

[273] Council Decision 88/591 of October 24, 1988 establishing a Court of First Instance of the European Communities [hereinafter: CFI Decision], [1988] O.J. L319/1, and L 241 (republished as amended by corrigenda in [1989] O.J. C215/1). By that decision, the Council, acting unanimously at the request of the Court of Justice and after consulting the Commission and the European Parliament, established a Court of First Instance of the European Communities pursuant to Art. 32d of the ECSC Treaty, Art. 168a of the EEC Treaty and Art. 140a of the EAEC Treaty. The EU Treaty rooted the existence of the Court of First Instance in the EC Treaty itself (see Art. 225(1)).

[274] In the first place, it was envisaged to cover disputes between the Community and its servants (see Declaration (No. 16) annexed to the Treaty of Nice) and disputes relating to the application of acts which create Community industrial property rights.

[275] See already the proposals of December 23, 2003 for a Council Decision establishing the European Civil Service Tribunal (COM (2003) 705 final) and for a Council Decision establishing the Community Patent Court and concerning appeals before the Court of First Instance (COM (2003) 828 final).

[276] Protocol on the Statute of the Court of Justice, annexed by the Treaty of Nice to the EU Treaty, the EC Treaty and the EAEC Treaty ([2001] O.J. C80/53), pursuant to Art. 245 of the EC Treaty and Art. 160 of the EAEC Treaty. The provisions of the Statute have the same normative force as Treaty articles (see Art. 311 of the EC Treaty and Art. 207 of the EAEC Treaty), although the Council, acting unanimously at the request of the Court of Justice and after consulting the European Parliament and the Commission, or at the request of the Commission and after consulting the European Parliament and the Court of Justice, may amend the provisions of the Statute, with the exception of Title I (on the status of Judges and Advocates General): see EC Treaty, Art. 245, and EAEC Treaty, Art. 160. The new Statute replaces the CFI Decision and the respective Protocols relating to the Statute of the Court of Justice which were annexed to the EC Treaty, the EAEC Treaty and the ECSC Treaty, with the exception of a number of provisions remaining in force for the Court of Justice and the Court of First Instance in matters relating to the ECSC (Treaty of Nice, Arts 7–10).

relating to the Court of Justice are to apply to the Court of First Instance and the judicial panels.[277]

1. Jurisdiction

Decentralised enforcement of Community law. The Court of Justice and the Court of First Instance ensure, each within its jurisdiction, that in the interpretation and application of the Treaties the law is observed (EC Treaty, Art. 220, and EAEC Treaty, Art. 136). This does not mean that the Court of Justice and the Court of First Instance automatically hear and determine all disputes whose outcome depends on the correct application of Community law. The founding fathers of the Communities opted for a system under which enforcement of Community law was left in principle to the national courts. A dispute relating to Community law may be brought before the Court of Justice or the Court of First Instance (including the judicial panels) only if this is permitted under one of the procedures prescribed by the Treaties.[278] Exceptionally, the Court of Justice has interpreted its own jurisdiction in a manner exceeding the literal scope of a given procedure, *inter alia* in order to fill a lacuna in the system of legal protection or to secure the coherence of the Community's legal order.[279] **10–073**

Possible actions. The procedures provided for in the Treaties enable the Court of Justice to carry out a four-fold task.[280] **10–074**

> (1) First, the Court decides disputes between Community institutions and bodies, both directly following the bringing of an action for annulment or of an action for failure to act, and indirectly pursuant to other procedures. The European Parliament, the Council, the Commission and—if the action seeks to safeguard their prerogatives—the Court of Auditors and the ECB are entitled to

---

[277] The provisions of the Statute are also to apply to the judicial panels unless the decision establishing the judicial panel provides otherwise. See EC Treaty, Art. 224, sixth para., and Art. 225a, sixth para.

[278] See ECJ, Case 66/76 *CFDT v Council* [1977] E.C.R. 305, para. 8.

[279] See ECJ, Case 294/83 *Les Verts v European Parliament* [1986] E.C.R. 1339, paras 23–25, and ECJ, Case C–70/88 *European Parliament v Council* [1990] E.C.R. I–2041, paras 11–27 (recognition of the fact that the Parliament may be a defendant or an applicant in proceedings, respectively, despite the wording of Art. 173, first para., of the EEC Treaty, for the sake of institutional balance; para. 13–011, *infra*); ECJ, Case C–2/88 Imm. *Zwartveld* [1990] E.C.R. I–3365, paras 15–26 (interpretation of the privileges and immunities of the Communities in the light of the duty of Community good faith or sincere co-operation within the meaning of Art. 10 of the EC Treaty, para. 5–053, *supra*); ECJ, Case 314/85 *Foto-Frost* [1987] E.C.R. 4199, paras 12–17 (where it was held that national courts have no power to declare Community acts invalid in spite of the limitation of the obligation to make references for preliminary rulings to national courts of last instance). See Lenaerts, "The Legal Protection of Private Parties under the EC Treaty: A Coherent and Complete System of Judicial Review?" in *Scritti in onore di Giuseppe Federico Mancini* (Dott. A. Giuffrè Editore, Milan, 1998), II, at 591–623.

[280] For further details, see Lenaerts and Arts, *Procedural Law of the European Union*.

bring an action for annulment under Art. 230 of the EC Treaty against acts of the European Parliament and the Council jointly, the Council, the Commission, the ECB (if the contested act is not a recommendation or an opinion) or the European Parliament (if the contested act has legal effects on third parties).[281] The European Parliament, the Council, the Commission, the Court of Auditors and the ECB may bring an action for failure to act under Art. 232 of the EC Treaty against the European Parliament, the Council, the Commission or the ECB. A dispute between institutions may be raised incidentally where institutions intervene in proceedings[282] or submit observations to the Court of Justice where a national court has put a question for a preliminary ruling on the validity of an act of the institutions or the ECB[283] or where the Court of Justice gives an opinion on a proposed international agreement pursuant to Art. 300(6) of the EC Treaty.

(2) Secondly, the Court determines disputes between the Community and the Member States. The Commission may bring a claim against a Member State which has failed to fulfil its Treaty obligations in accordance with the procedure set out in Arts 226 and 228 of the EC Treaty.[284] A Member State may bring an action for annulment against any act mentioned in the preceding paragraph or an action for failure to act against the European Parliament, the Council, the Commission or the ECB. Equally, a dispute between the Community and a Member State may be raised before the Court of Justice indirectly, given that Member States have the same right as the institutions to intervene or to submit observations in pending cases (they tend especially to submit observations in connection with requests for preliminary rulings on the interpretation of Community law from which it may ensue that national law is in breach of Community law).[285]

---

[281] The Commission is further entitled to bring proceedings against acts of the Board of Governors or the Board of Directors of the EIB and the EIB's Board of Directors to bring proceedings against acts of the Board of Governors (EC Treaty, Art. 237(b) and (c)). In this way, the Commission may bring proceedings against all acts adopted by the EIB falling within the Board of Governor's sphere of competence, even if the act in question was adopted by another organ: ECJ, Case C–15/00 *Commission v European Investment Bank* [2003] E.C.R. I–7281, paras 73–74.

[282] ECJ Statute, Art. 40. Institutions may intervene, *inter alia*, in order to defend an act adopted by them against which an objection of illegality has been raised (EC Treaty, Art. 241).

[283] ECJ Statute, Art. 23. See also EU Treaty, Art. 35(4)).

[284] See also EC Treaty, Art. 88(2), second subpara., Art. 95(9) and Art. 298. The Board of Directors of the EIB and the Board of the ECB have the same powers in respect of the fulfilment of obligations by Member States under the EIB Statute or the EC Treaty and the ESCB Statute: see EC Treaty, Art. 237(a) and (d), respectively.

[285] See Granger, "When governments go to Luxembourg . . .: the influence of governments on the Court of Justice" (2004) E.L.R. 3–31. See also the procedure set out in Art. 300(6) of the EC Treaty.

(3) The Court also has to hear and determine cases between Member States, but this is a fairly rare occurrence. Article 292 of the EC Treaty provides that Member States may not submit a dispute concerning the interpretation or application of the Treaty to any method of settlement other than those provided for in the Treaty.[286] A Member State may bring an alleged infringement of the Treaty by another Member State before the Court of Justice (EC Treaty, Art. 227). Member States may also bring a dispute before the Court of Justice under a special agreement (EC Treaty, Art. 239). In addition, disputes between Member States may be determined indirectly in all the aforementioned procedures.

(4) Lastly, the Court affords legal protection to natural and legal persons where a national court or tribunal makes a reference for a preliminary ruling on the interpretation of Treaty provisions or on the validity or interpretation of acts of the institutions or the ECB (EC Treaty, Art. 234) or where such persons bring an action against a Community institution or body. Natural or legal persons may bring an action for annulment against binding acts of such an institution or body which are addressed or of direct and individual concern to them under Art. 230, fourth para., of the EC Treaty or may bring an action for failure to act under Art. 232, third para., of that Treaty. In this way, the EC Treaty seeks to establish a complete system of legal remedies and procedures to permit the Court of Justice to review the legality of measures adopted by the Community institutions.[287] Where natural or legal persons cannot, by reason of the conditions for admissibility laid down in the fourth para. of Art. 230 of the EC Treaty, directly challenge Community measures of general application, they are able, depending on the case, either indirectly to plead the invalidity of such acts before the Community Courts by way of an objection of illegality (EC Treaty, Art. 241) or to do so before the national courts and ask them, since they have no jurisdiction themselves to declare those measures invalid,[288] to make

---

[286] This means that a dispute between Member States may be laid before an international tribunal only where the dispute relates to rights and obligations which do not flow from the EC Treaty. For an application, see the proceedings brought by Ireland against the UK in the International Tribunal for the Law of the Sea, in which an order granting provisional measures was given on December 3, 2001 *Ireland v UK (The MOX Case)* (available from the website *www.itlos.org*). The Commission has brought infringement proceedings against Ireland on the ground that, by bringing these proceedings, that Member State disregarded the exclusive jurisdiction of the Court of Justice: Case C–459/03, [2003] O.J. C7/14.

[287] ECJ, Case 294/83 *Les Verts v European Parliament* [1986] E.C.R. 1339, para. 23; ECJ, Case C–50/00 P *Unión de Pequeños Agricultores v Council and Commission* [2002] E.C.R. I–6677, paras 40–42; ECJ, Case C–491/01 *British American Tobacco (Investments) and Imperial Tobacco* [2003] E.C.R. I–11453, para. 39; ECJ (judgment of April 1, 2004), Case C–236/02 P *Commission v Jégo-Quéré*, not yet reported, paras 29–32.

[288] ECJ, Case 314/85 *Foto-Frost* [1987] E.C.R. 4199, para. 20 (n.279, *supra*).

a reference to the Court of Justice for a preliminary ruling on validity. In addition, the Court of Justice determines damages claims brought against the Community (EC Treaty, Art. 235 and Art. 288), disputes between the Community and its officials and other servants (EC Treaty, Art. 236) and disputes submitted to it pursuant to an arbitration clause (EC Treaty, Art. 238). The provisions establishing a number of Community bodies and agencies confer jurisdiction on the Court of Justice to hear and determine disputes pursuant to an arbitration clause contained in an agreement concluded by the body or agency in question and disputes relating to the non-contractual liability of that body or agency.[289] In future, the Court of Justice may also obtain jurisdiction to hear and determine disputes as between individuals with regard to Community industrial property rights.[290]

10–075 Jurisdiction under Title IV EC Treaty. The Court of Justice exercises its powers in respect of disputes which come within the scope of the provisions of the EC Treaty and the EAEC Treaty. As far as the provisions of Title IV of the EC Treaty (visas, asylum, immigration and other policies related to free movement of persons) are concerned, the Court has jurisdiction under the conditions laid down in that Title of the Treaty.[291] Unlike Art. 234 of the EC Treaty, Art. 68(1) confers on the Court of Justice jurisdiction to give preliminary rulings only on questions referred by a national court or tribunal against whose decisions there is no judicial remedy under national law.[292] The Council, the Commission or a Member State may request the Court of Justice to give a ruling on a question of interpretation of Title IV or of acts of Community institutions based thereon. Such preliminary rulings do not apply to judgments of national courts or tribunals which have become *res judicata* (EC Treaty, Art. 68(3)).

10–076 Limited jurisdiction under EU Treaty. As far as non-Community policy areas are concerned, the Court's jurisdiction is limited by Art. 46 of the EU

---

[289] See, *e.g.* ESCB Statute, Arts 35.3 and 35.4.

[290] To this end, the Council, acting unanimously on a proposal from the Commission and after consulting the European Parliament, has to adopt provisions to confer jurisdiction on the Court of Justice and the Member States have to adopt them in accordance with their respective constitutional requirements (EC Treaty, Art. 229a).

[291] See Fennelly, " 'The Area of Freedom, Security and Justice' and the European Court of Justice—A Personal View" (2000) I.C.L.Q. 1, at 4–8; Knapp, "Die Garantie des effektiven Rechtsschutzes durch den EuGH im 'Raum der Freiheit, der Sicherheit und des Rechts' " (2001) D.ö.V. 12–21; Arnull, "Les incidences du traité d'Amsterdam sur la Cour de justice des Communautés européennes" (2000) R.A.E. 223–230. As regards measures or decisions taken pursuant to Art. 62(1), the Court of Justice has no jurisdiction to rule on any measure or decision relating to the maintenance of law and order and the safeguarding of internal security (Art. 68(2); see para. 5–163, *supra*).

[292] Consequently, in this context the EC Treaty precludes preliminary references from "inferior" courts; see ECJ (order of March 18, 2004), Case C–45/03 *Dem'Yanenko*, not yet reported; ECJ (order of March 31, 2004), Case C–51/03 *Georgescu*, not yet reported; ECJ (order of June 10, 2004), Case C–555/03 *Warbecq*, not yet reported. *cf.* Art. 35(3) of the EU Treaty, which leaves it to the Member States to decide whether to allow lower courts to make references for preliminary rulings (see para. 10–077, *infra*).

Treaty. That article provides that, alongside the Community Treaties, the Court's jurisdiction extends to Title VI of the EU Treaty (police and judicial co-operation in criminal matters) and Title VII of that Treaty (enhanced co-operation) under the conditions provided for by Art. 35 of the EU Treaty, Art. 11 and Art. 11a of the EC Treaty and Art. 40 of the EU Treaty, respectively.[293] In so far as the Court of Justice has jurisdiction under the Community Treaties or the EU Treaty, it may review acts of the institutions in the light of Art. 6(2) of the EU Treaty (respect for fundamental rights; see para. 17–076). The Court also reviews compliance with the procedural provisions of Art. 7 of the EU Treaty (see para. 9–012). Lastly, the Court has jurisdiction over the final provisions of the EU Treaty (Arts 46 to 53). Accordingly, Art. 46 of the EU Treaty rules out judicial review by the Court of Justice in respect of provisions relating to the common foreign and security policy (Title V of the EU Treaty; see para. 18–021).

Judicial review in PJCC. As a result of the introduction of Art. 35 of the **10–077** EU Treaty, the Treaty of Amsterdam made judicial review by the Court of Justice possible in the (non-Community) field of police and judicial co-operation in criminal matters (PJCC). Already in the context of co-operation in the fields of justice and home affairs, the Council had conferred jurisdiction on the Court of Justice in various conventions concluded under the former Title VI of the EU Treaty to rule on disputes between Member States or between Member States and the Commission concerning the interpretation and application of the convention in question and enabled Member States to opt to confer jurisdiction on the Court to give preliminary rulings on interpretation of conventions at the request of a national court (see para. 18–009). The revision of Title VI by the Amsterdam Treaty introduced these arrangements for framework decisions, decisions, conventions and measures implementing them adopted by the Council pursuant to police and judicial co-operation in criminal matters.

Subject to the conditions laid down in Art. 35 of the EU Treaty,[294] the Court has jurisdiction to review the legality of framework decisions and decisions in actions brought by a Member State or the Commission, to rule on any dispute between Member States regarding the interpretation or the application of PJCC acts,[295] and to rule on any dispute between Member

---

[293] For EU Treaty, Art. 35, see para. 10–077, *infra*; for judicial review of enhanced co-operation, see para. 9–009, *supra*; Classen, "Die Jurisdiktion des Gerichtshofs der Europäischen Gemeinschaften nach Amsterdam" (1999) EuR. Beiheft 1, 73–90.

[294] Thus, the Court of Justice has no jurisdiction to review the validity or proportionality of operations carried out by the police or other law enforcement services of a Member State or the exercise of the responsibilities incumbent upon Member States with regard to the maintenance of law and order and the safeguarding of internal security (Art. 35(5)).

[295] Art. 35(7) refers in some language versions to *decisions* "adopted under Art. 34(2)"; it is clear from the other versions, however, that all acts referred to in Art. 34(2) are meant and not only "decisions". In order for the Court to have this power, the Council must have failed in settling the dispute within six months of its being referred to that institution by one of its members (EU Treaty, Art. 35(7), second sentence).

States and the Commission regarding the interpretation or the application of PJCC conventions (Art. 35(6) and (7)). A Member State may also accept the Court's jurisdiction to give preliminary rulings on the validity and interpretation of framework decisions and decisions, the interpretation of conventions and the validity and interpretation of measures implementing them (Art. 35(1) to (3)). Member States themselves determine whether only those courts or tribunals against whose decisions there is no judicial remedy[296] or any national court or tribunal may request a preliminary ruling (Art. 35(3)).[297] In this way, the Court of Justice may rule on PJCC provisions, including the provisions of the Schengen *acquis* which have been transposed into 'Union law'.[298]

10–078 Jurisdiction under conventions. The Court of Justice also has jurisdiction to give preliminary rulings at the request of national courts and tribunals on the interpretation of conventions which the Member States have concluded amongst themselves where a protocol to the convention confers jurisdiction on the Court; an example is the Brussels I or Judgments Convention (see para. 18–008).

10–079 Jurisdiction of Court of First Instance. Since October 31, 1989, part of the jurisdiction of the Court of Justice has been transferred to the Court of First Instance. The Court of First Instance was set up in order to lighten the Court of Justice's case-load and to assign specific tasks to each of the two courts, thereby improving the quality of judicial review.[299] All actions brought by natural or legal persons against Community institutions or

---

[296] Spain has accepted the jurisdiction of the Court of Justice under this condition, see [1999] O.J. L114/56.

[297] A declaration to this effect has been made by Austria, Belgium, Finland, Germany, Greece, Italy, Luxembourg, the Netherlands, Portugal and Sweden (see [1999] O.J. L114/56), France (*J.O.R.F.* No.165 of July 19, 2000, p.11073), and the Czech Republic (Declaration No.26 annexed to the 2003 Act of Accession on Art. 35 of the EU Treaty, [2003] O.J. L236/980). When making such a declaration, Member States may reserve the right to make provisions in their national law to the effect that, where a question is raised in a case before a national court or tribunal against whose decision there is no judicial remedy under national law, that court or tribunal will be *required* to refer the matter to the Court of Justice: Declaration (No.10) on Article 35 of the Treaty on European Union, [1997] O.J. C340/133. In their declarations, Austria, Belgium, the Czech Republic, France, Germany, Italy, Luxembourg, the Netherlands and Spain reserved that right, *ibid.* See Fennelly (n.291, *supra*), at 8–12; Knapp (n.291, *supra*), at 13–14. The German law in fact obliges a court whose decision is not amenable to appeal to make a reference for a preliminary ruling; see the opinion of Advocate General Ruiz-Jarabo Colomer in ECJ, Joined Cases C–187/01 and C–385/01 *Gözütok and Brügge* [2003] E.C.R. I–1345, point 32.

[298] The first time was by ECJ, Joined Cases C–187/01 and C–385/01 *Gözütok and Brügge* [2003] E.C.R. I–1345 (interpretation of the *ne bis in idem* principle enshrined in Art. 54 of the Convention of June 19, 1990 implementing the Schengen Agreement). For the incorporation of the Schengen *acquis*, see para. 5–164.

[299] See Lenaerts, "Le Tribunal de première instance des Communautés européennes: regard sur une décennie d'activités et sur l'apport du double degré d'instance au droit communautaire" (2000) C.D.E. 323–411.

bodies must be brought in the Court of First Instance.[300] There is a right of appeal to the Court of Justice against decisions of the Court of First Instance on points of law only. Until recently, the Treaty reserved to the Court of Justice jurisdiction over references for preliminary rulings. All actions brought by Member States and Community institutions and bodies also fell within the jurisdiction of that court. The amendments made by the Treaty of Nice to Art. 225 of the EC Treaty however entail increased jurisdiction for the Court of First Instance.[301]

In the first place, jurisdiction at first instance, subject to an appeal to the Court of Justice on points of law only, is extended to cover all actions referred to in Arts 230, 232, 235, 236 and 238 of the EC Treaty, with the exception of those assigned to a judicial panel and those reserved in the Statute for the Court of Justice (EC Treaty, Art. 225(1)). Art. 51 of the Statute of the Court provides, as from June 1, 2004, that jurisdiction shall be reserved to the Court of Justice in the actions referred to in Arts 230 and 232 of the EC Treaty when they are brought by a Member State against an act of or failure to act by the European Parliament or the Council (except for some acts of a clearly executive nature[302]), by both institutions acting jointly, or by the Commission under Art. 11a of the EC Treaty (on enhanced co-operation) and when they are brought by one Community institution or the ECB against another Community institution

---

[300] There has been an incremental transfer of jurisdiction, first by Art. 3 of the CFI Decision ([1988] O.J. L319/1, which came into force as a result of Art. 13 on October 31, 1989), as amended by Council Decision 93/350 of June 8, 1993 ([1993] O.J. L144/21, which took effect on August 1, 1993), by Council Decision 94/149 of March 7, 1994 ([1994] O.J. L66/29, which entered into force on March 15, 1994) and Decision 1999/291/EC, ECSC, Euratom of April 26, 1999 ([1999] O.J. L114/52, which entered into force on May 16, 1999). The CFI Decision was repealed at the entry into force on February 1, 2003 of the new ECJ Statute (n.276, *supra*).

[301] ECJ Statute, Art. 51, as amended by Council Decision 2004/407/EC, Euratom of April 26, 2004 ([2004] O.J. L132/5; corrigendum: [2004] O.J. L194/3). For the changes to the judicial system, see Tizzano, "La Cour de justice après Nice: le transfert de compétences au Tribunal de première instance" (2002) R.D.U.E. 665–685; Craig, "The Jurisdiction of the Community Courts Reconsidered" (2001) Texas International Law Journal 555–586; Johnston, "Judicial Reform and the Treaty of Nice" (2001) C.M.L.R. 499–523; Tambou, "Le système juridictionnel communautaire revu et corrigé par le traité de Nice" (2001) R.M.C.U.E. 164–170; Ruiz-Jarabo Colomer, "La réforme de la Cour de justice opérée par le traité de Nice et sa mise en oeuvre" (2001) R.T.D.E. 705–725; Lenz, "Die Gerichtsbarkeit in der Europäischen Gemeinschaft nach dem Vertrag von Nizza" (2001) Eu.GR.Z. 433–441; Lipp, "Europäische Justizreform" (2001) N.J.W. 2657–2663; Kapteyn, "De rechterlijke organisatie van de Europese Unie en de Intergouvernementele Conferentie 2000" (2001) N.J.B. 1–6; Fierstra, "Een nieuw toekomstperspectief voor het Hof van Justitie: de tussenstand na het Verdrag van Nice" (2001) N.T.E.R. 95–103; Lenaerts and Desomer, "Het Verdrag van Nice en het 'post-Nice'-debat over de toekomst van de Europese Unie" (2001–2002) R.W. 73, at 78–81; Dubos, "Quel avenir pour le Tribunal de première instance après le traité de Nice?" (2000) R.A.E. 426–440.

[302] ECJ Statute, Art. 51, first para., subs.(a). The Council decisions against which actions are not reserved to the Court of Justice are "—decisions taken by the Council under the third subpara. of Art. 88(2) of the EC Treaty;—acts of the Council adopted pursuant to a Council regulation concerning measures to protect trade within the meaning of Art. 133 of the EC Treaty;—acts of the Council by which the Council exercises implementing powers in accordance with the third indent of Art. 202 of the EC Treaty".

or the ECB.[303] This means that, alongside all actions brought by natural and legal persons against Community institutions and bodies, the Court of First Instance will hear all actions brought by Member States against all acts of or failures to act by the Commission (with the one exception mentioned), the acts of or failures to act by the Council in the cases mentioned above, as well as against the acts of or failures to act by any Community body.

Secondly, the Court of First Instance has jurisdiction to hear and determine actions or proceedings brought against decisions of the judicial panels (EC Treaty, Art. 225 (2)).

Thirdly, the Court of First Instance has jurisdiction to hear and determine questions referred for a preliminary ruling under Art. 234 of the EC Treaty in specific areas laid down by the Statute, unless it considers that the case requires a decision of principle likely to affect the unity or consistency of Community law, when it may refer the case to the Court of Justice for a ruling (Art. 225(3)). The present Statute has not yet conferred any areas on the Court of First Instance in which it may give preliminary rulings.

Whenever the Court of First Instance will hear and determine actions or proceedings brought against decisions of judicial panels or give preliminary rulings, its decisions may only exceptionally be subject to review by the Court of Justice, namely where there is a serious risk of the unity or consistency of Community law being affected.[304] The aim of this reordering of jurisdiction is that the Court of Justice should concentrate on its function as the highest court guaranteeing the unity and consistency of Community law.[305]

2. Composition

10–080 Judges and Advocates General. The Court of Justice consists of one judge for each Member State (since May 1, 2004, 25 in all), assisted by 8 Advocates General and a Registrar. The Advocates General, "acting with complete impartiality and independence", assist the Court of Justice by making, in open court, reasoned submissions prior to the Court's

---

[303] ECJ, Art. 51, first para., subs.(b) (referring, more precisely, to "actions brought by an institution of the Communities or by the European Central Bank against an act of or failure to act by the European Parliament, the Council, both those institutions acting jointly, or the Commission, or brought by an institution of the Communities against an act of or failure to act by the European Central Bank").

[304] See EC Treaty, Art. 225(2), second subpara., and (3), third subpara. This may occur where the First Advocate General puts this proposition to the Court of Justice within one month of delivery of the decision by the Court of First Instance: ECJ Statute, Art. 62. It is stated in Declaration (No.13) annexed to the Treaty of Nice that the essential provisions of the review procedure should be defined in the Statute of the Court of Justice (in particular as regards the effect of the Court of Justice decision on the dispute between the parties).

[305] For further discussion of the jurisdiction of the two courts, see Lenaerts and Arts, *Procedural Law of the European Union*.

deliberations.[306] The Council may, by unanimous vote, increase the number of Members (EC Treaty, Art. 221, first para., Art. 222, first para., and Art. 223, fifth para.). The Court of First Instance has at least one Judge for each Member State (since May 1, 2004 25 in all) and a Registrar. No Advocates General are appointed to the Court of First Instance, but the Statute may provided for that Court to be assisted by Advocates General (EC Treaty, Art. 224, first para.).[307]

The EC Treaty does not require Members of the Court of Justice or the Court of First Instance to be nationals of a Member State. The Treaty does not allocate the number of Advocates General among the Member States. Until the changes made by the Treaty of Nice, the EC Treaty contained a fixed number of Judges, but it did not allocate them either among the Member States.[308] In practice, to date each Member State has had one Judge. As far as the Advocates General are concerned, one comes from each of the five largest Member States and the other three come in turn from the remaining Member States.[309]

---

[306] EC Treaty, Art. 222, second para. The Court of Justice considers that the fact that the parties may not submit observations in response to the Advocate General's opinion is not in conflict with Art. 6 of the ECHR: ECJ (order of February 4, 2000), Case C–17/98 *Emesa Sugar (Free Zone) and Aruba* [2000] E.C.R. I–665, paras 10–18; rightly criticised in Lawson (2000) C.M.L.R. 983–990; Maes, "Is drie keer tegenspraak voor het EHRM geen scheepsrecht voor het H.v.J.?" (2001) T.B.P. 179–184; Benoît-Rohmer, "L'affaire *Emesa Sugar*: l'institution de l'avocat general de la Cour de justice des Communautés européennes à l'épreuve de la jurisprudence *Vermeulen* de la Cour européenne des droits de l'homme" (2001) C.D.E. 403–426. It appears that the European Court of Human Rights takes another view: see the judgment of June 7, 2001 in *Kress v France* (2001) S.E.W. 440–444, with a case note by Lawson; (2001) R.T.D.E. 809–819, with a case note by Benoît-Rohmer. See also Lenaerts, "Rechter en partijen in de rechtspleging voor Hof en Gerecht" (2002) S.E.W. 231–237.

[307] Art. 49 of the Statute of the Court of Justice nevertheless retains the existing rule that one of the Members of the Court of First Instance may be called upon to perform the task of an Advocate General.

[308] Where there was an even number of Member States, the Court of Justice generally had one Judge more than the number of Member States in order to ensure that the Court might sit with an uneven number of Judges (as required by Art. 17 of the Statute of the Court of Justice). In order to have an uneven number, the accession of four Member States in 1973 was to have increased the original number of seven judges to 11 (1972 Act of Accession, Art. 17; [1972] O.J. L73), but this number was reduced to 9 when Norway decided not to join the Community (Art. 4 of the Council Decision of January 1, 1973, [1973] O.J. L2). Following the accession of Greece, the Court of Justice had at first 10 judges (Art. 16 of the 1979 Act of Accession, [1979] O.J. L291, and Council Decision of December 22, 1980, [1980] O.J. L380/6). Subsequently, the Council increased the number to 11 by Decision of March 31, 1981 ([1981] O.J. L100/20). After the accession of Portugal and Spain there were 13 judges (Art. 17 of the 1985 Act of Accession, [1985] O.J. L302). The additional judge was appointed in turn from the largest Member States. Thus, most recently, the "13th Judge" came in turn from France, Germany, Spain and Italy. After the accession of Austria, Sweden and Finland, the Court of Justice had 15 judges.

[309] The 2003 Act of Accession has made no changes in the number of Advocates General. According to the Joint Declaration on the Court of Justice of the European Communities ([2003] O.J. L236/971), the new Member States will be integrated into the existing system for the appointment of Advocates General. Upon the accession of new Member States in 1973, the original number of Advocates General was raised from two to four (Art. 1 of the

10–081 Appointment. The Judges and Advocates General of the Court of Justice and the Judges of the Court of First Instance are appointed by common accord of the national governments for a six-year term.[310] Membership is partially renewed every three years, although retiring Members are eligible for reappointment (EC Treaty, Art. 223 and Art. 224).[311] Members of the judicial panels are appointed by the Council, acting unanimously (EC Treaty, Art. 225a, fourth para.).

10–082 Conditions for appointment. Judges and Advocates General of the Court of Justice and Judges of the Court of First Instance as well as Members of the Judicial Panels are "chosen from persons whose independence is beyond doubt". The EC Treaty further requires Members of the Court of Justice to "possess the qualifications required for appointment to the highest judicial offices in their respective countries" or to be "jurisconsults of recognised competence" (EC Treaty, Art. 223, first para.); Judges of the Court of First Instance must "possess the ability required for appointment to high judicial office" (EC Treaty, Art. 224, second para.); Members of Judicial Panels must "possess the ability required for appointment to judicial office" (EC Treaty, Art. 225a, fourth para.).

10–083 Duties. Before taking up their duties, each judge and Advocate General has to take up an oath in open court to perform his or her duties impartially and conscientiously and to preserve the secrecy of the deliberations of the Court (ECJ Statute, Arts 2, 8 and 47). Members may not hold any political or administrative office and are subject to the same requirements as Members of the Commission as regards engaging in any other occupation and the acceptance of appointments and benefits. A judge or Advocate General may be deprived of his or her office only if, in the unanimous opinion of the other judges and Advocates General, he or she

---

Council Decision of January 1, 1973, [1973] O.J. L2/29) and divided among the four largest Member States. Following the accession of Greece, a fifth such post was created (Council Decision of March 30, 1981, [1981] O.J. L100/21), which was to go to one of the smaller Member States. Their number was increased to six after the accession of Portugal and Spain (Art. 18 of the 1985 Act of Accession, [1985] O.J. L302). Art. 20 of the 1994 Act of Accession provided for eight Advocates General ([1994] O.J. C241/25). As agreed in a Joint Declaration annexed to the Act of Accession (*ibid.*, at p.381), the accession of an uneven number of new Member States (following Norway's decision not to accede) resulted in the "thirteenth Judge" being made into a ninth Advocate General for the remainder of his term of office (*i.e.* until October 6, 2000). See the Joint Declaration on Art. 31 of the Decision adjusting the instruments concerning the accession of the new Member States to the European Union ([1995] O.J. L1/221).

[310] For the fact that the Council as an institution is not involved in appointing members of the Court, see the Council's answer of December 20, 1995 to question P–2529/95 (Vandemeulebroecke), [1996] O.J. C56/24.

[311] See ECJ Statute, Art. 9 (for the Court of Justice). According to Art. 46(2)(a) and (b) of the 2003 Act of Accession, the term of office of five of the 10 Judges of the Court of Justice and of five of the 10 of the Court of First Instance appointed on May 1, 2004 is to expire on October 6, 2006 and August 31, 2004 respectively. The term of office of the other judges will expire on October 6, 2009 and August 31, 2007. Naturally, they may be reappointed.

no longer fulfils the requisite conditions or meets the obligations arising from his or her office (ECJ Statute, Arts 6, 8 and 44).[312] If the office of judge or Advocate General becomes vacant before the end of the term of office as a result of death or voluntary or compulsory retirement, the successor is appointed for the remainder of his or her predecessor's term of office (ECJ Statute, Art. 7).

3. Procedure

Rules of Procedure. The Court of Justice operates in accordance with the procedure laid down in the Treaties, the Statute and the Rules of Procedure, which the Court itself adopts but has to submit to the Council for its unanimous approval.[313] Procedure before the Court of First Instance is determined by the Statute of the Court of Justice, in so far as it is stated to be applicable to the Court of First Instance, and by its Rules of Procedure, which, under Art. 224, fifth para., of the EC Treaty, it establishes in agreement with the Court of Justice. Those Rules also have to be approved by the Council.[314] The procedure of the judicial panels is based on the Statute of the Court of Justice and on their own Rules of Procedure, which, under Art. 225a, fifth para., of the EC Treaty, they are to establish in agreement with the Court of Justice. Those rules have to be approved by the Council. **10–084**

1. Internal organisation

Chambers. Both in the Court of Justice and in the Court of First Instance, the judges elect their President from among their number for a term of three years. The President may be re-elected. Both Courts appoint their Registrar and lay down the rules governing his service (EC Treaty, Arts 223, third and fourth paras, and 224, third and fourth paras). The Court of Justice sits in chambers of three or five judges or in a Grand Chamber (13 judges) or, exceptionally, as a full Court.[315] The Court of First Instance sits in chambers of three or five judges. In certain cases it may sit as a full court or in a Grand Chamber (13 judges) or be constituted by a **10–085**

---

[312] In the case of Judges of the Court of First Instance, that Court must be heard (ECJ Statute, Art. 47).

[313] For the consolidated text of the Rules of Procedure of the Court of Justice of the European Communities (ECJ Rules of Procedure), see [2003] O.J. C193/1. For procedure before the Court, see Lenaerts and Arts, *Procedural Law of the European Union*, Chapters 21–24.

[314] See Arts 47–62 of the ECJ Statute and the consolidated text of the Rules of Procedure of the Court of First Instance of the European Communities (CFI Rules of Procedure) in [2003] O.J. C193/41. See Lenaerts and Arts, *ibid.*

[315] EC Treaty, Art. 221, second para., and ECJ Statute, Arts 16 and 17. Decisions of the full court shall be valid only if 15 judges are sitting (ECJ Statute, Art. 17, fourth para.). The Grand Chamber is presided over by the President of the Court and consists of the Presidents of the Chambers of five Judges, the Judge Rapporteur and such judges as are necessary to bring the number to 13 (ECJ Rules of Procedure, Art. 11b).

single judge.[316] The Court of Justice and the Court of First Instance employ some 1,100 staff.[317] When the Court of Justice was established by the ECSC Treaty, its seat was fixed in Luxembourg,[318] which is also where the Court of First Instance is based.[319]

5. Changes proposed in the EU Constitution

10–086 Jurisdiction and appointment. Under the EU Constitution, the "Court of Justice of the European Union" will be made up not only of the Court of Justice itself and the Court of First Instance (which is to be renamed the "General Court") but also of "specialised courts". In order to underscore the fact that enforcement of Union law falls above all to the national courts, the EU Constitution provides that Member States must provide rights of appeal sufficient to ensure effective legal protection in the fields covered by Union law (Art. I–29(1)).

As far as the jurisdiction of the Court of Justice is concerned, the EU Constitution adds the European Council to the institutions against which an action for annulment may be brought and the European Council and the European Central Bank to those against which an action for failure to act may be brought.[320] The Committee of the Regions will be included among the institutions that may bring an action for annulment for the purpose of protecting their prerogatives.[321] The EU Constitution also confirms the competence of the Court of Justice to review the legality of acts of bodies, offices or agencies of the Union which are intended to produce legal effects *vis-à-vis* third parties.[322] In addition, the EU Constitution will alter the requirements which natural or legal persons have to satisfy in order to bring

---

[316] ECJ Statute, Art. 50; CFI, Rules of Procedure, Arts 10 and 11.

[317] As at December 31, 2003, the two Courts had 1,140 posts: *General Report on the Activities of the European Union 2003* (n.122, *supra*), at 509. The judges and Advocates General are assisted by law clerks, known as legal secretaries or *référendaires*.

[318] Para. 10–145, *infra*.

[319] Sole Article, para. (d), of the Protocol on Seats (para. 10–146, *infra*). Art. 3 of the Decision on Provisional Location of April 8, 1965 (para. 10–145, *infra*) itself provided that existing and future judicial and quasi-judicial bodies set up under the Community Treaties should have their seat in Luxembourg. See also the Declaration to the Decision of October 29, 1993 (n.622 to para. 10–147, *infra*). In a unilateral declaration by Luxembourg, of which the Conference took note in signing the Treaty of Nice ([2001] O.J. C80/87), that Member State undertook not to claim the seat of the Boards of Appeal of the Office for Harmonisation in the Internal Market (trade marks and designs), even if those Boards were to become judicial panels within the meaning of Art. 220 of the EC Treaty.

[320] EU Constitution, Art. III–365(1) (which will put the European Council on an equal footing with the European Parliament insofar as the legality may be reviewed of acts intended to produce legal effects *vis-à-vis* third parties) and Art. III–367, first para. (which puts the European Council and the ECB on an equal footing with the European Parliament, the Council and the Commission).

[321] *ibid.*, Art. III–365(3) (which will put the Committee of the Regions on an equal footing with the Court of Auditors and the ECB).

[322] *ibid.*, Art. III–365(1) *in fine*, (action for annulment) and Art. III–367, first para., *in fine* (action for failure to act); for this principle, see paras 14–064—14–066, *infra*. The acts setting up bodies, offices and agencies of the Union may lay down specific conditions and arrangements concerning such actions (EU Constitution, Art. III–365(5)).

an action for annulment.[323] The jurisdiction of the Court of Justice will no longer be restricted as regards police and judicial co-operation in criminal matters[324] but it will continue to have no jurisdiction with regard to the CFSP (although it may review the legality of European decisions providing for restrictive measures against natural or legal persons, see Art. III–376 of the EU Constitution and para. 18–022).[325]

The appointment of the Judges and Advocates General of the Court of Justice will continue to be a matter for the governments of the Member States, deciding by common accord. However, the Member States will first be given an opinion on candidates' suitability to perform such duties by a panel composed of former members of the Court of Justice and the General Court, members of national supreme courts and lawyers of recognised competence (EU Constitution, Art. III–357).

E. THE COURT OF AUDITORS

History. The Court of Auditors[326] is the youngest of the institutions, since **10–087** it was brought into being by the Second Treaty on Budgetary Provisions of July 22, 1975, which established the present budgetary procedure.[327] At the request of the Commission and the European Parliament, the Member States set up the Court of Auditors as an independent supervisory body.[328] That body took over the task which the ECSC Treaty conferred on auditors and the EEC Treaty and the EAEC Treaty on an Audit Board, which the Merger Treaty also made responsible for the ECSC budget.[329] The EU Treaty put the Court of Auditors on an equal footing with the other four

---

[323] Under Art. III–365(4) of the draft EU Constitution, any natural or legal person will be able to institute proceedings against an act which is addressed to that person or is of direct and individual concern to that person, and against a regulatory act which is of direct concern to the person in question and does not entail implementing measures. Under Art. III–365(5), an action against acts of bodies, offices and agencies of the Union may be subject to such specific conditions as are laid down in the act setting up the relevant body, office or agency.

[324] The Court of Justice will, however, continue to have no jurisdiction to review the validity or proportionality of operations carried out by the police or other law enforcement services of a Member State or the exercise of the responsibilities incumbent upon Member States with regard to the maintenance of law and order and the safeguarding of internal security (Art. III–377 of the EU Constitution).

[325] See also the Report of March 15, 2004 on "the Future Role of the European Court of Justice" of the House of Lords' European Union Committee (HLP 46, 6th report of the session 2003–04); Louis, "La fonction juridictionnelle de Nice à Rome" (2003) J.T.D.E. 257–263.

[326] For the website of the Court of Auditors, see *www.eca.eu.int/*.

[327] Treaty of July 22, 1975 amending certain financial provisions of the Treaties establishing the European Communities and of the Treaty establishing a Single Council and a Single Commission of the European Communities, [1977] O.J. L359/1 (para. 10–130, *infra*).

[328] See EEC Treaty, Art. 4(3) and Art. 206, and EAEC Treaty, Art. 3(3) and Art. 180 (before the EU Treaty).

[329] Art. 78 of the ECSC, Art. 206 of the EEC Treaty and Art. 180 of the EAEC Treaty were replaced as a result of the Merger Treaty by Arts 78e–78g of the ECSC Treaty, Arts 206–206b of the EEC Treaty and Arts 180–180b of the EAEC Treaty, which have since been amended or repealed.

institutions.[330] On December 9, 1993, the Court decided to take the name of "European Court of Auditors".[331]

1. Powers

10–088 **External audit.** The Court of Auditors examines the accounts of all revenue and expenditure of the Community. The external audit of the budget which it carries out results in an annual report which is forwarded to all the institutions and published (EC Treaty, Art. 248; see para. 10–142). In addition, the Court may submit observations, particularly in the form of special reports, on specific questions (EC Treaty, Art. 248(4), second subpara.). It transmits such special reports to the institution or body concerned and to the European Parliament and the Council; it may publish them.[332] The Court of Auditors may also deliver opinions at the request of one of the Community institutions[333] and is consulted on legislation relating to the budget and accounts.[334] The Court of Auditors also assists the European Parliament and the Council in supervising and implementing the budget (see para. 10–142).

2. Composition

10–089 **Appointment.** The Court of Auditors consists of one national from each Member State (EC Treaty, Art. 247(1)).[335] Members of the Court of Auditors are not appointed by the governments of the Member States but by the Council by a qualified majority vote (following the Treaty of Nice), after consulting the European Parliament (EC Treaty, Art. 247(3)). Prospective Members must belong or have belonged in their respective countries to external audit bodies or be especially qualified for that office.

---

[330] See EC Treaty, Art. 7(1) and EAEC Treaty, Art. 3(1). The EU Treaty renumbered the provisions relating to the Court of Auditors as Arts 246–248 of the EC Treaty and Arts 160a–160c of the EAEC Treaty. The Court of Auditors was already equated in fact to an institution before as regards the status of its Members, officials and other servants.

[331] (1993) 12 EC Bull. point 1.7.41. For a survey, see Kok, "The Court of Auditors of the European Communities: 'The Other European Court in Luxembourg'" (1989) C.M.L.R. 345–367; O'Keeffe, "The Court of Auditors" in *Institutional Dynamics of European Integration. Essays in Honour of Henry G. Schermers* (n.214, *supra*), at 177–194; Inghelram, "The European Court of Auditors: Current Legal Issues" (2000) C.M.L.R. 129–146; Engwirda and Moonen, "De Europese Rekenkamer: positie, bevoegdheden en toekomstperspectief" (2000) S.E.W. 246–257.

[332] See Financial Regulation (n.338, *infra*), Art. 144(1).

[333] EC Treaty, Art. 248(4), second subpara. Under Art. 144(2) of the Financial Regulation, it may publish the opinion after consulting the institution concerned.

[334] EC Treaty, Art. 279.

[335] Before the Treaty of Nice, Art. 247 of the EC Treaty provided for a fixed number of Members. Thus, the original membership of nine was increased following the accession of new Member States to 10 (Art. 18 of the 1979 Act of Accession, [1979] O.J. L291), 12 (Art. 20 of the 1985 Act of Accession, [1985] O.J. L302) and 15 (Art. 22 of the 1994 Act of Accession, as amended by Council Decision of January 1, 1995, [1995] O.J. L1/4). As a result of Art. 47 of the 2003 Act of Accession, ten new Members joined the existing fifteen on May 1, 2004.

Their independence must be beyond doubt (EC Treaty, Art. 247(2)). Before their appointment, candidates nominated as Members are invited by the European Parliament to make a statement before the committee responsible and answer questions put by MEPs.[336] The Members are appointed for a renewable six-year term (EC Treaty, Art. 247(3)).

Independence. As in the case of Commissioners, Members of the Court of **10–090** Auditors have to be completely independent in the performance of their duties in the general interests of the Community. They are subject to the same rules with regard to occupations incompatible with their office and their professional duties as Commissioners (see EC Treaty, Art. 247(4) and (5)). When they take up office they solemnly undertake to respect those obligations.[337] The independence of the Court of Auditors is made clear by the fact that its Members may not be removed before the end of their term of office except at the request of the Court of Auditors itself if the Court of Justice finds that the Member concerned no longer fulfils the requisite conditions or meets the obligations arising from his or her office (EC Treaty, Art. 247(6) and (7)).

3. Operation

Rules of Procedure. The Court of Auditors acts collectively in accordance **10–091** with the Treaties, the Financial Regulation[338] and its Rules of Procedure, which it draws up subject to the approval of the Council.[339] It may establish internal chambers in order to adopt certain categories of reports or opinions (EC Treaty, Art. 248(4), third subpara.). The Members of the Court of Auditors elect from among their number a President to serve a three-year term (EC Treaty, Art. 247(3), fourth subpara.). He or she convenes and chairs meetings of the Court, which are not open to the public.[340] The Court adopts its reports and opinions by a majority of its

---

[336] EP Rules of Procedure, r.101(1). If the Parliament's opinion on an individual nomination is negative, it will request the Council to submit a new nomination: r.101(4). In May 2004, negative opinions on two candidates prompted one candidate to withdraw his candidacy but did not prevent the other candidate from being appointed: *Europe*, No. 8700, May 6, 2004, p.8.

[337] As in the case of members of the Commission, they take an oath, "the solemn undertaking provided for in the Treaties" (Rules of Procedure of the Court of Auditors, Art. 3), at a solemn sitting of the Court of Justice.

[338] Financial Regulation of June 25, 2002 applicable to the general budget of the European Communities, [2002] O.J. L248/1 (para. 10–116, *infra*).

[339] EC Treaty, Art. 248(4), fifth subpara. Before the Treaty of Nice added this legal basis to the EC Treaty, the Court of Auditors used to adopt its Rules of Procedure on the basis of its powers of internal organisation. See at present the Rules of Procedure of January 31, 2002, [2002] O.J. L210/1 (adopted on the basis of Arts 5 and 246 to 248 of the EC Treaty). For the collective nature of the Court of Auditors, see Art. 1 of the Rules.

[340] See Arts 20 and 23 of the Rules of Procedure of the Court of Auditors.

Members.[341] For the purposes of carrying out its auditing duties, the Court of Auditors forms audit groups which share out their respective responsibilities and have the task of preparing the deliberations of the Court.[342]

4. Internal organisation

10–092 **Staff.** The Court of Auditors has been based in Luxembourg since it was first set up.[343] A Secretary-General appointed by the Court of Auditors itself is responsible for its secretariat and for personnel policy and administration.[344] The Court of Auditors has a staff of around 500, employed in its administrative departments and audit groups.[345]

III. Bodies Established by or Pursuant to the Community Treaties

A. Advisory committees

1. The European Economic and Social Committee

10–093 **Advisory tasks.** The Treaties make provision for representative interest groups to make their views known on committees advising on Community decision-making. In this way, the ECSC Treaty set up a Consultative Committee consisting of producers, workers, consumers and dealers in order to assist the High Authority. The EC and EAEC Treaties created the Economic and Social Committee, in order to advise the Council and the Commission (EC Treaty, Art. 7(2)). This committee consists of representatives of the various economic and social components of organised civil society, and in particular representatives of producers, farmers, carriers, workers, dealers, craftsmen, professional occupations, consumers and the general interest (EC Treaty, Art. 257).[346] The EC Treaty

---

[341] Art. 22 of the Rules of Procedure. The Court of Auditors determines which decisions are to be adopted by a majority of the Members of the Court; other decisions are to be taken by a majority vote of the Members present (Art. 22(1) and (2)), possibly by a written procedure (Art. 22(5)).

[342] Rules of Procedure, Art. 12.

[343] Decision of the Representatives of the Governments of the Member States of April 5, 1977 on the provisional location of the Court of Auditors, [1977] O.J. L104/40, as confirmed by the Protocol on Seats, Sole Article, para. (e), para. 10–146, *infra*.

[344] Art. 13(1), (3) and (5) of the Rules of Procedure.

[345] See Art. 16(2) of the Rules of Procedure. As at December 31, 1999, the Court of Auditors' establishment plan comprised 552 posts: European Commission, *General Report on the Activities of the European Union 2000*, Brussels/Luxembourg, at 412.

[346] See also EAEC Treaty, Art. 3(2) and Art. 165. The EU Constitution leaves it to the Council to determine the composition of the Committee (Art. III–389), but provides that it is to consist of representatives of organisations of employers, of the employed, and of others representative of civil society, notably in socio-economic, civic, professional and cultural circles (Art. I–32(3)). See also Ferté and Roncin, "Quel avenir pour le Comité économique et social européen?" (2001) R.M.C.U.E. 52–59. For the website of the European Economic and Social Committee, see *www.ces.eu.int/*.

and the EAEC Treaty list the matters in respect of which an opinion has to be sought from the Committee before a decision is taken.[347] In addition to obligatory consultation, the Commission and the Council may also request an opinion if they consider it desirable. The Committee may also deliver opinions on its own initiative[348] and may be consulted by the European Parliament (EC Treaty, Art. 262, first and fourth paras).

Composition. The European Economic and Social Committee may have **10–094** no more than 350 members (at present it has 317), each Member State having a predetermined proportion (see EC Treaty, Art. 258, first and second paras).[349] Members are appointed by the Council by a qualified majority vote on proposals from the Member States (EC Treaty, Art. 259(1)). The Council consults the Commission and may obtain the opinion of European bodies which are representative of the various economic and social sectors to which the activities of the Community are of concern (EC Treaty, Art. 259(2)). Members are appointed for a renewable four-year term (EC Treaty, Art. 259(1)).[350] Because members are appointed personally, in principle—just like MEPs—they may not be bound by any mandatory instructions, but must be completely independent in the performance of their duties, in the general interest of the Community, just like Members of the Commission or the Court of Auditors (EC Treaty, Art. 258, third para.).

Operation. The European Economic and Social Committee adopts its own **10–095** rules of procedure.[351] Twice during their term of office, the Members of the Committee are to elect a President and a Bureau, which is required to

---

[347] See the obligation for the Commission to consult laid down in EC Treaty, Art. 37(2) and Art. 137, third para.; for the Council in Art. 40; Art. 44(1), first subpara., and (2); Art. 52(1) and (2); Art. 71(1) and (3); Art. 75(3), first subpara.; Art. 93; Art. 94; Art. 95(1); Art. 128(2); Art. 129, first para.; Art. 137(2), second subpara.; Art. 140, third para.; Art. 141(3); Art. 148; Art. 149(4); Art. 150(4); Art. 152(4); Art. 153(2); Art. 156, first and third paras; Art. 157(3), first subpara.; Art. 159, third para.; Art. 161, first, second and third paras; Art. 162, first para.; Art. 166(1) and (4); Art. 172, first and second paras; Art. 175(1), (2) and (3). See in the EAEC Treaty the obligation for the Commission to consult laid down in Art. 9, first para.; Art. 31, first para.; Art. 32, first para.; Art. 40; Art. 41, second para.; Art. 96, second para.; and Art. 98, second para.

[348] The EU Treaty introduced this possibility in Art. 262, first para., of the EC Treaty, although the Committee's Rules of Procedure already provided for it. The Commission submits its three-yearly report on economic and social cohesion to the European Economic and Social Committee (EC Treaty, Art. 159, second para.).

[349] See the most recent amendment by Art. 14 of the 2003 Act of Accession. In Declaration (No.20) annexed to the Treaty of Nice on the enlargement of the Union (n.93, *supra*), the then Member States determined the composition of the European Economic and Social Committee for the candidate States (with the exception of Turkey) to be adopted by common position during the accession negotiations.

[350] The EU Constitution will extend the term of office to five years, which brings it into line with that of Members of the European Parliament (Art. III–390, first para.).

[351] See the Rules of Procedure adopted pursuant to the second para. of Art. 260 of the EC Treaty (which, since the EU Treaty, no longer have to be approved by the Council); the latest version was adopted on July 17, 2002 ([2002] O.J. L268/1).

reflect the sectors represented on the Committee itself.[352] The Chairman convenes the Committee at the request of the Commission, the Council or its Bureau.[353] The Committee has set up specialist sections for the principal fields covered by the Treaty.[354] Although the Council and the Commission may only consult the Committee as such, the opinion of the relevant specialised section is always forwarded to them along with that of the Committee itself.[355] The seat of the European Economic and Social Committee is in Brussels.[356] It has a staff of about 500 officials.[357]

2. The Committee of the Regions

10–096 **Advisory tasks.** Since the entry into force of the EU Treaty, representatives of regional and local bodies also have a right to be consulted in the decision-making process.[358] The EC Treaty established a Committee of the Regions,[359] which, in the same way as the Economic and Social Committee, is entitled to be consulted by the Council and the Commission where the Treaty so provides[360] and may issue an opinion on its own initiative where it considers such action appropriate (EC Treaty, Art. 265, first and fifth paras). The Committee of the Regions may also be consulted by the Commission or the Council in all other cases, in particular those which concern cross-border co-operation, in which one of those two institutions

---

[352] EC Treaty, Art. 260, first para., and ESC Rules of Procedure, Art. 3.

[353] EC Treaty, Art. 260, third para., and ESC Rules of Procedure, Art. 29. Under that article, the Committee may be convened on a proposal from its Bureau, with the approval of the majority of its members.

[354] The Committee sets up its sections at the inaugural session following each four-yearly renewal (ESC Rules of Procedure, Art. 14).

[355] EC Treaty, Art. 261, third para., and Art. 262, third para. The Treaty also provides that subcommittees may be set up within the ESC to prepare draft opinions on specific questions or in specific fields (EC Treaty, Art. 261, fourth para.).

[356] Sole Article, paragraph (f), of the Protocol on Seats, para. 10–146, *infra*. The ECSC Consultative Committee was based in Luxembourg.

[357] As at December 31, 2003, the Committee had 180 permanent and temporary posts by way of its own staff and 337 in the services shared with the Committee of the Regions: *General Report on the Activities of the European Union 2003* (n.122, *supra*), at 514.

[358] By Decision of June 24, 1988 ([1988] O.J. L247/23), the Commission set up a Consultative Council of Regional and Local Authorities, which was wound up after the Committee of the Regions started its work (Commission Decision of April 21, 1994, [1994] O.J. L103/28).

[359] Kottmann, "Europe and the regions: sub-national entity representation at Community level" (2001) E.L.R. 159–176; Wiedmann, "Der Ausschuss der Regionen nach dem Vertrag von Amsterdam" (1999) EuR. 49–86; Ingelaere, "Het Comité van de Regio's" (1995) S.E.W. 383–398; Bassot, "Le Comité des Régions—Régions françaises et Länder allemands face à un nouvel organe communautaire", (1993) R.M.C.U.E. 729–739; Wuermeling, "Das Ende der 'Länderblindheit': Der Ausschuß der Regionen nach dem neuen EG-Vertrag" (1993) EuR. 196–206. For the website of the Committee of the Regions, see *www.cor.eu.int/*.

[360] See Art. 71(1) (transport); Art. 128(2) and Art. 129, first para. (employment); Art. 137(2), second subpara., and Art. 148 (social policy); Art. 149(4), first indent (education); Art. 150(4) (vocational training); Art. 151(5), first indent (culture); Art. 152(4) (public health); Art. 156, first and third paras (trans-European networks); Art. 159, third para., Art. 161, first, second and third paras, and Art. 162, first para. (economic and social cohesion); Art. 175(1), (2) and (3) (environment).

considers it appropriate; it may also be consulted by the European Parliament (EC Treaty, Art. 265, first and fourth paras). The Committee is informed of every request for an opinion made to the European Economic and Social Committee with a view to its delivering an opinion on the matter if it considers that specific regional aspects are involved (EC Treaty, Art. 265, third para.).[361] The EU Constitution will confer on the Committee of the Regions *locus standi* to bring an action for annulment before the Court of Justice for the purpose of protecting its prerogatives or to denounce an infringement of the principle of subsidiarity.[362]

Composition. The Committee of the Regions may have no more than 350 **10–097** members (at present it has 317), who are distributed among the Member States in the same way as the members of the European Economic and Social Committee (EC Treaty, Art. 263, second and third paras).[363] The members consist of representatives of regional and local bodies who either hold a regional or local authority electoral mandate or are politically accountable to an elected assembly.[364] The members of the Committee are appointed by the Council by a qualified majority vote in accordance with the proposals made by each Member State, together with an equal number of alternate members (EC Treaty, Art. 263, fourth para.). Consequently, the Member States themselves decide which domestic levels of administration they wish to have represented on the Committee, one of the reasons being that the status and powers of regional and local bodies differ greatly from one Member State to another.[365] As in the case of their counterparts at the European Economic and Social Committee, members of the Committee of the Regions are appointed for a renewable four-year

---

[361] Conversely, every act requiring an opinion of the Committee of the Regions is also submitted to the European Economic and Social Committee for its opinion (except as regards culture) and to the European Parliament. The Committee of the Regions also receives the three-yearly report on economic and social cohesion provided for in Art. 159, second para., of the EC Treaty.

[362] See Art. III–365(3) of the EU Constitution and Art. 7 of the Protocol annexed to the draft EU Constitution on the application of the principles of subsidiarity and proportionality, by virtue of which the Committee will be able to bring an action under Art. III–365 of the Constitution on grounds of infringement of the principle of subsidiarity—irrespective of whether or not such action is intended to protect its prerogatives—in respect of legislative acts for the adoption of which the Constitution provides that it be consulted.

[363] See the most recent amendment in Art. 15 of the 2003 Act of Accession. In Declaration (No.20) annexed to the Treaty of Nice on the enlargement of the Union (n.93, *supra*), the then Member States determined the composition of the Committee of the Regions for the candidate States (with the exception of Turkey) to be adopted by common position during the accession negotiations.

[364] The requirement that the proposed members must have an electoral mandate was introduced by the Treaty of Nice. Before, each Member State decided whether to put forward (indirectly) elected representatives.

[365] For the Belgian representation, see Ingelaere (n.359, *supra*), at 387; for the Netherlands, see Hessel and Mortelmans, *Het recht van de Europese Gemeenschappen en de decentrale overheden in Nederland* (Tjeenk Willink, Deventer, 1997), 67 pp.

term,[366] may not be bound by any mandatory instructions and have to be completely independent in the performance of their duties in the general interest of the Community (EC Treaty, Art. 263, fourth and fifth paras).

10–098 Operation. The Committee of the Regions adopts its own rules of procedure.[367] Twice during their term of office, the members are to elect a President, who convenes it on his or her own initiative or at the request of the Council or the Commission (Art. 264).[368] The Committee's Bureau has to reflect the geographical balance of the Community.[369]

The Committee of the Regions shares certain services with the European Economic and Social Committee.[370] As a result, the Committee of the Regions is also based in Brussels.[371]

3. Other committees

10–099 Consultative bodies. In a number of policy areas, the Treaty involves national civil servants, representatives of interest groups and independent experts in the decision-making process by means of committees created for that purpose. Pursuant to Art. 209 of the EC Treaty, the Council adopts the rules governing committees provided for in the Treaty (by a simple majority vote) after receiving the opinion of the Commission. Examples are the Advisory Committee on Transport, consisting of experts designated by the national governments, attached to the Commission (EC Treaty, Art. 79) and the Committee of the European Social Fund, composed of representatives of governments, trade unions and employers' associations and presided over by a member of the Commission, which assists the Commission in administering the Fund (EC Treaty, Art. 147).[372] The Treaty of Amsterdam created the Employment Committee, to which each Member State and the Commission appoint two members (EC Treaty, Art. 130).[373] That committee consults management and labour in order to

---

[366] The EU Constitution will also extend the term of office of members of the Committee of the Regions to five years (Art. III–386, second para.).

[367] Rules of Procedure adopted by the Committee of the Regions on May 10, 2004 ([2004] O.J. L175/1), replacing previous versions of April 9, 2003 ([2003] O.J. L189/53), of May 17 and 18, 1994 ([1994] O.J. L132/49) and of November 18, 1999 ([2000] O.J. L18/22).

[368] The President has to convene the Plenary Assembly at least once every three months and is under a duty to hold an extraordinary meeting if requested by at least a quarter of the members (Rules of Procedure, r.14).

[369] See Rules of Procedure, r.28.

[370] As at December 31, 2003, the Committee had 124 permanent and temporary posts by way of its own staff and 128 in the services shared with the European Economic and Social Committee: *General Report on the Activities of the European Union 2003* (n.122, *supra*), at 516.

[371] Sole Article, para. (g), of the Protocol on Seats, para. 10–146, *infra*.

[372] Rules of the Transport Committee, adopted by the Council on September 15, 1958, [1952–1958] O.J. Spec. Ed. 72; Rules of the Committee of the European Social Fund, adopted by the Council on August 25, 1960, [1959–1962] O.J. Spec. Ed. 65.

[373] Council Decision 2000/98/EC of January 24, 2000 establishing the Employment Committee, [2000] O.J. L29/21.

perform its task of formulating opinions and contributing (together with Coreper) to the preparation of Council proceedings (see para. 10–051). A similar task has been conferred on the Social Protection Committee, enshrined in the Treaty by the Treaty of Nice, to which each Member State and the Commission appoint two members (EC Treaty, Art. 144).

An important role is played by the Economic and Financial Committee, which keeps under review the economic and financial situation of the Member States and the Community and reports in particular on financial relations with third countries and international institutions (EC Treaty, Art. 114(2), second indent).[374] It reports on these matters to the Council and the Commission and advises those institutions at their request or on its own initiative. It prepares (together with Coreper) certain Council proceedings, reports to the Council and the Commission on free movement of capital and freedom of payments and carries out such other advisory and preparatory tasks as the Council should entrust to it (EC Treaty, Art. 114(2), third and fourth indents). The Committee also keeps under review the monetary and financial situation and the general payments system of Member States with a derogation (Art. 114(4)). The Member States, the Commission and the ECB each appoint no more than two members of the Committee (Art. 114(2), third subpara.).[375]

Other committees. A number of Community acts have set up advisory **10–100** committees, the Council being deemed to have the power to determine their rules by virtue of Art. 209 of the EC Treaty. This also applies to the advisory, management and regulatory committees which supervise the Commission's implementing powers under the various comitology procedures (see para. 14–043). Each such committee consists of representatives of the Member States and one representative of the Commission. Just as in the case of committees created by the EC Treaty itself, the Commission pays for the costs of these committee meetings out of its budget.[376]

---

[374] Statutes of the Economic and Financial Committee as revised by the Council on June 18, 2003, [2003] O.J. L158/58. This committee is the successor of the Monetary Committee, which kept under review the monetary and financial situation of the Member States and the Community and advised the Council and the Commission (see EC Treaty, Art. 114(1)). Under Art. 6 of the Decision on Provisional Location of April 8, 1965 (para. 10–145, *infra*), the Committee was to meet in Brussels and Luxembourg.

[375] The two members appointed by the Member States comprise one senior official from the administration and one from the national central bank, see Council Decision 98/743/EC of December 21, 1998 on the detailed provisions concerning the composition of the Economic and Financial Committee, [1998] O.J. L358/109. The members of the national central banks do not attend all meetings; see Art. 4 of the Statute of the Economic and Financial Committee.

[376] See the list of some 400 committees in Final adoption of the general budget for the European Union for the financial year 2004, [2004] O.J. C105, Part II/1391.

B. THE EUROPEAN CENTRAL BANK

10–101 Independent body. The European Central Bank (ECB)[377] is an independent Community body with legal personality.[378] It performs the tasks entrusted to it by the EC Treaty within the European System of Central Banks, which has managed Economic and Monetary Union (EMU) since the start of its third stage (January 1, 1999 for the Member States which adopted the euro as their currency unit).

On June 1, 1998 the ECB took over the tasks which the EC Treaty had entrusted to the European Monetary Institute (EMI), an independent body with legal personality, since the start of the second stage of EMU. The EMI itself had replaced the Committee of Governors of the central banks and the European Monetary Co-operation Fund.[379] Since, prior to the third stage of EMU, monetary policy remained in the hands of the Member States, national central banks constituted the members of the EMI and the EMI was directed and managed by a Council, consisting of a President and the governors of the national central banks.[380] The EMI operated in accordance with its Statute, adopted in the form of a Protocol annexed to the EC Treaty,[381] and its Rules of Procedure, which the Council of the EMI adopted independently. The EMI's seat was established at Frankfurt by the national governments at the level of Heads of State or Government.[382]

10–102 Tasks. Under Art. 108 of the EC Treaty, the ECB—just like the national central banks—exercises its powers and carries out its tasks and duties completely independently of the political authorities of the Community and the Member States or any other body. That independence does not mean that the ECB is separated entirely from the Community but seeks to shield the ECB from political influences in exercising the specific tasks attributed

---

[377] For the ECB website, see *www.ecb.int/*.

[378] EC Treaty, Art. 107(2). For the independent status and the place occupied by the ECB in the institutional structure of the Community, see paras 10–102 and 14–066, respectively. For the ECB as a Community body, see ECJ, Case C–11/00 *Commission v European Central Bank* [2003] E.C.R. I–7147, paras 89–96. See, in general, Zilioli and Selmayer, *The Law of the European Central Bank* (Hart Publishing, Oxford, 2001), 268 pp.

[379] See EC Treaty, Art. 117(1), first subpara., and (2), fifth indent. All the assets and liabilities of the European Monetary Co-operation Fund passed automatically to the EMI. Under Art. 123(2) of the EC Treaty, the assets and liabilities of the EMI were transferred to the ECB, which liquidated the EMI.

[380] EC Treaty, Art. 117(1), first subpara.; Louis, "L'Institut monétaire européen", *Reflets et Perspectives de la vie économique* (Recherche et diffusion économiques, Brussels, 1993), at 285–299; Slot, "The Institutional Provisions of the EMU", *Institutional Dynamics of European Integration. Essays in Honour of Henry G. Schermers* (n.214, *supra*), at 229–249. Baron A. Lamfalussy was appointed President of the EMI (from the start of the second stage of EMU—January 1, 1994 until June 30, 1997). He was followed by W.F. Duisenberg (July 1, 1997 until the start of the ECB).

[381] EC Treaty, Art. 117(1), third subpara., and Protocol (No.19) annexed to the EC Treaty on the Statute of the European Monetary Institute, annexed to the EC Treaty by the EU Treaty (EMI Statute), [1992] O.J. C224/115.

[382] See EMI Statute, Art. 13, and the Second Decision on the Seats of the Institutions of October 29, 1993, para. 10–147, *infra*.

to it.[383] The Statute of the European System of Central Banks (ESCB) governs the financial and administrative independence of the ECB.[384] That statute is set out in a Protocol annexed to the EC Treaty, together with that of the ECB.[385] The ECB ensures that it and the national central banks (of Member States taking part in EMU without a derogation) carry out the tasks which the EC Treaty confers on the ESCB (see para. 5–231).[386] The ECB is entitled to impose fines and periodic penalty payments on undertakings for failure to comply with obligations imposed by its regulations and decisions (EC Treaty, Art. 110(3)).[387] In addition, the ECB supervises the national central banks to make sure that they comply with their obligations and may bring a central bank before the Court of Justice if it finds that there has been an infringement (EC Treaty, Art. 237(d)).[388] The central bank concerned is under a duty to take the necessary measures to comply with the Court's judgment finding that it has failed to fulfil its obligations, but cannot be fined if it persists in the infringement.[389]

Internal organisation. The decision-making bodies of the ECB govern the **10–103** ESCB (EC Treaty, Art. 107(3)). Accordingly, the ECB's Governing Council is made up of the governors of the central banks of Member States without a derogation and the members of the ECB's Executive Board. The

---

[383] ECJ, Case C–11/00 *Commission v European Central Bank* [2003] E.C.R. I–7147, paras 134–135. For the substance of that independence, see *ibid.*, paras 130–132. See also Elderson and Weenink, "The European Central Bank redefined? A landmark judgment of the European Court of Justice" (2003) Euredia 273–301; Lavranos, "The limited, functional independence of the ECB" (2004) E.L.R. 115–123.

[384] See, *inter alia*, Art. 27 (independent audit of accounts), Art. 28 (capital of the ECB) and Art. 36 (staff) of the ESCB Statute.

[385] EC Treaty, Art. 8 and Art. 107(4) and Protocol (No.18) annexed to the EC Treaty on the Statute of the European System of Central Banks and of the European Central Bank [ESCB Statute], [1992] O.J. C224/104. Notwithstanding the status of that Protocol as part of the Treaty (see EC Treaty, Art. 311), some of its articles may be amended by the Council, provided that the European Parliament gives its assent. Where an amendment is recommended by the ECB (by unanimous vote of the Governing Board), the Council takes its decision by qualified majority after consulting the Commission. If a proposal is made by the Commission, the Council has to act unanimously to adopt it, after consulting the ECB (EC Treaty, Art. 107(5) and ESCB Statute, Art. 41).

[386] ESCB Statute, Art. 9.2.

[387] The ECB exercises this power within the limits and under the conditions laid down in Council Regulation (EC) No. 2532/98 of November 23, 1998 concerning the powers of the European Central Bank to impose sanctions, [1998] O.J. L318/4. For the applicable infringement procedure, see European Central Bank Regulation (EC) No. 2157/1999 of September 23, 1999 [1999] O.J. L264/21. See Fernández Martín and Texieira, "The imposition of sanctions by the European Central Bank" (2000) E.L.Rev. 391–407.

[388] Art. 237(d) confers on the Council of the ECB the same powers as are conferred on the Commission by Art. 226 of the EC Treaty. See also ESCB Statute, Art. 35.6 and Gaiser, "Gerichtliche Kontrolle im Europäischen System der Zentralbanken" (2002) EuR. 517, at 520–523. Remarkably, Art. 14.2 of the ESCB Statute makes provision for proceedings to be brought in the Court of Justice against a decision relieving a governor of a central bank from his or her office by the Governing Council of the ECB or by the governor concerned. See Gaiser, *ibid.*, at 523–524.

[389] *cf.* Art. 237(d), last sentence, with Art. 228 of the EC Treaty. See Slot (n.380, *supra*), at 246.

Executive Board consists of the President, the Vice-President and four (or fewer) members.[390] The governments of the Member States at the level of Heads of State or Government appoint the Executive Board by common agreement for a non-renewable eight-year term on a recommendation from the Council, after consulting the European Parliament and the ECB's Governing Council.[391] Member States with a derogation have no voting rights.[392] Candidates for office must be nationals of Member States without a derogation and of recognised standing and professional experience in monetary or banking matters (see EC Treaty, Art. 112(1) and (2)). Before their appointment, the European Parliament invites the nominees for President, Vice-President and other Executive Board Members of the ECB to make a statement before the committee responsible and answer questions put by MEPs.[393] Board members perform their duties on a full-time basis and may be compulsorily retired only by the Court of Justice on application by the Governing Council or the Executive Board.[394]

The Governing Council formulates the Community's monetary policy; the Executive Board implements that policy and gives the necessary directions to the national central banks.[395] The Executive Board is responsible for the preparation of meetings of the Governing Council and for current business of the ECB.[396] As a rule, the President represents the ECB externally.[397] To the extent deemed possible and appropriate, the ECB has recourse to the national central banks to carry out operations forming part of the ESCB's tasks.[398]

As long as there are Member States with a derogation, the governors of the central banks of all the Member States, together with the President and Vice-President of the ECB, will have certain responsibilities as the General Council of the ECB (EC Treaty, Art. 123(3)).[399]

---

[390] See EC Treaty, Art. 123(1), second indent.

[391] See the first Decision (98/345/EC) taken by common accord of the Governments of the Member States adopting the single currency at the level of Heads of State or Government of May 26, 1998 appointing the President, the Vice-President and the other members of the Executive Board of the European Central Bank, [1998] O.J. L154/33 (Duisenberg was appointed President).

[392] EC Treaty, Art. 122(4).

[393] EP Rules of Procedure, r.102(1) and (5). If the Parliament's opinion on a nominee is negative, it will request the Council to submit a new nomination: r.102(4).

[394] ESCB Statute, Arts 11.1 and 11.4. Art. 11.4 makes it possible for a Board member to be retired (as in the case of a Member of the Commission) if he or she no longer fulfils the conditions required for the performance of his or her duties or if he or she has been guilty of serious misconduct. The Code of Conduct for the members of the Governing Council may be found in [2002] O.J. C123/9.

[395] ESCB Statute, Art. 12.1, first and second subparas. The second subpara. also provides that the Governing Council may delegate powers to the Board.

[396] *ibid.*, Arts 11.6 and 12.2.

[397] *ibid.*, Art. 13.2.

[398] *ibid.*, Art. 12.1, third subpara.

[399] For those responsibilities, see ESCB Statute, Art. 47.

Operation. The EMI's seat at Frankfurt has been taken over by the **10–104** ECB.[400] The President of the Council and a Member of the Commission may take part, without any voting rights, in meetings of the Governing Council, moreover, the President of the Council may submit a motion for deliberation (EC Treaty, Art. 113(1)). The proceedings are confidential.[401] In principle, both the Governing Council and the Executive Board take their decisions by a simple majority vote, although in some cases the Governing Council has to act by a qualified majority of votes weighted according to the national central banks' shares in the ECB's subscribed capital.[402] The operation of the Governing Council may be amended by the Council meeting in the composition of the Heads of State or Government by a unanimous vote, subject to ratification by the Member States in accordance with their respective constitutional requirements.[403] In this way, a system was introduced on the accession of the new Member States in 2004 to the effect that not all governors of Central Banks would all have the same voting rights.[404] Depending on the size of the share of their Member State in the aggregate GDP of the Member States which have adopted the euro and in the total aggregated balance sheet of the monetary financial institutions of those Member States, the national central banks are allocated to groups within which the right to vote rotates.[405] The national central banks are the only shareholders in the ECB.[406] The key for subscription to shares in the ECB takes account of each Member State's share of the population of the Community and of its GDP.[407] The internal

---

[400] Second Decision on the Seats of the Institutions of October 29, 1993, taken over by the Protocol on Seats, Sole Article, paragraph (i); para. 10–147, *infra*. See ESCB Statute, Art. 37, and Heim, "The European Central Bank: Was it not bound to go to Luxembourg?" (1994) E.L.R. 48–55.

[401] ESCB Statute, Art. 10.4. Under this provision, the Governing Council may decide, however, to make the outcome of its deliberations public.

[402] For the Governing Council, see ESCB Statute, Arts 10.2 and 10.3 (qualified majority); for the Executive Board, see ESCB Statute, Art. 11.5.

[403] ESCB Statute, Art. 10.6, added by Art. 5 of the Treaty of Nice. See Servais, Vigneron and Ruggeri, "Le Traité de Nice. Son impact sur l'Union économique et monétaire" (2000) Euredia 477, at 489–493.

[404] Decision 2003/223/EC of the Council meeting in the composition of the Heads of State or Government of March 21, 2003 on an amendment to Art. 10.2 of the Statute of the European System of Central Banks and of the European Central Bank, [2003] O.J. L83/66.

[405] *ibid.*, Art. 1. See Heisenberg, "Cutting the Bank Down to Size: Efficient and Legitimate Decision-making in the European Central Bank After Enlargement" (2003) J.C.M.S. 397–420.

[406] ESCB Statute, Art. 28.2.

[407] *ibid.*, Art. 29.1. For the most recent subscription key, see Decision BCE/2004/4 of the European Central Bank of April 22, 2004 ([2004] O.J. L205/5); for the measures necessary for the paying-up of the capital of the ECB, see most recently Decision BCE/2004/6 of the ECB of April 22, 2004 ([2004] O.J. L205/7—for participating Member States) and Decision BCE/2004/10 of April 23, 2004 ([2004] O.J. L205/19—for non-participating Member States). See also Art. 30 of the ESCB Statute as regards the transfer of foreign reserve assets to the ECB and Arts 26 and 27 as regards financial accounts and auditing. For permitted increases in the ECB's capital, see Council Regulation (EC) No. 1009/2000 of May 8, 2000, [2000] O.J. L115/1.

organisation of the ECB is determined by its Rules of Procedure, adopted by the Governing Council.[408]

C. THE EUROPEAN INVESTMENT BANK

10–105 Tasks. The European Investment Bank[409] (EIB) is an independent Community body endowed with legal personality.[410] Its task is to finance, by recourse to the capital market and utilising its own resources, private and public investment projects fostering the balanced and steady development of the Community (EC Treaty, Art. 267). Together with the Structural Funds and other financial instruments, the EIB seeks in this way to promote economic and social cohesion within the Community.[411] In addition, as part of the Community's development policy, it may finance projects to be carried out in non-Community countries.[412]

10–106 Operation. The members of the EIB are the Member States (EC Treaty, Art. 226, second para.), each subscribing fixed amounts of its capital.[413] General directives for the EIB's credit policy and important decisions such as increases in capital are adopted by the Board of Governors, which consists of ministers designated by the Member States (in practice, the Finance Ministers).[414] The Board of Governors approves the Bank's Rules of Procedure[415] and therefore has the power to organise internal matters and is authorised to take the appropriate measures in order to ensure the internal operation of the EIB in conformity with the interests of its good administration.[416] It takes its decisions in accordance with the same rules on majority voting as the Council, except that the majority must represent at

---

[408] ESCB Statute, Art. 12.3 and the ECB's Rules of Procedure adopted pursuant thereto on February 19, 2004 ([2004] O.J. L80/33), replacing the first Rules of April 22, 1999 ([1999] O.J. L125/34), as amended on October 7, 1999 ([1999] O.J. L314/32). The Rules of Procedure of the Executive Board of the ECB were adopted by ECB Decision of October 12, 1999 ([1999] O.J. L314/34). For the Rules of Procedure of the General Council of the ECB of June 17, 2004, see [2004] O.J. L230/61.

[409] For the website of the EIB, see *www.eib.eu.int/*.

[410] See EC Treaty, Arts 9, 266 and 267, and the Protocol on the Statute of the European Investment Bank (EIB Statute). For the EIB as a Community body, see ECJ, Case 110/75 *Mills v European Investment Bank* [1976] E.C.R. 955, paras 7–14, and ECJ, Case C–15/00 *Commission v European Investment Bank* [2003] E.C.R. I–7281, para. 75; for the extent of its financial and institutional independence, see ECJ, Case 85/86 *Commission v European Investment Bank* [1988] E.C.R. 1281, paras 28–30; ECJ, Case C–370/89 *SGEEM v European Investment Bank* [1992] E.C.R. I–6211, paras 12–17; ECJ, Case C–15/00 *Commission v European Investment Bank* [2003] E.C.R. I–7281, paras 101–110. For further details, see Dunnett, "The European Investment Bank: Autonomous Instrument of Common Policy?" (1994) C.M.L.R. 721–763.

[411] For economic and social cohesion, see EC Treaty, Art. 159, first para. (para. 5–247, *supra*); see also EC Treaty, Arts 154 and 155 on Trans-European Networks.

[412] See EIB Statute, Art. 18(1).

[413] *ibid.*, Arts 4 and 5.

[414] *ibid.*, Art. 9(1) and (2).

[415] *ibid.*, Art. 9(3)(h).

[416] ECJ, Case C–15/00 *Commission v European Investment Bank* [2003] E.C.R. I–7281, paras 67–81.

least 50 per cent of the subscribed capital.[417] The Board of Directors takes decisions in respect of granting loans and guarantees and raising loans.[418] It also ensures that Member States fulfil their obligations under the EIB Statute.[419] The Board of Directors consists of 26 directors, of whom the Member States and the Commission nominates one each. They are then appointed by the Board of Governors for a five-year term.[420] The Board of Directors generally takes its decisions by at least one-third of the members with voting rights representing at least 50 per cent of the capital; where a qualified majority is required, 18 votes in favour and 68 per cent of the capital are needed.[421] Responsibility for the current business of the Bank lies with the Management Committee, which consists of a President and eight Vice-Presidents, who are appointed for a six-year term by the Board of Governors on a proposal from the Board of Directors.[422] Members of the Board of Directors and of the Management Committee perform their duties in complete independence and may be dismissed only by the Board of Governors.[423] The European Investment Bank has its seat in Luxembourg.[424]

D. The European Ombudsman

Task. The EU Treaty introduced a European Ombudsman[425] to look into **10–107** complaints of maladministration in the activities of Community institutions or bodies, with the exception of the Court of Justice and the Court of First Instance acting in their judicial role (EC Treaty, Art. 195(1)).[426] According

---

[417] EIB Statute, Art. 10, which provides that voting by the Board of Governors is to be in accordance with Art. 205 of the EC Treaty.

[418] *ibid.*, Art. 11(1).

[419] EC Treaty, Art. 237(a), which gives the Board of Directors the same powers as are enjoyed by the Commission under Art. 226 of the EC Treaty.

[420] EIB Statute, Art. 11(2).

[421] *ibid.*, Art. 12.

[422] *ibid.*, Art. 13.

[423] *ibid.*, Art. 11(2), last subpara., Art. 11(3) and Art. 13(8). Members of the Management Committee may be retired only on a proposal from the Board of Directors (EIB Statute, Art. 13(2)).

[424] Protocol on Seats, Sole Article, para. (h), 460, *infra*. See Art. 1 of the EIB Statute, which was implemented by Art. 5 of the Decision on Provisional Location of April 8, 1965, 459, *infra*.

[425] For the Ombudsman's website, see *www.euro-ombudsman.eu.int/*.

[426] Pierucci, "Le médiateur européen" (1993) R.M.C.U.E. 818–822; Marias, *The European Ombudsman*, (European Institute of Public Administration, Maastricht, 1994), 150 pp.; Pliakos, "Le médiateur de l'Union européenne" (1994) C.D.E. 563–606. In principle, there is nothing to prevent the Ombudsman from investigating a complaint concerning the activities of Community institutions and bodies which fall outside the ambit of the Community Treaties. The Ombudsman has taken the view that he may rule on a refusal by the Council to give a citizen access to documents, regardless of the subject-matter, see European Ombudsman, *Annual Report 1997* (Office for Official Publications of the EC, Luxembourg), at 23–24. Art. 41(1) of the EU Treaty expressly declares that Art. 195 applies to PJCC. Nevertheless, Art. 28(1) and Art. 41(1) of the EU Treaty preclude the powers of investigation provided for in Art. 193 of the EC Treaty in connection with action pursuant to the CFSP and PJCC, respectively.

to the Ombudsman, there is "maladministration" if a public authority fails to observe a rule or principle which is binding on it.[427] The regulations and general conditions governing the performance of the European Ombudsman's duties are laid down by the European Parliament in accordance with a special procedure, under which the Commission delivers an opinion and the Council grants its approval by a qualified majority (EC Treaty, Art. 195(4)).[428] The Parliament appoints the European Ombudsman, who operates as an independent watchdog *vis-à-vis* the Community authorities.

The European Ombudsman conducts inquiries into maladministration by Community institutions and bodies either on his or her own initiative or on the basis of complaints submitted to him or her directly or through an MEP.[429] Such a complaint may be made by any citizen of the Union or any natural or legal person residing or having its registered office in a Member State.[430] The Ombudsman will not investigate a complaint if the facts have been known to the complainant for more than two years[431] or if the facts are or have been the subject of legal proceedings.[432] This means that a complainant must decide whether to bring judicial proceedings or to bring a complaint before the Ombudsman (which does not cause time for bringing judicial proceedings to stop running).[433] Community institutions and bodies must supply any information requested and give access to any documents in their possession. They may refuse to do so only on duly substantiated grounds of secrecy.[434] The Ombudsman may not divulge

---

[427] See the 1997 Annual Report (n.426, *supra*), at p.22. For the broad interpretation given to this expression in practice, see recent annual reports and Yeng-Seng, "Premier bilan de l'activité du médiateur européen: d'une politique des petits pas à une pratique consolidée" (2003) R.M.C.U.E. 326, at 329–330.

[428] Decision of the European Parliament of March 9, 1994 on the regulations and general conditions governing the performance of the Ombudsman's duties, [1994] O.J. L113/15 [Ombudsman Regulations], appended to the EP Rules of Procedure as Annex X. See also rr.192–194 of the EP Rules of Procedure. On July 8, 2002, the European Ombudsman issued new implementing provisions, which are published in Annex X to the EP Rules of Procedure ([2003] O.J. L61/107).

[429] EC Treaty, Art. 195(1), second subpara. See Yeng-Seng (n.427, *supra*), at 331–332.

[430] EC Treaty, Art. 195(1), first subpara. Naturally, other persons may place facts before the European Ombudsman in order to induce him or her to carry out an inquiry on his or her own initiative. "The European Ombudsman. How to complain" is set out in [1996] O.J. C157/1, and on the Internet ([1998] O.J. C44/14).

[431] Ombudsman Regulations, Art. 2(4).

[432] EC Treaty, Art. 195(1), second subpara. In addition, prior to making a complaint the appropriate administrative approaches must have been made to the institution or body concerned (Ombudsman Regulations, Art. 2(4)). An official or other servant of the Communities may make a complaint concerning work relationships with a Community institution or body only if all the possibilities for the submission of internal administrative requests and complaints under the Staff Regulations have been exhausted and the relevant time-limits have expired (Ombudsman Regulations, Art. 2(8)).

[433] CFI, Case T–209/00 *Lamberts v European Ombudsman* [2002] E.C.R. II–2203, paras 65–66, upheld by ECJ (judgment of March 23, 2004), Case C–234/02 P *European Ombudsman v Lamberts*, not yet reported.

[434] Ombudsman Regulations, Art. 3(2).

information or documents obtained in the course of inquiries.[435] The national authorities must provide the Ombudsman with any information requested which may help to clarify instances of maladministration by Community institutions or bodies unless provision of the said information is precluded by national law.[436] Provided that he or she complies with the applicable national law, the Ombudsman may co-operate with similar authorities in Member States.[437]

The Ombudsman's first task is to try to seek a solution with the institution or body concerned.[438] If the Ombudsman finds that there has been maladministration, he or she informs the institution concerned—which then has three months to inform him or her of its views—and may make recommendations for resolving the matter.[439] At this point, the Ombudsman forwards a report to the European Parliament and to the institution concerned. The Ombudsman keeps the complainant informed of the outcome of the inquiries[440] and also reports to the responsible committee of the European Parliament.[441] If necessary, the European Parliament will be in the best position to take the requisite steps, since it also receives an annual report from the Ombudsman on the outcome of his or her inquiries.[442]

Appointment. The connection between the European Ombudsman and the **10–108** directly elected European Parliament emerges from the rules on his or her appointment and possible dismissal (EC Treaty, Art. 195(2)). After its election, the European Parliament appoints an Ombudsman for the

---

[435] *ibid.*, Art. 4(1). If he or she learns of facts which he or she considers might relate to criminal law, the competent national authorities must be notified. The Ombudsman must inform the institution with authority over the official or other servant and may do so if he or she discovers facts calling into question the conduct of the staff member from the disciplinary point of view (Ombudsman Regulations, Art. 4(2)).

[436] *ibid.*, Art. 3(3).

[437] *ibid.*, Art. 5.

[438] *ibid.*, Art. 3(5).

[439] EC Treaty, Art. 195(1), second subpara., and Ombudsman Regulations, Art. 3(6). For the Ombudsman's discretion to close a case or to reach a friendly settlement, see ECJ (judgment of March 23, 2004), Case C–234/02 P *European Ombudsman v Lamberts*, not yet reported, para. 82, and the case confirmed thereby: CFI, Case T–209/00 *Lamberts v European Ombudsman* [2002] E.C.R. II–2203, paras 78–85.

[440] Ombudsman Regulations, Art. 3(7).

[441] EP Rules of Procedure, r.193(3). It is not possible to bring an action for failure to act against the Ombudsman on account of his or her refusal to initiate an inquiry, see CFI (order of May 22, 2000), Case T–103/99 *Associazione delle cantine sociali Venete v European Ombudsman and the European Parliament* [2000] E.C.R. II–4165.

[442] EC Treaty, Art. 195(1), second and third paras. For recent annual reports, see the website cited in n. 425 (for earlier reports, see [1998] O.J. C380/11 (1997), [1999] O.J. C300/1 (1998) and [2000] O.J. C260/1 (1999).

duration of its term of office.[443] The Ombudsman may be dismissed by the Court of Justice only at the request of the European Parliament.[444] He or she has to be completely independent in the performance of his or her duties, which are to be carried out on a full-time basis.[445] The Ombudsman is assisted by his or her own secretariat.[446] The Ombudsman's seat is that of the European Parliament.[447]

E. OTHER COMMUNITY BODIES

10–109 Separate offices. In order effectively to carry out certain tasks, various sectors of the administration have a degree of independence. Examples, on a interinstitutional footing, are the Office for Official Publications of the European Communities,[448] the European Communities Personnel Selection Office (EPSO)[449] and, for those answerable to the Commission, the Statistical Office (Eurostat),[450] the Office for the administration and payment of individual entitlements,[451] the Offices for infrastructure and logistics[452] and the Office for Veterinary and Plant-Health Inspection and

---

[443] EC Treaty, Art. 195(2), first subpara. The Ombudsman has to be a Union citizen, have full civil and political rights, offer every guarantee of independence and meet the conditions required for the exercise of the highest judicial office in his or her country or have the acknowledged competence and experience to undertake the duties of Ombudsman (Ombudsman Regulations, Art. 6(2)). Since the responsible parliamentary committee was unable to reach agreement on the first candidate to be approved by the plenary session, the EP Rules of Procedure were amended so as to enable several nominations to be put forward (see now r.192). The plenary session then chooses between them. For the appointment procedure, see CFI, Case T–146/95 *Bernardi v European Parliament* [1996] E.C.R. II–769 (action for annulment held to be unfounded).

[444] The Ombudsman may be dismissed if he or she no longer fulfils the conditions required for the performance of his or her duties or if he or she is guilty of serious misconduct (EC Treaty, Art. 195(2), second subpara.).

[445] EC Treaty, Art. 195(3); Ombudsman Regulations, Art. 9 and Art. 10(1).

[446] Ombudsman Regulations, Art. 11(1).

[447] Ombudsman Regulations, Art. 13.

[448] Decision 2000/495/EC, ECSC, Euratom of the European Parliament, the Council, the Commission, the Court of Justice, the Court of Auditors, the Economic and Social Committee and the Committee of the Regions of July 20, 2000, [2000] O.J. L183/12. The Office is based in Luxembourg as a result of Art. 8 of the Decision on Provisional Location (para. 10–145, *infra*).

[449] Decision 2002/620/EC of the European Parliament, the Council, the Commission, the Court of Justice, the Court of Auditors, the Economic and Social Committee, the Committee of the Regions and the European Ombudsman of July 25, 2002, [2002] O.J. L197/53; for its operation and internal organisation, see Decision 2002/621/EC of the Secretaries-General of those institutions and committees and of the Representative of the European Ombudsman of July 25, 2002, [2002] O.J. L197/56.

[450] Based in Luxembourg as a result of Art. 9(a) of the Decision on Provisional Location; see now the Protocol on Seats, Sole Article, para. (c) (para. 10–145, *infra*). For the role played by Eurostat in the production of Community statistics, see the Commission's decision of April 21, 1997, [1997] O.J. L112/56.

[451] Established by the Commission by decision of November 6, 2002, [2003] O.J. L183/30. The Office is responsible for determining, calculating and paying pecuniary entitlements of staff of the Community.

[452] The Commission established these offices in Brussels and Luxembourg by decisions of November 6, 2002, [2003] O.J. L183/35 and 40, respectively.

Control.[453] The European Anti-Fraud Office (OLAF) set up by the Commission carries out powers of investigation in complete independence.[454] The European Data-Protection Supervisor, introduced pursuant to Art. 286 of the EC Treaty, also operates completely independently (see para. 10–162). Article 8 of the EAEC Treaty provides for the establishment by the Commission of a Joint Nuclear Research Centre (JRC).[455] Contrary to what their titles might suggest, the Community "Funds" are not separate bodies, but operate as normal administrative departments of the Commission.[456]

It is also worth mentioning at this juncture that a number of international agreements concluded by the Community—Association Agreements especially—have created joint consultative bodies and joint decision-making bodies.[457]

Independent legal persons. Some Community bodies take the form of **10–110** separate legal persons under the name of agencies, foundations, centres or offices. They have a measure of independence in regard to their budgets and personnel policies. Their special status does not prevent their acts from being subject in many cases to the Commission's administrative supervision and invariably subject to judicial review (see para. 14–064).

---

[453] The Commission approved the establishment of the Office by Decision of December 18, 1991, (1991) 12 EC Bull. point 1.2.201. The "Food and Veterinary Office" (FVO) is part of the Directorate-General for Health and Consumers and based in Grange (Ireland). The Second Decision on the Seats of the Institutions of October 29, 1993 (para. 10–147, *infra*) provided that its seat was to be determined by the Irish Government.

[454] Commission Decision 1999/352/EC, ECSC, Euratom of April 28, 1999 establishing the European Anti-fraud Office (OLAF), [1999] O.J. L136/20 (para. 10–156, *infra*). The Director of OLAF is nominated by the Commission, after consulting the European Parliament and the Council: Art. 5(1) of Decision 1999/352 and Art. 12(2) of Regulation (EC) No. 1073/1999 of the European Parliament and of the Council of May 25, 1999 concerning investigations conducted by the European Anti-Fraud Office (OLAF), [1999] O.J. L136/1). The members of OLAF's Supervisory Committee are appointed by common accord of the European Parliament, the Council and the Commission: Art. 11(2) of Regulation No. 1073/1999. See Kuhl and Spitzer, "Das Europäische Amt für Betrugsbekämpfung (OLAF)" (2000) EuR. 671–685. For the Rules of Procedure adopted by OLAF's Supervisory Committee on November 17, 1999, see [2000] O.J. L41/12.

[455] See Commission Decision 85/593/Euratom of November 20, 1985 on the reorganisation of the Joint Research Centre (JRC), [1985] O.J. L373/6. The Council defined the JRC's role in its conclusions of April 26, 1994, [1994] O.J. C126/1. See also Commission Decision 96/282/Euratom of April 10, 1996 on the reorganisation of the Joint Research Centre, [1996] O.J. L107/12.

[456] European Social Fund: DG Employment and Social Affairs (see also EC Treaty, Art. 268, first para.); European Agricultural Guidance and Guarantee Fund (EAGGF or FEOGA): DG Agriculture; European Development Fund (EDF): the EuropeAid Co-operation Office; European Regional Development Fund (ERDF) and Cohesion Fund: DG Regional Policy.

[457] For further details, see paras 20–009 and 20–019, *infra*. Admittedly, such bodies are not "Community" bodies as such, but their decisions may sometimes be enforced as part of Community law: see para. 17–094, *infra*.

The EAEC Treaty established a Supply Agency, which has legal personality and financial autonomy and operates under the Commission's supervision (EAEC Treaty, Arts 52–56). Article 45 of the EAEC Treaty and Art. 171 of the EC Treaty make it possible to set up joint undertakings for research and development.[458] In addition, pursuant to the Protocol on the Statute of the EIB, the EIB's Board of Governors has set up a European Investment Fund.[459] On a more general note, the Community is entitled to set up an independent body whenever this squares with action pursuant to a specific Treaty article or Art. 308 of the EC Treaty (see paras 14–062—14–063). In this way, it has created the European Centre for the Development of Vocational Training (Cedefop),[460] the European Centre for the Improvement of Living and Working Conditions[461] and the European Agency for Co-operation.[462] A series of bodies were able to start operation once the Member States decided on the location of their seats on October 29, 1993[463]: the European Environmental Agency[464]; the European Training Foundation[465]; the European Monitoring Centre for Drugs and Drug Addiction[466]; the European Medicines

---

[458] See, *e.g.* the Joint European Torus (JET) joint undertaking set up by Council Decision of May 30, 1978 at Culham, [1978] O.J. L151/10. (For the UK, see European Community (Definition of Treaties) (No. 5) (Joint European Torus) Order 1978.) The undertaking's statutes are appended to that decision. See also the Galileo Joint Undertaking (on satellite radio-navigation), set up by Council Regulation (EC) No. 876/2002 of May 21, 2002, [2002] O.J. L138/1, whose statutes are annexed to that regulation. Not all members of JET's staff are officials of the EAEC: see ECJ, Joined Cases 271/83, 15, 36, 113, 158 and 203/84 and 13/85 *Ainsworth v Commission and Council* [1987] E.C.R. 167, paras 19–23.

[459] Statutes of the European Investment Fund, adopted on June 14, 1994 and June 19, 2000, amended by the general meeting, [2001] O.J. C225/2. Shareholders in the Fund are the Community, the European Investment Bank and a group of financial institutions.

[460] Council Regulation (EEC) No. 337/75 of February 10, 1995, [1975] O.J. L39/1 (para. 5–240, *supra*). For its nature as a Community body, see ECJ, Case 16/81 *Alaimo v Commission* [1982] E.C.R. 1559, paras 7–12, at 1566–1567. As agreed when the seats of various new bodies were allocated on October 29, 1993, the Council has moved the Centre's seat from Berlin to Thessalonika: Council Regulation (EC) No. 1131/94 of May 16, 1994, [1994] O.J. L127/1.

[461] Council Regulation (EC) No. 1365/75 of May 26, 1994, [1975] O.J. L139/1 (see n.1107 to para. 5–236, *supra*). Its seat is in Ireland (Art. 4(2)), more specifically in Dublin.

[462] Council Regulation (EEC) No. 3245/81 of October 26, 1981, O.J. 1981 L328/1. The Agency should deal with personnel policy and recruitment as regards staff which the Community makes available as part of its financial and technical co-operation with developing countries but has never become operational.

[463] By the Second Decision on the Seats of the Institutions of October 29, 1993, para. 10–147, *infra*. The regulations setting up these bodies provided that they were to enter into force on the day following the date on which the competent authorities took a decision as to where they were to be based. They therefore entered into force on October 30, 1993 (see the notice in O.J. 1994 L294/29).

[464] Council Regulation (EEC) No. 1210/90 of May 7, 1990, O.J. 1990 L120/1. The Agency's seat is in the Copenhagen area.

[465] Council Regulation (EEC) No. 1360/90 of May 7, 1990, O.J. 1990 L131/1, as amended on several occasions (para. 5–240, *supra*). Its seat is at Turin.

[466] Council Regulation (EEC) No. 302/93 of February 8, 1993, O.J. 1993 L36/1. The Centre's seat is at Lisbon.

Agency[467]; the European Office for Harmonisation in the Internal Market (Trade Marks and Designs),[468] and the European Agency for Health and Safety at Work.[469] In addition, the Council set up a Community Plant Variety Office,[470] a Translation Centre for Bodies of the European Union,[471] a European Monitoring Centre on Racism and Xenophobia[472] and the European Agency for Reconstruction.[473] In 2002 the European Parliament and the Council further established the European Food Safety Authority,[474] the European Maritime Safety Agency and the European

---

[467] Regulation (EC) No. 726/2004 of the European Parliament and of the Council of March 31, 2004 laying down Community procedures for the authorisation and supervision of medicinal products for human and veterinary use and establishing a European Medicines Agency, O.J. 2004 L136/1, replacing Council Regulation (EEC) No. 2309/93 of July 22, 1993, O.J. 1993 L214/1 (which had established the European Agency for the Evaluation of Medicinal Products, the name of which was changed to European Medicines Agency by Regulation 726/2004). The Agency's seat is in London.

[468] Council Regulation (EC) No. 40/94 of December 20 1993 on the Community trademark, O.J. 1994 L11/1. The Office is responsible for organising procedures for applying for and using the Community trademark and the Community design. It has a Board of Appeal, against whose decisions an action may be brought in the Court of Justice. The Second Decision on the Seats of the Institutions of October 29, 1993 provided that the Office was to have its seat in Spain. The Spanish Government decided that it was to be located in Alicante. See the declaration of the Council and the Commission annexed to the regulation, O.J. 1994 L11/36.

[469] Council Regulation (EC) No. 2062/94 of July 18, 1994, O.J. 1994 L216/1. Pursuant to the Second Decision on the Seats of the Institutions of October 29, 1993, the Spanish Government determined that its seat would be at Bilbao: see the declaration of the Council and the Commission annexed to the regulation.

[470] Council Regulation (EC) No. 2100/94 of July 27, 1994 on Community plant variety rights, O.J. 1994 L227/1, as amended by Council Regulation (EC) No. 2506/95 of October 25, 1995, O.J. 1995 L258/3 (introduction of a procedure before the Court of First Instance against decisions of Boards of Appeal by analogy with the appeal procedures in respect of the Community trademark). The Office is responsible for organising procedures relating to applications for and the use of Community plant variety rights. The Office is based in Angers (France): see the Decision taken by common accord of the representatives of the governments of the Member States of December 6, 1996, O.J. 1997 C36/1.

[471] Council Regulation (EC) No. 2965/94 of November 28, 1994, O.J. 1994 L314/1, as amended by Council Regulation (EC) No. 2610/95 of October 30, 1995, O.J. 1995 L268/1. The Centre, which is based in Luxembourg, provides translation services for the aforementioned six bodies whose seats were determined on October 29, 1993, for Europol and the Europol Drugs Unit and for institutions and bodies of the Union which have their own translation services should they wish to make use of the Centre's services. For the implementing provisions necessary to ensure the confidentiality of certain activities of the Translation Centre, see O.J. 1999 C295/3.

[472] Council Regulation (EC) No. 1035/97 of June 2, 1997, O.J. 1997 L151/1. The Centre is based in Vienna (Decision of the representatives of the governments of the Member States of June 2, 1997, O.J. 1997 C194/4). The Centre's terms of reference have been enlarged to cover all violations of human rights.

[473] Council Regulation (EC) No. 2454/1999 of November 15, 1999 (O.J. 1999 L299/1), as amended by Council Regulation (EC) No. 2667/2000 of December 5, 2000 on the European Agency for Reconstruction (O.J. 2000 L306/7). The Agency's operational centre is located at Pristina, its seat in Thessaloniki.

[474] Regulation (EC) No. 178/2002 of the European Parliament and of the Council of January 28, 2002 laying down the general principles and requirements of food law, establishing the European Food Safety Authority and laying down procedures in matters of food safety, O.J. 2002 L31/1 (see para. 5–243). After operating provisionally in Brussels, the Authority's seat

Aviation Safety Agency.[475] The locations of these three agencies were not determined until December 13, 2003 by the Third Decision on Seats, which also decided on the locations of the European Network and Information Security Agency,[476] the European Centre for Disease Prevention and Control,[477] the European Railway Agency[478] and some other agencies still to be established.[479] In addition, for the purposes of managing Community programmes, the Commission may set up executive agencies with legal personality.[480] As part of the accession process, candidate countries may be authorised to participate in Community agencies.[481]

10–111 **Connected bodies.** The Member States have also set up a number of bodies which fall outside the framework of the Communities, yet are closely connected with them. These are the European University Institute in Florence[482] and the various European Schools.[483] The Communities are

---

was established in Parma (Italy) by the Third Decision on Seats. See Petit, "L'autorité alimentaire de sécurité des aliments (A.E.S.A.) et la nouvelle approche alimentaire communautaire" (2002) J.T.D.E. 209–214; Vos, "Naar een Europese FDA? De nieuwe Europese Autoriteit voor Voedselveiligheid" (2003) N.T.E.R. 177–181.

[475] Regulation (EC) No. 1406/2002 of the European Parliament and of the Council of June 27 2002 establishing a European Maritime Safety Agency, O.J. 2002 L208/1, and Regulation (EC) No. 1592/2002 of the European Parliament and of the Council of July 15, 2002 on common rules in the field of civil aviation and establishing a European Aviation Safety Agency, O.J. 2002 L240/1. The Maritime Safety Agency has its seat in Lisbon, the Aviation Agency in Cologne (see the Third Decision on Seats).

[476] Regulation (EC) No. 460/2004 of the European Parliament and of the Council of March 10, 2004 establishing the European Network and Information Security Agency, O.J. 2004 L77/1. The Third Decision on Seats provides that it is to be located in Greece in a town to be determined by the Greek government.

[477] Regulation (EC) No. 851/2004 of the European Parliament and of the Council of April 21, 2004 establishing a European Centre for disease prevention and control, O.J. 2004 L142/1. The Third Decision on Seats provides that it will have its seat in Stockholm.

[478] Regulation (EC) No. 881/2004 of the European Parliament and of the Council of April 29, 2004 establishing a European Railway Agency (Agency Regulation), O.J. 2004 L164/1 (republished with corrigendum: O.J. 2004 L220/3). The Third Decision on Seats provided that it is to be located in Lille-Valenciennes (France).

[479] Accordingly, the Third Decision on Seats announced the establishment of a European Chemicals Agency (having its seat in Helsinki). In adopting the decision on December 13, 2003, it was also made known that a future Community Fisheries Control Agency would be set up in Spain and that the European Public Prosecutor's Office, if established, will be located in Luxembourg.

[480] On the basis of Council Regulation (EC) No. 58/2003 of December 19, 2002 laying down the statute for executive agencies to be entrusted with certain tasks in the management of Community programmes, O.J. 2003 L11/1.

[481] See, e.g. the agreements on the participation of each of the candidate countries in the European Environment Agency and the European environment information and observation network, [2001] O.J. L213.

[482] Convention of April 19, 1972 setting up a European University Institute, [1976] O.J. C29/1 [the Convention]. Art. 9 of the EAEC Treaty, which provides for the establishment of "an institution of university status", has never been implemented.

[483] See the establishment of a European School in Luxembourg by the Statute of the European School of April 12, 1957 and in other places of work of institutions and bodies by the Protocol on the establishment of European Schools of April 13, 1962 adopted pursuant to that Statute. For the UK, see the European Communities (European Schools) Order 1972,

represented in the management of those bodies and the EU budget covers costs not paid by the Member States.[484] As a result of the latter aspect, a Member State which acts in breach of the Statute of the European Schools thereby producing a burden on the EU budget, also infringes Art. 10 of the EC Treaty.[485]

III. OTHER BODIES OF THE UNION

Non-Community bodies. The non-Community provisions of the EU Treaty **10–112** refer to a number of bodies, which may conveniently be classed as "bodies of the Union". First, there is the European Council (EU Treaty, Art. 4; see paras 10–003—10–007), which is not an institution or body of the Communities, but supported administratively as an inter-governmental body by the Member State which holds the Presidency of the Council for the time being. In addition, the EU Treaty set up two committees, which prepare the Council's work in the areas of the CFSP and PJCC, respectively: the Political and Security Committee and the Coordinating Committee (see para. 10–051).

Under the CFSP, a number of bodies have been set up with legal personality to take over structures already existing within the framework of the Western European Union (WEU). For instance, the Council has set up pursuant to Art. 14 of the EU Treaty an Institute for Security Studies[486] and a European Union Satellite Centre.[487]

The provisions of the EU Treaty on co-operation in the fields of justice and home affairs envisaged the creation of a European Police Office (Europol), which was ultimately set up by a convention concluded between

---

the European Communities (Definition of Treaties) (European School) Order 1990 and the European Communities (Privileges of the European School) Order 1990. The 1962 protocol has been replaced by the Convention of June 21, 1994 defining the Statute of the European Schools, [1994] O.J. L212/3 [the Statute] (this Convention was concluded between the Member States and the three Communities; it was ratified on behalf of the EC and the EAEC by a Council decision of June 17, 1994 pursuant to Art. 235 [now Art. 308] of the EC Treaty and Art. 203 of the EAEC Treaty and on behalf of the ECSC by a Commission decision based on the first para. of Art. 95 of the ECSC Treaty).

[484] See the representative of the Communities on the High Council of the European University Institute (Convention, Art. 6(3); the representative does not have voting rights) and the Community representative on the Board of Governors of the European Schools (Statute, Art. 8(1); that representative does have the right to vote) and the Community's contribution towards operating costs (provided for in Art. 19(2) of the Convention and Art. 25(2) of the Statute).

[485] ECJ, Case 44/84 *Hurd v Jones* [1986] E.C.R. 29, paras 36–45; ECJ, Case C–6/89 *Commission v Belgium* [1990] E.C.R. I–1595 (para. 5–055, *supra*).

[486] Council Joint Action 2001/554/CFSP of July 20, 2001 on the establishment of a European Union Institute for Security Studies, [2001] O.J. L200/1. The institute has its seat in Paris.

[487] Council Joint Action 2001/555/CFSP of July 20, 2001 on the establishment of a European Union Satellite Centre, [2001] O.J. L200/5. The centre is established at Torrejón de Ardoz (Spain). Denmark is not taking part in those activities of the centre which have implications for defence policy.

the Member States[488] and at present carries out tasks in the context of PJCC (see para. 6–008). Europol has legal personality.[489] Each Member State has a representative on its Management Board with one vote and virtually all its decisions have to be taken unanimously.[490] The Commission is invited to take part in its meetings, but has no vote.[491] A Director is responsible for day-to-day administration and for representing Europol.[492] The Second Decision on the Seats of the Institutions of October 29, 1993 provided that Europol and the existing Europol Drugs Unit were to have their seat at The Hague.[493] Legal personality has also been given to the European Police College (see para. 6–008).

The Treaty of Nice amended the JHA provisions of the EU Treaty so as to attribute tasks to Eurojust, an entity which was set up by the Council as a body with legal personality even before the Treaty of Nice entered into force.[494] Eurojust is composed of one national member seconded by each Member State in accordance with its legal system, being a prosecutor, judge or police officer of equivalent competence.[495] The national members form a college under the chairmanship of a member chosen from amongst their number. Each national member has one vote and votes are taken in accordance with the rules of procedure.[496] As in the case of Europol, the Commission is to be fully associated with the work of Eurojust and the daily management is ensured by an Administrative Director.[497] The seat of Eurojust is likewise located at The Hague.[498]

IV. Administrative Organisation

A. The position of the Union/Communities under the domestic legal systems of the Member States

10–113 Representation of the Communities. The existing Treaties confer legal personality on each of the Communities (EC Treaty, Art. 281; EAEC

---

[488] Convention of July 26, 1995, based on the former Art. K.3 of the Treaty on European Union, on the establishment of a European Police Office (Europol Convention), [1995] O.J. C316/2, as amended by Council Act of November 28, 2002 ([2002] O.J. C312/1) and Council Act of November 27, 2003 ([2004] O.J. C2/1).

[489] *ibid.*, Art. 26(1).

[490] *ibid.* Art. 28(1), (2), (7) and (10).

[491] *ibid.*, Art. 28(4).

[492] *ibid.*, Art. 29. For the internal organisation of Europol, see Gless, "Kontrolle über Europol und seine Bedienstete" (1998) EuR. 748–766.

[493] See now the Protocol on Seats, Sole Article, para. (j).

[494] Council Decision 2002/187/JHA of February 28, 2002 setting up Eurojust with a view to reinforcing the fight against serious crime ([2002] O.J. L63/1).

[495] *ibid.*, Art. 2.

[496] *ibid.*, Arts 10, 28 and 29. For the Rules of Procedure of May 30, 2002, see [2002] O.J. C286/1.

[497] *ibid.*, Art. 11.

[498] See Art. 1(c) of the Third Decision on Seats (para. 10–147, *infra*). From the outset, it carried out its activities in that city on a provisional basis in accordance with recital 17 in the preamble to the decision establishing Eurojust.

Treaty, Art. 184; see also ECSC Treaty, Art. 6), but not on the European Union. This means in the first place that the Communities are subjects of international law (see para. 19–002). Secondly, they enjoy the most extensive legal capacity accorded to legal persons governed by public law[499] under the laws of the Member States, in particular to acquire or dispose of property and to be a party to legal proceedings (EC Treaty, Art. 282; EAEC Treaty, Art. 185). The EC and the EAEC have to be represented by the Commission to this end. In practice, however, the other institutions also engage in domestic legal transactions, in particular pursuant to their power to engage in expenditure authorised under the budget (see para. 10–140).

The fact that the Communities have legal capacity and the capacity to enter into transactions means that they may also sue and be sued. Thus, the Communities may appear before the national courts, except in disputes which, under the Treaties, have to be brought before the Court of Justice, In this way, the Community Courts have exclusive jurisdiction to entertain damages claims for non-contractual liability based on the second para. of Art. 288 of the EC Treaty.[500] Since the national courts have no jurisdiction to entertain such claims, they are likewise not entitled to prescribe, with regard to one of the institutions, any interim measure or measure of inquiry (*e.g.* commissioning an expert report) whose purpose is to establish the role of that institution in the events which allegedly caused damage.[501] Although, in principle, the Commission is empowered to act before the national courts, it may authorise another institution to do so.[502]

When the EU Constitution enters into force, the "new" European Union will replace both the existing Community and the existing Union and will have legal personality in its own right (EU Constitution, Art. I–7).[503] The Union will be the sole legal person in international legal transactions (see para. 19–004) and will enjoy the most extensive legal capacity in the domestic legal order of the Member States. The Union will continue to be represented, in principle, by the Commission. Pursuant to the EU Constitution, however, it may also be represented by each of the institutions, by virtue of their administrative autonomy, in matters relating to their respective operation.[504] The European Atomic Energy Community

---

[499] See ECJ, Joined Cases 43/59, 45/59 and 48/59 *Von Lachmüller v Commission* [1960] E.C.R. 463, at 472; ECJ, Case 44/59 *Fiddelaar v Commission* [1960] E.C.R. 535, at 543.

[500] In addition to the jurisdiction of the Court of Justice to entertain claims for damage caused by Community institutions or the ECB or their servants (non-contractual liability: EC Treaty, Art. 235 and Art. 288, second para.), there are also staff disputes (EC Treaty, Art. 236) and disputes brought before the Court pursuant to arbitration clauses (EC Treaty, Art. 238). See in this connection Lenaerts and Arts, *Procedural Law of the European Union*, Chs 11, 16 and 17.

[501] ECJ, Case C–275/00 *Frist and Franex* [2002] E.C.R. I–10943, paras 43–48.

[502] For details of the Commission's involvement in legal proceedings, see the Commission's answer of July 11, 1988 to Question 2/88 (Dury), [1989] O.J. C24/10.

[503] Under Art. IV–438 of the EU Constitution, the European Union will constitute the successor to the existing European Union and European Community.

[504] Art. III–426.

will continue to exist as an entity with its own legal personality (see para. 4–005).

10–114 Privileges and immunities. In common with other international organisations, the Communities enjoy privileges and immunities with a view to their being able to carry out their tasks undisturbed. Under the EU Constitution, the privileges and immunities will be taken over by the Union itself. These privileges and immunities—enshrined in a Protocol appended to the EC Treaty by the Member States in accordance with Art. 291 of that Treaty[505]—have a purely functional character: they are intended to avoid any interference with the functioning and independence of the Communities.[506] In addition to conferring privileges and immunities on members of the institutions and on officials and other servants of the Communities,[507] the Protocol provides that the Communities' premises, buildings and archives are inviolable, exempt from search, requisition, confiscation or appropriation and not to be the subject of any administrative or legal measure of constraint without the authorisation of the Court of Justice (Arts 1 and 2).[508] In addition, the Communities are exempt from customs duties and restrictions on imports and exports (Art. 4) and direct taxes (Art. 3, first para.). Under bilateral arrangements with Member States, appropriate measures are to be taken to remit or refund indirect taxes paid on certain purchases (see Art. 3, second para.). These provisions are limited to purchases made by the Communities for their official use. The salaries which the Communities pay to their staff are not subject to national tax but taxed by the Communities themselves (see para. 10–152).

10–115 Position of independent bodies. Community bodies and agencies with legal personality in their own right take part in domestic legal transactions in the Member States independently. They may participate in legal proceedings before the competent national courts, provided that the disputes do not

---

[505] Protocol (No. 36) to the Community Treaties on the Privileges and Immunities of the European Communities (enacted in the UK by the European Communities Act 1972). For the text of the Protocol, see European Union, Selected instruments taken from the Treaties, Office for Official Publications of the EC, Luxembourg, 1995, Book I, Vol.I, at 717. See Schmidt, "Le Protocole sur les privilèges et immunités des Communautés européennes" (1991) C.D.E. 67–99. Art. 291 of the EC Treaty takes over the wording of Art. 28 of the Merger Treaty as a result of the simplification introduced by the Treaty of Amsterdam.

[506] ECJ, Case C–2/88 Imm. *Zwartveld* [1990] E.C.R. I–3365, paras 19–20.

[507] For the status of members of the institutions, see paras 10–149—10–151, *infra*; for the status of officials and other servants of the Communities, see paras 10–152—10–153, *infra*.

[508] As far as garnishee orders are concerned, the jurisdiction of the Court of Justice is confined to considering whether such a measure is likely to interfere with the proper functioning and the independence of the European Communities: ECJ (order of June 17, 1987), Case 1/87 SA *Universal Tankship* [1987] E.C.R. 2807, para. 3; ECJ, Case 1/88 SA *Générale de Banque v Commission* [1989] E.C.R. 857, para. 15 (the case numbers include the initials SA for the French "*saisie-arrêt*"). For the rest, the garnishee procedure is governed by the applicable national law.

come within the jurisdiction of the Court of Justice.[509] Thus disputes based on non-contractual liability are generally governed by the system of liability determined by the second para. of Art. 288 of the EC Treaty.[510]

In order to secure their independence, the EIB, the ECB and other Community bodies with legal personality are also covered by the Protocol on Privileges and Immunities.[511] As a result of their connection with the Communities, the EIB and the ECB do not have the same status as other similar international organisations.[512]

As far as Europol[513] and other non-Community bodies[514] are concerned, the necessary privileges and immunities are laid down in an agreement concluded between the Member States. This also applies to the military and civilian personnel whom the Member States make available for CFSP activities of the European Union.[515]

B. THE BUDGET OF THE UNION

General budget. Each year a general budget is drawn up,[516] which since **10–116** 1994 has been entitled the "general budget of the European Union". This is done in accordance with specific Treaty articles and with the Financial Regulation which the Council adopted pursuant to Art. 279 of the EC

---

[509] See, *e.g.* EIB Statute, Art. 29; ESCB Statute, Art. 35.
[510] See, *e.g.* Art. 35.3 of the ESCB Statute and Art. 21(2) of Regulation No. 58/2003 (n.480, *supra*).
[511] For the EIB and the ECB, see EC Treaty, Art. 291, and Arts 22 and 23 of the Protocol (Art. 23 having been added to the Protocol by Art. 9(5) of the Amsterdam Treaty) and Art. 40 of the ESCB Statute. Art. 23 of the Protocol was initially added upon the entry into force of the EU Treaty by a Protocol annexed to the EC Treaty, [1993] O.J. C224/122, which was repealed by the Amsterdam Treaty. For the executive agencies set up pursuant to Regulation No. 58/2003 (n.480, *supra*), see Art. 17 of that Regulation. As far as other bodies and agencies are concerned, see the regulations establishing them referred to in para. 10–111, *supra*.
[512] See Schermers (1988) C.M.L.R. 617, at 625–626 (note to ECJ, Case 85/86 *Commission v European Investment Bank* [1988] E.C.R. 1281 concerning the tax levied on EIB salaries which should accrue to the Communities, para. 10–153, *infra*).
[513] Protocol of June 19, 1997 on the privileges and immunities of Europol, the members of its organs, the deputy directors and employees of Europol ([1997] O.J. C221/2), drawn up, on the basis of the former Art. K.3 of the EU Treaty and Art. 41 of the Europol Convention (n.488, *supra*), to be adopted by the Member States in accordance with their respective constitutional requirements. For a critical view, see Ellermann, "Von Sammler zu Jäger—Europol auf dem Weg zu einem 'europäischen FBI'?" (2002) Z.Eu.S. 561, at 580–582.
[514] For the European Institute for Security Studies, see Art. 15 of Council Joint Action 2001/554/GFSP of July 20, 2001 (n.486, *supra*); for the Satellite Centre, see Art. 16 of Council Joint Action 2001/555/CFSP of July 20, 2001 (n.487, *supra*).
[515] See the agreement between the EU Member States of November 17, 2003, [2003] O.J. C321/6.
[516] See Art. 9(6) of the Treaty of Amsterdam which takes over Art. 20(1) of the Merger Treaty.

Treaty and Art. 183 of the EAEC Treaty.[517] The European Parliament and the Council work together in drawing up the budget, thereby constituting together the "budgetary authority".

1. Content of the budget

a. General principles

10–117 Scope of the budget. In principle, all items of revenue and expenditure for each financial year are to be included in estimates and shown in the budget (EC Treaty, Art. 268, first para.). Since the ECSC financed its expenditure out of levies on the coal and steel sectors, its budget was divided into administrative expenditure, which came under the general budget, and operating expenditure, which was covered by a separate budget. The same applies at present to the implementation of the CFSP and PJCC, where administrative expenditure is always charged to the general budget (see EC Treaty, Art. 268, second para., in conjunction with EU Treaty, Art. 28(2) and Art. 41(2); the EU Constitution will retain this system for the CFSP[518]). According to Art. 28(3) and Art. 41(3) of the EU Treaty, operational expenditure is also to be charged to the general budget, unless the Council decides otherwise by a unanimous vote.[519] Operational expenditure arising from operations having military or defence implications is always borne by the Member States (EU Treaty, Art. 28(3), first subpara.). Where expenditure is charged to the Member States, it is allocated in accordance with the GNP scale, unless the Council decides otherwise by a unanimous vote (EU Treaty, Art. 28(3), first subpara., and Art. 41(3)).[520] Member States which have abstained by formal declaration from CFSP decisions under the second subpara. of Art. 23(1) are not obliged to contribute to the financing of operations having military or defence implications (EU Treaty,

---

[517] Financial Regulation applicable to the general budget of the European Communities, as most recently laid down by Council Regulation (EC, Euratom) No. 1605/2002 of June 25, 2002, [2002] O.J. L248/1 (corrigendum in [2003] O.J. L25/43). For general discussions of this subject, see Van Craeyenest and Saarilahti, "Le nouveau règlement financier applicable au budget général de l'Union européenne: un maillon essentiel dans la réforme de la Commission" (2004) R.M.C.U.E. 30–51; Walder, *The Budgetary Procedure of the European Economic Community*, (Böhlau, Vienna, 1992), 122 pp; Strasser, *The Finances of Europe* (Office for Official Publications of the EC, Luxembourg, 1991), 439 pp.

[518] Art. III–313(1)–(2).

[519] In 1992 the EU Treaty determined, as far as the CFSP and JHA co-operation (EU Treaty, former Art. J.11 and former Art. K.8) was concerned, that operational expenditure could be charged to the EU budget *only if* the Council so decided by unanimous vote. In practice, the Council decided virtually always that it should be so charged with the result that in fact operational expenditure was invariably charged to the budget unless the Council decided otherwise. As far as the CFSP is concerned, the European Parliament, the Council and the Commission concluded an interinstitutional agreement on July 16, 1997 on provisions regarding the financing of the CFSP (1997) 7/8 EU Bull. point 2.3.1; para. 10–127, *infra*.

[520] Reference is made to the GNP scale in Art. 23 of Council Decision 2004/197/CFSP of February 23, 2004 establishing a mechanism ("ATHENA") to administer the financing of the common costs of European Union operations having military or defence implications ([2004] O.J. L63/68).

Art. 28(3), second subpara.).[521] Furthermore, Member States are only obliged to pay their share of the institutions' administrative costs in some instances in which the Treaties authorise them not to take part in the operations in question.[522]

Separate budgets. A further exception to the "unity" of the budget is loans **10–118** incurred or made by the Communities and the activities of the European Central Bank,[523] the European Investment Bank,[524] the Supply Agency and the EAEC Joint Undertakings.[525] Bodies and agencies having legal personality in their own right have their own budgets, which may be mentioned in the general budget as an explanation for the subsidy granted to such bodies and agencies by the Commission.[526] Europol and other non-Community bodies have own budget, financed by contributions from the Member States[527]; however, the budget of Eurojust is partially financed out of the EU budget.[528] Since the Financial Regulation adopted pursuant to Art. 279 of the EC Treaty provides for consultation of the European Parliament on the determination of Community expenditure, the Parliament exercises supervision to make sure that such expenditure is actually incorporated in the budget.[529] In the case of other expenditure assumed by the Member States, such as expenditure of the European Development Fund, the States operate by mutual agreement and there is nothing to prevent them from using procedural steps drawing on the rules applicable to Community expenditure and from associating the Community institutions with the procedure thus set up.[530]

---

[521] This applies in any case to Denmark under Art. 6 of the Protocol (No. 5) to the EU Treaty and the EC Treaty on the position of Denmark, [1997] O.J. C340/101. See, *e.g.* the exception for Denmark in Council Decision 2004/197/CFSP of February 23, 2004 (n.520, *supra*) and in respect of the Member States' contributions for the satellite centre: Art. 12(3) of Council Joint Action 2001/555/CFSP of July 20, 2001 (n.487, *supra*).

[522] Thus, there is no obligation for Member States to contribute towards the financing of expenditure in respect of enhanced co-operation if they do not participate therein, with the exception of the administrative costs entailed for the institutions, unless the Council, acting unanimously, decides otherwise (EU Treaty, Art. 44(2)). By the same token, Art. 5 of Protocol (No. 4) to the EU Treaty and the EC Treaty on the position of the UK and Ireland ([1997] O.J. C340/99), provides that a Member State not bound by a measure adopted pursuant to Title IV of the EC Treaty is to bear no financial consequences of that measure other than administrative costs entailed for the institutions.

[523] ESCB Statute, Arts 26 and 27.

[524] See EIB Statute, Art. 9(3)(f) and Art. 14.

[525] EAEC Treaty, Art. 171(2) and (3).

[526] See the acts establishing those bodies and agencies mentioned in paras 10–110—10–111, *supra*, as amended by the Council on July 22, 2003 ([2003] O.J. L245); for the executive agencies set up pursuant to Regulation No. 58/2003 (n.480, *supra*), see Art. 12 of that regulation.

[527] Europol Convention, Art. 35; n.488, *supra*.

[528] See Art. 34 and recital 4 of Council Decision 2002/187/JHA (n.494, *supra*), as supplemented by the Council on July 22, 2003 ([2003] O.J. L245/44).

[529] See ECJ, Case C–316/91 *European Parliament v Council* [1994] E.C.R. I–625, paras 16–19.

[530] *ibid.*, paras 38–42. For the European Development Fund, see paras 20–016 and 20–023, *infra*. The European Parliament considers that the EDF should be incorporated into the Union budget: see the resolution of July 12, 1995, [1995] O.J. C249/68.

10–119 **Structure of the budget.** In accordance with the annual nature of the budget, it contains the revenue resulting from the amounts collected during the financial year[531] and the expenditure authorised for the financial year in question.[532] The financial year runs from January 1 to December 31.[533] The general budget of the Union is published annually in a voluminous issue of the *Official Journal*. The expenditure of Union institutions is set out in separate sections of the budget.[534] The revenue and expenditure of other bodies are fully covered by the budgetary sections of the Commission.[535] Under the chapters of each section, expenditure is grouped into items according to its nature or purpose and subdivided in accordance with the Financial Regulation.[536] The budget is drawn up in euros,[537] even though the financial transactions are not necessarily carried out in euros.

10–120 **Budgetary principles.** The budget is otherwise constructed in accordance with the classical rules governing public finances. Revenue is to be used without distinction to finance all expenditure entered in the budget (the so-called universality principle).[538] In addition, revenue and expenditure may not be adjusted against each other.[539] Expenditure must be carried out in accordance with the classification into budget items approved by the budgetary authority (the so-called principle of specialisation). Accordingly, any transfer of appropriations from one title to another and from one chapter to another is subject in principle to the budgetary authority's approval.[540] Lastly, the Treaties require the budget to be in balance as to revenue and expenditure.[541] If at the end of the financial year, there is a

---

[531] Financial Regulation, Art. 8(1).

[532] EC Treaty, Art. 271, first para. Under the first and second paras of that provision, the Financial Regulation provides for exceptions for unexpended appropriations and appropriations spread over more than one year.

[533] EC Treaty, Art. 272(1).

[534] See EC Treaty, Art. 271, fourth para., as elaborated in Arts 40–45 of the Financial Regulation, which provides for separate sections for all institutions (and thus unlike Art. 271 also for the Court of Auditors) and, by virtue of Art. 1 of the Financial Regulation, also for the European Economic and Social Committee, the Committee of the Regions, the European Ombudsman and the Data protection Supervisor.

[535] Financial Regulation, Arts 171–176.

[536] EC Treaty, Art. 271, third para.

[537] Financial Regulation, Art. 16.

[538] Art. 6 of the Fifth Decision on Own Resources (para. 10–121, *infra*) and Art. 17 of the Financial Regulation. Exceptions to that principle are contained in that article of the Decision on Own Resources and in Art. 18 of the Financial Regulation.

[539] Financial Regulation, Art. 17. Exceptions to that principle are contained, in particular, in Art. 2(3) of the Fifth Decision on Own Resources and in Art. 20 of the Financial Regulation.

[540] Financial Regulation, Art. 24. Nevertheless, the Financial Regulation provides for a degree of flexibility of management so as to permit the assignment of financial and administrative means by purpose ("activity based budgeting"); see Arts 22 and 23 of the Financial Regulation.

[541] EC Treaty, Art. 268, third para., and Art. 272(10).

shortfall or a surplus of revenue over expenditure, the deficit or the surplus is carried over to the subsequent year's budget.[542]

b. Revenue

Own resources. The revenue side of the budget covers the Communities' **10–121** own resources. The ECSC operated from the outset with its own resources, consisting of levies on the production of coal and steel. In common with most international organisations, the EEC and the EAEC initially only had financial contributions from the Member States, although the Treaties put the Commission under a duty to investigate a system of own resources.[543] Such a system eventually resulted from the First Decision on Own Resources of April 21, 1970, which, in accordance with the third para. of Art. 201 of the EEC Treaty, was laid down by the Council on a proposal from the Commission after consulting the European Parliament and then adopted by the Member States in accordance with their respective constitutional provisions.[544] Since that system meant that considerable financial resources were taken outside the scope of national supervision, its adoption was coupled with the grant of budgetary powers to the European Parliament. To this end, the First Treaty on Budgetary Provisions of April 22, 1970 amended the Communities' budgetary procedure.[545] The system was adjusted by the Second Decision on Own Resources of May 7, 1985,[546] by the Third Decision on Own Resources of June 24, 1988,[547] by the Fourth Decision on Own Resources of October 31, 1994[548] and lastly by the Fifth Decision on Own Resources of September 29, 2000, which entered into

---

[542] Financial Regulation, Art. 15. That budgetary principle, which is also expressed in Art. 7 of the Fifth Decision on Own Resources, takes priority over the provision of the First Decision on Own Resources according to which a percentage of the VAT basis of assessment is to accrue to the Community as own resources. Where a surplus in revenue is carried over in full to the next financial year this increases the revenue for that financial year, which means that a lower rate may be applied to the VAT basis of assessment: ECJ, Case C–284/90 *Council v European Parliament* [1992] E.C.R. I–2277, para. 31; note by Van den Bossche (1994) C.M.L.R. 653–668.

[543] See EEC Treaty, Art. 201, and EAEC Treaty, Art. 173 (old version).

[544] Council Decision 70/243/ECSC/EEC/Euratom of April 21, 1970 on the replacement of financial contributions from Member States by the Communities' own resources, [1970] O.J. Spec. Ed. I, 224.

[545] Treaty of April 22, 1970 amending Certain Budgetary Provisions of the Treaties establishing the European Communities and of the Treaty establishing a Single Council and a Single Commission of the European Communities; for the text in English, see Treaties establishing the European Communities, Office for Official Publications of the EC, Luxembourg, 1978, at 855.

[546] Council Decision 85/257 of May 7, 1985 on the system of the Communities' own resources, [1985] O.J. L128/15. For the UK, see the European Communities (Finance) Act 1985.

[547] Council Decision 88/376 of June 24, 1988 on the system of the Communities' own resources. For the UK, see the European Communities (Finance) Act 1988.

[548] Council Decision 94/728 of October 31, 1994 on the system of the Communities' own resources, [1994] O.J. L293/9. For the UK, see the European Communities (Finance) Act 1995.

force on January 1, 2001.[549] The amended version of Art. 269 of the EC Treaty provides that, without prejudice to other revenue, the budget is to be financed wholly from own resources.

Under the EU Constitution, the same procedure will be applicable to the European law laying down the Union's system of own resources, which may establish new categories of resources or abolish an existing category. Implementing measures of the Union's own resources system will be laid down by the Council, acting by a qualified majority after obtaining the consent of the European Parliament (EU Constitution, Art. I–54(3) and (4)).

10–122 Revenue sources. The Communities' own resources consist of four sources of revenue:

(1) levies and import duties established within the framework of the common agricultural policy and the common organisation of the markets in sugar;

(2) Common Customs Tariff duties in respect of trade with non-member countries and anti-dumping duties;

(3) the application of a uniform rate to the VAT assessment base, not exceeding 50 per cent of the GNP of each Member State; and

(4) the application of a rate to be determined pursuant to the budgetary procedure to the sum of all the Member States' GNP.[550]

10–123 Correction mechanism. Unlike the first two "traditional" sources, the third source was not introduced until after the Sixth VAT Directive of May 17, 1977 harmonised the VAT basis of assessment throughout the Community.[551] After the United Kingdom repeatedly complained that it was paying much more into the budget than the Communities spent in that country, a hard-won compromise was reached by the European Council meeting at Fontainebleau on June 25 and 26, 1984 whereby the British VAT contribution was reduced and the contributions of other Member States increased, although Germany benefited by a more advantageous regime as it refused to finance the concession to the United Kingdom in full. The "correction of budgetary imbalances" was incorporated in the Second Decision on Own Resources, subsequently extended and amended

---

[549] Council Decision 2000/597/EC, Euratom of September 29, 2000 on the system of the Communities' own resources, [2000] O.J. L253/42. See the earlier report of the Commission on the operation of the system of own resources, "Agenda 2000—Financing the European Union" (1998) EU Bull. Suppl.2; Griese, "Die Finanzierung der Europäischen Union" (1998) EuR. 462–477.

[550] Fifth Decision on Own Resources, Art. 2(1).

[551] Sixth Council Directive 77/388/EEC of May 17, 1977 on the harmonisation of the laws of the Member States relating to turnover taxes—Common system of value added tax: uniform basis of assessment, [1977] O.J. L145/1.

by the Fifth Decision on Own Resources so as to diminish the share of Community financing, not only for Germany, but also for Austria, the Netherlands and Sweden. The maximum rate applied to the VAT assessment base was to be reduced from 1 per cent in 2001 to 0.75 per cent in 2002 and to 0.50 per cent in 2004.[552] The fourth category of own resources was introduced by the Third Decision on Own Resources in order to cope with rising expenditure on the part of the Communities. The rate of the contribution is determined under the budgetary procedure in the light of all other revenue from other sources and of the expenditure anticipated in the financial year. The correction mechanism also applies to this source of resources. The total amount of own resources assigned to the Communities came in 1999 to 1.27 per cent of the aggregate GNP of all the Member States and, since the Fifth Decision on Own Resources, has been limited by a formula intended to result in an equivalent amount.[553]

Other revenue. In addition, there is miscellaneous revenue, such as the **10–124** proceeds of the Community tax on officials' salaries[554] and the fines imposed by the Commission for contraventions of the competition rules.[555]

c. Expenditure

Compulsory and non-compulsory expenditure. The Communities' **10–125** expenditure is divided into compulsory and non-compulsory expenditure. Compulsory expenditure is expenditure necessarily resulting from the Treaties or from acts adopted in accordance therewith. All other expenditure is non-compulsory. The distinction is important in so far as the European Parliament has the last word on non-compulsory expenditure (EC Treaty, Art. 272(6); see para. 10–130 *et seq.*). This gives the Parliament a say in matters over which it would not otherwise have much influence, for instance where the Union charges action under the CFSP or PJCC to the EU budget. Given the political stake, the Parliament and the Council have often been at loggerheads about the classification of expenditure.

Classification of expenditure. In a Joint Declaration of June 30, 1982, the **10–126** European Parliament, the Council and the Commission set out a classification of expenditure and a procedure for reaching agreement on the classification of new budget items.[556] As far as expenditure under the CFSP

---

[552] Fifth Decision on Own Resources, Art. 4(4).

[553] Fifth Decision on Own Resources, Art. 3.

[554] See Art. 13 of the Protocol on Privileges and Immunities, the regulations on the emoluments of members of the institutions, the Staff Regulations and the Rules applicable to other servants and Regulation No. 260/68 on the tax for the benefit of the European Communities, para. 10–152, *infra*.

[555] See, *inter alia*, Arts 17 and 18 of Regulation No. 11/60, Arts 23 and 24 of Regulation No. 1/2003 and Arts 14 and 15 of Regulation No. 139/2004 (paras 5–198—5–200, *supra*).

[556] Joint Declaration by the European Parliament, the Council and the Commission of June 30, 1982 on various measures to improve the budgetary procedure, [1982] O.J. C194/1.

is concerned, the European Parliament and the Council decided on June 16, 1997 to classify such expenditure as non-compulsory expenditure.[557] These agreements were incorporated in the Interinstitutional Agreement between the European Parliament, the Council and the Commission of May 6, 1999.[558] That agreement defines compulsory expenditure as "such expenditure as the budgetary authority is obliged to enter in the budget by virtue of a legal undertaking entered into under the Treaties or acts adopted by virtue of the said Treaties".[559] As far as new budget items are concerned, the European Parliament and the Council are to examine the classification in the budget on the basis of the classification of expenditure appended to the Interinstitutional Agreement.[560] For CFSP expenditure, the European Parliament and the Council are to secure each year agreement on the amount and its distribution within the relevant budget chapter. In the absence of agreement, the amount contained in the previous budget for the CFSP is to be taken over unless the Commission proposes a lower amount.[561] The agreement provides for a collaboration procedure with trilogue meetings between delegations from the institutions led by the President of the Council responsible for budgets, the Chair of the European Parliament's Committee on Budgets and the Member of the Commission with responsibility for the budget.[562]

10–127 **Budgetary discipline.** In order to keep expenditure under control, the European Council decided in 1988 to impose strict budgetary discipline. The practical upshot of this was a Council Decision and an Interinstitutional Agreement between the European Parliament, the Council and the Commission.[563] A new Interinstitutional Agreement laid down a "financial perspective" extending until 1999 in the form of annual ceilings for expenditure.[564] The Interinstitutional Agreement of May 6, 1999

---

[557] Interinstitutional Agreement of July 16, 1997 on the financing of the CFSP (1997) 7/8 EU Bull. point 2.3.1; see also [1997] O.J. C286/80, point B. This applies both to administrative and policy expenditure.

[558] Interinstitutional Agreement of May 6, 1999 between the European Parliament, the Council and the Commission on budgetary discipline and improvement of the budgetary procedure, [1999] O.J. C172/1.

[559] *ibid.*, point 30.

[560] *ibid.*, point 31 and Annex IV.

[561] *ibid.*, point 39, which largely takes over the wording of the 1997 Interinstitutional Agreement. Whenever it adopts a decision in the field of CFSP entailing expenditure, the Council is under a duty immediately and in each case to send the European Parliament an estimate of the costs envisaged.

[562] *ibid.*, Annex III.

[563] Interinstitutional Agreement of June 29, 1988 on budgetary discipline and improvement of the budgetary procedure, [1988] O.J. L185/33; Council Decision 88/377/EEC of June 24, 1988 on budgetary discipline, [1988] O.J. L185/29.

[564] Interinstitutional Agreement of October 29, 1993 on budgetary discipline and improvement of the budgetary procedure, [1993] O.J. C331/1.

laid down the financial perspectives for 2000–2006.[565] Together with every new Decision on Own Resources, the Council adopts a decision or regulation on budgetary discipline.[566] Apart from technical adjustments, the financial perspective may be revised only by agreement between the European Parliament and the Council on a proposal from the Commission.[567] In this way, the financial perspective for the period 2004–2006 was adjusted to take account of the enlargement of the Union to 25 Member States.[568] The European Parliament was given an undertaking that there would be no revision of compulsory expenditure in the financial perspective which would lead to a reduction in the amount available for non-compulsory expenditure,[569] since this would reduce the Parliament's room for manoeuvre.

Such interinstitutional agreements facilitate decision-making, but do not affect the respective budgetary powers of the institutions as laid down in the EC Treaty.[570] The constraints resulting from the financial perspective adopted make the distinction between compulsory and non-compulsory expenditure less important in practical terms. Nevertheless, disputes still

---

[565] Interinstitutional Agreement between the European Parliament, the Council and the Commission (n.558 *supra*), Part I. See Godet, "Le nouveau 'code de procédure budgétaire' de l'Union européenne" (2000) R.T.D.E. 273–298; Chevalier, "L'accord interinstitutionnel du 6 mai 1999 et les perspectives financiers 2000–2006: de nouvelles ambitions pour l'Union européenne" (2000) R.M.C.U.E. 441–460 and 524–532. This agreement was supplemented by the Interinstitutional Agreement of November 7, 2002 between the European Parliament, the Council and the Commission on the financing of the European Union Solidarity Fund ([2003] O.J. C2831). See also the Interinstitutional Agreement of February 28, 2002 on the financing of the Convention on the future of the European Union ([2002] O.J. C54.1; extended by Interinstitutional Agreement of December 12, 2002, [2002] O.J. C320/1).

[566] Council Decision 94/729/EC of October 31, 1994 on budgetary discipline, [1994] O.J. L293/14; Council Regulation (EC) No. 2040/2000 of September 26, 2000 on budgetary discipline, [2000] O.J. L244/27. For the first application of this regulation, see Grossir, "La procédure budgétaire pour 2001: un long fleuve tranquille?" (2001) R.M.C.U.E. 374–396.

[567] Point 20 of the Interinstitutional Agreement of May 6, 1999 refers to the majority voting rules laid down in EC Treaty, Art. 272(9), fifth subpara. However, any revision of the financial perspective above 0·03 per cent of the Community GNP within the margin for unforeseen expenditure is to be taken jointly by the two arms of the budgetary authority, with the Council acting unanimously. Permitted technical adjustments are those made to the financial perspective to take account of movements in GNP and prices and adjustments relating to the implementation of the budget. *E.g.* Decision 2001/692/EC of the European Parliament and of the Council of May 3, 2001 on the adjustment of the financial perspective to take account of the conditions of implementation ([2001] O.J. L246/28) and Decision 2003/430/EC of the European Parliament and the Council of May 19, 2003 on the revision of the financial perspective ([2003] O.J. L147/31), which is connected with the perspective having regard to enlargement (n.568, *infra*). For possible new sources of revenue designed to avoid a deficit, see Storr, "Die Bewältigung defizitärer Haushaltslagen in der EU" (2001) EuR. 846–871.

[568] Decision 2003/429/EC of the European Parliament and of the Council of May 19, 2003 on the adjustment of the financial perspective for enlargement ([2003] O.J. L147/25), which, in accordance with point 25 of the Interinstitutional Agreement of May 6, 1999, was adopted under the procedure laid down in the fifth subpara. of Art. 272(9) of the EC Treaty.

[569] Interinstitutional Agreement of May 6, 1999, point 21, sixth para.

[570] *ibid.*, point 3.

arise between the institutions from time to time in connection with the classification of budgetary expenditure.[571]

10–128 Limits on expenditure. With a view to maintaining budgetary discipline, Art. 270 of the EC Treaty debars the Commission from making any proposal for a Community act, from altering its proposals or from adopting any implementing measure if this is likely to increase expenditure appreciably and the expenditure cannot be financed out of the Communities' own resources.

10–129 Constitution. As regards budgetary discipline, the EU Constitution will introduce a new system aimed at ensuring that Union expenditure develops in an orderly manner and within the own resources limits. The present system of multiannual financial perspectives will be replaced by a multiannual financial framework determining the amounts of the annual ceilings of appropriations for commitments by category of expenditure for a period of at least five years (EU Constitution, Arts I–55(1) and III–402). The Union's annual budget must comply with the multiannual financial framework. The Council will lay down this financial framework, acting unanimously after obtaining the consent of the European Parliament. The European Council, acting unanimously, may adopt a decision allowing the Council to lay down the financial framework by a qualified majority (EU Constitution, Art. I–55(2) and (4)). In addition, the European Parliament, the Council and the Commission are to ensure that the financial means are made available to allow the Union to fulfil its legal obligations in respect of third parties (EU Constitution, Art. III–413). The introduction of this new system allows for the distinction between obligatory and non-obligatory expenditure to be abandoned and for the budgetary procedure to be simplified, whilst extending the European Parliament's final say to all categories of expenditure (see para. 10–139).

2. Adoption of the budget

10–130 Procedure. Article 272 of the EC Treaty governs the unwieldy procedure for adopting the budget.[572] The budget is adopted in stages, with the Council placing drafts before the European Parliament on two occasions.

---

[571] See ECJ, Case C–41/95 *Council v European Parliament* [1995] E.C.R. I–4411, paras 1–31: as long as there was disagreement between the Council and the Parliament as to the classification of certain expenditure as non-compulsory, the Parliament could not assume that the two institutions were in agreement as to the maximum rate of increase (see para. 10–135, *infra*), which made the act declaring the final adoption of the budget unlawful.

[572] For the origins of this provision, see the Treaty of April 22, 1970 amending Certain Budgetary Provisions (n.545, *supra*) (First Treaty on Budgetary Provisions); and the Treaty of July 22, 1975 amending Certain Budgetary Provisions of the Treaties establishing the European Communities and of the Treaty establishing a Single Council and a Single Commission of the European Communities [Second Treaty on Budgetary Provisions], [1977] O.J. L359/1.

After the first reading by the Parliament, the Council already has the last word on compulsory expenditure. The Parliament takes the definitive decision on non-compulsory expenditure at the second reading.

Draft budget. Each institution draws up estimates of its expenditure for the **10–131** following year before July 1.[573] The Commission consolidates these estimates in a "preliminary draft budget", attaching thereto an opinion which may contain different estimates. The preliminary draft containing an estimate of revenue and expenditure must be placed before the Council no later than September 1 of the year preceding the year in which the budget is to be implemented (EC Treaty, Art. 272(2) and (3), first subpara.). At that stage, the Council establishes the "draft budget" by a qualified majority vote. If it intends to depart from the preliminary draft budget, the Council has to consult the Commission and any other institutions concerned (Art. 272(3), second and third subparas). The draft budget must be placed before the European Parliament by no later than October 5 (Art. 272(4), first subpara.). It should be noted, however, that interinstitutional agreements provide for tripartite dialogue ("trilogue") between the Commission, the Parliament and the Council even before the Commission establishes the preliminary draft budget and likewise before and after the European Parliament's first reading of the budget.[574]

---

[573] Under Art. 39 of the Financial Regulation, the Commission and the budgetary authority may agree to bring forward certain dates in the procedure provided that this does not have the effect of reducing or delaying the periods allowed for considering the relevant texts.

[574] See the interinstitutional collaboration in the budgetary sector provided for in Annex III to the Interinstitutional Agreement of May 6, 1999, n. 558, *supra*.

Figure 3: Procedure for adoption of the EU budget (Art. 272 EC Treaty)

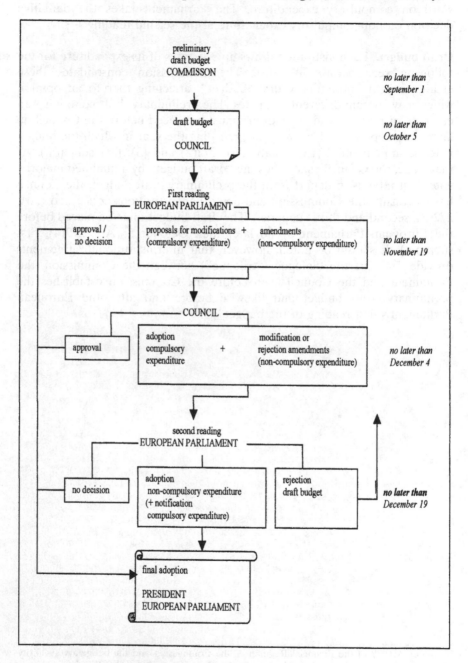

First reading. The European Parliament has 45 days to pronounce on the **10–132** draft budget in the first reading (*i.e.* until November 19). If the Parliament approves the draft budget within that period, the budget stands as finally adopted. If the Parliament simply does not amend the budget or propose any modifications (see below) to it, the budget is deemed to have been finally adopted (EC Treaty, Art. 272(4), third subpara.). The Parliament is entitled to change the draft budget. In the case of non-compulsory expenditure, the Parliament is entitled to "amend" the draft budget, acting by a majority of its Members, whilst, in the case of compulsory expenditure, it may propose "modifications" to the draft budget, acting by an absolute majority of the votes cast. The draft budget incorporating the amendments and proposed modifications is then forwarded to the Council (EC Treaty, Art. 272(4), second and fourth subparas).

Discussion in Council. Next, the Council discusses the draft budget with **10–133** the Commission and, where appropriate, the other institutions concerned. Within 15 days of the draft being placed before it (*i.e.* by December 4), the Council has to take a view on the Parliament's amendments and modifications in accordance with the conditions set out in Art. 272(5) of the EC Treaty.

The Council may modify amendments (relating to non-compulsory expenditure) by a qualified majority vote.

As far as proposed modifications (relating to compulsory expenditure) are concerned, the procedure differs depending on whether or not a given modification proposed by the Parliament has the effect of increasing the total expenditure of an institution. If a proposed modification would not have that effect because, for instance, it is compensated for by a proposed reduction in other expenditure, the proposed modification stands as accepted, unless the Council, acting by a qualified majority, rejects it within the prescribed period. If, in contrast, a proposed modification has the effect of increasing the total expenditure of an institution, it will be accepted only if the Council expressly agrees to do so by a qualified majority vote. If the Council cannot muster a sufficient majority within the prescribed period, the proposed modification is deemed to be rejected. If the Council rejects a modification proposed by the Parliament (expressly in the first procedure or impliedly in the second), it is entitled to retain the amount initially shown in the draft budget or fix another amount by a qualified majority vote.

If, within the prescribed period, the Council modifies one or more of the amendments adopted by the European Parliament or if the modifications proposed by the Parliament are rejected or modified, the modified draft budget must be forwarded to the Parliament. The Council has to inform that institution of the results of its deliberations.

Second reading. The European Parliament's second reading (*i.e.* the **10–134** reading of the draft budget modified by the Council, which has to be concluded within 15 days, *i.e.* by December 19) deals with the non-compulsory expenditure provided for in the budget (see EC Treaty, Art. 272(6)). As far as compulsory expenditure is concerned, the Parliament is merely "notified" of the action taken on its proposed modifications. As far as non-compulsory expenditure is concerned, the Parliament, acting by a majority of its Members and three-fifths of the votes cast, may amend or reject the modifications to its amendments made by the Council and adopt the budget accordingly. If the European Parliament does not act within the 15-day period, the budget is deemed to have been definitively adopted. It is only in that event that the last version of the budget as regards non-compulsory expenditure emanates from the Council.

10–135 Constraints. In exercising its decision-making powers with regard to non-compulsory expenditure, the European Parliament has to take account of the constraints imposed upon its powers by Art. 272(9) and (10) of the EC Treaty. In the first place, Parliament has to maintain a balance between expenditure and revenue (EC Treaty, Art. 272(10)).[575] Secondly, any increase in non-compulsory expenditure over and above the level of the preceding financial year may not exceed the maximum percentage determined by the Commission before May 1 each year from three macro-economic factors (EC Treaty, Art. 272(9)).[576] Nevertheless, the maximum percentage may be exceeded in two ways. First, the Parliament has some leeway if the actual rate of increase in non-compulsory expenditure in the Council's draft budget is over half the maximum rate, when it may, by amendment, further increase the total amount of such expenditure to a limit not exceeding half the maximum rate (EC Treaty, Art. 272(9), fourth subpara.). Secondly, the Parliament, acting by a majority of its Members and three-fifths of the votes cast, may fix another rate by agreement with the Council (acting by qualified majority) (EC Treaty, Art. 272(9), fifth subpara.).[577] Failure to comply with this procedure in the event of overshooting the maximum percentage fixed by the Commission has already resulted in two judgments annulling the act of the President of the Parliament finding that the budget had been finally adopted.[578]

---

[575] Infringement of the principle that the budget must be in equilibrium constitutes a ground for annulling the act of the President of the Parliament declaring that the budget has been finally adopted. See ECJ, Case C–284/90 *Council v European Parliament* [1992] E.C.R. I–2277, paras 32–33 (n.542, *supra*).

[576] The factors are the trend, in terms of volume, of GNP within the Community, the average variation in the budgets of the Member States and the trend of the cost of living during the preceding financial year.

[577] In point 12 of the Interinstitutional Agreement of May 6, 1999, the two arms of the budgetary authority agreed to accept the maximum rates of increase for non-compulsory expenditure deriving from the budgets established within the ceilings set by the financial perspective (para. 10–127, *supra*).

[578] ECJ, Case 34/86 *Council v European Parliament* [1986] E.C.R. 2155, paras 39 and 45; ECJ, Case C–41/95 *Council v European Parliament* [1995] E.C.R. I–4411, paras 23–37.

Revenue side. It is not clear from Art. 272 of the EC Treaty whether the **10–136** European Parliament is also entitled to amend the revenue side of the draft budget. Even though the Decision on Own Resources gives little scope for this, it may nevertheless be important for the Parliament to make amendments to the revenue side which ensue from amendments made in respect of non-compulsory expenditure or where the Parliament and the Council disagree about the correct application of the Decision on Own Resources.[579]

Adoption of budget. When the procedure provided for in Art. 272 of the **10–137** EC Treaty has been completed, the President of the European Parliament declares that the budget has been finally adopted (Art. 272(7)). That declaration endows the budget with binding force *vis-à-vis* the institutions and the Member States.[580] However, the Parliament, acting by a majority of its Members and two-thirds of the votes cast, may reject the draft budget for "important reasons" and ask for a new draft to be submitted to it (Art. 272(8)). This gives the Parliament an opportunity to express dissatisfaction about the Council's final decision on compulsory expenditure. Owing to the fact that the budget has to be in balance, that decision affects the amount of leeway the Parliament has with regard to non-compulsory expenditure. The Parliament has used this power on three occasions to date.[581]

Amending budget. If, in the event of unavoidable, exceptional or **10–138** unforeseen circumstances, expenditure or revenue is not in accordance with the estimates, the Council decides on whether it is necessary to adopt an amending budget.[582] The amending budget is adopted in accordance with the procedure laid down in Art. 272 of the EC Treaty.[583]

Article 273 of the EC Treaty deals with the situation where the budget has not yet been voted at the beginning of the financial year (for instance, if the European Parliament has rejected the budget). In that event, the Commission may in principle undertake monthly expenditure of one-twelfth of the relevant budgetary appropriations for the preceding financial year, provided that the monthly expenditure does not exceed

---

[579] For the latter case, see ECJ, Case C–284/90 *Council v European Parliament* [1992] E.C.R. I–2277 (n.542, *supra*). Although the Court of Justice did not discuss the European Parliament's right to make amendments to the revenue side of the draft budget, it did pronounce on whether or not the amendments made to the revenue side were lawful in the particular circumstances, which would appear to constitute implied recognition of that right of amendment.

[580] ECJ, Case 34/86 *Council v European Parliament* [1986] E.C.R. 2155, para. 8.

[581] See the resolutions of the European Parliament of December 13, 1979 ([1980] O.J. C4/37), December 16, 1982 ([1983] O.J. C13/67) and December 13, 1984 ([1985] O.J. C12/90).

[582] Financial Regulation, Art. 37. Prior to the Financial Regulation of June 25, 2002, there was a formal distinction between amending and supplementary budgets, but this was abolished as it served no practical purpose.

[583] Financial Regulation, Art. 38. See, *e.g.* amending Budget Nos 1 to 6 of the European Union for the financial year 2004 ([2004] O.J. L128, L147 and L148).

one-twelfth of the appropriations provided for in the (preliminary) draft budget.[584]

10–139 Constitution. As indicated above, the EU Constitution will significantly simplify the procedure for adopting the budget. Under Art. III–404 of the EU Constitution, the draft budget will be established by the Commission and will be subject to one reading only by the Council and the European Parliament. If the European Parliament, acting by a majority of its members, proposes amendments, a Conciliation Committee will be convened. This Committee is modelled on the conciliation committee which may be convened in the course of the co-decision procedure, which will become the ordinary legislative procedure. Representatives of the European Parliament and the Council will attempt to reach agreement on a joint text, which is then to be approved by the Parliament (acting by a simple majority) and the Council (acting by qualified majority). If, within the fixed deadline, the Conciliation Committee does not approve a joint text, or if the European Parliament, acting by a majority of its members, rejects it, the Commission is to submit a new draft budget. If, within that same deadline, the European Parliament approves the joint text whilst the Council rejects it, the European Parliament may, acting by a majority of its members and three-fifths of the votes cast, impose its amendments on the Council. Since the procedure for the adoption of the budget will no longer distinguish between obligatory and non-obligatory expenditure, the European Parliament will thus have the final say over all expenditure. However, the budget must remain within the limits of the multiannual financial framework established by the Council (see para. 10–129). If no budget law has been adopted at the beginning of a financial year, it will still be possible to incur expenditure on a monthly basis subject to certain conditions.[585]

3. Implementation of the budget

10–140 Implementation of expenditure. The Commission implements the budget on its own responsibility and within the limits of the appropriations, having regard to the principles of sound financial management (EC Treaty, Art. 274, first para.). Its power to implement the budget is separate from its power to implement legislative measures. Accordingly, the Commission's power to implement the budget is not such as to modify the rules on the implementation of acts of the Council laid down in the third indent of Art. 202 of the EC Treaty (see para. 14–051 et seq.).[586] Consequently, any

---

[584] EC Treaty, Art. 273, first para., in conjunction with Art. 13(2) of the Financial Regulation. The Council may decide to authorise an increase in the "provisional twelfths". If the decision relates to non-compulsory expenditure, the European Parliament may adopt a different decision as far as that expenditure is concerned (EC Treaty, Art. 273, second and third paras).

[585] EU Constitution, Art. III–405.

[586] ECJ, Case 16/88 Commission v Council [1989] E.C.R. 3457, paras 16–19.

implementation of expenditure by the Commission presupposes, in addition to the entry of the relevant appropriation in the budget, an act of secondary legislation from which the expenditure derives.[587] Prior adoption of such a "basic act" is not required only where budgetary appropriations are implemented for non-significant Community action.[588] Such action is defined in the Financial Regulation on the basis of the Interinstitutional Agreement concluded between the European Parliament, the Council and the Commission on October 13, 1998.[589]

The Commission confers the necessary powers to implement their own sections of the budget on the European Economic and Social Committee, the Committee of the Regions, the European Ombudsman and the European Data-protection Supervisor (EC Treaty, Art. 274, second para.; Financial Regulation, Art. 50). Nevertheless, it retains responsibility for financial management, even where the implementation of the budget is entrusted to national authorities or to the Community and the Member States jointly. On the basis of the information provided to it by the institutions by March 1 each year, the Commission draws up annual accounts for the Communities, a financial statement of assets and liabilities and a report on budgetary and financial management and forwards them to the European Parliament, the Council and the Court of Auditors (EC Treaty, Art. 275; Financial Regulation, Arts 121–128).

4. Budgetary control

Internal audit. The uptake and utilisation of Community funds is subject **10–141** to internal and external controls. Each institution entrusts authorising officers with implementing revenue and expenditure in accordance with the principles of sound financial management. The authorising officers are responsible for ensuring that the requirements of legality and regularity are complied with and introduce appropriate procedures for management and internal audit.[590] An internal auditor is charged with verifying the proper operation of budgetary implementation systems and procedures and reporting to his or her institution thereon.[591] The external controls are

---

[587] The EU Constitution will lay down this principle in Art. I–53(4).

[588] See ECJ (order of the President of September 24, 1996), Joined Cases C–239/96 R and C–240/96 R *UK v Commission* [1996] E.C.R. I–4475, paras 41–46; ECJ, Case C–106/96 *UK v Commission* [1998] E.C.R. I–2729, paras 21–37 (annulment of a Commission decision to carry out expenditure for which the Council had not adopted a basic act).

[589] Interinstitutional Agreement on legal bases and implementation of the budget ([1998] O.J. C344/1; see also (1998) 7/8 EU Bull. point 1.6.1), as taken over in points 36 and 37 of the Interinstitutional Agreement of May 6, 1999 (n.558, *supra*) and in Art. 49(2) of the Financial Regulation. It is a question of appropriations for pilot schemes, preparatory actions and specific or indefinite actions carried out by the Commission by virtue of its prerogatives (other than the right of initiative) and appropriations intended for the internal administration of each institution.

[590] EC Treaty, Art. 279(c); Financial Regulation, Arts 59 and 60.

[591] Financial Regulation, Arts 85 and 86. For the recent changes in terms of internal audits, see Craig, "The constitutionalisation of Community administration" (2003) E.L.R. 840, at 845–846.

carried out in the first instance by the Court of Auditors and subsequently by the European Parliament, working together with the Council.

10–142 **External audit.** The Court of Auditors examines the accounts of all revenue and expenditure of the Community. It examines not only the general budget, but also the accounts of all bodies set up by the Community in so far as the relevant constituent instrument does not preclude such examination (EC Treaty, Art. 248(1), first subpara.).[592] The purpose of the audit is to establish that all revenue has been received and all expenditure incurred in a lawful and proper manner having regard to financial regulations and the substantive provisions on the basis of which the operations were carried out.[593] The Court of Auditors also verifies that the financial management has been sound[594] and accordingly that resources have been utilised efficiently.[595] In particular, the Court is to report on any cases of irregularity.[596]

The external audit is carried out after operations have been performed, but does not have to wait until the accounts for the relevant financial year have been closed (EC Treaty, Art. 248(2)). The Court of Auditors is entitled to have access to all necessary decisions and information, which Community institutions, any bodies managing revenue or expenditure on behalf of the Community, any natural or legal person in receipt of payments from the budget and national audit bodies or the relevant national departments are under a duty to provide on request. Where necessary, it will carry out its inspections on the spot in Community institutions and on the premises of the aforementioned bodies and natural or legal persons. Where investigations are carried out in Member States, the Court of Auditors works in liaison with national audit bodies or competent departments, provided that they wish to take part in the audit. The Court and the national audit bodies are to co-operate in a spirit of trust while maintaining their independence.[597]

After the close of each financial year, the Court of Auditors draws up an annual report which is forwarded to the other institutions and published,

---

[592] Art. 14 of the EIB Statute sets up a special committee to verify the Bank's operations and accounts. However, the Court of Auditors does examine expenditure of Community funds carried out by the EIB on the Commission's instructions. Art. 248(3), third subpara., of the EC Treaty refers to the Court of Auditors' right of access to information held by the EIB, which is to be governed by an agreement between the Court of Auditors, the EIB and the Commission.

[593] See EC Treaty, Art. 248(2), and Financial Regulation, Art. 140(1).

[594] EC Treaty, Art. 248(2), first subpara.

[595] For the methods which the Court of Auditors has developed against a background of different auditing traditions in the Member States, see O'Keeffe (n.331, *supra*), at 186–191.

[596] EC Treaty, Art. 248(2), first subpara. For the right of persons mentioned in reports to be heard, see ECJ, Case C–315/99 P *Ismeri Europa v Court of Auditors* [2001] E.C.R. I–5281, paras 27–35, and the discussion by Inghelram in (2001) C.D.E. 707–728.

[597] See EC Treaty, Art. 248(3). See, in this connection, Flizot, "Les rapports entre la Cour des comptes européenne et les institutions supérieures de contrôle des Etats membres. Quelle application du principe du subsidiarité?" (2002) R.M.C.U.E. 112–121.

together with their replies to the Court's observations, in the *Official Journal* (EC Treaty, Art. 248(4), first subpara.).

Discharge. The European Parliament is empowered to give a discharge to **10–143** the Commission in respect of the implementation of the budget: it acts on a recommendation from the Council, acting by qualified majority. The European Parliament decides by a majority of the votes cast.[598] The Council and the European Parliament take their decisions in the light of the accounts and the financial statement submitted by the Commission, the annual report of the Court of Auditors,[599] the statement of the Court of Auditors of assurance as to the reliability of the accounts and the legality and regularity of the underlying transactions[600] and any relevant special reports of that institution (EC Treaty, Art. 276(1)). The EU Treaty reinforced the accountability of the Commission. Before giving a discharge to that institution, the European Parliament may ask the Commission to give evidence with regard to the execution of expenditure or the operation of financial control systems and to provide any necessary information (EC Treaty, Art. 276(2)). As in the case of the Council's recommendation, the decision giving discharge may be accompanied by observations on the implementation of the budget. The Commission has to take all appropriate steps to act on those observations and to report to the European Parliament and the Council on measures taken (EC Treaty, Art. 276(3)). The discharge is a decision which formally closes the accounts. Although it has no effect on the Commission's legal position, the Parliament's refusal to discharge it in full or in part is a powerful political signal.[601] Nevertheless,

---

[598] See Art. 5 of the Procedure for the consideration and adoption of decisions on the granting of discharge in Annex V to the EP Rules of Procedure.

[599] EC Treaty, Art. 248(4), first subpara.

[600] EC Treaty, Art. 248(1), second subpara. The statement is submitted to the European Parliament and the Council and published in the *Official Journal*.

[601] The European Parliament refused to give the Commission a discharge for the 1982 financial year on November 14, 1984 ([1984] O.J. C337/23; subsequently, discharge was given for purposes of closure of the accounts by resolution of March 15, 1985, [1985] O.J. C94/153); it provisionally refused to give a discharge on April 7, 1987 ([1987] O.J. C125/45, discharge eventually being given on January 19, 1988, [1988] O.J. C49/26). See Baziadoly, "Le refus de la décharge par le Parlement européen" (1992) R.M.C.U.E. 58–73. The European Parliament refused to give the Commission a discharge in respect of the 1990 financial year ("on account of persistent problems in relation to budgetary discipline, management of own resources and financial control": resolution of October 27, 1993, [1993] O.J. C315/89) and for the 1992 financial year (see the resolution of April 21, 1994, [1994] O.J. C128/322; discharge was granted by decision of April 5, 1995, [1995] O.J. L141/51; see also [1995] O.J. C109/51). The grant of a discharge was also postponed for the 1997 financial year, see the resolution of May 4, 1999, [1999] O.J. C279/119 (discharge was granted by decision of January 19, 2000, [2000] O.J. L45/36) and for the 1998 financial year, see the resolution of April 13, 2000, [2000] O.J. C40/381 (discharge was granted by resolution of July 6, 2000, A5–0190/2000). For the 1996 financial year, the grant of a discharge was definitively refused: resolution of May 4, 1999, [1999] O.J. C279/115 (the reasons, which were adopted on December 17, 1998, are appended thereto: see Beurdeley, "Les motifs du refus de décharge relatif au budget général de l'Union européenne" (2000) R.M.C.U.E. 696–702).

the Commission may be dismissed only if a motion of censure is passed by the Parliament (see para. 10–017).

10–144 **Combating fraud.** More than half of Community resources are utilised by national authorities, for which the Commission has set up control systems in a number of policy areas. Under Art. 280 of the EC Treaty, the Community and the Member States are to counter fraud and any other illegal activities affecting the financial interests of the Community through deterrent measures affording effective protection in the Member States.[602] The investigative duties conferred on the Commission by Community legislation are now performed by the European Anti-Fraud Office (OLAF, see para. 10–109), which may undertake both internal investigations in Community institutions and bodies and external investigations in the Member States.[603] Protection of the Community's financial interests signifies combating fraud and other irregularities at all levels at which those interests are liable to be affected, both within the Member States and at the level of the Community institutions and bodies.[604] As far as combating fraud at the Community level is concerned, Community bodies may not introduce their own systems to prevent and combat fraud in place of the general power of investigation vested in OLAF by Community legislation.[605]

Since the Community has no criminal jurisdiction, the prosecution of financial fraud is left principally to the Member States. The Member States

---

[602] See White, *Protection of the Financial Interests of the European Communities: The Fight against Fraud and Corruption* (Kluwer Law International, Deventer, 1998) 244 pp.

[603] See Regulation No. 1073/1999 adopted by the European Parliament and the Council on May 25, 1999 under Art. 280 of the EC Treaty concerning investigations conducted by the European Anti-Fraud Office (OLAF) ([1999] O.J. L136/1) and the Interinstitutional Agreement of May 25, 1999 between the European Parliament, the Council and the Commission concerning internal investigations by the European Anti-Fraud Office (OLAF) ([1999] O.J. L136/15). For the terms and conditions for internal investigations in relation to the prevention of fraud, corruption and any illegal activity detrimental to the Communities' interests, see amongst others, Council Decision 1999/394/EC, Euratom of May 25, 1999, [1999] O.J. L149/36, the Commission Decision of June 2, 1999, [1999] O.J. L149/57, and the Decision of the European Parliament of November 18, 1999 appended as Annex XI to the EP Rules of Procedure, [2003] O.J. L61/112. See Combeaud, "L'Olaf et les autorités judiciaires: quelle répression contre la fraude communautaire?" (2001) R.M.C.U.E. 695–702. See also n. 629 with regard to the discussion as to whether Members of the European Parliament may invoke parliamentary immunity in the context of an OLAF investigation.

[604] ECJ, Case C–11/00 *Commission v European Central Bank* [2003] E.C.R. I–7147, paras 103–104, and ECJ, Case C–15/00 *Commission v European Investment Bank* [2003] E.C.R. I–7281, paras 134–135.

[605] According to the Court of Justice, the expression "financial interests of the Community" covers the use by the ECB and the EIB of their own resources, even though they are managed autonomously: ECJ, Case C–11/00 *Commission v European Central Bank* [2003] E.C.R. I–7147, paras 89–97, and ECJ, Case C–15/00 *Commission v European Investment Bank* [2003] E.C.R. I–7281, paras 120–136. The fact that these bodies are subject to Community legislation on combating fraud does not detract from their functional independence: see para. 14–066. See also Marchegiani, "La BEI et l'OLAF, un conflit de nature constitutionnelle" (2000) R.M.C.U.E. 690–695.

are under a duty to co-ordinate their action aimed at protecting the Community's financial interests against fraud and to take the same measures to counter fraud affecting those financial interests as they take in respect of their own financial interests (Art. 280(2) and (3)). In order to make combating fraud more effective, common legal rules have been created for all areas covered by Community policies which are applicable to the administrative penalties provided for by Community law.[606] Under Art. 280(4), the European Parliament and the Council are to adopt, in accordance with the procedure laid down in Art. 251, after consulting the Court of Auditors, the necessary measures in the field of the prevention of and the fight against fraud affecting the Community's financial interests.[607] As has already been mentioned, this covers the fight against fraud at both the Community and the national levels. However, Community measures may not concern the application of national criminal law or the national administration of justice.[608] National provisions of criminal law were harmonised through conventions established by the Council pursuant to Title VI of the EU Treaty (PJCC) in which general rules and a common definition of fraud were formulated.[609] When the EU Constitution is in force, there will no longer be any legal differences between the latter field of co-operation and the areas of Community competence. Consequently, there will no longer be any bar on Community measures concerning the application of national criminal law or the national administration of justice (see Art. III–415 of the EU Constitution).

---

[606] Council Regulation (EC, Euratom) No. 2988/95 of December 18, 1995 on the protection of the European Communities' financial interests, [1995] O.J. L312/1. See Lenaerts, "Sanktionen der Gemeinschaftsorgane gegenüber natürlichen und juristischen Personen" (1997) EuR. 17–46; Michiels, "Nieuwe instrumenten ter bescherming van de financiële belangen van de Europese Gemeenschappen" (1996) S.E.W. 362–371; Wolfgang and Ulrich, "Schutz der finanziellen Interessen der Europäischen Gemeinschaften" (1998) EuR. 616–647.

[607] See, e.g. Decision 804/2004/EC of the European Parliament and of the Council of April 21, 2004 establishing a Community action programme to promote activities in the field of the protection of the Community's financial interests (Hercule programme), [2004] O.J. L143/9.

[608] Art. 280(4) of the EC Treaty. As to whether Community measures on fraud prevention may lead to a harmonisation of national criminal law, see Veldt Foglia, "(Nog) geen strafrecht in de Eerste Pijler?" (2002) S.E.W. 162–169.

[609] Convention of July 26, 1995 on the protection of the Communities' financial interests, [1995] O.J. C316/48 (explanatory report in [1997] O.J. C191/1). When consulted by the Council, the European Parliament came out against the Commission's proposal for this convention on the ground that the matter would be better dealt with by a directive based on Arts 95 and 280 of the EC Treaty, see the resolution of March 15, 1995, [1995] O.J. C89/82. See further the additional protocols to the above Convention of September 27, 1996 ([1996] O.J. C313/2; explanatory report in [1998] O.J. C11/5) and June 19, 1997 ([1997] O.J. C221/11). See Korte, "Der Schutz der finanziellen Interessen der Europäischen Gemeinschaften mit den Mitteln des Strafrechts—Das 'Zweite Protokol'" (1998) N.J.W. 1464–1466. See also the Convention drawn up on the basis of the former Art. K.3 of the EU Treaty on the fight against corruption involving officials of the European Communities or officials of Member States of the European Union (adopted by Council Act of May 26, 1997, [1997] O.J. C195/1). For the interpretation by the Court of Justice of these conventions and the protocols thereto, see para. 18–009, *infra*.

C. THE SEATS OF THE INSTITUTIONS AND BODIES

10–145 Provisional locations. Article 289 of the EC Treaty puts the national governments under a duty to determine the seat of the institutions by common accord (see also EAEC Treaty, Art. 189).[610] When the ECSC Treaty entered into force, the Foreign Ministers agreed that the High Authority and the Court of Justice would start work in Luxembourg and that the Assembly would hold its first session at Strasbourg, where the Council of Europe hemicycle was available. The Council met in Luxembourg, where the departments of the institutions, including the secretariat of the Assembly, were located. Following the entry into force of the EEC and EAEC Treaties, the two Commissions held their meetings in Brussels on grounds of convenience. The EEC and EAEC Councils also met in Brussels, followed by the committees of the Assembly, which continued to operate in Strasbourg and Luxembourg.

Concurrently with the establishment by the Merger Treaty of a single Council and a single Commission, the representatives of the national governments adopted the Decision on Provisional Location of April 8, 1965 pursuant to power conferred by that Treaty to settle "certain problems peculiar to the Grand Duchy of Luxembourg".[611] The Decision declared that Luxembourg, Brussels and Strasbourg were to remain the provisional places of work of the institutions of the Communities (Art. 1). As far as the institutions were concerned, the decision provided that during the months of April, June and October, the Council would hold its sessions in Luxembourg (Art. 2), that the Court of Justice would remain in Luxembourg (Art. 3) and that the General Secretariat of the Assembly and its departments would remain in Luxembourg (Art. 4), together with certain departments of the Commission (Arts 5–9). Since the governments were unable to reach agreement on the seats of the institutions,[612] the institutions remained free to determine their internal organisation within the confines of the decision. Thus, the European Parliament was entitled to decide to hold its plenary sessions in Strasbourg, meetings of political groups and parliamentary committees in Brussels—with the gradual transfer of some members of staff required for this purpose[613]—and special

---

[610] ECJ, Case 230/81 *Luxembourg v European Parliament* [1983] E.C.R. 255, para. 35.

[611] Decision of the Representatives of the Governments of the Member States on the provisional location of certain institutions and departments of the Communities (*Treaties establishing the European Communities*, Office for Official Publications, Luxembourg, 1978 at 837), adopted pursuant to Art. 37 of the Merger Treaty.

[612] On June 30, 1981 a Conference of Representatives of the Governments convened for this purpose in 1980 merely confirmed the Member States' power and maintained the *status quo* (as agreed at the European Council held in Maastricht on March 23 and 24, 1981; (1981) 3 EC Bull. point 1.1.8).

[613] ECJ, Case 230/81 *Luxembourg v European Parliament* [1983] E.C.R. 255, paras 37–58; ECJ, Joined Cases C–213/88 and C–39/89 *Luxembourg v European Parliament* [1991] E.C.R. I–5643, paras 35–38, 42–44 and 54–58. The division of staff must not be such, however, as to mean that the secretariat is no longer based in Luxembourg: ECJ, Case 108/83 *Luxembourg v European Parliament* [1984] E.C.R. 1945, para. 31. See Neville Brown, "The Grand Duchy Fights Again: Comment on Joined Cases C–213/88 and C–39/89" (1993) C.M.L.R. 599–611.

or additional plenary sessions in Brussels during the weeks during which the political groups and parliamentary committees met.[614]

Seats of institutions. By the First Decision on the Seat of the Institutions **10-146** of December 12, 1992,[615] the national governments at last acted upon Art. 289 of the EC Treaty.[616] The decision fixed a seat for each institution without altering the *status quo*: the European Parliament was to have its seat in Strasbourg, but was to continue to work in Brussels and Luxembourg (see para. 10-027); the Council was to have its seat in Brussels, but to continue to hold its meetings in April, June and October in Luxembourg; the Commission was to have its seat in Brussels, but its departments located in Luxembourg were to remain there; the Court of Justice, the Court of First Instance and the Court of Auditors were to continue to have their seats in Luxembourg. Consequently, the Community institutions have no common seat and indeed most of them have more than one place of work.[617] Above all the fact that the European Parliament is obliged to meet in Strasbourg, whilst the institutions with which it collaborates institutionally operate principally in Brussels, makes for needless costs and inconvenience for all those concerned. The Treaty of Amsterdam, however, enshrined those arrangements in a Protocol annexed to the Treaties (the "Protocol on Seats"),[618] which means that they can only be changed by means of the procedure for amending the Treaties.

Seats of other bodies. A decision of the national governments was required **10-147** to fix the seats of the EIB, the EMI and the ECB.[619] In order to determine the locations of other bodies, it is sufficient for a decision to be taken of the same legal nature as the one which set up the body in question or, failing this, a decision taken by the body itself pursuant to its power to determine its internal organisation.[620] Nevertheless, by the Decision on Provisional Location of April 8, 1965 the national governments did fix the working places of a number of bodies and departments. By the same token, the Heads of State or Government, acting under Art. 289 of the EC Treaty,

---

[614] ECJ, Joined Cases 358/85 and 51/86 *France v European Parliament* [1988] E.C.R. 4821, paras 29–41.

[615] Decision of December 12, 1992 taken by common agreement between the Representatives of the Governments of the Member States on the location of the seats of the institutions and of certain bodies and departments of the European Communities, [1992] O.J. C341/1.

[616] ECJ, Case C–345/95 *France v European Parliament* [1997] E.C.R. I–5215, para. 23.

[617] Although the European Parliament argued that this practice was contrary to Arts 10, 199 and 289 of the EC Treaty (see the position taken by the Parliament on April 20, 1993, [1993] O.J. C150/26), the Court of Justice endorsed maintaining several places of work for that institution in ECJ, Case C–345/95 *France v European Parliament* [1997] E.C.R. I–5215.

[618] Protocol (No. 8) annexed to the EU Treaty and the Community Treaties on the location of the seats of the institutions and of certain bodies and departments of the European Communities and Europol, [1997] O.J. C340/112.

[619] EIB Statute, Art. 1; EMI Statute, Art. 13; ESCB Statute, Art. 37.

[620] See, *e.g.* the regulation establishing the European Agency for Reconstruction, para. 10–110, *supra*.

fixed the definitive location of certain bodies and departments by, *inter alia*, the First Decision on the Seat of the Institutions of December 12, 1992,[621] the Second Decision on the Seat of the Institutions of October 29, 1993[622] and the Third Decision on Seats of December 13, 2003.[623] The executive agencies responsible for managing Community programmes on behalf of the Commission are established where the Commission has its seat.[624]

D. STATUS OF MEMBERS OF INSTITUTIONS AND BODIES

10–148 **Independent status.** Apart from the members of the Council, the status of members of the institutions in performing their duties is one of independence. Following their appointment by the national governments or the Council, they cannot be compelled to stand down except by the Court of Justice acting at the request of their particular institution.[625] Members of the European Parliament are answerable only to the electorate in their constituencies. Members of the other two political institutions are answerable to parliamentary assemblies: Ministers who sit in the Council to their national or regional parliaments; Members of the Commission collectively to the European Parliament, which approves their appointment.[626]

10–149 **Duties and immunities.** Members of the institutions are under a duty not to disclose information of the kind covered by the obligation of professional secrecy laid down by Art. 287 of the EC Treaty. Members of the

---

[621] n.615, *supra*. The Decision fixed the seat of the Economic and Social Committee at Brussels and the seats of the Court of Auditors (at that time still not an "institution") and of the European Investment Bank in Luxembourg (Art. 1(e)–(g)).

[622] Decision of October 29, 1993 taken by common agreement between the Representatives of the Governments of the Member States, meeting at Head of State and Government level, on the location of the seats of certain bodies and departments of the European Communities and of Europol, [1993] O.J. C323/1. See the bodies and departments mentioned in para. 10–110, *supra*. See also the Decision by common accord of the representatives of the Governments of the Member States of December 6, 1996 determining the seat of the Community Plant Variety Office ([1997] O.J. C36/1). However, in determining the seat of the European Monitoring Centre on Racism and Xenophobia, the representatives of the national governments based their decision of June 2, 1997 ([1997] O.J. C194/4), not on Art. 289 of the EC Treaty, but simply on the regulation establishing that body (para. 10–110, *supra*).

[623] Decision 2004/97/EC, Euratom taken by common agreement between the Representatives of the Member States, meeting at Head of State or Government level, of December 13, 2003 on the location of the seats of certain offices and agencies of the European Union, [2004] O.J. L29/15. See the bodies and agencies mentioned in para. 10–110.

[624] Art. 5 of Regulation No. 58/2003 (n.480, *supra*).

[625] For the Court of Justice and the Court of First Instance, see para. 10–083, *supra*; for the Court of Auditors, see para. 10–090, *supra*. The Council may also request that a Member of the Commission be compulsorily retired (para. 10–066, *supra*); the Commission may be made to resign as a body if the European Parliament passes a motion of censure (para. 10–017, *supra*).

[626] For the position to be given to the Union Minister for Foreign Affairs under the EU Constitution, see para. 10–071, *supra*.

Commission, the Court of Justice, the Court of First Instance and the Court of Auditors enjoy the privileges and immunities which the Protocol on Privileges and Immunities confers on officials and other servants of the Communities in respect of the performance of their official duties.[627] Members of the European Parliament enjoy privileged free movement and may not be the subject of proceedings in respect of opinions which they express in the performance of their duties.[628] During the session of the European Parliament, MEPs enjoy immunity from any measure of detention and legal proceedings in other Member States and the immunities accorded to MPs of the national parliament in their own Member States. This parliamentary immunity may not be claimed if an MEP is found in the act of committing an offence and may be waived by the European Parliament.[629] As "representatives of Member States taking part in the work of the institutions of the Communities", members of the Council enjoy the "customary privileges, immunities and facilities" in the performance of their duties and during their travel to and from the place of meeting.[630]

Financial status. The Council, acting by a qualified majority, is empowered **10–150** to determine the salaries, allowances and pensions of Members of the Commission, the Court of Justice, the Court of First Instance[631] and the Court of Auditors.[632] The payments are subject only to a tax for the benefit

---

[627] For the Commission, see Protocol on Privileges and Immunities (para. 10–114, *supra*), Art. 20; for the Court of Justice and the Court of First Instance, Art. 21; for the Court of Auditors, see EC Treaty, Art. 247(9).

[628] Protocol on Privileges and Immunities, Arts 8 and 9 of the Chapter formerly entitled "Members of the Assembly" also apply to directly elected Members of the European Parliament, as confirmed by Art. 6(2) of the Act on the Direct Election of the European Parliament (para. 10–022, *supra*).

[629] Protocol on Privileges and Immunities, Art. 10, and EP Rules of Procedure, rr.5 to 7. For a critical commentary on the European Parliament's interpretation of MEPs' immunities in the absence of any harmonisation, see Sieglerschmidt, "Das Immunitätsrecht der Europäischen Gemeinschaft. Seine Anwendung durch das Europäische Parlament und seine notwendige Weiterentwicklung" (1986) Eu.GR.Z. 445–453. For the possibility of invoking immunity in connection with an investigation carried out by the Community Anti-Fraud Office OLAF (n.603, *supra*), see CFI (order of the President of May 2, 2000), Case T–17/00 R *Rothley v European Parliament* [2000] E.C.R. II–2085; CFI, Case T–17/00 *Rothley v European Parliament* [2002] E.C.R. II–2085, as upheld by ECJ (judgment of March 30, 2004), Case C–167/02 *Rothley v European Parliament*, not yet reported. See Thym, "Europaabgeordnete gegen Europaparlement—der erste Akt des Streits um OLAF" (2000) EuR. 990–998.

[630] Protocol on Privileges and Immunities, Art. 11, first para.

[631] EC Treaty, Art. 210 (before the EU Treaty: Art. 6 of the Merger Treaty). See Regulation No. 422/67/EEC, No. 5/67/Euratom of the Council of July 25, 1967 determining the emoluments of the President and Members of the Commission and of the President, Judges, Advocates General and Registrar of the Court of Justice, [1967] O.J. Spec. Ed. 99, as amended, *inter alia* by Council Regulation (ECSC, EEC, Euratom) No. 4045/88 of December 19, 1988 laying down the emoluments of the President, Members and Registrar of the Court of First Instance of the European Communities, [1988] O.J. L356/1.

[632] EC Treaty, Art. 247(8). See Council Regulation (EEC/Euratom/ECSC) No. 2290/77 of October 18, 1977 determining the emoluments of members of the Court of Auditors, [1977] O.J. L268/1.

of the Communities.[633] The financial status of Members of the European Parliament is not yet determined by the Council.[634] Accordingly, the Member States fix their MEPs' remuneration. All the same, MEPs receive lump-sum expenses paid by the Communities. In order not to impair the internal functioning of the European Parliament and MEPs' privileged free movement, Member States may not tax those expenses.[635]

10–151 **Members of other bodies.** The board members of the ECB, who are appointed by the national governments, also have an independent status.[636] As in the case of the European Ombudsman (appointed by the European Parliament) and the European Data-protection Supervisor (appointed by the European Parliament and the Council), they may be compelled to retire only by the Court of Justice.[637] The Protocol on Privileges and Immunities applies to the European Ombudsman, the ECB, the EIB, the European Data-protection Supervisor and the other Community bodies and agencies with legal personality.[638] Members of advisory bodies enjoy privileges and immunities in the performance of their duties and during their travel to and from the place of meeting.[639] Europol and members of its organs enjoy the usual privileges and immunities by virtue of a special protocol (see para. 10–105). Bodies and agencies having legal personality in their own right fix the salaries of members of their management boards.[640] The European Ombudsman has the same financial status as Members of the Court of Justice.[641] Any payments made instead of remuneration to members of

---

[633] See privileges of officials, para. 10–152, infra.

[634] Uniform rules for the remuneration and social security status of MEPs have been proposed in the Draft Statute for Members of the European Parliament (and the annex thereto) adopted by the Parliament on December 3, 1998 (n.102, supra).

[635] ECJ, Case 208/80 Lord Bruce of Donington [1981] E.C.R. 2205, paras 15–20. The lump sum paid in respect of expenses might be subject to national tax if it were to be shown that it was excessively high and in reality constituted disguised remuneration, a question which would be a matter of Community law alone: ibid. para. 21.The European Parliament is currently working on rules for the uniform payment of MEPs and a system of reimbursement of costs actually incurred, together with a flat rate for general monthly expenses, the daily allowance and travel using own vehicles. For the problems associated with the system of flat-rate reimbursement of MEPs' expenses, see Special Report No. 10/98 of the Court of Auditors concerning the expenses and allowances of the Members of the European Parliament together with the replies of the European Parliament, [1998] O.J. C243/1.

[636] para. 10–103, supra.

[637] paras 10–108 and 10–110, supra. As regards the European Data-protection Supervisor, an application to this effect may be made not only by the European Parliament, but also by the Council or the Commission: Regulation No. 45/2001, Art. 42(6) (n.718, infra).

[638] For the European Ombudsman, see Ombudsman Regulations, Art. 10(3); for the EIB and the ECB, see Arts 22 and 23 of the Protocol on Privileges and Immunities and Art. 40 of the ESCB Statute. For the (Assistant) Data protection Supervisor, see Art. 42(7) and (8) of Regulation (EC) No. 45/2001 (n.718, infra). See also the regulations establishing the other bodies and agencies with legal personality, para. 10–110, supra.

[639] Protocol on Privileges and Immunities, Art. 11, second para.

[640] See, e.g. ESCB Statute, Art. 11.3 (Executive Board of the ECB); EIB Statute, Art. 13(5) (Management Committee).

[641] Ombudsman Regulations, Art. 10(2).

advisory bodies are determined by the Council pursuant to Art. 210 of the EC Treaty.[642]

E. STATUS OF OFFICIALS AND OTHER SERVANTS

Staff Regulations. The institutions and bodies of the European Union **10–152** employ more than 30,000 officials.[643] Under Art. 24 of the Merger Treaty (now EC Treaty, Art. 283), the Council, acting by a qualified majority on a proposal from the Commission and after consulting the other institutions concerned, is to lay down the Staff Regulations of officials of the European Communities and the Conditions of Employment of other servants of those Communities.[644] There has recently been a reform of the Staff Regulations and Conditions of Employment.[645] The reform was designed to meet the changing needs of the institutions and their staff, whilst respecting a Community administrative culture and tradition based on the principle of service to the citizen.[646] Formerly, officials' posts were classified in four categories (A (LA in the case of the language service), B, C, D) in descending order of rank (for instance A 1 to A 8).[647] From May 1, 2004, the established staff is organised in two function groups: administrators (AD), corresponding to administrative, advisory, linguistic and scientific duties, and assistants (AST), corresponding to executive, technical and clerical duties. Within each function group, officials are classified in grades in ascending hierarchical order.[648] In this way, a Director-General (AD 16 or AD 15), possibly assisted by a Deputy Director-General, will have under him or her Directorates run by Directors (AD 15 or AD 14). In turn, each Directorate is divided into administrative units in which administrators

---

[642] See EC Treaty, Art. 258, fourth para., as regards the European Economic and Social Committee.

[643] See the Commission's answer of April 3, 2003 to question E–0015/03 (Huhne), [2003] O.J. C242E/87 (stating that in 2002 all the institutions taken together employed 31,861 established officials and temporary staff, of whom 70.58 per cent worked for the Commission).

[644] Regulation (EEC, Euratom, ECSC) No. 259/68 of the Council of February 29, 1968, laying down the Staff Regulations of Officials and the Conditions of Employment of Other Servants of the European Communities and instituting special measures temporarily applicable to officials of the Commission [1968] O.J. Spec. Ed. I, 30, (Staff Regulations; Conditions of Employment of Other Servants).

[645] Council Regulation (EC, Euratom) No. 723/2004 of March 22, 2004 amending the Staff Regulations of officials of the European Communities and the Conditions of Employment of other servants of the European Communities, [2004] O.J. L124/1.

[646] *ibid.*, recital 1 in the preamble.

[647] Under the former system, Category A (eight grades) comprised staff engaged in administrative and advisory duties (university education or equivalent experience); category B (five grades) executive duties (advanced level of secondary education); category C (five grades) clerical duties (secondary education); category D (five grades) manual or service duties; L A (six grades) translating and interpreting each grade was divided into a number of salary steps. The system of salary steps still applies under the revised Staff Regulations.

[648] See Art. 5 of the amended Staff Regulations. In order to be recruited in function group AD it is necessary to have a university degree or equivalent professional experience; for function group AST, the requirement is for a diploma of post-secondary education or a diploma of secondary education and appropriate professional experience of at least three years.

work under Heads of Unit (AD 14 to AD 9). Each administration has one or more appointing authorities. In principle, officials are appointed following an open competition.[649] Normally, only nationals of Member States are recruited, the aim being to achieve the broadest possible geographical basis.[650]

Officials are obliged to carry out their duties and conduct themselves solely with the interests of the Communities in mind.[651] Officials must refrain from any unauthorised disclosure of information received in the line of duty, even after they have left the service, unless that information has already been made public or is accessible to the public.[652] They enjoy certain privileges and immunities in this connection.[653] Since those privileges and immunities are conferred on officials solely in the interests of the Communities, each institution is required to waive the immunity of an official or other servant wherever it considers that such waiver is not contrary to the Communities' interests (Protocol on Privileges and Immunities, Art. 18). Article 13 of the Protocol provides that officials and other servants are to be exempt from national taxes on salaries, wages and emoluments paid to them by the Communities and have to pay a tax for the benefit of the Communities on their Community salaries.[654] This tax is intended to secure the independent operation of the Communities and to place staff from different Member States on an equal footing.[655] Anyone deriving rights from the Staff Regulations (for instance, dependants, persons taking part in open competitions) may bring proceedings in the Court of First Instance after submitting a complaint to the appointing authority which has been rejected expressly or by implication.[656] Alongside the Staff Regulations, there are special rules applying to staff employed by the Communities under contract.[657] Officials and other staff are to act in

---

[649] *ibid.*, Art. 29(1). A different procedure may be employed for the recruitment of senior officials (Directors-General or their equivalent in grade AD 16 or AD 15 and Directors or their equivalent in grade AD 15 or AD 14) and, in exceptional cases, also for recruitment to posts which require special qualifications (Art. 29(2)). Recruitment has recently been entrusted to the European Communities Personnel Selection Office (see para. 10–109).

[650] *ibid.*, Art. 27. Under Art. 28(a), an official may be appointed only if "he is a national of one of the Member States of the Communities, unless an exception is authorised by the appointing authority, and enjoys his full rights as a citizen".

[651] *ibid.*, Art. 11.

[652] *ibid.*, Art. 17; see also EC Treaty, Art. 287.

[653] Protocol on Privileges and Immunities (para. 10–114, *supra*).

[654] See Regulation (EEC, Euratom, ECSC) No. 260/68 of the Council of February 29, 1968 laying down the conditions and procedure for applying the tax for the benefit of the European Communities, [1968] O.J. English Spec. Ed. I, 37. It does not empower the Community to make freelance interpreters subject to Community tax: CFI, Joined Cases T–202/96 and T–204/96 *Von Löwis and Alvarez-Cotera v Commission* [1998] E.C.R. II–2829, paras 51–58.

[655] ECJ, Case 85/86 *Commission v European Investment Bank* [1988] E.C.R. 1281, para. 23.

[656] See Staff Regulations, Art. 90 (administrative procedure) and Art. 91 (appeal to the Court of Justice). For the jurisdiction of the Court of First Instance, see Art. 3(1)(a) of the CFI Decision. For further particulars, see Lenaerts and Arts, *Procedural Law of the European Union*, Ch.16.

[657] The Conditions of Employment of Other Servants apply to temporary staff, auxiliary staff, contract staff, local staff and special advisers.

accordance with such codes of conduct as the institutions and bodies shall determine.[658]

Scope of Staff Regulations. The Staff Regulations and the Conditions of **10–153** Employment of Other Servants apply to the institutions, the European Economic and Social Committee, the Committee of the Regions, the European Ombudsman, the European Data-protection Supervisor and all bodies to which the Staff Regulations apply under the Community acts establishing them.[659] Some Community bodies may adopt their own staff regulations,[660] but in any case the Court of First Instance has jurisdiction to hear and determine any disputes.[661] More often, however, the decision setting up a new body or agency provides that the Staff Regulations and Conditions of Employment of Other Servants are to apply to it.[662] This also

---

[658] *e.g.* Code of Conduct of officials and other servants of the European Parliament ([2000] O.J. C97/1), of the General Secretariat of the Council ([2001] O.J. C189/1), of the Commission ([2000] O.J. L267/63), the European Central Bank ([2001] O.J. C76/12), the European Investment Bank ([2001] O.J. C17/26), the Community Plant Variety Office ([2000] O.J. C371/14), the European Environment Agency ([2000] O.J. L216/15) and the European Foundation for the Improvement of Living and Working Conditions ([2000] O.J. L316/69). Codes of Conduct for the Court of Auditors, the European Training Foundation, the European Agency for the Evaluation of Medicinal Products and the Translation Centre for the Bodies of the European Union may be found on their websites. See Martinez Soria, "Die Kodizes für gute Verwaltungspraxis" (2001) EuR. 682–705.

[659] Staff Regulations, Art. 1 to 1b; Conditions of Employment of Other Servants, Art. 6.

[660] See the independence in staff matters granted by EIB Statute, Art. 13(7), and ESCB Statute, Art. 36.1. The contractual employment relationship between the ECB and its staff does not prevent the ECB from adjusting the employment relationship in the interests of the service: CFI, Joined Cases T–178/00 and T–341/00 *Pflugradt v ECB* [2002] E.C.R. II–4035, paras 48–54.

[661] See ESCB Statute, Art. 36.2 (see CFI, Case T–333/99 *X. v ECB* [2001] E.C.R. II–3021, paras 36–44) and the conditions of employment drawn up for the staff of the European Training Foundation (see Art. 14 of the regulation establishing that body, para. 10–110, *supra*), the European Foundation for the Improvement of Living and Working Conditions (Art. 44 of Council Regulation (ECSC, EEC, Euratom) No. 1860/76 of June 29, 1976, [1976] O.J. L214/24) and the European Agency for Co-operation (Art. 18(1), second subpara., of the regulation setting up the agency, para. 10–110, *supra*); for the EIB, see ECJ, Case 110/75 *Mills v European Investment Bank* [1976] E.C.R. 955, paras 5–18. As regards the character of a "Community body", see ECJ, Case 16/81 *Alaimo v Commission* [1982] E.C.R. 1559, paras 7–12 (where it was accepted that the European Centre for the Development of Vocational Training was such a body) and CFI (order of December 16, 1994), Case T–177/94 *Altmann v Commission* [1994] E.C.R. II–1245, paras 41–44 (where it was held that the JET Joint Undertaking (n.458, *supra*) was not part of the Community; this does not preclude Community legal protection for JET officials: CFI, Joined Cases T–177/94 and T–377/94 *Altmann v Commission* [1996] E.C.R. II–2041, and CFI, Case T–99/95 *Stott v Commission* [1996] E.C.R. II–2227).

[662] This is true of the European Ombudsman's secretariat (Ombudsman Regulations, Art. 11(2)) and, by virtue of the regulations establishing them (for the references see para. 10–110, *supra*), the secretariat of the European Data protection Supervisor (Art. 43), the European Centre for the Development of Vocational Training (Art. 13), the European Office for Harmonisation in the Internal Market (Art. 112(1)), the European Environment Agency (Art. 17, first para.), the European Monitoring Centre for Drugs and Drug Addiction (Art. 15, first para.), the European Medicines Agency (Art. 75), the European Training Foundation (Art. 14), the European Agency for Health and Safety at Work (Art.

applies to Eurojust,[663] but not to Europol and other non-Community bodies, where the Council lays down specific staff regulations.[664] The executive agencies responsible for managing Community programmes operate partly with officials of the institutions and partly with contract staff.[665]

If the Protocol on Privileges and Immunities applies to a Community body or agency, the salaries of its staff are exempt from national tax.[666] Although a body with legal personality, such as the European Investment Bank, has institutional and financial independence, because it is closely linked to the Community the tax collected on staff salaries accrues to the general budget of the European Union.[667]

F. RULES GOVERNING LANGUAGES

10–154 Treaty languages. When the EEC and EAEC Treaties were signed, it was provided that the text in each official language of the Contracting Parties was equally authentic (EEC Treaty, Art. 248; EAEC Treaty, Art. 225). As a result of the successive accession treaties, authentic Czech, Danish, English, Estonian, Finnish, Greek, Hungarian, Irish, Latvian, Lithuanian, Maltese, Polish, Portuguese, Slovak, Slovenian, Spanish and Swedish texts of the EEC and EAEC Treaties and of the amending and supplementing treaties came into being alongside the Dutch, French, German and Italian texts.[668] All subsequent amending treaties provide that the text in each Treaty language is equally authentic.[669] As a result, the Treaties on which the

---

20), the Community Plant Variety Office (Art. 31), the Translation Centre (Art. 17(1)), the European Agency for Reconstruction (Art. 10), the European Food Safety Authority (Art. 48), the European Maritime Safety Agency (Art. 6), the European Aviation Safety Agency (Art. 20), the European Network and Information Security Agency (Art. 19) the European Centre for Disease Prevention and Control (Art. 29) and the European Railway Agency (Art. 24). In these cases, of course, the Court of First Instance has jurisdiction to hear and determine any disputes.

[663] See Art. 30 of Council Decision 2002/187/JHA (n.494, *supra*).

[664] Accordingly, Art. 30(3) of the Europol Convention (n.488, *supra*) leaves the staff regulations to be adopted by the Council, see the Council Decision of December 3, 1998, [1999] O.J. C26/23. For the European Union Institute for Security Studies, see Arts 7 and 8 of Joint Action 2001/554/CFSP (n.486, *supra*) and Art. 9 of Joint Action 2001/555/CFSP, which confer the status of contract staff on its personnel. For their staff regulations, see [2002] O.J. L39/18 and 44, respectively.

[665] Art. 17 of Regulation No. 58/2003 (n.480, *supra*).

[666] Protocol on Privileges and Immunities, Art. 13. For the bodies and agencies to which it applies, see para. 10–115, *supra*.

[667] ECJ, Case 85/86 *Commission v European Investment Bank* [1988] E.C.R. 1281, paras 28–30.

[668] EC Treaty, Art. 314, and EAEC Treaty, Art. 225, as most recently amended by the second para. of Art. 61 of the 2003 Act of Accession. In 1984, Letzeburgisch, which is not a Treaty language, became an official language of the Grand Duchy of Luxembourg (alongside French and German).

[669] See Single European Act, Art. 34; EU Treaty, Art. 53; Amsterdam Treaty, Art. 15; Treaty of Nice, Art. 13; see also Art. IV–448 of the EU Constitution. It is noted that the language regime for intergovernmental conferences is determined by the participating States; see, *e.g.*, the Commission's answer of December 20, 2002 to question P–3442/02 (Dehousse), [2003] O.J. C110E/213.

Union is based exist in 21 authentic languages. Only the French text of the ECSC Treaty was authentic (ECSC Treaty, Art. 100), but there were official translations in the other Treaty languages.[670] The EU Constitution may be translated also into any other languages as determined by Member States among those which, in accordance with their constitutional order, enjoy official status in all or part of their territory.[671]

Official languages of the Community. Every citizen of the Union may write **10–155** to any of the institutions, the European Economic and Social Committee, the Committee of the Regions and the European Ombudsman in one of the Treaty languages and have an answer in the same language (EC Treaty, Art. 21, third para.). The rules governing the languages of the institutions are determined by the Council, acting unanimously, without prejudice to the Statute of the Court of Justice (EC Treaty, Art. 290; EAEC Treaty, Art. 190, which before the Treaty of Nice referred to the "Rules of Procedure" of the Court of Justice). In Art. 1 of Regulation No. 1, the Council declares 20 languages (*i.e.* excluding Irish) to be official languages and working languages of the Community.[672] A Member State or one of its nationals may write to Community institutions in any Community language and the reply has to be drawn up in the same language (Art. 2 of Regulation No. 1). Documents sent by a Community institution to a Member State or to one of its nationals must be drafted in the official language of that State (Art. 3)[673] and, where the Member State has more than one official language, the

---

[670] The Decisions of Accession to the ECSC were authentic in all versions (*i.e.* in the Treaty languages at the time of accession). 1972, 1979 and 1985 Decisions of Accession (ns to para. 1–021, *supra*), Art. 3.

[671] Art. IV–448(2) of the EU Constitution. This possibility could be used, *e.g.* for Catalan, which is an official language in Catalonia (Spain).

[672] Regulation No.1 determining the languages to be used by the European Economic Community, [1952–1958] O.J. Spec. Ed. 59, as amended upon the accession of each new Member State (referring now in Art. 1 to languages "of the Union"). Since citizens are now entitled to use any Treaty language, the institutions must also be prepared to use Irish. See also Yvon, "Sprachenvielfalt und europäische Einheit—Zur Reform des Sprachenregimes der Europäischen Union" (2003) EuR. 681–695; Yasue, "Le multilinguisme dans l'Union européenne et la politique linguistique des Etats membres" (1999) R.M.C.U.E. 277–283. The "language policy" of the European Union should also be concerned with the clarity of the communication, see Aziz, "Mainstreaming the Duty of Clarity and Transparency as part of the Good Administrative Practice in the EU" (2004) E.L.J. 282–295; see also para. 16–019, *infra*.

[673] An irregularity in this respect which does not have harmful consequences capable of vitiating the administrative procedure does not affect the legality of the document in question: ECJ, Case 41/69 *ACF Chemiefarma v Commission* [1970] E.C.R. 661, paras 48–52. Where versions of an instrument in other, non-authentic languages are also sent to the person concerned, this does not affect its legality: ECJ, Joined Cases 40–48, 54–56, 111, 113–114/73 *Suiker Unie v Commission* [1975] E.C.R. 1663, paras 114–115. Whereas procedural documents, such as a decision and a statement of objections defining the institution's position must be sent to their addressee in the language of the case, annexes thereto which do not emanate from the institution must be regarded as supporting documentation and must be brought to the addressee's attention as they are: CFI, Case T–77/92 *Parker Pen v Commission* [1994] E.C.R. II–549, paras 70–74; CFI, Case T–148/89 *Tréfilunion v Commission* [1995] E.C.R. II–1063, paras 19–21.

language to be used is to be governed by the general rules of its law, if the Member State so requests (Art. 8). Regulations and other documents of general application must be drafted in all the official languages (Art. 4) and the *Official Journal* must be published in all official languages (Art. 5). There are, however, temporary derogations in respect of Maltese.[674] The versions of secondary legislation in all the official languages are therefore equally authentic.[675] As a result of the need for uniform interpretation of Community law, texts are not considered in isolation, but in cases of doubt are interpreted and applied in the light of the other authentic language versions.[676] In the case of divergence between versions, the provision in question must be interpreted by reference to the purpose and general scheme of the rules of which it forms a part.[677] For the sake of legal certainty, the words of a given version of a text should be given their natural and usual meaning and points at issue should, if possible, be resolved without giving preference to any one of the versions.[678] In principle, all the authentic language versions have the same weight and it makes no difference what proportion of the population of the Community the language in question represents.[679] Individual decisions do not necessarily have to be drawn up in all the official languages. Even if an individual decision is published in the *Official Journal* and is therefore translated into all the languages for the information of citizens, only the language used in the relevant procedure will be authentic and will be used to interpret that decision.[680]

---

[674] See Council Regulation (EC) No. 930/2004 of May 21, 2004 on temporary derogation measures relating to the drafting in Maltese of the acts of the institutions of the European Union, [2004] O.J. L169/1. Owing to the lack of qualified translators, the institutions are not bound to draft all acts in Maltese (except for regulations adopted under the co-decision procedure) for three years beginning on May 1, 2004. This derogation may be extended for a further year.

[675] In order to secure legal certainty, all existing acts which are translated into a new official language upon the accession of a new Member State are also authentic as from the date of accession: 1972 Act of Accession, Art. 155; 1979 Act of Accession, Art. 147; 1985 Act of Accession, Art. 397; 1994 Act of Accession, Art. 170; 2003 Act of Accession, Art. 58.

[676] ECJ, Case 19/67 *Bestuur van de Sociale Verzekeringsbank* [1967] E.C.R. 345, at 354. For an example, see ECJ, Case C–327/91 *France v Commission* [1994] E.C.R. I–3641, para. 35; see also the (somewhat amusing) question No.1896/92 (McCubbin) and the Commission's answer of September 3, 1993, [1994] O.J. C251/1.

[677] ECJ, Case 30/77 *Bouchereau* [1977] E.C.R. 1999, para. 14; see, more recently, ECJ, Case C–72/95 *Kraaijeveld* [1996] E.C.R. I–5403, paras 28–31; ECJ, Joined Cases C–267/95 and C–268/95 *Merck and Beecham* [1996] E.C.R. I–6285, paras 21–24.

[678] ECJ, Case 80/76 *Kerry Milk* [1977] E.C.R. 425, para. 11; CFI, Case T–42/89 *Yorck von Wartenburg v European Parliament* [1990] E.C.R. II–31, paras 16–18, and CFI, Case T–42/89 OPPO *European Parliament v Yorck von Wartenburg* [1990] E.C.R. II–299, paras 10–13. See also Van Calster, "The EU's Tower of Babel—The Interpretation by the Court of Justice of Equally Authentic Texts Drafted in More than One Official Language" (1997) Y.E.L. 363–393 and Sevón, "Languages in the Court of Justice of the European Communities" (1998) Rivista di diritto europeo 533–546.

[679] ECJ, Case C–296/95 *EMU Tobacco* [1998] E.C.R. I–1605, para. 36.

[680] CFI (judgment of September 9, 2003), Case C–361/01 P *Kik v Office for Harmonisation in the Internal Market*, not yet reported, para. 87.

Linguistic regime in Court of Justice. For the rules on the use of languages **10–156** before the Court of Justice Art. 7 of Regulation No. 1 refers to the ECJ Rules of Procedure.[681] The Rules of Procedure of the Court of Justice and the Court of First Instance provide that any of the Treaty languages may be used as the language of the case, which is to be chosen by the applicant.[682] However, where the defendant is a Member State or a national of a particular Member State, the applicant must opt for the official language (or one of the official languages) of that State.[683] Questions referred for a preliminary ruling are dealt with in the language of the court which made the reference.[684] Although in principle all documents are translated into the language of the case and the parties plead in that language, the Rules of Procedure provide for exceptions. Member States are entitled to use their official language (at their election) and the President may conduct the hearing in a language other than the language of the case. By the same token, Judges and Advocates General may put questions in another official language and the latter generally deliver their Opinions in their native tongue.[685] In order to avoid the use of interpreters, the two Courts use French as their working language. Judgments, orders intended for publication and Opinions (of the Court or Advocates General) are reported in all official languages.[686] The texts of documents drawn up in the language of the case or in any other language authorised by the Court are authentic.[687]

Linguistic regime in other institutions. Article 6 of Regulation No. 1 **10–157** provides that the Community institutions may stipulate in their rules of procedure which of the official languages are to be used in specific cases.

---

[681] Following on from Art. 290 of the EC Treaty, which refers as regards the rules governing languages to the Statute of the Court of Justice, Art. 64 of that Statute states that until the rules governing the language arrangements applicable at the Court of Justice and the Court of First Instance have been adopted in the Statute, the provisions of the Rules of Procedure of the Court of Justice and of the Court of First Instance governing language arrangements are to continue to apply.

[682] ECJ Rules of Procedure, Art. 29(1); CFI Rules of Procedure, Art. 35(1). Nevertheless, at the joint request of the parties or at the request of one of the parties (provided that it is not a Community institution), and after the opposite party and the Advocate General have been heard, the Court may authorise an official language other than the language of the case to be used (ECJ Rules of Procedure, Art. 29(2)(b) and (c); CFI Rules of Procedure, Art. 35(2)). Witnesses and experts may be authorised to use another language, even a language other than the language of the case (ECJ Rules of Procedure, Art. 29(4); CFI Rules of Procedure, Art. 35(4)).

[683] ECJ Rules of Procedure, Art. 29(2)(a). This situation may arise where the Court of Justice adjudicates pursuant to an arbitration clause contained in a contract concluded with Community institutions or bodies (EC Treaty, Art. 238).

[684] ECJ Rules of Procedure, Art. 29(2), second subpara.

[685] The Registrar arranges for translation into the language of the case (ECJ Rules of Procedure, Art. 29(3)–(5); CFI Rules of Procedure, Art. 35(3)–(5)).

[686] ECJ Rules of Procedure, Art. 30(2); CFI Rules of Procedure, Art. 36(2). Since January 1, 1994 an exception has been made for staff cases, where the judgment is generally published only in the language of the case. See the introduction to the source material.

[687] ECJ Rules of Procedure, Art. 31; CFI Rules of Procedure, Art. 37.

Thus, the European Parliament works on the basis that each Member is entitled to use his or her official language and provides that documents are to be drawn up in and speeches interpreted into all the official languages.[688] Consequently, knowledge of languages is not required in order to stand for election to the European Parliament.[689] In other institutions, it is not practicable for all the official languages to be on an equal footing as working languages. The Council deliberates and takes decisions "only on the basis of documents and drafts drawn up in the languages specified in the rules in force governing languages", but may decide otherwise by unanimous vote on grounds of urgency.[690] The Commission has to annex instruments adopted by it at a meeting or by the written procedure in the authentic language or languages to the minutes of the meeting at which they were adopted.[691] In the Court of Auditors, reports, opinions, observations and statements of assurance must be drafted in all the official languages.[692] Whilst these rules on the use of languages are complied with, in practice French, English and (to a lesser extent) German are used as working languages within the administration.[693]

10–158 Linguistic regime in other bodies. The Treaties do not contain any provision on the use of languages by other Community bodies and agencies, which means that their power of internal organisation is not restricted in

---

[688] EP Rules of Procedure, r.137; see the resolution of the European Parliament of May 6, 1994 on the right to use one's own language, [1994] O.J. C205/528. Speeches in Parliament may also be interpreted into any other language the Bureau may consider necessary; interpretation is provided in committee and delegation meetings for the official languages used and requested by the members (EP Rules of Procedure, r.137(2) and (3)). Furthermore, r.139 of the EP Rules of Procedure provides that account is to be taken, with regard to the official languages of the countries which acceded to the European Union on May 1, 2004, as of that date and until December 31, 2006, of the availability of the requisite interpreters and translators. An exception to the normal rule on the use of languages is made for recommendations within the framework of the CFSP (EP Rules of Procedure, r.90(3)).

[689] Resolution of the European Parliament of October 14, 1982 on multilingualism of the European Community, [1982] O.J. C292/96.

[690] Council Rules of Procedure, Art. 14(1). Declaration (No.29) annexed to the EU Treaty confirms the rules in force on the use of languages in the field of the CFSP, that is that meetings at official level and exchanges of information among Member States are conducted in English and French. See the Council's answer of October 8, 2000 to question E–1212/01 (Marchiani), [2002] O.J. C40E/25. The previous EPC practice continues to apply to the simplified written procedure (COREU). This consists in using only English and French as working languages: see the answer of the Presidency of November 6, 1985 to Question No. 1673/84 (Formigoni) (1985) 2 EPC Bulletin doc. 85/242, 140. In practice, English and French are chiefly used for communications within the Council, the exception being meetings of the Council itself.

[691] Commission Rules of Procedure, Art. 18, first para. Instruments adopted by the written procedure, the delegation procedure and by way of subdelegation (para. 10–068, *supra*) are to be attached, in the authentic language or languages, in such a way that they cannot be separated, to a day note noted in the minutes (Commission Rules of Procedure, Art. 18, second to fourth paras).

[692] Rules of Procedure of the Court of Auditors, Art. 30(1).

[693] For discussions of the language regime, under which English is increasingly obtaining the upper hand, see Fenet, "Diversité linguistique et construction européenne" (2001) R.T.D.E. 235–269; Oppermann, "Reform der Sprachenregelung?" (2001) N.J.W. 2663–2668.

this respect. The Council has made the rules governing the use of languages by the institutions applicable when setting up certain bodies.[694] Those rules also apply in Europol and Eurojust.[695] In Regulation No. 40/94 establishing the Office for Harmonisation in the Internal Market (trade marks and designs), the Council broke away from the principle that all the official languages are on an equal footing by providing that only English, French, German, Italian and Spanish are to be the languages of the Office.[696] The Office arranges for the translation of trade-mark applications submitted in other official languages of the Community (Regulation No. 40/94, Art. 115(3), second subpara.). In proceedings before the Office, so long as the applicant is the sole party to proceedings before the Office, the language used for filing the application for registration remains the language of proceedings (Art. 115(4)) and all documents necessary for dealing with the application will be drawn up in that language.[697] In opposition, revocation or invalidity proceedings, the language of the proceedings is such language of the Office as the applicant chooses (Art. 115(3), first subpara., and (5)), unless the parties agree to use another official language (Art. 115(7)).[698] Applications for the registration of designs are subject to similar rules.[699] The Court of Justice has held that the choice to limit the languages to those which are most widely known in the European Community is an

---

[694] See the regulations establishing the European Centre for the Development of Vocational Training (Art. 15), the European Foundation for the Improvement of Living and Working Conditions (Art. 19), the European Agency for Health and Safety at Work (Art. 17), the Community Plant Variety Office (Art. 34(1)), the European Maritime Safety Agency (Art. 9) and the European Network and Information Security Agency (Art. 22). The regulation establishing the European Training Foundation provides that the governing board is to determine the rules governing the languages of the Foundation "taking into account the need to ensure access to, and participation in, the work of the Foundation by all interested parties" (Art. 5(5)). In the case of the European Agency for Reconstruction, the regulation establishing it provides only that the Governing Board shall determine by unanimous decision the "rules governing the languages used by the Agency" (Art. 4(8); similar arrangements apply in the European Aviation Safety Agency (Art. 24(2)(k) in conjunction with Art. 28(1)) and the European Railways Agency (Art. 35(1)), where the Management Board/Administrative Board is to decide on the linguistic arrangements for the Agency by a unanimous vote.

[695] Europol Convention, Art. 33 (n.488, *supra*) and Art. 31 of Council Decision 2002/187/JHA (n.494, *supra*). Spain considers that these rules have been broken by the establishment of English and French as de facto working languages and has brought an action against notices of vacancy requiring knowledge of those languages in Case C–160/03 *Spain v Eurojust*, [2003] O.J. C124/15 (republished in [2003] O.J. 146/30).

[696] Art. 115(2) of Regulation No. 40/94 on the Community trade mark, [1994] O.J. L11/1. *Cf.* the equality of official languages in dealings with the Community Plant Variety Office (Art. 34(2) and (3) of Regulation No. 2100/94). See Gundel, "Zur Sprachenregelung bei den EG-Agenturen—Abschied auf Raten von der Regel der 'Allsprachigkeit' der Gemeinschaft im Verkehr mit dem Bürger?" (2001) EuR. 776–783.

[697] CFI, Case T–120/99 *Kik v Office for Harmonisation in the Internal Market* [2001] E.C.R. II–2235, para. 61, as upheld by ECJ (judgment of September 9, 2003), Case C–361/01 P *Kik v Office for Harmonisation in the Internal Market*, not yet reported, paras 44–49.

[698] See also CFI Rules of Procedure, Art. 131, for the language regime applicable to disputes relating to intellectual property rights.

[699] Art. 98 of Regulation No. 6/2002 of December 12, 2003 on Community designs ([2002] O.J. L3/1).

appropriate and proportionate linguistic solution to the difficulties arising where parties with different languages cannot agree on the language to be used. In so far as direct proceedings between the Office and the applicant can be conducted in the language of the applicant, the rules on use of languages in the Office are therefore not in breach of the principle of equal treatment.[700]

G. Transparency and Access to Documents

10–159 **Transparency.** According to Art. 1, second para., of the EU Treaty, decisions in the Union are "taken as openly as possible". Openness of decision-making applies as regards the operation of the European Parliament and, to a lesser extent, of the Council and the Commission (see paras 16–015–16–016). As far as officials of Community institutions are concerned, the recent reform of the Staff Regulations has replaced the general duty of confidentiality by a prohibition of the unauthorised disclosure of information received in the line of duty unless that information has already been made public or is accessible to the public (see para. 10–152).

10–160 **Access to documents.** Since 1991 the debate on the need for the Union to be "transparent" has concentrated on citizens' ability to have access to documents issued by the institutions or in their possession.[701] As a result of the Treaty of Amsterdam, access to documents was enshrined in Treaty law. Article 255 of the EC Treaty gives any citizen of the Union and any natural or legal person residing or having its registered office in a Member State a right of access to European Parliament, Council and Commission documents. General principles and limits on grounds of public or private interest governing this right of access are determined in Regulation No. 1049/2001 adopted by the European Parliament and the Council in accordance with Art. 251 of the EC Treaty.[702] That regulation builds upon

---

[700] CFI, Case T–120/99 *Kik v Office for Harmonisation in the Internal Market* [2001] E.C.R. II–2235, paras 62–63, as upheld by ECJ (judgment of September 9, 2003), Case C–361/01 P *Kik v Office for Harmonisation in the Internal Market*, not yet reported, paras 82–96.

[701] See Declaration (No.17) to the EU Treaty on the right of access to information and the Birmingham Declaration of October 16, 1992—A Community close to its citizens (1992) 10 EC Bull. point I.8 (see para. 16–015). For a general discussion, see Bradley, "La transparence de l'Union européenne: une évidence ou un trompe l'oeil?" (1999) C.D.E. 283–360; Curtin, "Citizens' fundamental right of access to EU information: an evolving digital *passepartout*?" (2000) C.M.L.R. 7–41; Harden, "Citizenship and Information" (2001) E.Publ.L 165–193.

[702] Regulation (EC) No. 1049/2001 of the European Parliament and the Council of May 30, 2001 regarding public access to European Parliament, Council and Commission documents, [2001] O.J. L145/43. See De Leeuw, "The Regulation on public access to European Parliament, Council and Commission documents in the European Union: are citizens better off?" (2003) E.L.R. 324–348; Schram, "Openbaarheid van Europese bestuursdocumenten" (2003) N.J.Wb. 581–592; Bartelt and Zeitler, "Zugang zu Dokumenten der EU" (2003) EuR. 487–503; Schauss, "L'accès du citoyen aux documents des institutions

the access to documents regulated by the Council and the Commission by a joint code of conduct and internal decisions,[703] on which the Community Court has repeatedly had occasion to rule, in particular in order to determine whether, in exercising their discretion, the institutions had genuinely balanced the interests of citizens in gaining access to their documents against any interest of their own in maintaining the confidentiality of their deliberations.[704] The regulation also applies to bodies with legal personality established pursuant to the EC Treaty.[705]

Refusal of access. As far as documents drawn up or received by an **10–161** institution and in its possession[706] are concerned, Regulation No. 1049/2001 provides that the institutions and bodies are to refuse access to a document

---

communautaires" (2003) J.T.D.E. 1–8; Kranenenborg, "De Eurowob in de hand, de EU transparant?" (2002) S.E.W. 447–456; Daalder, "Net op de valreep: de Europese Unie stelt de Eurowob vast" (2001) N.J.B. 1419–1425; Wägenbaur, "Der Zugang zu EU-Dokumenten—Transparenz zum Anfassen" (2001) Eu.Z.W. 680–685. When the European Parliament, the Council and the Commission act in pursuance of the EAEC Treaty, they should draw guidance from the regulation; see recital 5 in the preamble to the regulation and Declaration (No.41) annexed to the Treaty of Amsterdam on the provisions relating to transparency, access to documents and the fight against fraud, [1997] O.J. C340/140. For the importance of the right of access to documents, see the earlier case, ECJ, C–58/94 *Netherlands v Council* [1996] E.C.R. I–2169, paras 34–37. Since Art. 255 of the EC Treaty requires further implementing measures, that article does not have direct effect: CFI, Case T–191/99 *Petrie v Commission* [2001] E.C.R. II–3677, paras 34–35.

703 Code of Conduct of December 6, 1993 concerning public access to Council and Commission documents, [1993] O.J. L340/41 (corrigendum in [1993] O.J. L23/34; for its legal force, see ns to para. 17–149, *infra*); Council Decision 93/731/EC of December 20, 1993 ([1993] O.J. L340/43), Council Decision 2001/320/EC of April 9, 2001 ([2001] O.J. L111/29) and Commission Decision 94/90/ECSC, EC, Euratom of February 8, 1994 ([1994] O.J. L46/58).

704 See, *e.g.* CFI, Case T–194/94 *Carvel and Guardian Newspapers v Council* [1995] E.C.R. II–2765, paras 62–80; CFI, Case T–105/95 *WWF UK v Commission* [1997] E.C.R. II–313, para. 59; ECJ, Case C–353/99 P *Council v Hautala* [2001] E.C.R. I–9565, paras 21–31. For the obligation to state the reason for which access is refused, see, in particular, CFI, Case T–105/95 *WWF UK v Commission* [1997] E.C.R. II–313, paras 66–78; CFI, Case T–124/96 *Interporc v Commission* [1998] E.C.R. II–231, paras 46–57; CFI, Case T–174/95 *Svenska Journalistförbundet v Council* [1998] E.C.R. II–2289, paras 109–127 (annulment of insufficiently reasoned decisions); for confirmation that Decision 93/731 also applied to Council documents relating to non-Community activities, see CFI, Case T–174/95 *Svenska Journalistförbundet v Council* [1998] E.C.R. II–2289, paras 81–86.

705 See the amendments made by the Council to this effect on July 22, 2003 in the various regulations establishing such bodies ([2003] O.J. L245).

706 See Art. 2(3) of Regulation No.1049/2001. Under the former rules, access to a document of which the institution itself was not the originator had to be sought from its author, see CFI, Case T–92/98 *Interporc v Commission* [1999] E.C.R. II–3521, paras 65–72, upheld by ECJ, Case C–41/00 P *Interporc v Commission* [2003] E.C.R. I–2125, paras 34–59. Under the regulation, a Member State may request the Commission or the Council not to disclose a document originating from that Member State without its prior agreement: Regulation No.1049/2001, Art. 4(5). The public's right of access to documents does not imply a duty on the part of the institution to reply to any request for information from an individual: CFI (order of October 27, 1999), Case T–106/99 *Meyer v Commission* [1999] E.C.R. II–3273, para. 35. If a document has already been released and is easily accessible, it is sufficient for the institution to inform the applicant how to obtain the requested document: Regulation No.1049/2001, Art. 10(2). See also CFI (order of October 27, 1999), Case T–106/99 *Meyer v Commission* [1999] E.C.R. II–3273, para. 39 (access to documents is not applicable where the documents have already been published in the *Official Journal*).

so as to protect certain interests, namely: (a) the public interest as regards public security, defence and military matters, international relations or the financial, monetary or economic policy of the Community or a Member State, and (b) privacy and the integrity of the individual.[707] Unless there is an overriding public interest in disclosure, access to a document is also to be refused where disclosure would undermine the protection of: (a) commercial interests of a natural or legal person, including intellectual property, (b) court proceedings and legal advice,[708] or (c) the purpose of inspections, investigations and audits.[709] An institution or body may also refuse access to internal and preparatory documents if disclosure of the document would seriously undermine the institution's decision-making process, unless there is an overriding public interest in disclosure.[710] Those

---

[707] Regulation No. 1049/2001, Art. 4(1). As regards international relations, see the earlier decision in CFI, Case T–204/99 *Mattila v Council and Commission* [2001] E.C.R. II–2265, paras 63–69.

[708] Regulation No. 1049/2001, Art. 4(2). As far as the exception for "court proceedings" is concerned, access cannot be precluded generally for documents that have been drawn up by an institution for specific judicial proceedings. Where the Commission has received a request for access to documents which it has supplied to a national court in the context of its co-operation with national courts in applying competition law, it must verify whether those documents constitute legal or economic analyses drafted on the basis of data supplied by the national court and whether their disclosure would constitute an infringement of national law. In the event of doubt, it must consult the national court and refuse access only if that court objects to disclosure of the documents: ECJ, Joined Cases C–174/98 P and C–189/98 P *Kingdom of the Netherlands and Van der Wal v Commission* [2000] E.C.R. I–1, paras 20–33. *cf.* CFI, Case T–92/98 *Interporc v Commission* [1999] E.C.R. II–3521, paras 40–42 (exception for "court proceedings" covers documents drawn up solely for specific judicial proceedings). See also CFI (order of the President of March 3, 1998), T–610/97 R *Carlsen v Council* [1998] E.C.R. II–485, paras 43–53 (on account of the maintenance of legal certainty and stability of Community law, access may be refused to internal legal opinions).

[709] Regulation No. 1049/2001, Art. 4(2). See CFI, Case T–20/99 *Denkavit Nederland v Commission* [2000] E.C.R. II–3011 (refusal of access to an inspection document connected with an investigation not yet concluded by the Commission). In order to safeguard the aim of inspections and investigations, no access may be granted to documents which undertakings provide to the Commission on condition that they are kept confidential. In order to prevent a breach of confidentiality affecting the proper functioning of infringement proceedings under Art. 226 of the EC Treaty, the Court of First Instance has held that access to documents relating to the investigation must be refused: CFI, Case T–105/95 *WWF UK v Commission* [1997] E.C.R. II–313, para. 63; CFI, Case T–309/97 *The Bavarian Lager Company v Commission* [1999] E.C.R. II–3217, paras 45–46 (refusal during the inspection and investigation stage); CFI, Case T–191/99 *Petrie v Commission* [2001] E.C.R. II–3677, paras 67–69 (refusal after institution of proceedings in the Court of Justice). For criticism of the lack of access to the finding of an infringement and the reasoned opinion, see Krämer, "Access to Letters of Formal Notice and Reasoned Opinions in Environmental Law Matters" (2003) E.Env.L.Rev. 197–203.

[710] Regulation No. 1049/2001, Art. 4(3). Accordingly, an institution cannot refuse to grant access to documents pertaining to its deliberations merely on the basis that they contain information relating to positions taken by representatives of the Member States: CFI, Case T–111/00 *British American Tobacco International v Commission* [2001] E.C.R. II–2997, paras 52–57.

exceptions apply only where the risk of the public interest being undermined is reasonably foreseeable and not purely hypothetical.[711]

Where a document includes items of information falling within one of the grounds for refusing access, the principle of proportionality requires the institutions or bodies to consider granting access to the items for which those exceptions do not apply.[712] Within 15 working days of receipt of a written application, the institution or body must either grant access or refuse it totally or partially. If an application for access is refused or unanswered, the applicant must seek, by means of a confirmatory application, a formal refusal, against which an action for annulment will lie and/or a complaint may be made to the European Ombudsman.[713] The regulation requires each institution or body to keep a register and also provides for special treatment for sensitive documents.[714] Each institution or body is to elaborate in its own Rules of Procedure specific provisions regarding access to its documents.[715]

In principle, the exceptions relating to access to documents apply for a maximum period of 30 years. In the case of documents covered by the exceptions relating to privacy or commercial interests and in the case of sensitive documents, the exceptions may, if necessary, continue to apply after this period.[716] Subject to these limitations, documents of historical or administrative value of the institutions and bodies may be consulted after the expiry of the 30-year period in the institutions' historical archives.[717]

---

[711] CFI, Case T–211/00 *Kuijer v Council* [2002] E.C.R. II–485, paras 56–70 (adverse reports about human rights in third countries are not necessarily prejudicial to the Union's relations with those countries).

[712] ECJ, Case C–353/99 P *Council v Hautala* [2001] E.C.R. I–9565, paras 21–31, upholding CFI, Case T–14/98 *Hautala v Council* [1999] E.C.R. II–2489, paras 75–88, and ECJ (judgment of January 22, 2004), Case C–353/01 P *Mattila v Council and Commission*, not yet reported, paras 29–32.

[713] Regulation No. 1049/2001, Arts 6, 7 and 8.

[714] Art. 9 of Regulation No. 1049/2001 provides for the classification of documents as "top secret", "secret" or "confidential". See to that effect the earlier Council Decision 2000/527/EC of August 14, 2000 ([2000] O.J. L212/9) and Council Decision 2001/264/EC of March 19, 2001 adopting the Council's security regulations ([2001] O.J. L101/1).

[715] See Art. 255(3) of the EC Treaty and, for bodies with legal personality, the various regulations establishing them (as amended; n.705, *supra*). For the implementation thereof, see Art. 97 of the EP Rules of Procedure and the Decision of the Bureau of the European Parliament of November 28, 2001 ([2001] O.J. C374/1); Council Decision 2001/840/EC adding as Annex III (now Annex II) to the Rules of Procedure specific provisions regarding public access to Council documents ([2001] O.J. L313/40); the provisions appended as an annex to the Rules of Procedure adopted by the Commission by Decision of December 5, 2001 ([2001] O.J. L345/94); Decision 2003/603/EC of the European Economic and Social Committee of July 1, 2003 ([2003] O.J. L205/19), Decision No.64/2003 of the Committee of the Regions of February 11, 2003 ([2003] O.J. L160/96) and the rules on public access to documents of the European Central Bank ([2004] O.J. L80/42) and of the European Investment Bank ([2002] O.J. C292/10).

[716] Regulation No. 1049/2001, Art. 4(7).

[717] See Council Regulation (EEC, Euratom) No. 354/83 of February 1, 1998 concerning the opening to the public of the historical archives of the European Economic Community and the European Atomic Energy Community ([1983] O.J. L431), as radically amended by Regulation (EC, Euratom) 1700/2003, ([2003] O.J. L243/1). See the introduction to the source material.

THE INSTITUTIONS AND BODIES OF THE UNION

H. Protection of personal data

10–162 European Data-protection Supervisor. Community legislation provides protection for all persons with regard to the processing and free movement of their personal data.[718] Pursuant to Art. 286 of the EC Treaty, an independent supervisory body, the European Data-protection Supervisor, monitors compliance with this legislation on the part of the institutions and bodies of the Community.[719] The European Parliament and the Council appoints by common accord the European Data-protection Supervisor, who is to act completely independently, assisted by a secretariat.[720]

---

[718] See the harmonisation of national law effected on the basis of Art. 95 of the EC Treaty by Directive 95/96/EC of the European Parliament of the Council of October 24, 1995 on the protection of individuals with regard to the processing of personal data and on the free movement of such data ([1995] O.J. L281/31) and Directive 2002/58/EC of the European Parliament and of the Council of July 12, 2002 concerning the processing of personal data and the protection of privacy in the electronic communications sector (Directive on privacy and electronic communications) ([2002] O.J. L201/37) as well as, with regard to Community institutions and bodies, Regulation (EC) No. 45/2001 of the European Parliament and of the Council of December 18, 2000 on the protection of individuals with regard to the processing of personal data by the Community institutions and bodies and on the free movement of such data, adopted on the basis of Art. 286 of the EC Treaty ([2001] O.J. L8/1). See Feral, "Un pas supplémentaire vers la reconnaissance et la protection d'un droit fondamental dans l'Union européenne: le règlement (CE) n° 45/2001" (2001) R.M.C.U.E. 475–485; Brühann, "La protection des données à caractère personnel et la Communauté européenne" (1999) R.M.C.U.E. 328–341; Maiani, "Le cadre réglementaire des traitements de données personnelles effectués au sein de l'Union européenne" (2002) R.T.D.E. 283–309.

[719] Arts 41 et seq. of Regulation 45/2001 (n.718, supra); see also the obligation to this effect in Art. 8 of the Charter of Fundamental Rights of the European Union.

[720] For the regulations governing the duties of the Brussels-based European Data-protection Supervisor and the appointment procedure, see also Decision 1247/2002/EC of the European Parliament, the Council and the Commission of July 1, 2002, [2002] O.J. L183/1. The website is *www.edps.eu.int/*.

CHAPTER 11

THE MEMBER STATES OF THE UNION

National authorities. After the establishment of the European **11–001**
Communities and the European Union, the national authorities remain
continuously involved in the adoption, implementation and enforcement of
decisions, both within the institutions of the Union and as a result of the
exercise of their own functions.

I. THE MEMBER STATES AS CONSTITUENT AUTHORITY

Requirement of ratification. The Treaties on which the Union is founded **11–002**
were concluded by representatives of the national governments. In each
Member State, the Parliament has to approve the Treaties (sometimes after
a referendum) before the government can deposit the instrument of
ratification. Moreover, any amendment of the Treaties is determined by
common accord between the representatives of the Member States and
does not enter into force until it has been ratified by all Member States "in
accordance with their respective constitutional requirements".[1] The
Treaties also prescribe this procedure for a number of decisions with
"constitutional" status at Community level.[2] Accordingly, each Member
State's constituent authority determines who is to decide on membership of
the Union and on the related transfer of national powers.[3]

Domestic organisation of ratification. Since the subject-matter of the **11–003**
decision is the outcome of negotiations between the national governments,
the decision is confined to approval or rejection and there is no possibility
of making any changes. If a Member State rejects the proposed text, that
text may be amended only by common accord between the national

---

[1] EU Treaty, Art. 48. See the discussion of the entry into effect of the Treaties and of
amending Treaties (paras 7–001 and 7–004—7–008, *supra*); see also the procedure for
acceding to the Union (EU Treaty, Art. 49; para. 8–009, *supra*).
[2] These include the Acts on the direct election of the European Parliament and the
Communities' own resources (see para. 7–008, *supra*).
[3] It is a question as to by which (direct or representative) manner, by which (legislative or
executive) body and at which (national or possibly devolved) level the decision is taken. For
the question as to whether Community law subjects that ultimate right of decision of the
Member States (*Kompetenz-Kompetenz*) to formal and substantive constraints, see
paras 7–010—7–011, *supra*.

governments and whether it is ultimately adopted depends on its being approved in all the Member States. A Member State is at liberty to frame its constitutional law in such a way that the government has to consult the national parliament before approving the proposed text[4] or—conversely—that certain "constituent" decisions are deemed to have been already approved by a government act.[5] By the same token, a Member State may make ratification of a Treaty amendment dependent upon the approval of all the federated States or regions competent to that end.[6] In practice, some Member States hold a referendum which has to have a favourable outcome before constituent acts, such as Treaty amendments, can be ratified.[7] Applicant Member States have in many cases held a referendum on the Treaty by which they accede to the Union[8] and likewise Member States not wishing to take a major decision with regard to the activities of the Union without the express approval of the people.[9]

II.   The Member States as Actors in Decision-Making

A.   The role of the national governments

11–004 **Interaction between administrations.** Decision-making in the context of the Union (and the Communities) is based on action by the Member States.

---

[4] See Lepka and Terrebus, "Les ratifications nationales, manifestations d'un projet politique européen—la face cachée du Traité d'Amsterdam" (2003) R.T.D.E. 365, at 382–386. Generally, the national parliament has at most the right to be informed during the negotiations and to have cognisance of the draft Treaty before it is signed. See Art. 168 of the Belgian Constitution and the commentary by Ingelaere, "De Europeesrechtlijke raakvlakken van de nieuwe wetgeving inzake de internationale bevoegdheid van de Belgische Gemeenschappen en Gewesten" (1994) S.E.W. 67, at 79–81; Louis and Alen, "La Constitution et la participation à la Communauté européenne" (1994) B.T.I.R. 81, at 84.

[5] Thus under UK constitutional law, the government may ratify Treaties without parliamentary approval being needed. However, under the European Parliamentary Elections Act 1978, an Act of Parliament is required in order to ratify any Treaty which confers additional powers on the European Parliament: Denza, "La ratification du Traité de Maastricht par le Royaume-Uni" (1994) R.M.C.U.E. 172, at 173.

[6] This was the case in Belgium as regards the ratification of the EU Treaty (para. 3–011, *supra*), the Treaty of Amsterdam (para. 3–018, *supra*) and the Treaty of Nice (para. 3–023, *supra*). This does not mean of itself that the regions are part of the "constituent authority". If the national government ratifies a Treaty amendment without awaiting the requisite approvals, the Member State is bound as a party to the Treaty. For the involvement of decentralised bodies in the negotiations resulting in the Treaty of Nice, see Wiedmann, "Der Vertrag von Nizza—Genesis einer Reform" (2001) EuR. 185, at 196–202.

[7] In this way, referendums were held to approve the Single European Act (para. 3–006, *supra*), the EU Treaty (para. 3–011, *supra*), the Treaty of Amsterdam (para. 3–018, *supra*) and the Treaty of Nice (para. 3–023, *supra*). In some cases, the decision to ratify a Treaty was subjected to a referendum; in others, the referendum related to the amendment to the Constitution which was required in order to ratify; see Lepka and Terrebus (n.4, *supra*), at 378–382.

[8] para. 1–021, *supra*.

[9] See the referendum held in Italy on June 18, 1989 on the status of Italian Members of the European Parliament and the referendums held in Denmark on September 28, 2002 and in Sweden on September 14, 2003 on the introduction of the single currency (paras 5–222 and 5–233, *supra*). For a study of the various referendums, see Roberts-Thomson, "EU Treaty referendums and the European Union" (2001) European Integration 105–137.

Ministers in national (or regional)[10] governments, in their capacity as members of the Council, take the main decisions both in the context of the Communities and as far as intergovernmental forms of policy and co-operation are concerned. National civil servants and Community officials meet in order to carry out preparatory work for decision-making in the Council (see paras 10–0148—10–052). This gives rise to a relationship which facilitates the subsequent implementation of acts of the Council. In many cases, the same national civil servants are members of committees which supervise *ex post* the way in which the Commission or other Community bodies implement those acts, or they may prepare the necessary implementing measures themselves. The implementation of acts adopted by the Council on an inter-governmental basis even falls mainly to the Member States. This interaction between national civil servants and Community officials gives the lie to the widespread idea that decision-making is in the hands of "Eurocrats".[11]

In the case of some acts, the Community Treaties and the EU Treaty make express recourse to the "governments of the Member States".[12] In such a case, the representatives of the national governments[13] adopt the act in question, yet in coming together to adopt it they do not constitute a body of the Union· Consequently, a meeting of the representatives of the governments of the Member States at the level of Heads of State or Government has to be distinguished from the European Council (see para. 10–039).

B. THE ROLE OF THE NATIONAL PARLIAMENTS

Indirect involvement. The national (or regional) parliaments are not **11–005** directly involved in the formulation of acts of the Union (or of the Communities). Nevertheless in some respects they do play a role of their own before such acts obtain their full force. This is true in the first place of a number of acts having constitutional status (see para. 11–002). Next there is the case of directives, where the choice of the form and methods of

---

[10] For the involvement of devolved public authorities, see paras 11–013—11–016, *infra*.

[11] See Schockweiler, "La dimension humaine et sociale de la Communauté européenne" (1993) 4 R.M.U.E. 11, at 35–36. For an assessment from a "democratic" standpoint, see para. 16–004 *et seq.* See also Buitendijk and Van Schendelen, "Brussels Advisory Committees: A Channel for Influence", (1995) E.L.R. 37–56.

[12] See the references to the "governments of the Member States" (EC Treaty, Art. 79; Art. 214(2) and (3); Art. 215, second para. ; Art. 223, first para. ; Art. 225(3); Art. 289), a "conference of representatives of the governments of the Member States" (EU Treaty, Art. 48) and the "governments of the Member States at the level of Heads of State or Government" (EC Treaty, Art. 112(2)(b); Art. 117(1), second subpara. ; ESCB Statute, Art. 37). See also EC Treaty, Art. 37(1), which refers to a "conference of the Member States".

[13] The representatives of the governments do not have to be members of government. For instance, on April 27, 1994 the governments left it to the Permanent Representatives to appoint a Member of the Commission for the remainder of his predecessor's term of office (Decision 94/282 of April 27, 1994, [1994] O.J. L121/41; corrigendum L131/26): see *Europe*, No.6220, April 28, 1994, 5. See also EC Treaty, Art. 207(1).

attaining the result to be achieved is left to the "national authorities" (EC Treaty, Art. 249, third para.).[14] It often falls to national (or regional) parliaments to transpose a directive into national law (see para. 11–011). PJCC framework decisions also leave the choice of the form and methods of achieving the intended result to the "national authorities" (EU Treaty, Art. 34(2)(b)).

11–006 **Scrutiny of governmental action in the Council.** Furthermore, national parliaments may nevertheless influence decision-making at Union level by bringing pressure to bear on members of the Council, who are answerable to them. In practice, the influence of the national parliament varies greatly depending on the Member State considered. Most parliaments have a standing committee to scrutinise "European" business. In bicameral systems, each of the chambers of Parliament may have its own committee[15] or the two chambers may jointly set up a common committee.[16] In other parliaments the normal departmental committees deal with the adoption, transposition and subsequent implementation of acts of the Union.

In any event, parliamentary scrutiny of the role played by the national government in decision-making is possible only if:

(1) the parliament is in possession of the necessary information concerning the activities of the Union;

(2) influence may actually be brought to bear on a member of the Council; and

---

[14] ECJ, Case 102/79 *Commission v Belgium* [1980] E.C.R. 1473, para. 12. For the legal force of a directive in the event that a Member State fails to implement it, see para. 17–024 *et seq.*

[15] See, *e.g.* the commitees set up in Austria by the *Nationalrat* and the *Bundesrat*, in France by the *Assemblée nationale* and the *Sénat*, in Germany by the *Bundesrat* and *Bundesrat* (set up in the wake of the discussion about the EU Treaty pursuant to amendments to the Basic Law: Arts 45 and 52(3)(a), respectively) and in the UK by the House of Commons (Select Committee on European Legislation) and the House of Lords (Select Committee on the European Union). In the UK, according to the First Special Report of the House of Commons Select Committee on Modernisation of November 1, 1999 (HC 865), major changes have begun to be implemented in the process of scrutiny of European legislation. The Committee on European Legislation of the House of Commons has been replaced by the European Scrutiny Committee with enlarged terms of reference. The European Scrutiny Committee is appointed to examine European Union documents and: (a) to report its opinion on the legal and political importance of each such document and, where it considers appropriate, to report also on the reasons for its opinion and on any matters of principle, policy or law which may be affected; (b) to make recommendations for the further consideration of any such document pursuant to Standing Order No.119 (European Standing Committees); and (c) to consider any issue arising upon any such document or group of documents, or related matters. See "The European Scrutiny System in the House of Commons, A short guide for Members of Parliament by the staff of the European Scrutiny Committee", which is available, in the same way as all Select Committee reports, on the internet at *www.parliament.uk.*

[16] See, for instance, the committee set up by the two chambers of the Parliament jointly in Belgium, in Ireland and in Spain. In the Netherlands, only the *Tweede Kamer* has created a European affairs committee; see Del Grosso, *Parlement en Europese integratie* (Kluwer, Deventer, 2000), 293 pp. Furthermore, a standing committees on European affairs has been set up by the Danish *Folketing,* by the Finnish, Greek and Portuguese Parliament, and by the Swedish *Riksdag.*

(3) that member may be called to account for how he or she voted in the Council.

As far as all these matters are concerned, the impact of a given national parliament will depend on what powers are conferred upon it under domestic law. That having been said, the parliamentary scrutiny exercised at national level plays a part in determining the democratic character of the operation of the Union (see para. 16–004). The EU Constitution will therefore introduce mechanisms designed to ensure effective scrutiny by national parliaments of the positions adopted by the national governments within the Council.[17]

(1) **Right of national parliament to be informed.** Where the Commission **11–007** presents a legislative proposal to the Council, it will generally already have contacted the Member States. A Protocol to the Treaty of Amsterdam provides that all Commission consultation documents (green and white papers and communications) are to be promptly forwarded to the national parliaments.[18] Commission proposals for legislation are to be made available in good time "so that the government of each Member State may ensure that its national parliament receives them as appropriate".[19] Yet this does not give the national parliament any autonomous right of information. In some Member States, the government is bound under domestic law to provide the national parliament or the competent parliamentary committee with all Commission proposals[20] and to inform

---

[17] In addition, national parliaments may give their opinion as to whether the draft legislative acts comply with the respect of the principle of subsidiarity, see para. 5–035, *supra*. See Weatherill, "Using national parliaments to improve scrutiny of the limits of EU action" (2003) E.L.R. 909–912.

[18] Protocol (No.9) to the EU Treaties and the Community Treaties on the role of national parliaments in the European Union, annexed by the Amsterdam Treaty to those Treaties, [1997] O.J. C340/113, point 1. This gives binding force to Declaration (No.13) annexed to the EU Treaty on the role of national parliaments in the European Union, under which the national governments are to ensure that national parliaments receive Commission proposals for legislation in good time for information or possible examination.

[19] *ibid.*, point 2 (which provides that legislation is as defined by the Council in accordance with Art. 207(3) of the EC Treaty). In addition, the national parliaments may put their views across through the Conference of European Affairs Committees (COSAC), *ibid.* points 4–7 (see para. 16–012, *infra*). On January 27, 2003, COSAC adopted guidelines for relations between governments and Parliaments on Community issues, see [2003] O.J. C154/1.

[20] In Belgium, the government has entered into such an obligation *vis-à-vis* both chambers of the parliament and the parliaments of the Communities and Regions (Art. 92 *quater* of the special law of August 8, 1980 on institutional reform, see Louis and Alen, n.4, *supra*, at 84–85). Commission legislative proposals are also made available to the Danish *Folketing*, the German *Bundesrat* (para. 2 of the *Gesetz zur EEA, BGBl.* II, 1986, 1102), the House of Commons and the House of Lords, both Chambers of the Austrian Parliament, the Netherlands *Tweede Kamer*, the French *Sénat* and *Assemblée* (Law of May 10, 1990 and Art. 88–4 of the Constitution), the Italian Parliament (*Legge-Fabbri* of April 16, 1987), the Portuguese Parliament (Law No.20/94 of June 15, 1994) and the Finnish Parliament. For the practice in Belgium, see Gilliaux, *Les directives européennes et le droit belge* (Huylant, Brussels, 1997) 105–110 ; for the Netherlands, see Hessel and Mortelmans, *Het recht van de*

parliament of the stance which it intends to take in the Council. In the United Kingdom, all "European Union documents" must be laid before Parliament within two working days of their arrival at the Foreign and Commonwealth Office.[21] In 1998 the Leader of the UK House of Commons published measures to ensure more effective scrutiny of "laws being negotiated in Brussels" as part of a string of measures to modernise the work of the House of Commons. These included closer examination of initiatives under the CFSP, action in the field of JHA co-operation and measures signed up to by Heads of Government at European Councils.[22] As a result, texts of CFSP statements, declarations, common positions and joint actions are also to be made available to both Houses.[23] In the Netherlands, the government has to publish draft decisions to be taken under Title IV of the EC Treaty or Title VI of the EU Treaty and submit them to the parliament before they are adopted.[24] In several of the Member States which recently acceded to the Union, the Constitution was amended

Europese Gemeenschappen en de decentrale overheden in Nederland (Tjeenk Willink, Deventer, 1997) at 95–97; for France, see Sauron, "Le contrôle parlementaire de l'activité gouvernementale en matière communautaire en France" (1999) R.T.D.E. 171–200.

[21] The expression 'European Union document' covers: (i) any proposal under the Community Treaties for legislation by the Council or the Council acting jointly with the European Parliament; (ii) any document which is published for submission to the European Council, the Council or the European Central Bank; (iii) any proposal for a common strategy, a joint action or a common position under Title V of the Treaty on European Union which is prepared for submission to the Council or to the European Council; (iv) any proposal for a common position, framework decision, decision or a convention under Title VI of the Treaty on European Union which is prepared for submission to the Council; (v) any document (not falling within (ii), (iii) or (iv) above) which is published by one Union institution for or with a view to submission to another Union institution and which does not relate exclusively to consideration of any proposal for legislation; (vi) any other document relating to European Union matters deposited in the House by a Minister of the Crown. See the House of Commons Standing Order No.143.

[22] News Release of the President of the Council and the Leader of the House of Commons of January 27, 1998, ref. CAB 14/98.

[23] But in the vast majority of cases it is not deemed appropriate to lay drafts of CFSP documents before the House unless they fall within existing scrutiny guidelines. Documents not subject to confidentiality considerations and meeting one of the following three criteria might also be laid before Parliament at an early stage: (a) those deemed significant, particularly where the rights and duties of individuals may be affected; (b) those which give rise to an eventual need for UK legislation; and (c) those which impose legally binding commitments on the UK. As regards Title VI of the EU Treaty, the Government is committed to providing parliament with the first full text of any convention which, if agreed, would give rise to UK primary legislation. It will also provide other "significant" documents (subject to security or operational considerations).

[24] Arts 3 and 4 of the *Rijkswet* of December 19, 2001 ratifying the Treaty of Nice, *Stb.*, 2001, 617 (see, previously Art. 3(1) of the *Rijkswet* of December 17, 1992 ratifying the EU Treaty, *Stb.*, 1992, 692, and Art. 3 of the *Rijkswet* of December 24, 1998 ratifying the Treaty of Amsterdam, *Stb.*, 1998, 737). If, on account of exceptional circumstances of an imperative nature, the content of the draft is secret or confidential, it is only laid before the parliament for its confidential information: *ibid.*, Art. 3(2). As far as Title IV of the EC Treaty is concerned, such notification is not obligatory for acts adopted by the European Parliament and the Council under the co-decision procedure or for acts adopted pursuant to Art. 67(3) of the EC Treaty: *ibid.*, Art. 4(1). For parliamentary involvement in JHA co-operation, see Curtin and Pouw, "Samenwerking op het gebied van justitie en binnenlandse zaken in de Europese Unie: pre-Maastricht-nostalgie?" (1995) S.E.W. 579, at 596–599.

not only to allow for accession but also to impose on the national governement a duty to inform the national parliament in advance on the decisions to be taken at the level of the Union.[25] In any case, the duty to inform the national parliaments results in numerous documents being sent to these parliaments, where the information may be sifted by the general "European" committee or by the normal departmental committees (which is often more effective).

The EU Constitution will confer on the national parliaments an autonomous right to receive legislative proposals. Under a Protocol annexed to the EU Constitution, all proposals and other draft legislative acts presented to the European Parliament and to the Council must simultaneously be sent to (both chambers of) the national parliaments.[26] In addition, the national parliaments must be informed in advance if the Commission is to submit a proposal for application of the flexibility clause (corresponding to the current Art. 308 of the EC Treaty)[27] or if the European Council intends to make use of the possibility to introduce, in a given field, applicability of qualified majority voting or applicability of the ordinary legislative procedure.[28]

(2) Influence on the national government. In order to allow national **11–008** parliaments to take a position on legislative proposals to be discussed in the Council, a six-week period must elapse between the legislative proposal being made available and the date when it is placed on an agenda for the Council (see para. 14–016). As to the influence of parliamentary scrutiny on the position taken by the government, Denmark has organised its governmental structure in such a way that a Minister must defend in the Council the point of view approved by the parliamentary committee on European affairs.[29] The Finnish and Swedish Governments are placed under a similar obligation *vis-à-vis* their national parliaments.[30] In order to defend the interests of the *Länder*, the German *Bundesrat* may commit the

---

[25] See Art. 10b of the Czech Constitution, Art. 35/A of the Hungarian Constitution, Art. 3a of the Slovak Constitution and Arts 3–4 of the Constitutional Act on the Membership of Lithuania in the European Union.

[26] Art. 2 of the Protocol annexed to the EU Constitution on the role of national parliaments in the European Union.

[27] Art. I–18(2) of the EU Constitution.

[28] Art. 6 of the Protocol on the role of national parliaments in the European Union (n.26, *supra*), which refers to the powers that Art. IV–444 of the EU Constitution confers on the European Council in that respect.

[29] The Minister submits a draft negotiating mandate to the parliamentary committee, in which each Member has the same number of votes as the number of Members of parliament which he or she represents. That mandate constitutes only a political undertaking; see Hagel-Sørensen and Rasmussen, "The Danish Administration and its Interaction with the Community Administration" (1985) C.M.L.R. 273, at 279–286; Rasmussen, "Über die Durchsetzung des Gemeinschaftsrechts in Dänemark" (1985) EuR. 66–74.

[30] Aalto, "Accession of Finland to the European Union: First Remarks" (1995) E.L.R. 625–626; Bernitz, "Sweden and the European Union: On Sweden's Implementation and Application of European Law" (2001) C.M.L.R. 903, at 915.

Federal Government to follow its opinion in certain circumstances.[31] In Austria, depending on whether the matter comes within the competence of the *Länder* or the federal authorities, the Council representative is bound by a common position adopted by the *Länder* or one of the federal legislative chambers.[32] The Netherlands parliament has to agree to acts of the Council to be adopted under Title IV of the EC Treaty and Title VI of the EU Treaty.[33]

---

[31] Depending on whether the Federal State has exclusive competence, whether it has actually exercised a non-exclusive power in this respect or whether, in contrast, the *Länder* have exclusive competence, Art. 23(5) and (6) of the Basic Law (*Grundgesetz*, as amended prior to ratification of the EU Treaty) provides for a simple opinion of the *Bundesrat*, for an opinion with which the Federal Government has to comply in essential respects (*"massgeblich zu berücksichtigen"*), or for direct participation of a representative of the *Länder* in the Council proceedings. As far as the second type of opinion is concerned, the implementing law of March 12, 1993 (*Gesetz über die Zusammenarbeit von Bund und Ländern in Angelegenheiten der Europäischen Union*) provides that, in the event that there continues to be disagreement with the Federal Government, the *Bundesrat* may resolve by a two-thirds majority to confirm the opinion, whereupon the Federal Government will be bound thereby. It may then adopt a position conflicting with that opinion in the Council only if such action is required in the overriding interests of the State. Some German commentators consider that a binding mandate is contrary to the Basic Law. Since it makes it more difficult to reach a compromise in the Council, it is also argued by some that it is contrary to the Community principle of co-operation in good faith: see Ress, "Die Europäischen Gemeinschaften und der deutsche Föderalismus" (1986) Eu.GR.Z. 549, at 552–554; Wiedmann, "Föderalismus als europäische Utopie. Die Rolle der Regionen aus rechtsvergleichender Sicht. Das Beispiel Deutschlands und Frankreichs" (1992) A.ö.R. 46, at 62; Everling, "Überlegungen zur Struktur der Europäischen Union und zum neuen Europa-Artikel des Grundgesetzes" (1993) D.Vbl. 936, at 946; Badura, "Willensbildung und Beschlußverfahren in der Europäischen Union" (1994) EuR. Beiheft 1, 9, at 16–17 (together with the discussion at 41–42). See also the works cited in n.32 to para. 3–011, *supra*, concerning the amendment of the German Basic Law prior to ratification of the EU Treaty. For a critical commentary of the present arrangements, see Herdegen, "After the TV Judgment of the German Constitutional Court: Decision-making within the EU Council and the German *Länder*" (1995) C.M.L.R. 1369–1384.

[32] In matters coming within the legislative competence of the *Länder*, the representative in the Council is bound in principle by a position on which the *Länder* have reached agreement among themselves. That position may be departed from only on compelling grounds relating to foreign policy and integration. A similar obligation exists with regard to positions adopted by the lower house (*Nationalrat*) in matters coming under the legislative competence of the federal authorities and by the upper house (*Bundesrat*) as regards Community measures having to be implemented by a constitutional law. In discussing measures which would result in an amendment to Austrian constitutional provisions, the Austrian Minister may diverge from the position adopted by the national parliament only if the *Nationalrat* does not intimate its opposition within a specified time. See Seidl-Hohenveldern, "Constitutional Problems involved in Austria's Accession to the EU" (1995) C.M.L.R. 727, at 735–736; Griller, "Verfassungsfragen der österreichischen EU-Mitgliedschaft" (1995) Z.f.RV. 89, at 102–107; Thun-Hohenstein and Cede, *Europarecht—Das Recht der Europäischen Union unter besonderer Berücksichtigung des EU-Beitritts Österreichs* (Manz, Vienna, 1995) 235–237; Egger, "L'Autriche—Etat membre de l'Union européenne. Les effets institutionnels" (1996) R.M.C.U.E. 380, at 383. For the (limited) impact of the binding opinions of the *Nationalrat* in practice, see Pollak and Slominski, "Influencing EU Politics? The Case of the Austrian Parliament" (2003) J.C.M.S. 707–729.

[33] See Art. 3(3) of the *Rijkswet* of December 17, 1992, the *Rijkswet* of December 24, 1998 and the *Rijkswet* of December 19, 2001 (n.24, *supra*), under which the act is deemed to have

In other Member States, the parliament does not have the power to confer a specific mandate on the national government but has a right to be consulted on certain issues before the government defines its position.[34] For example, in the United Kingdom Parliament, pursuant to a House of Commons resolution of October 24, 1990 (which also applies to the House of Lords), Ministers should not give agreement to any proposals for Community legislation which have not been cleared by the European Scrutiny Committee or on which, when they have been recommended by the Committee for debate, the House has yet to reach a resolution.[35] The UK Government has agreed to deposit any JHA document and submit an explanatory memorandum on the same timescale as for deposited EC documents. It does not consider that a formal scrutiny reserve is appropriate in the case of JHA matters, given in particular the need for decisions to be taken rapidly.[36]

(3) Accountability of national government. Even if a government is not **11–009** specifically obliged to inform the national parliament or to take account of its views, the parliament may hold it politically answerable for the positions which it takes up within the Council. One difficulty here is that voting within the Council is secret. As far as its legislative work is concerned, however, the Council has agreed to disclose the outcome of votes (see para. 10–043). As a result, even where decisions are taken by a majority vote in the Council, the national parliaments may see how government ministers have acted.[37] In this connection, the EU Constitution recalls that the governments representing the Member States in the European Council and the Council are "themselves democratically accountable either to their national parliaments, or to their citizens" (Art. I–46(2)).

been approved if, within 15 days of the proposed act being laid before the parliament, one of the Chambers does not express the wish that the proposal be subject to express approval (Art. 3(4)). As far as Title IV of the EC Treaty is concerned, there is no such requirement as regards acts adopted by the European Parliament and the Council under the co-decision procedure or acts adopted by the Council under Art. 67(3) of the EC Treaty: Art. 4(1) of the *Rijkswet* of December 24, 1998 and December 19, 2001. See Besselink, "An Open Constitution and European Integration: The Kingdom of the Netherlands" (1996) S.E.W. 192, at 196; Van Traa, "De rol van het Nederlandse parlement bij de procedures van Titel V en VI van het Verdrag van de Europese Unie", in T.M.C. Asser Instituut, *Diversiteit van de besluitvorming van de Europese Unie* (T.M.C. Asser Instituut,The Hague, 1995), 68–75.

[34] *e.g.* this is true of the German *Bundestag* (Basic Law, Art. 23(3), and the implementing law of March 12, 1993) and of the House of Commons and the House of Lords (see following ns). The former French Prime Minister Balladur entered into a similar undertaking: see *Europe*, No.6264, July 1, 1994, 4; see now the "circulaire du Premier ministre du 13 décembre 1999 relative à l'application de l'article 88–4 de la Constitution"; for an application, see *Europe*, No.6334, October 10–11 1994, 4, and No.6335, October 12, 1994, 1.

[35] The scrutiny reserve resolution is printed with the House's Standing Orders, which are available at *www.parliament.uk.*

[36] See also Newman, "Parliamentary Scrutiny of European Legislation" (1991) E.Bus.L.Rev. 223–227; Denza, "La Chambre des Lords: vingt années d'enquêtes communautaires" (1993) R.M.C.U.E. 740–745; Birkinshaw and Ashbiagbor, "National Participation in Community Affairs: the UK Parliament and the EU" (1996) C.M.L.R. 499–529.

[37] For the limitations to this democratic control, see paras 16–008—16–010, *infra.*

11–010 Scrunity of implementing acts. The option available to national parliaments of securing influence by controlling their government's position in the Council continues in practice to be limited to the legislative activity of the Union. It is impossible for national parliaments to monitor the numerous acts by which the Commission or the Council execute Community legislation.[38] To a certain extent, however, such control is being exercised by civil servants from the various national ministerial departments who monitor the Commission's executive activities under the "comitology" system (see paras 14–054 et seq.).

III. THE MEMBER STATES' ROLE IN IMPLEMENTING TREATY PROVISIONS AND ACTS

11–011 Executing Community and Union law. The Member States are responsible for implementing Community law except where the task has been expressly assigned to a Community institution or body (see para. 14–047). Each Member State itself determines which bodies are to implement Community law (including the transposition of directives) and at what level of authority this is to take place (see para. 14–048). In many Member States this has resulted in changes in the domestic legal system, affecting both the organisation of the national administration and internal constitutional relationships.[39] For instance, in many cases the executive has been entrusted with the task of implementing directives.[40] When new Member

---

[38] In a memorandum dated January 19, 1998 from the President of the Council (the UK having the Presidency at the material time), the UK Government considered that the Commission's implementing legislation does not lend itself to detailed scrutiny because it is too voluminous and often technical, administrative or ephemeral, but that arrangements should be made to maintain an overview of the Commission's delegated legislative role. There could also be more involvement of individual Departmental Select Committees. In its seventh Report, the House of Commons Select Committee on Modernisation considers that scrutiny of Commission legislation is "fine in principle provided that no excessive burden is imposed" thereby. In practice such scrutiny "would operate 2 or 3 times a year" (*i.e.* on a limited scale).

[39] See Snyder, "The Effectiveness of European Community Law: Institutions, Processes, Tools and Techniques" (1993) M.L.R. 19, at 38–39. See especially the position of devolved authorities; para. 11–016, *infra*.

[40] Thus in France the incorporation of numerous directives is left to the executive as a result of the narrow interpretation put on the scope of "*lois*" and the broad interpretation given to the scope of "*règlements*" (Constitution, Arts 34 and 37): Laprat, "Réforme des traités; le risque du double déficit démocratique. Les Parlements nationaux et l'élaboration de la norme communautaire" (1991) R.M.C. 710, at 713. For the practice in Belgium, see Gilliaux (n.20, *supra*). Sometimes, too, the national parliament authorises the government to implement directives. This is the case in Italy, Portugal and Spain: Laprat, *ibid.*, at 713. Under the La Pergola law of March 9, 1989, the Italian Parliament passes an annual "*legge comunitaria*" authorising the government to take the necessary measures in order to transpose Community obligations into national legislation; see Tizzano, "La nouvelle loi italienne pour l'exécution des obligations communautaires" (1990) R.M.C. 532–540; Zampini, "L'Italie, en amont du manquement . . . Un problème de compétences entre l'exécutif, le parlement et les régions" (1994) R.T.D.E. 195–228. *Cf.* the use of orders in council in the UK.

States accede to the Union, the task of adjusting national law to Community law is sometimes left to the national government to carry out by means of subordinate legislation.[41] Article 10 of the EC Treaty puts the Member States under a duty, not only to take all necessary implementing measures, but also to adjust domestic law so as to ensure the effectiveness (*"effet utile"*) of Community law (see para. 5–051). Various public bodies are also caught by that obligation in view of their close organisational or functional connection with the public authorities.[42] However, at Community level it is only the "Member State", represented by the national government, which is liable for any breaches of the obligation to implement Community law.

The execution of non-Community acts also invariably falls to the Member States. But this is an obligation under international law and may not be enforced under Community law (see paras 15–006 and 15–013).

IV. RESOLUTION OF DISPUTES IN THE MEMBER STATES IN CONNECTION WITH THE IMPLEMENTATION AND ENFORCEMENT OF TREATY PROVISIONS AND ACTS

Judicial enforcement of Community law. The national courts play an **11–012** essential part in dealing with Community law. They determine, for instance, all disputes arising in each Member State in relation to the application of Community law.[43] As a result of the decentralised enforcement of Community law, each national court is a "Community court". If necessary, national courts may, and in some circumstances, must make a reference for a preliminary ruling to the Court of Justice.[44] If national judicial authorities

---

[41] In Spain, Law No.47/85 of December 27, 1985 authorised the government to adopt all such *"decretos legislativos"* as were necessary in order to implement Community law; see Arpio Santacruz, "Spanish Adaptation to Community Law: 1986–1988" (1991) E.L.R. 149, at 150. In Ireland, after the High Court held in *Meagher v Minister for Agriculture and Food and the Attorney General* that s.3(2) of the European Communities Act 1972 was unconstitutional for empowering the executive to enact subordinate legislation amending or repealing primary legislation in order to implement Community law, the Supreme Court set the decision aside on the basis of Art. 29.4.5 of the Constitution, according to which no provisions of the Constitution invalidate laws enacted, acts done or measures adopted by the State necessitated by membership of the Communities. In some cases, it held, it was proper for Community obligations to be discharged by administrative rather than legislative procedures (*Meagher v Minister for Agriculture and Food and the Attorney General* [1994] 2 C.M.L.R. 654–657 and 663–680). See "Application of Community law by national courts", Annex VI to the Commission's eleventh annual report to the European Parliament on monitoring the application of Community law—1993, [1994] O.J. C154/176.

[42] As far as the direct effect of directives is concerned, see para. 17–127, *infra*; for a study of the instrumental approach to the concept of the "State", see Hecquard-Théron, "La notion d'Etat en droit communautaire" (1990) R.T.D.E. 693–711.

[43] This is because only specific forms of action may be brought before the Court of Justice and the Court of First Instance, see paras 10–073—10–079, *supra*.

[44] See Lenaerts and Arts, *Procedural Law of the European Union*, Ch.2. An information note on references by national courts for preliminary rulings may be found on the website of the Court of Justice under "Texts governing procedure"; see also (1997) C.M.L.R. 1319–1322.

apply national law in a way which is contrary to Community law, this may in certain circumstances found an action by the Commission against the Member State in question for infringement of Community law.[45] A sufficiently serious breach of Community law by a judicial authority ruling at last instance may give rise to entitlement to reparation for the damage resulting from that breach (see para. 17–012).

As far as non-Community acts of the Union are concerned, the role played by the national courts depends on the status of those acts in the national legal order (see paras 18–014 *et seq.*).

V. THE ROLE PLAYED BY DEVOLVED AUTHORITIES

11–013 **Decentralisation within the Member States.** Most Member States have one form or another of geographical decentralisation, as a result of which real decision-making powers are vested in regional or local authorities. In those Member States described as "federal" (Austria, Belgium, Germany) or "regionalised" (Italy), the Constitution allows the regions to take certain decisions independently with regard to particular spheres. Some Member States confer less extensive powers on their regions (France) or provide for a form of decision-making autonomy for specific parts of the national territory (Finland, Portugal, United Kingdom). In other Member States still, (territorial) decentralisation is limited to giving powers of their own to local authorities and purely administrative units. Except for the case of Germany, the devolution of powers to a regional level of authority has occurred only in recent decades; in some Member States the question of devolution is completely off the agenda,[46] although the position has completely changed in the United Kingdom as a result of the recent creation of a Scottish Parliament and a Welsh Assembly (Scotland Act 1998; Government of Wales Act 1998).[47] In view of the different forms of territorial decentralisation in the Member States, it is impossible to define the intermediate level of authority in a uniform way with a view to involving

---

[45] See ECJ (judgment of December 9, 2003), Case C–129/00 *Commission v Italy*, not yet reported, paras 29–33 (not isolated or numerically insignificant judicial decisions but a widely-held judicial construction which has not been disowned by the supreme court, but rather confirmed by it, would be covered).

[46] See Van Ginderachter, "Le rôle des régions dans la construction européenne" (1992) R.M.C.U.E. 777–780. For the question of territorial decentralisation in the Netherlands, see Besselink, Albers and Eijsbouts, "Subsidiarity in Non-Federal Contexts: The Netherlands and the European Union" (1994) S.E.W. 275–320.; Hessel and Mortelmans (n.20, *supra*), 504 pp.

[47] As far as the UK is concerned, see s.29 (Legislative Competence) and s.57(2) of the Scotland Act 1998 and s.29 (Implementation of Community Law) of the Government of Wales Act 1998. Other relevant provisions are Sch.4 on Reserved Matters (especially para. 7(2)) and Schedule 4 on Enactments Protected from Modification of the Scotland Act and s.106 of the Government of Wales Act.

citizens more closely in action taken by the Union and the Communities.[48] Since the Treaties govern only the relationship between the Member States (and their nationals) and the relationship between the Communities and the Member States (and their nationals), regional and local authorities, as "parts" of the national authority, are subject to the same duty to implement and apply Community law (see para. 5–047).[49]

Involvement of regional authorities. The Communities' policies are **11–014** attuned in many instances to the regions. In various areas, the EC Treaty requires the Community to take account of specific regional situations.[50] (It should be noted that the draft EU Constitution will require the Union to respect the fundamental political and constitutional structures of the Member States as regards "regional and local self-government").[51] In addition, the Community grants aid to certain regions as part of its action to strengthen economic and social cohesion (see para. 5–247). In so far as the Member States concerned make the necessary internal arrangements to this effect, regional authorities are involved in implementing that aid policy.[52] Furthermore, the Community is increasingly empowered to conduct policies in areas which in federal systems are predominantly dealt with at the regional level of authority (the environment and matters affecting people, such as education, culture and public health). It is then the regions which have to implement the policies. As a result, they are increasingly asking for a say in Community formulation of the policies, in like manner to members of the national government and national civil servants.[53] However, direct participation of the regions in Community

---

[48] This is one of the aims of the EU Treaty; para. 3–012, *supra*. See also Scott, Peterson and Millar, "Subsidiarity: A 'Europe of the Regions' v the British Constitution" (1994) J.C.M.S. 47–67.

[49] *cf.* the Statement by the Kingdom of Belgium on the signing of treaties by the Kingdom of Belgium as a Member State of the European Union ([1998] O.J. C351/1), in which that Member State declares that, irrespective whether a Federal, Regional or Community Minister signs a treaty for Belgium, the Kingdom as such will in all cases be bound, in respect of its whole territory, by the provisions of the treaty and that the Kingdom alone, as such, will bear full responsibility for compliance with the obligations entered into in the treaties concerned.

[50] See Art. 33(2)(a) ("structural and natural disparities between the various agricultural regions"); Art. 40(d) ("employment in the various regions"); Art. 76(2) ("appropriate regional economic policy"); Art. 151(1) ("regional diversity" of culture); Art. 174(2) and (3) (diversity of situations and environmental situations in the various regions).

[51] See the discussion of the principle of proportionality, para. 5–046, *supra*; for the extent to which the principle of subsidiarity requires account to be taken of devolved authorities, see paras 5–031 and 5–035, *supra*. Even now, some commentators infer from Art. 10 of the EC Treaty an obligation for the Community to take account of the federal structure of Member States; see Epiney, "Gemeinschaftsrecht und Föderalismus: 'Landes-Blindheit' und Pflicht zur Berücksichtigung innerstaatlicher Verfassungsstrukturen" (1994) EuR. 301–324; *cf.* Van Nuffel, *De rechtsbescherming van nationale overheden in het Europees recht* (Kluwer, Deventer, 2000) at 288–294.

[52] See Hessel and Mortelmans, "Decentralised Government and Community Law: Conflicting Institutional Developments" (1993) C.M.L.R. 905, at 920–925 and 932–934.

[53] Reich, "Zum Einfluss des europäischen Gemeinschaftsrechts auf die Kompetenzen der deutschen Bundesländer" (2001) Eu.GR.Z. 1–18.

decision-making is difficult to arrange given the great disparities as between Member States in this area of the structure of the State.[54]

11–015 Participation of regions in EU decision-making. In order to involve the responsible regional ministers in decision-making, Art. 203 of the EC Treaty allows them to represent their Member State in the Council, provided that they are authorised to commit the national government (see paras 10–039–10–040). Regional ministers may avail themselves of this possibility if the national legal system makes provision for such authorisation. Such an authorisation may be granted to Ministers of regional authorities for individual Council meetings or by a general authority.[55]

At the same time, it has to be agreed who is to sit in the Council and how the Member State's votes are to be cast, especially where the regions' views

---

[54] Commentators have tended to concentrate on the position of the German *Länder* and other regions, see, for instance, Speer, "Innerstaatliche Beteiligung in europäischen Angelegenheiten—Der Fall Spanien" (2000) D.ö.V. 895–905; Garcia, "La Corse dans l'Union européenne" (2001) R.M.C.U.E. 314–322; Feral, "Les incidences de l'intégration européenne sur les collectivités territoriales françaises" (1994) R.M.C.U.E. 53–57; Neßler, "Die 'neue Ländermitwirkung' nach Maastricht" (1994) EuR. 216–229; Vaucher, "Réalité juridique de la notion de région communautaire" (1994) R.T.D.E. 525–550; Bassot, "Le Comité des Régions—Régions françaises et Länder allemands face à un nouvel organe communautaire", (1993) R.M.C.U.E. 729–739; Wuermeling, "Das Ende der 'Länderblindheit': Der Ausschuß der Regionen nach dem neuen EG-Vertrag" (1993) EuR. 196–206; Kalbfleisch-Kottsieper, "Fortentwicklung des Föderalismus in Europa—vom Provinzialismus zur stabilen politischen Perspektive?" (1993) D.ö.V. 541–551; Ress, "La participation des Länder allemands à l'intégration européenne" (1993) R.F.D.C. 657–662; Zuleeg, "Die Stellung der Länder und Regionen im europäischen Integrationsprozeß" (1992) D.Vbl. 1329–1337; Biancarelli, "CEE et collectivités territoriales. La dynamique institutionnelle" (1991) A.J.D.A. 835–845; Petersen, "Zur Rolle der Regionen im künftigen Europa" (1991) D.ö.V. 278–285. For the status of local authorities, see Hobe, Biehl and Schroeter, "Der Einfluß des Rechts der Europäischen Gemeinschaften/Europäischen Union auf die Struktur der kommunalen Selbstverwaltung" (2003) D.ö.V. 803–812; Schmidt, "Sind die EG und die EU an die Europäischen Charta der kommunalen Selbstverwaltung gebunden?" (2003) EuR. 936–948; Ehlers, "Kommunalaufsicht und europäisches Gemeinschaftsrecht" (2001) D.ö.V. 412–417; Le Mire, "Les répercussions de la construction européenne sur les collectivités locales" (1991) R.M.C. 785–796.

[55] A general authority is given in Belgium by Art. 81(6) of the special law of August 8, 1980 on institutional reform, which empowers the governments of the Belgian Communities and Regions to commit the State in the Council where one of their members represents Belgium pursuant to a co-operation agreement. See Ingelaere (n.4, *supra*), at 69–72; Louis and Alen (n.4, *supra*), at 93–96. As for representing the interests of the German and Austrian *Länder*, see n.31 and n.32, *supra*, respectively. For the participation of Scottish Ministers and Welsh Secretaries, see the White Papers, *Scotland's Parliament* (Cm.3658) and *A Voice for Wales*. See also Clark, "Scottish Devolution and the European Union" (1999) Pub.L. 504–524, Evans, "Regional Dimensions to European Governance" (2003) I.C.L.Q. 21–51 and "UK devolution and EU law" (2003) E.L.R. 475–492 and Stumpf, "Mitglieder von Regionalregierungen im EU-Ministerrat. Ein Vergleich zwischen den Rahmenbedingungen nach europäischem, deutschem und britischem Recht" (2002) EuR. 275–290. For the (not yet realised right of participation of) Spanish *Comunidades autónomas* in comparison with Scotland, see Ross and Salvador Crespo, "The effect of devolution on the implementation of European Community law in Spain and in the UK" (2003) E.L.R. 210–230. In Italy, Art. 117(5) of the Constitutional Law of October 18, 2001 provides for the participation of the regions and autonomous provinces in decisions regarding the elaboration of legislative acts at Community level.

differ.[56] This also applies to the representation of the "Member State" within the numerous working parties and committees which prepare the Council's work and within the committees which assist the Commission with the implementation of Community law. In this connection, too, a Member State may designate members of regional authorities, provided that it is understood that those persons represent the Member State as a whole.[57] Given that the regions therefore depend in the first instance on whether a compromise can be reached within their Member State, the system of direct representation in the Council and other bodies cannot always be used to defend their interests.[58] Moreover, even if a federal State—with one vote—defends the interests of its regions, the views of Member States of a more centralised persuasion may yet win the day in the Council or the relevant body.[59]

Regional authorities may have their say in decision-making directly through the Committee of the Regions (EC Treaty, Arts 263–265; see para. 10–096). The Committee's terms of reference are purely advisory, but it may nevertheless bring specific interests of the regions to the attention of the institutions which have a determinative influence on decision-making (Commission, Council and, sometimes, the European Parliament). The EU Constitution will also give the Committee the right to bring legal proceedings against acts of the institutions for infringement of the principle of subsidiarity. Despite its title, however, the Committee also has representatives of local authorities among its members and hence its positions also take account of their special interests.

Participation of regions in implementation. The Member States are at **11–016** liberty to leave implementation of some aspects of Community law to devolved bodies. If a Member State is held liable for the conduct or failure to act of such a body, it is not entitled, however, to hide behind the domestic division of powers or federal structure in order to avoid the Court

---

[56] In this way, the Belgian federal authority and the Belgian Communities and Regions concluded a co-operation agreement on March 8, 1994 pursuant to Art. 92*bis*(4*bis*) of the special law of August 8, 1980 on the representation of the Kingdom of Belgium in the Council of Ministers of the European Union, *Belgisch Staatsblad/Moniteur belge*, November 17, 1994; see Lejeune, "Le droit fédéral belge des relations internationales" (1994) 3 R.G.D.I.P. 578, at 610–615. For more details on the possibility of participation by decentralised authorities, see Van Nuffel (n.51, *supra*), at 472–488.

[57] See the Commission's answer of April 10, 2003 to question E–0777/03 (Bautista Ojeda), [2003] O.J. C11E/116.

[58] The fact that two compromises have to be reached (domestically and within the Council) has, of course, implications for the political control which can be exercised within a given region by the representative assembly over the regional government.

[59] Wiedmann (n.31, *supra*), at 47.

of Justice making a finding of an infringement[60] or to escape its obligation to bring such infringement to an end.[61] Consequently, a Member State may not rely on the defence that, under national constitutional law, the federal executive has no authority to give instructions to a devolved legislative authority which is in breach of its Treaty obligations.[62] Each Member State must ensure that individuals obtain reparation for damage caused to them by non-compliance with Community law, whichever public authority is responsible for the breach and whichever public authority is in principle, under the law of the Member State concerned, responsible for making reparation.[63] The constitutional system of each Member State must ensure that Treaty obligations are complied with.[64] In some Member States, the national authorities may take the place of the region in breach and do what is necessary in order to bring infringements of the Treaty to an end.[65] Furthermore, the national authorities may sometimes recover from the region concerned all costs incurred as a result of the infringement

---

[60] See already ECJ, Case 69/81 *Commission v Belgium* [1982] E.C.R. 153, para. 5 (and the parallel judgments delivered on the same day): "According to the established case law of the Court a Member State may not plead provisions, practices or circumstances in its internal legal system to justify failure to comply with obligations under Community directives". See, more recently, ECJ, Case C–247/98 *Commission v Spain* [2000] E.C.R. I–2823, para. 20; ECJ, Case C–383/00 *Commission v Germany* [2002] E.C.R. I–4219, para. 18; ECJ, Case C–388/01 *Commission v Italy* [2003] E.C.R. I–721, paras 25–26.

[61] ECJ, Case 96/81 *Commission v Netherlands* [1982] E.C.R. 1791, para. 12; ECJ, Joined Cases 227–230/85 *Commission v Belgium* [1988] E.C.R. 1, paras 9–10.

[62] ECJ, Case C–323/96 *Commission v Belgium* [1998] E.C.R. I–5063, paras 40–42 (in which judgment was given against Belgium because the Flemish Parliament had infringed Community rules on the award of public contracts).

[63] ECJ, Case C–302/97 *Konle* [1999] E.C.R. I–3099, para. 62 (a territorial decentralised body may be held liable); ECJ, Case C–424/97 *Haim* [2000] E.C.R. I–5123, paras 61–62 (a functionally decentralised body may be held liable); ECJ (judgment of September 30, 2003), Case C–224/01 *Köbler*, not yet reported, paras 44–47 and 50 (the Member State must designate the court competent to determine disputes concerning the reparation of damage resulting from judicial decisions). See Anagnostaras, "The allocation of responsibility in State liability actions for breach of Community law: a modern Gordian knot?" (2001) E.L.R. 139–158. As to calling into account a Belgian regional authority, see Verhoeven, "The application in Belgium of the duties of loyalty and co-operation" (2000) S.E.W. 328, at 331–332.

[64] Section 35 of the Scotland Act 1998 provides that if a Scottish Bill contains provisions which the Secretary of State has reasonable grounds to consider incompatible with international obligations or affects reserved matters, he may make an order preventing submission of the Bill for Royal Assent. For the transposition of directives in Belgium, see Gilliaux (n.20, *supra*), at 16–31.

[65] Pursuant to Art. 169 of the consolidated Belgian Constitution, Art. 16(3) of the special law of August 8, 1980 on institutional reform provides that the State shall act instead of a Belgian Community or Region where judgment is given against the State by an international or supranational court following a failure on the part of the Community or Region concerned to comply with an international or supranational obligation. For that substitution mechanism, see Ingelaere (n.4, *supra*), at 76–79; Lejeune (n.56, *supra*), at 619–621; for the limits to the State's ability to act in the place of the Community or Region, see Louis and Alen (n.4, *supra*), at 99–103.

(including any damages which have had to be paid).[66] Just as the Commission may bring an action for failure to fulfil Treaty obligations only against the national authorities, only the national authorities may rely upon procedural possibilities which are available to a "Member State" in order to challenge a Community act.[67]

Although the Treaties do not impose any obligation to "rule on the division of competences by the institutional rules proper to each Member State, or on the obligations which may be imposed on federal and [federated] authorities respectively", they do impose requirements with regard to the effectiveness of the domestic arrangements, that is to say, as to "whether the supervisory and inspection procedures established according to the arrangements within the national legal system are in their entirety sufficiently effective to enable the Community requirements to be correctly applied".[68] To this end, domestic law often has to be adapted. Thus the requirement to notify the Commission of all implementing measures already adopted puts the Member State under a duty not merely to rely on a general principle of loyalty towards the federation (*e.g.* the German *Grundsatz des bundesfreundlichen Verhaltens*) but expressly to require the States belonging to the federation to notify the measures they take to it.[69] On the other hand, decentralised authorities should apply Community provisions having direct effect even if this means refraining from applying provisions emanating from a superior authority within their Member State.[70]

---

[66] For Belgium, see Ingelaere (n.4, *supra*), at 78, and Lejeune (n.56, *supra*), at 611–622; for the substitution of the State and the recovery of costs in Austria, see Schäffer "Europa und die österreichische Bundesstaatlichkeit" (1994) D.ö.V. 181, at 192; for Germany, see Härtel, "Durchsetzbarkeit von Zwangsgeld-Urteilen des EuGH gegen Mitgliedstaaten" (2001) EuR. 617, at 628–630; for the possibility of substitution (in the broad sense) in Spain and the UK, see Ross and Salvador Crespo (n.55, *supra*), at 218–227.

[67] ECJ (order of March 21, 1997), Case C–95/97 *Région Wallonne v Commission* [1997] E.C.R. I–1787, paras 6–8. For this issue, see Van Nuffel, "What's in a Member State? Central and Decentralised Authorities before the Community Courts" (2001) C.M.L.R. 871–901.

[68] ECJ, Case C–8/88 *Germany v Commission* [1990] E.C.R. I–2321, para. 13.

[69] ECJ, Case C–237/90 *Commission v Germany* [1992] E.C.R. I–5973, paras 23, 25 and 29.

[70] ECJ, Case 103/88 *Fratelli Costanzo* [1989] E.C.R. 1839, paras 31–33.

CHAPTER 12

THE CITIZENS OF THE UNION

Personal jurisdiction. The scope *ratione personae* of the Treaties covers, **12–001** generally speaking, all who come under the jurisdiction of the Member States. Initially, however, the Treaties conferred rights of free movement only on Member State nationals who were engaged in an economic activity. But Community legislation and case law have extended enjoyment of those rights to some Member State nationals who are not engaged in an economic activity and to nationals of non-member countries who are dependants of economically active nationals of Member States (see paras 12–002–12–003). On top of this, there has been an increasing tendency to associate the status of national of the supranational entity itself with a specific legal position. As a result, the EU Treaty introduced the idea of citizenship of the Union (EC Treaty, Arts 17–22), conferring specific rights on all Member State nationals (see paras 12–004–12–013). Citizenship of the Union raises the question of the legal position of third-country nationals who come within the scope of application of Union and Community law (see para. 12–014).

I. The Legal Subjects of The Community

Individuals. The Community addresses itself directly to legal subjects. **12–002** Accordingly, all kinds of Community provisions are "directly applicable" in the Member States.[1] At the same time, legal subjects who are "Community nationals" make a direct contribution to decision-making through their representatives in the European Parliament and advisory bodies.[2] In the field of legal redress, the Court of Justice has developed general principles of law on the basis of Art. 220 of the EC Treaty with which Community institutions must always comply *vis-à-vis* all persons, regardless of their nationality.[3] Individuals may invoke Community law in domestic courts

---

[1] See EC Treaty, Art. 249, and the discussion of regulations and decisions, paras 17–115 and 17–137, *infra*; for the "direct effect" of Community provisions, see paras 17–047 *et seq.*

[2] For the connection between the direct effect of Community law and the involvement of Community "nationals" in decision-making, see ECJ, Case 26/62 *Van Gend & Loos* [1963] E.C.R. 1, at 12 (referred to in para. 1–018, *supra*). In addition, they have an indirect influence on decision-making through their national parliaments, which can monitor and scrutinise action taken by members of the Council; para. 11–006, *supra*.

[3] See the discussion of the general principles of Community law, including fundamental rights, in paras 17–065 *et seq.*

against other persons or against authorities of their own or another Member State.[4] Provided that they satisfy the requirements of the fourth para. of Art. 230 of the EC Treaty, individuals may contest acts of Community institutions by bringing an action in the Court of First Instance. If they do not satisfy those requirements, they are entitled to challenge the validity of the act in question in their domestic courts.[5]

12–003 Economically active persons. In addition, the Treaties create special rights for Member State nationals engaged in an economic activity: employees, self-employed persons and providers and recipients of services are entitled to remain in another Member State and take part in legal transactions there on the same terms as nationals of the host State. In order to ensure that such persons enjoy the fullest possible mobility, the Community institutions have adopted legislation: (a) extending enjoyment of the relevant rights to persons who are not yet engaged in an economic activity (job seekers) or have ceased to be so engaged (unemployed persons, persons unfit for work, pensioners), and (b) conferring tributary rights on members of the family of persons enjoying the rights in question.[6] The Court of Justice has made it clear that such nationals of other Member States are not only entitled to equal treatment in the exercise of their occupations, *e.g.* from the point of view of the economic and social benefits attaching thereto, but also may not be discriminated against on account of any transaction into which they enter in the host Member State, such as renting accommodation or bringing an action at law.[7] They have the same right as nationals of the host State to be active in trade unions and other organisations for the defence of their occupational or professional interests, to take part in the administration of public bodies and to hold public office. A Member State may preclude them only from carrying out activities involving the exercise of public authority or safeguarding the general interests of the State.[8] The (potential) economic activity invariably constitutes the requisite connecting factor with Community law. Nevertheless, by putting a broad interpretation on the expression

---

[4] For a survey of the legal position of Community nationals, see Everling, "Die Stellung des Bürgers in der Europäischen Gemeinschaft" (1992) Z.f.RV. 241–256. However, in principle an individual may not rely on the Treaty provisions on the free movement of persons against authorities in his or her own State unless, in exercising free movement, he or she finds himself or herself in a situation equivalent to that of a national of another Member State: paras 5–068—5–070, *supra*.

[5] See Lenaerts and Arts, *Procedural Law of the European Union*, Chs 7 and 10.

[6] See the discussion of the free movement of persons, paras 5–115—5–149, *supra*, and of the free movement of services, paras 5–169—5–179, *supra*.

[7] See the prohibition of discrimination in connection with free movement of persons, pars 5–128—5–149, *supra*, and free movement of services, para. 5–173, *supra*.

[8] For participation in elections to occupational guilds, see ECJ, Case C–213/90 *ASTI* [1991] E.C.R. I–3507, paras 15–20, and ECJ, Case C–118/92 *Commission v Luxembourg* [1994] E.C.R. I–1891, paras 5–7; for employment in the public service, see ECJ, Case 149/79 *Commission v Belgium* [1980] E.C.R. 3881, paras 10–15. For permissible restrictions on the free movement of persons, see paras 5–139—5–144, *supra*.

"vocational training", the Court of Justice has held that nationals of a Member State are entitled to have access to higher or university education elsewhere in the Community on the same terms as nationals of the host State and to reside in that country whilst they are studying.[9] In addition, it appears that anyone who travels to another country falls within the field of application of Community law in so far as he or she is a potential recipient of services or consumer.[10]

The economic objective of the principle of free movement of persons was overtly discarded for the first time by Directive 90/364, which allows any national of a Member State who is covered by sickness insurance and has sufficient resources to reside in another Member State.[11] Members of the family of such a person have the right to reside in the host Member State as well, and to engage in any activity, gainful or otherwise, even if they do not have the nationality of a Member State.[12]

II. CITIZENSHIP OF THE UNION

A. THE RELATIONSHIP BETWEEN THE UNION AND ITS CITIZENS

Steps towards citizenship. Through the introduction of the concept of **12–004** citizenship of the Union, the first subpara. of Art. 17(1) of the EC Treaty created a legal relationship between the Union and its nationals, to which the EC Treaty attaches specific rights and duties (EC Treaty, Art. 17(2)).[13]

---

[9] For access to education, see para. 5–239, *supra*; for the right of residence, see ECJ, Case C–357/89 *Raulin* [1992] E.C.R. I–1027, paras 34–43, and Directive 93/96 on the right of residence for students, [1993] O.J. L317/59 (para. 5–128, *supra*). For a survey of the access of Member State nationals to services and advantages provided by the public authorities in the host State, see von Wilmowsky, "Zugang zu den öffentlichen Leistungen anderer Mitgliedstaaten (Das Integrationskonzept des EWG-Vertrags in der Leistungsverwaltung)" (1990) Z.ä.o.R.V. 231–281.

[10] For the extent of the class of recipients of services, see ECJ, Joined Cases 286/82 and 26/83 *Luisi and Carbone* [1984] E.C.R. 377, para. 16; ECJ, Case 186/87 *Cowan* [1989] E.C.R. 195, paras 15–17 (para. 5–171, *supra*); for the freedom of movement of consumers as a corollary of the free movement of goods, see ECJ, Case C–362/88 *GB-INNO-BM* [1990] E.C.R. I–667, para. 8. See also Everling, "Von der Freizügigkeit der Arbeitnehmer zum Europäischen Bürgerrecht?" (1990) EuR. Beiheft 1, 81–103; Fallon, "Les droits accessoires à l'exercice des activités économiques de la personne dans la Communauté" (1993) Ann. Dr. Louv. 235–253.

[11] Council Directive 90/364/EEC of June 28, 1990 on the right of residence, [1990] O.J. L180/26 (para. 5–128, *supra*).

[12] *ibid.*, Art. 2(2). For a survey of the rights of EU nationals, see also Reich, *Bürgerrechte in der Europäischen Union* (Nomos, Baden-Baden, 1999), 462 pp.

[13] For general discussions of citizenship of the Union, see Kovar and Simon, "La citoyenneté européenne" (1993) C.D.E. 285–316; Marias (ed.), *European Citizenship* (European Institute for Public Administration, Maastricht, 1994) 276 pp.; O'Leary, *The Evolving Concept of Community Citizenship. From the Free Movement of Persons to Union Citizenship* (Kluwer Law International, The Hague, 1996) 347 pp.; Kostakopoulou, "Nested 'Old' and 'New' Citizenships in the European Union: Bringing out the Complexity" (1999) Col.J.E.L. 389–413. For a somewhat critical commentary, see Shaw, "The Interpretation of European Union Citizenship" (1998) M.L.R. 293–317; Reich, "Union Citizenship—Metaphor or Source of Rights?" (2001) E.L.J. 4–23.

The idea of conferring certain rights on Member State nationals as citizens of the supranational entity grew up in parallel with proposals to bring together the various integration paths into a single European Union (see paras 3–001–3–015).[14] At the instigation of the Paris Summit (December 1974), the Tindemans Report on European Union (1975) considered possible ways of strengthening the protection of citizens' rights and of making European solidarity tangible by means of external signs.[15] Also on the instructions of the Paris Summit, the Commission brought out reports on the feasibility of introducing a uniform passport, establishing a passport union and conferring special rights on citizens of the Member States, *inter alia*, so as to allow them to vote and stand as a candidate in municipal and, possibly also, regional elections and to hold public office at those levels.[16]

12–005 **Symbols of the Union.** However, citizens did not start to become more involved in the integration process until the first direct elections to the European Parliament in 1979. In 1985, the Adonnino Committee set up by the European Council produced two reports containing further proposals on how to attain a people's Europe.[17] The proposals received a positive reception at the Milan European Council of June 28 and 29, 1985[18] and have since either largely been translated into measures securing free movement of persons and mobility for students or resulted in the conferral of new competences on the Community in the social and cultural spheres by the Single European Act and the EU Treaty.[19] As the Adonnino Committee had proposed, the Community's image and identity have been strengthened through the adoption of the flag and the anthem of the Council of Europe[20] and the introduction of a Community driving licence.[21]

---

[14] For a survey, see the Commission's communication to the European Parliament of June 24, 1988 entitled "A people's Europe" (1988) EC Bull. Suppl.2.

[15] (1976) EC Bull. Suppl.1, 29–31. For the Paris Summit, see (1974) 12 EC Bull. point 1104, No.13.

[16] Towards European citizenship, "A Passport Union" and "The granting of special rights", reports presented by the Commission in implementation of points 10 and 11, respectively, of the final communiqué issued at the European Summit held in Paris on December 9 and 10, 1974, (1975) EC Bull. Suppl.7.

[17] A People's Europe, Reports from the *ad hoc* Committee (1985) EC Bull. Suppl.7 (reports of March 29–30 and June 28–29, 1985). For the Committee's terms of reference, see para. 3–005, *supra*.

[18] (1985) 6 EC Bull. point 1.4.8. In the *Erasmus* judgment, the Court of Justice referred to "achievement of a people's Europe" as one of the Community's general objectives: ECJ, Case 242/87 *Commission v Council* [1989] E.C.R. 1425, para. 29.

[19] See Schockweiler, "La dimension humaine et sociale de la Communauté européenne" (1993) 4 R.M.U.E. 11–45, especially at 14–35.

[20] The official flag of the Community is rectangular in form and blue in colour and has at its centre a circle of 12 five-pointed gold stars (the number 12 symbolises perfection and entirety and hence is not linked to the number of Member States; see the Commission's answer of November 22, 1993 to question No. E–1701/93 (Von Wechmar), [1994] O.J. C219/31); its anthem is the music of the Ode to Joy from the fourth movement of Beethoven's Ninth Symphony (both printed in (1986) 4 EC Bull. 52–53). See the request contained in the European Parliament's resolution of April 11, 1983 ([1983] O.J. C128/18),

The Member States also agreed amongst themselves to introduce a passport of uniform pattern.[22] The flag and the anthem have developed into symbols of the European Union, together with the euro, the motto "United in diversity" and May 9 as "Europe Day".[23]

Creation of Union citizenship. The threads leading to the grant of political **12–006** rights to Member State nationals were not woven together until it was decided to give such persons the status of "citizens of the Union". At Spain's instigation, the 1990–1991 Intergovernmental Conference decided to introduce citizenship of the Union concurrently with the establishment of the European Union.[24] As the EU Treaty inserted the provisions on citizenship (Arts 17–22) as "Part Two" of the EC Treaty, they form part of Community law. Since, the introduction of citizenship has provided the justification for the Community, acting under Art. 308 of the EC Treaty, to support organisations promoting "active European citizenship" (*e.g.* through the twinning of local authorities).[25]

---

the approval of the Adonnino Committee's proposal by the European Council ((1985) 6 EC Bull. points 1.4.7 and 1.4.8), and the declaration of the Presidents of the Council and the other institutions ((1986) 4 EC Bull. point 2.1.8.1). See also Bieber, "Die Flagge in der EG", in Fiedler and Ress (eds), *Verfassungsrecht und Völkerrecht. Gedächtnisschrift für Wilhelm Karl Geck* (Heymanns, Cologne, 1989), at 59–77. Further particulars on the flag as the European emblem may be found in CFI (judgment of April 21, 2004), Case T–127/02 *Concept v Office for Harmonisation in the Internal Market*, not yet reported (on the prohibition to register trade marks on account of their similarity to the European emblem).

[21] First Council Directive 80/1263/EEC of December 4, 1980 on the introduction of a Community driving licence, [1980] O.J. L375/1; Council Directive 91/439/EEC of July 29, 1991 on driving licences, [1991] O.J. L237/1. See also para. 5–133, *supra*.

[22] See the resolutions adopted on June 23, 1981 and June 30, 1982 by the representatives of the governments of the Member States, meeting within the Council ([1981] O.J. C241/1, and [1982] O.J. C179/1, respectively), confirmed by the European Council at Fontainebleau on June 25 and 26, 1984 (1984) 6 EC Bull. points 1.1.9 and 3.5.1), on July 14, 1986 ([1986] O.J. C185/1) and on July 10, 1995 ([1995] O.J. C200/1). See Denza, "Le passeport europeen" (1982) R.M.C. 489–493.

[23] See Art. I–8 of the EU Constitution. The celebration of 9 May refers to the day in 1950 on which Robert Schuman pronounced the declaration containing the proposal that led to the creation of the ECSC (see para. 1–003). For these symbols, see Röttinger, "Die Hoheitszeichen der Europäischen Union—ein paar vielleicht nicht nur theoretische Rechtsfragen" (2003) EuR. 1095–1108; Favret, "L'Union européenne: 'l'unité dans la diversité'—Signification et pertinence d'une devise" (2003) R.T.D.E. 657–660.

[24] See Solbes Mira, "La citoyenneté européenne" (1991) R.M.C. 168–170; Closa, "The Concept of Citizenship in the Treaty on European Union" (1992) C.M.L.R. 1137, at 1153–1157. For the first worked-out proposal, see the text submitted to the Intergovernmental Conference by the Spanish delegation on September 24, 1990, reproduced in Laursen and Vanhoonacker (eds), *The Intergovernmental Conference on Political Union* (European Institute of Public Administration/Martinus Nijhoff, Maastricht, 1992), at 328–332.

[25] See Council Decision of January 26, 2004 establishing a Community action programme to promote active European citizenship (civic participation), [2004] O.J. L30/6. In the preamble, reference is made to the call to bring citizens closer to the European design and the European institutions as formulated in the Declaration of Laeken (see para. 4–001, *supra*).

B. Definition of Citizenship

12–007 **Nationality of Member State.** A citizen of the Union is defined as any person holding the nationality of a Member State (EC Treaty, Art. 17(1)).[26] Citizenship of the Union complements and does not replace national citizenship (*ibid.*).[27] Whether a person has the nationality of a Member State is to be determined solely by reference to the nationality rules of the Member State concerned.[28] This is because what underlies the bond of nationality is a "special relationship of allegiance to the State and reciprocity of rights and duties".[29] Where having the nationality of a Member State is a condition for enjoyment of a Community right, Community law requires Member States to recognise the nationality of another Member State without imposing any other condition (*e.g.* residence in the territory of the Member State whose nationality is relied on).[30] This

---

[26] The European Parliament used the same definition in its Declaration of fundamental rights and freedoms of April 12, 1989 ([1989] O.J. C120/51), Art. 25(3) of which states that a Community citizen shall be "any person possessing the nationality of one of the Member States".

[27] The Treaty of Amsterdam added this provision so as to make it absolutely clear that Union citizenship is complementary. See also Closa, "Citizenship of the Union and Nationality of Member States" (1995) C.M.L.R. 487–518.

[28] This principle of international law is confirmed by Declaration (No.2), annexed to the EU Treaty, on nationality of a Member State and the Decision of the Heads of State or Government, meeting within the European Council on December 11 and 12, 1992, concerning certain problems raised by Denmark on the Treaty on European Union (Section A, "Citizenship", [1992] O.J. C348/2). Declaration No.2 states that Member States may declare, for information, who are to be considered their nationals. See the declaration made upon signature of the EEC Treaty by the Government of the Federal Republic of Germany on the definition of the expression "German national", which stated that all Germans as defined in the Basic Law (hence including nationals of the German Democratic Republic) were to be regarded as German nationals, and the declaration made on the accession of the UK by the British Government on the definition of the term "nationals" ([1972] O.J. L73/196), replaced by a Declaration of 1982 ([1983] O.J. C23/1: "As to the UK . . ., the terms 'nationals', 'nationals of Member States' or 'nationals of Member States and overseas countries and territories', wherever used in the [Treaties] or in any of the Community acts deriving from those Treaties, are to be understood to refer to: (a) British citizens; (b) persons who are British subjects by virtue of Part IV of the British Nationality Act 1981 and who have the right of abode in the UK and are therefore exempt from UK immigration control; (c) British Dependent Territories citizens who acquire their citizenship from a connection with Gibraltar"). These declarations have to be taken into account in interpreting the Treaty: ECJ, Case C–192/99 *Kaur* [2001] E.C.R. I–1237, paras 19–27; CFI, Case T–230/94 *Farrugia v Commission* [1996] E.C.R. II–195, paras 16–31. See also Simmonds, "The British Nationality Act 1981 and the Definition of the Term 'National' for Community Purposes" (1984) C.M.L.R. 675–686. For Netherlands nationals from overseas territories, see Staples, "Wie is burger van de Unie?" (2001) N.T.E.R. 109–112.

[29] ECJ, Case 149/79 *Commission v Belgium* [1980] E.C.R. 3881, para. 10.

[30] ECJ, Case C–369/90 *Micheletti* [1992] E.C.R. I–4239, paras 10–11 (on freedom of establishment), with a critical note by Jessurun d'Oliveira (1993) C.M.L.R. 623–637; ECJ, Case C–122/96 *Saldanha and MTS* [1997] E.C.R. I–5325, para. 15. This is not the case where a Member State has to do with a worker who has both the nationality of that Member State and that of a third country with which the Community has concluded an association agreement: ECJ, Case C–179/98 *Mesbah* [1999] E.C.R. I–7955, paras 29–41 (the Member State concerned may regard the worker solely as being one of its own nationals and consequently preclude a member of the worker's family from invoking rights under the association agreement).

means therefore that Member States must unconditionally accept the citizenship of the Union conferred by another Member State (through bestowal of the nationality of that State). In this way, Community law diverges from international law where a State may refuse to recognise the nationality of a person if it was granted contrary to international law and, in the case of a person having plural nationality (of two or more foreign States), may have regard to the "master" nationality.[31] A Member State cannot therefore preclude the application of Community law by relying, with regard to nationals of another Member States who are residing on their territory—and hence fall within the scope of application of Community law, on the fact that the persons concerned also have the nationality of the Member State of residence.[32] Since citizenship depends on a person's having the status of a national of a Member State, the Union differs fundamentally from federal States, in which nationality invariably falls within the jurisdiction of the federal authority.[33]

C. SUBSTANCE OF CITIZENSHIP

Rights associated with citizenship. Citizens of the Union enjoy the rights **12–008** conferred by the EC Treaty and are subject to the duties imposed thereby (EC Treaty, Art. 17(2)). Among the rights which Art. 17(2) associates with the status of Union citizen, is the right enshrined in Art. 12 of the EC Treaty not to be discriminated against on grounds of nationality within the scope of application of the Treaty (see paras 5–059–5–060).[34] More generally, every citizen of the Union has the right to equal treatment within the scope of Community law, in particular exercising the freedoms guaranteed by the EC Treaty.[35] Inequality of treatment may be justified

---

[31] See Kovar and Simon (n.13, *supra*), at 291–292, and especially Zimmermann, "Europäisches Gemeinschaftsrecht und Staatsangehörigkeit der Mitgliedstaaten unter besonderer Berücksichtigung der Probleme mehrfacher Staatsangehörigkeit" (1995) EuR. 54–70. The Court of Justice points out that the Hague Convention of April 12, 1930 on certain questions relating to the conflict of nationality laws (League of Nations Treaty Series, Vol.179, p.89) does not impose an obligation but simply provides an option, in the case of dual nationality, for the contracting parties to give priority to their own nationality over any other: ECJ (judgment of October 2, 2003), Case C–148/02 *Garcia Avello*, not yet reported, para. 28. In view of the rights which Community law connects with nationality of a Member State, however, a person cannot be deprived of his or her nationality in breach of general principles of Community law, see Hall, "Loss of Union Citizenship in Breach of Fundamental Rights" (1996) E.L.R. 129–143.

[32] ECJ (judgment of October 2, 2003), Case C–148/02 *Garcia Avello*, not yet reported, para. 28.

[33] Kovar and Simon (n.13, *supra*), at 294.

[34] ECJ, Case C–85/96 *Martínez Sala* [1998] E.C.R. I–2691, para. 62; case note by O'Leary (1999) E.L.R. 68–79.

[35] ECJ, Case C–224/98 *D'Hoop* [2002] E.C.R. I–6191, paras 27–40; ECJ (judgment of October 2, 2003), Case C–148/02 *Garcia Avello*, not yet reported, paras 30–45 (exercise of the freedom enshrined in Art. 18 of the EC Treaty to move and reside within the territory of the Member States); ECJ (judgment of March 23, 2004), Case C–138/02 *Collins*, not yet reported, para. 61 (exercise of the right enshrined in Art. 39 of the EC Treaty to seek employment in another Member State). For (indirect) discrimination on grounds of nationality, see para. 5–060.

only if it is based on objective considerations independent of the nationality of the persons concerned and is proportionate to the legitimate aim of the national provisions.[36]

Articles 18 to 21 of the EC Treaty enumerate the rights that the EC Treaty associates with citizenship of the Union citizens. Those articles not only codify rights recognised by Community law even before the EU Treaty entered into force (right to move and reside, right of petition), but also create rights of considerable political importance (right to vote and stand as a candidate in European and municipal elections; diplomatic protection; right to apply to the European Ombudsman).[37] These rights are vested in citizens of the Union in their capacity of nationals of a Member State and therefore as Union citizens even if they are not in gainful employment or self-employed. In the Charter of Fundamental Rights of the European Union, the rights of citizens of the Union are enshrined in the chapter entitled "Citizenship".[38] As in the case of the EC Treaty, the Charter extends some rights to natural and legal persons who reside or have their corporate seat in a Member State (access to documents and to the European Ombudsman and the right of petition) and reserves other rights to Union citizens (the right to vote and stand for election, diplomatic and consular protection). The other rights which the Charter confers only on citizens are the right to engage in work and to pursue a freely chosen or accepted occupation, to exercise the right of establishment and to provide services in any Member State and the right to move and reside freely within the territory of the Member States.[39]

The first para. of Art. 22 of the EC Treaty requires the Commission to report every three years on the application of the provisions on citizenship, taking into account the "development of the Union". In addition, the Council, acting unanimously on a proposal from the Commission and after consulting the European Parliament, may adopt provisions supplementing the rights provided for in the EC Treaty.[40] Consequently, the Treaty permits the Council only to extend, not to restrict, those rights. Any provisions so adopted are to be recommended to the Member States for

---

[36] *D'Hoop*, para. 36; *Garcia Avello*, para. 31.

[37] For a survey, see Staeglich, "Rechte und Pflichten aus der Unionsbürgerschaft" (2004) Z.Eu.S. 485–531.

[38] See Arts 39–46 of the Charter. For the fact that citizenship confers rights on persons regardless of their economic activity, see ECJ, Case C–413/99 *Baumbast and R.* [2002] E.C.R. I–7091, paras 81–84.

[39] Charter, Art. 15(2) and Art. 45(1). Where nationals of third countries are authorised to work in the territories of the Member States, they are entitled to working conditions equivalent to those of citizens of the Union (Charter, Art. 15(3)); Freedom of movement and residence may be granted, in accordance with the Treaty establishing the European Community, to nationals of third countries legally resident in the territory of a Member State (Charter, Art. 45(2)). Under the heading of "citizenship", the right to good administration is stated to be applicable to everyone (and hence not just to citizens) (Charter, Art. 41).

[40] Under the EU Constitution, the Council will have to obtain the "consent" of the European Parliament (Art. III-129, second para.).

adoption in accordance with their respective constitutional requirements (EC Treaty, Art. 22, second para.; see para. 7–008).

Residence rights. In the first place, citizenship of the Union entails the **12–009** right "to move and reside freely within the territory of the Member States, subject to the limitations and conditions laid down in this Treaty and by the measures adopted to give it effect" (EC Treaty, Art. 18(1)). Community law grants freedom of movement and residence in connection with the free movement of persons and services to qualifying persons and members of their families. In addition, it has created a general right of residence for Member State nationals and members of their families.[41] As a result, Art. 18 is primarily important in so far as it enshrines those rights in the Treaty. The provision is framed sufficiently precisely and unconditionally so as to confer direct effect on the rights in question.[42] Art. 18(1) does not prevent Member States from imposing restrictions on the right of movement and residence pursuant to Art. 39(3) and Arts 46 and 55 of the EC Treaty—*i.e.* in connection with the free movement of persons and services—on grounds of public policy, public security or public health. In addition, Community legislation may make the exercise of the right of residence subject to still other conditions, provided that they can be reconciled with the wording of Art. 18(1) of the EC Treaty. Since the right of residence is derived directly from the Treaty, such restrictions and conditions must be applied having regard to the general principles of Community law, such as the principle of proportionality.[43]

The European Parliament and the Council may adopt provisions under the co-decision procedure with a view to facilitating the exercise of the right to move and reside freely within the territory of the Member States. Such provisions may be adopted if "action by the Community should prove necessary to attain this objective and [the] Treaty has not provided the necessary powers" although they may not apply to provisions on passports, identity cards, residence permits or any other such document or to provisions on social security or social protection (see EC Treaty, Art. 18(2) and (3)). This constraint will disappear when the EU Constitution is in

---

[41] paras 5–127—5–128, *supra.*

[42] ECJ, Case C–413/99 *Baumbast and R.* [2002] E.C.R. I–7091, paras 80–86. For the implications of the fact that the right of residence ensues directly from the Treaty, see Dougan and Spaventa, "Educating Rudy and the (non-)English Patient—A double-bill on residency rights under Article 18 EC" (2003) E.L.R. 699–712. For an application of Art. 18 together with Arts 39 and 42 of the EC Treaty, see ECJ, Case C–135/99 *Elsen* [2000] E.C.R. I–1049, paras 33–36.

[43] ECJ, Case C–413/99 *Baumbast and R.* [2002] E.C.R. I–7091, paras 85–94; CFI, Case T–66/95 *Kuchlenz-Winter v Commission* [1997] E.C.R. II–637, paras 47–48. As regards the requirement for students of having sufficient resources: ECJ, Case C–184/99 *Grzelczyk* [2001] E.C.R. I–6193, paras 37–46; for the latitude available to Member States in implementing the right of residence for the various categories of beneficiaries (and members of their families): ECJ, Case C–424/98 *Commission v Italy* [2000] E.C.R. I–4001, paras 20–48. See Scheuing, "Freizügigkeit als Unionsbürgerrecht" (2003) EuR. 744–792.

force, since it will empower the Council, acting unanimously after consulting the European Parliament, to lay down other measures concerning passports, identity cards, residence permits or any other such document and measures concerning social security or social protection (Art. III–125(2)).

In April 2004, the various Community instruments dealing with the right of residence of citizens of the Union were simplified and merged in one Directive 2004/38/EC of the European Parliament and of the Council on the right of citizens of the Union and their family members to move and reside freely within the territory of the Member States.[44] Directive 2004/38 confers on Union citizens the right of residence on the territory of another Member State for a period of up to three months without any conditions or any formalities other than the requirement to hold a valid identity card or passport (Art. 6(1)). Union citizens and their family members enjoy this right as long as they do not become an unreasonable burden on the social assistance system of the host Member State (Art. 14(1)). Article 7(1) of the Directive grants the right of residence for a period of longer than three months to:

(a) Union citizens who are workers or self-employed persons in the host Member State;

(b) all other Union citizens who have sufficient resources for themselves and their family members not to become a burden on the social assistance system of the host Member State during their period of residence and comprehensive sickness insurance cover in that State;

(c) Union citizens following a course of study in the host Member State, if they have comprehensive sickness insurance cover in that State and assure the relevant authority that they have sufficient resources in the above sense; and

(d) the family members accompanying or joining a Union citizen who satisfies the conditions of Art. 7(1)(a), (b) or (c).[45]

The right of residence for a period longer than three months exists as long as the Union citizens and their family members meet the conditions set in

[44] Directive 2004/38/EC of the European Parliament and of the Council of April 29, 2004 on the right of the citizen of the Union and their family members to move and reside freely within the territory of the Member States amending Regulation (EEC) No. 1612/68 and repealing Directives 64/221/EEC, 68/360/EEC, 72/194/EEC, 73/148/EEC, 74/34/EEC, 75/35/EEC, 90/364/EEC, 90/365/EEC and 93/96/EEC, [2004] O.J. L158/77 (adopted on the basis of Arts 12, 18, 40, 44 and 52 of the EC Treaty). The Directive has to be implemented by April 30, 2006.

[45] A Union citizen who is no longer a worker or self-employed person is to retain that status in the circumstances listed in Art. 7(3) of the Directive. For the scope of the term "family members", see para. 5–127, supra. With respect to persons meeting the conditions under Art. 7(1)(c), Art. 7(4) of the Directive limits qualifying "family members" to the spouse or registered partner and dependent children.

Art. 7 of the directive (Art. 14(2)). However, an expulsion measure should not be the automatic consequence of recourse to the social assistance system (see Art. 14(3)). The host Member State should examine whether it is a case of temporary difficulties and take into account the duration of residence, the personal circumstances and the amount of aid granted in order to consider whether the beneficiary has become an unreasonable burden on its social assistance system and to proceed to his or her expulsion.[46] In no case—except on grounds of public policy or public security—should an expulsion measure be adopted against workers, self-employed persons or job-seekers with genuine chances of being engaged (Art. 14(4)). In the case of residence for periods longer than three months, a Member State may require Union citizens to register. A "residence card" will be issued only to family members who are not nationals of a Member State.[47] Furthermore, the directive grants Union citizens who have resided legally for a continuous period of five years in the host Member State the right of permanent residence there (Art. 16). The freedom of movement and residence of Union citizens and their family members may be restricted on grounds of public policy, public security and public health (Art. 27; see paras 5–139–5–140).

Subject to such specific provisions as are expressly provided for in the Treaty and secondary law, all Union citizens residing on the basis of Directive 2004/38 in the territory of the host Member State are to enjoy equal treatment with the nationals of that Member State within the scope of the Treaty (Art. 24(1); see also EC Treaty, Art. 12 and paras 5–059–5–060). Nonetheless, Directive 2004/38 does not require a Member State to confer entitlement to social assistance during the first three months of residence (or the longer period during which a citizen continues to seek employment with genuine chances of being engaged) nor, prior to the acquisition of the right of permanent residence, to grant maintenance aid for studies consisting in student grants or student loans to persons other than workers, self-employed persons, persons who retain such status and members of their families (Art. 24(2)).

Right to participate in municipal and European elections. Every citizen of **12–010** the Union residing in a Member State of which he or she is not a national has the right to vote and to stand as a candidate in municipal and European Parliament elections in the Member State in which he or she resides, under the same conditions as nationals of that State (EC Treaty, Art. 19(1) and (2)). The Treaty goes on to provide that those rights are to be "exercised subject to detailed arrangements to be adopted . . . by the Council, acting unanimously on a proposal from the Commission and after consulting the European Parliament; these arrangements may provide for derogations when warranted by problems specific to a Member State".

---

[46] Recital 16 in the preamble to Directive 2004/38.
[47] Directive 2004/38, Arts 8 and 9.

These rights may be regarded as applications of the prohibition of discrimination on grounds of nationality in the exercise of political rights fostering the integration of Member State nationals who have made use of their right freely to reside in other Member States.[48] Prior to the EU Treaty, it appeared impossible to provide in a Community measure for the right to vote and stand as a candidate in municipal elections[49] and in elections to the European Parliament.[50] Pursuant to Art. 19(2) of the EC Treaty, which refers to "detailed arrangements" with regard to the right to vote and stand as a candidate in elections to the European Parliament, the Council adopted Directive 93/109 on December 6, 1993.[51] Then, acting under Art. 19(1) of the EC Treaty, which provides for "detailed arrangements" for the exercise of the right to vote and stand as a candidate in municipal elections, the Council adopted Directive 94/80 on December 19, 1994.[52] The only reservation is that a Member State may provide that

---

[48] At the same time, the direct relationship between the Union and its citizens is powerfully reflected by the fact that any given MEP is not necessarily elected solely by nationals of one particular Member State. This makes it legitimate for MEPs to carry out their mandate independently of their nationality; para. 10–025, *supra*. See also Pliakos, "La nature juridique de l'Union européenne" (1993) R.T.D.E. 187, at 194.

[49] With a view to giving nationals of other Member States voting rights in local elections, the Commission had submitted a proposal pursuant to Art. 235 [now Art. 308] of the EC Treaty as long ago as June 24, 1988, but it was not adopted by the Council ([1988] O.J. C246/3, also published with additional explanatory material in (1988) EC Bull. Suppl.2, 29–44). For the discussion as to whether the EEC Treaty afforded a sufficient legal basis for the proposal, see Closa (n.24, *supra*), at 1147–1150; D'Argent, "Le droit de vote et d'éligibilité aux élections municipales et européennes comme attribut de la citoyenneté de l'Union" (1993) Ann. Dr. Louv. 221, at 222–226. Despite this, however, several Member States already gave voting rights in local elections to foreigners, in particular Denmark, Ireland and the Netherlands. Irish nationals resident in Great Britain already had the right to vote and stand as candidates in British elections, although there were stricter local residence requirements for both British subjects and Irish nationals in Northern Ireland. See Silvestro, "Le droit de vote et d'éligibilité aux élections municipales" (1993) R.M.C.U.E. 612–614. For a survey of the demographical, legal and political situation in the Member States, see the October 1986 report from the Commission to the European Parliament, "Voting rights in local elections for Community nationals" (1986) EC Bull. Suppl.7.

[50] This is because the Council failed to determine a uniform election procedure for the European Parliament pursuant to Art. 138(3) of the EEC Treaty on a proposal from the European Parliament (para. 10–022, *supra*). The power to recommend such a procedure for adoption by the Member States continues to exist, since Art. 19(2) of the EC Treaty introduces the right to vote "without prejudice to Art. 190(4) and to the provisions adopted for its implementation".

[51] Council Directive 93/108/EC of December 6, 1993 laying down detailed arrangements for the exercise of the right to vote and stand as a candidate in elections to the European Parliament for citizens of the Union residing in a Member State of which they are not nationals, [1993] O.J. L329/34 (see also para. 10–024, *supra*). See Taschner, "Droit de vote et d'éligibilité pour les citoyens de l'Union européenne" (1994) 1 R.M.U.E. 13–23; Oliver, "Electoral Rights under Art. 8b [now Art. 19] of the Treaty of Rome" (1996) C.M.L.R. 473–498.

[52] Council Directive 94/80/EC of December 19, 1994 laying down detailed arrangements for the exercise of the right to vote and to stand as a candidate in municipal elections by citizens of the Union residing in a Member State of which they are not nationals, [1994] O.J. L368/38. In a statement for the minutes, Spain declared that if the UK decided to extend the application of Directive 94/80 to Gibraltar, such application would be deemed to be without prejudice to Spain's position with regard to Gibraltar.

only its own nationals may hold the office of head, deputy or member of a municipal administration.[53]

The two Directives are designed to make the right to vote independent of nationality and require non-nationals to be subject to the same conditions, if any, as apply to nationals, in particular as regards duration of residence and evidence of residence in the constituency. A voter is entitled to exercise the right to vote if he or she has expressed the wish to do so.[54] If voting is compulsory in the Member State of residence, Community nationals on the electoral role are also obliged to vote[55]; once their names have been entered on the electoral roll, voters are to remain thereon under the same conditions as voters who are nationals.[56] Both Directives provide for derogations for any Member State in which the proportion of Union citizens of voting age who reside in it but are not nationals of it exceeds 20 per cent (in practice, Luxembourg). In such a Member State, Union citizens having the nationality of another Member State may be made subject to specific residence conditions which do not apply to its own nationals.[57] At the same time, measures may be taken with regard to the composition of lists of candidates in order to avoid polarisation between lists of national and non-national candidates.[58] In view of the specific features and balances linked to the fact that its Constitution provides for three different languages and a territorial division into regions and communities, Belgium is entitled to apply a similar specific residence condition in respect of voting in municipal elections in a limited number of local government units, the

---

[53] Directive 94/80 allows Member States to provide that only their own nationals may hold the office of "elected head, deputy or member of the governing college of the executive of a basic local government unit" (Art. 5(3), first subpara.) and to restrict the temporary or interim performance of such office to their own nationals (second subpara.). In addition, Member States may also stipulate that Union citizens elected as members of a representative council shall take part in neither the designation of delegates who can vote in a parliamentary assembly nor the election of the members of such an assembly (Art. 5(4)). In Belgium, the derogation applies to *burgemeesters/bourgmestres* and *schepenen/échevins*. In France, Art. 88–3 of the Constitution, which was amended with a view to ratification of the EU Treaty, expressly excludes non-French citizens from holding the offices of *"maire"* or *"adjoint"* and from appointment to the electoral college which nominates members of the *Sénat* and from taking part in their election. See Kovar and Simon (n.13, *supra*) and Oliver (n.51, *supra*), at 494–496. For the position in the UK, see the Local Government Elections (Changes to the Franchise and Qualifications of Members) Regulations 1995.

[54] Directive 93/109, Art. 8(1); Directive 94/80, Art. 7(1).

[55] Directive 93/109, Art. 8(2); Directive 94/80, Art. 7(2).

[56] Directive 93/109, Art. 9(4); Directive 94/80, Art. 8(3).

[57] Directive 93/109, Art. 14(1), first subpara. ; Directive 94/80, Art. 12(1)(a) and (b).

[58] Directive 93/109, Art. 14(1), second subpara. ; Directive 94/80, Art. 12(1)(c). That provision was incorporated despite criticism from the European Parliament to the effect that it was contrary to the spirit and the letter of the prohibition of discrimination enshrined in Art. 12 of the EC Treaty: see point 5 of the resolution of November 17, 1993, [1993] O.J. C329/130. See Oliver (n.51, *supra*), at 487.

names of which are to be notified in advance.[59] The Commission has to report regularly on whether the reasons for the above-mentioned derogations still apply in the Member States concerned.[60]

12–011 Diplomatic protection. In the territory of non-member countries in which their Member State is not represented, Union citizens are entitled to protection by the diplomatic or consular authorities of any Member State on the same conditions as nationals of that State (EC Treaty, Art. 20). Although diplomatic and consular missions in non-member countries co-ordinate their activities to some extent (see EU Treaty, Art. 16), diplomatic and consular protection is among the powers which each Member State exercises with the greatest freedom in regard to the policies pursued. Art. 20 of the EC Treaty does not introduce any Community rules on diplomatic protection and does not confer any more rights to protection from another Member State on Community nationals than are enjoyed by nationals of that Member State. Art. 20 provides that the Member States are to "establish the necessary rules among themselves and start the international negotiations required to secure this protection".[61] Since the Treaty does not provide for any role to be played by Community institutions, the implementing rules are based on intergovernmental agreements and, more recently, on Titles V and VI of the EU Treaty.[62]

12–012 Contacts with Union institutions. The first and second paras of Art. 21 of the EC Treaty give every Union citizen the right, respectively, to petition the European Parliament in accordance with Art. 194 and to apply to the

---

[59] Directive 94/80, Art. 12(2). This is justified by the penultimate recital in the preamble. In a statement for the minutes, Belgium declared that it would apply that derogation only in "some of the local government units in which the number of [Union] voters [not of Belgian nationality] exceeded 20 per cent of all voters where the Belgian Federal Government regarded the specific situation as justifying an exceptional derogation of that kind", [1994] O.J. L368/46. The European Parliament deplored the fact that it was not consulted on this derogation from the right to vote: resolution of April 5, 1995, [1995] O.J. C109/40. For the substance of this potential derogation, see Foubert, "Gemeentekiesrecht voor EU-burgers" (1998) T.B.P. 79–84. Belgium failed to implement the directive within the prescribed period: ECJ, Case C–323/97 *Commission v Belgium* [1998] E.C.R. I–4281. In the end, no use was made of this derogation.

[60] Directive 93/109, Art. 14(3); Directive 94/80, Art. 12(4). See the Commission's reports of January 7, 1998 on the application of Directive 93/109 ((1998) 1/2 EU Bull. point 1.1.1.) and of November 22, 1999 on the application of Directive 94/80/EC ((1999) 11 EU Bull. Point 1.1.1.).

[61] For the context of such "rules", see Kovar and Simon (n.13, *supra*), at 312–315; for the existing "Guidelines for the protection of unrepresented EC nationals by EC missions in third countries", see the Commission's answer of May 4, 1994 to question No. E–822/94 (Kostopoulos), [1994] O.J. C362/50.

[62] See the Decisions of the representatives of the governments of the Member States, meeting within the Council, of December 19, 1995 regarding protection for citizens of the European Union by diplomatic and consular representations (Decision 95/553/EC, [1995] O.J. L314/73) and of June 25, 1996 on the establishment of an emergency travel document (Decision 96/409/CFSP, [1996] O.J. L168/4, adopted under Title V of the EU Treaty). See Szczekalla, "Die Pflicht der Gemeinschaft *und* der Mitgliedstaaten zum diplomatischen und konsularischen Schutz" (1999) EuR. 352–342.

European Ombudsman established under Art. 195. Union citizens are entitled to exercise those rights even if they reside in a non-member country. The same rights likewise accrue to all other natural or legal persons residing or having their registered office in a Member State (see paras 10–012 and 10–107). Accordingly, any person, regardless of his or her political rights as a national of a Member State or a third country, who has been affected by a Community institution or body may have his or her situation reviewed by petitioning the European Parliament or making a complaint to the Ombudsman. Under Art. 255(1) of the EC Treaty, any person also has a right of access to European Parliament, Council and Commission documents (see para. 10–160). Furthermore, the third para. of Art. 21 of the EC Treaty empowers any "citizen of the Union" to write to any of the institutions in any of the Treaty languages and receive an answer in that language.[63]

Fundamental rights and freedoms. Whereas the Constitutions of most **12–013** Member States proclaim the fundamental rights and freedoms of citizens, the EC Treaty does not list the fundamental rights and freedoms which they may invoke in their relations with Community or national authorities. According to Art. 6(2) of the EU Treaty, the Union must respect fundamental rights, as guaranteed by the European Convention for the Protection of Human Rights and Fundamental Freedoms (ECHR) signed in Rome on November 4, 1950 and as they result from the constitutional traditions common to the Member States, as general principles of Community law. Within the field of application of Community law, the Court of Justice and the Court of First Instance have developed case law on protection of human rights on the basis of Art. 220 of the EC Treaty (see paras 17–073–17–090). They draw on the ECHR and the Charter of Fundamental Rights of the European Union and sometimes afford individuals more extensive protection of their rights.[64] Furthermore, Art. 6(2) of the EU Treaty puts the Member States and Community institutions under a duty to apply the same standard as regards human rights when acting in the fields of the CFSP and PJCC as when they act pursuant to Community powers.[65] In the event of a serious and persistent breach of fundamental rights by a Member State, certain of the rights deriving from the application of the Treaties for that State may be suspended (EU Treaty, Art. 7; see para. 9–012).

The incorporation in the EU Constitution of the Charter of Fundamental Rights will provide the Union, for the first time, with a catalogue of "rights,

---

[63] See para. 10–155, *infra*. Under Declaration (No.4) to the Treaty of Nice, the institutions of the Union, the European Economic and Social Committee, the Committee of the Regions and the European Ombudsman are to ensure that the reply to any written request by a citizen of the Union is made within a reasonable period.

[64] See Lenaerts, "Fundamental Rights to be Included in a Community Catalogue" (1991) E.L.R. 367, at 381–384.

[65] For the enforceability of the protection of fundamental rights, see para. 17–179, *infra*.

freedom and principles" that must be respected by the Union (see para. 17–086). Part I of the EU Constitution contains separate references to the Union's fundamental rights and Union citizenship,[66] thus confirming that the protection of fundamental rights is a separate matter from citizenship of the Union: this is because, by their nature, fundamental rights benefit Union citizens and third-country nationals coming within the scope of the Treaties in the same way.[67]

III. THE STATUS OF NATIONALS OF NON-MEMBER COUNTRIES

12–014 Third-country nationals. Until recently, nationals of non-Community countries did not enjoy any uniform status under Community law which determined their access to the territory of the Member States, their rights of residence and the activities they are allowed to carry on there. Some non-Community nationals are entitled to assert rights in these respects by virtue of conventions concluded between their countries and the Communities. In addition, nationals from non-Community countries may enjoy tributary rights of free movement which accrue to them as members of a Community national's family.[68] As a result of the abolition of checks carried out on persons at the Community's internal borders, the Member States had to agree on uniform rules on third-country nationals entering and residing in their territory. Since the Treaty of Amsterdam, the Community has initiated a common policy in the field of visas, asylum, immigration and other policies related to free movement of persons pursuant to Title IV of the EC Treaty (see para. 5–158 *et seq.*). In this way, third-country nationals are subject to common rules as to the entry to and residence within the territories of the Member States. However, some Member States do not take part in the adoption of these rules and are not bound by them.[69]

Nationals of third countries may enforce the rights which they derive from Community law before the Court of Justice and the Court of First

---

[66] See EU Constitution, Arts I–9 and I–10.

[67] See Weiler, "Thou Shalt Not Oppress a Stranger: On the Judicial Protection of the Human Rights of Non-EC Nationals—A Critique" (1992) E.J.I.L. 65–90; O'Leary, "The Relationship Between Community Citizenship and the Protection of Fundamental Rights in Community Law" (1995) C.M.L.R. 519–554; Davis, "Citizenship of the Union . . . rights for all?" (2002) E.L.R.; 122–137. Accordingly, the rights listed in the Charter of Fundamental Rights of the European Union are not reserved for nationals of the Member States, with the exception of certain civic rights (n.39, *supra*).

[68] paras 5–120, 5–157 and 12–003, *supra*. For the extent to which nationals of third countries might rely on more rights than EU nationals, see Weiss, "Gibt es eine EU-Inländerdiskriminierung? Zur Kollision von Gemeinschaftsrecht mit Welthandelsrecht und Assoziationsrecht" (1999) EuR. 499–516.

[69] See the special position of Denmark, para. 5–165, *supra*, and the exceptional status of Ireland and the UK, para. 5–166, *supra*. See also Staples, *The legal status of third country nationals resident in the European Union* (Kluwer, The Hague, 1999) 418 pp.; Rannou, "Le citoyenneté européenne et l'immigration" (2000) R.A.E. 38–56.

Instance on the same terms as citizens of the Union.[70] As has already been seen, third-country nationals with the right of residence in a Member State are entitled to access to documents of the European Parliament, the Council and the Commission and the right to petition the European Parliament or to make a complaint to the European Ombudsman (see para. 12–012). When third-country nationals exercise rights which they derive from Community law, they enjoy the benefit of the protection of fundamental rights conferred by Community law in their dealings with Community and national authorities. As far as non-Community action of the Union—carried out by Community institutions or Member States—is concerned, they likewise enjoy the protection of fundamental rights guaranteed by Art. 6(1) and (2) of the EU Treaty, although, in common with citizens of the Union, they are likely to find that that protection is not enforceable by court action.[71] Even after the EU Constitution has entered into force, the action of the Union and the Member States in the field of the CFSP will be amenable to review by the Court of Justice only exceptionally (see para. 18–022). In the field of CFSP, judicial enforcement of fundamental rights remains therefore to be left mainly to the domestic legal order of the Member States (which are bound in any case by the ECHR).

---

[70] EC Treaty, Arts 230, fourth para., and Art. 232, third para., refer to "any natural or legal person"; para. 10–074, *supra*. See the rights recognised with regard to "Justice" in Chapter VI of the Charter of Fundamental Rights of the European Union. More generally, see Lenaerts and Arts, *Procedural Law of the European Union*, Ch.7 (see the discussion of the requirements as to the admissibility relating to the persons).

[71] As regards the CFSP, this is the case as a result of Art. 46 of the EU Treaty; as regards PJCC, access to the Court of Justice may be had under the terms of Art. 35 of that Treaty; para. 10–077, *supra*; see also para. 18–021, *infra*.

CHAPTER 13

THE RELATIONSHIP BETWEEN THE ACTORS

Interaction. The European Union constitutes a level of administration in **13–001** its own right at which the institutions of the Union draw up legislation which has to be implemented and complied with within the Member States by the national authorities and their citizens. For the sound functioning of the Union, it is therefore important to have clear rules on the relationship between acts adopted at Union level, on the one hand, and national law, on the other. From the administrative point of view, however, what is important is not only the relationship between the Union and the Member States, but equally the way in which the various interests existing both within the Member States and across borders are reconciled through the interplay of Community and non-Community decision-making. In this connection, attention may be paid to the specific interests of each of the institutions of the Union and to the balance between institutions required by the Treaties. The same State functions which maintain the Member States in equilibrium as State authorities are also reflected at Union level.

I. RELATIONSHIP BETWEEN THE INSTITUTIONS OF THE UNION AND THE MEMBER STATES

Primacy of Union law. Both the provisions of the Community Treaties and **13–002** the secondary legislation based on it have primacy over the rules of national law of each of the Member States. This primacy arises out of the case law of the Court of Justice, according to which the objectives of the Treaty could not be achieved uniformly and effectively if the effect of Community law differed from Member State to Member State on the basis of national law (see paras 17–003–17–014). In order to secure compliance with Community law, the Court of Justice has recognised the right of citizens (and other legal subjects) to rely directly on provisions of Community law as against national authorities (see paras 17–047–17–050). These principles of "primacy" and "direct effect" have now been generally accepted within the national legal systems (see paras 17–015–17–046).

For other Treaty provisions and legislation not based on the Community Treaties, the relationship with national rules generally emerges from the form and content of the relevant provisions. The Court of Justice has only limited jurisdiction with respect to non-Community legislation (see paras 10–076–10–077). In the national legal systems, non-Community provisions have the (superior) position attributed to other rules of international law (see paras 18–001–18–023).

13–003 **Co-operation in good faith.** The corollary of Art. 10 of the EC Treaty is the general principle that the Member States should do everything necessary to ensure fulfilment of their obligations under Community law and to abstain from any measure which might jeopardise the attainment of the objectives of the Treaties. The Court of Justice considers that this principle of "co-operation in good faith" or "loyal co-operation" also holds good for the Community institutions, which must co-operate in good faith with the Member States and amongst each other in attaining the objectives of the Treaty (see paras 5–047–5–055). In addition, the Member States' national policy sphere is protected by the principle that the Community has only the powers conferred on it by the Treaties and also by the principles of subsidiarity and proportionality (EC Treaty, Art. 5; see paras 5–009–5–044). Those principles also apply to non-Community action by the Union, although they not always enforceable by the Court of Justice in this context (see para. 6–003).

13–004 **Confirmation inthe Constitution.** Most of these principles arising from the case law of the Court of Justice will be explicitly codified in the EU Constitution, in particular the principles governing the division of powers (see paras 5–009 and 5–027), the principle of sincere co-operation (see para. 5–049) and the principle of the primacy of Union law (see para. 17–002).

II. REPRESENTATION OF INTERESTS THROUGH INSTITUTIONS AND MEMBER STATES

13–005 **Representation of interests.** The Member States are not only the object of European decision-making but, as a result of the involvement of the national governments in the Council, also one of the actors involved in decision-making. Citizens, too, are not only the "objects" of European legislation, but, in electing the members of the European Parliament, they determine the composition of one of the actors participating in the Union's decision-making process. In contradistinction to traditional inter-governmental organisations, the interests of European citizens are defended not only by international action on the part of national authorities, but also by a directly representative institution—the European Parliament—and by other institutions and bodies which carry out their tasks independently of national interests in the general interest of the Union.[1]

Community and national interests. It emerges from the structure of the **13–006** Treaties that every time action on the part of the Union significantly affects the interests of the Member States, the relevant decision is reserved for the governments in the Council. Where the involvement of the Council as a Community institution is undesired, decisions are taken by the national governments among themselves or at the level of the Heads of State or Government in the European Council. In the case of certain "constitutive" acts, such as, of course, amendments to the Treaties, the matter is ultimately decided by the national parliaments or even by referendum, where the Treaties refer to the "constitutional requirements" of each Member State.

As a counterbalance to the defence of "national" interests, the Treaties provide for the involvement of the other Community institutions with a view to identifying and defending the "common" interest. Thus, the Commission takes views on the basis of its independent position and the European Parliament voices the majority views of its directly elected Members. The remaining Community institutions and bodies likewise perform tasks intended to safeguard particular common interests.[2]

It is no surprise therefore that Community decision-making is designed to reconcile "national" and "common" interests through interaction between the Council, the Commission and the European Parliament. Where decisions are taken by intergovernmental procedures, the Council's large degree of independence in reaching a decision results in a compromise being struck between purely "national" positions. Where the common interest prevails, the Treaties place the power in the hands of an independent Community institution. Accordingly, the Commission acts alone in monitoring compliance with Treaty obligations.

Individual interests. When it comes to the representation of interests **13–007** specific to citizens of the Union (and other individuals), the Treaties rely, on the one hand, on the ways in which individuals may make their voices heard in their own Member States and, on the other, on the say which individuals and interest groups have at Union level, namely involvement in decision-making via the European Parliament and through administrative and judicial remedies. "Democratic scrutiny" of Union policy is therefore exercised both at national and at Union level (see paras 16–004–16–019).

---

[1] For an outstanding analysis, see Jacqué, "Cours général de droit communautaire", *Collected Courses of the Academy of European Law I*, 1990, 237, at 289.
[2] See, *e.g.* compliance with the law (Court of Justice); due and proper management of the Communities' resources (Court of Auditors); maintenance of price stability (ECB).

III. Balance between the Institutions

13–008 Institutional balance. Since the institutions (and bodies) of the Communities act as a mouthpiece for national or common interests, the allocation of powers among the institutions is based on a delicate balance between the interests which they represent. That "institutional balance" is based on "a system for distributing powers among the different Community institutions, assigning to each institution its own role in the institutional structure of the Community and the accomplishment of the tasks entrusted to the Community".[3] The rule set out in the second subpara. of Art. 7(1) of the EC Treaty that "[e]ach institution shall act within the limits of the powers conferred upon it by this Treaty" must be read in the light of the principle of institutional balance. This means that each institution:

(1) has the necessary independence in exercising its powers;

(2) may not unconditionally assign its powers to other institutions or bodies; and

(3) must pay due regard to the powers of the other institutions.

It must be possible to impose a sanction for any failure to observe that institutional balance. This is why the Court of Justice is prepared to review the institutions' compliance with their powers.[4] The principle of co-operation in good faith (EC Treaty, Art. 10; see paras 5–047 *et seq.*) also puts the Member States under a duty to comply with the principle of institutional balance, while, in turn, requiring the institutions to have due regard to the powers of the Member States. The "balance" which has to be guaranteed does not necessarily mean that the most "balanced" relationship between the different interests at stake has to be achieved, but reflects the balance of power laid down in the Treaties.[5]

13–009 (1) Power of internal organisation. Each institution is empowered to determine its own organisation and manner of operation within the limits of the rules laid down in the Treaties.[6] In order to enable it to function

---

[3] ECJ, Case C–70/88 *European Parliament v Council* [1990] E.C.R. I–2041, para. 21.

[4] *ibid.*, paras 22–23; ECJ, Case 294/83 *Les Verts v European Parliament* [1983] E.C.R. 1339, para. 25. Examples are the Court's judgments in litigation on the correct legal basis for Community acts (see paras 5–009—5–027, *supra*) or on the extent of powers to adopt implementing acts (see paras 14–060—14–061, *infra*).

[5] See Jacqué (n.1, *supra*), at 292. See the appraisal of those relationships from the point of view of the separation of powers in paras 13–012—13–014, *infra*, and from the democratic standpoint in para. 16–004 *et seq.*

[6] This is true even if the act establishing the institution does not make express provision to this effect. The Court of Auditors was a case in point before the addition of the fifth subpara. of Art. 248(4) of the EC Treaty (see n.340 to para. 10–091, *supra*). However, the Council has to approve the Rules of Procedure of the Court of Justice and of the Court of First Instance (EC Treaty, Art. 223, sixth para., and Art. 224, fifth para.) and, at present, also the Rules of Procedure of the Court of Auditors (EC Treaty, Art. 248(4), fifth subpara.). For the extent of this power, see ECJ, Case C–58/94 *Netherlands v Council* [1996] E.C.R. I–2169, paras 37–43.

smoothly an institution is entitled to introduce its own internal decision-making procedure and establish procedures for monitoring whether its internal operations are in order. In so doing, an institution must take care to comply with principles enshrined in the Treaty.[7] Even Community bodies such as the European Central Bank and the European Investment Bank must comply with the limits which Community law places on the power of internal organisation. According to the Court of Justice, the ECB and the EIB exceeded those limits by introducing their own systems for combating fraud which precluded the investigatory powers conferred on the independent body OLAF by the Community legislature with regard to all Community institutions and bodies.[8] The institutions' independence is protected by privileges and immunities granted to them and their Members (see paras 10–114 and 10–149). What is more, Art. 10 of the EC Treaty requires Member States to abstain from any measure which might interfere with the internal functioning of the Community institutions.[9] Article 10 also prescribes a reciprocal duty to co-operate in good faith on the part of the institutions and the Member States. This means, for instance, that in their internal organisation the institutions have to take account of the powers of the Member States and of the other institutions. Accordingly, it has been held that in its resolutions on the question of its places of work the European Parliament has to respect the national governments' power to determine the seats of the institutions, together with the existing provisional decisions and the definitive decision on the location of the seats of the institutions.[10] The institutions are not entitled to rely on their privileges and immunities in order to neglect their duty to co-operate with the national authorities in view of the purely functional character of those rights conferred on the Communities.[11]

---

[7] With regard to the decision-making procedure, see ECJ, Case 5/85 *AKZO Chemie v Commission* [1986] E.C.R. 2585, paras 37 and 40, and the other judgments with regard to the principle of collective responsibility as it affects the Commission; para. 10–068, *supra*; with regard to monitoring internal operations, see ECJ, Case C–15/00 *Commission v European Investment Bank* [2003] E.C.R. I–7281, paras 67–68.

[8] ECJ, Case C–11/00 *Commission v European Central Bank* [2003] E.C.R. I–7147, paras 172–182; ECJ, Case C–15/00 *Commission v European Investment Bank* [2003] E.C.R. I–7281, paras 67–68.

[9] See ECJ, Case 208/80 *Lord Bruce of Donington* [1981] E.C.R. 2205, paras 14 and 19 (see para. 10–150, *supra*); ECJ, Case 230/81 *Luxembourg v European Parliament* [1983] E.C.R. 255, para. 37. See also ECJ, Case C–345/95 *France v European Parliament* [1997] E.C.R. I–5215, para. 32.

[10] ECJ, Case 230/81 *Luxembourg v European Parliament* [1983] E.C.R. 255, para. 38; ECJ, Case C–345/95 *France v European Parliament* [1997] E.C.R. I–5215, para. 31. See also para. 10–151, *supra*. See also ECJ, Case 294/83 *Les Verts v European Parliament* [1986] E.C.R. 1339, para. 25 and paras 51–55 (the European Parliament had introduced a scheme for the reimbursement of election campaign expenses unlawfully since the Act on the Direct Election of the European Parliament left such matters to the Member States to determine).

[11] ECJ, Case C–2/88 Imm. *Zwartveld* [1990] E.C.R. I–3365, para. 21. For the nature of the privileges and immunities, see para. 10–114, *supra*.

13–010 **(2) Limits to the delegation of powers.** An institution may not upset the institutional balance by assigning the powers conferred on it to other bodies. The Court of Justice has explained this principle by reference to Art. 3 of the ECSC Treaty, which entrusted the tasks of the ECSC to the "institutions of the Community . . . within the limits of their respective powers, in the common interest". The Court held that "there can be seen in the balance of powers which is characteristic of the institutional structure of the Community a fundamental guarantee granted by the Treaty in particular to the undertakings and associations of undertakings to which it applies. To delegate a discretionary power, by entrusting it to bodies other than those which the Treaty has established to effect and supervise the exercise of such power each within the limits of its own authority, would render that guarantee ineffective".[12] This does not preclude an institution from delegating "implementing" powers to other bodies in circumstances not detracting from the balance between the institutions (see para. 14–063).

13–011 **(3) Respect for each other's independence.** In their relationship with each other and in exercising their powers, the institutions must take care not to jeopardise each other's independence.[13] The practice adopted by an institution may not have the effect of depriving other institutions of a prerogative granted to them by the Treaties themselves.[14] This is true in particular of the European Parliament's power to take part in the Community's legislative process, which constitutes "an essential factor in the institutional balance intended by the Treaty".[15] The reason is that "[a]lthough limited, it reflects at Community level the fundamental democratic principle that the peoples should take part in the exercise of power through the intermediary of a representative assembly".[16] As has already been noted, institutional balance requires a sanction to be able to be brought to bear on any practice by which an institution exercises its powers without due regard for the other institutions' powers. Yet, before the EC Treaty was amended by the EU Treaty, the European Parliament, according to the wording of Art. 173 of the EEC Treaty, had no right to bring an action for annulment against acts of the Council or the Commission in order to safeguard its prerogatives. In a 1990 judgment the Court of Justice held that the absence of such a right "may constitute a procedural gap, but it cannot prevail over the fundamental interest in the

---

[12] ECJ, Case 9/56 *Meroni v High Authority* [1957 and 1958] E.C.R. 133, at 152. See Lenaerts, "Regulating the Regulatory Process: 'Delegation of Powers' in the European Community" (1993) E.L.R. 23, at 40–49.

[13] See ECJ, Case 25/70 *Köster* [1970] E.C.R. 1161, paras 4 and 8–9; ECJ, Opinion 1/59 *Procedure for amendment pursuant to the third and fourth paras of Art. 95 of the ECSC Treaty* [1959] E.C.R. 259, point (e), at 273.

[14] ECJ, Case 149/85 *Wybot* [1986] E.C.R. 2391, para. 23.

[15] ECJ, Case 138/79 *Roquette Frères v Council* [1980] E.C.R. 3333, para. 33, and ECJ, Case 139/79 *Maïzena v Council* [1980] E.C.R. 3393, para. 34.

[16] *ibid.*

maintenance and observance of the institutional balance laid down in the Treaties establishing the European Communities".[17] It went on to hold that an action for annulment brought by the Parliament against an act of the Council or the Commission would be admissible provided that the action sought only to safeguard the Parliament's prerogatives and was founded only on submissions alleging their infringement.[18] Consequently, the need to preserve the institutional balance laid down in the Treaties may exceptionally move the Court to take corrective action by way of an interpretation of the relevant provisions of the Treaty.[19] As far as the judiciary is concerned, institutional balance does not impede the courts from interpreting the Treaty as giving natural and legal persons a general right to compensation from the State for damage resulting from an infringement of Community law.[20]

IV. THE ALLOCATION OF THE CLASSICAL FUNCTIONS OF A STATE

Checks and balances. Community decision-making gives rise to both **13–012** legislative and implementing acts (see para. 14–003); additionally, it often requires legislative or implementing action in the Member States (see para. 14–048). The judicial resolution of disputes arising in connection with the application of Community law falls in principle to the national courts, but in certain clearly defined cases is entrusted to the Court of Justice and the Court of First Instance (see paras 10–073–10–079). Within the national legal systems, the principle of separation of powers (at least in theory) requires the legislative, executive and judicial functions to be allocated to different organs of the State in order to avoid citizens having to face an administration which holds all the powers without their exercise being subject to any political or judicial review. That principle does not signify that each function has to be carried out completely independently by a single public authority. Instead it is effectuated through a system of checks and balances designed to ensure that public authorities are required to co-operate with each other or to supervise each other. The question arises as to how that system is constituted in the Community legal order.[21]

---

[17] ECJ, Case C–70/88 *European Parliament v Council* [1990] E.C.R. I–2041, para. 26. See also ECJ, Case C–106/96 *UK v Commission* [1998] E.C.R. I–2729, paras 21–37 (annulment of a Commission decision implementing expenditure for which the Council had not adopted a basic act on the ground that the Commission had thereby infringed Art. 7(1) of the EC Treaty; see also para. 10–140, *supra*).

[18] *ibid.*, para. 27. In this connection the Court reversed its ruling in ECJ, Case 302/87 *European Parliament v Council* [1988] E.C.R. 5638, paras 8–28. See the discussion in n.79 to para. 10–021, *supra*, and the amendments which have since been made to the following articles of the Treaties: EC Treaty, Art. 230, third para.; EAEC Treaty, Art. 146, third para.

[19] Jacqué (n.1, *supra*), at 294.

[20] ECJ, Joined Cases C–46/93 and C–48/93 *Brasserie du Pêcheur and Factortame (Factortame IV)* [1996] E.C.R. I–1029, paras 24–30.

[21] For an analysis of the Community legal order in the light of that principle, see Lenaerts, "Some Reflections on the Separation of Powers in the European Community" (1991) C.M.L.R. 11–35.

13–013 Legislative and executive powers. Community institutions have a legislative function where the Treaty provides a legal basis; sometimes the Treaty also requires action on the part of national institutions (see para. 11–005). The European Parliament is generally involved in the Community legislative process in one way or another. Nevertheless, the process is largely determined by the Commission and the Council, both of which also have executive powers. Given that the power to take legislative decisions virtually always lies with the Council, it does not square with the principle of separation of powers that it should also perform executive tasks yet not be subject to effective political supervision (see paras 14–060–14–061). In contrast, the executive function performed by the Commission is completely compatible with that institution's role in the legislative process in so far as it consists principally of its right to initiate legislation, a right which in systems characterised by separation of powers is likewise generally vested in the executive.

Where national authorities are involved in the adoption of Community legislation, the constitutional rules of each Member State determine whether legislative or executive bodies are responsible for the necessary decision-making. An example is the transposition of directives into national law.

13–014 Judicial powers. The independence of the judiciary is guaranteed in the Community legal order. The Community's political institutions have no influence on the course of pending proceedings; they are, however, under a duty to co-operate with judicial authorities.[22] In view of the principle of the primacy of Community law, both the Community and national courts have frequently to rule on the compatibility of national law with Community law. When national courts have to make such rulings, Art. 10 of the EC Treaty puts them under a duty to set aside legislative measures which are incompatible with Community law even if the court hearing the case normally has no jurisdiction to review whether such measures are constitutional under domestic law. Furthermore, the Treaty gives natural and legal persons the right to obtain compensation before national courts for damage caused to them by a Member State as a result of breaches of Community law, even if the national legislature was responsible for the breach in question.[23] In this way, Community law has an influence on the scope of the division of powers under the national legal systems.[24] At

---

[22] For the duty to co-operate as far as Community institutions are concerned, see ECJ, Case C–2/88 Imm. *Zwartveld* [1990] E.C.R. I–3365, paras 21–22 (para. 5–053, *infra*).

[23] ECJ, Joined Cases C–46/93 and C–48/93 *Brasserie du Pêcheur and Factortame (Factortame IV)* [1996] E.C.R. I–1029, paras 31–36.

[24] See the judgments cited in the discussion of the duty to co-operate in good faith, nn.181–184 to paras 5–051 and 5–054, *supra* and the associated text. See also Barav, "Omnipotent Courts", in Curtin and Heukels (eds), *Institutional Dynamics of European Integration. Essays in Honour of Henry G. Schermers*, Vol.II (Martinus Nijhoff, Dordrecht, 1994) at 265–302.

Community level, the requirement for adequate legal protection entails that all acts of Community institutions, regardless whether they are of a legislative or executive nature, must be able to be reviewed for conformity with the Community Treaties. Since the Community is intended to be a "Community based on the rule of law", "neither its Member States nor its institutions can avoid a review of the question whether the measures adopted by them are in conformity with the basic constitutional charter, the Treaty".[25] Consequently, the principle of separation of powers does not preclude judicial review of measures adopted by the European Parliament.[26]

---

[25] ECJ, Case 294/83 *Les Verts v European Parliament* [1986] E.C.R. 1339, para. 23.
[26] *ibid.*, paras 24–25. See in particular ECJ, Case 230/81 *Luxembourg v European Parliament* [1983] E.C.R. 255, paras 14, 16 and 19.

Part IV

THE DECISION-MAKING PROCESS
WITHIN THE EUROPEAN UNION

CHAPTER 14

COMMUNITY DECISION-MAKING

Community and non-Community decision-making. Decision-making 14–001
within the European Union is based on interaction between the European
Parliament, the Council and the Commission. The Treaties prescribe
different decision-making procedures depending on the extent to which the
Contracting Parties have agreed in each given field that the national
governments—represented in the Council—will share their power of
decision with the Commission and the European Parliament. In this
connection, a distinction should be made between decision-making
pursuant to a provision of the Community Treaties ("Community
decision-making": this chapter), on the one hand, and decision-making
pursuant to a provision of Title V or Title VI of the EU Treaty (common
foreign and security policy and police and judicial co-operation in criminal
matters) and other forms of arrangements concluded among the Member
States (Chapter 15). Following the description of the various
decision-making procedures, some factors designed to legitimate the
decision-making process are analysed, in particular from the point of view
of its efficiency and the extent to which it is democratic and transparent in
nature (Chapter 16).

The EU Constitution will make further progress towards providing
decision-making in the Union with a stronger democratic foundation in so
far as the European Parliament will participate in it on an equal footing
with the Council. The EU Constitution will also simplify decision-making
considerably, since the Community system of decision-making will be
extended to all fields of action of the Union with the sole exception of the
common foreign and security policy (see para. 15–009).

I. The Distinction between Legislation and the Implementation of Legislation

No formal distinction. Acts adopted at Community level include not only 14–002
rules of a legislative nature but also detailed provisions which make it
possible to implement legislative provisions in practice and decisions which
apply legislative and other general rules to individual situations. The Treaty
distinguishes between "legislative" and "implementing" acts, in so far as

Art. 207(3) of the EC Treaty provides that the Council must define the cases "in which it is to be regarded as acting in its legislative capacity" with a view to allowing greater public access to documents in those cases. Nevertheless, in the Community legal order it is not easy to make a formal distinction between legislation and implementation of legislation. The Treaties did not set up separate legislative and executive institutions: the legislative function is spread over the Council, the European Parliament and the Commission (see para. 14–008), whilst the Commission and the Council also perform executive functions (see para. 14–051). Furthermore, it is impossible to classify the acts which those institutions adopt as legislative or implementing measures on the basis of their form. Both types of act are adopted in the form of any one of the legal instruments mentioned in Art. 249 of the EC Treaty.

14–003 Legislative measures. The distinction between legislation and implementation of legislation is therefore determined in the first place by the type of provision which serves as the legal basis for the Community act in question. If the act is based on an article of the Treaty, it may be regarded as a "legislative act", at least in so far as its content is also formulated in general, abstract terms. In contrast, implementing acts are involved where they are based on legislative acts (or on earlier implementing acts). The Court of Justice has stated as follows in this connection: "The concept of implementation for the purposes of [Article 145, now Article 202, of the EC Treaty] comprises both the drawing up of implementing rules and the application of rules to specific cases by means of acts of individual application".[1]

14–004 Implementing measures. Implementing provisions are necessary where legislative acts cannot determine every aspect of a particular policy. For example, the Commission may validly adopt a regulation implementing a basic regulation—in the manner prescribed in the latter regulation—which the Council adopted pursuant to the third subpara. of Art. 37(2) of the EC Treaty (on agriculture). The legislative procedure laid down by that article has no role to play any more in the adoption of the implementing measure. The only condition is that the Commission's implementing regulation must not go beyond implementation of the principles of the basic regulation.[2] Where a regulation empowers an institution to adopt general implementing provisions, this means, for example, that that institution is not empowered to alter the temporal scope of the regulation by that means.[3] Once an institution has adopted a general provision, it is contrary to the Community's legislative system to apply those general rules to individual

---

[1] ECJ, Case 16/88 *Commission v Council* [1989] E.C.R. 3457, para. 11.
[2] ECJ, Case 25/70 *Köster* [1970] E.C.R. 1161, paras 6 and 7.
[3] ECJ, Case C–93/00 *European Parliament v Council* [2001] E.C.R. I–10119, paras 39–43.

cases with a special procedure that derogates from these rules.[4] An implementing regulation cannot derogate from the provisions of a basic regulation,[5] unless such derogation is expressly provided for in the basic regulation and consistent with its general system and essential elements.[6] On the same grounds, an institution may not fail to comply in a decision with the conditions which it itself laid down in an earlier decision upon which that decision is based.[7] An act is invalid where it conflicts with the act on the basis of which it was adopted.

The fact that an implementing measure is subordinate to a legislative measure forms part of the general hierarchy of Community rules, which, unlike the hierarchical relationship of norms under the constitutional systems of most Member States, is not organised on formal lines, but substantively determined by the content of the rule (see para. 17–054). In the same way that a constitutional rule of Community law always ranks higher than a legislative measure, a legislative measure takes precedence over an implementing measure.

Constitution—Formal distinction to be introduced. The EU Constitution **14–005** will introduce a clear distinction between legislative and other acts of the Union with the aim of making decision-making at Union level more democratic and transparent. To that end, the EU Constitution uses the expression "legislative act" solely for acts which are formulated in general and abstract terms and adopted pursuant to a provision of the Constitution under the co-decision procedure or, in specific cases, under a "special legislative procedure" (EU Constitution, Art. I–34; see para. 14–013). Once the Constitution enters into force, legislative acts will be framed either as "European laws" or as "European framework laws" (see para. 17–146).

It follows that legislative acts will be formally distinguished from other acts adopted by the institutions of the Union, that is to say—alongside "implementing acts" adopted by the Commission or the Council to implement other binding acts—acts adopted by the Council or the Commission in specific cases to execute a provision of the Constitution[8] and acts adopted by the Commission pursuant to an explicit delegation by the legislator. For these purposes, the institutions are to make use of "European regulations" or "European decisions" (see para. 17–147). Accordingly, whereas the present practice is to use regulations and

---

[4] ECJ, Case 113/77 *NTN Toyo Bearing Company v Council* [1979] E.C.R. 1185, para. 21. See also ECJ, Case C–313/90 *CIRFS v Commission* [1993] E.C.R. I–1125, para. 44 (an individual decision may not impliedly amend a measure of general application); ECJ, Joined Cases C–246–249/94 *Co-operativa Agricola Zootecnica S. Antonio* [1996] E.C.R. I–4373, paras 30–31.

[5] ECJ, Case 38/70 *Tradax* [1971] E.C.R. 145, para. 10.

[6] ECJ, Case 230/78 *Eridania* [1979] E.C.R. 2749, para. 8. See also ECJ, Case 100/74 *C.A.M. v Commission* [1975] E.C.R. 1393, paras 27–28.

[7] *E.g.* ECJ, Case C–393/01 *France v Commission* [2003] E.C.R. I–5403, paras 40–60.

[8] For an example of the EU Constitution specifying both the power to enact legislation and the power to adopt executive acts, see Art. III–231(2) and (3) (agricultural policy).

directives for both legislative and executive action, under the EU Constitution there will be different instruments for the legislative and the executive function. The category of the non-legislative acts will continue to encompass both implementing measures of a general nature and decisions applying those general rules to individual cases.

II. LEGISLATION

A. BASIC OUTLINE

14–006 Legislative procedure. The Community Treaties do not prescribe a general procedure for the adoption of legislative acts. Instead, each Treaty article which provides for action by the Community lays down how that action is to be carried out. A general procedure exists only for Community participation in international agreements (EC Treaty, Art. 300; see paras 21–002 *et seq.*). As has already been mentioned, the EU Constitution will introduce the co-decision procedure as the "ordinary legislative procedure" for all fields of action of the Union, except for the common foreign and security policy. This procedure will however not be of universal application and will continue to co-exist with various "special legislative procedures" (see para. 14–013).

14–007 Duty to legislate. The power to legislate is not associated with a correlative duty to do so. A duty to legislate does arise, however, where the Treaty commits an institution to adopting a particular act within a specified time.[9] If the substance of the obligation is sufficiently clearly defined in the Treaty, a failure to comply with it will constitute an omission against which an action for failure to act will lie.[10] If neither the Council nor the European Parliament is under a duty to act, those institutions are in principle not bound to any time at which they must take a decision on a Commission proposal.[11]

---

[9] For time-limits prescribed for action on the part of the Council, see: EC Treaty, Arts 61, 62 and 63 and Art. 67; Art. 104(14), third subpara.; Art. 255(2); Art. 286(2). With a view to simplification of the Treaties, Arts 6, 7 and 8 of the Amsterdam Treaty repealed a number of provisions laying down time-limits and deleted the time-limit from others. Art. 10(1) of the Amsterdam Treaty emphasises that the repeal or deletion of such provisions does not bring about any change in their legal effects, in particular those arising from the time-limits prescribed therein. For an obligation to act, see, *inter alia*, EC Treaty, Art. 301; para. 20–051, *infra*.

[10] For such an obligation on the part of the Council, see ECJ, Case 13/83 *European Parliament v Council* [1985] E.C.R. 1513, para. 64 (concerning the obligation arising under Art. 71(2) of the EC Treaty; see para. 5–194, *supra*).

[11] See the Commission's answer of November 20, 1998 to question P–3242/98 (Jarembowski), [1999] O.J. C297/62. For a commentary, see Schorkopf, "Die Untätigkeit des Rates der Europäischen Union im Gesetzgebungsverfahren" (2000) EuR. 365–379.

Interaction between institutions. The majority of Community legislative **14–008** procedures involve the Commission, the Council and the European Parliament. Where a Treaty article confers the power to adopt an act on the Council or on the European Parliament and the Council jointly, the institutions are, as a general rule, entitled to act only if the Commission exercises its right of initiative (see para. 13–007). In so far as the co-decision procedure between the European Parliament and the Council does not apply, the European Parliament virtually always has some say in decision-making (see paras 14–020 *et seq.*). In addition, there are a number of advisory committees, consultation of which may or may not be compulsory (see para. 14–044). The upshot of the various permutations of institutions and bodies having some competence in the legislative field is that the Community adopts acts in accordance with a variety of different procedures.[12]

Role of Member States. The Member States as such are not involved in the **14–009** Community legislative process. Only some Community measures approximating to an amendment of the Treaties have to be approved also by the national parliaments in order for them to obtain the force of law (see paras 7–004—7–008). The Community is not entitled simply to delegate its legislative power to the Member States.[13] In areas where the Community has exclusive competence, Member States may be entrusted only with implementing policy options which have already been formulated by the Community.[14] Where the Community has already legislated in other areas, any decision as to whether to leave the matter henceforth entirely or partly to the Member States is subject to the requirements of Art. 5 of the EC Treaty (legal basis, subsidiarity and proportionality) and may be revoked at any time.[15]

Impact of voting requirements. In respect of matters on which the **14–010** European Parliament does not "co-decide" and the Council has the last word, the legislative process is dominated by the national governments collectively. Where a Treaty article requires an act of the Council to be adopted unanimously, each Member State has a decisive say in the outcome of the legislative process: either the Council adopts a piece of legislation to

---

[12] See the list set out in Piris, "After Maastricht, are the Community Institutions More Efficacious, More Democratic and More Transparent?" (1994) E.L.R. 449–487. For a schematic overview of the procedure by article of the Treaty, see Raworth, *The Legislative Process in the European Community* (Kluwer, Deventer, 1993) at 129–149, Ortúzar Andéchaga, "La posible extensión de la votación per mayoría cualificada en el Consejo, tema de estudio obligado de la próxima conferencia intergubernamental, impuesto por el Consejo Europea de Helsinki" (2001) 192 Not.U.Eur. 31–43.

[13] Lenaerts, "Regulating the Regulatory Process: 'Delegation of Powers' in the European Community" (1993) E.L.R. 23, at 28–32.

[14] In this connection, the institutions may confer specific authorisation to act on a Member State. para. 5–026, *supra*.

[15] paras 5–009–5–044, *supra*, especially para. 5–024.

which each Member State can reconcile itself, or no text at all. Where, in contrast, the Council takes its decision by a qualified majority vote, the interaction with the Commission and the European Parliament ensures that there is a genuine three-way dialogue. In such a case, the Commission (by means of a proposal)—and possibly the European Parliament (by means of amendments and the possible use of its veto in the co-decision procedure)—is in a position to present to the Council a legislative text which does not necessarily meet with the approval of every Member State.

B. DECISION-MAKING POWER

14-011 Council. The Council is the chief legislating institution. The majority of articles of the EC Treaty provide for acts of a general nature to be adopted by the Council either unanimously[16] or by a qualified majority[17] (for details

---

[16] See the acts to be adopted on a proposal from the Commission pursuant to Art. 13; Art. 18(2); Art. 19(1) and (2); Art. 22, second para.; Art. 42; Art. 47(2), second sentence; Art. 57(2), second sentence; Art. 67(1) and (2); Art. 71(2); Art. 93; Art. 94; Art. 104(14), second subpara.; Art. 105(6); Art. 107(5); Art. 117(7); Art. 123(4) and (5); Art. 133(5), second and third subparas, and (7); Art. 137(2), second subpara.; Art. 139(2), *in fine*; Art. 151(5), first and second indents; Art. 161, first and second paras; Art. 175(2) and (3), second subpara.; Art. 181a(2); Art. 202, third indent; Art. 229a; Art. 269, second para.; Art. 279; Art. 296(2); Art. 300(2), second sentence; Art. 308. See also the acts to be adopted by the Council on its own initiative (EC Treaty, Art. 144; Art. 187, second para.; Art. 290), on a recommendation from the Commission or the ECB (EC Treaty, Art. 111(1), first sentence), on a proposal from the European Parliament (EC Treaty, Art. 190(4), second subpara., and Art. 190(5)) or on an application from a (would-be) Member State (EC Treaty, Art. 88(2), third subpara., and EU Treaty, Art. 49, first para.). See, in addition, the decisions relating to the appointment of members of institutions or bodies or concerning the statutes of institutions or bodies referred to in ns. to para. 10–045.

[17] See the acts adopted on a proposal from the Commission under the co-operation and co-decision procedures provided for in Arts 252 and 251 of the EC Treaty, respectively (n.93 and n.104, *infra*, respectively) and under EC Treaty, Art. 11(2), first subpara.; Art. 14(3); Art. 26; Art. 37(2), third subpara.; Art. 45, second para.; Art. 49, second para.; Art. 52(1); Art. 57(2), first sentence; Art. 59; Art. 60(1) and (2), second subpara.; Art. 64(2); Art. 67(3); Art. 75(3); Art. 80(2); Art. 83(1); Art. 87(3)(e); Art. 89; Art. 92; Art. 96, second para.; Art. 100(1) and (2); Art. 100(2); Art. 104(14), third subpara.; Art. 107(6); Art. 111(4); Art. 114(3); Art. 117(6), second subpara.; Art. 128(2); Art. 132(1); Art. 133(2) and (4); Art. 139(2); Art. 149(4), second indent; Art. 152(4), second subpara.; Art. 161, third para.; Art. 166(4); Art. 172, first para.; Art. 175(2), second subpara.; Art. 181a(2); Art. 283; Art. 299(2); Art. 300(2), first sentence; Art. 301; EU Treaty, Art. 7(2) and (3). See also the acts to be adopted by the Council on a recommendation from the Commission (EC Treaty, Art. 99(4); Art. 111(3); Art. 119(2); Art. 121(2); Art. 128(2) and (4); Art. 133(3) and (4); Art. 300(1)), from the ECB (EC Treaty, Art. 107(5) and (6)), from either one of those two institutions (Art. 111(1), second sentence, and (2)), on an opinion of the Commission (EC Treaty, Art. 120(3)), on the basis of conclusions of the European Council (EC Treaty, Art. 99(2), third subpara.), on its own initiative (EC Treaty, Art. 11(2), second subpara.; Art. 119(3), second subpara.; Art. 210; Art. 214(2), first subpara.; Art. 215, second subpara.; Art. 247(8); Art. 258, fourth para.; Art. 309(2) and (3)) or following proposals from the Member States (EC Treaty, Art. 214(2), second and third paras). See also a number of preparatory acts adopted on a recommendation from the Commission (EC Treaty, Art. 99(2), first subpara.; Art. 104(6)), the decisions relating to the transition to the third stage of EMU (EC Treaty, Art. 121(3) and (4); on a recommendation and on a proposal, respectively, from the Commission: Art. 122(1) and (2)), the decision of approval provided for by Art. 195(4) of the EC Treaty and acts adopted in the course of the budgetary procedure (EC Treaty, Art. 272(3), third subpara., (5) and (9), fifth subpara.; Art. 273, second para.; Art. 276(1)).

of voting on the Council, see para. 10–045). In order to enable all necessary measures to be adopted during the transitional period provided for by the EC Treaty, a number of articles provided for decision-making to be carried out in stages, with decisions having to be taken unanimously in the first or in the first and second stages and by a qualified majority vote thereafter.[18]

The requirement for a unanimous vote does not only make it more difficult for agreement to be reached between the Member States in the Council, it also deprives the Commission of the room for manoeuvre which its right to make proposals affords in a procedure requiring only a qualified majority vote (see para. 14–017). The reason for this is that under such a procedure the Council has to vote unanimously on any amendment which it makes to the proposal from the Commission (EC Treaty, Art. 250(1)), whereas only a qualified majority is required to adopt the proposal. By the same token, a requirement for a unanimous vote tends to diminish the influence which the European Parliament can bring to bear directly or indirectly (where the Commission accepts its amendments). In exceptional cases, the Treaty requires some other majority[19] and, where no specific voting requirement is laid down, a simple majority of votes of members of the Council suffices.[20] A simple majority vote is needed for some preparatory acts[21] and for acts relating to internal organisation or relations with other institutions.[22]

European Parliament and Commission. The European Parliament and the **14–012** Council share legislative power under the procedure provided for in Art. 251 of the EC Treaty ("co-decision" procedure) within the scope *ratione materiae* of that procedure (see para. 14–030). The European Parliament (acting alone) has the power to adopt rules which are generally binding

---

[18] The relevant articles (or the clause on the transitional period) were repealed by the Treaty of Amsterdam as part of the exercise of simplifying the Treaties. The system is retained, however, in Art. 67(1) and (2) (whereby, after five years, the Council was to determine the field covered by the co-decision procedure, entailing voting by qualified majority) and Art. 67(4) of the EC Treaty (automatic application of the co-decision procedure after that period).

[19] See EC Treaty, Art. 104(13) (majority of two-thirds of the votes of the members, excluding those of the Member State concerned, weighted in accordance with Art. 205(2)) and Art. 122(5) (suspension of voting rights of Member States with a derogation); EU Treaty, Art. 7(1) (majority of four-fifths of the Members) and (5) (qualified majority in the same proportion of the weighted votes of the members of the Council concerned as laid down in Art. 205(2)). See also the procedures referred to in paras 14–059 14–063, *infra*.

[20] In accordance with EC Treaty, Art. 205(1).

[21] EC Treaty, Art. 112(2)(b), first subpara.; EU Treaty, Art. 48, second para.

[22] EC Treaty, Art. 115; Art. 196, second para.; Art. 207(2), second subpara., and (3); Art. 208; Art. 209; Art. 213(2), third subpara. (and Art. 216); Art. 218(1); Art. 221, third para.; Art. 230, second para.; Art. 232, first para.; Art. 248(4), second subpara.; Art. 260, third para.; Art. 262, first para.; Art. 264, third para.; Art. 265, first para.; Art. 284; Art. 300(6). See nevertheless the power to "legislate" under Art. 284 of the EC Treaty: ECJ, Case C–426/93 *Germany v Council* [1995] E.C.R. I–3723, paras 10–22.

only with a view to its internal organisation.[23] The Commission is empowered to adopt acts of a general nature within the limits of a power conferred on it to that end by a Treaty provision.[24] As far as acts concerning relations between the institutions are concerned, the Treaty sometimes provides for agreement to be reached between the institutions on the measure to be taken.[25]

14–013 Constitution. The EU Constitution will enlarge the field in which legislation is adopted "jointly by the European Parliament and the Council" under the co-decision procedure—which will in future be known as the "ordinary legislative procedure" (EU Constitution, Art. I–34(1); see para. 14–030). Article I–34(2) of the EU Constitution regards the instances in which the Council will not decide jointly with the European Parliament as "special legislative procedures", that is to say those cases in which legislation is to be adopted "by the European Parliament with the participation of the Council" or "by the latter with the participation of the European Parliament". The second option is the more frequent: in this case the Council will have the power of decision, acting unanimously or by a qualified majority, whilst the European Parliament will be consulted[26] or will have to give its consent.[27] It should be noted that the European Council may decide—on its own initiative and by a unanimous vote—that in some cases where the Constitution provides for legislation to be adopted under a special legislative procedure or where the Constitution provides for the Council to act unanimously in a given area, decisions will in future be taken under the ordinary legislative procedure or by qualified majority vote, as the case may be (EU Constitution, Art. IV–444).

---

[23] The European Parliament does lay down the regulations and general provisions governing the performance of the European Ombudsman's duties, but has to seek the opinion of the Commission first and needs the approval of the Council (EC Treaty, Art. 195(4)). The European Parliament is to lay down by the same procedure the regulations and general conditions governing the performance of the duties of its Members (EC Treaty, Art. 190(5)).

[24] ECJ, Joined Cases 188–190/80 *France, Italy and UK v Commission* [1982] E.C.R. 2545, paras 4–7 (following an application of EC Treaty, Art. 86(3); see para. 5–201, *supra*). For the field of application of the Commission's power to take decisions, see para. 10–059, *supra*.

[25] Provision is made for agreement to be reached between the Council and the European Parliament in EC Treaty, Art. 272(9), fifth subpara., and in the temporal provisions set out in Art. 251(7); Art. 252(g), and Art. 300(3), third subpara. EC Treaty, Art. 193, third para., provides for provisions to be determined by common accord between the Council, the European Parliament and the Commission, whilst Art. 248(3) provides for agreement to be reached between the Court of Auditors, the European Investment Bank and the Commission on the right of access of the Court of Auditors to information held by the EIB.

[26] See, *e.g.* EU Constitution, Arts III–125(2), III–126, III–176, III–269(3), III–275(3) and III–277, where the Council is to decide unanimously, and Art. III–127, where the Council is to decide by a qualified majority vote.

[27] See, *e.g.* EU Constitution, Arts III–124(1), III–129, III–270(2)(d) and III–274(1), where the Council is to decide unanimously.

C. RIGHT OF INITIATIVE

Right falling to the Commission. Under the ECSC system, the **14–014** Commission was empowered to adopt acts itself, except in exceptional cases where the Council took the decision on a proposal from the Commission.[28] In contrast, under the procedures provided for in the EC and EAEC Treaties, the Commission is generally the only institution empowered to submit a proposal for legislation, with the result that the other institutions cannot legislate in the absence of a prior proposal from the Commission. Generally, a formal "proposal" is needed, but sometimes a recommendation[29] or some other initiative[30] suffices. The Council may adopt an act without any input from the Commission,[31] at the initiative of a Member State[32] or at the proposal of the European Parliament[33] only by way of exception. In addition, the Council deals with some matters connected with the composition and organisation of other Community institutions and bodies at their request or on their recommendation.[34]

No right of initiative for the Council or European Parliament. The **14–015** Community Treaties provide for a right of initiative only for the Commission, which, as an independent expert institution, has the capacity to ensure that every legislative initiative is technically correct and also in the interest of the Community. If the Council itself had the right to initiate legislation, the Member States in that institution would be able to take a step backwards in the integration process and thereby damage the nucleus

---

[28] See, *e.g.* ECSC Treaty, Art. 59(2) and (5).

[29] See for authorisation to conduct international negotiations: EC Treaty, Art. 133(3), first subpara.; Art. 300(1). See also EC Treaty, Art. 99(2), first subpara., and (4), first subpara.; Art. 104(6) to (9) and (11) to (13); Art. 111(1), (2) and (3); Art. 119(1), second subpara.; Art. 120(2); Art. 121(2); Art. 122(1) (economic and monetary provisions); Art. 128(4) (employment).

[30] EC Treaty, Art. 116(2)(b) (report); Art. 120(3) (opinion).

[31] EC Treaty, Art. 144; Art. 187; Art. 210; Art. 247(8); Art. 258, fourth para.; Art. 309(2) and (3). See also Art. 2(1), second subpara., (4), second subpara., (6) and (7) of Protocol (No.2) to the EU Treaty and the EC Treaty integrating the Schengen *acquis* into the framework of the European Union, [1997] O.J. C340/93 (para. 5–164, *supra*).

[32] EC Treaty, Art. 67(1) (on a proposal from the Commission or on the initiative of a Member State, but only during a transitional period of five years following the entry into force of the Amsterdam Treaty, after which the Council is invariably to act on a proposal from the Commission; see Art. 67(2)); and Art. 88(2), third subpara. (at the request of a Member State), and EU Treaty, Art. 7(1) (on a proposal by one-third of the Member States, the European Parliament or the Commission) and (2) (on a proposal from one-third of the Member States or the Commission).

[33] EU Treaty, Art. 7(1).

[34] See the decisions taken on the basis of a proposal from the European Parliament (EC Treaty, Art. 190(4), and Act on the Direct Election of the European Parliament, Art. 14), at the request of the Court of Justice (EC Treaty, Art. 222, first para.; Art. 225a, first para., and Art. 245, second para.), on a recommendation from the ECB (EC Treaty, Art. 107(5) and (6); Art. 111(1) and (2)), at the request of the EIB (EC Treaty, Art. 266, third para.). Decisions to be taken at the request or on a recommendation of the Court of Justice, the ECB or the EIB may also be taken at the initiative of the Commission after consulting the institutions concerned.

of the *acquis communautaire*. The fact that initially the European Parliament was given little or no part to play in the legislative process, meant that it obtained no right of initiative.[35] In view of the democratic legitimacy of the directly elected European Parliament, it would seem justified to confer a right of initiative also on the European Parliament.[36]

14–016 **Formulating proposals.** The right to propose legislation means, in the first place, that the Commission can decide whether or not the Community should act and, if so, on what legal basis, in what legal form (if the legal basis permits a choice) and what content and implementing procedures the proposal should embody. Especially, where the adoption of a legislative act is characterised by a wide discretion, the Commission itself decides when it is appropriate to formulate and submit legislative proposals.[37]

Usually, the Commission makes contact with interest groups affected and the administrative authorities in the Member States before it adopts its proposal.[38] In so doing, it adheres to an annual legislative programme drawn up in consultation with the European Parliament and the Council.[39]

---

[35] The European Parliament has such a right only under EC Treaty, Art. 195(4) (Ombudsman Regulations) and Art. 190(5) (laying down the regulations and general conditions governing the performance of the duties of its Members). See also the discussion of Art. 192 of the EC Treaty (para. 14–018, *infra*).

[36] After repeated calls (see the resolutions of July 9, 1981 ([1981] O.J. C234/64), October 8, 1986 ([1986] O.J. C283/39) and March 14, 1990 ([1990] O.J. C96/114), the European Parliament is at present no longer pressing for such a right of initiative; see Lenaerts and De Smijter, "On the Democratic Representation through the European Parliament, the Council, the Committee of the Regions, the Economic and Social Committee and the National Parliaments", in Winter, Curtin, Kellermann and De Witte (eds), *Reforming the Treaty on European Union—The Legal Debate*, (T.M.C. Asser Institute/Kluwer, The Hague, 1996) 173, at 182.

[37] CFI, Case T–571/93 *Lefebvre v Commission* [1995] E.C.R. II–2379, paras 32–39.

[38] For a description of how the Commission formulates a proposal, see Raworth (n.12, *supra*), at 29–34. For the contacts made with approximately 3,000 interest groups and the intention of the European Parliament and the Commission to introduce a register and a code of conduct for lobbying organisations, see the Commission's communication, "An open and structured dialogue between the Commission and special interest groups", [1993] O.J. C63/2, and the European Parliament's code of conduct regarding interest groups (amendments to the EP Rules of Procedure of May 13, 1997; Annex IX to the Rules, Provisions governing the application of r.9(2)—Lobbying in Parliament): [1997] O.J. C167/20. See Rideau, "Les groupes d'intérêt dans le système institutionnnel communautaire", (1993) 3 R.A.E. 49–73; McLaughlin, Jordan and Maloney, "Corporate Lobbying in the European Community" (1993) J.C.M.S. 191–212. For studies of lobbying in practice, see Pedler and Van Schendelen (eds), *Lobbying the European Union* (Dartmouth, Aldershot, 1994) 311 pp.

[39] See the Interinstitutional Agreement between the European Parliament, the Council and the Commission of December 16, 2003 on better law-making, points 3 *et seq.* ([2003] O.J. C321/1). As far as the Parliament is concerned, the matter is governed by r.33 of the EP Rules of Procedure. The current procedure is that the Commission draws up the legislative programme and the European Parliament and the Council give their views on it (in a resolution and a declaration, respectively). Lastly, the European Parliament and the Commission adopt a joint declaration on the legislative programme. For this co-operation and the timetable for the legislative programme, see Annex XIV to the EP Rules of Procedure. As far compliance with the programme is concerned, see the undertaking given

According to the Protocol on the application of the principles of subsidiarity and proportionality, the Commission has to consult widely before proposing legislation and, where appropriate, publish consultation documents.[40] It must justify the relevance of its proposals with regard to the principle of subsidiarity and, whenever necessary, the explanatory memorandum accompanying a proposal is to give details in this respect.[41] In the case of major proposals for legislation, the Commission may carry out a prior impact assessment.[42] In some cases, the Commission may decide to have recourse to self-regulation by the economic operators, social partners or associations concerned.[43] In response to the demand for democracy, transparency and subsidiarity, the Commission increasingly issues consultative documents, "green papers", in order to encourage political debate. Packages of related proposals for legislation are published in the form of "white papers".[44]

The Commission formulates each proposal which it wishes to submit as a text ready to be adopted, and publishes it in the *Official Journal* (part C). Such proposals and other preparatory documents on general matters which have been approved within the Commission are referred to as "COM documents". If they are not already available on the Commision's website, they may be obtained on request.[45] According to the Protocol on the role of

by the Commission in point 2 of the specific agreement on the legislative process (Annex I) attached to the framework agreement on relations between Parliament and the Commission of July 5, 2000 ([2001] O.J. C121/122, and (2000) 7/8 EU Bull., point 2.2.1), which is appended to the EP Rules of Procedure as Annex XIII.

[40] Protocol (No.30) to the EC Treaty on the application of the principles of subsidiarity and proportionality, annexed by the Amsterdam Treaty to the EC Treaty ([1997] O.J. C340/105), point 9 (which makes an exception for "cases of particular urgency or confidentiality").

[41] *ibid.*, second indent. An explanation is to be given for the financing of Community action in whole or in part from the Community budget. At the same time, the Protocol requires the Commission to take duly into account the need for any burden, whether financial or administrative, falling upon the Community, national governments, local authorities, economic operators and citizens to be minimised and proportionate to the objective to be achieved: *ibid.*, third indent (see also the discussion of the principles of subsidiarity and proportionality in paras 5–028—5–044, *supra*).

[42] According to Declaration (No.12) annexed to the Treaty of Amsterdam on environmental impact assessments, the Commission undertakes to prepare environmental impact assessment studies when making proposals which may have significant environmental implications. In the case of major items of draft legislation, the Commission is to implement an integrated impact-assessment process, combining in one single evaluation the impact assessments relating inter alia to social, economic and environmental aspects: point 29 of the Interinstitutional Agreement of December 16, 2003 on better-lawmaking (see n. 39, *supra*). Where the co-decision procedure applies, the European Parliament and Council may, on the basis of jointly defined criteria and procedures, also have impact assessments carried out prior to the adoption of any substantive amendment: *ibid.*, point 30.

[43] Criteria for the application of self-regulation or co-regulation (by which a Community act leaves achievement of its aims to the parties concerned; para. 14–046, *infra*) are set out in points 16 to 25 of the Interinstitutional Agreement of December 16, 2003 (n.39, *supra*).

[44] Thus, the Commission's White Paper on European Governance contains proposals designed to get more people and organisations involved in shaping and delivering Union policy: [2001] O.J. C287/1.

[45] Documents published by the Commission's general secretariat (SEC documents) may not be so requested, although these are now issued as far as possible in the form of COM documents.

national parliaments in the European Union, all Commission documents (green and white papers and communications) are to be promptly forwarded to national parliaments.[46] Commission proposals for legislation are to be made available in good time so that the government of each Member State may ensure that its own national parliament receives them as appropriate.[47] In order to allow enough time for discussion of the proposals, the Protocol requires that there be a six-week period between the time when a Commission proposal is made available in all languages to the European Parliament and the Council and the date when it is placed on a Council agenda for decision (adoption of an act or of a common position under the procedure laid down in Art. 251 or 252 of the EC Treaty).[48] Before making any legislative initiative, the Commission is invariably to notify the European Parliament.[49] Moreover, in all fields where the European Parliament acts in a legislative capacity, or as a branch of the budgetary authority, it is to be informed, on a par with the Council, at every stage of the legislative and budgetary process.[50]

14–017 Amending or withdrawing a proposal. When the Commission is entitled to submit a formal "proposal", it has a significant influence over the course of decision-making. So long as the Council has not reached a decision, the Commission is entitled to amend its proposal at any time during the procedure leading to adoption of a Community act (EC Treaty, Art. 250(2)). It may therefore amend its proposal at any time while it is under discussion in the Council (and before that in the working parties and Coreper). In view of the flexibility demanded by the legislative procedure with a view to achieving a convergence of views between the institutions, no formalities have to be complied with in order to amend a proposal and amendments do not have to be made in writing.[51] Thus, an "amendment of a proposal" may consist in a Member of Commission's approving a compromise proposal put forward by the Presidency of the Council, even if it involves a significant change to the original proposal.[52] Since the right not

---

[46] Protocol (No.9) to the EU Treaty and the Community Treaties on the role of national parliaments in the European Union ([1997] O.J. C340/113), point 1.

[47] *ibid.*, point 2 (which refers to "Commission proposals for legislation as defined by the Council in accordance with Article 207(3)" of the EC Treaty).

[48] *ibid.*, point 3; see Art. 3(3) of the Council Rules of Procedure. This applies to legislative proposals or proposals for measures to be adopted under Title VI of the EU Treaty, subject to "exceptions on grounds of urgency, the reasons for which shall be stated in the act or common position". For such an exception (in a decision not adopted on the initiative of the Commission), see recital 14 in the preamble to the Council Decision of July 16, 2003 on the granting of aid by the Belgian Government to certain co-ordination centres established in Belgium ([2003] O.J. L184/17).

[49] Framework agreement on relations between Parliament and the Commission of July 5, 2000 (n.39, *supra*), point 13.

[50] *ibid.*, point 12.

[51] ECJ, Case C–280/93 *Germany v Council* [1994] E.C.R. I–4973, para. 36.

[52] ECJ, Case 445/00 *Austria v Council* [2003] E.C.R. I–1461, paras 16–17 and 44–47.

to submit a proposal is a corollary of the right of initiative, the Commission may also withdraw its proposal at any time.[53]

As has been noted, where the Council has to adopt an act on a proposal from the Commission, the former may amend the proposal only by a unanimous vote (except in the conciliation phase of the co-decision procedure: see EC Treaty, Art. 250(1)). Consequently, as soon as one Member State is in agreement with a Commission proposal, the Council has to reach agreement on the proposal which has been submitted and which may be constantly amended by the Commission until it obtains the support of a sufficient majority. If the Council is unanimous in wishing to adopt an act which differs in some way from the Commission's proposal, the latter may deprive the Council of its power of decision by withdrawing the proposal. The Commission's room for manoeuvre is significantly greater where the Council has to act by a qualified majority than when it is required to take a unanimous decision. In the first case, the Commission will amend its proposal during the negotiations in the Council just sufficiently in order to obtain the number of votes required; in the second case, the Commission has to comply with the wishes of all the Member States, either by amending its proposal itself or by adhering to its proposal and seeing the Council possibly alter it by a unanimous vote. If the Council wishes to depart from the Commission's proposal, it cannot introduce just any provision. The Council will not exceed its power to make amendments if the changes it makes remain within the scope of the act as defined in the original Commission proposal.[54]

In those policy areas where the Treaty gives the Commission the initiative in the form of a recommendation, it does not have the same influence on decision-making. When the Council has received the recommendation, it can still decide by the same majority even if it does not take up the recommendation and the power to take the decision cannot be removed from it.[55]

No obligation. In principle, the Commission cannot be compelled to **14–018** submit a proposal, although, in some instances, the EC Treaty requires the Commission to examine whether it should submit a proposal.[56] In addition,

---

[53] See the Commission's answer of January 23, 1987 to question 2422/86 (Herman), [1987] O.J. C220/6. The Commission is to give the European Parliament and the Council prior notification before withdrawing its proposals: point 9 of the specific agreement on the legislative process (Annex I) appended to the framework agreement of July 5, 2000 (n.39, *supra*).

[54] ECJ, Case C–408/95 *Eurotunnel* [1997] E.C.R. I–6315, paras 37–39; see also ECJ, Case 355/87 *Commission v Council* [1987] E.C.R. 1517, paras 42–44 (amendments tested against the "subject-matter" and the "objective" of the proposal).

[55] ECJ (judgment of July 13, 2004), Case C–27/04 *Commission v Council*, not yet reported, para. 80 (where Commission recommendations—and not proposals—are placed before the Council, it may modify the measure recommended by the majority required for the adoption of that measure). See also *ibid.* para. 92 (Council decision taken on a recommendation from the Commission cannot be modified without a fresh recommendation from the Commission).

[56] EC Treaty, Art. 95(7) and (8).

Art. 208 of the EC Treaty does empower the Council (acting by a simple majority vote) to "request the Commission to undertake any studies the Council considers desirable for the attainment of the common objectives, and to submit to it any appropriate proposals", whilst Art. 192 confers on the European Parliament "acting by a majority of its Members" the right to "request the Commission to submit any appropriate proposal on matters on which it considers that a Community act is required for the purpose of implementing this Treaty". Because the Commission's right to make proposals is essentially in the nature of a "power", no general obligation for the Commission to submit proposals at the request of the Council or the Parliament may be inferred from those Articles.[57] This is also true of a request made by a Member State for the Commission to submit a proposal for the implementation of Title IV of the EC Treaty, it being provided that the Commission "shall examine" any such request (EC Treaty, Art. 67(2), first indent).[58]

An obligation to submit a proposal does exist in those exceptional cases in which the Treaty imposes an obligation to legislate (see para. 14–007). In such case, a refusal on the part of the Commission to submit a proposal may be challenged by an action for failure to act (EC Treaty, Art. 232). The Commission is also bound to "submit its conclusions to the Council without delay" in the event that the Council or a Member State requests it to make a recommendation or a proposal pursuant to Art. 115 of the EC Treaty in order to enable the Council to legislate on specific matters relating to EMU. Having regard to the cautious wording of that article, it does not require the Commission formally to submit a proposal.

Neither the Council nor a Member State can compel the Commission to submit a proposal. Nevertheless, the Commission has to fulfil its duty to co-operate with the Council (see EC Treaty, Art. 218(1)).[59] The European Parliament can call the Commission to account for any abuse of its right to submit proposals when it makes the Commission answer for its policy (see

---

[57] See to this effect Lauwaars, *Lawfulness and Legal Force of Community Decisions* (Sijthoff, Leyden, 1973) at 108–109; for a different view, see Harnier, in von der Groeben, Thiesing and Ehlermann (eds), *Kommentar zum EWG-Vertrag* (Nomos, Baden-Baden, 1991) at 4307. However, the Commission has given the European Parliament and the Council an undertaking to take account of any requests made and to reply rapidly and appropriately to the parliamentary committees concerned and to the Council's preparatory bodies: point 4 of the framework agreement of July 5, 2000 (n.39, *supra*) and point 9 of the interinstitutional agreement of December 16, 2003 on better law-making (n.39, *supra*); see formerly point 3.3 of the Code of Conduct agreed between the European Parliament and the Commission on March 15, 1995, [1995] O.J. C89/69. For action taken by the Commission on the European Parliament's first four legislative initiatives, see its answer of August 1, 1996 to question E–1859/96 (Schleicher), [1996] O.J. C345/110.

[58] See also EC Treaty, Art. 11(2), third subpara., which requires Member States intending to establish enhanced co-operation to address a request to the Commission; if the Commission fails to submit a proposal to the Council, "it shall inform the Member States concerned of the reasons for not doing so".

[59] In practice, formal recourse to Art. 208 of the EC Treaty is replaced by dialogue between the two institutions. See the Council's answer of May 14, 1992 to question No. 607/92 (Dury), [1992] O.J. C159/64.

para. 10–017). Since the Treaties conferred the right of initiative on the Commission alone and the task of proposing legislation falls to it in its own right, it would seem inappropriate for the European Parliament to compel it to use that right in a particular way by threatening it with a motion of censure.[60] In this light, the European Parliament's legitimate pretension to a right of initiative to supplement its right to request a proposal under Art. 192 of the EC Treaty militates in favour of amendment of the Treaty.

Right of initiative under the Constitution. The EU Constitution will **14–019** confirm the Commission's right of initiative in so far as it will extend the application of the "ordinary legislative procedure" (the present co-decision procedure), which is dependent upon the Commission's submitting a proposal.[61] Apart from the CFSP, the Commission's right of initiative will cover all the fields of competence of the Union. As regards police and judicial co-operation in criminal matters, the Commission will continue to share the right of initiative with the Member States, which may submit an initiative provided that it emanates from a group consisting of at least a quarter of the Member States.[62] In principle, the Commission is the only institution entitled to submit proposals for legislation and neither the European Parliament nor the Council may force it to submit a proposal.[63] A remarkable innovation is the possibility for a group of citizens to invite the Commission to initiate legislation. At the initiative of at least one million citizens coming from a significant number of Member States, the Commission may be invited to submit "any appropriate proposal" on matters where citizens consider that a legal act of the Union is required for the purpose of implementing the Constitution (EU Constitution, Art. I–47(4)). The European Parliament and the Council, acting in accordance with the co-decision procedure, are to establish the procedures and conditions required for such a citizens' initiative, including the minimum number of Member States from which it must come.[64] However, the Constitution does not seem to oblige the Commission to comply with such a request.

---

[60] Compare the reasoning of the Court of Justice in conferring a right on the European Parliament to bring an action for annulment in the event of a breach of its prerogatives (now also recognised by EC Treaty, Art. 230) so as not to have to rely on forcing the Commission to bring an action: ECJ, Case C–70/88 *European Parliament v Council* [1990] E.C.R. I–2041, paras 19–27; see Lenaerts, "Some Reflections on the Separation of Powers in the European Community" (1991) C.M.L.R. 11, at 23–25.

[61] Para. 14–030, *infra*. In certain fields in which the ordinary legislative procedure applies, an initiative may however also emanate from a group of Member States, see para. 14–030, *infra*.

[62] EU Constitution, Art. I–34(3), and Art. III–264. See para. 15–011, *infra*, for the current PJCC procedure (any Member State may submit a proposal on an individual basis).

[63] Unlike the existing Arts 192 and 208 of the EC Treaty, Arts III–332 and III–345 of the EU Constitution require the Commission to inform the European Parliament and the Council, respectively, of its reasons if it does not submit a proposal.

[64] EU Constitution, Art. I–47(4), *in fine*.

In contrast, the EU Constitution expressly requires the Commission to carry out broad consultations with parties concerned.[65] More generally, the Union institutions are placed under an obligation to maintain a dialogue with representative associations and civil society (see para. 14–045). The Protocol annexed to the EU Constitution on the role of national parliaments in the European Union reinforces the existing rule that sufficient time should elapse between the date at which a legislative proposal is made available and the time when it is placed on the agenda of the Council.[66] Moreover, national parliaments are entitled to issue opinions on the extent to which legislative proposals comply or do not comply with the principle of subsidiarity (see para. 5–035).

D. ROLE OF THE EUROPEAN PARLIAMENT

1. No uniform input from the Parliament

14–020 Degrees of involvement. Notwithstanding its direct democratic legitimacy, the European Parliament does not invariably take part in the legislative process. The European Parliament's actual say in decision-making differs substantially depending on the subject-matter of the act being adopted. Various procedures co-exist, each entailing different degrees of involvement: optional opinion, obligatory opinion, co-operation, co-decision, and assent (see EC Treaty, Art. 192, first para.). In addition, there are some other forms of participation in decision-making and some Treaty articles which provide for no input of the Parliament in decision-making but simply for it to be informed of the measures adopted. Even after the EU Constitution enters into force, different degrees of participation of the European Parliament in decision-making will co-exist.

14–021 Increasing involvement. It was not until the 1980s that the European Parliament succeeded in increasing its say in Community decision-making.[67] For a long time, the Parliament's only right was to be consulted in certain cases and to deliver a non-binding opinion.[68] Grant of decision-making power in the budgetary procedure in 1970 gave the Parliament a means of blocking other institutions' decisions with financial implications. One year after the first direct elections to the European Parliament, the Court of Justice clarified for the first time in the isoglucose cases the scope of the Parliament's right to be consulted (see para. 14–025). In 1987 the Single

---

[65] *ibid.*, Art. I–47(3).

[66] *Cf.* the Protocol annexed to the EU Constitution on the role of national parliaments in the European Union, Arts 4–5, with the existing Protocol, para. 14–016, *supra*.

[67] For a survey of the increasing parliamentary involvement in decision-making, see Corbett, Jacobs and Shackleton, "The European Parliament at Fifty: A View from the Inside" (2003) J.C.M.S. 353–373; De Gucht with the collaboration of Keukeleire, *Besluitvorming in de Europese Unie* (Maklu, Antwerp, 1994) at 44–59.

[68] The ECSC Treaty also required the European Parliament to give its approval in the "minor amendment" procedure provided for in Art. 95 (*cf.* para. 7–009, *supra*).

European Act then increased Parliament's say by introducing co-operation and assent procedures and extending majority voting in the Council, which enlarged the Commission's scope for taking over parliamentary amendments.[69] The co-operation procedure, which enables the Parliament to have a real influence on decision-making through amendments proposed by it, was applied mainly to measures adopted with a view to achieving the internal market (see para. 14–027). Assent, which gives the European Parliament a veto, was introduced for the accession of new Member States and the conclusion of association agreements (see para. 14–038). In 1993, the EU Treaty introduced the co-decision procedure, which affords the European Parliament more of a say by coupling the right to propose amendments with a right of veto. At the same time, that Treaty reordered the field of application of the various legislative procedures so as to increase parliamentary involvement across the board. In various policy areas, a procedure involving a greater say on the part of the Parliament, sometimes even the new co-decision procedure, replaced a procedure under which the Parliament had no or only a small say. The fact that the Parliament's role has been increased piecemeal in stages means that its say in the legislative process differs from case to case, which makes it difficult to have a clear insight into its legislative role.[70] Where, in addition, the different aspects of a given policy area are governed by different procedures, there is also a threat to the coherence of the policy concerned.[71] The Treaty of Amsterdam improved matters in this respect by confining the co-operation procedure to aspects of EMU and largely replacing it by co-decision. The EU Constitution will abolish the co-operation procedure and the co-decision procedure will become the "ordinary legislative procedure" (see para. 14–030).

Democratic principle. The European Parliament's participation in **14–022** Community rule-making reflects at Community level the fundamental democratic principle that the peoples should take part in the exercise of power through the intermediary of a representative assembly. It was on this ground that the Court of Justice held that procedures providing for the involvement of the Parliament were essential procedural requirements for the adoption of legislative acts and that if those procedures were disregarded the acts in question could be declared void.[72] The European

---

[69] paras 14–011 and 14–017, *supra*. In addition to the general commentaries on the Single European Act (n.12 to para. 3–006, *supra*), see Domestici-Met, "Les procédures législatives communautaires après l'Acte unique" (1987) R.M.C. 556–571; Bieber, "Legislative Procedure for the Establishment of the Single Market" (1988) C.M.L.R. 711–724.

[70] See the criticism of Boest, "Ein langer Weg zur Demokratie in Europa. Die Beteiligungsrechte des Europäischen Parlaments bei Rechtsetzung nach dem Vertrag über die Europäische Union" (1992) EuR. 182, at 191.

[71] De Gucht with the collaboration of Keukeleire (n.67, *supra*), at 58.

[72] ECJ, Case 138/79 *Roquette Frères v Council* [1980] E.C.R. 3333, para. 33, and ECJ, Case 139/79 *Maïzena v Council* [1980] E.C.R. 3393, para. 34 (quoted in para 13–011, *supra*); ECJ, Case C–300/89 *Commission v Council* [1991] E.C.R. I–2867, para. 20.

Parliament's prerogatives are infringed where an act is wrongly adopted on a legal basis which does not provide for consultation of the Parliament, even if the institution which adopted the act has opted to consult it.[73] As more and more Treaty articles require the European Parliament to be involved in decision-making and the various legislative procedures call for different degrees of involvement, the Parliament is keeping an increasingly steady eye on the choice of legal basis made by the Commission and—in the second place—by the Council.[74] This explains the rising number of cases brought before the Court of Justice by the Parliament.[75]

2. Survey of procedures

a. Optional consultation

14–023 Consultation. An initial series of Treaty articles provides for no involvement of the European Parliament in the legislative process.[76] In such a case, the Council (or the Commission) may validly act without consulting the Parliament. Nevertheless, an institution may still seek its opinion.[77] It may even undertake to consult the European Parliament as much as possible.[78]

14–024 Preparing the position of the Parliament. Where the Commission or the Council consults the Parliament, the President of the Parliament refers the matter to the competent parliamentary committee (EP Rules of Procedure, r.40).[79] The committee verifies whether the proposed act has the correct

---

[73] ECJ, Case C–316/91 *European Parliament v Council* [1994] E.C.R. I–625, para. 16.

[74] The Commission undertakes to take the utmost account of all changes to the legal bases of its proposals contained in the European Parliament's amendments: point 4 of the specific agreement on the legislative process (Annex I) appended to the framework agreement of July 5, 2000 (n.39, *supra*).

[75] Now under EC Treaty, Art. 230, third para. See ECJ, Case C–70/88 *European Parliament v Council* [1990] E.C.R. I–2041; ECJ, Case C–70/88 *European Parliament v Council* [1991] E.C.R. I–4529; ECJ, Case C–295/90 *European Parliament v Council* [1992] E.C.R. I–4193; ECJ, Case C–316/91 *European Parliament v Council* [1994] E.C.R. I–625; ECJ, Case C–187/93 *European Parliament v Council* [1994] E.C.R. I–2857; ECJ, Case C–360/93 *European Parliament v Council* [1996] E.C.R. I–1195; ECJ, Case C–271/94 *European Parliament v Council* [1996] I–1689; ECJ, Case C–303/94 *European Parliament v Council* [1996] E.C.R. I–2943; ECJ, Case C–259/95 *European Parliament v Council* [1997] E.C.R. I–5303; EJC, Case C–22/96 *European Parliament v Council* [1998] E.C.R. I–3231; ECJ, Case C–42/97 *European Parliament v Council* [1999] E.C.R. I–869; ECJ, Joined Cases C–164–165/97 *European Parliament v Council* [1999] E.C.R. I–1139.

[76] See the measures adopted by the Council pursuant to EC Treaty, Art. 26; Art. 45, second para.; Art. 49, second para.; Art. 57(2); Art. 59; Art. 60(1); Art. 64(2); Art. 75(3); Art. 87(3)(e); Art. 92; Art. 96, second para.; Art. 100(1); Art. 104(6) to (9); Art. 119(1); Art. 144; Art. 187; Art. 209; Art. 210. See also all the Treaty articles conferring a power of decision on the Commission (para. 10–059, *supra*).

[77] ECJ, Case 165/87 *Commission v Council* [1988] E.C.R. 5545, para. 20.

[78] See the Commission's communication to the European Parliament of June 8, 1973 ((1973) 6 EC Bull. point 1201) and the Council's answer of May 25, 1984 to question 2277/83 (Lady Elles), [1984] O.J. C173/17; see also para. 14–039.

[79] For a detailed discussion of the course of all legislative procedures within the European Parliament and the Council, see Raworth (n.12, *supra*), at 45–56 (first reading) and 83–109 (second reading).

legal basis, whether it respects the principles of subsidiarity and proportionality and fundamental rights and whether sufficient financial resources are provided (EP Rules of Procedure, rr.34 to 36). Generally, the committee adopts a report comprising any draft amendments, a draft legislative resolution and an explanatory statement (EP Rules of Procedure, r.42), on which the Parliament holds a vote at the plenary session (EP Rules of Procedure, r.51).[80] The Commission is requested to state its position on draft amendments at the committee stage (EP Rules of Procedure, r.50) and after the vote at the plenary session (EP Rules of Procedure, rr.52 and 53). If the Commission declares that it is not prepared to accept all the amendments or that it is not prepared to withdraw a proposal not approved by the Parliament, the Parliament may prolong the consultative procedure by postponing the vote.[81] In order for the Parliament to give its opinion more expeditiously, its President, a parliamentary committee, a political group, at least 40 MEPs, the Commission or the Council may request that a debate on a proposal be treated as urgent. In the event that the Parliament accepts such a request, the consultation is placed on the agenda as a priority item and debate may take place at the plenary session without a (written) report from the responsible committee (EP Rules of Procedure, r.133).

b. Compulsory consultation

Duty to consult. Several Treaty articles require the Council to consult the **14–025** European Parliament.[82] In such case, the Council requests an opinion, which is adopted in accordance with the procedure described above. In the

---

[80] r.43 of the EP Rules of Procedure sets out two simplified procedures which the chair of a committee may follow provided that no objection is made by at least one-tenth of the Members of the responsible committee. First, he or she may move that the committee approve a proposal without amendments (r.43(1)). Secondly, he or she may move that the chair draw up a report including amendments, which is deemed to have been adopted if no objection is made. In the latter case, the draft legislative resolution is put to a vote in the plenary session without debate (r.43(2)). Furthermore, under r.130 any legislative proposal adopted in committee with fewer than one-tenth of the members of the committee voting against is placed on the draft agenda of Parliament for a single vote without amendment, unless political groups or one tenth of the Members of Parliament have requested in writing that the item be open to amendment. Such items are without debate unless Parliament decides otherwise on a proposal from the Conference of Presidents, or if requested by a political group or at least forty Members.

[81] See EP Rules of Procedure, rr.35(6) and 50(2) (postponement of the vote in the competent committee), 52(3) (referral of the matter back to the competent committee by the Parliament) and 53(2) (postponement of the final vote by the Parliament and referral of the matter back to the responsible committee). See Nicoll, "Le dialogue législatif entre le Parlement européen et la Commission. La procédure de renvoi en commission du Parlement européen" (1988) R.M.C. 240–242. However, the European Parliament cannot block the decision-making process by refusing to give an opinion: Raworth, "A Timid Step Forward: Maastricht and the Democratisation of the European Community" (1994) E.L.R. 16, at 19. If it attempts to do so, it acts in breach of the principle of co-operation in good faith *vis-à-vis* the Council: ECJ, Case C–65/93 *European Parliament v Council* [1995] E.C.R. I–643, paras 23–28 (para. 5–053, *supra*; see also para. 14–025, *infra*).

[82] See the acts adopted on a proposal from the Commission: EC Treaty, Art. 11(2), first

judgments of October 29, 1980 in the isoglucose cases, the Court of Justice held that consultation of the Parliament constituted an essential procedural requirement and annulled a regulation which the Council had adopted without consulting the Parliament.[83]

The fact that it is compulsory to consult the Parliament means that the Council must exhaust all the possibilities of obtaining its opinion in time.[84] The Court of Justice adverted to the possibility for the Council to request the Parliament to declare the consultation a matter of urgency (see para. 14–024) or for a request to be made for the Parliament to meet in extraordinary session (EC Treaty, Art. 196, second para.). Before the Parliament has delivered its opinion, the Council may consider the Commission's proposal or attempt to arrive at a common approach or even a common position within the Council provided that it does not adopt its final position before it is apprised of the Parliament's opinion.[85]

For its part, the Parliament is under a duty to co-operate in good faith with the Council. Accordingly, the Parliament was not entitled to challenge the Council for adopting a regulation on December 21, 1992 which had to be adopted for political and technical reasons before the end of 1992, without waiting for the Parliament to give its opinion. The Parliament had decided to deal with the proposal for a regulation as a case of urgency on December 18, 1992, during its last session of the year. However, the Parliament decided to adjourn that session without having debated the proposal and it was impossible to convene an extraordinary session of the Parliament before the end of the year.[86]

---

subpara.; Art. 13; Art. 19(1) and (2); Art. 22, second para.; Art. 37(2), third subpara.; Art. 52(1); Art. 67(1), (2) and (3); Art. 71(2); Art. 83(1); Art. 89; Art. 93; Art. 94; Art. 104(14), second and third subparas; Art. 107(6); Art. 117(6) and (7); Art. 122(2); Art. 128(2); Art. 130; Art. 133(7); Art. 137(2), second subpara.; Art. 166(4); Art. 172, first para.; Art. 175(2); Art. 181a(2); Art. 202, third indent; Art. 229a; Art. 269, second para.; Art. 279; Art. 283; Art. 299(2); Art. 300(3), first subpara.; Art. 308. See also the acts adopted under EC Treaty, Art. 111(1), first sentence; Art. 112(2)(b); Art. 117(1), second subpara., first sentence; Art. 121(2) and (4); Art. 144; Art. 225(2); Art. 245, second para.; Art. 247(3), first subpara.; EU Treaty, Art. 40a; Art. 44a; Art. 48, second para.

[83] ECJ, Case 138/79 *Roquette Frères v Council* [1980] E.C.R. 3333, paras 33–37, and ECJ, Case 139/79 *Maïzena v Council* [1980] E.C.R. 3393, paras 34–38.

[84] *ibid.*, paras 36 and 37.

[85] ECJ, Case C–417/93 *European Parliament v Council* [1995] E.C.R. I–1185, para. 10. The Commission is to ensure that the Council bodies are reminded in good time not to reach a political agreement on its proposals before the European Parliament has given its opinion. It is to ask for discussion to be concluded at ministerial level only after a reasonable period has been given to the members of the Council to examine the European Parliament's opinion: point 7(i) of the specific agreement on the legislative process (Annex I) appended to the framework agreement of July 5, 2000 (n.39, *supra*); see formerly the Code of Conduct agreed between the European Parliament and the Commission on March 15, 1995 (n.57, *supra*), point 3.4.

[86] ECJ, Case C–65/93 *European Parliament v Council* [1995] E.C.R. I–643, paras 24–28 (in which an action for annulment of Council Regulation No. 3917/92 extending into 1993 the application of generalised tariff preferences in respect of products originating in developing countries, [1992] O.J. L396/1, was dismissed); see Van Nuffel (1995) Col.J.E.L. 504, at 511–515. See also the discussion of the duty to co-operate in good faith in para. 5–052, *supra*.

The Council is bound to consult the Parliament and to allow it a reasonable time to deliver its opinion, but it is not under any duty to state in what way, if any, it took account of it. It is sufficient that the act adopted by the Council refers to the opinion requested (EC Treaty, Art. 253; see para. 17–109).

Preparing the position of the Parliament. If the European Parliament is **14–026** consulted at an early stage in the legislative process, it is possible that the proposal on which it delivered its opinion will be amended in the course of further discussion in Council working groups and Coreper. Further consultation will then be unnecessary if the amended proposal as a whole corresponds essentially to the original proposal (*e.g.* amendments made regarding only technical aspects or methods)[87] or where the amendments made modified the proposal essentially in the manner indicated by the Parliament.[88] It cannot be argued, however, that the amendments were essentially in line with what the Parliament was proposing on the basis of opinions not adopted by the Parliament as a whole but only by parliamentary committees.[89]

Since proper consultation of the European Parliament in the cases provided for by the Treaty constitutes one of the means enabling it to play an effective role in the legislative process of the Community, the Council cannot avoid reconsulting the Parliament on the ground that it was sufficiently informed as to the Parliament's opinion on the essential points at issue.[90] If it could, this would seriously undermine the maintenance of the institutional balance intended by the Treaty and would amount to disregarding the influence that due consultation of the Parliament can have on adoption of the measure in question.[91] If the Council fails to reconsult

---

[87] ECJ, Case 41/69 *ACF Chemiefarma v Commission* [1970] E.C.R. 661, paras 68–70; ECJ, Case 817/79 *Buyl v Commission* [1982] E.C.R. 245, paras 23–24; ECJ, Case 828/79 *Adam v Commission* [1982] E.C.R. 269, paras 24–25; ECJ, Case 1253/79 *Battaglia v Commission* [1982] E.C.R. 297, paras 24–25. See, *e.g.* ECJ, Case C–280/93 *Germany v Council* [1994] E.C.R. I–4973, paras 38–42; ECJ, Case C–417/93 *European Parliament v Council* [1995] E.C.R. I–1185, paras 16–26; see Van Nuffel (n.86, *supra*), at 505–509. A change in the legal form of a measure (directive rather than a regulation) does not constitute in itself a substantial change, see CFI, Joined Cases T–125/96 and T–152/96 *Boehringer Ingelheim Vetmedica v Council and Commission* [1999] E.C.R. II–3427, para. 133.

[88] ECJ, Case C–331/88 *Fedesa* [1990] E.C.R. I 4023, para. 39; ECJ, Joined Cases C–13 to C–16/92 *Driessen* [1993] E.C.R. I–4751, paras 23–25; ECJ, Case C–408/95 *Eurotunnel* [1997] E.C.R. I–6315, paras 46–63. The European Parliament itself has determined that the Council may reconsult it "where, through the passage of time or changes in circumstances, the nature of the problem with which the proposal is concerned substantially changes" (EP Rules of Procedure, r.55).

[89] ECJ, Case C–388/92 *European Parliament v Council* [1994] E.C.R. I–2067, para. 17.

[90] ECJ, Case C–21/94 *European Parliament v Council* [1995] E.C.R. I–1827, paras 24–26.

[91] *ibid.*, para. 26; see also ECJ, Case C–392/95 *European Parliament v Council* [1997] E.C.R. I–3213, para. 22. The Commission is to ensure that the Council adheres to the rules developed by the Court of Justice requiring the European Parliament to be reconsulted if the Council substantially amends a Commission proposal: point 7(ii) of the specific agreement on the legislative process (Annex I) appended to the framework agreement of July 5, 2000 (n.39, *supra*); see formerly the Codes of Conduct of 1990, (1990) 4 EC Bull. point I.6.1, and 1995 (n.57, *supra*), points 2 and 3.6.

the Parliament on a proposal after substantial amendment, the act in question will not have been lawfully adopted and may be annulled.[92]

c. Co-operation (EC Treaty, Art. 252)

14–027 Co-operation procedure. A number of Treaty provisions relating to EMU provide that the Council has to act in accordance with the procedure laid down in Art. 252 of the EC Treaty.[93] This procedure is known as the "co-operation procedure"[94] and was introduced by the Single European Act in order to increase the European Parliament's involvement in the Community's legislative process[95] and to make it possible for the Council to act by a qualified majority rather than by a unanimous vote. The move to qualified majority voting made for the flexibility which was considered necessary in order to adopt the substantial corpus of legislation for achieving the internal market (see paras 5–077–5–078).

14–028 Two stages. The Art. 252 procedure is made up of two stages. In the first stage, the Commission submits a proposal, the European Parliament delivers an opinion and the Council adopts a "common position" by a qualified majority vote (EC Treaty, Art. 252(a)). The common position is a draft act determined in the aforementioned consultation procedure and published in the *Official Journal*.[96]

In the second stage, the European Parliament may take three possible decisions on the common position, although in each case the final decision invariably lies with the Council.

First, the Parliament may approve the common position. If it does not take a decision within three months, the common decision is deemed to have been approved (Art. 252(b), second para.). In either event, the Council adopts the common position as the definitive act.

Secondly, the Parliament may propose amendments to the common position by an absolute majority of its component Members (Art. 252(c), first para.). Whether the Parliament's amendments are accepted by the Council depends on whether the Commission is prepared to take them over in an amended version of its proposal. This is because the Treaty provides that the Council, acting by a qualified majority, is to adopt the proposal as re-examined by the Commission (Art. 252(e), first para.); in order to adopt amendments not taken over by the Commission or to amend the proposal

---

[92] *e.g.* ECJ, Case C–65/90 *European Parliament v Council* [1992] E.C.R. I–4593, paras 20–21; ECJ, Case C–388/92 *European Parliament v Council* [1994] E.C.R. I–2067; ECJ, Case C–21/94 *European Parliament v Council* [1995] E.C.R. I–1827, paras 17–28; ECJ, Case C–392/95 *European Parliament v Council* [1997] E.C.R. I–3213, paras 14–24. See also CFI, Case T–164/97 *Busaca v Court of Auditors* [1998] E.C.R. -SC II–1699, paras 79–102.
[93] EC Treaty, Art. 99(5); Art. 102(2); Art. 103(2); Art. 106(2).
[94] The EEC Treaty provided that in such a case the Council was to act "by a qualified majority on a proposal from the Commission in co-operation with the European Parliament".
[95] ECJ, Case C–300/89 *Commission v Council* [1991] E.C.R. I–2867, para. 20.
[96] Council Rules of Procedure, Art. 17(1)(c).

as re-examined by the Commission, the Council's decision has to be unanimous (Art. 252(e), second para.).

Thirdly, the Parliament may decide, by a majority of its component Members, to reject the common position (Art. 252(c)). If it does so, the Council may still adopt the common position as a definitive act under the co-operation procedure by a unanimous vote.[97]

From co-operation to co-decision. Under the co-operation procedure, the **14–029** Commission and the Parliament can effectively influence the content of a legislative act if they succeed in getting a number of Member States behind them. The key element of the co-operation procedure consists precisely in the fact that the Council may adopt by a qualified majority a text containing amendments moved by the Parliament and accepted by the Commission, whilst it obliges the Council to take a unanimous decision in order to adopt a common position rejected by the Parliament or to amend a proposal which has been re-examined by the Commission.[98] Where the legal basis for a measure prescribes co-operation with the Parliament, that measure cannot also be based on a Treaty article requiring a unanimous vote on the part of the Council. If it could be, the Council would always have to act by a unanimous vote, which would divest the co-operation procedure of its very substance.[99]

The Parliament's say in this procedure, however, is weak in two respects: it cannot submit its amendments directly to the Council (with a view to their being approved by a qualified majority)[100] and cannot prevent an act which it views with disfavour from being adopted.[101].

In order to give the European Parliament a greater say in precisely those two respects, the EU Treaty introduced the co-decision procedure (EC

---

[97] EC Treaty, Art. 252(c), second para. In the framework agreement of July 5, 2000 (n.39, *supra*) the Commission undertakes, if appropriate, to withdraw a legislative proposal in that event unless there are important reasons for not doing so, which it is to provide in a statement before the European Parliament: point 7(iii) of the specific agreement on the legislative process (Annex I) appended to the framework agreement; see formerly point 3.8 of the code of conduct of March 15, 1995 (n.57, *supra*). In the first seven cases in which the Parliament rejected a Council common position, the Council adopted three common positions by a unanimous vote; on one occasion, the Commission withdrew its proposal and replaced the original one by new proposals: see the Commission's answer of August 5, 1996 to question E–1861/96 (Schleicher), [1996] O.J. C356/106. For a case study, see Earnshaw and Judge, "The European Parliament and the Sweeteners Directive: From Footnote to Inter-Institutional Conflict" (1993) J.C.M.S. 103–116.
[98] ECJ, Case C–300/89 *Commission v Council* [1991] E.C.R. I–2867, para. 19.
[99] *ibid.*, paras 17–20. In that judgment, the Court of Justice held that the directive could not be based on both Art. 130s of the EEC Treaty (Council to decide unanimously after merely consulting the European Parliament) and on Art. 100a (Council to decide in co-operation with the European Parliament). See also para. 5–014, *supra*.
[100] Except where the Parliament expressly or impliedly approves the common position, the Commission may assert its own policy judgment against the majority of the component Members of the Parliament. In such case, the Parliament's amendments will only be successful in the Council if no Member State opposes them.
[101] If the Commission does not withdraw its proposal, the Council may still adopt by a unanimous vote a common position rejected by the Parliament.

Treaty, Art. 251). In most policy areas where the co-operation procedure was in force, the Amsterdam Treaty replaced it by co-decision. Since the Contracting Parties refused to alter the provisions governing EMU, the co-operation procedure provided for in Art. 252 remains in force in that area. It will not be until the EU Constitution enters into force that the co-operation procedure will be entirely replaced by the co-decision procedure[102] or the consultation procedure[103]

d. Co-decision (EC Treaty, Art. 251)

14–030 **Two institutions co-deciding.** The procedure laid down in Art. 251 of the EC Treaty manifestly gives the European Parliament a greater say than the co-operation procedure. It introduces direct dialogue between the European Parliament and the Council and makes adoption of acts dependent upon the approval of both institutions. Since the Treaty of Amsterdam, the "co-decision" procedure applies to a major part of the policy areas in which Community legislation is adopted.[104] If the institutions reach agreement, the final act is adopted as a regulation, directive or decision of both the European Parliament and the Council, signed by both Presidents (see EC Treaty, Art. 254(1)).

Once the EU Constitution enters into force, the co-decision procedure (set out in Art. III–396) will be the "ordinary legislative procedure" for the adoption of legislative acts. The EU Constitution proposes to extend the application of this procedure to virtually all fields of action of the Union where the Council has to decide by qualified majority.[105] Co-decision will still not apply in the context of the CFSP.[106] The upshot is that the

---

[102] EU Constitution, Art. III–179(6); *cf.* EC Treaty, Art. 99(5).

[103] EU Constitution, Arts III–183(2) and III–186(2); *cf.* EC Treaty, Arts 102(2), 103(2) and 106(2).

[104] See EC Treaty, Art. 12: Art. 13(2); Art. 18(2); Art. 40; Art. 44(2); Art. 46(2); Art. 47(1) and (2); Art. 67(5); Art. 71(1); Art. 95(1); Art. 129; Art. 135; Art. 137(2); Art. 141(2); Art. 148; Art. 149(4), first indent; Art. 150(4); Art. 151(5), first indent; Art. 152(4), first subpara.; Art. 153(2); Art. 156, first para.; Art. 157(3); Art. 159, third para.; Art. 162; Art. 166(1); Art. 172, second para.; Art. 175(1) and (3), first subpara.; Art. 179(1); Art. 191, second para. ; Art. 225(2); Art. 280(4); Art. 285(1); Art. 286(2). The extension of the scope of the co-decision procedure was already contemplated by the former Art. 189b(8) of the EC Treaty; see the report from the Commission of July 3, 1996 provided for in that provision, (1996) 7/8 EU Bull. point 2.3.1. and the resolution of the European Parliament of November 14, 1996, [1996] O.J. C362/267. For an assessment, see Boyron, "Maastricht and the Codecision Procedure: A Success Story" (1996) I.C.L.Q. 293–318; Silvestro and Albani Liberali, "La codécision a été un succès, il faut aller de l'avant" (1997) R.M.C.U.E. 166–169. See the European Parliament's resolution of July 16, 1998 on the new co-decision procedure after Amsterdam, [1998] O.J. C292/140. For the limited extension of the scope of the co-decision procedure resulting from the Treaty of Nice, see Dashwood, "The Constitution of the European Union after Nice: law-making procedures" (2001) E.L.R. 215–238.

[105] There will be exceptions where European laws are to be adopted after obtaining the consent of the European Parliament, see *e.g.* EU Constitution, Art. I–54(4).

[106] The procedure set out in Art. III–396 of the EU Constitution will apply where the Constitution calls for the adoption of European laws or framework laws. Under Art. I–40(6), *in fine*, of the EU Constitution, European laws and framework laws may not be adopted in the field of the common foreign and security policy.

co-decision procedure will also be applicable in certain cases where the European Parliament and the Council adopt acts, not on a proposal of the Commission, but on the initiative of a group of Member States.[107]

First reading. Just as in the case of the co-operation procedure, the **14–031** co-decision procedure begins with a stage in which the European Parliament delivers an opinion on a Commission proposal submitted to the Parliament and the Council (Art. 251(2), first subpara.). In this "first reading", the Parliament proceeds in accordance with the aforementioned consultation procedure and may put forward amendments in its opinion.

If the Council approves all the amendments contained in the European Parliament's opinion, it may adopt the proposed act as amended by a qualified majority (Art. 251(2), second subpara., first indent). If the Parliament does not propose any amendments, the proposed act may also be adopted by a qualified majority (Art. 251(2), second subpara., second indent).[108] As far as the Commission is concerned, this means that, at this stage, it cannot oppose an act on which the Parliament and the Council are in full agreement.[109] Even though no provision to this effect is contained in the Treaty or in the Rules of Procedure of the Parliament, an informal "trilogue" may take place between the European Parliament, the Council and the Commission before or after the vote in the responsible parliamentary committee, which may allow a proposal to be adopted at first reading.[110]

Otherwise, the Council adopts a common position by a qualified majority for submission to the European Parliament. The Council is to inform the Parliament fully of the reasons which led it to adopt the common position

---

[107] See, for example, EU Constitution, Arts III–269—III–277 in conjunction with Art. III–264. For the adjustment to the procedure required in such cases, see Art. III–396(15) of the EU Constitution (where a law or a framework law is adopted at the initiative of a group of Member States, on a recommendation by the ECB or at the request of the Court of Justice or the European Investment Bank). In that case, the Commission may not compel the Council to take its decision by unanimity by issuing a negative opinion (*cf.* para. 14–0134, *infra*), although the Commission will continue to be closely involved in the functioning of the Conciliation Committee.

[108] In that respect, the Treaty of Amsterdam has simplified the procedure which, in the version provided for in the original EU Treaty, invariably required both an opinion of the European Parliament and a common position (former Art. 189b(2), second subpara.). Under that procedure, final approval of the Council was possible only in the second stage, after the Parliament had approved the common position or failed to pronounce upon it in time (former Art. 189b(2), third subpara., points (a) and (b)).

[109] Once the Council has adopted an act, the Commission of course can no longer withdraw its proposal; see EC Treaty, Art. 250(2). According to the joint declaration of the European Parliament, the Council and the Commission on practical arrangements for the new co-decision procedure (Art. 251 of the EC Treaty) [1999] O.J. C148/1), the Commission is to "exercise its right of initiative in a constructive manner with a view to making it easier to reconcile the positions of the European Parliament and the Council". The Commission has stated that withdrawal of a proposal during the first reading would be "counterproductive" (point I.3).

[110] For an example, see Directive 2004/48/EC of the European Parliament and of the Council of April 29, 2004 on the enforcement of intellectual property rights, [2004] O.J. L157/45.

and the Commission is to apprise it fully of its position (Art. 251(2), second subpara., third indent). The common position and the statement of reasons are published in the *Official Journal*.[111] When the President of the Parliament announces the common position at the plenary session, it is deemed to have been referred to the committee responsible at first reading, which draws up a recommendation for the second reading on behalf of the plenary session (EP Rules of Procedure, r.59). The recommendation may propose that the Parliament approves the common position, adopts amendments or rejects it.[112]

It should be noted that, in some policy areas, the Council does not decide by a qualified majority, but by a unanimous vote throughout the procedure.[113] As far as the time-limits for co-decision are concerned, all three-month periods may be extended by a maximum of one month and all six-week periods by no more than two weeks at the initiative of the European Parliament or the Council (EC Treaty, Art. 251(7)).

14–032 Adoption or rejection at second reading. If, within three months of the communication of the common position by the Council, the European Parliament approves it or has not taken a decision, the act in question is deemed to have been adopted in accordance with the common position (Art. 251(2), third subpara., point (a)). Within that period, the European Parliament may, however, decide to reject the common position. If it does so decide by an absolute majority of its component Members, the proposed act is deemed not to have been adopted (Art. 251(2), third subpara., point (b)).[114]

14–033 Amendments at second reading. Within the same three-month period, the European Parliament may also propose amendments to the common position by an absolute majority of its component Members (Art. 251(2), third subpara., point (c)). In its Rules of Procedure, the Parliament has limited its right to move amendments to those which seek to restore wholly or in part the position adopted by the Parliament in its first reading, to

---

[111] Council Rules of Procedure, Art. 17(1)(c).

[112] A proposal to amend or reject a common position may also be made by a political group or by at least 40 MEPs (EP Rules of Procedure, rr.61 and 62, first paras).

[113] This is so where the Council takes its decision under EC Treaty, Art. 42 (social security); Art. 47(2), second sentence (access to professions) and Art. 151(5) (incentive measures in the field of culture). Although this restricts to a considerable extent the leeway for reaching agreement between the institutions, it means that the Treaty does not regard the requirement for unanimity as being incompatible with the co-decision procedure. *cf.* the incompatibility found by the Court of Justice in the case of the co-operation procedure, para 14–029, *supra*. See Dashwood, "Community Legislative Procedures in the Era of the Treaty on European Union" (1994) E.L.R. 343, at 362.

[114] The Treaty of Amsterdam abolished the possibility for the Council to convene a meeting of the Conciliation Committee in these circumstances. The proposed act was then only deemed not to have been adopted if the European Parliament rejected it again by an absolute majority of its component Members (EC Treaty, former Art. 189b(2)(c)).

Figure 4: Co-Decision Procedure (Art. 251 EC Treaty)

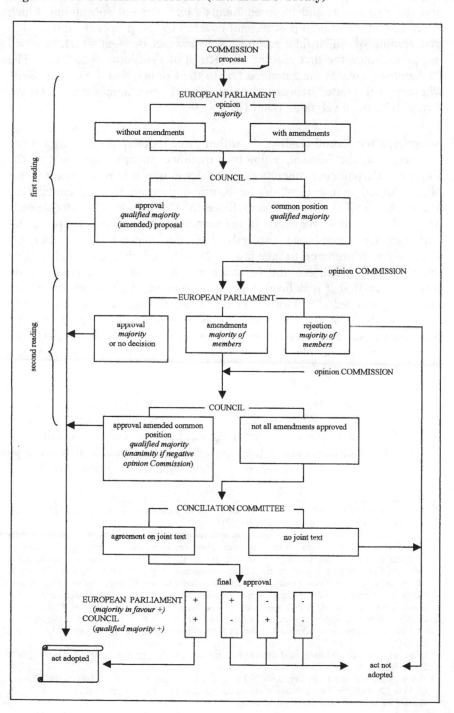

compromise amendments representing an agreement between the Council and the Parliament and to amendments which are not substantial, which alter parts of a common position not covered by the proposal submitted in first reading or which take account of a new fact or legal situation which has arisen since the first reading (EP Rules of Procedure, r.62(2)).[115] The Parliament forwards the amended text to the Council and the Commission, whereupon the latter delivers an opinion on the amendments (EC Treaty, Art. 251(2), third subpara., point (c)).

14–034 **Adoption after second reading.** If, within three months of the matter being referred to it, the Council, acting by a qualified majority, approves all the European Parliament's amendments, the act in question is deemed to have been adopted in the form of the common position thus amended (EC Treaty, Art. 251(3), first sentence). Since the Council does not decide on a proposal from the Commission in the second reading, whether a particular parliamentary amendment succeeds does not depend on whether the Commission is prepared to take it over. Nonetheless, in the second reading the Commission still has the influence which it has in the co-operation procedure in that if it delivers a negative opinion, the Council has to act unanimously (*ibid.*).[116] Moreover, the Commission is still entitled to withdraw its proposal, thereby bringing the whole decision-making procedure to an end.[117] As in first reading, an informal trilogue may take place so as to enable the Council to accept all the Parliament's second-reading amendments.[118]

14–035 **Conciliation Committee.** If the Council is minded not to adopt all the amendments, the President of the Council, in agreement with the President of the Parliament, convenes within six weeks a Conciliation Committee, composed of the members of the Council or their representatives and an equal number of representatives of the Parliament (EC Treaty, Art. 251(3),

---

[115] The President of Parliament may waive these rules if new elections have taken place since first reading, EP Rules of Procedure, r.62(3).

[116] The Commission undertakes to take the utmost account of parliamentary amendments unless there are important grounds for not doing so, in which case it has to explain its decision: point 5 of the framework agreement of July 5, 2000 (n.39, *supra*): At the same time, the Commission is to keep the relevant parliamentary committee regularly informed of the principal positions emerging from discussions within Council bodies and of any Commission amendments to the original proposal: point 6 of the specific agreement on the legislative processes (Annex I) appended to the framework agreement. If the Commission does not deliver an opinion within a reasonable time, the Council is entitled in the absence of a negative opinion to take its decision by a qualified majority: Dashwood (n .113, *supra*), at 354.

[117] Glaesner, "Willensbildung und Beschlussverfahren in der Europäischen Union" (1994) EuR. Beiheft 1, 25, at 26–27. See also n.46, *supra*.

[118] For an example, see Directive 2001/29/EC of the European Parliament and of the Council of May 22, 2001 on the harmonisation of certain aspects of copyright and related rights in the information society, [2001] O.J. L167/10.

second sentence, and (4), first sentence).[119] The Conciliation Committee addresses the Council's common position on the basis of the amendments proposed by the Parliament (Art. 251(4), third sentence) and has the task of "reaching agreement on a joint text" within six weeks of its being convened (EC Treaty, Art. 251(4), first sentence).[120] Agreement is reached by a qualified majority of members of the Council or their representatives and a majority of the representatives of the Parliament. The Commission takes part in the Conciliation Committee's deliberations and takes all necessary initiatives with a view to reconciling the positions of the Parliament and the Council (EC Treaty, Art. 251(4), second sentence). This means that the Commission is not entitled to withdraw its proposal at this stage.[121]

If the Conciliation Committee approves a joint text, the act has to be finally adopted in a third reading by the European Parliament by an absolute majority of the votes cast and by the Council by a qualified majority. If one of the two institutions fails to approve the proposed act within six weeks of its approval by the Committee, it is deemed not to have been adopted (EC Treaty, Art. 251(5)).[122] If the Conciliation Committee fails to reach agreement within the time-limit, the proposed act is deemed not to have been adopted (Art. 251(6)). Consequently, neither the Council nor the European Parliament can force through an act which has not been approved by the other institution.[123]

---

[119] The Conciliation Committee does not constitute a delegation of the Council as an institution but represents the views of the "members of the Council". See the joint declaration of the European Parliament, the Council and the Commission on practical arrangements for the new co-decision procedure (n.109, *supra*). For the composition (on the European Parliament side) and the mode of operation of the committee, see para. 10–028, *supra*.

[120] In its negotiations, the committee is not restricted to what is set out in the Council's common position or in the Commission's proposal; in order to safeguard the Commission's right of initiative, the joint text should, however, have the same subject-matter as the original Commission proposal: Dashwood (n.113, *supra*), at 358.

[121] Glaesner (n.117, *supra*), at 26 (who maintains however that this may be inferred from Art. 250(1) of the EC Treaty).

[122] See the negative outcome on March 1, 1995 of the vote in the plenary session of the European Parliament on a joint text of a directive on legal protection of biotechnological inventions on which agreement had already been reached between the European Parliament and Council delegations in the Conciliation Committee, [1995] O.J. C68/26.

[123] Under the first version of the co-decision procedure, the Council was entitled to confirm, by a qualified majority vote, the common position to which it had agreed before the conciliation procedure was initiated, possibly with amendments proposed by the Parliament. In that event, the act was finally adopted unless, within six weeks of the date of confirmation by the Council, the European Parliament rejected the text by an absolute majority of its component Members, in which case the proposed act was deemed not to have been adopted (see EC Treaty, former Art. 189b(6), second sentence). For an example, see the decision of the European Parliament of July 19, 1994 rejecting the text on the application of open network provision (OPN) to voice telephony which the Council had confirmed following conciliation in accordance with Art. 189b(6) of the EC Treaty, [1994] O.J. C261/13.

14–036 Commission acting as broker. The tortuous co-decision procedure has the merit of enabling the European Parliament to defend its point of view directly to the Council. After it has submitted its proposal, the Commission has only a limited role to play, although it does act in practice as an honest broker in formal and informal conciliation procedures. The Commission formally determines the course of the procedure only if it delivers a negative opinion in the second reading on the amendments proposed by the Parliament, hence making the Council's adoption of those amendments conditional upon its approving them by a unanimous vote. Accordingly, the Commission's position will prevail—provisionally—if at least one Member State agrees with it. There would appear to be little likelihood of the Commission's withdrawing its proposal as it would thereby openly put the Parliament out of play. If the Commission does not withdraw its proposal, it disqualifies itself from opposing the result of the decision-making process at a later stage. This is because once the Council fails to adopt all the Parliament's amendments, the President of the Council is obliged to convene the Conciliation Committee. The Commission does take part in the proceedings of that committee, but its final judgment of the "joint text" approved by the committee if the conciliation process is successful has no influence on the necessary majorities which need to be mustered in the Council and the Parliament in order to adopt the definitive act "in accordance with the joint text" and cannot prompt it to withdraw its proposal in order to bring the decision-making process to an end (see para. 14–035).

14–037 Success of co-decision. In theory, the Parliament occupies a strong negotiating position *vis-à-vis* the Council in that it may bring an end to the decision-making process by rejecting the common position. Nevertheless, the Parliament does not exercise its right to reject the common position lightly.[124] Rejection requires a majority vote of the Parliament's component Members. What is more, it serves no purpose for the Parliament to reject a common position when the Parliament would like the Community to legislate in the area concerned: in such case, the Parliament is obliged to "co-decide" with the Council. The decisive influence exercised by the Parliament is not based solely on its "negative" veto.[125] The Council cannot in fact adopt any act which has not been expressly or impliedly approved by the Parliament. The Conciliation Committee has developed into a successful way of striking compromises between the two legislative chambers.[126]

---

[124] For the first two cases, see nn.122 and 123, *supra*.

[125] This was the case with the procedure laid down in Art. 189b of the EC Treaty as introduced by the original EU Treaty; n.123, *supra*.

[126] In the German federal legislative process, a *Vermittlungsauschuss* (conciliation committee), which negotiates as between the directly elected *Bundestag* and the *Bundesrat*, consisting of representatives of the *Länder* governments, operates with some success. The Community conciliation system was modelled on the German system, but is not completely comparable with it since the directly-elected *Bundestag* retains the principal legislative powers. See Foster, "The New Conciliation Committee under Article 189b EC" (1994) E.L.R. 185–194.

e. Assent

Parliament's veto right. Since the Single European Act, a number of **14–038**
Treaty articles have required proposed acts to be given the assent of the
European Parliament. This means that the act only comes into being if the
Parliament approves it. The Parliament takes its decision on the basis of a
report from the responsible parliamentary committee recommending that
the proposal as a whole be adopted or rejected (EP Rules of Procedure,
r.75(1)). Given that no amendments may be proposed, assent constitutes *de
facto* a right of veto. Initially, assent was required outside the legislative
process proper only for the accession of new Member States and the
conclusion of association agreements.[127] Exceptionally, the Parliament
succeeded in having a real influence on the Community's external policy by
attaching conditions to its assent.[128] At present, the Parliament's assent is
required for important international agreements, including association
agreements (EC Treaty, Art. 300(3), second subpara.; see para. 21–013)
and for the accession of new Member States, where an absolute majority of
its component Members is required (EU Treaty, Art. 49). The Parliament
has reserved the right to adopt recommendations at any stage of the
international negotiations (EP Rules of Procedure, rr.82(4) and 83(5)).
Parliamentary assent also forms part of the procedure for the adoption of
some "organic" acts[129] and of the procedure for temporarily suspending the
rights of a Member State.[130] In this case, too, the Parliament may adopt
recommendations for modification of the proposal in the course of the
procedure (EP Rules of Procedure, r.75(3)). The EU Constitution will
preserve the "assent" procedure although it will be referred to in terms of
the Council's having to obtain the "consent" of the European Parliament.

f. Other conciliation procedures

Interinstitutional agreements. In addition, the European Parliament has a **14–039**
claim to be involved in decision-making where other institutions have
committed themselves to allowing it to play a part. In some cases, the EC
Treaty leaves the formulation of the mode of interaction between the
institutions to an "interinstitutional agreement" (to be determined by
"common accord").[131] Also outside those provisions, various

---

[127] See EEC Treaty, Arts 237 and 238.
[128] See the discussion of the part played by the European Parliament in the procedure for the
conclusion of international agreements in para. 21–014, *infra*.
[129] See, where a simple majority applies, EC Treaty, Art. 105(6); Art. 107(5); Art. 161, first,
second and third para., and, where a majority of its component Members has to be
obtained, EC Treaty, Art. 190(4), second subpara.
[130] EU Treaty, Art. 7(1), (2) and (6) (with a majority of three-fifths of the votes cast and a
majority of the Members).
[131] See EC Treaty, Art. 193, third para., concerning detailed provisions governing the exercise
of the right of inquiry; Art. 218(1); Art. 248(3), third subpara.; Art. 272(9), fifth subpara.
Art. 195(4) empowers the European Parliament to lay down the regulations and general
conditions governing the performance of the European Ombudsman's duties after seeking
an opinion from the Commission and subject to the Council's approval.

interinstitutional agreements have been concluded in which the European Parliament, the Council and the Commission enter into obligations which are binding upon them in so far as they do not infringe provisions of the Treaty or detract from the institutional balance sought thereby.[132] Such agreements may flesh out decision-making procedures or simplify them. Accordingly, in a 1975 Joint Declaration the three institutions agreed on a "conciliation procedure" between the Council and the European Parliament with the active assistance of the Commission for "Community acts of general application which have appreciable financial implications and of which the adoption is not required by virtue of acts already in existence".[133] Conciliation is to be initiated at the request of the Parliament or the Council if the Council is minded to depart from the Parliament's opinion.[134] It is conducted in a conciliation committee composed of representatives of the two institutions, meeting in the same way as its counterpart in the co-decision procedure.[135] Although this type of conciliation takes place only sporadically, it is expressly declared to be applicable in some Community measures[136] and, according to the European Parliament, also during the first reading under the co-operation and co-decision procedures.[137] The EU Constitution will continue to allow the European Parliament, the Council and the Commission to conclude interinstitutional agreements (see para. 17–148).

g. Information

14–040 Information. Lastly, a number of provisions on financial and economic matters require the Council (or the Commission) to inform the European Parliament of certain acts.[138] The Council has undertaken to inform the

---

[132] See the arrangements relating to the budgetary procedure (paras 10–126—10–127, *supra*) and the various agreements fleshing out the Treaties, more specifically the agreement on procedures for implementing the principle of subsidiarity (para. 5–028, *supra*) and the joint declaration on practical arrangements for the new co-decision procedure (n.109, *supra*). See Reich, "La mise en oeuvre du Traité sur l'Union européenne par les accords interinstitutionnels" (1994) R.M.C.U.E. 81–85; Monar, "Interinstitutional Agreements: The Phenomenon and Its New Dynamics After Maastricht" (1994) C.M.L.R. 693–719.

[133] Joint Declaration of the European Parliament, the Council and the Commission of March 4, 1975 ([1975] O.J. C89/1), points 1 and 2.

[134] *ibid.*, points 3 and 4.

[135] EP Rules of Procedure, r.56(3). Before the Art. 251 Conciliation Committee was set up, a committee with the same name and the same membership operated on an ad hoc basis.

[136] See Financial Regulation, Art. 184, for amendments to that Regulation (conciliation procedure if requested by the European Parliament) and the implementing measures based on Art. 14 of the Act on the Direct Election of the European Parliament (see the declaration relating to that article). See also the statement of intent to extend its field of application in the Solemn Declaration of Stuttgart on European Union of June 19, 1983 (1983) 6 EC Bull. point 1.6.1, No 2.3.6.

[137] See the resolution on the consultation procedure of February 16, 1989 ([1989] O.J. C69/51) and r.56 in conjunction with r.40(1), fifth subpara., of the EP Rules of Procedure.

[138] See the obligation for the Council under EC Treaty, Art. 99(2), third subpara., and for its President under Art. 60(2), second subpara.; Art. 99(4), second subpara. (which also puts the Commission under a duty), Art. 100(2); Art. 104(11), second subpara.; Art. 111(1), third sentence; Art. 114(3).

Parliament about trade agreements concluded pursuant to Art. 133 of the EC Treaty.[139] In such cases, the European Parliament is informed only after the measure has been adopted and therefore can have no influence on decision-making. The Commission has undertaken to ensure, within its means, that the European Parliament is kept informed and is fully associated with the preparation and conduct of intergovernmental conferences[140] and the preparation, negotiation and conclusion of international agreements and accession negotiations.[141]

E. ROLE OF THE SOCIAL PARTNERS

Dialogue between management and labour. From the outset, workers' and **14–041** employers' representatives have had an advisory role in Community decision-making as members of the European Economic and Social Committee (EC/EAEC) and of the ECSC Consultative Committee (see paras 10–093—10–094). The advisory Employment Committee and the Social Protection Committee have to consult "management and labour" in fulfilling their mandates (EC Treaty, Art. 130, second para., and Art. 144, second para.). The social partners meet regularly for "tripartite consultation" with representatives of the Council and the Commission.[142] The consultation of workers or their representatives is a general principle of labour law which is common to all the Member States and also applies to Community institutions and bodies.[143] At the same time, collective bargaining between employers and workers, together with the right of association, constitute matters in respect of which the Community is to encourage co-operation between the Member States (see EC Treaty, Art. 140), in particular through the establishment of a European works council in undertakings and groups with a Community dimension (see para. 5–236).

Since the Single European Act, the Community has also sought to facilitate dialogue between management and labour, which may potentially lead to "contractual relations".[144] The last-mentioned method of decision-making was developed in the Social Agreement (see para. 5–235), the provisions of which were incorporated into the EC Treaty by the Treaty of Amsterdam. Under Art. 138 of the EC Treaty, when the Commission is minded to submit proposals in the social policy field, it has to consult

---

[139] See the Luns-Westerterp procedures, paras 21–004 and 21–006, *infra*.
[140] Point 6 of the framework agreement of July 5, 2000 (n.39, *supra*).
[141] Point 15 of and Annex II ("Forwarding to the European Parliament information on international agreements and enlargement, and involvement of the European Parliament in this respect") to the framework agreement of July 5, 2000 (n.39, *supra*).
[142] This consultation is ongoing and culminates in a "Social Summit" held prior to meetings of the European Council, see Council Decision 2003/174/EC of March 6, 2003 establishing a Tripartite Social Summit for Growth and Employment ([2003] O.J. L70/31).
[143] CFI, Case T–192/99 *Dunnett v European Investment Bank* [2001] E.C.R. II–813, paras 85, 89 and 90.
[144] EC Treaty, Art. 139. In this connection, the EU Constitution stresses that the Union must take into account the diversity of national systems and facilitate dialogue between the social partners while respecting their autonomy (Art. I–48).

management and labour twice: for the first time, on the possible direction of Community action and, for the second time, if it considers Community action advisable, on the content of the envisaged proposal (Art. 138(2) and (3)). On the occasion of such consultation, management and labour may inform the Commission of their wish to deal with the matter by agreement or by other contractual relations. They have nine months to conclude the procedure, although an extension may be decided upon jointly with the Commission (Art. 138(4)). However, the Commission is not obliged to take account of the advice given by management and labour or of their wish to deal with a particular matter amongst themselves.[145] According to the Interinstitutional Agreement between the European Parliament, the Council and the Commission on better law-making, regulation may be entrusted to the social partners where it has represents added value for the general interest, but not where fundamental rights or important political options are at stake or in situations where the rules must be applied in a uniform fashion in all Member States. Furthermore, the principles of competition and the unity of the internal market must not be affected.[146]

14–042 Negotiating agreements. In the event that management and labour wish to negotiate an agreement, the negotiation stage is left solely to them. The EC Treaty itself does not determine between which social partners negotiations are to be conducted at Community level.[147]

The EC Treaty provides that if management and labour conclude an agreement, it may be implemented by the Community or by the Member States. The Community is empowered to implement such an agreement if the signatory parties make a joint request to that effect, provided that it relates to matters covered by Art. 137 of the EC Treaty (EC Treaty, Art. 139(2), first subpara.). In that event, the Council is to act by a qualified majority on a proposal from the Commission; if, however, the agreement contains one or more provisions relating to one of the areas for which Art. 137(2) requires unanimity, the Council has to decide by a unanimous vote (Art. 139(2), second subpara.). The Council implemented the first agreements concluded by management and labour by means of directives.[148]

---

[145] Watson, "Social Policy After Maastricht" (1993) C.M.L.R. 481, at 503. See also the discussion of the principle of subsidiarity, para. 5–063, *supra*.

[146] These principles, together with those of transparency and representativeness, are stipulated for "co-regulation" and self-regulation" in point 17 of the Interinstitutional Agreement of December 16, 2003 on better law-making (n.39, *supra*).

[147] CFI, Case T–135/96 *UEAPME v Council* [1998] E.C.R. II–2335, paras 75–79. The Commission did decide, however, to set up Sectoral Dialogue Committees (composed of equal numbers of representatives of the two sides of industry) promoting dialogue between the social partners at European level; see its Decision of May 20, 1998, [1998] O.J. L225/27. As far as the "tripartite social summit" is concerned, the Council has provided a number of guidelines on the composition of delegations of workers' and employers' representatives; see Art. 3(2) of Decision 2003/174/EC (n.142, *supra*).

[148] At the inter-trade level, see Council Directive 96/34/EC of June 3, 1996 on the Framework Agreement on parental leave concluded by UNICE, CEEP and the ETUC, [1996] O.J.

As a result, the provisions of the agreements are binding on Member States as regards the result to be achieved, but they retain the power to determine the form and methods.[149] The Commission and the Council are in no case obliged to implement agreements at the request of signatory parties. However, the Council has no power to amend an agreement concluded as between the social partners; it merely decides whether a Community-level agreement is to have legislative status. In the absence of any direct involvement of the European Parliament, the democratic legitimacy of such legislation rests on the role played by the social partners as well as on the necessary approval by the Council of the outcome of the negotiations.[150] In order to secure compliance with the principle of democracy, the Commission and the Council must check the representative nature of the social partners concerned in the light of the content of each agreement.[151]

L145/4 (agreement of December 14, 1995 annexed thereto) and Council Directive 97/81/EC of December 15, 1997 concerning the Framework Agreement on part-time work concluded by UNICE, CEEP and the ETUC, [1998] O.J. L14/9 (agreement of June 6, 1997 annexed thereto). Both of these directives are based on Art. 4(2) of the Social Agreement [now EC Treaty, Art. 139(2)]. See also Council Directive 1999/70/EC of June 28, 1999 concerning the framework agreement on fixed-term work concluded by ETUC, UNICE and CEEP, [1999] O.J. L175/43 (agreement of March 18, 1999 appended as an annex), which was based on Art. 139(2) of the EC Treaty. The parties to the agreements in question are the umbrella organisations for workers (ETUC) and employers in the private (UNICE) and public (CEEP) sectors. The following sectoral instruments are based on Art. 139(2) of the EC Treaty: Council Directive 1999/63/EC of June 21, 1999 concerning the Agreement on the organisation of working time of seafarers concluded by the European Community Shipowners' Association (ECSA) and the Federation of Transport Workers' Unions in the European Union (FST), [1999] O.J. L167/33 (agreement of September 30, 1998 appended as an annex) and Council Directive 2000/79/EC of November 27, 2000 concerning the European Agreement on the Organisation of Working Time of Mobile Workers in Civil Aviation concluded by the Association of European Airlines (AEA), the European Transport Workers' Federation (ETF), the European Cockpit Association (ECA), the European Regions Airline Association (ERA) and the International Air Carrier Association (IACA), [2000] O.J. L302/57 (agreement of March 22, 2000 appended as an annex).

[149] The directives in question provide that the social partners themselves may introduce the necessary implementing measures by agreement (cf. para. 14–048, infra).

[150] CFI, Case T–135/96 UEAPME v Council [1998] E.C.R. II–2335, paras 88–89. For a critical view of the democratic legitimacy of management and labour, see Betten, "The Democratic Deficit of Participatory Democracy in Community Social Policy" (1998) E.L.R. 20–36; Langenbucher, "Zur Zulässigkeit parlamentersetzender Normgebungsverfahren im Europarecht" (2002) Z.Eu.P. 265–286. Indeed, democratic legitimacy requires the involvement of Community institutions, see Britz and Schmidt, "Die institutionalisierte Mitwirkung der Sozialpartner an der Rechtsetzung der Europäischen Gemeinschaft—Herausforderung des gemeinschaftsrechtlichen Demokratieprinzips" (1999) EuR. 467–498. See EP Rules of Procedure, r.78, by which the Parliament seeks to play some role in this procedure.

[151] CFI, Case T–135/96 UEAPME v Council [1998] E.C.R. II–2335, para. 89. The Commission set out criteria to that effect in its communication on the application of the Agreement on Social Policy of December 14, 1993 (COM (93) 600 final), as mentioned in the judgment in UEAPME v Council. In that judgment, the Court of First Instance declared inadmissible an action brought for annulment of Directive 96/34/EC (n.148, supra) by the European Union of Crafts and Small and Medium-sized Enterprises (UEAPME), which was not involved in the negotiations on the framework agreement on parental leave.

If the Council does not adopt an implementing decision, the agreement in question is to be implemented in accordance with the procedures and practices specific to management and labour and the Member States (see para. 14–048). This was the case with the agreement concluded by the social partners in July 2002 on teleworking.[152] In the absence of implementation by Community legislation, the legal force of agreements concluded between management and labour at Community level remains uncertain, particularly because the question of the framework for the negotiations leading up to the conclusion of such agreements, including guarantees as to the representative nature of the negotiators for the workers and employers concerned, is not regulated.[153]

F. INPUT FROM OTHER BODIES AND GROUPS

14–043 Contacts with Commission. Before the Commission formulates and submits a proposal, it proceeds to carry out wide-ranging consultation of potentially affected groups (see para. 14–016). Representatives of interest groups themselves regularly contact Members of the Commission or its administration and Members of the European Parliament. As a result of its right of initiative, the Commission has a great influence on the content of Community legislation. In some cases where the Council does not have to decide on a Commission proposal, it has nonetheless to "consult" the Commission.[154]

14–044 Compulsory consultation. In various areas, the decision-making process involves compulsory consultation of especially constituted bodies. In the first place, there are the economic and social interest groups, which can make their views known through the European Economic and Social

---

[152] Framework Agreement of July 16, 2002 concluded by UNICE/UEAPME, the CEEP and the ETUC on telework (available from the website of the Commission's DG for Employment and Social Affairs).

[153] See Vigneau, "Etude sur l'autonomie collective au niveau communautaire" (2002) R.T.D.E. 653–683, and, earlier, the issues adumbrated by Vandamme, "Quel espace contractuel pour les partenaires sociaux après le traité de Maastricht" (1992) R.M.C.U.E. 788–792; Nyssen, "Le rôle des partenaires sociaux dans l'élaboration et la mise en oeuvre du droit communautaire" (1993) Ann. Dr. Louv. 319, at 328–331; Watson (n.145, *supra*), at 506–509; Gadbin, "L'association des partenaires économiques et sociaux organisés aux procédures de décision en droit communautaire" (2000) R.T.D.E. 1–46.

[154] EC Treaty, Art. 107(5) and (6); Art. 225(2); Art. 245, second para.; Art. 259(2); EU Treaty, Art. 40(2), first subpara.; Art. 48, second para., and Art. 49, first para.; Act on the Direct Election of the European Parliament, Art. 14. As far as application of Art. 259 of the EC Treaty is concerned (appointment of members of the European Economic and Social Committee), the Court of Justice has held that it is sufficient for the Commission to be present at the Coreper meeting at which consensus is reached on a decision submitted to the Council as a Part A item of the agenda: ECJ, Case 297/86 *CIDA v Council* [1988] E.C.R. 3531, paras 27–30. A Commission opinion is also required by Art. 209 of the EC Treaty and in one case constitutes the legislative initiative (n.30, *supra*). The European Parliament lays down regulations and general conditions after seeking the "opinion" of the Commission under Art. 190(5) (performance of MEPs' duties) and Art. 195(4) of the EC Treaty (Ombudsman Regulations).

Committee. Various Treaty articles require the Council or the Commission to consult that committee before adopting an act (see para. 10–093). The EU Treaty recognised the specific interests of regional and local authorities and set up the Committee of the Regions, which has to be consulted by the Council on certain matters. These matters are ones in respect of which policy is conducted in several Member States by decentralised authorities pursuant to rules on the devolution of powers (see para. 10–096). The opinions of those committees are in no way binding. Nevertheless, they do influence decision-making, especially where the views they contain are taken up by the Commission and/or the European Parliament, which normally has a say in decision-making on the matters in question.[155] Where the body concerned is composed of democratically elected representatives and it is consulted in order to enable the interests to be expressed of those at whom the eventual legal provision is aimed, the obligation to obtain an opinion may make it necessary to carry out a fresh consultation if the original proposal undergoes major changes not corresponding to changes recommended by the body in question.[156]

In economic and monetary matters, some Treaty articles require the Commission or the Council to seek the opinion of the Economic and Financial Committee,[157] whilst other articles oblige the Council to consult the ECB.[158] In one case, the opinion of the ECB is so crucial that the consultation has to endeavour to reach a "consensus" between the Council and the ECB (EC Treaty, Art. 111(1), first sentence). In relation to these matters, however, the Commission does not have its full right to submit proposals and the European Parliament is not generally involved in the decision-making process.[159]

Constitution—Participatory democracy. The EU Constitution states that **14–045** the democratic life of the Union relies, not only on the principle of "representative democracy" (in other words, the participation of the citizens through their representatives in the European Parliament and in the national parliaments), but also on the principle of "participatory democracy" (Arts I–46 and I–47). To that end, the EU Constitution will

---

[155] Only where decisions are taken under Art. 75(3) and Art. 144 of the EC Treaty is the European Economic and Social Committee and not the Parliament involved.

[156] The Court of First Instance applied the obligations to consult the European Parliament (see para. 14–026, *supra*) in a case where Art. 24 of the Merger Treaty required the Commission to consult the Staff Regulations Committee on any proposal to amend the Staff Regulations: CFI, Case T–164/96 *Busaca v Court of Auditors* [1998] E.C.R. II–1699, paras 79–102.

[157] For the Commission, see EC Treaty, Art. 104(4) and Art. 119(1), second subpara.; for the Council, see EC Treaty, Art. 114(3) and Art. 120(3).

[158] For the ECB, see the general obligation under EC Treaty, Art. 105(4), and the specific obligations under Art. 59; Art. 104(14), second subpara.; Art. 105(6); Art. 106(2), Art. 107(5) and (6); Art. 111(1) to (4); Art. 114(3); Art. 123(4) and (5), and EU Treaty, Art. 48, second para.

[159] See the cases where the Commission makes a "recommendation" (para. 14–014, *supra*) and the European Parliament is merely "informed" (para. 14–040, *supra*).

require the Union institutions to give citizens and representative associations the opportunity to make known and exchange their views publicly in all areas of Union action (Art. I–47(1)). The institutions are to "maintain an open, transparent and regular dialogue with representative associations and civil society" (Art. I–47(2)), in particular with the social partners[160] and with churches, religious associations and communities and philosophical and non-confessional organisations.[161] This appeal to dialogue is specifically reflected in the obligation imposed on the Commission to carry out broad consultations with parties concerned and to take note of any initiative put forward by a significant number of citizens (see para. 14–019). In addition, participation of civil society will have to be ensured in so far as the Union institutions, bodies, offices and agencies are to function "as openly as possible" (EU Constitution, Art. I–50(1); see para. 10–159 *et seq.*).

III. THE IMPLEMENTATION OF LEGISLATION

14–046 Duty to implement. The Treaties did not set up a uniform system for the implementation of Community legislation: where necessary, each act determines its implementation procedures itself; where the act in question does not do so, the principle applies in any event that "Member States shall take all appropriate measures, whether general or particular, to ensure fulfilment of the obligations arising out of this Treaty or resulting from action taken by the institutions of the Community" (EC Treaty, Art. 10, first para.). Accordingly, Community law is implemented as a rule by *administration communautaire indirecte.* In some policy areas, specific provisions entrust Community institutions and bodies with implementing tasks (*administration communautaire directe*). In both cases, the enforcement of legislative and implementing rules of Community law and the imposition of sanctions for breaches thereof fall primarily to the national administrative and judicial authorities. The Commission is empowered to conduct administrative inquiries itself and to fine individuals only very exceptionally.[162] The following sections discuss implementation by the Member States and implementation by Community institutions and bodies.

---

[160] EU Constitution, Art. I–48 (referring to "the diversity of national systems" and "their autonomy").

[161] *ibid.*, Art. I–52(3) ("[r]ecognising their identity and their specific contribution"). Under Art. 52(1)–(2), the Union must respect the status under national law of churches and religious associations or communities and that of philosophical and non-confessional organisations. See Hölscheidt and Mund, "Religionen und Kirchen im europäischen Verfassungsverbund" (2003) EuR. 1083–1094.

[162] paras 5–197—5–200, *supra* (competition cases). For the allocation of powers of implementation, see Möllers, "Durchführung des Gemeinschaftsrechts" (2002) EuR. 483–516.

It is also possible for Community legislation to leave it to the sectors or parties concerned to bring about the objectives sought by that legislation. According to what to the European Parliament, the Council and the Commission agreed in the Interinstitutional Agreement of December 2003, the Commission has to verify whether or not the Community legislation is being implemented and, if necessary, to propose an amendment to the legislative act or any other appropriate legislative measure.[163]

A. IMPLEMENTATION BY THE MEMBER STATES

Executive federalism. Article 10 of the EC Treaty puts Member States **14–047** under a duty to implement provisions of Community law so as to ensure fulfilment of the obligations contained therein. Where a piece of Community legislation makes no specific provision, its implementation is a matter in the first place for the Member States.[164] In this respect the Community exhibits characteristic features of a federal system in which legislative power is assigned to the central authority, but executive power is vested in authorities in the federated States (*executive federalism, Vollzugsföderalismus*). The Treaties expressly establish such a system with regard to directives, which, after adoption by the Community legislature, are binding on the Member States as to the result to be achieved, but leave the choice of the form and methods by which they are incorporated into national law to the national authorities (EC Treaty, Art. 249, third para.). Although in theory, therefore, directives leave certain policy choices to the Member States, in practice they are often formulated in such detail that the Member States are left only with the task of implementing them mechanically. The obligation to implement Community legislation also applies where it is cast in a different form (*e.g.* that of a regulation) but its substance needs specifying or it has to be applied in individual cases in order for it to be effective.[165] In many cases, Member States also have to legislate in order to be able to apply and enforce implementing rules adopted by Community institutions and bodies themselves and in order to be able to impose sanctions in the event of their breach.[166] The EU Constitution sets forth this obligation in general terms as a duty imposed on

---

[163] See points 18 to 21 on "co-regulation" in the Interinstitutional Agreement of December 16, 2003 on better law-making (n.39, *supra*). An example is the implementation of Community legislation by the social partners (para. 14–042, *supra*).

[164] See CFI, Cases T–492/93 and T–492/93 R *Nutral v Commission* [1993] E.C.R. II–1023, para. 26, upheld by ECJ, Case C–476/93 P *Nutral v Commission* [1995] E.C.R. I–4125, para. 14.

[165] See, *e.g.* ECJ, Case 30/70 *Scheer* [1970] E.C.R. 1197, para. 10; ECJ, Case 137/80 *Commission v Belgium* [1981] E.C.R. 2393, paras 3–9 (a Member State is under a duty to adopt the necessary implementing measures so as to apply the regulation establishing the Staff Regulations of Community officials).

[166] See Curtin and Mortelmans, "Application and Enforcement of Community Law by the Member States: Actors in Search of a Third Generation Script", in Curtin and Heukels (eds), *Institutional Dynamics of European Integration. Essays in Honour of Henry G. Schermers*, Vol.II (Martinus Nijhoff, Dordrecht, 1994) at 423–466.

Member States "to adopt all measures of national law necessary to implement legally binding Union acts" (Art. I–37(1)).[167]

14–048 Domestic organisation of implementation. The Member States carry out their task of implementing Community law in accordance with their particular constitutional traditions. Accordingly, depending on the subject-matter, the implementation of a Community provision may fall within the remit of legislative or executive bodies at national or regional level.[168] Each such body is under a duty to amend domestic law so as to make it conform with Community law.[169] The division of powers within a Member State does not preclude a breach of the duty to implement Community legislation from being invariably imputed to the State itself at Community level "whatever the agency of the State whose action or inaction is the cause of the failure to fulfil its obligations, even in the case of a constitutionally independent institution".[170]

In social matters, Member States may leave the implementation of Community provisions to be agreed between management and labour.[171] Art. 137(3) of the EC Treaty provides that a Member State may entrust management and labour, at their joint request, with the implementation of directives adopted pursuant to that article. In such case, the Member State is to ensure that management and labour introduce the necessary measures by agreement within the period prescribed for transposing the directive in question, and must take any necessary measure enabling it at any time to be in a position to guarantee the results imposed by the directive (Art. 137(3), second subpara.). Accordingly, the national authorities must see to it that workers who do not benefit from the protection of the directive by other means, in particular where they are not members of a trade union, where they are not covered by a collective agreement or where such an agreement does not fully guarantee the protection in question, are in fact covered.[172]

---

[167] See also Dubey, "Administration indirecte et fédéralisme d'exécution en Europe" (2003) C.D.E. 87–133.

[168] ECJ, Case 96/81 *Commission v Netherlands* [1982] E.C.R. 1791, para. 12.

[169] See ECJ, Joined Cases 314–316/81 and 83/82 *Waterkeyn* [1982] E.C.R. 4337, para. 14 (bodies exercising legislative power and the judiciary); ECJ, Case C–8/88 *Germany v Commission* [1990] E.C.R. I–2321, para. 13 (federated States and other territorial authorities). For judicial bodies, see para. 5–051, *supra*.

[170] ECJ, Case 77/69 *Commission v Belgium* [1970] E.C.R. 237, para. 15; ECJ, Case 8/70 *Commission v Italy* [1970] E.C.R. 961, para. 9. See also ECJ, Case 30/72 *Commission v Italy* [1973] E.C.R. 161, para. 11 (a Member State must take account in its domestic legal system of the consequences of its adherence to the Community and, if need be, adapt its budgetary procedures accordingly); ECJ, Case C–423/00 *Commission v Belgium* [2002] E.C.R. I–593 (Member State held to be in breach because a co-operation agreement between the federal authority and part States was required for implementation and could not be approved by those entities in time). For liability on the part of Member States for decentralised/devolved authorities, see para. 11–016, *supra*.

[171] See Steyger, "European Community Law and the Self-Regulatory Capacity of Society" (1993) J.C.M.S. 171–190.

[172] ECJ, Case 143/83 *Commission v Denmark* [1985] E.C.R. 427, para. 8. See Adinolfi, "The Implementation of Social Policy Directives Through Collective Agreements?" (1988) C.M.L.R. 291–316.

Also in the case of agreements concluded by management and labour at Community level, if the Council does not adopt an implementing act, such an agreement is to be implemented "in accordance with the procedures and practices specific to management and labour and the Member States" (Art. 139(2), first subpara.). The EC Treaty gives no indication as to whether or not there is an obligation to implement on the part of the Member States. It appears from a declaration on that provision of the Treaty that this was not the intention of the Contracting Parties.[173]

Uniform and full application of Community law. In the absence of **14–049** common rules in the matter, the Member States act, when implementing Community law, in accordance with the procedural and substantive rules of their own national law. In so doing, however, they must always pay due regard to the requirements of the uniform application of Community law.[174] The implementation of Community law may not create unequal treatment as between persons. The need to ensure that Community law is fully applied requires Member States not only to bring their legislation into conformity with Community law but also to do so by adopting rules of law capable of creating a situation which is sufficiently precise, clear and transparent to allow individuals to know the full extent of their rights and rely on them before the national authorities.[175] Where national legislation has been the subject of different relevant judicial constructions, some leading to the application of that legislation in compliance with Community law, others leading to the opposite application, it must be held that, at the very least, such legislation is not sufficiently clear to ensure its application in compliance with Community law.[176]

In order to ensure the uniform and full application of Community law, the Community legislature may indicate precisely what implementing measures the Member States must adopt and for what sanctions they must provide. In the absence of any provision in the Community rules laying down specific sanctions, the Member States are free to adopt such sanctions

---

[173] Declaration (No.27) on Art. 118b [now Art. 139](2) of the Treaty establishing the European Community, which was annexed to the Final Act of the Treaty of Amsterdam, envisages the "first" of the arrangements for application of the agreements between management and labour as taking the form of collective bargaining according to the rules of each Member State and involving "no obligation on the Member States to apply the agreements directly or to work out rules for their transposition, nor any obligation to amend national legislation in force to facilitate their implementation" ([1997] O.J. C340/136). This declaration takes over the wording of Declaration (No.2) on Art. 4(2) of the Social Agreement (the wording of which was taken over by Art. 139 of the EC Treaty).

[174] ECJ, Joined Cases 205–215/82 *Deutsche Milchkontor v Germany* [1983] E.C.R. 2633, para. 17.

[175] ECJ, Case C–162/99 *Commission v Italy* [2001] E.C.R. I–541, para. 22; ECJ, Case C–313/99 *Mulligan* [2002] E.C.R. I–5719, paras 46–54. The obligation to implement has been clarified in the case law principally with regard to directives; para. 17–122, *infra*.

[176] ECJ (judgment of December 9, 2003), Case C–129/00 *Commission v Italy*, not yet reported, para. 33, with annotations by Peerbux-Beaugendre (2004) R.T.D.E. 201–215; Mortelmans and van der Gronden (2004) A.Ae. 192–205.

as appear to them to be appropriate, including criminal sanctions.[177] In any event, the Member States must ensure that infringements of Community law are penalised under conditions, both procedural and substantive, which are analogous to those applicable to infringements of national law of a similar nature and importance and make the penalty effective, proportionate and dissuasive.[178] Moreover, the national authorities must proceed, with respect to infringements of Community law, with the same diligence as that which they bring to bear in implementing corresponding national laws.[179] Where national law contains a general principle according to which everyone is presumed to know the law, that principle may also be applied in the case of sanctions for infringements of Community law.[180]

Conversely, Community law requires Member States to provide for judicial review of the acts of their authorities which collaborate administratively in the production of a decision of a Community institution (see para. 17–077).

14–050 **Defective implementation.** The Commission may bring an action under Art. 226 of the EC Treaty against a Member State which fails to fulfil its obligations to implement Community law. If the Court of Justice finds that the Member State has indeed failed to fulfil its obligations, the State will be required to take the necessary measures to comply with the Court's judgment, failing which the Court may impose a flat-rate fine or a periodic penalty payment if second proceedings are brought (EC Treaty, Art. 228(1) and (2)). As the Court held in 1963 in *Van Gend & Loos* (see para. 1–018), individuals who have a direct interest in the correct implementation of Community law may make sure that Member States fulfil their obligations in respect of the implementation of Community law.[181] This is because,

---

[177] ECJ, Case 50/76 *Amsterdam Bulb* [1977] E.C.R. 137, paras 32–33. For the extent to which Member States may (not) be obliged to enforce Community rules *via* criminal law, see Comijs, "Communautair strafrecht?" (2001) N.T.E.R. 267–271; Veldt Foglia, "(Nog) geen strafrecht in de Eerste Pijler?" (2002) S.E.W. 162–169; Labayle, "Entre désir et réalité: Quelle voie pour une répression pénale des violations du droit communautaire?" (2003) R.M.C.U.E. 293–303; Corstens, "Criminal law in the First Pillar?" (2003) European Journal of Crime 131–144. For a critical view on the usefulness of criminal sanctions in environmental law, see Faure, "European Environmental Criminal Law: Do we really need it?" (2004) E.Env.L.Rev. 18–29.

[178] ECJ, Case 68/88 *Commission v Greece* [1989] E.C.R. 2965, para. 24; ECJ, Case C–326/88 *Hansen* [1990] E.C.R. I–2911, para. 17. As far as the ECSC was concerned, this followed from Art. 86 of the ECSC Treaty: ECJ, Case C–341/94 *Allain* [1996] E.C.R. I–4631, paras 23–24. See also the requirement for sanctions for unlawful discrimination to be effective and to have a deterrent effect, ECJ, Case 14/83 *Von Colson and Kamann* [1984] E.C.R. 1891, paras 23–24. For sanctions based on violations of humanitarian international law and human rights, see ECJ, Case C–84/95 *Bosphorus* [1996] E.C.R. I–3953, para. 26.

[179] *Commission v Greece*, cited n.178, *supra*, para. 25.

[180] ECJ, Case C–262/99 *Louloudakis* [2001] E.C.R. I–5547, paras 76–77. Where determination of the arrangements applicable has given rise to difficulties, however, account must be taken of the good faith of the offender when determining the penalty actually imposed on him: *ibid.*

[181] See Timmermans, "Judicial Protection Against the Member States: Arts 169 and 177 Revisited", *Institutional Dynamics of European Integration. Essays in Honour of Henry G. Schermers* (n.166, *supra*), 391, at 397–400.

under Art. 10 of the EC Treaty, the national courts are under a duty to secure the effectiveness (*effet utile*) of Community law. Individuals deriving rights from that law may have them enforced in a non-discriminatory manner by the courts. Since the 1991 judgment in *Francovich*, they may claim damages from a Member State whose breach of Community law causes them to suffer loss or damage. For the sake of the uniform application of Community law, this holds good irrespective as to whether the breach committed within the national legal order is attributable to the legislature, the executive or the judiciary (see para. 17–012).

B. IMPLEMENTATION BY INSTITUTIONS OR BODIES OF THE COMMUNITIES

1. Implementation by the Commission or the Council

a. General principles

Conferral of implementing powers on Commission. It falls to the **14–051** Community institutions to implement Community law only when that task has been expressly conferred upon them. According to the third indent of Art. 202 of the EC Treaty—added by the Single European Act—, the Council is to "confer on the Commission, in the acts which the Council adopts, powers for the implementation of the rules which the Council lays down" and "may impose certain requirements in respect of the exercise of these powers". The procedures in question must be "consonant with principles and rules to be laid down in advance by the Council, acting unanimously on a proposal from the Commission and after obtaining the opinion of the European Parliament". As a result, the Commission is given in principle the executive role to play in Community legislative measures, which may or may not be subject to conditions laid down by the Council (together with the European Parliament in matters coming under the co-decision procedure). Those conditions must comply with the "principles" and "rules" laid down by the Council in the "Comitology Decision" (see para. 14–054). The third indent of Art. 202 further provides that the Council "may also reserve the right, in specific cases, to exercise directly implementing powers itself". If it takes this step, however, it must state in detail the grounds for its decision.[182]

In this way, the third indent of Art. 202 of the EC Treaty confirms the former practice whereby the Council, acting under Art. 211 of the EC Treaty, conferred implementing powers on the Commission to be exercised in accordance with detailed rules laid down by the Council and subject to its right to reserve the decision for itself where necessary.[183] It must be

---

[182] ECJ, Case 16/88 *Commission v Council* [1989] E.C.R. 3457, para. 10. See also the action brought by the Commission against the Council for having unlawfully reserved implementing powers to itself and for not stating any reasons for doing so: Case C–257/01, [2001] O.J. C245/15.

[183] The Court of Justice approved this system as long ago as ECJ, Case 25/70 *Köster* [1970] E.C.R. 1161, para. 9.

noted that the Commission now takes precedence as the holder of implementing power, whereas prior to the Single European Act the Commission and the Council were on an equal footing.[184] One implementing power which the Treaty reserves for the Council is the power to implement agreements concluded between management and labour (Art. 139(2); see para. 14–042).

14–052 Wide interpretation of "implementation". An implementing power will be validly conferred only if it is sufficiently specific, in the sense that its bounds must be clearly specified.[185] Implementing powers encompass both regulatory powers[186] and the power to apply rules to specific cases by means of individual decisions.[187] Moreover, the term "implementation" has to be given a wide interpretation. In complex areas such as the organisation of the market in agricultural products, the Council may be forced to confer wide powers of discretion and action on the Commission.[188] Even where the Commission has no express power to this effect, its implementing provisions may impose penalties, which, within the context of the policy in question, are designed to secure the proper financial management of Community funds.[189] A measure intended to harmonise national legislation may confer powers on the Commission to compel the Member States to take temporary measures if otherwise the aims of the harmonisation would be jeopardised.[190]

14–053 Reorganisation of implementing powers by the Constitution. The EU Constitution proposes to reorganise the way in which implementing powers are conferred on the Council and the Commission in the light of the new distinction between situations where the institutions adopt legislative acts (European "laws" and "framework laws") and situations where the institutions adopt legally binding acts which are not legislative acts (European "regulations" or "decisions"). In the latter situation, the EU Constitution distinguishes between three sets of cases.

---

[184] Bradley, "Comitology and the Law: Through a Glass, Darkly" (1992) C.M.L.R. 693–721. See also the commentaries on the introduction of the Treaty article and the Comitology Decision adopted pursuant thereto: Blumann, "Le pouvoir exécutif de la Commission à la lumière de l'Acte unique européen" (1988) R.T.D.E. 23–59; Ehlermann, "Compétences d'exécution conférées à la Commission—La nouvelle décision-cadre du Conseil" (1988) R.M.C. 232–239; Blumann, "La Commission, agent d'exécution du droit communautaire. La comitologie", in Louis and Waelbroeck (eds), *La Commission au coeur du système institutionnel des Communautés européennes* (Editions de l'Université de Bruxelles, Brussels, 1989) at 49–77.

[185] ECJ, Case 291/86 *Central-Import Münster* [1988] E.C.R. 3679, para. 13.

[186] ECJ, Case 41/69 *ACF Chemiefarma v Commission* [1970] E.C.R. 661, paras 60–62.

[187] ECJ, Case 16/88 *Commission v Council* [1989] E.C.R. 3457, para. 11.

[188] ECJ, Case 23/75 *Rey Soda v Cassa Conguaglio Zucchero* [1975] E.C.R. 1279, paras 10–11.

[189] ECJ, Case C–240/90 *Germany v Commission* [1992] E.C.R. I–5383, paras 35–42. See also the earlier case ECJ, Case 25/70 *Köster* [1970] E.C.R. 1161, para. 7.

[190] ECJ, Case C–359/92 *Germany v Council* [1994] E.C.R. I–3681, paras 30–39 (252, *supra*).

The first case is the existing situation where legally binding acts of the Union need uniform conditions for their implementation and therefore confer implementing powers on the Commission or the Council. In principle, in these circumstances, the power of implementation is to be conferred on the Commission. Union acts may confer implementing powers on the Council only "in duly justified specific cases" and in the field of the CFSP (EU Constitution, Art. I–37(2)). As is at present the case under the Comitology Decision (which was adopted by the Council), the European Parliament and the Council, acting under the co-decision procedure, are to lay down the rules and general principles for mechanisms for control by Member States of the Commission's exercise of implementing powers (EU Constitution, Art. I–37(3)). Implementing acts of the Commission and the Council are to take the form of European "implementing regulations" or "implementing decisions" (EU Constitution, Art. I–37(4)).

Secondly, the EU Constitution will enable the European Parliament and the Council[191] to adopt European laws or framework laws delegating to the Commission the power to supplement these laws or framework laws or to amend certain of their non-essential elements by way of "delegated regulations". In such cases, the European law or framework law must explicitly define the objectives, content, scope and duration of the delegation, which may not cover the essential elements of an area (EU Constitution, Art. I–36(1)). Moreover, the European law or framework law must explicitly determine the conditions of application to which the delegation is subject. For example, it may be provided that a delegated regulation may enter into force only if no objection has been expressed by the European Parliament or by the Council within a given period, or that the European Parliament or the Council may revoke the delegation (EU Constitution, Art. I–36(2)). Under this type of delegated powers, the Commission is not subject to "comitology" control by the Member States as mentioned in Art. I–37 (see paras 14–054 *et seq.*). As a legally binding act, a delegated regulation of the Commission may in turn determine the conditions under which it needs further implementation pursuant to the second and fourth paras of Art. I–37 of the EU Constitution.

Finally, the EU Constitution mentions certain cases in which a provision of the Constitution explicitly provides that the Commission or the Council may adopt a "European regulation" or "European decision", thereby conferring on the institution in question an "implementing power" directly

---

[191] Art. I–36 of the EU Constitution mentions delegation by "European laws and European framework laws". It follows that the delegation can also be given by the Council (or by the European Parliament) acting alone where that institution adopts legislation in accordance with a "special legislative procedure".

based on authority given by the Constitution itself.[192] In certain cases, the Constitution also provides for the European Council and the European Central Bank to adopt "European regulations" or "European decisions" directly based on the Constitution.[193] Since those acts are legally binding, they may in turn determine the conditions under which the Commission or the Council may take further implementing acts in accordance with Art. I–37 of the EU Constitution.

b. Supervision of implementation by the Commission: "comitology"

14–054 Comitology Decision. As already mentioned, in conferring implementing powers on the Commission, the Council (and where the co-decision procedure applies, the European Parliament) may impose certain requirements (EC Treaty, Art. 202, third indent). In general, the European Parliament and the Council impose requirements on the Commission with a view to its carrying out its implementing function by means of a particular form of collaboration with a committee set up by them. In order to improve the efficiency of the Community decision-making process, the Council adopted the First Comitology Decision on July 13, 1987, which limited and enumerated the number of implementing procedures.[194] On June 28, 1999 the Council adopted the Second Comitology Decision, which, to a limited extent, responded to the European Parliament's wish to be able to exercise control over the implementation of acts adopted by co-decision.[195] The

---

[192] See, for instance, the European regulations or decisions to be adopted by the Council with a view to fixing Common Customs Tariff duties (Art. III–151(6)), for the application of the principles of the Union's competition policy (Arts III–163 and III–169) and in the fields of agriculture and fisheries (Art. III–231(3)); see also the European regulations to be adopted by the Commission so as to provide for "block exemptions" in the exercise of its competition policy (Arts III–165(3) and III–168(4)) and the European decisions to be adopted by the Commission with respect to public undertakings and undertakings to which Member States grant special or exclusive rights and with respect to State aid (Arts III–166(3) and III–168).

[193] e.g. the European Council in the field of CFSP (Arts I–40 and III–293) and the ECB in monetary matters (Art. III–190).

[194] Council Decision 87/373/EEC of July 13, 1987 laying down the conditions for the exercise of implementing powers conferred on the Commission, [1987] O.J. L197/33. The Council may not introduce any other procedures: ECJ, Case 16/88 *Commission v Council* [1989] E.C.R. 3457, para. 14.

[195] Council Decision 1999/468/EC of June 28, 1999 laying down the procedures for the exercise of implementing powers conferred on the Commission, [1999] O.J. L184/23. See Lenaerts and Verhoeven, "Comitologie en scheiding der machten. Enige kanttekeningen bij het Raadsbesluit van 28 juni 1999" (2000) S.E.W. 394–423; Mensching, "Der neue Komitologie-Beschluss des Rates" (2000) EU.Z.W. 268–271; Moteira González, "Änderung des normativen Rahmens der Komitologie" (2003) Z.Eu.S. 561–588. See also the 31st Report House of Lords: Select Committee on the European Union, Reforming Comitology (2002–03) HL 135. For a list of all the committees, see [2000] O.J. C225/2 for the adjustment of procedures provided for in existing legislation in the light of the Second Comitology Decision, see Regulation No. 1882/2003, [2003] O.J. L254/1. For the conflict between the European Parliament and the Commission preceding the adoption of the Second Comitology Decision, see Blumann, "Le Parlement européen et la comitologie: une complication pour la Conférence intergouvernementale de 1996" (1996) R.T.D.E. 1–24; Nuttens, "La 'comitologie' et la Conférence intergouvernementale" (1996) R.M.C.U.E. 314–327.

Comitology Decision sets out the "principles and rules" with which the Community legislator should comply in adopting legislative acts that confer implementing powers on the Commission.[196] As in the case of the first decision, the Second Comitology Decision classifies the committees into three groups, depending on whether they have advisory, management or regulatory powers. The decision sets out criteria on the basis of which the legislator may choose a committee procedure.[197] Although those criteria are not binding, they oblige the Community legislator to state reasons in the legislative act for any departure from those criteria.[198] It should first be noted that all the committees are made up of representatives of the Member States and chaired by a representative of the Commission, who has no vote. The latter submits to the committee a draft of the measures to be taken and may lay down a time-limit within which the committee must deliver its opinion according to the urgency of the matter. The new Comitology Decision requires each committee to adopt its own rules of procedure on the basis of standard rules of procedure[199] and to allow the public to have access to its documents (Comitology Decision, Art. 7(1) and (2)).[200] The Commission is to inform the European Parliament of committee proceedings on a regular basis (Comitology Decision, Art. 7(3)). The European Parliament receives in particular draft measures submitted to the committees for the implementation of instruments adopted by the co-decision procedure. If the European Parliament indicates, in a resolution setting out the grounds on which it is based, that draft implementing measures would exceed the implementing powers provided for in the basic instrument, the Commission must re-examine the draft

---

[196] ECJ, Case C–378/00 *Commission v European Parliament and Council* [2003] E.C.R. I–937, paras 40–42.

[197] Unlike the first decision, the Second Comitology Decision no longer provides for two variants of the management committee and the regulatory committee. Art. 2 of the Decision sets out criteria on which the choice of procedure is to be based. Management measures, such as those relating to the application of the common agricultural and common fisheries policies, or to the implementation of programmes with substantial budgetary implications, should be adopted by use of the management procedure. Measures of general scope designed to apply essential provisions of basic instruments, including measures concerning the protection of the health or safety of humans, animals or plants, should be adopted by use of the regulatory procedure. The regulatory procedure should also be used where a basic instrument stipulates that certain non-essential provisions of the instrument may be adapted or updated by way of implementing procedures. As for the advisory procedure, the Second Comitology Decision provides that it is to used "in any case in which it is considered to be the most appropriate", without prejudice to the use of the management or regulatory procedure. In addition, Art. 6 of the Second Comitology Decision describes the procedure which may be applied where the basic instrument confers on the Commission the power to decide on safeguard measures.

[198] ECJ, Case C–378/00 *Commission v European Parliament and Council* [2003] E.C.R. I–937, paras 43–55 (an unreasoned choice departing from those criteria was declared void).

[199] For the standard rules of procedure, see [2001] O.J. C38/3.

[200] CFI, Case T–188/97 *Rothmans v Commission* [1999] E.C.R. II–2463 (as far as access to its documents are concerned, a committee comes under the Commission).

measures and inform the European Parliament of the action which it intends to take on its resolution (Comitology Decision, Art. 8).[201]

14–055 **Advisory committee.** Where the Council has set up an advisory committee, the Commission must obtain its opinion, but is not bound by it. It must take the utmost account of its opinion, however, and inform it of the manner in which its opinion has been taken into account (Comitology Decision, Art. 3).

14–056 **Management committee.** Where the Council has established a management committee, the Commission must likewise seek its opinion. The committee delivers its opinion by a qualified majority as laid down in Art. 205(2) of the EC Treaty for decisions which the Council is required to adopt on a proposal from the Commission. The Commission then adopts the implementing measures, but has to communicate to the Council forthwith any measures which are not in accordance with the committee's opinion. In that event, the Commission may defer application of the measures which it has decided on for a period to be laid down in each basic instrument but which must in no case exceed three months (Comitology Decision, Art. 4(3)). The Council, acting on its own initiative by a qualified majority, may take a different decision within that period (Comitology Decision, Art. 4(4)).If the Council fails to reach a decision within that time-limit, the Commission's measures enter into force definitively.

A negative opinion from a management committee *ipso facto* gives the Council an opportunity to adopt a decision differing from the measures proposed by the Commission. Yet the fact that the management committee has delivered a negative opinion does not necessarily mean that every delegation has the same difficulties in accepting the Commission's measures, as a result of which the Council cannot always muster a sufficient majority in favour of different measures. In practice, the procedure does not often produce negative opinions, since the Commission ensures that its implementing function is conducted smoothly by negotiating with the delegations on the management committee beforehand.[202]

14–057 **Regulatory committee.** Where the Council sets up a regulatory committee, the Commission likewise submits a draft of the measures to be taken. If the committee votes by a qualified majority (determined in the same way as in the case of a management committee) in favour of the measures envisaged, they are adopted by the Commission. If, in contrast, the committee cannot

---

[201] See in this connection the agreement between the European Parliament and the Commission on procedures for implementing Council Decision 1999/468/EC of June 28, 1999 laying down the procedures for the exercise of implementing powers conferred on the Commission, [2000] O.J. L256/19.

[202] For the role played by management committees in agricultural policy, see Trotman, "Agricultural Policy Management: A Lesson in Unaccountability" (1995) C.M.L.R. 1385–1406.

muster a sufficient majority for a favourable opinion, or if no opinion is delivered, the Commission must submit the measures envisaged to the Council as a formal proposal and inform the European Parliament (Comitology Decision, Art. 5(3), (4) and (5)).[203] Next, the Council may adopt the proposal by a qualified majority (or amend it by a unanimous vote: see EC Treaty, Art. 250(1)), within a period to be laid down in each basic instrument but which may in no case exceed three months from the date of referral to the Council. If within that period the Council has indicated by a qualified majority that it opposes the proposal, the Commission must re-examine it. It may then submit an amended proposal to the Council, re-submit its proposal or present a legislative proposal on the basis of the Treaty. If on the expiry of that period the Council has neither adopted the proposed implementing act nor indicated its opposition to the proposal for implementing measures, the proposed implementing act is to be adopted by the Commission (Comitology Decision, Art. 5(6)).[204]

Consultation of expert committees. In implementing legislation, not only **14–058** does the Commission have to have regard to the politically sensitive nature of certain measures, but scientific and technical problems also arise. For this reason, various Community measures provide for the involvement of a scientific or technical committee with a view to their implementation. Where such a committee is set up, it must be consulted even if the instrument to be implemented does not say so in so many words, because such consultation constitutes the only guarantee that a Community measure is necessary and adapted to the objective pursued.[205] An infringement of internal procedural rules of such a committee which are intended to ensure that Member States' representatives have the time necessary to consult the different national administrative authorities, experts or professional organisations may constitute an infringement of essential procedural requirements and result in the annulment of the measure concerned.[206]

---

[203] Where the basic act does not specify precisely the period within which the Commission must submit a proposal to the Council, the Commission is entitled to seek additional advice before presenting an amended proposal, in particular where it is faced with a measure which is scientifically and politically highly complex and sensitive: ECJ, Case C–151/98 P *Pharos v Commission* [1999] E.C.R. I–8157, paras 20–27.

[204] This procedure is comparable to variant (a) (the "*filet*") under the First Comitology Decision which did not however allow the Council to reject the proposed measures by a qualified majority. Under variant (b) (the "*contrefilet*") provided for in the First Comitology Decision, the Commission was in a weaker position, since it enabled the Council to reject the proposal by a simple majority. For the differences between these variants, see ECJ, Case C–417/93 *European Parliament v Council* [1995] E.C.R. I–1185, para. 26, and the Opinion of Advocate General P. Léger, point 92. Compare the case note by Van Nuffel (1995) Col.J.E.L. 504, at 508, with Bradley, "Institutional Aspects of Comitology: Scenes from the Cutting Room Floor" in Joerges, *EU Committees: Social Regulation, Law and Politics*, (Hart Publishing, Oxford, 1999) 71, at 76–79.

[205] ECJ, Case C–212/91 *Angelopharm* [1994] E.C.R. I–171, paras 31–38.

[206] ECJ, Case C–263/95 *Germany v Commission* [1998] E.C.R. I–441, paras 31–32.

14–059 **Continuum.** The Council can control the Commission's implementing role to a greater or lesser extent depending on what sort of committee it sets up. In fact, the Comitology Decision is the expression of a continuum, ranging between the two options provided for in the third indent of Art. 202 of the EC Treaty, namely autonomous implementation by the Commission and implementation by the Council itself. Hence, an advisory committee does not really have any effect on the Commission's executive role, whilst a management committee or a regulatory committee can result in intervention on the part of the Council.[207]

14–060 **Control of implementation by Commission.** The European Parliament has often claimed that the task of implementation should be entrusted fully to the Commission. The reason is that this would enable both the Council and the European Parliament itself to supervise the Commission by virtue of their constitutional prerogatives. Both institutions should check that the Commission does not exceed the implementing power conferred on it. If it does, the European Parliament and the Council—and also any Member State—can bring an action for annulment of Commission measures in the Court of Justice.[208] In addition, the European Parliament may hold the Commission to account politically for the way in which it fulfils its executive role (see para. 10–017). In some circumstances, individuals, too, may obtain a court ruling on the legality of an implementing measure.[209]

---

[207] In judgments predating the Single European Act, the Court of Justice raised no objection to procedures involving a management committee or a regulatory committee: ECJ, Case 25/70 *Köster* [1970] E.C.R. 1161, para. 9 (management committee); ECJ, Case 5/77 *Tedeschi* [1977] E.C.R. 1555, paras 51–56 (regulatory committee). For the importance of the choice of the type of committee, see ECJ, Case C–417/93 *European Parliament v Council* [1995] E.C.R. I–1185, paras 24–26 (para. 14–057, *supra*).

[208] For cases which were successfully brought by a Member State, see ECJ, Case C–366/88 *France v Commission* [1990] E.C.R. I–3571, paras 17–25; ECJ, Case C–303/90 *France v Commission* [1991] E.C.R. I–5315, paras 27–35; ECJ, Case C–325/91 *France v Commission* [1993] E.C.R. I–3283, paras 14–17; ECJ, Case C–159/96 *Portugal v Commission* [1998] E.C.R. I–7379, paras 25–50; ECJ, Joined Cases C–289/96, C–293/96 and C–299/96 *Denmark, Germany and France v Commission* [1999] E.C.R. I–1541, paras 53–103; ECJ, Case 89/96 *Portugal v Commission* [1999] E.C.R. I–8377, paras 12–14; ECJ, Case C–393/01 *France v Commission* [2003] E.C.R. I–5405, paras 40–60; ECJ (judgment of September 30, 2003), Case C–239/01 *Germany v Commission*, not yet reported, paras 54–76. The power of implementation was not considered to have been exceeded in ECJ, Joined Cases C–296/93 and C–307/93 *France and Ireland v Commission* [1996] E.C.R. I–795, paras 11–24; ECJ, Joined Cases C–9/95, C–23/95 and C–156/95 *Belgium and Germany v Commission* [1997] E.C.R. I–645, paras 21–41; ECJ, Case C–285/94 *Italy v Commission* [1997] E.C.R. I–3519, paras 20–46. Before the broadening of its right to bring an action for annulement (see para. 10–021, *supra*), the European Parliament could do so where the Commission measure at issue infringed a legislative act adopted under a procedure providing for the involvement of the Parliament. See, *e.g.* ECJ, Case C–156/93 *European Parliament v Commission* [1995] E.C.R. I–2019, paras 12–13.

[209] For some examples, see ECJ, Case 22/88 *Vreugdenhil* [1989] E.C.R. 2049, paras 17–25; ECJ, Case C–212/91 *Angelopharm* [1994] E.C.R. I–171, paras 31–38 (n.169, *supra*, and associated text); ECJ, Case C–244/95 *Moskof* [1997] E.C.R. I–6441, paras 27–105; ECJ, Case C–106/97 *Dutch Antillian Diary Industry* [1999] E.C.R. I–5983, paras 65–66.

Control of implementation by Council. Where, in contrast, the Council **14–061** itself undertakes implementation or makes it subject to a comitology procedure which results in the power of implementation reverting to it, it is not possible for the European Parliament to exercise political control to the same extent. This appears justified where the Council takes decisions not based on a measure adopted by itself, such as where it appoints the members of a committee.[210] However, as far as general implementing measures are concerned, there is a danger of the Council's evading involvement of the European Parliament in the legislative process by adopting a vague piece of legislation and then giving it a completely different scope. Although the Court of Justice may find against such a practice,[211] the European Parliament lacks the necessary means of political control *vis-à-vis* the Council. It is virtually confined to the right to ask parliamentary questions (see para. 10–018). All that can be genuinely done about this problem is to allow the European Parliament a power of co-decision on the substance of the provision adopted in the legislative process, including the way in which it is implemented. In matters on which the Council "co-decides" with the European Parliament under the procedure set out in Art. 251 of the EC Treaty, the implementation procedures are in fact determined by consensus between the two institutions.

2. Implementation by other bodies

Independent executive bodies. In increasing numbers of policy areas, the **14–062** Community legislature has entrusted specific bodies with executive functions. In some cases, the legislature assigns tasks to specialised departments of the Commission (see para. 10–109). In others, executive tasks are conferred on bodies, offices or agencies with legal personality in their own right and powers of their own,[212] such as the European Agency for Co-operation, the European Office for Harmonisation in the Internal Market, the Community Plant Variety Office and the European Agency for Reconstruction (see para. 10–110). Delegation of the management of Community programmes to executive agencies allows the Commission to outsource certain of its own management tasks.[213] In many cases, bodies

---

[210] Beutler, Bieber, Pipkorn and Streil, *Die Europäische Union. Rechtsordnung und Politik* (Nomos, Baden-Baden, 1993) at 128.

[211] See, *e.g.* ECJ, Case C–303/94 *European Parliament v Council* [1996] E.C.R. I–2943, paras 21–33, and ECJ, Case C–93/00 *European Parliament v Council* [2001] E.C.R. I–10119, paras 35–44, and the inquiry carried out by the Court of Justice in ECJ, Case 46/86 *Romkes* [1987] E.C.R. 2671, paras 15–20, and ECJ, Case C–417/93 *European Parliament v Council* [1995] E.C.R. I–1185, paras 28–33.

[212] See ECJ, Case 9/56 *Meroni v High Authority* [1957 and 1958] E.C.R. 133, at 146 *et seq.*, and the parallel judgment ECJ, Case 10/56 *Meroni v High Authority* [1957 and 1958] E.C.R. 157.

[213] Council Regulation (EC) No. 58/2003 of December 19, 2002 laying down the statute for executive agencies to be entrusted with certain tasks in the management of Community programmes, [2003] O.J. L11/1.

with legal personality (known as offices, agencies, centres and foundations) perform executive functions in co-ordinating or supplementing action taken by the Member States. In that case, they collect and disseminate information, set up machinery for co-ordinating action on the part of the competent national authorities and carry out studies with a view to developing policy further.[214] Generally what is involved is a genuine amalgam of *administration communautaire directe* and *indirecte*[215] in which Community and national experts administer policy areas in collaboration with interest groups.[216]

14–063 Limits on delegation. Delegation of powers to an independent executive body may be effected in a legislative measure based on a specific provision of the Treaty, provided that the delegation is confined to the aims and means set out in that provision.[217] That constraint is less important where the body in question is set up to "attain . . . one of the objectives of the Treaty" under Art. 308 of the EC Treaty.[218] But, even then, it may be entrusted only with clearly defined executive tasks. The reason for this is that if the body had discretionary powers, the policy choices would no longer lie with the institutions which have the political responsibility under the Treaties. This would detract from the institutional balance on which the

---

[214] See the tasks assigned to other Community bodies and agencies with legal personality mentioned in para. 10–110, *supra*.

[215] Lenaerts (n.13, *supra*), at 46–47.

[216] See Chiti, "The Emergence of a Community Administration: The Case of European Agencies" (2000) C.M.L.R. 309–343; Vos, "Reforming the European Commission: What Role to Play for EU Agencies?" (2000) C.M.L.R. 1113–1134.

[217] See Council Regulation (EC) No. 881/2004 of the European Parliament and of the Council of April 29, 2004 establishing a European Railway Agency ([2004] O.J. L164/1; re-published with corrigendum : [2004] O.J. L220/3), adopted on the basis of Art. 71(1) of the EC Treaty; Council Regulation (EC) No. 1406/2002 of the European Parliament and of the Council of June 27, 2002 establishing a European Maritime Safety Agency ([2002] O.J. L208/1), and Council Regulation (EC) No. 1592/2002 of the European Parliament and of the Council of July 15, 2002 on common rules in the field of civil aviation and establishing a European Aviation Safety Agency ([2002] O.J. L240/1), both adopted on the basis of Art. 80(2) of the EC Treaty; Council Regulation (EC) No. 851/2004 of the European Parliament and of the Council of April 21, 2004 establishing a European Centre for disease prevention and control ([2004] O.J. L142/1), adopted on the basis of Art. 152(4)(b) of the EC Treaty; Council Regulation (EEC) No. 1210/90 of the European Parliament and of the Council of of May 7, 1990 on the establishment of the European Environment Agency and the European Environment Information and Observation Network ([1990] O.J. L120/1), adopted on the basis of Art. 175 of the EC Treaty. See also Council Regulation (EEC) No. 460/2004 of the European Parliament and of the Council of March 10, 2004 establishing the European Network and Information Security Agency ([2004] O.J. L77/1), adopted on the basis of Art. 95 of the EC Treaty, and Council Regulation (EC) No. 726/2004 of the European Parliament and of the Council of March 31, 2004 laying down Community procedures for the authorisation and supervision of medicinal products for human and veterinary use and establishing a European Medicines Agency ([2004] O.J. L136/1), adopted on the basis of Arts 95 and 152(4)(b) of the EC Treaty.

[218] See most of the bodies mentioned in para. 10–110, *supra*, with the exception of the agencies mentioned in the preceding n.

Community is based.[219] Accordingly, the Commission may not delegate the execution of a Community programme to an executive agency where this would involve "discretionary powers in translating political choices into action".[220]

Other conditions for delegation. Neither may an institution delegate more **14–064** powers than it possesses itself. Accordingly, independent executive bodies are subject to the same obligations in regard to adequate legal protection as the Community institutions. Their decisions must state the reasons on which they are based (EC Treaty, Art. 253) and be brought to the notice of the persons to whom they are addressed (EC Treaty, Art. 254). In addition, decisions which produce legal effects must be amenable to judicial review.[221]

To this end, some legislative acts expressly provide for a review mechanism. A Member State, a member of the governing board of the body and any other person directly and individually concerned may have the legality of an act of the body in question reviewed by the Commission.

The Commission's express or implied approval or disapproval of the act will then constitute an act amenable to judicial review.[222] In other cases, the person concerned must first apply to a board of appeal, against whose

---

[219] ECJ, Case 9/56 *Meroni* [1957 and 1958] E.C.R. 133, at 151 *et seq.* (cited in para. 13–010, *supra*). See also ECJ, Case 98/80 *Romano* [1981] E.C.R. 1241, para. 20 (a commission set up by the Council does not have the power to adopt acts having the force of law in view of the implementing powers vested in the Commission by Art. 211 of the EC Treaty).

[220] See recitals 4 and 5 in the preamble to Regulation No. 58/2003 and Art. 6(1) thereof (n.213, *supra*). For this constraint on the delegation of executive tasks by the Commission, see Remmert, "Die Gründung von Einrichtungen der mittelbaren Gemeinschaftsverwaltung" (2003) EuR. 134–145; Craig, "The constitutionalisation of Community administration" (2003) E.L.Rev. 840, at 848–854. A plea for more autonomous executive agencies may be found in Majone, "Delegation of Regulatory Powers in a Mixed Polity" (2002) E.L.J. 319–339.

[221] ECJ, Case 9/56 *Meroni* [1957 and 1958] E.C.R. 133, at 149–151. See, *e.g.* CFI, Joined Cases T–369/94 and T–85/95 *DIR International Film v Commission* [1998] E.C.R. II–357, paras 110–122 (review of a decision taken by the European Film Distribution Office).

[222] See, *e.g.* CFI, Joined Cases T–369/94 and T–85/95 *DIR International Film v Commission* [1998] E.C.R. II–357, paras 52–55 (decision of the European Film Distribution Office attributed to the Commission). See also the regulations (references in para. 10–110, *supra*) establishing the European Centre for the Development of Vocational Training (Cedefop) (Art. 18), the European Foundation for the Improvement of Living and Working Conditions (Art. 22), the European Agency for Co-operation (Art. 19), the European Agency for Health and Safety at Work (Art. 22), the Community Plant Variety Office (Art. 44), the European Office for Harmonisation in the Internal Market (Art. 118, which does not allow an act to be submitted by a member of the Administrative Board to the Commission but provides for general supervision by the Commission) and the European Centre for Disease Prevention and Control (Art. 28). See further Art. 22 of Regulation No. 58/2003 with regard to executive agencies entrusted with certain tasks in the management of Community programmes (n.213, *supra*) and Craig (n.220, *supra*), at 849–851.

decision an appeal will lie to the Community Court.[223] In some cases, a direct action will lie in the Community Court against the decision of abody.[224] If the act establishing the body does not provide for such a mechanism, it may be inferred from the fact that the Community is a "Community based on the rule of law" that, in any event, the validity of acts of all Community bodies must be amenable to judicial review where those acts produce legal effects.[225] This guarantee will be expressly mentioned in the text of the Constitution (para. 10–086).

14–065 Tasks conferred on international bodies. The same restrictions apply where the Community delegates tasks to international bodies.[226] The distribution of powers as between the institutions and between the Community and the Member States requires that the policy choices are laid down in the act establishing the body (the international agreement), which has to have been adopted by means of the appropriate procedure, with the result that the newly established body has executive powers only.[227] Where the body adopts acts which are binding on the Community as a party to the agreement, decision-making generally takes place by mutual agreement between all the contracting parties.[228] In principle acts of such a body may

---

[223] *Cf.* the Board of Appeal of the Office for Harmonisation in the Internal Market (Art. 130 of the regulation establishing the Office), the Community Plant Variety Office (Art. 45 of the regulation establishing the Office as amended by Council Regulation (EC) No. 2506/95 of October 25, 1995, [1995] O.J. L258/3) and the European Aviation Safety Agency (Arts 31–42 of the regulation establishing the Agency and Commission Regulation No. 104/2004 of January 22, 2004, [2004] O.J. L16/20) and the Complaints Board dealing with certain disputes arising under the Convention defining the status of the European Schools, established by Art. 27 of the Convention (alongside the exclusive jurisdiction of the Court of Justice over disputes between Contracting Parties relating to the interpretation and application of the Convention: Art. 26), [1994] O.J. L212/9. For legal redress under the former statute of the European Schools, see Henrichs, "Zur rechtlichen Stellung der Europäischen Schulen und ihrer Lehrer" (1994) EuR. 358–363; for the present situation, see the Commission's answer of May 22, 1997 to question E–1435/97 (Lehne), [1997] O.J. C/130.

[224] For acts of the European Monitoring Centre for Drugs and Drug Addiction and of the European Monitoring Centre on Racism and Xenophobia, see Art. 17 and Art. 15(3), respectively, of the regulations establishing those bodies. For judicial review of decisions of the European Data-protection Supervisor, see Art. 32(2) of the regulation establishing the supervisor (para. 10–110, *supra*).

[225] See ECJ, Case 294/83 *Les Verts v European Parliament* [1986] E.C.R. 1339, paras 23–25. *Cf.* CFI (order of June 8, 1998), Case T–148/97 *Keeling v Office for Harmonisation in the Internal Market* [1998] E.C.R. II–2217, paras 26–34.

[226] See Lenaerts (n.13, *supra*), at 37–40.

[227] See ECJ, Opinion 1/76 *Draft Agreement establishing a European laying-up fund for inland waterway vessels* [1977] E.C.R. 741, para. 5 and 15–16.

[228] See, *e.g.* the Council of Ministers set up by the ACP-EC Partnership Agreement (para. 20–024, *infra*) and the institutions of the European Economic Area (para. 23–010, *infra*). Nevertheless, some bodies set up by multilateral agreements take their decisions by majority vote: see Gilsdorf, "Les organes institués par des accords communautaires: effets juridiques de leurs décisions. Observations à propos notamment de l'arrêt de la Cour de justice des Communautés européennes dans l'affaire C–192/89" (1992) R.M.C.U.E. 328, at 332–333.

not escape any form of judicial review either.[229] The international agreement may share powers as between the Community and the other contracting parties only if this does not change the nature of the powers of the Community and of its institutions as conceived in the EC Treaty.[230] An international agreement between the Community and third States may devolve dispute settlement to a specific dispute-resolution system. However, in order to preserve the autonomy of the Community legal order, that dispute-resolution system may not have the effect of binding the Community and its institutions, in the exercise of their internal powers, to a particular interpretation of the rules of Community law.[231]

Delegation of powers in the Treaties. The Treaties themselves have **14–066** entrusted the performance of certain tasks to independent bodies with discretionary powers. Institutionally, this is a comparatively recent development, since the Member States held on for a long time to the institutional structure to which they were accustomed and which allowed them to exercise a measure of control over decision-making and implementation.[232] As independent bodies, the European Investment Bank and the European Central Bank have substantial latitude with regard to policy within the confines of the powers which they derive from the EC Treaty and the statutes appended thereto (EC Treaty, Arts 8 and 9). The ECB has similar legislative powers to those of the Council and is under an express obligation to act independently of any political influence.[233] That independent status may be unpicked only by means of an amendment to

---

[229] For the interpretation by the Court of Justice of such acts, see ECJ, Case C–192/89 *Sevince* [1990] E.C.R. I–3461, paras 10–11 (para. 17–096, *infra*).

[230] ECJ, Opinion 1/92 *Draft agreement between the Community, on the one hand, and the countries of the European Free Trade Association, on the other, relating to the creation of the European Economic Area* [1992] E.C.R. I–2821, para. 41; ECJ, Opinion 1/00 *Proposed agreement between the European Community and non-Member States on the establishment of a European Common Aviation Area* [2002] E.C.R. I–3493, paras 12 and 15–27. See Castillo de la Torre (2002) C.M.L.R. 1373–1393.

[231] ECJ, Opinion 1/00, paras 13 and 27–45 and Castillo de la Torre (n.230, *supra*), at 1396–1387. If the international agreement sets up its own system of case law, this may raise problems for the autonomy of the Community judicial system: see ECJ, Opinion 1/76 *Draft Agreement establishing a European laying-up fund for inland waterway vessels* [1977] E.C.R. 741, paras 21–22; ECJ, Opinion 1/91 *Draft agreement between the Community, on the one hand, and the countries of the European Free Trade Association, on the other, relating to the creation of the European Economic Area* [1991] E.C.R. I–6079, paras 37–53.

[232] Dehousse, "Integration v Regulation? On the Dynamics of Regulation in the European Community" (1992) J.C.M.S. 383, at 389–391. Under the CFSP there is a delegation of powers in the second and third paras of Art. 25 of the EU Treaty, under which the Council may authorise the Political and Security Committee to direct crisis management operations (see para. 15–007, *infra*).

[233] See the list of the ECB's regulatory instruments in Art. 110 of the EC Treaty and its independent status guaranteed by Art. 108 (para. 10–102, *supra*). See also the editorial, "Executive Agencies within the EC: The European Central Bank—A Model?" (1996) C.M.L.R. 623–631; Zilioli and Selmayr, "The European Central Bank: An Independent Specialised Organisation of Community Law" (2000) C.M.L.R. 591–644; Schütz, "Die Legitimation der Europäischen Zentralbank zur Rechtsetzung" (2001) EuR. 291–305.

the Treaty.[234] Nevertheless, the acts of the EIB and the ECB are also subject to judicial supervision[235] and the ECB is also under certain duties to report to the political authorities.[236] The Court of Justice has made it clear that the functional independence enjoyed by those bodies does not have the consequence of separating them entirely from the European Community and exempting them from every rule of Community law.[237] The fact that they are independent does not preclude the Community legislature from adopting legislative measures applying to them, for instance relating to the prevention of fraud.[238]

IV. Decision-making Restricted to Particular Member States

14–067 Non-participation of Member States. In two policy areas, the EC Treaty formulates a system of decision-making under which not all Member States take part in the adoption of acts: (1) visas, asylum, immigration and other policies related to free movement of persons (EC Treaty, Title IV; see paras 14–068–14–070); and (2) Economic and Monetary Union (EC Treaty, Title VII; see para. 14–071).

On top of this, the system of enhanced co-operation affords an opportunity for Community acts to be adopted as between a number of Member States only (see para. 14–072). Whenever decision-making is limited to certain Member States, the Council has to adapt voting requirements accordingly. In principle, the other Community institutions and bodies take part in the decision-making with the same composition and manner of operation as in the case of decision-making involving all the Member States. The rationale is that Members of the Commission, the European Parliament and other bodies do not represent particular Member States. The Court of Justice, too, has the same composition when it

---

[234] For some critical reservations, see Gormley and De Haan, "The democratic deficit of the European Central Bank" (1996) E.L.R. 95–112; cf. Brentford, "Constitutional Aspects of the Independence of the European Central Bank" (1998) I.C.L.Q. 75–116; Amtenbrink and De Haan, "The European Central Bank: An Independent Specialised Organisation of Community Law—A Comment" (2002) C.M.L.R. 65–76.

[235] For the ECB, see Arts 230, 232 and 234 of the EC Treaty; for the EIB, see Art. 237(b) and (c) of the EC Treaty and ECJ, Case C–15/00 *Commission v European Investment Bank* [2003] E.C.R. I–7281, para. 75. However, monetary policy relies to only a limited extent on legally binding decisions: Slot, "The Institutional Provisions of the EMU", *Institutional Dynamics of European Integration. Essays in Honour of Henry G. Schermers* (n.166, *supra*), 229, at 231.

[236] See the European Parliament's resolution of April 2, 1998 on democratic accountability in the third phase of EMU ([1998] O.J. C138/177) and Magnette, "Towards 'Accountable Independence'? Parliamentary Controls of the European Central Bank and the Rise of a New Democratic Model" (2000) E.L.J. 326–340.

[237] ECJ, Case C–11/00 *Commission v European Central Bank* [2003] E.C.R. I–7147, para. 135, and ECJ, Case C–15/00 *Commission v European Investment Bank* [2003] E.C.R. I–7281, para. 102.

[238] *ibid.*, paras 136–144 and 103–109, respectively.

adjudicates in disputes on the interpretation and application of acts adopted under these systems of decision-making.

A. APPLICATION OF TITLE IV OF THE EC TREATY

Adjusted decision-making. When the Council adopts measures under Title **14–068** IV of the EC Treaty concerning visas, asylum, immigration and other policies related to free movement of persons, in principle the decision-making proceeds without the participation of Denmark, Ireland and the United Kingdom, which have been granted special status by Protocol (see paras 5–165–5–166). The provisions of Title IV, measures adopted pursuant to that title, together with international agreements concluded by the Community pursuant to that title, and decisions of the Court of Justice interpreting such provisions or measures are not binding upon, or applicable in, those Member States.[239] Adjusted voting requirements apply in the case of Council acts adopted by a qualified majority[240]; the composition and method of work of the other institutions and bodies remain unchanged. This also applies to measures or conventions adopted pursuant to Title IV which build upon the Schengen *acquis*.[241] It should be noted that Iceland and Norway are to be associated with the further development of the Schengen *acquis*.[242]

Specific procedural rules. As far as the adoption of measures pursuant to **14–069** Title IV is concerned, Art. 67 of the EC Treaty lays down procedural rules which changed automatically five years after the entry into effect of the

---

[239] Art. 2 of Protocol (No.4) to the EU Treaty and the EC Treaty on the position of the UK and Ireland ([1997] O.J. C340/99) and Art. 2 of Protocol (No.5) to the EU Treaty and the EC Treaty on the position of Denmark (*ibid.*, p.101).

[240] Art. 1 of the Protocol on the position of the UK and Ireland and Art. 1 of the Protocol on the position of Denmark define a qualified majority as the same proportion of the weighted votes of the members of the Council concerned as laid down in Art. 205(2) of the EC Treaty. Where, for instance, the Council acts without those three States, a qualified majority is 201 out of 278 votes; where it acts without Denmark (or Ireland) and the UK, the majority is 206 out of 285 votes; non-participation of the UK alone would mean that the qualified majority required would be 211 out of 292 votes and non-participation of Denmark (or Ireland) would make the requisite majority 227 out of 314 votes.

[241] See Art. 5(1), first subpara., of Protocol (No.2) to the EU Treaty and the EC Treaty integrating the Schengen *acquis* into the framework of the European Union ([1997] O.J. C340/93). For the integration of the Schengen *acquis*, see para. 5–164, *supra*. In the event that Denmark should nevertheless participate in the adoption of measures building upon the Schengen *acquis* pursuant to Title IV, the measures concerned will not constitute "Community law" as far as Denmark is concerned, but will create an obligation under international law; see Art. 3 of the Protocol integrating the Schengen *acquis* into the framework of the European Union and Art. 5 of the Protocol on the position of Denmark.

[242] Appropriate procedures were to be agreed with these countries in an agreement concluded by the Council by a unanimous vote (not counting the UK and Ireland): Art. 6 of the Protocol integrating the Schengen *acquis* into the framework of the European Union. See para. 5–164, *supra*.

Treaty of Amsterdam (*i.e.* as from May 1, 2004). During that transitional period, the initiative for action under Title IV was to ensue either from the Commission (by means of a "proposal") or from a Member State (by means of an "initiative") (Art. 67(1)) and the Council acted unanimously after consulting the European Parliament. After the transitional period, the Council is invariably to act on a proposal from the Commission, which, however, is to examine any request made by a Member State that it submit a proposal (Art. 67(2), first indent). Furthermore, the co-decision procedure governed by Art. 251 of the EC Treaty is to apply to all or parts of the areas coming under Title IV, provided that the Council so decides by a unanimous vote after consulting the European Parliament (Art. 67(2), second indent).[243] The Treaty of Nice of Nice amended these provisions by also making the co-decision procedure applicable to measures on refugees and displaced persons, provided that the Council has previously adopted Community legislation defining the common rules and basic principles governing these issues, and to measures in the field of judicial co-operation in civil matters with the exception of aspects relating to family law (EC Treaty, Art. 67(5)).[244] As from May 1, 2004 the co-decision procedure likewise applies in any event to some measures relating to policy on visas (EC Treaty, Art. 67(4) in conjunction with Art. 62(2)(b)(ii) and (iv)).

A different procedure applies to measures relating to policy on visas which already came within the competence of the Community before the Treaty of Amsterdam, namely the list of third countries whose nationals must be in possession of visas when crossing the external borders and the uniform format for visas (Art. 62(2)(b)(i) and (iii)). In order to adopt such measures, the Council acts, since the entry into force of the Amsterdam Treaty, by a qualified majority on a proposal from the Commission after consulting the European Parliament (Art. 67(3)).

14–070 Specific conditions of non-participation. Denmark, Ireland and the United Kingdom remain outside Community policy pursuant to Title IV of the EC Treaty in somewhat different ways.

In principle, Denmark does not take part in the adoption by the Council of acts pursuant to Title IV; it participates solely in the adoption of the

---

[243] In Declaration (No.5) annexed to the Treaty of Nice, the Member States agreed that, from May 1, 2004, the co-decision procedure would be applicable to the adoption of the measures referred to in Art. 62(3) and Art. 63(3)(b) and that it would also apply to the adoption of the measures referred to in Art. 62(2)(a) from the date on which agreement was reached on the scope of the measures concerning the crossing by persons of the external borders of the Member States. The Council would, moreover, endeavour to make the co-decision procedure applicable from May 1, 2004 or as soon as possible thereafter to the other areas covered by Title IV or to parts of them.

[244] At the same time, however, the commitment to extend the co-decision procedure was mitigated for measures referred to in Art. 66 of the EC Treaty in that the Protocol on Art. 67 of the EC Treaty annexed by the Treaty of Nice to the EC Treaty ([2001] O.J. C80/699) provides that from May 1, 2004, the Council is to act on such measures by a qualified majority, on a proposal from the Commission and after consulting the European Parliament.

aforementioned measures relating to the determination of third countries whose nationals require visas and the uniform format for visas.[245] In principle, Ireland and the United Kingdom also do not take part in the adoption of acts by the Council under Title IV. Nevertheless, they are entitled so to take part if they notify the President of the Council in writing within three months after a proposal or an initiative has been presented to the Council that they wish to take part in the adoption and application of the proposed measure.[246] If, after a "reasonable" period has elapsed, such a measure cannot be adopted with the United Kingdom or Ireland taking part, the Council may adopt it without their participation.[247]

As has already been mentioned, if Denmark, Ireland and/or the United Kingdom do not take part, the Council adopts its measures by an adjusted majority and the resultant measures are not applicable in the non-participating State(s). All the same, Ireland and the United Kingdom may at any time notify their intention to the Council and the Commission that they wish to accept such a measure; in such case the procedure provided for in the EC Treaty for Member States wishing to take part in an existing form of enhanced co-operation applies *mutatis mutandis* (Art. 11(3); see para. 14–072).[248] Denmark and Ireland may abandon the special status conferred on them by Protocol by simple notification.[249]

B. Economic and Monetary Union

Adjusted decision-making. As far as Economic and Monetary Union is **14–071** concerned, the Community has a system of decision-making which is restricted to the 12 Member States taking part in the third stage of EMU because they satisfied the conditions laid down to that end (see para. 5–222). Under a Protocol to the EC Treaty, Denmark and the United Kingdom are in a special situation in that they are not under an obligation to take part in the third stage of EMU (see para. 5–233).

All the Member States took part in the decision by which the Council determined which of them satisfied those conditions (EC Treaty, Art. 121(4) and Art. 122(1)). Accordingly, even the United Kingdom and Denmark, which availed themselves of their special position in order not to participate, took part in the voting. Under Art. 122 of the EC Treaty, Member States which did not satisfy the conditions were given a derogation, as a result of which important provisions relating to EMU do not apply to them (see para. 5–232). Initially, Greece and Sweden had such

---

[245] Protocol on the position of Denmark, Art. 4.
[246] Protocol on the position of the United Kingdom and Ireland, Art. 3(1).
[247] *ibid.*, Art. 3(2).
[248] *ibid.*, Art. 4.
[249] Art. 7 of the Protocol on the position of Denmark (the other Member States have to be informed) and Art. 8 of the Protocol on the position of the UK and Ireland (the President of the Council has to be notified in writing). No such possibility is provided for in the case of the UK.

a derogation; since January 1, 2001, only Sweden remains in that position. The opt-out granted to Denmark means that it is regarded as a Member State with a derogation in the third stage.[250] The position of the United Kingdom is different from that of a Member State with a derogation but has the same implications for decision-making in the Council and the ECB.[251]

The voting rights of Member States with a derogation are to be suspended in respect of Council acts based on provisions relating to EMU which do not apply to them (EC Treaty, Art. 122(5)). The number of votes required to attain a qualified majority has been adjusted as a result.[252] In a resolution of the European Council, it has been confirmed that the ministers of the States participating in the Euro area may meet informally amongst themselves to discuss issues connected with their shared specific responsibilities for the single currency.[253] Whenever matters of common interest are concerned, they are to be discussed by ministers of all Member States; however, decisions are to be taken by the Council in accordance with the procedures determined by the Treaty.[254] A meeting of the ECOFIN Council comprising only representatives of participating Member States is known as the "Euro Council".[255]

In principle, Member States with a derogation do not take part in decision-making in the ECB. They are not involved in the appointment of members of the ECB's Executive Board, do not have a member on the board or do not have the Governor of their central bank sit on the Governing Council.[256] Since the ECB carries out some tasks regarding the central banks of Member States with a derogation and is to deliver opinions concerning them,[257] those Member States are nevertheless involved in the decision-making in those respects. It is for this reason that the ECB has a General Council, consisting of the President and Vice-President of the

---

[250] Art. 2 of Protocol (No.26) to the EC Treaty on certain provisions relating to Denmark.

[251] See Arts 7, 8 and 9 of Protocol (No.25) to the EC Treaty on certain provisions relating to the United Kingdom of Great Britain and Northern Ireland, [1993] O.J. C224/113 (para. 5–233, *supra*).

[252] The qualified majority is two-thirds of the votes weighted in accordance with Art. 205(2) (EC Treaty, Art. 122(5)). In view of the three Member States not taking part, a qualified majority is 199 out of 275 votes.

[253] Resolution of the European Council of December 13, 1997 on economic policy co-ordination in stage 3 of EMU and on Treaty Arts 111 and 113, [1998] O.J. C35/1 (also published in (1997) 12 EU Bull. points I.9 and I.19).

[254] *ibid.*

[255] The first such meeting was held on June 5, 1998 and was chaired, not by the British Chancellor of the Exchequer (representing the Member State occupying the Presidency of the Council), but by the Austrian Finance Minister (representing the Member State which was to take over the Presidency on July 1, 1998), see *Europe*, No.7235, June 5, 1998, 6.

[256] EC Treaty, Art. 112(2)(b) in conjunction with Art. 122(4); ESCB Statute, Arts 10.1 and 11.2 in conjunction with Art. 43.

[257] For instance, the authorities of a Member State with a derogation are obliged under Art. 105(4) of the EC Treaty to consult the ECB on any proposed act in the latter's fields of competence.

ECB and the Governors of all the national central banks, to take the necessary decisions in this regard.[258] The composition and operation of the other institutions and bodies, including the Economic and Financial Committee, will remain unchanged regardless as to whether the decisions to be taken affect all the Member States or only those without a derogation.

C. ENHANCED CO-OPERATION

Adjusted decision-making. Within the confines of Community **14–072** competences, the Council may, subject to certain conditions, authorise Member States to establish enhanced co-operation amongst themselves (see paras 9–005—9–006). Where Member States embark on enhanced co-operation, they may make use of the institutions, procedures and mechanisms laid down in the EC Treaty and the EU Treaty (See EU Treaty, Art. 43(1)). For the purpose of the adoption of the acts and decisions necessary for the implementation of enhanced co-operation, the relevant institutional provisions of the EC Treaty apply (see EC Treaty, Art. 11(3) in conjunction with EU Treaty, Art. 44(1)).

As far as enhanced co-operation in areas falling within the competence of the Community is concerned, this means that the procedure to be followed is that prescribed in the provision of the EC Treaty constituting the legal basis. Although all members of the Council may take part in the relevant deliberations, only those representing participating Member States may take part in the adoption of decisions (EU Treaty, Art. 44(1)). The number of votes required to adopt a decision by a qualified majority will be adapted.[259] Member States participating in enhanced co-operation are bound to apply the acts and decisions adopted for its implementation; non-participating Member States are under a duty not to impede its implementation (EU Treaty, Art. 44(2)).

Any Member State wishing to become a party to an existing form of enhanced co-operation falling within the field of application of the EC Treaty is to notify its intention to the Council and the Commission, which has to give an opinion thereon to the Council. Within four months of the date of notification, the Commission is to decide on the request and on such specific arrangements as it may deem necessary (EC Treaty, Art. 11a).

The same principles will apply to enhanced co-operation as provided for in the EU Constitution (see Art. I–44). Member States participating in enhanced co-operation are to apply amongst themselves the relevant provisions of the Constitution, while applying the necessary adjustments to voting requirements in the Council in cases where those decisions have to

---

[258] ESCB Statute, Arts 45–47.
[259] Art. 44(1) of the EU Treaty defines a qualified majority as the same proportion of the weighted votes of the members of the Council concerned as laid down in Art. 205(2) of the EC Treaty.

be taken by a qualified majority vote.[260] If a Member State requests to participate in an existing form of enhanced co-operation, it will be up to the Commission to evaluate whether the conditions for participation have been fulfilled and, if necessary, whether participation should be delayed (EU Constitution, Art. III–420(1)).

---

[260] EU Constitution, Art. I–44(3).

CHAPTER 15

NON-COMMUNITY DECISION-MAKING

Non-Community decision-making. The Community institutions and the **15–001**
Member States are involved in various forms of decision-making which are
sometimes complementary to Community decision-making, yet formally do
not constitute part of it. The Treaty provision conferring the power to
adopt the relevant act determines whether or not it is a Community act.
The fact that institutions of the Communities participate in the adoption or
implementation of acts is therefore not sufficient to render them
Community acts.[1] Accordingly, decision-making pursuant to Title V of the
EU Treaty (common foreign and security policy; see paras 15–002–15–008)
or pursuant to Title VI of the EU Treaty (police and judicial co-operation
in criminal matters, see paras 15–010–15–014) does not result in acts of
Community law. This is also true of agreements enshrined in conventions
concluded by the Member States amongst themselves or in decisions taken
by the governments of the Member States "meeting in the Council" (see
paras 15–016–15–018). As will be explained below, the distinction between
Community and non-Community decision-making will no longer apply once
the EU Constitution has entered into force. Separate rules for
decision-making will however continue to apply with respect to the CFSP
(see para. 15–009). Furthermore, there will continue to be nothing to
prevent the national governments from concluding conventions amongst
themselves or adopting decisions which, albeit closely connected with the
activities of the Union, are not based on the Constitution.

I. DECISION-MAKING UNDER THE COMMON FOREIGN AND
SECURITY POLICY (CFSP)

A. POLICY-MAKING IN THE CFSP

Decision-making. All acts that the Union wishes to adopt under the **15–002**
common foreign and security policy (CFSP; EU Treaty, Title V) emanate

---

[1] See ECJ, Joined Cases C–181/91 and C–248/91 *European Parliament v Council* [1993] E.C.R.
I–3685, paras 16–25; note by Van der Woude (1994) S.E.W. 442–444.

from the European Council and the Council.[2] The European Council defines the "principles" and "general guidelines" for the CFSP and decides on "common strategies to be implemented by the Union" (EU Treaty, Art. 13(1) and (2)). The Council adopts "joint actions", "common positions" or other decisions or concludes international agreements (see paras 18–015 *et seq.*); it does so on the basis of the principles and general guidelines defined by the European Council and in particular with a view to implementing the common strategies decided on by the European Council (EU Treaty, Art. 13(3)).

Accordingly, the policy guidelines are defined by the European Council by consensus between the Heads of State or Government. In principle, the Council has to act unanimously, although abstention does not prevent unanimity from being attained (EU Treaty, Art. 23(1), first subpara.). An abstaining member of the Council may qualify the abstention by making a formal declaration under the second subpara. of Art. 23(1) of the EU Treaty. If it makes such a declaration, the Member State is not obliged to apply the decision in question, but must accept that it binds the Union. This is termed "constructive abstention". Article 23 of the EU Treaty provides that, in a spirit of mutual solidarity, the Member State concerned is to refrain from any action likely to conflict with or impede Union action based on the decision in question, and that the other Member States are to respect its position. If the members of the Council qualifying their abstention in this way represent more than one-third of the votes, the decision is not adopted.[3]

By way of derogation, the Council decides by a qualified majority when adopting joint actions, common positions or other decisions on the basis of a common strategy,[4] when adopting a decision or an agreement implementing a joint action or a common position[5] and when appointing a

---

[2] For a description of decision-making in this area, see Müller-Brandeck-Bocquet, "The New CFSP and ESDP Decision-Making System of the European Union" (2002) E.For.Aff.Rev. 257–282; Pernice and Thym, "A New Institutional Balance for European Foreign Policy?" (2003) E.For.Aff.Rev. 369, at 374–380; For a discussion of the procedure and practice, see Keukeleire, *Het buitenlands beleid van de Europese Unie* (Kluwer, Deventer, 1998) 273–302.

[3] Art. 23(1), first subpara., *in fine*, refers to the votes being weighted in accordance with Art. 205(2) of the EC Treaty.

[4] *e.g.* Council Joint Action 1999/878/CFSP of December 17, 1999 establishing a European Union Co-operation Programme for Non-proliferation and Disarmament in the Russian Federation ([1999] O.J. L331/11), adopted pursuant to Common Strategy 1999/414/CFSP of the European Union of June 4, 1999 on Russia ([1999] O.J. L157/1) and on the basis of Arts 14 and 23(2) of the EU Treaty. The Council may also conclude international agreements by a qualified majority vote in pursuance of a common strategy. This follows from Art. 24(2) of the EU Treaty, which requires a unanimous vote only where the agreement covers issues for which unanimity is required for internal decisions.

[5] *e.g.* Council Decision 1999/729/CFSP of November 15, 1999 implementing Council Common Position 1999/728/CFSP concerning EU support for the implementation of the Lusaka ceasefire agreement and the peace process in the Democratic Republic of Congo and Council Decision 1999/730/CFSP of November 15, 1999 implementing Joint Action 1999/34/CFSP with a view to a European Union contribution to combating the destabilising accumulation and spread of small arms and light weapons in Cambodia, [1999] O.J. L294/4 and 5, respectively.

special representative (EU Treaty, Art. 23(2), first subpara.). Votes of members of the Council are weighted in the manner prescribed by Art. 205(2) of the EC Treaty for acts which do not have to be adopted on a proposal from the Commission.[6] If, however, a member of the Council declares that, for important and stated reasons of national policy, it intends to oppose the adoption of a decision to be taken by a qualified majority, no vote is taken and the Council, acting by a qualified majority, may request that the matter be referred to the European Council for decision by unanimity (EU Treaty, Art. 23(2), second subpara.). Where the Council authorises Member States to embark on enhanced co-operation, it also decides by a qualified majority and there is the same possibility to refer the matter to the European Council (see para. 15–008). In any event, no decision having military or defence implications may be taken by a qualified majority.[7]

The Council takes decisions relating to procedural questions by a simple majority vote (EU Treaty, Art. 23(3)).

Initiative and preparatory tasks. Any Member State or the Commission **15–003** may submit a proposal to deal with a particular question (EU Treaty, Art. 22(1)). The Council may request the Commission to submit proposals to it relating to the CFSP to ensure the implementation of a joint action (EU Treaty, Art. 14(4)). The Council is assisted by its Secretary-General, who, as High Representative for the CFSP, has the task of contributing to the formulation, preparation and implementation of policy decisions (EU Treaty, Art. 26). The Political and Security Committee (PSC) advises the Council and is the privileged interlocutor of the High Representative for the CFSP.[8] According to the EU Treaty, the Commission is to be "fully associated" with the work carried out in the field of the CFSP (Art. 27) and generally attends all meetings of the Council, Coreper and the PSC. However, it does not have an exclusive right of initiative or the prerogatives associated with that right in the ambit of the Community: amendment or withdrawal of a proposal has no effect on the manner in which decisions are taken in the Council.[9] In any event, the Commission is more closely

---

[6] See EU Treaty, Art. 23(2), third subpara. From November 1, 2004, the same changes made by the Protocol annexed by the Treaty of Nice to the EU Treaty and the Community Treaties on the enlargement of the Union ([2001] O.J. C80/49) and by the 2003 Act of Accession to Art. 205(2) of the EC Treaty apply as regards acts not adopted by the Council on the basis of a Commission proposal (see para. 10–045).

[7] EU Treaty, Art. 23(2), fourth subpara.

[8] EU Treaty, Art. 25, first para.

[9] The Commission may take the view, however, that a question falls within the competence of the Communities and submit a proposal based on the EC Treaty (*e.g.* for a measure under the common commercial policy or under Community development co-operation policy). Heukels and De Zwaan suggest that in such a case Art. 10 of the EC Treaty restricts a Member State's options to adopt an initiative at the same time under Title V of the EU Treaty or likewise under Title VI if the Commission proposes to deal with a matter coming within the field of police and judicial co-operation under the EC Treaty: Heukels and De

involved than it formerly was in European Political Co-operation (EPC), since the activities of the Foreign Ministers are no longer organised by a separate secretariat outside the Council. The conferral of tasks on the High Representative for the CFSP and the PSC in relation to the preparation and implementation of policy restricts, however, the Commission's ability to put its stamp on the CFSP. In any event, in military matters the activities of the Council and the PSC are prepared by a Military Committee (EUMC) on which the Chiefs of Defence sit. The EUMC is assisted by the Military Staff (EUMS), which is part of the General Secretariat of the Council.[10]

The Political and Security Committee meets at the place where the Council has its seat, one week before the Council meets or, if the Council so requests, together with the Council. The PSC's position also appears on the agenda for Coreper meetings.[11] The Council has accelerated means of decision-making at its disposal. Thus the PSC monitors the international situation on a permanent basis in areas covered by the CFSP (EU Treaty, Art. 25). The Military Staff performs early warning, situation assessment and strategic planning tasks.[12] In addition, the Presidency is entitled to convene a meeting of the Council at very short notice of its own motion or at the request of the Commission or a Member State (EU Treaty, Art. 22(2)).[13]

15–004 Involvement of European Parliament. The Council is entitled to act without seeking the opinion of the European Parliament, although the Presidency must be sure to consult the Parliament on the main aspects and the basic choices of the CFSP.[14] The President must ensure that the

---

Zwaan, "The Configuration of the European Union: Community Dimensions of Institutional Interaction", in Curtin and Heukels (eds), *Institutional Dynamics of European Integration. Essays in Honour of Henry G. Schermers*, Vol.II (Martinus Nijhoff, Dordrecht, 1994) 195, at 217.

[10] See the manner of operation and organisation set out in annexes to Council Decision 2001/79/CFSP of January 22, 2001 setting up the Military Committee of the European Union ([2001] O.J. L27/4) and to Council Decision 2001/80/CFSP of January 22, 2001 on the establishment of the Military Staff of the European Union ([2001] O.J. L27/7). The Military Staff consists of seconded military personnel headed by a three-star flag officer. The Military Committee is chaired by a four-star flag officer on appointment. See also Council Decision 2001/496/CFSP of June 25, 2001 on the rules applicable to national military staff on secondment to the General Secretariat of the Council in order to form the European Union Military Staff, [2001] O.J. L181/1.

[11] See the annex to Council Decision 2001/78/CFSP of January 22, 2001 setting up the Political and Security Committee ([2001] O.J. L27/1).

[12] See the annex to Council Decision 2001/80/CFSP of January 22, 2001 on the establishment of the Military Staff of the European Union ([2001] O.J. L27/7).

[13] The simplified written procedure (COREU) may be used in implementing the CFSP (Council Rules of Procedure, Art. 12(4); n.00 to para. 10–048, *supra*).

[14] According to the Interinstitutional Agreement on budgetary discipline and improvement of the budgetary procedure, signed by the European Parliament, the Council and the Commission on May 6, 1999, the Presidency is to consult the European Parliament on a yearly basis on a document established by the Council on the main aspects and basic choices of the CFSP, including the financial implications for the Communities' budget: [1999] O.J. C172/9, point 40.

Parliament's views are "duly taken into account". The President and the Commission are to keep the Parliament regularly informed of the development of the CFSP (see EU Treaty, Art. 21, first para.). The Commission has undertaken to keep the European Parliament fully and promptly informed about its CFSP initiatives.[15] Agreements have been reached between the European Parliament and the Council on the way in which the Parliament is given access to sensitive information in the field of security and defence policy.[16]

For its part, the Parliament may make recommendations to the Council (EU Treaty, Art. 21, second para.). The parliamentary committee responsible for the CFSP prepares any recommendations and may be authorised by the President of the Parliament to draw them up using an urgency procedure (EP Rules of Procedure, Rule 90(1) and (2)). The European Parliament may adopt such recommendations relatively quickly, since they do not have to be translated into all the official languages for the committee stage in urgent cases and are deemed to have been adopted at the next plenary session if no objection is made by at least 40 of the Parliament's component Members (EP Rules of Procedure, Rule 90(3) and (4)).

B. IMPLEMENTATION OF THE CFSP

Implementation by Council and Member States. A "common position", of **15–005** the Union commits the Member States in the positions they adopt and in the conduct of their activity (EU Treaty, Art. 14(3)). When the Council has adopted a common position, they are to ensure that their national policies conform thereto (EU Treaty, Art. 15). They are to uphold the common position in international organisations and at international conferences (Art. 19(1)).[17]

The Council determines the way in which a joint action is to be implemented (EU Treaty, Art. 14(1)). In so far as the Council does not do this, implementation of the CFSP is left to the Member States, which are to support the CFSP "actively and unreservedly in a spirit of loyalty and mutual solidarity" and "refrain from any action which is contrary to the interests of the Union or is likely to impair its effectiveness as a cohesive force in international relations" (EU Treaty, Art. 11(2)). In order to enable

---

[15] Framework agreement on relations between Parliament and the Commission of July 5, 2000 ([2001] O.J. C121/122, and (2000) 7/8 EU Bull., point 2.2.1; appended to the EP Rules of Procedure as Annex XIII), point 12. The Commission is also to take measures to improve the involvement of the European Parliament: *ibid.*, point 16.

[16] Interinstitutional Agreement of November 20, 2002 between the European Parliament and the Council concerning access by the European Parliament to sensitive information of the Council in the field of security and defence policy ([2002] O.J. C298/1), together with the Decision of the European Parliament of October 23, 2002 on the implementation of that agreement ([2002] O.J. C298/4), appended as Annex VII (B and C respectively) to the EP Rules of Procedure.

[17] For the international representation of the Union, see para. 19–011 *et seq.*, *infra*.

prior consultations to take place within the Council, a Member State has to provide prompt information of any plan to take action pursuant to a joint action, except in the case of measures constituting merely a national implementation of Council decisions. Only in cases of "imperative need arising from changes in the situation" may a Member State take the necessary measures as a matter of urgency in the absence of a Council decision and inform the Council immediately afterwards (EU Treaty, Art. 14(5) and (6)). If a Member State has major difficulties in implementing a joint action, it must refer them to the Council. The Council is then to seek appropriate solutions consistent with the objectives of the joint action which do not impair its effectiveness (EU Treaty, Art. 14(7)). In third countries and international conferences, the diplomatic and consular missions of the Member States and Commission Delegations are to co-operate in ensuring that the policy adopted by the Council is implemented (EU Treaty, Art. 20). Consequently, both the Council and the Commission are to help co-ordinate national measures for the implementation of the CFSP.

15–006 Execution and financing. The Presidency of the Council, assisted by the High Representative for the CFSP, is responsible for implementing CFSP decisions (EU Treaty, Art. 18(2) and (3)). The Presidency acts as the Union's spokesman, leads the negotiations and sometimes takes care of the practical implementation of CFSP decisions. Frequently, it is the Commission who provides it with administrative, financial and legal assistance.[18] Whenever it deems it necessary, the Council may appoint a special representative with a mandate in relation to particular policy issues (EU Treaty, Art. 18(5)).

The Presidency has to keep the European Parliament informed and ensure that its views are taken into account. The European Parliament may call the Council to account but may not impose sanctions upon it for the conduct of its policy in view of its limited supervisory powers over that institution. However, under the budgetary procedure, the Parliament is entitled to refuse to charge certain administrative or operational expenditure to the general budget.[19] In an Interinstitutional Agreement of July 16, 1997, the Council and the Commission came to an understanding with the European Parliament on the financing of the CFSP, which was taken over in the interinstitutional agreement of May 6, 1999.[20] Each time it adopts a decision in the field of the CFSP entailing expenses, the Council will immediately communicate an estimate of the costs envisaged (*fiche*

---

[18] For the practical aspects of implementation, see Keukeleire (n.2, *supra*), at 302–315. For example, the policy for the restructuring of Kosovo was carried out by the Commission in collaboration with the European Agency for Reconstruction (see para. 10–110).

[19] See EU Treaty, Art. 28(4) (paras 10–117 and 10–125, *supra*).

[20] Interinstitutional Agreement of July 16, 1997 (1997) EU Bull. point 2.3.1 and Interinstitutional Agreement of May 6, 1999, n.14, *supra*.

financière) to the European Parliament.[21] The Commission is to inform the budgetary authority about the execution of CFSP action and the financial forecasts for the remaining period of the year on a quarterly basis.[22] Since the Court of Justice has no jurisdiction with regard to the provisions of Title V of the EU Treaty, it may not review acts of the Council or the Member States which are based thereon.[23] In any event, the Commission does not have the power to supervise that national implementing measures comply with the obligations imposed on Member States by Title V of the EU Treaty.[24] As a result, parliamentary or judicial supervision of national measures implementing the CFSP takes place primarily in the Member States. At Union level, supervision of the implementation of the CFSP consists chiefly of mutual political supervision within the Council, which, as an institution, has a duty to ensure that the policy is properly implemented by the Member States (EU Treaty, Art. 11(2), third subpara.). That supervision may also be carried out within the Political and Security Committee (EU Treaty, Art. 25, first para., *in fine*).

Military operations. As far as security and defence policy is concerned, the **15–007** Union relies on the operational capacity of Member States to deploy military forces capable of the tasks referred to in Art. 17(2) of the EU Treaty (see para. 20–045). In order to formulate and implement Union decisions and measures with implications in the defence sphere, the Union uses the Political and Security Committee (PSC), assisted by the Military Committee and the Military Staff.[25] The PSC exercises political control and strategic direction of crisis management operations (EU Treaty, Art. 25, second paragraph). The operations themselves are carried out by units made available by the Member States.

Under the third para. of Art. 25 of the EU Treaty, the Council may authorise, for the purpose and duration of a crisis management operation, the PSC to take the relevant decisions concerning the political control and strategic direction of the operation.[26] In this way, the PSC has, for example,

---

[21] *ibid.*, point M. The *fiche financière* is to relate, *inter alia*, to the time-frame, staff employed, use of premises and other infrastructure, transport facilities, training requirements and security arrangements (*ibid.*).

[22] *ibid.*, point N.

[23] See EU Treaty, Art. 46; for a possible qualification in connection with the enforcement of fundamental rights, see para. 18–021, *infra*.

[24] Neither Art. 211 nor Art. 226 of the EC Treaty applies to the provisions of Title V of the EU Treaty. Because the Commission has no determinative influence on the CFSP, the European Parliament cannot pass a motion of censure under Art. 201 of the EC Treaty in respect of its role in this policy: see Art. 28(1) of the EU Treaty, which lists the articles of the EC Treaty that apply in the context of Title V of the EU Treaty; it does not include Art. 201.

[25] For their operation and organisation, see the annexes to Council Decisions 2001/79/CFSP and 2001/80/CFSP of January 22, 2001 (n.10, *supra*).

[26] Österdahl, "The EU and its Member States, Other States and International Organisations—The Common European Security and Defence Policy after Nice" (2001) Nordic J.I.L. 341, at 346–348. What is involved therefore is a delegation by Treaty of discretionary powers; see also para. 14–066.

directed military operations of the European Union in the Former Yugoslav Republic of Macedonia and in Congo.[27]

The Union's security and defence policy takes account of existing forms of military co-operation and of specific positions of particular Member States (EU Treaty, Art. 17(1), second subpara., and (4)). By virtue of a Protocol to the EC Treaty and the EU Treaty, Denmark does not participate in the elaboration and implementation of decisions and actions of the Union which have defence implications.[28] In that Protocol, however, Denmark has undertaken not to obstruct the development of enhanced co-operation between Member States in this area. When it holds the Presidency of the Council, Denmark renounces its right to exercise that office in each case involving the elaboration and implementation of decisions and actions of the Union which have defence implications and as far as the international representation of the Union is concerned.[29]

C. ENHANCED CO-OPERATION IN THE CFSP

15–008 Functioning of enhanced co-operation. Since the Treaty of Nice, enhanced co-operation among Member States, which is governed by Title VII of the EU Treaty (see para. 9–005), has also been available for the CFSP (see EU Treaty, Arts 27a to 27e; see para. 9–007). Member States participating in enhanced co-operation may make use of the institutions, procedures and mechanisms provided for in the EU Treaty. The institutional provisions set out in Title V of the EU Treaty apply for the purpose of the adoption of the acts and decisions necessary for the implementation of such enhanced co-operation (EU Treaty, Art. 27a(2) and Art. 44(1)). In the Council, all members may take part in the deliberations, but only those representing participating Member States may participate in the decision-making (EU Treaty, Art. 44(1)). In the case of acts requiring to be adopted by a

---

[27] See Art. 4 of Council Joint Action 2003/92/CFSP of January 27, 2003 on the European Union military operation in the Former Yugoslav Republic of Macedonia, [2003] O.J. L34/26, and Arts 7 and 10 of Council Joint Action 2003/423/CFSP of June 5, 2003 on the European Union military operation in the Democratic Republic of Congo, [2003] O.J. L143/50. Examples of decisions taken by the PSC pursuant to those joint actions are to be found in [2003] O.J. L170/15–19. Before the entry into force of the changes made to the EU Treaty by the Treaty of Nice, the PSC was already responsible for the political control and strategic direction of the EU police mission in Bosnia-Herzegovina; see Art. 7 of Council Joint Action 2002/210/CFSP of March 11, 2002, [2002] O.J. L70/1.

[28] Art. 6 of Protocol (No.5) to the EU Treaty and the EC Treaty on the position of Denmark ([1997] O.J. C340/101), confirming Part C of the Decision of the Heads of State and Government, meeting within the European Council, concerning certain problems raised by Denmark on the Treaty on European Union, [1992] O.J. C348/2. See Howarth, "The Compromise on Denmark and the Treaty on European Union: A Legal and Political Analysis" (1994) C.M.L.R. 765, at 776–779. For applications, see para. 20–047, *infra*.

[29] See the Declarations of the European Council of December 11–12, 1992, [1992] O.J. C348/2. Other Member States which are not members of the WEU and have not sought such an arrangement may undertake their normal duties as the Presidency in defence matters, *cf.* Curtin and Van Ooik, "De bijzondere positie van Denemarken in de Europese Unie" (1993) S.E.W. 675, at 686 (who make this observation in respect of Ireland).

qualified majority, the calculation of the requisite majority is to be adjusted.[30] Just as in the case of enhanced co-operation in the Community context, Member States participating in the co-operation must apply acts and decisions adopted for its implementation, whilst non-participating States must not impede its implementation (EU Treaty, Art. 44(2)).

Any Member State wishing to become a party to enhanced co-operation in respect of CFSP matters has to notify its intention to the Council and the Commission, which is to give an opinion to the Council. Within four months of the date of that notification, the Council is to decide on the request and on such specific arrangements as it deems necessary (EU Treaty, Art. 27e). The procedure for adopting that decision is noteworthy. The decision is deemed to be taken unless the Council, acting by a qualified majority within the four-month time limit, decides to hold it in abeyance[31]; in such case, the Council must state the reasons for its decision and set a deadline for re-examining it (EU Treaty, Art. 27e, first para., *in fine*).

D. DECISION-MAKING UNDER THE EU CONSTITUTION

Modifications to the CFSP. In "specific provisions relating to the common **15–009** foreign and security policy", the EU Constitution largely preserves the existing rules on decision-making in so far as it provides for decisions to be taken in principle by the European Council and the Council acting unanimously. The European Parliament has merely a general advisory role. The most important innovation is the creation of a Union Minister for Foreign Affairs (see para. 10–071), who will perform tasks now conferred on the Commission (right of initiative) and the President of the Council (chairing the Council, implementation and external representation), as presently assisted by the High Representative for the CFSP.

The Council defines and frames the CFSP on the basis of general guidelines and strategic lines defined by the European Council.[32] The EU Constitution makes the European Council responsible for identifying the strategic interests and objectives of the Union for both the CFSP and all other areas of external policy.[33] The principle that the Council is to decide by unanimity (with or without "constructive abstention" of some Member States) continues to apply, except where the Council implements a European decision of the European Council or a European decision defining a CFSP action or position or where it appoints a special

---

[30] Under Art. 44(1) of the EU Treaty, a qualified majority is defined as the same proportion of the weighted votes and the same proportion of the members of the Council as laid down in Art. 23(2), second and third subparas, of the EU Treaty (which is the majority laid down in Art. 205(2) of the EC Treaty for acts not adopted on the basis of a Commission proposal), but only the participating Member States are taken into account (see also n.6, *supra*).

[31] The votes of members of the Council are counted in accordance with Art. 23(2), third subpara., of the EU Treaty (n.30, *supra*).

[32] EU Constitution, Art. I–40(2) and III–295.

[33] *ibid.*, Art. III–293.

representative. In those cases, the Council is to decide by qualified majority. Under the EU Constitution, qualified majority voting will also apply where the Council adopts a European decision defining an action or position on a proposal put to it by the Union Minister for Foreign Affairs following a specific request made to him or her by the European Council.[34] In addition, the European Council may decide by a unanimous vote that the Council will decide in future by a qualified majority in other cases.[35] Unanimity remains the rule however for all decisions having military or defence implications.[36] Any proposal for CFSP action may be submitted by a Member State, by the Union Minister for Foreign Affairs acting alone, or by that Minister with the Commission's support.[37] Whereas in other areas of external policy the powers of initiative, implementation and representation are vested in the Commission, acting as a College, the Commission's role in CFSP matters is confined to supporting proposals submitted by the Union Minister for Foreign Affairs, who, it will be recalled, is a member of the College. In areas concerning both the CFSP and other fields of external action the Commission and the Minister may submit joint proposals.[38]

The implementation of CFSP decisions remains principally in the hands of the Member States and the Council, with the Union Minister for Foreign Affairs being responsible for securing their implementation. The Political and Security Committee preserves its existing powers of consultation and co-ordination.

The existing rules will largely be preserved with respect to enhanced co-operation between Member States in CFSP matters. In this connection, the Commission will share its advisory role with the Union Minister for Foreign Affairs.[39] Whenever a Member State makes a request to participate in an existing form of enhanced co-operation, the Council is to determine whether the conditions for participation are fulfilled and may, if necessary, delay such participation.[40]

II. DECISION-MAKING RELATING TO POLICE AND JUDICIAL CO-OPERATION IN CRIMINAL MATTERS (PJCC)

A. POLICY-MAKING WITH RESPECT TO PJCC

15–010 Role of the Council. The Council is to take measures and promote police and judicial co-operation in criminal matters (PJCC) using the appropriate

---

[34] *ibid.*, Art. III–300(2)(b).
[35] *ibid.*, Art. I–40(7) and Art. III–300(3).
[36] *ibid.*, Art. III–300(4).
[37] *ibid.*, Art. I–40(6) and Art. III–299(1).
[38] *ibid.*, Art. III–293(2). *e.g.* adoption of economic sanctions (Art. III–322(1)) and implementation of the solidarity clause (Art. III–329(2)).
[39] EU Constitution, Art. III–419(2).
[40] *ibid.*, Art. III–420(2).

form and procedures set out in Title VI of the EU Treaty (EU Treaty, Art. 34(2)).[41] The Council may adopt common positions, framework decisions and decisions, establish conventions and conclude international agreements (see para. 18–015 *et seq.*).

The Council acts by unanimous vote, except on procedural matters, where it decides by a majority of its members (EU Treaty, Art. 34(2) and (4)). Measures needed to implement PJCC decisions are adopted by a qualified majority vote, with the votes weighted in the manner prescribed by Art. 205(2) of the EC Treaty for acts not adopted by the Council on a Commission proposal (EU Treaty, Art. 34(2)(c) and Art. 34(3)).[42] This is also the procedure which the Council must follow where it concludes international agreements covering an issue for which a qualified majority is required for internal decisions or measures (EU Treaty, Art. 24(2)). Measures implementing conventions concluded between Member States are adopted by the Council by a majority of two-thirds of the Contacting Parties (EU Treaty, Art. 34(2)(d)).

Initiative and co-ordination. The Commission or any Member State may **15–011** propose initiatives for co-operation (EU Treaty, Art. 34(2)).[43] In principle, a six-week period should elapse between a proposal being made available in all languages to the European Parliament and the Council by the Commission and the date when it is placed on a Council agenda for decision.[44] Initiatives for PJCC measures and acts adopted by the Council under Art. 34(2) are published in the *Official Journal*, in accordance with the relevant Rules of Procedure of the Council and the Commission.[45] A co-ordinating committee advises the Council and assists it in preparing its

---

[41] Unlike under Title V of the EU Treaty, the European Council is not expressly involved in decision-making under Title VI. Nevertheless, in this case, too, under Art. 4, first para., of the EU Treaty it is to define the "general political guidelines".

[42] From November 1, 2004, the same changes made by the Protocol on the enlargement of the Union (n.6, *supra*) and by the 2003 Act of Accession to Art. 205(2) of the EC Treaty apply as regards acts not adopted by the Council on the basis of a Commission proposal (see para. 10–045).

[43] In connection with JHA co-operation, initiatives often—but not invariably—appeared to stem from the Member State occupying the Presidency; see, for instance, as regards the period July 1, 1996 to June 30, 1997 the Council's answer of November 17, 1997 to question E–2405/97 (Nassauer), [1998] O.J. C102/39.

[44] Protocol (No.9) to the EU Treaty and the Community Treaties on the role of the national parliaments in the European Union ([1997] O.J. C340/113), point 3. This protocol, however, does provide for exceptions "on grounds of urgency", for which reasons must be given. Points 5 and 6 of the Protocol confirm that the Conference of European Affairs Committees (COSAC) may make contributions concerning the Union's legislative activities, in particular in relation to the establishment of an area of freedom, security and justice.

[45] Council Rules of Procedure, Art. 17(1) (publication of framework decisions, decisions and agreements). Common positions and Member State initiatives are published in the *Official Journal*, unless decided otherwise (Council Rules of Procedure, Art. 17(2)). The Council or Coreper decides, on a case-by-case basis and taking account of possible publication of the basic act, whether implementing measures should be published (Council Rules of Procedure, Art. 17(4)). See also Declaration (No.9) on Art. 34(2) of the Treaty on European Union ([1997] O.J. C340/133).

discussions (Art. 36(1); see para 10–051), whilst the Commission is entitled to be "fully associated" with the work of the co-ordinating committee and the Council (including Coreper) (see Art. 36(2)).[46]

The Council consults the European Parliament before adopting a common position, a framework decision or a decision and before establishing a convention (EU Treaty, Art. 34(2) and Art. 39(1)). The European Parliament deals with the consultation in the same way as it does when it is consulted pursuant to the EC Treaty (see para. 14–024). It is to deliver its opinion within a time-limit laid down by the Council, which may not be less than three months. If the Parliament fails to deliver an opinion within the prescribed period, the Council is entitled to act (EU Treaty, Art. 39(1)). Accordingly, the Parliament's competence in the case of PJCC exceeds its prerogatives in the case of the CFSP—which, moreover, it also has in the area of PJCC -, namely to be regularly informed and consulted and to put questions and recommendations to the Council.[47] As in the case of the CFSP, the Commission has undertaken to keep the European Parliament informed about its PJCC initiatives.[48]

Lastly, the Council, acting unanimously on the initiative of the Commission or a Member State after consulting the European Parliament, may decide that PJCC action should come within the competence of the Community (EC Treaty, Title IV). A decision to this effect will not have the force of law until such time as it is adopted by the several Member States in accordance with their respective constitutional requirements (EU Treaty, Art. 42).[49] The Council may further decide by a qualified majority to authorise Member States to establish enhanced co-operation amongst themselves (see para. 15–014). Such authorisation already exists for the integration and further development of parts of the Schengen *acquis* pursuant to Title VI of the EU Treaty (see para. 15–014).

B. IMPLEMENTATION OF THE PJCC

15–012 **Executive tasks.** Common positions adopted by the Council pursuant to PJCC define the Union's approach to a particular matter and Member States are to defend them within international organisations and at international conferences (EU Treaty, Art. 37, first para.).

---

[46] See also the remark concerning the Commission's right of initiative in n.9, *supra*.

[47] See EU Treaty, Art. 39(2) and (3). The EP Rules of Procedure provide the same possibilities for having a recommendation which has been drawn up by a committee adopted rapidly by the plenary session but do not allow for a derogation from the rules on the use of languages (EP Rules of Procedure, compare r.94 and 90).

[48] See para. 15–004 and n.15, *supra*.

[49] In a declaration, Denmark has indicated the constitutional requirements applicable in that country to approval of any decision involving a transfer of sovereignty: see the Declaration by Denmark on Art. K.14 [now Art. 42] of the Treaty on European Union ([1997] O.J. C340/143); Denmark thereby confirmed its declarations on the former Art. K.9 of the EU Treaty which was associated to the Danish Act of ratification of the Treaty on European Union and of which the eleven other Member States took cognisance—Declaration on co-operation in the fields of justice and home affairs, [1992] O.J. C348/4.

Union framework decisions and decisions pursuant to PJCC are binding upon the Member States. According to Art. 34(2)(b) of the EU Treaty, framework decisions are binding upon the Member States as to the result to be achieved, but leave to the national authorities the choice of form and methods. Consequently, the EU Treaty provides that the Member States are to implement framework decisions. As far as decisions (other than framework decisions) are concerned, the EU Treaty refers only to implementing decisions of the Council. The Council is to adopt, by a qualified majority, measures necessary to implement such decisions at the level of the Union (Art. 34(2)(c)). In practice, the Commission is involved in implementing the measures.[50] For the development of the Schengen Information System, which is based both on Title IV of the EC Treaty and on Title VI of the EU Treaty, a Council PJCC decision is even implemented by the Commission in accordance with the Community comitology procedure.[51] This does not prevent Member States from adopting measures themselves in order to implement PJCC decisions, which, in common with PJCC framework decisions, "shall not entail direct effect" (Art. 34). In implementing PJCC measures, Member States can invoke the responsibilities incumbent upon them with regard to the maintenance of law and order and the safeguarding of internal security (EU Treaty, Art. 33).

In the event that the Council establishes conventions pursuant to PJCC, it is to recommend them for adoption by the Member States in accordance with their respective constitutional requirements. They are to begin the applicable procedure within a time-limit to be set by the Council (EU Treaty, Art. 34(2)(d)). Unless otherwise provided in the conventions, they are to enter into force once they have been adopted by at least half of the Member States as far as those Member States are concerned. The Council is to adopt measures implementing such conventions by a majority of two-thirds of the Contracting Parties (EU Treaty, Art. 34(2)(d)).

Parliamentary and judicial control. As far as supervising the **15–013** implementation of PJCC is concerned, there is not just mutual supervision by the Member States with parliamentary and judicial control being left to domestic provisions as was the case with co-operation in the field of justice

---

[50] See, *e.g.* the Commission's involvement with the committees which assist with the execution of the programmes referred to in n. to para. 6–008: answer of the Commission of March 3, 2000 to question E–2183/99 (Busk), [2001] O.J. C26E/2.

[51] Council Decision 2001/886/JHA of December 6, 2001 on the development of the second generation Schengen Information System (SIS II) ([2001] O.J. L328/1), Arts 5 and 6 of which involve a management committee and a regulatory committee, respectively, by analogy with the provisions of the Comitology Decision, to which reference is made in the parallel instrument, Council Regulation (EC) No. 2424/2001 of December 6, 2001, ([2001] O.J. L328/4).

and home affairs.[52] The European Parliament has powers under the budgetary procedure in order to scrutinise administrative and operational expenditure charged to the EU budget.[53] In addition, Art. 35 of the EU Treaty determines the procedures under which the Court of Justice may give preliminary rulings on the validity or interpretation of PJCC Acts, review the legality of framework decisions and decisions and rule on disputes between Member States regarding the interpretation or application of PJCC acts and on disputes between Member States and the Commission on the interpretation or application of PJCC conventions (see para. 10–077). It is clear, however, that at the level of the Union the PJCC is not yet submitted to the same degree of democratic and judicial control as the Community decision-making.[54]

C. Enhanced co-operation with respect to PJCC

15–014 Functioning of enhanced co-operation. Enhanced co-operation among Member States, which is governed by Title VII of the EU Treaty (see para. 9–004), was made available from the outset for PJCC (see EU Treaty, Arts 40–40b; see para. 9–008). Member States participating in enhanced co-operation may make use of the institutions, procedures and mechanisms provided for in the EU Treaty. The institutional provisions set out in Title VI of the EU Treaty apply for the purpose of the adoption of the acts and decisions necessary for the implementation of such enhanced co-operation (EU Treaty, Art. 40(2) and Art. 44(1)). In the Council, all members may take part in the deliberations, but only those representing participating Member States may participate in the decision-making (EU Treaty, Art. 44(1)). In the case of decisions having to be taken by a qualified majority vote, the voting requirements are adjusted.[55] Just as in the case of enhanced co-operation in the Community context and in the field of the CFSP, Member States participating in the co-operation must apply acts and decisions adopted for its implementation, whilst non-participating States must not impede its implementation (EU Treaty, Art. 44(2)).

Any Member State wishing to become a party to enhanced co-operation in respect of PJCC matters has to notify its intention to the Council and the Commission, which is to give an opinion to the Council possibly accompanied by a recommendation for such specific arrangements as it may deem necessary for that Member State to become a party to the

---

[52] Under JHA co-operation, the Court of Justice had only jurisdiction to interpret provisions of a convention concluded by the Member States and rule on any disputes relating thereto if the convention so provided: see EU Treaty, former Art. K.3(2)(c), third subpara. (see para. 18–009, *infra*).

[53] EU Treaty, Art. 41(4).

[54] See the criticism by Douglas-Scott, "The rule of law in the European Union—putting the security into the 'area of freedom, security and justice' " (2004) E.L.R. 219–242.

[55] Under Art. 44(1) of the EU Treaty, the qualified majority is defined as the same proportion of the weighted votes and the same proportion of the number of the Council members concerned as laid down in Art. 205(2) of the EC Treaty.

co-operation in question. Within four months of the date of that notification, the Council is to decide on the request (EU Treaty, Art. 40b). As in the case of CFSP co-operation, the decision is deemed to be taken unless the Council, acting by a qualified majority, decides to hold it in abeyance; in such case, the Council must state the reasons for its decision and set a deadline for re-examining it (EU Treaty, Art. 40b). Schengen co-operation is an existing example of enhanced co-operation of the PJCC type as far as Ireland and the United Kingdom are concerned, which, by virtue of their special position, are not taking part in the integration and further development of the Schengen *acquis* (see paras 5–164 and 5–166). Those Member States may at any time request to take part in some or all of the provisions of the *acquis* (Schengen Protocol, Art. 4).[56] The Council is to decide on such a request by a unanimous vote of the Schengen States and of the State concerned.[57] As far as building upon the Schengen *acquis* is concerned, these Member States may notify the President of the Council within a reasonable period that they wish to take part.[58] Under the Schengen Protocol, if only one or neither of those States makes such notification, the authorisation referred to in Art. 40a is to be deemed to have been granted to the Member States engaging in further co-operation.[59]

D. DECISION-MAKING UNDER THE EU CONSTITUTION

Changes with respect to existing rules. Under the EU Constitution, police **15–015** and judicial co-operation in criminal matters, together with the current provisions of Title IV of the EC Treaty, will be part of a single chapter on the area of freedom, security and justice. In this area, the Union will act by means of European laws and European framework laws, which means that measures are to be adopted by the European Parliament and the Council under the co-decision procedure, *i.e.* by a qualified majority vote in the Council. The Council is to decide by unanimity after obtaining the consent of the European Parliament on some important decisions with respect to

---

[56] For the UK, see Council Decision 2000/365/EC of May 29, 2000 concerning the request of the UK of Great Britain and Northern Ireland to take part in some of the provisions of the Schengen *acquis*, [2000] O.J. L131/43; for Ireland, see Council Decision 2002/192/EC of February 28, 2002 concerning Ireland's request to take part in some of the provisions of the Schengen acquis, [2002] O.J. L64/20.

[57] Schengen Protocol, Art. 4, second para. In Declaration (No.45) on that provision, annexed to the Treaty of Amsterdam ([1997] O.J. C340/140), the High Contracting Parties invite the Council to seek the Commission's opinion before taking such a decision (this was done in the case of Decisions 2000/365/EC and 2002/192/EC) and undertake to make their best efforts with a view to allowing Ireland and the UK to make use of the provisions of Art. 4 if they so wish. For the special position with regard to the further development of the Schengen *acquis* (which also applies to Denmark), see para. 14–070, *supra*).

[58] See Schengen Protocol, Art. 5(1), second subpara.

[59] *ibid.*

judicial co-operation,[60] whilst some sensitive aspects of police co-operation require the Council to decide by unanimity after consulting the European Parliament.[61] In PJCC matters, the Member States retain the possibility to submit proposals for action, alongside the Commission's right of initiative, even though in future such proposals will have to emanate from a group of at least a quarter of the Member States (EU Constitution, Art. III–264). The EU Constitution furthermore stresses that national parliaments may exercise control over compliance with the principle of subsidiarity (Art. III–259, first para.; see para. 5–035). The co-ordinating committee of senior national officials will continue to exercise its advisory function (EU Constitution, Art. III–261).

As far as judicial co-operation in criminal matters is concerned, the Intergovernmental Conference inserted in the EU Constitution an "alarm bell procedure", enabling any Member State which considers that a draft European framework law would affect fundamental aspects of its criminal justice system, to request that the draft framework law be referred to the European Council.[62] In that event, the co-decision procedure will be suspended for a period of up to four months, during which the European Council may either refer the draft back to the Council to have the decision-making procedure resumed, or request the Commission or the group of Member States from which the draft framework law emanates to submit a new draft (EU Constitution, Arts III–270(3) and III–271(3)). If the European Council has not taken any action by the end of that period or if, within twelve months from the submission of a new draft framework law, that draft has not been adopted, and at least one-third of the Member States wish to proceed on the basis of that draft, the authorisation to proceed with enhanced co-operation shall be deemed to be granted (Arts III–270(4) and III–271(4)).

European laws and framework laws with respect to PJCC will be implemented either by action of the Member States or by action taken by the Commission or the Council in accordance with the different options provided for in the Constitution to this end (see para. 14–053). In addition, the EU Constitution provides for specific forms of parliamentary control over the Union's policy in the area of freedom, security and justice. The European Parliament and the national parliaments are to be associated in the objective and impartial evaluation of the implementation of the Union's policies at national level which is to be conducted by the Member States in collaboration with the Commission (EU Constitution, Art. III–260).

---

[60] See, *e.g.* any extension of the scope of application of judicial co-operation to aspects of criminal procedure not currently mentioned in the Constitution (Art. III–270(2)(d)), the identification of additional other areas of crime in respect of which minimum rules may be established (Art. III–271(1), third subpara.) and the establishment of a European Public Prosecutor's Office (Art. III–274(1)).

[61] See, *e.g.* operational co-operation between police authorities (Art. III–275(3)) and operations on the territory of another Member State (Art. III–277).

[62] This procedure did not appear in the initial version of the EU Constitution.

Moreover, European laws will have to determine arrangements for involving the European Parliament and national parliaments in the evaluation of the activities of Eurojust and Europol (Arts III–273(1), third subpara., and III 276(2), second subpara.). In common with the legislative role of the European Parliament, these arrangements seek to counter criticism that there is at present no satisfactory degree of parliamentary control over PJCC activities in view of its intergovernmental nature.

Under the EU Constitution, enhanced co-operation in the field of PJCC will be subject to the same procedural provisions which apply to enhanced co-operation in other fields (para. 14–072).

III. Conventions Concluded between Member States

Negotiations between Member States. In some areas, the EC Treaty **15–016** requires the Member States to enter into negotiations so as to lay down rules by mutual agreement.[63] The most important basis for such agreements is Art. 293 of the EC Treaty, which leaves the achievement of certain objectives to conventions to be concluded between the Member States.[64] The negotiations take place between representatives of the Member States with or without the assistance of the Community institutions. Generally speaking, the European Parliament is not involved in drawing up such conventions. They receive the force of law when they have been ratified by the Member States. The Court of Justice may interpret such a convention only if it (or a protocol thereto) expressly gives it jurisdiction to do so.[65] Accordingly, the convention as such is not Community law (see paras 18–008–18–009). When new Member States join the Community, they do not automatically become parties to such conventions. A separate convention between all participating Member States is required.[66]

---

[63] EC Treaty, Art. 20 and Art. 293.

[64] This provision no longer appears in the EU Constitution since in all the areas concerned the Union is now empowered to act on the basis of other Treaty provisions. Naturally, this does not prevent Member States from concluding conventions amongst themselves in other areas.

[65] For references, see para. 18–008, *infra*.

[66] See Art. 63 of the Brussels Convention of September 27, 1968 (Brussels Convention or Judgments Convention, see para. 5–151, *supra*). Consequently, the Brussels Convention and the Protocol of June 3, 1971 on its interpretation (see para. 18–008, *infra*) have been amended upon the accession of new Member States by conventions of October 9, 1978 ([1978] O.J. L304/1), October 25, 1982 ([1982] O.J. L388/1), May 26, 1989 ([1989] O.J. L285/1) and November 29, 1996 ([1997] O.J. C15/1); for a consolidated version, see [1998] O.J. C27/1. For the UK, see the Civil Jurisdiction and Judgments Act 1982. See also the Brussels Convention of July 23, 1990 on the elimination of double taxation in connection with the adjustment of profits of associated enterprises ([1990] O.J. L225/10). For the amendment of this convention by the Convention of December 21, 1995 following the accession of new Member States, see [1996] O.J. C26/1. It was extended by the Protocol amending the Convention of July 23, 1990 on the elimination of double taxation in connection with the adjustment of profits of associated enterprises, concluded under Title VI of the EU Treaty ([1999] O.J. C202/1).

15–017 Duty to negotiate. In view of the harmonisation sought by Art. 293 of the EC Treaty, any convention drawn up pursuant thereto must be signed and ratified by all the Member States before it may enter into force.[67] If this is not possible, the Member States may possibly adopt the convention outside the ambit of Art. 293.[68] Since Art. 293 requires Member States, as far as necessary, to enter into negotiations,[69] the Commission may act pursuant to its power of supervision against Member States which refuse to enter into negotiations, but not against any which have merely not proceeded to ratify the convention to which the negotiations gave rise.[70]

IV.　OTHER DECISIONS OF MEMBER STATE GOVERNMENTS

15–018 Other decisions. Lastly, reference should be made to the practice whereby the national governments, without conforming with any particular procedural requirements, make use of meetings in the context of the Union or intergovernmental co-operative forums jointly to take decisions, pass resolutions or make declarations (see paras 2–019 and 18–011–18–013).

---

[67] Under Art. 62 of the Brussels Convention on jurisdiction and enforcement of judgments, the Convention was to enter in force "on the first day of the third month following the deposit of the last instrument of ratification by the last Signatory State to take this step" (for the original six Member States, this was February 1, 1973; the Civil Jurisdiction and Judgments Act 1982 implementing the Convention in the UK entered into force on July 13, 1982); the same provision was adopted in Art. 18 of the Brussels Convention of July 23, 1990 (see n. 66, *supra*); this instrument, known as the "Arbitration Convention", entered into force in the UK on January 1, 1995—notice in the *London Gazette* of February 23, 1995.

[68] See, *e.g.* the Rome Convention of June 19, 1980 (Rome Convention, see para. 5–152, *supra*; ratified in the UK by the Contracts (Applicable Law) Act 1990), which entered into force on "the first day of the third month following the deposit of the seventh instrument of ratification, acceptance or approval" (Art. 29(1); this was on April 1, 1991) and, in the case of signatory States depositing such instrument at a later date, "on the first day of the third month following the deposit of its instrument of ratification, acceptance or approval" (Art. 29(2); the Convention entered into force in the UK on April 1, 1991 as a result of the Contracts (Applicable Law) Act 1990 (Commencement No. 1) Order 1991).

[69] ECJ, Case 12/76 *Tessili* [1976] E.C.R. 1473, para. 9.

[70] See the Commission's answer of May 8, 1985 to question 2171/84 (Thome-Patenôtre), [1985] O.J. C189/41.

CHAPTER 16

LEGITIMACY OF DECISION-MAKING

I. EFFICIENCY OF DECISION-MAKING

Conflicting elements. Substantial numbers of national and Community civil **16–001**
servants work to achieve the aims of the Union smoothly and efficiently. To
this end, decisions must be able to be taken quickly. In addition, they must
be applied and, if necessary, enforced. These two aspects are essential for
efficient decision-making. However, in the design of the decision-making
procedure they may sometimes be in conflict with each other.[1]

Impediments to swift decision-making. The establishment of a single **16–002**
institutional framework for all policy areas of the Union is designed to
enable the whole range of decisions to be adopted smoothly.[2] The extension
of majority voting in the Council has the same end in mind.
  On the other hand, there is concern that the Union's acts should be
accepted by the Member States and their nationals. This is the only means
of ensuring effective application and enforcement. As a result, the
Commission often engages in dialogue with affected interest groups before
drawing up a proposal for an act (see para. 14–016). In matters which the
Contracting Parties recognise as being politically sensitive, in particular the
CFSP, all Member States must consent—that is, not cast their votes against
(EC Treaty, Art. 205(3))—in order to reach a decision. Where the EU
Treaty nevertheless allows a vote to be taken by a qualified majority for the
CFSP, the Council, acting by that majority, may request that the matter be
referred to the European Council—which decides by consensus—if a
Member State opposes the adoption of the measure in question "for
important and stated reasons of national policy".[3] Further constraints flow
from the decentralised implementation of many acts. It is often possible to
implement them in practice only if national civil servants have had an input

---

[1] See the discussions of efficiency in, for instance, Piris, "After Maastricht, are the Community
Institutions More Efficacious, More Democratic and More Transparent?" (1994) E.L.R. 449,
at 454–455; Snyder, "The Effectiveness of European Community Law: Institutions,
Processes, Tools and Techniques" (1993) M.L.R. 19–54.
[2] See the preamble to the EU Treaty, in which the Contracting Parties declare their wish "to
enhance further the democratic and efficient functioning of the institutions so as to enable
them better to carry out, within a single institutional framework, the tasks entrusted to
them".
[3] See EU Treaty, Art. 23(2) and Art. 40(2).

in drawing them up so as to take account of specific situations in the Member States. In many instances, the implementation of the principle of subsidiarity has a constraining effect on legislating at Union level in so far as it may leave certain aspects of the matter concerned to regulation by the Member States or the sectors concerned, which, overall, makes the law-making picture more complex. Lastly, involvement of representatives of the people makes it easier to gain acceptance for decisions: it is partly for this reason that decision-making should be legitimised by the contribution of the European Parliament or the national parliaments, even if this does diminish the Council's leeway to muster a sufficient majority by negotiation in order to get decisions adopted (see para. 16–004 *et seq.*)

16–003 **Impediments flowing from federal principles.** The accession of new Member States likewise poses an increasing challenge to the efficiency of decision-making. Not only where a unanimous vote is required, but also in discussions leading up to a majority vote, the number of interlocutors is likely to make it more difficult to reach compromises.[4] In enlarging and adjusting the institutions and their bureaucratic machinery, considerations of efficiency often have to give way to federal principles such as the protected minimum representation of small Member States (see para. 16–006) and the principle of equality of the various official languages (see paras 10–155 *et seq.*).

II. DEMOCRATIC CONTENT OF DECISION-MAKING

A. SUBSTANCE OF DEMOCRATIC LEGITIMACY

16–004 **Expressions of democracy.** Democracy is one of the principles upon which the Union is founded (EU Treaty, Art. 6(1); see also EU Constitution, Art. I–2). The basic premise of democracy is that all public authority emanates from the people. The European Parliament has interpreted this premise as follows: "Every public authority must be directly elected or answerable to a directly elected parliament".[5] The principle that the people should take part in, or supervise, decision-making underpins the public authority in every Member State and, in order for a country to be a member of the European Union, it therefore must be a parliamentary

---

[4] See Ungerer, "Institutional Consequences of Broadening and Deepening the Community: the Consequences for the Decision-Making Process" (1993) C.M.L.R. 71–83; Fastenrath, "Die Struktur der erweiterten Europäischen Union", and Lautenschlager, "Die Struktur der erweiterten Europäischen Union" (1994) EuR. Beiheft 1, 101–126 and 127–146, respectively (and see the discussion in 147–150, *ibid.*).
[5] Art. 17(2) of the Declaration of Fundamental Rights and Freedoms, adopted by the European Parliament on April 12, 1989, [1989] O.J. C120/51.

democracy.[6] Under Art. 7 of the EU Treaty, certain of a Member State's rights may be suspended in the event of its seriously and persistently breaching the principle of democracy.[7]

The part played by the European Parliament in decision-making also reflects at Community level the "fundamental democratic principle that the peoples should take part in the exercise of power through the intermediary of a representative assembly".[8] The importance attached to this by the Member States is reflected in the fact that all recent amendments to the Treaties have bolstered the role played by the European Parliament.[9] Where the European Parliament does not take part in the adoption of an act, the people's participation in the exercise of power may be secured in another manner. In this connection, the EU Constitution gives the following definition of the "principle of representative democracy": "Citizens are directly represented at Union level in the European Parliament. Member States are represented in the European Council by their Heads of State or Government and in the Council by their governments, themselves democratically accountable either to their national parliaments, or to their citizens" (Art. I–46(2)). According to Art. I–46(3) of the EU Constitution, every citizen has the right to participate in the democratic life of the Union. Alongside the "principle of representative democracy" so defined, the EU Constitution mentions the "principle of participatory democracy".[10] This refers to dialogue which the institutions of the Union are to maintain with citizens, their representative associations and civil society and the right for a significant number of citizens to submit an initiative to the Commission (EU Constitution, Art. I–47).[11]

---

[6] Art. 49 of the EU Treaty refers to the principles "which are common to the Member States" as set out in Art. 6(1); for a precursor, see the declaration of the European Council meeting at Copenhagen on April 7 and 8, 1978 (1978) 3 EC Bull. 5 (cited among the substantive requirements for accession to the Union, para. 8–007, *supra*).

[7] See Verhoeven, "How Democratic need European Union Members be? Some Thoughts after Amsterdam" (1998) E.L.R. 217–234.

[8] ECJ, Case 138/79 *Roquette Frères v Council* [1980] E.C.R. 3333, para. 33, and ECJ, Case 139/79 *Maïzena v Council* [1980] E.C.R. 3393, para. 34. It would not be compatible with the principle of democracy if the conditions under which MEPs exercise their mandate were to be affected by the fact that they do not belong to a political group to an extent exceeding what is necessary for the attainment of the legitimate objectives pursued by the Parliament through its organisation in political groups: CFI, Joined Cases T–222/99, T–327/99 and T–329/99 *Martinez v European Parliament* [2001] E.C.R. II–2823, para. 202, confirmed on the merits by ECJ (order of November 11, 2003), Case C–488/01 P *Martinez v European Parliament*, not yet reported, and set aside, as to the admissibility of the action brought by a political party, by ECJ (judgment of June 29, 2004), Case C–486/01 P *Front National v European Parliament*, not yet reported.

[9] Schockweiler, "La dimension humaine et sociale de la Communauté européenne" (1993) 4 R.M.U.E. 11, at 19.

[10] See also Peters, "European Democracy after the 2003 Convention" (2004) C.M.L.R. 37–85.

[11] para. 14–045, *supra*. For the involvement of management and labour, see already CFI, *UEAPME v Council* [1998] E.C.R. II–2335, para. 89 (see para. 14–042, *supra*). For other forms of democratic supervision (*e.g. via* the Internet), see Weiler, "The European Union belongs to its Citizens: Three Immodest Proposals" (1997) E.L.R. 150–156; Curtin, *Postnational Democracy. The European Union in Search of a Political Philosophy* (Kluwer Law International, The Hague, 1997) 62 pp.

16–005 Democracy versus federalism. Nevertheless, decision-making in the Union does not take place in the same democratic manner as it does within a State.[12] This is because the Union organises relations between States and their peoples and has to respect the national identity of each Member State (see EU Treaty, Art. 6(3); EU Constitution, Art. I–5(1)). As a result, the decision-making process has to embody "federal" guarantees.[13] For instance, owing to the concern to secure an adequate representation for the small Member States, the distribution of seats in the European Parliament and of votes in the Council does not completely mirror each Member State's share of the total population of the Union. On the other hand, decisions taken at Community level often affect the control of decision-making which the people in each Member State carry out through their national representative assembly. For reasons of efficiency, it would be inconceivable for such decisions to be subjected to the scrutiny and approval of all the national parliaments. It would seem that the resultant vacuum may be filled only by securing a sufficient parliamentary role in European decision-making itself.

16–006 Rule of law and transparency. Modern democracy does not only comprise participation of representative assemblies in public authority and supervision by such assemblies of public authority; it is also based on the principles of the rule of law and the correlative requirements of legal protection.[14] Accordingly, the democratic content of decision-making in the Union has to do not only with the way in which power is exercised, but also with the protection afforded to legal subjects pursuant to the rule of law.[15] This is all the more important given that many decisions of the Union are formulated by Community and national officials in the interaction between the Commission and the Council. Just as in the Member States, the growing influence of the executive inevitably goes hand in hand with a burgeoning

---

[12] See Verhoeven, *The European Union in Search of a Democratic and Constitutional Theory* (Kluwer Law International, The Hague, 2002) 365 pp.

[13] For the relationship between democracy and integration, see Weiler, "Parlement européen, intégration européenne, démocratie et légitimité", in Louis and Waelbroeck (eds), *Le Parlement européen dans l'évolution institutionnelle* (Editions de l'Université de Bruxelles, Brussels, 1988) 325–348, especially at 335–339. For the correlation between the degree of integration of international organisations and the demand for democratisation, see Stein, "International integration and democracy: no love at first sight" (2001) A.J.I.L. 489–534.

[14] See also Art. 6(1) of the EU Treaty, which refers to "the principles of liberty, democracy, respect for human rights and fundamental freedoms, and the rule of law". The definition of the principle of democracy in the European Parliament's Declaration on Fundamental Rights and Freedoms (n.5, *supra*) reads as follows: "All public authority emanates from the people and must be exercised in accordance with the principles of the rule of law" (Art. 17(1)).

[15] For a qualified assessment based on a teleological approach to the question of democracy, see De Smijter, "De verschijningsvormen van de democratie in de Europese Gemeenschappen: een nuancering van het democratische tekort van de Europese Gemeenschappen", *Democratie op het einde van de 20ste eeuw* (Belgian Royal Academy of Sciences, Letters and Fine Arts, Brussels, 1994), at 27–53.

number of tasks attributed to the public authorities.[16] This makes supervision by the courts necessary in order that, in the absence of effective parliamentary control, executive action can at least be compelled to comply with superior law.

In addition, it is equally important for the democratic content of decision-making that information should be available about policy and that policy should be open and transparent, since this is apt to increase public interest and confidence in the exercise of power.[17] To that effect, the EU Constitution declares that "[i]n order to promote good governance and ensure the participation of civil society, the Union institutions, bodies, offices and agencies shall conduct their work as openly as possible" (Art. I–50(1); see paras 16–015 et seq.).

B. Participation in and Supervision of Decision-Making

1. Transparency of the division of powers

Complex picture. In order to involve the people in the exercise of power, it **16–007** is a requirement of the democratic principle that a representative assembly, if not directly participating in decision-making, at least is able to supervise it. The members of the representative assembly (and their electors) may have an effective influence over decision-making only if it is clear in whom decision-making powers are vested and which particular powers are involved. As far as decision-making within the Union is concerned, this means that it must be clearly distinguishable whether a power is vested in the Union or in the Member States, which institution has the ultimate power of decision and which decision-making procedure has to be followed. The coexistence of two Communities, together with non-Community forms of policy and co-operation, itself witnesses to the fact that this sort of transparency is not an attribute of Union decision-making at present. The EU Constitution seeks to clarify the situation by eliminating the distinction between Community and non-Community action, although different rules will continue to exist with respect to the CFSP. Moreover, as far as Community powers are concerned, the diversity of legislative procedures makes decision-making an extremely complex matter. It would certainly be beneficial for the purposes of democratic supervision if Community legislation could be adopted in a more uniform manner, with the role played by each institution and the allocation of tasks as between the European Parliament and the national parliaments being made clearer for

---

[16] See the articles in Flinterman, Heringa and Waddington, *The Evolving Role of Parliaments in Europe/L'évolution du rôle des parlements en Europe* (Maklu/Nomos, Antwerp, 1994) 111 pp.

[17] De Smijter (n.15, *supra*), at 42–43. For the "social legitimacy" of public authority, which extends beyond its democratic aspect, see Weiler (n.13, *supra*), at 333–335. See also the European Parliament's resolution of December 10, 1996 on participation of citizens and social players in the European Union's institutional system, [1997] O.J. C20/31.

everyone.[18] In this connection, too, the EU Constitution proposes to simplify matters by introducing an "ordinary legislative procedure" allowing the European Parliament and the Council to co-decide; nevertheless, other procedures of decision-making will continue to co-exist.

2. Role of parliamentary bodies

16–008 Parliamentary control at Union level. In the light of the powers of the European Parliament, commentators often refer to a "democratic deficit" in the context of decision-making within the Union. What is meant is the consequences of the transfer of powers from the national to the Union level in terms of the intensity of parliamentary control of decision-making. Matters which used to come within the competence of the national parliament or in respect of which the national government was accountable to the national parliament now come within the sphere of the Union, where the European Parliament does not invariably have a decisive say in decision-making. The European Parliament may not "co-decide" with the Council on Community legislation in all cases; in others, the Council can take a decision against the wishes of the European Parliament (see paras 14–020–14–040). Furthermore, MEPs have no right to submit proposals for legislation: only the Commission has the right of initiative (see para. 14–015). As new powers are assigned to the Union, the democratic deficit would seem to grow if the gradual, piecemeal increase in the European Parliament's powers does not keep pace with the expansion of the Union's powers.[19] However, as has already been observed, the democratic content of decision-making at Union level cannot be reduced to the degree to which the European Parliament has a say.[20]

16–009 Parliamentary control at national level. When legislative measures are adopted by the Council on a proposal from the Commission, whether or

---

[18] See Lenaerts, "Some Reflections on the Separation of Powers in the European Community" (1991) C.M.L.R. 11, at 20; Piris (n.1, *supra*), at 469–470. A clear indication of the competent institution is also beneficial for all who wish to enter into contact with the Communities (*e.g.* non-member countries wishing to conclude agreements with Community institutions).

[19] See the resolution of the European Parliament of June 17, 1988 on the democratic deficit in the European Community, [1988] O.J. C187/229. See also the following learned articles: Boest, "Ein langer Weg zur Demokratie in Europa. Die Beteiligungsrechte des Europäischen Parlaments bei Rechtsetzung nach dem Vertrag über die Europäische Union" (1992) EuR. 182–200; Reich, "Le traité sur l'Union européenne et le Parlement européen" (1992) R.M.C.U.E. 287–292; Schockweiler (n.9, *supra*), at 35–44; Zuleeg, "Demokratie in der Europäischen Gemeinschaft" (1993) J.Z. 1069–1074; Classen, "Europäische Integration und demokratische Legitimation" (1994) A.ö.R. 238–260; Raworth, "A Timid Step Forward: Maastricht and the Democratisation of the European Community" (1994) E.L.R. 16–33; Ress, "Democratic Decision-making in the European Union and the Role of the European Parliament", in Curtin and Heukels (eds), *Institutional Dynamics of European Integration. Essays in Honour of Henry G. Schermers*, Vol.II (Martinus Nijhoff, Dordrecht, 1994) at 153–176; Bleckmann, "Das europäische Demokratieprinzip" (2001) J.Z. 53–58.

[20] See also Moravcsik, "In Defence of the 'Democratic Deficit': Reassessing Legitimacy in the European Union" (2002) J.C.M.S. 603–624.

not after consulting the European Parliament—that is to say, in the remaining instances in which legislation is not adopted by co-decision as between the Council and the Parliament -, they do not emanate from a representative assembly but from members of central or regional governments. This practice need not necessarily be undemocratic, provided that members of government are subject to effective parliamentary control. Whether that control takes place at the Union level or at the national level has more to do with the "federal" nature of decision-making than with its democratic content.[21]

It is a fact that, as a minister, each member of the Council is accountable to his or her national parliament. Consequently, decision-making exhibits an absolute democratic deficit only in so far as the Member States themselves do not provide for parliamentary scrutiny of action taken by members of government in the Council.[22] The national legal system can ensure that the national parliament is given the necessary information about the Council's activities and may, possibly, constrain the responsible national minister to comply with the brief given to him or her by the national parliament (see paras 11–006–11–009).

In order to have effective parliamentary control at national level, of course, the position taken by each member of the Council and the way he or she votes must be disclosed (see para. 16–016).[23] Where, however, the Council acts by a majority vote, this form of political control affords no guarantee that every national parliament's view will be reflected in Community acts. It is only where the Council acts unanimously, which by and large it has to do in the case of non-Community forms of policy and co-operation, that ministers may be called to account to their national parliament for every act adopted. Moreover, there is another ground on which national parliamentary control is still defective in vesting democratic legitimacy in Community and non-Community action of the Union. This is that national parliaments have neither a mandate nor the expertise to take account of the common interest in Council decision-making.

Reconciling different concepts of democracy. For those reasons, **16–010** commentators tend to argue that the European Parliament should be given fully-fledged powers to initiate legislation and co decide with the Council. The European Parliament itself urges that the whole decision-making

---

[21] De Smijter (n.15, *supra*), at 45.

[22] This also applies to regional ministers who act in the Council (by agreement) and have to answer to their representative assemblies.

[23] Some argue that openness of Council meetings may result in the real decision-making being carried out in working parties behind closed doors or at informal meetings: Dashwood, "The Role of the Council in the European Union", *Institutional Dynamics of European Integration. Essays in Honour of Henry G. Schermers* (n.19, *supra*), 117, at 132–133. In view of the great importance in practice of the committees which prepare Council meetings, it is at least as relevant to have their deliberations made public, see Van Schendelen, "'De Raad beslist'. Beslist de Raad?" (1995) S.E.W. 706, at 717–718.

process should be based on the dual legitimacy of the directly elected European Parliament—to defend the common interest—and of the Council, whose members are accountable to their national parliaments for the way in which they defend the national position.[24] Where the European Parliament co-decides on legislative measures, those measures reflect the will of a representative assembly at least at Union level, but, in cases involving majority voting on the Council, not necessarily the will of each national parliament.

Whether the European Parliament's involvement confers sufficient democratic legitimacy on decision-making at Union level depends on whether the representation of the people in that body is considered to be representative of European public opinion.[25] Depending on the view taken of the European Parliament, commentators argue for democratising decision-making in the Union either through stricter national parliamentary control or by means of a greater say for the European Parliament. In this way in its judgment of October 12, 1993 (the "*Maastricht-Urteil*"), the German *Bundesverfassungsgericht* (Constitutional Court) held that although, as European integration stands, the European Parliament constitutes a supplementary democratic support for the European Union, the Union still obtains its actual democratic legitimacy from the control which the national parliaments exercise over it.[26] In the view of the European Court of Human Rights, however, the European Parliament, which derives democratic legitimation from the direct elections by universal suffrage, must be seen as reflecting concerns as to "effective political democracy" within the European Union.[27]

16–011 Dual democratic legitimacy. The changes to the decision-making process envisaged by the EU Constitution build on the idea of the dual democratic legitimacy of the Union.[28] In those cases where the Council decides by a qualified majority vote, the ordinary legislative procedure will normally apply and therefore the European Parliament will have a decisive say (see para. 14–030). In those cases where the Council decides by unanimity, the

---

[24] See the resolution of the European Parliament of June 17, 1988 (n.19, *supra*), point 19, and its resolution of June 12, 1997 on the relations between the European Parliament and national parliaments, [1997] O.J. C200/153.

[25] For arguments in favour, see Ress (n.19, *supra*), at 174–175; for arguments against, see Schockweiler (n.9, *supra*), at 41–42. See also Weiler (n.13, *supra*), at 347; von Simson, "Was heisst in einer europäischen Verfassung 'das Volk'?" (1991) EuR. 1–18; De Smijter (n.15, *supra*), at 47–48.

[26] See paras 39–45 of that judgment (for references to the text of the judgment and commentaries, see para. 17–019, *infra*). See also the call for a debate on the role of national parliaments in the European system in Declaration (No.23) on the future of the Union annexed to the Treaty of Nice ([2001] O.J. C80/85).

[27] European Court of Human Rights, judgment of February 18, 1999, *Matthews v UK*, No.24833/94, para. 52.

[28] See Sommermann, "Verfassungsperspektiven für die Demokratie in der erweiterten Europäischen Union: Gefahr der Entdemokratisierung oder Fortentwicklung im Rahmen europäischer Supranationalität?" (2003) D.ö.V. 1009–1017.

ordinary legislative procedure will generally not apply, but the national parliament will be able to exercise control over the position which the national government adopts in the Council. In this connection, the EU Constitution will reinforce the mechanisms which facilitate control by national parliaments over the activities of their respective governments (see para. 11–006). In any event, the national parliaments will be entitled to exercise direct control over compliance with the principle of subsidiarity (see para. 5–035).

Contacts between European and national parliaments. Members of **16–012** national parliaments and MEPs regularly hold meetings on their own initiative to exchange information and ideas, both at national[29] and Community level.[30] Meetings are regularly held of national parliamentary European affairs committees (COSAC).[31] Representatives from the national parliaments and the European Parliament have met to discuss changes in the Union's institutional structure as the "Conference of Parliaments" or "assizes".[32] In order to guarantee the legitimacy and independence of the participating parliaments, such contacts have not been institutionalised.[33]

Other forms of representation. The EC Treaty also gives citizens an **16–013** additional say in decision-making through the institutional representation

---

[29] Thus, Members of the European Parliament meet national colleagues within the domestic party structure and they may be invited to attend meetings of national parliamentary committees. In several Member States, MEPs may take part in the proceedings of the advisory committees on European affairs set up by the national parliament, although generally they may not vote.

[30] The European political parties are based on national parties represented in the national parliaments. See Scoffoni, "Les relations entre le Parlement européen et les parlements nationaux et le renforcement de la légitimité démocratique de la Communauté" (1992) C.D.E. 22–41; Bonnamour, "Les relations entre Parlement européen et Parlements nationaux à la veille de la Conférence intergouvernementale de 1996" (1995) R.M.C.U.E 637–646.

[31] The Conference of European Affairs Committees of the Parliaments of the European Union (COSAC, standing for *Conférence des organes spécialisés en affaires communautaires*), established in Paris on November 16–17, 1989, may examine any legislative text or initiative and may address to the European Parliament, the Council and the Commission any contribution which it deems appropriate on the legislative activities of the Union, notably in relation to the application of the principle of subsidiarity, the area of freedom, security and justice and questions regarding fundamental rights: see Protocol (No.9) to the EU Treaty and the Community Treaties on the role of national parliaments in the European Union ([1997] O.J. C340/113, point 1), points 4–6. Contributions made by COSAC do not bind the national parliaments: *ibid.*, point 7. For COSAC's Rules of Procedure, approved on May 5 and 6, 2003, see [2003] O.J. C235/1. For the European Parliament's delegation to COSAC, see EP Rules of Procedure, r.123.

[32] See Declaration (No. 14) to the EU Treaty on the Conference of Parliaments. Such "assizes" met at Rome on November 27–30, 1990 (1990) 11 EC Bull. point 2.3.1. See also r.124 of the EP Rules of Procedure.

[33] See the resolution of the European Parliament of July 12, 1990 on the preparation of the meeting with the national parliaments to discuss the future of the Community (the "Assizes"), [1990] O.J. C231/165, and Scoffoni (n.30, *supra*), at 39–40.

657

of their interests as members of economic and social groups (European Economic and Social Committee) and of regional and local communities (Committee of the Regions).[34] However, those bodies do not have the same direct legitimacy as parliamentary bodies and merely have an advisory say in the Community's decision-making process (see para. 14–044). Representatives of management and labour (the "social partners") may conclude agreements with each other on which the Community institutions may confer the force of legislation (see para. 14–042). In practice, a variety of interest groups have a critical influence on decision-making as a result of the specific information and expertise with which they provide the Commission at an early stage of the decision-making process (see para. 14–016). Better involvement of various persons and organisations in the framing and execution of Union policy is one of the aims of the Commission's White Paper on European governance.[35]

16–014 Democratic control on implementation. The democratic control which is exerted over the execution of acts adopted within the Union differs depending on the authority responsible for implementation. The implementation of non-Community acts falls in the first place to the national governments and hence is subject to parliamentary supervision in as much as the Member States provide for it. The same is true where the Member States implement Community acts. In this case, however, national parliamentary scrutiny is coupled with supervision by the Commission and—in some instances—the European Parliament's powers of inquiry. The latter system will be extended in the EU Constitution to all fields of action of the Union with the exception of the CFSP.

It is impossible for the national parliaments to scrutinise the quantity of measures which are adopted by the institutions in order to implement acts of the Union. The only effective forum for conducting such scrutiny would seem to be the European Parliament. In view of the limited ability of the European Parliament to supervise the Council, the most democratic procedure is to confer implementing power on the Commission, since it is accountable to the Parliament (see para. 14–060). For that reason, too, independent Community bodies may be given only clearly defined executive tasks which do not detract from the Commission's political accountability (see para. 14–063). The position is different only where the Treaties themselves confer a particular position on a specific body, such as the European Central Bank, for important reasons (see para. 14–066).

---

[34] Lenaerts and De Smijter, "On the Democratic Representation through the European Parliament, the Council, the Committee of the Regions, the Economic and Social Committee and the National Parliaments", in Winter, Curtin, Kellermann and De Witte (eds), *Reforming the Treaty on European Union—The Legal Debate* (T.M.C. Asser Institute/Kluwer, The Hague, 1996) 173–197.

[35] European governance—A White Paper, [2001] O.J. C287/1; Dutheil de la Rochère, "Quelques réflexions à propos du livre blanc de la Commission 'gouvernance européenne' " (2002) R.M.C.U.E. 10–15.

3. Transparency of decision-making

"As open as possible". In order to enable political scrutiny of the Union **16–015** institutions' action to take place, the scrutinizing institutions must be able to have sufficient insight into on-going and proposed administrative activities. Moreover, the democratic character of the institutions and public confidence in the administration is reinforced by having a transparent decision-making process.[36] In a Declaration entitled "A Community close to its citizens", the European Council undertook to open up decision-making so as to make it more transparent and to ensure better-informed public debate on the Community's activities.[37] The Treaty of Amsterdam took this a stage further by declaring that decisions are "taken as openly as possible" in the Union (EU Treaty, Art. 1, second para.). The EU Constitution confirms this objective (see Art. I–50).

Openness of procedure. Most of the steps which the institutions have taken **16–016** since have been designed to bring about greater openness both in the preparation of decisions and during the actual decision-making process.[38] Accordingly, alongside its legislative programme, the Commission now publishes an annual work programme with a view to broader discussions, also in the national parliaments, and enables interest groups affected by a particular proposal to take part more extensively in its preparation.[39] The Council is providing more background information both before and after it adopts measures and may initiate public debate on a particular proposal for legislation.[40] In principle, the results of votes on proposals for legislation are published,[41] as are statements in the minutes of the Council.[42] The Council is however reluctant to publish minutes recording the negotiations

---

[36] See Declaration (No.17) to the EU Treaty on the right of access to information.

[37] Birmingham Declaration (October 16, 1992) A Community close to its citizens (1992) 10 EC Bull. point I.8.

[38] For a critical discussion, see Curtin and Meijers, "The Principle of Open Government in Schengen and the European Union: Democratic Retrogression?" (1995) C.M.L.R. 391–442. See also Blanchet, "Le Traité d'Amsterdam. Transparence et qualité de la législation" (1997) R.T.D.E. 915–928.

[39] See the communication on increased transparency in the work of the Commission ([1993] O.J. C63/8) and the communication of June 2, 1993 to the Council, the Parliament and the Economic and Social Committee: Openness in the Community, [1993] O.J. C166/4. See the discussion of the right of initiative in para. 14–016, *supra*.

[40] Transparency—Implementation of the Birmingham declaration, Annex 3 to Part A of the Conclusions of the European Council held in Edinburgh on December 11 and 12, 1992 (1992) 12 EC Bull. point I.24, as developed in the Council's Rules of Procedure (para. 10–043, *supra*).

[41] For the amendments of December 6, 1993 to the Council's Rules of Procedure and the consequent publication of votes, see para. 10–043, *supra*. For public access to documents, see Annex II to the Council's Rules of Procedure ([2002] O.J. L230/21).

[42] See the Council Code of Conduct of October 2, 1995 on public access to the minutes and statements in the minutes of the Council acting as legislator ((1995) 10 EU Bull. point 1.9.1) and the comments made thereon by the European Parliament in its resolution of October 12, 1995 on the transparency of Council decisions and the Community's legislative procedures ([1995] O.J. C287/179).

in the Council, since a majority of Member States take the view that confidentiality is necessary in order to be able to reach compromises.[43] Neither are documents disclosed relating to the deliberations of the committees which do the preparatory work for Council meetings.[44] For the same reasons, there is no obligation to disclose the proceedings of inter-governmental conferences on amendments of the Treaties.[45] In contrast, the Convention set up in 2002 to consider the future of the Union met in complete openness. The EU Constitution will require the European Parliament to "meet in public, as shall the Council when considering and voting on a draft legislative act" (Arts I–24(6) and I–50(2); see also para. 10–054). It remains to be seen whether this will result in obligations above and beyond those which the Council imposes on itself at present.

16–017 Access to information. The largest possible access for citizens to information strengthens the democratic character of the institutions and the public's trust in the administration.[46] Transparency of decision-making should therefore be coupled with easy public access to policy documents (see paras 10–159–10–161).

4. Easier access to legislation

16–018 Access to legislation. In order to make it easier to find Community legislation, the European Council proposes to undertake official codification or unofficial consolidation of legislation at an earlier stage and to improve computerised data bases.[47] Access may be had *via* the Internet to a variety of documents of the Community institutions and bodies and to data bases.[48] On December 20, 1994, the European Parliament, the Council and the Commission agreed on an accelerated working method for codifying legislative texts without altering their substantive content.[49]

---

[43] See the Council's Code of Conduct of October 2, 1995, *ibid.* (in which the Council states that it is committed to "endeavouring to incorporate the content of . . . statements [in the minutes] in the legislative act itself"); see also the Council's position in CFI, Case T–194/94 *Carvel and Guardian Newspapers v Council* [1995] E.C.R. II–2765, para. 52. For the restricted openness to the public of Council meetings, see para. 10–043, *supra;* for the disclosure of internal documents, see para. 10–160, *supra.*

[44] See also n.23.

[45] See Curtin, "The Constitutional Structure of the Union: A Europe of Bits and Pieces" (1993) C.M.L.R. 17, at 18.

[46] CFI, Case T–174/95 *Svenksa Journalistförbundet v Council* [1998] E.C.R. II–2289, para. 66.

[47] Transparency—Implementation of the Birmingham declaration (n.40, *supra*), point I.29.

[48] See the introduction to the source material.

[49] Interinstitutional Agreement of December 20, 1994, [1996] O.J. C102/2 (see also [1995] O.J. C43/42). In an interpretative declaration, the European Parliament has stated that, where there was an amendment either to the legal basis or to the procedure for adopting the text in question, it would have to reserve its view as to whether the codification was desirable (see the resolution of January 18, 1995, [1995] O.J. C43/41). See Dragone, "La codification communautaire: technique et procédures" (1998) 1 R.M.U.E. 77–94. See further the interinstitutional agreement between the European Parliament, the Council and the Commission of November 28, 2001 on a more structured use of the recasting technique for legal acts, [2002] O.J. C77/1.

Simplifying legislation. On the substantive side, access to Community acts **16–019** would undoubtedly be improved if they were classified in a more transparent manner. Accordingly, it was long proposed that acts should be classified either as "legislative" acts or as, more detailed, subordinate "implementing measures"—a proposal which has now been taken up in the EU Constitution (see para. 17–145). Further, there will always—and rightly—be a plea for simpler, clearer legislation.[50] In December 1998, the European Parliament, the Council and the Commission adopted guidelines for improving the drafting quality of Community legislation.[51] In December 2003, those institutions concluded a new agreement on better law-making which contains not only agreements on the co-ordination of the legislative process and on the use of alternative modes of regulation, but also commitments with regard to improving the quality of legislation, simplifying it and reducing its volume.[52] Lastly, in order to improve the accessibility of the Treaties, the Treaty of Amsterdam simplified the texts and renumbered the articles of the EU Treaty and the EC Treaty (see para. 3–021).

---

[50] See, for instance, the European Council in its declaration "Transparency—Implementation of the Birmingham declaration", Annex 3 to Part A of the Conclusions of the European Council held in Edinburgh on December 11 and 12, 1992 (1992) 12 EC Bull., point I.28.

[51] Interinstitutional Agreement of December 22, 1998 on common guidelines for the quality of drafting of Community legislation ([1999] O.J. C73/1), giving effect to Declaration (No.39), annexed to the Amsterdam Treaty, on the quality of the drafting of Community legislation ([1997] O.J. C340/139). See De Wilde, "Deficient European Legislation is in Nobody's Interest" (2000) E.J.L.R 293–319 and "Gebrekkige Europese regelgeving kent alleen maar verliezers—Het interinstitutioneel akkord van 1998: geen eindstation maar eerste tussenstation op weg naar verbetering Europese regelgeving" (2000) S.E.W. 401–413; Xanthaki, "The Problem of Quality in EU Legislation: What on Earth is Really Wrong?" (2001) C.M.L.R. 651–676. See also the Council Resolution of June 8, 1993 on the quality of drafting of Community legislation, [1993] O.J. C166/1, and Timmermans, "How Can One Improve the Quality of Community Legislation" (1997) C.M.L.R. 1229–1257. A possible instrument for improving quality has been suggested by Van Damme, "Naar een Europese Raad van State?" (2001) T.B.P. 519–523.

[52] Interinstitutional Agreement of December 16, 2003 on better law-making, [2003] O.J. C321/1. Pursuant to the principles of subsidiarity and proportionality, the Commission has also undertaken to simplify existing Community legislation: para. 5–033, *supra*. On the (limited) impact of the EU Constitution on the simplification of legislation, see Sandström, "Knocking EU Law into Shape" (2003) C.M.L.R. 1307–1313.

Part V

SOURCES OF LAW OF THE EUROPEAN UNION

CHAPTER 17

COMMUNITY LAW

I. FORMS OF COMMUNITY LAW

Community law. "Community law" encompasses the rules enshrined in the **17–001** Community Treaties and acts adopted pursuant thereto, as applied and interpreted by the national courts and the Court of Justice. The majority of those acts take the form of specific instruments of Community law (see, *inter alia*, Art. 249 of the EC Treaty). In addition, there are international agreements concluded by the Community.

Depending on the origin of the provisions, a distinction may be made between constitutive norms which come into being as a result of action on the part of the Member States themselves (primary Community law), rules created by Community institutions and bodies (secondary or "derived" Community law) and other rules which have been accepted by case law as being general principles of the Community's legal order.

Community law will become "Union law" when the EU Constitution replaces the EC Treaty and the distinction between Community and non-Community action of the Union will no longer exist (see para. 18–002, *infra*). When that happens, the Constitution will be the main source of "primary" or "constitutional" Union law. Secondary or "derived" Union law will then consist of the legislative and other acts of the Union. Under the Constitution, those acts will be categorised and designated differently (see para. 17–145, *infra*). The other sources of Community law will continue to exist as sources of Union law.

II. EFFECT IN THE NATIONAL LEGAL SYSTEMS

Principles. The status of Community law in the national legal systems is a **17–002** matter of Community law itself.[1] This means that Community law differs from the classical rule of international law that a State itself determines, apart from the limitations to which it expressly commits itself, the status of international commitments in its legal system. The case law of the Court of Justice relating to the primacy and the possible direct effect of Community law has made it clear that Community law *as such* has effect in the national

---

[1] ECJ, Case 26/62 *Van Gend & Loos* [1963] E.C.R. 1, at 10–12.

legal system. Both the Community and individuals are entitled to enforce the proper application of Community law. On the ground of the need to secure the full effect of Community law, the Court of Justice has developed in its case law other requirements with which the national legal order must comply in order to secure the primacy of Community law in practice.[2] After the EU Constitution has been adopted, those requirements will in principle apply to all forms of Union law. The Constitution will expressly provide that "[t]he Constitution and law adopted by the institutions of the Union in exercising competences conferred on it, shall have primacy over the law of the Member States" (Art. I–6).

A. THE PRINCIPLES OF THE PRIMACY AND FULL EFFECTIVENESS OF COMMUNITY LAW

1. Formulation on the basis of Community law

a. The principle of the primacy of Community law

17–003 **Primary and secondary Community law.** In its 1964 judgment in *Costa v ENEL* the Court of Justice first articulated the principle that Community law takes precedence over the domestic law of the Member States. The Court held that "the law stemming from the Treaty, an independent source of law, could not, because of its special and original nature, be overridden by domestic provisions, however framed, without being deprived of its character as Community law and without the legal basis of the Community itself being called into question".[3] The Court derived the primacy of Community law from the specific nature of the Community legal order, referring to the danger that, if the effect of Community law could vary from Member State to Member State in deference to subsequent national laws, this would be liable to jeopardise the attainment of the objectives set out in Art. 10 of the EC Treaty and give rise to discrimination prohibited by Art. 12 (see para. 1–019). The case was concerned with the primacy of a number of provisions of primary Community law. The Court subsequently also upheld the primacy of secondary Community law on the same grounds.[4]

17–004 **Precedence over any rule of national law.** As long ago as *Costa v ENEL*, the Court held that Community law could not be overridden by "domestic legal provisions, however framed".[5] Consequently, Community law takes

---

[2] In addition, the Member States are under a duty to take all necessary measures to implement provisions of Community law; see para. 14–047, *supra*.

[3] ECJ, Case 6/64 *Costa v ENEL* [1964] E.C.R. 585, at 594; for the further development of the primacy of Community law, see De Witte, "Le retour à *Costa*. La primauté du droit communautaire à la lumière du droit international" (1984) R.T.D.E. 425–454; Beljin, "Die Zusammenhänge zwischen dem Vorrang, den Instituten der innerstaatlichen Beachtlichkeit und der Durchführung des Gemeinschaftsrechts" (2002) EuR. 351–376.

[4] ECJ, Case 14/68 *Wilhelm* [1969] E.C.R. 1, para. 6; ECJ, Case 11/70 *Internationale Handelsgesellschaft* [1970] E.C.R. 1125, para. 3; ECJ, Case 249/85 *Albako* [1987] E.C.R. 2345, para. 14.

[5] ECJ, Case 6/64 *Costa v ENEL* [1964] E.C.R. 585, at 594.

precedence over any rule of domestic law, including "principles of a national constitutional structure".[6] This is because important principles which are common to the constitutional traditions of the Member States are subscribed to by the Community itself, notably respect for democracy (see paras 15–011 *et seq.*) and fundamental rights (see paras 17–063 *et seq.*).[7]

Conflict. The primacy of Community law signifies that national legal rules **17–005** must give way to conflicting provisions of Community law. In order to determine whether such a conflict exists, the aim and purpose of the Community provision must be assessed in the light of what it contains and what—deliberately or not—it does not contain. The national provision continues to be effective solely for those aspects which the Community provision has left unaffected.[8] Often the question arises as to how far a Community act allows the Member States to adopt measures with regard to partial aspects not dealt with in the Community act. In such case, it must be inferred from the aims and purpose of the Community act whether that act governs the area exhaustively or whether it still leaves some latitude for regulation by Member States. A matter not dealt with by the Community provision may be regulated by the Member States provided that they do not thereby undermine the aims and objects of the Community provision.[9] In the same way, it has to be determined whether a Community harmonisation measure allows Member States to impose obligations stricter than those provided for by the Community measure (see para. 5–208). In some fields, action by the Community may preclude any competence on the part of the Member States (see para. 5–023).

b. The principle of interpretation in conformity with Community law

Avoiding conflict. The primacy of Community law is a conflict rule which **17–006** applies where a legal relationship is governed by conflicting national and Community rules. Where the application of a national rule is likely to result

---

[6] ECJ, Case 11/70 *Internationale Handelsgesellschaft* [1970] E.C.R. 1125, para. 3 (which referred in particular to "fundamental rights as formulated by the constitution of [the] State", but see Community protection of fundamental rights: para. 17–063 *et seq., infra*). An example may be found in ECJ, Case C–285/98 Kreil [2000] E.C.R. I–69 (see n.253 to para. 5–063). See also ECJ, Case 30/72 *Commission v Italy* [1973] E.C.R. 161, para. 11 (precedence over "budgetary legislation or practice").

[7] For further details, see De Witte, "Community Law and National Constitutional Values" (1991) 2 L.I.E.I. 1–22.

[8] For examples in the case law, see in particular ECJ, Case 40/69 *Hauptzollamt Hamburg v Bollmann* [1970] 69, paras 4–5; ECJ, Case 50/76 *Amsterdam Bulb* [1977] E.C.R. 137, paras 9–30; ECJ, Case 111/76 *Van den Hazel* [1977] E.C.R. 901, paras 13–27; ECJ, Case 255/86 *Commission v Belgium* [1988] E.C.R. 693, paras 8–11; ECJ, Case 60/86 *Commission v UK* [1988] E.C.R. 3921, para. 11; ECJ, Case 190/87 *Moorman* [1988] E.C.R. 4689, paras 11–13.

[9] ECJ, Case C–355/00 *Freskot AE* [2003] E.C.R. I–5263, paras 18–33; ECJ (judgment of November 20, 2003), Case C–416/01 *ACOR*, not yet reported, paras 21–62.

in a conflict with a Community rule, it must first be determined whether the rules cannot be interpreted and applied in such a way as to avoid a conflict. Naturally, the Community rule must be interpreted in a uniform way in all Member States. As far as the interpretation of national law is concerned, the Court of Justice considers that Art. 10 of the EC Treaty places all public authorities, and therefore also judicial authorities, under a duty to interpret the national law which they have to apply as far as possible in conformity with the requirements of Community law.[10] The court must therefore consider whether national law (legislation and case law[11]) can be interpreted or applied in such a way that there is no conflict with Community law. This applies to all rules of Community law, including fundamental rights, general principles of Community law and rules of international law which are applicable in Community law.[12] Where national law is interpreted in conformity with the provisions of a directive, this practice is referred to as interpretation consistent with a directive (see para. 17–131). This duty to interpret national law in conformity with Community law is, however, limited by general principles of Community law, such as the principle of legal certainty, the principle of legality and the prohibition of retroactivity.[13] Interpreting national law in conformity with Community law may enable public authorities to avoid situations in which national rules have to be set aside on account of a conflict with Community law.[14]

c. Duty to set aside conflicting national rules

17–007 **Inapplicability of conflicting national rules.** In the 1978 judgment in *Simmenthal* ("*Simmenthal II*"), the Court of Justice held that "in accordance with the principle of the precedence of Community law, the relationship between provisions of the Treaty and directly applicable measures of the institutions on the one hand and the national law of the Member States on the other is such that those provisions and measures not only by their entry into force render automatically inapplicable any conflicting provision of current national law but—in so far as they are an integral part of, and take precedence in, the legal order applicable in the

---

[10] See ECJ, Case C–106/98 *Marleasing* [1990] E.C.R. I–4135, para. 8; ECJ, Case C–262/97 *Engelbrecht* [2000] E.C.R. I–7321, para. 39; ECJ (judgment of January 7, 2004), Case C–60/02 *Criminal proceedings against X*, not yet reported, paras 59–60 (para. 5–051, *supra*).

[11] See ECJ, Case C–456/98 *Centrosteel* [1998] E.C.R. I–6007, paras 16–17.

[12] For the interpretation and application of national law in the light of fundamental rights, see paras 17–077–17–078, *infra*); for the interpretation and application of national law in the light of rules of international law, see paras 17–092 and 17–095, *infra*).

[13] ECJ (judgment of January 7, 2004), Case C–60/02 *Criminal proceedings against X*, not yet reported, paras 61–63. See para. 17–119, *infra* (on regulations) and para. 17–131, *infra* (on directives).

[14] Interpretation in conformity with Community law also makes the question of the direct effect of Community law unnecessary (*i.e.* "can the provision of Community law be relied upon by the person seeking redress?"). See Betlem, "The Doctrine of Consistent Interpretation—Managing Legal Uncertainty" (2002) Oxford Journal of Legal Studies 397–418.

territory of each of the Member States—also preclude the valid adoption of new national legislative measures to the extent to which they would be incompatible with Community law".[15] Consequently, Member States are under a duty not only to avoid adopting a measure conflicting with Community law and to change any existing conflicting measure,[16] but also—so long as the offending measure has not been amended—to refrain from applying it.[17] In the judgment in *Simmenthal II*, the Court of Justice held that:

"every national court must, in a case within its jurisdiction, apply Community law in its entirety and protect rights which the latter confers on individuals and must accordingly set aside any provision of national law which may conflict with it, whether prior or subsequent to the Community rule".[18]

The duty to set aside conflicting rules applies not only to national courts, but also to public bodies, including administrative bodies.[19] In order to comply with that duty, inferior administrative authorities, such as local authorities, must refrain of their own motion from applying provisions adopted by a higher authority in breach of Community law.[20] Likewise, national authorities may not apply provisions of agreements concluded between Member States if they conflict with Community law.[21] A national measure will not only be inapplicable if it is substantively incompatible with a provision of Community law, but it may also be inapplicable if it was adopted contrary to a procedure laid down by Community law.[22] The incompatibility of national legislation with Community provisions can be

---

[15] ECJ, Case 106/77 *Simmenthal* [1978] E.C.R. 629, para. 17.

[16] See also ECJ, Case 159/78 *Commission v Italy* [1979] E.C.R. 3247, para. 22.

[17] See ECJ, Case 48/71 *Commission v Italy* [1972] E.C.R. 529, paras 6–8. *A fortiori*, a Member State is debarred from adopting specific measures to extend a provision found to be contrary to Community law: ECJ, Case C–101/91 *Commission v Italy* [1993] E.C.R. I–191, paras 22–23.

[18] ECJ, Case 106/77 *Simmenthal* ("*Simmenthal II*") [1978] E.C.R. 629, para. 21. See also ECJ, Case 249/85 *Albako* [1987] E.C.R. 2345, para. 17; ECJ, Case C–262/97 *Engelbrecht* [2000] E.C.R. I–7321, para. 40. For directives, see also para. 17–117.

[19] ECJ, Case 103/88 *Fratelli Costanzo* [1989] E.C.R. 1839, para. 31. See, *e.g.* national competition authorities; para. 5–195, *supra*).

[20] ECJ, Case 103/88 *Fratelli Costanzo* [1989] E.C.R. 1839, para. 31.

[21] ECJ, Case C–469/00 *Ravil* [2003] E.C.R. I–5053, para. 37.

[22] ECJ, Case C–194/94 *CIA Security International* [1996] E.C.R. I–2201, paras 45–54; ECJ, Case C–443/98 *Unilever Italia* [2000] E.C.R. I–7535, paras 31–52; ECJ, Case C–159/00 *Sapod Audic* [2002] E.C.R. I–5031, paras 48–52 (concerning Council Directive 83/189/EEC of March 28, 1983; see para. 5–212, *supra*); Candela Castillo, "La confirmation par la Cour du principe de non-opposabilité aux tiers des règles techniques non notifiées dans le cadre de la directive 83/189/CEE: un pas en avant vers l'intégration structurelle des ordres juridiques nationaux et communautaire" (1997) R.M.C.U.E. 51–59; Voinot, "Le droit communautaire et l'inopposabilité aux particuliers des règles techniques nationales" (2003) R.T.D.E. 91–112. A technical provision which has not been notified to the Commission will be inapplicable only if it constitutes a barrier to trade: ECJ, Case C–226/97 *Lemmens* [1998] E.C.R. I–3711, para. 35.

definitively remedied only by means of national provisions that are binding and have the same legal force as those that have to be modified.[23]

17–008 Simmenthal. In *Simmenthal II* the Court of Justice was seised of a question referred to it for a preliminary ruling by an Italian court, which, after obtaining a preliminary ruling on an earlier question,[24] had held that the imposition of certain inspection fees was incompatible with Community law and had therefore ordered the Italian tax authorities to repay them. The tax authorities appealed, relying on case law of the Italian Constitutional Court to the effect that a national law which conflicted with Community law was also incompatible with the Italian Constitution. On this view, the national court could not set aside the law in question until such time as it had been declared unlawful by the Constitutional Court. The Court of Justice ruled that:

> "a national court which is called upon, within the limits of its jurisdiction, to apply provisions of Community law is under a duty to give full effect to those provisions, if necessary refusing of its own motion to apply any conflicting provision of national legislation, even if adopted subsequently, and it is not necessary for the court to request or await the prior setting aside of such provisions by legislative or constitutional means".[25]

17–009 Factortame. The Court of Justice went even further in the 1990 judgment in *Factortame I*, in which the House of Lords asked whether an English court had the power under Community law to grant an interim injunction against the Crown where a party claimed to be entitled to rights under Community law.[26] The problem had arisen after the Divisional Court of the Queen's Bench Division had applied to the Court of Justice for a preliminary ruling on the compatibility with Community law of nationality requirements imposed by the 1988 Merchant Shipping Act and the 1988 Merchant Shipping (Registration of Fishing Vessels) Regulations in order to put an end to the practice of "quota hopping" by which foreign vessels without any genuine link with the United Kingdom were using its fishing quotas. The House of Lords had to decide whether that court could suspend the relevant part of the 1988 Act and the 1988 Regulations by way of interim relief, the Court of Appeal having determined that under common law the courts had no power to suspend the application of Acts of Parliament in that way. Starting out from its judgment in *Simmenthal II* and the principle of co-operation enshrined in Art. 10 of the EC Treaty, the Court of Justice ruled that:

---

[23] See ECJ, Case-145/99 *Commission v Italy* [2002] E.C.R. I–2235, paras 37–39.
[24] ECJ, Case 35/76 *Simmenthal ("Simmenthal I")* [1976] E.C.R. 1871.
[25] ECJ, Case 106/77 *Simmenthal* [1978] E.C.R. 629, para. 24.
[26] ECJ, Case C–213/89 *Factortame ("Factortame I")* [1990] E.C.R. I–2433, paras 14–15.

"the full effectiveness of Community law would be impaired if a rule of national law could prevent a court seised of a dispute governed by Community law from granting interim relief in order to ensure the full effectiveness of the judgment to be given on the existence of the rights claimed under Community law. It follows that a court which in those circumstances would grant interim relief, if it were not for a rule of national law, is obliged to set aside that rule".[27]

By so ruling, the Court safeguarded rights derived by individuals from Community law against action of a public authority, even where it had not been finally determined that the action in question was incompatible with Community law.[28]

Full effectiveness. In the judgments in *Simmenthal II* and *Factortame I*, the **17–010** Court of Justice linked the primacy of Community law with the duty of the national court to secure the full effectiveness (*effet utile*) of Community law, even at the expense of the legal tradition of its own Member State. Just as the primacy principle was associated with Art. 10 of the EC Treaty in *Costa v ENEL*, that duty on the part of the national court was also derived from the principle of co-operation in good faith enshrined in that article (see para. 5–054). Over time, the Court of Justice has gradually specified more precisely the requirements which Art. 10 of the EC Treaty imposes on Member States with a view to securing the "full effectiveness" in the national legal system of rights derived from Community law.[29]

---

[27] *ibid.*, para. 21. On October 11, 1990, the House of Lords affirmed the interlocutory injunction against the Secretary of State. See Barav and Simon, "Le droit communautaire et la suspension provisoire des mesures nationales—Les enjeux de l'affaire *Factortame*" (1990) R.M.C. 591–597.

[28] That the UK legislation was indeed incompatible with Community law was only determined following the Court's judgment giving a preliminary ruling on questions which had already been referred in ECJ, Case C–221/89 *Factortame* ("*Factortame II*") [1991] E.C.R. I–3905 and the judgment given on an action brought by the Commission under Art. 226 of the EC Treaty, ECJ, Case C–246/89 *Commission v UK* [1991] E.C.R. I–4585. In the latter case, the President of the Court had already granted an application from the Commission for an interim order requiring the UK to suspend the nationality requirements of the legislation at issue: ECJ (order of the President of October 10, 1989), Case C–246/89 R *Commission v UK* [1989] E.C.R. I–3125. This was followed by the case concerning State liability for the breach of Community law: ECJ, Joined Cases C–46/93 and C–48/93 *Brasserie du Pêcheur and Factortame* ("*Factortame IV*") [1996] E.C.R. I–1029 (para. 17–012, *infra*).

[29] The relevant case law is only discussed in outline in the following sections. For a more exhaustive discussion, see Lenaerts and Arts, *Procedural Law of the European Union*, Ch.3. cf. Delicostopoulos, "Towards European Procedural Primacy in National Legal Systems" (2003) E.L.J. 599–613; Temple Lang, "The Duties of National Courts under Community Constitutional Law" (1997) E.L.R. 3–18; Bebr, "Court of Justice: Judicial Protection and the Rule of Law", in Curtin and Heukels (eds), *Institutional Dynamics of European Integration. Essays in Honour of Henry G. Schermers*, Vol.II (Martinus Nijhoff, Dordrecht, 1994), at 303–333; Fitzpatrick and Szyszczak, "Remedies and Effective Judicial Protection in Community Law" (1994) M.L.R. 434–441; Snyder, "The Effectiveness of European Community Law: Institutions, Processes, Tools and Techniques" (1993) M.L.R. 19, at 40–47; Steiner, "From Direct Effects to Francovich: Shifting Means of Enforcement of Community Law" (1993) E.L.R. 3–22.

17–011 Remedies under national law. In the first place, Community law requires that the national rules governing claims by which an individual seeks to enforce his or her Community rights "must not be less favourable than those relating to similar domestic claims" (principle of equality) and must not embody requirements and time-limits "such as in practice to make it impossible or excessively difficult" to exercise those rights (principle of effectiveness).[30] It appears from *Factortame I* and a number of other judgments that the national court must, where necessary, refrain from applying the normal national legal rules in order to secure the full effectiveness of Community law.[31] As far as national procedural rules are concerned, account must be taken of their role in the procedure, its progress and its special features, viewed as a whole, before the various national instances, and of the basic principles of the domestic judicial system, such as protection of the rights of the defence, the principle of legal certainty and the proper conduct of procedure. Accordingly, national courts

---

[30] ECJ, Case 33/76 *Rewe* [1976] E.C.R. 1989, para. 5, and ECJ, Case 45/76 *Comet* [1976] E.C.R. 2043, paras 13–16; see also ECJ, Case 68/79 *Just* [1980] E.C.R. 501, paras 25–26; ECJ, Case 199/82 *San Giorgio* [1983] E.C.R. 3595, paras 12–17. See Girerd, "Les principes d'équivalence et d'effectivité: encadrement ou désencadrement de l'autonomie procédurale des Etats membres?" (2000) R.T.D.E. 75–102.

[31] See, *e.g.* ECJ, Case C–377/89 *Cotter and McDermott* [1991] E.C.R. I–1155, paras 20–22 and 26–27 (married women held entitled to benefits/compensatory payments paid to married men in respect of a spouse deemed to be dependent even though this was contrary to a prohibition of unlawful enrichment laid down by Irish law); ECJ, Case C–208/90 *Emmott* [1991] E.C.R. I–4269, paras 23–24 (Irish authorities held not entitled to rely on procedural rules relating to time-limits for bringing proceedings in an action brought against them by an individual in order to protect rights directly conferred upon him by a Community directive so long as Ireland had not properly transposed the directive into national law); ECJ, Case C–271/91 *Marshall v Southampton and South West Hampshire Area Health Authority ("Marshall II")* [1993] E.C.R. I–4367, paras 30 and 34–35 (Ms Marshall had succeeded in her claim for unlawful sex discrimination under the equal treatment directive following ECJ, Case 152/84 *Marshall v Southampton and South West Area Health Authority ("Marshall I")* [1986] E.C.R. 723; the Court held that the limit imposed on any damages claim which might be awarded by an Industrial Tribunal under the 1975 Sex Discrimination Act was unlawful), see the note by Curtin (1994) C.M.L.R. 631–652; ECJ, Case C–188/95 *Fantask* [1997] E.C.R. I–6783, paras 35–41 (concerning the claim that the recovery of charges levied contrary to a directive may be precluded on account of excusable error); ECJ, Case C–246/96 *Magorrian and Cunningham* [1997] E.C.R. I–7153, paras 36–47, and ECJ, Case C–326/96 *Levez v Jennings* [1998] E.C.R. I–7835, paras 18–33 (limitation of a claim based on Art. 141 to a period starting to run from a point in time two years prior to the commencement of proceedings); ECJ, Case C–62/00 *Marks & Spencer* [2002] E.C.R. I–6325, paras 33–47 (concerning national legislation retroactively curtailing the period within which repayment may be sought of sums collected in breach of the relevant directive); ECJ (judgment of October 2, 2003), Case C–147/01 *Weber's Wine World*, not yet reported, paras 86–92 (a retroactive restriction on the right to repayment of duty levied but not due was contrary to Art. 10 of the EC Treaty where that restriction specifically related to a duty which the Court of Justice held to be contrary to Community law). But see ECJ, Case C–338/91 *Steenhorst-Neerings* [1993] E.C.R. I–5475, para. 24, and ECJ, Case C–410/92 *Johnson* [1994] E.C.R. I–5483, paras 22–23, with a case note by Docksey (1995) C.M.L.R. 1447–1459 (where a rule of general application limiting the period for which arrears of social security benefits could be claimed was held not to be unlawful), see Szyszczak, "Making Europe More Relevant to its Citizens: Effective Judicial Process" (1996) E.L.R. 351–377; Hoskins, "Tilting the Balance: Supremacy and National Procedural Rules" (1996) E.L.R. 365–377. See also para. 17–014, *infra*.

are not required to raise of their own motion an issue concerning the breach of provisions of Community law where examination of that issue would oblige them to abandon the passive role assigned to them by going beyond the ambit of the dispute defined by the parties themselves and relying on facts and circumstances other than those on which the party with an interest in application of those provisions bases his or her claim.[32] However, where, pursuant to national law, a court may raise of its own motion pleas in law based on a binding national rule which were not put forward by the parties, it must examine of its own motion whether the national legislative or administrative authorities implementing a directive remained within the limits of their discretion.[33] In principle, Community law does not involve itself in the resolution of questions of jurisdiction to which the classification of legal situations based on Community law may give rise in the national judicial system. However, where a directive imposes an obligation to establish a suitable right of appeal and only a national jurisdictional rule prevents the national court from protecting the rights ensuing from the directive, the national court must disapply that rule.[34] Administrative bodies, too, must disapply conflicting procedural rules in order to give full effect to Community law.[35]

On the other hand, Community law does not preclude a national court from suspending enforcement of a national administrative measure adopted to implement a Community regulation which is alleged to be unlawful, provided that certain conditions laid down by Community law are satisfied, so as to ensure the uniform application of that law.[36]

---

[32] ECJ, Joined Cases C–430/93 and C–431/93 *Van Schijndel and Van Veen* [1995] E.C.R. I–4705, paras 19–22; *cf.* the judgment of the same date in ECJ, Case C–312/93 *Peterbroeck* [1995] E.C.R. I–4599, paras 14–21 (where it was held that the national court's refusal to entertain pleas not already raised before the tax authorities was contrary to Community law); see case notes by Heukels (1996) C.M.L.R. 337–353 and Pertegás Sender (1995/96) Col.J.E.L. 179–185; see also Prechal, "Community Law in National Courts: The Lessons from *Van Schijndel*" (1998) C.M.L.R. 681–706.

[33] ECJ, Case C–72/95 *Kraaijeveld* [1996] E.C.R. I–5403, para. 60. See also ECJ, Case C–126/97 *Eco Swiss China Time* [1999] E.C.R. I–3055, paras 31–34 (where a national court is required to grant an application for annulment of an arbitration award founded on failure to observe national rules of public policy, it must also do so if it considers that the award in question is contrary to Art. 81 of the EC Treaty). See Weyer, "Gemeinschaftsrechtliche Vorgaben für das nationale Zivilverfahren" (2000) EuR. 145–166; De Muynck, "De openbare orde en het mededingingsrecht" (2001) N.T.E.R. 253–257. For situations in which a directive obliges the court to apply Community law of its own motion, see ECJ, Joined Cases C–240/98 and C–244/98 *Océano Grupo Editorial* [2000] E.C.R. I–4941, paras 21–29; ECJ, Case C–473/00 *Cofidis* [2002] E.C.R. I–10875, paras 32–38.

[34] ECJ, Case C–462/99 *Connect Austria Gesellschaft für Telekommunikation* [2003] E.C.R. I–5197, paras 35–42.

[35] ECJ, Case C–118/00 *Larsy* [2001] E.C.R. I–5063, paras 50–53.

[36] ECJ, Joined Cases C–143/88 and C–92/89 *Zuckerfabrik Süderdithmarschen and Zuckerfabrik Soest* [1991] E.C.R. I–415, paras 14–33. Broadly, those conditions are: (1) the national court must entertain serious doubts as to the validity of the measure; (2) if the question of its validity has not already been brought before the Court of Justice, the national court should refer a question for a preliminary ruling; (3) there must be urgency and a threat of serious and irreparable damage to the applicant; and (4) the national court must take due account of the Community's interest. See the other decided cases discussed in Lenaerts and Arts, *Procedural Law of the European Union*, Ch.3.

d. Liability of the Member State for damage arising out a breach of Community law

17–012 *Francovich.* Pursuant to the principle of co-operation in good faith enshrined in Art. 10 of the EC Treaty, the Member States are required to nullify the unlawful consequences of a breach of Community law.[37] Such an obligation is owed, within the sphere of its competence, by every organ of the Member State concerned.[38] The Court of Justice has further held in *Francovich* that:

> "[t]he full effectiveness of Community rules would be impaired and the protection of the rights which they grant would be weakened if individuals were unable to obtain redress when their rights are infringed by a breach of Community law for which a Member State can be held responsible".[39]

The Court went on to state that "the principle whereby a State must be liable for loss and damage caused to individuals as a result of breaches of Community law for which the State can be held responsible is inherent in the system of the Treaty" and that a further basis for the obligation of Member States to make good such loss and damage is to be found in Art. 10 of the EC Treaty.[40] In *Factortame IV*, the Court of Justice made it clear that the right of reparation exists whether or not the relevant provision of Community law has direct effect.[41] What is more, the principle of State liability for loss and damage caused to individuals as a result of breaches of

---

[37] ECJ, Joined Cases C–6/90 and C–9/90 *Francovich* [1991] E.C.R. I–5357, para. 36; see earlier with regard to the corresponding provision of Art. 86 of the ECSC Treaty: ECJ, Case 6/60 *Humblet* [1960] E.C.R. 559, at 569. Accordingly, the national court must determine, for example, whether consent granted unlawfully may be revoked or suspended: ECJ (judgment of January 7, 2004), Case C–201/02 *Wells*, not yet reported, paras 64–70.

[38] Case C–8/88 *Germany v Commission* [1990] E.C.R. I–2321, para. 13; ECJ (judgment of January 7, 2004), Case C–201/02 *Wells*, not yet reported, para. 64.

[39] ECJ, Joined Cases C–6/90 and C–9/90 *Francovich* [1991] E.C.R. I–5357, para. 33. The principle is therefore intended both to protect the rights of individuals and to maintain the primacy of Community law; see Aboudrar-Ravanel, "Responsabilité et primauté, ou la question de l'efficience de l'outil" (1999) R.M.C.U.E. 544–558. Among numerous studies, see Schockweiler, "Die Hafting der EG-Mitgliedstaaten gegenüber dem einzelnen bei Verletzung des Gemeinschaftsrechts" (1993) EuR. 107–133; Van Gerven, "Bridging the Unbridgeable: Community and National Tort Laws after *Francovich* and *Brasserie*" (1996) I.C.LQ. 507–544; Wissink, "De Nederlandse rechter en overheidsaansprakelijkheid krachtens *Francovich* en *Brasserie du Pêcheur*" (1997) S.E.W. 78–90; Dantonel-Cor, "La violation de la norme communautaire et la responsabilité extracontractuelle de l'Etat" (1998) R.T.D.E. 75–91; Tridimas, "Liability for Breach of Community Law: Growing Up and Mellowing Down?" (2001) C.M.L.R. 301–332. Some commentators consider that Community law also puts individuals under a duty to make good damage resulting from a breach of Community law; see Kremer, "Die Haftung Privater für Verstösse gegen Gemeinschaftsrecht" (2003) EuR. 696–705. This is true of competition law; see para. 5–197.

[40] ECJ, Joined Cases C–6/90 and C–9/90 *Francovich* [1991] E.C.R. I–5357, paras 35–36.

[41] ECJ, Joined Cases C–46/93 and C–48/93 *Brasserie du Pêcheur and Factortame* [1996] E.C.R. I–1029, paras 18–23, with case notes by Foubert (1996) Col.J.E.L. 359–372 and Oliver (1997) C.M.L.R. 635–680.

Community law for which it can be held responsible holds good for any case in which a Member State breaches Community law, whatever be the organ of the State whose act or omission was responsible for the breach.[42] Consequently, an individual may bring a damages claim in the national courts on account of an act or omission of a legislative organ[43] or on account of decisions of judicial bodies adjudicating at last instance.[44]

Conditions for liability. The conditions under which that liability gives rise **17–013** to a right to reparation from the State depend on the nature of the breach of Community law giving rise to the loss and damage.[45] The Court of Justice made it clear in *Factortame IV* that the conditions under which the State may incur liability for damage caused to individuals by a breach of Community law cannot, in the absence of particular justification, differ from those governing the liability of the Community in like circumstances.[46] Where a national legislative or administrative organ has a wide discretion, Community law confers a right of reparation with regard to an act or omission of the legislature or executive in breach of that law where three conditions are met:

(1) the rule of law infringed must be intended to confer rights on individuals;

(2) the breach must be sufficiently serious; and

(3) there must be a direct causal link between the breach of the obligation resting on the State and the damage sustained by the injured parties.[47]

---

[42] *ibid.*, para. 32.

[43] *ibid.*, paras 34–36.

[44] ECJ (judgment of September 30, 2003), Case C–224/01 *Köbler*, not yet reported, paras 30–59. See Breuer (2004) E.L.R. 243–254; Wegener (2004) EuR. 84–91, and for a somewhat critical view, Wattel (2004) C.M.L.R. 177–190, and Steyger (2004) N.T.E.R. 18–22. For earlier discussions of this question, see Anagnostaras, "The Principle of State Liability for Judicial Breaches: The Impact of European Community Law" (2001) E.Pub.L. 281–305; Blanchet, "L'usage de la théorie de l'acte clair en droit communautaire: une hypothèse de mise en jeu de la responsabilité de l'Etat français du fait de la fonction juridictionnelle?" (2001) R.T.D.E. 397–438; for a critical view, see Wegener, "Staatshaftung für die Verletzung von Gemeinschaftsrecht durch nationale Gerichte?" (2002) EuR. 785–800. For discussions of implications for the domestic legal systems, see also Tezcan, "La responsabilité des Etats membres vis-à-vis des particuliers pour violation du droit communautaire et sa mise en oeuvre par les juridictions nationales" (1996) B.T.I.R. 517–558; Convery, "State Liability in the UK after *Brasserie du Pêcheur*" (1997) C.M.L.R. 603–634; Hatje, "Die Haftung der Mitgliedstaaten bei Verstossen des Gesetzgebers gegen europäisches Gemeinschaftsrecht" (1997) EuR. 297–310.

[45] ECJ, Joined Cases C–6/90 and C–9/90 *Francovich* [1991] E.C.R. I–5357, para. 38.

[46] ECJ, Joined Cases C–46/93 and C–48/93 *Brasserie du Pêcheur and Factortame* [1996] E.C.R. I–1029, paras 40–42.

[47] *ibid.*, paras 50–51; ECJ, Case C–392/93 *British Telecommunications* [1996] E.C.R. I–1631, para. 39. These rules have applied to legislative acts of the Community since ECJ, Case 5/71 *Zuckerfabrik Schöppenstedt v Council* [1971] E.C.R. 975, para. 11: see Lenaerts and Arts,

In any event, the existence and scope of the discretion available to the Member State must be determined by reference to Community law and not by reference to national law.[48] The same three conditions apply to State liability for damage resulting from the decision of a judicial body adjudicating at last instance.[49] According to the Court of Justice, this does not mean that the State cannot incur liability for acts of the legislature, executive or the judiciary under less strict conditions on the basis of national law.[50]

A breach of Community law will clearly be "sufficiently serious" if it has persisted despite a judgment of the Court of Justice from which it is clear that the conduct in question constituted an infringement.[51] Moreover, although the national courts have jurisdiction to decide how to characterise the breaches of Community law at issue, the Court of Justice will indicate a number of circumstances which the national courts might take into account,[52] and it will even characterise the breach itself if it has all the information necessary to that end.[53] The national court must take account of the clarity and precision of the rule infringed, whether the infringement and the damage caused was intentional or involuntary, whether any error of law was excusable or inexcusable, and the fact that the position taken by a Community institution may have contributed towards the adoption or maintenance of national measures or practices contrary to Community

---

Procedural Law of the European Union, Ch.11. For the parallel with the rules on liability applying to the Community, see ECJ, Case C–352/98P *Laboratoires pharmaceutiques Bergaderm and Goupil* [2000] E.C.R. I–5921, paras 38–44; for breaches of fundamental rights, see Van Gerven, "Remedies for Infringements of Fundamental Rights" (2004) E.Pub.L. 261–284.

[48] ECJ, Case C–424/97 *Haim* [2000] E.C.R. I–5123, para. 40.

[49] ECJ (judgment of September 30, 2003), Case C–224/01 *Köbler*, not yet reported, paras 51–53.

[50] ECJ, Joined Cases C–46/93 and C–48/93 *Brasserie du Pêcheur and Factortame* [1996] E.C.R. I–1029, para. 66; ECJ (judgment of September 30, 2003), Case C–224/01 *Köbler*, not yet reported, para. 57. See, *e.g.* in Belgium with respect to the regulatory activity of the administration: Cass. January 14, 2000, *Arr. Cass.*, 2000, No. 33, referred to in the Eighteenth Annual Report on monitoring Community law, COM (2001) 309 final. According to this "Evobus" judgment, any ordinary breach of Community law by an administrative authority may constitute a "fault" for which the State can be held liable. See also Cass. December 8, 1994, *Arr. Cass.* 1994, No. 541 (the second "Anca" judgment, in which the State was held to be liable for a breach of Community law by a judicial body); see Vuye, "Overheidsaansprakelijkheid wegens schending van het Europees Gemeenschapsrecht" (2003) T.B.H. 743–763.

[51] ECJ, Joined Cases C–46/93 and C–48/93 *Brasserie du Pêcheur and Factortame* [1996] E.C.R. I–1029, para. 57. However, the right of reparation does not depend on the existence of a prior judgment of the Court of Justice: *ibid.* paras 91–96.

[52] *ibid.*, paras 56 and 58–64, likewise paras 75–80 (the existence of fault may be taken into account only in order to determine whether the breach is sufficiently serious). For further clarification, see ECJ, Joined Cases C–94/95 and C–95/95 *Bonfaci and Berto* [1997] E.C.R. I–3969.

[53] See ECJ, Case C–392/93 *British Telecommunications* [1996] E.C.R. I–1631, para. 41; ECJ, Case C–118/00 *Larsy* [2001] E.C.R. I–5063, paras 40–49; ECJ (judgment of September 30, 2003), Case C–224/01 *Köbler*, not yet reported, paras 101–126.

law.[54] As far as liability for judicial decisions is concerned, the national court must take account of non-compliance by the court adjudicating at last instance with its obligation to make a reference for a preliminary ruling under the third para. of Art. 234 of the EC Treaty.[55] It follows from the foregoing that the incorrect transposition of provisions of a directive which are capable of bearing several interpretations and on which neither the Court nor the Commission has given any guidance does not constitute a sufficiently serious breach (see para. 17–134). An incorrect application of Community law by a judicial body adjudicating at last instance does not constitute a sufficiently serious breach where the answer to the question is not expressly covered by Community law, not provided by the case law of the Court of Justice and not obvious.[56] Where, however, at the time when it committed the infringement, a legislative or administrative organ of the Member State in question was not called upon to make any legislative choices and had only considerably reduced discretion, or even none at all, the mere infringement of Community law may be sufficient to establish the existence of a sufficiently serious breach.[57] As it appears from *Francovich*, there will be a sufficiently serious breach where a Member State fails to take any of the measures necessary to achieve the result prescribed by a directive within the period it lays down.[58]

Reparation for loss and damage. Provided that these conditions, **17–014** prescribed by Community law itself, are met, it is on the basis of the rules of national law on liability that the State must make reparation for the consequences of the loss and damage caused.[59] Naturally, the conditions laid down by national law must not be less favourable than those relating to similar domestic claims and must not be such as in practice to make it impossible or excessively difficult to obtain compensation.[60] It is the

---

[54] ECJ, Case C–118/00 *Larsy* [2001] E.C.R. I–5063, para. 39; ECJ (judgment of September 30, 2003), Case C–224/01 *Köbler*, not yet reported, para. 55.

[55] ECJ (judgment of September 30, 2003), Case C–224/01 *Köbler*, not yet reported, para. 55.

[56] *ibid.*, paras 121–122. This position is not altered by the fact that the national court should have made a reference for a preliminary ruling: *ibid.*, para. 123.

[57] ECJ, Case C–5/94 *Hedley Lomas* [1996] E.C.R. I 2553, para. 28 (infringement of Art. 29 of the EC Treaty, which prohibits quantitative restrictions on exports).

[58] ECJ, Joined Cases C–178/94, C–179/94, C–188/94, C–189/94 and C–190/94 *Dillenkofer* [1996] E.C.R. I–4845, paras 22–26. For the three conditions required to be met in order for a failure to transpose a directive to give rise to a right to damages, see para. 17–134, *infra*.

[59] ECJ, Joined Cases C–6/90 and C–9/90 *Francovich* [1991] E.C.R. I–5357, paras 42–43.

[60] See para. 17–011, *infra*, and, for the transposition of directives, para. 17–134, *infra*. Thus, it has been held that the following conditions for State liability should be set aside on the ground that they would impede effective judicial protection: a condition making reparation dependent upon the legislature's act or omission being referable to an individual situation, a condition requiring proof of misfeasance in public office (ECJ, Joined Cases C–46/93 and C–48/93 *Brasserie du Pêcheur and Factortame* [1996] E.C.R. I–1029, paras 67–73) and a rule totally excluding loss of profit as a head of damage (*ibid.*, para. 87). For the national courts' subsequent decisions in the *Brasserie du Pêcheur* and *Factortame* litigation, see the judgment of the *Bundesgerichtshof* of October 24, 1996, III ZR 127/91 (1996) Eu.Z.W. 761 (State held

national legal order which determines against what (central or decentralised) authority the claim must be made (see para. 11–016) and designates the judicial authority competent to determine disputes relating to compensation for damage.[61]

2. Incorporation in the Member States' legal systems

17–015 **Monist and dualist systems.** The principle of the primacy of Community law formulated by the Court of Justice was not automatically applied by each Member State in its domestic legal system. This was possible in the "monist" Member States, which give international legal norms as such precedence over domestic law. On that ground, those Member States accepted that Community law took precedence in its own right in the domestic legal system.[62] In contrast, in "dualist" systems, international legal provisions do not form part of the domestic legal system unless and until they have been incorporated therein by a provision of national law. If the principle of the primacy of Community law is given no legal force superior to the provision incorporating it, the process of incorporation does not secure primacy for Community law.[63] In some Member States, the courts base the primacy of Community law not on the specific nature of the Community legal order, but on the provision of the national Constitution which recognises the primacy of international law or which authorises the

---

not liable in *Brasserie du Pêcheur* because of the lack of a causal link) and the judgment of the Queen's Bench Division of July 31, 1997 in *R.* v *Secretary of State for Transport, Ex p. Factortame (No. 5)* [1997] T.L.R. 482 and (1998) R.T.D.E. 93–95 (State held liable for a serious breach). Cases in which damages have been granted in Member States for breaches of Community law are reported in the survey of the application of Community law by national courts annexed to the annual report of the Commission on monitoring the application of Community law which is available at the "europa" website (under "Documents of the Commission", see "Application of Community law") and the website of the Court of Justice (under "European Union law in Europe", see "National and international case law"). In determining the loss or damage for which reparation may be granted, the national court may always inquire whether the injured person showed reasonable care so as to avoid the loss or damage or to mitigate it (ECJ, Joined Cases C–178/94, C–179/94, C–188/94, C–189/94 and C–190/94 *Dillenkofer* [1996] E.C.R. I–4845, para. 72). See further Emiliou, "State Liability under Community Law: Shedding More Light on the *Francovich* Principle?" (1996) E.L.R. 399–411; Fines, "Quelle obligation de réparer pour la violation du droit communautaire? Nouveaux développements jurisprudentiels sur la responsabilité de 'l'Etat normateur'" (1997) R.T.D.E. 69–101; Ehlers, "Grundlagen einer gemeinschaftsrechtlich entwickelten Staatshaftung" (1997) EuR. 376–398. See also ECJ, Case C–66/95 *Sutton* [1997] E.C.R. I–2163, paras 28–35; ECJ, Case C–90/96 *Petrie* [1997] E.C.R. I–6527, para. 31; ECJ, Case C–127/95 *Norbrook Laboratories* [1998] E.C.R. I–1531, paras 106–112.
[61] ECJ (judgment of September 30, 2003), Case C–224/01 *Köbler*, not yet reported, paras 44–47 and 50 (concerning compensation for damage resulting from a judicial decision conflicting with Community law).
[62] *e.g.* the Benelux countries; see paras 17–016 and 17–026—17–027, *infra*. See, more recently, Cyprus, the Baltic States and Poland, paras 17–037, 17–040, 17–041—17–042 and 17–044.
[63] *cf.* Ireland, para 17–028, *infra*, with the UK and Denmark, paras. 17–028—17–029, *infra*. See, more recently, Hungary and Malta, paras 17–039 and 17–043; previously also the Czech Republic and the Slovak Republic, paras 17–038 and 17–045.

transfer of powers to a supranational authority.[64] This is often the case in the Member States which more recently acceded to the European Union and where the precedence of Community law has been embraced as part of the *acquis communautaire* to which the Member States subscribed upon accession.

As will be seen hereinafter,[65] it is particularly in Member States that provide for a system of constitutional review that the question arises as to whether Community law must be regarded as being subordinate to the national Constitution and whether provisions of Community law may be tested against the national Constitution. From the point of view of Community law, it is irrelevant what method a given Member State uses in order to provide a basis for the primacy of Community law within its domestic legal system, provided that that law actually is given precedence over domestic law. This remark also applies to the reluctance which some Constitutional Courts have shown in accepting the primacy of Community law.[66]

a. Original Member States

(1) *Belgium*

Franco-Suisse Le Ski. In 1970, the Belgian Constitution of 1831 was **17–016** amended to take account of the establishment of the Communities by the addition of Art. 25*bis* (Consolidated Constitution, Art. 34), which provides that "the exercise of certain powers may be conferred by treaty or by statute on international institutions".

Even before then, it had been argued that international law, including Community law, took precedence over domestic law. In the judgment of

---

[64] See paras 17–017—17–025 and 17–031—17–033, *infra*. For clauses governing the transfer of powers, see Lepka and Terrebus, "Les ratifications nationales, manifestations d'un projet politique européen—la face cachée du Traité d'Amsterdam" (2003) R.T.D.E. 365–388.

[65] For a more extensive survey of the primacy of Community law in the national legal systems, see Pescatore, "L'application judiciaire des traités internationaux dans la Communauté européenne et dans ses Etats membres", *Etudes de droit des Communautés européennes. Mélanges offerts à P. H. Teitgen* (Pedone, Paris, 1984), at 355–406; Henrichs, "Gemeinschaftsrecht und nationale Verfassungen. Organisations- und verfahrensrechtliche Aspekte einer Konfliktlage" (1990) Eu.GR.Z. 413–423; Bonichot and others, "L'application du droit communautaire dans les différents Etats membres de la Communauté économique européenne" (1990) R.F.D.A. 955–986. For the most significant judgments of national courts relating to the application of Community law, see the survey annexed to each annual report of the Commission on monitoring the application of Community law.

[66] In addition to the commentators cited above, see Darmon, "Juridictions constitutionnelles et droit communautaire" (1988) R.T.D.E. 217–251; Schermers, "The Scales in Balance: National Constitutional Courts v Court of Justice" (1990) C.M.L.R. 97–105; Rodríguez Iglesias, "Tribunales constitucionales y derecho comunitario", *Hacia un nuevo orden internacional y europeo. Estudios en homenaje al Profesor Don Manuel Díez de Velasco* (Tecnos, Madrid, 1993), at 1175–1200; Kortmann, "Secundair gemeenschapsrecht en de nationale constituties" (1999) S.E.W. 82–88. The Belgian *Arbitragehof/Cour d'Arbitrage* was the first constitutional court of a Member State to refer a question to the Court of Justice for a preliminary ruling: ECJ, Case C–93/97 *Fédération Belge des Chambres Syndicales de Médecins* [1998] E.C.R. I–4837.

May 27, 1971 in *Franco-Suisse Le Ski*, the *Hof van Cassatie/Cour de Cassation* accepted that view in confirming that a law could not prohibit the repayment of charges collected contrary to Art. 12 of the EEC Treaty on the ground that:

"where there is a conflict between a domestic provision and a provision of international law which has direct effects in the domestic legal order, the rule laid down by the treaty must prevail; that priority follows from the very nature of international law laid down by treaty; this applies *a fortiori* where, as in this case, the conflict arises between a provision of domestic law and a provision of Community law; this is because the treaties which brought Community law into being established a new legal order by virtue of which the Member States limited the exercise of their sovereign powers in the areas defined in those treaties; . . . it follows from the foregoing that the Judge was obliged to refrain from applying the provisions of domestic law which conflict with [Article 12 of the EEC Treaty]".[67]

Consequently, Belgian law followed the Court of Justice in deriving the primacy of Community law from the very nature of that law.[68]

As far as acceptance of the primacy of Community law over provisions of constitutional law is concerned, the state of Belgian law has become less clear since the *Arbitragehof/Cour d'Arbitrage* held that it has jurisdiction to assess the constitutionality of laws ratifying a treaty and treaties themselves.[69] Nevertheless, it may be argued that because of its particular nature, Community law must continue to have precedence over the Constitution.[70] Moreover, the *Raad van State/Conseil d'Etat* has held to this effect that Art. 34 of the consolidated Constitution does not only afford the

---

[67] Cass., May 27, 1971, *Arr. Cass.*, 959; (1972) S.E.W. 42.

[68] See Lenaerts, "The Application of Community Law in Belgium" (1986) C.M.L.R. 253–286; Wytinck, "The Application of Community Law in Belgium (1986–1992)" (1993) C.M.L.R. 981–1020.

[69] *Arbitragehof/Cour d'Arbitrage*, October 16, 1991, No. 26/91, *B.S./M.B.*, November 23, 1991, *A.A.*, 1991, 271; see also *Arbitragehof/Cour d'Arbitrage*, February 3, 1994, No. 12/94, *B.S./M.B*, March 11, 1994, *A.A.*, 1994, 211; *Arbitragehof/Cour d'Arbitrage*, April 26, 1994, No. 33/94, *B.S./M.B.*, June 22, 1994, *A.A.*, 1994, 419. See the critical commentary by Velu, "Toetsing van de grondwettigheid en toetsing van de verenigbaarheid met verdragen" (1992–93) R.W. 481, at 487–516; Popelier, "Ongrondwettige verdragen: de rechtspraak van het Arbitragehof in een monistisch tijdsperspectief" (1994–95) R.W. 1076–1080; Louis, "La primauté, une valeur relative?" (1995) C.D.E. 23–28; for an approving commentary, see Brouwers and Simonart, "Le conflit entre la Constitution et le droit international conventionnel dans la jurisprudence de la Cour d'arbitrage" (1995) C.D.E. 7–22; Melchior and Vandernoot, "Contrôle de constitutionnalité et droit communautaire dérivé" (1998) R.B.D.C. 3–45.

[70] This view also inspired the amendment which took away the jurisdiction of the *Arbitragehof/Cour d'Arbitrage* to give preliminary rulings on laws ratifying a constituent treaty relating to the European Union; see Vanden Heede and Goedertier, "Eindelijk een volwaardig Grondwettelijk Hof? Een commentaar op de Bijzondere Wet van 9 maart 2003" (2003) T.B.P. 458, at 468.

constitutional basis for the transfer of powers to the European Union but also for the jurisdiction of the Court of Justice to ensure the uniform interpretation of Community law, even though this limits the legal effects of national constitutional provisions.[71]

(2) *France*

Constitutional framework. The recognition of the primacy of Community **17–017** law in the French legal order is more complicated than Art. 55 of the 1958 French Constitution would suggest. According to that article, treaties which are approved and ratified in accordance with the relevant rules have legal force as from their publication superior to that of statutes, subject to the proviso that each treaty is complied with by the other party or parties. However, since Art. 54 of the Constitution provides that a treaty which the *Conseil Constitutionnel* declares unconstitutional may be approved and ratified only following an amendment of the Constitution,[72] treaties are subordinated to the Constitution. In this respect, Community law is equated with treaties in general. Initially, the French courts considered that the above-mentioned provisions of the Constitution did not allow them to give precedence to Community law. If they had to review the compatibility of a given statute with Community law, its compatibility with Art. 55 of the Constitution would in fact have been tested, whilst Art. 61 of the Constitution provided that (prior) review of constitutionality was reserved to the *Conseil Constitutionnel*. Thus, the *Conseil d'Etat*, the highest court of administrative law, refused to rule on the compatibility of a number of ministerial decrees with Community law thereby following the opinion of the *Commissaire du gouvernement*, who had argued that such a ruling would be tantamount to reviewing the constitutionality of the statutes on which the decrees were based.[73]

Reversal in case law of *Conseil d'Etat*. In 1975, however, the *Conseil* **17–018** *Constitutionnel* cleared the way for reviewing the compatibility of statutes with Community law when it held in the course of reviewing the constitutionality of a given statute that it would not give a view on its compatibility with a treaty on the ground that this was a different species of review, since a law contrary to a treaty does not for that reason violate the Constitution.[74] This prompted the *Cour de Cassation* to accept the primacy of Community law on the basis of Art. 55 of the Constitution and the

---

[71] *Raad van State/Conseil d'Etat*, November 5, 1996, No. 62.621 (*Goosse*) and No. 69.922 (*Orfinger*), discussed in "Annex VI—Application of Community law by national courts" to the Fourteenth Annual Report on monitoring the application of Community law (1996), [1997] O.J. C332/202.

[72] For the review of constitutionality by the *Conseil Constitutionnel*, see Boulouis, "Le juge constitutionnel français et l'Union européenne" (1994) C.D.E. 505–522.

[73] Judgment of March 1, 1968 *Syndicat général des Fabricants de semoules de France* (1968) Rec.C.E. 149; for the opinion, see (1968) A.J.D.A. 235.

[74] Judgment of January 15, 1975 (1975) Rec.Con.const. 19; (1975) Rec.Dalloz Jurispr. 529.

specific nature of Community law.[75] Yet, the primacy of Community law could find no foothold in administrative case law so long as the *Conseil d'Etat* did not agree to revise its jurisprudence. The reversal eventually came in 1989 when, in the *Nicolo* case, the *Conseil d'Etat* reviewed the law on the organisation of the European elections in the light of Art. 227(1) of the EEC Treaty.[76] Subsequently, the *Conseil d'Etat* held in *Boisdet* that a statute conflicted with a Community regulation and annulled a ministerial decree based thereon.[77]

17–019 Status of directives. The French courts give precedence to acts of secondary Community law likewise pursuant to Art. 55 of the Constitution by reference to the implied "ratification" of such acts operated through Art. 249 of the EC Treaty. Admittedly, the *Conseil d'Etat* still has some reservations about the primacy of directives. Since directives are binding only as to the result to be achieved on each Member State to which they are addressed, no reliance may be placed upon provisions of a directive in challenging an individual administrative act.[78] However, it appears from later judgments that a claim that administrative[79] or statutory[80] provisions on which an individual administrative act is based conflict with a directive may nevertheless be raised where the provisions are intended to implement the directive[81] and even when the directive has not yet been transposed into national law.[82]

17–020 On-going debate. Following the ratification of the EU Treaty and the Treaty of Amsterdam, Art. 88 relating to France's participation in the

---

[75] Judgment of May 24, 1975, *Administration des Douanes v Société des Cafés Jacques Vabre & Société Weigel et Cie* (1975) Rec.Dalloz Jurispr., 497, translated in [1975] 2 C.M.L.R. 336.

[76] Judgment of October 30, 1989 *Nicolo* (1989) Rec.C.E. 190, translated in [1990] 1 C.M.L.R. 173.

[77] Judgment of September 24, 1990, *Boisdet* (1990) Rec.C.E. 250, translated in [1991] 1 C.M.L.R. 3. See Manin, "The *Nicolo* Case of the *Conseil d'Etat*: French Constitutional Law and the Supreme Administrative Court's Acceptance of the Primacy of Community Law over Subsequent National Statute Law" (1991) C.M.L.R. 499–519; Oliver, "The French Constitution and the Treaty of Maastricht" (1994) I.C.L.Q. 1–25; Roseren, "The Application of Community Law by French Courts from 1982 to 1993" (1994) C.M.L.R. 315–376.

[78] Judgment of December 22, 1978, *Ministre de l'Intérieur v Cohn-Bendit* (1978) Rec.C.E. 524; (1979) Rec. Dalloz Jurispr., 155; translated in [1980] 1 C.M.L.R. 543.

[79] Judgment of July 8, 1991, *Palazzi* (1991) Rec.C.E. 276.

[80] Judgment of February 28, 1992, *Rothmans International France* and *Arizona Tobacco Products* (1992) Rec.C.E. 78 and 80; see also (1992) A.J.D.A. 224–226; [1993] 1 C.M.L.R. 253.

[81] Dal Farra, "L'invocabilité des directives communautaires devant le juge national de légalité" (1992) R.T.D.E. 631–667; Simon, "Le Conseil d'Etat et les directives communautaires: du gallicanisme à l'orthodoxie?" (1992) R.T.D.E. 265–283. For a survey, see Tomlinson, "Reception of Community Law in France" (1995) Col.J.E.L. 183–231.

[82] Judgment of February 6, 1998, *Tête e.a.* (1998) Rec.C.E. 30. The national provision may nevertheless only be contested if it is "incompatible" with Community law; see, *e.g.* the judgment of July 27, 2001, *Compagnie générale des eaux* (2001) Droit administratif—Juris classeur 33 and Favret, "Le rapport de compatibilité entre le droit national et le droit communautaire" (2001) A.J.D.A. 727–730.

European Community and the European Union was added to the French Constitution.[83] That article, however, does not refer to the status of Community law in the French legal order and, in particular, leaves open the question whether Community law takes precedence over the Constitution. As far as international law is concerned, in recent judgments both the *Conseil d'Etat* and the *Cour de Cassation* have suggested that international obligations do not automatically have precedence over the Constitution.[84] There is some discussion in the literature as to whether this case law also applies to Community law or whether the adoption of Art. 88 of the Constitution has not placed Community law at least on an equal footing with the Constitution.[85]

(3) *Germany*

Acceptance of primacy. Article 24(1) of the German Basic Law **17–021** (*Grundgesetz*) of 1949 provides that the federation may by enactment transfer powers to "inter-State institutions". Nevertheless, such a transfer of powers is subject to the structural principles of the German constitutional system as enshrined in Art. 79(3) of the Basic Law. For the purposes of the approval of the EU Treaty, a provision was added to the Basic Law declaring that the Federal Republic is to co-operate in developing the European Union, which is subject to democratic, social and federal principles, to the principle of the State governed by the rule of law, to the principle of subsidiarity and to protection of fundamental rights

---

[83] For the introduction of this article, see the literature in notes concerning the ratification of the EU Treaty and the Treaty of Amsterdam; paras 3–011 and 3–018, *supra*.

[84] See the judgment of the *Conseil d'Etat* of October 30, 1998 in *Sarran e.a.* (1998) Rec.C.E. 1081, (1998) A.J.D.A. 962, (2000) Rec. Dalloz Jurispr. 152, and the judgment of the *Cour de Cassation* of June 2, 2000 in *Fraisse* (2000) 4 Bulletin des arrêts 7, (2000) Rec. Dalloz Jurispr. 865. According to some commentators, however, this does not mean, that the Constitution invariable takes precedence over international agreements; see Kronenberger, "A New Approach to the Interpretation of the French Constitution in respect to International Conventions: From hierarchy of norms to conflicts of competence" (2000) N.I.L.R. 323–358; Ondoua, "La Cour de cassation et la place respective de la Constitution et des traités dans la hiérarchie des normes" (2000) R.G.D.I.P. 985–1001.

[85] The separate status of Community law is supported by the fact that in the judgment in *Fraisse* the *Cour de cassation* did not consider that Community law was applicable. However, since then the *Conseil d'Etat* has emphasised the supremacy of the Constitution in its judgment of December 3, 2001 in the *SNIP* case (*Syndicat national de l'industrie pharmaceutique*, (2002) R.F.D.A. 166; (2002) A.J.D.A. 1219; see Chaltiel, "La boîte de Pandore des relations entre la Constitution française et le droit communautaire" (2002) R.M.C.U.E. 595–599; Spiegels, "Das Verhältnis des Gemeinschaftsrechts zum französischen Recht—Nationale Souveränität und europäische Integration" (2003) EuR. 119–133. Yet, in the same judgment, the *Conseil d'Etat* confirmed the binding nature of general principles of Community law; see Castaing, "L'extension du contrôle de conventionnalité aux principes généraux du droit communautaire" (2003) R.T.D.E. 197–228. In its recent decisions of June 10 and July 1, 2004 (Nos 2004/496 and 2004/497), the *Conseil constitutionnel* relies on Art. 88-1 of the Constitution to conclude that, unless the Constitution provides otherwise, the act transposing a Community directive into French law cannot be reviewed on its conformity with Community law.

which is essentially comparable to that afforded by the Basic Law (Art. 23(1)).[86] The *Bundesverfassungsgericht* (Federal Constitutional Court) has accepted the primacy of Community law by virtue of domestic statutes approving the Community Treaties, hence only in so far as Community law remains within the bounds set by the Basic Law.[87]

17–022 *Solange* **judgments.** This was not sufficient to guarantee the primacy of Community law, however, when a Community measure was challenged in a German court on the ground that it violated fundamental rights enshrined in the Basic Law. Although the Court of Justice answered a question referred for a preliminary ruling by the court concerned by saying that the measure did not infringe any fundamental right,[88] the national court deemed it necessary also to bring the matter before the *Bundesverfassungsgericht*. That court held that the transfer of sovereignty to the Community made under Art. 24 of the Basic Law could not result in Community legislation detracting from the essential structure of the Basic Law. Despite the judgment of the Court of Justice and the primacy of Community law, the *Bundesverfassungsgericht* considered that it was necessary to conduct a second review of the Community legislation in the light of the fundamental rights guaranteed by the Basic Law *so long as* the Community legal order lacked a democratically elected parliament with legislative powers and powers of scrutiny and a codified catalogue of fundamental rights.[89] In order to guarantee the uniform application of Community law, the Court of Justice confirmed for its part that observance of fundamental rights formed part of the requirements which Community acts had to satisfy in order to be valid and therefore had to be enforced within the context of Community law itself.[90] In 1986, after considering the case law of the Court of Justice, the *Bundesverfassungsgericht*, referring to the importance that the Community institutions attached to the protection of fundamental rights and democratic decision-making, declared that an additional review of Community legislation in the light of the fundamental rights guaranteed by the Basic Law was no longer necessary *so long as* the

---

[86] For commentaries, see the works listed in ns concerning the ratification of the EU Treaty: para. 3–018, *supra*.

[87] Hanf, "Le jugement de la Cour constitutionnelle fédérale allemande sur la constitutionnalité du Traité de Maastricht" (1994) R.T.D.E. 391, at 395–398.

[88] ECJ, Case 11/70 *Internationale Handelsgesellschaft* [1970] E.C.R. 1125, paras 3–20.

[89] The judgment in question is the so-called (first) *Solange* judgment of May 29, 1974, BVerfGE 37, at 271; for an English translation, see [1974] 2 C.M.L.R. 540; see Ipsen, "BVerfG versus EuGH *re* 'Grundrechte'" (1975) EuR. 1–19.

[90] ECJ, Case 44/79 *Hauer* [1979] E.C.R. 3727, paras 13–16 (in which reference is made to the judgments in *Internationale Handelsgesellschaft* and *Nold* and to the fact that the institutions recognised "that conception" in the Joint Declaration of April 5, 1977; para. 17–074, *infra*).

case law of the Court of Justice continued to afford the level of protection found.[91]

Maastricht-*Urteil*. The *Bundesverfassungsgericht* confirmed its conditional 17–023 acceptance of the primacy of Community law on October 12, 1993 when it ruled on the constitutionality of the law ratifying the EU Treaty.[92] The *Bundesverfassungsgericht* declared once again that it secured the essential substance of the fundamental rights guaranteed by the Basic Law also with regard to action of the Community, while making it clear that the Court of Justice ensured respect for fundamental rights—within the Community field of competence—in each individual case and that the *Bundesverfassungsgericht* could therefore confine itself to a general guarantee that the standard of protection of fundamental rights would be undiminished.[93] It added that German law accepted acts of the "European institutions and bodies" only in so far as they remained within the bounds of the Treaty provisions approved by the ratification law, and made it plain that it would itself review whether such acts remained within those bounds.[94]

Recent case law. It appears from subsequent cases, however, that the 17–024 *Bundesverfassungsgericht* considers that the Court of Justice sufficiently guarantees the protection of fundamental rights and is returning to the

---

[91] Judgment of October 22, 1986 (*Solange II*) (1986) BVerfGE 73 at 339; for an English translation, see [1987] 3 C.M.L.R. 225; see the commentary by Frowein (1988) C.M.L.R. 201–206. The *Bundesverfassungsgericht* referred to the Joint Declaration of April 5, 1977 and the Declaration of the European Council of April 7 and 8, 1978 on democracy (1978) 3 EC Bull. 5. For the ensuing debate, see, among others, Everling, "Brauchen wir 'Solange III'?" (1990) EuR. 195–227; Tomuschat, "Aller guten Dinge sind III?" (1990) EuR. 340–361; Ehlermann, "Zur Diskussion um einen 'Solange III'-Beschluss: Rechtspolitische Perspektiven aus der Sicht des Gemeinschaftsrechts" (1991) EuR. Beiheft 1, 27–38.

[92] The "*Maastricht-Urteil*"; for the text, see (1993) Eu.GR.Z. 429; (1993) EuR. 294; [1974] 1 C.M.L.R. 57. For the conditional nature of that acceptance, see Zuleeg, "The European Constitution under Constitutional Constraints: The German Scenario" (1997) E.L.R. 19–34.

[93] Point B.2, under b, [1994] 1 C.M.L.R. 80.

[94] Points C.I.3. and C.II.2., under b, *ibid.*, 89 and 94, respectively. Among the many commentaries on that judgment, see Tomuschat, "Die Europäische Union unter der Aufsicht des Bundesverfassungsgerichts" (1993) Eu.GR.Z. 489–496; Hahn, "La Cour constitutionnelle fédérale d'Allemagne et le Traité de Maastricht" (1994) R.G.D.I.P. 107–126; Herdegen, "Maastricht and the German Constitutional Court: Constitutional Restraints for an 'Ever Closer Union'" (1994) C.M.L.R. 235–249; Ipsen, "Zehn Glossen zum Maastricht Urteil" (1994) EuR. 1–21; Kokott, "Deutschland im Rahmen der Europäischen Union—zum Vertrag von Maastricht" (1994) A.ö.R. 207–237; Meessen, "Maastricht nach Karlsruhe" (1994) N.J.W. 549–554; Schroeder, "Alles unter Karlsruher Kontrolle? Die Souveränitätsfrage im Maastricht-Urteil des BVerfG" (1994) Z.f.RV. 143–157; Schwarze, "La ratification du Traité de Maastricht en Allemagne, l'arrêt de la Cour constitutionnelle de Karlsruhe" (1994) R.M.C.U.E. 293–303. For the role which the Court of Justice could play in this connection by giving preliminary rulings at the request of the German Constitutional Court, see Grimm, "The European Court of Justice and National Courts: The German Constitutional Perspective after the Maastricht Decision" (1997) Col.J.E.L. 229–242.

position it took in 1986.[95] In a judgment of January 9, 2001, the *Bundesverfassungsgericht* held that the highest federal administrative court (*Bundesverwaltungsgericht*) fell short of its obligations in respect of the legal protection guaranteed by the Basic Law by refusing to make a reference to the Court of Justice for a preliminary ruling on a matter in respect of which that Court had not been able to secure complete clarity. The highest administrative court had breached constitutional obligations in so far as it had failed to take account of a general principle of Community law, namely the principle of equal treatment of men and women.[96]

(4) *Italy*

17–025 Italy. Community law has its place within the Italian legal order by virtue of the transfer of competence to international organisations authorised by Art. 11 of the 1947 Constitution.[97] Initially, the Italian Constitutional Court held that a law which conflicted with Community law was also unconstitutional. In order to give precedence to Community law, Italian courts therefore had to raise the issue of constitutionality first before the Constitutional Court in the event of a conflict between a national statute and Community law (see para. 17–008). It was not until the 1984 judgment in *Granital* that the Constitutional Court changed its view and declared that, in the event that a court found that a national provision conflicted with a rule of Community law having direct effect, it should refrain from

---

[95] Judgment of February 17, 2000 (*Alcan*) 2 BvR 1915/91, (2000) Eu.GR.Z. 17 and above all the order of June 7, 2000 (on the Community organisation of the market in bananas), BVerfGE 102, 147, (2000) EuR. 799–810; (2000) Eu.Z.W. 702–704; (2000) Eu.GR.Z. 328; (2000) N.J.W. 3124. See Grewe, "Le 'traité de paix' avec la Cour de Luxembourg: l'arrêt de la Cour constitutionnelle allemande du 7 juin 2000 relatif au règlement du marché de la banane" (2001) R.T.D.E. 1–17; Hoffmeister (2001) C.M.L.R. 791–804; Pernice, "Les bananes et les droits fondamentaux; la Cour constitutionnelle allemande fait le point" (2001) C.D.E. 427–440; Elbers and Urban, "The Order of the German Federal Constitutional Court of June 7, 2000 and the Kompetenz-Kompetenz in the European Judicial System" (2001) E.Pub.L. 21–32; Mayer, "Grundrechtsschutz gegen europäische Rechtsakte durch das BVerfG: Zur Verfassungsmässigkeit der Bananenmarktordnung" (2000) Eu.Z.W. 685–690; for a critical commentary, see Schmid, "All Bark and No Bite: Notes on the Federal Constitutional Court's 'Banana Decision'" (2001) E.L.J. 95–113.

[96] Judgment of January 9, 2001 (2001) Eu.GR.Z. 150–153; (2001) N.J.W. 1267; (2001) D.ö.V. 379; (2001) J.Z. 923; see Classen (2002) C.M.L.R. 641–652. Already in *Solange II* the *Bundesverfassungsgericht* had held that the refusal of the highest revenue court to make a reference for a preliminary ruling was in breach of the principle of the "gesetzliche Rechter" enshrined in Art. 101 of the Basic Law ("No one may be removed from the jurisdiction of his lawful judge."). With respect to prospects for the future, see Nickel, "Zur Zukunft des Bundesverfassungsgerichts im Zeitalter der Europäisierung" (2001) J.Z. 625–632.

[97] See Adinolfi, "The Judicial Application of Community Law in Italy (1981—1997)" (1998) C.M.L.Rev 1313, at 1322; Luciani, "La Constitution italienne et les obstacles à l'intégration européenne" (1992) R.F.D.C. 663, at 664.

applying the domestic provision without raising the question of constitutionality.[98]

Nevertheless, the Constitutional Court finds that there are still two situations in which it itself must give judgment. First, ever since the 1973 judgment in *Frontini*,[99] the Constitutional Court has held that it has jurisdiction to give a ruling where a rule of Community law purportedly breaches fundamental principles of the Italian legal order or inviolable human rights.[100] Secondly, the Constitutional Court reviews the constitutionality of domestic rules which allegedly are expressly intended to prevent compliance with essential obligations under the Treaties.[101] In 1994, however, the Constitutional Court refused to rule on the constitutionality of a national law in a case in which the lower court requested the ruling without first considering whether the law was compatible with Community law.[102]

(5) *Luxembourg*

Luxembourg. Luxembourg law recognised the primacy of Community law **17–026** unconditionally as an application of the priority of international law over domestic law which has been accepted since 1954.[103] Just as in Belgian law, precedence is given to international law on the ground of its very nature, with the result that the primacy of Community law is regarded as being the outcome of the specific nature of the Community legal order.[104] In this respect, the authorisation to transfer the exercise of competences to an international organisation (Constitution, Art. 49*bis*) is of no importance (here, too, the analogy with Belgium holds good).[105]

---

[98] Judgment No. 170/84 of June 8, 1984; for an English translation, see [1994] C.M.L.R. 756; see Barav, "Cour constitutionelle italienne et droit communautaire: le fantôme de *Simmenthal*" (1985) R.T.D.E. 313–341. More recently, see Gaja, "New Developments in a Continuing Story: The Relationship Between EEC Law and Italian Law" (1990) C.M.L.R. 83–95; Daniele, "Après l'arrêt *Granital*: droit communautaire et droit national dans la jurisprudence récente de la Cour constitutionnelle italienne" (1992) C.D.E. 3–21.

[99] Judgment No. 183/73 of December 27, 1973; for an English translation, see [1974] 2 C.M.L.R. 383.

[100] There was an initial application of this principle in judgment No. 232/89 of April 21, 1989 in *Fragd*; see Gaja (n.98, *supra*), at 94; Daniele (n.98, *supra*), at 16.

[101] For applications of this principle, see Daniele (n.98, *supra*), at 18–19; Adinolfi (n.97, *supra*), at 1318.

[102] Order of June 19, 1994, No. 244/94; see Adinolfi (n.97, *supra*), at 1317. In considering the constitutionality of a referendum to be held, the Constitutional Court itself even analysed the extent to which the referendum was in keeping with the Member State's obligations to give effect to its Community obligations; see the judgment of February 7, 2000, reported in the Eighteenth Annual Report on monitoring the application of Community law , COM (2001) 309 fin.

[103] *Cour de cassation*, July 14, 1954, *Pas.lux.*, Vol.16, 150.

[104] *Conseil d'Etat*, November 21, 1984, *Pas.lux.*, Vol.26, 174. See Thill, "La primauté et l'effet direct du droit communautaire dans la jurisprudence luxembourgeoise" (1990) R.F.D.A. 978–980.

[105] With respect to this clause governing the transfer of powers, see Lepka and Terebus (n.64, *supra*) at 368–369.

(6) *The Netherlands*

17–027 Netherlands. The primacy of Community law also found immediate acceptance in the Netherlands legal system. This was because it already recognised the principle of the supremacy of international law even before it was codified in the 1953 Constitution. The 1983 Constitution reads as follows:

> "Legal provisions valid within the Kingdom shall not be applied if to do so would not be compatible with provisions of treaties and acts of international organisations which are binding on any person" (Art. 94).

Since Art. 12 of the EEC Treaty therefore had precedence in domestic law in so far as it was "binding on any person", the court hearing *Van Gend & Loos* had only to ascertain through the preliminary reference to the Court of Justice whether the provision was capable of having legal effects on individuals (see 649).[106] In the Netherlands, too, acceptance of the primacy of Community law is based on recognition of the special nature of Community law.[107] Article 192 of the Constitution allows powers to be transferred to international organisations.[108]

b. Member States having acceded subsequently

(1) *Ireland, the United Kingdom and Denmark*

17–028 Ireland. In common with the two other States which acceded to the Community in 1973, Ireland belonged to the "dualist" school, according to which provisions of international law obtain the force of law only after they have been incorporated into the national legal system (Constitution, Art. 29.6). Consequently, in order to ensure the legal force of Community law, it

---

[106] Prechal, "La primauté du droit communautaire aux Pays-Bas" (1990) R.F.D.A. 981–982.

[107] See Kapteyn and VerLoren van Themaat, *Het recht van de Europese Unie en van de Europese Gemeenschappen* (Kluwer, Deventer, 2003), at 443; Kellermann, "Supremacy of Community Law in the Netherlands" (1989) E.L.R. 175–185; Brouwer, "Nederlandse gedachten over de Grondwet en het verdrag" (1992–93) R.W. 1366–1370. Nevertheless, from time to time, the articles of the Constitution relating to international law are relied upon before the Netherlands courts: see Lauwaars, Lyklema and Kuiper, "De Nederlandse jurisprudentie met betrekking tot de algemene leerstukken van het recht der Europese Gemeenschappen" (1973) S.E.W. 3, at 19; see also *Raad van State*, Administrative Disputes Division, judgments of November 11, 1991 (1992) N.J./A.B. No. 50, and February 17, 1993 (1993) N.J./A.B. No. 424. The primacy of Community law holds good irrespective of whether the Community provision at issue has direct effect: *Raad van State*, Administrative Disputes Division, judgment of July 7, 1995, *Metten v Minister van Financiën*, No. R01.93.0067, N.J.B.-Rechtspraak 426 (for an English translation, see (1996) M.J.E.C.L. 179–184); see Besselink, "Curing a 'Childhood Sickness'? On Direct Effect, Internal Effect, Primacy and Derogation from Civil Rights (The Netherlands Council of State Judgment in the *Metten* Case)" (1996) M.J.E.C.L. 165–184; Besselink, "An Open Constitution and European Integration: The Kingdom of the Netherlands" (1996) S.E.W. 192–206.

[108] If an international treaty contains provisions at variance with the Constitiution, the national parliament has to ratify it with a two-thirds majority (Constitution, Art. 91(3)).

was deemed necessary not only to adopt a law of accession, but also to adopt what is known as the third amendment to the Constitution.[109] As a result, Art. 29.4.5 of the Constitution provides that none of its provisions preclude national measures necessary for implementing Treaty obligations or prevent Community measures from having the force of law.[110] The Irish courts have inferred the primacy of Community law from this, even where a rule of Community law conflicts with a statutory or even a constitutional provision.[111] The Supreme Court has recently indicated, however, that it wishes to consider how Community law should be applied where it affects a right guaranteed by the Constitution.[112]

United Kingdom. In the United Kingdom, Community law obtains its legal **17–029** force from an Act of Parliament. This is because British law adheres to the principle of parliamentary sovereignty, which is tantamount to saying that the legislature is subject to no limitation, apart from its inability to restrict its own sovereignty.[113] Consequently, the legal force of primary and secondary Community law is based upon s.2(1) of the 1972 European Communities Act. As far as the relationship with domestic law is concerned, although s.2(4) does not recognise the primacy of Community law as such, it does provide that any enactment passed or to be passed shall be construed and have effect subject to the "foregoing provisions" of that section, which include s.2(1), the effect of which is to incorporate the whole of Community law into the law of the United Kingdom. Consequently, Community law takes precedence by virtue of the 1972 Act and the courts presume that Parliament does not intend to legislate contrary to Community law. Thus, the courts will construe a statute implementing a directive in conformity with the directive and are prepared in principle to abandon the normal canons of construction so as to enforce rights derived

---

[109] Collins and O'Reilly, "The Application of Community Law in Ireland 1973–1989" (1990) C.M.L.R. 315, at 323.

[110] See Hogan, "The Implementation of European Union Law in Ireland: The *Meagher* Case and the Democratic Deficit" (1994) Ir.J.E.L. 190–202. For the Supreme Court's reliance on Art. 29.4.5 of the Constitution in the *Meagher* case, see n.00 to para. 11–011, *supra*.

[111] Walsh, "Reflections on the Effects of Membership of the European Communities in Irish Law", in Capotorti, Ehlermann, Frowein, Jacobs, Joliet, Koopmans and Kovar (eds), *Du droit international au droit de l'intégration. Liber Amicorum P. Pescatore* (Nomos, Baden-Baden, 1987), at 806–820.

[112] Judgment of December 19, 1989, *Society for the Protection of Unborn Children Ireland v Grogan*, opinion of Finlay, J., [1990] 1 C.M.L.R. 689. The matter in question was Art. 40.3.3 of the Constitution concerning the right to life of the unborn child introduced by the eighth amendment; for the relationship of that provision to Community law and its subsequent application, see the discussion of free movement of services in n.737 to para. 5–170, *supra*. In a concurring opinion, Walsh, J., considered that an amendment to the Constitution could affect the legal effects of an earlier amendment, as a result of which it would appear that the primacy of Community law as a principle does not rank above the Constitution.

[113] Collins, *European Community Law in the UK* (Butterworths, London, 5th ed., 1998); Kinder-Gest, "Primauté du droit communautaire et droit anglais ou comment concilier l'impossible" (1991) R.A.E. 19–34.

from Community law against the wording of the statute.[114] Yet, the courts shirk at interpreting national law in conformity with Community law when it is a question of interpreting a statute which was not enacted to give effect to Community law.[115] If Parliament "deliberately passes an Act with the intention of repudiating . . . any provision in [the Treaty] or intentionally of acting inconsistently with it and says so in express terms", it would seem that United Kingdom courts would consider themselves under a duty to follow the statute.[116] However, it would appear from the *Factortame* litigation that British courts are increasingly prepared to disapply national law where it conflicts with directly enforceable Community law. The judgment of the Court of Justice holding that where necessary national courts must suspend the application of a domestic statute (see para. 17–009) was accepted by the House of Lords as a consequence of the obligations accepted by the United Kingdom when the European Communities Act was passed.[117] Meanwhile, the High Court has considered that the European Communities Act is a constitutional statute that cannot be impliedly repealed. It held that Community law, through its incorporation into UK law by the European Communities Acts, ranks supreme in the sense that anything in UK substantive law inconsistent with any of rights and obligations flowing from Community law is abrogated or must be modified to avoid the inconsistency, even if contained in primary legislation. Only in the event that a Community measure would be repugnant to a fundamental or constitutional right guaranteed by the law of England, would the question arise as to whether the general words of the European Communities Act were sufficient to incorporate the measure and give it overriding effect in domestic law.[118]

---

[114] *Pickstone v Freemans Plc* [1989] A.C. 66, where Lord Oliver stated that "a construction which permits the section [of the 1983 Equal Pay (Amendment) Regulations adopted to implement the directive on equal pay] to operate as a proper fulfilment of the UK's obligation under the Treaty involves not so much doing violence to the language of the section as filling a gap by an implication which arises, not from the words used, but from the manifest purpose of the Act and the mischief it was intended to remedy" (at 125). See also *Litster v Forth Dry Dock* [1989] 2 C.M.L.R. 194. See in this regard Collins (n.113, *supra*); de Búrca, "Giving Effect to European Community Directives" (1992) M.L.R. 215–240.

[115] See the judgment of the House of Lords in *Duke v Reliance Systems Ltd* [1988] A.C. 618, where it had been sought to construe the provisions of the 1975 Sex Discrimination Act consistently with the directive on equal treatment prior to entry into force of the 1986 Sex Discrimination Act giving the directive effect in the UK.

[116] See *Macarthy's Ltd v Smith* [1979] 3 All E.R. 325, at 329 (*per* Lord Denning M.R.).

[117] *R. v Secretary of State for Transport, Ex p. Factortame* (No. 2) [1991] 2 A.C. 603. See Tatham, "The Sovereignty of Parliament after Factortame" (1993) EuR. 188–196; Akehurst, "Parliamentary Sovereignty and the Supremacy of Community Law" (1989) B.Y.I.L. 351–357. For the way in which British courts have subsequently given effect to Community law, see Chalmers, "The Application of Community Law in the United Kingdom, 1994–1998" (2000) C.M.L.R. 83–128; Dutheil de la Rochère, Grief and Saulnier, "L'application du droit communautaire par les juridictions britanniques" (2001) R.T.D.E. 439–466 (period 1999–2000) and (2003) R.T.D.E. 471–488 (period 2001–2002).

[118] Judgment of February 18, 2002 in *Thoburn v Sunderland City Council* [2003] Q.B. 151.

Denmark. In Denmark, delegation of powers to international bodies is **17–030** made possible by Art. 20 of the 1953 Constitution. Also under the Danish system, primary and secondary Community law is given force by the statute on accession to the European Communities. Although this does not result in Community law having force superior to domestic law, the Danish courts interpret national law on the presumption that the legislature intended to act in conformity with Community law and to give preference to interpretations consistent with Community law. However, just as in the case of the United Kingdom, it cannot be taken for granted that Danish courts would give precedence to Community law if they were faced with a statutory provision which intentionally and expressly conflicted with Community law.[119] It further appears from a judgment of the Danish Supreme Court of April 6, 1998 that, in principle, the courts must comply with rulings of the Court of Justice unless they find themselves in the "exceptional situation" in which they are certain that a Community act held by the Court of Justice to be lawful or an interpretation by the Court of Justice of rules or principles of Community law exceeds the limits of the Danish law on accession to the EC/EU adopted under Art. 20 of the Constitution. In such a case, the national courts must disapply the act, rules or principles in question.[120]

(2) Greece

Greece. As a rule, Greek courts give precedence to Community law, often **17–031** on the ground of both the specific nature of the Community legal order and Art. 28 of the 1975 Greek Constitution, para. 1 of which confers superior force on international, as compared to domestic, law.[121] It should be noted, however, that, under the Constitution, the conferral of powers on an international organisation may limit the "exercise of national sovereignty" only in so far as this does not encroach upon "human rights and the foundations of the democratic system" (Art. 28(6)).[122]

---

[119] Gangsted-Rasmussen, "Primauté du droit communautaire en cas de conflit avec le droit danois" (1975) R.T.D.E. 700–707; Rasmussen, "Denmark in face of her Community Obligations" (1982) C.M.L.R. 601, at 622–623; von Holstein, "Le droit communautaire dans le système juridique danois" (1990) R.F.D.A. 962–964.

[120] For a short appraisal of this judgment, see K.L., "Redactionele signalen" (1998) S.E.W. 181. See the commentaries by Høegh (1999) E.L.R. 80–90; Hofmann (1999) Eu.GR.Z. 1–5. See also Biering, "The Application of EU Law in Denmark: 1986 to 2000" (2000) C.M.L.R. 925, at 928–932.

[121] Kerameus and Kremlis, "The Application of Community Law in Greece 1981–1987" (1988) C.M.L.R. 141–175; a critical view is taken of reliance on Art. 28 of the Constitution by Ioannou, "Recent Developments in the Application of Community Law in Greece" (1989) E.L.R. 461–469, and Konstadinidis, "Five Years of Application of Community Law in Greece" (1986) 2 L.I.E.I. 101–124.

[122] See Konstadinidis (n.121, *supra*), at 106.

(3) Portugal and Spain

17–032 Portugal. Before Portugal acceded to the European Communities in 1986, Art. 8 of the 1976 Portuguese Constitution was supplemented by a third paragraph giving effect to Community law in the domestic legal system. In the same way as the Constitution recognises the force in the domestic legal system of international treaty law (Art. 8(2)) and thereby gives that law precedence over national legislation, the primacy of Community law is inferred from Art. 8(3).[123] However, the highest administrative court refused to recognise the primacy of a Commission decision which ordered the withdrawal of a national court judgment conflicting with the Concentration Regulation on the ground that such primacy would jeopardise the independence of the judiciary.[124] Community law would therefore appear not to be hierarchically superior to the Constitution.[125]

17–033 Spain. In the Spanish legal order, the legal force of Community law derives from Art. 93 of the 1978 Constitution, which authorises the transfer of certain powers to an international organisation or institution.[126] The Constitutional Court has made it clear that a national provision which is contrary to Community law is not by virtue of that fact unconstitutional. It therefore leaves the resolution of such conflicts to the ordinary courts.[127] Generally, the courts give priority to Community law on the ground of the special nature of the Community legal order, but sometimes they do invoke Art. 93 of the Constitution.[128] The status of Community law *vis-à-vis* the Constitution is unclear, since the Constitution imposes limits on the transfer of powers to the Communities.[129] Nevertheless, the Constitutional Court has not yet gone behind the principle of primacy and has invariably

---

[123] Pinto, "L'application du droit communautaire au Portugal" (1990) R.F.D.A. 983–984; Cruz Vilaça, Pais Antunes and Piçarra, "Droit constitutionnel et droit communautaire: le cas portugais" (1991) Riv.D.E. 301–310; Botelho Moniz, "The Portuguese Constitution and the Participation of the Republic of Portugal in the European Union" (1998) E.Pub.L. 465–478.

[124] Supremo Tribunal Administrativo; October 27, 1999, Case 45389-A.

[125] Miranda, "La Constitution portugaise et le traité de Maastricht" (1992) R.F.D.C. 679, at 681; Botelho Moniz (n.123, *supra*), at 476–477; see also Gonçalves, "Quelques problèmes juridiques que pourra poser l'application du droit communautaire dans l'ordre interne portugais face à la Constitution de 1976" (1980) R.T.D.E. 662–693.

[126] Liñán Nogueras and Roldán Barbero, "The Judicial Application of Community Law in Spain" (1993) C.M.L.R. 1135–1154.

[127] *Tribunal Constitucional*, February 14, 1991, *ibid.*, at 1139. See, prior to that judgment, Sobrina Heredia, "La réception et la place dans l'ordre juridique espagnol des normes conventionnelles internationales et des actes normatifs des organisations internationales" (1990) R.F.D.A. 965–968.

[128] *cf.* Santaolalla Gadea and Martínez Lage, "Spanish Accession to the European Communities: Legal and Constitutional Implications" (1986) C.M.L.R. 11, at 22–23. For the first application of the principle of primacy by the highest ordinary court, in a judgment of June 13, 1991, see Abele, "Der Vorrang des Gemeinschaftsrechts in der Rechtsprechung des *Tribunal Supremo*" (1992) Eu.Z.W. 305–308.

[129] *Tribunal Constitucional*, July 1, 1992 (*declaración* concerning the constitutionality of the EU Treaty, which stood to be ratified); see the references in ns to para 3–018, *supra*.

refused to review Community acts directly in the light of fundamental rights enshrined in the Constitution.[130]

(4) *Austria, Finland and Sweden*

Austria. In Austria, Art. 9(2) of the Constitution enables specific **17–034** competences to be transferred to international organisations. Since accession to the European Union was regarded as a total revision of the Constitution, it had, in accordance with the procedure laid down in Art. 44(3) thereof, to be approved in a referendum and cast in a law on accession.[131] In view of the "monist" approach taken by Austrian law with regard to provisions of international law, commentators accept that all provisions of Community law adopted after accession also enjoy primacy.[132] There is a possibility that a conflict may arise in Austria as a result of the role played by the *Verfassungsgerichtshof* in guaranteeing its own standard of fundamental rights.[133]

Finland. The Finnish Constitution makes no mention of delegating **17–035** competence to any international organisation. Since the Finnish Parliament considered that, in some respects, accession to the European Union was incompatible with the Constitution, it adopted the 1994 law on accession under a procedure which also amended the Constitution.[134] Under the Finnish legal system, provisions of international law obtain the force of law only by formal incorporation. The 1994 law on accession to the Union incorporated the primacy and potential direct effect of Community law into Finnish law as parts of the *acquis communautaire*.[135]

---

[130] Liñán Nogueras and Roldán Barbero (n.126, *supra*), at 1141–1144.

[131] Seidl-Hohenveldern, "Constitutional Problems Involved in Austria's Accession to the EU" (1995) C.M.L.R. 727–731; Griller, "Verfassungsfragen der österreichischen EU-Mitgliedschaft" (1995) Z.f.RV. 89–115; Herbst, "Austrian Constitutional Law and Accession to the European Union" (1995) E.Pub.L. 1–7; Egger, "L'Autriche—Etat membre de l'Union européenne. Les effets institutionnels" (1996) R.M.C.U.E. 380–387.

[132] Egger (n.131, *supra*), at 382; Seidl-Hohenveldern (n.131, *supra*), at 737–740. Initially, the *Verwaltungsgerichtshof* raised questions as to the application of the principle of primacy; see ECJ, Case C–224/97 *Ciola* [1999] E.C.R. I–2517, paras 21–34.

[133] Griller, "Wird Österreich das dreizehnte EG-Mitglied? Neutralität und Grundprinzipien des österreichischen Bundesverfassungsrechts als Prüfsteine des Beitrittsantrags" (1991) Eu.Z.W. 679, at 689; Egger (n.131, *supra*), at 385. In practice, no problems have arisen; see Fischer and Lengauer, "The Adaptation of the Austrian Legal System Following EU Membership" (2000) C.M.L.R. 763, at 772–774; Peyrou-Pistoulet, "Droit constitutionnel et droit communautaire: l'exemple autrichien" (2001) R.F.D.C. 237, at 254–255.

[134] Aalto, "Accession of Finland to the European Union: First Remarks" (1995) E.L.R. 618, at 620–623. The four Basic Laws making up the Finnish Constitution have been replaced since March 1, 2000 by a single text. See Kulovesi, "International Relations in the New 'Constitution of Finland'" (2000) J.I.L. 513–522.

[135] For the application of these principles, see Jääskinen, "The Application of Community Law in Finland: 1995–1998" (1999) C.M.L.R. 407–411; Ojanen, "The Impact of EU Membership on Finnish Constitutional Law" (2004) E.Pub.L. 531–564. Compare this implicit incorporation with the express formulation of primacy and direct effect in the law ratifying the EEA Agreement, *ibid.*, at 626–627. For the precedence of EEA rules, see para. 23–010, *infra*.

17–036 Sweden. Sweden, in common with Finland, applies a "dualist" approach with regard to the position of international legal provisions. Art. 10:5 of the Swedish Constitution affords a basis for the primacy of Community law. Along the lines of the case law of the German *Bundesverfassungsgericht*, that provision makes it possible to transfer decision-making power to the Community in so far as (*sålänge*) the latter affords protection of fundamental rights commensurate with that of the Constitution and the ECHR.[136] Pursuant to that provision, the Swedish Parliament has passed a law confirming the validity in Sweden of existing and future Community law and the legal effects attributed to that law by the Treaties, thereby incorporating the principle of the primacy of Community law.[137]

(5) *The Member States having acceded in 2004*

17–037 Cyprus. The establishment of the Republic of Cyprus as an independent and sovereign State was the result of the Zurich and London Agreements which led to the signing in 1960 of the Constitution and three Treaties,[138] two of which are incorporated into the Constitution.[139] The Cypriot legal system is considered to be "monist" in the sense that duly ratified and published treaties acquire superior force to any municipal law.[140] According to Art. 179(1) of the Constitution of Cyprus, the Constitution remains nonetheless the supreme law of the Republic. The case law of the Supreme Court has recognised that self-executing international agreements are directly applicable as an integral part of the domestic legal order.[141] It has

---

[136] *Regeringsform*, Art. 10:5, first subpara., in force since November 1, 1994.
[137] For a discussion as to whether the Swedish courts may consider whether the Community has acted within its competence, see Andersson, "Remedies for Breach of EC Law before Swedish Courts", in Lonbay and Biondi (eds), *Remedies for Breach of EC Law* (John Wiley & Sons, Chichester, 1997), 203, at 204–206. In practice, Swedish courts recognise unconditionally the primacy of Community law; see Bernitz, "Sweden and the European Union: On Sweden's Implementation and Application of European Law" (2001) C.M.L.R. 903, at 925–927.
[138] These are the Treaty of Establishment, between the Republic of Cyprus, Greece, Turkey and the UK, the Treaty of Guarantee by which Greece, Turkey and the UK recognise and guarantee, *inter alia*, the independence, territorial integrity and security of the Republic of Cyprus and also the state of affairs established by the Basic Articles of the Constitution and, finally, the Treaty of Military Alliance between the Republic of Cyprus, Greece, Turkey and the UK.
[139] Under Art. 181 of the Constitution, the Treaty of Guarantee and the Treaty of Military Alliance are incorporated into the Constitution as Annexes I and II thereto. Continued exercise by the State of its legislative, executive, judicial and administrative functions, following the non-participation of Turkish Cypriots in the State organs of the Republic Cyprus since 1964, has been achieved without constitutional amendment concerning the bi-communal structure of the State, by taking temporary measures justified by the doctrine of necessity, enabling State functions and services to continue unimpeded while the above abnormal situation continues (on the partitioning of Cyprus, see n.5 to para. 8–001).
[140] Emiliou,"The Constitutional impact of enlargement at EU and national level: the case of the Republic of Cyprus" in Kellermann, de Zwaan and Czuczai (eds), *EU Enlargement—The Constitutional Impact of the Enlargement at EU and National Level* (T.M.C. Asser, The Hague, 2001) 243, at 245.
[141] *Malachtou v Armefti* (1987) 1 C.L.R. 207, at 235.

further adopted the rule that international agreements must be interpreted in accordance with international law and in conformity with the international obligations of the Republic.[142] According to some commentators, all this bodes well for the reception of Community law into the Cypriot legal order.[143]

Czech Republic. The Czech Republic, in common with Hungary, Malta **17–038** and the Slovak Republic, used to embrace a "dualist" system with respect to the incorporation of rules of international law.[144] Accordingly, treaty provisions were incorporated into the internal legal order only by express reference in a domestic rule of law. In practice, Czech courts were willing to interpret national law in the light of directly applicable provisions of the association agreement between the Czech Republic and the Community, even in the absence of any explicit reference to these provisions in domestic law.[145] Nonetheless, important constitutional amendments have been necessary to allow for the accession of the Czech Republic to the European Union.[146] According to Art. 10 of the Czech Constitution, as amended in 2002, international agreements which have been ratified, approved and promulgated and which are binding upon the Czech Republic are to constitute part of the Czech legal order. Should an international agreement make provision contrary to a domestic law, the international agreement shall be applied. This not only turns the Czech legal order into a "monist" system, but also paves the way for the precedence of Community and Union law. The new Art. 10a of the Czech Constitution authorises the transfer of powers to an international organisation or institution.[147] Article 95 of the Czech Constitution declares that national courts are bound by laws and international agreements constituting part of the legal order and may assess the conformity of any domestic regulation with the law or with such international agreement.[148]

---

[142] *ibid.*; see also *Shipowners Union v The Registrar of Trade Marks* (1988) 3 C.L.R 457.

[143] Emiliou,"Cyprus" in Ott and Inglis (eds), *Handbook on European Enlargement—A Commentary on the Enlargement Process,* (T.M.C. Asser, The Hague, 2002) 239, at 249.

[144] Balaš, "Legal and quasi-legal thresholds of the accession of the Czech Republic to the EC" in *EU Enlargement—The Constitutional Impact of the Enlargement at EU and National Level* (n.140, *supra*) 267–277.

[145] See the judgment of the High Court in *Olomouc* (nr.2.A 6/96), interpreting national competition law in the light of the former Art. 86 [now Art. 82] of the EC Treaty and Art. 64 of the Europe Agreement (which required practices to be assessed under the former Arts 85, 86 and 92 of the EEC Treaty; on the agreement, para. 23–027 *et seq., infra*). The Czech Constitutional Court confirmed this judgment (nr. III.US 31/97). See Týč, "Czech Republic" in *Handbook on European Enlargement—A Commentary on the Enlargement Process* (n.143, *supra*) 229, at 231.

[146] Týč (n.145, *supra*), at 236.

[147] According to Art. 10a(2) of the Czech Constitution, this transfer should take place by means of an international agreement which must be approved by Parliament unless a constitutional law requires approval by means of a referendum.

[148] Týč (n.146, *supra*), at 237.

17–039 Estonia. In Estonia, the primacy of Community law seems to be based both upon the precedence of international norms in general and upon the recent amendment to the 1992 Estonian Constitution. In common with the other Baltic states and Poland, Estonia has a "monist" legal system. With respect to the position of international law, it follows from Arts 3 and 123 of the Estonian Constitution that international agreements which have been ratified by the national parliament are part of the national legal order and, consequently, must be applied by the national courts.[149] According to Art. 123(2) of the Constitution, in the event of conflict between Estonian laws and international treaties ratified by the national parliament, the provisions of the treaty shall apply.[150] The same provision states, in its first paragraph, however, that the Republic of Estonia shall not conclude international treaties which are in conflict with the Constitution. In order to avoid such a conflict, the Constitution was amended in 2003 as a result of the same referendum by which the population gave its approval to accession to the European Union. According to the Amendment Act, "the Constitution of the Republic of Estonia applies taking account of the rights and obligations arising from the Accession Treaty".[151]

17–040 Hungary. Hungary is considered to belong to the "dualist" school as far as the integration of international law into the national legal order is concerned.[152] According to Art. 7(1) of the Hungarian Constitution of 1949, the Hungarian legal order "accepts the generally respected rules of international law, and guarantees the conformity of accepted international obligations with domestic law". Prior to Hungary's accession to the European Union, the Hungarian Constitution did not allow for the transfer of competence to international organisations. Moreover, the Hungarian legal order recognised the direct applicability of international norms only through the incorporation of such norms into domestic law.[153] Therefore, the Constitution was supplemented by Art. 2/A, according to which

---

[149] Pärn, "Estonia" in *Handbook on European Enlargement—A Commentary on the Enlargement Process* (n.143, *supra*) 251–255.

[150] *ibid.*, at 251–252.

[151] For the referendum, see para. 1–021, *supra*. For some cases in which Estonian courts relied on the association agreement with the Community and principles of EU law, *ibid.*, at 253–254 and Kerikmäe, "Estonian Constitutional Problems in Accession to the EU" in *EU Enlargement—The Constitutional Impact of the Enlargement at EU and National Level* (n.140, *supra*) 291, at 299–300.

[152] Vàrhelyi, "Hungary" in *Handbook on European Enlargement—A Commentary on the Enlargement Process* (n.143, *supra*) 257–265.

[153] Accordingly, the Constitutional Court held in Decision No. 30/1998 (VI.25) that it was not sufficient for Art. 62 of the association agreement with the Community to refer to rules of Community law (Arts 85, 86 and 92 [now Arts 81, 82 and 87] of the EC Treaty) in order for the Hungarian authorities to be bound, or even allowed, to apply these rules. It was considered a breach of sovereignty if Hungary were to apply rules emanating from an organisation of which it was not a member. See Vàrhelyi, *ibid.*, at 262–264; Volkai, "The Application of the Europe Agreement and European Law in Hungary: The Judgement of an Activist Constitutional Court on Activist Notions" (Harvard Jean Monnet Working Paper 8/99, Cambridge, 1999) 39 pp.

Hungary, "in its capacity as a Member State of the European Union, may exercise certain constitutional powers jointly with other Member States to the extent necessary in connection with the rights and obligations conferred by the Treaties on the foundation of the European Union and the European Communities", whereby "these powers may be exercised independently and by way of the institutions of the European Union". It remains to be seen whether the Hungarian Constitutional Court will follow the case law of the German *Bundesverfassungsgericht* in the interpretation of the term "to the extent necessary".

Latvia. Before the accession of Latvia to the European Union, Art. 68 of 17–041 the Latvian Constitution of 1922 was supplemented so as to allow for membership of the European Union, which had to be approved by a national referendum.[154] This provision forms the basis for the delegation of part of Latvia's state competences to the Union. In the Latvian legal order, once an international agreement has been approved by the Parliament, the provisions of the international agreement will prevail in case of conflict with rules of national law. Nonetheless, the Constitution is to take precedence over international agreements.[155] Even though the relationship between Community law and Latvian constitutional law has not been explicitly defined, Latvian courts are expected to give due effect to the primacy of Community law.[156]

Lithuania. The Constitution of Lithuania of 1992 contains a clause 17–042 allowing the Republic of Lithuania to participate in international organisations provided that they do not contradict the interests and independence of the State (Art. 136). On July 13, 2004, the Constitution was supplemented with a Constitutional Act according to which Lithuania is to share with and delegate competencies to the European Union.[157]

Article 2 of the Constitutional Act provides that the norms of the Union *acquis* shall be an integral part of the Lithuanian legal order and will apply directly when they are based on the founding Treaties of the Union. Furthermore, it expressly states that in any case of conflict of norms the

---

[154] According to Art. 68(4), substantial changes in the conditions of Latvia's membership of the European Union shall also be decided by a national referendum if such referendum is requested by at least one-half of the members of the Parliament (*Saeima*).

[155] See Luters-Thümmel, "Latvia" in *Handbook on European Enlargement—A Commentary on the Enlargement Process* (n.143, *supra*) 267, at 268–272.

[156] See, to that effect, also Ušacka, "The Impact of the European integration process on the Constitution of Latvia" in *EU Enlargement—The Constitutional Impact of the Enlargement at EU and National Level* (n.140, *supra*) 337, at 346.

[157] Constitutional Act of July 13, 2004, on the Membership of the Republic of Lithuania in the European Union. On the proposed Act, see Vadapalas and Jarukaitis, "Lithuania" in *Handbook on European Enlargement—A Commentary on the Enlargement Process* (n.143, *supra*), at 288.

norms of the Union *acquis* shall prevail over the laws of the Republic of Lithuania.[158]

17–043 Malta. The Maltese legal system distinguishes, in a "dualist" manner, between the national and international legal orders and does not accord international norms any legal force on their own in the domestic legal order.[159] Article 6 of the Maltese Constitution of 1964 provides that "if any other law is inconsistent with this Constitution, this constitution shall prevail and the other law, to the extent of the inconsistency, shall be void". Moreover, the Ratification of Treaties Act states that "[n]o provision of a treaty shall become, or be enforceable as, part of the law of Malta except by or under an Act of Parliament".[160] The Maltese Constitution was amended in 2003 to take account of accession to the European Union in the definition of the powers of the national parliament.[161] It took an Act of Parliament to ensure the legal force and primacy of Community and Union law in the Maltese legal order. Pursuant to the European Union Act, the Treaties as well as "existing and future acts adopted by the European Union" shall be part of the domestic law of Malta (Art. 3(1)), whereas any provision of domestic law which is incompatible with Malta's obligations under the Treaties will be without effect and unenforceable (Art. 3(2)).[162]

17–044 Poland. In 1997, Poland adopted a new Constitution, which allows for the transfer of certain sovereign powers to the European Union. According to Art. 90(1) of the Constitution, "the Republic of Poland may, by virtue of international agreements, delegate to an international organisation or international institution the competence of organs of State authority in relation to certain matters".[163] According to Art. 91(1) of the Constitution, a ratified international agreement shall constitute part of the domestic legal order and shall be applied directly, unless its application depends on the

---

[158] Commentators had argued earlier that the rule according to which international treaties have supremacy over domestic laws and secondary legal acts (based on Art. 138 of the Constitution and Art. 11(2) of the Law on international treaties) would also apply to Community and Union law: Vadapalas, "Delimitation of competences between the European Union and the Member States: a look from a candidate country" in Melissas and Pernice (eds), *Perspectives of the Nice Treaty and the Intergovernmental Conference in 2004* (Nomos, Baden-Baden, 2002), at 25.

[159] Frendo and Piscopo, "Malta" in *Handbook on European Enlargement—A Commentary on the Enlargement Process* (n.143, *supra*) 291–297.

[160] See Xuereb, "Constitutional questions raised by the proposed accession of Malta to the European Union in the general context" in *EU Enlargement—The Constitutional Impact of the Enlargement at EU and National Level* (n.140, *supra*) 229, at 230–236.

[161] Pursuant to Art. 65(1) of the Constitution of Malta, "Parliament may make laws for the peace, order and good government of Malta in conformity with full respect for human rights, generally accepted principles of international law and Malta's international and regional obligations in particular those assumed by the Treaty of Accession to the European Union signed in Athens on the 16th April, 2003".

[162] See the European Union Act of July 16, 2003: *www.legal-malta.com/law/laws-of-malta.htm*.

[163] See Jankowska-Gilberg, "Verfassungsrechtliche Grundlagen des Beitritts und der Mitgliedschaft Polens in der Europäischen Union" (2003) EuR. 417, at 418–427.

enactment of a statute. Moreover, Art. 91(3) of the Constitution provides that "[i]f an agreement, ratified by the Republic of Poland, establishing an international organization so provides, the laws established by it shall be applied directly and have precedence in the event of a conflict of laws". These provisions form a legal basis for the precedence of Community and Union law over provisions of national law. Since Art. 8(1) of the Constitution states that "[t]he Constitution shall be the supreme law of the Republic of Poland", it is still debated whether the precedence of Community law over provisions of national constitutional law needs to be explicitly confirmed in the Polish legal order.[164]

Slovak Republic. On the way to EU membership, the Slovak Republic had **17–045** its Constitution of 1992 thoroughly amended in 2001 so as to specify the rules by which powers were to be delegated to the European Union as well as the status of Community and Union law in the Slovak legal order, which was considered to be of a "dualist" nature.[165] As a result, Art. 7(2) of the Constitution states that the Slovak Republic may, by means of an international treaty ratified and promulgated in accordance with the law, or on the basis of such a treaty, transfer the exercise of part of its sovereign powers to the European Communities and the European Union.[166] The same provision introduces the primacy of European law into the Slovak legal order where it provides that "legally binding acts of the European Communities and of the European Union shall have precedence over laws of the Slovak Republic".[167] The constitutional amendments turned the Slovak legal order in a "monist" system.[168]

Slovenia. Pursuant to the Slovene Constitution of 1991, international **17–046** treaties which are ratified and published are part of the domestic legal order, ranking just below the Constitution.[169] Since it was considered not to

---

[164] *ibid.*, at 427–439; Lazowski, "Poland" in *Handbook on European Enlargement—A Commentary on the Enlargement Process* (n.143, *supra*) 299, at 306–307; Justynski, "The impact of the European integration process on the creation of the broad lines of the Constitution of the Republic of Poland and on the political practices of the country" in *EU Enlargement—The Constitutional Impact of the Enlargement at EU and National Level* (n.140, *supra*) 279–290 (all mentioning that Arts 90 and 91 of the Constitution do not give Community law precedence over the Constitution). Art. 188 of the Constitution of Poland empowers the Constitutional Tribunal to adjudicate on the "conformity of statutes and international agreements to the Constitution".

[165] Kunová,"Constitutional aspects of the accession of the Slovak republic to the European Union" in *EU Enlargement—The Constitutional Impact of the Enlargement at EU and National Level* (n.140, *supra*) 327, at 329. The Constitutional amendments were introduced by Constitutional Act No. 90/2001 Coll.

[166] Boháčik,"The Slovak Republic" in *Handbook on European Enlargement—A Commentary on the Enlargement Process* (n.143, *supra*) 323, at 325.

[167] *ibid.*, at 325 and 329. Art. 7(2) of the Constitution further specifies that "the transposition of legally binding acts which require implementation shall be realised through a law or a regulation of the Government [. . .]".

[168] *ibid.*, at 325.

[169] Vehar and Ilešič, "Slovenia" in *EU Enlargement—The Constitutional Impact of the Enlargement at EU and National Level* (n.140, *supra*) 331–339.

allow for any transfer of sovereign rights to an international organisation,[170] the Slovene Constitution has been supplemented in 2003 with a new Art. 3a, according to which "Slovenia may transfer the exercise of part of its sovereign rights to international organisations which are based on respect for human rights and fundamental freedoms, democracy and the principles of the rule of law and may enter into a defensive alliance with States which are based on respect for these values". According to the same provision, "[l]egal acts and decisions adopted within international organisations to which Slovenia has transferred the exercise of part of its sovereign rights shall be applied in Slovenia in accordance with the legal regulation of these organisations". This would seem to incorporate the principle of primacy of Community law in the Slovene legal order.

B. THE DIRECT EFFECT OF COMMUNITY LAW

17–047 *Van Gend & Loos.* Ever since the 1963 judgment in *Van Gend & Loos*, it is clear that individuals may derive rights directly from Community law.[171] In that judgment, the Court of Justice gave a preliminary ruling on a question raised by the Netherlands Tariefcommissie as to whether individuals might derive rights from Art. 12 of the EEC Treaty which the courts had to protect. The Court of Justice held that "[t]o ascertain whether the provisions of an international treaty extend so far in their effects it is necessary to consider the spirit, the general scheme and the wording of those provisions".[172] The Court inferred from the special nature of the Community legal order that Community law is "intended to confer upon [individuals] rights which become part of their legal heritage" (see para. 1–0018). The Court stated that "[t]hese rights arise not only where they are expressly granted by the Treaty, but also by reason of obligations which the Treaty imposes in a clearly defined way upon individuals as well as upon the Member States and upon the institutions of the Community". After inquiring into the substance and wording of Art. 12 of the EEC Treaty, the Court held that the prohibition laid down in that article on Member States increasing import duties or charges having equivalent effect which they already applied in their trade with each other had direct effect.[173]

17–048 **Conditions for direct effect.** The decisive test for determining whether or not a given provision has direct effect is its content. The Court of Justice has consistently held that a provision produces direct effects only if it is "clear and unconditional and not contingent on any discretionary implementing measure".[174] Although the Court has not invariably

---

[170] *ibid.*, at 338–339; Vehar, "Constitutional problems in the period of pre-accession in the Republic of Slovenia" in *EU Enlargement—The Constitutional Impact of the Enlargement at EU and National Level* (n.140, *supra*) 369, at 370.

[171] ECJ, Case 26/62 *Van Gend & Loos* [1963] E.C.R. 1, at 11–13.

[172] *ibid.*, at 12.

[173] *ibid.*, at 12–13.

[174] ECJ, Case 44/84 *Hurd* [1986] E.C.R. 29, para. 47.

formulated that test in the same way, it refers to a provision which requires no further implementation (involving a margin of discretion) by Community or national authorities in order to achieve the effect sought in an effective manner.[175] The standstill provision of Art. 12 of the EEC Treaty afforded a plain example of a provision which affords the Member States no discretion. A provision which puts an authority under a duty to act does not confer any rights on individuals which national courts may enforce if the authority has discretion.[176]

The judgment in *Van Gend & Loos* had already held that a provision did not lack clarity simply on the ground that the national court deemed it necessary to make a reference to the Court of Justice on the interpretation of the provision in question. A provision has direct effect where the court is able, without the operation of other implementing measures, to reach an interpretation which may be applied to the case at issue, as a result of which individuals may enforce the rights derived from that provision.[177] In *Van Gend & Loos*, the Court of Justice indicated that "an illegal increase may arise from a rearrangement of the tariff resulting in the classification of the product under a more highly taxed heading and from an actual increase in the rate of customs duty". That interpretation allowed the Netherlands court to apply the prohibition set out in Art. 12 of the EEC Treaty to the benefit of an undertaking.[178] Accordingly, Art. 39 of the EC Treaty (free movement of workers) is not prevented from having direct effect because para. 3 of that article contains a reservation with regard to limitations justified on grounds of public policy, public security or public health. This is because "the application of those limitations is . . . subject to judicial control".[179]

Direct effect of primary law. The Court of Justice has repeatedly had to **17–049** rule on whether provisions of the EC Treaty have direct effect.[180] The same test is applied in the case of the other Community Treaties.[181] The

---

[175] See the Opinion of Advocate General W. Van Gerven in ECJ, Case C–128/92 *Banks* [1994] E.C.R. I–1209, at I–1236–1237.

[176] ECJ, Case 28/67 *Molkerei-Zentrale Westfalen* [1968] E.C.R. 143, at 153; ECJ, Case 13/68 *Salgoil* [1968] E.C.R. 453, at 461.

[177] See, *e.g.* ECJ, Case 12/81 *Garland* [1982] E.C.R. 359, paras 14–15.

[178] ECJ, Case 26/62 *Van Gend & Loos* [1963] E.C.R. 1, at 14–15.

[179] ECJ, Case 41/74 *Van Duyn* [1974] E.C.R. 1337, para. 7. See, with regard to Art. 56 (free movement of capital), ECJ, Joined Cases C–163/94, C–165/94 and C–250/94 *Sanz de Lera* [1995] E.C.R. I–4821, para. 43.

[180] According to the list drawn up by Schermers and Waelbroeck, the following articles of the EC Treaty appear to have direct effect: Art. 12; Art. 23; Art. 25; Arts 28, 29 and 30; Art. 31(1) and (2); Arts 39–55 in general, and particularly Arts 39, 43, 49 and 50; Art. 81(1); Art. 82; Art. 86(1) and (2); Art. 88(3), last sentence; Art. 90, first and second paras; and Art. 141. See Schermers and Waelbroeck, *Judicial Protection in the European Union* (Kluwer, The Hague, 2001), para. 359, at 183–185. This is also true for EC Treaty, Art. 81(3) (see para. 5–197, *supra*). The Court of Justice has denied direct effect to the following provisions: EC Treaty, Art. 2; Art. 10; Art. 87(1); and Art. 97. *ibid.*, para. 360, at 185. Art. 293 of the EC Treaty has also been held not to have direct effect: ECJ, Case C–336/96 *Gilly* [1998] E.C.R. I–2793, paras 14–17; likewise Art. 1 of the EU Treaty and

application of the Community Treaties in the Member States does not depend on whether they have been transposed into the national legal system. Where a Treaty provision is recognised as having direct effect, an individual may therefore rely upon it both against Community and national authorities (vertically) and against other individuals (horizontally).[182] Such a provision has direct effect from the time when it enters into force or, as the case may be, from the end of the transitional period. In exceptional cases, however, the Court of Justice may place limitations on the temporal effect of a judgment recognising the direct effect of a provision (see para. 17–153).

17–050 **Direct applicability and effect of secondary law.** Alongside provisions of the Community Treaties, provisions contained in acts of Community institutions may be invoked by individuals. In principle, whether such provisions have direct effect depends on the same substantive criteria that apply to Treaty provisions.[183] As far as international agreements concluded by the Community are concerned, however, it must always be ascertained whether the possible direct effect of their provisions is consistent with the spirit, the general scheme and the terms of the agreement.[184] Under Art. 249 of the EC Treaty, regulations are "directly applicable" and are therefore binding, without any need for transposition, on all within the national legal order who are substantively affected thereby. Where a provision of a regulation has direct effect, an individual may rely upon it also against other individuals.[185] There is no such horizontal direct effect in the case of provisions of directives, which, if they satisfy the requirements for direct effect, can embody only obligations for State bodies.[186] In indicating that a provision has direct effect, the Court of Justice uses the expressions "direct applicability" and "direct effect" interchangeably. Some

---

Art. 255 of the EC Treaty: CFI, Case T–191/99 *Petrie v Commission* [2001] E.C.R. II–3677, paras 34–35.

[181] See ECJ, Case C–128/92 *Banks* [1994] E.C.R. I–1209, paras 15–19 (Arts 4(d), 65 and 66(7) of the ECSC Treaty held *not* to have direct effect); *cf.* the Opinion of Advocate General W. Van Gerven in that case, at I–1232–1243. See also ECJ, Case C–18/94 *Hopkins* [1996] E.C.R. I–2281, paras 26–29 (Art. 4(b) and Art. 63(1) of the ECSC Treaty held not to have direct effect) and ECJ, Case C–390/98 *Banks* [2001] E.C.R. I–6117 (Art. 4(b) held to have direct effect as far as discrimination between producers is concerned, but not Art. 4(c) of the ECSC Treaty).

[182] See, *e.g.* ECJ, Case 36/74 *Walrave* [1974] E.C.R. 1405, paras 17–25 (EC Treaty, Articles 12, 39 and 49); ECJ, Case 43/75 *Defrenne* [1976] E.C.R. 455, para. 39 (EC Treaty, Art. 119 [now Art. 141]); ECJ, Case C–281/98 *Angonese* [2000] E.C.R. I–4139, paras 30–36 (EC Treaty, Art. 48 [now Art. 39]).

[183] See ECJ, Case 9/70 *Grad* [1970] E.C.R. 825, paras 5–6. For a survey of the direct effect of various provisions of Community law, see Pescatore, "The Doctrine of 'Direct Effect': An Infant Disease of Community Law" (1983) E.L.R. 155–177; Prinssen and Schrauwen, (eds), *Direct Effect. Rethinking a Classic of EC Legal Doctrine* (Europa Law, Groningen, 2002), 300 pp.

[184] para. 17–093, *infra.*

[185] para. 17–119, *infra.*

[186] para. 17–124 *et seq.*, *infra.* For decisions, see para. 17–137, *infra.*

commentators consider that these expressions are not strictly defined and use both of them in referring to the possibility for an individual to rely upon a provision.[187] For a clearer understanding of the effect of Community law, it is nevertheless more illuminating to make a distinction between "direct applicability" (whether a provision requires implementation *as a legal instrument*) and "direct effect" (whether the *substance* of a provision may be relied upon).[188]

III. Sources of Community Law

Primary and secondary law. Community law encompasses rules which arise 17–051 as a result of action both by the Member States and by Community institutions and bodies. As has already been mentioned, the sources of Community law may therefore be divided into primary and secondary (or derived) Community law, the latter consisting of (international and autonomous) acts of institutions and bodies, as supplemented by the general principles recognised in the Community legal order. The discussion of the sources of Community law will be based upon this distinction, starting with the ranking order of the various types of provisions. The case law of the Court of Justice and the Court of First Instance is a separate source of Community law and plays an important part in constructing the Community legal order, even though the tasks of the two courts are formally limited to the interpretation and application of each of the other legal sources.

A. Hierarchy of Sources of Law

Hierarchy. As for the primacy of Community law, the relationship between 17–052 its various sources is not expressly laid down in the Treaties. Not even the EU Constitution makes any attempt to define a hierarchy or ranking order of sources of Union law. Nevertheless, the authors of the Treaties always assumed the existence of a hierarchy of norms. This emerges from Art. 230 of the EC Treaty, under which an action may be brought—in the Court of Justice or in the Court of First Instance—for the annulment of acts of Community institutions, *inter alia*, on the ground of "infringement of this Treaty or of any rule of law relating to its application" (see also ECSC Treaty, Art. 33, and EAEC Treaty, Art. 146). Consequently, judicial review extends to examining whether the acts in question are compatible with all superior rules of law.

---

[187] See, for instance, Lauwaars and Timmermans, *Europees recht in kort bestek* (Kluwer, Deventer, 2003), at 22–24 and 107–109; Barents and Brinkhorst, *Grondlijnen van Europees recht* (Kluwer, Deventer, 2003), at 52; see also Prechal, "Does Direct Effect Still Matter?" (2000) C.M.L.R. 1047–1069.

[188] See already Winter, "Direct Applicability and Direct Effect: Two Distinct and Different Concepts in Community Law" (1972) C.M.L.R. 425–438.

17–053 Primary law. At the top of that hierarchy, there are the provisions of "primary" Community law (see paras 17–056—17–064), including the general principles of law which the Court of Justice ensures are observed pursuant to Art. 220 of the EC Treaty (see paras 17–065—17–090). Since the institutions and bodies have to act within the powers conferred upon them by the Community Treaties, "secondary" or "derived" Community law is subordinate to those primary norms. The general principles of law play a role in the interpretation and application of Treaty provisions and other rules of Community law. General legal principles of a constitutional nature must be complied with in the case of secondary Community law; in contrast, "administrative" legal principles are supplementary in nature and apply only to the execution of Community law (see paras 17–066—17–067).

17–054 Secondary law. In the field of secondary Community law, it is not the form of a given measure, but its nature which determines its place within the legal order. Thus, legislative measures take precedence over implementing provisions, even though both may take the form of one of the instruments listed in Art. 249 of the EC Treaty (see para. 17–113).

Special priority attaches to international law in the Community legal order. Some principles of international law enshrined in treaties or having the force of customary law take precedence as general principles of Community law (see para. 17–103). The legal force of treaties concluded by the Community is superior to that of other "derived" Community acts (see para. 17–092).

There is no predetermined ranking order of the various forms of act which the institutions may adopt. Nevertheless, a number of acts of the Council stand out as being organic in character (see para. 17–141). In so far as other acts are based upon such an organic act, they may not depart from it unless it is expressly amended.[189]

Agreements concluded between institutions are binding upon the institutions concerned by virtue of the principle that an authority is bound by rules which it has itself adopted (*patere legem quam ipse fecisti*; see para. 17–149).

In addition, as regards the relationship between equivalent provisions of Community law, the principle applies that a later provision (*lex posterior*) prevails over an earlier one and a specific provision (*lex specialis*) over a more general one.[190]

---

[189] *E.g.* with regard to the Second Comitology Decision: ECJ, Case C–378/00 *Commission v European Parliament and Council* [2003] E.C.R. I–937, paras 40–42.

[190] But, in order for this to be so, the more specific or later provision must intend to limit or replace the general or earlier provision respectively; see, *e.g.* ECJ, Case C–481/99 *Heininger and Heininger* [2001] E.C.R. I–9945, paras 36–39; ECJ, Case C–444/00 *Mayer Parry Recycling* [2003] E.C.R. I–6163, paras 49–57. See also CFI, Case T–6/99 *ESF Elbe-Stahlwerke Feralpi v Commission* [2001] E.C.R. II–1523, para. 102 (ECSC Treaty as a *lex specialis*).

National law. In each Member State, Community law is applied in **17–055** conjunction with the applicable rules of national law. Consequently, the application of Community law relies in practice on national legislative and implementing provisions and on the interpretation and application given to Community law by national case law. These national sources of law do not as such form a source of Community law, although they influence the recognition of general principles of law in Community law (see para. 17–065 *et seq.*). In some cases, the Court of Justice and the Court of First Instance have to apply national law.[191] This occurs, for example, in disputes brought before the Community Court pursuant to an arbitration clause (EC Treaty, Art. 238) concerning a contract governed by the law of a particular Member State.[192] In the absence of an express reference to national law, the application of Community law may necessitate a reference to the laws of the Member States only where the Community Courts cannot identify in Community law or in the general principles of Community law, criteria enabling them to define the meaning and scope of such a provision by way of independent interpretation.[193]

B. PRIMARY COMMUNITY LAW

1. Status of primary Community law

Constitutional law. Primary Community law consists of those provisions **17–056** which were adopted directly by the Member States in their capacity as "constituent authority", meaning in the first place the Community Treaties and the Treaties amending or supplementing them. Together with the general principles of law, these Treaty provisions constitute the "constitutional" provisions of Community law.[194] This is because they serve as the legal basis for action on the part of the Communities and unquestionably take precedence over the law of the Member States.[195] Where such provisions satisfy the test formulated by the Court of Justice for direct effect, they may as such confer rights on individuals (see para. 17–049).

---

[191] See Lenaerts, "Interlocking Legal Orders in the European Union and Comparative Law" (2003) I.C.L.Q. 873–906; Kohler and Knapp, "Nationales Recht in der Praxis des EuGH" (2002) Z.Eu.P. 701–726.

[192] See Van Nuffel, "De contractuele aansprakelijkheid van de Europese Gemeenschap: een bevoegdheidskluwen ontward" (2000–2001) A.J.T. 157–162.

[193] See CFI, Case T–43/90 *Díaz García v European Parliament* [1992] E.C.R. II–2619, para. 36; CFI (Judgment of April 21, 2004), Case T–172/01 *M. v Court of Justice*, not yet reported, para. 71.

[194] See ECJ, Case 294/83 *Les Verts v European Parliament* [1986] E.C.R. 1339, para. 23 ("the basic constitutional charter, the Treaty").

[195] For the "constitutional" nature of primary Community law, see Heintzen, "Hierarchisierungsprozesse innerhalb des Primärrechts der Europäischen Gemeinschaft" (1984) EuR. 35, at 40, and the commentators cited in para. 1–020, *supra*. For the precedence of primary law over secondary Community law, see, *e.g.* CFI, Case T–144/99 *Institute of Professional Representatives before the European Patent Office v Commission* [2001] E.C.R. II–1087, paras 50–54; ECJ (order of the President of February 23, 2001), Case C–445/00 R *Austria v Council* [2001] E.C.R. I–1461, paras 82–93.

17–057 **Adoption and amendment.** Primary Community law comes into being by mutual agreement as between the Member States and may be amended only in accordance with the proper procedure. In the case of the Treaties, that procedure is the amendment procedure prescribed by Art. 48 of the EU Treaty and some simplified procedures, which in any event are based on approval by the Member States in accordance with their respective constitutional traditions.[196] At the same time, the provisions of the Acts of Accession and the adjustments of secondary legislation annexed to those Acts themselves and ensuing therefrom constitute provisions of primary law, which, unless otherwise provided, may be amended or repealed only by recourse to the procedures prescribed for amending the original Treaties.[197] In some cases, a rule of primary law provides that it may be amended by the Community institutions acting on their own.[198] However, in the absence of express authority, provisions of secondary legislation cannot detract from provisions of primary law, such as a protocol annexed to an Act of Accession.[199]

17–058 **Judicial review.** The Court of Justice has no jurisdiction to rule on the validity of primary Community law. It may merely give preliminary rulings on the interpretation of the Treaties (see EC Treaty, Art. 234(a)). Since the Treaties and the amendments thereto do not constitute acts of the institutions within the meaning of Arts 7 and 230 of the EC Treaty, the Court of Justice has no power to consider their legality.[200] This means that provisions constituting an integral part of the Acts of Accession are also not subject to judicial review by the Court of Justice.[201]

2. Survey of primary Community law

17–059 **Community Treaties.** Primary Community law comprises, first and foremost, the Community Treaties (the EC Treaty and the EAEC Treaty; before July 23, 2002 also the ECSC Treaty). Since in principle the broad field of competence of the EC Treaty also embraces the atomic-energy sector, the EC Treaty governs the interrelationship between that treaty and the EAEC Treaty. Art. 305 of the EC Treaty provides that the provisions of

---

[196] For these procedures, see paras 7–003—7–008, *supra*.

[197] See, *e.g.* Art. 7 of the 2003 and 1994 Acts of Accession, Art. 6 of the 1985 Act of Accession and ECJ, Joined Cases 31–35/86 *LAISA v Council* [1988] E.C.R. 2285, para. 12.

[198] For the procedures in question, see para. 7–009, *supra*. For an application after the introduction in 1993 of a common organisation of the market in bananas, which was the subject of a special "protocol on bananas" annexed to the EEC Treaty, see ECJ, Case C–280/93 *Germany v Council* [1994] E.C.R. I–4973, paras 113–118.

[199] ECJ (judgment of September 11, 2003), Case C–445/00 *Austria v Commission*, not yet reported, paras 57–64.

[200] ECJ, Joined Cases 31–35/86 *LAISA v Council* [1988] E.C.R. 2285, para. 12; CFI (order of July 14, 1994), Case T–584/94 *Roujansky v Council* [1994] E.C.R. II–585, para. 15, upheld by ECJ (order of January 13, 1995), Case C–253/94 P *Roujansky v Council* [1995] E.C.R. I–7.

[201] *LAISA v Council* (see preceding n.), paras 13–18.

the EC Treaty "shall not derogate" from those of the EAEC Treaty. As far as the atomic energy sector is concerned, this means that the EC Treaty therefore does not apply whenever the EAEC Treaty contains a derogating provision.[202] Where the EAEC Treaty does not lay down rules on a particular matter coming under the atomic energy sector, the matter in question falls within the EC Treaty.[203] Thus, the EC rules on the free movement of workers apply to all employees in the nuclear energy sector who are not in "skilled employment" within the meaning of Art. 96 of the EAEC Treaty. In this way, EC law operates as the *lex generalis*, supplementing, where necessary, the *lex specialis* (EAEC law).

For the sake of the coherence of Community law, the Court of Justice often looks for assistance, when interpreting Treaty provisions, from a comparison of provisions of the other Treaties which have resolved the question at issue more clearly[204] or explicitly.[205] Sometimes the Court holds that principles formulated in the context of one of the Treaties are of

---

[202] See Cusack, "A Tale of Two Treaties: An Asssessment of the Euratom Treaty in Relation to the EC Treaty" (2003) C.M.L.R. 117–142. This was also true of the ECSC Treaty as a result of the Art. 305 of the EC Treaty, which provided that the EC Treaty should "not affect" the ECSC Treaty: see, *e.g.* ECJ, Joined Cases 27 to 29/58 *Compagnie des Hauts Fournaux et Fonderies de Givors v High Authority* [1960] E.C.R. 241, at 255; ECJ, Joined Cases 188 to 190/80 *France, Italy and UK v Commission* [1982] E.C.R. 2545, paras 30–31; ECJ, Case 239/84 *Gerlach* [1985] E.C.R. 3507, paras 10–11; ECJ, Case C–18/94 *Hopkins v National Power and PowerGen* [1996] E.C.R. I–2281, paras 11–24.

[203] ECJ, Joined Cases 188 to 190/80 *France, Italy and UK v Commission* [1982] E.C.R. 2545, para. 32 (the application of a directive based on Art. 86(3) of the EC Treaty to public undertakings in the atomic energy sector does not derogate from the EAEC Treaty); ECJ, Opinion 1/94 *Agreement establishing the World Trade Organisation* [1994] E.C.R. I–5267, para. 24 (in the absence of any EAEC provision relating to external trade, agreements concluded pursuant to Art. 133 of the EC Treaty also extend to EAEC products).

[204] ECJ, Case 13/60 *Geitling v High Authority* [1962] E.C.R. 83, at 102 (interpretation of Art. 65 of the ECSC Treaty by analogy with Art. 81 of the EC Treaty); ECJ, Case 294/83 *Les Verts v European Parliament* [1986] E.C.R. 1339, para. 24 (argument based on Art. 38 of the ECSC Treaty in an interpretation of Art. 173 of the EEC Treaty recognising that an action for annulment could be brought against the European Parliament). In *Continental Can*, the Court refused to take account, in interpreting Art. 82 of the EC Treaty, of an *a contrario* argument based on the wording of Art. 66 of the ECSC Treaty: ECJ, Case 6/72 *Europemballage and Continental Can v Commission* [1973] E.C.R. 215, para. 22.

[205] ECJ, Case 9/56 *Meroni v High Authority* [1957 and 1958] E.C.R. 133, at 140–141 (reasoning by analogy from Art. 241 of the EC Treaty and Art. 156 of the EAEC Treaty in interpreting Art. 36 of the ECSC Treaty) (see also Case 10/56 *Meroni v High Authority* [1957 and 1958] E.C.R. 157, at 162–163, and Case 15/57 *Compagnie des Hauts Fourneaux de Chasse v High Authority* [1957 and 1958] E.C.R. 211, at 224–225, delivered on the same day); Case 266/82 *Turner v Commission* [1984] E.C.R. 1, para. 5 (reference to the second para. of Art. 34 of the ECSC Treaty in applying Art. 233 of the EC Treaty). See also ECJ, Case 314/85 *Foto-Frost* [1987] E.C.R. 4199, paras 13–18 (determination of the duty of courts, not being courts of last instance, to make a reference for a preliminary ruling under Art. 234 of the EC Treaty by analogy with Art. 41 of the ECSC Treaty) and the converse case in ECJ, Case C–221/88 *Busseni* [1990] E.C.R. I–495, paras 10–16 (reference made to Art. 234 of the EC Treaty and Art. 150 of the EAEC Treaty in order to determine the scope of Art. 41 of the ECSC Treaty).

general validity.[206] Where, however, a treaty provision introduces a divergent rule, that rule must be complied with.[207]

The unity of Community law is further underpinned by the single nature of the institutions (see para. 1–011). The Court of Justice has interpreted the provisions concerning the institutions in the various Treaties in conjunction with each other, and where necessary, reconciling them.[208] Where an institution lays down rules on its internal functioning, it necessarily acts in the field of all the Treaties. Accordingly, Art. 38 of the ECSC Treaty afforded Luxembourg a sufficient legal basis to bring an action for annulment against a European Parliament resolution in which it decided to hold its meetings in Brussels and Strasbourg. The Parliament argued that the application was inadmissible on the ground that the resolution was based on all three Treaties and therefore could not be contested pursuant to the ECSC Treaty alone. The Court held, however, that the action would lie precisely because the measure related simultaneously and indivisibly to the sphere of the three Treaties.[209]

17–060 **Amending Treaties.** In so far as later Treaties (such as the Single European Act, the EU Treaty, the Treaty of Amsterdam and the Treaty of Nice) amended and supplemented the Community Treaties, their provisions likewise constitute primary Community law. Some parts of these treaties, however, are not part of Community law, namely the provisions contained in Titles V and VI of the EU Treaty.[210] In so far as the latter provisions

---

[206] ECJ, Ruling 1/78 *Draft Convention of the International Atomic Energy Agency on the Physical Protection of Nuclear Materials, Facilities and Transport* [1978] E.C.R. 2151, para. 15 (reference to the EC Treaty in order to emphasise the general scope of the provisions of the EAEC Treaty relating to the common market), and para. 36 (application of the principle that there should be harmony between international action by the Community and the distribution of internal powers, which emerged from the case law on the EC Treaty, to situations governed by the EAEC Treaty); ECJ, Case C–221/88 *Busseni* [1990] E.C.R. I–495, paras 21 and 39 (alignment of the effects of recommendations adopted under Art. 14 of the ECSC Treaty with those of directives adopted under Art. 249 of the EC Treaty); ECJ, Case C–341/94 *Allain* [1996] E.C.R. I–4631, paras 23–25 (interpretation of obligations arising under Arts 14 and 86 of the ECSC Treaty by reference to the case law on Art. 10 of the EC Treaty); ECJ, Case C–390/98 *Banks* [2001] E.C.R. I–6117, paras 70 and 73–75.

[207] ECJ, Joined Cases 16 and 17/62 *Confédération nationale des producteurs de fruits et légumes v Council* [1962] E.C.R. 471, at 478 (second para. of Art. 173 of the EEC Treaty relating to the *locus standi* of legal or natural persons to bring an action for annulment interpreted restrictively despite the broader provisions of the ECSC Treaty); ECJ, Case C–327/91 *France v Commission* [1994] E.C.R. I–3641, paras 37–39 (the third para. of Art. 101 of the EAEC Treaty manifestly confers on the Commission different powers at the international level than Art. 300 of the EC Treaty).

[208] ECJ, Case 101/63 *Wagner* [1964] E.C.R. 195, at 200–201.

[209] ECJ, Case 230/81 *Luxembourg v European Parliament* [1983] E.C.R. 255, paras 14–20. For the unity of the Staff Regulations of the various institutions, see CFI, Case T–164/97 *Busaca v Court of Auditors* [1998] E.C.R.-SC II–1699, paras 48–61 (upheld on appeal, see ECJ, Case C–434/98 P *Council v Busaca and Court of Auditors* [2000] E.C.R. I–8577).

[210] Paras 3–014—3–015, *supra*; this also applies partially to Title I of the EU Treaty and to the (largely abrogated) Titles II and III of the Single European Act (paras 3–007–3–008, *supra*).

cannot be enforced by the Community Courts, their legal effects in a Member State will be dependent upon the status given to rules of international law in the legal order of that Member State.

Protocols. Primary law also includes the "protocols annexed to [the **17–061** Treaties] by common accord of the Member States", which form "an integral part" thereof (EC Treaty, Art. 311, and EAEC Treaty, Art. 207).[211] Consequently, the statutes of the EIB and the ECB, which are contained in protocols, have the same legal status as the EC Treaty. A protocol may therefore make changes in the Treaty and other provisions of primary law.[212] Where particular Member States are given a special position diverging from the rules of the Treaty, it is often formulated in a protocol.[213] Such protocols may not derogate from basic provisions of the Treaty to which they are annexed.[214] This means that they must always be interpreted in a manner which accords with such basic provisions.[215]

Accession Treaties. As has already been mentioned, primary Community **17–062** law encompasses all provisions which have been agreed between the Member States and the acceding State with regard to the conditions of accession and the resultant adjustments to the Treaties, namely the Accession Treaty, the Act of Accession and provisions forming an integral part thereof. In interpreting those provisions, regard must be had to the foundations and system of the Community, as established by the original Treaties.[216]

Declarations. In signing each of the Community Treaties and the Treaties **17–063** amending them, the Member States, as an "intergovernmental conference", adopted declarations or took note of unilateral declarations made by Member States, which are annexed to the final act of the intergovernmental

---

[211] CFI, Joined Cases T–164/99, T–37/00 and T–38/00 *Leroy v Council* [2001] E.C.R. II–1819, para. 58.

[212] *ibid.*, para. 67.

[213] Important examples are Protocol (No. 25) to the EC Treaty on certain provisions relating to the UK of Great Britain and Northern Ireland and Protocol (No. 26) to the EC Treaty on certain provisions relating to Denmark, annexed by the EU Treaty to the EC Treaty (special position with regard to EMU), as well as Protocol (No. 4) to the EU Treaty and the EC Treaty on the position of the UK and Ireland and Protocol (No. 5) to the EU Treaty and the EC Treaty on the position of Denmark, annexed by the Amsterdam Treaty to the EC Treaty and the EU Treaty (special position with regard to, *inter alia*, to the application of Title IV of the EC Treaty).

[214] ECJ, Case C–280/93 *Germany v Council* [1994] E.C.R. I–4973, para. 117.

[215] In case of doubt, a protocol must be interpreted so as to avoid a conflict with general principles of law, such as the principle of equal treatment: CFI, Case T–333/99 *X v ECB* [2001] E.C.R. II–3021, para. 38. For a case in which the protocol itself provides that its application squares with fundamental principles of the internal market and free movement, see ECJ (judgment of September 11, 2002), Case C–445/00 *Austria v Council*, not yet reported, paras 65–75.

[216] ECJ, Case 231/78 *Commission v UK* [1979] E.C.R. 1447, para. 12; ECJ, Case C–233/97 *KappAhl Oy* [1998] E.C.R. I–8068, paras 18–21.

conference.[217] Unlike protocols, such declarations are not binding.[218] Declarations which are signed by all the Member States may nevertheless be taken into account by the Court of Justice in interpreting provisions of the Treaties,[219] at least in so far as they do not conflict with those provisions.[220]

17–064 **Constitutional acts.** Some acts which the Council adopts pursuant to the Community Treaties may be regarded as being primary Community law because their entry into force depends upon their being adopted by the Member States in accordance with their respective constitutional requirements. This category of acts consists, for the present, of the Decision of September 20, 1996 and the appended Act, adopted pursuant to Art. 190(4) of the EC Treaty, concerning the direct election of the European Parliament and the "own resources" decisions adopted under Art. 269, second paragraph, of that Treaty (see para. 7–008). Although they may possibly not be subject to judicial review by the Court of Justice,[221] the Court does not shirk from subordinating their provisions to the general principles enshrined in the Treaties.[222]

---

[217] Such declarations are sometimes made after signature; see, *e.g.* the Declaration of May 1, 1992 of the High Contracting Parties interpreting Protocol (No. 7) annexed to the EU Treaty and the Community Treaties (n.737 mode to para. 5–170, *supra*) and the declarations made by the European Council and the unilateral declarations made by Denmark at the European Council held on December 11 and 12, 1992 on the occasion of the Danish ratification of the EU Treaty ([1992] O.J. C348; para. 3–011, *supra*).

[218] Toth, "The Legal Status of the Declarations Annexed to the Single European Act" (1986) C.M.L.R. 803, at 812; see also the Commission's answer of December 1, 1997 to question No E–3008/97 (Hager), [1998] O.J. C134/56.

[219] See Art. 31(2)(b) of the Vienna Convention of May 23, 1969 on the law of treaties (see n.454, *infra*), which for the purpose of interpreting a treaty considers its context to be, *inter alia*, any instrument which was made by one or more parties in connection with the conclusion of the treaty and accepted by the other parties as an instrument related to the treaty. See Schermers, "The Effect of the Date December 31, 1992" (1991) C.M.L.R. 275, at 276.

[220] See also the discussion of non-Community action on the part of the Union in para. 18–013, *infra*. See, in addition, ECJ, Case C–233/97 *KappAhl Oy* [1998] E.C.R. I–8068, paras 22–23 (declaration made during the accession negotiations not to be used in interpreting the Act of Accession as it was not reflected in the wording of the Act).

[221] In any event, the European Court of Human Rights assumed in the judgment in *Matthews* that the 1976 Act on the direct election of the European Parliament as "a treaty within the Community legal order" could not be challenged before the Court of Justice: European Court of Human Rights, February 18, 1999, *Matthews v UK*, No. 24833/94, para. 33. On the basis of this finding, the UK was found to have violated Art. 3 of the First Protocol to the ECHR by excluding Gibraltar from the election of the European Parliament (see para. 17–081, *infra*).

[222] See with regard to the Third Decision on Own Resources, ECJ, Case C–284/90 *Council v European Parliament* [1992] E.C.R. I–2227, para. 31. See for further particulars Arnauld, "Normenhierarchien innerhalb des primären Gemeinschaftsrechts—Gedanken im Prozess der Konstitutionalisierung Europas" (2003) EuR. 191–216.

C. GENERAL PRINCIPLES OF COMMUNITY LAW

1. General principles of law

a. Status

Source of general principles. According to Art. 220 of the EC Treaty, the **17–065**
Court of Justice and the Court of First Instance ensure that "in the
interpretation and application of this Treaty the law is observed" (see also
EAEC Treaty, Art. 136, and the EU Constitution, Art. I–29(1)).
Recognition of "the law" as a source of Community law has enabled the
Court of Justice to have recourse to general principles of law in interpreting
and applying Community law.[223] The Court applies principles which it finds,
if not expressly, at least implicitly in the legal traditions of the Member
States.[224] Several principles of law are moreover supported by the Charter
of Fundamental Rights of the European Union.[225] These principles form
part of the Community legal order and hence infringement of them
constitutes an "infringement of this Treaty or of any rule of law relating to
its application" within the meaning of the second paragraph of Art. 230 of
the EC Treaty.[226]

Administrative principles. Some legal principles afford guidance for the **17–066**
administration where it encounters ambiguities or *lacunae* in Community
legislation which it has to apply ("principles of administrative law").[227] By
the same token, Art. 288 of the EC Treaty (EAEC Treaty, Art. 188) puts
the Community under a duty to make good any damage caused by its
institutions or by its servants in the performance of their duties "in
accordance with the general principles common to the laws of the Member
States" (this being the Community regime for non-contractual liability).
The general principle thus expressed that an unlawful act or omission gives
rise to an obligation to make good the damage caused also reflects the

---

[223] Expressly mentioned in ECJ, Joined Cases C–46/93 and C–48/93 *Brasserie du Pêcheur and Factortame ("Factortame IV")* [1996] E.C.R. I–1029, paras 24–30. See also Schermers, "Algemene rechtsbeginselen als bron van gemeenschapsrecht" (1983) S.E.W. 514–527.

[224] Schwarze, "Tendances vers un droit administratif commun en Europe" (1993) R.T.D.E. 235–245; for an outstanding survey with numerous references to learned articles and textbooks, see Schermers and Waelbroeck, *Judicial Protection in the European Union* (Kluwer, The Hague, 2001), paras 53–258, at 28–132; Tidimas, *The General Principles of EC Law*, (Oxford, Oxford University Press, 1999) 377 pp.; Usher, *General Principles of EC Law* (Longman, London, 1998), 167 pp.; Bernitz and Nergelius (eds), *General Principles of European Community Law* (Kluwer Law International, The Hague, 2000), 244 pp. See also Lenaerts, "Le droit comparé dans le travail du juge communautaire" (2001) R.T.D.E. 487–528 and "Interlocking Legal Orders in the European Union and Comparative Law" (n.191, *supra*).

[225] See CFI, Case T–54/99 *max.mobil.Telekommunikation Service v Commission* [2002] E.C.R. II–313, paras 48 and 57 (concerning the right to sound administration and the right to an effective remedy before a tribunal).

[226] ECJ, Case 112/77 *Töpfer v Commission* [1978] E.C.R. 1019, para. 19.

[227] Schwarze, *European Administrative Law* (Sweet and Maxwell, London, 1992), at 68–71 (which contains an extended discussion of the main principles and their status).

obligation on public authorities to make good damage caused in the performance of their duties.[228]

17–067 Constitutional principles. Other legal principles are constitutional in nature and the Community institutions must comply with them even when issuing legislative measures. If so far as they are applicable, they apply not only to acts of the institutions but also to measures adopted by Member States in implementing Community law.[229] The Court of Justice includes among constitutional principles also fundamental rights (see para. 17–073) and general principles of international law (see para. 17–103). Some of these principles are set out in the EC Treaty itself, such as the principles of subsidiarity (Art. 5, second para.; see paras 5–028 *et seq.*), proportionality (Art. 5, second and third paras.; see paras 5–036 *et seq.*) and institutional balance (Art. 7; see paras 13–008 *et seq.*), the duty to co-operate in good faith (Art. 10; see paras 5–047 *et seq.*) and the principle of non-discrimination (*inter alia*, Art. 12; see paras 5–056 *et seq.*); others are recognised by other provisions of primary Community law.[230] In one case, the Court of Justice has even applied a constitutional principle against the wording of the Treaty itself.[231] The principle was that of democracy, which is recognised by Art. 6(1) of the EU Treaty, together with the principles of liberty, respect for human rights and fundamental freedoms and the rule of law, as a principle common to the Member States on which the Union is founded. If the Council should determine the existence of a serious and persistent breach by a Member State of those principles, certain of the rights deriving from the Treaties may be suspended as far as the Member State in question is concerned (EU Treaty Art. 7; see para. 9–012).

17–068 National constitutional traditions. The Court of Justice often recognises general principles of law as forming part of the Community legal order without expressly referring to the constitutional traditions of the Member States. A legal principle is usually put forward where it is impliedly associated with the concepts applying in the field in the Member States. Where, however, the existence and substance of a legal principle and any

---

[228] ECJ, Joined Cases C–46/93 and C–48/93 *Brasserie du Pêcheur and Factortame* (*"Factortame IV"*) [1996] E.C.R. I–1029, paras 28–29.

[229] See, for instance, ECJ, Case 77/81 *Zuckerfabrik Franken* [1982] E.C.R. 681, paras 22–29 (principles of legal certainty and proportionality); ECJ, Joined Cases 201–202/85 *Klensch* [1986] E.C.R. 3477, paras 8–10 (principle of equal treatment; for this principle see also para. 5–060, *supra*); ECJ, Case C–197/91 *FAC* [1993] E.C.R. I–2639, paras 23–25; with regard to fundamental rights, see also para. 17–077, *infra*. See Temple Lang, "The Sphere in which Member States are obliged to comply with the General Principles of Law and Community Fundamental Rights Principles" (1991) L.I.E.I. 23–35.

[230] See, *e.g.* the budgetary principles set out in the Financial Regulation and the Decisions on Own Resources (paras 10–117–10–120, *supra*).

[231] ECJ, Case C–70/88 *European Parliament v Council* [1990] E.C.R. I–2041, paras 26–27 (discussed in connection with institutional balance in para. 13–011, *supra*). For the principle of democracy, see also para. 16–005.

possible derogations from such a principle are less clear, the Court of Justice makes more exhaustive inquiries into its status in the national legal systems or in treaties which the Member States have signed.[232] This does not prevent the Court from recognising a principle of law which can be derived neither from common national constitutional traditions nor from treaties. One example is the right of a legal person not to be forced to give evidence against itself in a procedure under competition law.[233]

b. Survey

Principles of sound administration. According to the Charter of **17–069** Fundamental Rights, every person has the right to have his or her affairs handled impartially, fairly and within a reasonable time by the institutions and bodies of the Union.[234] Among the principles of law classed as "principles of sound administration",[235] a prominent place is occupied by the principle of legal certainty, according to which legal rules must be clear and their application foreseeable for all interested parties.[236] This means in

---

[232] See, e.g. ECJ, Case 155/79 *AM & S v Commission* [1982] E.C.R. 1575, paras 18–22 (confidentiality of exchange of letters between lawyer and client; para. 17–071, *infra*); ECJ, Joined Cases 46/87 and 227/88 *Hoechst v Commission* [1989] E.C.R. 2859, paras 17–19, and the parallel judgments ECJ, Case 85/87 *Dow Benelux v Commission* [1989] E.C.R. 3137, paras 28–30, and ECJ, Joined Cases 97–99/87 *Dow Chemical Ibérica v Commission* [1989] E.C.R. 3165, paras 14–16 (the Court of Justice found that the legal systems of all the Member States provided protection against arbitrary or disproportionate intervention by public authorities in the sphere of a natural or legal person's private activities, but did not extend the fundamental right to inviolability of the home to business premises; para. 17–089, *infra*).

[233] ECJ, Case 374/87 *Orkem v Commission* [1989] E.C.R. 3283, paras 32–35, and the parallel judgment ECJ, Case 27/88 *Solvay v Commission* [1989] E.C.R. 3355 (this right is not derived from the common constitutional traditions of the Member States, from Art. 6 of the ECHR or from Art. 14 of the International Covenant on Civil and Political Rights, but arises out of the rights of the defence: para. 17–107, *infra*). Community law does not require that principle to be respected in national proceedings which concern exclusively private relations between individuals and cannot lead directly or indirectly to the imposition of a penalty by a public authority: ECJ, Case C–60/92 *Otto* [1993] E.C.R. I–5683, paras 11–17.

[234] Charter of Fundamental Rights, Art. 41(1). See CFI, Case T–54/99 *max.mobil.Telekommunikation Service v Commission* [2002] E.C.R. II–313, paras 48 and 53.

[235] See in the Charter of Fundamental Rights of the European Union in particular the right to good administration (Art. 41), the right of access to documents (Art. 42), the right to an effective remedy and to a fair trial (Art. 47), the presumption of innocence and right of the defence (Art. 48), the principles of legality and proportionality of criminal offences (Art. 49) and the right not to be punished twice in criminal proceedings for the same offence (Art. 50). See Lais, "Das Recht auf eine gute Verwaltung unter besonderer Berücksichtigung der Rechtsprechung des Europäischen Gerichtshofs" (2002) Z.Eu.S. 447–482; Kanska, "Towards Administrative Human Rights in the EU—Impact of the Charter of Fundamental Rights" (2004) E.L.J. 296–326. For the UK, see Wade & Forsyth, *Administrative Law* (Oxford University Press, Oxford, 9th ed. 2004), 1030 pp. See also Popelier, "Legal Certainty and Principles of Proper Law Making" (2000) European Journal of Law Reform 321–342.

[236] ECJ, Case C–325/91 *France v Commission* [1993] E.C.R. I–3283, para. 26. For the application of legal rules interpreted by the Court of Justice, see ECJ, Case 43/75 *Defrenne* [1976] E.C.R. 455, paras 71–7; ECJ, Case C–143/93 *Van Es Douane Agenten* [1996] E.C.R. I–431, paras 27–33; ECJ, Case C–177/96 *Banque Indosuez* [1997] E.C.R. I–5659, paras 26–31.

the first place that every Community act intended to have legal effects must be based on a provision of superior law which is expressly stated to be its legal basis (see paras 5–009–5–012). Legal certainty also requires certain requirements to be fulfilled, such as the requirement for acts to state the reasons on which they are based (see para. 17–109) and to be notified to interested parties in a language which they understand.[237] Every measure of the institutions having legal effects must be clear and precise and must be brought to the notice of the person concerned in such a way that he or she can ascertain exactly the time at which the measure comes into being and starts to have legal effects.[238] Further expressions of the principle of legal certainty include respect for acquired rights,[239] the requirement for measures imposing penalties to have an unambiguous legal basis (*nulla poena sine lege*)[240]—which is the principle of legality in relation to crime and punishment and signifies that a provision of criminal law may not be applied extensively to the detriment of the defendant,[241]—the fact that measures having adverse effect on individuals may not be retroactive,[242] the existence of time-limits for challenging (Community) administrative acts[243] and the limitation period imposed for the imposition of sanctions.[244]

Individuals may also rely on the principle of protection of legitimate expectations. That principle protects any legitimate expectations created by the Community authorities.[245] The existence of a mere Commission proposal for a measure[246] or the fact that the Commission remained for a

---

[237] ECJ, Case 66/74 *Farrauto* [1975] E.C.R. 157, para. 6.

[238] CFI, Case T–115/94 *Opel Austria v Council* [1997] E.C.R. II–39, para. 124; ECJ (judgment of April 29, 2004), Case C–470/00 P *European Parliament v Ripa di Meana*, not yet reported, paras 65–71.

[239] ECJ, Case 12/71 *Henck* [1971] E.C.R. 743, paras 4–5 (where the law is subsequently changed, the provision in question must be interpreted in the light of the law as it was at the time when the provision was applied).

[240] ECJ, Case 117/83 *Könecke* [1984] E.C.R. 3291, para. 11.

[241] ECJ, Joined Cases C–74/95 and C–129/95 *Criminal proceedings against X* [1996] E.C.R. I–6609, para. 25; ECJ (judgment of January 7, 2004), Case C–60/02 *Criminal proceedings against X*, not yet reported, paras 61–63.

[242] ECJ, Case 63/83 *Kirk* [1984] E.C.R. 2689, para. 22. A new rule may, however, be applied to future effects of situations which arose under earlier rules: ECJ, Case 84/78 *Tomadini* [1979] E.C.R. 1801, para. 21. For the retroactive entry into effect of Community measures, see para. 17–111, *infra*.

[243] ECJ (judgment of January 13, 2004), Case C–453/00 *Kühne & Heitz* , not yet reported, para. 24. In exceptional cases, however, an administrative body with the *power* to reopen a decision that has become final may be placed under an *obligation* to do so if that decision was based on an incorrect application of Community law : ibid., paras 25–28 (para. 5–051, *supra*).

[244] ECJ, Case 48/69 *ICI v Commission* [1972] E.C.R. 619, para. 49.

[245] ECJ, Case 112/77 *Töpfer v Commission* [1978] E.C.R. 1019, paras 18–20; for example, see ECJ, Case 120/86 *Mulder* [1988] E.C.R. 2321, and Case 170/86 *von Deetzen* [1988] E.C.R. 2355; CFI, Case T–203/96 *Embassy Limousines & Services v European Parliament* [1999] E.C.R. -II 4239, paras 73–88. The principle of protection of legitimate expectations is often relied on in staff cases, see CFI, Case T–123/89 *Chomel v Commission* [1990] E.C.R. II–131, paras 25–31. The principle of good faith is the corollary in public international law of the principle of protection of legitimate expectations: CFI, Case T–115/94 *Opel Austria v Council* [1997] E.C.R. II–39, para. 93 (para. 21–006, *infra*).

[246] ECJ, Joined Cases C–13 to C–16/92 *Driessen* [1993] E.C.R. I–4751, para. 33.

long time without taking any action after delivering a reasoned opinion before bringing an action in the Court under Art. 226 of the EC Treaty[247] does not create a legitimate expectation. On account of the principle of protection of legitimate expectations, a legal measure cannot unconditionally be retroactively withdrawn. The retroactive withdrawal of an unlawful measure is permissible provided that the withdrawal occurs within a reasonable time and that the institution from which it emanates has had sufficient regard to how far the beneficiaries of the measure might have been led to rely on its lawfulness.[248] However, a lawful measure which has conferred individual rights or similar benefits may not at all be retroactively withdrawn .[249] In any event, by virtue of the principle of protection of legitimate expectations, a Community institution cannot be forced to apply Community rules *contra legem*.[250]

Other general principles. The Court of Justice also has to rule very **17–070** frequently on whether institutions and Member States have complied with the principles of equal treatment (see para. 5–056) and proportionality (see para. 5–036 *et seq.*). The principle of proportionality, too, has several aspects, such as the need for sanctions to be proportional to the seriousness of the infringement found[251] and for no greater burdens to be imposed on individuals than is reasonably necessary to attain the policy aim intended.[252] Under the Community legal order there is also a prohibition of the abuse of law.[253] Accordingly, an advantage granted by Community rules may not be obtained where the conditions laid down for obtaining it are created artificially and it appears from a combination of objective circumstances that, despite formal observance of the conditions laid down by those rules, the purpose of those rules has not been achieved. The Community Court also recognises the principle of unjust enrichment.[254] In addition, the Court of Justice has recognised *force majeure* as an exceptional ground for

---

[247] ECJ, Case C–317/92 *Commission v Germany* [1994] E.C.R. I–2039, para. 4.

[248] Joined Cases 7/56 and 3/57 to 7/57 *Algera v Common Assembly of the ECSC* [1957] E.C.R. 81, 116; Case 14/81 *Alpha Steel v Commission* [1982] E.C.R. 749, para. 10; Case 15/85 *Consorzio cooperative d'Abruzzo v Commission* [1987] E.C.R. 1005, para. 12; CFI, T–251/00 *Lagardère and Canal+ v Commission* [2002] E.C.R. II–4825, paras 138–152.

[249] Joined Cases 7/56 and 3/57 to 7/57 *Algera v Common Assembly of the ECSC* [1957] E.C.R. 81, 115; ECJ, Case 159/82 *Verli-Wallace* [1983] E.C.R. 2711, para. 8. See Lübbig, "Die Aufhebung (Rücknahme und Widerruf) von Verwaltungsakten der Gemeinschaftsorgane" (2003) Eu.Z.W. 233–236.

[250] CFI, Case T–2/93 *Air France v Commission* [1994] E.C.R. II–323, para. 102.

[251] ECJ, Case 240/78 *Atalanta* [1979] E.C.R. 2137, para. 15.

[252] ECJ, Case 9/73 *Schlüter* [1973] E.C.R. 1135, para. 22.

[253] ECJ, Case C–110/99 *Emsland-Stärke* [2000] E.C.R. I–11569, paras 50–54. See Triantafyllou, "L'interdiction des abus de droit en tant que principe général du droit communautaire" (2002) C.D.E. 611–632; Lagondet, "L'abus de droit dans la jurisprudence communautaire" (2003) J.D.D.E. 8–12; Weber (2004) L.I.E.I. 43–55.

[254] CFI, Case T–171/99 *Corus UK v Commission* [2001] E.C.R. II–2967, paras 55–56 (in repaying amounts undue, the interest on those amounts must also be repaid). See also Jones, *Restitution and European Community Law* (Mansfield Press, London, 2000), 206 pp.

escaping the legal consequences of failing to fulfil an obligation.[255] In the field of the common agricultural policy, *force majeure* may be relied upon in the case of abnormal and unforeseen circumstances beyond the control of the person concerned, the consequences of which could not have been avoided in spite of the exercise of all due care.[256]

In recent case law, the Community Court has also described the precautionary principle as a general principle of Community law requiring the competent authorities to take appropriate measures to prevent specific potential risks to public health, safety and the environment by giving precedence to the requirements related to the protection of those interests over economic interests.[257] It follows from the precautionary principle that where there is uncertainty as to the existence or extent of risks to human health, protective measures may be taken without having to wait until the reality and seriousness of those risks become fully apparent.[258]

17–071 Procedural rights. In areas in which the Community has a wide discretion, the Court of Justice is strict in supervising that procedural requirements designed to ensure that individuals' interests have been duly taken into

---

[255] ECJ, Case 4/68 *Schwarzwaldmilch* [1968] E.C.R. 377, at 385–387; ECJ, Case 68/77 *IFG v Commission* [1978] E.C.R. 353, para. 11.

[256] See ECJ, Case C–347/93 *Boterlux* [1994] E.C.R. I–3933, para. 34.

[257] CFI, Case T–13/99 *Pfizer Animal Health* [2003] E.C.R. II–3305, paras 113–115 and Case T–70/99 *Alpharma v Council* [2003] E.C.R. II–3495, paras 134–136; CFI, Joined Cases T–74/00, T–76/00, T–83 to T–85/00, T–132/00, T–137/00 and T–141/00 *Artegodan v Commission* [2002] E.C.R. II–4945, paras 182–184 (upheld on appeal: ECJ, Case C–39/03 P *Commission v Ategodan* [2003] E.C.R. I–7885). See da Cruz Vilaça, "The Precautionary Principle in EC Law" (2004) E.Pub.L. 369–406; MacMaoláin, "Using the precautionary principle to protect human health: *Pfizer v Council*" (2003) E.L.R. 723–734; De Sadeleer, "Le principe de précaution—Un nouveau principe général du droit" (2003) J.T.D.E. 129–134 and "Le statut juridique du principe de précaution en droit communautaire: du slogan à la règle" (2001) C.D.E. 91–132; Icard, "Le principe de précaution: exception à l'application du droit communautaire?" (2002) R.T.D.E. 471–497; Corcelle, "La perspective communautaire du principe de précaution" (2001) R.M.C.U.E. 447–454; Alemanno, "Le principe de précaution en droit communautaire" (2001) R.T.D.E 917–953; Fisher, "Is the precautionary principle justiciable?" (2001) J.Env.L. 315–334; Douma, "The Precautionary Principle in the European Union" (2000) R.E.C.I.E.L. 132–143. See also Daemen, "The European Community's Evolving Precautionary Principle—Comparisons with the United States and Ramifications for Doha Round Trade Negotiations" (2003) E.Env.L.Rev. 6–19; Ladeur, "The introduction of the precautionary principle into EU law: a Pyrrhic victory for environmental and public health law? Decision-making under conditions of complexity in multi-level political systems" (2003) C.M.L.R. 1455–1479.

[258] ECJ (judgment of September 9, 2003), Case C–236/01 *Monsanto Agricoltura Italia*, not yet reported, paras 111–112, referring to CFI, Case T–13/99 *Pfizer Animal Health* [2003] E.C.R. II–3305, paras 113–115 and Case T–70/99 *Alpharma v Council* [2003] E.C.R. II–3495, paras 134–136; CFI, Joined Cases T–74/00, T–76/00, T–83 to T–85/00, T–132/00, T–137/00 and T–141/00 *Artegodan v Commission* [2002] E.C.R. II–4945, paras 182–184 (upheld on appeal: ECJ, Case C–39/03 P *Commission v Ategodan* [2003] E.C.R. I–7885). See also EFTA Court, Case E–3/00 *EFTA Surveillance Authority v Norway* [2000–2001] EFTA Court Report, 73, para. 25, and formerly, in connection with the principle of proportionality, ECJ, Case C–180/96 *UK v Commission* [1998] E.C.R. I–2265, paras 99–100; Case C–180/96 *National Farmers' Union* [1998] E.C.R. I–2211, paras 63–34.

account have been complied with.[259] The Court takes the view that in all proceedings in which sanctions, in particular fines or penalty payments, may be imposed, the right to be heard is a fundamental principle of Community law which must be respected even in the absence of any provision relating to the procedure in question.[260] The upshot of this is that when any administrative body adopts a measure which is liable to prejudice the interests of individuals, it is bound to put them in a position to express their point of view.[261] In order to enable them effectively to exercise the right to defend themselves, each of them must, where necessary, be informed clearly and in good time of the objections raised against them.[262] Also as regards the rights of the defence, the Commission may not compel an undertaking to provide it with answers which might involve an admission on its part of the existence of the infringement which it is incumbent on the Commission to prove.[263] Moreover, the Commission has to conclude an administrative procedure within a reasonable time.[264] The Court further recognises the "fundamental legal principle" that an official against whom disciplinary proceedings have been brought is entitled to be assisted by a lawyer, who must be allowed access to the file.[265] Letters exchanged between a lawyer and his or her client are confidential if the communications were made for the purposes and in the interests of the client's right of defence and emanate from an "independent" (that is to say, not an "in-house") lawyer.[266]

---

[259] Lenaerts and Vanhamme, "Procedural Rights of Private Parties in the Community Administrative Process" (1997) C.M.L.R. 531–569; Drabek, "A Fair Hearing Before EC Institutions" (2001) E.Rev.Priv.L. 529–563.

[260] ECJ, Case 85/76 *Hoffmann-La Roche v Commission* [1979] E.C.R. 461, para. 9; see also ECJ, Case C–135/92 *Fiskano v Commission* [1994] E.C.R. I–2885, para. 39. The principle of the right to a fair hearing, to which the principle of the right to be heard is closely linked, applies also to the Member States, in particular in the context of proceedings brought against them, such as those concerning the review of State aid or the monitoring of Member State conduct as regards public enterprises; see ECJ, Case C–3/00 *Denmark v Commission* [2003] E.C.R. I–2643, paras 45–46.

[261] ECJ, Case 121/76 *Moli v Commission* [1977] E.C.R. 1971, para. 20; ECJ, Case 322/81 *Michelin v Commission* [1983] E.C.R. 3461, para. 7; CFI, Case T–346/94 *France-aviation v Commission* [1995] E.C.R. II–2841, paras 28–40; CFI, Case T–42/96 *Eyckeler and Malt v Commission* [1998] E.C.R. II–401, paras 76–88.

[262] ECJ, Case 17/74 *Transocean Marine Paint v Commission* [1974] E.C.R. 1063, para. 15; see also CFI, Joined Cases T–39/92 and T–40/92 *CB and Europay v Commission* [1994] E.C.R. II–49, paras 46–61.

[263] ECJ, Case 374/87 *Orkem v Commission* [1989] E.C.R. 3283, paras 32–35 (n.233, *supra*); CFI, Case T–112/98 *Mannesmannröhren-Werke v Commission* [2001] E.C.R. II–729, paras 59–79.

[264] CFI, Joined Cases T–213/95 and T–18/96 *SCK and FNK v Commission* [1997] E.C.R. II–1739, para. 56.

[265] ECJ, Case 115/80 *Demont v Commission* [1981] E.C.R. 3147, paras 11–12. For access to the file in competition cases, see CFI, Case T–30/91 *Solvay v Commission* [1995] E.C.R. II–1775; CFI, Case T–36/91 *ICI v Commission* [1995] E.C.R. II–1847; CFI, Case T–37/91 *ICI v Commission* [1995] E.C.R. II–1901.

[266] ECJ, Case 155/79 *AM & S v Commission* [1982] E.C.R. 1575, paras 18–22; CFI (order of April 4, 1990), Case T–30/89 *Hilti v Commission* [1990] E.C.R. II–163, paras 13–18.

The principle *ne bis in idem* means that a person cannot be adjudged or sentenced for something for which he or she was already unappealably acquitted or sentenced and, for example, precludes the Community, in competition matters, from finding an undertaking guilty or bringing proceedings against it a second time on the grounds of anti-competitive conduct in respect of which it has been penalised or declared not liable by a previous unappealable Community decision.[267] Where proceedings at Community level are carried on concurrently with national proceedings with a different aim, two sanctions are not necessarily ruled out, although "a general requirement of natural justice" demands that any previous punitive decision must be taken into account in determining any sanction which is to be imposed.[268] The *ne bis in idem* principle does not preclude the Community from imposing sanctions on a person for the same facts for which he has already been sentenced or tried outside the Community unless this is precluded by an international agreement.[269] Accordingly, under the Schengen Agreement a person whose case has been finally disposed of in a Member State may not be prosecuted again on the same facts in another Member State.[270]

In a number of cases, the Court has taken into account such principles as "natural justice", "fairness" and "equity".[271] In relations between

---

[267] CFI, Joined Cases T–305/94, T–306/94, T–307/94, T–313/94, T–314/94, T–315/94, T–316/94, T–318/94, T–325/94, T–328/94, T–329/94 and T–335/94 *Limburgse Vinyl Maatschappij NV v Commission ("PVC II")* [1999] E.C.R. II–931, paras 86–97, as upheld on appeal (ECJ, Joined Cases C–238/99 P, C–244/99 P, C–245/99 P, C–247/99 P, C–250–252/99 P and C–254/99 P *Limburgse Vinyl Maatschappij NV v Commission* [2002] E.C.R. I–8375, paras 59–63). See also ECJ, Joined Cases 18/65 and 35/65 *Gutmann v Commission* [1966] E.C.R. 103, at 119 (the principle prevents the Community from imposing two disciplinary measures for a single offence and from holding disciplinary proceedings more than once with regard to a single set of facts).

[268] ECJ, Case 14/68 *Wilhelm* [1969] E.C.R. 1, para. 11.

[269] CFI (judgment of July 9, 2003), Case T–223/00 *Kyowa Hakko Kogyo and Kyowa Hakko Europe v Commission*, not yet reported, paras 96–105, and CFI (judgment of July 9, 2003), Case T–224/00 *Archer Daniel Midland Company and Archer Daniel Midland Ingredients v Commission*, not yet reported, paras 85–94; CFI (judgment of April 29, 2004), Joined Cases T–236/01, T–239/01, T–244/01–T–246/01, T–251/01 and T–252/01, *Tokai Carbon v Commission*, not yet reported, paras 130–148.

[270] ECJ, Joined Cases C–187/01 and C–385/01 *Criminal proceedings against Hüseyin Gözütok and Klaus Brügge* [2003] E.C.R. I–1345, paras 25–48 (the *ne bis in idem* principle laid down in Art. 54 of the Convention implementing the Schengen Agreement also applies to procedures whereby further prosecution is barred, such as the procedures at issue in the main actions by which the Public Prosecutor in a Member State discontinues, without the involvement of a court, a prosecution brought in that State once the accused has fulfilled certain obligations and, in particular, has paid a certain sum of money determined by the Public Prosecutor). See Ongena, "De *ne bis in idem*'-regel en de Schengenlanden" (2003) N.J.Wb. 762–768; Fletcher, "Some Developments to the *ne bis in idem* Principle in the European Union: *Criminal proceedings against Hüseyin Gözütok and Klaus Brügge*" (2003) Mod.L.Rev. 769–780.

[271] For "fairness" and "equity", see ECJ, Case 31/75 *Costacurta v Commission* [1975] E.C.R. 1563, para. 4; ECJ, Case 94/75 *Süddeutsche Zucker v Hauptzollamt Mannheim* [1976] E.C.R. 153, para. 5; for other principles of law, see Schermers and Waelbroeck, *Judicial Protection in the European Union* (Kluwer, The Hague, 2001), paras 185–242, at 103–126.

Community institutions and bodies and their personnel, the Community Court applies general principles of employment law.[272]

Access to the law. In connection with the principle of open administration, **17–072** Community law recognises an obligation to publish or notify binding acts to the parties concerned (see paras 17–110–17–111). The right of access to documents held by public authorities, which exists in most Member States in the form of a constitutional or legislative principle, now also exists *vis-à-vis* the Community institutions.[273]

2. Fundamental rights

a. Status

(1) Fundamental rights as general principles of Community law

General principles. Ever since 1969 it has been clear that "fundamental **17–073** human rights [are] enshrined in the general principles of Community law and protected by the Court".[274] Consequently, under Art. 220 of the EC Treaty, the Court of Justice and the Court of First Instance guarantee that fundamental rights (fundamental rights and freedoms; human rights) are respected within the ambit of Community law. Article 6(2) of the EU Treaty enshrines protection of fundamental rights in the following terms:

> "The Union shall respect fundamental rights, as guaranteed by the European Convention for the Protection of Human Rights and Fundamental Freedoms signed in Rome on November 4, 1950 and as they result from the constitutional traditions common to the Member States, as general principles of Community law".[275]

---

[272] CFI, Case T–192/99 *Dunnett v European Investment Bank* [2001] E.C.R. II–813, paras 85 and 89–90 (employees' right to be consulted about the withdrawal of a financial advantage).

[273] ECJ, Case C–58/94 *Netherlands v Council* [1996] E.C.R. I–2169, paras 34–40. The right of access to documents must be regarded as being a general principle of Community law, see in particular Broberg, "Access to documents: a general principle of Community law" (2002) E.L.R. 194–205. For access to documents, see para. 10–160, *supra*.

[274] ECJ, Case 29/69 *Stauder* [1969] E.C.R. 419, para. 7; see also ECJ, Case 11/70 *Internationale Handelsgesellschaft* [1970] E.C.R. 1125, para. 4.

[275] There is extensive literature on this subject; for some general articles, see Zuleeg, "Der Schutz der Menschenrechte im Gemeinschaftsrecht" (1992) D.ö.V. 937–944; Coppel and O'Neill, "The European Court of Justice: Taking Rights Seriously?" (1992) C.M.L.R. 669–692, and above all the reply from Weiler and Lockhart, "'Taking Rights Seriously' Seriously: The European Court and its Fundamental Rights Jurisprudence" (1995) C.M.L.R. 51–94 and 579–627; Rodriguez Iglesias, "The Protection of Fundamental Rights in the Case Law of the Court of Justice of the European Communities" (1995) Col.J.E.L. 169–181; Lenaerts, "Le respect des droits fondementaux en tant que principe constitutionnel de l'Union européenne", in *Mélanges Michel Waelbroeck* (Bruylant, Brussels, 1999), at 423–457; Alston and Weiler, "An 'Ever Closer Union' in Need of a Human Rights Policy" (1998) E.J.I.L. 658–723; Lenaerts, "Fundamental Rights in the European Union" (2000) E.L.R. 575–600; Von Bogdandy, "The European Union as a Human Rights Organisation? Human Rights and the Core of the European Union" (2000) C.M.L.R. 1307–1338.

In setting their policy, the Community and the Member States "have in mind" fundamental social rights (see EC Treaty, Art. 136).[276]

17–074 Increased importance. The EC Treaty makes no express mention of fundamental rights, although a fundamental right to equal treatment does underlie the prohibition of discrimination on grounds of nationality (EC Treaty, Art. 12) and the principle of equal pay for men and women for equal work (EC Treaty, Art. 141) (see para. 5–056). Initially, the Court of Justice merely held that it could not rule on the compatibility of Community measures with fundamental rights guaranteed by the Constitution of a Member State.[277] In the 1970 judgment in the *Internationale Handelsgesellschaft* case, the Court added, however, that the protection of fundamental rights, "whilst inspired by the constitutional traditions common to the Member States, must be ensured within the framework of the structure and objectives of the Community".[278] In *Nold*, the Court then specified that:

"[i]n safeguarding these rights, the Court is bound to draw inspiration from constitutional traditions common to the Member States, and it cannot therefore uphold measures which are incompatible with fundamental rights recognised and protected by the Constitutions of those States. Similarly, international treaties for the protection of human rights on which the Member States have collaborated or of which they are signatories, can supply guidelines which should be followed within the framework of Community law".[279]

The European Parliament, the Council and the Commission associated themselves with that case law in a Joint Declaration of April 5, 1977 by expressing the "prime importance" which they attached to the protection of fundamental rights "as derived in particular from the constitutions of the Member States and the European Convention for the Protection of Human Rights and Fundamental Freedoms".[280] The formulation of Community protection for fundamental rights was prompted by the Constitutional

---

[276] The first para. of Art. 136 of the EC Treaty refers to the fundamental social rights set out in the European Social Charter, which was signed at Turin under the auspices of the Council of Europe on October 18, 1961 (which has been ratified by all the Member States; for the text, see ETS No.35. It is also available from the Council of Europe website at *www.conventions.coe.int/*.) This provision also refers to the 1989 Community Charter of the Fundamental Social Rights of Workers (para. 5–235, *supra*). The Treaty of Amsterdam added a reference to fundamental social rights to the preamble of the EU Treaty, but not to the preamble of the EC Treaty.

[277] ECJ, Case 1/58 *Stork* [1959] E.C.R. 17, at 26.

[278] ECJ, Case 11/70 *Internationale Handelsgesellschaft* [1970] E.C.R. 1125, para. 4.

[279] ECJ, Case 4/73 *Nold v Commission* [1974] E.C.R. 491, para. 13.

[280] Joint Declaration of the European Parliament, the Council and the Commission, [1977] O.J. C103/1; see Forman, "The Joint Declaration on Fundamental Rights" (1977) E.L.R. 210–215.

Courts of some Member States, especially Germany and Italy (see paras 17–018 and 17–025).

Guiding sources. As we have seen, in protecting fundamental rights, the **17–075** Court is to be guided by the constitutional traditions of the Member States and by treaties on human rights. Art. 6(2) of the EU Treaty confirms that the European Convention for the Protection of Human Rights and Fundamental Freedoms (ECHR) signed in Rome on November 4, 1950 (ECHR, see para. 2–004) is especially important in this regard.[281] The legal position of the Member States with regard to the ECHR is identical inasmuch as they are all bound thereby and by the individual right to make an application to the European Court of Human Rights (see para. 2–004). There is an increasing tendency for the Court of Justice to review the interpretation and application of Community law in the light of provisions of the ECHR and, in so doing, it refers to an ever greater extent to the case law of the European Court of Human Rights.[282] Even in a situation in

---

[281] CFI, Case T–10/93 *A. v Commission* [1994] E.C.R. II–179, paras 48–49; ECJ, Case C–415/93 *Bosman* [1995] E.C.R. I–4921, para. 79; see also the earlier case ECJ, Case 222/84 *Johnston* [1986] E.C.R. 1651, para. 18. The recognition now given in the EU Treaty to the ECHR is the culmination of increasingly strong support for the case law of the Court of Justice, first in the Joint Declaration of the European Parliament, the Council and the Commission (see preceding n.280, *supra*) and secondly in the preamble to the Single European Act; see ECJ, Case 249/86 *Commission v Germany* [1989] E.C.R. 1263, para. 10; see Pipkorn, "La Communauté européenne et la Convention européenne des droits de l'homme" (1994) A.D. 463, at 464. For the status of the ECHR in the Member States, see Chryssogonos, "Zur Inkorporation der Europäischen Menschenrechtskonvention in den nationalen Rechtsordnungen der Mitgliedstaaten" (2001) EuR. 49–61.

[282] ECJ, Case 374/87 *Orkem v Commission* [1989] E.C.R. 3283, para. 30; ECJ, Joined Cases 46/87 and 227/88 *Hoechst v Commission* [1989] E.C.R. 2859, para. 18 (same form of words in *Dow Benelux v Commission* and *Dow Chemical Ibérica v Commission*, cited in n.232, *supra*); ECJ, Case C–13/94 *P. v S.* [1996] E.C.R. I–2143, para. 16; ECJ, Joined Cases C–74/95 and C–129/95 *Criminal Proceedings against X* [1996] E.C.R. I–6609, para. 25; ECJ, Case C–368/95 *Familiapress* [1997] E.C.R. I–3689, para. 26; ECJ, Case C–249/96 *Grant* [1998] E.C.R. I–621, paras 33–34; ECJ, Case C–185/95 P *Baustahlgewebe v Commission* [1998] E.C.R. I–8417, para. 29; ECJ, Case C–199/92 *Hüls v Commission* [1999] E.C.R. I–4287, para. 150, and Case C–235/92 P *Montecatini v Commission* [1999] E.C.R. I–4539, paras 175–176; ECJ (order of February 4, 2000), Case C–17/98 *Emesa Sugar (Free Zone) and Aruba* [2000] E.C.R. I–675, para. 14; ECJ, Case C–7/98 *Krombach* [2000] E.C.R. I–1935, para. 39; ECJ, Case C–274/99 P *Connolly v Commission* [2001] E.C.R. I–1611, paras 39–49; ECJ, Case C–60/00 *Carpenter* [2002] E.C.R. I–6279, para. 42; ECJ, Joined Cases C–238/99 P, C–244/99 P, C–245/99 P, C–247/99 P, C–250–252/99 P and C–254/99 P *Limburgse Vinyl Maatschappij NV v Commission* [2002] E.C.R. I–8375, paras 182, 234 and 274–275; ECJ, Case C–94/00 *Roquette Frères* [2002] E.C.R. I–9011, paras 29 and 52; ECJ, Joined Cases C–465/00, C–138/01 and C–139/01 *Rechnungshof v Österreichischer Rundfunk* [2003] E.C.R. I–4948, paras 77 and 83; ECJ (judgment of March 25, 2004), C–71/02 *Herbert Karner Industrie-Auktionen*, not yet reported, para. 52; see also Joined Cases T–213/95 and T–18/96 *SCK and FNK v Commission* [1997] E.C.R. II–1739, para. 57; CFI, Joined Cases T–222/99, T–327/99 and T–329/99 *Martinez v European Parliament* [2001] E.C.R. II–2823, para. 232, confirmed on the merits by ECJ (order of November 11, 2003), Case C–488/01 P *Martinez v European Parliament*, not yet reported, and set aside, as to the admissibility of the action brought by a political party, by ECJ (judgment of June 29, 2004), Case C–486/01 P *Front National v European Parliament*, not yet reported.

which Community law is not applicable, the Court of Justice has recently referred to the applicable case law of the Court of Human Rights.[283] The Court of Justice will also have regard to the International Covenant on Civil and Political Rights of December 19, 1966 (ICCPR)[284] and other international agreements,[285] in order to determine the precise scope of a Community fundamental right. Following the proclamation of the Charter of Fundamental Rights of the European Union by the Presidents of the European Parliament, the Council and the Commission on December 7, 2000 (see paras 17–083–17–085), the Community Courts also seek guidance from the provisions of that charter. This is because the Charter must be regarded as confirming the general principles that are observed in a State governed by the rule of law and that are common to the constitutional traditions of the Member States.[286] When the EU Constitution enters into force, the incorporation of the Charter of Fundamental Rights in Part II of the Constitution will give it full legal force (see para. 17–086). At the same time, the EU Constitution confirms that fundamental rights as guaranteed by the ECHR and as resulting from the constitutional traditions common to the Member States constitute "general principles of the Union's law".[287]

---

[283] See ECJ (judgment of September 23, 2003), Case C–109/01 *Akrich*, not yet reported, paras 58–60 (concerning the right to respect for family life in a situation in which Community law does not confer on a national of a non-member country who is married with a national of an EU State right of residence in that Member State).

[284] See ECJ, Case 374/87 *Orkem v Commission* [1989] E.C.R. 3283, para. 31; ECJ, Joined Cases C–297/88 and C–197/89 *Dzodzi* [1990] E.C.R. I–3763, para. 68; ECJ, Case C–249/96 *Grant* [1998] E.C.R. I–621, paras 43–47; CFI, Case T–48/96 *Acme Industry v Council* [1999] E.C.R. II–3089, para. 30. The International Covenant on Civil and Political Rights of December 19, 1966 (UNTS, Vol.99, p.171) has been ratified by all the Member States.

[285] See ECJ, Case 149/77 *Defrenne* [1978] E.C.R. 1365, para. 28 (1961 European Social Charter and 1958 ILO Convention No.III).

[286] See CFI, Case T–54/99 *max.mobil.Telekommunikation Service v Commission* [2002] E.C.R. II–313, paras 48 and 57; CFI, Case T–177/01 *Jégo-Quéré v Commission* [2002] E.C.R. II–2365 (set aside on appeal: ECJ (judgment of April 1, 2004), Case C–263/02 P *Commission v Jégo-Quéré*, not yet reported). The Advocates General of the Court of Justice also refer in their opinions to fundamental rights as they are set forth in the Charter: see, *e.g.* the opinions of Advocate General A. Tizzano for ECJ, Case C–173/99 *BECTU* [2001] E.C.R. I–4881, points 26–28; Advocate General P. Léger for Case C–353/99 P *Council v Hautala* [2001] E.C.R. I– 9565, points 77–89; Advocate General C. Stix-Hackl for ECJ, Case C–131/00 *Nilsson* [2001] E.C.R. I–10165, point 18; Advocate General F. Jacobs for ECJ, Case C–50/00 P *Unión de Pequenos Agricultores v Council* [2002] E.C.R. I–6677, point 39; Advocate General L.A. Geelhoed for ECJ, Case C–413/99 *Baumbast* [2002] E.C.R. I–7091, points 59, 93, 110 and 124; Advocate General D. Ruiz-Jarabo Colomer for ECJ, Case C–208/00 *Überseering* [2002] E.C.R. I–9919, point 59, and Advocate General Mischo for ECJ, Joined Cases C–20/00 and C–64/00 *Booker Aquaculture and Hydro Seafood GSP* [2003] E.C.R. I–7411, points 125–126. The European Court of Human Rights has referred to the Charter in its judgment of July 11, 2002 in *Goodwin v UK*, No.28957/95, para. 100.

[287] EU Constitution, Art. I–9(3).

(2) *Protection* vis-à-vis *Community institutions*

Community institutions and bodies. Community acts which violate **17–076** fundamental rights are unlawful.[288] The consequence of the fact that the ECHR is applied in the Community legal order is that the principles derived from Art. 6 of the ECHR apply to actions brought in the Court of Justice and the Court of First Instance.[289] It does not mean, however, that the Commission is regarded as a tribunal within the meaning of Art. 6 of the ECHR in procedures imposing sanctions.[290] It follows from Art. 6(2) of the EU Treaty that non-Community action on the part of Community institutions—under the CFSP or police and judicial co-operation in criminal matters (PJCC)—must also respect fundamental rights. Under Art. 46 of the EU Treaty, the Court of Justice may carry out judicial review in respect of compliance with this obligation "in so far as the Court has jurisdiction under the [Community and EU] Treaties".[291] As far as PJCC is concerned, Art. 35 of the EU Treaty determines the jurisdiction of the Court; as far as the CFSP is concerned, it is not clear whether that obligation may be judicially enforced (see para. 18–021).

(3) *Protection* vis-à-vis *Member States*

Member States acting within the scope of Community law. Fundamental **17–077** rights are an integral part of the Community legal order. As a result of the primacy of Community law, any action on the part of the Member States taken within the scope of Community law has to comply with Community requirements with regard to the protection of fundamental rights.[292] In a 1989 judgment, the Court held that "[s]ince those requirements are also binding on the Member States when they implement Community rules, the Member States must, as far as possible, apply those rules in accordance with those requirements".[293] The Member States act "within the scope of Community law" where they apply Treaty provisions[294] or implement Community acts, in particular where applying or implementing

---

[288] See, *e.g.* ECJ, Case C–404/92 P *X. v Commission* [1994] E.C.R. I–4737, paras 17–25, with a case note by De Smijter (1995) Col.J.E.L. 332–338.

[289] ECJ, Case C–185/95 P *Baustahlgewebe v Commission* [1998] E.C.R. I–8417, paras 20–21.

[290] ECJ, Joined Cases 209–215/78 and 218/78 *Van Landewyck v Commission* [1980] E.C.R. 3125, para. 81. See Wils, "La compatibilité des procédures communautaires en matière de concurrence avec la Convention européenne des droits de l'homme" (1996) C.D.E. 329–354; Zampini, "Convention européenne des droits de l'homme et droit communautaire de la concurrence" (1999) R.M.C.U.E. 628–647.

[291] See Wachsmann, "Le Traité d'Amsterdam. Les droits de l'homme" (1997) R.T.D.E. 883, at 888; Wölker, "Grundrechtsschutz durch den Gerichtshof der Europäischen Gemeinschaften und nationale Gerichte nach Amsterdam" (1999) EuR. Beiheft 1, 99–116.

[292] ECJ, Case 222/84 *Johnston* [1986] E.C.R. 1651, para. 18. See also Art. 51(1) of the Charter of Fundamental Rights of the European Union (para. 17–084, *infra*).

[293] ECJ, Case 5/88 *Wachauf* [1989] E.C.R. 2609, para. 19.

[294] ECJ, Case 222/86 *Heylens* [1987] E.C.R. 4097, paras 14–16 (EC Treaty, Art. 39).

regulations[295] or transposing directives into national law.[296] This also applies where a measure constitutes a necessary step in the procedure for adoption of a Community measure and the Community institutions have only a limited or non-existent discretion with regard to that measure.[297] The Court of Justice refuses to consider the compatibility with fundamental rights of a national measure which lies "outside the scope of Community law".[298] Thus, Community law had nothing to say about a deprivation of liberty after a sentence under provisions of national criminal law which were not designed to secure compliance with rules of Community law. Whilst any deprivation of liberty may impede the person concerned from exercising his or her right to free movement, a purely hypothetical prospect of exercising that right does not establish a sufficient connection with Community law.[299]

17–078 Interpretation by the Court of Justice. Where national rules fall within the scope of Community law and reference is made to the Court of Justice for a preliminary ruling, the Court considers that it must provide all the criteria of interpretation needed by the national court to determine whether the rules are compatible with fundamental rights.[300] National rules fall within the scope of Community law if they obstruct the exercise of freedoms guaranteed by the Treaty. Where a Member State then relies on a justificatory ground available under Community law, that ground must be interpreted in the light of the general principles of law and in particular of fundamental rights.[301] In this way, a provision of national law which

---

[295] ECJ, Case 5/88 *Wachauf* [1989] E.C.R. 2609, paras 16–22; ECJ, Case C–2/92 *Bostock* [1994] E.C.R. I–955, paras 16–27.

[296] ECJ, Case 222/84 *Johnston* [1986] E.C.R. 1651, paras 13–21; ECJ, Joined Cases C–465/00, C–138/01 and C–139/01 *Rechnungshof v Österreichischer Rundfunk* [2003] E.C.R. I–4948, paras 68–91; Joined Cases C–20/00 and C–64/00 *Booker Aquaculture and Hydro Seafood GSP* [2003] E.C.R. I–7411, paras 88–92.

[297] ECJ, Case C–97/91 *Oleificio Borelli v Commission* [1992] E.C.R. I–6313, paras 9–14; ECJ, Case C–269/99 *Carl Kühne* [2001] E.C.R. I–9517, paras 57–58.

[298] ECJ, Case 12/86 *Demirel* [1987] E.C.R. 3719, para. 28; ECJ, Case C–159/90 *Society for the Protection of Unborn Children Ireland v Grogan* [1991] E.C.R. I–4685, para. 31; ECJ, Case C–177/94 *Perfili* [1996] E.C.R. I–161, para. 20; ECJ, Case C–144/95 *Maurin* [1996] E.C.R. I–2909, para. 12; ECJ, Case C–309/96 *Annibaldi* [1997] E.C.R. I–7493, paras 10–25; see also the earlier judgment ECJ, Joined Cases 60–61/84 *Cinéthèque v Fédération nationale des cinémas français* [1985] E.C.R. 2605, para. 26 ("an area which falls within the jurisdiction of the national legislator").

[299] ECJ, Case C–299/95 *Kremzow* [1997] E.C.R. I–2629, paras 16–18.

[300] ECJ, Case C–260/89 *ERT* [1991] E.C.R. I–2925, para. 42; ECJ, Case C–159/90 *Society for the Protection of Unborn Children Ireland v Grogan* [1991] E.C.R. I–4685, para. 31; ECJ, Case C–2/92 *Bostock* [1994] E.C.R. I–955; ECJ, Case C–112/00 *Schmidberger* [2003] E.C.R. I–5659, para. 75.

[301] *ERT* (preceding n.), para. 43; ECJ, Case C–62/90 *Commission v Germany* [1992] E.C.R. I–2575, para. 23; ECJ, Case C–368/95 *Familiapress* [1997] E.C.R. I–3689, paras 24–25; see Waelbroeck, "La protection des droits fondamentaux à l'égard des Etats membres dans le cadre communautaire", *Mélanges F. Dehousse. II. La construction européenne* (Nathan/Labor, Paris/Brussels, 1979), at 333–335; Weiler, "The European Court at a Crossroads: Community Human Rights and Member State Action", in Capotorti, Ehlermann, Frowein, Jacobs, Joliet, Koopmans and Kovar (eds), *Du droit international au droit de l'intégration. Liber Amicorum P. Pescatore* (Nomos, Baden-Baden, 1987), at 821–842.

obstructs the exercise of the freedom to provide services can "fall under the exceptions provided for by the combined provisions of Articles 56 [now Article 46] and 66 [now Article 55] only if they are compatible with the fundamental rights the observance of which is ensured by the Court".[302] More generally, this applies to any hindrance of the freedoms guaranteed by Arts 28, 39, 43, 49 and 56 of the EC Treaty, which may be justified on grounds of a mandatory requirement in the public interest recognised by case law or listed in Art. 30, 39(3), 46 or 58 of the EC Treaty, as the case may be.[303] If such a national provision violates a fundamental right, it will not be covered by a potential justificatory ground and will constitute a prohibited obstruction of the free movement of goods, persons, services or capital. The Court of Justice has likewise made it clear that respect for fundamental rights may constitute in itself a ground for restricting the freedoms guaranteed by the Treaty.[304] In such case, the competent authorities enjoy a wide margin of discretion in order to determine whether the restrictions placed upon intra-Community trade are proportionate in the light of the protection of fundamental rights.[305] The Court of Justice will also review the question of respect for fundamental rights in interpreting the Brussels Convention.[306]

Non-Community areas. As far as action undertaken by the Member States **17–079** pursuant to the CFSP is concerned, Art. 46 of the EU Treaty precludes any review by the Court of Justice. Consequently, in that connection the Court of Justice cannot rule on whether the Member States have complied with fundamental rights, to which Art. 6(2) of the EU Treaty refers only as "general principles of Community law". Protection of fundamental rights in

---

[302] *ERT* (preceding n.), para. 43.
[303] *e.g.* ECJ, Case C–60/00 *Carpenter* [2002] E.C.R. I–6279, paras 42–46 (hindrance of freedom to provide services tested against—and found in breach of—the right to respect for family life within the meaning of ECHR, Art. 8). See as far back as ECJ, Case 36/75 *Rutili* [1975] E.C.R. 1219, paras 26–32 (application of Art. 39(3) of the EC Treaty in conjunction with implementation of Council Regulation No.1612/68 of October 15, 1968, para. 5–131, *supra*, and Council Directive 64/221/EEC of February 25, 1964, para. 5–139, *supra*). See the balancing of an impediment to the provision of services (prohibition on providing information about abortion clinics abroad) against freedom of expression conducted in Advocate General W. Van Gerven's Opinion in ECJ, Case C–159/90 *Society for the Protection of Unborn Children Ireland v Grogan* [1991] E.C.R. I–4685, points 30–38. *cf.* Lenaerts, "Le respect des droits fondementaux en tant que principe constitutionnel de l'Union européenne (n.275, *supra*), at 430, and Duikersloot, "Nationale maatregelen, communautaire grondrechten en de vrij verkeersjurisprudentie" (1997) S.E.W. 218, at 221–224. It is for the national court to determine as a matter of fact whether the national legislation at issue is covered by derogations provided for in the ECHR with regard to particular fundamental rights (*e.g.* ECJ, Case C–368/95 *Familiapress* [1997] E.C.R. I–3689, paras 26–33), although the Court of Justice may itself apply the criterion of proportionality (*e.g.* ECJ, Case C–60/00 *Carpenter* [2002] E.C.R. I–6279, paras 42–43).
[304] ECJ, Case C–112/00 *Schmidberger* [2003] E.C.R. I–5659, paras 69–94.
[305] *ibid.*, para. 82.
[306] ECJ, Case C–7/98 *Krombach* [2000] E.C.R. I–1935, paras 35–45 (a national court may refuse to enforce a judgment on public policy grounds where there was a breach in another Contracting State of the right to defend oneself).

the context of that non-Community action on the part of the Member States therefore rests on the protection afforded by the national legal systems under the supervision of the institutions set up by the ECHR. The same is also true of action taken by Member States in connection with PJCC, where Art. 35 of the EU Treaty does not expressly provide for judicial supervision of their action. When the Court of Justice interprets PJCC framework decisions, decisions, conventions or measures implementing them,[307] or rules on disputes between Member States regarding the interpretation or application of PJCC acts or on disputes between Member States and the Commission on the interpretation or application of PJCC conventions,[308] it is possible that it will indicate how such interpretation and application can be kept compatible with fundamental rights. A serious and persistent breach of fundamental rights on the part of a Member State may result, under the procedure introduced by Art. 7 of the EU Treaty, in the suspension of certain of the rights which derive from the application of the Treaties (see para. 9–012).

17–080 Limited jurisdiction. Some commentators argue that the Court of Justice should provide for uniform protection of human rights against all measures affecting nationals of a Member State where they exercise their right of free movement or freedom to provide services.[309] In the case of non-Community nationals, a sufficient connection with Community law and the fundamental rights secured thereby would be present if the person concerned had been admitted to the territory of the Community.[310] However, such extension of Community protection of fundamental rights would make for a generalisation of the supervision exercised by the Court of Justice over action undertaken by Member States—even outside the substantive scope of Community law—which might affect the division of powers as between the Member States and the Community.[311]

(4) *Strengthening the protection of fundamental rights*

17–081 The European Court of Human Rights. The Community has committed itself to respecting fundamental rights, including the ECHR, but is not a

---

[307] See EU Treaty, Art. 35(1).

[308] See EU Treaty, Art. 35(7).

[309] See the Opinion of Advocate General F.G. Jacobs in ECJ, Case C–168/91 *Konstantinidis* [1993] E.C.R. I–1191, point 46.

[310] O'Leary, "A Case Study of the Community's Protection of Human Rights, with Particular Reference to the Free Movement of Persons" (1994) A.D. 431, at 488–460; see also Weiler, "Thou Shalt Not Oppress a Stranger: On the Judicial Protection of the Human Rights of Non-EC Nationals—A Critique" (1992) E.J.I.L. 65–90.

[311] For a comparison with the protection of fundamental rights in the United States, which is based on "federalisation", see Lenaerts, "Fundamental Rights to be included in a Community Catalogue" (1991) E.L.R. 367, at 368–376. See further Ruffert, "Die Mitgliedstaaten der Europäischen Gemeinschaft als Verpflichtete der Gemeinschaftsgrundrechte" (1995) Eu.GR.Z. 518–530.

party to that Convention.[312] The European Commission of Human Rights
(now abolished, see para. 2–004) considered that a petition would not lie
against Community institutions.[313] Since the Community legal order itself
guarantees respect for the ECHR, the European Commission of Human
Rights took the view that a complaint made against a Member State which
was merely implementing a judgment of the Court of Justice was
inadmissible.[314]

The European Court of Human Rights has confirmed that acts of the
Community cannot be tested against the ECHR, because the Community is
not a party to the Convention,[315] but an indirect review may nevertheless be
carried out by testing the act by which a Member State gives effect to
Community provisions against the Convention.[316] The European Court of
Human Rights has held that the fact that the Member States have
transferred powers to the Community does not, in principle, release them
from their obligations to comply with the ECHR. That Court has declared
that it is competent to review acts adopted in the framework of the
Community/Union against the ECHR in so far as the Community legal
order itself does not afford equivalent protection.[317] In *Matthews v United
Kingdom* such protection was clearly not secured since the complaint
related to the exclusion of inhabitants of Gibraltar from the direct election
of the European Parliament, as laid down in the Act on the direct election
of the European Parliament, which, as an act of primary law, could not be
reviewed by the Court of Justice.[318] In other cases, the European Court will

---

[312] Schermers, "The European Communities Bound by Fundamental Human Rights" (1990)
C.M.L.R. 249–258; Lawson, *Het EVRM en de Europese Gemeenschappen*, (Kluwer,
Deventer, 1999) 569 pp.

[313] European Commission of Human Rights, July 10, 1978, *CFDT v EEC*, No.8030/77, D.R.,
Vol.13, 231.

[314] European Commission of Human Rights, February 9, 1990, *M. & Co. v Germany*,
No.13258/87, ECHR Y., 1990, 46 (complaint about the implementation by Germany of a
judgment given by the Court of Justice under Art. 256 of the EC Treaty; declared
inadmissible). In another case, however, the implementation by a Member State of a
Community agricultural regulation was tested against the ECHR: European Commission
of Human Rights, July 1, 1993, *Procola v Luxembourg*, No.1450/89, D.R. Vol 75, 5.

[315] Judgment of the European Court of Human Rights of February 18, 1999 in *Matthews v UK*,
No 24833/94, para. 32.

[316] Judgment of the European Court of Human Rights of November 15, 1996 in *Cantoni v
France*, No.17862/91, para. 30 (review in the light of the ECHR not precluded by the fact
that the national provision was based almost word for word on a Community directive).

[317] Judgment of the European Court of Human Rights of February 18, 1999 in *Matthews v UK*,
No 24833/94, paras 33–34. A complaint from Basque organisations against all the Member
States with regard to CFSP common positions was declared inadmissible without the Court
of Human Rights having to rule on whether the complainants had exhausted domestic
remedies within the Union: judgment of the European Court of Human Rights of May 23,
2002 in *SEGI and Gestoras Pro-Amnistía v Belgium*, Nos 6422/02 and 9916/02.

[318] In *Matthews*, the UK was held to have violated the right to free elections enshrined in Art.
3 of the First Protocol to the ECHR. For further particulars, see De Schutter and L'Hoest,
"La Cour européenne des droits de l'homme juge du droit communautaire: Gibraltar,
l'Union européenne et la Convention européenne des droits de l'homme" (2000) C.D.E.
141–214; Winkler, "Der Europäische Gerichtshof für Menschenrechte, das Europäisches

have to decide whether lodging a complaint against all the Member States makes it possible to review Community acts in the light of the ECHR.[319]

In so far as a complaint cannot be lodged in the Court of Human Rights against the Community institutions, the only protection of fundamental rights provided *vis-à-vis* the Community institutions consists of a review at last instance by the Court of Justice. If the issue raised has not yet been considered by the European Court of Human Rights, it is possible that the Community Court will put a different construction on the scope of the ECHR than that Court would have done.[320] Where there is conflicting case law of the Court of Justice and the European Court of Human Rights concerning the scope of the ECHR, national (and Community) authorities are liable to be squeezed between the primacy of Community law, on the one hand, and their obligations under the ECHR, on the other.[321]

17–082 **Accession to the ECHR.** That problem could be resolved by allowing the Court of Justice and the Court of First Instance to make references for preliminary rulings to the European Court of Human Rights.[322] This would require agreement between all the signatory States of the ECHR. However, the Commission would like to go further and has resurrected a proposal for

---

Parlament and der Schutz der Konventionsgrundrechte im Europäischen Gemeinschaftsrecht" (2001) Eu.GR.Z. 18–27. For the Act, see para. 10–022, *supra*; for the status of provisions of primary law, see paras 17–056—17–064. The implementation of the judgment in the UK has been contested by Spain, see n.96 to para. 10–024.

[319] See the applications in Cases 38837/97 (Lenz) and 56672/00 (Senator Lines). By judgment of July 4, 2000 (No.51717/99) the Court of Human Rights dismissed a complaint brought by Guérin Automobiles against all the Member States for an alleged violation by the Community Court of Arts 6 and 13 of the ECHR without ruling on its jurisdiction *ratione personae*. See Tulkens, "L'Union européenne devant la Cour européenne des droits de l'homme" (2000) R.U.D.H. 50–57. Conversely, the Community Court of First Instance manifestly lacks jurisdiction to entertain an application to annul a decision of the Commission of Human Rights: CFI (order of November 16, 1995), Case T–201/95 *Zanone v Council of Europe and France*, unreported; appeal rejected by ECJ (order of May 23, 1996), Case C–9/96 P *Zanone v Council of Europe and France*, unreported.

[320] *cf.* ECJ, Joined Cases 46/87 and 227/88 *Hoechst v Commission* [1989] E.C.R. 2859, paras 17–18 (inviolability of the home under Art. 8 of the ECHR held not to extend to business premises) and European Court of Human Rights (judgment of December 16, 1992), *Niemietz v Germany*, Series A, Vol.251–B, 23; European Court of Human Rights (judgment of April 16, 2002), *Colas v France*, No.37971/97 (ECHR, Art. 8 also applies to business premises). Since then, the Court of Justice seems to accept that Art. 8 of the ECHR applies to business premises; see ECJ, Case C–94/00 *Roquette Frères* [2002] E.C.R. I–9011, para. 29. See Lienemeyer and Waelbroeck (2003) C.M.L.R. 1481–1497; Kranenborg, "Article 8 EVRM en de verificatiebevoegdheden van de Commissie" (2003) S.E.W. 49–57.

[321] See further Callewaert, "Het EVRM en het communautair recht: een Europese globalisering?" (2001) N.T.E.R. 259–267; Krüger and Polakiewicz, "Vorschläge für ein kohärentes System des Menschenrechtsschutzes in Europa: Europäische Menschenrechtskonvention und EU-Grundrechtcharta" (2001) Eu.GR.Z. 92–105.

[322] Lenaerts, "Fundamental Rights to be included in a Community Catalogue" (1991) E.L.R. 367, at 380–381.

the Community to accede to the ECHR.[323] This would mean that individuals could contest alleged violations of fundamental rights by acts of the Community institutions before the European Court of Human Rights. The fact that domestic remedies must have been exhausted before a matter may be brought before the Strasbourg Court would mean, as far as the Community is concerned, that the Court of Justice would have to give judgment before a complaint could be considered.[324] Before the Community could accede, the ECHR would have to be amended, as the ECHR as it stands at present is open to accession only by the Member States of the Council of Europe. In an opinion, the Court of Justice declared that accession of the Community to the ECHR would entail a substantial change in the Community system for the protection of human rights and have fundamental implications for the Community and the Member States. In view of the constitutional significance of such a change, it could be brought about only by way of an amendment of the EC Treaty.[325] Alongside the Commission, the European Parliament continues to advocate accession of the Community/Union to the ECHR. It will become possible for the Union to accede to the ECHR when the EU Constitution enters into force. Article I–9(2) of the EU Constitution provides that the Union "shall accede" to the ECHR, whilst making it clear that such accession "shall not affect the Union's competences as defined in

---

[323] Commission communication of November 19, 1990, SEC (90) 2087 final, supported by the European Parliament in its resolution of January 18, 1994, [1994] O.J. C44/32; see, previously, the Commission's memorandum of April 4, 1979 on the accession of the European Communities to the Convention for the Protection of Human Rights and Fundamental Freedoms (1979) EC Bull. Suppl.2.

[324] Pipkorn (n.281, *supra*), at 474–479; see also Cohen-Jonathan, "La problématique de l'adhésion des Communautés européennes à la Convention européenne des droits de l'homme", *Etudes de droit des Communautés européennes. Mélanges offerts à P.-H. Teitgen* (Pedone, Paris, 1984), at 81–108.

[325] ECJ, Opinion 2/94 *Accession by the Communities to the Convention for the Protection of Human Rights and Fundamental Freedoms* [1996] E.C.R. I–1759, paras 34–35, with notes by Bernaerts (1996) Col.J.E.L. 372–381; Gaja (1996) C.M.L.R. 973–989. For (in many respects well-directed) criticism, see De Schutter and Lejeune, "L'adhésion de la Communauté à la Convention européenne des droits de l'homme. A propos de l'avis 2/94 de la Cour de justice des Communautés" (1996) C.D.E. 555–606; Vedder, "Die 'verfassungsrechtliche Dimension'—die bisher unbekannte Grenze für Gemeinschaftshandeln? Anmerkung zum Gutachten 2/94, EMRK, des EuGH" (1996) EuR. 309–319; Wachsmann, "L'avis 2/94 de la Cour de justice relatif à l'adhésion de la Communauté européenne à la Convention de sauvegarde des droits de l'homme et des libertés fondamentales" (1996) R.T.D.E. 467–491; Waelbroeck, "La Cour de justice et la Convention européenne des droits de l'homme" (1996) C.D.E. 549–553. See also Curtin and Klerk, "De Europese Unie en het Europees Verdrag voor de Rechten van de Mens. Een nieuwe fase in een lat-relatie?" (1997) N.J.B. 202–210; Chaltiel, "L'Union européenne doit-elle adhérer à la Convention européenne des droits de l'homme?" (1997) R.M.C.U.E. 34–50; Benoît-Rohmer, "L'adhésion de l'Union à la Convention européenne des droits de l'homme" (2000) R.U.D.H. 57–61; Salinas Alcega, "Desarrolos recentes en la protección de los derechos humanos en Europa. Nuevos elementos en una vieja controversia: la adhesión de las Comunidades Europeas a la Convención europea de salvaguarda de los derechos humanos y las libertades fundamentales" (2001) 199 Not.U.Eur. 9–36. A Finnish proposal for the revision of the Treaties (see (2000) Eu.GR.Z. 572) was not accepted by the 2000 IGC.

the Constitution".[326] As a result, accession to the ECHR will not only be a possibility—as soon as the ECHR is framed in such a way as to allow the Union to accede—but also an obligation.

17–083 European catalogue of rights. It has long been considered in academic writings that the EC Treaty should have its own catalogue of fundamental rights which individuals could invoke directly in the Community law context. Some commentators considered that such a catalogue could include rights not enshrined in the ECHR, namely economic and social fundamental rights and fundamental rights peculiar to the Community legal order.[327] The European Parliament formulated such a proposal in its Declaration of fundamental rights and freedoms of April 12, 1989,[328] although it was not followed through to any great extent.

The impetus for a genuine catalogue of fundamental rights of the European Union came from the Cologne European Council of June 1999,[329] which conferred the task of drawing up a Charter of Fundamental Rights to a "forum" (later called a "convention"). This body started work on February 1, 2000 under the presidency of the former German President Roman Herzog with representatives of national governments, the European Parliament and national parliaments and a representative of the President of the Commission. Representatives of the Court of Justice and the Council of Europe, including the European Court of Human Rights, were present as observers.[330] This unique formula inspired the Convention which was set

---

[326] A Protocol annexed to the EU Constitution relating to Art. I-9(2) provides that the agreement relating to the accession of the Union to the ECHR is to make provision for preserving the "specific characteristics of the Union and Union law", in particular with regard to the Union's participation in the control bodies of the ECHR and the "mechanisms necessary to ensure that proceedings by non-Member States and individual applications are correctly addressed to the Member States and/or the Union as appropriate". For the position of the European Parliament on accession to the ECHR, see resolution of March 16, 2000 on the drafting of a European Union Charter of Fundamental Rights ([2000] O.J. C377/332), point 15. See also Krüger and Polakiewicz, "Proposals for a Coherent Human Rights Protection System in Europe" (2001) R.U.D.H. 1–14.

[327] Lenaerts (n.322, *supra*), at 376–390; Hilf, "Ein Grundrechtskatalog für die Europäische Gemeinschaft" (1991) EuR. 19–30; Pipkorn (n.281, *supra*), at 480–481. For a different view of the relationship between the EC/EU and the ECHR, see Toth, "The European Union and Human Rights: The Way Forward" (1997) C.M.L.R. 491–529; Besselink, "Entrapped by the Maximum Standard: On Fundamental Rights, Pluralism and Subsidiarity in the European Union" (1998) C.M.L.R. 629–680.

[328] [1989] O.J. C120/51; discussed by Weiler, Lenaerts, Vanhamme and Bieber in Bieber, De Gucht, Lenaerts and Weiler (eds), *Au nom des peuples européens/In the name of the peoples of Europe* (Nomos, Baden-Baden, 1996), at 171–364. Although some rights were reserved for "Community citizens", the declaration sought to afford in principle protection for "every citizen in the field of the application of Community law".

[329] Annex IV to the conclusions of the European Council held at Cologne on June 3 and 4, 1999, (1999) 6 EU Bull. point I–64.

[330] The composition and manner of operation of the forum was determined by the European Council held at Tampere on October 15 and 16, 1999 (1999) 10 EU Bull. point I.2. In addition to various governmental and non-governmental organisations, the Committee of the Regions, the Economic and Social Committee and the European Ombudsman were also heard. For its establishment, see De Búrca, "The drafting of the European Union Charter of fundamental rights" (2001) E.L.R. 126–138; Desomer, "Het Handvest van de grondrechten van de Europese Unie" (2001) T.B.P. 671, at 671–673.

up after the Treaty of Nice to reflect on the future of the Union (see para. 4–001). In September 2000 the Convention arrived at a consensus on a draft Charter which was subsequently approved by the European Council, the European Parliament and the Commission.[331] On December 7, 2000 the Charter of Fundamental Rights was solemnly proclaimed at Nice by the Presidents of the European Parliament, the Council and the Commission.[332]

Charter of Fundamental Rights. The Charter of Fundamental Rights of **17–084** the European Union[333] brings together rights which ensue out of the common constitutional traditions and the international obligations of the Member States, namely the EU Treaty and Community law, the ECHR and the European Social Charter, the case law of the Court of Justice and the European Court of Human Rights, the Charter of Fundamental Social Rights of Workers and Community legislation on data protection and worker participation. In addition to the preamble,[334] the Charter is composed of six chapters setting out rights which cut across the traditional division between political and civil rights and economic and social rights (see para. 17–088). Apart from some rights connected with citizenship of the Union (see para. 12–008), the fundamental rights set forth in the Charter may be invoked in the context of Community law or EU law by anyone, including persons who are not nationals of Member States.

The provisions of the Charter are addressed to the institutions and bodies of the Union and to the Member States when they are implementing Union law (Art. 51(1)). This means that the provisions of the Charter only apply to national authorities in so far as they act within the scope of

---

[331] (2000) 10 EU Bull. point I.2.I and (2000) 11 EU Bull. point I.2.1.

[332] (2000) 12 EU Bull. point I.2.2. Its proclamation preceded the meeting of the European Council held at Nice on December 7–9, 2000 and the conclusion on December 10, 2000 of the Intergovernmental Conference which reached agreement on the Treaty of Nice.

[333] The text of the Charter of Fundamental Rights of the European Union may be found in [2000]O.J. C364/1 and (2000) 12 EU Bull. Point 2.2.1. For the Charter on the web, see *www.europarl.eu.int/charter/pdf/text—en.pdf.* For an analysis of the content, see Ashiagbor, "Economic and Social Rights in the European Charter of Fundamenal Rights" (2004) E.H.R.L.R. 62–72; Lenaerts and De Smijter, "A 'Bill of Rights' for the European Union" (2001) C.M.L.R. 273–300; Bribosia and De Schutter, "La Charte des droits fondamentaux de l'Union européenne" (2001) J.T. 281–293; Tettinger, "Die Charta der Grundrechte der Europäischen Union" (2001) N.J.W. 1010–1015; Hirsch Ballin, "Het Handvest van de Grondrechten van de Europese Unie: het eerste hoofdstuk van een Europese constitutie?" (2001) A.A. 88–93; Vitorino, "La Charte des droits fondamentaux de l'Union européenne" (2001) R.D.U.E. 27–64; Rodriguez Bereijo, "La carta de los derechos fundamentales de la Unión Europea" (2001) 192 Not.U.Eur. 9–20; Burgorgue-Larsen, "La charte des droits fondamentaux de l'Union européenne racontée au citoyen européen" (2001) R.A.E. 398–409; Goldsmith, "A Charter of Rights, Freedoms and Principles" (2001) C.M.L.R. 1201–1216; Betten, "The EU Charter of Fundamental Rights: a Trojan Horse or a Mouse?" (2001) Int'l J. Comp.Lab.Ind.Rel. 151–164; Pache, "Die Europäische Grundrechtscharta—ein Ruckschritt für den Grundrechtsschutz in Europa?" (2001) EuR. 475–494; Simon, "Les droits du citoyen de l'Union" (2000) R.U.D.H. 22–27.

[334] See Busse, "Eine kritische Würdigung der Präambel der Europäischen Grundrechtecharta" (2002) Eu.GR.Z. 559–576.

Community law or non-Community provisions of the Union.[335] In so far as rights recognised by the Charter are based on the Community Treaties or the EU Treaty they have to be exercised under the conditions and within the limits defined by those Treaties (Art. 52(2)).[336]

In so far as the Charter contains rights which correspond to rights guaranteed by the ECHR, the meaning and scope of those rights is the same as those laid down by that convention, but this does not prevent Union law from providing more extensive protection (Art. 52(3)).[337] In addition, the Charter provides that its provisions may not be interpreted as restricting or adversely affecting human rights and fundamental freedoms as recognised, in their respective fields of application, by EU law and international law, by international agreements and by the Member States' constitutions (Art. 53).[338] Consequently, in applying the Charter, the norm affording the highest level of protection prevails. The Charter formulates fundamental rights, but does not lay down any rules concerning the relationship between the Community and the national legal orders. The reference to the Member States' constitutions does not mean therefore that the primacy of Community over national law has been relinquished.[339]

17–085 Legal status of Charter. The Charter consists of precise formulations of fundamental rights and their field of application. Nevertheless it has not been incorporated in the Treaties and its provisions have not been expressly given force of law in any other way. On the contrary, in 2000 the discussion about the status of the Charter was postponed to a subsequent inter-governmental conference.[340] Nonetheless this has not prevented the

---

[335] This does not, however, prevent national legal systems from giving direct effect to the provisions of the Charter. For a well-reasoned argument in favour of giving a strict interpretation to the term "implementing", see Eeckhout, "The EU Charter of Fundamental Rights and the Federal Question" (2002) C.M.L.R. 945–994.

[336] Eeckhout (n.335, *supra*), at 979–991.

[337] For the relationship between the Charter and the ECHR, see Drzemczewski, "The Council of Europe's Position with Respect to the EU Charter of Fundamental Rights" (2001) Human Rights L.J. 14–32; Callewaert, "Die EMRK und die EU-Grundrechtecharta" (2003) EU.GR.Z. 198–206. Where a provision of the Charter affords a broader protection than the ECHR (*e.g.* the right to marry in Art. 9 of the Charter, which, unlike Art. 12 of the ECHR, does not refer to the gender of the partners), the provision in question may provide support for deriving broader protection from the ECHR; see European Court of Human Rights, July 11, 2002, *Goodwin v UK*, No.28957/95, paras 94–104, more specifically para. 100.

[338] See Alonso Garcia, "The General Provisions of the Charter of Fundamental Rights of the European Union" (2002) E.L.J. 492–514.

[339] See Liisberg, "Does the EU Charter of Fundamental Rights Threaten the Supremacy of Community Law?" (2001) C.M.L.R. 1171–1199; Douglas-Scott, "The Charter of Fundamental Rights as a Constitutional Document" (2004) E.H.R.L.R. 37–50.

[340] See the call for a debate on the status of the Charter in Declaration (No.23) annexed to the Treaty of Nice on the future of the Union ([2001] O.J. C80/85) and the Laeken Declaration ((2001) 12 EU Bull. point I.27, where it is stated that "Thought would also have to be given to whether the Charter of Fundamental Rights should be included in the Basic Treaty" ("and to whether the European Community should accede to the European Convention on Human Rights").

Charter from being regarded as being an authoritative catalogue of fundamental rights, having regard to the broad participation in drawing up the text and its subsequent approval by the national governments (within the European Council), the European Parliament and the Commission. The institutions and bodies of the Union and likewise the Member States may therefore be already bound to respect the Charter.[341] The Community Court rightly regards the Charter as confirming the general principles of the State governed by the rule of law which are common to the constitutional traditions of the Member States (see para. 17–075). This way, the Charter has become seamlessly incorporated into the system of protection of fundamental rights which the Court of Justice has developed since the 1970s.

Incorporation in the Constitution. The EU Constitution will indubitably **17–086** confer binding force on the Charter as a result of its incorporation in Part II of the Constitution as a catalogue of rights, freedoms and principles that must be respected by the Union and by the Member States when implementing Union law (Art. I–9(1) and Art. II–111(1)). The EU Constitution also clarifies a number of questions relating to the application of the Charter. First, it inserts in the preamble to the Charter a call for all courts of the Union and the Member States to interpret the provisions of the Charter "with due regard to the explanations prepared under the authority of the Praesidium of the Convention which drafted the Charter and updated under the responsibility of the Praesidium of the European Convention" (see also Art. II–112(7)). In addition, the EU Constitution makes it clear that the Charter does not confer any new powers on the institutions of the Union, which may act only within the limits of the powers conferred on them by the Constitution.[342] To the extent that provisions of the Charter do not embody rights or freedoms but "principles", Art. II–112(5) restricts judicial enforcement of those provisions to the interpretation and the review of the legality of acts adopted by the institutions of the Union and by the Member States—within the limits of their respective powers—with a view to implementing those principles. This does not mean, however, that acts other than those directly implementing

---

[341] For the view that the Community institutions "bound themselves" to the European Charter, see Alber, "Die Selbstbinding der europäischen Organen an die Europäischen Charta der Grundrechte" (2000) Eu.GR.Z. 349–353; Hirsch Ballin, "Eén wezenlijke maatstaf voor alle actoren in de Gemeenschap" (2001) S.E.W. 330–337. See also the communication from the Commission on the legal nature of the Charter of fundamental rights of the European Union, COM (2000) 644 final.

[342] See the passages inserted to that effect in Art. II–111(1) and (2) and Art. II–112(5) of the EU Constitution.

the Charter may not be indirectly reviewed for compliance with the principles enshrined therein.[343]

b. Survey

17–087 Fundamental rights. As already mentioned, fundamental rights enshrined in the European Convention for the Protection of Human Rights and Fundamental Freedoms (ECHR), the International Covenant on Civil and Political Rights and other international conventions or following from the constitutional traditions of the Member States may be invoked in the context of Community law and EU law.

17–088 Rights enshrined in the Charter. The Charter of Fundamental Rights (see para. 17–084) brings those and other fundamental rights together into six chapters, recognising both political and civil rights and economic and social rights.

The first chapter "dignity" confirms human dignity (Art. 1), the right to life (Art. 2), the right to integrity of the person (Art. 3), the prohibition of torture and inhuman or degrading treatment or punishment (Art. 4) and the prohibition of slavery and forced labour (Art. 5).

By way of "freedoms", Chapter II sets forth: the right to liberty and security (Art. 6); respect for private and family life (Art. 7); protection of personal data (Art. 8); the right to marry and found a family (Art. 9); freedom of thought, conscience and religion (Art. 10); freedom of expression and information (Art. 11); freedom of assembly and of association (Art. 12); freedom of the arts and sciences (Art. 13); the right to education (Art. 14); freedom to choose an occupation and the right to engage in work (Art. 15); freedom to conduct a business (Art. 16); the right to property (Art. 17); the right to asylum (Art. 18); and protection in the event of removal, expulsion or extradition (Art. 19).

Under the heading "equality", Chapter III recognises: equality before the law (Art. 20); non-discrimination (Art. 21); cultural, religious and linguistic diversity (Art. 22); equality between men and women (Art. 23); the rights of the child (Art. 24); the rights of the elderly (Art. 25); and integration of persons with disabilities (Art. 26).

Under "solidarity", Chapter IV covers: workers' right to information and consultation within the undertaking (Art. 27); the right of collective bargaining and action (Art. 28); the right of access to placement services

---

[343] See, *e.g.* the obligation for the Union to ensure consistency between its various policies and activities "taking all of its objectives into account" (draft EU Constitution, Art. III–115; see para. 5–007, *supra*). For the status of fundamental rights in the draft EU Constitution, see Williams, "EU human rights policy and the Convention on the Future of Europe: a failure of design?" (2003) E.L.R. 794–813; Mayer, "La Charte européenne des droits fondamentaux et la Constitution européenne" (2003) R.T.D.E. 175–196; Turpin, "L'intégration de la Charte des droits fondamentaux dans la Constitution européenne" (2003) R.T.D.E. 615–636.

(Art. 29); protection in the event of unjustified dismissal (Art. 30); fair and just working conditions (Art. 31); prohibition of child labour and protection of young people at work (Art. 32); family and professional life (Art. 33); social security and social assistance (Art. 34); health care (Art. 35); access to services of general economic interest (Art. 36); environmental protection (Art. 37); and consumer protection (Art. 38).

Chapter V "citizens' rights" enshrines: the right to vote and to stand as a candidate at elections to the European Parliament (Art. 39); the right to vote and to stand as a candidate at municipal elections (Art. 40); the right to good administration (Art. 41); the right of access to documents (Art. 42); the European Ombudsman (Art. 43); the right to petition (Art. 44); freedom of movement and of residence (Art. 45); and diplomatic and consular protection (Art. 46).

Under the heading "justice", Chapter VI recognises: the right to an effective remedy and to a fair trial (Art. 47); the presumption of innocence and the right of defence (Art. 48); the principles of legality and proportionality of criminal offences and penalties (Art. 49); and the right not to be tried or punished twice in criminal proceedings for the same criminal offence (Art. 50).

Rights elaborated in the case law. The Court of Justice and the Court of **17–089** First Instance have ruled on the following fundamental rights:

— the principle of equal treatment[344];

— the right to a fair hearing (ECHR, Art. 6)[345] including the right to effective judicial control (*i.e.* existence of a judicial remedy; see also ECHR, Art. 13),[346] the right to legal process within a reasonable

---

[344] Para. 5-056, *supra*.

[345] ECJ, Case 98/79 *Pecastaing* [1980] E.C.R. 691, paras 21–22; CFI, Case T–535/93 *F. v Council* [1995] E.C.R. -SC II–163, paras 32–35, English abstract at I–A–49. *cf.* CFI, Case T–83/96 *Van der Wal v Commission* [1998] E.C.R. II–545, paras 45–47, set aside on appeal by ECJ, Joined Cases C–174/98 P and C–189/89 P *Netherlands and Van der Wal v Commission* [2000] E.C.R. I–1, paras 17–18.

[346] ECJ, Case 222/84 *Johnston* [1986] E.C.R. 1651, para. 18; ECJ, Case 222/86 *Heylens* [1987] E.C.R. 4097, para. 14; ECJ, Case C–97/91 *Oleificio Borelli v Commission* [1992] E.C.R. I–6313, paras 13–14; ECJ, Case C–269/99 *Carl Kühne* [2001] E.C.R. I–9517, paras 57–58; ECJ, Case C–185/97 *Coote* [1998] E.C.R. I–5199, paras 20–22; CFI, Case T–177/01 *Jégo-Quéré v Commission* [2002] E.C.R. II–2365, para. 41 (set aside on appeal: ECJ (judgment of April 1, 2004), Case C–263/02 P *Commission v Jégo-Quéré*, not yet reported). This fundamental right does not require a court to grant interim measures with regard to the right of residence: ECJ, Joined Cases C–297/88 and C–197/89 *Dzodzi* [1990] E.C.R. I–3763, para. 68. See also Art. 47 of the Charter of Fundamental Rights of the EU, applied in CFI, Case T–177/01 *Jégo-Quéré v Commission* [2002] E.C.R. II–2365, paras 41–51; *cf.* ECJ, Case C–50/00 P *Unión de Pequenos Agricultores v Council and Commission* [2002] E.C.R. I–6677, paras 32–45, ECJ (judgment of April 1, 2004), Case C–263/02 P *Commission v Jégo-Quéré*, not yet reported (different approach to the completeness of the Community system of legal remedies and procedures by reference to Arts 6 and 13 of the ECHR).

time,[347] the right of reply in adversarial proceedings,[348] the presumption of innocence,[349] the right to be defended[350] and the right to call witnesses[351];

— the principle that provisions of criminal law may not have retroactive effect (ECHR, Art. 7)[352];

— retroactive imposition of a lighter penalty (ICCPR, Art. 15)[353];

— the principle *ne bis in idem* (Art. 4 of the Seventh Protocol to the ECHR)[354];

— the right to human dignity[355];

— respect for private life,[356] family life,[357] the home and correspondence (ECHR, Art. 8),[358] in particular respect for a

---

[347] See the application (as a general principle of law, but applying Art. 6 of the ECHR by analogy) in CFI, Joined Cases T–213/95 and T–18/96 *SCK and FNK v Commission* [1997] E.C.R. II–1739, paras 53–64, and the application of the principle of law derived from Art. 6 of the ECHR to proceedings before the Court of First Instance in ECJ, Case C–185/95 P *Baustahlgewebe v Commission* [1998] E.C.R. I–8417, paras 20–22 and 26–48; ECJ, Case C–238/99 P, C–244/99 P, C–245/99 P, C–247/99 P, C–250–252/99 P and C–254/99 P *Limburgse Vinyl Maatschappij NV v Commission* [2002] E.C.R. I–8375, paras 164–235.

[348] ECJ (order of February 4, 2000, Case C–17/98 *Emesa Sugar (Free Zone) and Aruba* [2000] E.C.R. I–665, paras 10–18 (where the Court of Justice held that the fact that a party may not submit observations in response to the Advocate General's opinion does not conflict with the right of all persons in adversarial proceedings to a fair hearing; see para. 10–080, *supra*).

[349] ECJ, Case C–199/92 P *Hüls v Commission* [1999] E.C.R. I–4287, paras 149–150, and ECJ, Case C–235/92 P *Montecatini v Commission* [1999] E.C.R. I–4539, paras 175–176. The right not to be compelled to testify against oneself (enshrined as regards criminal matters in Art. 14(3)(g) of the ICCPR) has until now been enforced only in connection with complying with the rights of the defence; n.263, *supra*).

[350] ECJ, Case C–7/98 *Krombach* [2000] E.C.R. I–1935, paras 35–46.

[351] CFI, Case T–9/99 *HFB Holding für Fernwärmetechnik Beteiligungsgesellschaft mbH & Co. KG v Commission* [2002] E.C.R. II–1487, paras 389–392.

[352] For the possibility to impose penalties: ECJ, Case 63/83 *Kirk* [1984] E.C.R. 2689, para. 22; ECJ, Joined Cases C–74/95 and C–129/95 *Criminal proceedings against X* [1996] E.C.R. I–6609, para. 25 (para. 17–069, *supra*); for the penalty: CFI, Case T–23/99 *LR AF 1998 v Commission* [2002] E.C.R. II–1705, paras 218–238.

[353] CFI, Case T–48/96 *Acme Industry v Council* [1999] E.C.R. II–3089, para. 30.

[354] ECJ, Case C–238/99 P, C–244/99 P, C–245/99 P, C–247/99 P, C–250–252/99 P and C–254/99 P *Limburgse Vinyl Maatschappij NV v Commission* [2002] E.C.R. I–8375, paras 59–63 (see para. 17–071, *supra*).

[355] ECJ, Case C–337/98 *Netherlands v European Parliament and Council* [2001] E.C.R. I–7079, paras 70–77.

[356] See ECJ, Case 165/82 *Commission v UK* [1983] E.C.R. 3431, para. 13, although this judgment makes no reference to the ECHR. For the protection of personal data, see ECJ, Case C–369/98 *Fisher and Fisher* [2000] E.C.R. I–6751, paras 32–38; ECJ, Joined Cases C–465/00, C–138/01 and C–139/01 *Rechnungshof v Österreichischer Rundfunk* [2003] E.C.R. I– 4989, paras 73–90.

[357] ECJ, Case 249/86 *Commission v Germany* [1989] E.C.R. 1263, para. 10. See in particular with regard to family reunification, ECJ, Case 12/86 *Demirel* [1987] E.C.R. 3719, para. 28; ECJ, Case C–60/00 *Carpenter* [2002] E.C.R. I–6279, paras 40–46; ECJ (judgment of September 23, 2003), Case C–109/01 *Akrich*, not yet reported, paras 58–60.

[358] With regard to the Commission's powers to carry out investigations in supervising compliance with the competition rules, see ECJ, Case 136/79 *National Panasonic v Commission* [1980] E.C.R. 2033, paras 19–20; ECJ, Case 5/85 *AKZO Chemie v Commission* [1986] E.C.R. 2585, paras 25–27.

person's physical integrity,[359] the right to keep one's state of health private,[360] medical confidentiality[361] and the right to inviolability of one's home[362];

— freedom to manifest one's religion (ECHR, Art. 9)[363];

— freedom of expression (ECHR, Art. 10)[364];

— freedom of association (ECHR, Art. 11)[365] and freedom of peaceful assembly,[366] in particular the right to be a member of a trade union and to take part in trade union activities[367];

---

[359] CFI, Joined Cases T–121/89 and T–13/90 *X. v Commission* [1992] E.C.R. II–2195, paras 53–59, set aside on appeal by ECJ, Case C–404/92 P *X. v Commission* [1994] E.C.R. I–4737, paras 17–24, in which it was held that the Commission had violated Art. 8 of the ECHR in that, although a would-be official had refused an AIDS test, the Commission had nevertheless had a test performed on him from which the presence of the disease could be inferred; see also CFI, Case T–10/93 *A. v Commission* [1994] E.C.R. II–179, paras 47–51; ECJ, Case C–377/98 *Netherlands v European Parliament and Council* [2001] E.C.R. I–7079, paras 70 and 78–80.

[360] CFI, Case T–176/94 *K. v Commission* [1995] E.C.R. -SC II–621, para. 31, English abstract at I–A-203.

[361] ECJ, Case C–62/90 *Commission v Germany* [1992] E.C.R. I–2575, para. 23.

[362] ECJ, Joined Cases 46/87 and 227/88 *Hoechst v Commission* [1989] E.C.R. 2859, paras 17–18 (same form of words in *Dow Benelux v Commission* and *Dow Chemical Ibérica v Commission*, cited in n.232, *supra*) and ECJ, Case C–94/00 *Roquette Frères* [2002] E.C.R. I–9011, paras 22–99 (see n.320, *supra*).

[363] ECJ, Case 130/75 *Prais v Council* [1976] E.C.R. 1589, paras 6–19.

[364] ECJ, Joined Cases 43 and 63/82 *VBVB and VBBB v Commission* [1984] E.C.R. 19, para. 34; ECJ, Joined Cases 60–61/84 *Cinéthèque* [1985] E.C.R. 2605, paras 25–26; ECJ, Case C–159/90 *Society for the Protection of Unborn Children Ireland v Grogan* [1991] E.C.R. I–4685, paras 30–31; ECJ, Case C–260/89 *ERT* [1991] E.C.R. I–2925, para. 44; ECJ, Case C–219/91 *Ter Voort* [1992] E.C.R. I–5485, paras 35–38; ECJ, Case C–23/93 *TV10* [1994] E.C.R. I–4795, paras 23–25; ECJ, Case C–368/95 *Familiapress* [1997] E.C.R. I–3689, paras 18 and 25–33; ECJ, Case C–112/00 *Schmidberger* [2003] E.C.R. I–5659, paras 79–80; ECJ (judgment of March 25, 2004), Case C–71/01 *Herbert Karner Industrie-Auktionen*, not yet reported, paras 50–51. For the relationship with the obligations imposed by the Staff Regulations of officials, see ECJ, Case C–150/98 P *Economic and Social Committee v E* [1999] E.C.R. I–8877, paras 12–18; ECJ, Case C–274/99 P *Connolly v Commission* [2001] E.C.R. I–1611, paras 37–56; ECJ, Case C–340/00 P *Commission v Cwik* [2001] E.C.R. I–10269, paras 17–28. See also ECJ, Case C–100/88 *Oyowe and Traore v Commission* [1989] E.C.R. 4285, para. 16, which makes no reference to the ECHR. For further particulars, see Apt, "On the Right to Freedom of Expression in the European Union" (1998) Col.J.E.L. 69–123.

[365] ECJ, Case C–415/93 *Bosman* [1995] E.C.R. I–4921, para. 79; CFI, Joined Cases T–222/99, T–327/99 and T–329/99 *Martinez v European Parliament* [2001] E.C.R. II–2823, paras 230–235 (confirmed on the merits by the ECJ, see n.282, *supra*).

[366] ECJ, Case C–235/92 P *Montecatini v Commission* [1999] E.C.R. I–4539, para. 137; ECJ, Case C–112/00 *Schmidberger* [2003] E.C.R. I–5659, paras 79–80. See Mann and Ripke, "Überlegungen zur Existenz und Reichweite eines Gemeinschaftsgrundrechts der Versammlungsfreiheit" (2004) Eu.GR.Z. 125–133.

[367] ECJ, Case 36/75 *Rutili* [1975] E.C.R. 1219, paras 31–32 (where Arts 8, 9, 10 and 11 of the ECHR are mentioned in one breath; see also ns 371 and 373, *infra*). For officials' freedom of association recognised by the Staff Regulations, as interpreted in the light of "general principles of labour law" (with no reference to the ECHR), see ECJ, Case 175/73 *Union Syndicale v Council* [1974] E.C.R. 917, paras 14–15; ECJ, Joined Cases C–193 and C–194/87 *Maurissen v Court of Auditors* [1990] E.C.R. I–95, paras 13–38.

— rights of ownership or the right to property as protected by constitutional law in all Member States[368] and Art. 1 of Protocol No. 1 to the ECHR[369];

— freedom to carry on an economic activity (trade or profession)[370]; and

— the right of everyone lawfully within the territory of a State to liberty of movement therein (Art. 2 of Protocol No. 4 to the ECHR).[371]

17–090 Balancing fundamental rights. It appears from the case law that these fundamental rights are not unfettered prerogatives, but must be viewed in the light of their social function. The Community may subject the enjoyment of fundamental rights to restrictions, provided that the restrictions "in fact correspond to objectives of general interest pursued by the Community and that they do not constitute a disproportionate and intolerable interference which infringes upon the very substance of the right guaranteed".[372] Such restrictions must therefore be properly proportionate to the public-interest aim pursued (see paras 5–036 *et seq.*). The ECHR declares that certain fundamental rights are to be subject to no restriction "except such as is in accordance with the law and is necessary in a democratic society in the interests of national security, public safety or the

---

[368] ECJ, Case 4/73 *Nold v Commission* [1974] E.C.R. 491, para. 14.
[369] ECJ, Case 44/79 *Hauer* [1979] E.C.R. 3727, paras 17–30; see the following cases not making any reference to the Protocol: ECJ, Joined Cases 41, 121 and 796/79 *Testa* [1980] E.C.R. 1979, paras 17–22; ECJ, Case 59/83 *Biovilac v EEC* [1984] E.C.R. 4057, paras 21–23; ECJ, Case 265/87 *Schräder* [1989] E.C.R. 2237, paras 15–17; ECJ, Case 5/88 *Wachauf* [1989] E.C.R. 2609, paras 17–23; ECJ, Case C–177/90 *Kühn* [1992] E.C.R. I–35, paras 16–17; ECJ, Case C–280/93 *Germany v Council* [1994] E.C.R. I–4973, paras 77–80; ECJ, Joined Cases C–20/00 and C–64/00 *Booker Aquaculture and Hydro Seafood* [2003] E.C.R. I–7411, para. 67.
[370] ECJ, Case 230/78 *Eridania* [1979] E.C.R. 2749, paras 20–22; ECJ, Case 240/83 *ADBHU* [1985] E.C.R. 531, paras 9–13; ECJ, Case C–200/96 *Metronome Musik* [1998] E.C.R. I–1953, para. 21. This fundamental right has generally been raised before the Court of Justice together with the right to property, in which case the Court has considered them together (see *Nold*, n.368, *supra*, and *Biovilac*, *Wachauf* and *Kühn*, n.369, *supra*) or considered the right to carry on a trade or profession and the right to property one after another (see the following judgments cited in n.369, *supra*: *Hauer*, paras 31–32, *Schräder*, para. 18, and *Germany v Council*, paras 81–87).
[371] ECJ, Case 36/75 *Rutili* [1975] E.C.R. 1219, para. 32.
[372] ECJ, Case 265/87 *Schräder* [1989] E.C.R. 2237, para. 15; ECJ, Case C–200/96 *Metronome Musik* [1998] E.C.R. I–1953, para. 21; see also ECJ, Case 44/79 *Hauer* [1979] E.C.R. 3727, paras 23 and 30, and the other cases cited in n.369, *supra*. The balancing of interests carried out in Case C–280/93 *Germany v Council* has come in for criticism; see Everling, "Will Europe Slip on Bananas? The Banana Judgment of the Court of Justice and National Courts" (1996) C.M.L.R. 401, at 416–419. For the limitations of fundamental rights resulting from economic sanctions imposed by the Community, see ECJ, Case C–84/95 *Bosphorus* [1996] E.C.R. I–3953, paras 21–26, and the critical article by Canor, "'Can Two Walk Together, Except They Be Agreed?' The Relationship between International Law and European Law: The Incorporation of United Nations Sanctions against Yugoslavia into European Community Law through the Perspective of the European Court of Justice" (1998) C.M.L.R. 137, at 161–187.

economic well-being of the country, for the prevention of disorder or crime, for the protection of health or morals, or for the protection of the rights and freedoms of others" (ECHR, Art. 8 para. 2; see to the same effect Arts 9 para. 2, 10 para. 2 and 11 para. 2).[373] To the same effect, the Charter of Fundamental Rights of the European Union states that any limitation on the exercise of the rights and freedoms recognised therein must be provided for by law and respect the essence of those rights and freedoms and that, subject to the principle of proportionality, limitations may be made only if they are necessary and genuinely meet objectives of general interest recognised by the Union or the need to protect the rights and freedoms of others (Art. 52(1)).[374]

D. INTERNATIONAL LAW

1. International agreements concluded by the Community

a. Legal force and direct effect of international agreements

Binding force. Article 300 of the EC Treaty lays down the procedure by **17–091** which the Community concludes agreements with non-member countries or international organisations (see paras 21–002 *et seq.*). Agreements concluded under the conditions set out in that article are binding on the Community institutions and on Member States (EC Treaty, Art. 300(7); see also EU Constitution, Art. III–323(2)).[375] The provisions of such agreements form an integral part of the Community legal order from the

---

[373] See ECJ, Case 36/75 *Rutili* [1975] E.C.R. 1219, para. 32; ECJ, Case 136/79 *National Panasonic v Commission* [1980] E.C.R. 2033, para. 19; ECJ, Case C–219/91 *Ter Voort* [1992] E.C.R. I–5485, para. 38. Compare ECJ, Case C–112/00 *Schmidberger* [2003] E.C.R. I–5659, paras 79, and ECJ (judgment of March 25, 2004), Case C–71/01 *Herbert Karner Industrie-Auktionen*, not yet reported, paras 50–51 (balance of interests performed by the Court of Justice having regard to the authority's margin of appreciation) with ECJ, Case C–368/95 *Familiapress* [1997] E.C.R. I–3689, paras 26–33 (balance of interests left to the national legal system). See also the balancing of interests conducted in CFI, Case T–176/94 *K v Commission* [1995] E.C.R. -SC II–621, paras 33–45, English abstract at I–A–203.

[374] For these and other restrictions on the rights recognised by the Charter, see Triantafyllou, "The European Charter of Fundamental Rights and the 'Rule of law': Restricting Fundamental Rights by Reference" (2002) C.M.L.R. 53–64.

[375] The difference in terminology in some language versions of the Treaty (*e.g.* "akkoord"/"overeenkomst" in the Dutch) has no significance in this connection (see para. 21–002). For a survey of the status of international law in the Community legal order, see Vanhamme, *Volkenrechtelijke beginselen in het Europees recht* (Europa Law, Groningen, 2001), 435 pp. See also EC Treaty, Art. 111(3), second subpara., in which it is provided that agreements concluded in accordance with Art. 109(3) are binding on Community institutions, the ECB and Member States. It may not be inferred from this that other agreements concluded by the Community are not binding on the ECB: Slot, "The Institutional Provisions of the EMU", in Curtin and Heukels (eds), *Institutional Dynamics of European Integration. Essays in Honour of Henry G. Schermers*, Vol.II (Martinus Nijhoff, Dordrecht, 1994), 229, at 247.

time when they enter into force.[376] This is in accordance with the "monist" approach: agreements concluded by the Community form part of the Community legal order without there being any necessity to transpose them into internal provisions of Community law.[377] Agreements not concluded by the Community but by the Member States also have binding force if the Community has assumed, under the EC Treaty, the powers previously exercised by the Member State in the field to which the agreement applies.[378] This was the case with the General Agreement on Tariffs and Trade (GATT; see para. 20–010), since the powers in connection with the application of that agreement were conferred on the Community by the EC Treaty and the Community itself subsequently took part in the tariff negotiations.[379] An agreement concluded by the Member States is also binding on the Community when the Treaty provides that the Community must exercise its powers in accordance therewith. Examples are provided by the Geneva Convention and the Protocol relating to the status of refugees and other relevant treaties, which are binding on the Community in the matter of asylum policy (EC Treaty, Art. 63(1)).

17–092 **Precedence over secondary law.** Furthermore the rules ensuing from agreements binding on the Community rank higher than acts of the Community institutions. This can be seen from the fact that the Court of Justice considers itself bound to "examine whether [the] validity [of acts of the institutions] may be affected by reason of the fact that they are contrary to a rule of international law".[380] In view of the fact that international

---

[376] ECJ, Case 181/73 *Haegeman* [1974] E.C.R. 449, para. 5; ECJ, Case 104/81 *Kupferberg* [1982] E.C.R. 3641, paras 11–13. For obligations entered into by the Community under international law through mere signature, see para. 21–006, *infra*. As far as the temporal effect of international agreements is concerned, unless otherwise provided, an international agreement applies to the future effects of situations which arose before the agreement entered into force: ECJ, Case C–162/00 *Pokrzeptowicz-Meyer* [2002] E.C.R. I–1049, paras 48–51.

[377] Although the Court of Justice derives its jurisdiction to review such agreements from their nature as "acts of institutions", see Rideau, "Les accords internationaux dans la jurisprudence de la Cour de Justice des Communautés européennes: Réflexions sur les relations entre les ordres juridiques international, communautaire et nationaux" (1990) R.G.D.I.P. 289, at 308–312. See also Bourgeois, "Effects of International Agreements on European Community Law: Are the Dice Cast?" (1984) Mich.L.Rev. 1250–1273; Pescatore, "L'application judiciaire des traités internationaux dans la Communauté européenne et dans ses Etats membres", *Etudes de droit des Communautés européennes. Mélanges offerts à P. H. Teitgen* (Pedone, Paris, 1984), at 355–406 (who also surveys the situation in the Member States; see also in this connection para. 17–015 *et seq., supra*).

[378] ECJ, Case C–379/92 *Peralta* [1994] E.C.R. I–3453, para. 16.

[379] ECJ, Joined Cases 21–24/72 *International Fruit Company* [1972] E.C.R. 1219, paras 10–17 (para. 20–010, *infra*). Likewise, the Community replaced the Member States with respect to commitments arising from the Convention of December 15, 1950 on the Nomenclature for the Classification of Goods in Customs Tariffs and from the Convention of the same date establishing a Customs Co-operation Council: ECJ, Case 38/75 *Nederlandse Spoorwegen* [1975] E.C.R. 1439, para. 21.

[380] ECJ, Joined Cases 21–24/72 *International Fruit Company* [1972] E.C.R. 1219, para. 6.

agreements concluded by the Community rank higher than provisions of secondary Community legislation, such provisions must, so far as is possible, be interpreted in a manner that is consistent with those agreements.[381] Since agreements concluded by the Community are binding on the Member States, their provisions also take precedence over national law. The Court of Justice takes the view that:

"[i]t follows from the Community nature of such provisions that their effect in the Community may not be allowed to vary according to whether their application is in practice the responsibility of the Community institutions or of the Member States and, in the latter case, according to the effects in the internal legal order of each Member State which the law of that State assigns to international agreements concluded by it".[382]

Accordingly, the supervision exercised by the Commission in ensuring that Member States comply with Community law also extends to making sure that they comply with international agreements binding on the Community. In giving effect to Community law, the Member States must apply national rules as far as possible in the light of the wording and the purpose of such agreements.[383] In practice, it is exceptional for the Court of Justice to find that a national provision is incompatible with an agreement concluded by the Community.[384] Moreover, the European Court has only once as yet found an act of a Community institution to be incompatible with such an agreement.[385]

---

[381] ECJ, Case C–61/94 *Commission v Germany* [1996] E.C.R. I–3989, para. 52; ECJ, Case C–284/95 *Safety High Tech* [1998] E.C.R. I–4301, para. 22; ECJ, Case C–341/95 *Bettati* [1998] E.C.R. I–4355, para. 20; CFI, Case T–256/97 *BEUC v Commission* [2000] E.C.R. II–101, paras 65–73.

[382] ECJ, Case 104/81 *Kupferberg* [1982] E.C.R. 3641, para. 14. See also ECJ, Case 38/75 *Nederlandse Spoorwegen* [1975] E.C.R. 1439, para. 16.

[383] ECJ, Case C–53/96 *Hermès International* [1998] E.C.R. I–3603, para. 28.

[384] See, *e.g.* ECJ, Joined Cases 194 and 241/85 *Commission v Greece* [1988] E.C.R. 1037 (infringement of the Second EEC-ACP Convention); ECJ, Case C–469/93 *Chiquita Italia* [1995] E.C.R. I–4533, paras 54–63 (infringement of Protocol No.5 to the Fourth ACP-EEC Convention); ECJ, Case C–61/94 *Commission v Germany* [1996] E.C.R. I–3989, paras 18–58 (infringement of the International Dairy Arrangement concluded under the GATT). For the failure to fulfil an obligation arising under the EEA Agreement to accede to an international convention, see ECJ, Case C–13/00 *Commission v Ireland* [2002] E.C.R. I–2943, paras 14–23.

[385] See CFI, Case T–115/94 *Opel Austria v Council* [1997] E.C.R. II–39, paras 122–123 (the regulation in question was annulled because it breached the EEA Agreement and that constituted an infringement of the legitimate expectations of the undertaking concerned, para. 21–006, *infra*).

17–093 Direct effect. In judicial proceedings, individuals may rely on a provision of an agreement concluded by the Community only if the provision in question has direct effect.[386] The test is whether, "regard being had to its wording and the purpose and nature of the agreement itself, the provision contains a clear and precise obligation which is not subject, in its implementation or effects, to the adoption of any subsequent measure".[387] Accordingly, a provision of an agreement concluded by the Community will have direct effect if it fulfils the general Community law requirements for direct effect (see para. 17–048), and where, in addition, direct effect is compatible with the purpose and nature (sometimes expressed as "the spirit, the general scheme and the terms"[388]) of the agreement in question. It may also have been indicated in the agreement what effect its provisions are to have in the internal legal order of the Contracting Parties.[389] The Court has in many cases held the following to have direct effect: provisions of association agreements concluded by the Community,[390] free trade agreements[391] and co-operation agreements.[392] A provision is not prevented

---

[386] ECJ, Joined Cases 21–24/72 *International Fruit Company* [1972] E.C.R. 1219, para. 8. In this connection, see Cheyne, "International Agreements and the European Community Legal System" (1994) E.L.R. 581–598; Manin, "A propos de l'accord instituant l'Organisation mondiale du commerce et de l'accord sur les marchés publics: la question de l'invocabilité des accords internationaux conclus par la Communauté européenne" (1997) R.T.D.E. 399, at 416–422 ; Vanhamme, "Inroepbaarheid van verdragen en volkenrechtelijke beginselen voor de Europese rechter: stand van zaken" (2001) S.E.W. 247–256 (and the articles cited in para. 17–050, *supra*).

[387] ECJ, Case 12/86 *Demirel* [1987] E.C.R. 3719, para. 14.

[388] See ECJ, Joined Cases 21–24/72 *International Fruit Company* [1972] E.C.R. 1219, para. 20; ECJ, Case 87/75 *Bresciani* [1976] E.C.R. 129, para. 16.

[389] ECJ, Case 104/81 *Kupferberg* [1982] E.C.R. 3641, para. 17.

[390] See ECJ, Case 87/75 *Bresciani* [1976] E.C.R. 129, paras 16–25 (1963 Yaoundé Convention, Art. 2(1)); ECJ, Case 17/81 *Papst & Richarz* [1982] E.C.R. 1331, paras 25–27 (Association Agreement concluded with Greece, Art. 53(1)); ECJ, Case C–432/92 *Anastasiou* [1994] E.C.R. I–3087, paras 23–27 (provisions of a Protocol to the Association Agreement concluded with Cyprus); ECJ, Case C–469/93 *Chiquita Italia* [1995] E.C.R. I–4533, paras 30–36 and 57 (Fourth ACP-EC Convention and Protocol No.5 thereto); CFI, Case T–115/94 *Opel Austria v Council* [1997] E.C.R. II–39, para. 102 (EEA Agreement, Art. 10); ECJ, Case C–63/99 *Gloszcuk and Gloszcuk* [2001] E.C.R. I–6369, paras 29–38, and ECJ, Case C–62/00 *Pokrzeptowicz-Meyer* [2002] E.C.R. I–1049, paras 20–30; ECJ, Case C–235/99 *Kondova* [2001] E.C.R. I–6427, paras 30–39; ECJ, Case C–257/99 *Barkoci and Malil* [2001] E.C.R. I–6557, paras 30–39; ECJ (judgment of May 8, 2003), Case C–438/00 *Kolpak* [2003] E.C.R. I–4135, paras 24–30 (articles on establishment in Europe Agreements with Poland, Bulgaria, the Czech Republic and Slovakia, respectively).

[391] See ECJ, Case 104/81 *Kupferberg* [1982] E.C.R. 3641, para. 26 (Agreement concluded with Portugal, Art. 21, first para.).

[392] See ECJ, Case C–18/90 *Kziber* [1991] E.C.R. I–199, paras 15–23 (Agreement concluded with Morocco, Art. 41(1); confirmed by ECJ, Case C–58/93 *Yousfi* [1994] E.C.R. I–1353, paras 16–19); and ECJ, Case C–126/95 *Hallouzi-Choho* [1996] E.C.R. I–4807, paras 19–20, and ECJ, Case C–416/96 *El-Yassini* [1999] E.C.R. I–1209, paras 25–32 (Agreement concluded with Morocco, Art. 40); ECJ, Case C–103/94 *Krid* [1995] E.C.R. I–719, paras 21–24 (Agreement concluded with Algeria, Art. 39(1); upheld in ECJ, Case C–113/97 *Babahenini* [1998] E.C.R. I–183, para. 17); ECJ, Case C–162/96 *Racke* [1998] E.C.R. I–3655, paras 30–36 (Agreement concluded with Yugoslavia, Art. 22(4)); ECJ, Case C–37/98 *Savas* [2000] E.C.R. I–2927, paras 46–55 (Additional Protocol of the Agreement concluded with Turkey, Art. 41(1)).

from having direct effect on the ground that such effect is recognised unilaterally by the Community, but not by the other party to the agreement.[393] Neither is direct effect ruled out on the ground that the agreement provides for a special institutional framework for consultations and negotiations in relation to the implementation of the agreement or for safeguard clauses enabling the parties to derogate from certain provisions of the agreement in specific circumstances.[394] Even if an agreement concluded by the Community contains provisions which do not have direct effect, in the sense that they do not create rights which individuals can rely on directly before the courts, that fact does not preclude review by the courts of compliance with the obligations incumbent on the Community as a party to that agreement.[395]

b. Legal force and direct effect of decisions adopted by organs set up by international agreements

International organs. The Court of Justice has further held that the legal **17–094** force and possible direct effect of international agreements also apply to decisions adopted by institutions set up by the agreement which are responsible for implementing it. In Opinion 1/91 the Court noted that "international agreements concluded by means of the procedure set out in Article 228 [now Article 300] of the Treaty are binding on the institutions of the Community and its Member States and that, as the Court of Justice has consistently held, the provisions of such agreements and the measures adopted by institutions set up by such agreements become an integral part of the Community legal order when they enter into force".[396] The Court thereby confirmed that such provisions and measures are directly applicable. The Court had in fact previously held that decisions adopted by an association council set up by an association agreement were directly applicable on the ground that they were "directly connected with the Association Agreement".[397] That consideration generally holds good for decisions of institutions set up by any agreement concluded by the

---

[393] See ECJ, Case 104/81 *Hauptzollamt Mainz v Kupferberg* [1982] E.C.R. 3641, para. 18.

[394] *ibid.*, paras 20–21; see also ECJ, Case C–192/89 *Sevince* [1990] E.C.R. I–3461, para. 25; ECJ, Case C–469/93 *Chiquita Italia* [1995] E.C.R. I–4533, para. 36. For GATT and the WTO, see, however, para. 17–095, *infra*.

[395] ECJ, Case C–377/98 *Netherlands v European Parliament and Council* [2001] E.C.R. I–7079, para. 54.

[396] ECJ, Opinion 1/91 *Draft agreement between the Community, on the one hand, and the countries of the European Free Trade Association, on the other, relating to the creation of the European Economic Area* [1991] E.C.R. I–6079, para. 37. This applies in principle for new EU Member States as from the date of accession; see the Council's answer of February 13, 1997 to question No.E–1794/96 (Balfe), [1997] O.J. C105/3.

[397] ECJ, Case 30/88 *Greece v Commission* [1989] E.C.R. 3711, para. 13, *in fine*; ECJ, Case C–192/89 *Sevince* [1990] E.C.R. I–3461, para. 9.

Community, such as decisions of a joint committee established by a trade agreement.[398]

Provisions of such decisions have direct effect if they satisfy the requirements which provisions of the agreement itself must meet in order to have direct effect.[399] In this way, the Court of Justice has held that a number of provisions of decisions of the Association Council set up by the EEC-Turkey Agreement have direct effect.[400]

An international agreement may further provide for its own system of courts, including a court with jurisdiction to settle disputes between the Contracting Parties to the agreement, and, as a result, to interpret its provisions.[401] In such a case, the decisions of such a court will be binding on Community institutions, including the Court of Justice.[402]

c. Status of agreements concluded within the framework of the GATT/WTO

17–095 GATT and WTO. The superior legal force of international agreements concluded by the Community causes them to fetter the freedom of action of the Community institutions and the Member States. The situation is somewhat different as regards the international rules which arise within the framework of the General Agreement on Tariffs and Trade (GATT; see para. 20–010) and the World Trade Organisation (WTO; see paras

---

[398] Nevertheless, it is often the practice in the Community to transpose into Community law decisions taken by a joint committee set up by an agreement or by a co-operation or association council: see, *e.g.* Art. 1 of Regulations Nos 2229/91, 2230/91 and 2231/91 on the application of Decisions Nos 1/91, 2/91 and 3/91, respectively, of the EEC-Israel Co-operation Council ([1991] O.J. L211): "Decision No. 1/91 [2/91 or 3/91] of the EEC-Israel Co-operation Council shall apply in the Community". See Gilsdorf, "Les organes institués par des accords communautaires: effets juridiques de leurs décisions. Observations à propos notamment de l'arrêt de la Cour de justice des Communautés européennes dans l'affaire C–192/89" (1992) R.M.C.U.E. 328, at 331–334. For the EEA Agreement, see para. 23–010, *infra*.

[399] ECJ, Case C–192/89 *Sevince* [1990] E.C.R. I–3461, para. 14. For acts of bodies set up by multilateral agreements (under which the Community does not always have a right of veto), implementing measures are, however, generally still required: see Gilsdorf (n.398, *supra*), at 336–337.

[400] *ibid.*, paras 17–26; ECJ, Case C–237/91 *Kus* [1992] E.C.R. I–6781, paras 27–36; ECJ, Case C–355/93 *Eroglu* [1994] E.C.R. I–5113, paras 11 and 17; ECJ, Case C–171/01 *Wählergruppe Gemeinsam* [2003] E.C.R. I–4301, paras 54–67. In the case of Decision No. 3/80, direct effect was not accepted for those provisions requiring implementing measures: *cf.* ECJ, Case C–227/94 *Taflan-Met* [1996] E.C.R. I–4085, paras 23–38, and ECJ, Case C–262/96 *Sürül* [1999] E.C.R. I–2685, paras 48–74.

[401] ECJ, Opinion 1/91 *Draft agreement between the Community, on the one hand, and the countries of the European Free Trade Association, on the other, relating to the creation of the European Economic Area* [1991] E.C.R. I–6079, paras 39–40.

[402] *ibid.*, para. 39. In that Opinion, the Court held, however, that the system of court machinery provided for in the (first) draft agreement creating the European Economic Area was contrary to Art. 220 of the EC Treaty and, more generally, to the foundations of the Community; ns to para. 23–018, *infra*. In interpreting a provision of Community law, the Court of Justice will take a lead from the construction put on it by the EFTA Court (where the provision also applies in the EFTA States by virtue of the EEA Agreement): see para. 23–017, *infra*). For another example, see the dispute-settlement machinery of the World Trade Organisation: para. 20–013, *infra*.

20–011–20–014), which do not have the same effect in the Community legal order.

As far as GATT is concerned, the Court has held that "an obligation to recognise them as rules of international law which are directly applicable in the domestic legal systems of the Contracting Parties cannot be based on the spirit, general scheme or terms of GATT".[403] The Court further stated that "GATT, which according to its preamble is based on the principle of negotiations undertaken on the basis of 'reciprocal and mutually advantageous arrangements', is characterised by the great flexibility of its provisions, in particular those conferring the possibility of derogation, the measures to be taken when confronted with exceptional difficulties and settlement of conflicts between the Contracting Parties".[404]

Because of these special features, the Court has never held any GATT rule to have direct effect.[405] According to the Court, such direct effect is necessary, not only in order to derive rights from the rules, but also to serve as a condition so as to enable individuals to rely on them in order to contest the validity of Community acts or the application of national provisions.[406] Commentators had assumed that Member States and Community institutions could in fact invoke for that purpose GATT provisions without direct effect.[407] In the meantime, however, the Court of Justice has made it clear that the special features of GATT also preclude the Court from taking account of GATT rules in assessing the legality of a regulation in annulment proceedings brought by a Member State under Art. 230 of the EC Treaty.[408]

---

[403] ECJ, Case C–280/93 *Germany v Commission* [1994] E.C.R. I–4973, para. 110.

[404] *ibid.*, para. 106; for the first such *dictum*, see ECJ, Joined Cases 21–24/72 *International Fruit Company* [1972] E.C.R. 1219, para. 21.

[405] ECJ, Joined Cases 21–24/72 *International Fruit Company* [1972] E.C.R. 1219, paras 19–27; ECJ, Case 9/73 *Schlüter* [1973] E.C.R. 1135, paras 29–30; ECJ, Case 266/81 *SIOT* [1983] E.C.R. 731, para. 28; ECJ, Joined Cases 267–269/81 *SPI and SAMI* [1983] E.C.R. 801, para. 23; ECJ, Case C–469/93 *Chiquita Italia* [1995] E.C.R. I–4533, paras 26–29.

[406] See Rideau (n.377, *supra*), at 356–362. *cf.* regulations or directives without direct effect which may nevertheless be sufficiently clear to warrant at least a review of the compatibility of a national provision with their provisions (paras 17–119 and 17–132, *infra*, respectively). In a solitary case, the Court of Justice did dismiss a claim that a number of regulations were incompatible with provisions of GATT on substantive grounds without raising the question as to whether those provisions had direct effect: ECJ, Case 112/80 *Dürbeck* [1981] E.C.R. 1095, paras 45–46.

[407] See Petersmann, "Application of GATT by the Court of Justice of the European Communities" (1983) C.M.L.R. 397, at 415–437; Hahn and Schuster, "Zum Verstoss von gemeinschaftlichem Sekundärrecht gegen das GATT—Die gemeinsame Marktorganisation für Bananen vor dem EuGH" (1993) EuR. 261, at 280–281.

[408] ECJ, Case C–280/93 *Germany v Commission* [1994] E.C.R. I–4973, para. 109, with a case note by Foubert (1995) Col.J.E.L. 312–319. For a critical view, see Petersmann, "Proposals for a New Constitution for the European Union: Building-Blocks for a Constitutional Theory and Constitutional Law of the EU" (1995) C.M.L.R. 1123, at 1164–1170; Everling (n.372, *supra*), at 421–423; for a less critical view, see Dony, "L'affaire des bananes" (1995) C.D.E. 461, at 487–491. The Court of Justice does accept that the Commission may bring an action under Art. 226 of the EC Treaty against a Member State which infringes an agreement concluded in connection with GATT, see ECJ, Case C–61/94 *Commission v Germany* [1996] E.C.R. I–3989, para. 52, with a case note by Eeckhout (1998) C.M.L.R. 557–566.

Likewise, the Court of Justice will not review the legality of Community acts in the light of agreements concluded under the auspices of the WTO.[409] Although the WTO Agreement replaced GATT with stringent dispute-settlement machinery, the Court of Justice has refused to recognise the WTO accords as rules binding on the Community institutions so as to allow the institutions every latitude to resolve disputes with trading partners within the framework of the WTO, possibly through negotiation.[410] For those reasons, it is also not possible to review Community acts in the light of rulings of the WTO Dispute Settlement Body (see para. 20–014) on the compatibility of Community acts concerned with WTO obligations.[411]

---

[409] ECJ, Case C–149/96 *Portugal v Council* [1999] E.C.R. I–8395, paras 34–52; see also ECJ, Joined Cases C–300/98 and C–392/98 *Parfums Christian Dior* [2000] E.C.R. I–11307, paras 41–44; ECJ (order of May 2, 2001), Case C–307/99 *OGT Fruchthandelsgesellschaft* [2001] E.C.R. I–3159, paras 24–28; ECJ, Case C–377/98 *Netherlands v European Parliament and Council* [2001] E.C.R. I–7079, para. 52; ECJ, Joined Cases C–27/00 and C–122/00 *Omega Air* [2002] E.C.R. I–2569, paras 89–97; CFI, Case T–2/99 *T. Port v Council* [2001] E.C.R. II–2093 and Case T–3/99 *Bananatrading v Council* [2001] E.C.R. II–2123, paras 51 and 43, respectively. For a relatively approving view of the case law commencing with Case C–146/96 *Portugal v Council*: Rosas, (2000) C.M.L.R. 797–816; Berrod, "La Cour de justice refuse l'invocabilité des accords OMC: essai de régulation de la mondialisation" (2000) R.T.D.E. 419–450; Mengozzi, "La Cour de justice et l'applicabilité des règles de l'OMC en droit communautaire à la lumière de l'affaire Portugal c. Conseil" (2000) R.D.U.E. 509–522; Von Bogdandy, "Rechtsgleichheit, Rechtssicherheit und Subsidiarität im transnationalen Wirtschaftsrecht" (2001) Eu.Z.W. 357–365; Pischel, "Trade, Treaties and Treason: Some Underlying Aspects of the Difficult Relationship Between the EU and the WTO" (2001) E.For.Aff.Rev. 103–133; for a critical view: Bronckers, "La jurisprudence des juridictions communautaires relatives à l'OMC demande réparation: plaidoyer pour les droits des Etats membres" (2001) C.D.E. 3–14; Royla, "WTO-Recht—EG-Recht: Kollision, Justiziabilität, Implementation" (2001) EuR. 495–521; Ott, "Der EuGH and das WTO Recht: Die Entdeckung der politischen Gegenseitigkeit—altes Phänomen oder neuer Ansatz?" (2003) EuR. 504–521. In favour of a possibility of reviewing Community law in the light of WTO provisions, see, in particular, Beneyto, "The EU and the WTO. Direct Effect of the New Dispute Settlement System?" (1996) Eu.Z.W. 295–299; for a somewhat more cautious view, see Kuijper, "The New WTO Dispute Settlement System: The Impact on the European Community" (1995) J.W.T. 49, at 62–64; Eeckhout, "The Domestic Legal Status of the WTO Agreement: Interconnecting Legal Systems" (1997) C.M.L.R. 11–58; Manin (n.386, *supra*), at 399–428; Trachtman, "Bananas, Direct Effect and Compliance" (1999) E.J.I.L. 655–678.

[410] Case C–149/96 *Portugal v Council*, cited in n.409, *supra*, paras 36–46.

[411] ECJ, Case C–104/97 P *Atlanta v Council and Commission* [1999] E.C.R. I–6983, para. 20; CFI, Case T–254/97 *Fruchthandelsgesellschaft Chemnitz v Commission* [1999] E.C.R. II–2743, paras 28–30; CFI, Case T–18/99 *Cordis Obst und Gemüse Großhandel v Commission* [2001] E.C.R. II–913, paras 44–60, CFI, Case T–30/99 *Bocchi Food Trade International v Commission* [2001] E.C.R. II–943, paras 49–65, and CFI, Case T–52/99 *T. Port* [2001] II–981, paras 44–60; CFI (judgment of February 10, 2004), Joined Cases T–64/01 and T–65/01 *Afrikanische Frucht-Compagnie and Internationale Fruchtimport Gesellschaft Weichert & Co v Council and Commission*, not yet reported, paras 139–142. See in this connection, Lavranos, "Die Rechtswirkung von WTO panel reports im Europäischen Gemeinschaftsrecht sowie im deutschen Verfassungsrecht" (1999) EuR. 289–308; Rosas, "Implementation and Enforcement of WTO Dispute Settlement Findings: An EU Perspective" (2001) J.I.E.L. 131–144; Zonnekeyn, "The Status of Adopted Panel and Appellate Body Reports in the European Court of Justice and the Court of First Instance" (2000) J.W.T. 93–108. Nevertheless, the Court of Justice has held that the Court of First Instance should provide separate reasons as to why the legality of an act could not be

The Court of Justice considers itself under an obligation to review the legality of a contested Community act in the light of the GATT/WTO rules in two circumstances only.[412] First, it will conduct such a review where the Community intended to implement a particular obligation entered into within the framework of the GATT/WTO, which is the case, for example, with the anti-dumping regulation adopted in order to comply with the international obligations assumed by the Community as a result of Article VI of GATT and the GATT Anti-Dumping Code adopted for the purpose of implementing that Article.[413] Secondly, a Community act will be reviewed in the light of the GATT/WTO rules where it expressly refers to specific GATT/WTO provisions.[414] Accordingly, a measure adopted by the Community in order to comply with reports adopted under the WTO dispute settlement machinery cannot be reviewed in the light of those reports if the measure does not refer expressly to specific obligations ensuing from those reports.[415]

The fact that provisions of an agreement do not have direct effect does not release national courts from their obligation to apply national rules as far as possible in the light of the wording and purpose of those provisions and does not preclude the legal order of a Member State from according to

---

reviewed in the light of a decision of the WTO Dispute Settlement Body; see ECJ (judgment of September 30), 2003, Case C–93/02 P *Biret International v Council*, not yet reported, paras 51–66, and ECJ (judgment of September 30, 2003), Case C–94/02 P *Etablissements Biret v Council*, not yet reported, paras 54–69 (making it clear that the legality of a Community act may not be affected in any event by such a decision before the expiry of the reasonable time which the Community has to comply with its WTO obligations). See Wiers in (2004) L.I.E.I. 143–151.

[412] ECJ, Case C–280/93 *Germany v Commission* [1994] E.C.R. I–4973, para. 111; ECJ, Case C–149/96 *Portugal v Council* [1999] E.C.R. I–8395, para. 49.

[413] ECJ, Case C–69/89 *Nakajima* [1991] E.C.R. I–2069, paras 29–31; ECJ, Case C–76/00 P *Petrotub and Republica v Council* [2003] E.C.R. I–79, paras 52–63; CFI, Case T–162/94 *NMB France v Commission* [1996] E.C.R. II–427, paras 99–107. See Desmedt, "L'accès des particuliers aux droits et obligations de l'OMC dans la CE" (2003) T.B.H. 357–372; Zonnekeyn, "The ECJ's *Petrotub* Judgment: Towards a Revival of the "*Nakajima* Doctrine"?" (2003) L.I.E.I. 249–266. See also the review of a regulation whereby the Community gave effect to GATT provisions by adopting a regulation after concluding agreements with third countries in accordance with those provisions: ECJ, Case C–352/96 *Italy v Council* [1998] E.C.R. I–6937, paras 19–21.

[414] ECJ, Case 70/87 *Fediol v Commission* [1989] E.C.R. 1781, paras 18–22, at 1830 (GATT rules invoked as part of international law with a view to a finding whether conduct constituted an illicit trade practice within the meaning of Regulation No. 2641/84; for that regulation, see para. 20–008, *infra*).

[415] CFI, Case T–18/99 *Cordis Obst und Gemüse Großhandel v Commission* [2001] E.C.R. II–913, paras 57–59 (and corresponding passages in CFI, Case T–30/99 *Bocchi Food Trade International v Commission* [2001] E.C.R. II–943, and CFI, Case T–52/99 *T. Port* [2001] II–981). See Peers, "WTO dispute settlement and Community law" (2001) E.L.R. 605–610; Zonnekeyn, "The Latest on Indirect Effect of WTO Law in the EU Legal Order. The *Nakajima* case law misjudged?" (2001) J.I.E.L. 597–608. Such a review is possible at most with regard to Community rules which are amended on the basis of Regulation No. 1515/2001, ([2001] O.J. L201/10), which permits the Council to bring Community anti-dumping and anti-subsidy measures into line with a report drawn up by the Dispute Settlement Procedure by means of a simplified procedure (see para. 20–013).

individuals the right to rely directly on those provisions or from obliging the courts to apply those provisions of their own motion.[416]

d. Interpretation and reviewing the legality of international agreements

17–096 **Judicial review.** Where the Community acts externally by means of international agreements, that action itself is subject to judicial supervision. Before it is concluded, the "agreement envisaged" may be referred to the Court of Justice for its opinion (EC Treaty, Art. 300(6); see paras 21–020–21–021). When the agreement enters into force, it becomes *ipso facto* part of the Community legal order. However, as an "act of the institutions", the agreement comes within the jurisdiction of the Court to give preliminary rulings on its interpretation and validity under Art. 234 of the EC Treaty.[417] The interpretative jurisdiction applies only as far as the Community is concerned.[418] According to the Court of Justice, it is also possible to bring an action for annulment under Art. 230 of the EC Treaty against the act whereby the Commission sought to conclude an agreement.[419] However, the annulment of such an act does not release the Community from its international obligations. In order to guarantee the rights of the contracting parties, the law of treaties confines the possibilities

---

[416] ECJ, Joined Cases C–300/98 and C–392/98 *Parfums Christian Dior* [2000] E.C.R. I–11307, paras 45–49, ECJ, Case C–98/99 *Schieving-Nijstadt* [2001] E.C.R. I–5851, paras 54–73. For the indirect force of WTO rules in the Community legal order, see Snyder, "The Gatekeepers: The European Courts and WTO law" (2003) C.M.L.R. 313–367.

[417] For the first instance in the case law, see ECJ, Case 181/73 *Haegeman* [1974] E.C.R. 449, paras 4–6. This also applies to mixed agreements (para. 21–016, *infra*), even to provisions which are to be implemented by the Member States in accordance with the internal division of powers between the Community and the Member States: ECJ, Case 12/86 *Demirel* [1987] E.C.R. 3719, paras 8–12; ECJ, Case C–53/96 *Hermès International* [1998] E.C.R. I–3603, paras 22–29; ECJ, Joined Cases C–300/98 and C–392/98 *Parfums Christian Dior* [2000] E.C.R. I–11307, paras 32–40. See Lenaerts and Arts, *Procedural Law of the European Union*, Ch.6 (interpretation) and Ch.10 (rulings on validity); Heliskoski, "The Jurisdiction of the European Court of Justice to Give Preliminary Rulings on the Interpretation of Mixed Agreements" (2000) Nordic J.Int'l Law 395–412; Van Nuffel and Vanovermeire, "Over de bevoegdheid van het Hof van Justitie tot uitlegging van TRIPs en de directe werking van artikel 50 lid 6 TRIPs" (2001) T.B.H. 445–454; Neframi, "La compétence de la Cour de justice pour interpréter l'Accord TRIPS selon l'arrêt 'Parfums Christian Dior'" (2001) R.D.U.E. 491–519; Koutrakos, "The Interpretation of Mixed Agreements under the Preliminary Reference Procedure" (2002) E.For.Aff.Rev. 25–52.

[418] See for the EEA Agreement, ECJ, Case C–321/97 *Andersson and Andersson* [1999] E.C.R. I–3551, paras 26–33; ECJ, Case C–140/97 *Rechberger and Greindl* [1999] E.C.R. I–3499, paras 37–38; ECJ, Case C–300/01 *Salzmann* [2003] E.C.R. I–4899, paras 65–71.

[419] ECJ, Case C–327/91 *France v Commission* [1994] E.C.R. I–3641, paras 14–17; ECJ, Opinion 3/94 *Framework Agreement on Bananas* [1995] E.C.R. I–4577, para. 22; ECJ, Case C–360/93 *European Parliament v Council* [1996] E.C.R. I–1195; ECJ, Case C–122/95 *Germany v Council* [1998] E.C.R. I–973, para. 42; see also the earlier case ECJ, Opinion 1/75 *Draft Understanding on a Local Cost Standard drawn up under the auspices of the OECD* [1975] E.C.R. 1355, at 1361. For criticism, see Kaddous, "L'arrêt *France c. Commission* de 1994 (accord concurrence) et le contrôle de la 'légalité' des accords externes en vertu de l'art. 173 CE: la difficile réconciliation de l'orthodoxie communautaire avec l'orthodoxie internationale" (1996) C.D.E. 613–633; Leray and Potteau, "Réflexions sur la cohérence du système de contrôle de la légalité des accords internationaux conclus par la Communauté européenne" (1998) R.T.D.E. 535–571.

of annulment to cases in which the Community's consent was expressed in circumstances involving a manifest violation of a rule regarding competence which is of fundamental importance.[420] It is therefore advisable that the Community Court should invariably accompany the annulment of consent to an international agreement with a declaration that its legal effects remain unaffected.[421] In order to secure uniform application of Community law, the Court of Justice likewise has jurisdiction to give preliminary rulings—subject to the same conditions—on the validity and interpretation of decisions of authorities established by agreements concluded by the Community.[422]

2. International agreements concluded by Member States with non-member countries

a. Agreements concluded after the Community Treaties entered into force

Member States' agreements. The Community Treaties do not preclude **17–097** international competence on the part of the Member States in respect of matters which do not fall within the exclusive competence of the Communities. In respect of matters for which the Community has exclusive competence, a Member State can no longer conclude agreements with non-member States unless it has a special authorisation (see with regard to the common commercial policy, para. 20–004).

Agreements which Member States conclude with non-member countries or international organisations are not binding on the Communities.[423] The Court of Justice has no jurisdiction to give rulings on the interpretation of provisions of international law which are binding on Member States outside the framework of Community law[424] and has no power to determine whether a national provision is compatible with such an agreement.[425] Agreements concluded by Member States are binding on the Community, however, where the Treaty refers to them or where, under the EC Treaty,

---

[420] See Art. 46(2) of the Vienna Convention of March 21, 1986 on the Law of Treaties between States and International Organisations or between International Organisations (n.454, *infra*).

[421] Vanhamme (n.375, *supra*), at 311–315, and Kapteyn, "Quelques réflexions sur le contrôle de la constitutionnalité des accords conclus par la Communauté avec des pays tiers" in Rodriguez Iglesias, Due, Schintgen and Elsen (eds), *Mélanges en hommage à Fernand Schockweiler* (Nomos, Baden-Baden, 1999), at 275–285, who refer in this connection to the possibilities afforded by Art. 231 of the EC Treaty.

[422] ECJ, Case C–192/89 *Sevince* [1990] E.C.R. I–3461, paras 10–11 (decision of an association council; see also the judgments cited in n.400, *supra*); ECJ, Case C–188/91 *Deutsche Shell* [1993] E.C.R. I–363, paras 17–18 (decision of a joint committee). As regards reviewing the validity of such decisions, see Lenaerts and Arts, *Procedural Law of the European Union*, Ch.10.

[423] For a discussion of agreements concluded as between Member States, see para. 18–007 *et seq.*, *infra*; for the legal force of agreements concluded by the Council on behalf of the Member States under the CFSP or PJCC, see para. 18–023, *infra*.

[424] ECJ, Case 130/73 *Vandeweghe* [1973] E.C.R. 1329, para. 2.

[425] ECJ, Case C–379/92 *Peralta* [1994] E.C.R. I–3453, paras 16–17.

the Community has taken over the powers formerly vested in the Member States with regard to the application of such agreements (see para. 17–091). In order to ensure that Community law is uniformly applied, the Court may interpret provisions of such agreements with effect from the time at which the Community was substituted for the Member States.[426]

The duty of co-operation in good faith places a Member State under a duty to exercise its international powers without detracting from Community law[427] or from its effectiveness (*effet utile*) (see para. 5–054). Accordingly, a Member State must implement its international obligations with non-member countries—or with other Member States—in such a way as to take account of the obligation to treat its own nationals and nationals of other Member States in the same way.[428]

b. Agreements concluded before the Community Treaties entered into force

17–098 Pre-existing international obligations. In establishing the Communities, the Member States sought to create reciprocal rights and obligations without detracting from their existing international obligations. For this reason, they assumed that agreements which they had concluded with non-member countries before the Community Treaties entered into force in principle were not set aside by provisions of the Treaties. Art. 307 of the EC Treaty and Arts 105–106 of the EAEC Treaty which were adopted to this end still apply to agreements concluded at an earlier date by which Member States continue to be bound and to agreements which new Member States entered into before accession.[429] Of course, this does not mean that all the advantages which the Treaties confer on the Member States, notably the introduction of a customs union, may be extended to third States as a result of the application of agreements concluded prior to accession (see EC Treaty, Art. 307, third para.). Article 306 of the EC

---

[426] ECJ, Joined Cases 267–269/81 *SPI and SAMI* [1983] E.C.R. 801, paras 14–19.

[427] See, *e.g.* ECJ, Joined Cases C–176/97 and C–177/97 *Commission v Belgium and Luxembourg* [1998] E.C.R. I–3557 (agreement held to be contrary to a Community regulation).

[428] ECJ, Case C–307/97 *Saint Gobain ZN* [1999] E.C.R. I–6161, paras 57–58; ECJ, Case C–55/00 *Gottardo* [2002] E.C.R. I–413, paras 33–34. This obligation does not apply where such equal treatment would call in question the balance and reciprocity of the relevant international agreement: *Saint Gobain ZN*, para. 59, and *Gottardo*, para. 36. See De Pauw, "Zijn bilaterale socialezekerheidsverdragen tussen EU-lidstaten en derde landen auomatisch van toepassing op alle EU-onderdanen?" (2002) J.T.T. 257–261.

[429] See most recently Art. 6(12) of the 2003 Act of Accession ; see also EU Constitution, Art. III–435. Art. 307 of the EC Treaty does not apply to a legal relationship with a third country which was not a party to the international agreement in question before the EC Treaty entered into force: ECJ, Joined Cases C–364/95 and C–365/95 *T Port v Commission* [1998] E.C.R. I–1023, paras 59–65.

Treaty provides for preference to be given to agreements connected with the Benelux Economic Union.[430]

Precedence of international obligations. The first para. of Art. 307 of the **17–099** EC Treaty gives precedence in principle to "[t]he rights and obligations arising from agreements concluded before the entry into force of this Treaty between one or more Member States on the one hand, and one or more third countries, on the other" by providing that they "shall not be affected by the provisions of this Treaty". This means that national courts must ensure that non-member countries' rights under earlier agreements are honoured and the correlative obligations of Member States fulfilled.[431] A Member State is not entitled to rely on Art. 307 in order to derive rights *vis-à-vis* other Member States, contrary to Community law, from agreements concluded before the EC Treaty entered into force.[432] In principle, this also holds good for multilateral agreements to which third countries—as well as Member States—are parties.[433] If, however, the multilateral agreement itself does not leave any room for the application of derogating provisions as between any States party to it, it may be that application of Community law as between Member States will "jeopardise non-member countries' rights"[434] under the agreement.[435] In such a case, the first para. of Art. 307 of the EC Treaty may perhaps result in the multilateral agreement being given precedence.[436]

Consequently, in the event of a conflict between any provision of Community law and an international obligation originating in a prior

---

[430] Art. 306 is designed to prevent the application of Community law from causing the disintegration of the Benelux Union or from hindering its development. Consequently, Benelux rules may be applied in derogation from Community rules only in so far as the Benelux Union is further advanced than the common market. Compare ECJ, Case 105/83 *Pakvries* [1984] E.C.R. 2101, para. 11 (priority given to Benelux customs arrangements) with ECJ, Case C–473/93 *Commission v Luxembourg* [1996] E.C.R. I–3207, paras 42–43 (priority given to Community law as it was held to "go further" than the relevant provision of the Benelux Treaty). See also EU Constitution, Art. IV–441.

[431] ECJ, Case 10/61 *Commission v Italy* [1962] E.C.R. 1, at 10. In any event, the international obligations in question must be obligations whose performance may still be required by the non-member country. See, *e.g.* in the case of a division of a non-member country: ECJ (judgment of November 18, 2003), Case C–216/01 *Budejovický Budvar*, not yet reported, paras 146–167.

[432] See, *e.g.* ECJ, Case C–475/93 *Thévenon* [1995] E.C.R. I–3813 (Regulation No. 1408/71 held to replace a convention between France and Germany).

[433] ECJ, Case 10/61 *Commission v Italy* [1962] E.C.R. 1, at 10 (concerning GATT); ECJ, Case 812/79 *Burgoa* [1980] E.C.R. 2787, para. 11; ECJ, Case 121/85 *Conegate v HM Customs and Excise* [1986] E.C.R. 1007, para. 25; ECJ, Case 286/86 *Deserbais* [1988] 4907, paras 17–18; ECJ, Case C–473/93 *Commission v Luxembourg* [1996] E.C.R. I–3207, paras 39–40.

[434] The expression is used by Advocate General J. Mischo in his Opinion in ECJ, Case C–221/89 *Factortame* ("*Factortame II*") [1991] E.C.R. I–3905, point 15.

[435] In his Opinion in *Factortame II*, cited in the preceding n., the Advocate General considered whether this was the case, but expressly dismissed this possibility: *ibid.*, point 16, last paragraph. See also ECJ, Case C–158/91 *Levy* [1993] E.C.R. I–4287, paras 13–22.

[436] For a discussion of this eventuality, see Lenaerts and De Smijter, "Some Reflections on the Status of International Agreements in the Community Legal Order", in *Mélanges en hommage à Fernand Schockweiler* (n.421, *supra*), 347, at 363.

agreement concluded between a Member State and a non-member country, Art. 307 of the EC Treaty ensures that the international obligation is complied with. By the same token, a provision of national law which is necessary in order to ensure the performance by the Member State concerned of such an international obligation must be applied even though it conflicts with a provision of Community law.[437] In such case, the national court has to determine the extent to which the international obligations of the Member State are compatible with Community law.[438] As far as possible, it must interpret those obligations in a manner compatible with Community law.[439] Where a treaty permits a Member State to take a measure which appears to conflict with Community law, yet does not put it under an obligation to do so, the Member State should refrain from such action.[440]

Article 307 of the EC Treaty does not alter the type of rights which arise out of agreements concluded by Member States.[441] This means that an individual cannot rely on that article of the Treaty in order to invoke a provision of an agreement which does not have direct effect.[442] In that sense, Art. 307 does not have the effect of conferring on individuals who rely on an agreement concluded prior to the entry into force of the Treaty rights which the national or the Community courts must protect.[443]

17–100 Impact on Community institutions. After entry into force of the Community Treaties, agreements concluded by Member States did not become binding on the Community save where the Treaty referred thereto or, exceptionally, where the Communities substituted themselves for the Member States (see para. 17–097). The first para. of Art. 307 of the EC Treaty refers only to obligations of Member States. Nevertheless, "it would not achieve its purpose if it did not imply a duty on the part of the institutions of the Community not to impede the performance of the obligations of Member States which stem from a prior agreement. However, that duty of the Community institutions is directed only to permitting the Member State concerned to perform its obligations under the prior agreement and does not bind the Community as regards the non-member country in question".[444] Consequently, although an institution

---

[437] ECJ, Case C–158/91 *Levy* [1993] E.C.R. I–4287, para. 22.
[438] *ibid.*, para. 21.
[439] De Smijter and Vanhamme, "Een analyse van het arrest *Levy* en zijn implicaties voor de interpretatie van artikel 234 EG-Verdrag" (1993–1994) R.W. 1387, at 1390.
[440] ECJ, Case C–324/93 *Evans Medical Ltd* [1995] E.C.R. I–563, para. 32; ECJ, Case C–124/95 *Centro-Com* [1997] E.C.R. I–81, paras 54–60.
[441] ECJ, Case 812/79 *Burgoa* [1980] E.C.R. 2787, para. 10.
[442] ECJ (order of May 2, 2001), Case C–307/99 *OGT Fruchthandelsgesellschaft* [2001] E.C.R. I–3159, paras 29–30.
[443] *ibid.*; CFI, Case T–2/99 *T. Port* [2001] II–2093, para. 83, and Case T–3/99 *Bananatrading* [2001] E.C.R. II–2123, para. 78.
[444] ECJ, Case 812/79 *Burgoa* [1980] E.C.R. 2787, para. 9.

cannot compel a Member State to back out of its obligations under a prior agreement, Art. 307 does not debar the Community from taking action at variance with those obligations.[445]

Obligation to eliminate incompatibilies. To the extent that agreements **17–101** concluded prior to the entry into force of the EC Treaty are not compatible with it, the second para. of Art. 307 requires the Member State(s) concerned to "take all appropriate steps to eliminate the incompatibilities established" and, where necessary, to "assist each other to this end" or to "adopt a common attitude". Accordingly, the Member State(s) in question must start negotiations with a view to adapting the prior agreement. If such negotiations are unsuccessful, the Member State(s) will have, if possible, to terminate the agreement.[446] A Member State which fails to take all necessary steps to eliminate incompatibilities will be in breach of its obligations under Community law. Despite this, the application of the prior agreement will continue to be assured under the first para. of Art. 307 since that provision is primarily designed to protect the rights of non-member countries.[447]

3. Other rules of international law

International law. It is clear from the provisions of Art. 307 of the EC **17–102** Treaty itself that it is the Community's intention to fit in with international law. The Court of Justice has declared that the Community must respect international law in the exercise of its powers[448] and will therefore examine whether the validity of acts of the Community institutions is affected by reason of the fact that they are contrary to "a rule of international law".[449] The EU Constitution includes "respect for the principles of the United Nations Charter and international law" among the objectives of the Union's external action.[450]

---

[445] Petersmann, "Artikel 234", in von der Groeben, Thiesing and Ehlermann (eds), *Kommentar zum EWG-Vertrag* (Nomos, Baden-Baden, 1991), 5738; for a case study, see Grimes, "Conflicts between EC Law and International Treaty Obligations: A Case Study of the German Telecommunications Dispute" (1994) Harv.I.L.J. 535, at 548–549.

[446] ECJ, Case C–62/98 *Commission v Portugal* [2000] E.C.R. I–5171, paras 49–50, and C–84/98 *Commission v Portugal* [2000] E.C.R. I–5215, paras 58–59. See Klabbers, "Moribund on the Fourth of July? The Court of Justice on prior agreements of the Member States" (2001) E.L.R. 187–197; Manzini, "The Priority of Pre-Existing Treaties of EC Member States within the Framework of International Law" (2001) E.J.I.L. 781–792.

[447] ECJ (judgment of November 18, 2003), Case C–216/01 *Budejovický Budvar*, not yet reported, para. 172.

[448] ECJ, Case C–286/90 *Poulsen and Diva Navigation* [1992] E.C.R. I–6019, para. 9.

[449] ECJ, Joined Cases 21–24/72 *International Fruit Company* [1972] E.C.R. 1219, para. 6 (quoted in para. 17–092, *supra*). For a survey, see Meessen, "The Application of Rules of Public International Law within Community Law" (1976) C.M.L.R. 485–501 and, more recently, Vanhamme (n.375, *supra*), at 255–330.

[450] EU Constitution, Art. III–292(1).

a. Customary international law and general principles of law

17–103 Principles of international law. Not only provisions of international agreements binding on the Communities act as sources of Community law. Mention has already been made of the general principles of law, among which the Court of Justice includes fundamental rights, *inter alia* as enshrined in treaties on human rights concluded by the Member States (see para. 17–075). In interpreting and applying Community law, the Court of Justice also takes customary international law into account[451] and principles of international law, such as the fact that a State is precluded from refusing its own nationals the right of entry to its territory[452] and the territoriality principle as limiting the extent of the Community's powers.[453] In considering the scope of obligations arising under international agreements, the Court of Justice complies with the rules of customary international law, a notable example being the rules of the "law of treaties" codified in the Vienna Conventions.[454] Thus, Community law applies the international-law principle of good faith, which debars a contracting party from taking any measure incompatible with an international agreement after it has been ratified but before it has entered into force,[455] and the rules concerning the suspension and termination of an agreement on the ground of a

---

[451] ECJ, Case C–286/90 *Poulsen and Diva Navigation* [1992] E.C.R. I–6019, paras 10, 13–16 and 25–29 (customary law in the context of the law of the sea). See also, by implication, ECJ, Case C–221/89 *Factortame ("Factortame II")* [1991] E.C.R. I–3905, paras 15–16.

[452] ECJ, Case 41/74 *Van Duyn* [1974] E.C.R. 1337, para. 22.

[453] ECJ, Joined Cases 89, 104, 114, 116–117 and 125–129/85 *Åhlström v Commission* [1988] E.C.R. 5193, para. 18; CFI, Case T–102/96 *Gencor v Commission* [1999] E.C.R. II–753, paras 89–108. For more on the territorial scope of the Treaties, see paras 8–001—8–005, *supra*.

[454] See the Vienna Convention of May 23, 1969 on the law of treaties (in force since January 27, 1980). Although this convention has not been ratified by all Member States (the UK has ratified it; for the text, see UNTS No. 58 (1980) Vol.III; Misc. 1971; Cmnd.4818), it is deemed to be a codification of customary international law. See also the Vienna Convention of March 21, 1986 on the Law of Treaties between States and International Organisations or between International Organisations, which also largely codifies customary international law; see Kuijper, "The Court and the Tribunal of the EC and the Vienna Convention on the Law of Treaties 1969" (1998) L.I.E.I. 1–23, and Manin, "The European Communities and the Vienna Convention on the Law of Treaties between States and International Organisations or between International Organisations" (1987) C.M.L.R. 457–481. For an application of the 1969 Convention, see ECJ, Opinion 1/91 *Draft agreement between the Community, on the one hand, and the countries of the European Free Trade Association, on the other, relating to the creation of the European Economic Area* [1991] E.C.R. I–6079, para. 14; ECJ, Case C–432/92 *Anastasiou* [1994] E.C.R. I–3087, paras 43 and 50; ECJ, Case C–466/98 *Commission v UK* [2002] E.C.R. I–9427, para. 24; and ECJ, Case C–268/94 *Portugal v Council* [1996] E.C.R. I–6177, paras 19 and 27, where it was referred to as "international law"; for the application of such a rule before codification, see ECJ, Case 10/61 *Commission v Italy* [1962] E.C.R. 1, at 10.

[455] Vienna Convention 1969, Art. 18(a) as applied in CFI, Case T–115/94 *Opel Austria v Council* [1997] E.C.R. II–39, paras 90–123 (with regard to an agreement concluded by the Community, see para. 21–006, *infra*); see also ECJ, Case C–27/96 *Danisco Sugar* [1997] E.C.R. I–6653, paras 20 and 31 (concerning an accession treaty concluded by a would-be Member State).

fundamental change of circumstances (*rebus sic stantibus* clause).[456] In connection with a question of the succession of States (following the break-up of Czechoslovakia), the Court of Justice referred to the international practice based on the continuity of treaties.[457] The Court sometimes finds it useful in interpreting provisions of Community law to refer to agreements concluded by the Member States[458] and decisions of international organisations,[459] although it does not treat them as binding.

b. Obligations in connection with the United Nations

United Nations. All the Member States of the Union are members of the **17–104** United Nations (UN). The United Nations Charter[460] provides that membership is open only to "States", which precludes the Community/Union from joining.[461] As members of the UN, all the Member States are represented in the General Assembly. In the Security Council, France and the United Kingdom have permanent membership and the right of veto (UN Charter, Art. 27(1) and (3)); other Member States may sit thereon as one of the ten non-permanent members. The Community may accede to an agreement concluded under the auspices of the UN where that agreement so permits.[462] Where Member States have to give effect to obligations arising for them under the UN Charter (*e.g.* binding

---

[456] Vienna Convention 1969, Art. 62, applied in ECJ, Case C–162/96 *Racke* [1998] E.C.R. I–3655, paras 37–60 (applied by the Council in suspending and denouncing the Co-operation Agreement with Yugoslavia). The Court of Justice conducts its review in the light only of provisions which may be regarded as a codification of existing customary law: *ibid.*, paras 24 and 59; see the case notes by Klabbers (1999) C.M.L.R. 179–189 and Berramdane (2000) C.D.E. 253–279.

[457] ECJ (judgment of November 18, 2003), Case C–216/01 *Budejovický Budvar*, not yet reported, paras 150–166.

[458] See ECJ, Case 92/71 *Interfood* [1972] E.C.R. 231, para. 6 (agreements concluded at the 1960 and 1961 Tariff Conferences). In particular, this applies to the international agreements which constituted the inspiration for the common customs tariff; see, *e.g.* ECJ, Case 38/77 *Enka* [1977] E.C.R. 2203, paras 24–29 (Convention of December 15, 1950 on the Valuation of Goods for Customs Purposes). See also ECJ, Case 24/86 *Blaizot* [1988] E.C.R. 379, para. 17 (1961 European Social Charter). This is not the case where an agreement conflicts with a higher principle of Community law: CFI, Case T–192/96 *Lebedef v Commission* [1998] E.C.R. -SC II–1047, para. 77 (English abstract at IA-363) (ILO Convention).

[459] For provisions of the FAO and the World Health Organisation, see ECJ, Case 92/74 *Van den Berg* [1975] E.C.R. 599, paras 2–9; ECJ, Case 178/84 *Commission v Germany* [1986] E.C.R. 1227, paras 44 and 52; for explanatory notes and classification opinions of the International Customs Co-operation Council, see ECJ, Case 14/70 *Bakels v Oberfinanzdirektion München* [1970] E.C.R. 1001, paras 6–11; for recommendations of the International Commission on Radiological Protection, see ECJ, Case C–376/90 *Commission v Belgium* [1992] E.C.R. I–6153, paras 21–26.

[460] United Nations Charter, signed at San Francisco on June 26, 1945 (*TS* 67 (1946); Cmd 7015; United Nations Act 1946).

[461] UN Charter, Arts 3 and 4.

[462] *e.g.* the Agreement of the United Nations Economic Commission for Europe concerning the adoption of uniform technical prescriptions for wheeled vehicles, equipment and parts which can be fitted to and/or be used on wheeled vehicles and the conditions for reciprocal recognition of approvals granted on the basis of these prescriptions, approved by Council Decision of November 27, 1997, [1997] O.J. L346/78.

resolutions of the Security Council), they cannot avoid those obligations by claiming that certain powers have been transferred to the Communities.[463] As far as such cases are concerned, the EC Treaty not only provides that in principle pre-existing international obligations take precedence (EC Treaty, Art. 307, first para.; see para. 17–099), but it also allows the Member States, after prior consultation, to waive Community obligations so as to enable a Member State to carry out "obligations it has accepted for the purpose of maintaining peace and international security" (EC Treaty, Art. 297; see para. 9–001).

17–105 **Legal status of UN obligations.** Since all EU Member States are bound by the obligations arising under the UN Charter, the question may be asked as to whether the Community itself is so bound.[464] Whatever the answer to that question, the Community institutions must put the Member States in a position to comply with their pre-existing international obligations (see para. 17–100). This also means that, where possible, Community law should be interpreted in conformity with those obligations (see para. 17–099). Community measures giving effect to a resolution of the UN Security Council therefore must be interpreted in accordance with the wording and the aim of the resolution.[465] Where only the Community has the power to give effect to UN obligations, for instance in order to impose economic sanctions, it should take the necessary steps to that effect.[466] Where the Community decides to implement a binding UN resolution, the damage resulting from the economic sanctions imposed by the resolution cannot be attributed to the Community.[467]

---

[463] See Art. 103 of the UN Charter, which provides that States' obligations under the Charter are to prevail over their obligations under any other international agreement, and Art. 48(2) of the Charter, which provides that Members of the UN are to carry out decisions for the maintenance of international peace and security "directly and through their action in the appropriate international agencies of which they are members". As far as UN obligations are concerned, the Communities cannot be regarded as having been substituted for the Member States; unlike in the case of GATT (para. 17–091, *supra*), all competence in that connection has not been transferred to the Communities and the Communities do not act as equal partners within the organisation. See Petersmann, "Internationale Wirtschaftssanktionen als Problem des Völkerrechts und des Europarechts" (1981) Z.Vgl.RW. 1, at 26; Stein, "European Political Co-operation (EPC) as a Component of the European Foreign Affairs System" (1983) Z.a.ö.RV. 49, at 66.

[464] According to Art. 2(6) of the UN Charter, "[t]he Organisation shall ensure that States which are not Members of the United Nations act in accordance with [the principles set out in that article] so far as may be necessary for the maintenance of international peace and security". Gilsdorf and other commentators consider that the legal effects of this provision on non-UN Members may mean that the Community is under a direct obligation to carry out UN obligations: Gilsdorf, "Les réserves de sécurité du traité CEE, à la lumière du traité sur l'Union européenne" (1994) R.M.C.U.E. 17, at 21.

[465] ECJ, Case C–177/95 *Ebony Maritime and Loten Navigation* [1997] E.C.R. I–1111, paras 20–21 and 31.

[466] Petersmann (n.463, *supra*), at 26–27.

[467] CFI, Case T–184/95 *Dorsch Consult v Council and Commission* [1998] E.C.R. II–667, para. 74.

Review in the light of UN obligations. Another question is whether, in **17–106** interpreting and applying provisions of Community law, the courts may test them against the UN Charter and resolutions adopted pursuant to that instrument. This is the case where a Community measure purports to give effect to a UN obligation (*e.g.* with a view to implementing sanctions imposed by the Security Council).[468] In addition, an individual may invoke obligations contained in provisions having direct effect, such as some Security Council resolutions imposing sanctions.[469] Furthermore, it would appear that the Court of Justice is prepared to take account of rulings of the International Court of Justice in interpreting Community law.[470]

E. AUTONOMOUS MEASURES ADOPTED BY INSTITUTIONS AND BODIES

Range of instruments. The first para. of Art. 249 of the EC Treaty states **17–107** that, in order to carry out their task and in accordance with the provisions of the Treaty, the European Parliament acting jointly with the Council, the Council, and the Commission are to make regulations and issue directives, take decisions, make recommendations or deliver opinions. The institutions may not choose between those instruments when exercising their powers, but have to be guided by the article of the Treaty which serves as the legal basis for the action to be taken (see para. 5–011).

Nevertheless, the institutions make use of instruments other than those listed in the second to the fifth paras of Art. 249 (see para. 17–140 *et seq.*). For one thing, interinstitutional agreements are in a special category (see para. 17–148). Moreover, Community bodies other than the institutions mentioned are empowered to adopt legislative measures (see para. 17–150). For its part, the EU Constitution will introduce a new classification and new designations for the Community instruments and there will be stricter rules on the choice of the instruments to be used in each particular case (see paras 17–145 *et seq.*).

The Treaty sets out a number of formal requirements to be satisfied by acts of the institutions, some of which—pursuant to general principles of

---

[468] ECJ, Case C–84/95 *Bosphorus* [1996] E.C.R. I–3953, paras 13–15. See Canor, "'Can Two Walk Together, Except They Be Agreed?' The Relationship between International Law and European Law: The Incorporation of United Nations Sanctions against Yugoslavia into European Community Law through the Perspective of the European Court of Justice" (1998) C.M.L.R. 137–187. More generally on the compatibility with international law of sanctions adopted by the Community, see Karagiannis, "Sanctions internationales et droit communautaire" (1999) R.T.D.E. 363–394.

[469] See Angelet, "La mise en oeuvre des mesures coercitives économiques des Nations-Unies dans la Communauté européenne" (1993) B.T.I.R. 500, at 502–505 and 528.

[470] ECJ, Case C–432/92 *Anastasiou* [1994] E.C.R. I–3087, para. 49; ECJ, Case C–162/96 *Racke* [1998] E.C.R. I–3655, paras 24 and 50. See Higgins, "The ICJ, the ECJ and the integrity of international law" (2003) I.C.L.Q. 1–20.

law—also apply to acts of other Community bodies.[471] These requirements will continue to apply under the EU Constitution.[472]

1. Formal requirements

a. Manner in which acts come into being

17–108 **Authentication.** In their respective rules of procedure, the institutions themselves have adopted provisions regarding the procedure which must be followed in order to adopt an act and the formal requirements with which the act must satisfy.[473] Some of those provisions may be regarded as being essential procedural requirements within the meaning of the second para. of Art. 230 of the EC Treaty, which, if infringed, may give rise to an action for annulment.[474] This is the case, for example, with the authentication procedures laid down in the rules of procedure of the Council and the Commission.[475] Article 15 of the Council Rules of Procedure provides that the text of acts adopted by the Council is to bear the signatures of the President-in-Office and the Secretary-General of the Council; acts adopted jointly with the European Parliament also have to be signed by the President of the Parliament (EC Treaty, Art. 254(1)). Authenticating a measure by dating it and appending the requisite signatures confirms that the terms of the authenticated instrument correspond to those of the act adopted and enables the competence of the authority issuing the measure to be verified.[476] Authentication renders the instrument enforceable and ensures that it is incorporated into the Community legal order.[477]

---

[471] For a general discussion of acts of the institutions and bodies, see Lauwaars, *Lawfulness and Legal Force of Community Decisions* (Sijthoff, Leiden, 1973), at 5–54 (discussion of legal instruments) and 148–176 (formal requirements); Louis, "Les actes des institutions", in Louis, Vandersanden, Waelbroeck and Waelbroeck, *Commentaire Mégret—Le droit de la CEE. 10. La Cour de justice. Les actes des institutions* (Editions de l'Université de Bruxelles, Brussels, 1993), at 475–540.

[472] See Arts I–38(2) (statement of reasons), I–39 (publication and entry into force) and III–401 (enforcement).

[473] For references to the rules of procedure of the various institutions, see the discussion of the operation of the European Parliament, the Council and the Commission in paras 10–026, 10–042 and 10–067, *supra*, respectively.

[474] See Lenaerts and Arts, *Procedural Law of the European Union*, Ch.7.

[475] ECJ, Case C–137/92 P *Commission v BASF* [1994] E.C.R. I–2555, para. 76 (requirement for authentication laid down in the Commission's Rules of Procedure). See more recently ECJ, Case C–107/99 *Italy v Commission* [2002] E.C.R. I–1091, paras 47–48.

[476] CFI, Joined Cases T–79/89, T–84/89, T–85/89, T–86/89, T–89/89, T–91/89, T–92/89, T–94/89, T–96/89, T–98/89, T–102/89 and T–104/89 *BASF v Commission* [1992] E.C.R. II–315, para. 75.

[477] *ibid.* In that case, the Court of First Instance considered that the defects of the relevant Commission decision, *inter alia*, on account of failure to comply with the authentication procedure, were so manifest and serious as to render the decision non-existent: *ibid.*, para. 96, at II–362. On an appeal brought by the Commission, the Court of Justice held that the irregularity was not of such obvious gravity that the decision had to be treated as legally non-existent; accordingly, the Court of Justice set aside the judgment and annulled the Commission decision at issue for infringement of essential procedural requirements: ECJ, Case C–137/92 P *Commission v BASF* [1994] E.C.R. I–2555, paras 48–55 and 75–78. See

Thereafter, a measure may be amended only in accordance with the rules on competence and procedure, apart from simple corrections of spelling and grammar.[478]

b. Statement of reasons

Obligation to state reasons. Regulations, directives and decisions adopted **17–109** jointly by the European Parliament and the Council and regulations, directives and decisions of the Council or the Commission must state the reasons on which they are based and refer to any proposals or opinions which were required to be obtained pursuant to the Treaty (EC Treaty, Art. 253). The obligation to state reasons for binding acts may also be found in Art. 162 of the EAEC Treaty.[479]

The duty to state reasons constitutes an essential procedural requirement within the meaning of the second para. of Art. 230 of the EC Treaty and may be raised by the Court of Justice or the Court of First Instance of its own motion.[480] If the Court finds the statement of reasons to be inadequate, it will annul the contested act.[481] The Court of Justice has held that the duty to state the reasons on which acts are based does not take "merely formal considerations into account but seeks to give an opportunity to the parties of defending their rights, to the Court of exercising its supervisory functions and to Member States and to all interested nationals of ascertaining the circumstances in which the [institution] has applied the Treaty".[482] To this end, the statement of reasons must "disclose in a clear and unequivocal fashion the reasoning followed by the Community authority which adopted the measure in question".[483] Although where a given decision follows a well-established line of decisions, the reasons on which it is based may be given in a summary manner, the Community authority must give an explicit account of its reasoning if the decision goes appreciably further than previous decisions.[484] It is a requirement of the principle of subsidiarity that an institution must state its grounds for considering that the objectives of its action cannot be sufficiently achieved by the Member States (EC Treaty,

---

also CFI, Joined Cases T–80/89, T–81/89, T–83/89, T–87/89, T–88/89, T–90/89, T–93/89, T–95/89, T–97/89, T–99/89, T–100/89, T–101/89, T–103/89, T–105/89, T–107/89 and T–112/89 *BASF v Commission* [1995] E.C.R. II–729, paras 108–126; CFI, Case T–32/91 *Solvay v Commission* [1995] E.C.R. II–1825, paras 49–54; CFI, Case T–37/91 *ICI v Commission* [1995] E.C.R. II–1901, paras 88–93.

[478] CFI, Joined Cases T–79/89, T–84/89, T–85/89, T–86/89, T–89/89, T–91/89, T–92/89, T–94/89, T–96/89, T–98/89, T–102/89 and T–104/89 *BASF v Commission* [1992] E.C.R. II–315, para. 35; see also ECJ, Case 131/86 *UK v Council* [1988] E.C.R. 905, paras 34–39.

[479] Art. 162 of the EAEC Treaty only omits any reference to acts adopted jointly by the European Parliament and the Council.

[480] ECJ, Case 18/57 *Nold v High Authority* [1959] E.C.R. 41, at 51–52. See Lenaerts and Arts, *Procedural Law of the European Union*, Ch.7.

[481] See, *e.g.* CFI, Case T–38/92 *AWS Benelux BV v Commission* [1994] E.C.R. II–213, paras 26–36.

[482] ECJ, Case 24/62 *Germany v Commission* [1963] E.C.R. 63, at 69.

[483] ECJ, Case C–350/88 *Delacre v Commission* [1990] E.C.R. I–395, para. 15.

[484] *ibid.*

Art. 5; see para. 5–033). Where the Community institutions have discretion (power of appraisal), sufficient reasoning is of even more fundamental importance in order to enable the Court to verify whether the factual and legal matters upon which the exercise of the power of appraisal depended were present.[485] The extent of the requirement to state reasons is also influenced by the type of instrument employed by the institution.[486] In the case of a measure of general application, the Court of Justice has held that the statement of reasons may be confined to indicating the general situation which led to its adoption and the general objectives which it is intended to achieve.[487]

In order to make it clear that an act was produced in accordance with the procedure prescribed for the adoption of acts of the type in question, Art. 253 of the EC Treaty provides that it must refer to any proposals or opinions required to be obtained, although there is no need to mention whether and why a given proposal or opinion was or was not followed.[488] In regulations, directives and decisions, the Council cites proposals submitted and "opinions obtained", which does not restrict it to opinions which it was required to obtain.[489]

c. Publication or notification—entry into effect

17–110 **Publication and notification.** Article 254(1) and (2) of the EC Treaty provides that regulations, directives and decisions adopted in accordance with the co-decision procedure (EC Treaty, Art. 251) have to be published in the *Official Journal*, together with regulations of the Council or the Commission and directives of those institutions which are addressed to all the Member States. Those acts are printed in Part L (Legislation) of the

---

[485] ECJ, Case C–269/90 *Technische Universität München* [1991] E.C.R. I–5469, paras 14 and 27.
[486] For regulations, see, for instance, ECJ, Case 5/67 *Beus* [1968] E.C.R. 83, at 95; for decisions, see ECJ, Case 16/65 *Schwarze* [1965] E.C.R. 877, at 888, and ECJ, Case C–350/88 *Delacre v Commission* [1990] E.C.R. I–395, para. 16. See also Lenaerts and Arts, *Procedural Law of the European Union*, Ch.7.
[487] ECJ, Case C168/98 *Luxembourg v European Parliament and Council* [2000] E.C.R. I–9131, paras 62–68.
[488] ECJ, Case 4/54 *ISA v High Authority* [1954 to 1956] E.C.R. 91, at 100 (concerning Art. 15 of the ECSC Treaty); ECJ, Case C–62/88 *Greece v Council* [1990] E.C.R. I–1527, para. 29 (concerning Art. 190 [now Art. 253] of the EC Treaty).
[489] See Council Rules of Procedure, Annex V, "Provisions concerning the forms of acts". Art. 253 of the EC Treaty does not require acts to refer to any subsequent amendment of the Commission proposal, unless the Commission withdrew its original proposal and replaced it by a new one: ECJ, Case C–280/93 *Germany v Council* [1994] E.C.R. I–4973, para. 37. Neither is there a requirement for a summary of the facts establishing that each of the institutions involved in the legislative procedure observed its procedural rules: ECJ, Case C–377/98 *Netherlands v European Parliament and Council* [2001] E.C.R. I–7079, paras 86–87.

Official Journal.[490] Other directives and decisions and recommendations have to be notified to those to whom they are addressed.[491] Unless the Council or Coreper decides otherwise, they are published in the *Official Journal.*[492]

Entry into effect. Acts which have to be published in the *Official* **17–111** *Journal* pursuant to Art. 254(1) and (2) of the EC Treaty enter into force on the date specified therein or, in the absence of such date, on the 20th day following that of their publication. Other directives and decisions take effect upon notification (Art. 254(3)). The Court of Justice has held that it is a fundamental principle of the Community legal order that a measure adopted by the public authorities shall not be applicable to those concerned before they have the opportunity to make themselves acquainted with it.[493] This means that proceedings cannot be brought against individuals for breach of an obligation arising under a regulation where it was not adequately brought to their attention.[494]

The unity and uniform application of Community law require that, save as otherwise expressly provided, a regulation should enter into force on the same date in all the Member States, regardless of any delays in the distribution of the *Official Journal*. In the absence of evidence to the contrary, a regulation is to be regarded as having been published throughout the Community on the date borne by the issue of the *Official Journal* containing the text of that regulation.[495] If an institution deliberately backdates an act, it infringes the principle of legal certainty.[496] In general, the principle of legal certainty precludes a Community measure from taking effect from a point in time before its publication. Exceptionally, a measure may so take effect on the dual condition that the purpose to be achieved so demands and the legitimate expectations of those concerned are duly respected.[497] In accordance with the principles of

---

[490] Before the amendment made by the EU Treaty to Art. 254 of the EC Treaty, directives did not have to be published. In practice, they were published in the *Official Journal*, Part L, under the heading "acts whose publication is not obligatory". Acts published pursuant to Art. 163 of the EAEC Treaty also appear in the *Official Journal*, likewise PJCC acts (under Declaration (No. 9) on Art. K.6 [now Art. 34](2) of the Treaty on European Union, [1997] O.J. C340/133). ECSC acts were also published in this way pursuant to Art. 15 of the ECSC Treaty. See the introduction to the source material.

[491] EC Treaty, Art. 254(3); Council Rules of Procedure, Art. 18(1) and (2)(a).

[492] Council Rules of Procedure, Art. 17(2)(d).

[493] ECJ, Case 98/78 *Racke* [1979] E.C.R. 69, para. 15; see also the parallel judgment of the same date in Case 99/78 *Decker* [1979] E.C.R. 101.

[494] ECJ, Case C–469/00 *Ravil* [2003] E.C.R. I–5053, paras 91 to 100, and ECJ, Case C–108/01 *Consorzio del Prosciutto di Parma* [2003] E.C.R. I–5121, paras 88–96. Such an obligation may be relied on against individuals where they may be deemed to have been aware of it in the light of the circumstances: *Ravil*, paras 101–103.

[495] ECJ, Case 98/78 *Racke* [1979] E.C.R. 69, paras 16–17.

[496] CFI, Case T–115/94 *Opel Austria v Council* [1997] E.C.R. II–39, paras 127–132 (see also para. 17–069, *supra*).

[497] ECJ, Case 98/78 *Racke* [1979] E.C.R. 69, para. 20; ECJ, Case C–110/97 *Netherlands v Council* [2001] E.C.R. I–8763, paras 151–157.

legal certainty and protection of legitimate expectations, new rules apply immediately to the future effects of a situation which arose under the old rules[498]; they can apply to situations existing before their entry into force only in so far as it clearly follows from their terms, objectives or general scheme that such effect must be given to them.[499] The same is true of the application of the Treaty (see para. 7–001) and of international agreements concluded by the Community (see para. 17–091).

d. Enforcement

17–112 Enforcement. The Community is not competent to enforce compliance with its acts itself. However, decisions of the Council or of the Commission which impose a pecuniary obligation on natural or legal persons, with the exception of States, are enforceable by virtue of the first para. of Art. 256. The same is true of judgments of the Court of Justice or the Court of First Instance, which Art. 244 declares enforceable under the conditions laid down in Art. 256.[500] The national authority designated for this purpose by each Member State must append an order for enforcement without any formality other than verification of the authenticity of the decision.[501] Enforcement then takes place in accordance with the applicable national rules of civil procedure (EC Treaty, Art. 256, second para.). Enforcement may be suspended only by an order of the Court of Justice or the Court of First Instance. However, supervising the manner of enforcement falls to the national courts (EC Treaty, Art. 256, fourth para.).

2. Acts of the institutions

a. Survey

17–113 Terminology. Article 249 of the EC Treaty defines the instruments available to the Council, the Commission and, under the co-decision procedure (Art. 251), the European Parliament and the Council jointly: regulations, directives, decisions, recommendations and opinions. Article 161 of the EAEC Treaty lists the same instruments for use by the Council and the Commission. Rules adopted under the ECSC Treaty could take the form of decisions, recommendations and opinions (ECSC Treaty, Art. 14),

---

[498] ECJ, Case 270/84 *Licata v Economic and Social Committee* [1986] E.C.R. 2305, para. 31; ECJ, Case C–160/00 *Pokrzeptowicz-Meyer* [2002] E.C.R. I–1049, para. 50.

[499] ECJ, Case 21/81 *Bout* [1982] E.C.R. 381, para. 13; ECJ, Case C–34/92 *GruSA Fleisch* [1993] E.C.R. I–4147, para. 22. For futher details, see Kaleda, "Immediate Effects of Community Law in the New Member States: Is there a Place for a Consistent Doctrine?" (2004) E.L.J. 102–122.

[500] See also Arts 164 and 159, respectively, of the EAEC Treaty.

[501] In the UK, application to append an order for enforcement to a judgment is made to the Secretary of State; the High Court in England or Wales or in Northern Ireland or the Court of Session in Scotland registers the judgment (Enforcement of Community Judgments) Order 1972, SI 1972/1590, Art. 3(1); see also European Communities Act, s.3(3).

but the terminology of the ECSC Treaty did not correspond to that of the later Community Treaties.[502] It is clear from the definitions given in the relevant articles that the instruments which they list do not have the same legal effects. Whether a given act is a "regulation" or a "decision" depends on its aim and content, not on the official title conferred on it by the institution which adopted it.[503] The five instruments listed are not the only acts by which the institutions can produce legal effects (see para. 17–140). When the EU Constitution enters into force, there will be a new range of legal instruments which will enable a distinction to be made between instruments, not only on the basis of their legal effects, but also on the basis of whether the instrument in question contains a legislative or an implementing act (see paras 17–145 et seq.).

Judicial review. The legality of a Community act which produces legal **17–114** effects may be reviewed by the Court of Justice or the Court of First Instance when a direct action is brought against it (EC Treaty, Art. 230), where an objection of illegality is raised (Art. 241) or where a national court makes a reference to the Court of Justice for a preliminary ruling on its validity (Art. 234, first para., indent (b)). In addition, the Court of Justice may rule on the interpretation of any "act of the institutions" (*ibid.*).[504]

b. Regulations

Definition. A regulation has general application and is binding in its **17–115** entirety and directly applicable in all the Member States (EC Treaty, Art. 249, second para.).

General application. The fact that a regulation has general application **17–116** means that it is "applicable to objectively determined situations and involves legal consequences for categories of persons viewed in a general

---

[502] ECSC *decisions* were binding in their entirety (ECSC Treaty, Art. 14, second para.) and could be general or individual in character (see ECSC Treaty, Art. 33, second para.). ECSC general decisions corresponded to EC and EAEC regulations and ECSC individual decisions to EC and EAEC decisions. ECSC *recommendations* were binding as to the aims to be pursued, but left the choice of the appropriate methods of achieving those aims to those to whom the recommendations were addressed (ECSC Treaty, Art. 14, third para.). They could therefore be equated with EC and EAEC directives (except that the latter may be addressed only to Member States). ECSC *opinions* had no binding force (ECSC Treaty, Art. 14, fourth para.) and hence corresponded to EC and EAEC recommendations and opinions.

[503] ECJ, Joined Cases 16–17/62 *Confédération Nationale des Producteurs de Fruits et Légumes v Council* [1962] E.C.R. 471, at 479; ECJ, Case 26/86 *Deutz and Geldermann v Council* [1987] E.C.R. 941, paras 6–7.

[504] For the system of legal redress, see ECJ, Case 294/83 *Les Verts v European Parliament* [1986] E.C.R. 1339, para. 23 *et seq.*, and the detailed discussion in Lenaerts and Arts, *Procedural Law of the European Union*, of actions for annulment (Ch.7), the objection of illegality (Ch.9) and the preliminary ruling procedure (Ch.6—interpretation—and Ch.10—review of validity).

and abstract manner".[505] The field of application of a regulation is not individually tailored to specific individuals or situations. A measure does not lose its "character as a regulation simply because it may be possible to ascertain with a greater or lesser degree of accuracy the number or even the identity of the persons to whom it applies at any given time as long as there is no doubt that the measure is applicable as the result of an objective situation of law or of fact which it specifies and which is in harmony with its ultimate objective".[506] The general scope of a regulation differentiates it from a decision whose "essential characteristics . . . arise from the limitation of the persons to whom it is addressed".[507] Whether a given act has general or individual scope determines whether a natural or legal person may bring an action for its annulment pursuant to the fourth para. of Art. 230 of the EC Treaty. This is because, according to that provision, an action for annulment may be brought by any natural or legal person "against a decision addressed to that person or against a decision which, although in the form of a regulation or a decision addressed to another person, is of direct and individual concern to the former".[508]

17–117 Binding in its entirety. A regulation is binding in its entirety, which means that, unlike a directive, it is intended to subject a situation to rules which are all-embracing and, where necessary, precise. Where a regulation is adopted under the Treaty as a "legislative" act,[509] it sometimes remains deliberately vague in conferring executive tasks (expressly) on the Community institutions or (implicitly or expressly) on the Member States. Regulations are generally adopted as implementing measures in areas in which Community legislation imposes extensive administrative tasks on the Community, such as the common agricultural policy and the application of the Common Customs Tariff.

17–118 Direct applicability. Regulations are directly applicable in all Member States. A regulation automatically forms part of the (highest) provisions of a Member State's legal order without it being necessary to transpose it in any way. Indeed, formal incorporation of provisions of a regulation into the national legal order is regarded as impermissible on the ground that it would bring into doubt "both the legal nature of the applicable provisions and the date of their coming into force".[510] Nevertheless, the direct

---

[505] ECJ, Case 6/68 *Zuckerfabrik Watenstedt v Council* [1968] E.C.R. 409, at 415.
[506] *ibid.*; ECJ, Case 101/76 *Koninklijke Scholten Honig v Commission* [1977] E.C.R. 797, para. 23.
[507] ECJ, Joined Cases 16–17/62 *Confédération Nationale des Producteurs de Fruits et Légumes v Council* [1962] E.C.R. 471, at 478.
[508] See the discussion in Lenaerts and Arts, *Procedural Law of the European Union*, Ch.7.
[509] Alongside other Treaty provisions which do not prescribe any specific normative instrument (para. 17–140, *infra*), Art. 39(3)(d) and Art. 89 of the EC Treaty require "regulations" to be used and Art. 37(2), third subpara., Art. 40, Art. 83(1) and Art. 110(1) provide for the possible use of regulations.
[510] ECJ, Case 39/72 *Commission v Italy* [1973] E.C.R. 101, paras 16–17; see also ECJ, Case 34/73 *Variola* [1973] E.C.R. 981, para. 11; ECJ, Case 50/76 *Amsterdam Bulb* [1977] E.C.R. 137, paras 4–7.

applicability of regulations does not preclude a power on the part of the Member States to take the necessary implementing measures.[511] Indeed, Member States are obliged to take such measures.

Direct effect. Individuals are always entitled to rely on any regulation **17–119** before the national courts with a view to having national law which is incompatible therewith disapplied. In addition, provisions of a regulation may have direct effect. The Court of Justice has held that "by reason of their nature and their function in the system of the sources of Community law, regulations have direct effect and are, as such, capable of creating individual rights which national courts must protect".[512] The case law does not always draw a distinction between direct applicability of a regulation and the direct effect of its provisions. Nevertheless, it may be taken that a provision of a regulation will have *direct effect* only if it satisfies the same requirements as apply to Treaty articles; in other words, it must be "clear and precise" and must not "leave any margin of discretion to the authorities".[513] The fact that a regulation is *directly applicable* means that it is applied "in favour of or against those subject to it" without having been transposed into national law.[514] Consequently, individuals may derive rights from a provision of a regulation which has *direct effect* as against both national authorities and individuals.[515] Even where on account of its content a regulation does not have direct effect, national provisions must nevertheless be interpreted as far as possible in the light of its wording and objectives.[516] This principle of consistent interpretation is limited, however, by the general principles of Community law, such as the principle of legal certainty, the principle of legality and the prohibition of retroactivity. Where a regulation empowers Member States to impose sanctions for infringements of the regulation, it cannot, of itself and independently of a national law adopted by a Member State for its implementation, have the effect of determining or aggravating the liability in criminal law of persons who act in contravention of the provisions of that regulation.[517] Moreover, a

---

[511] ECJ, Case 230/78 *Eridania* [1979] E.C.R. 2749, para. 35 (para. 14–047, *supra*).

[512] ECJ, Case 43/71 *Politi* [1971] E.C.R. 1039, para. 9; ECJ, Case 93/71 *Leonesio* [1972] E.C.R. 287, para. 5; see also paras 22–23.

[513] ECJ, Case 9/73 *Schlüter* [1973] E.C.R. 1135, para. 32, at 1158; ECJ, Case C–403/98 *Azienda Agricola Monte Arcosu* [2001] E.C.R. I–103, paras 26–28. See Bleckmann, "L'applicabilité directe du droit communautaire", in *Les recours des individus devant les instances nationales en cas de violation du droit européen: Communautés européennes et Convention des droits de l'homme* (Larcier, Brussels, 1978), 85, at 110; Easson, "The 'Direct Effect' of EEC Directives" (1979) I.C.L.Q. 319, at 321–322; for the debate amongst academics, see Louis (n.471, *supra*), at 493–496.

[514] ECJ, Case 34/73 *Variola* [1973] E.C.R. 981, para. 10. See also para. 17–128, *infra*.

[515] See ECJ, Case C–253/00 *Munoz and Superior Fruiticola* [2002] E.C.R. I–7289, paras 27–32, with a case note by Biondi (2003) C.M.L.R. 1243–1250.

[516] See the case note by Kronenberger to the judgment in ECJ, Case C–403/98 *Azienda Agricola Monte Arcosu* [2001] E.C.R. I–103 in (2001) C.M.L.R. 1545–1556.

[517] ECJ (judgment of January 7, 2004), Case C–60/02 *Criminal proceedings against X*, not yet reported, paras 61–63.

provision may be relied on against individuals only if they were capable of knowing about it.[518]

c. Directives

17–120 Definition. A directive is binding, as to the result to be achieved, upon each Member State to which it is addressed, but leaves to the national authorities the choice of form and methods (EC Treaty, Art. 249, third para.). The legal force of a directive is equivalent to that of a recommendation made pursuant to the ECSC Treaty,[519] although such a recommendation could be addressed to persons other than Member States (see ECSC Treaty, Art. 14, third para.). By leaving the Member States free to determine themselves the way in which the intended result is achieved within the national legal system, directives reflect the idea of subsidiarity.[520] Consequently, directives are an appropriate means of introducing Community rules which call for existing national provisions to be amended or fleshed out before the new rules can be applied.[521] A directive may also be addressed to only one Member State.[522]

(1) *The transposition of directives into national law*

17–121 Implementation. Unlike regulations, directives are not directly applicable in Member States' domestic legal systems. They obtain their full legislative status only after they have been implemented in national law.[523]

17–122 Requirements of legal certainty. The provisions of directives must be implemented with unquestionable binding force, and the specificity, precision and clarity necessary to satisfy the requirements of legal certainty.[524] For the purpose of considering whether a directive has been correctly implemented, the scope of national laws, rules or administrative

---

[518] para. 17–111, *supra.*

[519] ECJ, Case C–221/88 *Busseni* [1990] E.C.R. I–495, para. 21; ECJ, Case C–18/94 *Hopkins* [1996] E.C.R. I–2281, paras 25–29.

[520] For the directive as a possible instrument amenable to Member States, see Van Nuffel, *De rechtsbescherming van nationale overheden in het Europees* recht (Kluwer, Deventer, 2000), at 246–264. See further Prechal, *Directives in European Community Law. A Study on EC Directives and their Enforcement by National Courts* (Oxford University Press, Oxford, 1995) (which explains all aspects of directives).

[521] The EC Treaty requires directives to be used, *inter alia,* in Art. 44(1); Art. 46(2); Art. 47(1) and (2); Art. 52(1); Art. 94; Art. 96, second para.; Art. 137(2), first subpara., indent (b). Alongside other Treaty articles which do not prescribe the use of any particular legislative instrument (para. 17–140, *infra*), the following are among the articles of the EC Treaty which provide for the possible use of directives: Art. 37(2), third subpara.; Art. 40; Art. 83(1); Art. 86(3); Art. 119(2).

[522] See, *e.g.* Directive 79/174 concerning the flood protection programme in the Hérault Valley, [1979] O.J. L38/18 (based on Art. 43 [now Art. 37] of the EC Treaty and addressed only to France).

[523] ECJ, Case 102/79 *Commission v Belgium* [1980] E.C.R. 1473, para. 12.

[524] This is settled case law of the Court of Justice; see, *e.g.* ECJ, Case C–159/99 *Commission v Italy* [2001] E.C.R. I–4007, para. 32.

provisions must be assessed in the light of the interpretation given to them by national courts.[525] In order to secure the full application of directives in law and not only in fact, Member States must make sure that there is a clear legal framework for the area in question, even where there is no practice in the Member State which is incompatible with the directive in question[526] or an activity referred to in a directive does not (yet) exist in a Member State.[527] In this respect, a Member State does not fulfil its obligations by maintaining an administrative practice which, albeit consonant with the directive, may be changed as and when the authorities please and is not sufficiently publicised.[528] Nor is it sufficient to make a general reference to the applicable Community provisions and to the primacy of Community law.[529] In order to achieve the clarity and precision needed to meet the requirement of legal certainty, it is not sufficient that the settled case law of a Member State interprets the provisions of national law in a manner deemed to satisfy the requirements of a directive.[530] The principle of legal certainty requires appropriate publicity for the national implementing measures in such a way as to enable the persons concerned by such measures to ascertain the scope of their rights and obligations in the particular area governed by Community law.[531]

Nevertheless, transposition of a directive into national law does not necessarily require that "its provisions be incorporated formally and verbatim in express, specific legislation"; sometimes "a general legal context may, depending on the content of the directive, be adequate for the purpose provided that it does indeed guarantee the full application of the directive in a sufficiently clear and precise manner so that, where the directive is intended to create rights for individuals, the persons concerned can ascertain the full extent of their rights and, where appropriate, rely on them before the national courts".[532] Accordingly, the existence of general

---

[525] ECJ, Case C–382/92 *Commission v UK* [1994] E.C.R. I–2435, para. 36: ECJ, Case C–300/95 *Commission v UK* [1997] E.C.R. I–2649, para. 37. The legal framework will not be considered clear enough where the case law is not sufficiently settled, see, *e.g.* ECJ, Case C–372/99 *Commission v Italy* [2002] E.C.R. I–819, paras 20–28.

[526] ECJ, Case C–339/87 *Commission v Netherlands* [1990] E.C.R. I–851, para. 25 (which refers to a "specific legal framework").

[527] ECJ, Case C–372/00 *Commission v Ireland* [2001] E.C.R. I–10303, para. 11; ECJ, Case C–441/00 *Commission v UK* [2002] E.C.R. I–4699, para. 15. It is only where transposition of a directive is pointless for reasons of geography that it is not mandatory: *Commission v Ireland*, para. 13, *Commission v UK*, para. 17.

[528] ECJ, Case 102/79 *Commission v Belgium* [1980] E.C.R. 1473, para. 11. See Curtin, "Directives: The Effectiveness of Judicial Protection of Individual Rights" (1990) C.M.L.R. 709–739, especially, at 716–718.

[529] ECJ, Case C–96/95 *Commission v Germany* [1997] E.C.R. I–1653, paras 32–41.

[530] ECJ, Case C–144/99 *Commission v Netherlands* [2001] E.C.R. I–3541, paras 20–21.

[531] ECJ, Case C–415/01 *Commission v Belgium*, [2003] E.C.R. I–2081 paras 26–26 (duty to publish maps demarcating special protection areas in order to implement the directive on protection of birds).

[532] ECJ, Case 363/85 *Commission v Italy* [1987] E.C.R. 1733, para. 7; ECJ, Case C–131/88 *Commission v Germany* [1991] E.C.R. I–825, para. 6; ECJ, Case C–361/88 *Commission v Germany* [1991] E.C.R. I–2567, para. 15. Recent examples are afforded by ECJ, Case C–478/99 *Commission v Sweden* [2002] E.C.R. I–4147, paras 10–24, and ECJ, Case C–233/00 *Commission v France*, [2003] E.C.R. I–6625, paras 75–87.

principles of constitutional or administrative law may make transposition by means of statutory or administrative measures unnecessary.[533]

17–123 Time-limit for implementation. Generally, a directive will lay down a time-limit within which the Member States must put the necessary measures into effect.[534] As a result, a directive imposes an "obligation to achieve a result" (*obligation de résultat*), which must be fulfilled before the end of the period laid down by the directive.[535] A Member State cannot rely upon domestic difficulties or provisions of its national legal system, even of its Constitution, for the purpose of justifying a failure to comply with obligations and time-limits resulting from directives.[536] This is because the governments of the Member States participate in the preparatory work for directives and must therefore be in a position to prepare within the period prescribed the legislative provisions necessary for their implementation.[537] The fact that a directive is belatedly transposed into national law may not cause the date to be postponed by which the obligations imposed by the directive have to be fulfilled.[538] That provisions of a given directive qualify for direct effect does not release the Member State to which it is addressed from the obligation to adopt implementing measures satisfying the purpose of the directive in good time.[539] A Member State does not fulfil its obligation to implement a directive by merely relying on the duty of national courts to disapply conflicting national provisions.[540]

Before the period prescribed for implementing a directive has expired, there is no obligation for Member States to adopt transposition measures. However, as a result of Art. 10 of the EC Treaty, they must refrain from taking any measures liable seriously to compromise the result prescribed by the directive. It is for the national court to assess whether that is the case by

---

[533] ECJ, Case 29/84 *Commission v Germany* [1985] E.C.R. 1661, para. 23; for an application, see ECJ, Case 248/83 *Commission v Germany* [1985] E.C.R. 1459, paras 18–19 and 30. See Siems, "Effektivität und Legitimität einer Richtlinienumsetzung durch Generalklauseln" (2002) Z.Eu.P. 747–753.

[534] According to point 33 of the Interinstitutional Agreement between the European Parliament, the Council and the Commission of December 16, 2003 on better lawmaking ([2003] O.J. C321/1), the institutions will ensure that all directives include a binding time-limit for transposition that is as short as possible and generally does not exceed two years.

[535] ECJ, Case 8/81 *Becker v Finanzamt Münster-Innenstadt* [1982] E.C.R. 53, para. 18.

[536] ECJ, Case 100/77 *Commission v Italy* [1978] E.C.R. 879, para. 21.

[537] ECJ, Case 301/81 *Commission v Belgium* [1983] E.C.R. 467, para. 11; ECJ, Case C–319/99 *Commission v France* [2000] E.C.R. I–10439, para. 10. If the prescribed period proves too short, all that a Member State can do is take the appropriate initiatives at Community level with the responsible institutions in order to obtain the necessary extension of the period: ECJ, Case 52/75 *Commission v Italy* [1976] E.C.R. 277, para. 12/13.

[538] ECJ, Case C–396/92 *Bund Naturschutz in Bayern v Freistaat Bayern* [1994] E.C.R. I–3717, paras 18–19; see also ECJ, Case C–208/90 *Emmott* [1991] E.C.R. I–4269, paras 23–24 (n.31, *supra*).

[539] ECJ, Case 102/79 *Commission v Belgium* [1980] E.C.R. 1473, para. 12.

[540] ECJ, Case C–197/96 *Commission v France* [1997] E.C.R. I–1489, paras 13–16; ECJ, Case C–207/96 *Commission v Italy* [1997] E.C.R. I–6869, paras 26–27.

considering, in particular, the effects in practice of applying the incompatible provisions and of their duration in time.[541] If the provisions in issue are intended to constitute full and definitive transposition of the directive, their incompatibility might give rise to the presumption that the result prescribed by the directive will not be achieved within the period prescribed if it is impossible to amend them in time.[542] Incompatibility of national measures or non-transposition of certain provisions will not necessarily compromise the result required where a Member State adopts transitional implementing provisions or implements the directive in stages.[543] In any event, measures adopted before the period for transposition has expired in order to implement a directive must be interpreted as far as possible in conformity with that directive.[544]

(2) *The direct effect of provisions of an unimplemented or incorrectly implemented directive*

Conditions for direct effect. Since directives leave the choice of "form and **17–124** methods" to the Member States, they leave in principle the competent national authorities some discretion. All the same, they often contain clear, unconditional provisions necessitating no further implementation entailing any policy choices. If a Member State fails to transpose a directive into national law or fails to transpose it properly, the Court of Justice will hold that an individual may nevertheless derive rights from those of its

---

[541] ECJ, Case C–129/96 *Inter-Environnement Wallonie* [1997] E.C.R. I–7411, paras 45–47; ECJ, Case C–14/02 *ATRAL* [2003] E.C.R. I–4431, paras 58–60. See Prechal (n.520, *supra*), at 24–26; Gilliaux, *Les directives européennes et le droit belge*, (Brussels, Bruylant, 1997) at 142–145. The obligation not to take any measures which may seriously compromise the aims of a directive even before its transposition applies to national public authorities, but not to individuals: CFI, Joined Cases T–172/98, T–175/98 to T–176/98 *Salamander v European Parliament and Council* [2000] E.C.R. II–2487, para. 57.

[542] ECJ, Case C–129/96 *Inter-Environnement Wallonie* [1997] E.C.R. I–7411, para. 48. See in this connection Dal Farra, "L'invocabilité des directives communautaires devant le juge national de légalité" (1992) R.T.D.E. 631, at 643–645. It is not clear whether a national court is obliged to disapply such a conflicting national provision before the time limit for transposition has expired. According to the Court of Justice, no such obligation exists in procedures brought by individuals in reliance on the direct effect of a directive: ECJ (judgment of February 5, 2004), Case C–157/02 *Rieser Internationale Transporte and Asfinag*, not yet reported, para. 67.

[543] ECJ, Case C–129/96 *Inter-Environnement Wallonie* [1997] E.C.R. I–7411, para. 49.

[544] ECJ, Case 80/86 *Kolpinghuis Nijmegen* [1987] E.C.R. 3969, paras 15–16 read in conjunction with para. 12. See also Prechal (n.520, *supra*), at 24 and 207; Langenfeld, "Zur Direktwirkung von EG-Richtlinien" (1992) D.ö.V. 955, at 964; Ress, "Die richtlinienkonforme 'Interpretation' innerstaatlichen Rechts" (1994) D.ö.V. 489, at 492–493. After the expiry of the time-limit for implementation, the national court is under a duty also to interpret in the light of the directive rules of law not adopted specifically in order to transpose the directive (para. 17–131, *infra*), at least with respect to facts which occurred after the expiry of that time limit: ECJ, Case C–456/98 *Centrosteel* [1998] E.C.R. I–6007, para. 17. Pursuant to a principle of national law according to which more favourable provisions of criminal law have retroactive effect, national courts may set aside domestic provisions which conflict with a directive (whether transposed or not) in respect of offences which occurred before the period prescribed for transposition had expired: ECJ, Case C–230/97 *Awoyemi* [1998] E.C.R. I–6781, paras 32–45.

provisions which satisfy the substantive requirements which must be met in order for Treaty provisions to have direct effect, that is the provisions of the directive which are "unconditional and sufficiently precise" (see para. 17–048).[545] In this way, a credit negotiator was entitled to rely against the German tax authorities on a tax exemption provided for in the Sixth VAT Directive even though the directive had not yet been implemented in Germany.[546] In order for a provision of a directive to have direct effect, the Court of Justice has held that, in addition to the aforementioned substantive requirements, the following two conditions must be satisfied:

(i) the period prescribed for implementing the directive must have expired; and

(ii) the individual must rely upon the relevant provisions against a State body.

17–125 **(a) Expiry of time-limit.** A directive cannot have any direct effect until the period prescribed for implementing it in the national legal system has expired. Direct effect arises only at the end of the prescribed period, provided that the Member State is then in breach of its obligation to transpose the directive.[547] Sometimes a directive prescribes not only a date by which Member States must amend their national provisions, but also a date as from which the amended provisions must be applied. In such case, the directive cannot produce any effects enforceable by the national courts before the second date has gone by.[548] As soon as a Member State has implemented the directive, its effects reach individuals through the intermediary of the implementing measures, and there is no need to rely directly on its provisions,[549] unless the implementing measures are incorrect

---

[545] ECJ, Case 8/81 *Becker v Finanzamt Münster-Innenstadt* [1982] E.C.R. 53, para. 25; ECJ, Case 152/84 *Marshall v Southampton and South-West Hampshire Area Health Authority* ("*Marshall I*") [1986] E.C.R. 723, para. 46; ECJ, Case 103/88 *Fratelli Costanzo v Comune di Milano* [1989] E.C.R. 1839, para. 29. The basis of the case law has shifted from effectiveness (*effet utile*) to the principle *nemo auditur* (para. 17–126, *infra*), see Emmert and Pereira de Azevedo, "L'effet horizontal des directives. La jurisprudence de la CJCE: un bateau ivre?" (1993) R.T.D.E. 503, at 506–517. For the first cases in which the Court found that directives, in common with regulations, could have direct effects for individuals: ECJ, Case 9/70 *Grad* [1970] E.C.R. 825, para. 5, and ECJ, Case 33/70 *SACE* [1970] E.C.R. 1213, para. 15; for the subsequent finding that a directive is capable of having direct effects on relations between individuals and Member States because "the effectiveness [*effet utile*] of such a measure would be weakened if nationals of that State could not invoke it in the courts and if the national courts could not take it into consideration as part of Community law": ECJ, Case 41/74 *Van Duyn* [1974] E.C.R. 1337, para. 12.

[546] ECJ, Case 8/81 *Becker v Finanzamt Münster-Innenstadt* [1982] E.C.R. 53, para. 49. For more recent examples, see ECJ, Joined Cases C–388/00 and C–429/00 *Radiosistemi* [2002] E.C.R. I–4301, paras 49–66; ECJ, Joined Cases C–465/00, C–138/01 and C–139/01 *Rechnungshof v Österreichischer Rundfunk* [2003] E.C.R. I–4948, paras 99–100; ECJ (judgment of February 5, 2004), Case C–157/02 *Rieser Internationale Transporte and Asfinag*, not yet reported, para. 67.

[547] ECJ, Case 148/78 *Ratti* [1979] E.C.R. 1629, paras 43–44; see also ECJ, Joined Cases C–140/91, C–141/91, C–278/91 and C–279/91 *Suffriti* [1992] E.C.R. I–6337, paras 11–13.

[548] ECJ, Case C–316/93 *Vaneetveld* [1994] E.C.R. I–763, paras 18–19.

[549] ECJ, Case 270/81 *Felicitas* [1982] E.C.R. 2771, paras 24–26.

or inadequate.[550] Individuals are also entitled to rely directly on the provisions of a directive where national measures correctly implementing the directive are not being applied in such a way as to achieve the result sought by it.[551]

(b) Direct effect only against a Member State. An individual may invoke **17–126** directly effective provisions of a directive only against a Member State which either failed to implement the directive within the prescribed period or implemented it incorrectly. The Court of Justice has held that "a Member State which has not adopted the implementing measures required by the directive in the prescribed periods may not rely, as against individuals, on its own failure to perform the obligations which the directive entails".[552] The Court's aim is to "prevent the State from taking advantage of its own failure to comply with Community law"[553] and therefore reflects the civil law principle *nemo auditur turpitudinem suam allegans* and the common law doctrine of estoppel.[554]

Broad interpretation of term "Member State". In its judgment in *Marshall* **17–127** *I*, the Court held that "where a person involved in legal proceedings is able to rely on a directive as against the State he may do so regardless of the capacity in which the latter is acting, whether employer or public authority. In either case it is necessary to prevent the State from taking advantage of its own failure to comply with Community law".[555] By putting a broad construction on the term "State", the Court of Justice has considerably extended the situations in which an individual may rely on a directly effective provision of a directive. An individual may so rely against "organisations or bodies which were subject to the authority or control of the State or had special powers beyond those which result from the normal rules applicable to relations between individuals",[556] in particular against central and (geographically or functionally) decentralised authorities[557] and

---

[550] ECJ, Joined Cases C–253/96 to C–258/96 *Kampelmann* [1997] E.C.R. I–6907, paras 42–45.

[551] ECJ, Case C–62/00 *Marks & Spencer* [2002] E.C.R. I–6325, para. 27.

[552] ECJ, Case 148/78 *Ratti* [1979] E.C.R. 1629, para. 22.

[553] ECJ, Case 152/84 *Marshall v Southampton and South-West Hampshire Area Health Authority* ("*Marshall I*") [1986] E.C.R. 723, para. 49; ECJ, Case C–91/92 *Faccini Dori* [1994] E.C.R. I 3325, para. 22.

[554] See Van Gerven, "The Horizontal Effect of Directive Provisions Revisited: The Reality of Catchwords", *Institutional Dynamics of European Integration. Essays in Honour of Henry G. Schermers* (n.375, *supra*), 335, at 343–345.

[555] ECJ, Case 152/84 *Marshall I* [1986] E.C.R. 723, para. 49.

[556] ECJ, Case C–188/89 *Foster* [1990] E.C.R. I–3313, para. 18.

[557] *e.g.* tax authorities (ECJ, Case 8/81 *Becker* [1982] E.C.R. 53, para. 49, and ECJ, Case C–221/88 *Busseni* [1990] E.C.R. I–495, para. 30), local and regional authorities (ECJ, Case 103/88 *Fratelli Costanzo v Comune di Milano* [1989] E.C.R. 1839, paras 31–32; ECJ, Joined Cases C–253/96 to C–258/96 *Kampelmann* [1997] E.C.R. I–6907, paras 36–47), a constitutionally independent public authority charged with the maintenance of public order and safety (ECJ, Case 222/84 *Johnston* [1986] E.C.R. 1651, paras 56–57) and a public body responsible for the provision of health care (ECJ, Case 152/84 *Marshall I* [1986] E.C.R. 723, para. 49–50).

bodies, whatever their legal form, which have been made responsible, pursuant to a measure adopted by the State, for providing a public service under the control of the State.[558] It appears therefore that an individual may rely on rights derived from a directive regardless of the capacity of the body concerned or whether that body was entrusted with the implementation of the directive in national law.

17–128 No horizontal direct effect. Also in *Marshall I*, the Court of Justice made it clear that "a directive may not of itself impose obligations on an individual and that a provision of a directive may not be relied upon against such a person".[559] A directive may therefore have vertical but not horizontal direct effect. The Court based its view on the binding nature conferred by Art. 249 of the EC Treaty on a directive only in relation to "each Member State to which it is addressed".[560] Furthermore, the Court of Justice explained in *Faccini Dori* that:

> "[t]he effect of extending that case law [on the direct effect of directives] to the sphere of relations between individuals would be to recognise a power in the Community to enact obligations for individuals with immediate effect, whereas it has competence to do so only where it is empowered to adopt regulations".[561]

In *Faccini Dori*, the Court was faced with the fact that Italy had failed to transpose Directive 85/577 to protect the consumer in respect of contracts negotiated away from business premises. The Court held that a consumer could not rely upon her right to cancel a contract within seven days as against the trader with whom she had concluded it in Italy, even though the directive conferred that right unconditionally and sufficiently precisely.[562] It follows that a directly effective provision of a directive cannot be enforced by an individual as against another individual and, *a fortiori*, not by a public authority against an individual.[563] In addition, an individual may not rely on a directly effective provision of a directive against a public authority where

---

[558] ECJ, Case C–188/89 *Foster* [1990] E.C.R. I–3313, para. 20; ECJ (judgment of February 5, 2004), Case C–157/02 *Rieser Internationale Transporte and Asfinag*, not yet reported, para. 22–29. For a discussion of the criterion "public body", see the note to the judgment in *Foster* by Szyszczak (1990) C.M.L.R. 868–871; Prechal, "Remedies after *Marshall*" (1990) C.M.L.R. 451, at 457–462; Curtin, "The Province of Government: Delimiting the Direct Effect of Directives in the Common Law Context" (1990) E.L.R. 195–223.

[559] ECJ, Case 152/84 *Marshall I* [1986] E.C.R. 723, para. 48.

[560] *ibid.*

[561] ECJ, Case C–91/92 *Faccini Dori* [1994] E.C.R. I–3325, para. 24.

[562] *ibid.*, paras 18 and 30; see also ECJ, Case C–192/94 *El Corte Inglés* [1996] E.C.R. I–1281, paras 15–21.

[563] ECJ, Joined Cases 372–374/85 *Traen* [1987] E.C.R. 2141, para. 24; ECJ, Case 14/86 *Pretore de Salò v Persons Unknown* [1987] E.C.R. 2545, paras 19–20; ECJ, Case 80/86 *Kolpinghuis Nijmegen* [1987] E.C.R. 3969, paras 9–10; ECJ, Case C–168/95 *Arcaro* [1996] E.C.R. I–4705, paras 33–38; ECJ (order of September 19, 2001), Case C–18/00 *Perino*, not reported, paras 22–26.

this would directly lead to the directive imposing obligations on another individual.[564] Accordingly, the Court held in its judgment in *Wells* that an individual may not rely on a directive against a Member State where it is a matter of a State obligation directly linked to the performance of an obligation falling, pursuant to that directive, on a third party.[565] Mere adverse repercussions on the rights of third parties, even if the repercussions are certain, do not justify preventing an individual from invoking the provisions of a directive against the Member State concerned.[566]

Directive versus regulation. The fact that the rights enshrined in a directive **17–129** can be enforced only if the directive has been transposed or, in the absence of (correct) transposition, only against a public body hampers the uniform application through the Community of Community legislation adopted in the form of a directive. Whereas an individual can rely unconditionally as against another individual on rights conferred by a regulation, this is possible in the case of a directive only if the directive has been correctly implemented in the Member State in question. This means that individuals in Member States which have not transposed the directive correctly do not enjoy the same rights as individuals in the rest of the Community. Moreover, failure to transpose a directive may mean that it is applied to similar fact situations differently within a Member State, for instance where certain individuals may assert their rights by making a claim against a public authority (*e.g.* public-sector employees) whilst others may not enforce the same rights in a private legal relationship (*e.g.* private-sector employees).[567] Some commentators consider that it is necessary in the

---

[564] ECJ, Case C–97/96 *Daihatsu Deutschland* [1997] E.C.R. I–6843, paras 24–25. See also (with regard to an ECSC recommendation) ECJ, Case C–221/88 *Busseni* [1990] E.C.R. I–495, paras 23–26, in which the ECSC was equated with an individual for the purposes of invoking a provision according preferential treatment in proving certain debts owed to it by an insolvent undertaking. The Court noted that ECSC's claim on preferential treatment would affect the rights of all other creditors of the undertaking whose debts did not enjoy the same preferential status and therefore ruled that the ECSC's preferential status was not to prejudice the rights of creditors other than the State.

[565] ECJ (judgment of January 7, 2004), Case C–201/02 *Wells*, not yet reported, paras 56 and 58.

[566] *ibid.*, para. 57. In the case at hand, an individual challenged the decision by which national authorities had given permission for mining operations at a quarry without the environmental impact assessment laid down by a Community directive having first been carried out. The Court considered that the adjoining landowner could invoke the directive even if the fact that mining operations had to be halted to await the results of that assessment was a consequence of the belated performance of the State's obligations. It held that the obligation on the Member State to ensure that the competent authorities carried out the environmental impact assessment was not directly linked to the performance of any obligation which would fall on the quarry owners. *ibid.*, para. 58. See also para. 17–132, *infra.*

[567] The Court of Justice accepted that consequence in ECJ, Case 152/84 *Marshall I* [1986] E.C.R. 723, para. 51. The prohibition of discrimination laid down *in the Treaty* may well apply in relations between individuals because that prohibition has direct effect and, as a Treaty provision, is applicable without further qualification in the national legal systems: ECJ, Case 36/74 *Walrave* [1974] E.C.R. 1405, para. 18 *et seq.*

interest of uniform, equal application of Community law that an individual should be able to rely as against other individuals on clear and unconditional provisions of a directive which has not been (properly) implemented.[568] However, it appears from *Faccini Dori* that a directive does not acquire the same legal force as a regulation after the period prescribed for implementing it has run out.[569]

(3) *Other effects of an unimplemented or incorrectly implemented directive*

17–130 Principles ensuring effectiveness. Where a provision of a directive has not been (correctly) implemented, the absence of direct effect does not exclude this provision from having certain "effects" on the legal position of the authorities or individuals concerned. To that end, the case law has formulated a number of Community law principles.[570] Thus, the national courts must:

(a) construe national law as far as possible in a way which is consistent with the directive;

(b) in principle, give the directive in question precedence over conflicting rules of national law;

(c) Where, in spite of this, the result required to be obtained by the directive cannot be attained, the Member State will be required to make good the damage caused to individuals as a result of its failure to transpose the directive, provided that certain conditions are fulfilled.

---

[568] See the Opinion of Advocate General W. Van Gerven in ECJ, Case C–271/91 *Marshall* [1993] E.C.R. I–4367, point 12; the Opinion of Advocate General F.G. Jacobs in ECJ, Case C–316/93 *Vaneetveld* [1994] E.C.R. I–763, point 18 *et seq.*, and the Opinion of Advocate General C.O. Lenz in ECJ, Case C–91/92 *Faccini Dori* [1994] E.C.R. I–3325, points 43 *et seq.*; see also Emmert and Pereira de Azevedo (n.545, *supra*), and Barents, "Some Remarks on the 'Horizontal' Effects of Directives", in O'Keeffe and Schermers (eds), *Essays in European Law and Integration* (Kluwer, Deventer, 1982), at 97–104; Wyatt, "The Direct Effect of Community Social Law—Not Forgetting Directives" (1983) E.L.R. 241–248; for the contrary view, see Timmermans, "Directives: Their Effect within the National Legal Systems" (1979) C.M.L.R. 533, at 541–544; for arguments for and against, see Easson, "Can Directives impose Obligations on Individuals" (1979) E.L.R. 67–79.

[569] For a commentary on this judgment, see Tridimas, "Horizontal Effect of Directives: A Missed Opportunity" (1994) E.L.R. 621–636, and the note by Robinson (1995) C.M.L.R. 629–639. Even though this case law has been confirmed, the academic debate continues, see Betlem, "Medium Hard Law—Still No Horizontal Direct Effect of European Community Directives After *Faccini Dori*" (1995) Col.J.E.L. 469–496; Emmert and Pereira de Azevedo, "Les jeux sont faits: rien ne va plus ou une occasion perdue par la CJCE" (1995) R.T.D.E. 11–21.

[570] See Steiner (n.29, *supra*), at 3–22; Plaza Martin, "Furthering the Effectiveness of EC Directives and the Judicial Protection of Individual Rights Thereunder" (1994) I.C.L.Q. 26–54; Schockweiler, "Les effets des directives dans les ordres juridiques nationaux" (1995) 2 R.M.U.E. 9–26; Lenz, Sif Tynes and Young, "Horizontal What? Back to Basics" (2000) E.L.R. 509–522.

Where necessary, the national court should first refer to the Court of Justice for a preliminary ruling on the interpretation of the directive (EC Treaty, Art. 234).

(a) Interpretation in conformity with directive. In the first place, national **17–131** courts must make use of the methods of interpretation available to them under national law so as to interpret national law as far as possible in conformity with the directive. The Court of Justice has held that:

> "the Member States' obligation arising from a directive to achieve the result envisaged by the directive and their duty under Art. 10 of the Treaty to take all appropriate measures, whether general or particular, to ensure fulfilment of that obligation, is binding on all the authorities of Member States including, for matters within their jurisdiction, the courts. It follows that, in applying the national law . . ., national courts are required to interpret their national law in the light of the wording and the purpose of the directive in order to achieve the result referred to in the third paragraph of Art. 189 [now Article 249]".[571]

The Court has made it clear that this applies not only in applying "the provisions of a national law specifically introduced in order to implement" the directive[572] but "whether the provisions in question were adopted before or after the directive".[573] The national court must interpret national law "as far as possible" in conformity with the directive,[574] where necessary adjusting the existing case law. The relevant provision of national law must, however, be amenable to such interpretation.[575] The national court is therefore not obliged to make an interpretation *contra legem*.[576] The obligation to interpret national law in conformity with a directive is also "limited by the general principles of law which form part of Community law and in particular the principles of legal certainty and non-retroactivity".[577]

---

[571] ECJ, Case 14/83 *Von Colson and Kamann* [1984] E.C.R. 1891, para. 26; ECJ, Case 79/83 *Harz* [1984] E.C.R. 1921, para. 26.

[572] *ibid.*

[573] ECJ, Case C–106/89 *Marleasing* [1990] E.C.R. I–4135, para. 8. It is disputed whether national law must be interpreted consistently with a directive as regards facts which occurred before the deadline for implementation expired: see Betlem, "The Doctrine of Consistent Interpretation—Managing Legal Uncertainty" (2002) Oxford Journal of Legal Studies 397, at 403–406. For the obligation during the transposition period, see para. 17–124, *supra*.

[574] *ibid.*

[575] ECJ, Case C–334/92 *Wagner Miret* [1993] E.C.R. I–6911, para. 22.

[576] The national court may however be required in certain circumstances to disapply rules of national law which conflict with the provisions of the directive in question, para. 17–132, *infra*.

[577] ECJ, Case 80/86 *Kolpinghuis Nijmegen* [1987] E.C.R. 3969, para. 13; for an application, see ECJ, Case 14/86 *Pretore de Salò v Persons Unknown* [1987] E.C.R. 2545, para. 20; ECJ, Joined Cases C–74/95 and C–129/95 *Criminal proceedings against X* [1996] E.C.R. I–6609, paras 25 and 31. For the limits which national law may place on the ability to interpret

The obligation to interpret national law in conformity with directives holds good irrespective as to whether their provisions have direct effect. As a result of such an interpretation of national law, the provisions of the directive in question may also be effective *vis-à-vis* individuals.[578] In such case, there is no question of a non-implemented directive imposing obligations on individuals since any obligation falling on individuals would be based on the provisions of national law. The duty to interpret domestic law in conformity with Community law comes up against a limitation, however, where such an interpretation would mean that obligations imposed by a non-implemented directive could be relied upon as against an individual.[579] This is the case, for example, where such an interpretation would have the effect of determining or aggravating, on the basis of a directive (in the absence of a law adopted for its implementation), the liability in criminal law of persons acting in contravention of the directive's provisions.[580] Also, where criminal liability arises under legislation adopted for the specific purpose of implementing a directive, the national court must take account of the principle that criminal proceedings may not be brought in respect of conduct which is not clearly defined as culpable by law.[581]

17–132 (b) Disapplication of conflicting national law. Secondly, it follows from the primacy of Community law that the provisions of a directive must enjoy precedence over conflicting rules of national law. This applies in the first place to measures taken specifically with a view to implementing a

---

national law in conformity with a directive, see De Búrca (n.114, *supra*), at 215–240 (case law in the UK); Jarass, "Richtlinienkonforme bzw. EG-rechtskonforme Auslegung nationalen Rechts" (1992) EuR. 211, at 220–223. For national case law holding interpretation consistent with a directive to be possible/impossible, see Verhoeven, "The application in Belgium of the duties of loyalty and co-operation" (2000) S.E.W. 328, at 332–334.

[578] Interpreting national law in the light of the directive may result in an individual being held to comply with certain obligations under national law or in that individual being precluded from effectuating claims against another individual. See ECJ, Case C–106/89 *Marleasing* [1990] E.C.R. I–4135, paras 6–9; ECJ, Case C–421/92 *Habermann-Beltermann* [1994] E.C.R. I–1657, paras 8–10; ECJ, Case C–472/93 *Spano* [1995] E.C.R. I–4321, paras 17–18; ECJ, Case C–129/94 *Ruiz Bernáldez* [1996] E.C.R. I–1829, paras 1–26; ECJ, Joined Cases C–240/98 to C–244/98 *Océano Grupo Editorial* [2000] E.C.R. I–4941, paras 20–32; ECJ, Case C–456/98 *Centrosteel* [2000] E.C.R. I–6007, paras 13–18. See also Ress (n.544), at 489–496.

[579] See ECJ, Case C–355/96 *Silhouette International Schmied* [1998] E.C.R. I–4799, paras 32–37. In proceedings between individuals, it is up to the national court to determine whether, in the absence of direct effect, the provisions of national law can be interpreted to achieve the result claimed by the applicant (see, *e.g.* ECJ, Case C–343/98 *Collino and Chiaperro* [2000] E.C.R. I–6659, paras 20–24), if necessary by disapplying conflicting rules of national law (see, *e.g.* ECJ, Case C–456/98 *Centrosteel* [2000] E.C.R. I–6007, para. 17).

[580] ECJ, Case 14/86 *Pretore di Salò v Persons Unknown* [1987] E.C.R. 2545, para. 20; ECJ, Case 80/86 *Kolpinghuis Nijmegen* [1987] E.C.R. 3969, paras 13–14; ECJ, Case C–168/95 *Arcaro* [1996] E.C.R. I–4705, para. 42.

[581] ECJ, Joined Cases C–74/95 and C–129/95 *Criminal proceedings against X* [1996] E.C.R. I–6609, para. 25 (which refers to Art. 7 of the ECHR).

directive. The national court must consider "whether the competent national authorities, in exercising the choice which is left to them as to the form and the methods of implementing the directive, have kept within the limits as to their discretion set out in the directive".[582] If national law confers on courts and tribunals discretion to apply mandatory rules of law of their own motion, they must examine *ex proprio motu* whether the national authorities remained within the limits of their discretion under the directive.[583] However, the review to be conducted of national law in the light of the directive extends further than measures taken to implement it; it covers all rules governing the application of the directive in the national legal system, including rules which applied before the directive was adopted.[584] In this connection, a national court may also be obliged to disapply national procedural or jurisdictional rules which would impede the protection of rights contained in the directive (see para. 17–011).

Public authorities other than the courts must also refrain from applying national rules which conflict with a directive. For instance, a local authority has been held to be under a duty to refrain from applying conflicting provisions of a national law.[585] Moreover, all the authorities of a Member State must take, according to their respective powers, all the general and particular measures necessary to ensure that the result sought by the directive is achieved.[586]

In principle, the obligation to refrain from applying conflicting rules of national law exists only after the deadline for implementing the directive has expired.[587] This obligation arises because of the primacy of Community law and therefore holds good irrespective as to whether the provisions of the directive relied upon have direct effect. The provisions need only be sufficiently clear as to serve as a yardstick.[588]

The Court of Justice has clarified the obligation to disapply conflicting rules of national law in a number of cases where provisions of an unimplemented or incorrectly implemented directive have been invoked against a public authority. In such "vertical" context, the disapplication of

---

[582] ECJ, Case 51/76 *Verbond van Nederlandse Ondernemingen* [1977] E.C.R. 113, paras 22– 24; ECJ, Case 38/77 *Enka* [1977] E.C.R. 2203, paras 10 and 17–18. This is also true of individual decisions: ECJ, Case 36/75 *Rutili* [1975] E.C.R. 1219, paras 17–20.

[583] ECJ, Case C–72/95 *Kraaijeveld* [1996] E.C.R. I–5403, paras 57–58.

[584] ECJ, Case 21/78 *Delkvist* [1978] E.C.R. 2327, paras 13–16. For the inapplicability of rules adopted contrary to a duty of notification laid down by a directive, see n.22, *supra*.

[585] ECJ, Case 103/88 *Fratelli Costanzo* [1989] E.C.R. 1839, para. 33.

[586] ECJ, Case C–72/95 *Kraaijeveld* [1996] E.C.R. I–5403, para. 61; ECJ, Case C–435/97 *World Wildlife Fund* [1999] E.C.R. I–5613, para. 70.

[587] ECJ (judgment of February 5, 2004), Case C–157/02 *Rieser Internationale Transporte and Asfinag*, not yet reported, paras 67–68. For the situation during the period for implementation, see para. 17–123, *supra*.

[588] See ECJ, Case C–72/95 *Kraaijeveld* [1996] E.C.R. I–5403, paras 59–61; ECJ, Case C–435/97 *World Wildlife Fund* [1999] E.C.R. I–5613, paras 69–71; ECJ, Case C–287/98 *Linster* [2000] E.C.R. I–6917, paras 31–39. See also Manin, "L'invocabilité des directives: Quelques interrogations" (1990) R.T.D.E. 669–693; Langenfeld (n.544, *supra*), at 962–964; for the application of such a test in France, see para. 17–023, *supra*.

conflicting rules of national law may indirectly have repercussions on the position of third parties who infer rights from these rules or are exempted under these rules from certain obligations.[589] It is not yet clear, however, whether Community law would require a national judge to disapply conflicting rules of national law where an individual or a public authority invokes provisions of an unimplemented or incorrectly implemented directive against an individual.[590] In any event, the Court of Justice is not prepared to accept a situation in which the disapplication of national provisions would lead to the imposition on an individual, without any basis in national law, of an obligation laid down by a directive which has not been (correctly) implemented[591] or, more specifically, where it has the effect of determining or aggravating, on the basis of the directive and in the absence of a law enacted for its implementation, the liability in criminal law of persons who act in contravention of that directive's provisions.[592]

17–133 Effects in horizontal relations. It is clear from the foregoing that, to a certain extent, an individual may rely in relations with another individual on the provisions of a directive which has not been (properly) implemented, in particular where national law can be interpreted in the light of provisions of the directive. Yet it appears that a provision of a directive may not be relied upon if that would directly lead to the imposition on that individual of an

---

[589] This would be the case, *e.g.* where an individual challenges the legality of decisions (on grounds of incompatibility with a Community directive) by which national authorities approve private projects having an effect on the environment (*e.g.* the cases cited in the preceding n.; see also ECJ (judgment of January 7, 2004), Case C–201/02 *Wells*, not yet reported, cited in para. 17–127, *supra*) or grant a marketing authorisation to a competitor (*e.g.* ECJ, Case C–201/94 *Smith & Nephew and Primecrown* [1996] E.C.R. I–5819, paras 35–39). See also the inapplicability of rules adopted by national authorities contrary to a duty of notification: ECJ, Case C–194/94 *CIA Security International* [1996] E.C.R. I–2201, paras 32–55; ECJ, Case C–443/98 *Unilever Italia* [2000] E.C.R. I–7535, paras 45–51 (see also n.22). See Weatherill, "Breach of directives and breach of contract" (2001) E.L.R. 177–186.

[590] See the Opinion of April 27, 2004 of Advocate General Ruiz-Jarabo Colomer in Joined Cases C–397/01 to C–403/01 *Pfeiffer*, not yet reported (litigation between employees and private employer). It should be noted that the Court has often been asked to give a preliminary ruling on the interpretation of a Community directive with a view of having the referring court assess the legality of provisions of national law in the light of the directive, even in cases involving litigation between individuals, without the Court touching the issue whether or not Community law would require the referring court to disapply the conflicting provisions of national law. See, *e.g.* ECJ, Case C–85/94 *Piageme* [1995] E.C.R. I–2955, paras 1–31; ECJ, Case C–441/93 *Pafitis* [1996] E.C.R. I–1347, paras 1–70; ECJ, Case C–180/95 *Draehmpaehl* [1997] E.C.R. I–2195, paras 16–43; ECJ, Case C–215/97 *Bellone* [1998] E.C.R. I–2191, paras 9–18.

[591] See ECJ (order of October 24, 2002), Case 233/01 *Riunione Adriatica di Securtà* [2002] E.C.R. I–9411, paras 20–21 (interpretation cannot enable the national court to give judgment against an individual for the payment of a debt which the Court held not to be based on national law).

[592] ECJ, Case C–168/95 *Arcaro* [1996] E.C.R. I–4705, paras 39–43.

obligation laid down by an unimplemented or incorrectly implemented directive.[593]

(c) State liability for damages. An individual may obtain redress for loss or **17–134** damage sustained as the result of the non-transposition of a directive by bringing a damages claim against the Member State. The fate of the claim no longer depends on the extent to which national law recognises that the State may be liable for legislative action or inaction. Following the judgment in *Francovich* (see para. 17–012), Member States are bound under Community law to make good loss or damage suffered by individuals as a result of a failure to transpose a directive into national law provided that the following three conditions are satisfied: first, the result prescribed by the directive should entail the grant of rights to individuals; secondly, it should be possible to identify the content of those rights on the basis of the provisions of the directive; thirdly, there must be a causal link between the breach of the State's obligation and the loss and damage suffered by the injured parties.[594]

Liability for loss or damage caused by a breach of Community law constitutes a general principle of that law. Consequently, there is a right to damages also where a provision having direct effect is infringed and it is not confined to the situation in which directives have not been implemented (see para. 17–012). Sometimes, a directive leaves a degree of discretion to Member States, resulting in their having to make choices when legislating to transpose the directive. In such a case, a damages claim will not arise merely because the provision breached confers rights on individuals and there is a causal link between the breach and the damage, the Court of Justice further requires the breach to be "sufficiently serious" (see para. 17–013). This will be the case where the Member State manifestly and gravely disregarded the limits on the exercise of its discretion.[595] The incorrect transposition of provisions of a directive capable of bearing several interpretations on which neither the Court of Justice nor the Commission have given a ruling does not constitute a sufficiently serious breach.[596] Where a Member State fails to take any of the measures necessary to achieve the result prescribed by the directive within the period it lays down, this in itself will constitute a sufficiently serious breach of

---

[593] See also A[rnull], "Editorial: The Incidental Effect of Directives'" (1999) E.L.R. 1–2; Lackhoff and Nyssens, "Direct Effect of Directives in Triangular Situations" (1998) E.L.R. 397; Straetmans, *Consument en markt* (Kluwer, Deurne, 1998), 255–265; Stuyck (1996) C.M.L.R. 1261–1272.

[594] ECJ, Joined Cases C–6/90 and C–9/90 *Francovich* [1991] E.C.R. I–5357, paras 39–41; ECJ, Case C–91/92 *Faccini Dori* [1994] E.C.R. I–3325, para. 27.

[595] ECJ, Case C–392/93 *British Telecommunications* [1996] E.C.R. I–1631, paras 39–45

[596] *ibid.*, paras 42–46; see also ECJ, Joined Cases C–283/94, C–291/94 and C–292/94 *Denkavit* [1996] E.C.R. I–5063, paras 50–53; ECJ, Case C–319/96 *Brinkmann Tabakfabriken* [1998] E.C.R. I–5255, paras 30–31.

Community law.[597] There is no need for the existence of intentional fault or negligence on the part of the organ of the State for the breach to entail a right to damages, provided that the three aforementioned conditions are satisfied.[598] Nor is reparation dependent on a prior finding by the Court of Justice of an infringement of Community law attributable to the State.[599] Retroactive application in full of the measures implementing the directive constitutes proper reparation, unless the beneficiaries establish the existence of complementary loss resulting from failure to implement the directive in time, in which case such loss must also be made good.[600] Bringing a claim for damages may be made subject to a reasonable limitation period (such as one year commencing from the entry into force of the measure transposing the directive), provided that such procedural rule is not less favourable than those relating to similar domestic claims.[601]

The Court of Justice has indicated that it would be possible to bring a damages claim where an individual could not rely on the provisions of a non-implemented directive on the ground that such provisions required additional implementing measures and hence could not have direct effect,[602] that the national law could not be interpreted in conformity with the directive[603] or that the provisions—albeit satisfying the substantive requirements for direct effect—were invoked as against another individual.[604]

d. Decisions

17–135 Definition. A decision is binding in its entirety upon those to whom it is addressed (EC Treaty, Art. 249, fourth para.).

17–136 Individual scope. A decision will always be addressed to specific persons, therefore constituting, in contradistinction to a regulation, a measure of individual scope. This means that a decision is an appropriate normative

---

[597] ECJ, Joined Cases C–178/94, C–179/94, C–188/94, C–189/94 and C–190/94 *Dillenkofer* [1996] E.C.R. I–4845, para. 26; ECJ, Case C–150/99 *Stockholm Lindöpark* [2001] E.C.R. I–493, paras 36–41. Such a breach of Community law may exist on the basis of the wrong transposition of only one sufficiently clear provision of a directive: ECJ, Case C–140/97 *Rechberger and Greindl* [1999] E.C.R. I–3499, paras 51–53.

[598] For lack of a direct causal link between the infringement of Community law and the damage, see ECJ, Case C–319/96 *Brinkmann Tabakfabriken* [1998] E.C.R. I–5255, para. 29.

[599] *Dillenkofer*, cited in n.597, paras 27–28.

[600] ECJ, Joined Cases C–94–95/95 *Bonifaci and Berto* [1997] E.C.R. I–3969, paras 51–54; ECJ, Case C–373/95 *Maso* [1997] E.C.R. I–4051, paras 39–42.

[601] ECJ, Case C–261/95 *Palmisani* [1997] E.C.R. I–4025, paras 28–40.

[602] ECJ, Joined Cases C–6/90 and C–9/90 *Francovich* [1991] E.C.R. I–5357, paras 26–27.

[603] ECJ, Case C–334/92 *Wagner Miret* [1993] E.C.R. I–6911, para. 22; ECJ, Case C–111/97 *Evobus Austria* [1998] E.C.R. I–5411, paras 14–21.

[604] ECJ, Case C–91/92 *Faccini Dori* [1994] E.C.R. I–3325, para. 25; ECJ, Case C–192/94 *El Corte Inglés* [1996] E.C.R. I–1281, para. 22. *cf.* ECJ, Case C–97/96 *Daihatsu Deutschland* [1997] E.C.R. I–6843, paras 24–26 (where, with regard to a dispute between private legal persons, the Court of Justice did not consider it necessary to inquire into the direct effect of the directive and merely referred to the possibility of a damages claim) with ECJ, Joined Cases C–253/96 to C–258/96 *Kampelmann* [1997] E.C.R. I–6907, para. 46 (where, with regard to disputes between individuals and public undertakings, the Court inquired into direct effect and did not discuss the damages claim).

instrument for executive acts of the institutions. Accordingly, when supervising compliance with the competition rules, the Commission addresses decisions to the undertakings and Member States concerned.[605] A decision may be addressed to individuals and Member States alike. A decision addressed to all the Member States will often constitute a legislative act.[606] With regard to the persons to whom it is addressed, a decision is binding in its entirety. An innominate act addressed by an institution to a particular person may constitute a decision only if it is intended to produce legal effects.[607]

Binding force. Decisions addressed to the Member States are binding on **17–137** all institutions of the State concerned, including the judiciary. Accordingly, they are under a duty by virtue of the primacy of Community law to refrain from applying any national provisions which would be likely to hinder the implementation of a decision.[608] In certain circumstances the provisions of a decision may also have direct effect in the sense that an individual may rely on it in a dispute with a public authority.[609] The Court of Justice has held that "[p]articularly in cases where, for example, the Community authorities by means of a decision have imposed an obligation on a Member State or all the Member States to act in a certain way, the effectiveness (*'l'effet utile'*) of such a measure would be weakened if the nationals of that State could not invoke it in the courts and the national courts could not take it into consideration as part of Community law".[610] The Court added, in view of the individual scope of decisions, that "in each particular case, it must be ascertained whether the nature, background and wording of the provision in question are capable of producing direct effects in the legal relationship between the addressee of the act and third parties".[611] In the same way as provisions of a directive, provisions of a decision may have direct effect only if they are precise and unconditional and the period, if any, within which a Member State had to comply with it has expired.[612]

---

[605] See also the Treaty articles requiring the Commission to use a decision as a normative instrument: Art. 75(4); Art. 76(2), second subpara.; Art. 85(2) (sometimes "directives or decisions" are prescribed: Art. 86(3); for the Council, see Art. 119(2)). For the different powers of the Commission under Art. 86(3) of the EC Treaty depending on whether it adopts a directive or a decision, see ECJ, Joined Cases C–48/90 and C–66/90 *Netherlands v Commission* [1992] E.C.R. I–565, paras 26–27. Regulations laying down protective measures against dumped and subsidised imports are exceptions in that they provide that charges must always be imposed by regulation (para. 20–008, *infra*).

[606] See, *e.g.* Council Decision 98/415/EC of June 29, 1998 on the consultation of the European Central Bank by the national authorities on draft legislative provisions, [1998] O.J. L189/42 (adopted pursuant to Art. 105(4) of the EC Treaty and Art. 4 of the ESCB Statute). For decisions addressed to the Member States, see Mager, "Die staatengerichtete Entscheidung als supranationale Handlungsform" (2001) EuR. 661–681.

[607] See Lenaerts and Arts, *Procedural Law of the European Union*, Ch.7.

[608] ECJ, Case 249/85 *Albako* [1987] E.C.R. 2345, para. 17.

[609] *ibid.*, para. 10.

[610] ECJ, Case 9/70 *Grad* [1970] E.C.R. 825, para. 5.

[611] *ibid.*, para. 6. See also the parallel judgments ECJ, Case 20/70 *Lesage* [1970] E.C.R. 861, paras 5–6, and ECJ, Case 23/70 *Haselhorst* [1970] E.C.R. 881, paras 5–6.

[612] ECJ, Case C–156/91 *Hansa Fleisch Ernst Mundt* [1992] E.C.R. I–5567, paras 15–20.

e. Recommendations and opinions

17–138 **No binding force.** According to the fifth para. of Art. 249 of the EC Treaty, recommendations and opinions have no binding force. This was also true of ECSC opinions (ECSC Treaty, Art. 14, fourth para.), but not of ECSC recommendations (see para. 17–120). Some Treaty provisions restrict the institutions to making recommendations.[613] The Court of Justice has held that EC recommendations are "measures which, even as regards the persons to whom they are addressed, are not intended to produce binding effects", and "generally adopted by the institutions of the Community when they do not have the power under the Treaty to adopt binding measures or when they consider that it is not appropriate to adopt more mandatory rules".[614] They do not create rights upon which individuals may rely before a national court.[615]

17–139 **Some legal effect.** Nevertheless, a recommendation may not be regarded as having no legal effect at all. The Court of Justice has observed that "[t]he national courts are bound to take recommendations into consideration in order to decide disputes submitted to them, in particular when they cast light on the interpretation of national measures adopted in order to implement them or where they are designed to supplement binding Community provisions".[616] Where several interpretations of national or Community provisions are possible, it would appear that the duty of co-operation in good faith (EC Treaty, Art. 10) requires the national courts to adopt the interpretation which best corresponds to the aim of the recommendation.[617]

f. Other acts

17–140 **Other instruments.** The list of instruments in Art. 249 of the EC Treaty does not prevent the institutions from producing legal effects by means of other instruments.[618] Some Treaty provisions refer to a specific

---

[613] As regards the Council, see, *inter alia*, EC Treaty, Art. 99(2), third subpara., and (4), first subpara.; Art. 128(4); Art. 149(4), second indent; Art. 151(5), second indent; Art. 152(4), second subpara.; Art. 276(1); as a stage in a supervisory procedure: see EC Treaty, Art. 104(7); as regards the Commission: see para. 10–059, *supra* (participation in decision-making) and para. 14–014, *supra* (right of initiative).

[614] ECJ, Case C–322/88 *Grimaldi* [1989] E.C.R. 4407, paras 13 and 16.

[615] *ibid.*, para. 16.

[616] *ibid.*, para. 18.

[617] For other legal effects which may arise out of non-binding acts, see para. 17–143, *infra*.

[618] See ECJ, Case 22/70 *Commission v Council* [1971] E.C.R. 263, paras 41–42.

instrument[619] or, more generally, authorise the adoption of "provisions",[620] "measures,"[621] "rules" or "arrangements".[622] In addition, the institutions often have recourse to "decisions" (not in the strict sense, often referred to as *sui generis* decisions"), "resolutions", "declarations", "conclusions" and similar instruments, which are not always intended to have legal effects.[623] Thus the Commission is increasingly using "communications", "guidelines" and "codes of conduct" in which it sets out the way in which it intends to exercise its power of decision in particular sectors.[624] Such acts have legal effects if they create in individuals a legitimate expectation that the institution will adhere to this policy line.[625] This also applies in the relationship between institutions and the Member States.[626] In some cases, an institution is not empowered to adopt acts embodying obligations. Where it nevertheless adopts an act with legal effects, the Court of Justice

---

[619] *e.g.* international agreements; para. 20–031, *infra*. Before the Treaty of Amsterdam, the EC Treaty also referred to a "general programme" in Art. 54 [now Art. 44](1) and Art. 63 [now Art. 52](1). The "incentive measures" referred to in the EC Treaty (Art. 13(2); Art. 129; Art. 149(4), first indent; Art. 151(5), first indent; Art. 152(4)(c)) and "general orientations" (Art. 111(2)) or "guidelines" (Art. 99(2); Art. 128(2); Art. 155(1), first indent; see also Art. 300(1)) take the form in practice of decisions and action programmes (see paras 5–239 and 5–241, *supra*) or, in the case of guidelines, conclusions (see para. 5–224, *supra*).

[620] See, *inter alia*, EC Treaty, Art. 18(2); Art. 22, second para.; Art. 71(1)(d) and (2); Art. 75(3); Art. 93; Art. 99(5); Art. 190(4), second subpara. .

[621] See, *inter alia*, EC Treaty, Art. 13; Art. 14; Art. 42; Art. 57(2); Art. 60(1); Arts 61–66; Art. 71(1)(c); Art. 95(1); Art. 96, second para., *in fine*; Art. 100(1); Art. 135; Art. 137(2), third subpara.; Art. 141(3); Art. 152(4)(a) and (b); Art. 153(3); Art. 155(1), second indent; Art. 157(3), first subpara.; Art. 159, third para.; Art. 301.

[622] See, *inter alia*, EC Treaty, Art. 12, second para., and Art. 19(1) and (2); see also the reference to "rules" in Art. 71(1)(a).

[623] For the function of such informal acts, see Everling, "Zur rechtlichen Wirkung von Beschlüssen, Entschliessungen, Erklärungen und Vereinbarungen des Rates oder der Mitgliedstaaten der Europäischen Gemeinschaft", in Lüke, Ress and Will (eds), *Rechtsvergleichung, Europarecht und Staatenintegration. Gedächtnisschrift für L.-J. Constantinesco* (Heymann, Cologne, 1983), 133, at 144–147; Klabbers, "Informal Instruments before the European Court of Justice" (1994) C.M.L.R. 997, at 1003–1004. For their status in the national legal systems, see, *e.g.* Gautier, "Le Conseil d'Etat français et les actes 'hors nomenclature' de la Communauté européenne" (1995) R.T.D.E. 23–37.

[624] *e.g.* with regard to competition policy, see paras 5–198, 5–200 and 5–204, *supra*; see Cosma and Whish, "Soft Law in the Field of EU Competition Policy" (2003) E.Bus.L.Rev. 25–56.

[625] ECJ, Case C–313/90 *CIRFS v Commission* [1990] E.C.R. I–1125, paras 34 and 36; CFI, Case T–380/94 *AIUFFASS and AKT v Commission* [1996] E.C.R. II–2169, para. 57; CFI, Case T–105/95 *WWF UK v Commission* [1997] E.C.R. II–313, paras 53–55; CFI, Case T–149/95 *Ducros v Commission* [1997] E.C.R. II–2031, paras 61–62; CFI, Case T–23/99 *LR AF 1998 v Commission* [2002] E.C.R. II–1705, para. 274. See Tournepiche, "Les communications: instruments privilégiés de l'action administrative de la Commission européenne" (2002) R.M.C.UE. 55–62.

[626] Accordingly, the Commission is bound by the guidelines and notices that it issues in the area of supervision of State aid where they do not depart from the rules in the Treaty and are accepted by the Member States: ECJ, Case C–409/00 *Spain v Commission* [2003] E.C.R. I–1487, para. 95; ECJ (judgment of April 29, 2004), Case C–91/01 *Italy v Commission*, not yet reported, para. 45.

may declare it void.[627] The precise legal effects of an act must be determined in the light of its content. Accordingly, the Court held in the *AETR* judgment that the Council's "proceedings" of March 20, 1970 regarding the stance to be adopted by the national governments in negotiations on an international transport agreement "could not have been simply the expression or the recognition of a voluntary co-ordination, but were designed to lay down a course of action binding on both the institutions and the Member States".[628]

17–141 *"Sui generis" decisions.* When it uses a "decision" (termed in Dutch a *besluit* and in German a *Beschluss* and hence differing from the terms *beschikking* and *Entscheidung* used in Art. 249—in other words a *"sui generis* decision"), an institution generally intends to adopt a binding act. The Council often uses instruments so styled where it adopts a legislative Act on the basis of a Treaty provision, such as Art. 308 of the EC Treaty, which does not prescribe any particular instrument.[629] The Council has also used such instruments to amend certain provisions of the Treaties[630] and to adopt rules of an organic nature, such as the Comitology Decisions[631] and the Decision establishing the Court of First Instance.[632] Generally, too, the Community approves an international agreement by means of such a "decision".[633] Lastly, the institutions adopt various such decisions in connection with their internal organisation or in order to adopt the statutes of other bodies.[634]

---

[627] See ECJ, Case C–303/90 *France v Commission* [1991] E.C.R. I–5315, paras 15–35 (annulment of a Commission code of conduct); ECJ, Case C–325/91 *France v Commission* [1993] E.C.R. I–3283, paras 14–30 (annulment of a Commission communication on the ground that it did not state the legal basis from which it derived legal force); ECJ, Case C–57/95 *France v Commission* [1997] E.C.R. I–1627 (annulment of a communication by which the Commission purported to impose obligations not already contained in the EC Treaty).

[628] ECJ, Case 22/70 *Commission v Council* [1971] E.C.R. 263, para. 53.

[629] See, *e.g.* Council Decision 87/327/EEC of June 15, 1987 adopting the European Community Action Scheme for the Mobility of University Students (Erasmus), [1987] O.J. L166/20, which was based on Arts 128 and 235 of the EEC Treaty. It was replaced by Decision 89/663/EEC of December 14, 1989, based on Art. 128 of the EEC Treaty, [1989] O.J. L395/23. See also Council Decision 94/819/EC of December 6, 1994 establishing an action programme for the implementation of a European Community vocational training policy, [1994] O.J. L340/8, which was based on Art. 127 [now Art. 150] of the EC Treaty.

[630] para. 7-009, *supra*. Council decisions which have to be adopted by the Member States in accordance with their respective constitutional requirements constitute "primary Community law", para. 17–064, *supra*.

[631] Council Decision 87/373/EEC of July 13, 1987 laying down the conditions for the exercise of implementing powers conferred on the Commission, [1987] O.J. L197/33 and Council Decision 1999/468/EC of June 28, 1999 laying down the conditions for the exercise of implementing powers conferred on the Commission, [1999] O.J. L184/33 (para. 14–054, *supra*).

[632] Council Decision 88/591/ECSC, EEC, Euratom of October 24, 1988 establishing a Court of First Instance, [1988] O.J. L319/1 (para. 10–072, *supra*).

[633] See para. 21–007, *infra*.

[634] See, *e.g.* the Council's Rules of Procedure (para. 10–042, *supra*); see also the Ombudsman

Non-binding acts. As has been mentioned, the institutions may adopt **17–142** recommendations, opinions and other instruments if they wish to adopt a non-binding act. In many cases, such acts are published in the *Official Journal* (Part C). They form part of the "declarations or resolutions of, or other positions taken up by" the Council, in respect of which new Member States are placed "in the same situation as the [original] Member States" by virtue of the Act of Accession. New Member States undertake to "observe the principles and guidelines deriving from those declarations, resolutions or guidelines" and to take "such measures as may be necessary to ensure their implementation".[635] The Act of Accession itself "does not attach any additional legal effect" to those measures.[636]

Resolutions. A "resolution" generally contains a statement of intention **17–143** with regard to a policy programme which an institution wishes to have achieved.[637] In several cases, the Court of Justice has held that a given "Council resolution" had no binding force.[638] All the same, even non-binding acts can have some legal effects.[639] For one thing they may be useful for the purposes of interpreting Treaty provisions and binding acts of Community law,[640] although they cannot alter such provisions or acts.[641] Thus, the Court of Justice has had regard to Council resolutions in determining what matters are covered by a policy area assigned to the Community by the Treaty.[642] It is for this reason that, whenever they wish

---

Regulations adopted by the European Parliament (ns to para. 10–107, *supra*). See also the Council Decision of March 29, 1994 concerning the taking of [a] Decision by qualified majority by the Council ([1994] O.J. C105/1; the "Ioannina Compromise"), which, however, did not have any binding legal effects (para. 10–047, *supra*).

[635] 2003 Act of Accession, Art. 5(3); see the similarly worded Art. 3(3) of the 1972, 1979 and 1985 Acts of Accession and Art. 4(3) of the 1994 Act of Accession (for references, see para. 1–021, *supra*).

[636] ECJ, Case 44/84 *Hurd* [1986] E.C.R. 29, para. 30, at 79.

[637] See, *e.g.* the environment action programmes, the most recent of which was provided for in a resolution of February 1, 1993 of the Council of the European Communities and of the representatives of the governments of the Member States, meeting in the Council, [1993] O.J. C138/1. The Court of Justice has held that this action programme "does not lay down rules of a mandatory nature": ECJ, Case C–142/95 P *Associazione Agricoltori della Provincia di Rovigo* [1996] E.C.R. I–6669, paras 29–32. For the legal force of the "general programme" referred to in EC Treaty, former Arts 54(1) and 63(1), see Everling (n.623, *supra*), at 135.

[638] See ECJ, Joined Cases 90 91/63 *Commission v Luxembourg and Belgium* [1964] E.C.R. 625, at 631; ECJ, Case 9/73 *Schlüter* [1973] E.C.R. 1135, para. 40; ECJ, Case 59/75 *Manghera* [1976] E.C.R. 91, para. 21.

[639] See the survey produced by Borchardt and Wellens, "Soft law in het Gemeenschapsrecht" (1987) S.E.W. 663, at 700–709 (and the discussion of that survey in (1988) S.E.W. 243–248). Klabbers argues that there is a presumption that even 'informal' instruments are binding (n.623, *supra*), at 1019–1023.

[640] Everling, "Probleme atypischer Rechts- und Handlungsformen bei der Auslegung des europäischen Gemeinschaftsrechts", in Bieber and Ress (eds), *Die Dynamik des Europäischen Gemeinschaftsrechts/The dynamics of EC-Law* (Nomos, Baden-Baden, 1987), at 417–433.

[641] ECJ, Case 59/75 *Manghera* [1976] E.C.R. 91, para. 21.

[642] See ECJ, Case 293/83 *Gravier* [1985] E.C.R. 593, para. 22 (access to vocational training); ECJ, Joined Cases 281/85, 283–285/85 and 287/85 *Germany, France, Denmark and UK v Commission* [1987] E.C.R. 3203, para. 17 (migration policy).

to avoid a resolution having effects on the way in which the allocation of powers as between the Community and the Member States is interpreted, the members of the Council adopt the relevant act in the form of a "resolution of the Council and the representatives of the Governments of the Member States, meeting within the Council".[643] Only on one occasion has the Court of Justice held a Council resolution to have binding force, when it found that it was an application of the duty of co-operation imposed by Art. 10 of the EC Treaty. The resolution in fact determined the procedure whereby Member States wished to take the necessary conservation measures in respect of fishery resources in the North Sea.[644] In that case the resolution contributed to the legitimacy of the temporary measures which the Member States were authorised to take in the absence of a common fisheries policy.[645] More generally, a non-binding act by which an institution regards itself as being bound must be viewed as a rule of conduct from which the institution may diverge only if it gives reasons for doing so, on account of the principle of protection of legitimate expectations[646] and the principle of equal treatment.[647]

17–144 **Unilateral declarations.** The non-binding acts discussed above must be distinguished from declarations made in the minutes of meetings by institutions or Member States on the occasion of the adoption of Community acts. No reliance may be placed on a unilateral declaration of a Member State for the purposes of interpreting a Community act on the ground that "the objective scope of rules laid down by the common institutions cannot be modified by reservations or objections which Member States may have made at the time the rules were being formulated".[648] A declaration made by Member States or the institutions concerned cannot have any bearing on the objective scope of a Community act.[649] Such a

---

[643] *E.g.* the Resolution of the Council and of the representatives of the Governments of the Member States, meeting within the Council of February 26, 2001 on strengthening the capabilities of the European Union in the field of civil protection ([2001] O.J. C82/1). This does not happen only in the case of resolutions: *cf.* the Conclusions of the Council and the Representatives of the Governments of the Member States, meeting within the Council of December 4, 2000 on combating doping ([2000] O.J. C356/1).

[644] At issue was the Hague Resolution of November 3, 1976, see ECJ, Case 141/78 *France v UK* [1979] E.C.R. 2923, paras 8–11; ECJ, Case 32/79 *Commission v UK* [1980] E.C.R. 2403, para. 11 ("It is not contested that this resolution is binding on the Member States"); ECJ, Case 804/79 *Commission v UK* [1981] E.C.R. 1045, paras 23–31.

[645] See also ECJ, Case 61/77 *Commission v Ireland* [1978] E.C.R. 417, para. 66.

[646] ECJ, Case 81/72 *Commission v Council* [1973] E.C.R. 575, paras 10–11.

[647] ECJ, Case 148/73 *Louwage v Commission* [1974] E.C.R. 81, para. 12 (internal directive of the Commission); CFI, Case T–10/93 *A. v Commission* [1994] E.C.R. II–179, para. 60 (Conclusions of the Council and the Ministers for Health).

[648] ECJ, Case 143/83 *Commission v Denmark* [1985] E.C.R. 427, para. 13; see also ECJ, Case 38/69 *Commission v Italy* [1970] E.C.R. 47, para. 12. For the significance of such declarations in practical decision-making, see Everling (n.623, *supra*), at 134. For their use in interpreting Community acts, see Schønberg and Frick, "Finishing, refining, polishing: on the use of *travaux préparatoires* as an aid to the interpretation of Community legislation" (2003) E.L.R. 149–171.

[649] ECJ, Case 237/84 *Commission v Belgium* [1986] E.C.R. 1247, para. 17.

declaration may be used to interpret such an act only where reference is made to its content in the wording of the act in question,[650] since legislation is addressed to those affected by it and they must be able to rely on what it contains.[651] The Court of Justice may have regard to a joint declaration in order to "confirm" the interpretation having to be given to the Community act at issue.[652] Individual declarations of one or more Member States may have factual importance, in particular where they contain details of the manner in which the adoption of an act was discussed in the Council. In that event, the Court of Justice and the Court of First Instance may take the declarations into account in order to determine the content of the discussion and then to review it.[653] In view of the uncertainty to which such explanatory statements may lead, the European Parliament has asked that statements relating to legislative acts not be made.[654]

As far as the institutions' practice is concerned, the Court has plainly stated that "[a] mere practice on the part of the Council cannot derogate from the rules laid down in the Treaty. Such a practice cannot therefore create a precedent binding on Community institutions with regard to the correct legal basis".[655]

g. The EU Constitution and the introduction of a distinction between legislative acts and implementing acts

Distinguishing between legal instruments. Under the present system of **17–145** legal instruments, regulations and directives may be used both for basic acts directly based on a provision of the Treaties and for acts implementing those basic acts or implementing other implementing acts. With a view to improving transparency, it has long been proposed that a substantive distinction between legislative and implementing acts should also be

---

[650] See ECJ, Case C–292/89 *Antonissen* [1991] E.C.R. I–745, para. 18; ECJ, Case C–25/94 *Commission v Council* [1996] E.C.R. I–1469, para. 38; ECJ, Case C–329/95 *VAG Sverige* [1997] E.C.R. I–2675, para. 23. See also ECJ, Case C–368/96 *Generics* [1998] E.C.R. I–7967, paras 26–35 (general concept used in a directive interpreted in accordance with criteria set out in minutes of the Council).

[651] ECJ, Joined Cases C–283/94, C–291/94 and C–292/94 *Denkavit* [1996] E.C.R. I–5063, para. 29.

[652] ECJ, Case 136/78 *Auer* [1979] E.C.R. 437, para. 25 (declaration of the Council); ECJ, Case C–310/90 *Egle* [1992] E.C.R. I–177, para. 12 (joint declaration by the Commission and the Council). See also ECJ, Case 324/82 *Commission v Belgium* [1984] E.C.R. 1861, para. 33.

[653] CFI, Case T–194/94 *Carvel and Guardian Newspapers v Council* [1995] E.C.R. II–2765, paras 74–77.

[654] See the "declaration" appended to the Interinstitutional Agreement of December 22, 1998 on common guidelines for the quality of drafting of Community legislation ([1999] O.J. C73/1) (and a declaration to a different effect by the Council). See also the earlier resolution of the European Parliament of October 12, 1995 on the transparency of Council Decisions and the Community's legislative procedures, [1995] O.J. C287/179, and the Council's answer of December 21, 1995 to question No. P–2829/95 (Kristoffersen), [1996] O.J. C56/44.

[655] ECJ, Case 68/86 *UK v Council* [1988] E.C.R. 855, para. 24; ECJ, Case 131/86 *UK v Council* [1988] E.C.R. 905, para. 29. See also the articles in Bieber and Ress (eds), n.640, *supra*.

formally reflected in distinct legal instruments.[656] In this connection, the European Parliament generally proposed that it and the Council should be empowered to adopt legislative acts and the Commission to adopt implementing measures. The EU Constitution has responded to the call for a transparent system of legislative acts with an internal hierarchy,[657] as part of its general restructuring of the allocation of implementing powers to the Commission and the Council. To that effect, the EU Constitution provides for a limitative list of instruments which may be used by the institutions and bodies of the Union when adopting legislative and other acts. Where the EU Constitution reproduces provisions of the EC Treaty and the EU Treaty, in principle it replaces the existing instrument by an instrument taken from that list.[658]

17–146 Legislative acts. The EU Constitution defines two instruments for legislative action on the part of the Union. First, there will be the "European law", which is "a legislative act of general application" that "shall be binding in its entirety and directly applicable in all Member States" (Art. I–33(1), second subpara.). This means that European laws will correspond to what are now regulations. Next, there will be the "European framework law", defined as "a legislative act binding, as to the result to be achieved, upon each Member State to which it is addressed" and which is to "leave to the national authorities the choice of form and methods" (Art. I–33(1), third subpara.). European framework laws will therefore correspond to what are now directives. In addition, (non-binding) recommendations and opinions will continue to exist (Art. I–33(1), sixth subpara.).

Where the Constitution does not specify the type of act to be adopted, the institutions are to select the type of act on a case-by-case basis, in compliance with the applicable procedures and with the principle of proportionality (see EU Constitution, Art. I–38(1)). Where the European Parliament and the Council consider the adoption of draft legislative Acts, they must refrain from adopting acts not provided for by the relevant procedure in the area in question (EU Constitution, Art. I–33(2)). It would

---

[656] See as long ago as April 18, 1991 the resolution of the European Parliament on the nature of Community acts, [1991] O.J. C129/136, and, more recently, the resolution of the European Parliament of December 17, 2002 on the typology of acts and the hierarchy of legislation in the European Union, [2004] O.J. C31E/126.

[657] Previous Intergovernmental Conferences did not act upon the request to undertake such a discussion contained in Declaration (No. 16) annexed to the EU Treaty on the hierarchy of Community acts. See Tizzano, "La hiérarchie des normes communautaires" (1995) 3 R.M.U.E. 219–232; Monjal, "La Conférence intergouvernementale de 1996 et la hiérarchie des normes communautaires" (1996) R.T.D.E. 681–716; Kovar, "La déclaration No. 16 annexée au Traité sur l'Union européenne: chronique d'un échec annoncé?" (1997) C.D.E. 3–11.

[658] See Monjal, "Simplifiez, simplifiez, il en restera toujours quelque chose." (2003) R.D.U.E. 343–368. This has not yet been clarified in some cases, for example where the EU Constitution requires the adoption of "measures" (*e.g.* pursuant to Arts III–194 and III–196 in monetary matters).

seem to follow that institutions may no longer adopt legislation in another form, for example, by means of a "*sui generis* decision". Different rules apply as far as the CFSP is concerned. In that field, the EU Constitution does not allow for the adoption of legislative acts and leaves the institutions with the "European decision" as the instrument to be used (see para. 18–022, *infra*).

Non-legislative acts. Where the institutions do not take legislative action **17–147** but rather implementing measures, they may use a "European regulation" or a "European decision".

A European regulation is an act of general application for the implementation of legislative acts, other implementing acts and certain specific provisions of the Constitution.[659] It will be called a "delegated European regulation" where it is adopted (by the Commission) pursuant to a delegation of power from the legislator to supplement or amend certain legislative acts (Art. I–36, see para. 14–053). Where a European regulation implements other legally binding acts, it will be called an "implementing regulation" (Art. I–37(4)). A European regulation may either have legal effects similar to those of the existing regulation ("binding in its entirety and directly applicable in all Member States ") or have effects similar to those of a directive ("binding, as to the result to be achieved, upon each Member State to which it is addressed" but leaving "to the national authorities the choice of form and methods") (Art. I–33(1), fourth subpara.).

A European decision is an act "binding in its entirety". Where a decision specifies the persons to whom it is addressed, it will be binding only on them (Art. I–33(1), fifth subpara.). This means that acts which are now adopted in the form of decisions may in future be taken in the form of European decisions. Unlike existing decisions, European decisions will not necessarily be addressed to a specific person. Where a European decision implements other legally binding acts, it will be called an "implementing decision" (Art. I–37(4)).

As far as implementing acts are concerned, the institutions are under the same duty to select the type of act in compliance with the principle of proportionality, except where the Constitution specifies the type of act to be adopted. For example, the Constitution provides—as noted above—that acts in the field of CFSP must take the form of a European decision.

---

[659] Art. I–33(1), fourth subpara., of the EU Constitution does not expressly provide for European regulations to implement other implementing acts. This may however be inferred from Art. I–37(2) (referring in general terms to the implementation of all "legally binding Union acts").

3. Interinstitutional agreements

17–148 **Agreements between institutions.** Some Treaty provisions authorise the institutions concerned to determine relations *inter se* by "common accord" or by agreement.[660] The European Parliament, the Council and the Commission are increasingly concluding agreements, initially mainly to improve the flow of information to the Parliament and to increase its participation in decision-making.[661] In the meantime, agreements have been reached on other matters, institutional and otherwise.[662] The first agreements sometimes took the form of an exchange of letters between the institutions concerned; subsequently, they have generally been officially published. In a declaration annexed to the Treaty of Nice, the Intergovernmental Conference then in session spoke out against the practice of the European Parliament and the Commission concluding agreements between themselves, that is to say without involving the Council

---

[660] See EC Treaty, Art. 193, third para.; Art. 218(1); Art. 248(3), third subpara.; Art. 272(9), fifth subpara. .

[661] For the relationship between the Council and the European Parliament, see the (never officially published) Luns procedure of 1964 and the 1973 Westerterp procedure (para. 21–004, *infra*) and the Interinstitutional Agreement of November 20, 2002 concerning access by the European Parliament to sensitive information of the Council in the field of security and defence policy (see para. 15–004, *supra*). The following in particular have arisen as between the European Parliament, the Council and the Commission: the Joint Declaration of March 4, 1975 ([1975] O.J. C89/1, on the consultation procedure, para. 14–039, *supra*); the Joint Declaration of June 30, 1982 and the Interinstitutional Agreements of June 29, 1988, October 29, 1993, May 6, 1999 and November 7, 2002 on budgetary procedure (see paras 10–126 and 10–127, *supra*); the Joint Declaration on the implementation of the new co-decision procedure (n.109 to para. 14–031, *supra*), the Joint Declaration on the Socrates decision of March 4, 1995 (see n.1126 to para. 5–239, *supra*) and the Interinstitutional Agreement of July 16, 1997 on the financing of the CFSP (see para 15–006, *supra*). Between the European Parliament and the Commission codes of conduct were concluded in 1990 ((1990) 4 EC Bull. I.6.1) and on March 15, 1995 (see notes to para. 14–018, 14–025 *et seq.*, *supra*, and 21–004, *infra*) and a framework agreement on relations between the European Parliament and the Commision on July 5, 2000 ([2001] O.J. C121/122, and (2000) 7/8 EU Bull. point 2.2.1).

[662] See the Joint Declaration of the European Parliament, the Council and the Commission of April 5, 1977 on fundamental rights (see para. 17–074, *supra*); the Joint Declaration against racism and xenophobia of the European Parliament, the Council, the representatives of the Member States, meeting in the Council, and the Commission of June 11, 1986 ([1986] O.J. C158) and (as agreed between the European Parliament, the Council and the Commission) the Interinstitutional Declaration of October 25, 1993 on democracy, transparency and subsidiarity ([1993] O.J. C329/135, and (1993) 10 EC Bull. point 2.2.1); the Interinstitutional Agreement of December 20, 1994 on the codification of legislation and the Interinstitutional Agreement of November 28, 2001 on a more structured use of the recasting technique for legal acts (see para. 16–018, supra), the Interinstitutional Agreement of December 22, 1998 on common guidelines for the quality of drafting of Community legislation (see para. 16–019, *supra*), the Interinstitutional Agreement of May 25, 1999 concerning internal investigations by the European Anti-fraud Office (OLAF) ([1999] O.J. L136/15); the Interinstitutional Agreement of February 28, 2002 on the financing of the Convention on the future of the European Union ([2002] O.J. C54/1; extended by Interinstitutional Agreement of December 12, 2002, [2002] O.J. C320/1) and the Interinstitutional Agreement of December 16, 2003 on better law-making (see para. 16–019). As between the Commission and the Council, see the Code of Conduct of December 6, 1993 on public access to documents (see para. 10–160, *supra*).

in the agreement.[663] Other bodies also make use of agreements.[664] The EU Constitution will introduce an express legal basis for the European Parliament, the Council and the Commission to conclude interinstitutional agreements which may be of a binding nature.[665]

Legal force. The institutions can use an interinstitutional agreement to **17–149** simplify the implementation of procedures laid down in the Treaties, without actually amending those procedures or altering the balance as between the institutions.[666] Where the Treaty does not expressly provide for an agreement to be reached, the legal force of an agreement will depend on whether the institutions intended it to be binding.[667] An indication is afforded, in the first place, by the title chosen by the institutions: declaration, *modus vivendi*, code of conduct or agreement (which is stricter). The institutions may merely have intended to co-ordinate their positions as a first step towards the adoption of subsequent binding acts.[668] The fact that the content of an interinstitutional agreement is purely political may preclude its being binding,[669] whilst other agreements appear

---

[663] According to that declaration (No. 3) annexed to the Treaty of Nice, interinstitutional agreements "may be concluded only with the agreement of these three institutions". See Tournepiche, "La clarification du statut juridique des accords interinstitutionnels" (2002) R.T.D.E. 209–222.

[664] *e.g.* the agreement of December 13, 2001 between the ECB and Europol on combating counterfeiting ([2002] O.J. C23/9) and, for the same purpose, the co-operation agreement of March 29, 2004 between the ECB and the International Criminal Police Organisation (Interpol) ([2004] O.J. C134/9); the agreement of June 9, 2004 between Europol and Eurojust on information exchange (*Europe*, No. 8722, June 10, 2004, p.10).

[665] EU Constitution, Art. III–397.

[666] para. 13–008, *supra*); see also Declaration (No. 3) annexed to the Treaty of Nice on Art. 10 of the EC Treaty. That declaration states expressly that "[s]uch agreements may not amend or supplement the provisions of the Treaty". This reflects a lack of trust on the part of the Member States in connection with the agreement concluded between the Commission and the European Parliament on July 5, 2000 (see n.661, *supra*). According to that declaration, such an agreement should not be possible in the future, since it states that agreements "may be concluded only with the agreement of these three institutions". This gives the Council a veto.

[667] Monar, "Interinstitutional Agreements: The Phenomenon and its New Dynamics after Maastricht" (1994) C.M.L.R. 693, at 697–703. The Interinstitutional Agreement of December 22, 1998 on common guidelines for the quality of drafting of Community legislation (n.662, *supra*) expressly provides that the guidelines set out therein "are not legally binding".

[668] ECJ, Case C–58/94 *Netherlands v Council* [1996] E.C.R. I–2169, paras 23–27 (on the Code of Conduct concerning public access to Council and Commission documents; see para. 10–160, *supra*). However, an institution is bound by a code of conduct *vis-à-vis* third parties where it adopted the code by decision and thereby voluntarily assumed a series of obligations for itself (*patere legem quam ipse fecisti*), see CFI, Case T–105/95 *WWF UK v Commission* [1997] E.C.R. II–313, paras 53–55.

[669] See the assessment of the Joint Declaration on fundamental rights in the Commission's answer of June 1, 1977 to question No. 170/77 (Maigaard), [1977] O.J. C180/18, and the Council's answer of September 23, 1977 to question No. 128/77 (Dondelinger), [1977] O.J. C259/4, to the effect that, more generally, joint declarations are "political undertakings" and "in the final instance it would be for the Court of Justice to assess their legal implications" (see also the answer of the same date to question No. 169/77 (Maigaard, *ibid.*, concerning the conciliation procedure).

to lay down binding rules of conduct.[670] Academics have argued that, in certain circumstances, an interinstitutional agreement can be binding in so far as it is an expression of the duty of co-operation enshrined in Art. 10 of the EC Treaty (see also EC Treaty, Art. 218(1)).[671] There are indications in decided cases that the Court of Justice accepts in principle that interinstitutional agreements have binding force.[672] Sometimes such an agreement is referred to in order to confirm the Court's interpretation of Community law.[673]

4. Acts of other Community bodies

17–150 **European Central Bank.** Under Art. 110(1) of the EC Treaty, the ECB may make regulations, take decisions, make recommendations and deliver opinions. Article 110(2) defines those instruments in the same terms as Art. 249 of the EC Treaty (when the Constitution enters into force, these instruments will be European regulations, European decisions, recommendations and opinions[674]). Accordingly, with the exception of directives, the ECB may adopt the same instruments as the Council, the Commission, and the European Parliament jointly with the Council. Alongside "decisions", Art. 12.1 of the ESCB Statute refers to "guidelines" and "instructions to national central banks", which may also contain binding rules.[675] The requirements laid down by the EC Treaty with regard to stating reasons for and publishing or notifying acts of the institutions also apply to regulations and decisions of the ECB.[676] In addition, the ECB may decide to publish its decisions, recommendations and opinions.[677] It has in fact opted to publish these and other legal instruments (guidelines and decisions) in the *Official Journal.*[678] ECB regulations and decisions are

---

[670] Point 2 of the Interinstitutional Agreement of May 6, 1999 on budgetary discipline and improvement of budgetary procedure states that "the budgetary discipline is binding on all the institutions involved in its implementation for as long as the Agreement is in force"). This applies *a fortiori* to the agreement between the ECB and Europol of December 13, 2001 (n.664), since it provides in Art. 10 for dispute resolution by arbitration.

[671] Hilf, "Die rechtliche Bedeutung des Verfassungsprinzips der parlamentarischen Demokratie für den europäischen Integrationsprozess" (1984) EuR. 9, at 24–25; Monar (n.667, *supra*), at 700. Bieber derives this duty to co-operate from Art. 4 [now Art. 7] of the EC Treaty: Bieber, "The Settlement of Institutional Conflicts on the Basis of Art. 4 of the EEC Treaty" (1984) C.M.L.R. 505, at 520–521.

[672] See ECJ, Case 211/80 *Advernier v Commission* [1984] E.C.R. 131, para. 22 (reference to the Joint Declaration of March 4, 1975); ECJ, Case 34/86 *Council v European Parliament* [1986] E.C.R. 2155, para. 50 (reference to the Joint Declaration of June 30, 1982).

[673] Case 44/79 *Hauer* [1979] E.C.R. 3727, para. 15 (Joint Declaration on fundamental rights); CFI, Case T–194/94 *Carvel and Guardian Newspapers v Council* [1995] II–2765, para. 66 (Code of Conduct on public access to documents).

[674] EU Constitution, Art. III–190(1).

[675] Gaiser, "Gerichtliche Kontrolle im Europäischen System der Zentralbanken" (2002) EuR. 517, at 521–522 and 533–534. According to Art. 14.3 of the Statute of the European System of Central Banks, the national central banks "shall act in accordance with the guidelines and instructions of the ECB".

[676] EC Treaty, Art. 110(2), fourth subpara., which declares that Arts 253 and 254 are to apply.

[677] EC Treaty, Art. 110(2), fifth subpara.

[678] See the preamble to the Decision of the ECB of November 10, 2000 on the publication of certain legal acts and instruments of the ECB, [2001] O.J. L55/68.

enforceable in the same way and on the same terms as acts of the institutions.[679]

Other bodies. There is no catalogue of instruments which other **17–151** Community bodies must use in order to carry out the tasks conferred on them by the Treaties or specific Community acts or to regulate their internal organisation. In any event, the general principles apply. Acts of such bodies must state the reasons on which they are based and must be brought to the notice of their addressees and their legality must be subject to judicial review (see para. 14–064). As far as bodies set up by agreements concluded between the Community and non-member countries are concerned, the Council decides, when such an agreement is concluded, whether their decisions should be published in the *Official Journal.*[680]

Collective agreements. Article 139 of the EC Treaty refers to an **17–152** instrument which does not emanate from a Community body. Under paragraph 1 of that article, should management and labour so desire, the dialogue between them at Community level may lead to contractual relations, including agreements. At present, collective agreements do not have the same legal force throughout the Community in relation to the parties thereto, let alone third parties. Consequently, in the absence of Community provisions relating to this matter, the legal force of any collective agreements concluded as such at Community level remains unclear (see para. 14–042).

F. THE CASE LAW OF THE COURT OF JUSTICE AND THE COURT OF FIRST INSTANCE

Source of law. In the Community legal order, the case law of the Court of **17–153** Justice and the Court of First Instance constitutes an important source of law. Although they play a crucial role in extending this legal order, their task is formally limited to interpreting and applying each of the other sources of law discussed above. The EU Constitution recognises the role of the Community Court where it confirms that the case law of the Court of Justice and of the Court of First Instance on the interpretation and application of the existing Treaties and secondary law will remain "the source of interpretation of Union law and in particular of the comparable provisions of the Constitution".[681]

The interpretation which the two courts give to a rule of Community law defines the meaning and scope of that rule as it must be or ought to have

---

[679] EC Treaty, Art. 110(2), fourth subpara., provides that Art. 256 is to apply.

[680] Council Rules of Procedure, Art. 17(5). Some commentators consider that it is implicit in the Court of Justice's jurisdiction to interpret those decisions (para. 17–096, *supra*) that the Court may also rule on their legality in an action for annulment brought under Art. 230 of the EC Treaty: Bebr (n.29, *supra*), at 306.

[681] EU Constitution, Art. IV–438(4).

been understood and applied from the time of its coming into force.[682] It follows that a rule of Community law interpreted in this way must be applied to legal relationships which arose or were formed before the Court gave its ruling on the question on interpretation.[683] In practice, however, such an interpretation may have unexpected effects. A judicial ruling holding that a provision has direct effect may, for instance impose considerable burdens where authorities or individuals are faced with unforeseen claims from individuals. Accordingly, in exceptional cases, the Court of Justice will impose restrictions on grounds of legal certainty on the *ex tunc* effect of its preliminary rulings on Community law.[684] For instance, the Court may restrict the direct effect of a provision to claims relating to periods starting on the date on which its judgment was given.[685] It is clear from this alone that the interpretation which the two courts give to rules of Community Law is not merely declaratory, but contributes to the further development of Community law.[686]

---

[682] See Lenaerts and Arts, *Procedural Law of the European Union*, Ch.6.

[683] ECJ (judgment of January 13, 2004), *Kühne & Heitz*, not yet reported, paras 21–22.

[684] See in this connection, Bribosia and Rorive, "Le droit transitoire jurisprudentiel des juridictions européennes" (2002) R.D.ULB. 125–152.

[685] See, *e.g.* in connection with the direct effect of the interpretation given by the Court of Justice to Art. 141 of the EC Treaty, ECJ, Case 43/75 *Defrenne v Sabena* [1976] E.C.R. 455, paras 71–75. *cf.* ECJ, Case C–262/88 *Barber v Guardian Royal Exchange Insurance Group* [1990] E.C.R. I–1889, paras 40–45, in which the Court restricted its interpretation that pensions paid by contracted-out occupational pension schemes constituted "pay" within the meaning of Art. 141 to future pensions as well as to pensions in respect of which legal proceedings had been brought, or an equivalent claim had been made, before the date of the judgment. The EC Treaty has been supplemented by a Protocol (No. 17) concerning Art. 119 [now Art. 141] of the Treaty establishing the European Community ([1992] O.J. C224/104), which imposes a particular interpretation of the effects *ratione temporis* of the judgment in *Barber*. According to the Protocol, pensions so interpreted cover only benefits attributable to periods of employment after that date, except where claims have been made within the meaning of the judgment. For judgments delivered before the Protocol entered into force, see ECJ, Case C–109/91 *Ten Oever* [1993] E.C.R. I–4879, para. 19; and thereafter ECJ, Case C–152/91 *Neath v Steeper* [1993] E.C.R. I–6935, paras 13–18; ECJ, Case C–200/91 *Coloroll Pension Trustees* [1994] E.C.R. I–4389; ECJ, (no reference to the Protocol); ECJ, Case C–57/93 *Vroege* [1994] E.C.R. I–4541, paras 35–43; ECJ, Case C–128/93 *Fisscher* [1994] E.C.R. I–4583, paras 47–50; ECJ, Case C–147/95 *Evrenopoulos* [1997] E.C.R. I–2057, paras 30–40 (clarification of the Protocol). For a critical view of the technique whereby the Member States sought to "correct" the case law of the Court of Justice by means of a protocol, see Curti Gialdino, "Some Reflections on the *Acquis Communautaire*" (1995) C.M.L.R. 1089, at 1117–1120. The limitation of the possibility of relying on the direct effect of Art. 141 of the Treaty does not prevent claimants from relying on national provisions laying down a principle of equal treatment; see ECJ, Case C–50/96 *Schröder* [2000] E.C.R. I–743, paras 46–50; ECJ, Joined Cases C–234/96 and C–235/96 *Vick and Conze* [2000] E.C.R. I–799, paras 46–50, and ECJ, Joined Cases C–270/97 and C–271/97 *Sievers and Schrage* [2000] E.C.R. I–929, paras 48–52.

[686] For an account of case law as a source of law, see Schermers and Waelbroeck, *Judicial Protection in the European Union* (Kluwer, The Hague, 2001), paras 260–266, at 133–137.

CHAPTER 18

NON-COMMUNITY ACTS OF THE UNION

I. FORMS OF NON-COMMUNITY ACTS

Non-Community acts. The instruments of European integration do not **18–001** invariably take the form of acts of institutions or bodies based on the Community Treaties. Frequently, the Member States opt for non-Community methods in order to co-ordinate their action (see paras 2–010–2–019). In that connection, ministers or representatives of the national governments reach agreements which range from mere declarations to international conventions and are sometimes concluded when "meeting in the Council". Such agreements are also made by the Heads of State or Government of the Member States meeting as the European Council or otherwise. Since such acts are not based on the Community Treaties, the provisions relating to Community decision-making do not apply to them (see paras 15–016–15–018). The Council also adopts acts pursuant to the EU Treaty which do not constitute Community law, but arise pursuant to the provisions of Title V (common foreign and security policy, CFSP) and Title VI (police and judicial co-operation in criminal matters, PJCC) of that Treaty (see paras 15–002–15–014). This chapter examines the legal force of the various non-Community acts.

Union law. It should be noted that the EU Constitution will abolish the **18–002** distinction between Community and non-Community acts. Under the Constitution, the Union will adopt acts of "Union law" in all its policy areas. These acts will have the same legal force as present acts of Community law. As far as the CFSP and PJCC are concerned, the Union will adopt instruments which differ in no respect from the instruments used in its other fields of action (see para. 18–022). This will also be true of international agreements concluded in the fields of the CFSP and PJCC (see para. 18–024). The EU Constitution no longer provides for conventions to be concluded between the Member States as a means of taking legislative action (see para. 18–010). Nevertheless, the possibility cannot be ruled out that Member States will continue to conclude conventions amongst themselves or adopt—while "meeting in the Council"—decisions that are closely connected with the activities of the Union but not based on the Constitution (*cf.* paras 18–007–18–013). It will only be by examining their content and the circumstances in which they are adopted that the legal effects of these forms of action will be able to be determined, in particular whether or not the action should be regarded as an exercise of powers conferred by the Constitution on the Union. That appraisal will be carried out on the same basis as determining whether a given act is a Community or a non-Community act (*cf.* paras 18–003 and 18–006).

II. LEGAL FORCE OF NON-COMMUNITY ACTS

A. GENERAL APPRAISAL

18–003 Legal basis. In the first instance, the legal basis of a given act determines whether it is a Community or a non-Community act. The Court of Justice made this clear in the *AETR* judgment in holding that the Council's "proceedings" relating to the AETR negotiations (see para. 17–140) constituted an act against which an action for annulment would lie under the first para. of Art. 230 of the EC Treaty. It stated that:

"[t]o decide this point, it is first necessary to determine which authority was, at the relevant date, empowered to negotiate and conclude the AETR. The legal effect of the proceedings differs according to whether they are regarded as constituting the exercise of powers conferred on the Community, or as acknowledging a co-ordination by the Member States of the exercise of powers which remained vested in them".[1]

Where representatives of the Member States act, not in their capacity as members of the Council, but as representatives of their governments, and thus collectively exercise the powers of the Member States, their acts are not subject to judicial review by the Court of Justice under Art. 230 of the EC Treaty.[2] Since an action for annulment may be brought against all measures adopted by the institutions, whatever their nature or form, which are intended to have legal effects, it is not enough that an act should be described as a "decision of the Member States" for it to be excluded from review. In order for such an act to be excluded from review, it must be determined whether, having regard to its content and all the circumstances in which it was adopted, the act in question is a measure of the Member States or of the Council.[3]

18–004 Community basis. In some cases, the Member States act in order to carry out a task expressly conferred on the national governments by the Treaties.

---

[1] ECJ, Case 22/70 *Commission v Council* [1971] E.C.R. 263, paras 3–4.
[2] ECJ, Joined Cases C–181/91 and C–248/91 *European Parliament v Council* [1993] E.C.R. I–3685, para. 12.
[3] *ibid.*, paras 13–14 (where reference is made to the *AETR* judgment).

Alongside amendment of the Treaties, which is the task of a "conference of representatives of the governments of the Member States" (EU Treaty, Art. 48), decisions of the "governments of the Member States" are used chiefly to appoint members of the Court of Justice and the Court of First Instance[4] and members of certain bodies[5] and to fix the seats of institutions and bodies.[6] In view of the fact that such acts have their legal basis in the Treaty and are essentially connected with the functioning of the Communities, they must be regarded as being Community law, albeit probably not amenable to judicial review by the Court of Justice on account of their "primary" nature.[7]

Schengen-*acquis*. In areas in which not all Member States take part in **18–005** Community policy, acts may be adopted which do not apply to non-participating Member States[8] and are not binding on them.[9] Accordingly, following its integration into the framework of the European Union, the Schengen *acquis* is applicable to all the Member States with the exception of Ireland and the United Kingdom.[10] Depending on their subject matter, the necessary acts are adopted either under Title IV of the EC Treaty or under Title VI of the EU Treaty.[11] Those parts of the Schengen *acquis* whose legal basis is determined in Title IV of the EC Treaty form part of Community law. As far as those parts are concerned, Denmark "shall maintain the same rights and obligations in relation to the other [Schengen States] as before the said determination",[12] which means that they do not have the force of Community law in that Member State. In principle, Denmark is not to take part in the further adoption of acts

---

[4] See EC Treaty, Art. 223, first para. (Court of Justice) and Art. 224, second para. (Court of First Instance).

[5] See EC Treaty, Art. 79 (Advisory Committee on Transport); Art. 112(2)(b) (Executive Board of the ECB; referring to "the governments of the Member States at the level of Heads of State or Government").

[6] EC Treaty, Art. 289; ESCB Statute, Art. 37 (referring to "the governments of the Member States at the level of Heads of State or Government").

[7] para. 17–058, *supra*; see Schermers and Waelbroeck, *Judicial Protection in the European Union* (The Hague, Kluwer, 2001) para. 670, at 329–330.

[8] See EC Treaty, Art. 122(3) (economic and monetary provisions of the Treaty which do not apply to Member States with a derogation) and EU Treaty, Art. 44(2) (acts and decisions adopted for the implementation of enhanced co-operation between Member States "shall be binding only on those Member States which participate in such co-operation and, as appropriate, shall be directly applicable only in those States").

[9] See Art. 44(2) of the EU Treaty (see n.8, *supra*) and Art. 2 of Protocol (No.4) on the position of the UK and Ireland and Art. 2 of Protocol (No.5) on the position of Denmark, both annexed by the Treaty of Amsterdam to the EU and the EC Treaties ([1997] O.J. C340/99 and 101, respectively), which declare that the relevant Treaty provisions, measures adopted by the institutions and decisions of the Court of Justice shall not "form part of Community law" applicable to the Member States in question.

[10] Art. 2(1), first subpara., of Protocol (No.2) integrating the Schengen *acquis* into the framework of the European Union, annexed by the Amsterdam Treaty to the EU Treaty and the EC Treaty ([1997] O.J. C340/93).

[11] *ibid.*, Art. 2(1), second subpara. (see para. 5–164, *supra*).

[12] *ibid.*, Art. 3, first para.

pursuant to Title IV of the EC Treaty. In the event that it should nevertheless decide to transpose such acts into national legislation, this will "create an obligation under international law" between Denmark and the participating Member States.[13] The upshot will be that a given act of the Community institutions will be binding for all the Member States concerned, but, as far as Denmark is concerned, not as Community law.

18–006 International law. Acts adopted as between Member States but not on the basis of the Community Treaties, irrespective as to whether they are adopted in the Council, are in the nature of international law. Their legal effects depend on the originators, the form and the content of each act. Where such acts are closely connected with the objectives of the Communities or with Community acts, their legal effects are likely to be influenced by Community law, in particular the obligations imposed by the principle of co-operation in good faith on Member States also in respect of non-Community action (see para. 18–013). This will be the case, for instance, where the Member States involve the Community institutions in implementing an arrangement which they have adopted by mutual agreement. When they do so, the acts which the Community institutions take pursuant to the arrangement will be subject to the supervision of the Community Court. This is because the Court may in principle review the legality of any act of an institution which is intended to have legal effects "irrespective of whether the act was adopted by the institution pursuant to Treaty provisions".[14] Acts of the Member States which have no connection with Community law have to be appraised in the light of international law.[15]

B. CONVENTIONS CONCLUDED BETWEEN THE MEMBER STATES

18–007 Conventions. In matters coming within their competence, Member States may exercise their powers individually or collectively[16]; in so doing they may therefore conclude conventions amongst themselves.[17] Conventions signed between Member States may be published in the *Official Journal*.[18] The

---

[13] Protocol (No.5) annexed to the EU Treaty and the EC Treaty on the position of Denmark, Art. 5(1).

[14] ECJ, Case C–316/91 *European Parliament v Council* [1994] E.C.R. I–625, para. 9. For acts of the Council under Title V and Title VI of the EU Treaty, see paras 18–014—18–020, *infra*.

[15] Accordingly, Member States may in principle refer disputes relating to such acts to the International Court of Justice. According to Art. 292 of the EC Treaty, this is not possible in the case of "a dispute concerning the interpretation or application of this Treaty".

[16] ECJ, Joined Cases C–181/91 and C–248/91 *European Parliament v Council* [1993] E.C.R. I–3685, para. 16 (concerning humanitarian aid).

[17] For a survey, see De Witte, "Internationale verdragen tussen lidstaten van de Europese Unie" in (2001) Mededelingen van de Nederlandse Vereniging voor Internationaal Recht, at 79–131.

[18] Art. 17(1)(e) and (f) of the Council Rules of Procedure requires such publication for conventions between Member States which are signed on the basis of Art. 293 [ex Art. 220] of the EC Treaty or established by the Council in accordance with Art. 34(2) of the EU Treaty.

mere fact that a provision of Community law authorises Member States to co-operate is not enough to justify the view that an agreement concluded by Member States for that purpose forms an integral part of Community law whose interpretation falls within the jurisdiction of the Court of Justice.[19]

Interpretation of conventions. Article 293 of the EC Treaty sets out a **18–008** number of objectives which the Member States may achieve by mutual agreement. The Court of Justice has held that Art. 220 is "not intended to lay down a legal rule directly applicable as such, but merely defines a number of matters on which the Member States are to enter into negotiations with each other 'so far as is necessary'".[20] Conventions concluded in this way are not acts of the institutions, but agreements governed by international law to which Art. 234 of the EC Treaty does not apply.[21] However, the Member States may provide in the convention itself or in a protocol thereto for the Court of Justice to have jurisdiction to interpret its provisions, as is the case with the Brussels Convention, which was concluded pursuant to Art. 293.[22] According to the Court of Justice, provisions of a convention concluded on the basis of that article and within the framework defined by it are "linked to the E[E]C Treaty".[23] As a result, the Court of Justice reviewed a national provision of procedural law forming part of the provisions to which the Brussels Convention refers in the light of the prohibition of discrimination laid down in Art. 12 of the EC Treaty and found that the provision in question was contrary thereto.[24]

Although they are not part of Community law, conventions contemplated by Art. 293 of the EC Treaty and those that are "inseparable from the attainment of the objectives of the EC Treaty" as well as "the protocols on the interpretation of those conventions by the Court of Justice, signed by

---

[19] ECJ (order of November 12, 1998), Case C–162/98 *Hartmann* [1998] E.C.R. I–7083, paras 11–12, and ECJ (order of November 12, 1998), Case C–194/98 *Pörschke*, unreported, paras 11–12.

[20] ECJ, Case 137/84 *Mutsch* [1985] E.C.R. 2681, para. 11; ECJ, Case C–336/96 *Gilly* [1998] E.C.R. I–2793, para. 15.

[21] ECJ, Case 56/84 *Von Gallera* [1984] E.C.R. 1769, para. 4.

[22] Brussels Convention of September 27, 1968 on jurisdiction and the enforcement of judgments in civil and commercial matters (the Brussels Convention, often referred to as the Judgments Convention; see para. 5–151, *supra*). Questions on the interpretation and application of the Convention may be referred to the Court of Justice for a preliminary ruling pursuant to the Luxembourg Protocol of June 3, 1971 on its interpretation ([1978] O.J. L304/36. For the UK, see the Civil Jurisdiction and Judgments Act 1982.) For the courts and tribunals which may make references to the Court for a preliminary ruling, see Lenaerts and Arts, *Procedural Law of the European Union*, Ch.19. Provision was also made for the Court of Justice to interpret the Brussels Convention of February 29, 1968 on the mutual recognition of companies and bodies corporate (see n.560 to para. 5–137, *supra*) under a protocol of June 3, 1971 appended thereto, which, like the Convention itself, has not entered into force. The Court of Justice has no such jurisdiction in respect of the third convention adopted pursuant to Art. 293: Brussels Convention of July 23, 1990 on the elimination of double taxation in connection with the adjustment of profits of associated enterprises ([1990] O.J. L225/10; see n.00 to para. 15–016, *supra*).

[23] ECJ, Case C–398/92 *Mund & Fester* [1994] E.C.R. I–467, para. 12.

[24] *ibid.*, paras 13–22.

the present Member States of the Community" constitute part of the *acquis communautaire*.[25] New Member States undertake in the Act of Accession to accede to such conventions and to enter into negotiations with the other Member States in order to make the necessary adjustments thereto.[26] These conventions also include the 1980 Rome Convention, which the Member States concluded outside the framework of Art. 293. A protocol annexed to the Convention confers jurisdiction on the Court of Justice to interpret it.[27] New Member States must also accede to international agreements which this Community and the Member States have concluded jointly and to "internal" agreements which the Member States have concluded with each other for the purposes of implementing such international agreements.[28]

18–009 PJCC conventions. In addition, the Member States also conclude conventions with each other in areas which have no or only slight links with Community law.[29] Where such agreements relate to "the functioning of the Union or [are] connected with the activities thereof", new Member States undertake to accede to them.[30]

This applies in particular to conventions established by the Council in connection with PJCC under Art. 34(2)(d) of the EU Treaty, which the Council recommends to the Member States for adoption in accordance with their respective constitutional requirements.[31] Unless they provide otherwise, such conventions, once adopted by at least half of the Member States, enter into force for those Member States (EU Treaty, Art. 34(2)(d)). If the Member State concerned accepts the jurisdiction of the

---

[25] 2003 Act of Accession, Art. 5(2) and 1994 Act of Accession, Art. 4(2). The 1972 and 1979 Acts of Accession mentioned only the Art. 293 conventions, whilst Art. 3(2) of the 1985 Act of Accession also referred to conventions which "are inseparable from the attainment of the objectives of that Treaty and thus linked to the Community legal order" (for the references of the Acts of Accession, see para. 1–021, *supra*).

[26] *ibid.*

[27] Rome Convention of June 19, 1980 on the law applicable to contractual obligations (see para. 5–151, *supra*), the Protocol of December 19, 1988 on interpretation of the Convention by the Court of Justice ([1989] O.J. L48/1) and the Protocol of December 19, 1988 conferring on the Court of Justice of the European Communities certain powers to interpret the Convention ([1989] O.J. L48/17). For further particulars, see Lenaerts and Arts, *Procedural Law of the European Union*, Ch.19. See also the powers conferred on the Court by Arts 5 and 73 of the Luxembourg Convention for the European patent for the common market (Community Patent Convention), [1976] O.J. L17/1. That convention has been signed by nine Member States including the UK. Denmark and Ireland have been unable to ratify it.

[28] See Art. 6(2) to (6) and (11) of the 2003 Act of Accession; Art. 5(2) and (3) of the 1994 Act of Accession.

[29] See, *inter alia*, the conventions on police and judicial co-operation mentioned in para. 2–015, *supra*.

[30] Art. 5(1), *in fine*, of the 2003 Act of Accession; Art. 4(1), *in fine*, of the 1994 Act of Accession.

[31] For their implementation, see para. 15–012, *supra*. With reference to conventions in the sphere of justice and home affairs, the first indent of Art. 3(4) of the 2003 Act of Accession provides that they "are inseparable from the attainment of the objectives of the EU Treaty". See also Art. 3 of the 1994 Act of Accession.

Court of Justice, that court may give preliminary rulings on the interpretation of such conventions (EU Treaty, Art. 35(1)). In order to accept the Court's jurisdiction, the Member State must make a declaration specifying that it accepts the Court's interpretative jurisdiction either for all courts and tribunals or only for those against whose decisions there is no judicial remedy (EU Treaty, Art. 35(3); see para. 10–077). In any case, the Court is empowered to rule on any dispute between Member States regarding the interpretation or the application of such conventions whenever the dispute cannot be settled by the Council within six months of its being referred to that institution, and on any dispute between Member States and the Commission regarding the interpretation or the application of such conventions (EU Treaty, Art. 35(7)).

With the introduction of Art. 35 of the EU Treaty, the Treaty of Amsterdam confirmed the arrangements which had gradually evolved with regard to conventions in the sphere of justice and home affairs (JHA), in respect of which, under the former Art. K.3(2)(c) of the EU Treaty, the Council conferred jurisdiction on the Court of Justice to interpret provisions of conventions and to rule on any disputes regarding their application.[32] Most JHA conventions which recognise the jurisdiction of the Court of Justice provide for a first stage in which disputes between Member States about the interpretation and application of the convention are to be discussed in the Council. After six months, a party to the dispute may refer the case to the Court of Justice.[33] Furthermore, any dispute between one or more Member States and the Commission concerning the application of the convention which cannot be settled by negotiation may be brought before the Court of Justice. Each such convention (or a protocol thereto)

---

[32] See also the parallel between the limitation on the Court's jurisdiction, on the one hand, in Art. 35(5) of the EU Treaty and, on the other, in Art. 26(8) of the Convention of December 18, 1997 on mutual assistance and co-operation between customs administrations ([1998] O.J. C24/2), which provides that the Court "shall not have jurisdiction to check the validity or proportionality of operations carried out by competent law enforcement agencies under this Convention nor to rule on the exercise of responsibilities which devolve upon Member States for maintaining law and order and for safeguarding internal security".

[33] See Art. 27 of the Convention on the use of information technology for customs purposes ([1995] O.J. C316/42); Art. 8 of the Convention on the protection of the European Communities' financial interests ([1995] O.J. C316/51); Art. 8 of the Protocol of September 27, 1996 to the Convention on the protection of the European Communities' financial interests ([1996] O.J. C313/2); Art. 13 of the Second Protocol to the Convention on the protection of the European Communities' financial interests ([1997] O.J. C221/12); Art. 12(1) of the Convention on the fight against corruption involving officials of the European Communities or officials of Member States of the European Union ([1997] O.J. C195/2). Art. 40(2) of the Europol Convention (para. 6–008, *supra*) provides that if disputes are not settled within six months, the Member States party to the dispute are to decide, by agreement amongst themselves, the modalities according to which they are to be settled. It appears from a declaration on Art. 40(2) ([1995] O.J. C316/32) that all the Member States, with the exception of the UK, agree that in such cases they will systematically submit the dispute to the Court of Justice.

permits Member States to recognise the jurisdiction of the Court of Justice to give preliminary rulings on its interpretation.[34] Member States may elect to allow references for preliminary rulings to be made only by courts of last instance or by any court or tribunal.[35] Some JHA conventions confer on the Court of Justice the same interpretative jurisdiction as the Brussels and Rome Conventions by separate protocols. These conventions are the Convention on Jurisdiction and the Recognition and Enforcement of Judgments in Matrimonial Matters ("Second Brussels Convention")[36] and the Convention on the service in the EU Member States of judicial and extrajudicial documents in civil or commercial matters.[37]

JHA conventions are governed only by international law. Any implementing measures adopted by the Council or other implementing bodies[38] pursuant to such conventions in principle do not constitute acts of Community law. Where, however, the Court of Justice is given jurisdiction to interpret provisions of such conventions and to rule on any disputes relating to their application, it can secure consistency with Community law. This is especially true of PJCC conventions, which, as in the case of the Brussels and Rome Conventions, give shape to the Community legal order in a broader sense.[39]

---

[34] See the arrangements laid down in the Protocols on the interpretation, by way of preliminary rulings, by the Court of Justice of the European Communities of the Convention on the establishment of a European Police Office ([1996] O.J. C299/1), of the Convention on the protection of the European Communities' financial interests ([1997] O.J. C151/2; this protocol also being applicable to the Second Protocol to the Convention: [1997] O.J. C221/12) and of the Convention on the use of information technology for customs purposes ([1997] O.J. C151/16). Similar rules are set out in Art. 12(3)–(6) of the Convention of May 26, 1997 on the fight against corruption involving officials of the European Communities or officials of Member States of the European Union ([1997] O.J. C195/2) and Art. 26(3)–(7) of the Convention of December 18, 1997 on mutual assistance and co-operation between customs administrations ([1998] O.J. C24/2).

[35] As far as the Europol Convention is concerned, the first option has been chosen by France and Ireland, the second by, for instance, Belgium, the Netherlands and Sweden: see the declarations in [1996] O.J. C299/2, and (for Sweden) in [1997] O.J. C100/1. As regards the financial interests and customs information technology conventions, the first option has been chosen by Ireland and Portugal (and by France in the case of the latter convention) and the second by the Netherlands ([1997] O.J. C151/14 and p.28). In the case of the customs co-operation convention, Ireland has chosen the first option and Austria, Germany, Greece and Italy the second ([1998] O.J. C24/21).

[36] Convention of May 28, 1998 on Jurisdiction and the Recognition and Enforcement of Judgments in Matrimonial Matters ("Second Brussels Convention"; see para. 5–151, *supra*) and the Protocol on the interpretation by the Court of Justice of the European Communities of that Convention, [1998] O.J. C221/20 (explanatory report at [1998] O.J. C221/65).

[37] Convention of May 26, 1997 on the service in the Member States of the European Union of judicial and extrajudicial documents in civil or commercial matters (see para. 5–151, *supra*) and the Protocol on the interpretation by the Court of Justice of the European Communities of the Convention, [1997] O.J. C261/17 (explanatory report at [1997] O.J. C261/38).

[38] *e.g.* decisions of the committee set up by Art. 18 of the Dublin Convention; see para. 2–016, *supra*.

[39] See Van Houtte, "Het Europees Overeenkomstenverdrag" in Van Houtte and Pertegás Sender (eds), *Europese IPR-verdragen* (Acco, Leuven, 1997), at 190.

Constitution. The EU Constitution does not mention conventions between **18–010** Member States as a policy instrument of the Union. This will not prevent existing conventions from preserving their legal force, including any interpretative jurisdiction conferred on the Court of Justice.

C. OTHER ACTS OF MEMBER STATE GOVERNMENTS

Intergovernmental acts. Where the Member States conclude agreements as **18–011** between themselves which they do not wish to cast as a formal convention, they resort to acts of representatives of the governments of the Member States or the responsible ministers "meeting in the Council".[40] If competences are not clearly allocated as between the Community and the Member States, such acts are often issued by "the Council and the Ministers, meeting in the Council" (see para. 2–019).[41] The acts take various forms (acts, declarations, resolutions, findings), from which it is often clear that the Member States' intention is to adopt a non-binding act.[42]

Legal effects. International law determines whether—and if so what—legal **18–012** effects ensue from such acts. As already mentioned, the fact that new Member States accede by means of the Act of Accession to "decisions and agreements adopted by the Representatives of the Governments of the Member States meeting within the Council"[43] does not confer any additional legal effects on such acts.[44] Nevertheless, the Member States may lay down agreements in such acts which are binding under international law. In such a case, each Member State decides for itself whether the agreements in question are subject to the same ratification procedure as treaties and what legal force is to be given them under national law.[45] This

---

[40] One of the earliest instances of this was the adoption of the so-called "acceleration decisions" of May 12, 1960 and May 15, 1962, para. 5–076, *supra*.

[41] For the changing nature of these forms of decision in the sphere of education, see Van Craeyenest, "La nature juridique des résolutions sur la co-opération en matière d'éducation", in De Witte (ed.), *European Community Law of Education* (Nomos, Baden-Baden, 1989), at 127–133. For agreements concluded by the Member States outside the Council, see Mortelmans, "The Extramural Meetings of the Ministers of the Member States of the Community" (1974) C.M.L.R. 62–91.

[42] See, *e.g.* the Declaration by the Council and the representatives of the Governments of the Member States, meeting within the Council, of December 16, 1997 on respecting diversity and combating racism and xenophobia, [1998] O.J. C1/14.

[43] Art. 5(1) of the 2003 Act of Accession; Art. 4(1) of the 1994 Act of Accession.

[44] para. 17–142, *supra*; for the opposite view, see Schermers and Waelbroeck, *Judicial Protection in the European Union* (Kluwer, The Hague, 2001), paras 670–671, at 330 (who take the view that since the Act of Accession refers to those decisions, it recognises them as being Community law).

[45] Everling, "Zur rechtlichen Wirkung von Beschlüssen, Entschliessungen, Erklärungen und Vereinbarungen des Rates oder der Mitgliedstaaten der Europäischen Gemeinschaft", in Lüke, Ress and Will (eds), *Rechtsvergleichung, Europarecht und Staatenintegration. Gedächtnisschrift für L.-J. Constantinesco* (Heymann, Cologne, 1983), 133, at 136. For the Netherlands, see Besselink, "An Open Constitution and European Integration: The Kingdom of the Netherlands" (1996) S.E.W. 192, at 205.

is also true of acts adopted by the national governments at the level of the Heads of State or Government, whether meeting within the European Council[46] or as the European Council.[47]

18–013 Judicial enforcement. The obligations which the Member States assume in non-Community acts may not be enforced as such by the Court of Justice.[48] In common with joint declarations made in the Council, however, such acts do have interpretative value in "confirming" obligations arising for the Member States under Community law (see para. 17–144), although the acts in question cannot detract in any way from Treaty provisions.[49] In addition, the principle of co-operation in good faith requires Member States not to take any measure by such an act which "could jeopardise the attainment of the objectives of this Treaty" (EC Treaty, Art. 10, second para.; see paras 5–054 *et seq.*). This suggests that the Commission could bring an action under Art. 226 of the EC Treaty against acts by which the national governments detracted from their Treaty obligations.[50]

D. Acts of the European Council and the Council pursuant to the CFSP and PJCC

18–014 Range of instruments. In areas coming under the common foreign and security policy (CFSP; EU Treaty, Title V) or police and judicial co-operation in criminal matters (PJCC; EU Treaty, Title VI), the European Council and the Council may adopt acts with differing legal force. They often adopt declarations or positions containing merely a political assessment or a declaration of intent. Examples are the "principles", "general guidelines" and "common strategies" determined by the European Council in the context of the CFSP (EU Treaty, Art. 13(1) and (2)).[51] Some resolutions or recommendations of the Council, however,

---

[46] Decision of the Heads of State and Government, meeting within the European Council, concerning certain problems raised by Denmark on the Treaty on European Union ([1992] O.J. C348/2).

[47] Art. 5(3) of the 2003 Act of Accession and Art. 4(3) of the 1994 Act of Accession place "declarations or resolutions of, or other positions taken up by" the European Council on the same footing as those of the Council (para. 17–142, *supra*). For a commentary dealing specifically with the legal force of resolutions of the European Council, see Martenczuk, "Der Europäische Rat und die Wirtschafts- und Währungsunion" (1998) EuR. 151, at 155–157.

[48] For a study of their legal force, see Schermers, "Besluiten van de Vertegenwoordigers der Lid-Staten: Gemeenschapsrecht?" (1966) S.E.W. 545–579; Pescatore, "Remarques sur la nature juridique des 'décisions des représentants des Etats membres réunis au sein du Conseil'" (1966) S.E.W. 579–586; Everling (n.45, *supra*), at 147–156; Borchardt and Wellens, "Soft law in het Gemeenschapsrecht" (1987) S.E.W. 663–727.

[49] ECJ, Case 43/75 *Defrenne* [1976] E.C.R. 455, para. 57, at 478 (concerning a resolution of a conference of the Member States). In this way, the Court of Justice may also interpret the actual provisions of such acts.

[50] Schermers (n.48, *supra*), at 562 and 575.

[51] But a "common strategy" does have consequences as regards the procedure to be followed by the Council; see para. 15–002. For that instrument, see Spencer, "The EU and Common Strategies: The Revealing Case of the Mediterranean" (2001) E.For.Aff.Rev. 31–51. For a survey of CFSP instruments, see Dashwood, "External Relations Provisions of the Amsterdam Treaty" (1998) C.M.L.R. 1019, at 1030–1033.

set out detailed agreements.[52] Informal agreements at international level are also entered into by the President of the Council.[53]

The EU Treaty also prescribes specific instruments for Council action in the context of the CFSP (joint actions, common positions) and in that of PJCC (common positions, framework decisions, decisions), alongside the PJCC conventions which Member States may conclude amongst themselves (see para. 18–009) and agreements concluded by the Council at international level (see para. 18–023).[54] With the exception of conventions and agreements, such instruments are not subject to any special procedure of approval and ratification by the Member States.[55] They constitute instruments of international law, which, in principle, must be applied by each Member State as from their entry into force (for framework decisions, however, see para. 18–017). Whenever the Council adopts such acts, it may decide by unanimous vote to publish them in the *Official Journal*.[56] PJCC instruments are to be published in the *Official Journal* in any event.[57]

Common position. Common positions define the approach of the Union to a particular matter (EU Treaty, Art. 15 and Art. 34(2)(a)). In the case of the CFSP, the matter is referred to as being "of a geographical or thematic nature" and the EU Treaty specifies that Member States are to ensure that their national policies conform to common positions (Art. 15). In this connection, Member States are to "uphold" common positions in international organisations and at international conferences (Art. 19(1)). **18–015**

Joint action. Joint actions, as part of the CFSP, address specific situations where operational action of the Union is deemed to be required. They commit the Member States in the positions they adopt and in the conduct **18–016**

---

[52] See, *e.g.* in the context of JHA co-operation the recommendation concerning transit for the purposes of expulsion and the addendum thereto, both of which antedated the entry into force of the EU Treaty, but were published as annexes to the Council Recommendation of December 22, 1995 on concerted action and co-operation in carrying out expulsion measures, [1996] O.J. C5/3.

[53] See, *e.g.* Lopandic, "Les mémorandums d'entente: des instruments juridiques spécifiques de la politique étrangère et de sécurité de l'Union européenne—Le cas de l'ex-Yougoslavie" (1995) R.M.C.U.E. 557–562.

[54] See Van den Brink, "Besluiten in de tweede en derde pijler van de Europese Unie: van eigenheid naar eenvormigheid?" (2003) Rechtsgeleerd Magazijn Themis 243–253. Initially, both Title V (CFSP) and Title VI (JHA co-operation) of the EU Treaty referred to both common (or joint) positions (former Arts J.2 and K.2) and joint action (former Arts J.3 and K.3). The Treaty of Amsterdam replaced joint action in Title VI (henceforth PJCC) by framework decisions and decisions (see EU Treaty, Art. 34(2)).

[55] See also Art. 2 of the 1994 and 2003 Acts of Accession: "From the date of accession, the provisions of the original Treaties and the acts adopted by the institutions and the European Central Bank before accession shall be binding on the new Member States and shall apply in those States under the conditions laid down in those Treaties and in this Act".

[56] Council Rules of Procedure, Art. 17(3) and (4). The decisions are published in Part L of the *Official Journal*.

[57] Council Rules of Procedure, Art. 17(1)(d) and (e) (publication of framework decisions, decisions and agreements). See also para. 15–011.

of their activity (EU Treaty, Art. 14(3)).[58] Even if there is a change in circumstances having a substantial effect on a question subject to a joint action, the action is to stand until such time as the Council decides to review its principles and objectives (Art. 14(2)).

18–017 Framework decision. A framework decision is a PJCC instrument for the approximation of the laws and regulations of the Member States (EU Treaty, Art. 34(2)(b)). Framework decisions are binding upon Member States as to the result to be achieved but leave to the national authorities the choice of form and methods.[59] Article 34(2)(b) further provides that framework decisions do not entail direct effect.

18–018 Decision. No other acts are defined in the context of the CFSP.[60] The Member States, however, adopt familiar forms of act such as a "decision of the representatives of the Governments of the Member States".[61]

As far as PJCC is concerned, the EU Treaty empowers the Council to adopt "decisions" for any other purpose consistent with the objectives of Title VI, excluding any approximation of the laws and regulations of the Member States (Art. 34(2)(c)). Such decisions are binding and do not entail direct effect (*ibid.*). In addition, the EU Treaty refers to measures adopted by the Council (by a qualified majority of votes weighted in accordance with Art. 205(2) of the EC Treaty) to implement PJCC decisions; measures implementing PJCC conventions are adopted by a majority of two-thirds of the contracting parties.[62]

18–019 Legal effects. As for any non-Community act, the Member States determine the status and legal effects of CFSP and PJCC acts within their domestic legal systems.[63] In "monist" Member States (such as Belgium and the Netherlands), binding CFSP and PJCC acts may take precedence over domestic law as acts governed by international law. If their provisions have direct effect (under international law), they may be relied upon by

---

[58] See Münch, "Die gemeinsame Aktion im Rahmen des GASP: Inhalt, Rechtsnatur und Reformbedürftigkeit" (1996) EuR. 415–433.

[59] An analogy may be drawn with the description of directives in Art. 249 of the EC Treaty (para. 17–120, *supra*). For an appraisal of this instrument, see Monjal, "Le droit dérivé de l'Union européenne en quête d'identité" (2001) R.T.D.E. 335–369.

[60] The EU Treaty also refers to "decisions" without further particularisation, *inter alia*, in Art. 13(3), first subpara., and Art. 17(3), first and fourth subparas.

[61] See Decision (96/409/CFSP) of the representatives of the Governments of the Member States, meeting within the Council, of June 25, 1996 on the establishment of a temporary travel document, [1996] O.J. L168/4.

[62] EU Treaty, Art. 34(2)(c) and (d), second para., respectively.

[63] para. 18–012, *supra*. For the CFSP, see para. 22–009, *infra*; for the former JHA co-operation, see Müller-Graff, "The Legal Bases of the Third Pillar and its Position in the Framework of the Union Treaty" (1994) C.M.L.R. 493, at 508–509 (who observes that a JHA "joint position" has more the value of a joint declaration of the Member States). See also Griller, "Die Unterscheidung von Unionsrecht und Gemeinschaftsrecht nach Amsterdam" (1999) EuR. Beiheft 1 45, at 64–68.

individuals before domestic courts.[64] It was precisely in order to avoid this that the new Art. 34(2)(b) and (c) of the EU Treaty declares that PJCC framework decisions and decisions do not entail direct effect, apparently not even where their content lends itself to direct effect. Nevertheless, such framework decisions and decisions must be able to be invoked by interested parties before national courts. If they could not be so raised, it would be impossible to see how they could be the subject of a reference for a preliminary ruling (see EU Treaty, Art. 35(1)).[65]

Since supervision by the Commission and enforcement by the Court of Justice of the provisions of Titles V and VI of the EU Treaty are largely precluded (EU Treaty, Art. 46; see para. 10–076), the Court of Justice has no jurisdiction to review obligations arising for the Member States under CFSP or PJCC acts. All the same, the compatibility of national measures with PJCC acts may arise where the Court of Justice rules on disputes between Member States concerning the interpretation or the application of such acts (Art. 35(7), first sentence). Member States should first raise such a dispute with the Council (*ibid.*). The Court of Justice may also answer such a question where it gives a preliminary ruling on the interpretation of a framework decision, a decision or an implementing measure (Art. 35(1)),[66] if the Member State in question has accepted the Court's jurisdiction in this regard (Art. 35(3); see para. 10–077).[67] Moreover, in interpreting Community law, the Court may have regard to an act adopted pursuant to Title V or Title VI.[68]

Judicial review. Moreover, Council action under PJCC is subject to judicial **18–020** review by the Court of Justice by virtue of Art. 35 of the EU Treaty. Direct review will take place where a Member State or the Commission brings an action challenging the legality of framework decisions or decisions (Art. 35(6)). Indirect review is possible with respect to the validity of framework decisions, decisions and implementing measures where the Court of Justice gives a preliminary ruling on a question from a national court on the validity of such an act (Art. 35(1), (2) and (3)).

---

[64] For similar observations concerning the German legal system, see Meyring, "Intergovernmentalism and Supranationality: Two Stereotypes for a Complex Reality" (1997) E.L.R. 221, at 238–242.

[65] See Monjal, "La décision-cadre instaurant le mandat d'arrêt européen et l'ordre juridique français: la constitutionnalité du droit dérivé de l'Union européenne sous contrôle du Conseil d'Etat" (2003) R.D.U.E. 109, at 178–187.

[66] Art. 35(1) of the EU Treaty does not mention PJCC common positions, which are also excluded from judicial review under Art. 35(6), but may be the subject of a ruling on their interpretation or application under Art. 35(7), first sentence.

[67] However, the Court has no jurisdiction to review the validity or the proportionality of operations carried out by the police or other law enforcement services of a Member State or the exercise of the responsibilities incumbent upon Member States with regard to the maintenance of law and order and the safeguarding of internal security: EU Treaty, Art. 35(5).

[68] For the CFSP, see para. 22–005, *infra*.

18–021 **Relation with Community law.** Article 46 of the EU Treaty does not exclude the jurisdiction of the Court of Justice to ensure, under Art. 47 of that Treaty, that no provision in Title V or Title VI of the EU Treaty detracts from the Community Treaties. As a result, the Court still has the power to pronounce on action by the institutions or the Member States which is alleged to constitute an infringement of Community law even if the action is undertaken pursuant to the CFSP or PJCC.

It appears from the case law that the Court of Justice can examine, pursuant to the division of competence as between the Community and the Member States, whether a given act of the Member States ought to be regarded as being an action of the Council pursuant to the Community Treaties (see para. 18–003). Accordingly, the Court has held that it has jurisdiction under Art. 47 of the EU Treaty to examine whether an act of the Council which was formally based on Title V or VI of the EU Treaty, but related to a matter coming within the Community's competence, should not instead have been adopted on the basis of a provision of the Community Treaties and in accordance with the procedure prescribed thereby.[69]

As has been mentioned, the Court of Justice can rule on the legality of a Community act—that is to say, whether it is compatible with Community law—irrespective as to whether it was adopted pursuant to the Treaty or to an agreement concluded between the Member States (see para. 18–006). Under Art. 47 of the EU Treaty, the Court must give such a ruling also on any act of an institution adopted pursuant to Title V or VI of the EU Treaty where it is alleged that the act in question infringed Community law. This has been confirmed by Art. 46(d) of the EU Treaty as regards the supervision which the Court of Justice may carry out to ensure respect for fundamental rights as general principles of Community law (see EU Treaty, Art. 6(2)). Article 46(d) confers such a power on the Court with regard to action of the institutions in so far as it has jurisdiction under the Community Treaties or the EU Treaty (for instance, in relation to PJCC acts). The question arises as to whether the Court of Justice also has jurisdiction under Art. 47 of the EU Treaty in conjunction with Art. 220 of the EC Treaty to inquire whether a CFSP act of an institution respects fundamental rights.

Lastly, Art. 10 of the EC Treaty requires the Member States to abstain from "any measure" which could jeopardise the attainment of the objectives of that Treaty. This will therefore hold good also for

---

[69] ECJ, Case C–170/96 *Commission v Council* [1998] E.C.R. I–2763, paras 13–17 (action brought against the Joint Action (96/197/JHA) of March 4, 1996 adopted by the Council on the basis of the former Article K.3 of the EU Treaty on airport transit arrangements, [1996] O.J. L63/8). See also CFI (orders of June 7, 2004), Case T–333/02 *Gestoras Pro-Amnistía v Council* and case T–338/02 *Segi v Council* unreported. See Curtin and Van Ooik, "Een Hof van Justitie van de Europese *Unie?*" (1999) S.E.W. 24–38; Pechstein, "Die Justitabilität des Unionsrechts" (1999) EuR. 1–26. For a more general discussion, see Edward, "Is Art. L of the Maastricht Treaty Workable?" (1995) EuR. Beiheft 2, 23–25.

implementing measures taken by the Member States pursuant to obligations assumed by them under Title V or VI of the EU Treaty.[70] It is not clear whether any violation of fundamental rights committed in that context would also constitute an infringement of Art. 10 of the EC Treaty.[71]

Constitution. When the EU Constitution enters into force, the institutions **18–022** of the Union are to take action in the fields of the CFSP and PJCC by means of the instruments specified in the Constitution. As far as PJCC is concerned, this means that the European Parliament and the Council will adopt European laws and European framework laws, which may be implemented at Union level by the various acts that may be used for the implementation of legislative acts (see paras 17–146 and 17–147). PJCC "framework decisions" and "decisions" will therefore no longer exist. At the same time there will no longer be any difference in terms of judicial enforcement between Union acts adopted in the field of police and judicial co-operation in criminal matters and other Union acts (see para. 10–086).

Specific rules will continue to exist as far as the CFSP is concerned. Art. I–40(6) of the EU Constitution provides that European laws and framework laws are excluded in CFSP matters. The European Council and the Council are to adopt European decisions (Art. I–40(3)). This means that common positions and joint actions, together with all acts adopted for their implementation, will take the form of European decisions (see also EU Constitution, Art. III–294(3)(b)). As for the legal effects of CFSP acts, the EU Constitution makes no distinction between European decisions adopted within the framework of the CFSP and other European decisions. The principle of the primacy of Union law will therefore apply in full to any Union action within the framework of the CFSP (see para. 17–002). All the same, the Court of Justice does not have jurisdiction with respect to the provisions of the Constitution relating to the CFSP (EU Constitution, Art. III–376). It will therefore be up to the national courts, when asked to rule on national measures implementing CFSP acts, to determine the legal effects of the CFSP acts concerned and to resolve any conflict between those acts and other legal rules or principles. As far as the CFSP is concerned, the Court of Justice will have jurisdiction to rule only on actions for annulment brought by natural or legal persons against European decisions of the Council providing for restrictive measures against natural and legal persons.[72] In addition, the Court of Justice will continue to have jurisdiction to ensure that implementation of the CFSP does not affect the application of Union powers in other areas (EU Constitution, Art. III–308).

---

[70] See, for action of Member States pursuant to an EPC act, ECJ, Case C–124/95 *Centro-Com* [1997] E.C.R. I–81, paras 24–30, at I–123–124.
[71] See, however, O'Leary, "A Case Study of the Community's Protection of Human Rights, with Particular Reference to the Free Movement of Persons" (1994) A.D. 431, at 451; for protection of fundamental rights, see para. 17–079, *supra*.
[72] EU Constitution, Art. III–376, second para. For the restrictive measures in question, see para. 20–253, *infra*.

This supervisory competence corresponds to the review which the Court of Justice carries out now with respect to the division of powers between Community and non-Community action of the Union.

E. INTERNATIONAL AGREEMENTS CONCLUDED BY THE UNION IN CONNECTION WITH THE CFSP AND PJCC

18–023 **Agreements concluded by the Union.** The Council may conclude international agreements with one or more States or international organisations in connection with the CFSP and PJCC (EU Treaty, Art. 24 and Art. 38; see para. 21–019). Since the EU Treaty does not expressly confer legal personality on the Union, the question arises as whether in concluding such an agreement the Council does not simply enter into an international commitment on behalf of the Member States jointly.[73] However, all the agreements which the Council has since concluded on behalf of the EU refer to the European Union as one of the participating parties, which suggests that, internationally, the Union as such is bound by the agreement and not the EU Member States severally.[74] Article 24 of the EU Treaty provides that no agreement shall be binding on a Member State whose representative in the Council states that it has to comply with the requirements of its own constitutional procedure.[75] The other members of the Council may nevertheless agree that the agreement is to apply

---

[73] For an affirmative view, see Neuwahl, "A Partner with a Troubled Personality: EU Treaty-making in Matters of CFSP and JHA after Amsterdam" (1998) E.For.Aff.Rev. 177–195. *cf.* Des Nerviens, "Le Traité d'Amsterdam. Les relations extérieures" (1997) R.T.D.E. 801, at 806 (who regards the Union, rather than the Member States, as the party to such agreements).

[74] See, *e.g.* the Agreement of April 25, 2001 between the European Union and the Federal Republic of Yugoslavia (FRY) on the activities of the European Union Monitoring Mission (EUMM) in the FRY, approved by Council Decision 2001/352/CFSP of April 9, 2001 ([2001] O.J. L125/1), the Agreement between the European Union and Bosnia and Herzegovina on the activities of the European Union Police Mission (EUPM) in Bosnia and Herzogovina, approved by Council Decision 2002/845/CFSP of September 30, 2002 ([2002] O.J. L293/1) and the Agreement between the European Union and the Former Yugoslav Republic of Macedonia on the status and activities of the European Union Police Mission in the Former Yugoslav Republic of Macedonia (EUPOL Proxima), approved by Council Decision 2004/75/CFSP of December 11, 2003 ([2004] O.J. L16/66). This also applies to the Agreement between the European Union and the North Atlantic Treaty Organisation on the security of information, approved by Council Decision 2003/211/CFSP of February 24, 2003 ([2003] O.J. L80/35), the Agreements between the European Union and the United States of America on extradition and mutual legal assistance in criminal matters, approved by Council Decision 2003/516/EC of June 6, 2003 ([2003] O.J. L181/25) and the Agreement between the European Union and the Republic of Iceland and the Kingdom of Norway on the application of certain provisions of the Convention of May 29, 2000 on Mutual Assistance in Criminal Matters between the Member States of the European Union and the 2001 Protocol thereto, approved by Council Decision 2004/79/EC of December 17, 2003 ([2004] O.J. L26/1).

[75] Such a declaration was made, for example, by 12 Member States with regard to the agreements with the USA on extradition and mutual legal assistance in criminal matters (n.74, *supra*). See Genson, "Les accords d'extradition et d'entraide judiciaire signés le 25 juin 2003 à Washington entre l'Union européenne et les Etats-Unis d'Amérique" (2003) R.M.C.U.E. 427–432.

provisionally to them (EU Treaty, Art. 24(5)). Agreements concluded in accordance with Art. 24 of the EU Treaty are binding on the institutions of the Union (EU Treaty, Art. 24(6)).[76] Such agreements are published in the *Official Journal*, unless the Council decides otherwise.[77] Under Art. 46 of the EU Treaty, the Court of Justice has no jurisdiction to rule on the validity or interpretation of such agreements.[78]

Status under the Constitution. When the EU Constitution enters into **18–024** force, the general rules of the Constitution on the conclusion of international agreements will be applicable to agreements concluded by the Union in CFSP matters. This means that the special procedural features set out in Art. 24 of the EU Treaty will disappear. Since, in principle, the Court of Justice does not have jurisdiction with respect to action taken by the Union within the framework of the CFSP (see para. 18–022), international agreements concluded in that field will not be subject to the jurisdiction of the Court.

---

[76] However, the Agreement between the European Union and NATO on the Security of Information restricts its application as far as the EU is concerned to the Council of the European Union, the Secretary-General/High Representative and the General Secretariat of the Council and the Commission (Agreement, Art. 3; n.74, *supra*).

[77] Council Rules of Procedure, Art. 17(1)(h).

[78] Since the provisions of Art. 24 of the EU Treaty apply to such agreements in the sphere of PJCC, the Court of Justice also has no jurisdiction in regard to them. *cf.* Neuwahl (n.73, *supra*), at 193 (who refers to the possibility of agreeing to judicial review in this respect).

Part VI

THE EXTERNAL RELATIONS OF THE
EUROPEAN UNION

THE POSITION IN INTERNATIONAL LAW OF THE COMMUNITIES AND THE UNION

International position. The European Union has stated the express **19–001** objective of asserting its identity on the international scene (EU Treaty, Art. 2, second indent). In order to secure "cohesive force" for the Union in international relations,[1] the EU Treaty has created a framework for a common foreign and security policy (CFSP, Title V). Nevertheless, the European Communities have been taking part in international transactions pursuant to their respective competences ever since their establishment. The Union has set itself the task of ensuring the consistency of its external activities as a whole in the areas of Community policy and the common foreign and security policy (EU Treaty, Art. 3, second para.).

This part commences with a discussion of the position in international law of the Communities and the Union (this chapter), which is followed by a survey of the external powers of the Communities and of the Union (Chapter 20) and the Community and non-Community procedure for concluding international agreements (Chapter 21). Next, the consistency of the CFSP and Community action is reviewed (Chapter 22). Lastly, the action undertaken by the Union and its Member States *vis-à-vis* the other European States warrants a specific chapter (Chapter 23), since the Union has to be seen in the context of its resolve to "continue the process of creating an ever closer union among the peoples of Europe" (EU Treaty, preamble).

When the EU Constitution enters into force, the distinction between Community and non-Community action of the Union will no longer exist. The Constitution will create a single legal regime for all external action of the Union. Specific rules will however continue to exist for the CFSP. As a result, there will always be a need to ensure consistency between that field of action of the Union and the other areas of its external action.

I. INTERNATIONAL LEGAL PERSONALITY

Communities. By virtue of Art. 281 of the EC Treaty and Art. 184 of the **19–002** EAEC Treaty, both the European Community (EC) and the European

---

[1] See EU Treaty, Art. 11(2).

Atomic Energy Community (EAEC) have legal personality. Just like the Member States, each Community, as a legal person, has the capacity to exercise rights in international legal transactions and enter into obligations over the whole field of its objectives.[2] This means that the Communities may, in principle, conclude agreements with non-member countries and international organisations, be held liable under international law if they breach their obligations and may take action themselves where their rights are infringed. If a Community institution concludes an agreement, the agreement will be binding on the Communities and they will be liable for its performance.[3] The Communities' international capacity is governed by the rules of international law[4]; however, the division of powers as between the Communities and the Member States is a matter of Community law.[5]

19–003 **Union.** The EU Treaty does not expressly endow the European Union with legal personality. In order for an international organisation to have legal personality, it does not necessarily have to be expressly conferred on the organisation by the Treaty establishing it. Legal personality may be inferred from the powers and means whereby the contracting parties endow a given organisation with independent status.[6] In signing the EU Treaty, the Contracting Parties apparently did not intend to confer autonomy on the Union. Accordingly, the Union's objectives can be achieved only through action taken by the Communities and the Member States, either in accordance with the rules of Community law or in the form of action by the Member States and the Community institutions in accordance with the rules of Title V or Title VI of the EU Treaty.[7] However, it is pointed out in the literature that, in pursuing their non-Community activities, the

---

[2] See ECJ, Case 22/70 *Commission v Council* [1971] E.C.R. 263, paras 13–14; ECJ, Joined Cases 3, 4 and 6/76 *Kramer* [1976] E.C.R. 1279, para. 17/18.

[3] ECJ, Case C–327/91 *France v Commission* [1994] E.C.R. I–3641, paras 24–25. For the legal succession to the ECSC, see n.1 to para. 20–001.

[4] See, *inter alia*, the Vienna Convention of March 21, 1986 on the Law of Treaties between States and International Organisations or between International Organisations (para. 17–089, *infra*).

[5] ECJ, Ruling 1/78 *Draft Convention of the International Atomic Energy Agency on the Physical Protection of Nuclear Materials, Facilities and Transports* [1978] E.C.R. 2151, para. 35. See also Lachmann, "International Legal Personality of the EC: Capacity and Competence" (1984) L.I.E.I. 3–21; Groux and Manin, *The European Communities in the International Legal Order* (Office for Official Publications of the EC, Luxembourg, 1985), 163 pp.

[6] Schermers and Blokker, *International Institutional Law* (Martinus Nijhoff, The Hague, 1995), paras 1562–1570, at 976–981.

[7] Pliakos, "La nature juridique de l'Union européenne" (1993) R.T.D.E. 187, at 212–213; for the recognition of legal personality, see Ress, "Democratic Decision-Making in the European Union and the Role of the European Parliament", in Curtin and Heukels (eds), *Institutional Dynamics of European Integration. Essays in Honour of Henry G. Schermers*, Vol.II (Martinus Nijhoff, Dordrecht, 1994), 153, at 156; for a somewhat less categorical view, see Dörr, "Zur Rechtsnatur der Europäischen Union" (1995) EuR. 334–348; Pechstein, "Rechtssubjektivität für die Europäische Union?" (1996) EuR. 137–144; Von Bogdandy, "The Legal Case for Unity: The European Union as a Single Organisation with a Single Legal System" (1999) C.M.L.R. 887–910; Wessel, "The Inside Looking Out: Consistency and Delimitation in EU External Relations" (2000) C.M.L.R. 1135–1171.

Community institutions actually also act as institutions of the Union. This is true especially of the Council. Moreover, the Treaty of Amsterdam introduced in Art. 24 of the EU Treaty the power of the Council to conclude agreements with non-member countries and international organisations. In the first agreements concluded by the Council on behalf of the Union, the EU appears to be indicated as a participating party which is bound by the agreements (see para. 18–007). These factors suggest that the Union must also be regarded as having legal personality under international law.[8]

Constitution. The EU Constitution seeks to clarify this matter. Art. I–7 **19–004** expressly confers legal personality on the European Union that will be the successor of the European Community and the present European Union.[9] The EAEC will continue to exist as a separate entity with legal personality (see para. 4–005).

Membership of international organisations. As already stated, each **19–005** Community (EC and EAEC) has at present the capacity to conclude agreements, including multilateral agreements establishing an international organisation.[10] In some cases, the Community may conclude agreements only together with the Member States (see para. 20–037). It may likewise accede to an international organisation, provided that the statutes of the organisation permit non-States to join.[11] In some instances, the Community has taken the place of its Member States; generally, it becomes a member alongside the Member States, as in the case of certain commodities

---

[8] See to this effect Österdahl, "The EU and its Member States, Other States and International Organisations—The Common European Security and Defence Policy After Nice" (2001) Nordic J.I.L. 341–350; Wessel, "De Europese Unie in de internationale rechtsorde" (2001) Mededelingen van de Nederlandse Vereniging voor Internationaal Recht 11–37. For a cautious view, see Grard, "La condition internationale de l'Union européenne après Nice" (2000) R.A.E. 374, at 375–378. See also Tiilikainen, "To Be or Not to Be? An Analysis of the Legal and Political Elements of Statehood in the EU's External Identity" (2001) E.For.Aff.Rev. 223–241.

[9] For this succession and legal continuity, see Art. IV–438 of the EU Constitution. See Fassbender, "Die Völkerrechtssubjektivität der Europäischen Union nach dem Entwurf des Verfassungsvertrages" (2004) A. Völkerr. 26–43.

[10] ECJ, Opinion 1/76 *Draft Agreement establishing a European laying-up fund for inland waterway vessels* [1977] E.C.R. 741, para. 5. For internal limitations on powers in this connection, see para. 14–065, *supra*.

[11] Various international organisations, particularly those established before the Community, do not allow non-States to be members, but permit the Community to take part in their activities without voting rights as an "observer" or with some similar status. See, for instance, the Council of Europe (resolution of the Committee of Ministers of May 1951); the UN General Assembly (Resolution 3208 (XXIX) of October 11, 1974); the International Labour Organisation (ILO Constitution, Art. 12(2)). For representation at the UN, see the Council's answer of November 30, 2000 to question E–2810/00 (Titford), [2001] O.J. C113E/181. See also the website of the EU delegation to the UN: *www.europa-eu-un.org/*.

agreements,[12] the Food and Agricultural Organisation (FAO)[13] and the World Trade Organisation (WTO).[14] In the event that the Community becomes a member of an international organisation alongside the Member States, that organisation has to decide whether the Community should have voting rights of its own or whether it may exercise the Member States' rights on terms to be determined.[15] In the latter case, before any meeting of the organisation it will require a declaration to be made indicating whether competence lies with the Community or the Member States in respect of a particular item of the agenda and who is to exercise the right to vote.[16] The Community and the Member States have to co-ordinate their positions in advance (see para. 19–009). Where the Community is empowered under Community law to conclude an agreement in the context of the International Labour Organisation but cannot do so itself under the ILO Constitution, it may exercise its external competence through the medium of the Member States acting jointly in the Community's interest.[17]

19–006 **Liability under international law.** The Community is liable for consequences of its international action. A party which has been adversely affected thereby can sometimes obtain redress through Community judicial procedures. The Community institutions may also award it compensation pursuant to their own powers of decision. For its part, the Community is entitled to act where its rights under a treaty are infringed. For instance, it may adopt economic sanctions pursuant to its competence in the sphere of commercial policy (see para. 20–050). However, as a non-State, the Community is not entitled to bring proceedings in the International Court of Justice.[18] A dispute may only be resolved in the manner agreed by the

[12] Barents, "The European Communities and the Commodity Organisations" (1984) 1 L.I.E.I. 77–91.

[13] The Community acceded thereto in 1991. See Frid, "The European Economic Community: A Member of a Specialised Agency of the United Nations" (1993) E.J.I.L. 239–255; Schwob, "L'amendement à l'acte constitutif de la FAO visant à permettre l'admission en qualité de membre des organisations d'intégration économique régionale et la Communauté économique européenne" (1993) R.T.D.E. 1–38.

[14] See para. 20–014, *infra*. See also Leenen, "Participation of the EEC in International Environmental Agreements", and Koers, "The European Economic Community and International Fisheries Organisations" (1984) 1 L.I.E.I. 93–111 and 113–131, respectively.

[15] Govaere, Capiau and Vermeersch, "In-Between Seats: The Participation of the European Union in International Organisations" (2004) E.For.Aff.Rev. 155–187; Sack, "The European Community's Membership of International Organisations" (1995) C.M.L.R. 1227–1256; Neuwahl, "Shared Powers or Combined Incompetence? More on Mixity" (1996) C.M.L.R. 667–687.

[16] ECJ, Case C–25/94 *Commission v Council* [1996] E.C.R. I–1469. See Lenaerts and De Smijter, "The United Nations and the European Union: Living Apart Together" in Wellens (ed.), *International Law: Theory and Practice. Essays in Honour of Eric Suy*, (The Hague, Martinus Nijhoff, 1998) 439, at 443–447.

[17] ECJ, Opinion 2/91 *Convention No 170 of the International Labour Organisation concerning safety in the use of chemicals at work* [1993] E.C.R. I–1061, para. 5.

[18] Art. 34(1) of the Statute of the International Court of Justice, to which all members of the United Nations are party *ipso facto* (UN Charter, Art. 93(1); for the UN Charter, see para. 17–104, *supra*).

Contracting Parties or in accordance with the procedure provided for in the treaty in question, which will generally be based on negotiations or arbitration.[19] Since agreements concluded by the Community are binding on its institutions and on the Member States (EC Treaty, Art. 300(7)), it is incumbent on both the institutions and the Member States to ensure that the obligations arising under such agreements are complied with.[20] In so doing, the Member States fulfil "an obligation not only in relation to the non-member country concerned but also and above all in relation to the Community which has assumed responsibility for the due performance of the agreement".[21] It probably cannot be inferred from this that the Member States are vicariously liable under international law for obligations entered into by the Community.[22]

II. INTERNATIONAL REPRESENTATION

A. DIPLOMATIC RELATIONS OF THE UNION

Accreditations. Non-member countries wishing to maintain permanent **19–007** contacts with the European Union apply to the Union for accreditation of a diplomatic mission. The credentials of heads of missions from third countries accredited to the European Union are presented to the President of the Council and the President of the Commission, who meet for the occasion.[23] The Member State in whose territory the institutions of the Union are established accords such missions the "customary diplomatic immunities and privileges" (Protocol on Privileges and Immunities, Art. 17).[24] In addition to their normal diplomatic functions, those missions often represent their countries on the advisory bodies set up by trade or association agreements concluded with the Communities (see paras 20–009 and 20–019).[25]

---

[19] Groux and Manin (n.5, *supra*), at 161–168.

[20] ECJ, Case 104/81 *Kupferberg* [1982] E.C.R. 3641, para. 11 (for the legal force of agreements concluded by the Community, see para. 17–091, *supra*).

[21] *ibid.*, para. 13. Accordingly, the Commission may bring an action under Art. 226 of the EC Treaty against a Member State which has failed to fulfil its obligations under an agreement concluded by the Community: ECJ, Case C–13/00 *Commission v Ireland* [2002] E.C.R. I–2943, paras 14–20.

[22] Groux and Manin (n.5, *supra*), at 153–156; Manin, "L'article 228, paragraphe 2, du traité C.E.E.", *Etudes de droit des Communautés européennes. Mélanges offerts à P.-H. Teitgen*, (Pedone, Paris, 1984) 289, at 302–304.

[23] Luxembourg Compromise of 28 and January 29, 1966, Part a(3), (1966) 3 Bull.CE, 10. According to the latest information published in this connection, 166 diplomatic missions were accredited to the European Union in 1999. European Commission, General Report on the Activities of the European Union 1999, (Office for Official Publications of the EC, Brussels/Luxembourg, 2000) at 313.

[24] For that Protocol, see para. 10–114, *supra*.

[25] Louis, *The Community Legal Order* (Office for Official Publications of the EC, Brussels/Luxembourg, 1993), at 75–76.

19–008 Delegations. The Treaties do not expressly empower the Union/Communities to open their own diplomatic representations in third countries. The European Parliament purports to derive a "right to send diplomatic representation" from the fact that the Communities have international legal personality.[26] In practice, however, the Union/Communities do not set up diplomatic missions. Nevertheless, pursuant to its power of internal organisation and its power to conduct negotiations on agreements,[27] the Commission has established delegations in more than a hundred and fifty non-member countries and international organisations.[28] Whether or not under an agreement concluded with the Communities, such delegations are generally granted the customary diplomatic privileges and immunities.[29] For its part, the General Secretariat of the Council has set up liaison offices in Geneva and New York in order to maintain contacts with the international organisations based in those cities.

B. REPRESENTATION OF THE COMMUNITIES

19–009 Usual forms. The Treaties set out no general rules on the external representation of the Communities. The way in which the Communities manifest themselves externally coincides with the powers which each institution has to act externally. Accordingly, the Commission virtually always has the right to negotiate agreements which the Communities wish to conclude, even though it is the Council which concludes them.[30] Article 302 of the EC Treaty likewise charges the Commission with ensuring the maintenance of "all appropriate relations" with the organs of the United Nations and its specialised agencies, as well as "such relations as are appropriate" with all international organisations.[31]

In practice, there are various ways in which the Communities may be involved in international discussions. Where international discussions are concerned with subjects which fall within the competence of one of the Communities, a delegation from the Commission will normally attend. In

---

[26] Resolution of November 17, 1960, J.O. 1496/60; see also the resolution of April 14, 1989, [1989] O.J. C120/340.

[27] Sauvignon, "Les Communautés européennes et le droit de légation actif" (1978) R.M.C. 176, at 180; Stein, "External Relations of the European Community: Structure and Process"(1990) *Collected Courses of the Academy of European Law. I*, 1990, 115, at 134.

[28] European Commission, General Report on the Activities of the European Union 2001 (Office for Official Publications of the EC, Brussels/Luxembourg, 2002) at 405 (158 accreditations). See also Brinkhorst, "Permanent Missions of the EC in Third Countries: European Diplomacy in the Making" (1984) 1 L.I.E.I. 23–33.

[29] Groux and Manin (n.5, *supra*), at 36–38. For Commission delegations in the ACP States, see Protocol No 2 annexed to the ACP-EC Partnership Agreement on Privileges and Immunities, [2001] O.J. L317/281.

[30] See EC Treaty, Art. 133(3) and Art. 300(1), and EAEC Treaty, Art. 101, second and third para. s; see, however, EC Treaty, Art. 111(3) (paras 21–004—21–008, *infra*).

[31] The Commission and the Council consult each other on the desirability, the methods and the nature of such relations: Part a(5) of the Luxembourg Compromise (n.23, *supra*).

the event that the discussions also cover subjects within the competence of the Member States, they will generally insist on their own representatives being present. In such case, "unity in the international representation of the Community" requires there to be close co-operation between the Member States and the Community institutions, both in the process of negotiating and concluding agreements and in the fulfilment of the obligations entered into.[32] The Member States are invariably represented alongside the Communities in international organisations whose sphere of action is more broadly defined than the competences of the Communities.[33] In order to take part in the activities of such an organisation, the duty to co-operate, which is incumbent on the Community and its Member States, is reflected in practice in arrangements agreed upon by the Commission and the Council. Such arrangements primarily seek to achieve a common position on the part of the Community and the Member States and to formulate agreements as to how that position is to be represented in the organisation and how voting rights are to be exercised.[34] Accordingly, the Commission or the Presidency will act, depending on whether or not the common position relates principally to a subject coming within the exclusive competence of the Community. A breach of such an arrangement may result in the annulment of the decision by which the institution concerned determined its action in the organisation in question.[35]

In practice, representation is determined in accordance with the division of powers, internal agreements and the political sensitivity of the subject-matter in line with one of the following permutations.[36] In the first place, the Commission (together with officials of the Council) and representatives of the Member States may act in split delegations. The Commission delegation sometimes includes representatives of the Member State holding the Presidency of the Council for the time being (for example, at the General Assembly of the United Nations) or, possibly, representatives of all the Member States. In other cases, a delegation led by

---

[32] ECJ, Opinion 2/91 *Convention No.170 of the International Labour Organisation concerning safety in the use of chemicals at work* [1993] E.C.R. I–1061, para. 36, at I–1083; ECJ, Opinion 1/94 *Agreement establishing the World Trade Organisation* [1994] E.C.R. I–5267, para. 108; ECJ, Opinion 2/00 *Cartagena Protocol* [2001] E.C.R. I–9713, para. 18. See also ECJ, Ruling 1/78 *Draft Convention of the International Atomic Energy Agency on the Physical Protection of Nuclear Materials, Facilities and Transports* [1978] E.C.R. 2151, paras 34–36.

[33] See also where a Member State acts independently in the interest of an overseas territory, para. 19–014.

[34] Such arrangements may be enshrined in the decision by which the Community concludes the relevant international agreement; see, *e.g.* Art. 3 of Council and Commission Decision (98/181/EC, ECSC, Euratom) of September 23, 1997 on the conclusion, by the European Communities, of the Energy Charter Treaty and the Energy Charter Protocol on energy efficiency and related environmental aspects, [1998] O.J. L69/1; Art. 3 of Council Decision (98/216/EC) of March 9, 1998 on the conclusion, on behalf of the European Community, of the United Nations Convention of June 17, 1994 to combat desertification in countries seriously affected by drought and/or desertification, particularly in Africa, [1998] O.J. L83/1.

[35] ECJ, Case C–25/94 *Commission v Council* [1996] E.C.R. I–1469, paras 48–51.

[36] The survey is taken from Groux and Manin (n.5, *supra*), at 42. See also Sack (n.15, *supra*), at 1252–1256.

the Commission and including representatives of all the Member States and Commission and Council officials acts for the Communities and the Member States (for example, in GATT/WTO negotiations).

19–010 Economic and monetary affairs. The EC Treaty does govern the external representation of the Community "as regards issues of particular relevance to economic and monetary union" (Art. 111(4)). In this connection, the Council, acting on a proposal from the Commission and after consulting the ECB, is to decide on the Community's position at international level by a qualified majority vote.[37] The Council is also to decide, on the basis of the same procedure, on the Community's representation in accordance with the allocation of powers laid down in Arts 99 and 105 (Art. 111(4)). In this way the Council can carry out this representation itself or leave it to the Commission, the European Central Bank or, where the power lies with the Member States, to the Presidency of the Council or to those Member States belonging to a particular international organisation.[38]

C. REPRESENTATION OF THE UNION IN CONNECTION WITH ITS NON-COMMUNITY ACTION

19–011 Presidency. In matters coming within the CFSP and police and judicial co-operation in criminal matters (PJCC), the Union is represented by the Presidency of the Council, which expresses the Union's position in international organisations and international conferences (EU Treaty, Art. 18(1) and (2) and Art. 37, second para.). The Presidency is assisted by the Secretary-General of the Council—the High Representative for the CFSP—and, if need be, by the next Member State to hold the Presidency; the Commission is to be "fully associated in [those] tasks" (Art. 18(3) and (4)). Whenever it deems it necessary, the Council may appoint a special representative with a mandate in relation to particular policy issues (Art. 18(5)).[39] When it is necessary to conclude an agreement with one or more States or international organisations in implementation of Title V or Title VI, the Council may authorise the Presidency to open negotiations to that effect (EU Treaty, Art. 24(1) and Art. 38). The diplomatic and consular missions of the Member States and the Commission delegations in third countries and at international conferences, together with their representatives in international organisations, are to co-operate in ensuring

---

[37] See the arrangements relating to implementation of this Treaty provision in the Resolution of the European Council of December 13, 1997 on economic policy co-ordination in stage three of EMU and on Arts 111 and 113 of the EC Treaty ([1998] O.J. C35/1), Part II.

[38] Lebullenger, "La projection externe de la zone euro" (1998) R.T.D.E. 459–478; Weiss, "Kompetenzverteilung in der Währungspolitik und Aussenvertretung des Euro" (2002) EuR. 165–191; Herrmann, "Monetary Sovereignty over the Euro and External Relations of the Euro Area: Competences, Procedures and Practice" (2002) E.For.Aff.Rev. 1–24. For representation by the ECB, see ESCB Statute, Art. 6.

[39] The European Union has already appointed several "special envoys"; see the discussion of the CFSP in para. 20–043, *supra*.

that CFSP measures are complied with (EU Treaty, Art. 20, first para.). In view of the wide scope of "foreign policy" under Title V of the EU Treaty, this procedure covers, in principle, all matters in respect of which the Union acts externally outside the sphere of competence of the Communities. The usual ways in which the Member States and the Communities deal with their international representation in an area of shared competence may be used in order to "associate" the Commission in the CFSP.

Co-operation. Representation of the Union is based completely on **19–012** co-ordination of the existing representations of the Member States and the Communities. Under the second para. of Art. 20 of the EU Treaty, they are to step up their co-operation by exchanging information, carrying out joint assessments and contributing to the implementation of the diplomatic and consular protection of nationals of other Member States in accordance with Art. 20 of the EC Treaty (see para. 12–011). Already in the days of EPC, the Foreign Ministers had agreed on arrangements for co-operation in the form of regular meetings between diplomats and officials both *in situ* and in the Political Committee (now the Political and Security Committee).[40]

Co-ordination. Where not all the Member States are represented in a **19–013** particular international organisation or at a given international conference (and hence the Member State acting as President of the Council is not necessarily represented), the Member States so represented are to co-ordinate their action in any event and keep the others informed (EU Treaty, Art. 19(1), first subpara.). They are also to uphold any common positions which have been adopted, and are committed by any joint actions (EU Treaty, Art. 14(3) and Art. 19(1)). This also holds good for questions relating to PJCC (EU Treaty, Art. 37, second para.). Member States which are permanent Members of the UN Security Council are to ensure the defence of the Union's positions and interests "without prejudice to their responsibilities under the provisions of the United Nations Charter" (EU Treaty, Art. 19(2), second subpara.). This would appear to authorise those Member States to adopt a position independently in respect of matters on which the Union has not yet reached a common position where the Security Council is required to reach an urgent decision.[41]

---

[40] Decision of the Ministers of Foreign Affairs, meeting within the framework of European Political Co-operation, of February 28, 1986 (1986) 1 EPC Bulletin doc. 86/090, 108, II.

[41] Art. 103 of the UN Charter provides that the obligations of Members of the United Nations under the Charter are to prevail over their obligations under any other international agreement. Those obligations include "prompt and effective action by the United Nations", in respect of which Art. 24 of the UN Charter provides that "primary responsibility for the maintenance of international peace and security" is conferred on the Security Council. See Eaton, "Common Foreign and Security Policy" in O'Keeffe and Twomey (eds), *Legal Issues of the Maastricht Treaty* (Chancery, London, 1994), 215, at 223. For the priority of those obligations over Community obligations, see Art. 297 of the EC Treaty (para. 9–001, *supra*).

19–014 Overseas territories. Where an overseas territory comes under the jurisdiction of one of the Member States or the foreign relations of such a territory are taken care of by a Member State, in principle the representation of the Union also covers that territory.[42] However, in the case of certain territories, application of the EC Treaty is ruled out or subject to special arrangements.[43] In certain circumstances, divergences may arise between the interests of the Union and those of overseas countries and territories referred to in Art. 299(3) and (6)(a) and (b) of the EC Treaty. If the Council does not succeed in reconciling those interests, the Member States concerned may act separately in the interests of the overseas countries and territories concerned, "without affecting the Community's interests".[44] Where such a divergence of interests is likely to occur, the Member State concerned is to give notice to the Council and the Commission and make it clear that it is acting in the interests of an overseas territory.[45]

D. REPRESENTATION OF THE UNION UNDER THE EU CONSTITUTION

19–015 Towards single representation. As mentioned above, the EU Constitution will merge the Community and the European Union into a new European Union with legal personality. Article III–328 of the EU Constitution provides for "Union delegations" which are to represent the Union in third countries and at international organisations. Those delegations will be placed under the authority of the Union Minister for Foreign Affairs and act in close co-operation with Member States' diplomatic and consular missions.

It should be noted, however, that the rules governing the representation of the Union will differ depending on whether external action within the framework of the CFSP is involved or external action in one of the other policy areas of the Union. In CFSP matters, the Union is to be represented by the Union Minister for Foreign Affairs, who is to conduct political dialogue with third parties on the Union's behalf and express the Union's position in international organisations and at international conferences (EU Constitution, Art. III–296). The Minister will also chair the Council for Foreign Affairs (see para. 10–054). Member States will continue to be under a duty to co-ordinate their international action and to uphold the Union's positions, even in organisations or conferences in which not all

---

[42] See the territorial scope of the Treaties, para. 8–001, *supra*.

[43] para. 8–002, *supra*.

[44] Declaration (No.25) annexed to the EU Treaty on the representation of the interests of the overseas countries and territories referred to in Art. 227 [now Art. 299], para. (3) and [the former] para. (5)(a) and (b) of the EC Treaty. Besides overseas countries and territories covered by the association arrangements of Part Four of the EC Treaty, it used to cover Hong Kong and East Timor. However, Gibraltar, the Channel Islands and the Isle of Man are not covered. See Eaton (n.41 *supra*), at 223. According to the Declaration, it also applies to Macau.

[45] Declaration (No.25) annexed to the EU Treaty.

Member States participate (EU Constitution, Art. III–305). The Union Minister for Foreign Affairs will be responsible for organising that co-ordination. Moreover, Member States which are represented in international organisations or conferences in which not all Member States participate must keep the non-participating Member States and the Union Minister for Foreign Affairs informed of any matter of common interest. This also applies to the Member States which are members of the United Nations Security Council "without prejudice to their responsibilities under the United Nations Charter".[46] Alongside the Minister of Foreign Affairs, the President of the European Council will represent the Union in CFSP matters "at his or her level and in that capacity". This will probably be the case where the Union needs to be represented *vis-à-vis* foreign Heads of State or Government. In any event, the representation of the Union by the President of the European Council may not encroach upon the powers of the Union Minister for Foreign Affairs (Art. I–22(2), second subpara.).

In matters not falling within the framework of the CFSP, the present situation remains unchanged in so far as the EU Constitution does not expressly allocate the power of external representation.[47] To the extent that the Commission continues to have the power to establish contacts with international organisations and to negotiate agreements with third countries and organisations, it will retain its present powers of external representation. However, the general rules of the EU Constitution concerning international agreements leave it to the Council to choose a "negotiator" (see para. 21–015). In those matters where the Union shares competence with the Member States, the Union will have to have recourse to one of the various methods mentioned in para. 19–009 for organising its external representation.

The Union Minister of Foreign Affairs will be responsible in the Commission for its responsibilities in the sphere of external relations and for co-ordinating other aspects of the Union's external action. This means that, at the external level, the Union Minister for Foreign Affairs is to act in a dual capacity. On the one hand, the Minister will conduct the CFSP pursuant to the powers which the Constitution confers directly on him or her. On the other hand, the Minister will act as a Member of the Commission pursuant to the powers which the Constitution confers on the Commission (see also para. 10–071). Accordingly, both the Minister and the Commission will be responsible for establishing all appropriate forms of co-operation with the organs of the United Nations and the European international organisations.[48] In his or her dual capacity, the Union

---

[46] EU Constitution, Art. III–305(2), second para. (*cf.* para. 19–013, *supra*). When the Union has defined a position on a subject which is on the United Nations Security Council agenda, those Member States which sit on the Security Council are to request that the Union Minister for Foreign Affairs be asked to present the Union's position (Art. III–305(2), third subpara.).

[47] Art. III–196 provides for separate rules to apply in monetary matters (*cf.* para. 19–010).

[48] See Art. III–327 of the EU Constitution.

Minister for Foreign Affairs will be assisted by a European External Action Service, comprising officials from relevant departments of the General Secretariat of the Council and of the Commission as well as staff seconded from national diplomatic services.[49]

---

[49] Art. III–296(3) of the EU Constitution.

CHAPTER 20

THE EXTERNAL POWERS OF THE COMMUNITIES AND THE UNION

External powers. The Union's "external" policy is based on the external **20–001** powers of the Communities and action by the institutions and the Member States pursuant to the common foreign and security policy (CFSP). As far as the Community powers are concerned, the EC Treaty does not provide the Community with a general legal basis authorising it to act *vis-à-vis* non-member countries. The EC Treaty merely contains a number of specific external powers—each with its own objectives—the most important of which are those relating to the common commercial policy, the power to conclude association agreements and the powers with regard to development co-operation.[1] Within the confines of the powers conferred on it by the EAEC Treaty, however, the Community has a general power to conclude international agreements (see EAEC Treaty, Art. 101, first para.). The CFSP does not consist of a list of powers, but formulates aims and instruments with a view to pursuing a "foreign policy" alongside and in connection with Community action.

Both the Community's external policy and the Union's foreign policy consist, on the one hand, of "autonomous" measures of the Community or the Union having effects for non-member countries and their nationals and, on the other, of treaties and agreements concluded with non-member countries or international organisations ("contractual" acts).

The EU Constitution brings the external powers of the Union together in one Title relating to "the Union's external action". It sets out the principles

---

[1] See EC Treaty, Art. 26 (Common Custom Tariff), Art. 34(3), first subpara. (agriculture), Arts 57–60 (movements of capital and payments), Art. 71(1)(a) (transport), Art. 111 (monetary policy), Arts 131–134 (common commercial policy), Art. 149(3) (education), Art. 150(3) (vocational training), Art. 151(3) (culture), Art. 152(3) (public health), Art. 155(3) (trans-European networks), Arts 164(b) and 170 (research and technological development), Art. 174(4) (environment), Arts 177–181 (development co-operation), Art. 181a (economic, financial and technical co-operation), Arts 302–304 (relations with international organisations) and Art. 310 (association agreements). *cf.* Art. 71 *et seq.* of the ECSC Treaty (commercial policy); see ECJ, Opinion 1/94 *Agreement establishing the World Trade Organisation* [1994] E.C.R. I–5267, paras 25–27. From July 24, 2002, the European Community took over the rights and obligations arising under the international agreements concluded by the ECSC with non-member countries; see Decision 2002/595/EC of the Representatives of the Governments of the Member States, meeting within the Council, of July 19, 2002 and Council Decision 2002/596/EC of July 19, 2002 on the consequences of the expiry of the Treaty establishing the European Coal and Steel Community (ECSC) on the international agreements concluded by the ECSC, [2002] O.J. L194/35 and 36, respectively.

which are to guide the Union's external action and the objectives to be pursued.[2] At the same time, the EU Constitution underscores the need to ensure consistency not only between the different areas of its external action, but also between those areas and its other policies.[3] It will be up to the European Council to identify the strategic interests and objectives of the CFSP and other areas of the Union's external action.[4]

I. THE COMMON COMMERCIAL POLICY

A. SCOPE

20–002 Trade in goods. Following the abolition of national customs duties and charges of equivalent effect, the Council introduced a Common Customs Tariff and uniform customs rules for goods from or destined for non-member countries which are processed in the Community (see para. 5–095). In order to prevent Member States from putting their own undertakings at an advantage or otherwise introducing inequalities in the trade field, Title IX of the EC Treaty provides for the common market to be underpinned by a common commercial policy.

By way of measures required to be based on "uniform principles", Art. 133(1) of the EC Treaty mentions both autonomous measures (changes in tariff rates, achievement of uniformity in liberalisation measures, export policy and measures to protect trade) and the conclusion of tariff and trade agreements. This list, which is not exhaustive, does not rule out other methods of regulating external trade.[5] For the common commercial policy not to become nugatory in the course of time, it was considered not to be confined to trade liberalisation measures, which was the dominant idea at the time when the EEC Treaty was drafted, but also to encompass "more highly developed mechanisms".[6] Such mechanisms include commodity agreements, designed to regulate world trade and stabilise developing countries' export revenue,[7] and a system of generalised preferences for developing countries.[8] The fact that a measure takes account of environmental protection objectives does not remove it from the sphere of commercial policy.[9] Such measures will fall within the common commercial policy even if they may have effects on economic policy or other policy areas for which the Member States have competence.[10] Specific clauses in a

---

[2] EU Constitution, Art. III–292(1) and (2). For these principles, see Richardson, "The European Union in the World—a Community of Values" (2002) Fordham I.L.J. 12–35.

[3] EU Constitution, Art. III–292(3).

[4] *ibid.*, Art. III–293.

[5] ECJ, Opinion 1/78 *International Agreement on Natural Rubber* [1979] E.C.R. 2871, para. 45.

[6] *ibid.*, para. 44.

[7] *ibid.*, paras 42–44.

[8] ECJ, Case 45/86 *Commission v Council* [1987] E.C.R. 1493, paras 17–20. For that system, see para. 20–026, *infra*.

[9] ECJ, Case C–62/88 *Greece v Council* [1990] E.C.R. I–1527, paras 18–20.

[10] Opinion 1/78 *International Agreement on Natural Rubber* [1979] E.C.R. 2871, para. 49.

given agreement which affect the competence of the Member States but are of a subsidiary or ancillary nature do not alter the agreement's nature as a commercial policy agreement.[11] The Court of Justice takes the view that the common commercial policy may not be interpreted restrictively on the ground that to do so would risk causing disturbances in intra-Community trade by reason of the disparities which would then exist in certain sectors of economic relations with non-member countries.[12]

Accordingly, Art. 133 of the EC Treaty constitutes the legal basis for autonomous and contractual acts of the Community which specifically regulate trade, unless they are expressly contemplated by other provisions of the EC Treaty, such as Art. 26 (customs tariff) or Arts 179–181 (development co-operation). In addition, any act whose principal characteristic is its influence on the volume or flow of trade must be based on Art. 113.[13]

Trade in services and intellectual property. The common commercial 20–003 policy is not confined to the external protection of the customs union. International trade in services is increasingly accounting for a greater share than trade in goods. In the context of the GATT Uruguay Round, the Community and the Member States conducted negotiations on agreements for liberalising trade in goods and services and on trade-related aspects of intellectual property (see paras 20–011 et seq.). In an opinion, the Court of Justice has made it clear that Art. 133(1)–(4) does not cover all aspects of those agreements.[14] The Court held that those provisions of the EC Treaty covered services supplied across frontiers where neither the provider nor the recipient of the services moved to the other's country, but not services provided through the presence of natural persons or a commercial presence in the recipient's State or the case where the recipient travels to the provider's country.[15] As far as protection of intellectual property rights was

---

[11] *ibid.*, para. 56.

[12] *ibid.*, para. 45. For the differing scope attributed by the Commission and the Council to the common commercial policy, see *ibid.*, paras 38–39, and ECJ, Case 45/86 *Commission v Council* [1987] E.C.R. 1493.

[13] See the compromise view put forward by Ehlermann, "The Scope of Art. 113 of the EEC Treaty", *Etudes de droit des Communautés européennes. Mélanges offerts à P.-H. Teitgen* (Pedone, Paris, 1984), 145, at 152–156; Bourgeois, "Art. 113", in von der Groeben, Thiesing, Ehlermann (eds), *Kommentar zum EWG-Vertrag* (Nomos, Baden-Baden, 1991), at 3174. For an application of this principle, see ECJ, Opinion 1/94 *Agreement establishing the World Trade Organisation* [1994] E.C.R. I–5267, paras 28–34.

[14] ECJ, Opinion 1/94 *Agreement establishing the World Trade Organisation* [1994] E.C.R. I–5267; see Auvret-Finck (1995) R.T.D.E. 322–336; Bourgeois (1995) C.M.L.R. 763–787; Van Nuffel (1995) Col.J.E.L. 338–354; see also Dutheil de la Rochère, "L'ère des compétences partagées: A propos de l'étendue des compétences extérieures de la Communauté européenne" (1995) R.M.C.U.E. 461–470; Pescatore, "Opinion 1/94 on 'conclusion' of the WTO-Agreement: Is there an escape from a programmed disaster?" (1999) C.M.L.R. 387–405.

[15] *ibid.*, paras 44–47.

concerned, only measures designed to prevent the import of counterfeit goods came within the ambit of the common commercial policy.[16]

The Treaty of Amsterdam empowered the Council, acting unanimously, to extend the application of Art. 133 to international negotiations and agreements on services and intellectual property in so far as they were not already covered thereby.[17] Its scope was not extended until the amendments made by the Treaty of Nice, which provide that provisions relating to the common commercial policy are also applicable to the negotiation and conclusion of agreements in the fields of trade in services—regardless of whether or not the provider or the recipient of the services move—and the commercial aspects of intellectual property (EC Treaty, Art. 133(5)).[18] According to Art. 133(6) of the EC Treaty, international agreements relating to services in the transport sector do not come under the common commercial policy, but remain subject to the provisions of the EC Treaty relating to transport.[19] The Treaty confirms the principle that the Council may not conclude an agreement in the external sphere if it includes provisions which would go beyond the Community's internal powers, in particular by leading to harmonisation of the laws or regulations of the Member States in an area for which the Treaty rules out such harmonisation.[20] The second subpara. of Art. 133(6) mentions "in this regard" areas in which the Community has "shared competence" with the Member States: cultural and audiovisual services, educational services, and social and human health services.[21] The Council, acting unanimously on a proposal from the Commission and after consulting the European

---

[16] *ibid.*, paras 54–60.

[17] Blin, "L'article 113 CE après Amsterdam" (1998) R.M.C.U.E. 447–456; Neframi, "Quelques réflexions sur la réforme de la politique commerciale par le traité d'Amsterdam: le maintien du *statu quo* et l'unité de la répresentation internationale de la Communauté" (1998) C.D.E. 137–159. For a critical view of the utility of this power, see Dashwood, "External Relations Provisions of the Amsterdam Treaty" (1998) C.M.L.R. 1019, at 1021–1023.

[18] See Krenzler and Pitschas, "Progress or Stagnation?: The Common Commercial Policy After Nice" (2001) E.For.Aff.Rev. 291–313 (for the German version, see (2001) EuR. 442–461); Grard, "La condition internationale de l'Union européenne après Nice" (2000) R.A.E. 374–388); Vincent, "Les relations entre l'Union européenne et l'Organisation mondiale du commerce: du nouveau pour le praticien?" (2001) J.T.D.E. 105–110; Hermann, "Common Commercial Policy After Nice: Sisyphus Would Have Done a Better Job" (2002) C.M.L.R. 7–29; Neframi, "La politique commerciale commune selon le traité de Nice" (2001) C.D.E. 605–646.

[19] EC Treaty, Art. 133(6), third subpara. (referring to Title V of Part Three and Art. 300 of the EC Treaty). This exception confirms the case law of the Court of Justice in Opinion 1/94: ECJ, Opinion 1/94 *Agreement establishing the World Trade Organisation* [1994] E.C.R. I–5267, paras 48–49. Commercial policy measures may concern transport services if that aspect constitutes a necessary ancillary aspect of those measures: *ibid.*, para. 51.

[20] EC Treaty, Art. 133(6), first subpara. For areas in which the Treaty excludes such harmonisation (*e.g.* aspects of education and culture), see para. 5–013, *supra.*

[21] It should be noted in this connection, however, that in so far as a trade agreement results in harmonisation in areas where harmonisation is expressly precluded internally, the relevant external competence is vested according to the first subpara. of Art. 133(6) entirely in the Member States.

Parliament, may extend the application of Art. 133 to international negotiations and agreements on other aspects of intellectual property in so far as they are not covered by Art. 133(5) (EC Treaty, Art. 133(7)).

Exclusive competence. The definition of the common commercial policy is **20–004** of great importance for the external policy of the Community institutions and the Member States. This is because the Council is entitled to adopt autonomous and contractual commercial policy measures by a qualified majority vote (EC Treaty, Art. 133(4)). What is more, the common commercial policy—at least as regards goods—constitutes an area of competence which is vested exclusively in the Community and therefore excludes in principle any national measures from the outset.[22] Negotiations with one or more States or international organisations are conducted by the Commission in consultation with a special committee after the Council has authorised the Commission to open the necessary negotiations and has issued the necessary guidelines (EC Treaty, Art. 133(3)).[23] For the rest, the "relevant provisions" of Art. 300 apply (see para. 21–002 *et seq.*).

Nevertheless, the Court of Justice has acknowledged that there are situations in which Member States are entitled to take part in the negotiation and conclusion of a trade agreement alongside the Community.[24] The Member States may participate in an agreement where financing constitutes an essential element of the scheme established thereby and is to be borne out of their budgets.[25] Furthermore, national commercial policy measures are permissible by virtue of a "specific authorisation" of the Community.[26] In this way, the Council authorised the Member States

---

[22] ECJ, Opinion 1/75 *Draft Understanding on a Local Cost Standard drawn up under the auspices of the OECD* [1975] E.C.R. 1355 (quoted in para. 5–022, *supra*).

[23] The Treaty of Nice added as safeguards that the Commission must report regularly to the special committee on the progress of negotiations and that the Council and the Commission are responsible for ensuring that the agreements negotiated are compatible with internal Community policies and rules (EC Treaty, Art. 133(3), first and second subparas). See Krenzler and Pitschas (n.18, *supra*), at 448–450.

[24] Member States are also entitled to continue negotiations which they started at a time when they still had competence in the relevant field where a new distribution of powers as between the Community and the Member States threatens to jeopardise the successful outcome of the negotiations (ECJ, Case 22/70 *Commission v Council* [1971] E.C.R. 263, paras 86–90) or where their participation is required in order to secure the Community's participation in the relevant agreement (ECJ, Joined Cases 3, 4 and 6/76 *Kramer* [1976] E.C.R. 1279, paras 34–44/45).

[25] ECJ, Opinion 1/78 *International Agreement on Natural Rubber* [1979] E.C.R. 2871, para. 60.

[26] ECJ, Case 41/76 *Donckerwolcke* [1976] E.C.R. 1921, para. 32. For a controversial application of this principle, see ECJ, Case 174/84 *Bulk Oil v Sun International* [1986] E.C.R. 559, paras 31–33 (see the discussion of exclusive competence in para. 5–026, *supra*). Another application may be found in the Member States' power to adopt, by way of derogation from the Community export rules, measures restricting the export of dual-use goods: see para. 20–007, *infra*.

on a regular basis to renew or maintain certain bilateral agreements which they had concluded before the end of the transitional period.[27]

As regards agreements relating to trade in services and the commercial aspects of intellectual property, Art. 133 provides for certain decisions not to be taken by a qualified majority vote.[28] First, by way of derogation from Art. 133(4), the Council decides by unanimity in two cases: where an agreement includes provisions for which unanimity is required for the adoption of internal rules or where it relates to a field in which the Community has not yet exercised the powers conferred upon it by the Treaty by adopting internal rules (EC Treaty, Art. 133(5), second subpara.). Secondly, the Council decides by unanimous vote on "horizontal" agreements, that is to say, agreements which, alongside trade in services or commercial aspects of intellectual property, concern matters covered by the second subpara. of para. 5 or the second subpara. of para. 6 of Art. 133 (see para. 20–003).[29]

Unlike in the case of the common commercial policy relating to goods,[30] Community competence in respect of agreements on trade in services and the commercial aspects of intellectual property is not exclusive. Accordingly, in these areas the EC Treaty confirms the competence of the Member States to maintain and conclude agreements with third countries or international organisations in so far as such agreements comply with Community law and other relevant international agreements (EC Treaty, Art. 133(5), fourth subpara.). This means that the external action of the Member States is limited only if the Community has already adopted internal or external measures in the relevant fields or when it adopts such measures.[31] In addition, as far as trade in cultural and audiovisual services, educational services, and social and human health services is concerned, Art. 133(6) expressly declares that agreements relating thereto fall within the shared competence of the Community and its Member States. Where a

---

[27] Council Decision 69/494 of December 16, 1969 on the progressive standardisation of agreements concerning commercial relations between Member States and third countries and on the negotiation of Community agreements ([1969](II) English O.J. Spec. Ed. 603); the authorisation set out therein was renewed most recently by Council Decision 2001/855/EC of November 15, 2001 ([2001] O.J. L320/13).

[28] Qualified majority voting remains the rule, however, for agreements on the transborder provision of services and protection against the importation of counterfeit goods, which, according to the case law, come under Art. 133(1)–(4). For decision-making under paras 5 and 6, which were added by the Treaty of Nice, see Krenzler and Pitschas (n.18, *supra*), at 450–454.

[29] This is so even if the matter which may result in decision-taking by unanimous vote is only ancillary: Krenzler and Pitschas (n.18, *supra*), at 454.

[30] This includes agreements on crossborder trade in services and protection against the import of counterfeit goods (see n.28, *supra*).

[31] See para. 5–023, *supra*. In any event, international agreements concluded by the Community are binding on the Member States by virtue of Art. 300(7) of the EC Treaty (see para. 17–091, *supra*).

field falls with the competence of both the Community and the Member States, the Community's external action is categorised as mixed (see para. 21–016). This means that an agreement may come about only where it is concluded jointly by the Community and the Member States. Consequently, in addition to a Community decision (whether or not taken by a unanimous vote in the Council), the consent of all the Member States is required.[32]

Derogations. As long as all aspects of the common commercial policy are **20–005** not subject to uniform rules, disparities between national legislation may result in trade from or to the Community being concentrated in particular Member States or may bring about economic difficulties in some Member States. In such circumstances, the Commission may recommend co-operation between Member States and, where appropriate, authorise Member States to take the "necessary protective measures" subject to certain conditions (EC Treaty, Art. 134, first para.).[33] Because such authorisation constitutes not only an exception to the common commercial policy, but also a departure from the rule that there must be equal treatment of products coming from third countries which are in free circulation in Member States (EC Treaty, Art. 23(2)), it must be strictly interpreted in order to prevent the Member State concerned from introducing a measure of effect equivalent to a quantitative restriction.[34] In case of urgency, the Commission may authorise a Member State to take the necessary measures itself and inform the other Member States afterwards. The Commission is still entitled to ask the Member State concerned to abolish or amend such measures (EC Treaty, Art. 134, second para.).

Changes under the Constitution. The EU Constitution will clarify the **20–006** scope of the common commercial policy in so far as Art. III–315(1) refers to agreements relating to trade in services, the commercial aspects of intellectual property and foreign direct investment as areas of the common commercial policy. One innovation introduced by the EU Constitution lies in the fact that it provides that "European laws shall establish the measures defining the framework for implementing the common commercial policy"; in other words, measures are to be adopted by the European Parliament and the Council under the co-decision procedure (Art. III–315(2)). The general rules of Art. III–325 of the EU Constitution will apply to the

---

[32] Art. 133(6), second subpara., confirms these principles in the case of agreements relating to trade in cultural and audiovisual services, educational services, and social and human health services and, as far as the Community decision-making procedure is concerned, refers to Art. 300 of the EC Treaty (see para. 21–002 *et seq.*).

[33] For the applicable procedure, see Commission Decision 87/433/EEC of July 22, 1987 on surveillance and protective measures which Member States may be authorised to take pursuant to Art. 115 [now Art. 134] of the EC Treaty, [1987] O.J. L238/26.

[34] ECJ, Case 41/76 *Donckerwolcke* [1976] E.C.R. 1921, paras 29 and 38.

negotiation and conclusion of agreements with third countries or international organisations. Since the ordinary legislative procedure will apply for the adoption of internal measures, this means that the Council will decide by qualified majority after obtaining the consent of the European Parliament. The Commission is to conduct the negotiations pursuant to an authorisation from the Council (Art. III–315(3)). In some areas, however, the EU Constitution requires the Council to decide by unanimity on the negotiation or conclusion of international agreements. In the first place, this will apply to agreements in the fields of trade in services, the commercial aspects of intellectual property and foreign direct investment, where such agreements include provisions for which unanimity is required for the adoption of internal rules.[35] In addition, unanimity is required in the field of trade in cultural and audiovisual services where an agreement might prejudice the Union's cultural and linguistic diversity, and likewise in the field of trade in social, education or health services where an agreement might seriously disturb the national organisation of such services and prejudice the responsibility of Member States to deliver them.[36] It will no longer be possible for the Council to extend the scope of the common commercial policy to those aspects of intellectual property protection that are not yet covered. External action of the Union in those areas will have to be based on another provision of the Constitution.[37]

Unlike Art. 133 of the EC Treaty, which does not regard all areas of the common commercial policy as coming under the exclusive competence of the Community, Art. I–13 of the EU Constitution regards the entire field of the common commercial policy as constituting an exclusive competence of the Union. Article III–315(6) of the EU Constitution provides that the exercise of competence in this field may not affect the delimitation of competence between the Union and the Member States. This seems to confirm the principle that any external action of the Union in the field of the common commercial policy is to respect the restrictions which apply to the action of the Union at the internal level, for example, in terms of voting requirements in the Council. Accordingly, external action of the Union in the field of the common commercial policy may not lead to any harmonisation of national law where the Constitution rules out any such harmonisation.[38]

---

[35] EU Constitution, Art. III–315(4), second subpara. A comparison with Art. 133(5) of the EC Treaty shows that unanimity will no longer be required solely because the Union seeks to conclude an agreement in an area where it has not yet adopted internal measures or where a "horizontal" agreement is involved (*cf.* para. 20–004, *supra*).

[36] EU Constitution, Art. III–315(4), third subpara. Compared to Art. 133(5) of the EC Treaty, this means that unanimity will no longer be required for any single agreement that affects cultural, audiovisual, educational and social and human health services "horizontally" (*cf.* para. 20–004, *supra*).

[37] *e.g.* the "flexibility clause set out in Art. I–18 or the legal basis for intellectual property laid down in Art. III–176 of the EU Constitution.

[38] EU Constitution, Art. III–315(6).

B. AUTONOMOUS MEASURES

Import and export regime. Alongside the Common Customs Tariff, the **20–007** Council has adopted common rules for imports[39] and exports.[40]

Initially, the import rules allowed Member States to maintain quantitative restrictions in respect of some products. The rules which the Council adopted in March 1994 liberalised imports and provided only for potential supervisory and safeguard measures on the part of the Community. Exceptional rules apply to the (former) state-trading countries. In particular, quantitative restrictions and a surveillance system are in force for products from China.[41] Neither do the general import rules apply to textile products from third countries where imports are either governed by bilateral agreements concluded by the Community with countries accepting "voluntary" limitations on exports[42] or come under a specific import regime.[43] A special import regime has been introduced on the basis of Art. 133 of the EC Treaty in order to allow manufacturers to bring certain key medicines onto the market only in developing countries at prices lower than those in developed countries. Under this regime, the import of such "tiered priced" products into the Community is prohibited.[44]

The Community export rules provide that, in principle, exportation to third countries is free. However, they do allow Member States to apply restrictions in their trade relations with third countries in order to protect the interests listed in Art. 30 of the EC Treaty as justifying restrictions on intra-Community trade in goods.[45] Although the Member States have a degree of discretion, for instance in estimating a risk to their national security, such restrictions on freedom of exportation may not exceed what is appropriate and necessary in order to protect the interest in question.[46] A

---

[39] Council Regulation (EC) No. 3285/94 of December 22, 1994 on the common rules for imports and repealing Council Regulation (EC) No. 518/94, ([1994] O.J. L349/53). That regulation adjusted the rules set out in Regulation No. 518/94 of March 7, 1994 in the light of the Community's obligations under the 1994 Agreement establishing the World Trade Organisation: para. 20–011, *infra*.

[40] Regulation 2603/69 of the Council of December 20, 1969 establishing common rules for exports, [1969](II) O.J. English Spec. Ed. 590.

[41] Council Regulation 519/94 of March 7, 1994 on common rules for imports from certain third countries and repealing Regulations (EEC) Nos 1765/82, 1766/82 and 3420/83, [1994] O.J. L67/89.

[42] Galloway, "L'achèvement du marché intérieur pour le régime à l'importation des produits textiles dans la Communauté: politique de forteresse ou de la dissuasion" (1994) R.M.C.U.E. 362–371. Internally, the Commission manages the import regime in accordance with Council Regulation (EEC) No. 3030/93 of October 12, 1993, [1993] O.J. L275/1.

[43] Council Regulation (EC) No. 517/94 of March 7, 1994 on common rules for imports of textile products from certain third countries not covered by bilateral agreements, protocols or other arrangements, or by other specific Community import rules, [1994] O.J. L67/1.

[44] Council Regulation (EC) No. 953/2003 of May 26, 2003 to avoid trade diversion into the European Union of certain key medicines, [2003] O.J. L135/5.

[45] Regulation No. 2603/69 (n.40, *supra*), Arts 1 and 11.

[46] See ECJ, Case C–70/94 *Werner* [1995] E.C.R. I–3189, paras 8–29; ECJ, Case C–83/94 *Leifer* [1995] E.C.R. I–3231, paras 7–30 (dual-use goods).

Member State may no longer rely on this exception if the necessary protection of the interests in question is already ensured by a Community measure (*e.g.* a measure imposing sanctions).[47] At the same time, Member States must place trust in each other as far as concerns export checks made by other Member States and, where necessary, co-operate with other Member States and the Commission.[48] As far as goods which may be used for both civil and military purposes (dual-use goods) are concerned, the Council has now adopted Community rules on such export checks.[49]

Turning to agricultural products account must be taken of the instruments provided for under the common agricultural policy (see paras 5–187 *et seq.*).

20–008 **Protective measures.** In accordance with the rules agreed in the context of GATT and of the WTO, the Council has drawn up instruments under Art. 133 of the EC Treaty with a view to taking protective measures in respect of dumped or subsidised imports: products which are imported to the Community for an export price below their normal value (dumping) or whose export is subsidised in the country of origin, may have an anti-dumping or countervailing duty imposed on them where the marketing of the products concerned causes producers in the Community to suffer injury.[50] The Commission investigates whether dumping or subsidies are involved, together with the question of injury, and may impose a provisional duty where the Community interest so requires. Subsequently, the Council may impose a definitive duty within a specific time-limit,

---

[47] ECJ, Case C–124/95 *Centro-Com* [1997] E.C.R. I–81, para. 46.

[48] *ibid.*, paras 49 and 52.

[49] Council Regulation (EC) No. 1334/2000 of June 22, 2000 setting up a Community regime for the control of exports of dual-use items and technology, [2000] O.J. L159/1. See Karpenstein, "Die neue Dual-Use Verordnung" (2000) Eu.Z.W. 677–680; Koutrakos, "The Reform of Common Rules on Exports of Dual-Use Goods under the Law of the European Union" (2000) E.J.L.Ref 167–189; Hohmann, "Neufassung der Dual-Use Verordnung: Änderung für die Exportwirtschaft und für global agierende Dienstleistungsanbieter" (2002) Europäisches Wirtschafts und Steuerrecht 70–76. Previously there was an "integrated regime" consisting of a CFSP decision and an EC regulation (para. 22–007, *infra*); before that, such goods came within the general derogation clause of the Community export rules.

[50] Council Regulation (EC) No. 384/96 of December 22, 1995 on protection against dumped imports from countries not members of the European Community ([1996] O.J. L56/1, amended by Council Regulation (EC) No. 905/98 of April 27, 1998, [1998] O.J. L128/18) and Council Regulation (EC) No. 2026/97 of March 8, 2004 on protection against subsidised imports from countries not members of the European Community ([1997] O.J. L288/1), both recently amended by Regulation (EC) No. 461/2004 of March 8, 2004, [2004] O.J. L77/12. See Vander Schueren, "New Anti-Dumping Rules and Practice: Wide Discretion held on a Tight Leash?" (1996) C.M.L.R. 271–297; Stanbrook and Bentley, *Dumping and Subsidies* (Kluwer Law International, The Hague, 1996), 441 pp.; Bourgeois (ed.), *Subsidies and International Trade* (Kluwer, Deventer, 1991), 214 pp.

whereby a Commission proposal shall be deemed adopted unless the Council decides by a simple majority to reject it.[51]

In 1984, the Council introduced, also under Art. 133 of the EC Treaty, a "new commercial policy instrument", which enables the Community to take action against illicit commercial practices.[52] Following the conclusion of the Agreement establishing the World Trade Organisation in 1994 (see para. 20–011), the Council replaced that instrument by Regulation No.3286/94, which enables the Community to enforce its rights under international trade rules, in particular those established under the auspices of the World Trade Organisation.[53] Under the procedures laid down in that regulation, the Community may initiate, pursue and terminate international dispute settlement proceedings in the area of the common commercial policy. A further regulation affords the means for acting against goods infringing certain intellectual property rights.[54] The Community also provides protection against "extra-territorial" sanctions, whereby third countries affect activities of persons coming under the jurisdiction of Member States.[55]

---

[51] Arts 7 and 9 of Regulation 384/96 (as amended in 2004). Where the import of particular products is unnecessarily restricted by a combination of anti-dumping measures or anti-subsidy measures with safeguard tariff measures which may be imposed under Regulations Nos 519/94 (n.41, *supra*) and 3285/94 (n.39, *supra*) in order to obtain protection against sharply increased imports, the Council, acting by simple majority, may adjust the measures in question by virtue of Council Regulation (EC) No. 452/2003 of March 6, 2003 on measures that the Community may take in relation to the combined effect of anti-dumping or anti-subsidy measures with safeguard measures ([2003] O.J. L69/3).

[52] Council Regulation (EEC) No. 2641/84 of September 17, 1984 on the strengthening of the common commercial policy with regard in particular to protection against illicit trade practices, [1984] O.J. L252/1. See Steenbergen, "The New Commercial Policy Instrument" (1985) C.M.L.R. 421–439; Denton, "The New Commercial Policy Instrument and *AZKO v Dupont*" (1988) E.L.R. 3–27.

[53] Council Regulation (EC) No. 3286/94 of December 22, 1999 laying down Community procedures in the field of the common commercial policy in order to ensure the exercise of the Community's rights under international trade rules, in particular those established under the auspices of the World Trade Organisation, [1994] O.J. L349/71. For application of these rules, see Commission Decision 98/277/EC of April 16, 1998 concerning the failure of the United States of America to repeal its Antidumping Act of 1916, [1998] O.J. L126/36, and Commission Decision 98/731/EC of December 11, 1998 concerning section 110(5) of the Copyright Act of the United States of America, [1998] O.J. L346/60. See Sunberg and Vermulst, "The EC Trade Barriers Regulation" (2001) J.W.T. 989–1013. In addition, under Art. 133 of the EC Treaty, the Council may also adopt direct protective measures; see Council Regulation (EC) No. 2238/2003 of December 15, 2003 protecting against the effects of the application of the United States Anti-Dumping Act of 1916, and actions based thereon or resulting therefrom ([2003] O.J. L333/1). For its part, the Community may withdraw or amend its anti-dumping and anti-subsidy measures using a simplified procedure; see para. 20–013, *infra*.

[54] Council Regulation (EC) No. 1383/2003 of July 22, 2003 concerning customs action against goods suspected of infringing certain intellectual property rights and the measures to be taken against goods found to have infringed such rights, [2003] O.J. L196/7.

[55] Council Regulation (EC) No. 2271/96 of November 22, 1996 protecting against the effects of extra-territorial application of legislation adopted by a third country, and actions based thereon or resulting therefrom, [1996] O.J. L309/1 (adopted on the basis of Arts 57, 133 and 308 of the EC Treaty); see Hüber, "La réaction de l'Union européenne face aux lois américaines Helms-Burton et D'Amato" (1997) R.M.C.U.E. 301–308. See also para. 22–007, *infra*.

C. TRADE AGREEMENTS AND CO-OPERATION AGREEMENTS

20–009 Trade agreements. As a major economic power, the Community has trade relations with most countries in the world and makes use to this end of the powers conferred on it by Art. 133 and Arts 308 and 310 of the EC Treaty. A variety of agreements (trade agreements, free trade agreements, co-operation agreements, association agreements) often give rise to lasting co-operation, which is administered by bilateral co-operative bodies ("joint committees" or "joint commissions"). Pursuant to Art. 310 of the EC Treaty, the Community has concluded association agreements with the ACP States, most of the Mediterranean countries and the countries belonging to the European Economic Area (see para. 20–020). On the basis of Art. 133, trade agreements have been concluded with the EFTA countries[56] and with a number of other (especially developing) countries.[57] "Co-operation agreements" have been increasingly concluded under Arts 133 and 308 of the EC Treaty. Such agreements go beyond commercial co-operation, as they are also designed to secure economic co-operation or to afford a "framework" for both types of co-operation. Since the entry into force of the EU Treaty, the Community has concluded such agreements with developing countries on the basis of Arts 133 and 181 of the EC Treaty. Co-operation agreements have been concluded with Canada (the only western country to conclude such an agreement),[58] with a number of developing and other countries in Asia[59] and Latin

---

[56] para. 23–001, *infra*; for the Agreement on the European Economic Area, see para. 23–004, *infra*.

[57] See, *e.g.* the Agreement of July 15, 1975 with Mexico ([1975] O.J. L247/11), the Agreements on commercial co-operation of July 22, 1975 with Sri Lanka ([1975] O.J. L247/2) and of October 19, 1976 with Bangladesh ([1976] O.J. L319/2) and the commercial agreement in the form of an exchange of letters between the EEC and Andorra ([1990] O.J. L374/13). With regard to San Marino, the agreement concluded on December 16, 1991 on trade and customs union applies ([2002] O.J. L84/43); see also Mateu, "Dix ans de relations entre la Principauté d'Andorre et l'Union européenne, 1991–2001" (2001) R.M.C.U.E. 415–417.

[58] Framework Agreement of July 6, 1976 for commercial and economic co-operation, [1976] O.J. L260/2.

[59] See the agreements on commercial and economic co-operation of May 21, 1985 with China ([1985] O.J. L250/2) (preceded by a "classical" trade agreement) and of June 16, 1992 with Mongolia ([1993] O.J. L41/46); the co-operation agreements of March 7, 1980 with the member countries of the Association of South-East Asian Nations (ASEAN: Indonesia, Malaysia, the Philippines, Singapore and Thailand, [1980] O.J. L144/2; accession of Brunei: [1985] O.J. L81/2; extension to Vietnam: [1999] O.J. L117/30), of June 15, 1988 with the countries party to the Charter of the Co-operation Council for the Arab States of the Gulf (United Arab Emirates, Bahrein, Oman, Qatar, Saudi Arabia, and Kuwait, [1989] O.J. L54/3), of June 15, 1992 with Macao ([1992] O.J. L404/27), of December 20, 1993 with India ([1994] O.J. L223/24), of July 18, 1994 with Sri Lanka ([1995] O.J. L85/33), of July 17, 1995 with Vietnam ([1996] O.J. L136/29), of November 20, 1995 with Nepal ([1996] O.J. L137/15), of April 29, 1997 with Laos ([1997] O.J. L334/14) and Cambodia ([1997] O.J. C107/7), of November 25, 1997 with Yemen ([1998] O.J. L72/18, replacing the agreement of October 9, 1984, [1985] O.J. L26/2) and of November 24, 2001 with Pakistan (concluded only on April 29, 2004; replacing the agreement of July 23, 1985, [1986] O.J. L108/2); and the framework agreement concluded with South Korea on October 28, 1996 ([2001] O.J. L90/45).

America[60] and, in recent years, with the central and eastern European countries[61] and South Africa.[62] Following the entry into force of the Treaty of Nice, agreements on economic, financial and technical co-operation may also be concluded pursuant to Art. 181a of the EC Treaty (see para. 20–029).

The agreements concluded with the EFTA countries and the association agreements are preferential in nature and enable products from the non-member countries concerned to enter the Community at a zero or reduced rate of duty. The joint committees established by the agreements principally lay down rules on the origin of goods so as to determine which products may move within the free trade area unhampered by customs duties and quantitative restrictions.[63]

Multilateral trade and tariff agreements are principally negotiated in the context of the WTO (formerly GATT; see para. 20–010—20–014). In addition, the Community is a party to the Food Aid Convention[64] and has approved various commodity agreements negotiated in the United Nations Conference on Trade and Development (UNCTAD).[65]

---

[60] See the framework co-operation agreement concluded on February 22, 1993 with the Republics of Costa Rica, El Salvador, Guatemala, Honduras, Nicaragua and Panama ([1999] O.J. L63/38); the framework agreement concluded on April 23, 1993 with the Cartagena Agreement *and* its member countries, namely Bolivia, Colombia, Ecuador, Peru and Venezuela ([1998] O.J. L127/10) and the interregional framework co-operation agreement concluded on December 15, 1995 with the Southern Common Market ("Mercado Común del Sur" or "Mercosur") and its Party States (Argentina, Brazil, Paraguay and Uruguay) ([1999] O.J. L112/65). See Wehner, "EU und Mercosur: Auf dem Weg zur Freihandelszone?" (2000) R.I.W. 370–376. An economic partnership, political co-ordination and co-operation agreement of December 8, 1997 exists with Mexico ([2000] O.J. L276/45) and an association agreement was signed with Chile on November 18, 2002 ([2002] O.J. L352/1) following on from the framework co-operation agreement of June 21, 1996 ([1999] O.J. L42/46). The bulk of the trade chapter, the institutional framework and the trade-related co-operation provisions have been applied provisionally since February 1, 2003.

[61] paras 23–025 *et seq.* and 23–036, *infra.*

[62] Co-operation Agreement with the Republic of South Africa of October 10, 1994, [1994] O.J. L341. This agreement has been replaced by the association agreement "on trade, development and co-operation" signed on October 11, 1999 ([1999] O.J. L311/3), concluded by the Community by Council Decision 2004/441/EC of April 26, 2004 ([2004] O.J. L127/109).

[63] In a free-trade area where there is no common customs tariff, rules on origin are important because they prevent goods from entering the area from third countries *via* the country which applies the lowest rate of duty. For the compatibility of preferential regional trade agreements with the WTO regime, see Cremona, "Rhetoric and Reticence: EU External Commercial Policy in a Multilateral Context" (2001) C.M.L.R. 359–396; see also Bourgeois, "Het EG-beleid met betrekking tot vrijhandelszones. Kunst- en vliegwerk" (2002) S.E.W. 170–176.

[64] The Grains Trade Convention has been extended until June 30, 2001; a new Food Aid Convention 1999 was approved by the Council by Decision of June 13, 2000 ([2000] O.J. L163/37.

[65] See, *e.g.* Council Decision 2001/877/EC of September 24, 2001 on the signing and conclusion on behalf of the European Community of the International Coffee Agreement 2001 ([2001] O.J. L326/22), and Council Decision 2002/970/EC of November 18, 2002 concerning the conclusion on behalf of the European Community of the International Cocoa Agreement 2001 ([2002] O.J. L342/1).

D. Participation in GATT and the World Trade Organisation

1. The Community and GATT

20–010 GATT. All the Member States are party to the General Agreement on Tariffs and Trade (GATT),[66] under which the signatory States undertake to grant products from the other signatory States "most favoured nation" treatment and to refrain from imposing any non-tariff barriers to trade not included amongst the safeguard measures permitted by GATT. The EC customs union constitutes an exception to the most-favoured nation clause and is expressly authorised by Article XXIV of GATT (see para. 5–086).[67] The Community is not a GATT Contracting Party. Nevertheless, from the outset, it has regarded itself as bound by GATT and has taken part since the introduction of the Common Customs Tariff in the multilateral negotiating rounds for the gradual liberalisation of world trade, in which it is represented by the Commission. In the 1972 judgment in the *International Fruit* case, the Court of Justice held that the Member States could not withdraw from their obligations under GATT by concluding an agreement between them (the EEC Treaty), but, on the contrary, their desire to observe those undertakings followed from the very provisions of the EEC Treaty.[68] The Court went on to point out that the Community had assumed functions inherent in the trade and tariff policy and to hold that "[b]y conferring those powers on the Community, the Member States showed their wish to bind it by the obligations entered into under the General Agreement".[69] Accordingly, the Community succeeded *de facto* to the Member States in GATT, with the Commission defending the Community standpoint in the GATT organs, which operate on the basis of consensus. When agreements have been drawn up in the context of GATT, such as those reached during the Tokyo Round (1973–1979), the Community has therefore become a party to them, in some cases together with the Member States.[70] This practice is accepted by the other

---

[66] The General Agreement on Tariffs and Trade (GATT) was concluded in Geneva on October 30, 1947 by the Protocol of Provisional Application, UNTS, Vol.55, 194; Cmnd. 7258.

[67] For a survey of GATT and the status of the Community, see Petersmann, "The EEC as a GATT Member: Legal Conflicts between GATT Law and European Community Law", in Hilf, Jacobs and Petersmann (eds), *The European Community and GATT* (Kluwer, Deventer, 1986), 23, at 24–39.

[68] ECJ, Joined Cases 21–24/72 *International Fruit Company* [1972] E.C.R. 1219, paras 11–13.

[69] *ibid.*, paras 14–15. For the question as to whether GATT provisions may be pleaded, see para. 17–095, *supra*.

[70] See the Agreements on technical barriers to trade, government procurement, trade in civil aircraft, and interpretation and application of Articles VI, XVI and XXIII of the General Agreement on Tariffs and Trade, [1980] O.J. L71/29, 44, 58 and 72, respectively (the first and the third agreements are of the "mixed" type); for their approval, see the Council Decision of December 10, 1979, [1980] O.J. L71/1. The Commission disagreed with the categorisation of the agreements in question as "mixed"; see Bourgeois, "The Tokyo Round Agreements on Technical Barriers and on Government Procurement in International and EC Perspective" (1982) C.M.L.R. 5, at 21–22.

Contracting Parties, which, where necessary, address themselves to the Community in dispute-settlement procedures.

2. The Community and the World Trade Organisation

WTO Agreement. On September 20, 1986, the eighth multilateral **20–011** negotiating round began at Punta del Este (Uruguay Round). The negotiations were not concluded until December 15, 1993. The resulting Agreement establishing the World Trade Organisation (WTO) was signed on April 15, 1994 at Marrakesh by the GATT States and the Community and entered into force on January 1, 1995.[71]

WTO bodies. The World Trade Organisation replaced the GATT as a **20–012** fully-fledged international organisation with legal personality, which has its secretariat in Geneva.[72] A Ministerial Conference, which meets at least once every two years, takes the most important decisions and delegates tasks to a General Council. In addition, there is a Council for Trade in Goods, a Council for Trade in Services and a Council for Trade-Related Aspects of Intellectual Property Rights. Representatives of all members of the WTO sit on those bodies.[73] In principle, they take their decisions by consensus, although it is possible to adopt some decisions by a majority vote.[74]

Dispute settlement. The WTO constitutes the institutional framework for **20–013** trade relations in all areas covered by the agreements annexed to the WTO Agreement. First, there is the adjusted version of the General Agreement on Tariffs and Trade (GATT 1994), the General Agreement on Trade in Services (GATS) and the Agreement on Trade-Related Aspects of

---

[71] Agreement establishing the World Trade Organisation, including the Agreements set out in Annexes 1–4 thereto, approved by Council Decision 94/800/EC of December 22, 1994 concerning the conclusion on behalf of the European Community, as regards matters within its competence, of the agreements reached in the Uruguay Round multilateral negotiations (1986–1994), [1994] O.J. L336/1. The Commission had first sought the Court's opinion on the division of competence with regard to the conclusion of the WTO, see ECJ, Opinion 1/94 *Agreement establishing the World Trade Organisation* [1994] E.C.R. I–5267 (see the commentaries cited in n.14, *supra*). See Brittan, "Uruguay Round" (1994) C.M.L.R. 229–234. Since then, the Council has approved on behalf of the Community, as regards matters within its competence, the results of the WTO negotiations on financial services and the movement of natural persons (Decision 96/412/EC of June 25, 1996, [1996] O.J. L167/23), basic telecommunications services (Decision 97/838/EC of November 28, 1997, [1997] O.J. L347/45) and financial services (Decision 1999/61/EC of December 14, 1998, [1999] O.J. L20/38).
[72] For the WTO website, see *www.wto.org/*.
[73] WTO Agreement, Art. IV.
[74] WTO Agreement, Art. IX, para. 1 of which provides that where the Communities exercise their right to vote, they are to have a number of votes equal to the number of their Member States (which are WTO Members). According to a footnote to that provision, the Member States and the Communities together cannot cast more votes than the number of Member States.

Intellectual Property Rights (TRIPs).[75] The second and third annexes relate to the Rules and Procedures Governing the Settlement of Disputes and the Trade Policy Review Mechanism. Responsibility for these matters lies with the General Council, sitting as the Dispute Settlement Body (DSB) and the Trade Policy Review Body (TPRB). The DSB may remit a dispute to a Panel. Panel reports are automatically adopted by the DSB, unless it decides by consensus not to do so or a party to the dispute appeals to the Standing Appellate Body. Reports of the Standing Appellate Body are also taken over automatically by the DSB unless it decides by consensus not to do so. The final decision is binding and entitles a party to impose trade sanctions if the other party to the dispute does not comply with it.[76]

Within the Community legal order, the Community is at liberty to settle disputes with its trading partners within the framework of the WTO, possibly by negotiation. Consequently, where a report of a Panel or of the Standing Appellate Body finds that there is a conflict between a Community measure and WTO obligations, that report cannot in principle be pleaded before the Community Court in proceedings brought against the Community measure in question (see para. 17–095). In anti-dumping or anti-subsidy cases, however, there exists a simplified procedure which the Council can use in order to bring Community legislation into line with a report drawn up by the Dispute Settlement Body.[77]

20–014 **Division of powers.** The Member States and the Community are members of the WTO. Some matters within the scope of the WTO fall within the competence of the Member States (GATS and TRIPs), whilst others fall within the exclusive competence of the Community (see para. 20–003). As already mentioned, unity in the international representation of the Community requires there to be close co-operation between the Member States and the Community in applying the WTO Agreement. The duty to co-operate is all the more imperative where the Community or a Member

---

[75] See Weiss, "The General Agreement on Trade in Services 1994" (1995) C.M.L.R. 1177–1225 and Frid, "Multilateral Liberalisation of Trade in Services under the GATS" (1998) S.E.W. 410–416. See also n.71, *supra*.

[76] Understanding on Rules and Procedures Governing the Settlement of Disputes, Annex 2 to the WTO Agreement, [1994] O.J. L336/234. See Petersmann, "The Dispute Settlement System of the World Trade Organisation and the Evolution of the GATT Dispute Settlement System since 1948" (1994) C.M.L.R. 1157–1244; Kuijper, "The New WTO Dispute Settlement System: The Impact on the European Community" (1995) J.W.T. 49–71; Cottier, "Dispute Settlement in the World Trade Organisation: Characteristics and Structural Implications for the European Union" (1998) C.M.L.R. 325–378; Lebullenger, "La Communauté européenne face au procéssus de réexamen du système de règlement des différends de l'Organisation mondiale du commerce" (1998) R.M.C.U.E. 629–637; Rosas, "Implementation and Enforcement of WTO Dispute Settlement Findings: An EU Perspective" (2001) J.I.E.L. 131–144.

[77] Council Regulation (EC) No. 1515/2001 of July 23, 2001 on the measures that may be taken by the Community following a report adopted by the WTO Dispute Settlement Body concerning anti-dumping and anti-subsidy matters ([2001] O.J. L201/10). See Blanchard, "L'effet des rapports de l'Organe de règlement des différends de l'OMC à la lumière du règlement (CE) 1515/2001 du Conseil de l'Union européenne" (2003) R.M.C.U.E 37–48.

State is authorised to take cross-retaliation measures but can do so effectively only in an area for which the other is competent.[78]

II. ASSOCIATION

Association. The Community is entitled to involve certain countries and **20–015** territories closely in its operation by means of "association". Concerning the countries and territories which come under the sovereignty of a Member State but are not part of the Community, Art. 187 of the EC Treaty empowers the Council to determine the details and procedure of association. Furthermore, Art. 310 of the EC Treaty authorises the Community to conclude agreements with non-member countries or international organisations so as to establish an association. These powers will continue to exist in the EU Constitution,[79] which will supplement them by a clause enabling the Union to conclude specific agreements with neighbouring States.[80]

A. THE OVERSEAS COUNTRIES AND TERRITORIES

Overseas countries and territories. Association of the overseas countries **20–016** and territories is the subject of Part Four of the EC Treaty (Arts 182–188). Its purpose is to "promote the economic and social development of the countries and territories and to establish close economic relations between them and the Community as a whole" (EC Treaty, Art. 182, second para.).[81] To this end, association establishes a free trade area between the Community and the overseas countries and territories, whereby the Member States endeavour to apply to their trade with them the same treatment as they accord to each other, but the overseas countries and territories determine their trade policy *vis-à-vis* the Member States themselves, subject to the condition that they treat all the Member States in the same way (see Art. 183, points (1) and (2), and Art. 184). All the Member States contribute towards the development of the overseas

---

[78] ECJ, Opinion 1/94 *Agreement establishing the World Trade Organisation* [1994] E.C.R. I–5267, paras 108–109.

[79] See Arts III–286—III–292 (overseas countries and territories) and Art. III–324 (association agreements).

[80] Art. I–57 of the EU Constitution ("The Union and its neighbours") provides that such agreements, in common with association agreements, may contain reciprocal rights and obligations as well as the possibility of undertaking activities jointly.

[81] For the "advantages" which association confers on those countries and territories, see ECJ, Case C–430/92 *Netherlands v Commission* [1994] E.C.R. I–5197, para. 22. The association arrangements apply only to products originating in those countries and territories: ECJ, Case C–310/95 *Road Air* [1997] E.C.R. I–2229, paras 29–36. The application of the association regime does not bring a territory within the sphere of application of the EC Treaty; see ECJ, Case C–181/97 *van der Kooy* [1999] E.C.R. I–483, paras 32–42 (Netherlands Antilles held not to be part of the Community for the purposes of the application of the VAT Directive).

countries and territories through the European Development Fund set up for that purpose (Art. 183, point 3). A Convention annexed to the EC Treaty determined the substance of the association scheme for the first five years. Since then, the Council lays down provisions to this end unanimously "on the basis of the experience acquired under the association of the countries and territories with the Community and of the principles set out" in the EC Treaty (Art. 187). Accordingly, the Council has to reconcile the aims of association with the "principles"—likewise laid down in the Treaty—underlying the common agricultural policy. To this end, the Council has arranged matters so that agricultural products from overseas countries and territories are on an equal footing with EC products, but a safeguard clause enables the Community to react to a limited extent to difficulties to which free access of products originating in those countries and territories to the Community market may give rise.[82]

Since most areas colonised by the Member States became independent in the 1960s, this scheme now applies only to certain overseas countries and territories having special relations with Denmark, France, the Netherlands and the United Kingdom.[83] The scheme is now substantively identical to that of the association agreements which the Community has concluded under Art. 310 of the EC Treaty. Unlike those agreements, however, the association scheme does not require any institutions of its own on account of its autonomous nature.

B. ARTICLE 310 OF THE EC TREATY

1. Scope

20–017 **Association agreements.** Article 310 of the EC Treaty and Art. 206 of the EAEC Treaty provide the legal basis for the Community to "conclude with one or more States or international organisations agreements establishing

---

[82] Council Decision 2001/822/EC of November 27, 2001 on the association of the overseas countries and territories with the European Community, [2001] O.J. L314/1. That decision replaced Council Decision 91/482/EEC of July 25, 1991 on the association of the overseas countries and territories with the European Economic Community, [1991] O.J. L263/1 (subsequently amended by Council Decision 97/803/EC of November 24, 1997, [1997] O.J. L329/50, and extended by Council Decision 2000/169/EC of February 25, 2000, [2000] O.J. L55/67). The safeguard clause contained in that decision was declared lawful in CFI, Joined Cases T–480/93 and T–483/93 *Antillean Rice Mills v Commission* [1995] E.C.R. II–2305, paras 81–97, as confirmed on appeal by ECJ, Case C–390/95 P *Antillean Rice Mills v Commission* [1999] E.C.R. I–769. For the validity of Decision 97/803/EEC, see ECJ, Case C–17/98 *Emesa Sugar (Free Zone) and Aruba* [2000] E.C.R. I–675, paras 27–67.

[83] The countries and territories to which the provisions of Part Four of the Treaty are applicable (listed in Annex II to the EC Treaty): Greenland, the French T.O.M.s or *territoires d'outre mer* (New Caledonia and Dependencies, French Polynesia, French Southern and Antarctic Territories, Wallis and Futuna Islands, Mayotte and Saint Pierre and Miquelon), Aruba and the Netherlands Antilles (Bonaire, Curaçao, Saba, Sint Eustatius and Sint Maarten), Anguilla, Cayman Islands, Falkland Islands, South Georgia and the South Sandwich Islands, Monserrat, Pitcairn, Saint Helena and Dependencies, British Antarctic Territory, British Indian Ocean Territory, Turks and Caicos Islands, British Virgin Islands and Bermuda. For the special status of Greenland, Aruba and the Netherlands Antilles, see also para. 8–002, *supra*.

an association involving reciprocal rights and obligations, common action and special procedures". Because association is defined in this way, there is a need for a degree of institutionalisation of the international co-operation so as to make it possible for decisions to be taken in common. As the Court of Justice has held, an association agreement creates "special, privileged links with a non-member country which must, at least to a certain extent, take part in the Community system".[84]

Scope of agreements. The Community has the power to "guarantee **20–018** commitments towards non-member countries in all the fields covered by the Treaty".[85] As a result, it may conclude association agreements relating to any area coming under the EC or the EAEC Treaties.[86] Thus, an association agreement may cover free movement of workers who are nationals of the non-member country party to the agreement even though the power to adopt the necessary implementing measures is not vested in the Community.[87]

Bodies set up by association agreement. With a view to its implementation **20–019** and further development, each association agreement sets up a joint body composed, on the one hand, of members of the national governments or the members of the Council—generally supplemented by members of the Commission—and, on the other, of members of the government of each third country involved. That association council (sometimes called "council of ministers" or, to suit the title of the agreement, the "co-operation council") takes its decision by unanimous vote. Preparatory and executive powers may be delegated to the association (or co-operation) committee, which is made up of representatives of the members of the association council. Generally, each association engenders (by virtue of the agreement itself or of a decision of the association council) an advisory parliamentary body, consisting of Members of the European Parliament and of the parliament(s) of the non-member country or countries concerned. Generally, the association council has jurisdiction to rule on any disputes between the Contracting Parties relating to the interpretation or

---

[84] ECJ, Case 12/86 *Demirel* [1987] E.C.R. 3719, para. 9. "Reciprocal rights and obligations" does not mean equality of contractual obligations: ECJ, Case 87/75 *Besciani* [1976] E.C.R. 129, para. 22.

[85] *Demirel*, (n.84, *supra*), para. 9.

[86] For a discussion (and a comparison) of the content of association agreements, see Lenaerts and De Smijter, "The European Community's Treaty-Making Competence" (1996) Y.E.L. 1, at 19–47; Hummer, "Die räumliche Erweiterung des Binnenmarktrechts" (2002) EuR. Beiheft 1, 75–146.

[87] ECJ, Case 12/86 *Demirel* [1987] E.C.R. 3719, para. 10. On the Community side, the financing and other arrangements for implementing association agreements are often enshrined in an internal agreement concluded by the representatives of the governments of the Member States, meeting in the Council (see, for instance, in the case of the ACP-EC Partnership Agreement, n.111, *infra*).

application of the association agreement. If a settlement cannot be reached, it is possible to have recourse to arbitration.[88]

2. Association agreements

a. Survey

20–020 **Association agreements.** The first time the Community made use of Art. 310 of the EC Treaty [at that time Art. 238 of the EEC Treaty] was when it concluded agreements with Greece and Turkey to prepare them for possible accession.[89] The next association agreements with Cyprus and Malta looked forward to the gradual establishment of a customs union.[90] Since then, the Community has concluded agreements, often styled "co-operation agreements", under Art. 310 of the EC Treaty with virtually every country in the Mediterranean area. Accordingly, the Community currently has associations with each of the Maghreb countries (Algeria, Morocco and Tunisia),[91] the Mashreq countries (Egypt, Jordan, Lebanon and Syria)[92] and Israel.[93] Association agreements have also been signed

---

[88] For these bodies, see Ntumba, "Les institutions mixtes de gestion des accords conclus entre la CEE et les pays en voie de développement (PVD)" (1988) R.M.C. 481–486; Lenaerts and De Smijter (n.86, *supra*), at 47–57. A list of association and co-operation councils and of the representations of ACP States may be found in the pre-1997 annual *Council Guide* (Secretariat General of the Council of the European Union, Brussels).

[89] Agreement of September 12, 1963 establishing an Association between the EEC and Turkey (J.O. 3687/64; English text published in [1973] O.J. C113/1), with an Additional Protocol of November 23, 1970 (J.O. L293/73), as fleshed out by, *inter alia*, (internal) Agreement 64/737/EEC (J.O. 3705/64) and a number of decisions of the Association Council (such as Decisions 2/76 and 1/80 (unpublished) and 3/80, [1983] O.J. C110/60). The Agreement of July 9, 1961 with Greece (O.J. English Spec. Ed., Second Series, I. External Relations (1), p.3) lapsed when Greece acceded to the Communities.

[90] Agreement of December 5, 1970 between the EEC and Malta, 1971 J.O. L61/1; for the English text, see *Collection of the Agreements concluded by the European Community*, Luxembourg, Office for Official Publications of the European Community, Vol.1, Bilateral EEC-Europe 1958–1975, at 431; Agreement between the EEC and Cyprus, [1973] O.J. L133/1. Those agreements lapsed when both States acceded to the European Union.

[91] See the Co-operation Agreements of April 25, 1976 with Tunisia ([1978] O.J. L265/2), of April 26, 1976 with Algeria ([1978] O.J. L263/2) and of April 27, 1978 with Morocco ([1978] O.J. L264/2). Subsequently, the Community concluded "Euro-Mediterranean" Association Agreements on July 17, 1995 with Tunisia ([1998] O.J. L97/2), on February 26, 1996 with Morocco ([2000] O.J. L70/2) and on April 22, 2002 with Algeria ((2002) 4 EU Bull. point 1.6.51).

[92] See the Co-operation Agreements of January 18, 1977 with Egypt ([1978] O.J. L266/2), Jordan ([1978] O.J. L268/2) and Syria ([1978] O.J. L269/2) and of May 3, 1977 with Lebanon ([1978] O.J. L267/2). "Euro-Mediterranean" Association Agreements were signed with Jordan on November 24, 1997 ([2002] O.J. L129/1), with Egypt on June 25, 2001 ([2004] O.J. L304/39) and with Lebanon on June 17, 2002 ((2002) 6 EU Bull. point 1.6.75).

[93] See the "Euro-Mediterranean" Association Agreement of November 20, 1995 ([2000] O.J. L147/3). An association agreement had been concluded with Israel on May 11, 1975 pursuant to Art. 113 [now Art. 133] of the EC Treaty ([1975] O.J. L136/3), but the additional protocols (such as the fourth protocol, [1988] O.J. L327/36) and protocols on financial and technical co-operation (such as the most recent protocol of June 12, 1991, [1992] O.J. L94/46) were based on Art. 238 [now Art. 310] of the EC Treaty. For the way in which the European Parliament exercised its power of assent, see para. 21–014, *infra*.

with Chile and South Africa.[94] Political considerations play a part in determining whether such agreements are concluded and implemented (see, for instance, the repudiation of the co-operation agreement with Yugoslavia in 1991[95]).

In the same way as the initial agreements with Cyprus and Malta, all association agreements simplify access to the Community market for goods from the countries concerned and, at the same time, commit the Community to co-operate with them economically and financially. In all the agreements, save that concluded with Israel, the Community unilaterally grants a zero tariff or (in the case of "sensitive" products, such as textiles) a reduced tariff. The non-member countries undertake for their part to grant products from the Community most-favoured nation status and not to apply any fiscal discrimination. In the case of Israel, the Community has concluded an agreement based on reciprocal tariff reductions.[96] Turkey and the Community have constituted a customs union since January 1, 1996.[97] The agreements with the Maghreb countries and some decisions of the EC-Turkey Association Council require the Member States to treat nationals of those countries who are lawfully on their territory in the same way as their own nationals as regards conditions of employment, remuneration and social security (see para. 5–157). Pursuant to undertakings entered into by the Community at the Euro-Mediterranean Conference held in Barcelona on November 27 and 28, 1995,[98] the existing association agreements are gradually being replaced by agreements which are eventually to lead to the establishment of a Euro-Mediterranean Free Trade Area.[99] Henceforward, the Palestine Authority is to be involved.[100]

---

[94] See n.60, *supra* (Chile) and n.62 (South Africa—that agreement has already been concluded by the Community).

[95] Council Decision 91/602/EEC of November 25, 1991, [1991] O.J. L325/23. See Fransen, "The EEC and the Mediterranean Area: Associations and Co-operation Agreements" (1992) Leiden J.I.L. 215–243.

[96] For the content of these preferential agreements and their compatibility with the GATT, see Schoneveld, "The EEC and Free Trade Agreements: Stretching the Limits of GATT Exceptions to Non-Discriminatory Trade?" (1992) J.W.T. 59–78.

[97] Decision No. 1/95 of the EC-Turkey Association Council of December 22, 1995 on implementing the final phase of the Customs Union, [1996] O.J. L35/1.

[98] See the Barcelona Declaration and the programme of work (1995) 11 EU Bull. point 2.3.1.

[99] See the Euro-Mediterranean Agreements mentioned in n.91–93, *supra*. The structure for Community financial and technical aid is the Euro-Mediterranean partnership: Council Regulation (EC) No. 1488/96 of July 23, 1996 on financial and technical measures to accompany the reform of economic and social structures in the framework of the Euro-Mediterranean partnership (MEDA), [1996] O.J. L189/1. See Gaudissart, "Cinq ans après Barcelone. Etat et perspectives du Partnerariat euro-méditerranéen" in Dumoulin and Duchenne (eds), *L'Europe et la Méditerranée* (P.I.E. Peter Lang, Brussels, 2001), at 133–147.

[100] See the Euro-Mediterranean Interim Association Agreement of February 24, 1997 on trade and co-operation between the European Community, of the one part, and the Palestine Liberation Organisation (PLO) for the benefit of the Palestine Authority of the West Bank and the Gaza Strip, of the other part, [1997] O.J. L187/1. For the development of foreign policy through partnerships, see Keukeleire, *Het buitenlands beleid van de Europese Unie* (Kluwer, Deventer, 1998) at 375–412.

Since the Treaty of Nice, agreements on economic, financial and technical co-operation may also be concluded on the basis of Art. 181a of the EC Treaty (see para. 20–029).

Lastly, the ACP-EC Conventions (see para. 20–021) also took the form of association agreements, as did the Agreement on the European Economic Area (see para. 23–004) and the Europe Agreements concluded with central European countries (see para. 23–027).

b. The ACP-EC Partnership Agreement

20–021 **From Lomé to Cotonou.** After most of the colonised areas in Africa obtained their independence, the Community concluded the association agreements signed at Yaoundé (Cameroon) on July 20, 1963 and July 29, 1969 with the African States in question and Madagascar.[101] Following the accession of the United Kingdom, the Community entered into negotiations with a number of States in Africa, the Caribbean and the Pacific, which culminated in an association agreement being concluded with these "ACP States". The ACP-EC Convention was signed at Lomé (Togo) on February 28, 1975, following which it was renewed every five years.[102] A new ACP-EC Agreement was concluded at Cotonou (Benin) on June 23, 2000 by the Community, its Member States and 76 ACP States for a 20-year period starting on March 1, 2000.[103] This ACP-EC "Partnership Agreement" provides for co-operation with 77 ACP States and has since been extended to cover 78 States.[104]

---

[101] J.O. 1430/64, and [1970] O.J. L282. English version in O.J. Spec. Ed., Second Series I, External Relations (January 1974).

[102] ACP-EC Convention of February 28, 1975, [1976] O.J. L25; Second ACP-EC Convention of October 31, 1979, [1980] O.J. L347; Third ACP-EC Convention of December 8, 1984, [1986] O.J. L86; Fourth ACP-EC Convention of December 15, 1989, [1991] O.J. L229/3 (concluded for ten years and since revised by the Convention of Mauritius of November 4, 1995, [1998] O.J. L156/3).

[103] [2000] O.J. L317/3, approved by Council Decision 2003/159/EC of December 19, 2002 ([2003] O.J. L65/27). Under Art. 95, amendments may be made at the end of each five-year period. See Babarinde and Faber, "From Lomé to Cotonou: Business as Usual?" (2004) E.For.Aff.Rev. 27–47 ; Arts, "ACP-EU Relations in a New Era: The Cotonou Agreement" (2003) C.M.L.R. 95–116; Vincent, "L'entrée en vigueur de la convention de Cotonou" (2003) C.D.E. 157–176; Petit, "Le nouvel accord de partenariat ACP-UE" (2000) R.M.C.U.E. 215–219. The ACP-EC Partnership Agreement entered into force on April 1, 2003.

[104] Somalia is considered one of the (least developed) ACP States, even though it has not signed the Partnership Agreement. South Africa participates in the Partnership Agreement subject to the qualifications set out in Protocol 3 on South Africa (the general and institutional provisions and the co-operation strategies will apply to that country, but in principle not the provisions on financial assistance and trade co-operation); however, South Africa is linked to the EC by the co-operation agreement of October 11, 1999 (n.62, *supra*), which according to Protocol 3 takes precedence over the provisions of the Partnership Agreement. East Timor became the 78th State to accede to the Partnership Agreement, by virtue of Decision No. 1/2003 (2003/404/EC) of the ACP-EC Council of Ministers of May 16, 2003 ([2003] O.J. L141/25) adopted pursuant to Art. 94(1) of the Agreement. For a list of the other ACP States, see the tables in Arts (n.104, *supra*), at 113, and in Matambalya

Content of Partnership Agreement. The ACP-EC Partnership Agreement **20–022** is intended to promote and expedite the economic, cultural and social development of the ACP States, with a view to contributing to peace and security and to promoting a stable and democratic political environment (Art. 1, first para.). The key objectives are poverty eradication, sustainable development and the gradual integration of the ACP countries into the world economy. At the same time, the ACP-EC Partnership Agreement has a political dimension based on respect for human rights, democratic principles and the rule of law, and good governance. In the event that one of the parties fails to fulfil an obligation stemming from respect for human rights, democratic principles or the rule of law, a consultation procedure may be initiated which may result in "appropriate measures" being taken and, in the last resort, in the suspension of the Partnership Agreement.[105]

The ACP-EC Partnership Agreement seeks to gear the aid granted to the ACP States more to the degree of development of individual ACP countries or groups of countries. As far as the group of least-developed ACP States is concerned, the existing trade conditions remain largely unchanged. As regards the other ACP States, economic partnerships are to be concluded by the end of 2007. Until that time, the non-reciprocal trade preferences are to be maintained: products originating in the ACP States may be imported into the Community free of customs duties, with the exception of those coming under a common organisation of the market or specific rules of the common agricultural policy, for which the Community has introduced a favourable import regime.[106] For ACP States which are not in a position to enter into economic partnership agreements, the Community is to work out an alternative framework for trade.[107]

The ACP-EC Partnership Agreement does not include any provisions on the free movement of workers, but it does oblige the Member States and the ACP countries to accord each other's nationals who are legally employed in their respective territories treatment free from any discrimination based on nationality as regards working conditions,

---

and Wolf, "The Cotonou Agreement and the Challenges of Making the New EU-ACP Trade Regime WTO Compatible" (2001) J.W.T. 123, at 142. Cuba has not yet been admitted to accede to the Partnership Agreement, although it is accepted as a member by the group of ACP States.

[105] ACP-EC Partnership Agreement, Art. 96; see, *e.g.* as regards Liberia, Council Decision 2002/274/EC of March 25, 2002 ([2002] O.J. L96/23) and the partial suspension of the Partnership Agreement by Council Decision 2003/631/EC of August 25, 2003 ([2003] O.J. L220/3). A similar procedure was introduced by Art. 366a of the Fourth ACP-EC Convention, which provided for the possibility of suspending the application of the agreement for a State which failed to fulfil the obligation to respect human rights; see the procedure laid down in Council Decision 199/214/EC of March 11, 1999, [1999] O.J. L75/32, and its application, for instance, in 1999 in respect of Niger (*Europe*, No. 7447, April 17, 1999, p.8). Art. 97 of the ACP-EC Partnership Agreement provides for a similar consultation procedure for serious cases of corruption.

[106] ACP-EC Partnership Agreement, Art. 36, as enlarged upon in Annex V.

[107] ACP-EC Partnership Agreement, Art. 37(6).

remuneration and dismissal relative to their own nationals.[108] Each of the ACP States undertakes to accept the return and re-admission of any of its nationals who are illegally present on the territory of a Member State of the EU.[109]

20–023 Community assistance. In co-operating on development financing, the Community grants administrative, technical and financial assistance to projects in the ACP States. Since the ACP-EC Partnership Agreement was concluded by the Community together with the Member States, the corresponding financial obligation falls on the Community and the Member States considered together.[110] Since the Community does not have exclusive competence in this area, the Member States lawfully elected to finance the aid from national contributions made available to the European Development Fund, which is administered by the Commission.[111] In this way, the Commission grants aid directly to the ACP States and to the overseas countries and territories referred to in Part Four of the EC Treaty. The ACP States choose the projects to be financed and are responsible for formulating, negotiating and concluding contracts with undertakings. The intervention of Commission representatives is intended solely to determine whether the conditions for Community financing are satisfied.[112] The European Investment Bank may also grant loans and other financial assistance.

20–024 ACP bodies. Policy decisions with regard to the implementation of the ACP-EC Partnership Agreement are taken at least once a year by the Council of Ministers, consisting of the members of the Council and (one or more) members of the Commission, on the one hand, and a member of the government of each ACP State, on the other.[113] Tasks may be delegated to

---

[108] ACP-EC Partnership Agreement, Art. 13(3). Art. 274 of the Fourth ACP-EC Convention itself prohibited ACP States and EU Member States from discriminating as between nationals of different Member States or ACP States without putting them under an obligation to treat nationals of Member States and of ACP States identically: ECJ, Case 65/77 *Razanatsimba* [1977] E.C.R. 2229, paras 12–14. A Member State may reserve more favourable treatment to the nationals of a given ACP country in so far as such treatment results from the provisions of an international agreement comprising reciprocal rights and advantages: *ibid.*, para. 19.

[109] ACP-EC Partnership Agreement, Art. 13(5)(c).

[110] ECJ, Case C–316/91 *European Parliament v Council* [1994] E.C.R. I–625, paras 28–33.

[111] *ibid.*, paras 34–38; see the Internal Agreement between Representatives of the Governments of the Member States, meeting within the Council, on the Financing and Administration of Community Aid under the Financial Protocol to the Fifth ACP-EC Convention and the allocation of financial assistance for the Overseas Countries and Territories to which Part Four of the EC Treaty applies ([2000] O.J. L317/355), which establishes an Ninth Development Fund for the period 2000 to 2005.

[112] As a result, undertakings which tender for or are awarded contracts do not have any contractual relationship with the Community: ECJ, Case 126/83 *STS v Commission* [1984] E.C.R. 2769, paras 10–18.

[113] ACP-EC Partnership Agreement, Art. 15. For the Rules of Procedure of the ACP-EC Council of Ministers, see [2001] O.J. L43/20.

the Committee of Ambassadors, which meets on a regular basis. That committee consists of the Permanent Representatives of all the Member States and a representative of the Commission, on the one hand, and the head of each ACP State's mission to the EU, on the other.[114] In order to prepare for these meetings, both the members of the Council and the ACP States within their own group endeavour to reach a common position. The ACP States do so in the Council of ACP Ministers set up for this purpose and in the Committee of ACP Ambassadors, both of which are based in Brussels.[115] The ACP-EC bodies are chaired alternately by a Member State and an ACP State.[116] The Joint Parliamentary Assembly acts as a consultative body. It is made up of Members of the European Parliament and of Members of Parliament of the ACP States or representatives designated by them. It meets twice a year, alternatively in the Community and in an ACP State.[117]

Accession. A request to accede may be made only by States "whose **20–025** structural characteristics and economic and social situation are comparable to those of the ACP States" and has to be approved by the Council of Ministers.[118] Any new Member State of the European Union becomes a party to the ACP-EC Partnership Agreement from the date of accession if the act of accession so provides or, otherwise, by depositing an act of accession which is to be notified to all the ACP countries.[119]

III. DEVELOPMENT CO-OPERATION AND HUMANITARIAN AID

Development policy. Although competence in respect of development **20–026** co-operation was first incorporated in the EC Treaty by the EU Treaty, the Community had already been pursuing its own development policy for some considerable time. Thus, the scheme for overseas countries and territories (Part Four of the EC Treaty; see para. 20–016) and the association policy with regard to countries in the Mediterranean area and the ACP States (see paras 20–020–20–023) aimed primarily to promote those countries' economic and social development. In association therewith, various common commercial policy measures had development policy aspects without detracting from their commercial policy nature (see para.

---

[114] ACP-EC Partnership Agreement, Art. 16. For the Rules of Procedure of the ACP-EC Committee of Ambassadors, see [2001] O.J. L43/24.

[115] The ACP States agreed to this in the Georgetown Agreement of June 6, 1975; the Internal Agreement on measures and procedures to be followed for the implementation of the ACP-EC Partnership Agreement, [2000] O.J. L317/376, applies as between the Member States.

[116] ACP-EC Partnership Agreement, first para. of Arts 15(1) and 16(1).

[117] *ibid.*, Art. 17.

[118] *ibid.*, Art. 94(1); for its application, see para. 20–021, *supra*.

[119] *ibid.*, Art. 94(3), second subpara. For an example, see Art. 6(4) of the 2003 Act of Accession.

20–002). Above all, there were the multilateral commodity agreements, the Food-Aid Convention and the co-operation agreements concluded with developing countries (see para. 20–009). In addition, since 1971 the Council has granted, pursuant to an UNCTAD resolution of 1968, generalised tariff preferences by regulation for certain industrial, textile and agricultural products from developing countries for which the common commercial policy affords a sufficient legal basis.[120] By granting tariff preferences, the Community seeks to increase the beneficiary countries' export revenue, hence promoting their economic development. Since January 1, 1995, new rules are in force which aim gradually to concentrate preferences on the least developed countries.[121] Lastly, the Council has adopted measures pursuant to Art. 308 of the EC Treaty whose principal characteristic is development, namely financial and technical assistance granted to non-associated developing countries under co-operation agreements[122] and food aid.[123]

20–027 Specific powers. The powers provided for in Arts 177–181 of the EC Treaty are directed towards the economic and social development of the developing countries, their integration into the world economy and combating poverty in the developing countries. However, Community development policy must also contribute towards the development and consolidation of democracy and the rule of law, and respect for human rights.[124] The specific power with regard to development co-operation makes it superfluous to make reference to Art. 308 of the EC Treaty, both as far as concerns autonomous measures adopted by the Community pursuant to Art. 179 of the EC Treaty[125] and co-operation and

---

[120] ECJ, Case 45/86 *Commission v Council* [1987] E.C.R. 1493, paras 14–21.

[121] See Peers, "Reform of the European Community's Generalised System of Preferences: A Missed Opportunity" (1995) J.W.T. 79–96. See also the multiannual scheme of generalised tariff preferences (1995–2004), as applied for the period January 1, 2002 to December 31, 2005 by Council Regulation (EC) No. 2501/2001 of December 10, 2001, ([2001] O.J. L346/1) and extended by Council Regulation (EC) No. 2211/2003 of December 15, 2003, ([2003] O.J. L332/1).

[122] Council Regulation (EEC) No.443/92 of February 25, 1992 on financial and technical assistance to, and economic co-operation with, the developing countries in Asia and Latin America, [1992] O.J. L52/1.

[123] See Snyder, "The European Community's Food Aid Legislation: Towards a Development Policy", in his work *New Directions in European Community Law* (Weidenfeld, London, 1990), at 146–176. For the present system, see n.127, *infra*.

[124] The promotion of regional integration is not stated to be an objective in the EC Treaty, but is mentioned in Art. 1 of the ACP-EC Partnership Agreement (para. 20–022, *supra*). See Ntumba, *La Communauté économique européenne et les intégrations régionales des pays en développement* (Bruylant, Brussels, 1990), 541 pp.

[125] See, *e.g.* Council Regulations (EC) Nos 1734/94 and 1735/94 of July 11, 1994 on financial and technical co-operation with the Occupied Territories, [1994] O.J. L182/4 and 6, which followed Council Decision 91/408/EEC of July 22, 1991 on financial aid for Israel and the Palestinian population of the Occupied Territories, [1991] O.J. L227/33 (based on Art. 235 of the EEC Treaty [now Art. 308 of the EC Treaty]).

other agreements concluded pursuant, *inter alia*, to Art. 181 of the EC Treaty.[126]

In pursuance of these powers, the Community has introduced, for example, prevention and intervention systems for humanitarian aid, food aid, aid for uprooted people and aid for rehabilitation and reconstruction operations for developing countries.[127] Respect for human rights is a precondition for benefiting from tariff preferences[128] and plays an important role in agreements concluded by the Community in pursuance of its development co-operation policy.[129] Article 179 of the EC Treaty provides that co-operation with the ACP countries is "not to be affected". This does not prevent the Community from extending certain aspects of that co-operation to other developing countries.[130] The specific powers relating to development co-operation are to apply "[w]ithout prejudice to the other provisions of this Treaty" (Art. 179(1)) and therefore do not detract from the powers exercised by the Community in the context of the

---

[126] See, for instance, the Conventions with the United Nations Relief and Works Agency for Palestine Refugees (UNRWA) concerning aid to refugees in the countries of the Near East of 1993 ([1994] O.J. L9/17), 1996 ([1996] O.J. L282/69) and of 1999 ([1999] O.J. L261/36), concluded under Art. 181 in conjunction with Art. 300(3), first subpara., of the EC Treaty; a previous convention had been concluded pursuant to Art. 235 [now Art. 308] of the EC Treaty ([1990] O.J. L118/36). See also the co-operation agreements with India, Sri Lanka and South Africa (para. 20–009, *supra*) concluded under Arts 113 and 130y [now Arts 133 and 181] in conjunction with Art. 228 [now Art. 300](2), first sentence, and (3), first subpara., of the EC Treaty, instead of Arts 113 and 235 [now Arts 133 and 308] of the EC Treaty, on the basis of which previous co-operation agreements had been concluded. Consequently, a unanimous vote was not required.

[127] See, Council Regulation (EC) No. 1257/96 of June 20, 1996 concerning humanitarian aid, [1996] O.J. L163/1; Council Regulation (EC) No. 1292/96 of June 27, 1996 on food-aid policy and food-aid management and special operations in support of food security, [1996] O.J. L166/1; Council Regulation (EC) No. 2258/96 of November 22, 1996 on rehabilitation and reconstruction operations in developing countries, [1996] O.J. L306/1; Regulation (EC) No. 2130/2001 of the European Parliament and of the Council of October 29, 2001 on operations to aid uprooted people in Asian and Latin American developing countries, [2001] O.J. L287/3 (all based on Art. 179 of the EC Treaty). See Baroncini, "The Legal Framework of the European Community's Assistance towards Uprooted People" (2000) R.A.E. 139–166.

[128] *e.g.*, Council Regulation (EC) No. 552/97 of March 24, 1997 temporarily withdrawing access to generalised tariff preferences from the Union of Myanmar, [1997] O.J. L85/8 (access withdrawn on account of systematic use of forced labour in Myanmar (Burma)).

[129] ECJ, Case C–268/94 *Portugal v Council* [1996] E.C.R. I–6177, paras 23–29. The Court considers that references to respect for human rights in agreements in the field of development policy may be an important factor in the exercise of the right of the Community—on the basis of international law—to have the agreement suspended or terminated where the non-member country has violated human rights (*ibid.*, para. 27). See also para. 20–022, *supra*, and Ward, "Framework for Co-operation between the European Union and Third States: A Viable Matrix for Uniform Human Rights Standards?" (1998) E.For.Aff.Rev. 505–536; Fierro, "Legal Basis and Scope of Human Rights Clauses in EC Bilateral Agreements: Any Room for Positive Interpretation?" (2001) E.L.J. 41–68; Delaplace, "L'Union européenne et la conditionnalité de l'aide au développement" (2001) R.T.D.E 609–626.

[130] Flaesch-Mougin, "Le traité de Maastricht et les compétences externes de la Communauté européenne: à la recherche d'une politique externe de l'Union" (1993) C.D.E. 351, at 365. See, *e.g.* the possibility for the European Investment Bank to grant aid (EC Treaty, Art. 179(2)).

common commercial policy (EC Treaty, Art. 133). In view of the broad objectives pursued by development co-operation policy, it must be possible for a measure to cover a variety of specific matters. Where a measure contains clauses concerning several specific matters, the Treaty provisions on development co-operation afford a sufficient legal basis, provided that development co-operation is the essential object of the measure and the obligations contained in those clauses are not so extensive as to constitute in fact objectives distinct from those of development co-operation.[131]

Under Art. 179 of the EC Treaty, measures to further the Treaty objectives with regard to development co-operation, including possibly multiannual programmes, are adopted by the European Parliament and the Council under the co-decision procedure. Such measures may be financed by the Community and may also receive support for their implementation from the funds of the European Investment Bank.[132] Detailed rules for Community co-operation with non-member countries and competent international organisations may be incorporated in agreements between the Community and the countries or international organisations in question which are negotiated and concluded in accordance with Art. 300 of the EC Treaty.[133] This is without prejudice to Member States' competence to negotiate in international bodies and to conclude international agreements on development co-operation themselves (EC Treaty, Art. 181).[134] Development co-operation policy therefore does not constitute an exclusive competence of the Community; it is intended to be complementary to policies pursued by the Member States in this regard.[135] Nevertheless, Member States' action is limited by exclusive Community competence with regard to the common commercial policy and by arrangements adopted by the Community internally or agreed upon at international level.[136] The Community and the Member States are to co-ordinate their policies on development co-operation and consult each other on their aid programmes. They may undertake joint action and are to contribute if necessary to the

---

[131] ECJ, Case C–268/94 *Portugal v Council* [1996] E.C.R. I–6177, para. 39 (by analogy with Opinion 1/78 on the common commercial policy: para. 20–002, *supra*). This test was applied to drug abuse control clauses (paras 60–68) and clauses concerning the protection of intellectual property (paras 69–77).

[132] EC Treaty, Art. 179(2). The EIB grants such support in the context of the ACP-EC Convention (para. 20–023, *supra*).

[133] Under Art. 300, the Council decides in principle by a qualified majority vote after consulting the European Parliament or obtaining its assent (see para. 21–003 *et seq.*).

[134] Consequently, co-operation agreements include the following clause: "Without prejudice to the relevant provisions of the Treaties establishing the European Communities, neither this Agreement nor any action taken thereunder shall in any way affect the powers of the Member States of the Communities to undertake bilateral activities with [the non-member country] in the framework of economic co-operation or to conclude, where appropriate, new economic co-operation agreements with [the non-member country]" (see, for instance, Art. 25 of the co-operation agreement with India; n.100 to para. 20–009, *supra*).

[135] EC Treaty, Art. 177(1); see also ECJ, Case C–268/94 *Portugal v Council* [1996] E.C.R. I–6177, para. 36.

[136] See Declaration (No. 10) annexed to the EU Treaty, discussed in para. 20–036, *infra*).

implementation of Community aid programmes (EC Treaty, Art. 180(1)).[137] The Commission may take any useful initiative to promote the co-ordination of the policies of the Community and the Member States (Art. 180(2)). Frequently, aid programmes of public authorities in beneficiary countries require them to have the projects supported by the Community carried out by means of specific calls for tenders.[138]

Humanitarian aid. The EU Constitution will supplement the existing powers in the field of development co-operation by adding a specific legal basis for humanitarian aid, which is not restricted to developing countries. The Union may provide ad hoc assistance, relief and protection for people in third countries who are victims of natural or man-made disasters (EU Constitution, Art. III–321(1)). In this context, the EU Constitution also provides for the setting up of a European Voluntary Humanitarian Aid Corps (Art. III–321(5)). In matters of humanitarian aid, as in the field of development co-operation, the European Parliament and the Council will adopt European laws and framework laws, *i.e.* they are to act under the co-decision procedure. **20–028**

IV. ECONOMIC, FINANCIAL AND TECHNICAL CO-OPERATION WITH NON-MEMBER COUNTRIES

Co-operation with third countries. The Treaty of Nice has introduced a specific legal basis enabling the Community to adopt measures for economic, financial and technical co-operation with non-member countries. Art. 181a of the EC Treaty serves as the legal basis for a whole series of measures which were formerly adopted under Art. 308 of that Treaty, possibly in combination with Art. 133 (common commercial policy) or Art. 181 (development co-operation) (see paras 20–009, 20–020 and 20–027). Such measures are to be complementary to those carried out by the Member States and consistent with the development policy of the Community and must contribute to the general objective of developing and consolidating democracy and the rule of law and to the objective of respecting human rights and fundamental freedoms (Art. 181a(1)).[139] The arrangements for Community co-operation with non-member countries and international organisations may be the subject of agreements between the Community and the third parties concerned, which are to be negotiated and concluded in accordance with Art. **20–029**

---

[137] See also ECJ, Case C–316/91 *European Parliament v Council* [1994] E.C.R. I–625, paras 25–27; Flaesch-Mougin (n.130, *supra*), at 364.

[138] See Kalbe, "The award of contracts and the enforcement of claims in the context of EC external aid and development co-operation" (2001) C.M.L.R. 1217–1267.

[139] For the incorporation of human rights clauses, see the literature cited in n.129, *supra*. Sometimes trading partners are resistant to the incorporation of a human rights clause: see *Europe*, No. 6901, January 27–28, 1997, 10, and No. 6903, January 30, 1997, 9 (complaints from Australia).

300 (see paras 21–003 *et seq.*). This is without prejudice to the Member States' competence to negotiate in international bodies and to conclude international agreements (Art. 181a(3), second subpara.). Accordingly, policy on economic, financial and technical co-operation does not constitute an exclusive competence of the Community.

Whereas Art. 308 of the EC Treaty requires the Council to vote by unanimity, the Council acts on the co-operation provided for in Art. 181a by a qualified majority. However, a unanimous vote is required where the co-operation is to be based on an association agreement referred to in Art. 310 (see paras 20–017 *et seq.*) or on agreements to be concluded with the States which are candidates for accession to the Union (Art. 181a(2)). It is remarkable that the involvement of the European Parliament depends on the degree of development of the beneficiary countries: whereas development co-operation measures are adopted by the European Parliament and the Council under the co-decision procedure (see para. 20–027), the Council decides on co-operation with non-member countries under Art. 181a of the EC Treaty after merely consulting the Parliament. This anomaly will no longer exist when the EU Constitution is in force, as it will make the co-decision procedure applicable in this field.[140] As far as urgent financial aid is concerned, the Council, acting by a qualified majority, will be empowered to take decisions on its own.[141]

V. Other Community Powers

A. External Aspects of Internal Rules

20–030 **External aspects.** Community rules have external aspects where they are applicable to nationals of non-member countries or to situations which are partly connected with such countries. Thus, free movement of goods is applicable to goods from third countries which are in free circulation in the Member States (EC Treaty, Art. 23(2) and Art. 24); the Council adopts, with regard to third-country nationals, measures concerning external border controls, visas, asylum and immigration (EC Treaty, Arts 61–64); and the Community is empowered to lay down rules on international transport to or from Member States (EC Treaty, Art. 71(1)(a)). The common organisations of the agricultural markets not only regulate Community production but also establish an import regime to stabilise the markets and ensure sales of Community production.[142] Measures liberalising free movement of workers, the right of establishment and free movement of services within the common market also have implications for nationals of non-Community countries wishing to work, establish themselves or provide services in a Member State.[143]

---

[140] EU Constitution, Art. III–319(2).
[141] *ibid.*, Art. III–320.
[142] See ECJ, Case C–280/93 *Germany v Council* [1994] E.C.R. I–4973, para. 55.
[143] See, *e.g.* the measures with regard to freedom of establishment and freedom to provide services enumerated in ECJ, Opinion 1/94 *Agreement establishing the World Trade Organisation* [1994] E.C.R. I–5267, paras 90–94.

B. International Agreements Based on Internal Powers

Explicit treaty-making power. In some cases, the EC Treaty expressly **20–031** empowers the Community to conclude international agreements. The agreements in question are firstly those concerning the common commercial policy (Art. 133) and association agreements (Art. 310). In addition, the Community is empowered to conclude agreements on an exchange-rate system for the euro in relation to non-Community currencies (Art. 111(1)),[144] on research and technological development (Art. 170, second para.),[145] on development co-operation (Art. 181, first para.; see para. 20–027) and on the environment (Art. 174(4), first subpara.).[146] In these areas, both the Community and the Member States may co-operate with third countries or international organisations (see Art. 181, first para., and Art. 174(4), first subpara.). As a result, the Community's competence does not detract from the Member States' own powers to negotiate in international fora and conclude international agreements (see Arts 111(5), 174(4), second subpara., and 181, second para.).[147]

Implied treaty-making power. In addition, the Court of Justice has held **20–032** that "authority to enter into international commitments may not only arise from an express attribution by the Treaty, but may also flow implicitly from its provisions. The Court [has] concluded, in particular, that whenever Community law created for the institutions of the Community powers within its internal system for the purpose of attaining a specific objective, the Community [has] authority to enter into the international commitments necessary for the attainment of that objective even in the absence of an express provision in that connection".[148] In any event, such external authority flows by implication from measures adopted by the institutions in so far as it is necessary to secure the effectiveness of those measures.[149] The

---

[144] See the literature cited in n.38 to para. 19–010.

[145] See, *e.g.* the Agreement on scientific and technical co-operation between the European Community and the State of Israel, approved by Council Decision 2004/576/EC of April 29, 2004, [2004] O.J. L261/47.

[146] As regards the environment, see Thieme, "European Community External Relations in the Field of the Environment" (2001) E.Env.L.Rev. 252–264.

[147] With regard to exchange-rate questions, see the authorisations conferred on Member States pursuant to Art. 111(3) of the EC Treaty as mentioned in n.1070 to para. 5–231.

[148] ECJ, Opinion 2/91 *Convention No. 170 of the International Labour Organisation concerning safety in the use of chemicals at work* [1993] E.C.R. I–1061, para. 7; ECJ, Opinion 2/94 *Accession by the Communities to the Convention for the Protection of Human Rights and Fundamental Freedoms* [1996] I–1759, para. 26.

[149] Opinion 2/91, *ibid.*, para. 7; ECJ, Joined Cases 3, 4 and 6/76 *Kramer* [1976] E.C.R. 1279, para. 19/20.

Court of Justice held accordingly in the *AETR* judgment that the Community was empowered to accede to an international agreement on working conditions in international road transport on the ground that the Council had adopted a regulation internally on the harmonisation of certain social legislation relating to road transport.[150] In addition, where a power cannot be effectively exercised without involving non-member countries, the Community is entitled *ipso facto* to act externally, even if the first use made of the power is to conclude and implement an international agreement.[151] This was the case with an agreement on a European inland-waterways fund which could not be concluded without involving non-member countries whose vessels used the waterways in question.[152] In this situation, therefore, the Community has external competence because its internal competence may be exercised effectively only together with an external competence. It is implicit in these two situations that there is a limited parallelism between internal and external powers. On the basis of this reasoning, *e.g.* Art. 37 and Art. 71, respectively, of the EC Treaty constitute the basis for a number of fisheries and transport agreements

---

[150] See the *AETR* judgment of March 31, 1971, Case 22/70 *Commission v Council* [1971] E.C.R. 263, paras 16–29 (quoted in para. 5–015, *supra*). For later examples of international competence implicitly arising out of existing Community legislation, see ECJ, Opinion 1/92 *Draft Agreement between the Community, on the one hand, and the countries of the European Free Trade Association, on the other, relating to the creation of the European Economic Area* [1992] E.C.R. I–2821, paras 39–40; ECJ, Opinion 1/94 *Agreement establishing the World Trade Organisation* [1994] E.C.R. I–5267, para. 77. In so far as the judgments of the Court of Justice of November 5, 2002 on the bilateral "open-skies" agreements hold that Community legislation on air transport confers exclusive external competence in respect of some aspects (fares, booking systems and slot allocation) (n.161, *infra*), this also constitutes recognition of external powers arising for the Community out of internal legislation.

[151] ECJ, Opinion 1/94 *Agreement establishing the World Trade Organisation* [1994] E.C.R. I–5267, paras 82–85; ECJ, Opinion 2/92 *Third Revised Decision of the OECD on national treatment* [1995] E.C.R. I–521, paras 31–32.

[152] See ECJ, Opinion 1/76 *Draft Agreement establishing a European laying-up fund for inland waterway vessels* [1977] E.C.R. 741, para. 4. In Opinion 1/94, the Court of Justice held that such an external power did not exist for the provision of services, in respect of which the rules on freedom of establishment and freedom to provide services are not inextricably bound up with the status of nationals of a third country in the Community or of nationals of a Member State in a third country (Opinion 1/94, para. 85) or for intellectual property, in respect of which harmonisation at Community level does not necessarily have to be accompanied by agreements with non-member countries in order to be effective (*ibid.*, para. 100). However, the Treaty of Nice extended the common commercial policy to cover certain aspects of trade in services and intellectual property (see para. 20–003). In the judgments of November 5, 2002 on the bilateral "open skies" agreements, the Court of Justice considered that as regards freedom to provide services in the field of air transport external competence was not necessary in order to effectively exercise internal competence: ECJ, Case C–467/98 *Commission v Denmark* [2002] E.C.R. I–9519, paras 54–64; ECJ, Case C–468/98 *Commission v Sweden* [2002] E.C.R. I–9575, paras 51–61; ECJ, Case C–469/98 *Commission v Finland* [2002] E.C.R. I–9627, paras 55–65; ECJ, Case C–471/98 *Commission v Belgium* [2002] E.C.R. I–9681, paras 65–75; ECJ, Case C–472/98 *Commission v Luxembourg* [2002] E.C.R. I–9741, paras 59–69; ECJ, Case C–475/98 *Commission v Austria* [2002] E.C.R. I–9797, paras 65–75; ECJ, Case C–476/98 *Commission v Germany* [2002] E.C.R. I–9855, paras 80–90 (at the same time the Court of Justice recognised, however, that there was external Community competence on the basis of the *AETR* case law; see nn.150 and 161, *supra*).

which the Community has concluded with non-member countries.[153] Accordingly, too, the Community is entitled to conclude agreements on immigration with non-member countries pursuant to Art. 63 of the EC Treaty.[154] The judgment in *AETR* case also underscored that to the extent to which autonomous action on the part of the Member States at international level is likely to detract from Community legislation, the external competence of the Community that arises implicitly from internal legislation constitutes exclusive competence in the sense that it precludes any autonomous action on the part of the Member States (see para. 20–036).

Article 308 of the EC Treaty. Furthermore, the Community has an **20–033** additional power under the Treaty to conclude agreements if it takes "appropriate measures" under Art. 308 of the EC Treaty where action by the Community proves necessary to attain, in the course of the operation of the common market, one of the objectives of the Community.[155] Article 308 may, however, be used as a legal basis only if the Treaty has not provided the necessary powers, and hence cannot be employed where the means of acting externally are already present by implication in an internal power.[156]

---

[153] For an example of disputes on the definition of external powers, see Close, "External Relations in the Air Transport Sector: Air Transport Policy or the Common Commercial Policy?" (1990) C.M.L.R. 107–127. For the possible external competence ensuing from Art. 65 of the EC Treaty (judicial co-operation in civil matters), see Kotuby, "External Competence of the European Community in the Hague Conference on Private International Law: Community Harmonisation and Worldwide Unification" (2001) N.I.L.R. 1–30; Thoma, "La définition et l'exercice de compétences externes de la Communauté européenne au domaine de la co-opération dans les matières civiles ayant une incidence transfrontalière" (2002) ERPL/REDP 397–416. For the lack of external competence as regards social policy, see Novitz, " 'A Human Face' for the Union or More Cosmetic Surgery? EU Competence in Global Social Governance and Promotion of Core Labour Standards" (2002) M.J.E.C.L. 231–261.

[154] See, *e.g.* the Agreements concluded between the European Community (with the exception of Denmark, as far as the first agreement is concerned; with the exception of both Denmark and Ireland, as far as the second is concerned) and the Government of the Hong Kong Special Administrative Region of the People's Republic of China (PRC) and the Macao Special Administrative Region of the PRC on the readmission of persons residing without authorisation, approved by Council Decision 2004/80/EC of December 17, 2003 ([2004] O.J. L17/23) and 2004/424/EC of April 21, 2004 ([2004] O.J. L143/97), respectively; and the Memorandum of Understanding between the European Community (with the exception of Denmark, Ireland and UK) and the National Tourism Administration of the People's Republic of China on visa and related issues concerning tourist groups from the People's Republic of China (ADS) ([2004] O.J. L83/12).

[155] ECJ, Case 22/70 *Commission v Council* [1971] E.C.R. 263, para. 95. See, *e.g.* the seven bilateral agreements on co-operation in the field of education and training under the Erasmus Programme concluded between the EEC and Austria, Finland, Iceland, Norway, Sweden, Switzerland and Liechtenstein, respectively, approved by Council Decisions 91/611/EEC to 91/617/EEC of October 28, 1991 on the basis of Art. 235 of the EEC Treaty [now Art. 308 of the EC Treaty], [1991] O.J. L332/1–71.

[156] See Raux, "Le recours à l'article 235 du traité CEE en vue de la conclusion d'accords externes", *Etudes de droit des Communautés européennes. Mélanges offerts à P.-H. Teitgen* (Pedone, Paris, 1984), 407, at 428; Kovar, "Les compétences implicites: jurisprudence de la Cour et pratique communautaire", in Demaret (ed.), *Relations extérieures de la Communauté européenne et marché intérieur: aspects juridiques et fonctionnels* (College of Europe/Story, Bruges, 1988), 15, at 22–31.

859

20–034 **International co-operation.** In some areas, the EC Treaty declares that the Community and the Member States are empowered to foster co-operation with non-member countries and relevant international organisations without expressly conferring on the Community a power to conclude agreements. Examples are education (Art. 149(3)), vocational training (Art. 150(3)), culture (Art. 151(3)) and public health (Art. 152(3)). In such cases, international co-operation may take place *via* the "(incentive) measures" provided for in the articles in question, which are intended to be consonant with the complementary nature of the powers in question.[157] In the field of trans-European networks, the Community may decide to co-operate with third countries (Art. 155(3)) in accordance with the procedure laid down in Art. 156 of the EC Treaty. According to the case law referred to above, it is likewise possible to infer a power for the Community to conclude any necessary international agreements in these policy areas.[158]

20–035 **Constitution.** Under the EU Constitution, the Union may conclude international agreements not only in those cases where the Constitution so provides (environment, research and technological development, associations, common commercial policy, development co-operation, economic, financial and technical co-operation with third countries, humanitarian aid and monetary policy), but also "where the conclusion of an agreement is necessary in order to achieve, within the framework of the Union's policies, one of the objectives referred to in the Constitution, or is provided for in a legally binding Union act or is likely to affect common rules or alter their scope" (Art. III–323(1)). In this way, the EU Constitution codifies the external powers which—according to the case law of the Court of Justice—flow implicitly from the Community Treaties and secondary Community law (see paras 20–032–20–034).

C. Relationship to the Member States' international powers

20–036 **Pre-emption of national powers.** As some Treaty provisions explicitly recognise (see para. 20–031), the Community's non-exclusive external powers do not deprive Member States of the power to act externally. It follows, however, from Art. 10 of the EC Treaty that "to the extent to which Community rules are promulgated for the attainment of the objectives of the Treaty, the Member States cannot, outside the framework of the Community institutions, assume obligations which might affect those

---

[157] Flaesch-Mougin (n.130, *supra*), at 357–358.
[158] See the Agreements, concluded by the European Community in 1995 on the basis of Arts 149 and 150 of the EC Treaty, with the USA and Canada, respectively, establishing co-operation programmes in higher education and vocational training, renewed by Council Decisions of February 26, 2001 (2001/196/EC and 2001/197/EC, [2001] O.J. L17/7 and 15, respectively). See to this effect, Lenaerts, "Education in European Community Law after Maastricht" (1994) C.M.L.R. 7, at 39.

rules or alter their scope" (judgment in the *AETR* case).[159] This means that Member States retain their powers as long as the Community has not, or only partially, exercised its (non-exclusive) powers.[160] Where, however, the Community adopts a measure internally or internationally, the Member States should attune their international action in the light of that measure.[161] This would be the case if a Member State were to enter into international commitments falling within the scope of the Community rules, or in any event within an area which is already largely covered by such rules, even if there is no contradiction between those commitments and the Community rules.[162] Accordingly, the Member States retain the power to enter into international commitments (for instance, with regard to worker protection) where the Community has adopted only minimum requirements in the relevant field;[163] yet they may not enter into such

---

[159] ECJ, Case 22/70 *Commission v Council* [1971] E.C.R. 263, para. 22. In that judgment, the Court of Justice therefore held not only that Community competence *existed* (see para. 20–032) but also that the Member States could no longer act in that area and that, as a result, the Community had *exclusive* competence (para. 5–023, *supra*).

[160] See, *e.g.* ECJ, Opinion 1/94 *Agreement establishing the World Trade Organisation* [1994] E.C.R. I–5267, paras 88–89 and 101–105; see Van Nuffel (n.14, *supra*), at 348–351; ECJ, Opinion 2/00 *Cartagena Protocol* [2001] E.C.R. I–9713, paras 45–47. See Maubernard, "L' "intensité modulable" des compétences externes de la Communauté européenne et de ses Etats membres" (2003) R.T.D.E. 229–246. There is an exception where the internal Community power can only be exercised effectively together with the external power (para. 20–032, *supra*).

[161] See the judgments of November 5, 2002 in which bilateral agreements between Member States and the USA relating to access to air transport ('open skies' agreements) were held to be contrary to Community legislation on fares and booking systems: ECJ, Case C–467/98 *Commission v Denmark* [2002] E.C.R. I–9519, paras 75–112; ECJ, Case C–468/98 *Commission v Sweden* [2002] E.C.R. I–9575, paras 71–108; ECJ, Case C–469/98 *Commission v Finland* [2002] E.C.R. I–9627, paras 75–113; ECJ, Case C–471/98 *Commission v Belgium* [2002] E.C.R. I–9681, paras 88–126; ECJ, Case C–472/98 *Commission v Luxembourg* [2002] E.C.R. I–9741, paras 81–118; ECJ, Case C–475/98 *Commission v Austria* [2002] E.C.R. I–9797, paras 88–126; ECJ, Case C–476/98 *Commission v Germany* [2002] E.C.R. I–9855, paras 101–137. At the same time, the Court of Justice held that there had been an infringement of Art. 43 of the EC Treaty concerning establishment in those judgments and in ECJ, Case 466/98 *Commission v UK* [2003] E.C.R. I–9427. For those judgments, see Slot and Dutheil de la Rochère (2003) C.M.L.R. 697–713; Heffernan and McAuliffe, "External relations in the air transport sector: the Court of Justice and the open skies agreements" (2003) E.L.R. 601–619; Middeldorp and Van Ooik, "Van verdeelde *Open Skies* naar een uniform Europees extern luchtvaartbeleid" (2003) N.T.E.R. 1–9; Thym, "Der Binnenmarkt und die 'Freiheit der Lüfte'" (2003) EuR. 277–290; Grard, "La Cour de justice des Communautés européennes et la dimension externe du marché unique des transports aériens" (2003) C.D.E. 695–733; Stadlmeier, "Das Ende einer Ära? Die *Open Skies*-Urteile des EuGH" (2003) Z.ö.R. 163–195; Dehousse and Maczkovics, "Les arrêts *open skies* de la Cour de justice: l'abandon de la compétence externe implicite de la Communauté?" (2003) J.T.D.E. 225–236.

[162] ECJ, Case C–467/98 *Commission v Denmark* [2002] E.C.R. I–9519, para. 82 (and the parallel judgments in the "open skies" cases).

[163] ECJ, Opinion 2/91 *Convention No. 170 of the International Labour Organisation concerning safety in the use of chemicals at work* [1993] E.C.R. I–1061, paras 18–21; case notes by Emiliou (1994) E.L.R. 76–86 and Timmermans (1994) S.E.W. 622–627 (who emphasises that competence on the part of the Member States may be different where the international obligations themselves do not consist of minimum standards, as in the case of the ILO Convention at issue); Auvret-Finck (1995) C.D.E. 443–460.

commitments in an area which is already covered to a large extent by Community rules adopted with a view to achieving even fuller harmonisation.[164] Whenever the Community has included in its internal rules provisions relating to the treatment of nationals of non-member countries or has expressly conferred on its institutions powers to negotiate with non-member countries, it acquires an exclusive external competence in the spheres covered by those measures.[165] A Community measure may, however, authorise a Member State to conclude international agreements diverging from that measure.[166] The upshot is that the extent of the Member States' international competence depends on whether or not the Community has exercised its internal and external powers exhaustively.[167] The Member States have recognised this consequence of the judgment in the *AETR* case, even in those areas where the Treaty confirms in principle their international competence.[168] In this sense, the allocation of external powers as between the Community and the Member States changes with the intensity with which the Community exercises the power relating to the field in question.

20–037 **Transparency.** The allocation of powers as between the Community and the Member States in the field of external relations constitutes a purely internal matter as far as the Community is concerned (see para. 19–002). However, its changing nature makes contracting parties uncertain as to who is assuming the international obligations flowing from a given agreement. Indeed, other parties have made the conclusion of an international agreement on the part of the Community conditional upon its being signed

---

[164] Opinion 2/91, paras 25–26. See also ECJ, Opinion 2/92 *Third Revised Decision of the OECD on national treatment* [1995] E.C.R. I–521, paras 30–36.

[165] ECJ, Case C–467/98 *Commission v Denmark* [2002] E.C.R. I–9519, para. 83 (and the parallel judgments in the "open skies" cases).

[166] See, for instance, the authority granted by Council Decision 96/402/EC to Germany (pursuant to Council Directive 77/388/EEC on the harmonisation of the laws of the Member States relating to turnover taxes) to conclude an agreement with Poland containing measures derogating from that directive, [1996] O.J. L165/35.

[167] By the same token, Protocol (No. 31) to the EC Treaty on external relations of the Member States with regard to the crossing of external borders, annexed by the Amsterdam Treaty to the EC Treaty ([1997] O.J. C340/108) confirms that Member States have competence to conclude agreements with third countries "as long as they respect Community law and other relevant international agreements". For the operation of "pre-emption", see Lenaerts, "Les répercussions des compétences de la Communauté européenne sur les compétences externes des Etats membres et la question de la 'preemption'" in Demaret (ed.), *Relations extérieures de la Communauté européenne et marché intérieur: aspects juridiques et fonctionnels* (College of Europe/Story, Bruges, 1988), 39, at 54–62; for "pre-emption" generally, see para. 5–023, *supra*.

[168] See the Declaration annexed to the Single European Act on Art. 130r of the EEC Treaty and Declaration (No. 10) annexed to the EU Treaty, in which the Intergovernmental Conference considered that "the provisions of Art. 109 [now Art. 111](5), Art. 130r [now Art. 174](4), second subpara., and Art. 130y [now Art. 181] do not affect the principles resulting from the judgment handed down by the Court of Justice in the AETR case".

in parallel by the Member States.[169] It is for this reason, too, that multilateral agreements often require signatory international organisations to deposit a declaration as to the situation with regard to the internal division of powers.[170] In such a case, the Community is subject to an obligation of international law requiring it to submit a complete declaration of its competences. Where the Council authorises the Commission to accede to a convention, the duty to co-operate in good faith to which the institutions are subject requires the Council to enable the Commission to comply with international law by submitting a complete declaration of competences.[171]

Constitution. In order to ensure a transparent allocation of powers, the definition of the Union's exclusive competence in the EU Constitution refers also to cases where external action of the Union may prevent the Member States from acting at the international level on their own. Largely inspired by the *AETR* case law of the Court of Justice, Art. I–13(2) of the EU Constitution provides that the Union: **20–038**

> "shall also have exclusive competence for the conclusion of an international agreement when its conclusion is provided for in a legislative act of the Union or is necessary to enable the Union to exercise its internal competence, or in so far as its conclusion may affect common rules or alter their scope".

---

[169] See Arts 2 and 3 of Annex IX to the United Nations Convention of December 10, 1982 on the Law of the Sea ([1998] O.J. L179/113), which stipulated that the majority of the Member States had to accede thereto before the Community could accede. See Simmonds, "The Community's Participation in the U.N. Law of the Sea Convention", in O'Keeffe and Schermers (eds), *Essays in European Law and Integration* (Kluwer, Deventer, 1982), 141, at 179–195; Stein, "External Relations of the European Community: Structure and Process"(1990) *Collected Courses of the Academy of European Law. I*, 1990, 115, at 161–162. For the Convention, see para. 8–001, *supra*.

[170] See, *e.g.* Art. 5 of Annex IX to the United Nations Convention of December 10, 1982 on the Law of the Sea and the Community's Declaration concerning the competence of the European Community with regard to matters governed by the United Nations Convention of the Law of the Sea of December 10, 1982 and the Agreement of July 28, 1994 relating to the implementation of Part XI of the Convention ([1998] O.J. L179/129). See also Art. 47(2) of the Agreement for the implementation of the provisions of the United Nations Convention of the Law of the Sea of December 10, 1982 relating to the conservation and management of straddling stocks and highly migratory fish stocks, approved by the Community, together with the annexed declaration on competence, by Council Decision 98/414/EC of June 8, 1998, [1998] O.J. L189/39; Art. 13(3) of the Vienna Convention of March 22, 1985 for the Protection of the Ozone Layer, [1988] O.J. L297/10; Art. 22(3) of the United Nations Framework Treaty of May 9, 1992 on Climatical Change, [1994] O.J. L33/13; Art. 34 of the United Nations Convention of June 17, 1994 to combat desertification in countries seriously affected by drought and/or desertification, particularly in Africa, published together with the annexed declaration on competence ([1998] O.J. L83/34).

[171] ECJ, Case C–29/99 *Commission v Council* [2002] E.C.R. I–11221, paras 67–71.

VI. THE COMMON FOREIGN AND SECURITY POLICY (CFSP)

A. OBJECTIVES AND SCOPE OF THE CFSP

20–039 Objectives. Title V of the EU Treaty constitutes the framework for the common foreign and security policy (CFSP) which the Union conducts alongside—and in conjunction with—the external policy of the Communities.[172] Article 11(1) of the EU Treaty formulates specific objectives for the CFSP which supplement, the general objectives of Art. 2 of the EU Treaty:

(1) safeguarding the common values, fundamental interests, independence and integrity of the Union;

(2) strengthening the security of the Union in all ways;

(3) preserving peace and strengthening international security;

(4) promoting international co-operation; and

(5) developing and consolidating democracy and the rule of law, and respect for human rights and fundamental freedoms.[173]

In the case of the first objective, the EU Treaty stresses that the Union is to act in conformity with the principles of the United Nations Charter[174]; as far as preserving peace and strengthening international security are concerned, the EU Treaty also mentions the principles of the Helsinki Final Act and the objectives of the Paris Charter (with respect to the OSCE, see para. 2–006).

20–040 Scope. Unlike European Political Co-operation (EPC; see para. 2–013), the CFSP works not merely on the basis of inter-governmental co-operation

---

[172] For a general survey, see Baches Opi and Floyd, "A Shaky Pillar of Global Stability: The Evolution of the European Union's Common Foreign and Security Policy" (2003) Col.J.E.L. 299–332.

[173] For a discussion of CFSP objectives, see Keukeleire, *Het buitenlands beleid van de Europese Unie*, (Deventer, Kluwer, 1998) at 153–175. The last three objectives were already mentioned in the preamble to the Single European Act. The preamble to the EEC Treaty still clearly limited the Community to the (economic) sphere of interest of the European peoples and associated countries overseas. The objectives set out in Art. 11 of the EU Treaty are concerned more with political than with economic action: Dashwood, "External Relations Provisions of the Amsterdam Treaty" (1998) C.M.L.R. 1019, at 1029. Pursuant to these objectives, the Member States subscribed to the establishment of the International Criminal Court: Council Common Position 2001/443/CFSP of June 11, 2001 on the International Criminal Court, [2001] O.J. L155/19, as amended (after the ratification by all Member States of the Statute of the International Criminal Court) by Council Common Positions 2002/474/CFSP of June 20, 2002, [2002] O.J. L164/1, and 2003/444/CFSP of June 16, 2003, [2003] O.J. L150/67.

[174] For the United Nations Charter and the relationship with the EU/Community, see para. 17–104, *infra*. For the financial support provided by the Member States and the EU to the UN, see the Council's answer of November 21, 1997 to question E–1697/97 (Müller), [1998] O.J. C102/7.

between the Member States but is primarily shaped by measures adopted by the institutions of the Union. The CFSP covers "all areas of foreign and security policy" (EU Treaty, Art. 11(1)), including the possibility of a common defence policy. In this respect, too, the CFSP can no longer be compared to EPC, which initially avoided defence questions.[175] The Member States are to support the CFSP actively and unreservedly in a "spirit of loyalty and mutual solidarity"; to this end, they must work together and refrain from any action which is contrary to the interests of the Union (EU Treaty, Art. 11(2)). The measures which the institutions adopt under the CFSP do not, however, have the force of Community law; the binding force of those instruments therefore depends on the status that the national legal system confers on those commitments undertaken under international law (see paras 18–014—18–023).[176]

CFSP in the Constitution. As mentioned above, the EU Constitution will **20–041** bring the CFSP and the other external powers of the Union together in one Title relating to the Union's external action.[177] This means that the CFSP will be related to the same principles and objectives that have to guide the Union in the other areas of its external policy (see EU Constitution, Art. III–292(1) and (2)). Since the CFSP will have the same legal foundation as the other external powers of the Union, there will in principle no longer be any distinction between acts adopted within the framework of the CFSP and other acts of "Union law" in terms of their legal force. Accordingly, the CFSP will be subject to the principle that the Constitution, and law adopted by the Union's institutions in exercising competences conferred on it, is to have primacy over the law of the Member States (Art. I–6) and Member States must "comply" with the Union's action in the field of CFSP (Art. I–16(2)). Given that, in principle, the Court of Justice will not have any jurisdiction in the field of the CFSP, it will be up to the national courts to rule on the effects of CFSP acts when they are called upon to resolve conflicts between CFSP acts and national law (see para. 18–022). Furthermore, the EU Constitution contains "specific provisions" fleshing out some specific features of CFSP decision-making (see para. 15–009) and CFSP instruments (see para. 18–022).

---

[175] Initially, the exclusion of defence arose chiefly at the request of Ireland (not a member of NATO) and France (not part of the integrated military structure). In the Solemn Declaration of Stuttgart, however, the Heads of State or Government agreed to co-ordinate national positions as far as "political and economic aspects of security" were concerned (confirmed in Art. 30(6) of the Single European Act).

[176] For the legal constraints which the CFSP places on action by the Member States, see Mayer, "Angriffskrieg und europäisches Verfassungsrecht—Zu den rechtlichen Bindungen von Aussenpolitik in Europa" (2003) A.Völkerr. 394–418.

[177] See Cremona, "The Draft Constitutional Treaty: External Relations and External Action" (2003) C.M.L.R. 1347–1366; Pernice and Thym, "A New Institutional Balance for European Foreign Policy?" (2002) E.For.Aff.Rev. 369–400; Kugelmann, "'Kerneuropa' und der EU-Außenminister—die verstärkte Zusammenarbeit in der GSAP" (2004) EuR. 322–344.

B. SUBSTANCE OF THE COMMON FOREIGN AND SECURITY POLICY

20–042 **General framework.** The EU Treaty does not lay down any substantive rules with which the Union's policy must comply. The Member States are to judge themselves, in the context of the European Council and the Council, whether a matter should be covered by the common policy.[178] The Contracting Parties did not wish to give a list of matters which should fall entirely within the common policy. The Ministers of Foreign Affairs of the Member States did in fact indicate factors which should be taken into account, namely geographical proximity of a given country or region, an important interest for the Union in the political and economic stability of a region or country, and threats to the security interests of the Union.[179] Only questions of security policy are specified in the EU Treaty (see Art. 17(2)).

The Treaty provisions do, however, describe the procedures by which the CFSP is given shape. The Treaty of Amsterdam has streamlined these procedures, whilst defining the CFSP instruments in more precise terms.[180] The policy line for the CFSP is determined by the European Council, which is to define the principles and general guidelines and the common strategies to be pursued by the Union (Art. 13(1) and (2)).[181] The Council is to take decisions "on the basis of" the general guidelines defined by the European Council (Art. 13(3), first subpara.) or to "implement" common strategies (Art. 13(3), second subpara.). In principle, the Council takes its decision by a unanimous vote.[182] However, since the Treaty of Amsterdam, decisions can be taken in certain cases by a qualified majority vote. This will be so where the Council adopts a common position, a joint action or other decisions on the basis of a common strategy adopted (by consensus) by the European Council and where it adopts a decision implementing a joint

---

[178] See EU Treaty, Art. 13(2) and Art. 14(1). For a survey of recent years of the CFSP, see Hill, "Renationalising or Regrouping? EU Foreign Policy Since September 11, 2001" (2004) J.C.M.S. 143–163; for a substantive analysis of the initial years, see Keukeleire (n.173, *supra*), at 195–240, and other discussions in Ryba, "La politique étrangère et de sécurité commune (PESC). Mode d'emploi et bilan d'une année d'application (fin 1993–1994)" (1995) R.M.C.U.E. 14–35; Burghardt and Tebbe, "Die Gemeinsame Aussen- und Sicherheitspolitik der Europäischen Union—Rechtliche Struktur und politischer Prozess" (1995) EuR. 1–20; Willaert and Marqués-Ruiz, "Vers une politique étrangère et de sécurité commune: état des lieux" (1995) 3 R.M.U.E 35–95.

[179] See the Report of the Ministers of Foreign Affairs, approved by the European Council held at Lisbon on June 26 and 27, 1992, on the likely development of the CFSP (1992) 6 EC Bull. point I–31.

[180] For the decision-making procedure, see paras 15–002–15–007, *infra*; for a discussion of the various legal instruments, see paras 18–014–18–023, *infra*. Before the Amsterdam Treaty, the Council adopted common positions pursuant to the former Art. J.2 and joint actions pursuant to the former Art. J.3 of the EU Treaty.

[181] For the first, see Common Strategy 1999/414/CFSP of the European Union of June 4, 1999 on Russia, adopted by the European Council ([1999] O.J. L157/1) and subsequently Common Strategy 1999/877/CFSP of the European Council of December 11, 1999 on Ukraine ([1999] O.J. L331/1) and Common Strategy 2000/458/CFSP of the European Council of June 19, 2000 on the Mediterranean region ([2000] O.J. L183/5).

[182] EU Treaty, Art. 23(1), first subpara. For the possibility of "constructive abstention" of a Member State from implementing a CFSP decision, see para. 15–002, *infra*.

action or a common position.[183] Since a common strategy tends to consist of a list of specific actions, the possibility of deciding by a qualified majority is limited in practice to the technical implementation of matters on which there is agreement between all the Member States.[184]

In situations where operational action is deemed necessary, the Council is to adopt a joint action, laying down the objectives, scope, means to be made available, if necessary their duration, and the conditions for implementation (Art. 14(1)). The joint action so adopted may be reviewed in the light of a change in circumstances (Art. 14(2)).[185] The Council adopts common positions in order to define the Union's approach to particular matters of a geographical or thematic nature (Art. 15). Where necessary, the Council may conclude an agreement with one or more States or international organisations (Art. 24). The Member States are to consult one another on any matter of foreign and security policy of general interest (EU Treaty, Art. 16). A special instance of co-operation is the protection which diplomatic and consular missions of a Member State in third countries must afford to nationals of another Member State which is not represented in the country in question.[186]

Foreign policy of the Union. The introduction of a "common" foreign and **20–043** security policy has not prompted the Member States to take joint action in every sphere of foreign and security policy. The CFSP primarily affords the Member States an institutional framework which facilitates the framing and execution of a common policy in matters on which all of them agree there should be joint action.

By means of common positions, the Council has imposed economic sanctions against non-member States (see para. 20–051), formulated objectives and priorities for Union policy *vis-à-vis* non-member countries[187]

---

[183] EU Treaty, Art. 23(2), first subpara. The Treaty of Amsterdam also changed the CFSP from the point of view of its financing, which, in principle, is to be charged to the general budget of the Communities (see para. 10–116, *supra*), and with regard to the assistance which was formerly provided by the Presidency, but is now to be given by the Secretary-General of the Council as High Representative for the CFSP (see para. 15–003, *supra*). See Bonino, "La réforme de la politique étrangère et de sécurité commune: aspects institutionnels" (1995) 3 R.M.U.E. 261–266; P . des Nerviens, "Le Traité d'Amsterdam. Les relations extérieures" (1997) R.T.D.E. 801–812; Kugelmann, "Die Gemeinsame Aussen- und Sicherheitspolitik" (1998) EuR. Beiheft 2 at 99–123.

[184] See Pernice and Thym, "A New Institutional Balance for European Foreign Policy?" (2003) E.For.Aff.Rev. 369, at 375.

[185] *e.g.* Council Decision 94/308/CFSP of May 16, 1994 (n.194, *infra*).

[186] EU Treaty, Art. 20, second para., which refers to Art. 20 of the EC Treaty. See citizenship of the Union, para. 12–011, *supra*.

[187] See, for instance, the Common Positions on Afghanistan (the most recent being 2001/56/CFSP of January 22, 2001, [2001] O.J. L21/1), Albania (97/357/CFSP of June 2, 1997, [1997] O.J. L153/4), Angola (the most recent being 2002/495/CFSP of June 25, 2002, [2002] O.J. L167/9), Burma/Myanmar (96/635/CFSP of October 28, 1996, [1996] O.J. L287/1), Burundi (95/91/CFSP of March 24, 1995, [1995] O.J. L72/1), Cuba (96/697/CFSP of December 2, 1996, [1996] O.J. L322/1), East Timor (96/407/CFSP of June 25, 1996,

and defined a common stance of the Member States for international conferences[188] or the procedure for action on the part of the Union in international organisations.[189]

Council joint actions afford a basis for Union humanitarian aid actions,[190] for support for the restoration of democracy[191] or the peace process[192] in specific States and for intervention in crisis-stricken areas (*e.g.*, through the nomination of a Special Envoy of the European Union[193]). Accordingly, in

[1996] O.J. L168/2), Nigeria (the most recent being 2002/401/CFSP of May 27, 2002, [2002] O.J. L139/1), Rwanda (the most recent being 2001/779/CFSP of November 19, 2001, [2001] O.J. L303/1) and Ukraine (94/779/CFSP of November 28, 1994, [1994] O.J. L313/1). See also Common Position 98/350/CFSP of May 25, 1998 concerning human rights, democratic principles, the rule of law and good governance in Africa ([1998] O.J. L158/1) and Common Position 1999/691/CFSP of October 22, 1999 on support to democratic forces in the Federal Republic of Yugoslavia ([1999] O.J. L273/1).

[188] See, *e.g.* Common Position 95/379/CFSP of September 18, 1995, [1995] O.J. L227/3 (conference on conventional weapons), Common Positions 96/408/CFSP of June 25, 1996, [1996] O.J. L168/3, and 98/197/CFSP of March 4, 1998, [1998] O.J. L75/2 (conference on chemical weapons), Common Position 98/289/CFSP of April 23, 1998, [1998] O.J. L129/1 (conference on nuclear weapons), Common Position 2001/567/CFSP of July 23, 2001, [2001] O.J. L202/1 (fight against ballistic missile proliferation) and Common Position 2003/805/CFSP of November 17, 2003, [2003] O.J. L302/34 (instruments to combat the proliferation of weapons of mass destruction and means of delivery).

[189] *e.g.* Common Position 97/484/CFSP of July 24, 1997 on the Korean Peninsular Energy Development Organisation (KEDO), [1997] O.J. L213/1.

[190] *e.g.* support for the conveying of humanitarian aid in Bosnia and Herzegovina (Decision 93/603/CFSP of November 8, 1993, [1993] O.J. L286/1).

[191] *e.g.* the dispatch of a team of observers for the parliamentary elections in the Russian Federation (Decision 93/604/CFSP of November 9, 1993, [1993] O.J. L286/3), support for the transition towards a democratic and multi-racial South Africa (Decision 93/678/CFSP of December 6, 1993, [1993] O.J. L316/45), support for the democratic transition process in the Democratic Republic of Congo (Joint Actions 96/656/CFSP of November 11, 1996, [1996] O.J. L300/1, and 97/875/CFSP of December 19, 1997, [1997] O.J. L357/1) and support for the democratic process in Nigeria (Joint Action 98/735/CFSP of December 22, 1998, [1998] O.J. L354/1). See Youngs, "European Union Democracy Promotion Politics: Ten Years On" (2001) E.For.Aff.Rev. 355–373.

[192] See, for instance, the support given to the Middle East peace process (Decision 94/276/CFSP of April 19, 1994, [1994] O.J. L119/1, as supplemented, and Joint Action 97/289/CFSP of April 29, 1997 on an assistance programme to support the Palestine Authority in its efforts to counter terrorist activities emanating from the territories under its control, [1997] O.J. L120/2); participation of the Union in the implementing structures of the peace plan for Bosnia-Herzegovina (Joint Action 95/545/CFSP of 95/545/CFSP of December 11, 1995, [1995] O.J. L309/2, as subsequently supplemented and extended); support for the electoral process in Bosnia-Herzegovina (Joint Actions 96/406/CFSP of June 10, 1996, [1996] O.J. L168/1, as supplemented, and 98/302/CFSP of April 30, 1998, [1998] O.J. L138/3); support for the OAU peace process between Ethiopia and Eritrea (Council Common Position 2000/420/CFSP of June 29, 2000, [2000] O.J. L161/1); support for the conflict settlement process in South Ossetia (Council Joint Actions 2001/759/CFSP of October 29, 2001, [2001] O.J. L286/4, and 2003/473/CFSP of June 25, 2003, [2003] O.J. L157/72) and support for the implementation of the Lusaka Ceasefire Agreement and the peace process in the Democratic Republic of Congo (Common Position 2003/319/CFSP of May 8, 2003, [2003] O.J. L115/87).

[193] In this way, Special Envoys were appointed for the African Great Lakes Region (most recently Joint Action 2004/530/CFSP of June 28, 2004; [2004] O.J. L234/13), for the City of Mostar (Joint Action 96/442/CFSP of July 15, 1996, [1996] O.J. L185/2), for the Middle East peace process (most recently Joint Action 2003/873/CFSP of December 8, 2003, [2003]

1994 the European Union agreed, in connection with the conflict in Bosnia and Herzegovina, to take over the administration of the city of Mostar for two years.[194] Pursuant to a joint action, the Member States met with the Baltic and central and eastern European States in Paris on May 26 and 27, 1994.[195] This inaugural conference for a Stability Pact agreed to study measures to promote good neighbourliness at regional round table meetings.[196] At the final conference held on March 20 and 21, 1995 in Paris, the Stability Pact was signed, which has been followed up by the OSCE.[197] On the basis of joint actions adopted under Art. 14 of the EU Treaty, the Union has also established its own police and military missions. A joint action established a EU Police Mission which ensured the follow-on to the UN International Police Task Force from January 1, 2003 with the aim of establishing sustainable policing arrangements as part of support for the rule of law in Bosnia and Herzegovina.[198] In 2003 the European Union initiated the first military operations, first in the Former Yugoslav Republic of Macedonia (this operation has since been replaced by an EU police

---

O.J. L326/46), for the Federal Republic of Yugoslavia (Joint Action 98/375/CFSP of June 8, 1998, [1998] O.J. L165/2), for the Palestinian Authority (Joint Action 97/289/CFSP of April 29, 1997, [1997] O.J. L120/2), for South-East Europe (most recently Joint Actions 2002/964/CFSP of December 10, 2001 and 2003/449/CFSP of June 16, 2003, [2002] O.J. L334/9 and [2003] O.J. L150/74, respectively; corrigendum in [2003] O.J. L158/63), for Kosovo (Joint Action 1999/239/CFSP of March 30, 1999, [1999] O.J. L89/1), for the Former Yugoslavian Republic of Macedonia (FYROM) (most recently Joint Action 2004/565/CFSP of July 26, 2004; [2004] O.J. L251/18), for Afganistan (most recently Joint Action 2003/871/CFSP of December 8, 2003, [2003] O.J. L326/41), for Bosnia and Herzegovina (Joint Action 2002/211/CFSP of March 11, 2002, [2002] O.J. L70/7) and for the South Caucasus (Joint Action 2003/872/CFSP of December 8, 2003, [2003] O.J. L326/44). *cf.* EU Treaty, Art. 18(5).

[194] It did so on the basis of a memorandum of understanding concluded by the EU and the WEU with the local authorities ((1994) 7/8 EU Bull. point 1.3.2); see also Council Decision 94/308/CFSP of May 16, 1994 adapting and extending the application of Decision 93/603/CFSP (n.190, *supra*), [1994] O.J. L134/1, as amended and supplemented); for the phasing out of the EU administration of Mostar, see Joint Action 96/476/CFSP of July 26, 1996 ([1996] O.J. L195/1); for the phasing out of EU operations in Mostar, see Council Decision 96/744/CFSP of December 20, 1996 ([1996] O.J. L340/1).

[195] See Council Decision 93/728/CFSP of December 20, 1993 concerning the joint action adopted by the Council on the basis of Article J.3 of the Treaty on European Union on the inaugural conference of the Stability Pact ([1993] O.J. L339/1); continuation decided by Council Decision 94/367/CFSP of June 14, 1994 ([1994] O.J. L165/2).

[196] Concluding Document from the Inaugural Conference for a Pact on Stability in Europe (1994) 5 EU Bull. point 2.2.1.

[197] (1995) 3 EU Bull. point 1.4.4. See Benoît-Rohmer, "Conclusion du Pacte de stabilité en Europe" (1995) R.T.D.E. 273–277, and para. 23–031, *infra*. A Stability Pact is also contemplated for South-Eastern Europe, see Common Position 1999/345/CFSP of May 17, 1999 adopted by the Council on the basis of Art. 15 of the EU Treaty on European Union, [1999] O.J. L133/1. There is further co-operation with the OSCE on the basis of Council Joint Action 2000/456/CFSP of July 20, 2000 regarding a contribution of the European Union towards reinforcing the capacity of the Georgian authorities to support and protect the OSCE Observer Mission on the border of the Republic of Georgia with the Chechen Republic of the Russian Federation ([2000] O.J. L183/3).

[198] Council Joint Action 2002/210/ CFSP of March 11, 2002 on the European Union Police Mission, [2002] O.J. L70/1.

mission)[199] and subsequently in Congo and Bosnia and Herzegovina.[200] Whereas both military operations have been planned on the basis of a joint action adopted under Art. 14 of the EU Treaty, their actual launch was a matter of "security policy" decided on the basis of Art. 17(2) of the EU Treaty (see para. 20–045).

20–044 Constitution. The most striking amendment which the EU Constitution contemplates making to the existing framework is the creation of a Union Minister for Foreign Affairs, who will combine powers of initiative, representation and implementation (see para. 15–009). As far as the content of the CFSP is concerned, the EU Constitution provides only that it should be based on the development of mutual political solidarity among Member States, the identification of questions of general interest and the achievement of an ever-increasing degree of convergence of Member States' actions.[201] Important changes will however be made to the European Security and Defence Policy (see para. 20–046). Under the EU Constitution the Council will no longer act by means of a "common position" or a "joint action", but will adopt "European decisions" defining actions and positions of the Union and arrangements for their implementation.[202]

C. THE EUROPEAN SECURITY AND DEFENCE POLICY (ESDP)

20–045 Security policy of the Union. According to Art. 17(1) of the EU Treaty, the CFSP includes all questions relating to the security of the Union. The European Security and Defence Policy (ESDP) includes "the progressive framing of a common defence policy",[203] which relates to humanitarian and rescue tasks, peace-making tasks and tasks of combat forces in crisis management, including peace-making (the "Petersberg tasks" listed in Art.

---

[199] Council Joint Action 2003/92/CFSP of January 27, 2003 on the European Union military operation in the Former Yugoslav Republic of Macedonia ("Concordia"), [2003] O.J. L34/26, succeeded by Council Joint Action 2003/681/CFSP of September 29, 2003 on the European Union Police Mission in the Former Yugoslav Republic of Macedonia (EUPOL "Proxima"), [2003] O.J. L249/66.

[200] Council Joint Action 2003/423/CFSP of June 5, 2003 on the European Union military operation in the Democratic Republic of Congo ("ARTEMIS"), [2003] O.J. L143/50, and Council Joint Action 2004/570/CFSP of July 12, 2004 on the European military operation in Bosnia and Herzegovina ("ALTHEA"), [2004] O.J. L252/11.

[201] EU Constitution, Art. I–40(1).

[202] ibid., Art. III–294(3)(b).

[203] The EU Treaty originally referred to "the eventual framing of a common defence policy, which might in time lead to a common defence" (former Article B, second indent, and Art. J.4(1)). See Collet, "Le Traité de Maastricht et la Défense" (1993) R.T.D.E. 225–233. cf. the new version of Art. 2, second indent, of the EU Treaty.

17(2) of the EU Treaty).[204] The operational capacity to carry out such tasks was originally provided by the Western European Union (WEU; see para. 2–006). Since the Treaty of Nice, the WEU has been integrated into the European Union (even though not all the Member States belong to the WEU) and the European Union executes the security and defence policy itself.[205] In connection with its take-over of the WEU structures, the Council has set up by, joint actions, an Institute for Security Studies and a Satellite Centre.[206] For the purposes of implementing the ESDP, the EU has its own political and military structures (see para. 15–007), which, for example, have taken charge of the EU police mission in Bosnia-Herzegovina, the EU police mission and, subsequently, the (first) EU military operation in the Former Yugoslav Republic of Macedonia, and the EU military operations in Congo and Bosnia and Herzegovina.[207] The Member States have undertaken to be in a position to deploy within 60 days forces of 50,000–60,000 persons to carry out the tasks set out in Art. 17(2) of the EU Treaty and to sustain such a deployment for at least one year.[208] The EU can also have recourse to NATO assets and capabilities for

---

[204] The tasks listed in Art. 17(2) are known as the "Petersberg tasks" following the Petersberg Declaration made by the WEU States on June 19, 1992. The European Parliament distinguishes between "security" and "defence", with the concept of security including the Petersberg operations and the concept of defence covering territorial defence and the protection of the vital interests of the Member States, see its resolution of May 14, 1998 on the gradual establishment of a common defence policy for the European Union, [1998] O.J. C167/190. See Pagani, "A New Gear in the CFSP Machinery: Integration of the Petersberg Tasks in the Treaty on European Union" (1998) E.J.I.L. 737–749.

[205] Cammileri, "Le traité de Nice et la politique européenne de la défense" (2000) R.A.E 389–397; Duke, "CESP: Nice's Overtrumped Success?" (2001) E.For.Aff.rev. 155–175. The WEU continues to exist as an institution of collective defence in accordance with Art. V of the Treaty of Brussels (see para. 2–006, *supra*). For the former relationship between the WEU and the EU, see Cahen, "L'Union de l'Europe occidentale (UEO) et la mise en oeuvre de la future défense commune de l'Union européenne" (1996) R.M.C.U.E. 21–35.

[206] Council Joint Action 2001/554/CFSP of July 20, 2001 on the establishment of a European Union Institute for Security Studies, [2001] O.J. L200/1; Council Joint Action 2001/555/CFSP of July 20, 2001 on the establishment of a European Union Satellite Centre, [2001] O.J. L200/5. See also para. 10–112, *supra*.

[207] For the joint actions governing the EU police and military missions, see para. 20–043 ; for the actual launch of the military operations, see Council Decision 2003/202/CFSP of March 18, 2003 relating to the launch of the EU military operation in the Former Yugoslav Republic of Macedonia ([2003] O.J. L76/43) and Council Decision 2003/432/CFSP of June 12, 2003 on the launching of the European military operation in the Democratic Republic of Congo (OJ 2003 L 147/42), each adopted on the basis of Arts 17(1) and 25 of the EU Treaty but implementing Council Joint Action 2003/92/CFSP (n.199, *supra*) and Council Joint Action 2003/423/CFSP (n.200, *supra*), respectively. See Benoit, "Le lancement des premières opérations militaires de l'Union européenne" (2004) R.M.C.U.E. 235–240; Solana, "Politique européenne de sécurité et de défense: de l'opérationnalité aux opérations" (2003) R.M.C.U.E. 148–150; for a critical appraisal of the ESDP, see Dumoulin, Matthieu and Sarlet, "Six scénarios pour la PESD" (2002) R.M.C.U.E. 676–687.

[208] Conclusions of the Presidency of the European Council held in Helsinki on December 10–11, 1999 (1999) 12 EU Bull. point I.9.28; see also Annex IV thereto. The European Council has declared that this capacity is partially operational: Annex II to the conclusions of the European Council held in Laeken on December 14–15, 2001 (2001) 12 EU Bull. point I.28.

its operations[209] and invite non-EU allies to participate in its operations (see para. 20–048). If Member States consider it appropriate, the ESDP will be supported by co-operation in the field of armaments. To that effect, a European Defence Agency was established in July 2004.[210]

The progressive framing of a common defence policy might lead to a "common defence", should the European Council so decide. In this case, the European Council is to recommend to the Member States the adoption of a decision in accordance with their respective constitutional requirements (Art. 17(1), first subpara.). In order to further the objectives of Art. 17, its provisions will be reviewed, if necessary, in the course of an amendment of the Treaty (Art. 17(5)).

20–046 **Extension under the Constitution.** The EU Constitution seeks to further develop the common security and defence policy as an "integral part" of the CFSP. In the first place, it extends the list of tasks in the course of which the Union may use civilian and military means. The "Petersberg tasks" mentioned above will be supplemented by joint disarmament operations, military advice and assistance tasks and tasks of combat forces undertaken for crisis management, including peace-making and post-conflict stabilisation. All these tasks are also to contribute to the fight against terrorism, *inter alia* by supporting third countries in combating terrorism in their territories.[211] In addition, the EU Constitution confirms Member States' commitment to making civilian and military capabilities available to the Union for the implementation of the common security and defence policy, as well as to progressively improving their military capabilities.[212] In this connection, the European Defence Agency will have to assist the Council and the Member States, *e.g.* in identifying operational requirements and strengthening the industrial and technological base of the defence sector.[213] The EU Constitution empowers the Council to entrust

---

[209] Presidency Report on strengthening of the common European policy on security and defence, Annex III to the Presidency conclusions of the European Council held in Cologne on 3 and June 4, 1999 (1999) 6 EU Bull. point I.62. For the necessary arrangements with NATO, see para. 20–048, *infra*.

[210] Council Joint Action 2004/551/CFSP of July 12, 2004, on the establishment of the European Defence Agency, [2004] O.J. L245/17. The Agency is open to participation by all EU Member States (except for Denmark, which is not bound by the Joint Action) and will act in the field of defence capabilities development, research, acquisition and armaments. The Agency operates under the authority of the Council. It has its own legal personality and is based in Brussels. Co-operation in the field of armaments has existed since 1996 in the context of the Western European Armament Group. See also the common list of military equipment covered by the European Union code of conduct on arms export ([2003] O.J. C314/1), based on the list drawn up by the Council pursuant to Art. 296(2) of the EC Treaty (see para. 9–001, *supra*).

[211] EU Constitution, Art. III–309(1).

[212] *ibid.*, Art. I–41(3).

[213] *ibid.*, Art. I–41(3), second subpara., and Art. III–311.

the implementation of a task to a group of Member States which are willing and have the necessary capabilities for such as task.[214]

Under the EU Constitution, the common security and defence policy will continue to include "the progressive framing of a common Union defence policy" and hold out the prospect of establishing a genuine "common defence" if the European Council, acting unanimously, so decides.[215] For those Member States whose military capabilities fulfil higher criteria and which have made more binding commitments to one another in this area with a view to carrying out the most demanding missions, the EU Constitution will create a framework for establishing "permanent structured co-operation".[216] A Protocol annexed to the Constitution sets out the commitments in terms of the military capabilities required of Member States wishing to participate in that permanent structured co-operation.[217]

In any event, Art. I–41(7) of the EU Constitution provides that, if a Member State is the victim of armed aggression on its territory, the other Member States have an obligation towards it to provide aid and assistance by all the means in their power, in accordance with the United Nations Charter. The EU Constitution emphasises, however, that, for those States which are members of NATO, that organisation is to remain the foundation of their collective defence and the forum for its implementation. Further commitments and co-operation in this area must therefore be consistent with commitments under NATO.[218]

D. SPECIAL STATUS OF CERTAIN MEMBER STATES

Non-participation. The policy of the Union must not prejudice the specific **20–047** character of the security and defence policy of certain Member States (EU Treaty, Art. 17(1), second subpara.).[219] As has already been mentioned, not all the EU Member States are members of the WEU; at the same time, the CFSP decision-making procedure allows Member States to make a formal declaration that they abstain in a given vote. They will then not be obliged to apply the relevant decision (EU Treaty, Art. 23(1), see para. 15–002). Denmark has stated in a protocol that it does not participate in the elaboration and implementation of decisions and actions of the Union

---

[214] *ibid.*, Art. I–41(5) and Art. III–310.
[215] *ibid.*, Art. I–41(2), first subpara.
[216] *ibid.*, Art. I–41(6) and Art. III–312.
[217] Protocol on permanent structured co-operation established by Arts I–41(6) and III–312 of the Constitution.
[218] EU Constitution, Art. I–41(7), second para.
[219] For example, in a declaration (No. 35) annexed to the 2003 Act of Accession, Malta emphasises its neutrality.

which have defence implications, in particular the European security and defence policy (ESDP).[220]

20–048 Closer co-operation. The EU Treaty does not prevent the development of closer co-operation between two or more Member States on a bilateral level, "in the framework of the WEU and the Atlantic Alliance", provided that such co-operation does not impede co-operation within the Union (EU Treaty, Art. 17(4)). In this way, France and the Federal Republic of Germany set up a Franco-German brigade, with headquarters in Strasbourg, as long ago as January 12, 1989. Subsequently, Belgium, Luxembourg and Spain joined the "Eurocorps", in which national units are placed under a common command.

The collaboration existing between the majority of the Member States within NATO is still more important. The CFSP must respect the obligations of certain Member States under the North Atlantic Treaty Organisation and be compatible with the policy established within that framework (EU Treaty, Art. 17(1), second subpara.).[221] This means that an ESDP action could not be directed against a Member State of NATO.[222] There are to be permanent and continuing consultations with the non-EU European allies, covering the full range of security, defence and crisis management issues, in particular before decisions are taken on matters affecting their security interests.[223] Non-EU European allies may participate in an operation conducted by the EU for which NATO assets are deployed and should be invited to take part in operations conducted by the EU where no NATO assets are to be used.[224] The European Union aims to

---

[220] Art. 6 of Protocol (No. 5) on the position of Denmark, annexed by the Treaty of Amsterdam to the EC Treaty and the EU Treaty ([1997] O.J. C340/101). Pursuant to that protocol, Denmark is not participating, *e.g.* in the European Union's military operations in the Former Yugoslav Republic of Macedonia or in Congo (see recital 14 on the preamble to Joint Action 2003/92/CFSP and recital 13 in the preamble to Joint Action 2003/423/CFSP, nn.199 and 200, *supra*). Denmark had already adopted this stance upon the introduction of the CFSP in 1993; see para. 15–007. For applications, see Denmark's declarations relating to Council Decision 96/670/CFSP of November 22, 1996 on the implementation of a Joint Action by the Union in the Great Lakes Region ([1996] O.J. L312/3) and to Council Decision 98/547/CFSP of September 22, 1998 on the study of the feasibility of international police operations to assist the Albanian authorities ([1998] O.J. L263/1).

[221] For the North Atlantic Treaty (Washington Treaty), see para. 2–006, *supra*. See Kintis, "NATO-WEU: An Enduring Relationship" (1998) E.For.Aff.Rev. 537–562; Österdahl, "The EU and its Member States, Other States and International Organisations—The Common European Security and Defence Policy After Nice" (2001) Nordic J.I.L. 341–372.

[222] See the conclusions of the European Council held in Brussels on 24 and October 25, 2002 (2002) 10 EU Bull. point I.15, section 2.

[223] *ibid.*, point I.15, sections 3 to 5.

[224] *ibid.*, point I.15, sections 11 and 15. Accordingly, third countries have been invited to participate in the military operations of the European Union in the Former Yugoslav Republic of Macedonia (FYROM) and in Congo pursuant to agreements concluded on the basis of Art. 24 of the EU Treaty, see, e.g., the agreement between the European Union and Romania on the participation of Romania in the EU-led forces in the FYROM, concluded by Council Decision 2004/392/CFSP of May 19, 2003 ([2004] O.J. L120/61).

have a strategic partnership with NATO on the basis of which the two organisations may collaborate in crisis management while retaining their independence of decision-making. This collaboration is founded upon "permanent arrangements" between the EU and NATO.[225] These "Berlin plus" arrangements give the EU assured access to NATO's planning and logistics capabilities for its own military operations.[226]

Since the Treaty of Nice, Member States may embark upon enhanced co-operation relating to implementation of a joint action or a common position, but such co-operation may not relate to matters having military or defence implications (EU Treaty, Arts 27a to 27e; see para. 9–007).

Constitution. The EU Constitution continues to provide that Union policy **20–049** should not prejudice the specific character of the security and defence policy of certain Member States and also preserves the possibility for a Member State to have recourse to "constructive abstention".[227] At the same time, the EU Constitution makes it easier for those Member States wishing to co-operate more intensively amongst themselves to do so. This is because Member States will no longer be debarred from establishing enhanced co-operation in the field of military affairs and defence. As already mentioned, the Constitution goes so far as to organise a form of enhanced co-operation by setting out the conditions for "permanent structured co-operation" between Member States (see para. 20–046).

VII. ECONOMIC SANCTIONS

Initial way of action. Where the Union wishes to act internationally by **20–050** adopting economic sanctions, both CFSP and Community powers come into play. The status under Community law of economic sanctions has completely changed over the years.[228] Initially, a decision to impose

---

[225] These arrangements are to be found in the joint declaration by the European Union and the NATO of December 16, 2002 on the European Security and Defence policy (see NATO Press Release (2002) 142, available on the NATO website). NATO also concluded an agreement with the European Union on the security of information, based on Art. 24 of the EU Treaty (approved by Council Decision 2003/211/CFSP of February 24, 2003, [2003] O.J. L80/35).

[226] The terms "Berlin plus" refer to the ministerial meeting of the North Atlantic Council on June 3, 1996 in Berlin where it was agreed that a European Security and Defence Identity should be built within NATO. The European Council welcomed the "Berlin plus" arrangements in the conclusions of its meeting held in Thessaloniki on 19 and June 20, 2003 (2003) 6 EU Bull. point I.23, s.60.

[227] EU Constitution, Art. I–41(2), second subpara. and Art. III–300(1), second subpara., respectively.

[228] See Stein, "European Political Co-operation (EPC) as a Component of the European Foreign Affairs System" (1993) Z.a.ö.RV. 49–69; Vaucher, "L'évolution récente de la pratique des sanctions communautaires à l'encontre des Etats tiers" (1993) R.T.D.E. 39–59. For a discussion of the status under international law of sanctions imposed by the Community, see Kuyper, "Community Sanctions against Argentina: Lawfulness under Community and International Law" in O'Keeffe and Schermers (eds), *Essays in European Law and Integration* (Kluwer, Deventer, 1982), at 151–164; Sturma, "La participation de la Communauté européenne à des 'sanctions' internationales" (1993) R.M.C.U.E. 250, at 255–264.

economic sanctions on a non-member country came to be discussed only at meetings of the Foreign Ministers under the auspices of EPC. The sanctions were then adopted at the national level as an exercise of the exceptional power provided for in Art. 297 of the EC Treaty.[229] It was not until 1982 that the Council accepted that the Community could adopt economic sanctions itself pursuant to its powers under the common commercial policy,[230] although not all the Member States supported this view.[231] Except where economic sanctions were adopted pursuant to a resolution of the UN Security Council, such Community measures were generally preceded by a decision taken in the context of EPC.[232]

20–051 **Current procedure.** Since the EU Treaty, sanctions generally come under the CFSP (EU Treaty, Title V). Sometimes, sanctions agreed under the CFSP may be carried out directly by the Member States[233]; at other times, a CFSP sanction has to be supplemented by action by way of PJCC (EU Treaty, Title VI).[234] Frequently, however, a CFSP sanction has to be

---

[229] See the Council's answer of March 17, 1976 to question 526/75 (Patijn), [1976] O.J. C89/6; compare the Commission's answer of March 15, 1976 to question 527/75 (Patijn), which did not rule out a Community power (*ibid.*, C89/8). In this way, the Member States imposed sanctions against Rhodesia between 1966 and 1974, Iran in 1980 and South Africa in 1985–1986 (supplemented by two Community measures: an ECSC import ban and an EEC regulation). See Schröder, "Wirtschaftssanktionen der Europäischen Gemeinschaften gegenüber Drittstaaten, dargestellt am Beispiel des Iran-Embargos" (1980) G.Y.I.L. 111–125; Petersmann, "Internationale Wirtschaftssanktionen als Problem des Völkerrechts und des Europarechts" (1981) Z.Vgl.RW. 1–28; Raux, "Les sanctions de la Communauté européenne et des Etats membres contre l'Afrique du Sud pour cause d'apartheid" (1989) R.M.C. 33–34; and a number of case studies in (1984) B.T.I.R. 150–245.

[230] In this way, the EEC imposed sanctions against the USSR on account of the situation in Poland (1992), against Argentina on account of its occupation of the Falklands (1982), against South Africa (1986), against Iraq (1990), against Libya (1992), against Yugoslavia and, subsequently, against the Republics of Serbia and Montenegro (from 1991) and against Haiti (1993).

[231] Thus, some Member States declared, on the occasion of the extension of the sanctions against Argentina, that they would not implement the sanctions domestically (relying on Art. 297 of the EC Treaty) or would prolong them by means of national measures. See Kuyper (n.228, *supra*), at 142 and 149–151; Verhoeven, "Sanctions internationales et Communautés européennes. A propos des îles Falklands (Malvinas)" (1984) C.D.E. 259–290.

[232] UN Security Council resolutions required sanctions to be adopted against Rhodesia, Iraq, Libya, Yugoslavia and Haiti. For an inquiry into the relationship between those resolutions and the Community sanctions adopted in order to implement them, see Angelet, "La mise en oeuvre des mesures coercitives économiques des Nations-Unies dans la Communauté européenne" (1993) B.T.I.R. 500, at 501–517.

[233] See, *e.g.* the sanctions imposed pursuant to a UN Security Council resolution against Nigeria by Common Positions of November 20, 1995 (95/515/CFSP), [1995] O.J. L298/1, and December 4, 1995 (95/544/CFSP), [1995] O.J. L309/1) (restrictions on visas for, *e.g.* members of the Government and their families, sports boycott and arms embargo); see also the sanctions imposed against the Tabilan: CFI (order of the President of May 7, 2002) Case T–306/01 R *Aden v Council and Commission* [2002] E.C.R. II–2387, paras 59–60. For the implementation of sanctions in the Netherlands, see Wijmenga, "Internationale sanctieregimes en de gewijzigde Sanctiewet 1997" (2002) S.E.W. 42–51.

[234] *e.g.* Council Decision 2003/48/JHA of December 19, 2002 on the implementation of specific measures for police and judicial co-operation to combat terrorism in accordance with Art. 4 of Common Position 2001/931/CFSP (n.236, *infra*), [2003] O.J. L16/68.

implemented by a Community measure. Article 301 of the EC Treaty states that where it is provided, in a common position or a joint action adopted under Title V of the EU Treaty, for "an action by the Community to interrupt or to reduce, in part or completely, economic relations with one or more third countries", the Council is to take the "necessary urgent measures", acting by a qualified majority on a proposal from the Commission. This Treaty provision applies where it is "provided" in a CFSP act for an action by the Community. This will be the case where the Council adopts a decision under Title V of the EU Treaty pursuant to a superior international obligation, that is to say, binding resolutions of the UN Security Council. In principle, the Community may give effect to such resolutions directly.[235] Since the entry into force of the EU Treaty, the Council first adopts an act pursuant to Title V of the EU Treaty.[236]

The fact that the Community is bound to act in this context does not mean that the CFSP act determines the action to be taken by the institutions. It is true that the Commission is bound to propose the "necessary urgent measures" to the Council, but the latter determines what measures it deems necessary.[237] The Council is empowered to take measures "to interrupt or to reduce, in part or completely, economic relations with one or more third countries". Consequently, the Council's sanctions are not confined to measures taken by the Community under the common commercial policy, but may also relate to other economic matters.[238] Accordingly, Art. 60(1) of the EC Treaty reads as follows:

---

[235] See Angelet (n.232, *supra*), at 520.

[236] That act takes the form of a common position which used to be based on Art. 15 [formerly Art. J.2] of the EU Treaty. See, *e.g.* with regard to Burma/Myanmar, Council Common Position 2000/346/CFSP of April 26, 2000, based on Art. 15 of the EU Treaty, and the connected Council Regulation (EC) No. 1081/2000 of May 22, 2000 based on Arts 60 and 301 of the EC Treaty ([2000] O.J. L122/1 and 29, respectively) and, with regard to combating terrorism, Council Common Position 2001/931/CFSP of December 27, 2001 based on Art. 15 of the EU Treaty, and the connected Council Regulation (EC) No. 2580/2001 of December 27, 2001 on specific restrictive measures directed against certain persons and entities with a view to combating terrorism based on Arts 60, 301 and 308 of the EC Treaty ([2001] O.J. L344/93 and 70, respectively). Similar CFSP/EC sanctions were also adopted with regard to Libya (from 1993), Sudan (1994), Haiti (1994), the Federal Republic of Yugoslavia (Serbia and Montenegro) (from 1995), Iraq (from 1996), UNITA in Angola (from 1997), Sierra Leone (from 1997), Afghanistan (from 2000), Liberia (from 2001), Zimbabwe and Somalia (from 2002), the Transnistrian region of the Moldovan Republic (from 2003) and Belarus (from 2004).

[237] Neuwahl, "Foreign and Security Policy and the Implementation of the Requirement of 'Consistency' under the Treaty on European Union" in O'Keeffe and Twomey (eds), *Legal Issues of the Maastricht Treaty* (Chancery, London, 1994), 227, at 239.

[238] Gilsdorf, "Les réserves de sécurité du traité CEE, à la lumière du traité sur l'Union européenne" (1994) R.M.C.U.E. 17, at 25. In this way, the Council prohibited the satisfaction of claims with regard to contracts and transactions, the performance of which was affected by sanctions imposed by the UN Security Council against Iraq (ban imposed pursuant to Art. 235 of the EEC Treaty [now Art. 308 of the EC Treaty] by Regulation (EEC) No. 3541/92 of December 7, 1992, [1992] O.J. L361/1) and against Libya (ban imposed pursuant to Art. 228a of the EC Treaty [now Art. 301 of the EC Treaty] by Regulation (EC) No. 3275/93 of November 29, 1993, [1993] O.J. L295/4). The question

"If, in the cases envisaged in Article 301, action by the Community is deemed necessary, the Council may, in accordance with the procedure provided for in Article 301, take the necessary urgent measures on the movement of capital and on payment as regards the third countries concerned".[239]

The Council is to act by a qualified majority vote, which may mean that decisions may be adopted that could not be embodied in the CFSP, for which unanimity is required. As in the case of the procedure laid down in Art. 133 of the EC Treaty, the Art. 301 procedure does not provide for any involvement of the European Parliament in the decision-making.[240]

20–052 **Scope of Community measures.** Article 301 does not prevent the Community from imposing sanctions which go further than "the necessary urgent measures" on the basis of some other power-conferring provision. For instance, Community sanctions may still be based on Art. 133 of the EC Treaty. The Council does not first have to define a common position or joint action under Title V of the EU Treaty in order to adopt such sanctions.[241] Trade not subject to the Community sanction remains subject to the general rules on exports (see para. 20–007).

20–053 **Action by Member States.** At the same time, a Member State retains the power under Art. 297 of the EC Treaty to take measures "in order to carry out obligations it has accepted for the purpose of maintaining peace and international security". Article 297 requires Member States to "consult each other" in this connection in order to prevent the functioning of the common market from being affected. Since the entry into force of the EU Treaty, that obligation coincides with CFSP commitments (see para. 9–001). Only if sanctions imposed by a UN Security Council resolution were not implemented either by a CFSP act or by Community action within the prescribed period would a Member State be entitled to rely on Art. 297 in order to implement the resolution itself. On these lines, the Court of Justice has held that, in exercising their national competence to take measures of foreign and security policy, Member States must respect the rules of the common commercial policy.[242]

Without prejudice to Art. 297 and as long as the Council has not taken measures pursuant to Art. 60(1) of the EC Treaty, a Member State may

---

whether sanctions may be imposed pursuant to Art. 301 of the EC Treaty only against non-member countries or also against EU nationals in Member States is being raised in Case T–306/01 *Aden v Council and Commission* (see already CFI (order of the President of May 7, 2002) Case T–306/01 R *Aden v Council and Commission* [2002] E.C.R. II–2387, para. 65).

[239] For applications of this provision, see n.236, *supra*.
[240] For the sanctions procedure, see Auvret-Finck, "Les procédures de sanction internationale en vigueur dans l'ordre interne de l'Union et la défense des droits de l'homme dans le monde" (2003) R.T.D.E. 1–21.
[241] Gilsdorf (n.238, *supra*), at 25.
[242] ECJ, Case C–124/95 *Centro-Com* [1997] E.C.R. I–81, para. 27.

take unilateral measures against a third country with regard to capital movements and payments for serious political reasons and on grounds of urgency (EC Treaty, Art. 60(2), first subpara.). The Commission and the other Member States must be informed of such measures at the latest by the date on which they enter into force. The Council, acting by a qualified majority on a proposal from the Commission, may decide that the Member State concerned must amend or abolish the measures. The President of the Council is to inform the European Parliament of any such decision (EC Treaty, Art. 60(2), second subpara.). Even if the Council has already decided in a CFSP act to impose sanctions on a non-member country, Member States may act pursuant to Art. 60(2) until such time as the Council itself acts pursuant to Art. 60(1).[243]

Constitution. The EU Constitution will replace Arts 60 and 301 of the EC **20–054** Treaty by a single clause enabling the Council to interrupt or reduce, in part or completely, economic and financial relations with one or more third countries whenever a CFSP "European decision" so provides.[244] There will be an additional legal basis for the Council to adopt restrictive measures against natural or legal persons and non-State groups or bodies pursuant to a CFSP "European decision".[245] In that event, the Council will implement the relevant European decision by adopting European regulations or decisions, acting by a qualified majority on a joint proposal from the Union Minister for Foreign Affairs and the Commission. Even though the relevant European decisions will be taken under the CFSP, the Court of Justice will have jurisdiction to review their legality in so far as they provide for restrictive measures against natural or legal persons (see para. 18–022).

---

[243] Angelet (n.232, *supra*), at 522.
[244] EU Constitution, Art. III–322(1).
[245] *ibid.*, Art. III–322(2). In addition, Art. III–160 of the EU Constitution empowers the European Parliament and the Council to adopt European laws—with a view to preventing and combating terrorism and related activities—defining a framework for administrative measures with regard to capital movements and payments, such as the freezing of funds held by natural or legal persons, groups or non-State entities.

CHAPTER 21

THE COMMUNITY AND NON-COMMUNITY PROCEDURE FOR CONCLUDING AGREEMENTS

Framework. The Community treaties set out the procedure which the **21–001** Community must follow in concluding agreements with non-member countries or international organisations (paras 21–002–21–014). In some cases, not only the Community but also the Member States are party to such an agreement: this is the case with "mixed agreements" as they are termed (paras 21–016–21–018). The procedure for concluding non-Community agreements of the Union is laid down in Art. 24 of the EU Treaty (see para. 21–019). In order to avoid the Community concluding international agreements which exceed the limits of the Community treaties, these treaties—but not the EU Treaty—allow an opinion to be sought from the Court of Justice before concluding an agreement (paras 21–020–21–021). When the EU Constitution enters into force, the present Community procedure—as amended (see para. 21–015)—will apply to international agreements to be concluded by the Union in all areas of its external policy.

I. FIELD OF APPLICATION OF THE COMMUNITY PROCEDURE

Article 300 EC Treaty. Article 300 of the EC Treaty sets out the internal **21–002** procedure which the Community has to follow "[w]here this Treaty provides for the conclusion of agreements between the Community and one or more States or international organisations". That Treaty provision does not itself confer any power on the Community to act internationally, but applies whenever the Community wishes to conclude an agreement pursuant to a power contained expressly or impliedly in the Treaty.[1] The decision by which the Community approves a given agreement refers in its preamble not only to the Treaty provision constituting the substantive legal basis, but also to the provision of Art. 300 which sets out the applicable procedure. The term "agreement" is used here "in a general sense to

---

[1] See, expressly, EC Treaty, Art. 133(3), third subpara.; Art. 170, second para.; Art. 174(4), first subpara.; Art. 181, first para.; Art. 181a.

indicate any undertaking entered into by entities subject to international law which has binding force, whatever its formal designation".[2] Articles 101–106 of the EAEC Treaty set out detailed rules for the conclusion of agreements by that Community; no such rules were contained in the ECSC Treaty.

II. Community Procedure for the Negotiation and Conclusion of Agreements

21–003 General outline. Article 300 of the EC Treaty constitutes a general provision of "constitutional" import, since in conferring certain powers on the Community institutions it seeks to establish a balance between the institutions.[3] Broadly speaking, the balance consists in the fact that the Commission conducts the negotiations, the Council concludes the agreement and the European Parliament is (generally) consulted or (in some instances) has to give its assent. Article 300 sets out the procedure for negotiating and concluding agreements with third countries and international organisations, including tariff and trade agreements and association agreements.[4] The EU Constitution will modify to some extent the procedure for the negotiation and conclusion of international agreements (see para. 21–015).

The same procedural requirements apply to amendments of agreements and to additional or implementing protocols concluded together with or on the basis of the agreement itself.[5] In principle, the denunciation of an agreement also comes under Art. 300.[6] The same procedural requirements apply to the suspension of the application of an agreement (Art. 300(2), second subpara.), although the application of an agreement may also be suspended by and in accordance with the procedure for imposing economic

---

[2] ECJ, Opinion 1/75 *Draft Understanding on a Local Cost Standard drawn up under the auspices of the OECD* [1975] E.C.R. 1355, at 1359–1360. Art. 300 of the EC Treaty does not cover guidelines agreed with a non-member country which do not constitute a binding agreement: ECJ (judgment of March 23, 2004), Case C–233/02 *France v Commission*, not yet reported. In some language versions of the Treaty (in particular Dutch) two different terms are used, whereas the other versions employ only one ("agreement", "Abkommen", "accord"). This has no significance. According to Declaration (No. 5) annexed to the EU Treaty, the expression "formal agreements" in Art. 111(1) of the EC Treaty does not introduce a new category of international agreement.

[3] ECJ, Case C–327/91 *France v Commission* [1994] E.C.R. I–3641, para. 28.

[4] See EC Treaty, Art. 300(1).

[5] Accordingly, r.83 of the EP Rules of Procedure deals with the "conclusion, renewal or amendment of an international agreement".

[6] See, *e.g.* Council Decision 91/602/EEC of November 25, 1991 denouncing the Co-operation Agreement between the European Economic Community and the Socialist Federal Republic of Yugoslavia ([1991] O.J. L325/23), which was adopted in accordance with the procedure set out in Art. 238 of the EEC Treaty [now Art. 310 of the EC Treaty].

sanctions.[7] The same procedures also apply for the purpose of establishing the positions to be adopted on behalf of the Community in a body set up by an agreement when that body is called upon to adopt decisions having legal effects, with the exception of decisions supplementing or amending the institutional framework of the agreement (Art. 300(2), second subpara.).[8]

A. NEGOTIATIONS

Negotiation by Commission. Agreements with non-member countries or **21–004** international organisations are negotiated by the Commission.[9] It makes recommendations to this effect to the Council, which has to authorise it to open the necessary negotiations (Art. 300(1), first subpara., first sentence). So as to enable it to make effective recommendations, the Commission is empowered to conduct exploratory discussions with potential Contracting Parties.[10] The Commission conducts the negotiations in consultation with special committees appointed by the Council to assist it in this task and within the framework of such directives as the Council may issue to it (Art. 300(1), first subpara., second sentence). Since the Council has to approve the agreement ensuing from the negotiations, it is reasonable that the Council should be able to put across its views in this way at the outset and during the course of the negotiations. In exercising its powers under Art. 300(1), the Council acts by a qualified majority, except in the case of agreements which it has to approve by a unanimous vote (see Art. 300(2), first subpara., second sentence), where it also has to adopt all measures prior to approving a given agreement likewise by a unanimous vote (Art. 300(1), second subpara.). The European Parliament is keen for the Commission to apprise it of its recommendations and wishes to be informed by the Commission and the Council of the progress of

---

[7] See the discussion of Art. 301 of the EC Treaty, paras 20–051—20–053, *supra*. Accordingly, the trade concessions under the Co-operation Agreement with Yugoslavia were suspended (Council Regulation (EEC) No. 3300/91 of November 11, 1991, [1991] O.J. L315/1) and an embargo was brought in against Haiti by way of derogation from the Fourth ACP-EC Convention (Council Regulation (EEC) No. 1608/93 of June 24, 1993, [1993] O.J. L155/2) under Art. 133 of the EC Treaty. For the validity under international law of the suspension of the Co-operation Agreement with Yugoslavia, see ECJ, Case C–162/96 *Racke* [1998] E.C.R. I–3655 (see para. 17–103, *supra*).

[8] The European Parliament must be "immediately and fully informed" about any decision concerning the suspension (or the provisional application) of agreements or the establishment of the Community position in a body set up by an agreement: EC Treaty, Art. 300(2), third subpara. For the Commission's undertaking to this effect, see point 4 of Annex II ("Forwarding to the European Parliament information on international agreements and enlargement, and involvement of the European Parliament in this respect") to the Framework agreement on relations between Parliament and the Commission of July 5, 2000 ([2001] O.J. C121/122, and (2000) 7/8 EU Bull. point 2.2.1), annexed to the EP Rules of Procedure as Annex XIII.

[9] For the Commission's capacity to negotiate, see Keukeleire, *Het buitenlands beleid van de Europese Unie* (Kluwer, Deventer, 1998), 136–144.

[10] Flaesch-Mougin, "Le traité de Maastricht et les compétences externes de la Communauté européenne: à la recherche d'une politique externe de l'Union" (1993) C.D.E. 351, at 378.

international negotiations.[11] The Commission has undertaken to do so.[12] For its part, the Council has agreed under the Luns-Westerterp procedures that the European Parliament should hold a debate before negotiations are opened and that during the negotiations for association agreements the Commission should keep in close contact with the responsible parliamentary committee.[13] In its Rules of Procedure, the European Parliament has provided that in the case of any international agreement it may request the Council not to authorise the opening of negotiations until the Parliament has stated its position on the proposed negotiating mandate and that it may adopt recommendations to be taken into account before the relevant international agreement is concluded.[14] Such acts adopted by the European Parliament are not in any way binding on the Commission or the Council, but are important where the conclusion of the agreement in question is contingent on the Parliament's assent.

21–005 **Monetary affairs.** By way of derogation from Art. 300, there are special rules on negotiations "where agreements concerning monetary or foreign exchange regime matters need to be negotiated by the Community with one or more States or international organisations" (EC Treaty, Art. 111(3)). In such case, the Council is to decide on the arrangements for the negotiation and conclusion of the agreement in question by a qualified majority on a recommendation from the Commission and after consulting the European Central Bank. These arrangements are to ensure that the Community expresses a single position (Art. 111(3), first subpara.). Depending on the formula chosen by the Council, negotiations on these matters need not necessarily be entrusted to the Commission. The Commission is entitled, however, to be fully associated with the negotiations.[15]

---

[11] According to r.83(1) and (4) of the EP Rules of Procedure, the responsible parliamentary committee is to be informed, if necessary on a confidential basis.

[12] See points 2–5 of Annex II to the Framework Agreement of July 5, 2000 (n.8, *supra*); see formerly point 3.10 of the Code of Conduct agreed between the European Parliament and the Commission on March 15, 1995, [1995] O.J. C89/69.

[13] On March 24–25, 1964, the Council took the decision to provide information on association agreements following an exchange of letters between the President of the Council (Luns, the Dutch Foreign Minister) and the President of the European Parliament (Martino). After the then President of the Council (Westerterp) stated in November 1972 that he was prepared to make confidential information about trade agreements available to parliamentary committees, the Council laid down a number of procedural rules concerning trade agreements in a communication of October 16, 1973, which was notified to the European Parliament. These interinstitutional decisions were never published officially; for their wording, see Tomuschat, "Artikel 228", in von der Groeben, Thiesing, Ehlermann (eds), *Kommentar zum EWG-Vertrag* (Nomos, Baden-Baden, 1991), at 5666–5669; see also Rengeling, "Zu den Befugnissen des Europäischen Parlaments beim Abschluss völkerrechtlicher Verträge im Rahmen der Gemeinschaftsfassung", *Staatsrecht—Völkerrecht—Europarecht. Festschrift für H.-J. Schlochauer* (de Gruyter, Berlin, 1981), at 877–898.

[14] EP Rules of Procedure, r.83(2) and (5).

[15] EC Treaty, Art. 111(3), first subpara. In such matters, the Commission does not automatically represent the Community internationally; para. 19–010, *supra*. For cases in which negotiating mandates were conferred on the Member States, see the decisions cited in n.1070 to para. 5–231, *supra*.

B. Conclusion of Agreements

1. Initialling and signature

Division of powers. After the negotiations have closed, the text of the draft **21–006** agreement is initialled by the negotiators. The power to sign the agreement is vested in the Council, which takes a decision to that effect in accordance with the same procedure as for the conclusion of the agreement (Art. 300(2), first subpara.). At the same time, a decision may be adopted on the provisional application of the agreement before it enters into force (*ibid.*). The Council may give the Commission authorisation to act in this connection.[16] Where the agreement is concerned with a matter in respect of which both the Community and the Member States have competence, the Community and the Member States must determine together who has the right of signature. Since that right entails the power to take the final decision as to the content of the agreement and creates an impression in other subjects of international law as to the division of competence as between the Community and the Member States, the decision as to who has the right of signature is amenable to judicial review.[17]

Unlike in the case of initialling, which is intended only to fix the definitive text of the agreement, obligations ensue from signature for a contracting party, whether or not it signs subject to ratification. Until such time as it makes its intention clear not to become a party, a signatory State or international organisation is obliged to refrain from acts which would defeat the object and purpose of the agreement.[18] This international-law principle of good faith applies equally after the agreement has been ratified and during the period prior to its entry into force.[19] It applies to the Community institutions when an agreement has been approved by the Community, the date of its entry into force is known and the Community adopts acts conflicting with provisions of the agreement.[20] Individuals may challenge such acts in reliance on the principle of protection of legitimate expectations in so far as the acts in question conflict with provisions of the agreement which have direct effect for them following the agreement's entry into force.[21]

---

[16] See the opening words of the first subpara. of Art. 300(2); see also the "arrangements" for the conclusion of agreements covered by Art. 111 on which the Council is to decide pursuant to para. 3 of that article.

[17] ECJ, Case C–25/94 *Commission v Council* [1996] E.C.R. I–1469, paras 29–37.

[18] Art. 18, point (a), of the Vienna Convention of March 21, 1986 on the Law of Treaties between States and International Organisations or between International Organisations (para. 17–103, *supra*).

[19] *ibid.*, Art. 18, point (b).

[20] CFI, Case T–115/94 *Opel Austria v Council* [1997] E.C.R. II–39, paras 90–94.

[21] *ibid.*, para. 94 (the judgment in the *Opel Austria* case accordingly annulled a regulation imposing duties only a few days before the EEA Agreement prohibiting such duties entered into effect).

Under the Luns procedure, the Council agreed as long ago as 1964 to inform the responsible committee of the European Parliament confidentially and informally about each initialled association agreement before signing it. Then, the Treaty required the European Parliament to be consulted before the conclusion of such an agreement. Since the Single European Act, the Parliament has to give its assent. Moreover, from 1973 on, information has been provided about initialled trade agreements to the responsible parliamentary committee under the Westerterp procedure; the Parliament itself is not informed about the content of such agreements until they have been signed. The EC Treaty itself still does not provide for the European Parliament to play any role in concluding such agreements (Art. 300(3)). According to the Parliament, every draft agreement should be submitted to it before signature, at least in order to obtain its opinion.[22]

2. Power to conclude agreements

21–007 **Council.** Subject to the powers vested in the Commission in this field, the Council concludes agreements by a qualified majority vote on a proposal of the Commission. However, the Council has to take its decision by a unanimous vote where the agreement in question covers a field for which unanimity is required for the adoption of internal rules,[23] and where agreements referred to in Art. 310 (association agreements) are involved (Art. 300(2), first subpara.). There are also different rules in this respect for agreements relating to monetary and exchange-rate matters. In such cases, the Council does not decide on a proposal from the Commission but on a recommendation from the ECB or the Commission after consulting the ECB (EC Treaty, Art. 111(1)). Moreover, the conclusion of such agreements is subject to such arrangements as the Council decides upon pursuant to Art. 111(3) (see para. 21–005). In the case of agreements based on Art. 133 of the EC Treaty (common commercial policy), the Council decides in principle by a qualified majority vote; however, as far as agreements on trade in services or commercial aspects of intellectual property rights, unanimity is required in some cases (see para. 20–004).

The Council generally "concludes" an agreement by means of a decision (in the sense of a "*sui generis*" decision) concluding the agreement "on behalf of the Community". Where the Council adopts a regulation or a decision within the meaning of Art. 249 to this end, this does not deprive the agreement of its legal force as an international agreement concluded by the Community.[24] An agreement obtains the force of Community law after

---

[22] EP Rules of Procedure, r.83(6).

[23] See, *inter alia*, EC Treaty, Art. 111(1); Art. 174(4) in conjunction with Art. 175(2); Art. 308 and other Treaty articles implicitly conferring the power to conclude agreements and prescribing a unanimous vote in the Council. This rule is maintained in Art. 133(5), second subpara., of the EC Treaty.

[24] See Everling, "The Law of the External Economic Relations of the European Community" in Hilf, Jacobs and Petersmann (eds), *The European Community and GATT* (Kluwer, Deventer, 1986), 85, at 96; Tomuschat (n.13, *supra*), at 5671.

it has entered into effect internationally. Agreements concluded by the Community are published in the *Official Journal*.[25]

Commission. It appears from the wording of Art. 300(2) that the **21–008** Commission is sometimes vested with the power to conclude agreements. What is involved is a small number of administrative agreements.[26]

Internal Community powers vested in the Commission cannot alter the allocation of powers between the Council and the Commission with regard to the conclusion of international agreements. Consequently, the Commission has no power to conclude an agreement with a non-member country on the application of the competition rules, even though, internally, it does have the power to adopt individual decisions in that field.[27] Even when concluding non-binding guidelines with a non-member country, the Commission must take account of the division of powers and the institutional balance established by the Treaty.[28]

Article 300(4) allows the Council, when concluding an agreement, to authorise the Commission to approve modifications on behalf of the Community where the agreement provides for them to be adopted by a simplified procedure or by a body set up by the agreement. The Council may attach specific conditions to such authorisation.

3. Involvement of the European Parliament

a. Consultation

Duty to consult. The general rule laid down in the EC Treaty is that, **21–009** except in the case of agreements mentioned in Art. 133(3) (tariff and trade agreements), the Council concludes agreements after consulting the European Parliament, even where the agreement covers a field for which the co-decision procedure (Art. 251) or the co-operation procedure (Art. 252) is required for the adoption of internal rules (Art. 300(3), first

---

[25] Council Rules of Procedure, Art. 17(1)(g).
[26] See EC Treaty, Art. 302 (relations with international organisations) and Art. 7 of the Protocol on Privileges and Immunities (agreements for the recognition by non-member countries of Community *laissez-passer* as valid travel documents).
[27] ECJ, Case C–327/91 *France v Commission* [1994] E.C.R. I–3641, paras 40–43 (annulling the decision whereby the Commission sought to conclude the Agreement with the United States of America regarding the application of the competition laws of the European Communities and the United States, which was signed and entered into force on September 23, 1991). Agreements on co-operation in the field of competition have since been concluded by the Council pursuant to Art. 83 and—as far as mergers are concerned—Art. 308 of the EC Treaty; the Commission had to conclude such agreements only as far as the ECSC was concerned: see Council and Commission Decision 95/145/EC, ECSC of April 10, 1995, [1995] O.J. L95/45 (concluding again the 1991 agreement) and Council and Commission Decision 98/386/EC, ECSC of May 29, 1998, [1998] O.J. L173/26 (additional agreement with the United States); Council and Commission Decision 1999/445/EC, ECSC of April 29, [1999] O.J. L175/49 (agreement with Canada); Council Decision 2003/520/EC of June 16, [2003] O.J. L183/11 (agreement with Japan).
[28] ECJ (judgment of March 23, 2004), Case C–233/02 *France v Commission*, not yet reported, para. 40.

subpara., first sentence). The European Parliament also has to be consulted where no involvement whatsoever of the European Parliament is prescribed for the adoption of internal rules. As a result, the European Parliament is consulted on all external agreements with the exception of trade agreements, whilst for some agreements its assent is required (see paras 21–012–21–014). The European Parliament is not consulted, but must be "immediately and fully informed" in the event of the suspension of an agreement or the establishment of the Community position in a body set up by an association agreement when that body is called upon to adopt decisions having legal effects, with the exception of decisions supplementing or amending the institutional framework of the agreement (EC Treaty, Art. 300(2), second and third subparas).[29]

21–010 Opinion of the Parliament. The Council has to consult the European Parliament before it concludes the agreement in question. The Treaty does not provide that the Parliament's opinion must be sought before the agreement is signed, which is the view taken by the Parliament.[30] If the matter is urgent, the Council may lay down a commensurate time-limit within which the Parliament should deliver its opinion. If the Parliament fails to deliver an opinion within that time-limit, the Council may act (Art. 300(3), first subpara., second and third sentences).[31] The European Parliament adopts its opinion by a majority of votes cast. The Council is not bound in any way by that opinion. Nevertheless, if the opinion adopted by the Parliament is negative, the President of the Parliament requests the Council not to conclude the agreement in question.[32]

21–011 Trade agreements. Under the procedure for the conclusion of trade agreements under Art. 133, the EC Treaty makes no provision for any involvement of the European Parliament. Under the Westerterp procedure (see para. 21–004) it may only have cognisance of a signed agreement, after which it may, if it deems it appropriate, adopt an opinion on its own initiative. In this connection, it should be noted that the European Council nevertheless proposed as long ago as 1983 that the European Parliament should be consulted on the conclusion of all "significant international

---

[29] See Dashwood, "External Relations Provisions of the Amsterdam Treaty" (1998) C.M.L.R. 1019, at 1024–1028.

[30] See EP Rules of Procedure, r.83(6).

[31] Accordingly, the agreement between the EC and the USA on the processing and transfer of PNR data by Air Carriers to the United States Department of Homeland Security, Bureau of Customs and Border Protection, has been concluded by Council Decision 2004/496/EC of March 17, 2004 ([2004] O.J. L183/183), the European Parliament not being able to deliver an opinion within the time-limit laid down "in view of the urgent need to remedy the situation of uncertainty in which airlines and passengers found themselves, as well as to protect the financial interests of those concerned" (see point 3 of the preamble).

[32] EP Rules of Procedure, r.83(8).

agreements".[33] In any event, the European Parliament has more of a say where the agreement concerned falls within one of the categories of agreement discussed below for which it has to give its assent. Where the European Parliament has doubts whether a envisaged trade agreement is compatible with the EC Treaty it can—as in the case of other agreements—seek the opinion of the Court of Justice (see para. 21–020).

b. Assent

Duty to obtain assent. For four categories of agreements, the EC Treaty **21–012** makes their conclusion dependent upon the prior assent of the European Parliament (Art. 300(3), second subpara.). Here, too, the Parliament contends that, in the absence of any provision in the Treaty, it should have to give its assent before the agreement is signed.[34] The Council and the European Parliament may, in an urgent situation, agree upon a time-limit for the assent (Art. 300(3), third subpara.). The European Parliament gives its assent by a majority of the votes cast on the basis of a report from the responsible committee which may merely recommend either that the whole of the proposal be accepted or rejected; no amendments may be tabled.[35] If the European Parliament decides to withhold its assent, its President refers the agreement in question back to the Council for reconsideration.[36]

Four categories of agreements. The assent procedure applies, in the first **21–013** place, to association agreements within the meaning of Art. 310. The requirement for parliamentary assent for such agreements was introduced as long ago as the Single European Act. However, since the EU Treaty, assent has to be given by an absolute majority of the votes cast and no longer by a majority of the component Members of the European Parliament. Secondly, assent has to be obtained for other agreements establishing a specific institutional framework by organising co-operation procedures. Since most "co-operation agreements" establish bilateral bodies, this provision refers in all likelihood to agreements which establish a more complex institutional structure, yet are not concluded pursuant to Art. 310.[37] The third category of agreements requiring parliamentary assent

---

[33] Solemn Declaration of Stuttgart on European Union, June 19, 1983 (1983) 6 EC Bull. point 1.6.1. In practice, the Council generally requests an opinion; see, however, the European Parliament's resolution of February 1, 1996 on the failure to consult Parliament on the EU-Russia Interim Agreement, [1996] O.J. C47/26 (in which the Parliament refers to the failure to comply with a Council "undertaking"). For the European Parliament's limited influence in the case of trade agreements, see Bosse-Platière, "Le Parlement européen et les relations extérieures de la Communauté européenne après le Traité de Nice" (2002) R.T.D.E. 527–553.

[34] EP Rules of Procedure, r.83(6).

[35] *ibid.*, paras 6 and 7, which refer (except for the majority required) to the assent procedure under r.75 of the EP Rules of Procedure (para. 14–038, *supra*).

[36] *ibid.*, para. 9.

[37] Flaesch-Mougin (n.10, *supra*), at 385–386. A first instance is the WTO Agreement, para. 20–011, *supra*.

are those having "important budgetary implications" for the Community (now the EU).[38] The final category consists of agreements entailing amendment of an act adopted under the procedure laid down in Art. 251. Accordingly, the Council may not, by means of an international agreement, detract from internal legislation which the European Parliament and the Council adopted under the co-decision procedure. However, so long as no internal act has been adopted, the Council is entitled to conclude international agreements in the field in question after merely consulting the European Parliament (see para. 21–009).

Unlike the requirement as to majority voting in the Council (see para. 21–007), the requirement for parliamentary assent is no longer tied exclusively to the legal basis of the agreement in question (although the first category of agreements requiring parliamentary assent is still so tied). Criteria relating more to the importance of a given agreement (see, particularly, the third category) are now at least equally significant.[39] The upshot of all this will probably be differences of opinion as between the Council and the Parliament.[40]

21–014 **Political impact.** The power of assent enables the European Parliament to have a real say in the Community's foreign policy.[41] The European

---

[38] In order to ascertain whether an agreement has important budgetary implications, account must be taken of whether expenditure under the agreement is spread over several years, of a comparison of the expenditure under the agreement with the amount of the appropriations designed to finance the Community's external operations and, where the agreement relates to a particular sector, of a comparison between the expenditure entailed by the agreement and the whole of the budgetary appropriations for the sector in question, taking the internal and external aspects together. See ECJ, Case C–189/87 *European Parliament v Council* [1999] E.C.R. I–4741, paras 29–33.

[39] The possible procedures are:
    (1) unanimous vote in the Council following the assent of the European Parliament, in the case of association agreements and all agreements relating to an area for which a unanimous vote (in the Council) is required for internal provisions, which also: (a) give rise to a specific institutional framework, (b) have substantial budgetary implications, or (c) amend an act adopted under the co-decision procedure;
    (2) unanimous vote in the Council after consultation of the European Parliament, in the case of agreements relating to an area for which a unanimous vote is required for internal acts which do not fall under (a), (b) or (c);
    (3) qualified majority vote in the Council with no involvement of the European Parliament, in the case of tariff and trade agreements under Art. 133(3) of the EC Treaty;
    (4) qualified majority vote in the Council and assent of the European Parliament, in the case of an agreement relating to an area other than (1), (2) or (3), which also falls within either (a), (b) or (c);
    (5) qualified majority vote in the Council after consultation of the European Parliament, in the case of agreements falling within an area other than (1), (2) or (3) and not coming within (a), (b) or (c).

[40] Flaesch-Mougin (n.10, *supra*), at 387.

[41] See Bieber, "Democratic Control of European Foreign Policy" (1990) E.J.I.L. 148–173; for a survey of this competence in the overall context of the European Parliament's scrutiny of external policy: Robles Carrillo, *El control de la Política Exterior por el Parlamento Europeo* (Civitas, Madrid, 1994), 563 pp; Hilf and Schorkopf, "Das Europäische Parlament in den Aussenbeziehungen der Europäischen Union" (1999) EuR. 185–202.

Parliament has sometimes withheld its assent to additional protocols to association agreements until the negotiators agreed to provisions complying with the Parliament's wishes regarding, in particular, respect for human rights in the non-member country concerned.[42] Thus, in March 1988 the European Parliament withheld assent to additional protocols to the EEC-Israel Agreement until such time as Israel complied with the requirement under a Community regulation to afford agricultural products from the occupied territories direct access to the Community.[43] Assent gives the European Parliament a means of applying pressure with a view to its being more closely involved in the drawing up of agreements or of particular clauses therein. By this means, the European Parliament may obtain concessions from the Council with regard to the involvement of the Parliament going beyond the specific confines of a particular agreement.[44]

C. CHANGES TO THE PROCEDURE FOR THE CONCLUSION OF AGREEMENTS PROVIDED FOR IN THE EU CONSTITUTION

Single procedure. As has been mentioned, the EU Constitution will **21–015** establish a single procedure for the conclusion of international agreements in all policy areas of the Union. Any recommendation to the Council for the opening of negotiations will still emanate from the Commission, except where the envisaged agreement relates exclusively or principally to the common foreign and security policy, in which case it will be up to the Union Minister for Foreign Affairs to submit recommendations.[45] The Council is to nominate the Union negotiator (or leader of the Union's negotiating team), depending on the subject of the agreement envisaged.[46] On a proposal of the negotiator, the Council will adopt the decision authorising the signature and the conclusion of the agreement.[47] As far as the nomination of the negotiator is concerned, the Constitution will leave more latitude to the Council than Art. 300 of the EC Treaty, under which only the Commission is designated to act as a negotiator. Negotiations are reserved to the Commission only as regards agreements in the field of the

---

[42] See the European Parliament's refusal to give its assent to Protocols with Syria ([1992] O.J. C39/52 and 55) and Morocco ([1992] O.J. C39/54). Assent was ultimately given on October 28, 1992 (but not for one of the Protocols with Syria, [1992] O.J. C305/64); for the Protocols in question, see [1992] O.J. L352/14 (Morocco) and [1992] O.J. L352/22 (Syria). On December 15, 1987, the European Parliament deferred giving its assent to two financial protocols annexed to the EEC-Turkey Agreement on similar grounds ([1988] O.J. C13/28; it gave its assent thereto on January 20, 1988, [1988] O.J. C49/52).

[43] [1988] O.J. C94/55 (assent withheld on March 9, 1988; for the political reasons, see (1988) 3 EU Bull. points 2.4.13–15); [1988] O.J. C290/60 (assent given on October 12, 1988); Silvestro, "Les Protocoles financiers CEE-Israël à l'examen du Parlement européen" (1991) R.M.C.U.E. 462–464.

[44] Flaesch-Mougin (n.10, *supra*), at 385.

[45] EU Constitution, Art. III–325(3).

[46] *ibid.*

[47] *ibid.*, Art. III–325(5) and (6).

common commercial policy.[48] Nevertheless, the intention behind the EU Constitution seems to be that negotiations should be conducted, as far as the CFSP is concerned, by the Union Minister for Foreign Affairs, whereas, in all other areas, negotiations should be conducted by the Commission or by the Council itself. The EU Constitution takes over the rule that the Council is to decide on the signature and conclusion of an agreement by a qualified majority, except where the agreement covers a field for which, at the internal level, unanimity is required for the adoption of a Union act, and in the case of association agreements.[49] Separate rules will continue to exist for monetary affairs.[50]

As far as the participation of the European Parliament is concerned, the EU Constitution introduces an obligation for the Council at least to consult the European Parliament in all areas outside the CFSP. The European Parliament must give its "consent" to association agreements, agreements establishing a specific institutional framework and agreements with important budgetary implications, as well as to agreements covering fields to which either the ordinary legislative procedure applies[51]—such as the common commercial policy—or the special legislative procedure under which the Parliament's consent is required.[52]

III.   MIXED AGREEMENTS

21–016 Legal reasons. External action on the part of the Communities often takes the form of a mixed agreement, where both one of the Communities and the Member States are parties.[53] Most multilateral agreements to which the Community is a party and all the present association agreements fall into this category.[54] Close co-operation is required between the Member States and the Community institutions where the subject-matter of an agreement appears to fall partly within the competence of the Community and partly within that of the Member States (see paras 19–009, 20–004 and 20–014). In such a case, the agreement will be concluded both by the Community

---

[48] *ibid.*, Art. III–315(3).

[49] *ibid.*, Art. III–325(8) (which also mentions in this connection co-operation agreements concluded pursuant to Art. III–319 of the EU Constitution with States which are candidates for accession).

[50] *ibid.*, Art. III–326.

[51] This means that consent is no longer required only for agreements entailing amendments to an existing act adopted under the co-decision procedure.

[52] EU Constitution, Art. III–325(6) (which also requires "consent" to the agreement by which the Union is to accede to the European Convention of Human Rights).

[53] See, expressly, Art. 102 of the EAEC Treaty. For an extensive discussion, see the articles in O'Keeffe and Schermers (eds), *Mixed Agreements* (Kluwer, Deventer, 1983), 248 pp.; Leal-Arcas, "The European Community and Mixed Agreements" (2001) E.For.Aff.Rev. 483–513.

[54] For a survey, see O'Keeffe and Schermers (n.53, *supra*), at 207–215; Groux and Manin, *The European Communities in the International Legal Order* (Office for Official Publications of the EC, Luxembourg, 1985), at 68–72.

and by the Member States, unless the agreement does not allow international organisations such as the Community to sign and the Community exercises its external competence through the medium of the Member States.[55] The Court of Justice has also held that the Member States may participate in an agreement where the financing falls to them and constitutes an essential element of the agreement (see para. 20–004). Lastly, a Member State may participate in an international agreement alongside the Community as the international representative of certain dependent territories which are not part of the sphere of application of Community law.[56] Where the Community—possibly with its Member States—accedes to an organisation established by a multilateral treaty, complications arise not only from the allocation of competences, but also from the allocation and exercise of voting rights in organs of the organisation (see para. 19–005). Even under the EU Constitution, mixed agreements will continue to be useful in those areas where the Union shares competence with the Member States.

Political reasons. In practice, mixed agreements also come to the fore in **21–017** other circumstances for a variety of political reasons. The contracting parties may ask for the agreement to be concluded as a mixed agreement. In addition, Member States often choose to be party to the agreement. In this way, the conclusion of the agreement is not hampered by any disputes as to the extent of Community powers and the Member States remain in a position to take implementing measures themselves. In the case of an agreement which establishes institutions with powers of decision, the mixed form guarantees that the Member States keep their voting rights in those institutions or that the Community—in the event that the Member States do not exercise their voting rights themselves—has a number of votes equal to the number of Member States.[57] Since the Member States also commit themselves internationally by a mixed agreement, the Community, for its part, is secured as regards the funding or other implementing measures which the agreement requires the Member States to take.[58] Nevertheless, the fact that an agreement entails obligations and financial burdens for the Member States does not detract from the exclusive character of a

---

[55] ECJ, Opinion 2/91 *Convention No. 170 of the International Labour Organisation concerning safety in the use of chemicals at work* [1993] E.C.R. I–1061, para. 5.

[56] ECJ, Opinion 1/78 *International Agreement on Natural Rubber* [1979] E.C.R. 2871, para. 62 (for any conflicting interests, see para. 19–014, *supra*). The special position of the Member State concerned has no effect on the demarcation of spheres of competence within the Community: ECJ, Opinion 1/94 *Agreement establishing the World Trade Organisation* [1994] E.C.R. I–5267, paras 17–18.

[57] For voting rights and, more generally, participation in such bodies, see Groux and Manin (n.54, *supra*), at 91–96; Sack, "The European Community's Membership of International Organisations" (1995) C.M.L.R. 1227, at 1232–1256; Neuwahl, "Shared Powers or Combined Incompetence? More on Mixity" (1996) C.M.L.R. 667, at 678–687.

[58] Nevertheless, the Commission does not favour this form of action: see, *e.g.* n.70 to para. 20–010, *supra* (on the Tokyo Round Agreements).

Community competence.[59] Thus, participation of the Member States in an agreement does not as such result from their obligations to bear some of the expenses of an international organisation like the WTO, which has only an operating budget and not financial instruments.[60] Accession of the Member States to such an agreement could be regarded, however, as an action pursuant to special authorisation on the part of the Community.[61]

21–018 Consequences. In any event, a mixed agreement does not result in any shift in the respective powers of the Community and the Member States to give effect to the obligations arising for each of them out of the agreement. The conclusion of a mixed agreement possibly prevents the system for which it provides from being able to be regarded as an exercise of power by the Community which results in a policy area being taken outside the sphere of competence of the Member States.[62]

IV. NON-COMMUNITY PROCEDURE FOR THE CONCLUSION OF AGREEMENTS

21–019 Agreements concluded by the Union. Article 24 of the EU Treaty lays down the procedure which must be followed where the Union concludes an agreement with one or more non-member countries or an international organisation within the framework of Title V (common foreign and security policy, CFSP) or Title VI (police and judicial co-operation in criminal matters, PJCC) of that treaty.[63] In such case, the Council may authorise the Presidency, assisted by the Commission as appropriate, to open negotiations to that effect (EU Treaty, Art. 24(1)).[64] In practice, the Council has also authorised its Secretary General/High Representative for the CFSP to negotiate on behalf of the Presidency.[65]

---

[59] ECJ, Opinion 1/75 *Draft Understanding on a Local Cost Standard drawn up under the auspices of the OECD* [1975] E.C.R. 1355, at 1364.

[60] ECJ, Opinion 1/94 *Agreement establishing the World Trade Organisation* [1994] E.C.R. I–5267, para. 21.

[61] See Neuwahl, "Joint Participation in International Treaties and the Exercise of Power by the EEC and its Member States: Mixed Agreements" (1991) C.M.L.R. 717, at 733.

[62] *ibid.*, at 729–731. For liability in the case of "mixed" international obligations of the Community and its Member States, see Björklund, "Responsibility in the EC of Mixed Agreements—Should Non-Member Parties Care?" (2001) Nordic J.I.L. 373–402.

[63] See the CFSP and PJCC agreements referred to in para. 18–023, *supra*. For PJCC competence, see EU Treaty, Art. 24(4) and Art. 38.

[64] The use of the word "may" in Art. 24 of the EU Treaty suggests that negotiations may be conducted in some other manner, *e.g.* by the Commission or a Member State following the grant of authorisation by the Council.

[65] See the authorisation given to negotiate on behalf of the Presidency detailed arrangements regarding the participation of third States in the EU military operation in the Former Yugoslav Republic of Macedonia in Art. 8(3) of Council Joint Action 2003/92/CFSP of January 27, 2003 ([2003] O.J. L34/26). Previously, negotiations on behalf of the Union were invariably conducted by the Presidency.

Such agreements are concluded by the Council on a recommendation from the Presidency. The Council acts unanimously when the agreement covers a CFSP issue for which unanimity is required for the adoption of internal decisions. When the agreement is envisaged to implement a CFSP joint action or common position, the Council acts by a qualified majority (EU Treaty, Art. 24(2) and (3)). As far as PJCC (Title VI of the EU Treaty) is concerned; the Council acts by a qualified majority when the agreement in question covers an issue for which a qualified majority is required for the adoption of internal decisions or measures (EU Treaty, Art. 24(4)). Approval in the Council may be inferred from the decision authorising the Presidency to sign the agreement or have it signed.[66]

The EU Treaty allows Member States not to be bound by an agreement concluded on behalf of the Union before it is ratified in their national legal system. To that end, Art. 24(5) of the EU Treaty provides that no agreement is to be binding on a Member State whose representative in the Council states that it has to comply with the requirements of its own constitutional procedure. The other members of the Council may then agree that the agreement shall nevertheless apply provisionally.

When the EU Constitution enters into force, all agreements in the field of the CFSP and PJCC will be concluded in accordance with the same procedure applying to all other agreements to be concluded by the Union (see para. 21–015).

V. OPINION OF THE COURT OF JUSTICE

Objective. The European Parliament,[67] the Council, the Commission and **21–020** the Member States may obtain the opinion of the Court of Justice as to whether an envisaged agreement is compatible with the provisions of the EC Treaty. Where the Court's opinion is adverse, the agreement may enter into force only in accordance with the procedure for amending the Treaty laid down in Art. 48 of the EU Treaty (EC Treaty, Art. 300(6)). The procedure for obtaining the prior opinion of the Court is intended to avoid complications from arising as a result of a finding made in judicial proceedings that an international agreement which is binding on the Community is incompatible with provisions of the EC Treaty on account of its content or the procedure by which it was concluded. Such a judicial decision "could not fail to provoke, not only in a Community context but also in that of international relations, serious difficulties and might give rise to adverse consequences for all interested parties, including third

---

[66] This was the case with the first CFSP and PJCC agreements (para. 18–023, *supra*), where in the decisions approving the agreements the Council authorised the Presidency to indicate the person who was to sign the agreement so as to bind the Union.

[67] The European Parliament was given the right to obtain an opinion by the Treaty of Nice.

countries".[68] Article 103 of the EAEC Treaty provides for a similar review procedure with regard to agreements which Member States propose concluding with third States.[69] However, the EAEC Treaty does not allow the opinion of the Court of Justice to be sought on agreements concluded with third parties by the Commission on the basis of that treaty.[70] The EU Treaty does not confer jurisdiction on the Court of Justice to rule on the compatibility of CFSP or PJCC agreements with that Treaty.[71]

21–021 Conditions. The Court of Justice will accept as an "envisaged agreement" an agreement whose subject-matter is known, even if there is not yet agreement on the full text. Especially as regards a question of competence "it is clearly in the interests of all the States concerned, including non-member countries, for such a question to be clarified as soon as any particular negotiations are commenced".[72] In so far as the subject-matter of the envisaged agreement is known, questions of competence may be submitted to the Court of Justice before negotiations have formally begun.[73] On the other hand, no time-limit is prescribed for making a request for an opinion and, hence, such a request may be made after the negotiations have come to an end[74] and even after the agreement has been signed but before the Community's consent to be bound by the agreement is finally expressed.[75] Once the Community has concluded an international agreement, the Court of Justice no longer has jurisdiction to give an opinion on it.[76] In such proceedings, any issues may be raised which potentially cast doubt on the substantive or formal validity of the agreement having regard to the Treaty. Questions relating to the division of competence to conclude such an agreement as between the Community and

---

[68] ECJ, Opinion 1/75 *Draft Understanding on a Local Cost Standard drawn up under the auspices of the OECD* [1975] E.C.R. 1355, at 1361.

[69] See ECJ, Ruling 1/78 *Draft Convention of the International Atomic Energy Agency on the Physical Protection of Nuclear Materials, Facilities and Transports* [1978] E.C.R. 2151, paras 2–3.

[70] This does not prevent the Court of Justice from ruling, both under the EC Treaty and the EAEC Treaty, on an application for annulment of the decision by which such an agreement is approved (para. 17–096, *supra*): ECJ, Case C–29/99 *Commission v Council* [2002] E.C.R. I–11221, para. 54.

[71] For the exclusion of judicial review, see para. 18–023, *supra*.

[72] ECJ, Opinion 1/78 *International Agreement on Natural Rubber* [1979] E.C.R. 2871, para. 35.

[73] ECJ, Opinion 2/94 *Accession by the Communities to the Convention for the Protection of Human Rights and Fundamental Freedoms* [1996] E.C.R. I–1759, paras 16–18.

[74] ECJ, Opinion 1/75 *Draft Understanding on a Local Cost Standard drawn up under the auspices of the OECD* [1975] E.C.R. 1355, at 1361.

[75] ECJ, Opinion 1/94 *Agreement establishing the World Trade Organisation* [1994] E.C.R. I–5267, para. 12, at I–5392.

[76] ECJ, Opinion 3/94 *Framework Agreement on Bananas* [1995] E.C.R. I–4577, paras 8–23. This does not mean that an action for annulment cannot be brought against the decision by which the Community concluded the agreement: *ibid.*, para. 22; ECJ, Case C–122/95 *Germany v Council* [1998] E.C.R. I–973, para. 42 (see para. 17–096). See also Karagiannis, "L'expression 'accord envisagé' dans l'article 228 para. 6 du traité CE" (1998) C.D.E. 105–136.

the Member States are particularly liable to be raised.[77] Since the answer to such a question depends on the scope of Community powers, the Court will also rule on the correct legal basis for the Community to use in order to approve the agreement in question.[78] However, the procedure for obtaining an opinion is not intended to solve difficulties associated with implementation of an envisaged agreement which falls within shared Community and Member State competence.[79]

[77] ECJ, Opinion 1/75 (n.74, *supra*), at 1360; Ruling 1/78 (n.69, *supra*), para. 5; Opinion 1/78 (n.72, *supra*), para. 30; Opinion 2/91 (n.55, *supra*), para. 3; ECJ, Opinion 2/92 *Third Revised Decision of the OECD on national treatment* [1995] E.C.R. I–521, paras 13–14; Opinion 1/94 (n.75, *supra*) para. 9, at I–5391–5392. See also Art. 107(2) of the ECJ Rules of Procedure ("The Opinion may deal not only with the question whether the envisaged agreement is compatible with the provisions of the EC Treaty but also with the question whether the Community or any Community institution has the power to enter into that agreement"). For further details, see Lenaerts and Arts, *Procedural Law of the European Union*, Ch.12.

[78] ECJ, Opinion 2/92 (n.77, *supra*), paras 9–14; ECJ, Opinion 2/00 *Cartagena Protocol* [2001] E.C.R. I–9713, paras 5–12; for a critical view, see Maubernard, "L' 'intensité modulable' des compétences externes de la Communauté européenne et de ses Etats membres" (2003) R.T.D.E. 229–264. See also Gattinara, "La compétence consultative de la Cour de justice après les avis 1/00 et 2/00" (2003) R.D.U.E. 687–741.

[79] ECJ, Opinion 2/00 *Cartagena Protocol* [2001] E.C.R. I–9713, para. 17.

CHAPTER 22

CONSISTENCY BETWEEN THE COMMON FOREIGN AND SECURITY POLICY AND COMMUNITY ACTION ON THE PART OF THE UNION

I. CONSISTENCY BETWEEN THE COMMON FOREIGN AND SECURITY POLICY AND THE COMMUNITIES

A. PRINCIPLE

Consistency. The EU Treaty requires the Union to "ensure the consistency **22–001** of its external activities as a whole in the context of its external relations, security, economic and development policies" (Art. 3, second para., first sentence).[1] The structure of the Union is such that it acts externally either within the context of the Communities or within that of the "supplementary" common foreign and security policy provided for in Title V of the EU Treaty (CFSP).

The field of application of Community action on the part of the Union is determined by the powers of the Community institutions, as described above (see paras 20–001–20–034). In contrast, the scope of the CFSP extends to "all areas of foreign and security policy" (see para. 20–040). Where external action of the Union falls within the powers of the Communities, it is governed by Community law, namely the rules determining the relationship of Community action to any potential action on the part of the Member States. In contrast, action under Title V of the EU Treaty is based on the Member States' international powers. Alongside specific objectives for such action, Title V chiefly sets out procedural rules on consultation and the possible definition of common positions, joint actions or other decisions on the part of the Union (see paras 20–042–20–045).

The legal split between Community and CFSP action on the part of the Union does not square with what really happens at international level: economic decisions taken by States or organisations are often the reason for or a consequence of political decisions.[2] By the same token, Community

---

[1] For a general discussion of the need for consistency, see Gauttier, "Horizontal Coherence and the External Competences of the European Union" (2004) E.L.J. 23–41.

[2] Flaesch-Mougin, "Le traité de Maastricht et les compétences externes de la Communauté européenne: à la recherche d'une politique externe de l'Union" (1993) C.D.E. 351, at 373.

external relations have invariably pursued political objectives.[3] Consequently, when the Union wishes to express a policy with regard to the outside world, it is essential for its Community and CFSP action to be consistent. Besides, it was the need to defend Community interests more effectively through concerted action which underlay the co-ordination of Member States' foreign policies that developed into European Political Co-operation (EPC).[4] The Single European Act gave the Presidency of the Council and the Commission special responsibility for ensuring consistency between the external policy of the Community and the policies agreed upon in EPC.[5] The EU Treaty entrusts that task to the same institutions: the Council and the Commission are responsible for ensuring that consistency, for co-operating to that end, and for implementing the Union's external policy, each in accordance with its respective powers (Art. 3, second para., second and third sentences).[6] Even when Member States enter into enhanced co-operation, the Council and the Commission have to ensure the consistency of activities undertaken on that basis and the consistency of such activities with the policies of the Union and the Community (EU Treaty, Art. 45).

Since the EU Constitution will maintain the CFSP as a separate policy area alongside the other fields of the Union's external action, it will be necessary to ensure that there is consistency between that area and the other fields of action. This task will be conferred on the Council and the Commission, assisted by the Union Minister for Foreign Affairs.[7]

B. GUARANTEES OF CONSISTENCY

1. Objectives of the Union

22–002 **Uniform objectives.** The EU Treaty sets express objectives for the Union which are intended to secure consistency in its external action.[8] In the first place, the Union seeks to assert its identity on the international scene, in particular through the implementation of a common foreign and security policy, while maintaining in full and building upon the *acquis*

---

[3] See paras 20–002 (common commercial policy), 20–020—20–025 (association agreements) and 20–026—20–027 (development co-operation), *supra*.

[4] For the interaction between the EC and EPC as the *raison d'être* for EPC, see Lak, "Interaction between European Political Co-operation and the European Community (External)—Existing Rules and Challenges" (1989) C.M.L.R. 281, at 285–293; Nuttall, "Interaction between European Political Co-operation and the European Community" (1987) Y.E.L. 211–249.

[5] Single European Act, Art. 30(5).

[6] See also the discussion of the structure of the Union in paras 3–012—3–016; for the CFSP, see Kugelmann, "Die Gemeinsame Aussen- und Sicherheitspolitik" (1998) EuR. Beiheft 2, at 99–123.

[7] EU Constitution, Art. III–292(3), second subpara.

[8] Müller-Graff, "Einheit und Kohärenz der Vertragsziele von EG and EU" (1998) EuR. Beiheft 2, 67–80; see also Flaesch-Mougin (n.2, *supra*), at 373–374, and Pechstein, "Das Kohärenzgebot als entscheidende Integrationsdimension der Europäischen Union" (1995) EuR. 247–258.

communautaire (EU Treaty, Art. 2, second and fifth indents). In addition, Art. 6(1) and (2) of the EU Treaty refers to the principles of democracy, the rule of law and respect for human rights and fundamental freedoms, which are binding as regards Community action of the Union (see EC Treaty, Art. 177(2) and Art. 220) and to which the Union must have regard in the context of the CFSP (EU Treaty, Art. 11, fifth indent).[9] The EU Constitution will reflect the aim that the Union's external action is to pursue uniform objectives by bringing the CFSP and the other external policy areas together in a single Title with common objectives.[10]

2. A single institutional framework

Institutions. In order to secure consistency in its activities, the Union has a **22–003** single institutional framework (EU Treaty, Art. 3, first para.).[11] This is clear even at the stage of the preparation of policy decisions, where at present the Commission exercises the right of initiative in both Community and CFSP decision-making. Coordination is also provided for between Coreper, which carries out the preparatory work for Council decision-making generally, and the Political and Security Committee, which advises the Council in particular on CFSP matters (see para. 15–003).

Most acts exercising the external powers of the Communities and all CFSP acts are adopted by the Council, which proceeds in the same way in both cases. In so doing, it follows the general political guidelines provided by the European Council (EU Treaty, Art. 4, first para., and Art. 13). The fact that those taking part in the decision-making are the same ensures some degree of coherence between the Community and the CFSP action of the Union. In any event, Title V of the EU Treaty requires the Council to "ensure the unity, consistency and effectiveness of action by the Union" in defining and implementing the CFSP (EU Treaty, Art. 13(3), third subpara.).

The Council lays down the objectives, the scope, the means, if necessary, the duration, and the conditions for the implementation of any joint action under the CFSP (EU Treaty, Art. 14(1)) and can make sure that the implementing measures to be taken by the Council or the Member States do not run counter to Community policy. The requirement for the unity, consistency and effectiveness of any action may necessitate charging policy expenditure to the EU budget or carrying out its implementation

---

[9] See the Commission's communication, published as "The European Union and human rights in the world" (1995) EU Bull. Suppl.3; for a substantive appraisal of the policy of the European Union, see King, "Human Rights in European Foreign Policy: Success or Failure for Post-Modern Diplomacy" (1999) E.J.I.L. 313–337. See also the position with regard to human rights in connection with development co-operation, para. 20–027, *supra*.

[10] EU Constitution, Art. III–292(1) and (2).

[11] See Krenzler and Schneider, "Die Gemeinsame Aussen- und Sicherheitspolitik der Europäischen Union—Zur Frage der Kohärenz" (1994) EuR. 144, at 148–155; Wessel, "De 'tweede pijler' van de Europese Unie: een vreemde eend in de bijt?" (1995) S.E.W. 554, at 544–559.

exclusively *via* Community measures. The Commission has to take consistency into account when it proposes implementing measures by virtue of its right of initiative in the context of Community and CFSP decision-making. Where CFSP action necessitates the conclusion of international agreements, this may be done since the Treaty of Amsterdam by the procedure laid down in Art. 24 of the EU Treaty.[12]

As far as the international representation of the Union is concerned, Title V of the EU Treaty makes first recourse to the President of the Council; in contrast, the Commission is generally empowered to represent the Communities (see paras 19–009—19–014). In Community practice, various forms of international representation have emerged and are designed to secure unity in the external action of the Communities and the Member States (see para. 19–009). In addition, the EU Treaty lays down that the Commission must be fully associated with the work carried out in the CFSP field generally (Art. 18(4)).[13]

In order to strengthen consistency between the various fields of external action, the EU Constitution will require the European Council to identify the strategic interests and objectives of the Union's external action.[14] In addition, the introduction of a Union Minister for Foreign Affairs will mean that a number of tasks at present performed by the Commission, the Presidency of the Council and the High Representative for the CFSP will be combined together. Whereas the Union Minister for Foreign Affairs will be responsible, in his or her own capacity, for the preparation and the execution of the CFSP, that Minister will also be responsible, within the Commission, for the co-ordination of other aspects of the Union's external action.[15]

3. External supervision

22–004 **Parliamentary control.** Only limited parliamentary scrutiny is possible with a view to ensuring that the CFSP and Community policy are mutually consistent. The European Parliament may put questions to the Commission and the Council, but may not hold the Commission politically accountable for a CFSP action of the Union where that institution has no Community powers to influence decision-making and to supervise that the institutions and the Member States comply with their Treaty obligations (see paras 15–004 and 15–006). The entry into force of the EU Constitution will not bring any change in this situation.

---

[12] Previously, such international agreements could be concluded only on the basis of a Community power, see Wessel (n.11, *supra*), at 559.

[13] For a case in which the Council emphasised the duty to ensure consistency and the fact that the Commission had been fully associated with the work on the common position to be adopted, see Common Position 94/779/CFSP of November 28, 1994 defined by the Council on the basis of the former Article J.2 of the Treaty on European Union on the objectives and priorities of the European Union towards Ukraine, [1994] O.J. L313/1.

[14] EU Constitution, Art. III–293.

[15] See para. 10–071, *supra* (position of the Minister) and para. 15–009 (powers of the Minister).

Judicial review. The Court of Justice has no direct jurisdiction to rule on **22–005** the compatibility of a given Community action with the CFSP (EU Treaty, Art. 46). At most, the Court may take CFSP commitments into account when interpreting Community law.[16] In the case of a Community action closely connected with CFSP action, a breach of commitments arising for the institutions or the Member States under the latter might be regarded as a breach of co-operation in good faith.[17] Conversely, judicial review is of course possible in the event that CFSP action on the part of the Council, the Commission or the Member States infringes Community obligations (EU Treaty, Art. 47; see para. 18–011). In this area, too, the EU Constitution will introduce virtually no changes (see para. 18–022).

C. RELATIONSHIP BETWEEN THE COMMON FOREIGN AND SECURITY POLICY AND THE COMMUNITIES

Co-existence. The EU Treaty refers to Titles V and VI as forms of policy **22–006** and co-operation which have "supplemented" the European Communities (Art. 1, third para.).[18] Article 47 of the EU Treaty declares that the provisions of those titles are not to affect the Community Treaties. It follows that action pursuant to the Community Treaties is not subordinated to CFSP action on the part of the Union. In practice, both EC and CFSP actions serve as the expression of a consistent foreign policy.[19] Both forms of action coexist, however, as distinct instruments of the Union's external policy.[20]

Integrated approach. A CFSP act does not have the same legal force as a **22–007** Community act as far as the Community institutions are concerned. Admittedly, however, in exercising its right of initiative the Commission must ensure consistency in the external activities of the Union, but this does not for all that make it bound by provisions of a common position or a joint action of the Council which is based on Title V of the EU Treaty.[21]

---

[16] Neuwahl, "Foreign and Security Policy and the Implementation of the Requirement of 'Consistency' under the Treaty on European Union" in O'Keeffe and Twomey (eds), *Legal Issues of the Maastricht Treaty* (Chancery, London, 1994), 227, at 244.

[17] Krenzler and Schneider (n.11, *supra*), at 158; Pechstein (n.8, *supra*), at 257–258. This is conceivable in particular where a Member State's Community obligations under Arts 297 and 298 of the EC Treaty are at issue: see Gilsdorf, "Les réserves de sécurité du traité CEE, à la lumière du traité sur l'Union européenne" (1994) R.M.C.U.E. 17, at 24.

[18] In emphasising the supplementary nature of the CFSP *vis-à-vis* the Communities, this wording goes a step further than Art. 1 of the Single European Act (albeit never repealed), which provides that the EC and EPC have as their objective "to contribute *together* to making concrete progress towards European unity ['*Union*' in other language versions]" (emphasis supplied).

[19] See Keukeleire, *Het buitenlands beleid van de Europese Unie* (Kluwer, Deventer, 1998) at 331–361.

[20] Krenzler and Schneider (n.11, *supra*), at 152; see also Flaesch-Mougin (n.2, *supra*), at 375–376; Pechstein (n.8, *supra*), at 255–256, and Griller, "Die Unterscheidung von Unionsrecht und Gemeinschaftsrecht nach Amsterdam" (1999) EuR. Beiheft 1, at 45–72.

[21] See Glaesner, "Willensbildung und Beschlussverfahren in der Europäischen Union" (1994) EuR. Beiheft 1, 25, at 36.

Accordingly, the Council confines itself in CFSP acts to "noting" the Commission's intention to submit proposals for Community measures in support of CFSP objectives.[22]

The autonomy of the Communities does not preclude Community measures from being formulated after the Council has reached an agreement in the context of the CFSP or the Council from leaving the elaboration of a CFSP act to the Communities. In this way, rules have been adopted for the export of goods which may have both a civil and a military use (dual-use goods)[23] and for protection against the effects of the extra-territorial application of legislation adopted by a third country.[24] With regard to such matters, Community rules together with a CFSP decision are adopted as "an integrated system involving, in accordance with their own powers, the Council, the Commission and the Member States".[25] In the meantime, the system for the control of dual-use products and technology has been fully incorporated into a Community measure (see para. 20–007). At the same time, it is current practice for a CFSP act to be followed up by Community measures in the context of economic sanctions imposed on third countries or persons (see paras 20–050—20–052).

22–008 **Towards a single foundation.** When the EU Constitution enters into force, both the present Community powers and the CFSP will become "powers of the Union". The institutions of the Union will have to comply with binding CFSP acts of the European Council and of the Council in the same way that they have to comply with any other binding act of the Union. When the European Council and the Council adopt a European decision within the framework of the CFSP, that decision will be binding in its

---

[22] See Common Position 94/779/CFSP of November 28, 1994 (n.13, *supra*), where the Council "notes that the Commission will direct its action towards achieving the objectives and priorities of this common position by appropriate Community measures"; Joint Action 96/656/CFSP of November 11, 1996 in support of the democratic transition process in Zaire ([1996] O.J. L300/1), where the Council "notes" that the Commission "intends to propose measures to help achieve the objectives of this Joint Action, *inter alia*, under the European Development Fund"; Joint Action 98/117/CFSP of February 2, 1998 in support of the Bosnian Peace Process ([1998] O.J. L35/1), where the Council "notes that the Commission in support of the objectives of this joint action intends to come forward with proposals where appropriate for project assistance in support of the new Government" (it is stated in the preamble that additional Community measures should also be considered "in order to ensure the consistency of the Union's external activities").

[23] Council Decision 94/942/CFSP of December 19, 1994 on the joint action adopted by the Council (on the basis of the former Art. J.3 of the EU Treaty) concerning the control of exports of dual-use goods ([1994] O.J. L367/8) and Council Regulation (EC) No. 3381/94 of December 19, 1994 setting up a Community regime for the control of exports of dual-use goods ([1994] O.J. L367/1), which was meanwhile replaced by a single Community system (see para. 20–007).

[24] Joint Action 96/668/CFSP of November 22, 1996 and Council Regulation (EC) No. 2271/96 of November 22, 1996 (para. 20–008, *supra*), both of which are designed to provide protection against the effects of the extra-territorial application of legislation adopted by a third country and acts based thereon or resulting therefrom ([1996] O.J. L309/7 and 1, respectively).

[25] See Art. 1, fourth para., of Decision 94/942/CFSP (n.23, *supra*).

entirety on the persons to whom it is addressed.[26] As for the enforcement in practice of CFSP acts, account must be taken of the fact that the Court of Justice has no jurisdiction in this regard (see para. 18–022).

II. CONSISTENCY BETWEEN THE EXTERNAL ACTION OF THE UNION AND THAT OF THE MEMBER STATES

Sincere co-operation. The "consistency" in foreign policy required by the **22–009** EU Treaty is predicated on the unity which has to exist as between the action of the Union and that of its Member States.

As far as Community powers are concerned, that requirement appears to be embodied in the principle of sincere co-operation or co-operation in good faith which applies to the Member States and the institutions (EC Treaty, Art. 10): in principle, Member States may not act in an area which falls within the exclusive competence of the Community and they may not take or maintain any action in any other field which conflicts with Community law (see para. 20–036).

Article 11(2) of the EU Treaty emphasises the same principle in the context of the CFSP.[27] However, Title V of the EU Treaty does not affect the powers of the Member States. It merely contains an obligation for the Member States to consult each other and, if a common position or joint action is adopted, to uphold it and to act in accordance with it. Commission delegations in non-Community countries and at international conferences are also subject to these obligations (see para. 15–005). The consistency required in this connection is presently based on a commitment under international law and, as such, cannot be enforced by the Court of Justice (EU Treaty, Art. 46). It is improbable that a Member State would bring a breach of a CFSP commitment before the International Court of Justice. Whether individuals may challenge a breach by a Member State of commitments entered into under the CFSP depends on the legal force of such commitments in the national legal system. It follows that the consistency of the Member States' foreign and security policies with that of the Union has to be secured primarily within the Council (see Art. 11(2), third subpara.; Art. 13(3), third subpara.). The fact that national diplomats and civil servants are involved in preparing decisions, together with the unanimity required in order to adopt decisions, affords a certain guarantee that action by the Member States will not be at odds with the CFSP action decided upon by the Union.

Under the EU Constitution, any action of the Member States within the scope of the CFSP will be subject to the principles of sincere co-operation

---

[26] See Art. I–33(1), fifth subpara., of the EU Constitution.
[27] See also Art. 16 of the EU Treaty, which refers to "concerted and convergent action".

and the primacy of Union law. Lack of jurisdiction in the field of CFSP will impede the Community Court from securing compliance by the Member States with their CFSP obligations. In this respect, the consistency between the CFSP and other fields of external action will, in practice, be a matter for the political authorities.

CHAPTER 23

RELATIONS BETWEEN THE EUROPEAN UNION AND THE OTHER EUROPEAN STATES[1]

I. RELATIONS WITH MEMBER COUNTRIES OF THE EUROPEAN FREE TRADE ASSOCIATION

A. HISTORICAL INTERPRETATION

EFTA. Shortly after the EEC Treaty was signed, seven other European 23–001 States, at the instigation of the United Kingdom, decided to set up their own model of integration: the European Free Trade Area (EFTA; see para. 2–007). After the accession of Denmark, Ireland and the United Kingdom to the Communities, those former EFTA countries had to redefine their trade relations with the remaining EFTA members and treat their goods as if they came from any non-Community country. In order to avoid the resultant restrictions on trade, the Community concluded the first trade-liberalising agreements with the EFTA countries in July 1972 on the basis of Art. 113 of the EEC Treaty.[2]

Trade agreements. Each of those agreements created, by stages, a bilateral 23–002 free trade area for industrial goods between the parties. To this effect, customs duties and charges of equivalent effect, as well as quantitative restrictions and measures of equivalent effect were abolished in trade

---

[1] This chapter was contributed by Eddy De Smijter, administrator in the European Commission, and voluntary academic collaborator in the Institute for European Law of the K.U. Leuven.

[2] On July 22, 1972, bilateral trade agreements were concluded with Iceland ([1972] O.J. English Spec. Ed. 301, p.4,); Austria ([1972] O.J. Spec. Ed. L300, p.4), Portugal ([1972] O.J. English Spec. Ed. L301, p.166), Sweden ([1972] O.J. Spec. Ed. L300, p.99), and Switzerland ([1972] O.J. Spec. Ed. L300, p.191). The agreement with Switzerland also applies to Liechtenstein, which is in a customs union with that country pursuant to a Treaty of March 29, 1923 (see the Additional Agreement, [1972] O.J. English Spec. Ed. L300, p.283). Bilateral trade agreements were concluded with Norway on May 14, 1973 ([1973] O.J. L171/1) and with Finland on October 5, 1973 ([1973] O.J. L328/1). After being an associate member of EFTA since 1961, Finland became a full Member on January 1, 1986 in the course of the preparatory negotiations for the EEA Agreement (para. 23–004, *infra*). For the origin and particulars of the various trade agreements, see Wellenstein, "The Free Trade Agreements between the enlarged European Communities and the EFTA-Countries" (1973) C.M.L.R. 137–149.

between the two economic areas.[3] The provisions of the trade agreements took their inspiration from parallel provisions of the EEC Treaty, sometimes even taking them over virtually *verbatim*.[4] Nevertheless, it appears from the different context in which the provisions operated and from the particular objectives of the trade agreements, on the one hand, and the EC Treaty, on the other, that similar or identical provisions were not necessarily to be interpreted in the same way.[5]

The administration of the agreements and supervision as to their correct implementation was entrusted to a Joint Committee with equal numbers of representatives from each side. Where the agreement provided for the necessary powers, the Joint Committee could make recommendations and take decisions.[6]

23–003 Free trade area. Since the various countries with which the EEC concluded free trade agreements in 1972 themselves belonged to a free trade area, the Community and the EFTA countries formed a large free trade area given that all measures restricting trade as between States were abolished on January 1, 1984.[7] It was just at this time that the European countries were recovering from the economic crisis of the 1970s. For both parties, it was the right moment to review their economic relations. These were the circumstances in which the idea formed of arranging for more extensive economic co-operation in western Europe, namely through the establishment of a European Economic Area (EEA).

B. THE EUROPEAN ECONOMIC AREA

1. Origins

23–004 EEA Agreement. The expression "European Economic Area" occurred for the first time in the joint declaration made by the Member States of the EEC and of EFTA and the Commission on April 9, 1984 in Luxembourg on the occasion of their first multilateral meeting since the signature of the free trade agreements.[8] The declaration was concerned with consolidating

---

[3] These provisions were underpinned by: (1) the abolition of all restrictions on payments relating to trade in goods, (2) the prohibition of discriminatory tax measures and charges, and (3) rules on competition, state aid and dumping.

[4] Compare Arts 22, 13 and 20, 23 and 18, first para., of the Agreement between the EEC and Switzerland with the present Arts 10, 28 and 30, 81–82, and 90 of the EC Treaty.

[5] For an early application of this principle, see ECJ, Case 270/80 *Polydor* [1982] E.C.R. 329, paras 14 *et seq.* For a clear explanation of the *ratio* of the Court's judgment, see ECJ, Case C–312/91 *Metalsa* [1993] E.C.R. I–3751, paras 10–12. See, in addition, Bellis, "The Interpretation of the Free Trade Agreements between the EFTA Countries and the European Community" (1985) Swiss Rev.I.Comp.L. 21–30.

[6] For the legal force of decisions of Joint Committees, see para. 17–094, *supra*.

[7] For further details, see Friedrich, "Die Freihandelsabkommen der Europäischen Gemeinschaften mit den EFTA-Staaten" (1983) N.J.W. 1237–1242.

[8] (1984) 4 EC Bull. point I.2.1.

and strengthening trade relations on the continent of Europe; a dynamic "European economic space" was to be the medium for and the outcome of the co-operation. It was only in the course of the subsequent negotiations that the three-fold thrust of the future "dynamic and homogeneous"[9] integration model became clear: (1) there was to be a multilateral co-operative structure incorporating (2) a considerable proportion of the *acquis communautaire* and (3) having common institutions with autonomous decision-making and administrative powers.[10] After an adverse opinion from the Court of Justice on the compatibility of the system of judicial supervision envisaged in the draft EEA Agreement with provisions of the EEC Treaty, the Agreement was adjusted in that respect.[11] On May 2, 1992 the amended version of the Agreement on the European Economic Area was signed at Oporto.[12] It was approved by the Community as an association agreement under Art. 238 of the EEC Treaty [now Art. 310 of the EC Treaty]. The negative outcome of the Swiss referendum in December 1992[13] prevented the EEA Agreement from coming into force at the same time as the European internal market was completed on January 1, 1993. Ultimately, the EEA Agreement was to come into effect on January 1, 1994 between the European Community, the European Coal and Steel Community and their Member States, on the one hand, and Austria, Finland, Iceland, Norway and Sweden, on the other. The EEA Agreement did not come into effect as regards Liechtenstein until May 1, 1995 after the Principality had taken the necessary measures with regard to its

---

[9] The reaction of the Ministers of the EFTA countries to the Commission's White Paper on the completion of the internal market, and more specifically the determination of a target date for the achievement of the internal market (December 31, 1992), was that the European Economic Area should not only be "dynamic", but also "homogeneous", so as to avoid structural discrimination after 1992. In the same spirit, the EEC or EEC Member States concluded a number of multilateral agreements with the EFTA countries: (1) the Convention on the simplification of formalities in trade in goods (including the introduction of a single administrative customs document), [1987] O.J. L134/1, (2) a customs convention (on a common European transit procedure), [1987] O.J. L226/1, and (3) the Convention on jurisdiction and the enforcement of judgments in civil and commercial matters (the Lugano Convention, constituting a *de facto* extension of the territorial scope of the Brussels Convention of September 27, 1968, para. 5–151, *supra*), [1988] O.J. L319/9.

[10] See the Statement on the broad lines of Commission policy, presented by Jacques Delors, President of the Commission, to the European Parliament as the programme of work for the new Commission on January 17, 1989 ((1989) EC Bull. Suppl.1, 17–18). See also the Presidency's conclusions following the European Council held in Strasbourg on December 8 and 9, 1989 (1989) 12 EC Bull. point I.1.13. For further details of the negotiations which led to the conclusion of the Agreement on the European Economic Area, see the exhaustive discussion in Norberg, Hökborg, Johansson, Eliasson and Dedichen, *EEA Law. A Commentary on the EEA Agreement* (Kluwer, Deventer, 1993), at 47–70.

[11] Paras 23–017—23–018, *infra*.

[12] [1994] O.J. L1.

[13] On December 6, 1992, 50.3 per cent of the total population and 18 of the 26 cantons voted against Swiss ratification of the EEA Agreement.

regional union with Switzerland.[14] With a view to the accession of ten new Member States to the European Union, an agreement was signed in Luxembourg on October 14, 2003 so as to ensure their contemporaneous accession to the EEA Agreement on May 1, 2004.[15]

23–005 Membership. Following the accession of Austria, Finland and Sweden to the European Union in 1995, Iceland, Liechtenstein and Norway are left as the only non-EU Member States in the European Economic Area.[16] Since the Swiss Confederation has not ratified the EEA Agreement, relations between Switzerland and the European Communities are chiefly governed by the 1972 bilateral free trade agreement.[17] In order to supplement this free trade agreement, both parties concluded a number of sectoral agreements in 1999 in policy areas of common interest, namely free movement of persons, research, public procurement, reciprocal recognition of conformity assessments, access to the market in agricultural products and transport.[18] As a result of the outcome of the EEA referendum, Switzerland has also temporarily shelved its application to join the European Union (which goes back to May 1992).[19]

---

[14] On November 2, 1994, Liechtenstein (which had been a member of EFTA since September 1, 1991) amended its Customs Treaty of March 29, 1923 with Switzerland so as not to impair the sound functioning of the EEA Agreement (see Art. 1(2) of the Protocol adjusting the Agreement on the European Economic Area, [1994] O.J. L1/572). After a positive vote in a referendum held on April 9, 1995, the EEA Agreement entered into force as regards Liechtenstein on May 1, 1995 ([1995] O.J. L140/30; see Art. 7(1) of Decision No.1/95 of the EEA Council of March 10, 1995, [1995] O.J. L86/58).

[15] See the Agreement between the EC, the existing EEA States (the 15 EU Member States plus Liechtenstein, Iceland and Norway) and the 10 candidate Member States on the participation of the Czech Republic, the Republic of Estonia, the Republic of Cyprus, the Republic of Latvia, the Republic of Lithuania, the Republic of Hungary, the Republic of Malta, the Republic of Poland, the Republic of Slovenia and the Slovak Republic in the European Economic Area ([2004] O.J. L130/11). As from May 1, 2004, this EEA Enlargement Agreement is provisionally applicable (see Council Decision 2004/368/EC of March 30, 2004, [2004] O.J. L130/1). As far as the geographical coverage of the EEA Agreement is concerned, Art. 128(1) of the Agreement provides that "[a]ny European State becoming a member of the Community shall, and the Swiss Confederation or any European State becoming a member of EFTA may, apply to become a party to this Agreement".

[16] For the question of the *raison d'être* and viability of the European Economic Area, see Säilä, "L'Espace économique européen et l'élargissement de l'Union européenne" (1994) R.M.C.U.E. 5–11. See also the European Parliament's resolution of February 15, 1995 on the European Economic Area ([1995] O.J. C56/55). For the transitional powers of the EFTA institutions, see Tichy and Dedichen, "Securing a Smooth Shift between the Two EEA Pillars: Prolonged Competence of EFTA Institutions with respect to former EFTA States after their Accession to the European Union" (1995) C.M.L.R. 131–156.

[17] For that trade agreement, see n.2, *supra*.

[18] [2002] O.J. L114. For the bilateral sectoral agreements, see Breitenmoser, "Sectoral Agreements between the EC and Switzerland: Contents and Context" (2003) C.M.L.R. 1137–1186; Schwok and Levrat, "Switzerland's Relations with the EU after the Adoption of the Seven Bilateral Agreements" (2001) E.For.Aff.Rev. 335–354; Hummer, "Die räumliche Erweiterung des Binnenmarkts" (2002) EuR. Beiheft 1, 75, at 104–115. Since June 2001 both parties have been negotiating additional sectoral agreements.

[19] This does not mean that Switzerland has withdrawn its application for membership or that the Commission has given a negative opinion. It merely signifies that both parties consider that at present the time is not ripe to activate the application.

2. Substantive scope

Objective. Article 1 of the EEA Agreement provides that its aim is to **23–006** "promote a continuous and balanced strengthening of trade and economic relations between the Contracting Parties with equal conditions of competition, and the respect of the same rules, with a view to creating a homogeneous European Economic Area".

Selective duplicate of the Community. The EEA Agreement creates a **23–007** system of free movement of goods, persons, services and capital in which strict competition rules apply, and accompanying measures are to provide for closer co-operation in areas such as research and development, the environment, education and social policy. The legislative system created thereby is a selective duplicate of the Community legal order: the rules applying in those areas under Community law are mirrored, *mutatis mutandis*, in the EEA Agreement. The Agreement therefore takes part of the *acquis communautaire* and extends its territorial scope to cover the territory of the European Economic Area.[20]

As far as achievement of the four freedoms is concerned, the most important difference between Community law and the EEA Agreement is to be found in the area of free movement of goods. Unlike the EC Treaty, the EEA Agreement establishes not a customs union, but a free trade area. In other words, no customs charges are levied in the territory of the EEA for trade in goods as between the countries of the EEA, but each of the Contracting Parties is entitled to retain its own import and export duties for goods coming from and going to third States.[21] This also means that the

---

[20] By Decision (No.7/94) of March 21, 1994 amending Protocol 47 and certain Annexes to the EEA Agreement ([1994] O.J. L160/1), the EEA Joint Committee amended the EEA Agreement to reflect the way in which the Community legal order had changed between the conclusion of the EEA negotiations and the entry into effect of the EEA Agreement (it related, more specifically, to acts adopted by the European Community before January 1, 1994 and published after June 31, 1991). That decision synchronising the rules applicable in the EEA with those of the EC was necessary in order to make sure that the EEA legal order was homogeneous at the time when it came into effect. Decision of the EFTA Surveillance Authority No.3/94/COL of January 12, 1994 on the issuing of 10 notices and guidelines in the field of competition ([1994] O.J. L153) is to be construed in the same sense. The EFTA Surveillance Authority examines whether the EFTA countries and EFTA nationals have complied with their obligations under the EEA Agreement. Accordingly, the EFTA Surveillance Authority applies the provisions of the EEA Agreement relating to implementation of the competition rules applying to undertakings. The EEA Agreement puts the EFTA Surveillance Authority under a duty in performing that task to have regard to the principles which the Commission applies in the competition field (see Annex XIV to the EEA Agreement, [1994] O.J. L1/445). As a result, the EFTA Surveillance Authority takes over the Commission's competition notices and guidelines *mutatis mutandis*. See, *e.g.* the EFTA Surveillance Authority notice on co-operation between national competition authorities and the EFTA Surveillance Authority in handling cases falling within the scope of Arts 53 or 54 of the EEA Agreement ([2000] O.J. C307/6).

[21] In the absence of a common customs tariff, there is also no question of a common policy on external trade. The existence of a free trade area, in contrast, implies that there can be no anti-dumping measures against products originating in EFTA countries which come under

main question is whether given goods should be categorised as "internal" or "external" in origin. The rules on the origin of goods determine whether or not particular products qualify for free movement.[22] A further interesting distinction between the two legal orders has to do with the sensitive area of agricultural and fisheries products. Unlike Community law, which embodies a detailed common agricultural and fisheries policy, the EEA Agreement is confined in this area to mere commitments to use best endeavours. In order to fill the resultant gaps, bilateral sectoral agreements have been concluded between the EC and the various EFTA countries.[23]

23–008 Homogeneity. In order to reinforce their reciprocal economic relations, the Contracting Parties to the EEA Agreement committed themselves to achieving homogeneity (see para. 23–006).

In the first place, homogeneity requires that rules apply in the (territorial and substantive) field of application of the EEA Agreement which are identical to—or at least not in conflict with[24]—provisions of bilateral or multilateral agreements governing trade relations between two or more of the Contracting Parties.[25] For this reason, the EEA Agreement contains provisions whose content and wording are virtually identical to corresponding provisions of the EC Treaty (or the ECSC Treaty). The Agreement provides for a system for ensuring that, as far as possible, substantively identical provisions are uniformly interpreted.[26] In addition, certain protocols and principally the annexes set out the relevant acts adopted by the Community institutions pursuant to the EC Treaty (and the

---

the EEA Agreement and with regard to which the *acquis communautaire* has been completely incorporated in the EEA Agreement (see Art. 26 of the EEA Agreement and Regulation 5/94 on the suspension of the anti-dumping measures against EFTA countries, [1994] O.J. L3/1).

[22] Art. 9 of the EEA Agreement and Protocol 4 ([1994] O.J. L1/54) contain the rules on the origin of goods. From July 1, 1997, diagonal cumulation of origin may be applied as between the EC, the EFTA States, Bulgaria, the Czech Republic, Estonia, Hungary, Latvia, Lithuania, Poland, Romania, Slovenia and Slovakia in so far as the relevant free trade agreements concluded with the EC contained identical rules of origin (Commission communication, [1997] O.J. C291/10).

[23] For those bilateral agreements, see [1993] O.J. L109 and L346/14 *et seq.* See also Protocols 9 and 42 to the EEA Agreement ([1994] O.J. L1/160 and 209).

[24] In the event of a conflict between rules of the EEA Agreement and provisions of bilateral or multilateral agreements between two or more Contracting Parties governing the same matters, consistency may be secured by giving precedence to the rules of the EEA Agreement (see, *e.g.* Art. 120 of the EEA Agreement).

[25] This is true, of course, only in so far as the EEA Agreement itself does not provide for an exception. In this respect, Art. 121 of the EEA Agreement is very cautiously worded: "The provisions of this Agreement shall not preclude co-operation [within the framework of certain bilateral or multilateral agreements] to the extent that such co-operation does not impair the good functioning of this Agreement".

[26] See paras 23–017–23–019, *infra.* For the need to secure homogeneous interpretation of identically worded provisions, see ECJ, Opinion 1/91 *Draft Agreement between the Community, on the one hand, and the countries of the European Free Trade Association, on the other, relating to the creation of the European Economic Area* [1991] E.C.R. I–6079, paras 13–22, and CFI, Case T–115/94 *Opel Austria v Council* [1997] E.C.R. II–39, paras 106–110.

ECSC Treaty). They form an integral part of the Agreement.[27] In this way, secondary Community law is also applicable, *mutatis mutandis*, in the EEA.[28]

Apart from its rather static approach to having identical rules, the EEA Agreement provides for dynamic processes for ensuring on-going homogeneity. These cover both subsequent legislative activities of the Communities in a field of competence falling within the substantive scope of the Agreement and developments in the relevant case law of the Court of Justice.[29]

3. Institutional operation

Interaction of EC and EFTA. The EEA brings together the two largest **23–009** European economic organisations. The EC and EFTA are at the same time the founders and direct pillars of the EEA. This is reflected in the organisational coherence which exists between the EC, EFTA and the EEA: the institutions of the Community and EFTA[30] do not operate only within the field of application of the treaties by which they were established, they also play a role under the EEA Agreement. Alongside those two groups, the EEA Agreement has an institutional framework of its own. Decision-making, surveillance and dispute settlement in the EEA are the outcome of the interaction between those three institutional bases of the EEA.[31]

---

[27] EEA Agreement, Art. 119.

[28] Protocol 1 (on "horizontal adaptations") sets out the general rules applicable on adaptation of provisions of the acts listed with a view to applying them in the legal order of the EEA.

[29] See the decision-making procedure (para. 23–011 *et seq.*, *infra*), the surveillance procedure and the consistent interpretation of the EEA Agreement (para. 23–016 *et seq.*, *infra*).

[30] Following the signature of the EEA Agreement, the EFTA countries set up, by a number of agreements concluded amongst themselves, specific institutions in order to render the Agreement operational and, at the same time, to enable it to function within the EEA on an equal footing with the EC and its institutions. The EFTA Committee of Parliamentarians, the EFTA Standing Committee, the EFTA Surveillance Authority and the EFTA Court approximate for EFTA, *mutatis mutandis*, to the European Parliament, the Council, the Commission and the Court of Justice in the case of the European Union. For the Agreement between the EFTA States on the establishment of a Surveillance Authority and a Court of Justice, see [1994] O.J. L344/1. For the EFTA Court, see Norberg, "The EFTA Court" (1994) C.M.L.R. 1147–1156; Christiansen, "The EFTA Court" (1997) E.L.Rev. 539–553, and Baudenbacher, "Between Homogeneity and Independence: the Legal Position of the EFTA Court in the European Economic Area" (1997) Col.J.E.L. 169–227. For a survey of the EFTA Court's case law in its first years of operation, see Blanchet and Westman-Clément, "La Cour AELE—Un premier bilan" (1995) R.M.C.U.E. 496–501 and (1996) R.M.C.U.E 438–446; Forman, "The EEA Agreement five years on: dynamic homogeneity in practice and its implementation by the two EEA courts" (1999) C.M.L.R. 751–781; Van den Bossche, "Het EVA-Hof: convergente scheurmaker?" (2001) S.E.W. 257–266.

[31] For further details, see Reymond, "Institutions, Decision-Making Procedure and Settlement of Disputes in the European Economic Area" (1993) C.M.L.R. 449–480; Travers, "The European Economic Area and the European Communities: A Constitutional Dilemma Partially Resolved" (1994) Ir.J.E.L. 74–91.

a. Institutions

23–010 EEA Institutions. The institutions of the EEA are responsible for seeing that the EEA is dynamic and homogeneous. Among other things, they have to take care that the EEA evolves in parallel with every new development of Community law in matters covered by the EEA Agreement. The institutions' composition and operation are characterised by "consolidated bilateralism".[32] This emerges for instance from the decision-making procedure of the EEA Council and the EEA Joint Committee, whose decisions are always based on agreement between the Community, on the one hand, and the EFTA States, speaking with one voice, on the other.[33] The EEA Council consists of the members of the Council of the European Union and members of the Commission and one member of government of each of the EFTA States.[34] It is responsible for giving the political impetus and laying down the general guidelines for the implementation of the Agreement.[35] The EEA Joint Committee consists of representatives of the Contracting Parties[36]; it ensures the effective implementation and operation of the Agreement. In so doing, it performs its duties in the decision-making procedure, in guaranteeing the homogeneous interpretation of the EEA

---

[32] Jacot-Guillarmod uses the expression "consolidated bilateralism" to express the idea that the multilateral EEA amounts *de facto* to a bilateral agreement between a powerful Community, on the one hand, and a strengthened EFTA, on the other: Jacot-Guillarmod, "Expressions juridiques au sein du système européen de libre-échange, du rapprochement de l'AELE et de la Communauté", in Capotorti, Ehlermann, Frowein, Jacobs, Joliet, Koopmans and Kovar (eds), *Du droit international au droit de l'intégration. Liber Amicorum P. Pescatore* (Nomos, Baden-Baden, 1987), 299, at 318.

[33] For the EEA Joint Committee, see Art. 93(2) of the EEA Agreement. As for the decision-making procedure in the EEA Council, it is provided in the Agreed Minutes of the negotiations for the EEA Agreement *ad* Art. 90 of that Agreement that, when taking decisions, EFTA Ministers are to speak with one voice (see also Art. 4 of the Rules of Procedure of the EEA Council, [1994] O.J. L138/39). For the purposes of determining the position to be adopted by the Community in the EEA Council and in the EEA Joint Committee, procedural rules were adopted by Council Regulation (EC) No. 2894/94 of November 28, 1994 concerning arrangements for implementing the Agreement on the European Economic Area, [1994] O.J. L305/6. For an assessment of that consolidated bilateralism, see the European Parliament's resolution on economic and trade relations between the European Community and the EFTA countries in the European Economic Area, [1992] O.J. C305/586, point 17.

[34] EEA Agreement, Art. 90(1), first subpara. The office of President of the EEA Council is to be held alternately, for a six-month period, by a member of the Council of the European Union and a member of the government of an EFTA State. The EEA Council is convened twice a year by its President (EEA Agreement, Art. 91).

[35] See EEA Agreement, Art. 89. The function, composition and operation of the EEA Council as prescribed by Arts 89, 90 and 91 of the EEA Agreement resemble the role played by the European Council in the European Union. The legal/constitutional function performed by the EEA Council appears to be greater than that analogy might suggest. Art. 95(5), Art. 118 and Art. 128 of the EEA Agreement in turn set out provisions concerning the interaction between the EEA Council and the EEA Joint Parliamentary Committee, the role of the EEA Council in the procedure for amending the Agreement and its part in the procedure for the accession of new parties to the Agreement.

[36] EEA Agreement, Art. 93(1). Concerning the Community and the EU Member States, "Contracting Parties" means the EC, the ECSC and/or the EU Member States, depending on their respective competences under the EU Treaty (EEA Agreement, Art. 2(c)).

Agreement and in the dispute-settlement procedure.[37] Decisions taken by the EEA Joint Committee, unless otherwise provided in the Agreement, are "upon their entry into force . . . binding on the Contracting Parties which shall take the necessary steps to ensure their implementation and application".[38] In addition, there is the EEA Joint Parliamentary Committee and the EEA Consultative Committee, which are advisory bodies representing, respectively, the peoples of Europe and the social partners.[39] Their main objective is to promote understanding between the Contracting Parties. They express their views in the form of reports or resolutions.[40]

b. Decision-making procedure

Two categories. Decision-making under the EEA Agreement may be **23–011** divided into two categories: autonomous and hybrid decision-making.

---

[37] Arts 92, 93 and 94 of the EEA Agreement define the function, the composition and the operation of the EEA Joint Committee. The upshot is that the Joint Committee appears to be a *sui generis* institution: scarcely supervised by any other institution, it is the EEA's highest regulatory and supervisory body. For its role in decision-making, in guaranteeing the homogeneous interpretation of the EEA Agreement and in dispute settlement, see Arts 97–104, Arts 105 and 106 and Art. 111, respectively, of the Agreement. Additionally, the Joint Committee has a hand in the adoption of safeguard measures (Arts 113 and 114) and in the procedure for making (major) amendments to the Agreement (Art. 117). Lastly, the EEA Joint Committee also has powers under a number of substantive provisions of the Agreement (see, *e.g.* Art. 48, Art. 64(1), Art. 82(1)(c) and Art. 86). For the Rules of Procedure of the EEA Joint Committee, see [1994] O.J. L85/60.

[38] EEA Agreement, Art. 104. The precedence of such acts over national law within the Community is a consequence of the primacy of Community law (see ECJ, Opinion 1/91 *Draft Agreement between the Community, on the one hand, and the countries of the European Free Trade Association, on the other, relating to the creation of the European Economic Area* [1991] E.C.R. I–6079, para. 37). As far as the EFTA States are concerned, Protocol 35 to the EEA Agreement refers to the obligation for them to introduce, where necessary, a statutory provision that EEA rules prevail over national law. For the precedence and direct effect of EEA rules, see Reinisch, "Zur unmittelbaren Anwendbarkeit von EWR-Recht" (1993) Z.f.RV. 11–30; Van Gerven, "The Genesis of EEA Law and the Principles of Primacy and Direct Effect" (1992–1993) Fordham I.L.J. 955–989, and, for a conflicting view in many respects, Sevón, "Primacy and Direct Effect in the EEA. Some Reflections", in *Festskrift til Ole Due* (GEC Gads, Copenhagen, 1994), at 340–354. See also Sevón and Johannsson, "The Protection of the Right of Individuals under the EEA Agreement" (1999) E.L.R. 373–386.

[39] The EEA Joint Parliamentary Committee consists of 66 members, one half of whom are Members of the European Parliament, the other half Members of the Parliaments of the EFTA States (EEA Agreement, Art. 95(1) and Art. 2 of Protocol 36 on the Statute of the EEA Joint Parliamentary Committee). The EEA Consultative Committee consists of equal numbers of the Community's European Economic and Social Committee and of the EFTA Consultative Committee (EEA Agreement, Art. 96(2)).

[40] Art. 95 of the EEA Agreement and Protocol 36 on the Statute of the EEA Joint Parliamentary Committee and Art. 96 of the EEA Agreement lay down the composition and the function and operation of the EEA Joint Parliamentary Committee and the EEA Consultative Committee, respectively. They appear from these provisions to have a small role to play in comparison with their counterparts in the EC, namely the European Parliament and the European Economic and Social Committee. For the Rules of Procedure of the EEA Joint Parliamentary Committee, see [1994] O.J. L247/34; for those of the EEA Consultative Committee, see [1994] O.J. L310/10.

23–012 Autonomous decision-making. Autonomous decision-making has its basis directly in a provision of the EEA Agreement (or in a Protocol or annex thereto). In each case, the legal basis defines the decision-making procedure to be used and is often confined to a decision to be taken by the EEA Joint Committee.[41] As has already been mentioned, the EEA Joint Committee then decides on the basis of agreement between the Community, on the one hand, and the EFTA countries, speaking with one voice, on the other.

23–013 Hybrid decision-making. Although hybrid decision-making ultimately originates outside the EEA Agreement, it indubitably influences its legal order. What is covered by this expression is legislative initiatives taken by the Contracting Parties in a field of competence coming under the EEA Agreement. The domestic legislative process could result in discrepancies between the domestic law of (one of the) Contracting Parties and EEA law. In order to secure the homogeneity of the EEA, the EEA Agreement provides for parallel or consecutive decision-making at EEA level (EEA Agreement, Arts 97–104). Hybrid decision-making (and the associated decision-making procedure) typifies the legislative dynamic of the EEA as it is set in motion by legislative initiatives of (one of) the Contracting Parties.[42]

23–014 Constraints on national legislation. As far as new legislative initiatives on the part of an EU Member State or an EFTA State are concerned, the first indent of Art. 97 of the EEA Agreement provides that States are entitled to undertake such initiatives "if the EEA Joint Committee concludes that the legislation as amended does not affect the good functioning of this Agreement".[43] Consequently, even though the EEA Agreement does not transfer any legislative powers to an EEA institution,[44] EEA membership does to some extent limit national legislative sovereignty.[45]

---

[41] See, *e.g.* the substantive provisions of the EEA Agreement mentioned in n.37, *supra*, or Art. 31(2), last subpara., Art. 35 of Protocol 4 on the rules on the origin of goods, Art. 4 of Protocol 10 on simplification of inspections and formalities in respect of carriage of goods or Art. 7 of Protocol 38 on the Financial Mechanism.

[42] See Cremona, "The 'Dynamic and Homogeneous' EEA: Byzantine Structures and Variable Geometry" (1994) E.L.R. 508–526.

[43] In view of the substantive scope of the EEA Agreement, that scenario means that the first indent of Art. 97 of the Agreement chiefly contemplates amendments of the domestic legislation of the EFTA States. It may be deduced by contrary inference from the second indent of Art. 97 of the EEA Agreement in conjunction with Art. 98 that the first indent of Art. 97 does not cover the eventuality of new Community legislation.

[44] See the first recital in the preamble to Protocol 35 on the implementation of EEA rules.

[45] The first indent of Art. 97 fleshes out the principle of fidelity to the objectives of the EEA set out in Art. 3 of the EEA Agreement and, more generally, reflects the principle of international law that the hierarchical priority of international agreements determines the leeway open to the national legislature.

Following Community legislation. In order to keep the EEA homogeneous **23–015** in areas to which the EEA Agreement applies having regard to the dynamic nature of the Community legal order, Art. 98 of the Agreement provides for a procedure under which the EEA Joint Committee may take decisions amending the annexes and a number of Protocols to the EEA Agreement.[46] In this way, the EEA legal order may be synchronised with that of the Community. If the EEA Joint Committee cannot reach agreement with regard to amending an annex to the EEA Agreement in the light of new Community legislation, the relevant annex (or affected part thereof) is regarded as provisionally suspended.[47] The fact that an amending decision is not adopted at EEA level means that, for a time, the Contracting EFTA States will jointly fall behind legislative developments in EC law to some extent in an area within the competence of the EEA. In order to facilitate decision-making in the EEA Joint Committee and to avoid such adverse consequences,[48] the EEA Agreement provides for on-going consultations to take place during the Community legislative process.[49]

c. Surveillance procedure, settlement of disputes and consistent interpretation

Commission and EFTA Surveillance Authority. Supervision that **23–016** obligations under the EEA Agreement are complied with is effected by a dual surveillance mechanism. On the one hand, the Commission monitors the application of the EEA Agreement by the Communities and the Member States and persons within their jurisdiction.[50] The Community Treaties determine any subsequent steps to be taken in that surveillance procedure. On the other hand, the EFTA Surveillance Authority (ESA) monitors fulfilment of EEA obligations by the EFTA States and persons within their jurisdiction.[51] In parallel to the Community system of legal protection, the EFTA Court acts in this respect as the highest court in the event that an EFTA State fails to comply with decisions of the EFTA

---

[46] Art. 98 of the EEA Agreement refers in turn to Arts 93(1), 99, 100, 102 and 103, which set out in detail the procedure for amending annexes and Protocols to the EEA Agreement.

[47] EEA Agreement, Art. 102(5). Note that this provision refers only to amendments of an annex to the EEA Agreement. Only Art. 93(2) and Art. 103(1) of the Agreement apply to the amendment of a Protocol referred to in Art. 98.

[48] It is clear from the Agreed Minutes of the negotiations for the EEA Agreement that the consequences are regarded as objectionable. It is declared *ad* Art. 111 (and therefore also with regard to Art. 102(5) of the EEA Agreement) that "suspension is not in the interest of the good functioning of the Agreement and all efforts should be made to avoid it".

[49] Examples of that on-going consultation are Art. 99(1) (in preparing Community legislation, the Commission is to seek advice from experts of the EFTA States) and Art. 99(3) (continuous information and consultation process in the EEA Joint Committee).

[50] EEA Agreement, Art. 109(1). By this means the Commission carries out its Community supervisory duties (see EC Treaty, Art. 211; para. 10–057, *supra*).

[51] Art. 109 of the EEA Agreement and Arts 5, 22 and 31 of the Agreement between the EFTA States on the establishment of a Surveillance Authority and a Court of Justice. For the Rules of Procedure of the Surveillance Authority, see [1994] O.J. L113/19.

Surveillance Authority or where an EFTA State or a natural or legal person wishes to challenge the legality of such a decision.[52]

23–017   Court of Justice and EFTA Court. Dispute settlement is likewise differentiated according to whether the Community or EFTA is involved. As far as concerns disputes between persons subject to the Community legal order on the interpretation or the application of the EEA Agreement, the Court of Justice has jurisdiction at last instance.[53] Disputes of that nature between persons coming under the jurisdiction of EFTA fall to be determined by the EFTA Court.[54] In both legal systems, domestic courts and tribunals also have jurisdiction to rule on the interpretation and application of the EEA Agreement. Judges may[55] refer a question to the Court of Justice or the EFTA Court, as the case may be, in order to obtain a preliminary ruling on the interpretation of provisions of the EEA Agreement. Under Art. 234 of the EC Treaty, courts or tribunals of EU Member States may seek a preliminary ruling only from the Court of Justice.[56] Courts and tribunals of EFTA States may seek a preliminary ruling on the interpretation of the EEA Agreement from the EFTA Court.[57] Where, however, the question relates to an EEA rule which is

---

[52] Art. 108 of the EEA Agreement and Arts 31, 35, 36 and 37 of the Agreement between the EFTA States on the establishment of a Surveillance Authority and a Court of Justice. See Baudenbacher, "The EFTA Court—An Example of the Judicialisation of International Economic Law" (2003) E.L.R. 880–899. For the Rules of Procedure of the EFTA Court, adopted on January 4 and February 1, 1994, see [1994] O.J. L278/1. *Mutatis mutandis*, those rules are virtually identical to those of the Court of Justice of the European Communities, the main differences being that there are no Advocates General and no Chambers and that English is the only language of the case. The case law of the EFTA Court may be obtained from the following Internet site: *www.eftacourt.lu/*.

[53] In its Opinion of December 14, 1991, the Court of Justice declared once again that it had jurisdiction to give a ruling on an international agreement concluded in accordance with the procedure laid down in Art. 228 [now Art. 300] of the EC Treaty (*i.e.* to interpret it and supervise compliance by the EU Member States): ECJ, Opinion 1/91 *Draft Agreement between the Community, on the one hand, and the countries of the European Free Trade Association, on the other, relating to the creation of the European Economic Area* [1991] E.C.R. I–6079, paras 37–38. For the first application of a provision of the EEA Agreement by the European Court, see CFI, Case T–115/94 *Opel Austria v Council* [1997] E.C.R. II–39, paras 97–125.

[54] Arts 32 and 34 of the Agreement between the EFTA States on the establishment of a Surveillance Authority and a Court of Justice.

[55] Read "must" in the case of a court or tribunal of an EU Member State against whose decisions there is no remedy under national law (EC Treaty, Art. 234, third para.).

[56] The Court of Justice cannot, however, give a ruling on the interpretation of the EEA Agreement with regard to events which occurred when the State concerned was a party to the EEA Agreement but not yet a Member State of the EU: ECJ, Case C–140/97 *Rechberger and Greindl* [1999] E.C.R. I–3499, paras 38–39, and ECJ, Case C–321/97 *Andersson and Andersson* [1999] E.C.R. I–3551, paras 26–33 (concerning Austria and Sweden, respectively). This is because in such a case the Court of Justice had interpretative jurisdiction only if the (former) EFTA State had authorised its courts and tribunals to refer questions to the Court of Justice for a preliminary ruling.

[57] Art. 34 of the Agreement between the EFTA States on the establishment of a Surveillance Authority and a Court of Justice, which contains a relatively open-ended variant of the preliminary ruling procedure provided for in Art. 234 of the EC Treaty.

identical in substance to an EC rule, EFTA courts may refer a question for a preliminary ruling to the Court of Justice if the EFTA State in question has provided for this possibility.[58] In such case, the ruling of the Court of Justice will be binding on the court or tribunal of the EFTA State.[59]

Provisions of the EEA Agreement which are essentially identical to corresponding rules of primary or secondary Community law are interpreted by the EFTA Surveillance Authority and the EFTA Court[60] in accordance with the case law of the Court of Justice.[61] For its part, the Court of Justice sometimes refers to the case law of the EFTA Court.[62]

EEA Joint Committee. In the event of a conflict of interpretation as **23–018** between a person coming under the Community legal order, on the one hand, and an EFTA State, on the other, the Community or an EFTA State

---

[58] Art. 107 of the EEA Agreement and Protocol 34 to the Agreement.

[59] *Cf.* the Opinions of the Court of Justice on the compatibility with Community law of the draft versions of the EEA Agreement: ECJ, Opinion 1/91 *Draft Agreement between the Community, on the one hand, and the countries of the European Free Trade Association, on the other, relating to the creation of the European Economic Area* [1991] E.C.R. I–6079, paras 54–65, and ECJ, Opinion 1/92 *Draft Agreement between the Community, on the one hand, and the countries of the European Free Trade Association, on the other, relating to the creation of the European Economic Area* [1992] E.C.R. I–2821, paras 15–37. For the EEA judicial system and the role played by the highest courts in the EFTA States, see Sevón, "The EEA Judicial System and the Supreme Courts of the EFTA States" (1992) E.J.I.L. 329–340.

[60] See, *e.g.* EFTA Court, Case E–1/94 *Restamark* (January 1, 1994-June 30, 1995) Reports of the EFTA Court 15, paras 24, 32–33, 46–52, 56, 60, 64–66 and 79–80. See also Baudenbacher (n.52), at 889–899. For a critical appraisal of the EFTA Court's case law, see Kronenberger, "Does the EFTA Court interpret the EEA Agreement as if it were the EC Treaty? Some Questions raised by the *Restamark* judgment" (1996) I.C.L.Q. 198–212.

[61] Art. 6 of the EEA Agreement guarantees only that provisions of the Agreement identical in substance to corresponding rules of primary and secondary Community law will be interpreted in conformity with rulings of the Court of Justice given prior to the date of signature of the Agreement. Moreover, that article does not make it clear whether it applies to the whole of the case law of the Court of Justice. The Court of Justice objected to the wording of that article in its first Opinion on the EEA Agreement (Opinion 1/91 (n.59, *supra*), paras 23–29). The Contracting Parties dealt with the reservations expressed by the Court of Justice through the addition of Protocol 48 to the EEA Agreement and Art. 3(2) of the Agreement between the EFTA States on the establishment of a Surveillance Authority and a Court of Justice: see Opinion 1/92 (n.59, *supra*), paras 20–29. Further particulars of those two Opinions may be obtained from Barents, "The Court of Justice and the EEA Agreement—Between Constitutional Values and Political Realities" (1992) Riv.D.E. 751–767; Brandtner, "The 'Drama' of the EEA—Comments on Opinions 1/91 and 1/92" (1992) E.J.I.L. 300–328 and Auvret-Finck, "Les Avis 1–91 and 2–92 relatifs au projet d'accord sur la création de l'espace économique européen" (1993) C.D.E. 38–59.

[62] *e.g.* ECJ, Case C–13/95 *Süzen* [1997] E.C.R. I–1295, para. 10; ECJ, Joined Cases C–34–36/95 *De Agostini* [1997] E.C.R. I–3843, para. 37; ECJ, Case C–172/99 *Liikenne* [2001] E.C.R. I–745, para. 2; ECJ (judgment of April 1, 2004), Case C–286/02 *Bellio F.lli*, not yet reported, paras 34 and 57–60; CFI, Case T–115/94 *Opel Austria v Council* [1997] II–39, para. 108; CFI, Case T–13/99 *Pfizer Animal Health v Council* [2003] E.C.R. II–3305, paras 115 and 143, and CFI, Case T–70/99 *Alpharma v Council* [2003] E.C.R. II–3495, paras 136 and 156.

may bring the dispute before the EEA Joint Committee.[63] In reaching its interpretation, the EEA Joint Committee is to have every regard to the need to maintain the good functioning of the EEA Agreement.[64] One result of this is that, in interpreting EEA rules which are essentially the same as EC (or ECSC rules), the EEA Joint Committee will not depart from the case law of the Court of Justice, irrespective as to whether it dates from before or after the date of signature of the EEA Agreement.[65] This secures the homogeneity of the EEA also with regard to the evolving case law of the Court of Justice on the interpretation of (new) rules of law. This will be the case, *a fortiori*, where the Court of Justice is involved in determining the dispute.[66]

23–019 Other means of securing homogeneity. The EEA Agreement provides for yet other measures with a view to securing homogeneity in the surveillance and interpretation of the EEA Agreement. Thus there is a continuous exchange of information between the so-called surveillance bodies, namely the Commission and the EFTA Surveillance Authority, on the one hand, and between the Court of Justice, the EFTA Court and the highest courts in the EFTA States, on the other.[67] If, in spite of this formalised co-operation, major differences should arise in the supervisory action of the surveillance bodies or in the case law, the EEA Joint Committee will attempt to maintain uniformity in the surveillance or the interpretation of the EEA Agreement.[68] If the EEA Joint Committee fails to reach agreement on a solution, the relevant part of the EEA Agreement may be temporarily suspended.[69]

---

[63] EEA Agreement, Art. 111(1). Note that only the Community and the EFTA States are entitled to bring a dispute on interpretation before the EEA Joint Committee, not the EU Member States.

[64] EEA Agreement, Art. 111(2).

[65] See Protocol 48 to the EEA Agreement.

[66] Art. 111(3) of the EEA Agreement provides that if the EEA Joint Committee has not settled the dispute within three months, the Contracting Parties to the dispute may agree to request the Court of Justice to give a ruling on the interpretation of the relevant rules. If the EEA Joint Committee has not reached an agreed solution within six months or if, by then, the Contracting Parties to the dispute have not decided to seek a ruling from the Court of Justice, a Contracting Party may either apply for provisional suspension of part of the EEA Agreement or take unilateral safeguard measures in order to offset any situations of imbalance.

[67] EEA Agreement, Art. 109(2) and Art. 106, respectively.

[68] EEA Agreement, Art. 109(5) and Art. 105, respectively. According to Protocol 48 to the Agreement, decisions taken by the EEA Joint Committee under Art. 105 may not affect the case law of the Court of Justice. Consequently, in case of a discrepancy in the interpretation of EEA rules which are essentially identical to EC (ECSC) rules, the interpretation of the Court of Justice constitutes the standard to follow.

[69] EEA Agreement, Arts 105 and 109(5) in conjunction with Arts 111 and 102.

II. Relations with Central and Eastern European Countries

Historical background. Initially, the Community's trade policy with regard **23–020** to the countries of central and eastern Europe[70] was confined to preponderantly unilateral, and extremely restrictive, rules on imports and exports of goods from and to those countries.[71] The Council for Mutual Economic Assistance (CMEA), to which those countries belonged,[72] did not agree to their entering into direct trade relations with the Community, whilst the Community refused to recognise CMEA as a trading partner. It was only after the emergence of President Mikhail Gorbachev in the Soviet Union that the Community succeeded in pursuing an *Ostpolitik* based at the same time on a purely administrative working relationship with CMEA, on the one hand, and on trade and co-operation with the separate CMEA States, on the other. On June 25, 1988, the Community signed a Joint Declaration together with CMEA on the basis of Art. 235 of the EEC Treaty,[73] which marked the legal termination of the refusal of CMEA and its member countries to recognise the EEC. The declaration also afforded the central European countries an opportunity of going outside CMEA's closed trading circuit and of making a significant step towards the international economy. It was that very economic normalisation which was the key idea in the initial phase of relations between the EEC and the countries of central and eastern Europe following the raising of the Iron Curtain and it underlies both the western European unilateral aid programmes and the bilateral agreements concluded between the European Communities and those countries.

A. Unilateral Trade Measures

PHARE Programme. The seven most highly industrialised countries (the **23–021** Group of Seven or G–7) meeting at a summit conference in Paris on July 15 and 16, 1989, asked the Commission to act as co-ordinator of the various

---

[70] In the absence of a generally accepted definition, the expression "central Europe" is used here to denote the following States: Albania, Bosnia and Herzegovina, Bulgaria, Croatia, the Czech Republic, Estonia, Hungary, Latvia, Lithuania, Poland, Romania, Serbia and Montenegro, Slovakia, Slovenia and the former Yugoslav Republic of Macedonia. The expression "eastern Europe" covers Armenia, Azerbaijan, Belarus, Georgia, Kazakhstan, Kyrgyzstan, Moldova, Russia, Tajikistan, Turkmenistan, Ukraine and Uzbekistan. The central European States in the Balkans are also referred to as "south-eastern" European States (see paras 23–034—23–035).

[71] For the current rules, see the discussion of autonomous commercial measures in para. 20–007, *supra*.

[72] CMEA was set up by oral international agreement during an economic conference held in Moscow in January 1949, which was attended by representatives from Bulgaria, Czechoslovakia, Hungary, Poland, Romania and the Soviet Union. On December 14, 1959, the CMEA Charter was signed at Sofia. At the time when CMEA was wound up in early 1991, its membership included Cuba, the German Democratic Republic, the Mongolian People's Republic and Vietnam, in addition to its six original member countries.

[73] [1988] O.J. L157/35.

western European initiatives taken to support economic and political reform in Poland and Hungary. Within the Community, that assistance took the form of the PHARE Programme.[74] That programme for financing economic restructuring in certain countries in central Europe was subsequently extended so as to cover all the central European countries.[75] From the outset, the Commission made the inclusion of a given central European country on the list of PHARE beneficiaries dependent upon its fulfilling fundamental economic and political conditions.[76] By means of micro-economic financial and technical assistance, the PHARE Programme aims to create an administrative, legislative, financial and commercial/economic framework within which a free market can function in an adequate manner.[77] For the purposes of fund allocation, the Commission laid down a number of PHARE priorities in consultation with the OECD, the IMF and the World Bank. The actual assistance given, however, is relatively flexible in so far as it takes account of the specific needs of each country both separately from and together with the capacity of its economy and administration to take advantage of it.[78]

23–022 TACIS Programme. At the European Council held in Rome on December 14 and 15, 1990, it was agreed that the European Communities should also provide financial support for economic reform in the Soviet Union.[79] The TACIS Programme[80] set up for this purpose assists the transition from a centrally planned economy to a free-market economy in all the republics of

---

[74] Council Regulation (EEC) No. 3906/89 of December 18, 1989 on economic aid to the Republic of Hungary and the Polish People's Republic, [1989] O.J. L375/11 (repeatedly amended, most recently by Council Regulation (EC) No. 2500/2001 of December 17, 2001, [2001] O.J. L342/1). Alongside its symbolic meaning of "beacon", PHARE stands for *Pologne/Hongrie, Assistance pour la restructuration des économies*.

[75] As far as the countries of south-eastern Europe are concerned, the PHARE Programme has been replaced since 2001 by the CARDS Programme (*Community Assistance for Reconstruction, Development and Stabilisation*). That programme of assistance fits in with the stability and association process in which those countries are involved (see para. 23–034 *et seq.*). See Council Regulation (EC) No. 2666/2000 of December 5, 2000 on assistance for Albania, Bosnia and Herzegovina, Croatia, the Federal Republic of Yugoslavia and the Former Yugoslav Republic of Macedonia, [2000] O.J. L306/1. The CARDS Programme was introduced by the European Agency for Reconstruction (see para. 10–110). 4.65 billion Euro is earmarked for the CARDS Programme for the period 2000–2006.

[76] The dual "conditionality" is laid down in a communication from the Commission to the Council and the European Parliament of February 1, 1990, *The development of the Community's relations with the countries of central and eastern Europe*, SEC (90) 196 final.

[77] The financial aid consists both of (non-repayable) grants and loans. Technical assistance has taken the form, *inter alia*, of multilateral co-operative projects, such as the Trans-European Mobility Programme for University Studies (Tempus; see n.00 to para. 5–229, *supra*) and the European Training Foundation (para. 5–240, *supra*).

[78] For the procedure for tendering for PHARE projects, see the Commission's answer of March 13, 1997 to question E–0301/97 (Amadeo), [1997] O.J. C217/153.

[79] See the conclusions of the Presidency following the European Council held in Rome on December 14 and 15, 1990 (1990) 12 EC Bull. point I.30.

[80] TACIS stands for *Technical Assistance to the Commonwealth of Independent States*.

the former Soviet Union and in Mongolia.[81] Financial and technical assistance is mainly provided by subsidising co-operation agreements and technical networks set up with a view to the transfer of know-how. In order to maximise the impact of the operation, the Council has selected a number of sectors of the economy which qualify for funding.[82]

Loans. Additionally, the Community also provides loans through the **23–023** European Investment Bank (EIB). Loans are also provided indirectly through its participation in the European Bank for Reconstruction and Development (EBRD). The decision setting up the EBRD was taken in Paris on May 29, 1990.[83] It has 62 shareholder members, including the EC, the EU Member States and the EIB.[84] Since they hold the majority of the EBRD share capital, the EC, the EU Member States and the EIB together have an important position on its Board of Directors.[85] Using a system of preferential loans, the EBRD supports economic and political reforms in central and eastern Europe. On the one hand, it sets out, in consultation with the IMF and the World Bank, to improve the competitive position of the central and eastern European countries by promoting productive and competitive investment in the private sector, to foster the transition towards open market-oriented economies and to accelerate the necessary structural adjustments. On the other hand, the EBRD seeks to further the development of multiparty democracy, pluralism, protection of human rights and freedom of the press.[86]

---

[81] Council Regulation (EEC, Euratom) No. 2157/91 of July 15, 1991 concerning the provision of technical assistance to economic reform and recovery in the Union of Soviet Socialist Republics, [1991] O.J. L201/2 (1991–1992 period). For the period 2000–2006, Council Regulation (EC, Euratom) No. 99/2000 of December 29, 1999 concerning the provision of assistance to the partner States in Eastern Europe and Central Asia ([2000] O.J. L12/1) applies.

[82] For an assessment of the TACIS Programme, see the Opinion of the Economic and Social Committee in [1998] O.J. C214/75. Special Report No.6/97 of the Court of Auditors on TACIS subsidies to Ukraine (accompanied by the Commission's response), [1997] O.J. C171, is more critical.

[83] Agreement establishing the European Bank for Reconstruction and Development—EBRD, approved on behalf of the Community by Council Decision of November 19, 1990 ([1990] O.J. L372/4) and on behalf of the EIB by Decision of the Board of Governors of June 11, 1990 ([1990] O.J. L377/3). The EBRD started operations on April 15, 1991. The website of the EBRD is to be found at *www.ebrd.com/*.

[84] Alongside the EC, the EIB, the EU Member States, the (other) Member States of the OECD and the other central and eastern European countries, Egypt, Israel, Korea, Liechtenstein, Morocco and Mongolia are shareholder/members of the EBRD. See Dunnett, "The European Bank for Reconstruction and Development: A Legal Survey" (1991) C.M.L.R. 571–597.

[85] Art. 26 of the EBRD Agreement provides that 11 of the 23 members of the Board of Directors are to be elected by the Governors representing the EC, the EIB and the (then 15) EU Member States. See also the Council Decision of February 17, 1997 providing that the European Community should subscribe for extra shares as a result of the decision to double the capital of the European Bank for Reconstruction and Development, [1997] O.J. L52/15.

[86] See Art. 1 of the EBRD Agreement.

23–024 Generalised tariff preferences. As a complementary step, the Community adopted a set of autonomous aid measures designed to promote trading relations with the countries of central and eastern Europe. This chiefly involved the grant of generalised tariff preferences (GTPs) for central and eastern European products. Although the GTP system is primarily an instrument of development policy, since 1990, the Council has included a number of central and eastern European countries on the list of eligible beneficiaries with a view to assisting their transition to market economies. At the time of writing, only Albania (a beneficiary since 1992), the other south-eastern European States (some of which have been beneficiaries since 1997) and the eastern European countries (beneficiaries since 1993) still benefit from Community GTPs.[87] In view of the alternative nature of GTPs, countries with which the EC concludes a free trade agreement are taken off the list of countries qualifying for generalised tariff preferences.[88]

B. BILATERAL RELATIONS WITH CENTRAL AND EASTERN EUROPEAN COUNTRIES

1. Trade and co-operation agreements

23–025 Trade and co-operation. Even before the Joint Declaration of June 25, 1988 was signed (see para. 23–020), the Commission had started to negotiate bilateral trade agreements with a number of central European countries. The aim of the agreements was in the first instance to normalise trade relations with the central European members of GATT.[89] The first agreement was confined to trade in industrial products and was concluded on the basis of Art. 113 of the EEC Treaty.[90] Subsequent agreements were based on both Art. 113 and Art. 235 of the EEC Treaty,[91] since they contained an additional section on commercial and economic co-operation designed to provide structural stimulation for both capacity in the central and eastern European economies and the extent and variety of bilateral

---

[87] For the current generalised tariff preferences scheme, see para. 20–026, *supra*.

[88] See, *e.g.* Council Regulation (EEC) No. 1509/92 of June 5, 1992 withdrawing Hungary, Poland and Czechoslovakia from the list of beneficiaries of the Community generalised preferences scheme as from March 1, 1992 ([1992] O.J. L159/1).

[89] This is because the restrictive measures taken by the Community against these countries were manifestly at odds with the GATT most-favoured-nation clause (para. 5–086, *supra*). In 1988, Czechoslovakia (founding member since 1947), Poland (member since 1967), Romania (member since 1971) and Hungary (member since 1973) were members of GATT.

[90] This was the 1980 trade agreement with Romania ([1980] O.J. L352/1), which was subsequently replaced by a trade and co-operation agreement (see the following footnote).

[91] The Community concluded bilateral trade and co-operation agreements with Hungary (September 26, 1988, [1988] O.J. L327/2), Poland (September 19, 1989, [1989] O.J. L339/2), the Soviet Union (December 19, 1989, [1990] O.J. L68/3), Czechoslovakia (May 7, 1990, [1990] O.J. L291/29), Bulgaria (May 8, 1990, [1990] O.J. L291/8), Romania (October 22, 1990, [1991] O.J. L79/13), Albania (May 11, 1992, [1992] O.J. L343/1), Estonia (May 11, 1992, [1992] O.J. L403/2), Latvia (May 11, 1992, [1992] O.J. L403/11), Lithuania (May 11, 1992, [1992] O.J. L403/2) and the former Yugoslav Republic of Macedonia (April 29, 1997, [1997] O.J. L348/2).

trade between the Contracting Parties in the medium to long term.[92] Furthermore, the trade and co-operation agreements differed from the earlier trade agreements on account of their broader scope (they covered all goods with the exception of textiles, coal and steel) and of their strict timetable for the gradual, full abolition of Community quantitative restrictions on the import of certain central and eastern European goods. Another manifest change was the creation of an institutional supporting structure for each trade and co-operation agreement. The joint committees, composed of equal numbers of members from each side, met regularly in order to ensure that the agreements were functioning properly. Their practical recommendations were intended to facilitate the attainment of the aims set by the relevant agreement. In addition, the joint committees attuned the aims of the agreements to suit changing economic circumstances, thereby ensuring that the agreements were dynamic.

Two-track policy. The disintegration of the communist structures which **23–026** had secured economic and political stability in central and eastern Europe (CMEA and the Warsaw Pact in the spring of 1991, the Soviet Union towards the end of that year) left a dangerous power vacuum. Since the trade and co-operation agreements were insufficient to produce economic well-being and political stability, the Community designed a new two-track policy. The Community's bilateral relations with the central European countries took the form of association agreements which were to prepare them for accession at a later date (see paras 23–027 et seq.).[93] Bilateral relations with the eastern European countries are less far-reaching since there is no prospect, at present, of those countries joining the European Union. The Community has concluded partnership and co-operation agreements with those countries (see paras 23–036 et seq.).[94] Alongside those bilateral agreements, the European Communities have also adopted a number of multilateral initiatives. For instance, the Energy Charter Treaty affords the central and eastern European countries an opportunity of

---

[92] The co-operation extends, *inter alia*, to the exchange of economic information, setting up joint ventures, transfers of technical know-how and carrying out joint research activities.

[93] See para. 23–034 *et seq.* for the stabilisation and association agreements concluded with the south-eastern European countries. Relations with central European States with which association agreements have not been concluded are still principally governed by trade and co-operation agreements. The further development of those relations has been made to depend upon a series of political and economic conditions.

[94] For further information, see De Smijter, "De relaties tussen de Europese Unie en de landen van Centraal-Europa, een juridische visie", in Malfliet (ed.), *Alternatieven voor het teloorgegane communisme*, (Leuven, Garant, 1994) at 17–40. See also Toledano Laredo, "L'Union européenne, l'ex-Union Soviétique et les Pays de l'Europe centrale et orientale: un aperçu de leurs accords" (1994) C.D.E. 543–562, and Ryba, "L'Union européenne et l'Europe de l'Est—l'évolution des relations de la Communauté—devenue Union européenne—avec l'Europe de l'Est et les perspectives d'avenir" (1994) R.M.C.U.E. 564–582.

developing their potential as energy suppliers, whilst at the same time helping to improve guaranteed energy supplies.[95]

2. Europe Agreements with central European countries

23–027 Europe Agreements. Ten central European countries have concluded association agreements with the Communities and the Member States[96]: on December 16, 1991 the Visegrád countries—Hungary, Poland and Czechoslovakia (since divided into two[97]), on February 1, 1993 Romania, on March 8, 1993 Bulgaria, on June 12, 1995 the Baltic States Estonia, Latvia and Lithuania and on June 10, 1996 Slovenia.[98] The Europe Agreements gave characteristic expression to Community relations with the central European countries. They not only enabled the associated countries to partake of the substantive achievements of the Communities, but they also created a framework for regular political dialogue between the Contracting Parties.[99] This was because the Europe Agreements were

[95] The Energy Charter Treaty has been signed by the European Communities, the EU Member States, the countries of central and eastern Europe, the members of the OECD (with the exception of New Zealand), Cyprus, Liechtenstein and Malta. See the Council and Commission Decision of September 23, 1997 on the conclusion of the Energy Charter Treaty and the Energy Charter Protocol, n.34 to para. 19–009, *supra*.

[96] The Council and Commission decisions on the conclusion of Europe Agreements have a three-fold legal basis: (1) the ECSC Treaty, (2) Art. 238 [now Art. 310] in conjunction with Art. 228 [now Art. 300](3), second subpara., of the EC Treaty and (3) Art. 101, second para., of the EAEC Treaty.

[97] Following the dissolution of Czechoslovakia on December 31, 1992, the Community signed association agreements on October 4, 1993 with both the Czech and the Slovak Republics. For the question under international law of State succession in the case of an agreement between Czechoslovakia and Austria, see ECJ (judgment of November 18, 2003) Case C–216/01 *Budějovický Budvar*, not yet reported (see para. 17–103, *supra*); for a practical study of the Community agreements with Czechoslovakia, the Soviet Union and Yugoslavia, see Weiss, "Succession of States in respect of Treaties concluded by the European Communities" (1994) S.E.W. 661–679.

[98] The Europe Agreements with Hungary ([1993] O.J. L347/2) and Poland ([1993] O.J. L348/2) entered into force on February 1, 1994. The Europe Agreements with Romania ([1994] O.J. L357/2), Bulgaria ([1994] O.J. L358/3), Slovakia ([1994] O.J. L359/2) and the Czech Republic ([1994] O.J. L360/2) entered into force on February 1, 1995. The Europe Agreements with Estonia ([1998] O.J. L68/3), Latvia ([1998] O.J. L26/3) and Lithuania ([1998] O.J. L51/3) entered into force on February 1, 1998. The Europe Agreement with Slovenia ([1999] O.J. L51/3) entered into force on February 1, 1999.

[99] The Association Agreements with the central European countries are referred to as *Europe Agreements* "to mark the importance of the political initiative which they represent": see the communication from the Commission to the Council and the European Parliament of August 27, 1990, *Association Agreements with the countries of central and eastern Europe: A general outline*, COM (90) 398 final, 1. At the European Council held at Essen on December 9 and 10, 1994, it was decided to conduct the political dialogue in a multilateral framework. This "structured dialogue" was regarded as constituting political and technical preparation for the accession of the central European States to the European Union ((1994) 12 EU Bull. point I.13). For the political nature of the Europe Agreements, see also the clause incorporated in them on respect for democratic principles, human rights and the principles of the market economy: (1992) 5 EC Bull. point I.2.13; see Rose and Haerpfer, "Democracy and Enlarging the European Union Eastwards", *EUI Working Papers No.95/12* (European University Institute, Robert Schuman Centre, Florence, 1995), 45 pp., and King, "The European Community and Human Rights in Eastern Europe" (1996) 2 L.I.E.I. 93–125.

regarded as a preparatory stage for full membership of the European Union (see para. 23–031). Since the Communities had no competence with respect to that part of the agreements, the EU Member States had to conclude them as well. Following the accession of eight central European countries to the Union, the Europe Agreements remain of importance only for Bulgaria and Romania.

a. Substantive aspects

Contents. The Europe Agreements embody various liberalisation **23–028** measures, which are intended to lead after a maximum of ten years to the creation of a free trade area in industrial products[100] between the Community and the central European countries concerned.[101] The calendar for this is asymmetrical in that the EC was to open up its market to central European products faster than the association countries are to open their markets to Community goods. Within five years of the entry into force of a given Europe Agreement, the Community must abolish all import duties, together with any remaining non-specific quantitative restrictions on imports and measures having equivalent effect, whereas the central European partner State has 10 years to fulfil the same obligations.[102] In view of their (admittedly staggered) reciprocity and the highly vigorous nature of the measures to be taken, the Europe Agreements exhibit substantive differences in comparison with the trade and co-operation agreements. The incorporation of provisions relating to the liberalisation of the movement of workers, establishment and the provision of services is completely novel.[103] Despite their nature of a programme, these provisions constituted a major step in the gradual extension of the *acquis communautaire* to the central European countries.[104] In particular, the

---

[100] The Europe Agreements also contain a number of specific provisions on agricultural and fisheries products. Arrangements with regard to textiles, coal and steel are set out in Protocols and Additional Protocols to the respective Europe Agreements. See, *e.g.* the Council Decision of September 18, 1995 on the conclusion of additional protocols to the Europe Agreements on trade in textile products between the European Community and Bulgaria, Hungary, Poland, Romania and the Czech and Slovak Republics, respectively, [1997] O.J. L127/1.

[101] However, the Europe Agreements do not bring about a free-trade area or any other model of economic integration as between the various central European countries.

[102] The free trade area applies, of course, only to products which satisfy the origin rules. See para. 23–007, *supra*, and Priess and Pethke, "The Pan-European Rules of Origin: the Beginning of a New Area in European Free Trade" (1997) C.M.L.R. 773–809.

[103] On September 27, 2001 the Court of Justice ruled for the first time on the consequences of the right of nationals of central European States to enter and remain in the territory of the European Union. See, *e.g.* ECJ, Case C–257/99 *Barkoci and Malik* [2001] E.C.R. I–6557. For an interpretation of the provision prohibiting discrimination as regards free movement of workers, see ECJ, Case C–162/00 *Pokrzeptowicz-Meyer* [2002] E.C.R. I–1049.

[104] The articles relating to trade in services empower the relevant Association Council to take the necessary measures to implement the objectives set in this sphere in each Europe Agreement. As far as workers are concerned, the provisions of the Agreement are more specific: any form of discrimination on grounds of nationality is prohibited as far as conditions of employment are concerned. *cf.*, in this respect, the Association Agreements with the Maghreb States, para. 5–157, *supra*.

chapter on "approximation of legislation" is worth mentioning. Pursuant thereto, the associated partner is to endeavour to make its legislation compatible with that of the Community and the Community is to provide technical assistance in this connection.[105] In this respect, competition law in the central European countries is of decisive importance.[106] Eventually, the extent to which the two legal systems are compatible will have a decisive impact on the timescale for achieving the economic integration of the country concerned with the Community. In order to assist would-be Member States, the Commission drew up a non-binding white paper on May 3, 1995.[107] The white paper indicated the legislative measures which the central European countries should implement in areas of crucial importance for the functioning of the internal market (principally competition, social policy and environment management).[108]

23–029 Co-operation programme. The approach to economic, cultural and financial co-operation was more developed and diversified in the Europe Agreements than in the trade and co-operation agreements. The broadly conceived co-operation programme was intended to create a favourable socio-economic, legal and psychological climate for achieving the intended objective of each agreement.[109] The financing of the association, unlike that of most association arrangements, was not governed by a financial protocol annexed to the agreement (which was for a limited duration), since the Europe Agreements themselves contained provisions relating to financial assistance from the Community (to which no time-limit was set), which underscored the intention to support the reform of the central European economies on the basis of a solid plan extending over a period of years.

---

[105] Evans, "Voluntary Harmonisation in Integration between the European Community and Eastern Europe" (1997) E.L.R. 201–220.

[106] See the decisions of the various Association Councils adopting implementing rules for the application of the provisions on competition and State aid in the Europe Agreements (*e.g.* Decisions Nos 1/96 and 1/98 of the EC-Czech Republic Association Council, [1996] O.J. L31/21, and [1998] O.J. L195/21, respectively). For an analysis of these competition provisions, see Evans, "Contextual Problems of EU Law: State Aid Control under the Europe Agreements" (1996) E.L.R. 263–279 and Van den Bossche, "The Competition Provisions in the Europe Agreements. A Comparative and Critical Analysis", in Maresceau (ed.), *Enlarging the European Union. Relations between the EU and Central and Eastern Europe* (Longman, London, 1997), at 84–107. For the compatibility of the competition provisions with the Hungarian Constitution, see Volkai, "The Application of the Europe Agreement and European Law in Hungary: The Judgement of an Activist Constitutional Court on Activist Notions" (Harvard Jean Monnet Working Paper 8/99, Cambridge, 1999) 39 pp.

[107] White Paper—Preparation of the associated countries of central and eastern Europe for integration into the internal market of the Union, COM(95) 163 final, May 3, 1995.

[108] See also Gaudissart and Sinnaeve, "The Role of the White Paper in the Preparation of the Eastern Enlargement" in Maresceau (ed.), *Enlarging the European Union. Relations between the EU and Central and Eastern Europe* (Longman, London, 1997) at 41–71.

[109] Most Association Councils have taken decisions adopting the general terms and conditions for the participation of the central European country in question in Community programmes (see, *e.g.* [2002] O.J. L46/37). The co-operation is directed towards raising the central European level in the various flanking policy areas in which the Europe Agreements encourage co-operation.

b. Institutional dimension

Association bodies. Just as in the case of other association agreements, **23–030** each Europe Agreement created an institutional structure, consisting of an association council, an association committee and an association parliamentary committee. Within their respective spheres of competence, the three institutions are responsible for seeing that the agreement is implemented in a dynamic manner.[110] The institutions are composed, on the basis of the principle of parity, of an equal number of representatives of the two Contracting Parties. On the side of the Communities and the EU Member States, however, only members of the Council and the Commission sit on the institutions. The principle of parity also requires decisions of the association institutions to be taken by consensus.[111] As far as decision-making in the association council is concerned, this means that the Community may only put forward a common position. A Community procedure has been formulated for adopting such common positions.[112]

c. Aims

Initial prospects. An association agreement is the means *par excellence* of **23–031** preparing third countries adequately for future membership of the European Union, since such an agreement results in a partial extension to such countries of the *acquis communautaire* without its being coupled with any extension of the actual territory of the Union. Nevertheless, initially any prospect of the accession of the central European countries was ruled out.[113] This was because the primary aim of the Europe Agreements was to support the central European economies commercially, financially and technically, to underscore the common pan-European identity and to break down the isolation of the countries concerned by stimulating the achievement of political stability with a view to their returning to the heart of political and economic life in Europe and taking part in the broader process of differentiated European integration.[114] For their part, some

---

[110] In contradistinction to the joint committee set up by a trade and co-operation agreement, the association council has fully-fledged powers of decision, also in the matter of dispute settlement (see, *e.g.* Decision 3/96 of the EC-Poland Association Council of July 16, 1996, [1996] O.J. L208/31). The association committee ensures continuity between meetings of the association council and prepares its meetings. The association parliamentary committee may make recommendations to the association council and ask it to provide information.

[111] For the status of decisions of association councils (secondary association law) in the Community legal order, see para. 17–094, *supra*.

[112] See, *e.g.* the Decision of the Council and the Commission of December 13, 1993 on the conclusion of a Europe Agreement with Hungary ([1993] O.J. L347).

[113] For a very plain statement to this effect, see the communication from the Commission to the Council and the European Parliament of August 27, 1990 (n.99, *supra*), 3, *in fine*. Nevertheless, the central European countries succeeded in having the following passage incorporated in the preamble to the Europe Agreements: "HAVING IN MIND that the final objective of [the central European State concerned] is to become a member of the Community and that this association, in the view of the Parties, will help to achieve this objective".

[114] See the concluding document of the Inaugural Conference for a Pact on Security in Europe, [1994] O.J. L165/2 (see para. 20–043, *supra*).

central European countries, namely the Visegrád countries, expressly called on the Community in a joint memorandum of September 1992 to determine a timetable for accession and the conditions for membership.[115]

23–032 Preparation for EU membership. It was not until June 1993 that the European Council, meeting in Copenhagen, envisaged the accession of the central European countries and described the Europe Agreements as a preparation for membership.[116] Consequently, the Europe Agreements represented for both parties the appropriate legal framework for effectively preparing the central European countries for later membership of the European Union.[117] In December 1995, the Madrid European Council decided that the first stage of the accession negotiations would start six months after the conclusion of the 1996 Intergovernmental Conference. The Commission was to make the necessary proposals to this end.[118] On July 15, 1997 the Commission published Agenda 2000[119] and its opinions on the accession applications of ten associated central European countries.[120] The European Council held in Luxembourg decided to allow the enlargement process to commence on March 30, 1998 with the ten central

---

[115] See the summary of that joint memorandum of the Visegrád countries in *Europe*, October 23, 1992, 6. For more particulars, see Lippert and Schneider (eds), *Monitoring Association and Beyond: The European Union and the Visegrád States*, in *Europäische Schriften des Instituts für Europäische Politik*, Vol.74, (Europa Union Verlag, Bonn, 1995), 408 pp.

[116] European Council of June 21 and 22, 1993 (1993) 6 EC Bull. point I.13; see also the European Council held in Corfu on June 24 and 25, 1994 (1994) 6 EU Bull. point I–13. For Europe Agreements as preparation for the accession of the central European countries to the European Union, see Inglis, "The Europe Agreements compared in the light of their Pre-accession Reorientation" (2000) C.M.L.R. 1173–1210.

[117] See the detailed report made by the Council to the European Council held in Essen on December 9 and 10, 1994 on a strategy to prepare for the accession of the associated countries of central and eastern Europe ((1994) 12 EU Bull. points I–39 to I–54). For the European Parliament's resolution on that strategy, see [1994] O.J. C363/16. For the possible use of the European Economic Area as a subsequent step in preparing the central European countries for accession to the European Union, see Peers, "An Ever Closer Waiting Room? The Case for Eastern European Accession to the European Economic Area" (1995) C.M.L.R. 187–213.

[118] European Council of December 15 and 16, 1995 (1995) 12 EU Bull. point I.25.

[119] European Commission, "Agenda 2000—For a stronger and wider Union" (1997) EU Bull. Suppl.5. Agenda 2000 is in three parts. The first sets out a number of specific Commission proposals for reforming the internal policies of the Union, principally the common agricultural policy and economic and social cohesion (see the proposals set out in [1998] O.J. C176 and (1998) 3 EU Bull. points I.1. to I.25). The second part contains an intensified strategy for preparing for accessions, and the third part is a study on the effects of the enlargement of the Union on the various European policy spheres. For a brief assessment, see the editorial, "Agenda 2000: For a stronger and wider Union" (1998) C.M.L.R. 317–324.

[120] Supplements 6/97 to 15/97 to the EU Bulletin contain the Commission's opinions on the accession applications lodged by Hungary, Poland, Romania, the Slovak Republic, Latvia, Estonia, Lithuania, Bulgaria, the Czech Republic and Slovenia, respectively. The Commission considered that accession negotiations could be started with Estonia, Hungary, Poland, Slovenia and the Czech Republic.

European would-be Member States.[121] As part of this process, the intensified pre-accession strategy aimed at better preparing the would-be Member States for accession.[122] Accession partnership was the pivot of the pre-accession strategy.[123] The accession partnerships brought all forms of assistance to the central European States within a single framework.[124] In this context, screening of the incorporation of the *acquis communautaire* by the applicant States had been taking place since April 3, 1998.[125] Following on from the conclusions of the Luxembourg European Council, actual accession negotiations began on March 31, 1998 with (Cyprus and) five central European countries: the Czech Republic, Estonia, Hungary, Poland and Slovenia.[126] At its meeting in Helsinki on December 10 and 11, 1999, the European Council decided to open accession negotiations in February 2000 with the five remaining central Eastern States (and Malta).[127] This ultimately led to the accession on May 1, 2004 of Cyprus, Malta and eight central European countries (see para. 1–021); it is envisaged that Bulgaria and Romania will accede in 2007 (see also para. 8–011).

3. The pre-accession strategy with Turkey

Turkey. The Community and the Member States concluded an association **23–033** agreement with Turkey as long ago as 1963. This led to the establishment of a customs union as from 1996 (see para. 20–020). The European Council

---

[121] European Council of December 12 and 13, 1997 (1997) 12 EU Bull. point I.5. In parallel, the first meeting of the European Conference was held on March 12, 1998 ((1998) 3 EU Bull. point 1.3.50). This multilateral forum set out to consider questions of general interest for its participants ((1997) 12 EU Bull. point I.4). Apart from the ten central European countries, Cyprus and Turkey were also invited. Turkey did not attend.

[122] See, *e.g.* the Pre-accession Pact on organised crime between the Member States of the European Union and the applicant countries of Central and Eastern Europe and Cyprus ([1998] O.J. C220/1), approved by the Justice and Home Affairs Council on May 28, 1998.

[123] See Council Regulation (EC) No. 622/98 of March 16, 1998 on assistance to the applicant States in the framework of the pre-accession strategy, and in particular on the establishment of Accession Partnerships ([1998] O.J. L85/1) and Council Decisions 98/259/EC–98/268/EC of March 30, 1998 on the principles, priorities, intermediate objectives and conditions contained in the accession partnerships ([1998] O.J. L121). For the 10 accession partnerships, see [1998] O.J. C202. The accession partnerships were amended by Council Decisions 2002/83/EC–2002/94/EC of January 28, 2002 ([2002] O.J. L44) and, in the case of Bulgaria, Romania and Turkey, again by Council Decisions 2003/396/EC–2003/398/EC of May 19, 2003 ([2003] O.J. L145).

[124] See, *e.g.* the Decision of the Board of Governors of the European Investment Bank of January 28, 1998: EIB pre-accession facility, [1998] O.J. C116/10. See also the regulations adopted by the Council on June 21, 1999 on co-ordinating aid to the applicant countries in the framework of the pre-accession strategy and amending Regulation (EC) No. 3906/89 (Regulation (EC) No. 1266/1999; [1999] O.J. L161/68) and establishing an Instrument for Structural Policies for Pre-accession (Regulation 1267/1999; [1999] O.J. L161/73). For a survey of all pre-accession instruments, see Evtimov, "Die Osterweiterung der Europäischen Union und die Auswirkungen auf die Schweiz: Rechtliche Fragestellungen" (2001) 3 RSDIE/SZIER 289–323.

[125] (1998) 3 EU Bull. point I.3.51.

[126] (1998) 3 EU Bull. point I.3.52.

[127] (1999) 12 EU Bull. point I.3.10.

held in Luxembourg on December 12 and 13, 1997 confirmed Turkey's eligibility for accession to the European Union and that it would be judged on the basis of the same criteria as the other applicant States.[128] Since then, there exists a pre-accession strategy for Turkey which is modelled on the accession partnerships for Cyprus, Malta and the central European candidate countries.[129] No date has yet been set for opening accession negotiations.[130]

4. The stabilisation and association agreements with the south-eastern European countries

23–034 **Stabilisation and association process.** Since 1999, the European Union engages in a stabilisation and association process with regard to five countries in the western Balkans, namely Albania, Bosnia and Herzogovina, Croatia, the former Yugoslav Republic of Macedonia, and Serbia and Montenegro.[131] The stabilisation and association process has the aim of preparing these countries for accession to the European Union,[132] with the emphasis being placed on regional co-operation among the five countries.[133] This emerges in particular from the requirement that each country which concludes a stabilisation and association agreement with the European Communities must also conclude a bilateral regional co-operation agreement with the other south-eastern European countries which have

---

[128] (1997) 12 EU Bull. point I.6.31. See also the position expressed by the President of the Council at the meeting of the EC-Turkey Association Council of April 29, 1997 (1997) 4 EU Bull. point 1.4.74).

[129] See Council Regulation (EC) No. 390/2001 of February 26, 2001 on assistance to Turkey in the framework of the pre-accession strategy, and in particular on the establishment of an Accession Partnership ([2001] O.J. L58/1) and Council implementing Decisions 2001/235/EC and 2003/398/EC of March 8, 2001 and May 19, 2003 on the principles, priorities, intermediate objectives and conditions contained in the Accession Partnership with Turkey ([2001] O.J. L85/13, and [2003] O.J. L145/40, respectively).

[130] For a recent account of how matters stand, see the conclusions of the European Council held in Brussels on December 12, 2003, points 39 to 41. See also Örücü, "Turkey Facing the European Union—Old and New Harmonies" (2000) E.L.R. 523–537; for a historical survey, see Önis, "An Awkward Partnership: Turkey's Relations with the European Union in Comparative-Historical Perspective" (2001) Journal of European Integration History 105–119.

[131] See the conclusions of the General Affairs Council of June 21, 1999, based on the communication from the Commission to the Council and the European Parliament on the stabilisation and association process for countries of South-Eastern Europe of May 26, 1999 (COM(99)235). For a survey, see Pippan, "The Rocky Road to Europe: The EU's Stabilisation and Association Process for the Western Balkans and the Principle of Conditionality" (2004) E.For.Aff.Rev. 219–245.

[132] See the Presidency conclusions following the European Councils held at Santa Maria da Feira on June 19–20, 2000 ((2000) 6 EU Bull. point I.49.67) and at Nice on December 7–9, 2000 ((2000) 12 EU Bull. point I.36.60), where express reference is made to "potential candidates for EU membership" and "a clear prospect of accession".

[133] See the conclusions of the Zagreb summit of November 24, 2000 of the Heads of State or of Government of the EU Member States and the five south-eastern European countries ((2000) 11 EU Bull. point 1.6.57).

signed stabilisation and association agreements. In practice, this means that accession of a south-eastern European country to the European Union may be possible only once a close regional relationship has come about between the five south-eastern European States (see also para. 8–011).

Stabilisation and association agreements. The stabilisation and association **23–035** process is underpinned by financial assistance provided by the European Union through the CARDS Programme[134] and is crystallised in the stabilisation and association agreements concluded between the European Communities and their Member States, on the one hand, and each of the south-eastern countries, on the other. At the time of writing, stabilisation and association agreements have been signed with Croatia and with the Former Yugoslav Republic of Macedonia. Only the latter has already entered into force.[135] These agreements provide for the establishment of a bilateral free trade area between the European Communities and the south-eastern European country in question after a six-year transitional period. The agreements further include a chapter on political dialogue between the contracting parties[136] and provisions on free competition, protection of intellectual property rights and the right of establishment. Pending the entry into force of these multilateral stabilisation and association agreements, the European Communities are concluding interim agreements with the south-eastern European countries on trade and trade-related matters relating to the stabilisation and association agreements.[137] In addition, "European partnerships" are to be established to identify priorities for further action towards moving the western Balkan countries closer to the European Union while also serving as a checklist against which to measure progress.[138]

5. Partnership and co-operation agreements with eastern European countries

Partnership and co-operation agreements. Unlike the central European **23–036** countries, the eastern European States have never entertained the prospect

---

[134] For the CARDS Programme, see n.75, *supra*.
[135] The stabilisation and association agreement with the Former Yugoslav Republic of Macedonia was signed on April 9, 2001 and approved by the Community by decision of the Council and Commission of February 23, 2004 ([2004] O.J. L84/1—it entered info force on April 1, 2004: [2004] O.J. L85/26); the agreement with Croatia was signed on October 29, 2001.
[136] See the Joint declaration of the European Community and its Member States and the Republic of Croatia on political dialogue, [2001] O.J. C320/1.
[137] The Interim Agreement with Croatia ([2001] O.J. L330/3) entered into force on March 1, 2002.
[138] Council Regulation (EC) No. 533/2004 of March 22, 2004 on the establishment of European partnerships in the framework of the stabilisation and association process ([2004] O.J. L86/1).

of accession to the European Union in their relations with the Community. Neither have the Communities ever intended to conclude agreements with those States with a view to extending the principles of the internal market to parts of the former Soviet Union.[139] As a result, the Communities have elected to follow the 1989 trade and co-operation agreement concluded with the Soviet Union by partnership and co-operation agreements with a number of republics of the former Soviet Union.[140] Such agreements have entered into effect with Russia (December 1, 1997),[141] Ukraine (March 1, 1998),[142] Moldova (July 1, 1998) and Armenia, Azerbaijan, Georgia, Kazakhstan, Kyrgyzstan and Uzbekistan (the last six on July 1, 1999).[143] Partnership and co-operation agreements with Belarus (March 6, 1995) and Turkmenistan (May 25, 1998) have been signed but have not yet entered into effect. As in the case of relations with the central European countries, provision is made for the conclusion of an interim agreement on trade and related matters so that the provisions of the partnership and co-operation agreement may be applied provisionally before the latter enters into effect.[144]

---

[139] See the Commission's answer of December 21, 1993 to question E–2996/93 (Oomen-Ruijten, Herman, Von Habsburg and Elles), [1994] O.J. C310/47.

[140] See the resolution of the European Parliament on the partnership agreements with the NIS (New Independent States), [1995] O.J. C109/298. As far as concerns Tajikistan, Turkmenistan and Belarus, relations are still governed by the trade and co-operation agreement concluded with the Soviet Union (n.91, *supra*). For an overall picture, see Yakemtchouk, "L'Union européenne face aux nouveaux Etats indépendants issus de l'ancienne URSS" (1997) R.M.C.U.E. 444–453 and Hillion, "Institutional Aspects of the Partnership between the European Union and the Newly Independent States of the Former Soviet Union: Case Studies of Russia and Ukraine" (2000) C.M.L.R. 1211–1235.

[141] [1997] O.J. L327/3. See also the European Union's action plan for Russia ((1996) 5 EU Bull. point 2.3.1.) and the European Parliament's resolutions thereon ([1996] O.J. C347/155, and [1998] O.J. C138/166). For further particulars, see Van Eeckhaute, "De overeenkomst inzake partnership en samenwerking: een nieuw juridisch en politiek kader voor de betrekkingen tussen de Europese Unie en Rusland" (1994–1995) R.W. 1041–1052; Niedobitek, "Die Europäische Union und Russland—zum Stand der Beziehungen" (1997) EuR. 107–131 and Shemiatenkov, "The Relations between Russia and the EU" (1997) R.A.E. 277–289.

[142] [1998] O.J. L49/3. European Union policy *vis-à-vis* Ukraine is the subject of a Council Common Position of November 28, 1994 ([1994] O.J. L313/1) and a Common Strategy of the European Council of December 11, 1999 ([1999] O.J. L331/1). See also the European Union's action plan for Ukraine ((1996) 12 EU Bull. point 1.4.75), the European Parliament's resolution thereon ([1998] O.J. C104/226) and Yakemtchouk, "L'Union européenne et l'Ukraine" (2003) R.M.C.U.E. 443–441.

[143] The agreements are published in [1998] O.J. L181/3 (Moldova), [1999] O.J. L196/3 (Kazakhstan), [1999] O.J. L196/48 (Kyrgyzstan), [1999] O.J. L205/3 (Georgia), [1999] O.J. L229/3 (Uzbekistan), [1999] O.J. L239/3 (Armenia) and [1999] O.J. L246/3 (Azerbaijan).

[144] The interim agreements suspend the provisions of the trade and co-operation agreements relating to trade and commercial co-operation but provisionally do not affect their provisions on economic co-operation and institutional arrangements. On March 25, 1996 an interim agreement was signed with Belarus ((1996) 3 EU Bull. point 1.4.65) and on November 10, 1999 an interim agreement with Turkmenistan ((1999) 11 EU Bull. point 1.5.70). Those agreements have not yet entered into effect. The reason why no progress has been made in relations between Belarus and the European Union can be seen from the Council's conclusions on Belarus ((1997) 9 EU Bull. point 1.3.56).

Aims. The partnership and co-operation agreements build upon the forms **23–037** of co-operation introduced in the 1989 trade and co-operation agreement. They also contain more ambitious measures designed to liberalise trade.[145] The starting point of the measures is reciprocal most-favoured-nation treatment, and they may in time result in a free trade area.[146] The partnership and co-operation agreements also provide in one paragraph for structured political dialogue. Since this relates to an area within the Member States' competence, the partnership and co-operation agreements take the form of mixed agreements. The agreements are underpinned by an institutional structure, consisting of a co-operation council, a co-operation committee and a co-operation parliamentary committee. Those bodies have to ensure that the relevant agreement is properly implemented.[147]

---

[145] The agreements also include specific provisions for textile, coal and steel products. Hence, the European Communities often conclude sectoral agreements with eastern European countries in addition to partnership and co-operation agreements. See, *e.g.* the agreement between the ECSC and Russia ([1997] O.J. L300/51), which entered into force on October 13, 1997 and the agreement between the EC and Russia on trade in textile products ([1998] O.J. L169/1), which has been applied since May 1, 1998.

[146] See, for instance, the evolutive clause in Art.3 of the Partnership and Co-operation Agreement with Russia and the Decision of the Co-operation Council between the European Communities, and their Member States, of the one part, and the Russian Federation, of the other part, of March 6, 2002 to establish a joint High-Level Group to elaborate the concept of a common European economic space ([2002] O.J. L82/9).

[147] The fact that a specific institutional framework is created means that the Community has to approve the agreement pursuant to Arts 133 and 308 of the EC Treaty in conjunction with Art.300(3), second subpara. As a result, the European Parliament's assent is required.

INDEX

(all references are to paragraph numbers;
italics refer to references in footnotes)

THE AUTHORS

Koen Lenaerts

Born 1954; lic.iuris, Ph.D. in law (Katholieke Universiteit Leuven); Master of Laws, Master in Public Administration (Harvard University); Lecturer (1979–1983) subsequently Professor of European Law, Katholieke Universiteit Leuven (since 1983); legal secretary (*référendaire*) at the Court of Justice of the European Communities (1984–1985); Professor at the College of Europe, Bruges (1984–1989); Member of the Brussels Bar (1986–1989); Visiting Professor at the Harvard Law School (1989); Judge of the Court of First Instance of the European Communities (1989–2003). Judge of the Court of Justice of the European Communities.

Piet Van Nuffel

Born 1968; lic.iuris, Ph.D. in law (Katholieke Universiteit Leuven); Master of Laws (Harvard University); Teaching assistant and Research Fellow (Flanders Foundation for Scientific Research) at the Katholieke Universiteit Leuven (1993–1999); legal secretary (*référendaire*) at the Court of First Instance of the European Communities (1999 to 2001); Administrator at the European Commission, Directorate-General for Competition, Unit for general competition policy, economic and legal aspects (2001–2003). Legal secretary at the Court of Justice of the European Communities; Professor at the College of Europe, Natolin (as of 2004-2005).